Association for Computational Linguistics

6th Applied Natural Language Processing Conference

1st Meeting of the North American Chapter of the Association for Computational Linguistics

Proceedings of the Conferences

and

Proceedings of the ANLP-NAACL 2000 Student Research Workshop

April 29—May 4, 2000
Seattle, Washington, USA

Published by the Association for Computational Linguistics
http://www.acl.web.org/

Distributed by Morgan Kaufmann Publishers
http://www.mkp.com

Production and Manufacturing by
Omipress, Inc.
Post Office Box 7214
Madison, WI 53707-7314

Order copies of this and other ACL publications from:

Morgan Kaufmann Publishers
San Francisco

http://www.mkp.com
orders@mkp.com
1-800-745-7323
1-800-814-6418 (fax)

ANLP-NAACL 2000
ISBN: 1-55860-704-8

Preface

The year 2000 marks the launch of the North American chapter of the Association for Computational Linguistics (NAACL). The ACL Executive committee under the leadership of Phil Cohen used this as an opportunity to bring industry and researchers together to explore the full spectrum of computational linguistics and natural language processing by planning a joint conference, combining the 6th Applied Natural Language Processing Conference (ANLP) and the 1st Conference of NAACL. ANLP-NAACL2000 marks not only the first major ACL sponsored conference of the new millennium, but reflects a significant change in the field, as we see speech and language applications leave the laboratory and enter every day use.

The technical program covers all facets of the field, from theory and methodology to its application in commercial software. We chose to have two independent program chairs so that papers from each of these two perspectives could be evaluated independently and they appear in separate sections of the proceedings. Janyce Wiebe, New Mexico State University, was the NAACL Program Chair and Sergei Nirenburg, also from New Mexico State University, was the ANLP Program Chair. I would like to thank them and their program committees and teams of reviewers, whose hard work produced an exciting program with three parallel sessions, reflecting the breadth of quality research and application development being done throughout the world.

We were honored to have as invited speakers two industry leaders: Dave Nagel, President, AT&T Laboratories and AT&T Chief Technical Officer, speaking on "Voice access to information", and Rick Rashid, Vice President, Microsoft Research, speaking on "The Future - It isn't what it used to be". From the academic community, Leonard Talmy, State University of New York at Buffalo, an internationally recognized researcher in cognitive science, speaking on "How Language Structures Concepts". These plenary sessions have shown us how far the community has come in bringing speech and language to the marketplace and to remind us of the complexity of language and its relationship to human cognition.

As is traditional at ACL conferences, the program goes beyond the presentation of technical papers and plenary sessions. There are also tutorials aimed at helping participants broaden their knowledge, workshops for exploring an area in depth, demonstrations to show the software implementations behind the theories, and exhibits to display the commercial products that have come out of the research, much of which was presented at past ACLs. I would like to thank the Tutorial Chair: Jennifer Chu Carroll (Lucent Technologies), Workshop Chair: Scott Miller (BBN), Demonstrations Chair: Jeff Reynar (Microsoft) and Exhibits Chair: Deborah Dahl (Unisys), all of whom composed quality programs.

One of the most valuable aspects of ACL conferences is the opportunity it offers to students, who can get a broad perspective on the field and meet the people whose papers they read in their courses. They also have the opportunity to present their own research, both in the main sessions and in special student sessions designed to help those in the early stages of their research. This year, we tried a new approach with a Student Research Workshop held before the conference with panelists to provide feedback to students, for which we received NSF funding from the Knowledge and Cognitive Systems Program under Ephraim Glinert. I would like to thank Committee members Donna Byron (University of Rochester) and Peter Vanderheyden (University of Waterloo), Co-Chairs, and Mary Harper (Purdue University), Faculty Advisor and NSF Principal Investigator and all of the reviewers who contributed to an excellent program and provided feedback to the students on their research. I would also like to thank the students who submitted papers and attended the workshop. They are the future of our organization.

Rick Wojcik (Boeing) as Local Arrangements Chair took care of the myriad of arrangements that go into an event of this size. Kathy McCoy, Secretary-Treasurer of the ACL, and Priscilla Rasmussen, ACL Business Manager, provided unending support in the planning, decision making, and execution of all of the arrangements. Mark Maybury (Mitre), Publicity Chair, expanded the number of places we advertise the conference to help widen our audience. June Santeusanio and Russell Kenyon from GTE created and updated a terrific web site, bringing the information about the conference to a central place. Russell developed the on-line registration form and provided support throughout the registration process.

I would especially like to thank Gary Coen (Boeing), who was the Sponsorship Chair, and all of the commercial companies who contributed to the conference. We had the largest level of industry support of any ACL conference in the past. Microsoft, Boeing, Sun, Intel (China), Xerox PARC, Logos, Conversa, and General Electric all contributed funds to support various events, allowing us to have a commercial grade conference at a hotel facility while keeping the conference fees at their usual level to accommodate academic budgets. GTE (BBN), Answerlogic, IBM, and Inxight provided scholarships to allow more students to attend the conference.

There are many more people who deserve thanks for contributing in one way or another. ACL is an all volunteer organization and it is a credit to everyone who participates that we can put on an event of this size and scope, benefiting everyone who attends through the exchange of ideas and inspiration we get from seeing the leading edge of the field.

Marie Meteer
General Chair, ANLP-NAACL 2000
April 2000

CONFERENCE PROGRAM

TUTORIALS, Saturday 29 April 2000, 8:30AM-5:00PM

Information Retrieval, 8:30AM-12:00PM
James Allan, University of Massachusetts, Amherst

The State of the Art in Language Modeling, 8:30AM-12:00PM
Joshua Goodman, Microsoft Research

Finite-State Morphology/Phonology: Theory, Applications, and Recent Developments, 1:30PM-5:00PM
George Kiraz, Lucent Technologies Bell Labs

Machine Translation, 1:30PM-5:00PM
Kevin Knight, USC/ISI

Monday, May 1	**ANLP/NAACL TECHNICAL SESSIONS**	**PRELIMINARY PROGRAM**	
	NAACL	*ANLP*	
8:45	**Introductory Remarks**		
	Session 1	**Session 2**	**Session 3**
9:00	**Modelling Grounding and Discourse Obligations Using Update Rules** Colin Matheson, David Traum, Massimo Poesio	**BusTUC-A Natural Language Bus Route Oracle** Amble Tore	
9:25	**The Automatic Translation of Discourse Structures** Daniel Marcu, Lynn Carlson, Maki Watanabe	**Machine Translation Between Very Close Languages** Jan Hajic, Jan Hric, Vladislav Kubon	
9:50	**A Probabilistic Genre-independent Model of Pronominalization** Michael Strube, Maria Wolters	**Cross-Language Multimedia Information Retrieval** Sharon Flank	
10:15	**Advances in domain independent linear text segmentation** Freddy Y.Y. Choi	**Automatic Construction of Parallel English-Chinese Corpus for Cross-language Information Retrieval** Jiang Chen, Jian-Yun Nie	
10:40	*BREAK*		
	NAACL	*ANLP*	*NAACL*

11:05	**Bagging and boosting a Treebank Parser** John C. Henderson, Eric Brill	**Providing Customer Service Using Natural Language Dialog** Amit Bagga, Tomek Strzalkowski	**Encoding information on adjectives in an Italian semantic net for computational applications** Antonietta Alonge, Francesca Bertagna, Nicoletta Calzolari, Adriana Roventini
11:30	**Noun Phrase Recognition by System Combination** Erik F. Tjong Kim Sang	**Translation Using Dialogue Participants' Information** Setsuo Yamada, Eiichiro Sumita, Hideki Kashioka	**The FrameNet tagset for frame-semantic and syntactic coding of predicate-argument structure** Christopher Johnson, Charles Fillmore
11:55	**A Simple Approach to Building Ensembles of Naive Bayesian Classifiers for Word Sense Disambiguation** Ted Pedersen	**Distilling Dialogues: A Method Using Natural Dialogue Corpora for Dialogue Systems Development** Nils Dahlback, Arne Jonsson	**Generation in the Lambek Calculus Framework: an Approach with Semantic Proof Nets** Sylvain Pogodalla
12:20	*LUNCH*		
	NAACL	*ANLP*	*ANLP*
1:50	**Word-for-Word Glossing with Contextually Similar Words** Patrick Pantel, Dekang Lin	**Plan-Based Dialogue Management in a Physics Tour** Reva Freedman	**A Framework for MT and Multilingual NLG Systems Based on Uniform Lexico-Structural Transformations** Benoit Lavoie
2:15	**Arabic Morphology Generation Using a Concatenative Strategy** Violetta Cavalli-Sforza, Abdelhadi Soudi, Teruko Mitamura	**Talk'n'Travel: A Conversational System for Air Travel Planning** David Stallard	**REES: A Large-Scale Relation and Event Extraction System** Chinatsu Aone, Mila Ramos-Santacruz
2:40	**Morphological Tagging: Data vs. Dictionaries** Jan Hajic	**Analysing Speech Transcriptions** Mark Stevenson, Robert Gaizauskas	**DIP: Detector for Incorrect Presuppositions in Survey Questions** Katja Wiemer-Hastings, Peter Wiemer-Hastings, Sonya Rajan, Arthur C. Graesser, Roger J. Kreuz, Ashish Karnavat
3:05	*BREAK*		
3:30	**Voice Access to Information** **Dave Nagel,** *Invited Speaker*		
4:30	*BREAK*		
	NAACL	*ANLP*	
4:40	**The Effectiveness of Corpus-Induced Dependency Grammars for Post-processing Speech** Mary P. Harper, Christopher M. White, Wen Wang, Michael T. Johnson, Randall A. Helzerman	**MIMIC: An Adaptive Mixed Initiative Spoken Dialogue System for Information Queries** Jennifer Chu-Carroll	

5:05	**Analyzing Dependencies of Japanese Subordinate Clauses based on Statistics of Scope Embedding Preference** Takehito Utsuro, Shigeyuki Nishiokayama, Masakazu Fujio, Yuji Matsumoto	**Javox: A Toolkit for Building Speech Enabled Applications** Michael Fuklerson, Alan W. Biermann	
5:30	**Rapid Parser Development: A Machine Learning Approach for Korean** Ulf Hermjakob	**A Compact Architecture for Dialogue Management Based on Scripts** Manny Rayner, Beth Ann Hockey, Frankie James	
5:55	*Close*		

Tuesday, May 2	**ANLP/NAACL TECHNICAL SESSIONS**	**PRELIMINARY PROGRAM**	
	Session 1	**Session 2**	**Session 3**
	NAACL	*ANLP*	
9:00	**A Classification Approach to Word Prediction** Yair Even-Zohar, Dan Roth	**A Representation for Complex and Evolving Data Dependencies in Generation** Roger Evans, Mike Reape, Lynne Cahill, Christine Doran, Chris Mellish, Daniel Paiva, Donia Scott, Niel Tipper	
9:25	**A Maximum-Entropy-Inspired Parser** Eugene Charniak	**An Automatic Reviser: The TransCheck System** Jean-Marc Jutras	
9:50	**Detecting Grammatical Errors without Negative Evidence** Martin Chodorow, Claudia Leacock	**Unit Completion for a Computer-Aided Translation Typing System** Phillippe Langlais, George Foster, Guy Lapalme	
10:15	**Automatic Corpus Correction with Anomaly Detection** Eleazar Eskin	**Multilingual Coreference Resolution** Sanda Harabagiu Steven J. Maiorano	
10:40	*BREAK*		
	NAACL	*ANLP*	*ANLP*
11:05	**Exploiting Auxiliary distributions in stochastic unification-based grammars** Mark Johnson, Stefan Riezler	**Using Predictive Annotation to Rank Suspected Answers** Dragomir Radev, John Pranger, Varerie Sam	**Message Classification in the Call Center** Stephan Busemann, Sven Schmeier, Roman Georg Arens

11:30	**Ambiguity Packing in HPSG --- Practical Results** John Carroll, Stephan Oepen	**A Question Answering System Supported by Information Extraction** Rohini Srihari, Wei Li	**Categorizing Unknown Words: Using Decision Trees to Differentiate Names and Misspellings** Janine Toole
11:55	**Forest-Based Statistical Sentence Generation** Irene Langkilde	**Examining the Role of Statistical and Linguistic Knowledge Sources in a General-Knowledge Question Answering System** Claire Cardie, Vincent Ng, David Pierce, Chris Buckley	**Extracting Molecular Binding Relationships from Biomedical Text** Thomas Rindflesch, Jayant Rajan, Lawrence Hunter
12:20	*LUNCH*		
	NAACL	*ANLP*	*ANLP*
1:50	**Cut-and-Paste Based Text Summarization** Hongyan Jing, Kathleen R. McKeown	**Korean Compound Noun Segmentation Based on Lexical Data Extracted from Corpus** Juntae Yoon	**Experiments with Corpus-Based LFG Specialization** Nicola Cancedda, Christer Samuelsson
2:15	**Minimizing Word Error Rate in Textual Summaries of Spoken Language** Klaus Zechner, Alex Waibel	**A Tool for Automated Revision of Context-Free Grammars** Nanda Kambhatla, Wlodek Zadrozny	**Aggressive Morphology for Robust Lexical Coverage** William Woods
2:40	**Trainable methods for Surface natural Language Generation** Adwait Ratnaparkhi	**TnT-A Statistical Part-of-Speech Tagger** Thorsten Brants	**Language Independent Morphological Analysis** Tatuo Yamastia, Yuji Matsumoto
3:05	*BREAK*		
3:30	**How Language Structures Concepts** **Leonard Talmy,** *Invited Speaker*		
4:30	*BREAK*		
4:40	**Evaluating automatic dialogue stategy adaptation for a spoken dialogue system** Jennifer Chu-Carroll, Jill Suzanne Nickerson	**A Divide-and-Conquer Strategy for Shallow Parsing of German Free Texts** Christian Braun, Guenter Neumann, Jakub Piskorski	
5:05	**Learning to recognize probabilistic Situations in a Spoken Dialogue system: Experiments with 'How May I Help You?'** Marilyn Walker, Irene Langkilde, Jerry Wright, Allen Gorin, Diane Litman	**A Hybrid Approach for Named Entity and Sub-type Tagging** Rohini Srihari, Cheng Niu, Wei Li	

5:30	**Predicting Automatic Speech Recognition Performance Using Prosodic Cues** Diane J. Litman, Julia B. Hirschberg, Marc Swerts	**Spelling and Grammar Correction for Danish in SCARRIE** Patrizia Paggio	
5:55	*CLOSE*		

Wednesday, May 3	**ANLP/NAACL TECHNICAL SESSIONS**	**PRELIMINARY PROGRAM**	
	Session 1	**Session 2**	**Session 3**
9:00	Plenary (TBA)		
	NAACL	*ANLP*	
9:50	**A Novel Use of Statistical Parsing to Extract Information from Text** Scott Miller, Heidi Fox, Lance Ramshaw, Ralph Weischedel	**Linguistic Knowledge can Improve Information Retrieval** William Woods, Lawrence A. Bookman, Ann Houston, Robert J. Kuhns, Paul Martin	
10:15	**Assigning Function Tags to Parsed Text** Don Blaheta, Eugene Charniak	**Domain-Specific Knowledge Acquisition Using Word Net** Dan Moldovan, Roxana Girju, Vasile Rus	
10:40	*BREAK*		
	NAACL	*NAACL*	*NAACL*
11:05	**Mostly-Unsupervised Statistical Segmentation of Japanese** Rie Kubota Ando, Lillian Lee	**Removing Left Recursion from Context-Free Grammars** Robert C. Moore	**Using Semantic Preferences to Identify Verbal Participation in Role Switching Alternations** Diana McCarthy
11:30	**Tagging Sentence Boundaries** Andrei Mikheev	**Left-To-Right Parsing and BiLexical Context-Free Grammars** Mark-Jan Nederhof, Giorgio Satta	**Acknowledgments in Human-Computer Interaction** Karen Ward, Peter A. Heeman
11:55	*NAACL BUSINESS MEETING*		
12:20	*LUNCH*		
	NAACL	*ANLP*	*ANLP*

1:50	**A Better Algorithm for the Alignment of Phonetic Sequences** Grzegorz Kondrak	**Large-Scale Controlled Vocabulary Indexing for Named Entities** Mark Wasson	**Automatic Discovery of Scenario-Level Pattern for Information Extraction** Roman Yangarber, Ralph Grishman, Pasi Tapanainen, Silja Huttunen
2:15	**Finite-State Reduplication in One-Level Prosodic Morphology** Markus Walther	**Building Lists for Named Entity Recognition** Mark Stevenson, Robert Gaizauskas	**Answer Extraction** Steven Abney, Michael Collins, Amit Singhal
2:40	**A finite-state and data-oriented method for grapheme to phoneme conversion** Gosse Bouma	**Automatic Identification of Phrases for Browsing Electronic Documents** Nina Wacholder, Judith L. Klavans, David Kirk Evans	**Sentence Simplification in Automatic Text Summarization** Hongyan Jing
3:05	*BREAK*		
3:30	**The Future—It isn't what it used to be** **Rick Rashid,** *Invited Speaker*		
4:30	*BREAK*		
	NAACL	*ANLP*	
4:40	**A Framework for Robust Semantic Interpretation** Carolyn Penstein Rose	**Named Entity Extraction from Noisy Input: Speech and OCR** Ralph Weischedel, David Miller, Sean Boisen, Richard Schwartz, Rebecca Stone	
5:05	**Understanding each other** Claire Gardent, Karsten Konrad	**The Use of Instrumentation in Grammar Engineering** Norbert Broeker	
5:30	**An Empirical Assessment of Semantic Interpretation** Martin Romacker, Udo Hahn	**The Efficiency of Multimodal Interaction** Philip R. Cohen, David McGee	
5:55	*CLOSE*		

TUTORIALS

Saturday 29 April 2000, 8:30AM-5:00PM

Information Retrieval, 8:30AM-12:00PM
James Allan, University of Massachusetts, Amherst

This tutorial will examine the role of Natural Language Processing in Information Retrieval (IR). It will start with a historical overview of how NLP has been used and abused over the 40 years of IR research, attempting to illustrate why distrust of NLP was rampant in the IR community. We will next explore reasons that NLP might have been doomed to failure in early IR contexts--where basic IR techniques already captured some of what NLP might have offered, and NLP techniques with even small error rates were therefore unable to offer more. We will then focus on NLP/IR success stories--both past and present--that show how NLP can be (and has been) successfully used in some applications. The last portion of the tutorial will focus on very recent applications of NLP for retrieval and organization purposes. We will discuss the use of NLP and IR as part of Web applications, and as applied to Web pages. The tutorial will also include a discussion of the exciting Question and Answer track from TREC-8 (1999). That task results showed that a combination of IR and NLP was highly effective, creating a great opportunity for future collaboration between the two fields.

The State of the Art in Language Modeling, 8:30AM-12:00PM
Joshua Goodman, Microsoft Research

This tutorial will cover the state-of-the-art in language modeling. The goal of language models is to predict the probability of words; this is directly useful for speech recognition, handwriting recognition, spelling correction, and other areas. Because language modeling is one of the most explored areas of statistical modeling, the state of the art is relatively advanced. Techniques from language modeling may be of interest to anyone pursuing probabilistic modeling, including those interested in statistical parsing, information retrieval, machine translation, and compression. The tutorial should be accessible to anyone with an elementary knowledge of probability.

The most basic language models -- n-gram models -- essentially just count occurrences of words in training data. I will describe six improvements over this simple baseline: smoothing, caching, skipping, sentence-mixture models, clustering, and parsing-based models.

1) Smoothing addresses the problem of data sparsity: there is rarely enough data to accurately estimate the parameters of a language model. Smoothing gives a way to combine less specific, more accurate information with more specific, but noisier data. I will describe two classic techniques: deleted interpolation and Katz (or Good-Turing) smoothing, and one recent technique, Modified Kneser-Ney smoothing, which is the best available.
2) Caching is a widely used technique that uses the observation that recently observed words are likely to occur again. Models from recently observed data can be combined with more general models to improve performance.
3) Skipping models use the observation that even words that are not directly adjacent to the target word contain useful
information.
4) Sentence-mixture models use the observation that there are many different kinds of sentences. By modeling each sentence type separately, performance is improved.
5) Clustering is one of the most useful language modeling techniques. Words can be grouped together into clusters through various automatic techniques; then the probability of a cluster can be predicted instead of the probability of the word. Clustering can be used to make smaller models or better performing ones.
6) All of the previous techniques ignore the structure of language. Recently, Ciprian Chelba has shown that techniques from statistical parsing can be used for improved models.

Finally, I will also talk about some practical aspects of language modeling. I will describe how freely available, off-the-shelf tools can be used to easily build language models, and how to use methods such as count cutoffs to compress language models.

Those who attend the tutorial should walk away with a broad understanding of the current techniques, and the background needed to either build their own language models, or to apply some of these techniques to other fields.

Finite-State Morphology/Phonology:Theory,Applications,and Recent Developments, 1:30PM-5:00PM
George Kiraz, Lucent Technologies Bell Labs

Morphology and phonology are crucial components in any large scale NLP and/or speech system. Finite-state (FS) approaches to morphology/phonology are the state-of-the-art in the field; they aim at modeling the morphology/phonology of language with computational devices whose computational power does not exceed that of FS machines. Such machines are of interest because they are easy to implement, fast to run and mathematically elegant. The purpose of this tutorial is to give a comprehensive introduction to the field of computational morphology, with emphasis on recent developments and practical techniques to build real systems.

The first hour of the tutorial will be introductory, bringing all the participants to a common understanding of the prerequisites involved: (1) morphology from a linguistics perspective, (2) automata theory from a computer-science perspective, and (3) how the two fields make up 'FS computational morphology'.

The second hour will concentrate on the theory of FS morphology. The various popular formalisms and notations will be explained. Algorithms for compiling formalisms into FS machines (i.e., rule compilers) will be detailed with comprehensive step-by-step examples. Algorithms for interpreting the formalisms directly will be outlined. Recent developments in the field will be emphasized.

The third hour will concentrate on building practical applications. An introduction to the available tools (and how to build such tools) will be given. This will be followed by building simple grammars, moving to more complex grammars, including challenging morphological and morphotactic phenomena (e.g., long-distance dependencies, heavy agglutinative morphology, reduplications, Semitic root-and-pattern, etc.). The tutorial will demonstrate how various linguistic descriptions of morphology and phonology (segmental, Autosegmental, prosodic, templatic, optimality theory, etc.) can be modeled with FS approaches.

The tutorial will end with 'Open Questions' detailing some of the issues that await research.

Machine Translation, 1:30PM-5:00PM
Kevin Knight, USC/ISI

Mechanical translation of one human language into another is one of the oldest applications of computer science, with roots going back to the 1940s and 1950s. It did not work very well then, and it does not work very well now. But, people use it all the time! MT programs can translate email, web pages, and online chat; with human post editing, they can translate corporate and government documents. There has also been an explosion in the number of language pairs available. The major force that continues to drive machine translation research is the idea that if it did work, people would use it a lot more. MT also provides a gauge of the breadth and depth of our scientific understanding of human language, including both interpretation and generation aspects.

This tutorial will cover a number of practical and theoretical topics. Most of the tutorial will consist of an in-depth look at several radically different types of MT systems. This will include both special-purpose and general-purpose MT. We will discuss how various MT systems are constructed, and what their strengths and weaknesses are. We will describe the workings of an interlingua-based system, and we will give a gentle yet rigorous description of a corpus-based statistical MT system. We will go through examples during the tutorial and also distribute small-scale (one-hour to eight-hour) assignments that can be done after the tutorial. These assignments demonstrate basic principles without requiring extensive programming.

We will also discuss the evaluation of MT systems, the economics of machine translation (including existing products and services), and the management of both source-language and target-language texts. This last topic includes ways of authoring documents to reduce ambiguity ("controlled language"), ways of preserving unresolved ambiguities in output text, and issues concerning pre-editing and post-editing of documents.

Finally, we will briefly discuss the future of MT, taking special account of current research in integrating MT with other natural language technologies (cross-language information retrieval, speech-to-speech translation, multilingual summarization, etc). We will also look at how current research in NLP is likely to affect MT in the future.

Syllabus:
1. Introduction to MT. Why is MT important? History of MT research and commercial development. General-purpose vs. special-purpose MT. Architectures that have been used for MT.
2. Building MT Systems. Syntactic transfer: building a lexicon, transfer rules. Interlingua-based MT: domain-specific interlingua design, parsing, semantic interpretation, generation. Direct transfer: statistical algorithms trained on bilingual corpora, text alignment, transliteration, example-based MT.
3. Managing the Input, Managing the Output. Pre-editing. Reducing ambiguity through controlled-language source text. Post-editing. Ambiguity preservation.
4. Evaluation of MT Systems. Why it's hard. Metrics that have been proposed and used. Strengths and weaknesses.
5. The Economics of MT. Products and services available.
6. The Future of MT. Integrating MT with other natural language technologies: cross-language information retrieval, speech-to-speech MT, summarizing foreign-language documents. How current NLP research bears on MT.

Table of Contents

Association for Computational Linguistics

6th Applied Natural Language Processing Conference

Proceedings of the Conference

April 29—May 4, 2000
Seattle, Washington, USA

ANLP 2000–PREFACE

131 papers were submitted to ANLP-2000. 46 were accepted for presentation at the conference.

Papers came from 24 countries: fifty eight from the United States of America, eleven each from Germany and United Kingdom, nine from Canada, eight from Japan, four each from Italy and Spain, three each from France, Korea and Switzerland, two each from Australia, China, The Netherlands and Sweden and one each from Czech Republic, Denmark, Finland, Greece, India, Hong Kong, Malaysia, Norway, Russia and Taiwan.

40 papers were submitted from industry. 85 papers came from academia.
2 papers were submitted from government organizations and four submissions were combined.

The reviewing process was supported by a web-based reviewer interface developed by Elisha Kane at New Mexico State University's Computing Research Lab. Linda Fresques of CRL coordinated the refereeing process.

I would like to express my gratitude to and appreciation of the Program Committee members responsible for the six areas:

Lynn Carlson, Tools and Resources for Developing NLP Systems Subcommittee
Eduard Hovy, Integrated NLP Systems Subcommittee
Richard Kittredge, Multilingual Text Processing Subcommittee
Ray Perrault, Spoken Language Systems Subcommittee
Oliviero Stock, Monolingual Text Processing Systems Subcommittee
John White, Evaluation Subcommittee

The following colleagues did the bulk of the reviewing:

Doug Appelt	Igor Boguslavsky	David Carter
Fabio Ciravegna	Jim Cowie	Ido Dagan
Robert Dale	John Dowding	Andreas Eisele
Michael Elhadad	Jim Glass	Oren Glikman
Ralph Grishman	Jan Hajič	Donna Harman
Lynette Hirschman	Pierre Isabelle	Tanya Korelsky
Yuval Krymolowski	Alberto Lavelli	Chin-Yew Lin
Inderjeet Mani	Daniel Marcu	Paul Martin
Zvi Marx	David McDonald	Teruko Mitamura
Martha Palmer	Owen Rambow	Norbert Reithinger
Harold Somers	Tomek Strzalkowski	Beth Sundheim
Toshiyuki Takezawa	Kathryn B. Taylor	Hans Uszkoreit
Takehito Utsuro	Piek Vossen	Ralph Weischedel
Dekai Wu	Rémi Zajac	

We believe that the quality of the papers selected is rather high and hope that the conference will be a success.

Sergei Nirenburg
Chair, Program Committee
ANLP-2000

ANLP Table of Contents

Section 1: Applied Natural Language Processing Conference (ANLP)

BusTUC - A natural language bus route oracle

Tore Amble
Dept. of computer and information science
University of Trondheim
Norway, N-7491
amble@idi.ntnu.no

Abstract

The paper describes a natural language based expert system route advisor for the public bus transport in Trondheim, Norway. The system is available on the Internet,and has been intstalled at the bus company's web server since the beginning of 1999. The system is bilingual, relying on an internal language independent logic representation.

1 Introduction

A natural language interface to a computer database provides users with the capability of obtaining information stored in the database by querying the system in a natural language (NL). With a natural language as a means of communication with a computer system, the users can make a question or a statement in the way they normally think about the information being discussed, freeing them from having to know how the computer stores or processes the information.

The present implementation represents a a major effort in bringing natural language into practical use. A system is developed that can answer queries about bus routes, stated as natural language texts, and made public through the Internet World Wide Web (`http://www.idi.ntnu.no/bustuc/`).

Trondheim is a small city with a university and 140000 inhabitants. Its central bus systems has 42 bus lines, serving 590 stations, with 1900 departures per day (in average). That gives approximately 60000 scheduled bus station passings per day, which is somehow represented in the route data base.

The starting point is to automate the function of a route information agent. The following example of a system response is using an actual request over telephone to the local route information company:

```
Hi, I live in Nidarvoll and tonight i
must reach a train to Oslo at 6 oclock.
```

and a typical answer would follow quickly:

```
Bus number 54 passes by Nidarvoll skole
at 1710 and arrives at Trondheim Railway
Station at 1725.
```

In between the question and the answer is a process of lexical analysis, syntax analysis, semantic analysis, pragmatic reasoning and database query processing.

One could argue that the information content could be solved by an interrogation, whereby the customer is asked to produce 4 items: `station of departure, station of arrival, earliest departure timeand/or latest arrival time`. It is a myth that natural language is a better way of communication because it is "natural language". The challenge is to prove by demonstration that an NL system can be made that will be preferred to the interrogative mode. To do that, the system has to be correct, user friendly and almost complete within the actual domain.

2 Previous Efforts, CHAT-80, PRAT-89 and HSQL

The system, called BusTUC is built upon the classical system CHAT-80 (Warren and Pereira, 1982). CHAT-80 was a state of the art natural language system that was impressive on its own merits, but also established Prolog as a viable and competitive language for Artificial Intelligence in general. The system was a brilliant masterpiece of software, efficient and sophisticated. The natural language system was connected to a small query system for international geography. The following query could be analysed and answered in a split second:

```
Which country bordering the Mediterranean
borders a country that is bordered by a
country whose population exceeds the
population of India?
```

(*The answer 'Turkey' has become incorrect as time has passed. The irony is that Geography was chosen as a domain without time.*)

The ability to answer ridiculously long queries is of course not the main goal. The main lesson is that complex sentences are analysed with a proper understanding without sacrificing efficiency. Any superficial pattern matching technique would prove futile sooner or later.

2.1 Making a Norwegian CHAT-80, PRAT-89

At the University of Trondheim (NTNU), two students made a Norwegian version of CHAT-80,called PRAT-89 (Teigen and Vetland, 1988),(Teigen and Vetland, 1989). (Also, a similar Swedish project SNACK-85 was reported).

The dictionary was changed from English to Norwegian together with new rules for morphological analysis. The change of grammar from English to Norwegian proved to be amazingly easy. It showed that the langauges were more similar than one would believe, given that the languages are incomprehensible to each other's communities.

After changing the dictionary and grammar, the following Norwegian query about the same domain could be answered correctly in a few seconds.

```
Hvilke afrikanske land som har en
befolkning stoerre enn 3 millioner
og mindre enn 50 millioner og er nord
for Botswana og oest for Libya har en
hovedstad som har en befolkning stoerre
enn 100 tusen.
```

(*A translation is beside the point of being a long query in Norwegian.*)

2.2 HSQL - Help System for SQL

A Nordic project HSQL (Help System for SQL) was accomplished in 1988-89 to make a joint Nordic effort interfaces to databases.

The HSQL project was led by the Swedish State Bureau (Statskontoret), with participants from Sweden, Denmark, Finland and Norway (Amble et al., 1990). The aim of HSQL was to build a natural language interface to SQL databases for the Scandinavian languages Swedish, Danish and Norwegian. These languages are very similar, and the Norwegian version of CHAT-80 was easily extended to the other Scandinavian languages. Instead of Geography, a more typical application area was chosen to be a query system for hospital administration. We decided to target an SQL database of a hospital administration which had been developed already.

The next step was then to change the domain of discourse from Geography to hospital administration, using the same knowledge representation techniques used in CHAT-80. A semantic model of this domain was made, and then implemented in the CHAT-80 framework.

The modelling technique that proved adequate was to use an extended Entity Relationship (ER) model with a class (type) hierarchy, attributes belonging to each class, single inheritance of attributes and relationships.

Coupling the system to an SQL database.
After the remodelling, the system could answer queries in "Scandinavian" to an internal hospital database as well as CHAT-80 could answer Geography questions. HSQL produced a Prolog-like code FOL (First Order Logic) for execution. A mapping from FOL to the data base Schema was defined, and a translator from FOL to SQL was implemented. The example

```
Hvilke menn ligger i en kvinnes seng?
```

(*Which men lie in a woman's bed?*)

would be translated dryly into the SQL query:

```
SELECT DISTINCT
  T3.name,T1.sex,T2.reg_no,T3.sex,
  T4.reg_no,T4.bed_no,T5.hosp_no,T5.ward_no
FROM PATIENT T1,OCCUPANCY T2,PATIENT T3,
          OCCUPANCY T4,WARD T5
WHERE
    (T1.sex='f') AND
    (T2.reg_no=T1.reg_no) AND
    (T3.sex='m') AND
    (T4.reg_no=T3.reg_no) AND
    (T4.bed_no=T2.bed_no) AND
    (T5.hosp_no=T4.hosp_no) AND
    (T5.ward_no=T4.ward_no)
```

2.3 The The Understanding Computer

The HSQL was a valuable experience in the effort to make transportable natural language interfaces. However, the underlying system CHAT-80 restricted the further development.

After the HSQL Project was finished, an internal reseach project TUC (the Understanding Computer) was initiated at NTNU to carry on the results from HSQL. The project goals differed from those of HSQL in a number of ways, and would not be concerned with multimedia interfaces . On the other hand, portability and versatility were made central issues concerning the generality of the language and its applications. The research goals could be summarised as to

- Give computers an operational understanding of natural language.
- Build intelligent systems with natural language capabilities.
- Study common sense reasoning in natural language.

A test criterion for the understanding capacity is that after a set of definitions in a Naturally Readable Logic, NRL, the system's answer to queries in NRL should conform to the answers of an idealised rational agent.

```
Every man that lives loves Mary.
John is a man. John lives.
Who loves Mary?
==> John
```

NRL is defined in a closed context. Thus interfaces to other systems are in principle defined through simulating the environment as a dialogue partner.

TUC is a prototypical natural language processor for English written in Prolog. It is designed to be a general purpose easily adaptable natural language processor. It consists of a general grammar for a subset of English, a semantic knowledge base, and modules for interfaces to other interfaces like UNIX, SQL-databases and general textual information sources.

2.4 The TABOR Project

It so happened that a Universtity Project was starteded in 1996, called TABOR (" Speech based user interfaces and reasoning systems "), with the aim of building an automatic public transport route oracle, available over the public telephone. At the onset of the project, the World Wide Web was fresh, and not as widespread as today, and the telephone was still regarded as the main source of information for the public.

Since then, the Internet became the dominant medium, and it is as likeley to find a computer with Internet connection, as to find a local busroute table. (The consequtive wide spreading of cellular phones changed the picture in favour of the telephone, but that is another story).

It was decided that a text based information system should be built, regardless of the status of the speech rocgnition and speech synthesis effort, which proved to lag behind after a while.

The BusTUC system

The resulting system BusTUC grew out as a natural application of TUC, and an English prototype could be built within a few months (Bratseth, 1997).

Since the summer 1996, the prototype was put onto the Internet, and been developed and tested more or less continually until today. The most important extension was that the system was made bilingual (Norwegian and English) during the fall 1996.

In spring 1999, the BusTUC was finally adopted by the local bus company in Trondheim (A/S Trondheim Trafikkselskap), which set up a server (a 300 MHz PC with Linux).

Until today, over 150.000 questions have been answered, and BusTUC seems to stabilize and grow increasingly popular.

3 Anatomy of the bus route oracle

The main components of the bus route information systems are:

- A parser system, consisting of a dictionary, a lexical processor, a grammar and a parser.
- A knowledge base (KB), divided into a semantic KB and an application KB
- A query processor, containg a routing logic system, and a route data base.

The system is bilingual and contains a double set of dictionary, morphology and grammar. Actually, it detects which language is most probable by counting the number of unknown words related to each language, and acts accordingly. The grammars are surprisingly similar, but no effort is made to coalesce them. The Norwegian grammar is slightly bigger than the English grammar, mostly because it is more elaborated but also because Norwegian allows a freer word order.

3.1 Features of BusTUC

For the Norwegian systems, the figures give an indication of the size of the domain: 420 nouns, 150 verbs, 165 adjectives, 60 prepositions, etc.

There are 1300 grammar rules (810 for English) although half of the rules are very low level.

The semantic net described below contains about 4000 entries.

A big name table of 3050 names in addition to the official station names, is required to capture the variety of naming. A simple spell correction is a part of the system (essentially 1 character errors).

The pragmatic reasoning is needed to translate the output from the parser to a route database query language . This is done by a production system called Pragma, which acts like an advanced rewriting system with 580 rules.

In addition, there is another rule base for actually generating the natural language answers (120 rules).

The system is mainly written in Prolog (Sicstus Prolog 3.7), with some Perl programs for the communication and CGI-scripts.

At the moment, there are about 35000 lines of programmed Prolog code (in addition to route tables which are also in Prolog).

Average response time is usually less than 2 seconds, but there are queries that demand up to 10 seconds.

The error rate for single, correct, complete and relevant questions is about 2 percent.

3.2 The Parser System

The Grammar System

The grammar is based on a simple grammar for statements, while questions and commands are derived by the use of movements. The grammar formalism which is called Consensical Grammar, (CONtext SENSItive CompositionAL Grammar) is an easy to use variant of Extraposition Grammar (Pereira and Warren, 1980), which is a generalisation of Definite Clause Grammars. Compositional grammar means that the semantics of a a phrase is composed of the semantics of the subphrases; the basic constituents being a form of verb complements. As for Extraposition grammars, a grammar is translated to Definite Clause Grammars, and executed as such.

A characteristic syntactic expression in Consensical Grammar may define an incomplete construct in terms of a "difference " between complete constructs. When possible, the parser will use the subtracted part in stead of reading from the input, after a gap if necessary. The effect is the same as for Extraposition grammars, but the this format is more intuitive.

Examples of grammar rules.

```
statement(P) --->
   noun_phrase(X,VP,P),
   verb_phrase(X,VP).

statement(Q) --->
   verb_complements0(VC),
%% initial optional verb complements

   statement(Q) -...
       verb_complements0(VC).
%% may be inserted  after a gap

whoseq(P) --->    % whose dog barked?
   [whose],
   noun(N),
    whoq(P) -     %% without gap
       ([who],[has],[a],noun(N),[that]).


whoq(P) --->
   [who],
   whichq(P) - ([which],[person]).

whichq(which(X)::P) --->
   [which],
   statement(P) - the(X).
```

Example:

```
Whose dog barked?
```

is analysed as if the sentence had been

```
Who has a dog that barked?
```

which is analysed as

```
Which person has a dog that barked?
```

which is analysed as

```
for which X is it true that
the (X) person has a dog that barked?
```

where the last line is analysed as a `statement`.

Movement is easily handled in Consensical Grammar without making special phrase rules for each kind of movement. The following example shows how TUC manages a variety of analyses using movements:

```
Max said Bill thought
   Joe believed Fido Barked.

Who said Bill thought
   Joe believed Fido barked?  ==> Max

Who did Max say thought
   Joe believed Fido barked?  ==> Bill

Who did Max say Bill thought
   believed Fido barked?      ==> Joe
```

The parser

The experiences with Consensical grammars are a bit mixed however. The main problem is the parsing method itself, which is top down with backtracking. Many principles that would prove elegant for small domains turned out to be too costly for larger domains, due to the wide variety of modes of expressions, incredible ambiguities and the sheer size of the covered language.

The disambiguation is a major problem for small grammars and large languages, and was solved by the following guidelines:

- a semantic type checking was integrated into the parser, and would help to discard sematically wrong parses from the start.
- a heuristics was followed that proved almost irreproachable: The longest possible phrase of a category that is semantically correct is in most cases the preferred interpretation.
- due to the perplexity of the language, some committed choices (cuts) had to be inserted into the grammar at strategic places. As one could fear however, this implied that wrong choices being made at some point in the parsing could not be recovered by backtracking.

These problems also made it imperative to introduce a timeout on the parsing process of embarassing 10 seconds. Although most sentences, would be parsed within a second, some legal sentences of moderate size actually need this time.

3.3 The semantic knowledge base

Adaptability means that the system does not need to be reprogrammed for each new application.

The design principle of TUC is that most of the changes are made in a tabular semantic knowledge base, while there is one general grammar and dictionary. In general, the logic is generated automatically from the semantic knowledge base.

The nouns play a key role in the understanding part as they constitute the class or type hierarchy. Nouns are defined in an `a-kind-of` hierarchy. The hierarchy is tree-structured with single inheritance. The top level also constitute the top level ontology of TUC's world.

In fact, a type check of the compliances of verbs, nouns adjectives and prepositions is not only necessary for the semantic processing but is essential for the syntax analysis for the disambiguation as well. In TUC, the legal combinations are carefully assembled in the semantic network, which then serves a dual purpose.

These semantic definitions are necessary to allow for instance the following sentences

```
The dog saw a man with a telescope.
The man saw a dog with a telescope.
```

to be treated differently because `with telescope` may modify the noun `man` but not the noun `dog`, while `with telescope` modifies the verb `see`, restricted to `person`.

3.4 The Query Processor

Event Calculus

The semantics of the phrases are built up by a kind of verb complements, where the event play a central role.

The text is translated from Natural language into a form called TQL (Temporal Query Language/ TUC Query Language) which is a first order event calculus expression, a self contained expression containing the literal meaning of an utterance.

A formalism TQL that was defined, inspired by the Event Calculus by Kowalski and Sergot (Kowalski and Sergot, 1986).

The TQL expressions consist of predicates, functions, constants and variables. The textual words of nouns and verbs are translated to generic predicates using the selected interpretation. The following question

```
Do you know whether the bus goes
to Nidar on Saturday ?
```

would give the TQL expression below. Typically, the Norwegian equivalent

```
Vet du om bussen gaar
til Nidar paa soendag ?
```

gives exactly the same code.

```
test::                        % Type of question
 isa(real,program,tuc),      % tuc is a program
 isa(real,bus,A),            % A is a real bus
 isa(real,saturday,B),       % B isa saturday
 isa(real,place,nidar),      % Nidar is a place
 event(real,D),              % D is an event
 know(whether,tuc,C,D),      % C was known at D
 event(C,E),             % E is an event in C
 action(go,E),           % the action of E is Go
 actor(A,E),             % the actor of E is  A
 srel(to,place,nidar,E),% E is  to nidar
 srel(on,time,B,E). % E is on the saturday B
```

The event parameter plays an important role in the semantics. It is used for various purposes. The most salient role is to identify a subset of time and space in which an action or event occured. Both the actual time and space coordinates are connected to the actions through the event parameter.

Pragmatic reasoning

The TQL is translated to a route database query language (BusLOG) which is actually a Prolog program. This is done by a production system called Pragma, which acts like an advanced rewriting system with 580 rules.

In addition, there is another rule base for actually generating the natural language answers (120 rules).

4 Conclusions

The TUC approach has as its goal to automate the creation of new natural language interfaces for a well defined subset of the language and with a minimum of explicit programming.

The implemented system has proved its worth, and is interesting if for no other reason. There is also an increasing interest from other bus companies and route information companies alike to get a similar system for their customers.

Further work remains to make the parser really efficient, and much work remains to make the language coverage complete within reasonable limits.

It is an open question whether the system of this kind will be a preferred way of offering information to the public.

If it is, it is a fair amount of work to make it a portable system that can be implemented elsewhere, also connecting various travelling agencies.

If not, it will remain a curiosity. But anyway, a system like this will be a contribution to the development of intelligent systems.

References

Tore Amble, Erik Knudsen, Aarno Lehtola, Jan Ljungberg, and Ole Ravnholt. 1990. *Naturlig Språk och Grafik - nya vägar inn i databaser.*

Statskontoret. Rapport om HSQL, ett kunskapsbaseret hjälpsystem för SQL.

Jon S. Bratseth. 1997. BusTUC - A Natural Language Bus Traffic Informations System. Master's thesis, The Norwegian University of Science and Technology.

R. Kowalski and M. Sergot. 1986. A logic based calculus of events. *New Generation Computing*, 8(0):67–95.

F.C.N. Pereira and D.H.D. Warren. 1980. Definite clause grammar for language analysis. *Artificial Intelligence*, 0(3).

J. Teigen and V. Vetland. 1988. Syntax analysis of norwegian language. Technical report, The Norwegian Institute of Technology.

J. Teigen and V. Vetland. 1989. Handling reasonable questions beyond
the linguistic and conceptual coverage of
natural language interfaces. Master's thesis, The Norwegian Institute of Technology.

D.H.D Warren and F.C.N. Pereira. 1982. An efficient and easily adaptable system for interpreting natural language queries. *Computational Linguistics*, 8(3-4).

Machine Translation of Very Close Languages

Jan HAJIČ
Computer Science Dept.
Johns Hopkins University
3400 N. Charles St., Baltimore,
MD 21218, USA
hajic@cs.jhu.edu

Jan HRIC
KTI MFF UK
Malostranské nám.25
Praha 1, Czech Republic, 11800
hric@barbora.mff.cuni.cz

Vladislav KUBOŇ
ÚFAL MFF UK
Malostranské nám.25
Praha 1, Czech Republic, 11800
vk@ufal.mff.cuni.cz

Abstract

Using examples of the transfer-based MT system between Czech and Russian RUSLAN and the word-for-word MT system with morphological disambiguation between Czech and Slovak ČESÍLKO we argue that for really close languages it is possible to obtain better translation quality by means of simpler methods. The problem of translation to a group of typologically similar languages using a pivot language is also discussed here.

Introduction

Although the field of machine translation has a very long history, the number of really successful systems is not very impressive. Most of the funds invested into the development of various MT systems have been wasted and have not stimulated a development of techniques which would allow to translate at least technical texts from a certain limited domain. There were, of course, exceptions, which demonstrated that under certain conditions it is possible to develop a system which will save money and efforts invested into human translation. The main reason why the field of MT has not met the expectations of sci-fi literature, but also the expectations of scientific community, is the complexity of the task itself. A successful automatic translation system requires an application of techniques from several areas of computational linguistics (morphology, syntax, semantics, discourse analysis etc.) as a necessary, but not a sufficient condition. The general opinion is that it is easier to create an MT system for a pair of related languages. In our contribution we would like to demonstrate that this assumption holds only for really very closely related languages.

1. Czech-to-Russian MT system RUSLAN

1.1 History

The first attempt to verify the hypothesis that related languages are easier to translate started in mid 80s at Charles University in Prague. The project was called RUSLAN and aimed at the translation of documentation in the domain of operating systems for mainframe computers. It was developed in cooperation with the Research Institute of Mathematical Machines in Prague. At that time in former COMECON countries it was obligatory to translate any kind of documentation to such systems into Russian. The work on the Czech-to-Russian MT system RUSLAN (cf. Oliva (1989)) started in 1985. It was terminated in 1990 (with COMECON gone) for the lack of funding.

1.2 System description

The system was rule-based, implemented in Colmerauer's Q-systems. It contained a full-fledged morphological and syntactic analysis of Czech, a transfer and a syntactic and morphological generation of Russian. There was almost no transfer at the beginning of the project due to the assumption that both languages are similar to the extent that does not require any transfer phase at all. This assumption turned to be wrong and several phenomena were covered by the transfer in the later stage of the project (for example the translation of the Czech verb "být" [to be] into one of the three possible Russian equivalents: empty form, the form "byt6" in future tense and the verb "javljat6sja"; or the translation of verbal negation).

At the time when the work was terminated in 1990, the system had a main translation dictionary of about 8000 words, accompanied by so called transducing dictionary covering another 2000 words. The transducing dictionary was based on the original idea described in Kirschner (1987). It aimed at the exploitation of the fact that technical terms are based (in a majority of European languages) on Greek or Latin stems, adopted according to the particular derivational rules of the given languages. This fact allows for the "translation" of technical terms by means of a direct transcription of productive endings and a slight (regular) adjustment of the spelling of the stem. For example, the English words *localization* and *discrimination* can be transcribed into Czech as "lokalizace" and "diskriminace" with a productive ending –ation being transcribed to –ace. It was generally assumed that for the pair Czech/Russian the transducing dictionary would be able to profit from a substantially greater number of productive rules. This hypothesis proved to be wrong, too (see Bémová, Kuboň (1990)). The set of productive endings for both pairs (English/Czech, as developed for an earlier MT system from English to Czech, and Czech/Russian) was very similar.

The evaluation of results of RUSLAN showed that roughly 40% of input sentences were translated correctly, about 40% with minor errors correctable by a human post-editor and about 20% of the input required substantial editing or re-translation. There were two main factors that caused a deterioration of the translation. The first factor was the incompleteness of the main dictionary of the system. Even though the system contained a set of so-called fail-soft rules, whose task was to handle such situations, an unknown word typically caused a failure of the module of syntactic analysis, because the dictionary entries contained - besides the translation equivalents and morphological information - very important syntactic information.

The second factor was the module of syntactic analysis of Czech. There were several reasons of parsing failures. Apart from the common inability of most rule-based formal grammars to cover a particular natural language to the finest detail of its syntax there were other problems. One of them was the existence of non-projective constructions, which are quite common in Czech even in relatively short sentences. Even though they account only for 1.7% of syntactic dependencies, every third Czech sentence contains at least one, and in a news corpus, we discovered as much as 15 non-projective dependencies; see also Hajič et al. (1998). An example of a non-projective construction is "Soubor se nepodařilo otevřít." [lit.: File *Refl.* was_not_possible to_open. – It was not possible to open the file]. The formalism used for the implementation (Q-systems) was not meant to handle non-projective constructions. Another source of trouble was the use of so-called semantic features. These features were based on lexical semantics of individual words. Their main task was to support a semantically plausible analysis and to block the implausible ones. It turned out that the question of implausible combinations of semantic features is also more complex than it was supposed to be. The practical outcome of the use of semantic features was a higher ratio of parsing failures – semantic features often blocked a plausible analysis. For example, human lexicographers assigned the verb 'to run' a semantic feature stating that only a noun with semantic features of a human or other living being may be assigned the role of subject of this verb. The input text was however full of sentences with 'programs' or 'systems' running etc. It was of course very easy to correct the semantic feature in the dictionary, but the problem was that there were far too many corrections required.

On the other hand, the fact that both languages allow a high degree of word-order freedom accounted for a certain simplification of the translation process. The grammar relied on the fact that there are only minor word-order differences between Czech and Russian.

1.3 Lessons learned from RUSLAN

We have learned several lessons regarding the MT of closely related languages:

- The transfer-based approach provides a similar quality of translation both for closely related and typologically different languages
- Two main bottlenecks of full-fledged transfer-based systems are:

- complexity of the syntactic dictionary
- relative unreliability of the syntactic analysis of the source language

- Even a relatively simple component (transducing dictionary) was equally complex for English-to-Czech and Czech-to-Russian translation
- Limited text domains do not exist in real life, it is necessary to work with a high coverage dictionary at least for the source language.

2. Translation and localization

2.1 A pivot language

Localization of products and their documentation is a great problem for any company, which wants to strengthen its position on foreign language market, especially for companies producing various kinds of software. The amounts of texts being localized are huge and the localization costs are huge as well.
It is quite clear that the localization from one source language to several target languages, which are typologically similar, but different from the source language, is a waste of money and effort. It is of course much easier to translate texts from Czech to Polish or from Russian to Bulgarian than from English or German to any of these languages. There are several reasons, why localization and translation is not being performed through some pivot language, representing a certain group of closely related languages. Apart from political reasons the translation through a pivot language has several drawbacks. The most important one is the problem of the loss of translation quality. Each translation may to a certain extent shift the meaning of the translated text and thus each subsequent translation provides results more and more different from the original. The second most important reason is the lack of translators from the pivot to the target language, while this is usually no problem for the translation from the source directly to the target language.

2.2 Translation memory is the key

The main goal of this paper is to suggest how to overcome these obstacles by means of a combination of an MT system with commercial MAHT (Machine-aided human translation) systems. We have chosen the TRADOS Translator's Workbench as a representative system of a class of these products, which can be characterized as an example-based translation tools. IBM's Translation Manager and other products also belong to this class. Such systems uses so-called translation memory, which contains pairs of previously translated sentences from a source to a target language. When a human translator starts translating a new sentence, the system tries to match the source with sentences already stored in the translation memory. If it is successful, it suggests the translation and the human translator decides whether to use it, to modify it or to reject it.
The segmentation of a translation memory is a key feature for our system. The translation memory may be exported into a text file and thus allows easy manipulation with its content. Let us suppose that we have at our disposal two translation memories – one human made for the source/pivot language pair and the other created by an MT system for the pivot/target language pair. The substitution of segments of a pivot language by the segments of a target language is then only a routine procedure. The human translator translating from the source language to the target language then gets a translation memory for the required pair (source/target). The system of penalties applied in TRADOS Translator's Workbench (or a similar system) guarantees that if there is already a human-made translation present, then it gets higher priority than the translation obtained as a result of the automatic MT. This system solves both problems mentioned above – the human translators from the pivot to the target language are not needed at all and the machine-made translation memory serves only as a resource supporting the direct human translation from the source to the target language.

3. Machine translation of (very) closely related Slavic languages

In the group of Slavic languages, there are more closely related languages than Czech and Russian. Apart from the pair of Serbian and Croatian languages, which are almost identical and were

considered one language just a few years ago, the most closely related languages in this group are Czech and Slovak.
This fact has led us to an experiment with automatic translation between Czech and Slovak. It was clear that application of a similar method to that one used in the system RUSLAN would lead to similar results. Due to the closeness of both languages we have decided to apply a simpler method. Our new system, ČESÍLKO, aims at a maximal exploitation of the similarity of both languages. The system uses the method of direct word-for-word translation, justified by the similarity of syntactic constructions of both languages.
Although the system is currently being tested on texts from the domain of documentation to corporate information systems, it is not limited to any specific domain. Its primary task is, however, to provide support for translation and localization of various technical texts.

3.1 System ČESÍLKO

The greatest problem of the word-for-word translation approach (for languages with very similar syntax and word order, but different morphological system) is the problem of morphological ambiguity of individual word forms. The type of ambiguity is slightly different in languages with a rich inflection (majority of Slavic languages) and in languages which do not have such a wide variety of forms derived from a single lemma. For example, in Czech there are only rare cases of part-of-speech ambiguities (stát [to stay/the state], zena [woman/chasing] or tri [three/rub(imperative)]), much more frequent is the ambiguity of gender, number and case (for example, the form of the adjective *jarní* [spring] is 27-times ambiguous). The main problem is that even though several Slavic languages have the same property as Czech, the ambiguity is not preserved. It is distributed in a different manner and the "form-for-form" translation is not applicable.
Without the analysis of at least nominal groups it is often very difficult to solve this problem, because for example the actual morphemic categories of adjectives are in Czech distinguishable only on the basis of gender, number and case agreement between an adjective and its governing noun. An alternative way to the solution of this problem was the application of a stochastically based morphological disambiguator (morphological tagger) for Czech whose success rate is close to 92%. Our system therefore consists of the following modules:

1. Import of the input from so-called 'empty' translation memory
2. Morphological analysis of Czech
3. Morphological disambiguation
4. Domain-related bilingual glossaries (incl. single- and multiword terminology)
5. General bilingual dictionary
6. Morphological synthesis of Slovak
7. Export of the output to the original translation memory

Let us now look in a more detail at the individual modules of the system:

ad 1. The input text is extracted out of a translation memory previously exported into an ASCII file. The exported translation memory (of TRADOS) has a SGML-like notation with a relatively simple structure (cf. the following example):

Example 1. – A sample of the exported translation memory
<RTF Preamble>...</RTF Preamble>
<TrU>
<CrD>23051999
<CrU>VK
<Seg L=CS_01>Pomocí výkazu ad-hoc můžete rychle a jednoduše vytvářet rešerše.
<Seg L=SK_01>n/a
</TrU>

Our system uses only the segments marked by <Seg L=CS_01>, which contain one source language sentence each, and <Seg L=SK_01>, which is empty and which will later contain the same sentence translated into the target language by ČESÍLKO.

ad 2. The morphological analysis of Czech is based on the morphological dictionary developed by Jan Hajič and Hana Skoumalová in 1988-99 (for latest description, see Hajič (1998)). The dictionary contains over 700 000 dictionary entries and its typical coverage varies between

99% (novels) to 95% (technical texts). The morphological analysis uses the system of positional tags with 15 positions (each morphological category, such as Part-of-speech, Number, Gender, Case, etc. has a fixed, single-symbol place in the tag).

Example 2 – tags assigned to the word-form "pomocí" (help/by means of)

pomocí:
NFP2------A---- | NFS7------A---- | R--2----------
where :
N – noun; R – preposition
F – feminine gender
S – singular, P – plural
7, 2 – case (7 - instrumental, 2 - genitive)
A – affirmative (non negative)

ad 3. The module of morphological disambiguation is a key to the success of the translation. It gets an average number of 3.58 tags per token (word form in text) as an input. The tagging system is purely statistical, and it uses a log-linear model of probability distribution – see Hajič, Hladká (1998). The learning is based on a manually tagged corpus of Czech texts (mostly from the general newspaper domain). The system learns contextual rules (features) automatically and also automatically determines feature weights. The average accuracy of tagging is between 91 and 93% and remains the same even for technical texts (if we disregard the unknown names and foreign-language terms that are not ambiguous anyway).
The lemmatization immediately follows tagging; it chooses the first lemma with a possible tag corresponding to the tag selected. Despite this simple lemmatization method, and also thanks to the fact that Czech words are rarely ambiguous in their Part-of-speech, it works with an accuracy exceeding 98%.

ad 4. The domain-related bilingual glossaries contain pairs of individual words and pairs of multiple-word terms. The glossaries are organized into a hierarchy specified by the user; typically, the glossaries for the most specific domain are applied first. There is one general matching rule for all levels of glossaries – the longest match wins.

The multiple-word terms are sequences of lemmas (not word forms). This structure has several advantages, among others it allows to minimize the size of the dictionary and also, due to the simplicity of the structure, it allows modifications of the glossaries by the linguistically naive user. The necessary morphological information is introduced into the domain-related glossary in an off-line preprocessing stage, which does not require user intervention. This makes a big difference when compared to the RUSLAN Czech-to-Russian MT system, when each multiword dictionary entry cost about 30 minutes of linguistic expert's time on average.

ad 5. The main bilingual dictionary contains data necessary for the translation of both lemmas and tags. The translation of tags (from the Czech into the Slovak morphological system) is necessary, because due to the morphological differences both systems use close, but slightly different tagsets. Currently the system handles the 1:1 translation of tags (and 2:2, 3:3, etc.). Different ratio of translation is very rare between Czech and Slovak, but nevertheless an advanced system of dictionary items is under construction (for the translation 1:2, 2:1 etc.). It is quite interesting that the lexically homonymous words often preserve their homonymy even after the translation, so no special treatment of homonyms is deemed necessary.

ad 6. The morphological synthesis of Slovak is based on a monolingual dictionary of Slovak, developed by J.Hric (1991-99), covering more than 100,000 dictionary entries. The coverage of the dictionary is not as high as of the Czech one, but it is still growing. It aims at a similar coverage of Slovak as we enjoy for Czech.

ad 7. The export of the output of the system ČESÍLKO into the translation memory (of TRADOS Translator's Workbench) amounts mainly to cleaning of all irrelevant SGML markers. The whole resulting Slovak sentence is inserted into the appropriate location in the original translation memory file. The following example also shows that the marker <CrU> contains an information that the target language sentence was created by an MT system.

Example 3. – A sample of the translation memory containing the results of MT

<RTF Preamble>...</RTF Preamble>
<TrU>
<CrD>23051999
<CrU>MT!
<Seg L=CS_01>Pomocí výkazu ad-hoc můžete rychle a jednoduše vytvářet rešerše.
<Seg L=SK_01>Pomocí výkazov ad-hoc môžete rýchlo a jednoducho vytvárať rešerše.
</TrU>

3.2 Evaluation of results

The problem how to evaluate results of automatic translation is very difficult. For the evaluation of our system we have exploited the close connection between our system and the TRADOS Translator's Workbench. The method is simple – the human translator receives the translation memory created by our system and translates the text using this memory. The translator is free to make any changes to the text proposed by the translation memory. The target text created by a human translator is then compared with the text created by the mechanical application of translation memory to the source text. TRADOS then evaluates the percentage of matching in the same manner as it normally evaluates the percentage of matching of source text with sentences in translation memory. Our system achieved about 90% match (as defined by the TRADOS match module) with the results of human translation, based on a relatively large (more than 10,000 words) test sample.

4. Conclusions

The accuracy of the translation achieved by our system justifies the hypothesis that word-for-word translation might be a solution for MT of really closely related languages. The remaining problems to be solved are problems with the one-to many or many-to-many translation, where the lack of information in glossaries and dictionaries sometimes causes an unnecessary translation error.

The success of the system ČESÍLKO has encouraged the investigation of the possibility to use the same method for other pairs of Slavic languages, namely for Czech-to-Polish translation. Although these languages are not so similar as Czech and Slovak, we hope that an addition of a simple partial noun phrase parsing might provide results with the quality comparable to the full-fledged syntactic analysis based system RUSLAN (this is of course true also for the Czech-to-Slovak translation). The first results of Czech-to Polish translation are quite encouraging in this respect, even though we could not perform as rigorous testing as we did for Slovak.

Acknowledgements

This project was supported by the grant GAČR 405/96/K214 and partially by the grant GAČR 201/99/0236 and project of the Ministry of Education No. VS96151.

References

Bémová, Alevtina and Kuboň, Vladislav (1990). *Czech-to-Russian Transducing Dictionary*; In: Proceedings of the XIIIth COLING conference, Helsinki 1990

Hajič, Jan (1998). *Building and Using a Syntactially Annotated Coprus: The Prague Dependency Treebank*. In: Festschrift for Jarmila Panevová, Karolinum Press, Charles Universitz, Prague. pp. 106—132.

Hajič, Jan and Barbora Hladká (1998). *Tagging Inflective Languages. Prediction of Morphological Categories for a Rich, Structured Tagset.* ACL-Coling'98, Montreal, Canada, August 1998, pp. 483-490.

Hajič, Jan; Brill, Eric; Collins, Michael; Hladká Barbora; Jones, Douglas; Kuo, Cynthia; Ramshaw, Lance; Schwartz, Oren; Tillman, Christoph; and Zeman, Daniel: *Core Natural Language Processing Technology Applicable to Multiple Languages.* The Workshop'98 Final Report. CLSP JHU. Also at: http://www.clsp.jhu.edu/ws98/projects/nlp/report.

Kirschner, Zdeněk (1987). APAC3-2: *An English-to-Czech Machine Translation System*; Explizite Beschreibung der Sprache und automatische Textbearbeitung XIII, MFF UK Prague

Oliva, Karel (1989). *A Parser for Czech Implemented in Systems Q*; Explizite Beschreibung der Sprache und automatische Textbearbeitung XVI, MFF UK Prague

Cross-Language Multimedia Information Retrieval

Sharon Flank
eMotion, Inc.
2600 Park Tower Dr., Vienna, VA 22180 USA
sharon.flank@emotion.com

Abstract

Simple measures can achieve high-accuracy cross-language retrieval in carefully chosen applications. Image retrieval is one of those applications, with results ranging from 68% of human translator performance for German, to 100% for French.

1 Introduction

Information is increasingly global, and the need to access it crosses language barriers. The topic of this paper, cross-language information retrieval, concerns the automatic retrieval of text in one language via a query in a different language. A considerable body of literature has grown up around cross-language information retrieval (e.g. Grefenstette 1998, TREC-7 1999). There are two basic approaches. Either the query can be translated, or each entire document can be translated into the same language as the query. The accuracy of retrieval across languages, however, is generally not good. One of the weaknesses that plagues cross-language retrieval is that we do not have a good sense of who the users are, or how best to interact with them.

In this paper we describe a multimedia application for which cross-language information retrieval works particularly well. eMotion, Inc. has developed a natural language information retrieval application that retrieves images, such as photographs, based on short textual descriptions or captions. The captions are typically one to three sentences, although they may also contain strings of keywords. Typical queries are, as in most Web search applications, two to three words in length. At this point, all of the captions are in English. eMotion hosts a large database of images for sale and for licensing, PictureQuest. At least 10% of PictureQuest's user base is outside the United States. The tests were performed on the PictureQuest database of approximately 400,000 images.

Recent Web utilization data for PictureQuest indicate that of the 10% of users from outside the United States, a significant portion come from Spanish-speaking, French-speaking, and German-speaking countries. It is expected that adding appropriate language interfaces and listing PictureQuest in foreign-language search engines will dramatically increase non-English usage.

2 The Cross-Language Multimedia Retrieval Application

This paper offers several original contributions to the literature on cross-language information retrieval. First, the choice of application is novel, and significant because it simplifies the language problem enough to make it tractable. Because the objects retrieved are images and not text, they are instantly comprehensible to the user regardless of language issues. This fact makes it possible for users to perform a relevance assessment without the need for any kind of translation. More important, users themselves can select objects of interest, without recourse to translation. The images are, in fact, associated with caption information, but, even in the monolingual system, few users ever even view the captions. It should be noted that most of the images in PictureQuest are utilized for advertising and publishing, rather than for news applications. Users of history and news photos do tend to check the captions, and often users in publishing will view the captions. For advertising, however, what the image itself conveys is far more important than the circumstances under which it was created.

Another significant contribution of this paper is the inclusion of a variety of machine translation systems. None of the systems tested is a high-end machine translation system: all are freely available on the Web.

Another key feature of this paper is the careful selection of an accuracy measure appropriate to the circumstances of the application. The standard measure, percent of monolingual performance achieved, is used, with a firm focus on precision. In this application, users are able to evaluate only what they see, and generally have no idea what else is present in the collection. As a result, precision is of far more interest to customers than recall. Recall is, however, of interest to image suppliers, and in any case it would not be prudent to optimize for precision without taking into account the recall tradeoff.

The PictureQuest application avoids several of the major stumbling blocks that stand in the way of high-accuracy cross-language retrieval. Ballesteros and Croft (1997) note several pitfalls common to cross-language information retrieval:

(1) The dictionary may not contain specialized vocabulary (particularly bilingual dictionaries).

(2) Dictionary translations are inherently ambiguous and add extraneous terms to the query.

(3) Failure to translate multi-term concepts as phrases reduces effectiveness.

In the PictureQuest application, these pitfalls are minimized because the queries are short, not paragraph-long descriptions as in TREC (see, e.g., Voorhees and Harman 1999). This would be a problem for a statistical approach, since the queries present little context, but, since we are not relying on context (because reducing ambiguity is not our top priority) it makes our task simpler. Assuming that the translation program keeps multi-term concepts intact, or at least that it preserves the modifier-head structure, we can successfully match phrases. The captions (i.e. the documents to be retrieved) are mostly in sentences, and their phrases are intact. The phrase recognizer identifies meaningful phrases (e.g. *fire engine*) and handles them as a unit. The pattern matcher recognizes core noun phrases and makes it more likely that they will match correctly.

Word choice can be a major issue as well for cross-language retrieval systems. Some ambiguity problems can be resolved through the use of a part-of-speech tagger on the captions. As Resnik and Yarowsky (in press) observe, part-of-speech tagging considerably reduces the word sense disambiguation problem. However, some ambiguity remains. For example, the decision to translate a word as *car*, *automobile*, or *vehicle*, may dramatically affect retrieval accuracy. The PictureQuest system uses a semantic net based on WordNet (Fellbaum 1998) to expand terms. Thus a query for *car* or *automobile* will retrieve essentially identical results; *vehicle* will be less accurate but will still retrieve many of the same images. So while word choice may be a significant consideration for a system like that of Jang et al., 1999, its impact on PictureQuest is minimal.

The use of WordNet as an aid to information retrieval is controversial, and some studies indicate it is more hindrance than help (e.g. Voorhees 1993, 1994, Smeaton, Kelledy and O'Donnell 1995). WordNet uses extremely fine-grained distinctions, which can interfere with precision even in monolingual information retrieval. In a cross-language application, the additional senses can add confounding mistranslations. If, on the other hand, WordNet expansion is constrained, the correct translation may be missed, lowering recall. In the PictureQuest application, we have tuned WordNet expansion levels and the corresponding weights attached to them so that WordNet serves to increase recall with minimal impact on precision (Flank 2000). This tuned expansion appears to be beneficial in the cross-language application as well.

Gilarranz, Gonzalo and Verdejo (1997) point out that, for cross-language information retrieval, some precision is lost in any case, and WordNet is more likely to enhance cross-linguistic than monolingual applications.

In fact, Smeaton and Quigley (1996) conclude that WordNet is indeed helpful in image retrieval, in particular because image captions are too short for statistical analysis to be useful. This insight is what led us to develop a proprietary image retrieval engine in the first place: fine-grained linguistic analysis is more useful that a statistical approach in a caption averaging some thirty words. (Our typical captions are longer than those reported in Smeaton and Quigley 1996).

3 Translation Methodology

We performed preliminary testing using two translation methodologies. For the initial tests, we chose European languages: French, Spanish, and German. Certainly this choice simplifies the translation problem, but in our case it also reflects the most pressing business need for translation. For the French, Spanish, and German tests, we used Systran as provided by AltaVista (Babelfish); we also tested several other Web translation programs. We used native speakers to craft queries and then translated those queries either manually or automatically and submitted them to PictureQuest. The resulting image set was evaluated for precision and, in a limited fashion, for recall.

The second translation methodology employed was direct dictionary translation, tested only for Spanish. We used the same queries for this test. Using an on-line Spanish-English dictionary, we selected, for each word, the top (top-frequency) translation. We then submitted this word-by-word translation to PictureQuest. (Unlike AltaVista, this method spell-corrected letters entered without the necessary diacritics.) Evaluation proceeded in the same manner. The word-by-word method introduces a weakness in phrase recognition: any phrase recognition capabilities in the retrieval system are defeated if phrases are not retained in the input. We can assume that the non-English-speaking user will, however, recognize phrases in her or his own language, and look them up as phrases where possible. Thus we can expect at least those multiword phrases that have a dictionary entry to be correctly understood. We still do lose the noun phrase recognition capabilities in the retrieval system, further confounded by the fact that in Spanish adjectives follow the nouns they modify. In the *hombre de negocios* example in the data below, both AltaVista and Langenscheidt correctly identify the phrase as multiword, and translate it as *businessman* rather than *man of businesses*.

The use of phrase recognition has been shown to be helpful, and, optimally, we would like to include it. Hull and Grefenstette 1996 showed the upper bound of the improvements possible by using lexicalized phrases. Every phrase that appeared was added to the dictionary, and that tactic did aid retrieval. Both statistical co-occurrence and syntactic phrases are also possible approaches. Unfortunately, the extra-system approach we take here relies heavily on the external machine translation to preserve phrases intact. If AltaVista (or, in the case of Langenscheidt, the user) recognizes a phrase and translates it as a unit, the translation is better and retrieval is likely to be better. If, however, the translation mistakenly misses a phrase, retrieval quality is likely to be worse. As for compositional noun phrases, if the translation preserves normal word order, then the PictureQuest-internal noun phrase recognition will take effect. That is, if *jeune fille* translates as *young girl*, then PictureQuest will understand that *young* is an adjective modifying *girl*. In the more difficult case, if the translation preserves the correct order in translating *la selva africana*, i.e. *the African jungle*, then noun phrase recognition will work. If, however, it comes out as *the jungle African*, then retrieval will be worse. In the architecture described here, fixing this problem requires access to the internals of the machine translation program.

4 Evaluation

Evaluating precision and recall on a large corpus is a difficult task. We used the evaluation methods detailed in Flank 1998. Precision was evaluated using a crossing measure, whereby any image ranked higher than a better match was penalized. Recall per se was measured only with respect to a defined subset of the images. Ranking incorporates some recall measures into the precision score, since images ranked too low are a recall problem, and images marked too high are a precision problem. If there are three good matches, and the third shows up as #4, the bogus #3 is a precision problem, and the too-low #4 is a recall problem.

For evaluation of the overall cross-language retrieval performance, we simply measured the ratio between the cross-language and monolingual retrieval accuracy (C/M%). This is standard; see, for example, Jang et al. 1999.

Table 1 illustrates the percentage of monolingual retrieval performance we achieved for the translation tests performed. In this instance, we take the precision performance of the human-translated queries and normalize it to 100%, and adjust the other translation modalities relative to the human baseline.

Language	**Raw Precision (%)**	**C/M (%)**
French (Human)	80	100
French (AltaVista)	86	100
French (Transparent Language)	66	83

Language	Raw Precision (%)	C/M (%)
French (Intertran)	44	55
Spanish (Human)	90	100
Spanish (AltaVista)	53	59
Spanish (Langenscheidt Bilingual Dictionary)	63	70
German (Human)	80	100
German (AltaVista)	54	68

Several other factors make the PictureQuest application a particularly good application for machine translation technology. Unlike document translation, there is no need to match every word in the description; useful images may be retrieved even if a word or two is lost. There are no discourse issues at all: searches never use anaphora, and no one cares if the translated query sounds good or not.

In addition, the fact that the objects being retrieved were images greatly simplified the endeavor. Under normal circumstances, developing a user-friendly interface is a major challenge. Users with only limited (or nonexistent) reading knowledge of the language of the documents need a way to determine, first, which ones are useful, and second, what they say. In the PictureQuest application, however, the retrieved assets are images. Users can instantly assess which images meet their needs.

In conclusion, it appears that simple on-line translation of queries can support effective cross-language information retrieval, for certain applications. We showed how an image retrieval application eliminates some of the problems of cross-language retrieval, and how carefully tuned WordNet expansion simplifies word choice issues. We used a variety of machine translation systems, none of them high-end and all of them free, and nonetheless achieved commercially viable results.

5 Appendix: Data

Source	Example	Score
OrigSp	1. hombres reparando carretera	
Human	men repairing road	100
AV	men repairing wagon	0
Lang.	man repair road	100
OrigSp	2. mujer vestida de rojo comprando en una tienda	
Human	woman wearing red shopping in store	100
AV	woman dressed red buying in one tends	90 (2 of 20 bad)
Lang.	woman clothe red buy in shop	wearing red is lost 75 (5 of 20 bad)
OrigSp	3. carros manejando por la autopista	
Human	cars driving on the highway	100
AV	cars handling by the freeway	80 (4 of 20 bad)
Lang.	cart handle for the expressway	0
OrigSp	4. leones cazando en la selva africana	
Human	lions hunting in the African forest	80 (1 of 5 bad)
AV	lions hunting in the African forest	80 (1 of 5 bad)
Lang.	lion hunt in the jungle	45 (11 of 20 bad)
OrigSp	5. malabarista con usando bolas de colores	
Human	juggler using colorful balls	67 (1 of 3 bad)
AV	juggler with using balls of colors	50 (4 of 8 bad)
Lang.	juggler by means of use ball colour	(0; 1 should be there)
OrigSp	6. niños rubios jugando con canicas	

Source	Example	Score
Human	blonde children playing with marbles	90 (#3 should be #1; remainder of top 20 ok)
AV	blond children playing with marbles	90 (2 of 20 bad)
Lang.	young fair play by means of marble	50 (1 of 2 bad)
OrigSp	7. poder adquisitivo	
Human	buying power	
AV	spending power	45 (11 of 20 bad)
Lang.	purchasing power	100
OrigSp	8. exitoso hombre de negocios en oficina	
AV	successful businessman in office	60 (8 of 20 bad)
Lang.	successful businessman in office	6 (8 of 20 bad)
OrigSp	9. madre e hija horneando pan en la cocina	
Human	mother and daughter baking bread in the kitchen	100 (but no full matches)
AV	mother and daughter [horneando-removed] bread in the kitchen	30 (14 of 20 bad)
Lang.	mother and child bake bread in the kitchen	100 (but no full matches)
OrigSp	10. vejez y soledad	
Human	old age and loneliness	100
AV	oldness and solitude	0
Lang.	old age and loneliness	100

5.1 Spanish

Human translations, tested on PictureQuest: 90% (normalize to 100%)

AltaVista: 53% (59% normalized)

Langenscheidt, word-by-word: 63% (70% normalized)

5.1.1 AltaVista

For AltaVista, we left out the words that AltaVista didn't translate.

5.1.2 Langenscheidt

Langenscheidt, word-by-word: 63% (70% normalized)

For the Langenscheidt word-by-word, we used the bilingual dictionary to translate each word separately as if we knew no English at all, and always took the first translation. We made the following adjustments:

1. Left out "una," since Langenscheidt mapped it to "unir" rather than to either *a* or *one*

2. Translated "e" as *and* instead of *e*

5.2 French

Human translations, tested on PictureQuest: 80%

AltaVista: 86% (100% normalized)

Transparent Language (freetranslation.com): 66% (83% normalized)

Intertran (www.intertran.net:2000): 44% (55% normalized)

[French examples originally drawn from http://humanities.uchicago.edu/ARTFL/projects/academie/1835.searchform.html: French-French]

Source	Example	Score
OrigFr	1. signes du zodiaque	
Human	signs of the zodiac	100
AV	signs of the zodiac	100
TrLang	sign zodiaque	0
IntrTran	[signes] any zodiac	100
OrigFr	2. poisson dans l'eau	
Human	fish in water	30 (14 of 20 bad)
AV	fish in water	30 (14 of 20 bad)
TrLang	fish in water	30 (14 of 20 bad)
IntrTran	fish at water	30 (14 of 20 bad)
OrigFr	3. Les maux d'oreille	

Source	Example	Score
	douloureux	
Human	painful earaches	100
AV	Painful earaches	100
TrLang	the painful ear evil	0
IntrTran	the [maux] [doreille]' distressing	0
OrigFr	4. Prendre un lapin par les oreilles	
Human	to take a rabbit by the ears	65 (7 of 20 bad)
AV	To take a rabbit by the ears	65 (7 of 20 bad)
TrLang	take a rabbit by the ears	65 (7 of 20 bad)
IntrTran	capture a bunny by the ears	80 (1 of 5 bad)
OrigFr	5. Chat qui vit dans les bois	
Human	cat which lives in wood	45 (11 of 20 bad)
AV	Cat which lives in wood	45 (11 of 20 bad)
TrLang	cat that lives in wood	65 (7 of 20 bad)
IntrTran	cat thanksgiving lives at the forest	70 (6 of 20 bad)
OrigFr	6. Sortir d'une maison	
Human	to leave a house	60 (8 of 20 bad)
AV	To leave a house	60 (8 of 20 bad)
TrLang	to go out of a house	95 (1 of 20 bad)
IntrTran	come out dune' dwelling house	90 (18 of 20 bad)
OrigFr	7. Instrument de charpentier	
Human	carpenter's tool	95 (1 of 20 bad)
AV	Instrument of carpenter	100
TrLang	instrument of carpenter	100
IntrTran	implement any carpenter	35 (13 of 20 bad)
OrigFr	8. jouer du violon	
Human	to play the violin	100
AV	to play of the violin	100
TrLang	to play the violin	100
IntrTran	gamble any violin	0
OrigFr	9. Les plaisirs du corps	
Human	pleasures of the body	100
AV	Pleasures of the body	100
TrLang	the pleasures of the body	100
IntrTran	the delight any body	0
OrigFr	10. une jeune fille mange du fruit	
Human	a girl eats fruit	100
AV	a girl eats fruit	100
TrLang	a girl eats fruit	100
IntrTran	a girl am eating any fruit	65 (7 of 20 bad)

5.3 German

Human translations, tested on PictureQuest: 80% (100% normalized)

AltaVista 54% (68% normalized)

Source	Example	Score
OrigGr	1. Golfplatz	
Human	boys golf course	95
AV	golf course	95
OrigGr	2. künstliche Paradiese	
Human	artificial paradise	100
AV	artificial paradiese	0
OrigGr	3. Solarenergie für Autos	
Human	solar energy for automobiles	95
AV	solar energy for auto	95
OrigGr	4. wanderungen durch den Wald	
Human	hiking through the forest	90
AV	migrations by the forest	0
OrigGr	5. Elefanten im Zoo	
Human	an elephant in a zoo	25 (#17 should be #2)
AV	elephant in the zoo	100
OrigGr	6. die Synthese der Desoxynribonukleinsäure	
Human	the synthesis of desoxyribonucleic acid	100
AV	the synthesis of the Desoxynribonukleinsaeure	0
OrigGr	7. schwarze Autos	
Human	black cars	100
AV	black auto	100
OrigGr	8. jungen zusammen spielen	
Human	playing together	60
AV	young together play	35

Source	Example	Score
OrigGr	9. Damen im blau	
Human	women in blue	65
AV	Ladies in blue	75
OrigGr	10. Damen auf Arbeit	
Human	woman at work	65
AV	Ladies on work	40

6 Acknowledgements

I am grateful to Doug Oard for comments on an earlier version of this paper.

7 References

Ballesteros, Lisa, and W. Bruce Croft, 1997. "Phrasal Translation and Query Expansion Techniques for Cross-Language Information Retrieval," in *AAAI Spring Symposium on Cross-Language Text and Speech Retrieval*, Stanford University, Palo Alto, California, March 24-26, 1997.

Fellbaum, Christiane, ed., 1998. *WordNet: An Electronic Lexical Database.* Cambridge, MA: MIT Press.

Flank, Sharon. 2000. "Does WordNet Improve Multimedia Information Retrieval?" Working paper.

Flank, Sharon. 1998. "A Layered Approach to NLP-Based Information Retrieval," in *Proceedings of COLING-ACL, 36th Annual Meeting of the Association for Computational Linguistics*, Montreal, Canada, 10-14 August 1998.

Gilarranz, Julio, Julio Gonzalo and Felisa Verdejo. 1997. "An Approach to Conceptual Text Retrieval Using the EuroWordNet Multilingual Semantic Database," in AAAI Spring Symposium on Cross-Language Text and Speech Retrieval, Stanford University, , Palo Alto, California, March 24-26, 1997. (http://www.clis.umd.edu/dlrg/filter/sss/papers)

Grefenstette, Gregory, ed., 1998. *Cross-Language Information Retrieval.* Norwell, MA: Kluwer.

Hull, David A. and Gregory Grefenstette, 1996. "Experiments in Multilingual Information Retrieval," in *Proceedings of the 19th International Conference on Research and Development in Information Retrieval (SIGIR96)* Zurich, Switzerland.

Jang, Myung-Gil, Sung Hyon Myaeng, and Se Young Park, 1999. "Using Mutual Information to Resolve Query Translation Ambiguities and Query Term Weighting," in *Proceedings of 37th Annual Meeting of the Association for Computational Linguistics*, College Park, Maryland.

McCarley, J. Scott, 1999. "Should We Translate the Documents or the Queries in Cross-Language Information Retrieval?"

Resnik, Philip and Yarowsky, David, in press. "Distinguishing Systems and Distinguishing Sense: New Evaluation Methods for Word Sense Disambiguation," *Natural Language Engineering.*

Smeaton, Alan F., F. Kelledy and R. O'Donnell, 1995. "TREC-4 Experiments at Dublin City University: Thresholding Posting Lists, Query Expansion with WordNet and POS Tagging of Spanish," in Donna K. Harman (ed.) NIST Special Publication 500-236: *The Fourth Text REtrieval Conference (TREC-4)*, Gaithersburg, MD, USA: Department of Commerce, National Institute of Standards and Technology. (http://trec.nist.gov/pubs/trec4/t4_proceedings.html)

Smeaton, Alan F. and I. Quigley, 1996. "Experiments on Using Semantic Distances Between Words in Image Caption Retrieval," in *Proceedings of the 19th International Conference on Research and Development in Information Retrieval (SIGIR96)* Zurich, Switzerland.

Voorhees, Ellen M. 1994. "Query Expansion Using Lexical-Semantic Relations," in *Proceedings of the 17th International ACM SIGIR Conference on Research and Development in Information Retrieval*, pp. 61-70.

Voorhees, Ellen M. 1993. "Using WordNet to Disambiguate Word Senses for Text Retrieval," in *Proceedings of the 16th International ACM SIGIR Conference on Research and Development in Information Retrieval*, pp. 171-180.

Voorhees, Ellen M. and Donna K. Harman, editors, 1999. *The 7th Text Retrieval Conference (TREC-7).*

Automatic construction of parallel English-Chinese corpus for cross-language information retrieval

Jiang Chen and Jian-Yun Nie
Département d'Informatique et Recherche Opérationnelle
Université de Montréal
C.P. 6128, succursale CENTRE-VILLE
Montreal (Quebec), Canada H3C 3J7
{*chen, nie*}*@iro.umontreal.ca*

Abstract

A major obstacle to the construction of a probabilistic translation model is the lack of large parallel corpora. In this paper we first describe a parallel text mining system that finds parallel texts automatically on the Web. The generated Chinese-English parallel corpus is used to train a probabilistic translation model which translates queries for Chinese-English cross-language information retrieval (CLIR). We will discuss some problems in translation model training and show the preliminary CLIR results.

1 Introduction

Parallel texts have been used in a number of studies in computational linguistics. Brown et al. (1993) defined a series of probabilistic translation models for MT purposes. While people may question the effectiveness of using these models for a full-blown MT system, the models are certainly valuable for developing translation assistance tools. For example, we can use such a translation model to help complete target text being drafted by a human translator (Langlais et al., 2000).

Another utilization is in cross-language information retrieval (CLIR) where queries have to be translated from one language to another language in which the documents are written. In CLIR, the quality requirement for translation is relatively low. For example, the syntactic aspect is irrelevant. Even if the translated word is not a true translation but is strongly related to the original query, it is still helpful. Therefore, CLIR is a suitable application for such a translation model.

However, a major obstacle to this approach is the lack of parallel corpora for model training. Only a few such corpora exist, including the Hansard English-French corpus and the HKUST English-Chinese corpus (Wu, 1994). In this paper, we will describe a method which automatically searches for parallel texts on the Web. We will discuss the text mining algorithm we adopted, some issues in translation model training using the generated parallel corpus, and finally the translation model's performance in CLIR.

2 Parallel Text Mining Algorithm

The PTMiner system is an intelligent Web agent that is designed to search for large amounts of parallel text on the Web. The mining algorithm is largely language independent. It can thus be adapted to other language pairs with only minor modifications.

Taking advantage of Web search engines as much as possible, PTMiner implements the following steps (illustrated in Fig. 1):

1 Search for candidate sites – Using existing Web search engines, search for the candidate sites that may contain parallel pages;

2 File name fetching – For each candidate site, fetch the URLs of Web pages that are indexed by the search engines;

3 Host crawling – Starting from the URLs collected in the previous step, search through each candidate site separately for more URLs;

4 Pair scan – From the obtained URLs of each site, scan for possible parallel pairs;

5 Download and verifying – Download the parallel pages, determine file size, language, and character set of each page, and filter out non-parallel pairs.

2.1 Search for candidate Sites

We take advantage of the huge number of Web sites indexed by existing search engines in determining candidate sites. This is done by submitting some particular requests to the search engines. The requests are determined according to the following observations. In the sites where parallel text exists, there are normally some pages in one language containing links to the parallel version in the other language. These are usually indicated by those links' anchor texts [1]. For example, on some English page there may be a link to its Chinese version with the anchor text "Chinese Version" or "in Chinese".

[1] An anchor text is a piece of text on a Web page which, when clicked on, will take you to another linked page. To be helpful, it usually contains the key information about the linked page.

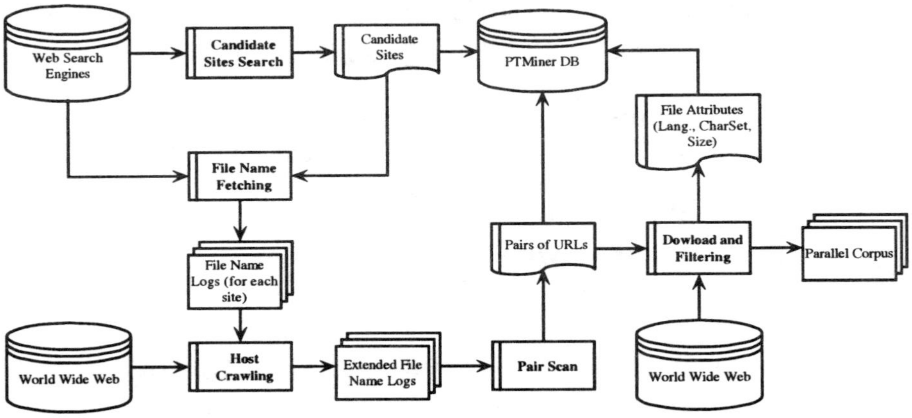

Figure 1: The workflow of the mining process.

The same phenomenon can be observed on Chinese pages. Chances are that a site with parallel texts will contain such links in some of its documents. This fact is used as the criterion in searching for candidate sites.

Therefore, to determine possible sites for English-Chinese parallel texts, we can request an English document containing the following anchor:

anchor : *"english version"* [*"in english"*, ...].

Similar requests are sent for Chinese documents.

From the two sets of pages obtained by the above queries we extract two sets of Web sites. The union of these two sets constitutes then the candidate sites. That is to say, a site is a candidate site when it is found to have either an English page linking to its Chinese version or a Chinese page linking to its English version.

2.2 File Name Fetching

We now assume that a pair of parallel texts exists on the same site. To search for parallel pairs on a site, PTMiner first has to obtain all (or at least part of) the HTML file names on the site. From these names pairs are scanned. It is possible to use a Web crawler to explore the candidate sites completely. However, we can take advantage of the search engines again to accelerate the process. As the first step, we submit the following query to the search engines:

host : *hostname*

to fetch the Web pages that they indexed from this site. If we only require a small amount of parallel texts, this result may be sufficient. For our purpose, however, we need to explore the sites more thoroughly using a host crawler. Therefore, we continue our search for files with a host crawler which uses the documents found by the search engines as the starting point.

2.3 Host Crawling

A host crawler is slightly different from a Web crawler. Web crawlers go through innumerable pages and hosts on the Web. A host crawler is a Web crawler that crawls through documents on a given host only. A breadth-first crawling algorithm is applied in PTMiner as host crawler. The principle is that when a link to an unexplored document on the same site is found in a document, it is added to a list that will be explored later. In this way, most file names from the candidate sites are obtained.

2.4 Pair Scan

After collecting file names for each candidate site, the next task is to determine the parallel pairs. Again, we try to use some heuristic rules to guess which files may be parallel texts before downloading them. The rules are based on external features of the documents. By external feature, we mean those features which may be known without analyzing the contents of the file, such as its URL, size, and date. This is in contrast with the internal features, such as language, character set, and HTML structure, which cannot be known until we have downloaded the page and analyzed its contents.

The heuristic criterion comes from the following observation: We observe that parallel text pairs usually have similar name patterns. The difference between the names of two parallel pages usually lies in a segment which indicates the language. For example, "file-ch.html" (in Chinese) vs. "file-en.html" (in English). The difference may also appear in the path, such as ".../chinese/.../file.html" vs. ".../english/.../file.html". The name patterns described above are commonly used by webmasters to help organize their sites. Hence, we can suppose that a pair of pages with this kind of pattern are probably parallel texts.

First, we establish four lists for English prefixes, English suffixes, Chinese prefixes and Chinese suffixes. For example: $English\ Prefix = \{e, en, e\_, en\_, e-, en-, ...\}$. For each file in one language, if a segment in its name corresponds to one of the language affixes, several new names are generated by changing the segment to the possible corresponding affixes of the other language. If a generated name corresponds to an existing file, then the file is considered as a candidate parallel document of the original file.

2.5 Filtering

Next, we further examine the contents of the paired files to determine if they are really parallel according to various external and internal features. This may further improve the pairing precision. The following methods have been implemented in our system.

2.5.1 Text Length

Parallel files often have similar file lengths. One simple way to filter out incorrect pairs is to compare the lengths of the two files. The only problem is to set a reasonable threshold that will not discard too many good pairs, i.e. balance recall and precision. The usual difference ratio depends on the language pairs we are dealing with. For example, Chinese-English parallel texts usually have a larger difference ratio than English-French parallel texts. The filtering threshold had to be determined empirically, from the actual observations. For Chinese-English, a difference up to 50% is tolerated.

2.5.2 Language and Character Set

It is also obvious that the two files of a pair have to be in the two languages of interest. By automatically identifying language and character set, we can filter out the pairs that do not satisfy this basic criterion. Some Web pages explicitly indicate the language and the character set. More often such information is omitted by authors. We need some language identification tool for this task.

SILC is a language and encoding identification system developed by the RALI laboratory at the University of Montreal. It employs a probabilistic model estimated on tri-grams. Using these models, the system is able to determine the most probable language and encoding of a text (Isabelle et al., 1997).

2.5.3 HTML Structure and Alignment

In the STRAND system (Resnik, 1998), the candidate pairs are evaluated by aligning them according to their HTML structures and computing confidence values. Pairs are assumed to be wrong if they have too many mismatching markups or low confidence values.

Comparing HTML structures seems to be a sound way to evaluate candidate pairs since parallel pairs usually have similar HTML structures. However, we also noticed that parallel texts may have quite different HTML structures. One of the reasons is that the two files may be created using two HTML editors. For example, one may be used for English and another for Chinese, depending on the language handling capability of the editors. Therefore, caution is required when measuring structure difference numerically.

Parallel text alignment is still an experimental area. Measuring the confidence values of an alignment is even more complicated. For example, the alignment algorithm we used in the training of the statistical translation model produces acceptable alignment results but it does not provide a confidence value that we can "confidently" use as an evaluation criterion. So, for the moment this criterion is not used in candidate pair evaluation.

3 Generated Corpus and Translation Model Training

In this section, we describe the results of our parallel text mining and translation model training.

3.1 The Corpus

Using the above approach for Chinese-English, 185 candidate sites were searched from the domain *hk*. We limited the mining domain to *hk* because Hong Kong is a bilingual English-Chinese city where high quality parallel Web sites exist. Because of the small number of candidate sites, the host crawler was used to thoroughly explore each site. The resulting corpus contains 14820 pairs of texts including 117.2Mb Chinese texts and 136.5Mb English texts. The entire mining process lasted about a week. Using length comparison and language identification, we refined the precision of the corpus to about 90%. The precision is estimated by examining 367 randomly picked pairs.

3.2 Statistical Translation Model

Many approaches in computational linguistics try to extract translation knowledge from previous translation examples. Most work of this kind establishes probabilistic models from parallel corpora. Based on one of the statistical models proposed by Brown et al. (1993), the basic principle of our translation model is the following: given a corpus of aligned sentences, if two words often co-occur in the source and target sentences, there is a good likelihood that they are translations of each other. In the simplest case (model 1), the model learns the probability, $p(t|s)$, of having a word t in the translation of a sentence containing a word s. For an input sentence, the model then calculates a sequence of words that are most probable to appear in its translation. Using a similar statistical model, Wu (1995) extracted a large-scale English-Chinese lexicon from the HKUST cor-

<s id="0000"> <HTML> <HEAD> <META HTTP-EQUIV="Content-type" CONTENT="text/html; charset=iso-8859-1"> <META HTTP-EQUIV="Content-language" CONTENT="Western"> </s>	<s id="0000"> <HTML> <HEAD> <META HTTP-EQUIV="Content-type" CONTENT="text/html; charset=big5"> <META HTTP-EQUIV="Content-language" CONTENT="zh"> </s>
<s id="0001"> <TITLE>Journal of Primary Education 1996, Vol., No. 1&2, pp. 19-27 </TITLE> </HEAD> </s>	<s id="0001"> <TITLE> Journal of Primary Education 1996, Vol., No. 1&2, Page 19-27 </TITLE> </HEAD> </s>
<s id="0002"> <BODY BACKGROUND="../gif/pejbg.jpg" TEXT="#000000" BGCOLOR="#ffffff"> <CENTER> </s> <s id="0003"> <H1>Journal of Primary Education </H1> </s> <s id="0004"> <HR> <B>Volume 6, No 1&2, pp. 19-27 (May, 1996) </B> <HR> </s>	<s id="0002"> <BODY BACKGROUND="../gif/pejbg.jpg" TEXT="#000000" BGCOLOR="#ffffff"> <A HREF="/en/pej/b2g_pej.phtml?URL=%2fen%2fp ej%2f0601%2f0601019c.htm"> <IMG SRC="/en/gif/kan.gif" ALT="简体" BORDER=0 ALIGN=R IGHT> </A> <CENTER> </s>
<s id="0005"> <H3>Principles for Redesigning Teacher Education </H3> Alan TOM </CENTER> </s>	<s id="0003"> <H2>初等教育学报</H2> </s> <s id="0004"> <HR>（一九九六年五月）第六卷. </s>
<s id="0006"> <P> <B> <I> Abstract </I> </B> </s>	<s id="0005"> 第一及二期19-27页 <HR> </s>

Figure 2: An alignment example using pure length-based method.

pus which is built manually. In our case, the probabilistic translation model will be used for CLIR. The requirement on our translation model may be less demanding: it is not absolutely necessary that a word t with high $p(t|s)$ always be a true translation of s. It is still useful if t is strongly related to s. For example, although "railway" is not a true translation of "train" (in French), it is highly useful to include "railway" in the translation of a query on "train". This is one of the reasons why we think a less controlled parallel corpus can be used to train a translation model for CLIR.

3.3 Parallel Text Alignment

Before the mined documents can be aligned into parallel sentences, the raw texts have to undergo a series of some preprocessing, which, to some extent, is language dependent. For example, the major operations on the Chinese-English corpus include encoding scheme transformation (for Chinese), sentence level segmentation, parallel text alignment, Chinese word segmentation (Nie et al., 1999) and English expression extraction.

The parallel Web pages we collected from various sites are not all of the same quality. Some are highly parallel and easy to align while others can be very noisy. Aligning English-Chinese parallel texts is already very difficult because of the great differences in the syntactic structures and writing systems of the two languages. A number of alignment techniques have been proposed, varying from statistical methods (Brown et al., 1991; Gale and Church, 1991) to lexical methods (Kay and Röscheisen, 1993; Chen, 1993). The method we adopted is that of Simard et al. (1992). Because it considers both length similarity and cognateness as alignment criteria, the method is more robust and better able to deal with noise than pure length-based methods. Cognates are identical sequences of characters in corresponding words in two languages. They are commonly found in English and French. In the case of English-Chinese alignment, where there are no cognates shared by the two languages, only the HTML markup in both texts are taken as cognates. Because the HTML structures of parallel pages are normally similar, the markup was found to be helpful for alignment.

To illustrate how markup can help with the alignment, we align the same pair with both the pure length-based method of Gale & Church (Fig. 2), and the method of Simard et al. (Fig. 3). First of all, we observe from the figures that the two texts are

<s id="0000"> <HTML> <HEAD> <META HTTP-EQUIV="Content-type" CONTENT="text/html; charset=iso-8859-1"> <META HTTP-EQUIV="Content-language" CONTENT="Western"> </s>	<s id="0000"> <HTML> <HEAD> <META HTTP-EQUIV="Content-type" CONTENT="text/html; charset=big5"> <META HTTP-EQUIV="Content-language" CONTENT="zh"> </s>
<s id="0001"> <TITLE>Journal of Primary Education 1996, Vol., No. 1&2, pp. 19-27 </TITLE> </HEAD> </s>	<s id="0001"> <TITLE> Journal of Primary Education 1996, Vol., No. 1&2, Page 19-27 </TITLE> </HEAD> </s>
<s id="0002"> <BODY BACKGROUND="../gif/pejbg.jpg" TEXT="#000000" BGCOLOR="#ffffff"> <CENTER> </s>	<s id="0002"> <BODY BACKGROUND="../gif/pejbg.jpg" TEXT="#000000" BGCOLOR="#ffffff"> <A HREF="/en/pej/b2g_pej.phtml?URL=%2fen%2fp ej%2f0601%2f0601019c.htm"> <IMG SRC="/en/gif/kan.gif" ALT="简体" BORDER=0 ALIGN=R IGHT> </A> <CENTER> </s>
<s id="0003"> <H1>Journal of Primary Education </H1> </s>	<s id="0003"> <H2>初等教育学报</H2> </s>
<s id="0004"> <HR> <B>Volume 6, No 1&2, pp. 19-27 (May, 1996) </B> <HR> </s>	<s id="0004"> <HR> （一九九六年五月） 第六卷. </s> <s id="0005"> 第一及二期19-27页 <HR> </s>
<s id="0005"> <H3>Principles for Redesigning Teacher Education </H3> Alan TOM </CENTER> </s>	<s id="0006"> <H3>革新教师教育的原则 </H3> Alan TOM </CENTER> </s>
<s id="0006"> <P> <B> <I> Abstract </I> </B> </s>	<s id="0007"> <P> <I> <B> 摘要 </B> </I> <P> </s>

Figure 3: An alignment example considering cognates.

divided into sentences. The sentences are marked by <s id="xxxx"> and </s>. Note that we determine sentences not only by periods, but also by means of HTML markup.

We further notice that it is difficult to align sentences 0002. The sentence in the Chinese page is much longer than its counterpart in the English page because some additional information (font) is added. The length-based method thus tends to take sentence 0002, 0003, and 0004 in the English page as the translation of sentence 0002 in the Chinese page (Fig. 2), which is wrong. This in turn provocated the three following incorrect alignments. As we can see in Fig. 3, the cognate method did not make the same mistake because of the noise in sentence 0002. Despite their large length difference, the two 0002 sentences are still aligned as a 1-1 pair, because the sentences in the following 4 alignments (0003 - 0003; 0004 - 0004, 0005; 0005 - 0006; 0006 - 0007) have rather similar HTML markups and are taken by the program to be the most likely alignments.

Beside HTML markups, other criteria may also be incorporated. For example, it would be helpful to consider strong correspondence between certain English and Chinese words, as in (Wu, 1994). We hope to implement such correspondences in our future research.

3.4 Lexicon Evaluation

To evaluate the precision of the English-Chinese translation model trained on the Web corpus, we examined two sample lexicons of 200 words, one in each direction. The 200 words for each lexicon were randomly selected from the training source. We examined the most probable translation for each word. The Chinese-English lexicon was found to have a precision of 77%. The English-Chinese lexicon has a higher precision of 81.5%. Part of the lexicons are shown in Fig. 4, where t/f indicates whether a translation is true or false.

These precisions seem to be reasonably high. They are quite comparable to that obtained by Wu (1994) using a manual Chinese-English parallel corpus.

3.5 Effect of Stopwords

We also found that stop-lists have significant effect on the translation model. Stop-list is a set of the most frequent words that we remove from the train-

English word	t/f	Translation	Probability	Chinese word	t/f	Translation	Probability
a.m.	t	上午	0.201472	办事处	t	office	0.375868
access	f	公开	0.071705	保护	t	protection	0.343071
adaptation	t	适应	0.179633	报告	t	report	0.358592
add	t	补充	0.317435	备	t	prepare	0.189513
adopt	t	采用	0.231637	本地	t	local	0.421837
agent	t	代理人	0.224902	便会	f	follow	0.023685
agree	t	同意	0.36569	标准	t	standard	0.445453
airline	t	航空公司	0.344001	补校	f	adult	0.044959
amendment	t	修订	0.367518	不足	t	inadequate	0.093012
appliance	t	用具	0.136319	部分	t	part	0.313676
apply	t	适用	0.19448	财经	t	financial	0.16608
attendance	t	列席	0.171769	参观	t	visit	0.309642
auditor	f	审核	0.15011	草案	t	bill	0.401997
average	t	平均	0.467646	车辆	t	vehicle	0.467034
base_on	f	计算	0.107304	储蓄	t	saving	0.176695

Figure 4: Part of the evaluation lexicons.

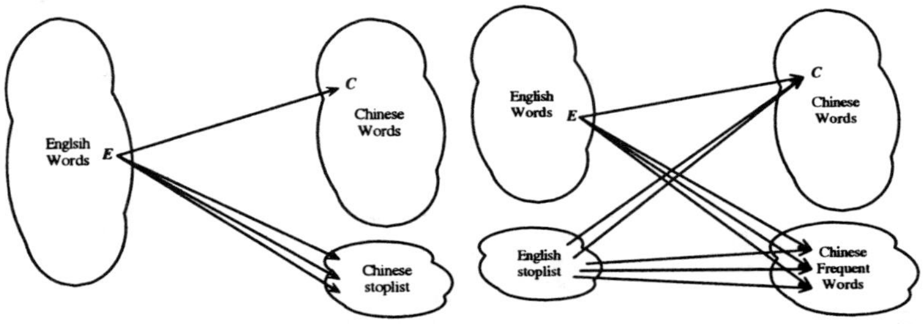

Figure 5: Effect of stop lists in C-E translation.

ing source. Because these words exist in most alignments, the statistical model cannot derive correct translations for them. More importantly, their existence greatly affects the accuracy of other translations. They can be taken as translations for many words.

A priori, it would seem that both the English and Chinese stop-lists should be applied to eliminate the noise caused by them. Interestingly, from our observation and analysis we concluded that for better precision, only the stop-list of the target language should be applied in the model training.

We first explain why the stop-list of the target language has to be applied. On the left side of Fig. 5, if the Chinese word C exists in the same alignments with the English word E more than any other Chinese words, C will be the most probable translation for E. Because of their frequent appearance, some Chinese stopwords may have more chances to be in the same alignments with E. The probability of the translation $E \rightarrow C$ is then reduced (maybe even less than those of the incorrect ones). This is the reason why many English words are translated to "的" (of) by the translation model trained without using the Chinese stop-list.

We also found that it is not necessary to remove the stopwords of the source language. In fact, as illustrated on the right side of Fig. 5, the existence of the English stopwords has two effects on the probability of the translation $E \rightarrow C$:

1 They may often be found together with the Chinese word C. Owing to the Expectation Maximization algorithm, the probability of $E \rightarrow C$ may therefore be reduced.

2 On the other hand, there is a greater likelihood that English stopwords will be found together with the most frequent Chinese words. Here, we use the term "Chinese frequent words" instead of "Chinese stopwords" because even if a stop-list is applied, there may still remain some common words that have the same effect as the stopwords. The coexistence of English and Chinese frequent words reduces the probability that the Chinese frequent words are the translations of E, and thus raise the probability of $E \rightarrow C$.

The second effect was found to be more significant than the first, since the model trained without the English stopwords has better precision than the model trained with the English stopwords. For the correct translations given by both models, the model

	C-E CLIR	E-C CLIR
Mono-Lingual IR	0.3861	0.3976
Translation Model	0.1504 (39.0%mono)	0.1841 (46.3%mono)
Dictionary	0.1530 (39.6%mono)	0.1427 (35.9%mono)
TM + DICT	0.2583 (66.9%mono)	0.2232 (56.1%mono)

Table 1: CLIR results.

trained without considering the English stopwords gives higher probabilities.

4 English-Chinese CLIR Results

Our final goal was to test the performance of the translation models trained on the Web parallel corpora in CLIR. We conducted CLIR experiments using the *Smart* IR system.

4.1 Results

The English test corpus (for C-E CLIR) was the AP corpus used in TREC6 and TREC7. The short English queries were translated manually into Chinese and then translated back to English by the translation model. The Chinese test corpus was the one used in the TREC5 and TREC6 Chinese track. It contains both Chinese queries and their English translations.

Our experiments on these two corpora produced the results shown in Tab. 1. The precision of monolingual IR is given as benchmark. In both E-C and C-E CLIR, the translation model achieved around 40% of monolingual precision. To compare with the dictionary-based approach, we employed a Chinese-English dictionary, CEDICT (Denisowski, 1999), and an English-Chinese online dictionary (Anonymous, 1999a) to translate queries. For each word of the source query, all the possible translations given by the dictionary are included in the translated query. The Chinese-English dictionary has about the same performace as the translation model, while the English-Chinese dictionary has lower precision than that of the translation model.

We also tried to combine the translations given by the translation model and the dictionary. In both C-E and E-C CLIR, significant improvements were achieved (as shown in Tab. 1). The improvements show that the translations given by the translation model and the dictionary complement each other well for IR purposes. The translation model may give either exact translations or incorrect but related words. Even though these words are not correct in the sense of translation, they are very possibly related to the subject of the query and thus helpful for IR purposes. The dictionary-based approach expands a query along another dimension. It gives all the possible translations for each word including those that are missed by the translation model.

4.2 Comparison With MT Systems

One advantage of a parallel text-based translation model is that it is easier to build than an MT system. Now that we have examined the CLIR performance of the translation model, we will compare it with two existing MT systems. Both systems were tested in E-C CLIR.

4.2.1 Sunshine WebTran Server

Using the Sunshine WebTran server (Anonymous, 1999b), an online English-Chinese MT system, to translate the 54 English queries, we obtained an average precision of 0.2001, which is 50.3% of the mono-lingual precision. The precision is higher than that obtained using the translation model (0.1804) or the dictionary (0.1427) alone, but lower than the precison obtained using them together (0.2232).

4.2.2 Transperfect

Kwok (1999) investigated the CLIR performance of an English-Chinese MT software called Transperfect, using the same TREC Chinese collection as we used in this study. Using the MT software alone, Kwok achieved 56% of monolingual precision. The precision is improved to 62% by refining the translation with a dictionary. Kwok also adopted pre-translation query expansion, which further improved the precison to 70% of the monolingual results.

In our case, the best E-C CLIR precison using the translation model (and dictionary) is 56.1%. It is lower than what Kwok achieved using Transperfect, however, the difference is not large.

4.3 Further Problems

The Chinese-English translation model has a far lower CLIR performance than that of the English-French model established using the same method (Nie et al., 1999). The principal reason for this is the fact that English and Chinese are much more different than English and French. This problem surfaced in many phases of this work, from text alignment to query translation. Below, we list some further factors affecting CLIR precision.

- The Web-collected corpus is noisy and it is difficult to align English-Chinese texts. The alignment method we employed has performed more poorly than on English-French alignment. This in turn leads to poorer performance of the translation model. In general, we observe a higher variability in Chinese-English translations than in English-French translations.

- For E-C CLIR, although queries in both languages were provided, the English queries were not strictly translated from the original Chinese ones. For example, 人权状况 (*human right situation*) was translated into *human right issue*. We cannot expect the translation model to translate *issue* back to 状况 (*situation*).
- The training source and the CLIR collections were from different domains. The Web corpus are retrieved from the parallel sites in Hong Kong while the Chinese collection is from *People's Daily* and *Xinhua News Agency*, which are published in mainland China. As the result, some important terms such as 最惠国 (*most-favored-nation*) and 一国两制 (*one-nation-two-systems*) in the collection are not known by the model.

5 Summary

The goal of this work was to investigate the feasibility of using a statistical translation model trained on a Web-collected corpus to do English-Chinese CLIR. In this paper, we have described the algorithm and implementation we used for parallel text mining, translation model training, and some results we obtained in CLIR experiments. Although further work remains to be done, we can conclude that it is possible to automatically construct a Chinese-English parallel corpus from the Web. The current system can be easily adapted to other language pairs. Despite the noisy nature of the corpus and the great difference in the languages, the evaluation lexicons generated by the translation model produced acceptable precision. While the current CLIR results are not as encouraging as those of English-French CLIR, they could be improved in various ways, such as improving the alignment method by adapting cognate definitions to HTML markup, incorporating a lexicon and/or removing some common function words in translated queries.

We hope to be able to demonstrate in the near future that a fine-tuned English-Chinese translation model can provide query translations for CLIR with the same quality produced by MT systems.

References

Anonymous. 1999a. Sunrain.net - English-Chinese dictionary. http://sunrain.net/r_ecdict_e.htm.

Anonymous. 1999b. Sunshine WebTran server. http://www.readworld.com/translate.htm.

P. F. Brown, J. C. Lai, and R. L. Mercer. 1991. Aligning sentences in parallel corpora. In *29th Annual Meeting of the Association for Computational Linguistics*, pages 89–94, Berkeley, Calif.

P. F. Brown, S. A. Della Pietra, V. J. Della Pietra, and R. L. Mercer. 1993. The mathematics of machine translation: Parameter estimation. *Computational Linguistics*, 19:263–311.

S. F. Chen. 1993. Aligning sentences in bilingual corpora using lexical information. In *Proceedings of the 31th Annual Meeting of the Association for Computational Linguistics*, pages 9–16, Columbus, Ohio.

Paul Denisowski. 1999. Cedict (chinese-english dictionary) project. http://www.mindspring.com/paul_denisowski/cedict.html.

William A. Gale and Kenneth W. Church. 1991. A program for aligning sentences in bilingual corpora. In *Proceedings of the 29th Annual Meeting of the Association for Computational Linguistics*, pages 177–184, Berkeley, Calif.

P. Isabelle, G. Foster, and P. Plamondon. 1997. SILC: un système d'identification de la langue et du codage. http://www-rali.iro.umontreal.ca/ProjetSILC.en.html.

M. Kay and M. Röscheisen. 1993. Text-translation alignment. *Computational Linguistics*, 19:121–142.

K. L. Kwok. 1999. English-chinese cross-language retrieval based on a translation package. In *Workshop of Machine Translation for Cross Language Information Retrieval, Machine Translation Summit VII*, Singapore.

P. Langlais, G. Foster, and G. Lapalme. 2000. Unit completion for a computer-aided translation typing system. In *Applied Natural Language Processing Conference (ANLP)*, Seattle, Washington, May.

Jianyun Nie, Michel Simard, Pierre Isabelle, and Richard Durand. 1999. Cross-language information retrieval based on parallel texts and automatic mining parallel texts from the Web. In *ACM SIGIR'99*, pages 74–81, August.

Philip Resnik. 1998. Parallel stands: A preliminary investigation into mining the Web for bilingual text. In *AMTA'98*, October.

Michel Simard, George F. Foster, and Pierre Isabelle. 1992. Using cognates to align sentences in bilingual corpora. In *Proceedings of TMI-92*, Montreal, Quebec.

Dekai Wu. 1994. Aligning a parallel English-Chinese corpus statistically with lexical criteria. In *ACL-94: 32nd Annual Meeting of the Assoc. for Computational Linguistics*, pages 80–87, Las Cruces, NM, June.

Dekai Wu. 1995. Large-scale automatic extraction of an English-Chinese lexicon. *Machine Translation*, 9(3-4):285–313.

PartsID: A Dialogue-Based System for Identifying Parts for Medical Systems

Amit BAGGA, Tomek STRZALKOWSKI, and G. Bowden WISE
Information Technology Laboratory
GE Corporate Research and Development
1 Research Circle
Niskayuna, USA, NY 12309
{bagga, strzalkowski, wisegb}@crd.ge.com

Abstract

This paper describes a system that provides customer service by allowing users to retrieve identification numbers of parts for medical systems using spoken natural language dialogue. The paper also presents an evaluation of the system which shows that the system successfully retrieves the identification numbers of approximately 80% of the parts.

Introduction

Currently people deal with customer service centers either over the phone or on the world wide web on a regular basis. These service centers support a wide variety of tasks including checking the balance of a bank or a credit card account, transferring money from one account to another, buying airline tickets, and filing one's income tax returns. Most of these customer service centers use interactive voice response (IVR) systems on the front-end for determining the user's need by providing a list of options that the user can choose from, and then routing the call appropriately. The IVRs also gather essential information like the user's bank account number, social security number, etc. For back-end support, the customer service centers use either specialized computer systems (example: a system that retrieves the account balance from a database), or, as in most cases, human operators.

However, the IVR systems are unwieldy to use. Often a user's needs are not covered by the options provided by the system forcing the user to hit 0 to transfer to a human operator. In addition, frequent users often memorize the sequence of options that will get them the desired information. Therefore, any change in the options greatly inconveniences these users. Moreover, there are users that always hit 0 to speak to a live operator because they prefer to deal with a human instead of a machine. Finally, as customer service providers continue to rapidly add functionality to their IVR systems, the size and complexity of these systems continues to grow proportionally. In some popular systems like the IVR system that provides customer service for the Internal Revenue Service (IRS), the user is initially bombarded with 10 different options with each option leading to sub-menus offering a further 3-5 options, and so on. The total number of nodes in the tree corresponding to the IRS' IVR system is quite large (approximately 100) making it extremely complex to use.

Some customer service providers have started to take advantage of the recent advances in speech recognition technology. Therefore, some of the IVR systems now allow users to say the option number (1, 2, 3, ..., etc.) instead of pressing the corresponding button. In addition, some providers have taken this a step further by allowing users to say a keyword or a phrase from a list of keywords and/or phrases. For example, AT&T, the long distance company, provides their users the following options: "Please say information for information on placing a call, credit for requesting credit, or operator to speak to an operator."

However, given the improved speech recognition technology, and the research done in natural language dialogue over the last decade, there exists tremendous potential in enhancing these customer service centers by allowing users to conduct a more natural human-like dialogue with an automated system to provide a customer-friendly system. In this paper we describe a system that uses natural language dialogue to provide customer service for a medical domain. The system allows field engineers to call and obtain identification numbers of parts for medical systems using natural language dialogue. We first describe some work done previously in using natural language dialogue for customer service applications. Next, we present the architecture of our system along with a description of each of the key components. Finally, we conclude by providing results from an evaluation of the system.

1. Previous Work

As mentioned earlier, some customer service centers now allow users to say either the option number or a keyword from a list of options/descriptions. However, the only known work which automates part of a customer service center using natural language dialogue is the one by Chu-Carroll and Carpenter (1999). The system described here is used as the front-end of a bank's customer service center. It routes calls by extracting key phrases from a user utterance and then by statistically comparing these phrases to phrases extracted from utterances in a training corpus consisting of pre-recorded calls where the routing was done by a human. The call is routed to the destination of the utterance from the training corpus that is most "similar" to the current utterance. On occasion, the system will interact with the user to clarify the user's request by asking a question. For example, if the user wishes to reach the loan department, the system will ask if the loan is for an automobile, or a home. Other related work is (Georgila et al., 1998).

While we are aware of the work being done by speech recognition companies like Nuance (www.nuance.com) and Speechworks (www.speechworks.com) in the area of providing more natural language dialogue-based customer service, we are not aware of any conference or journal publications from them. Some magazine articles which mention their work are (Rosen 1999 ; Rossheim 1999 ; Greenemeier 1999 ; Meisel 1999). In addition, when we tried out a demo of Nuance's systems, we found that their systems had a very IVRish feel to them. For example, if one wanted to transfer $50 from one account to another, the system would first ask the account that the money was coming from, then the account that the money was going to, and finally, the amount to be transferred. Therefore, a user could not say "I want to transfer $50 from my savings account to my checking account" and have the system conduct that transaction.

In addition to the works mentioned above, there have been several classic projects in the area of natural language dialogue like TRAINS/TRIPS project at Rochester (Allen et al., 1989, 1995, 1996), Duke's Circuit-Fixit-Shoppe and Pascal Tutoring System (Biermann et al., 1997; 1995), etc. While the Circuit-Fixit-Shoppe system helps users fix a circuit through a dialogue with the system, the TRIPS and the TRAINS projects allow users to plan their itineraries through dialogue. Duke's Pascal tutoring system helps students in an introductory programming class debug their programs by allowing them to analyze their syntax errors, get additional information on the error, and learn the correct syntax. Although these systems have been quite successful, they use detailed models of the domain and therefore cannot be used for diverse applications such as the ones required for customer service centers. Other related work on dialogue include (Carberry, 1990; Grosz and Sidner, 1986; Reichman, 1981).

2. PartsID: A System for Identification of Parts for Medical Systems

Initially, we were approached by the medical systems business of our company for help in reducing the number of calls handled by human operators at their call center. An analysis of the types of customer service provided by their call center showed that a large volume of calls handled by their operators were placed by field engineers requesting identification numbers of parts for various medical systems. The ID numbers were most often used for ordering the corresponding parts using an automated IVR system. Therefore, the system we have built

Figure 1. PartsID System Architecture

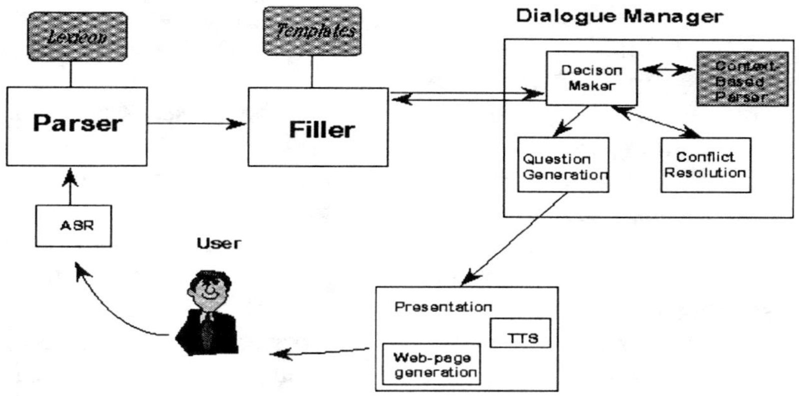

helps automate some percentage of these calls by allowing the engineer to describe a part using natural language. The rest of this section describes our system in detail.

2.1 Data

The database we used for our system was the same as the one used by the operators at the call center. This database consists of the most common parts and was built by the operators themselves. However, the data contained in the database is not clean and there are several types of errors including mis-spellings, use of non-standard abbreviations, use of several different abbreviations for the same word, etc.

The database consists of approximately 7000 different parts. For each part, the database contains its identification number, a description, and the product (machine type) that it is used in. The descriptions consist of approximately 60,000 unique words of which approximately 3,000 are words which either are non-standard abbreviations or are unique to the medical domain (example: collimator).

Due to the large size of the database, we did not attempt to clean the data. However, we did build several data structures based on the database which were used by the system. The primary data structures built were two inverted hash tables corresponding to the product, and the part description fields in the database. The inverted hash tables were built as follows:

1) Each product and part description field was split into words.
2) Stop-words (words containing no information like: a, the, an, etc.) were filtered.
3) Each remaining word was inserted as the index of the appropriate hash table with the identification number of the part being the value corresponding to the index.

Therefore, for each non-stop-word word used in describing a part, the hash table contains a list of all the parts whose descriptions contained that word. Similarly, the products hash table contains a list of all parts corresponding to each product word.

2.2 System Architecture

The architecture of the system is shown in Figure 1. The system was designed in a manner such that it could be easily ported from one application to another with minimal effort other than providing the domain-specific knowledge regarding the new application. Therefore, we decided to abstract away the domain-specific information into self-contained modules while keeping the other modules completely independent. The domain-specific modules are shown in the dark shaded boxes in Figure 1. The remainder of this section discusses each of the modules shown in the system architecture.

2.2.1 The Speech Recognition System (ASR)

Since customer service centers are meant to be used by a variety of users, we needed a user-independent speech recognition system. In addition, since the system could not restrict the manner in which a user asked for service, the speech recognition system could not be grammar-based. Therefore, we used a general purpose dictation engine for the system. The dictation system used was Lernout & Hauspie's VoiceXPress system (www.lhs.com). Although the system was general purpose, we did provide to it the set of keywords and phrases that are commonly used in the domain thereby enabling it to better recognize these domain-specific keywords and phrases. The keywords and phrases used were simply the list of descriptions and product names corresponding to each part in the database. It should be noted that the set of domain-specific keywords and phrases was provided to the speech recognition system as a text document. In other words, the training was not done by a human speaking the keywords and phrases into the speech recognition system. In addition, the speech recognition system is far from perfect. The recognition rates hover around 50%, and the system has additional difficulty in identifying product names which are most often words not found in a dictionary (examples: 3MlaserCam, 8000BUCKY, etc.).

2.2.2 Parser and the Lexicon

The parser is domain-driven in the sense that it uses domain-dependent information produced by the lexicon to look for information, in a user utterance, that is useful in the current domain. However, it does not attempt to understand fully each user utterance. It is robust enough to handle ungrammatical sentences, short phrases, and sentences that contain mis-recognized text.

The lexicon, in addition to providing domain-dependent keywords and phrases to the parser, also provides the semantic knowledge associated with each keyword and phrase. Therefore, for each content word in the inverted hash tables, the lexicon contains entries which help the system determine whether the word was used in a part description, or a product name. In addition, the lexicon also provides the semantic knowledge associated with the pre-specified actions which can be taken by the user like "*operator*" which allows the user to transfer to an operator, and "*stop*," or "*quit*" which allow the user to quit the system. Some sample entries are:

collimator => (description_word,collimator)
camera => (product_word, camera)
operator => (user action, operator)
etc.

The parser scans a user utterance and returns, as output, a list of semantic tuples associated with each keyword/phrase contained in the utterance. It is mainly interested in "key words" (words that are contained in product and part descriptions, user action words, etc.) and it ignores all the other words in the user utterance. The parser also returns a special tuple containing the entire input string which may be used later by the context-based parser for sub-string matching specially in cases when the DM has asked a specific question to the user and is expecting a particular kind of response.

2.2.3 The Filler and Template Modules

The filler takes as input the set of tuples generated by the parser and attempts to check off templates contained in the templates module using these tuples. The set of templates in the templates module contains most of remaining domain-specific knowledge required by the system. Each template is an internal representation of a part in the database. It contains for each part, its ID, its description, and the product which contains it. In addition, there are several additional templates corresponding to pre-specified user actions like "*operator*," and "*quit*." A sample template follows:

t1_1 = (
'product' => 'SFD',
'product_ids' => '2229005',
'product_descriptions' => 'IR RECEIVER PC BOARD CI104 BISTABLE MEMORY')

For each tuple input from the parser, the filler checks off the fields which correspond to the tuple. For example, if the filler gets as input *(description_word, collimator)*, it checks off the description fields of those templates containing *collimator* as a word in the field. A template is checked off *iff* one or more of its fields is checked off. In addition, the filler also maintains a list of all description and product words passed through the tuples (i.e. these words have been uttered by the user). These two lists are subsequently passed to the dialogue manager.

Although the filler does not appear to be very helpful for the current application domain, it is an important part of the architecture for other application domains. For example, the current PartsID system is a descendant from an earlier system which allowed users to process financial transactions where the filler was instrumental in helping the dialogue manager determine the type of transaction being carried out by the user (Bagga et al., 2000).

2.2.4 The Dialogue Manager (DM)

The DM receives as input from the filler the set of templates which are checked off. In addition, it also receives two lists containing the list of description words, and product word uttered by the user. The DM proceeds using the following algorithm:

1) It first checks the set of checked off templates input from the filler. If there is exactly one template in this set, the DM asks the user to confirm the part that the template corresponds to. Upon receipt of the confirmation from the user, it returns the identification number of the part to the user.
2) Otherwise, for each description word uttered by the user, the DM looks up the set of parts (or templates) containing the word from the descriptions inverted hash table. It then computes the intersection of these sets. If the intersection is empty, the DM computes the union of these sets and proceeds treating the union as the intersection.
3) If the intersection obtained from (2) above contains exactly one template, the DM asks the user to confirm the part corresponding to the template as in (1) above.
4) Otherwise, the DM looks at the set of product words uttered by the user. If this set is empty, the DM queries the user for the product name. Since the DM is expecting a product name here, the input provided by the user is handled by the context-based parser. Since most product names consist of non-standard words consisting of alpha-numeric characters (examples: AMX3, 8000BUCKY, etc.), the recognition quality is quite poor. Therefore, the context-based parser ranks the input received from the user using a sub-string matching algorithm that uses character-based unigram and bigram counts (details are provided in the next section). The sub-string matching algorithm greatly enhances the performance of the system (as shown in the sample dialogue below).
5) If the set of product words is non-empty, or if the DM has successfully queried the user for a product name, it extracts the set of parts (templates) containing each product word from the product words inverted hash table. It then computes an intersection of these sets with the intersection set of description words obtained from (2) above. The resulting intersection is the joint product and description intersection.
6) If the joint intersection has exactly one template, the DM proceeds as in (1) above. Alternatively, if the number of templates in the joint intersection is less than 4, the DM lists the parts corresponding to each of these and asks the user to confirm the correct one.
7) If there are more than 4 templates in the joint intersection, the DM ranks the templates based upon word overlap with the description words uttered by the user. If the number of resulting top-ranked templates is less than 4, the DM proceeds as in the second half of (6) above.
8) If the joint intersection is empty, or in the highly unlikely case of there being more than 4 top-ranked templates in (7), the DM asks the user to enter additional disambiguating information.

The goal of the DM is to hone in on the part (template) desired by the user, and it has to determine this from the set of templates input to it by the filler. It has to be robust enough to deal with poor recognition quality, inadequate information input by the user, and ambiguous data. Therefore, the DM is designed to handle these issues. For example, description words that are mis-recognized as other description words usually cause the intersection of the sets of parts corresponding to these words to be empty. The DM, in this case, takes a union of the sets of parts corresponding to the description words thereby ensuring that the template corresponding to the desired part is in the union.

The DM navigates the space of possibilities by first analyzing the intersection of the sets of parts corresponding to the description words uttered by the user. If no unique part emerges, the DM then checks to see if the user has provided any information about the product that the part is going to be used in. If no product was mentioned by the user, the DM queries the user for the product name. Once this is obtained, the DM then checks to see if a unique part corresponds to the product name and the part description provided by the user. If no unique part emerges, then the DM backs off and asks the user to re-enter the part description. Alternatively, if more than one part corresponds to the specified product and part description, then the DM ranks the parts based upon the number of words uttered by the user. Obviously, since the DM in this case uses a heuristic, it asks the user to confirm the part that ranks the highest. If more than one (although less than 4) parts have the same rank, then the DM explicitly lists these parts and asks the user to specify the desired part. It should be noted that the DM has to ensure that the information it receives is actually what the user meant. This is especially true when the DM uses heuristics, and sub-string matches (as in the case of product names). Therefore, the DM occasionally asks the user to confirm input it has received.

2.2.5 The Sub-String Matching Algorithm

When the dialogue manager is expecting a certain type of input (examples : product names, yes/no responses) from the user, the user response is processed by the context-based parser. Since the type of input is known, the context-based parser uses a sub-string matching algorithm that uses character-based unigram and bigram counts to match the user input with the expectation of the dialogue manager. Therefore, the sub-string matching module takes as input a user utterance string along with a list of expected responses, and it ranks the list of expected responses based upon the user response. Listed below are the details of the algorithm :

1) The algorithm first concatenates the words of the user utterance into one long string. This is needed because the speech recognition system often breaks up the utterance into words even though a single word is being said. For example, the product name AMX110 is often broken up into the string '*Amex 110*'.
2) Next, the algorithm goes through the string formed in (1) and compares this character by character with the list of expected responses. It assigns one point for every common character. Therefore, the expected response 'AMX3' gets three points for the utterance 'Amex110'.
3) The algorithm then compares the user utterance with the list of expected responses using 2 characters (bigrams) at a time. It assigns 2 points for each bigram match. For the example shown in (2), there are two bigram matches : the first is that the utterance starts with an 'A' (the previous character is this case is the null character), and the second is the bigram 'AM'.
4) The algorithm now compares the length of the user utterance string and the expected response. If the length of the two strings is the same, then it assigns 2 points to the expected response.
5) Finally, the algorithm calculates the number of unique characters in the expected response, and the user utterance string. If these characters are the same, then it assigns 4 points to the expected response.

The expected response which has the highest number of points is the most likely one. If two or more expected responses have the same number of points, then the system asks the user to confirm the correct one.

While we have not evaluated this sub-string matching algorithm independently, a brief evaluation in the context of the system resulted in about 90% accuracy.

2.2.6 The Presentation Module

The presentation module works in one of two possible modes: over the phone, and over the web. This module takes as input a string generated by the question-generation module and presents this string to the user in the appropriate mode of communication. If the speech option for the system is turned on, the speech-based output is generated using Lernout and Hauspie's RealSpeak text-to-speech system. Although the system currently cannot use both modes of communication simultaneously, we plan to incorporate this feature sometime in the future.

2.2.7 Robustness of the System

As with any dialogue system, it is extremely important for the system to be robust. Our system has the following two features which make it extremely robust:

1) The user can, at any given moment, say *operator* to transfer to an operator, *quit/stop* to exit, and *back/restart* to start afresh.
2) When expecting a response from the user, if the system does not receive an expected input, it repeats the question at most twice before transferring control to an operator.

3. Sample Dialogues

This section gives examples of two sample dialogues that occur during the testing of the system. The system's response is indicated by "S>", the user's response by "U>", and the recognition of the user's response by "V>".

S> Welcome to the PartsID Center. Please tell me the part that you want the ID for.
U> I need the ID for PCB Control.
V> I need the I the for PCB home thrown.

S> What product do you need this for?
U> COMPAX 40E
V> home fax for a 00 E

S> Is COMPAX 40E the product name that you said?
U> yes
V> gas

S> Do you want the ID for PCB Display SID or the PCB Control?
U> The second one.
V> The second home.

S> Do you need the ID for PCB Control used in product COMPAX 40E?
U> yes
V> yes

S> The ID for PCB Control used in product COMPAX 40E is 2168983. Do you wan to exit or find the ID for another part?
U> look up another part.

S> Welcome to the PartsID Center. Please tell me the part that you want the ID for.
U> I need cable data for cradle 2M long.
V> I needed cable date them for cradle to be loan.

S> Do you need this part for a ANGIXM2004, or a AFM?
U> AFM
V> a fan

S> Is AFM the product name that you said?
U> yes
V> yes

S> Do you want the ID for Cable Data for Cradle 2M long?
U> yes
V> yes

S> The ID for Cable Data for Cradle 2M long used in product AFM is 45438628. Do you wan to exit or find the ID for another part?
U> look up another part.

4. Evaluation and Results

The goal of our evaluation was to ensure that the system helped a user successfully identify parts irrespective of the performance of the speech recognition engine for the user. In other words, we wanted to see if the system was robust enough to conduct transactions with a diverse mix of users. We tested the system with 4 different users two of whom had foreign accents. For each user, we randomly selected 20 parts from the database. The results are summarized in Table 1.

These results show that the system was quite successful in handling requests from users with a variety of accents achieving varying recognition rates. Out of the 80 parts tested, only twice did the user feel that he/she had to transfer to an operator. The system successfully retrieved the identification numbers of 79% of the parts while transferring 19% of the cases to a human operator because of extremely bad

User	Parts successfully identified	Calls system transfers to operator	Calls user transfers to operator	System prompts per call	Relevant words recognized per part
1	15	3	2	3.7	2.5
2	18	2	0	3	2.35
3	13	7	0	2.5	1.65
4	17	3	0	2.9	2.7

Table 1: Summary of Results

recognition. We are planning on conducting a more elaborate test which a larger set of users.

Conclusions

In this paper we have described a robust system that provides customer service for a medical parts application. The preliminary results are extremely encouraging with the system being able to successfully process approximately 80% of the requests from users with diverse accents.

Acknowledgements

We wish to thank the GE Medical Systems team of Todd Reinke, Jim Tierney, and Lisa Naughton for providing support and funding for this project. In addition, we also wish to thank Dong Hsu of Lernout and Hauspie for his help on the ASR and the text-to-speech systems. Finally, we wish to thank the Information Technology Laboratory of GE CRD for providing additional funding for this project.

References

Allen, J. F. et al. (1995) *The TRAINS Project: A case study in building a conversational planning agent.* Journal of Experimental and Theoretical AI, (7) 7-48.

Allen, J. F., Miller, B. W.; Ringer, E. K.; and Sikorski, T. (1996) *A Robust System for Natural Spoken Dialogue.* 34th Annual Meeting of the ACL, Santa Cruz, 62-70.

Bagga, A., Stein G. C., and Strzalkowski, T. (2000) *FidelityXPress: A Multi-Modal System for Financial Transactions.* Proceedings of the 6th Conference on Content-Based Multimedia Information Access (RIAO'00).

Biermann, A.W.; Rodman, R.; Rubin, D.; and Heidlage, J.R. (1985) *Natural language with discrete speech as a mode for human to machine communication.* Communication of the ACM 18(6): 628-636.

Biermann, Alan W.; Guinn, Curry I.; Fulkerson, M.: Keim, G.A.; Liang, Z.; Melamed, D.M.; and Rajagopalan, K. (1997) *Goal-oriented Multimedia Dialogue with Variable Initiative.* Lecture Notes in Artificial Intelligence 1325; Springer-Verlag, New York; pp. 1-16.

Carberry, S. (1990) *Plan Recognition in Natural Language Dialogue.* Cambridge, Mass.: The MIT Press.

Chu-Carroll, J, and R. Carpenter. (1999) *Vector-Based Natural Language Call Routing.* Journal of Computational Linguistics, 25(30), pp. 361-388.

Georgila, K., A.Tsopanoglou, N.Fakotakis and G.Kokkinakis. (1998) *An Integrated Dialogue System for the Automation of Call Centre Services.* ICLSP'98, 5th International Conference on Spoken Language Processing, Sydney, Australia.

Grosz, B.J. and Sidner, C.L. (1986) *Attentions, intentions, and the structure of discourse.* Computational Linguistics 12(3): 175-204.

Greenemeier, L. (1999) *Voice-Recognition Technology Builds a Following.* Information Week, December 13.

Meisel, W. (1999) *Can Speech Recognition Give Telephones a New Face?* Business Communications Review, November 1.

Reichman, R.. (1981) Plain-speaking: *A theory and grammar of spontaneous discourse.* PhD thesis, Department of Computer Science, Harvard University, Cambridge, Massachusetts.

Rosen, C. (1999) Speech Has Industry Talking. Business Travel News, November.

Rossheim, J. (1999) *Giving Voice to Customer Service.* Datamation, November 1.

Translation using Information on Dialogue Participants

Setsuo Yamada, Eiichiro Sumita and Hideki Kashioka
ATR Interpreting Telecommunications Research Laboratories*
2-2, Hikaridai, Seika-cho, Soraku-gun,
Kyoto, 619-0288, JAPAN
{syamada, sumita, kashioka}@itl.atr.co.jp†

Abstract

This paper proposes a way to improve the translation quality by using information on dialogue participants that is easily obtained from outside the translation component. We incorporated information on participants' social roles and genders into transfer rules and dictionary entries. An experiment with 23 unseen dialogues demonstrated a recall of 65% and a precision of 86%. These results showed that our simple and easy-to-implement method is effective, and is a key technology enabling smooth conversation with a dialogue translation system.

1 Introduction

Recently, various dialogue translation systems have been proposed (Bub and others, 1997; Kurematsu and Morimoto, 1996; Rayner and Carter, 1997; Rosé and Levin, 1998; Sumita and others, 1999; Yang and Park, 1997; Vidal, 1997). If we want to make a conversation proceed smoothly using these translation systems, it is important to use not only linguistic information, which comes from the source language, but also extra-linguistic information, which does not come from the source language, but, is shared between the participants of the conversation.

Several dialogue translation methods that use extra-linguistic information have been proposed. Horiguchi outlined how "spoken language pragmatic information" can be translated (Horiguchi, 1997). However, she did not apply this idea to a dialogue translation system. LuperFoy et al. proposed a software architecture that uses "a pragmatic adaptation" (LuperFoy and others, 1998), and Mima et al. proposed a method that uses "situational information" (Mima and others, 1997). LuperFoy et al. simulated their method on man-machine interfaces and Mima et al. preliminarily evaluated their method. Neither study, however, applied its proposals to an actual dialogue translation system.

The above mentioned methods will need time to work in practice, since it is *hard to obtain the extra-linguistic information on which they depend.*

We have been paying special attention to "politeness," because a lack of politeness can interfere with a smooth conversation between two participants, such as a clerk and a customer. It is easy for a dialogue translation system to know which participant is the clerk and which is the customer from the interface (such as the wires to the microphones).

This paper describes a method of "politeness" selection according to a participant's social role (a clerk or a customer), which is easily obtained from the extra-linguistic environment. We incorporated each participant's social role into transfer rules and transfer dictionary entries. We then conducted an experiment with 23 unseen dialogues (344 utterances). Our method achieved a recall of 65% and a precision of 86%. These rates could be improved to 86% and 96%, respectively (see Section 4). It is therefore possible to use a "participant's social role" (a clerk or a customer in this case) to appropriately make the translation results "polite," and to make the conversation proceed smoothly with a dialogue translation system.

Section 2 analyzes the relationship between a particular participant's social role (a clerk) and politeness in Japanese. Section 3 describes our proposal in detail using an English-to-Japanese

*Current affiliation is ATR Spoken Language Translation Research Laboratories

†Current mail addresses are *{setsuo.yamada, eiichiro.sumita, hideki.kashioka}@slt.atr.co.jp*

translation system. Section 4 shows an experiment and results, followed by a discussion in Section 5. Finally, Section 6 concludes this paper.

2 A Participant's Social Role and Politeness

This section focuses on one participant's social role. We investigated Japanese outputs of a dialogue translation system to see how many utterances should be polite expressions in a current translation system for travel arrangement. We input 1,409 clerk utterances into a Transfer Driven Machine Translation system (Sumita and others, 1999) (TDMT for short). The inputs were closed utterances, meaning the system already knew the utterances, enabling the utterances to be transferred at a good quality. Therefore, we used closed utterances as the inputs to avoid translation errors.

As a result, it was shown that about 70% (952) of all utterances should be improved to use polite expressions. This result shows that a current translation system is not enough to make a conversation smoothly. Not surprisingly, if all expressions were polite, some Japanese speakers would feel insulted. Therefore, Japanese speakers do not have to use polite expression in all utterances.

We classified the investigated data into different types of English expressions for Japanese politeness, i.e., into honorific titles, parts of speech such as verbs, and canned phrases, as shown in Table 1; however, not all types appeared in the data. For example, when the clerk said "How will you be paying, Mr. Suzuki," the Japanese translation was made polite as "donoyouni oshiharaininarimasu-ka suzuki-sama" in place of the standard expression "donoyouni shiharaimasu-ka suzuki-san."

Table 1 shows that there is a difference in how expressions should be made more polite according to the type, and that many polite expressions can be translated by using only local information, i.e., transfer rules and dictionary entries. In the next section, we describe how to incorporate the information on dialogue participants, such as roles and genders, into transfer rules and dictionary entries in a dialogue translation system.

3 A Method of Using Information on Dialogue Participants

This section describes how to use information on dialogue participants, such as participants' social roles and genders. First, we describe TDMT, which we also used in our experiment. Second, we mention how to modify transfer rules and transfer dictionary entries according to information on dialogue participants.

3.1 Transfer Driven Machine Translation

TDMT uses bottom-up left-to-right chart parsing with transfer rules as shown in Figure 1. The parsing determines the best structure and best transferred result locally by performing structural disambiguation using semantic distance calculations, in parallel with the derivation of possible structures. The semantic distance is defined by a thesaurus.

```
(source pattern)
⇒
((target pattern 1)
 ((source example 1)
  (source example 2)
  ... )
 (target pattern 2)
 ... )
```

Figure 1: Transfer rule format

A transfer rule consists of a source pattern, a target pattern, and a source example. The source pattern consists of variables and constituent boundaries (Furuse and Iida, 1996). A constituent boundary is either a functional word or the part-of-speech of a left constituent's last word and the part-of-speech of a right constituent's first word. In Example (1), the constituent boundary $\langle V\text{–}CN \rangle$ is inserted between "accept" and "payment," because "accept" is a Verb and "payment" is a Common Noun. The target pattern consists of variables that correspond to variables in the source pattern and words of the target language. The source example consists of words that come from utterances referred to when a person creates transfer rules (we call such utterances closed utterances).

Figure 2 shows a transfer rule whose source pattern is (X $\langle V\text{–}CN \rangle$ Y). Variable X corresponds to x, which is used in the target pattern, and Y corresponds to y, which is also

Table 1: Examples of polite expressions

Type:	**verb, title**			
Eng:	How will you be paying, Mr. Suzuki			
Standard:	*donoyouni*	*shiharaimasu-ka*	*suzuki-san*	
Polite:	*donoyouni*	*oshiharaininarimasu-ka*	*suzuki-sama*	
Gloss:	`How`	`pay-QUESTION`	`suzuki-Mr.`	
Type:	**verb, common noun**			
Eng:	We have two types of rooms available			
Standard:	*aiteiru*	*ni-shurui-no*	*heya-ga*	*arimasu*
Polite:	*aiteiru*	*ni-shurui-no*	*oheya-ga*	*gozaimasu*
Gloss:	`available`	`two-types-of`	`room-TOP`	`have`
Type:	**auxiliary verb**			
Eng:	You can shop for hours			
Standard:	*suujikan*	*kaimono-wo*	*surukotogadekimasu*	
Polite:	*suujikan*	*kaimono-wo*	*shiteitadakemasu*	
Gloss:	`for hours`	`make-OBJ`	`can`	
Type:	**pronoun**			
Eng:	Your room number, please			
Standard:	*anatano*	*heya*	*bangou-wo*	*onegaishimasu*
Polite:	*okyakusamano*	*heya*	*bangou-wo*	*onegaishimasu*
Gloss:	`Your`	`room`	`number-sc obj`	`please`
Type:	**canned phrase**			
Eng:	How can I help you			
Standard:	*dou*	*shimashitaka*		
Polite:	*douitta*	*goyoukendeshouka*		
Gloss:	`How`	`can I help you`		

Example (1)

Eng:	We accept payment by credit card			
Standard:	*watashitachi-wa*	*kurejitto-kaado-deno*	*shiharai-wo*	*uketsukemasu*
Polite:	*watashidomo-wa*	*kurejitto-kaado-deno*	*oshiharai-wo*	*oukeshimasu*
Gloss:	`We-TOP`	`credit-card-by`	`payment-OBJ`	`accept`

used in the target pattern. The source example (("accept") ("payment")) comes from Example (1), and the other source examples come from the other closed utterances. This transfer rule means that if the source pattern is (X ⟨*V–CN*⟩ Y) then (y "wo" x) or (y "ni" x) is selected as the target pattern, where an input word pair corresponding to X and Y is *semantically the most similar in a thesaurus* to, or *exactly the same* as, the source example. For example, if an input word pair corresponding to X and Y is *semantically the most similar in a thesaurus* to, or *exactly the same* as, (("accept") ("payment")), then the target pattern (y "wo" x) is selected in Figure 2. As a result, an appropriate target pattern is selected.

After a target pattern is selected, TDMT creates a target structure according to the pattern

```
(X ⟨V–CN⟩ Y)
⇒
((y "wo" x)
 ((("accept") ("payment"))
  (("take") ("picture")))
 (y "ni" x)
 ((("take") ("bus"))
  (("get") ("sunstroke")))
)
```

Figure 2: Transfer rule example

by referring to a transfer dictionary, as shown in Figure 3. If the input is "accept ⟨*V–CN*⟩ payment," then this part is translated into "shiharai wo uketsukeru." "wo" is derived from the target pattern (y "wo" x), and "shiharai" and "uketsukeru" are derived from the transfer dictionary, as shown in Figure 4.

```
(source pattern)
⇒
(((target pattern 1_1) :pattern-cond 1_1
  (target pattern 1_2) :pattern-cond 1_2
  ...
  (target pattern 1_n) :default)
 ((source example 1)
  ... )
 (((source example 1) → (target word 1_1) :word-cond 1_1
   (source example 1) → (target word 1_2) :word-cond 1_2
   ...
   (source example 1) → (target word 1_m) :default)
  ... )
(((target pattern 2_1) :pattern-cond 2_1
 ... )))
```

Figure 5: Transfer rule format with information on dialogue participants

```
(((source word 1) → (target word 1_1) :cond 1_1
  (source word 1) → (target word 1_2) :cond 1_2
  ...
  (source word 1) → (target word 1_k) :default)
 ... )
```

Figure 6: Dictionary format with information on dialogue participants

```
((source word) → (target word)
 ... )
```

Figure 3: Transfer dictionary format

```
(("accept") → ("uketsukeru")
 ("payment") → ("shiharai"))
```

Figure 4: Transfer dictionary example

```
(X "sama")
⇒
((("Mr." x) :h-gender male
  ("Ms." x) :h-gender female
  ("Mr-ms." x))
 ((("case"))
  (("room number")))
)
```

Figure 7: Transfer rule example with the participant's gender

3.2 Transfer Rules and Entries according to Information on Dialogue Participants

For this research, we modified the transfer rules and the transfer dictionary entries, as shown in Figures 5 and 6. In Figure 5, the target pattern "target pattern 1_1" and the source word "source example 1" are used to change the translation according to information on dialogue participants. For example, if ":pattern-cond 1_1" is defined as ":h-gender male" as shown in Figure 7, then "target pattern 1_1" is selected when the hearer is a male, that is, "("Mr." x)" is selected. Moreover, if ":word-cond 1_1" is defined as ":s-role clerk" as shown in Figure 8, then "source example 1" is translated into "target word 1_1" when the speaker is a clerk, that is, "accept" is translated into "oukesuru." Translations such as "target word 1_1" are valid only in the source pattern; that is, a source example might not always be translated into one of these target words. If we always want to produce translations according to information on dialogue participants, then we need to modify the entries in the transfer dictionary like Figure 6 shows. Conversely, if we do not want to always change the translation, then we should not modify the entries but modify the transfer rules. Several conditions can also be given to ":word-cond" and ":pattern-cond." For example, ":s-role customer and :s-gender female," which means the speaker is a customer and a female, can be given. In Figure 5, ":default" means the default target pattern or word if no condition is matched. The condition is checked from up to down in order; that is, first, ":pattern-cond 1_1," second, ":pattern-cond 1_2," ... and so on.

```
(X ⟨V-CN⟩ Y)
⇒
((y "wo" x)
 ((("accept") ("payment"))
  (("take") ("picture")))
 ((("accept") → ("oukesuru") :s-role clerk
   ("accept") → ("uketsukeru")))
)
```

Figure 8: Transfer rule example with a participant's role

```
((("payment") → ("oshiharai") :s-role clerk
  ("payment") → ("shiharai"))
 (("we") → ("watashidomo") :s-role clerk
  ("we") → ("watashitachi")))
```

Figure 9: Transfer dictionary example with a speaker's role

Even though we do not have rules and entries for pattern conditions and word conditions according to another participant's information, such as ":s-role customer"(which means the speaker's role is a customer) and ":s-gender male" (which means the speaker's gender is male), TDMT can translate expressions corresponding to this information too. For example, "Very good, please let me confirm them" will be translated into "shouchiitashimasita kakunin sasete itadakimasu" when the speaker is a clerk or "soredekekkoudesu kakunin sasete kudasai" when the speaker is a customer, as shown in Example (2).

By making a rule and an entry like the examples shown in Figures 8 and 9, the utterance of Example (1) will be translated into "watashidomo wa kurejitto kaado deno oshiharai wo oukeshimasu" when the speaker is a clerk.

4 An Experiment

The TDMT system for English-to-Japanese at the time of the experiment had about 1,500 transfer rules and 8,000 transfer dictionary entries. In other words, this TDMT system was capable of translating 8,000 English words into Japanese words. About 300 transfer rules and 40 transfer dictionary entries were modified to improve the level of "politeness."

We conducted an experiment using the transfer rules and transfer dictionary for a clerk with 23 unseen dialogues (344 utterances). Our input was off-line, i.e., a transcription of dialogues, which was encoded with the participant's social role. In the on-line situation, our system can not infer whether the participant's social role is a clerk or a customer, but can instead determine the role without error from the interface (such as a microphone or a button).

In order to evaluate the experiment, we classified the Japanese translation results obtained for the 23 unseen dialogues (199 utterances from a clerk, and 145 utterances from a customer, making 344 utterances in total) into two types: expressions that had to be changed to more polite expressions, and expressions that did not. Table 2 shows the number of utterances that included an expression which had to be changed into a more polite one (indicated by "Yes") and those that did not (indicated by "No"). We neglected 74 utterances whose translations were too poor to judge whether to assign a "Yes" or "No."

Table 2: The number of utterances to be changed or not

Necessity of change	The number of utterances
Yes	104
No	166
Out of scope *	74
Total	344

* 74 translations were too poor to handle for the "politeness" problem, and so they are ignored in this paper.

The translation results were evaluated to see whether the impressions of the translated results were improved or not with/without modification for the clerk from the viewpoint of "politeness." Table 3 shows the impressions obtained according to the necessity of change shown in Table 2.

The evaluation criteria are recall and precision, which are defined as follows:

$$\text{Recall} = \frac{\text{number of utterances whose impression is better}}{\text{number of utterances which should be more polite}}$$

Example (2)

Eng:	Very good, please let me confirm them			
Standard:	*wakarimasita*	*kakunin*	*sasete*	*kudasai*
Clerk:	*shouchiitashimasita*	*kakunin*	*sasete*	*itadakimasu*
Customer:	*soredekekkoudesu*	*kakunin*	*sasete*	*kudasai*
Gloss:	very good	confirm	let me	please

Table 3: Evaluation on using the speaker's role

Necessity of change	Impression	The number of utterances
Yes (104)	better	68
	same	5
	worse	3
	no-diff	28
No (166)	better	0
	same	3
	worse	0
	no-diff	163

better: Impression of a translation is better.

same: Impression of a translation has not changed.

worse: Impression of a translation is worse.

no-diff: There is no difference between the two translations.

$$\text{Precision} = \frac{\text{number of utterances whose impression is better}}{\text{number of utterances whose expression has been changed by the modified rules and entries}}$$

The recall was 65% $(= 68 \div (68 + 5 + 3 + 28))$ and the precision was 86% $(= 68 \div (68 + 5 + 3 + 0 + 3 + 0))$.

There are two main reasons which bring down these rates. One reason is that TDMT does not know who or what the agent of the action in the utterance is; agents are also needed to select polite expressions. The other reason is that there are not enough rules and transfer dictionary entries for the clerk.

It is easier to take care of the latter problem than the former problem. If we resolve the latter problem, that is, if we expand the transfer rules and the transfer dictionary entries according to the "participant's social role" (a clerk and a customer), then the recall rate and the precision rate can be improved (to 86% and 96%, respectively, as we have found). As a result, we can say that our method is effective for smooth conversation with a dialogue translation system.

5 Discussion

In general, extra-linguistic information is hard to obtain. However, some extra-linguistic information can be easily obtained:

(1) One piece of information is the participant's social role, which can be obtained from the interface such as the microphone used. It was proven that a clerk and customer as the social roles of participants are useful for translation into Japanese. However, more research is required on another participant's social role.

(2) Another piece of information is the participant's gender, which can be obtained by a speech recognizer with high accuracy (Takezawa and others, 1998; Naito and others, 1998). We have considered how expressions can be useful by using the hearer's gender for Japanese-to-English translation.

Let us consider the Japanese honorific title "sama" or "san." If the hearer's gender is male, then it should be translated "Mr." and if the hearer's gender is female, then it should be translated "Ms." as shown in Figure 7. Additionally, the participant's gender is useful for translating typical expressions for males or females. For example, Japanese "wa" is often attached at the end of the utterance by females.

It is also important for a dialogue translation system to use extra-linguistic information which the system can obtain easily, in order to make a conversation proceed smoothly and comfortably for humans using the translation system. We expect that other pieces of usable information can be easily obtained in the future. For example, age might be obtained from a cellular telephone if it were always carried by the same person and provided with personal information. In this case, if the system knew the hearer was a child, it could change complex expressions into easier ones.

6 Conclusion

We have proposed a method of translation using information on dialogue participants, which is easily obtained from outside the translation component, and applied it to a dialogue translation system for travel arrangement. This method can select a polite expression for an utterance according to the "participant's social role," which is easily determined by the interface (such as the wires to the microphones). For example, if the microphone is for the clerk (the speaker is a clerk), then the dialogue translation system can select a more polite expression.

In an English-to-Japanese translation system, we added additional transfer rules and transfer dictionary entries for the clerk to be more polite than the customer. Then, we conducted an experiment with 23 unseen dialogues (344 utterances). We evaluated the translation results to see whether the impressions of the results improved or not. Our method achieved a recall of 65% and a precision of 86%. These rates could easily be improved to 86% and 96%, respectively. Therefore, we can say that our method is effective for smooth conversation with a dialogue translation system.

Our proposal has a limitation in that if the system does not know who or what the agent of an action in an utterance is, it cannot appropriately select a polite expression. We are considering ways to enable identification of the agent of an action in an utterance and to expand the current framework to improve the level of politeness even more. In addition, we intend to apply other extra-linguistic information to a dialogue translation system.

References

Thomas Bub et al. 1997. Verbmobil: The combination of deep and shallow processing for spontaneous speech translation. In *the 1997 International Conference on Acoustics, Speech, and Signal Processing: ICASSP 97*, pages 71–74, Munich.

Osamu Furuse and Hitoshi Iida. 1996. Incremental translation utilizing constituent boundary patterns. In *Proceedings of COLING-96*, pages 412–417, Copenhagen.

Keiko Horiguchi. 1997. Towards translating spoken language pragmatics in an analogical framework. In *Proceedings of ACL/EACL-97 workshop on Spoken Language Translation*, pages 16–23, Madrid.

Akira Kurematsu and Tsuyoshi Morimoto. 1996. *Automatic Speech Translation.* Gordon and Breach Publishers.

Susann LuperFoy et al. 1998. An architecture for dialogue management, context tracking, and pragmatic adaptation in spoken dialogue system. In *Proceedings of COLING-ACL'98*, pages 794–801, Montreal.

Hideki Mima et al. 1997. A situation-based approach to spoken dialogue translation between different social roles. In *Proceedings of TMI-97*, pages 176–183, Santa Fe.

Masaki Naito et al. 1998. Acoustic and language model for speech translation system ATR-MATRIX. In *the Proceedings of the 1998 Spring Meeting of the Acoustical Society of Japan*, pages 159–160 (in Japanese).

Manny Rayner and David Carter. 1997. Hybrid language processing in the spoken language translator. In *the 1997 International Conference on Acoustics, Speech, and Signal Processing: ICASSP 97*, pages 107–110, Munich.

Carolyn Penstein Rosé and Lori S. Levin. 1998. An interactive domain independent approach to robust dialogue interpretation. In *Proceedings of COLING-ACL'98*, pages 1129–1135, Montreal.

Eiichiro Sumita et al. 1999. Solutions to problems inherent in spoken-language translation: The ATR-MATRIX approach. In *the Machine Translation Summit VII*, pages 229–235, Singapore.

Toshiyuki Takezawa et al. 1998. A Japanese-to-English speech translation system: ATR-MATRIX. In *the 5th International Conference On Spoken Language Processing: ICSLP-98*, pages 2779–2782, Sydney.

Enrique Vidal. 1997. Finite-state speech-to-speech translation. In *the 1997 International Conference on Acoustics, Speech, and Signal Processing: ICASSP 97*, pages 111–114, Munich.

Jae-Woo Yang and Jun Park. 1997. An experiment on Korean-to-English and Korean-to-Japanese spoken language translation. In *the 1997 International Conference on Acoustics, Speech, and Signal Processing: ICASSP 97*, pages 87–90, Munich.

Distilling dialogues - A method using natural dialogue corpora for dialogue systems development

Arne Jönsson and Nils Dahlbäck
Department of Computer and Information Science
Linköping University
S-581 83, LINKÖPING
SWEDEN
nilda@ida.liu.se, arnjo@ida.liu.se

Abstract

We report on a method for utilising corpora collected in natural settings. It is based on distilling (re-writing) natural dialogues to elicit the type of dialogue that would occur if one the dialogue participants was a computer instead of a human. The method is a complement to other means such as Wizard of Oz-studies and un-distilled natural dialogues. We present the distilling method and guidelines for distillation. We also illustrate how the method affects a corpus of dialogues and discuss the pros and cons of three approaches in different phases of dialogue systems development.

1 Introduction

It has been known for quite some time now, that the language used when interacting with a computer is different from the one used in dialogues between people, (c.f. Jönsson and Dahlbäck (1988)). Given that we know that the language will be different, but not *how* it will be different, we need to base our development of natural language dialogue systems on a relevant set of dialogue corpora. It is our belief that we need to clarify a number of different issues regarding the collection and use of corpora in the development of speech-only and multimodal dialogue systems. Exchanging experiences and developing guidelines in this area are as important as, and in some sense a necessary pre-requisite to, the development of computational models of speech, language, and dialogue/discourse. It is interesting to note the difference in the state of art in the field of natural language dialogue systems with that of corpus linguistics, where issues of the usefulness of different samples, the necessary sampling size, representativeness in corpus design and other have been discussed for quite some time (e.g. (Garside et al., 1997; Atkins et al., 1992; Crowdy, 1993; Biber, 1993)). Also the neighboring area of evaluation of NLP systems (for an overview, see Sparck Jones and Galliers (1996)) seems to have advanced further.

Some work have been done in the area of natural language dialogue systems, e.g. on the design of Wizard of Oz-studies (Dahlbäck et al., 1998), on measures for inter-rater reliability (Carletta, 1996), on frameworks for evaluating spoken dialogue agents (Walker et al., 1998) and on the use of different corpora in the development of a particular system (The Carnegie-Mellon Communicator, Eskenazi et al. (1999)).

The question we are addressing in this paper is how to collect and analyse relevant corpora. We begin by describing what we consider to be the main advantages and disadvantages of the two currently used methods; studies of human dialogues and Wizard of Oz-dialogues, especially focusing on the ecological validity of the methods. We then describe a method called 'distilling dialogues', which can serve as a supplement to the other two.

2 Natural and Wizard of Oz-Dialogues

The advantage of using real dialogues between people is that they will illustrate which tasks and needs that people actually bring to a particular service provider. Thus, on the level of the users' general goals, such dialogues have a high validity. But there are two drawbacks here. First; it is not self-evident that users will have the same task expectations from a computer system as they have with a person. Second, the language used will differ from the language used when interacting with a computer.

These two disadvantages have been the major force behind the development of Wizard of Oz-methods. The advantage here is that the setting will be human-computer interaction. But there are important disadvantages, too. First, on the practical side, the task of setting up a high quality simulation environment and training the operators ('wizards') to use this is a resource consuming task (Dahlbäck et al., 1998). Second, and probably even more important, is that we cannot then observe real users using a system for real life tasks, where they bring their own needs, motivations, resources, and constraints to bear. To some extent this problem can be overcome using well-designed so called 'scenarios'. As pointed out in Dahlbäck (1991), on many levels of analysis the artificiality of the situation will not affect the language used. An example of this is the pattern of pronoun-antecedent relations. But since the tasks given to the users are often pre-described by the researchers, this means that this is not a good way of finding out *which* tasks the users actually want to perform. Nor does it provide a clear enough picture on how the users will act to find something that satisfies their requirements. If e.g. the task is one of finding a charter holiday trip or buying a TV-set within a specified set of constraints (economical and other), it is conceivable that people will stay with the first item that matches the specification, whereas in real life they would probably look for alternatives. In our experience, this is primarily a concern if the focus is on the users' goals and plans, but is less a problem when the interest is on lower-level aspects, such as, syntax or patterns of pronoun-antecedent relationship (c.f. Dahlbäck (1991)).

To summarize; real life dialogues will provide a reasonably correct picture of the way users' approach their tasks, and what tasks they bring to the service provider, but the language used will not give a good approximation of what the system under construction will need to handle. Wizard of Oz-dialogues, on the other hand, will give a reasonable approximation of some aspects of the language used, but in an artificial context.

The usual approach has been to work in three steps. First analyse real human dialogues, and based on these, in the second phase, design one or more Wizard of Oz-studies. The final step is to fine-tune the system's performance on real users. A good example of this method is presented in Eskenazi et al. (1999). But there are also possible problems with this approach (though we are not claiming that this was the case in their particular project). Eskenazi et al. (1999) asked a human operator to act 'computer-like' in their Wizard of Oz-phase. The advantage is of course that the human operator will be able to perform all the tasks that is usually provided by this service. The disadvantage is that it puts a heavy burden on the human operator to act as a computer. Since we know that lay-persons' ideas of what computers can and cannot do are in many respects far removed from what is actually the case, we risk introducing some systematic distortion here. And since it is difficult to perform consistently in similar situations, we also risk introducing non-systematic distortion here, even in those cases when the 'wizard' is an NLP-professional.

Our suggestion is therefore to supplement the above mentioned methods, and bridge the gap between them, by post-processing human dialogues to give them a computer-like quality. The advantage, compared to having people do the simulation on the fly, is both that it can be done with more consistency, and also that it can be done by researchers that actually know what human-computer natural language dialogues can look like. A possible disadvantage with using both Wizard of Oz-and real computer dialogues, is that users will quickly adapt to what the system can provide them with, and will therefore not try to use it for tasks they know it cannot perform. Consequently, we will not get a full picture of the different services they would like the system to provide.

A disadvantage with this method is, of course, that post-processing takes some time compared to using the natural dialogues as they are. There is also a concern on the ecological validity of the results, as discussed later.

3 Distilling dialogues

Distilling dialogues, i.e. re-writing human interactions in order to have them reflect what a human-computer interaction could look like involves a number of considerations. The main issue is that in corpora of natural dialogues one of the interlocutors is not a dialogue system. The system's task is instead performed by a human and the problem is how to anticipate the behaviour of a system that does not exist based on the performance of an agent with different performance characteristics. One important aspect is how to deal with human features that are not part of what the system is supposed to be able to handle, for instance if the user talks about things outside of the domain, such as discussing an episode of a recent TV show. It also involves issues on how to handle situations where one of the interlocuters discusses with someone else on a different topic, e.g. discussing the up-coming Friday party with a friend in the middle of an information providing dialogue with a customer.

It is important for the distilling process to have at least an outline of the dialogue system that is under development: Will it for instance have the capacity to recognise users' goals, even if not explicitly stated? Will it be able to reason about the discourse domain? What services will it provide, and what will be outside its capacity to handle?

In our case, we assume that the planned dialogue system has the ability to reason on various aspects of dialogue and properties of the application. In our current work, and in the examples used for illustration in this paper, we assume a dialogue model that can handle any relevant dialogue phenomenon and also an interpreter and speech recogniser being able to understand any user input that is relevant to the task. There is is also a powerful domain reasoning module allowing for more or less any knowledge reasoning on issues that can be accomplished within the domain (Flycht-Eriksson, 1999). Our current system does, however, not have an explicit user task model, as opposed to a system task model (Dahlbäck and Jönsson, 1999), which is included, and thus, we can not assume that the 'system' remembers utterances where the user explains its task. Furthermore, as our aim is system development we will not consider interaction outside the systems capabilities as relevant to include in the distilled dialogues.

The context of our work is the development a multi-modal dialogue system. However, in our current work with distilling dialogues, the abilities of a multi-modal system were not fully accounted for. The reason for this is that the dialogues would be significantly affected, e.g. a telephone conversation where the user always likes to have *the next connection, please* will result in a table if multi-modal output is possible and hence a fair amount of the dialogue is removed. We have therefore in this paper analysed the corpus assuming a speech-only system, since this is closer to the original telephone conversations, and hence needs fewer assumptions on system performance when distilling the dialogues.

4 Distillation guidelines

Distilling dialogues requires guidelines for how to handle various types of utterances. In this section we will present our guidelines for distilling a corpus of telephone conversations between a human information provider on local buses[1] to be used for developing a multimodal dialogue system (Qvarfordt and Jönsson, 1998; Flycht-Eriksson and Jönsson, 1998; Dahlbäck et al., 1999; Qvarfordt, 1998). Similar guidelines are used within another project on developing Swedish Dialogue Systems where the domain is travel bureau information.

We can distinguish three types of contributors: 'System' (i.e. a future systems) utterances, User utterances, and other types, such as moves by other speakers, and noise.

4.1 Modifying system utterances

The problem of modifying 'system' utterances can be divided into two parts: *how* to change and *when* to change. They are in some respects intertwined, but as the how-part affects the when-part more we will take this as a starting point.

- *The 'system' provides as much relevant information as possible at once.* This depends on the capabilities of the systems output modalities. If we have a screen or similar output device we present as much as possible which normally is all relevant information. If we, on the other hand, only have spoken output the amount of information that the hearer can interpret in one utterance must be considered when distilling. The system might in such cases provide less information. The principle of providing all relevant information is based on the assumption that a computer system often has access to all relevant information when querying the background system and can also present it more conveniently, especially in a multimodal system (Ahrenberg et al., 1996). A typical example is the dialogue fragment in figure 1. In this fragment the system provides information on what train to take and how to change to a bus. The result of distilling this fragment provides the revised fragment of figure 2. As seen in the fragment of figure 2 we also remove a number of utterances typical for human interaction, as discussed below.
- *System utterances are made more computer-like and do not include irrelevant information.* The latter is seen in S9 in the dialogue in figure 3 where the provided information is not relevant. It could also be possible to remove S5 and respond with S7 at once. This, however, depends on if the information grounded in S5-U6 is needed for the 'system' in order to know the arrival time or if that could be concluded from U4. This in turn depends on the system's capabilities. If we assume that the dialogue system has a model of user tasks, the information in S5-U6 could have been concluded from that. We will, in this case, retain S5-U6 as we do not assume a user task model (Dahlbäck and Jönsson, 1999) and in order to stay as close to the original dialogue as possible.

The next problem concerns the case when 'system' utterances are changed or removed.

- *Dialogue contributions provided by something or someone other than the user or the 'system' are removed.* These are regarded as not being part of the interaction. This means that if someone interrupts the current interaction, say that the telephone rings during a face-to-face interaction, the interrupting interaction is normally removed from the corpus.

  Furthermore, 'system' interruptions are removed. A human can very well interrupt another human interlocuter, but a computer system will not do that.

  However, this guideline could lead to problems, for instance, when users follow up such interruptions. If no information is provided or the interrupted sequence does not affect the dialogue, we have no problems removing the interruption. The problem is what to do when information from the 'system' is used in the continuing dialogue. For such cases we have no fixed strategy,

[1]The bus time table dialogues are collected at Linköping University and are available (in Swedish) on http://www.ida.liu.se/~arnjo/kfb/dialoger.html

U4: yes I wonder if you have any mm buses or (.) like express buses leaving from Linköping
to Vadstena (.) on sunday
*ja ville undra om ni hade några öh bussar eller (.) typ expressbussar som åkte från Linköping
till Vadstena (.) på sönda*
S5: no the bus does not run on sundays
nej bussen går inte på söndagar
U6: how can you (.) can you take the train and then change some way (.) because (.)
to Mjölby 'n' so
*hur kan man (.) kan man ta tåg å sen byta på nått sätt (.) för de (.)
till mjölby å så*
S7: that you can do too yes
de kan du göra också ja
U8: how (.) do you have any such suggestions
hur (.) har du nåra några såna förslag
S9: yes let's see (4s) a moment (15s) now let us see here (.) was it on the sunday you should travel
ja ska se här (4s) ett ögonblick (15s) nu ska vi se här (.) va de på söndagen du skulle åka på
U10: yes right afternoon preferably
ja just de eftermidda gärna
S11: afternoon preferable (.) you have train from Linköping fourteen twenty nine
eftermidda gärna (.) du har tåg från Linköping fjorton å tjugonie
U12: mm
mm
S13: and then you will change from Mjölby station six hundred sixty
å så byter du från Mjölby station sexhundrasexti
U14: sixhundred sixty
sexhundrasexti
S15: fifteen and ten
femton å tie

Figure 1: Dialogue fragment from a real interaction on bus time-table information

U4: I wonder if you have any buses or (.) like express buses going from Linköping
to Vadstena (.) on sunday
S5: no the bus does not run on sundays
U6: how can you (.) can you take the train and then change some way (.) because (.)
to Mjölby and so
S7: you can take the train from Linköping fourteen and twenty nine and then you will
change at Mjölby station to bus six hundred sixty at fifteen and ten

Figure 2: A distilled version of the dialogue in figure 1

the dialogue needs to be rearranged depending on how the information is to be used (c.f. the discussion in the final section of this paper).

- *'System' utterances which are no longer valid are removed.* Typical examples of this are the utterances S7, S9, S11 and S13 in the dialogue fragment of figure 1.
- *Remove sequences of utterances where the 'system' behaves in a way a computer would not do.* For instance jokes, irony, humor, commenting on the other dialogue participant, or dropping the telephone (or whatever is going on in S7 in figure 4). A common case of this is when the 'system' is talking while looking for information, S5 in the dialogue fragment of figure 4 is an example of this. Related to this is when the system provides its own comments. If we can assume that it has such capabilities they are included, otherwise we remove them.
- *The system does not repeat information that has already been provided unless explicitly asked to do so.* In human interaction it is not uncommon to repeat what has been uttered for purposes other than to provide grounding information or feedback. This is for instance common during

U4: 'n' I must be at Resecentrum before fourteen and thirty five (.) 'cause we will going to the interstate buses
å ja ska va på rececentrum innan fjorton å trettifem (.) fö vi ska till långfärdsbussarna

S5: aha (.) 'n' then you must be there around twenty past two something then
jaha (.) å då behöver du va nere strax efter tjuge över två nånting då

U6: yes around that
ja ungefär

S7: let's see here (11s) two hundred and fourteen Ryd end station leaves forty six (.) thirteen 'n' forty six then you will be down fourteen oh seven (.)
då ska vi se här (11s) tvåhundrafjorton Ryd ändhållplatsen går förtisex (.) tretton å förtisex då är du nere fjorton noll sju (.)

U8: aha
jaha

S9: 'n' (.) the next one takes you there (.) fourteen thirty seven (.) but that is too late
å (.) nästa är du nere (.) fjorton å trettisju (.) men de ä ju för sent

Figure 3: Dialogue fragment from a real interaction on bus time-table information

U2: Well, hi (.) I am going to Ugglegatan eighth
ja hej (.) ja ska till Ugglegatan åtta

S3: Yes
ja

U4: and (.) I wonder (.) it is somewhere in Tannefors
och (.) jag undrar (.) det ligger nånstans i Tannefors

S5: Yes (.) I will see here one one I will look exactly where it is one moment please
ja (.) jag ska se här ett ett jag ska titta exakt var det ligger ett ögonblick bara

U6: Oh Yeah
jarå

S7: (operator disconnects) (25s) mm (.) okey (5s) what the hell (2s)
(operator connects again) hello yes
((Telefonisten kopplar ur sig)) (25s) ähh (.) okey (5s) de va som faan (2s)
((Telefonisten kopplar in sig igen)) hallå ja

U8: Yes hello
ja hej

S9: It is bus two hundred ten which runs on old tannefors road that you have to take and get off at the bus stop at that bus stop named vetegatan
det ä buss tvåhundratio som går gamla tanneforsvägen som du får åka å gå av vid den hållplatsen vid den hållplatsen som heter vetegatan.

Figure 4: Dialogue fragment from a natural bus timetable interaction

search procedures as discussed above.

- *The system does not ask for information it has already achieved.* For instance asking again if it is on Sunday as in S9 in figure 1. This is not uncommon in human interaction and such utterances from the user are not removed. However, we can assume that the dialogue system does not forget what has been talked about before.

4.2 Modifying user utterances

The general rule is to change user utterances as little as possible. The reason for this is that we do not want to develop systems where the user needs to restrict his/her behaviour to the capabilities of the dialogue system. However, there are certain changes made to user utterances, in most cases as a consequence of changes of system utterances.

- *Utterances that are no longer valid are removed.* The most common cases are utterances whose request has already been answered, as seen in the distilled dialogue in figure 2 of the dialogue in figure 1.

S11: sixteen fifty five
sexton femtifem
U12: sixteen fifty five (.) aha
sexton femtifem (.) jaha
S13: bus line four hundred thirty five
linje fyrahundra trettifem

Figure 5: Dialogue fragment from a natural bus timetable interaction

- *Utterances are removed where the user discusses things that are in the environment.* For instance commenting the 'systems' clothes or hair. This also includes other types of communicative signals such as laughter based on things outside the interaction, for instance, in the environment of the interlocuters.
- *User utterances can also be added in order to make the dialogue continue.* In the dialogue in figure 5 there is nothing in the dialogue explaining why the system utters S13. In such cases we need to add a user utterance, e.g. *Which bus is that?*. However, it might turn out that there are cues, such as intonation, found when listening to the tapes. If such detailed analyses are carried out, we will, of course, not need to add utterances. Furthermore, it is sometimes the case that the telephone operator deliberately splits the information into chunks that can be comprehended by the user, which then must be considered in the distillation.

5 Applying the method

To illustrate the method we will in this section try to characterise the results from our distillations. The illustration is based on 39 distilled dialogues from the previously mentioned corpus collected with a telephone operator having information on local bus time-tables and persons calling the information service.

The distillation took about three hours for all 39 dialogues, i.e. it is reasonably fast. The distilled dialogues are on the average 27% shorter. However, this varies between the dialogues, at most 73% was removed but there were also seven dialogues that were not changed at all.

At the most 34 utterances where removed from one single dialogue and that was from a dialogue with discussions on where to find a parking lot, i.e. discussions outside the capabilities of the application. There was one more dialogue where more than 30 utterances were removed and that dialogue is a typical example of dialogues where distillation actually is very useful and also indicates what is normally removed from the dialogues. This particular dialogue begins with the user asking for the telephone number to 'the Lost property office' for a specific bus operator. However, the operator starts a discussion on what bus the traveller traveled on before providing the requested telephone number. The reason for this discussion is probably that the operator knows that different bus companies are utilised and would like to make sure that the user really understands his/her request. The interaction that follows can, thus, in that respect be relevant, but for our purpose of developing systems based on an overall goal of providing information, not to understand human interaction, our dialogue system will not able to handle such phenomenon (Jönsson, 1996).

The dialogues can roughly be divided into five different categories based on the users task. The discussion in twenty five dialogues were on bus times between various places, often one departure and one arrival but five dialogues involved more places. In five dialogues the discussion was one price and various types of discounts. Five users wanted to know the telephone number to 'the Lost property office', two discussed only bus stops and two discussed how they could utilise their season ticket to travel outside the trafficking area of the bus company. It is interesting to note that there is no correspondence between the task being performed during the interaction and the amount of changes made to the dialogue. Thus, if we can assume that the amount of distillation indicates something about a user's interaction style, other factors than the task are important when characterising user behaviour.

Looking at what is altered we find that the most important distilling principle is that the 'system' provides all relevant information at once, c.f. figures 1 and 2. This in turn removes utterances provided by both 'system' and user.

Most added utterances, both from the user and the 'system', provide explicit requests for information that is later provided in the dialogue, e.g. utterance S3 in figure 6. We have added ten utterances in all 39 dialogues, five 'system' utterances and five user utterances. Note, however, that we utilised the transcribed dialogues, without information on intonation. We would probably not have needed to add this many utterances if we had utilised the tapes. Our reason for not using information on intonation is that we do not assume that our system's speech recogniser can recognise intonation.

Finally, as discussed above, we did not utilise the full potential of multi-modality when distilling the dialogues. For instance, some dialogues could be further distilled if we had assumed that the system had presented a time-table. One reason for this is that we wanted to capture as many interesting aspects intact as possible. The advantage is, thus, that we have a better corpus for understanding human-

U2: Yees hi Anna Nilsson is my name and I would like to take the bus from Ryd center to Resecentrum in Linköping
jaa hej Anna Nilsson heter jag och jag vill åka buss från Ryds centrum till resecentrum i Linköping.

S3: mm **When do you want to leave?**
mm **När vill du åka?**

U4: 'n' I must be at Resecentrum before fourteen and thirty five (.) 'cause we will going to the interstate buses
å ja ska va på rececentrum innan fjorton å trettifem (.) fö vi ska till långfärdsbussarna

Figure 6: Distilled dialogue fragment with added utterance

computer interaction and can from that corpus do a second distillation where we focus more on multimodal interaction.

6 Discussion

We have been presenting a method for distilling human dialogues to make them resemble human computer interaction, in order to utilise such dialogues as a knowledge source when developing dialogue systems. Our own main purpose has been to use them for developing multimodal systems, however, as discussed above, we have in this paper rather assumed a speech-only system. But we believe that the basic approach can be used also for multi-modal systems and other kinds of natural language dialogue systems.

It is important to be aware of the limitations of the method, and how 'realistic' the produced result will be, compared to a dialogue with the final system. Since we are changing the dialogue moves, by for instance providing all required information in one move, or never asking to be reminded of what the user has previously requested, it is obvious that what follows after the changed sequence would probably be affected one way or another. A consequence of this is that the resulting dialogue is less accurate as a model of the entire dialogue. It is therefore not an ideal candidate for trying out the systems over-all performance during system development. But for the smaller sub-segments or sub-dialogues, we believe that it creates a good approximation of what will take place once the system is up and running. Furthermore, we believe distilled dialogues in some respects to be more realistic than Wizard of Oz-dialogues collected with a wizard acting as a computer.

Another issue, that has been discussed previously in the description of the method, is that the distilling is made based on a particular view of what a dialogue with a computer will look like. While not necessarily being a detailed and specific model, it is at least an instance of a class of computer dialogue models. One example of this is whether the system is meant to acquire information on the user's underlying motivations or goals or not. In the examples presented, we have not assumed such capabilities, but this assumption is not an absolute necessity. We believe, however, that the distilling process should be based on one such model, not the least to ensure a consistent treatment of similar recurring phenomena at different places in the corpora.

The validity of the results based on analysing distilled dialogues depends partly on how the distillation has been carried out. Even when using natural dialogues we can have situations where the interaction is somewhat mysterious, for instance, if some of the dialogue participants behaves irrational such as not providing feedback or being too elliptical. However, if careful considerations have been made to stay as close to the original dialogues as possible, we believe that distilled dialogues will reflect what a human would consider to be a natural interaction.

Acknowledgments

This work results from a number of projects on development of natural language interfaces supported by The Swedish Transport & Communications Research Board (KFB) and the joint Research Program for Language Technology (HSFR/NUTEK). We are indebted to the participants of the Swedish Dialogue Systems project, especially to Staffan Larsson, Lena Santamarta, and Annika Flycht-Eriksson for interesting discussions on this topic.

References

Lars Ahrenberg, Nils Dahlbäck, Arne Jönsson, and Åke Thurée. 1996. Customizing interaction for natural language interfaces. *Linköping Electronic articles in Computer and Information Science, also in Notes from Workshop on Pragmatics in Dialogue, The XIV:th Scandinavian Conference of Linguistics and the VIII:th Conference of Nordic and General Linguis-*

tics, Göteborg, Sweden, 1993, 1(1), October, 1. http://www.ep.liu.se/ea/cis/1996/001/.

Sue Atkins, Jeremy Clear, and Nicholas Ostler. 1992. Corpus design criteria. *Literary and Linguistic Computing*, 7(1):1–16.

Douglas Biber. 1993. Representativeness in corpus design. *Literary and Linguistic Computing*, 8(4):244–257.

Jean Carletta. 1996. Assessing agreement on classification tasks: The kappa statistic. *Computational Linguistics*, 22(2):249–254.

Steve Crowdy. 1993. Spoken corpus design. *Literary and Linguistic Computing*, 8(4):259–265.

Nils Dahlbäck and Arne Jönsson. 1999. Knowledge sources in spoken dialogue systems. In *Proceedings of Eurospeech'99, Budapest, Hungary.*

Nils Dahlbäck, Arne Jönsson, and Lars Ahrenberg. 1998. Wizard of oz studies – why and how. In Mark Maybury & Wolfgang Wahlster, editor, *Readings in Intelligent User Interfaces.* Morgan Kaufmann.

Nils Dahlbäck, Annika Flycht-Eriksson, Arne Jönsson, and Pernilla Qvarfordt. 1999. An architecture for multi-modal natural dialogue systems. In *Proceedings of ESCA Tutorial and Research Workshop (ETRW) on Interactive Dialogue in Multi-Modal Systems, Germany.*

Nils Dahlbäck. 1991. *Representations of Discourse, Cognitive and Computational Aspects.* Ph.D. thesis, Linköping University.

Maxine Eskenazi, Alexander Rudnicki, Karin Gregory, Paul Constantinides, Robert Brennan, Christina Bennett, and Jwan Allen. 1999. Data collection and processing in the carnegie mellon communicator. In *Proceedings of Eurospeech'99, Budapest, Hungary.*

Annika Flycht-Eriksson and Arne Jönsson. 1998. A spoken dialogue system utilizing spatial information. In *Proceedings of ICSLP'98, Sydney, Australia.*

Annika Flycht-Eriksson. 1999. A survey of knowledge sources in dialogue systems. In *Proceedings of IJCAI-99 Workshop on Knowledge and Reasoning in Practical Dialogue Systems, August, Stockholm.*

Roger Garside, Geoffrey Leech, and Anthony McEnery. 1997. *Corpus Annotation.* Longman.

Arne Jönsson and Nils Dahlbäck. 1988. Talking to a computer is not like talking to your best friend. In *Proceedings of the First Scandinavian Conference on Artificial Interlligence, Tromsø.*

Arne Jönsson. 1996. Natural language generation without intentions. In *Proceedings of ECAI'96 Workshop Gaps and Bridges: New Directions in Planning and Natural Language Generation*, pages 102–104.

Pernilla Qvarfordt and Arne Jönsson. 1998. Effects of using speech in timetable information systems for www. In *Proceedings of ICSLP'98, Sydney, Australia.*

Pernilla Qvarfordt. 1998. Usability of multimodal timetables: Effects of different levels of domain knowledge on usability. Master's thesis, Linköping University.

Karen Sparck Jones and Julia R. Galliers. 1996. *Evaluating Natural Language Processing Systems.* Springer Verlag.

Marilyn A. Walker, Diane J. Litman, Candace A. Kamm, and Alicia Abella. 1998. Paradise: A framework for evaluating spoken dialogue agents. In Mark Maybury & Wolfgang Wahlster, editor, *Readings in Intelligent User Interfaces.* Morgan Kaufmann.

Plan-Based Dialogue Management in a Physics Tutor

Reva Freedman
Learning Research and Development Center
University of Pittsburgh
Pittsburgh, PA 15260
freedrk+@pitt.edu
http://www.pitt.edu/~freedrk

Abstract

This paper describes an application of APE (the Atlas Planning Engine), an integrated planning and execution system at the heart of the Atlas dialogue management system. APE controls a mixed-initiative dialogue between a human user and a host system, where turns in the 'conversation' may include graphical actions and/or written text. APE has full unification and can handle arbitrarily nested discourse constructs, making it more powerful than dialogue managers based on finite-state machines. We illustrate this work by describing Atlas-Andes, an intelligent tutoring system built using APE with the Andes physics tutor as the host.

1 Introduction

The purpose of the Atlas project is to enlarge the scope of student interaction in an intelligent tutoring system (ITS) to include coherent conversational sequences, including both written text and GUI actions. A key component of Atlas is APE, the Atlas Planning Engine, a "just-in-time" planner specialized for easy construction and quick generation of hierarchically organized dialogues. APE is a domain- and task-independent system. Although to date we have used APE as a dialogue manager for intelligent tutoring systems, APE could also be used to manage other types of human-computer conversation, such as an advice-giving system or an interactive help system.

Planning is an essential component of a dialogue-based ITS. Although there are many reasons for using natural language in an ITS, as soon as the student gives an unexpected response to a tutor question, the tutor needs to be able to plan in order to achieve its goals as well as respond appropriately to the student's statement. Yet classical planning is inappropriate for dialogue generation precisely because it assumes an unchanging world. A more appropriate approach is the "practical reason" approach pioneered by Bratman (1987, 1990). According to Bratman, human beings maintain plans and prefer to follow them, but they are also capable of changing the plans on the fly when needed. Bratman's approach has been introduced into computer science under the name of *reactive planning* (Georgeff and Ingrand 1989, Wilkins et al. 1995).

In this paper we discuss the rationale for the use of reactive planning as well as the use of the hierarchical task network (HTN) style of plan operators. Then we describe APE (the Atlas Planning Engine), a dialogue planner we have implemented to embody the above concepts. We demonstrate the use of APE by showing how we have used it to add a dialogue capability to an existing ITS, the Andes physics tutor. By showing dialogues that Atlas-Andes can generate, we demonstrate the advantages of this architecture over the finite-state machine approach to dialogue management.

2 Integrated planning and execution for dialogue generation

2.1 'Practical reason' and the BDI model

For an ITS, planning is required in order to ensure a coherent conversation as well as to accomplish tutorial goals. But it is impossible to plan a whole conversation in advance when the student can respond freely at every turn, just as human beings cannot plan their daily lives in advance because of possible changes in conditions. Classical planning algorithms are inappropriate because the tutor must be able to change plans based on the

---

This research was supported by NSF grant number 9720359 to CIRCLE, the Center for Interdisciplinary Research on Constructive Learning Environments at the University of Pittsburgh and Carnegie-Mellon University.

student's responses.

For this reason we have adopted the ideas of the philosopher Michael Bratman (1987, 1990). Bratman uses the term "practical reason" to describe his analysis since he is concerned with how to reason about practical matters. For human beings, planning is required in order to accomplish one's goals. Bratman's key insight is that human beings tend to follow a plan once they have one, although they are capable of dropping an intention or changing a partial plan when necessary. In other words, human beings do not decide what to do from scratch at each turn.

Bratman and others who have adopted his approach use a tripartite mental model that includes *beliefs*, *desires* and *intentions* (Bratman, Israel and Pollack 1988, Pollack 1992, Georgeff et al. 1998), hence the name "BDI model." Beliefs, which are uninstantiated plans in the speaker's head, are reified by the plan library. Desires are expressed as the agent's goals. Intentions, or plan steps that the agent has committed to but not yet acted on, are stored in an agenda. Thus the agent's partial plan for achieving a goal is a network of intentions. A plan can be left in a partially expanded state until it is necessary to refine it further.

2.2 Implementation via reactive planning

Bratman's approach has been elaborated in a computer science context by subsequent researchers (Bratman, Israel and Pollack 1988, Pollack 1992, Georgeff et al. 1998). Reactive planning (Georgeff and Ingrand 1989, Wilkins et al. 1995), originally known as "integrated planning and execution," is one way of implementing Bratman's model. Originally developed for real-time control of the space shuttle, reactive planning has since been used in a variety of other domains. For the Atlas project we have developed a reactive planner called APE (Atlas Planning Engine) which uses these ideas to conduct a conversation. After each student response, the planner can choose to continue with its previous intention or change something in the plan to respond better to the student's utterance.

Like most reactive planners, APE is a hierarchical task network (HTN) style planner (Yang 1990, Erol, Hendler and Nau 1994). Hierarchical decomposition asserts that each goal can be achieved via a series of subgoals instead of relying on means-end reasoning. Hierarchical decomposition is more appropriate to dialogue generation for a number of reasons. First, decomposition is better suited to the type of large-scale dialogue planning required in a real-world tutoring system, as it is easier to establish what a human speaker will say in a given situation than to be able to understand why in sufficient detail and generality to do means-end planning. Second, Hierarchical decomposition minimizes search time. Third, our dialogues are task-oriented and have a hierarchical structure (Grosz and Sidner 1986). In such a case, matching the structure of the domain simplifies operator development because they can often be derived from transcripts of human tutoring sessions. The hierarchy information is also useful in determining appropriate referring expressions. Fourth, inter-leaved planning and execution is important for dialogue generation because we cannot predict the human user's future utterances. In an HTN-based system, it is straightforward to implement interleaved planning and execution because one only needs to expand the portion of the plan that is about to be executed. Finally, the conversation is in a certain sense the trace of the plan. In other words, we care much more about the actions generated by the planner than the states involved, whether implicitly or explicitly specified. Hierarchical decomposition provides this trace naturally.

3 Background: the Andes physics tutor

Andes (Gertner, Conati and VanLehn 1998) is an intelligent tutoring system in the domain of first-year college physics. Andes teaches via *coached problem solving* (VanLehn 1996). In coached problem solving, the tutoring system tracks the student as the latter attempts to solve a problem. If the student gets stuck or deviates too far from a correct solution path, the tutoring system provides hints and other assistance.

A sample Andes problem is shown in mid-solution in Figure 1. A physics problem is given in the upper-left corner with a picture below it. Next to the picture the student has begun to sketch the vectors involved using the GUI buttons along the left-hand edge of the screen. As the student draws vectors, Andes and the student cooperatively fill in the variable definitions in the upper-right corner. Later the student will use the space below to write equations connecting the variables.

In this example, the elevator is decelerating, so the acceleration vector should face the opposite direction from the velocity vector. (If the acceleration vector went the same direction as the velocity vector, the speed of the elevator would increase and it would crash into the ground.) This is an important issue in beginning physics; it occurs in five Andes problems.

When such errors occur, Andes turns the incorrect item red and provides hints to students in the lower-left corner of the screen. A sample of these hints, shown in the order a student would encounter them, is shown in Fig. 2. But hints are an output-only form of natural language; the student can't take the initiative or ask a question. In addition, there is no way for the system to ask the student a question or lead the student through a multi-step directed line of reasoning. Thus there is no way to use some of the effective rhetorical methods used by skilled human tutors, such as analogy and *reductio ad absurdum*. Current psychological research suggests that active methods, where students have to answer questions, will improve the performance of tutoring systems.

4 Structure of the Atlas Planning Engine

Figure 3 shows a sample plan operator. For legibility, the key elements have been rendered in English instead of in Lisp. The *hiercx* slot provides a way for the planner to be aware of the context in which a decomposition is proposed. Items in the *hiercx* slot are instantiated and added to the transient database only so long as the operator which spawned them is in the agenda.

To initiate a planning session, the user invokes the planner with an initial goal. The system searches the operator library to find all operators whose goal field matches the next goal on the agenda and whose filter conditions and precon-

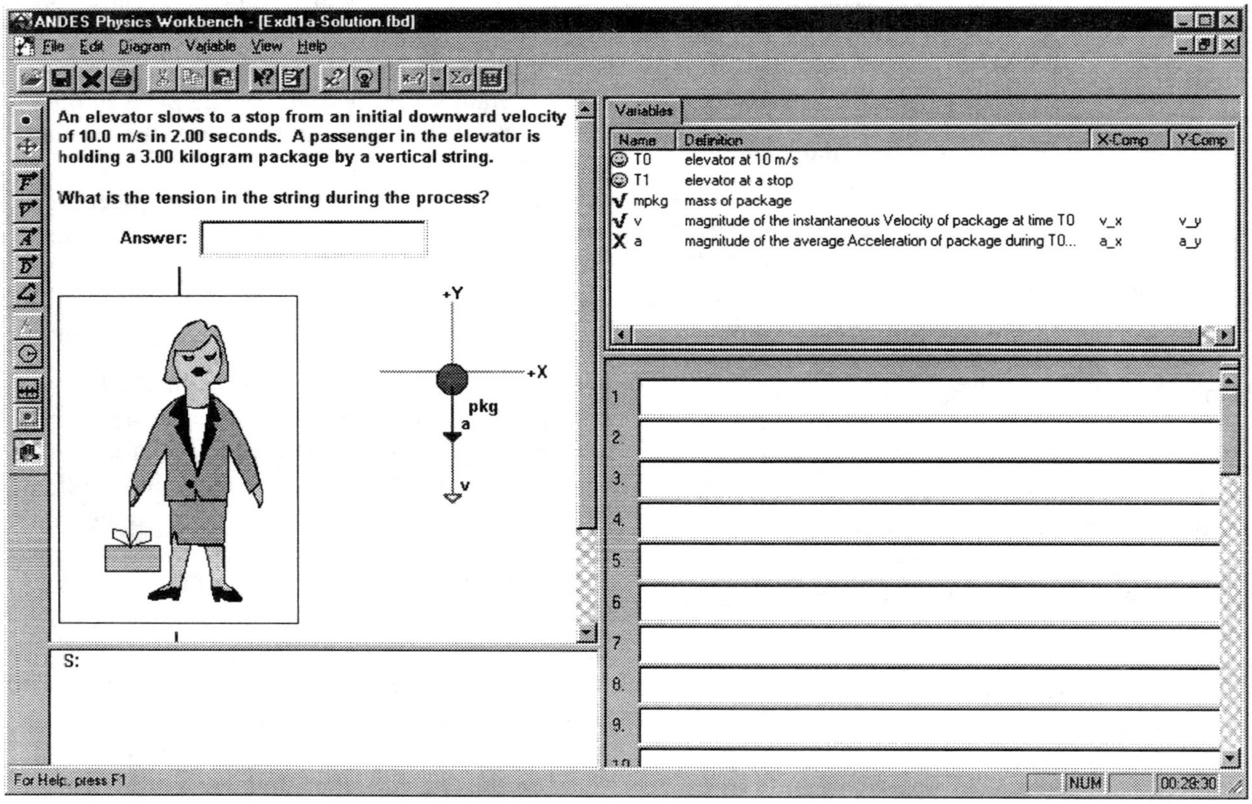

Figure 1: Screen shot of the Andes physics tutor

S: ⟨draws acceleration vector in same direction as velocity⟩
T: Wrong.
S: What's wrong with that?
T: Think about the direction of the acceleration vector.
S: Please explain further.
T: Remember that the direction of acceleration is the direction of the change in velocity.
S: Please explain further.
T: The direction of the acceleration vector is straight up.
S: ⟨draws acceleration vector correctly⟩

Figure 2: Andes hint sequence formatted as dialogue

ditions are satisfied. Goals are represented in first-order logic without quantifiers and matched via unification. Since APE is intended especially for generation of hierarchically organized task-oriented discourse, each operator has a multi-step recipe in the style of Wilkins (1988). When a match is found, the matching goal is removed from the agenda and is replaced by the steps in the recipe. APE has two kinds of primitive actions; one ends a turn and the other doesn't.

From the point of view of discourse generation, the most important APE recipe items are those allowing the planner to change the agenda when necessary. These three types of recipe items make APE more powerful than a classical planner.

• *Fact:* Evaluate a condition. If false, skip the rest of the recipe. *Fact* is used to allow run-time decision making by bypassing the rest of an operator when circumstances change during its execution. *Fact* can be used with *retry-at* to implement a loop just as in Prolog.

• *Retry-at:* The purpose of *retry-at* is to allow the planner to back up to a choice point and make a new decision. It removes goals sequentially from the top of the agenda, a full operator at a time, until the supplied argument is false. Then it restores the parent goal of the last operator removed, so that further planning can choose a new way to achieve it. *Retry-at* implements a Prolog-like choice of alternatives, but it differs from backtracking in that the new operator is chosen based on conditions that apply when the retry operation is executed, rather than on a list of possible operators formed when the original operator was chosen. For *retry-at* to be useful, the author must provide multiple operators for the same goal. Each operator must have a set of preconditions enabling it to be chosen at the appropriate time.

• *Prune-replace:* The intent of *prune-replace* is

```
(def-operator handle-same-direction
  :goal (...)
  :filter  ()
  :precond (...)
     ; We have asked a question about acceleration
     ; ... and the student has given an answer
     ; ... from which we can deduce that s/he thinks accel. and velocity go in
     ;     the same direction
     ; and we have not given the explanation below yet
  :recipe (...)
     ; Tell the student: "But if the acceleration went the same
        direction as the velocity, then the elevator would be speeding up."
     ; Mark that we are giving this explanation
     ; Tell the student that tutor is requesting another answer ("Try again.")
     ; Edit the agenda (using prune-replace) so that responding to another
        answer is at the top of the agenda
  :hiercx  ())
```

Figure 3: Sample plan operator

to allow the planner to remove goals from the agenda based on a change in circumstances. It removes goals sequentially from the top of the agenda, one at a time, until the supplied argument becomes false. Then it replaces the removed goals with an optional list of new goals. *Prune-replace* allows a type of decision-making frequently used in dialogue generation. When a conversation partner does not give the expected response, one would often like to remove the next goal from the agenda and replace it with one or more replacement goals. *Prune-replace* implements a generalized version of this concept.

APE is domain-independent and communicates with a host system via an API. As a partner in a dialogue, it needs to obtain information from the world as well as produce output turns. Preconditions on plan operators can be used to access information from external knowledge sources. APE contains a recipe item type that can be used to execute an external program such as a call to a GUI interface. APE also has recipe items allowing the user to assert and retract facts in a knowledge base. Further details about the APE planner can be found in (Freedman, 2000).

5 Implementation of Atlas-Andes

5.1 Architecture of Atlas-Andes

The first system we have implemented with APE is a prototype Atlas-Andes system that replaces the hints usually given for an incorrect acceleration vector by a choice of generated subdialogues. Figure 4 shows the architecture of Atlas-Andes; any other system built with APE would look similar. Robust natural language understanding in Atlas-Andes is provided by Rosé's CARMEL system (Rosé 2000); it uses the spelling correction algorithm devised by Elmi and Evens (1998).

5.2 Structure of human tutorial dialogues

In an earlier analysis (Kim, Freedman and Evens 1998) we showed that a significant portion of human-human tutorial dialogues can be modeled with the hierarchical structure of task-oriented dialogues (Grosz and Sidner 1986). Furthermore, a main building block of the discourse hierarchy, corresponding to the transaction level in Conversation Analysis (Sinclair and Coulthard 1975), matches the *tutoring episode* defined by VanLehn et al. (1998). A tutoring episode consists of the turns necessary to help the student make one correct entry on the interface.

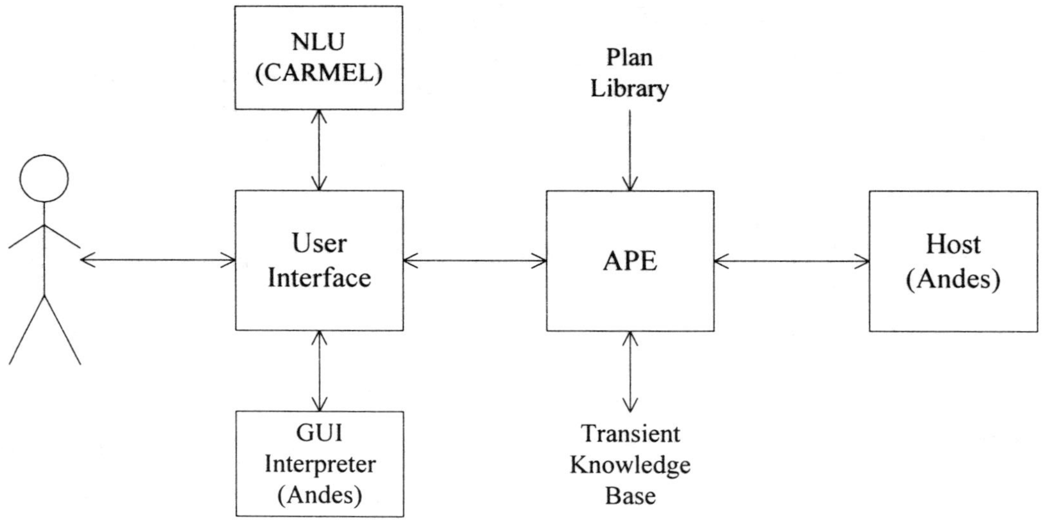

Figure 4: Interface between Atlas and host system

To obtain empirical data for the Atlas-Andes plan operators, we analyzed portions of a corpus of human tutors helping students solve similar physics problems. Two experienced tutors were used. Tutor A was a graduate student in computer science who had majored in physics; tutor B was a professional physics tutor.

The complete corpus contained solutions to five physics problems by 41 students each. We analyzed every tutoring episode dealing with the acceleration vector during deceleration, totaling 29 examples divided among 20 students and both tutors. The tutors had very different styles. Tutor A tended to provide encouragement rather than content, making those transcripts less useful for deriving an information-based approach. Tutor B used an information-based approach, but after one wrong answer tended to complete the solution as a monologue. Largely following tutor B's approach to sequence and content, we isolated six ways of teaching the student about direction of acceleration.

5.3 Sample output and evaluation

Figure 5 shows an example of text that can be generated by the Atlas-Andes system, showing an analogy-based approach to teaching this content. The operator library used to generate this text could generate a combinatorially large number of versions of this dialogue as well as selected examples of other ways of teaching about direction of acceleration.

This operator library used to generate this text contained 111 plan operators, divided as follows:

Tutoring schemata	4	4%
Switching between schemata	5	4%
API and GUI handling	33	30%
Answer handling	35	31%
Domain-dep. lex. insertion	24	22%
Domain-indep. lex. insertion	10	9%
TOTAL	111	100%

We are currently working on components that will allow us to increase the number of physics concepts covered without a corresponding increase in the number of operators. The schema switching operators prevent the tutor from repeating itself during a physics problem. They could be reduced or eliminated by a general discourse history component that tutoring schema operators could refer to. Domain-dependent lexical insertion refers to the choice of lexical items such as *car* and *east* in the sample dialogue, while domain-independent lexical insertion refers to items such as *OK* and *exactly*. Both categories could be eliminated, or at least severely reduced, through the use of a text realization package. Together that would provide a one-third reduction in the number of operators needed. As the set of API and GUI handling operators is fixed, that would reduce by half the number of application operators needed.

The largest remaining category of operators is the answer handlers. These operators handle a variety of answers for each of the five questions that the system can ask. The answers we recognize include categories such as "don't know" as well as specific answers (e.g. a direction perpendicular to the correct answer) which we recognize because the tutor has specific replies for them. In order to reduce the number of

S: ⟨draws acceleration vector in same direction as velocity⟩
T: What is the definition of acceleration?
S: Don't know.
T: OK, let's try this. If a car was driving along east, which way would you have to push on it to make it stop?
S: West.
T: Exactly. The opposite direction. So the net force goes the opposite direction, and so does the acceleration. Try to draw the acceleration vector again now.
S: ⟨draws acceleration vector correctly⟩

Figure 5: Example of generated dialogue

operators further, we must investigate more general methods of handling student errors. In particular, we plan to investigate error-classifying predicates that apply to more than one question as well as the use of intention-based predicates. Since the system only covers one rule of physics, albeit in a variety of ways, we plan to make some of these efficiency improvements before adding new rules of physics and testing it with users.

Preconditions for the operators in the plan library utilize discourse or interaction history, the current goal hierarchy, recent information such as the tutor's current goal and the student's latest response, shared information such as a model of objects on the screen, and domain knowledge. As an example of the latter, if the student draws an acceleration vector which is incorrect but not opposite to the velocity vector, a different response will be generated.

5.4 Discussion

Many previous dialogue-based ITSs have been implemented with finite-state machines, either simple or augmented. In the most common finite state model, each time the human user issues an utterance, the processor reduces it to one of a small number of categories. These categories represent the possible transitions between states. Thus history can be stored, and context considered, only by expanding the number of states. This approach puts an arbitrary restriction on the amount of context or depth of conversational nesting that can be considered. More importantly, it misses the significant generalization that these types of dialogues are hierarchical: larger units contain repeated instances of the same smaller units in different sequences and instantiated with different values. Furthermore, the finite-state machine approach does not allow the author to drop one line of attack and replace it by another without hard-coding every possible transition.

It is also clear that the dialogue-based approach has many benefits over the hint-sequence approach. In addition to providing a multi-step teaching methods with new content, it can respond flexibly to a variety of student answers at each step and take context into account when generating a reply.

6 Related work

Wenger (1987), still the chief textbook on ITSs, states that using a global planner to control an ITS is too inefficient to try. This is no longer true, if indeed it ever was. Vassileva (1995) proposes a system based on AND-OR graphs with a separate set of rules for reacting to unexpected events. Lehuen, Nicolle and Luzzati (1996) present a method of dialogue analysis that produces schemata very similar to ours. Earlier dialogue-based ITSs that use augmented finite-state machines or equivalent include CIRCSIM-Tutor (Woo et al. 1991, Zhou et al. 1999) and the system described by Woolf (1984). Cook (1998) uses levels of finite-state machines. None of these systems provides for predicates with variables or unification.

7 Conclusions

In this paper we described APE, an integrated planner and execution system that we have implemented as part of the Atlas dialogue manager. APE uses HTN-style operators and is based on reactive planning concepts. Although APE is intended largely for use in domains with hierarchical, multi-turn plans, it can be used to implement any conversation-based system, where turns in the 'conversation' may include graphical actions and/or text. We illustrated the use of APE with an example from the Atlas-Andes physics tutor. We showed that previous models based on finite-state machines are insufficient to handle the nested subdialogues and abandoned partial subdialogues that occur in practical applications. We showed how APE generated a sample dialogue that earlier systems could not handle.

Acknowledgments

We thank Abigail Gertner for her generous assistance with the Andes system, and Michael Ringenberg for indispensible programming support. Carolyn Rosé built the CARMEL natural language understanding component. Mohammed Elmi and Michael Glass of Illinois Institute of Technology provided the spelling correction code. We thank Pamela Jordan and the referees for their comments.

References

Bratman, M. E. 1987. *Intentions, Plans, and Practical Reason*. Cambridge, MA: Harvard.

Bratman, M. E. 1990. What is Intention? In P. R. Cohen, J. Morgan and M. E. Pollack, *Intentions in Communication*. Cambridge, MA: MIT Press.

Bratman, M. E., Israel, D. J. and Pollack, M. E. 1988. Plans and Resource-Bounded Practical Reasoning. *Computational Intelligence* 4(4): 349–355.

Cook, J. 1998. Knowledge Mentoring as a Framework for Designing Computer-Based Agents for Supporting Musical Composition Learning. PhD. diss., Computing Department, The Open University.

Elmi, M. A. and Evens, M. W. 1998. Spelling Correction using Context. In Proceedings of the 17th COLING/36th ACL (COLING–ACL '98), Montreal.

Erol, K., Hendler, J. and Nau, D. S. 1994. HTN Planning: Complexity and Expressivity. In Proceedings of the Twelfth National Conference on Artificial Intelligence (AAAI '94), Seattle.

Freedman, R. 2000 (to appear). Using a Reactive Planner as the Basis for a Dialogue Agent. In Proceedings of the Thirteenth Florida Artificial Intelligence Research Symposium (FLAIRS '00), Orlando.

Gertner, A. S., Conati, C. and VanLehn, K. 1998. Procedural Help in Andes: Generating Hints Using a Bayesian Network Student Model. In Proceedings of the Fifteenth National Conference on Artificial Intelligence (AAAI '98), Madison.

Georgeff, M. P. and Ingrand, F. F. 1989. Decision-Making in an Embedded Reasoning System. In Proceedings of the Eleventh International Joint Conference on Artificial Intelligence (IJCAI '89), Detroit.

Georgeff, M. P., Pell, B., Pollack, M. E., Tambe, M. and Wooldridge, M. 1998. The Belief-Desire-Intention Model of Agency. In N. Jenning, J. Muller, and M. Wooldridge (Eds.), *Intelligent Agents V*. Springer.

Grosz, B. J. and Sidner, C. L. 1986. Attention, Intentions, and the Structure of Discourse. *Computational Linguistics* 12(3): 175–204.

Kim, J., Freedman, R. and Evens, M. 1998. Responding to Unexpected Student Utterances in CIRCSIM-Tutor v. 3: Analysis of Transcripts. In Proceedings of the Eleventh Florida Artificial Intelligence Research Symposium (FLAIRS '98), Sanibel Island.

Lehuen, J., Nicolle, A. and Luzzati, D. 1996. Un modèle hypothético-expérimental dynamique pour la gestion des dialogues homme-machine. In Actes du dixième congrès de reconnaissance des formes et intelligence artificielle (RFIA '96), Rennes.

Pollack, M. E. 1992. The Uses of Plans. *Artificial Intelligence* 57(1): 43–69.

Rosé, C. P. 2000. A Framework for Robust Semantic Interpretation. In Proceedings of the First Annual Conference of the North American Chapter of the Association for Computational Linguistics (NAACL '00).

Sinclair, J. M. and Coulthard, R. M. 1975. *Towards an Analysis of Discourse: The English Used by Teachers and Pupils*. London: Oxford University Press.

VanLehn, K. 1996. Conceptual and Meta Learning during Coached Problem Solving. In *Intelligent Tutoring Systems: Third International Conference (ITS '96)*, Montreal. Berlin: Springer. LNCS 1086.

VanLehn, K., Siler, S., Murray, C. and Baggett, W. 1998. What Makes a Tutorial Event Effective? In Proceedings of the Twenty-first Annual Conference of the Cognitive Science Society, Madison. Hillsdale, NJ: Erlbaum.

Vassileva, J. 1995. Reactive Instructional Planning to Support Interacting Teaching Strategies. In Proceedings of the Seventh World Conference on AI and Education (AI–ED '95), Washington, D.C. Charlottesville, VA: AACE.

Wenger, E. 1987. *Artificial Intelligence and Tutoring Systems: Computational and Cognitive Approaches to the Communication of Knowledge*. San Mateo, CA: Morgan Kaufmann.

Wilkins, D. 1988. *Practical Planning: Extending the Classical AI Planning Paradigm*. San Mateo, CA: Morgan Kaufmann.

Wilkins, D., Myers, K., Lowrance, J. and Wesley, L. 1995. Planning and Reacting in Uncertain and Dynamic Environments. *Journal of Experimental and Theoretical Artificial Intelligence* 7: 121–152.

Woo, C., Evens, M. W., Michael, J. A. and Rovick, A. A. 1991. Dynamic Instructional Planning for an Intelligent Physiology Tutoring System. In Proceedings of the Fourth Annual IEEE Computer-Based Medical Systems Symposium, Baltimore.

Woolf, B. 1984. Context-Dependent Planning in a Machine Tutor. Ph.D. diss., Dept. of Computer and Information Science, University of Massachusetts at Amherst. COINS Technical Report 84–21.

Yang, Q. 1990. Formalizing planning knowledge for hierarchical planning. *Computational Intelligence* 6(1): 12–24.

Zhou, Y., Freedman, R., Glass, M., Michael, J. A., Rovick, A. A. and Evens, M. W. 1999. Delivering Hints in a Dialogue-Based Intelligent Tutoring System. In Proceedings of the Sixteenth National Conference on Artificial Intelligence (AAAI '99), Orlando, FL.

A Framework for MT and Multilingual NLG Systems Based on Uniform Lexico-Structural Processing

Benoit Lavoie
CoGenTex, Inc.
840 Hanshaw Road
Ithaca, NY
USA, 14850
benoit@cogentex.com

Richard Kittredge
CoGenTex, Inc.
840 Hanshaw Road
Ithaca, NY
USA, 14850
richard@cogentex.com

Tanya Korelsky
CoGenTex, Inc.
840 Hanshaw Road
Ithaca, NY
USA, 14850
tanya@cogentex.com

Owen Rambow *
ATT Labs-Research, B233
180 Park Ave, PO Box 971
Florham Park, NJ
USA, 07932
rambow@research.att.com

Abstract

In this paper we describe an implemented framework for developing monolingual or multilingual natural language generation (NLG) applications and machine translation (MT) applications. The framework demonstrates a uniform approach to generation and transfer based on declarative lexico-structural transformations of dependency structures of syntactic or conceptual levels ("uniform lexico-structural processing"). We describe how this framework has been used in practical NLG and MT applications, and report the lessons learned.

1 Introduction

In this paper we present a linguistically motivated framework for uniform lexico-structural processing. It has been used for transformations of conceptual and syntactic structures during generation in monolingual and multilingual natural language generation (NLG) and for transfer in machine translation (MT). Our work extends directions taken in systems such as Ariane (Vauquois and Boitet, 1985), FoG (Kittredge and Polguère, 1991), JOYCE (Rambow and Korelsky, 1992), and LFS (Iordanskaja et al., 1992). Although it adopts the general principles found in the above-mentioned systems, the approach presented in this paper is more practical, and we believe, would eventually integrate better with emerging statistics-based approaches to MT.

* The work performed on the framework by this co-author was done while at CoGenTex, Inc.

The framework consists of a portable Java environment for building NLG or MT applications by defining modules using a core tree transduction engine and single declarative ASCII specification language for conceptual or syntactic dependency tree structures[1] and their transformations. Developers can define new modules, add or remove modules, or modify their connections. Because the processing of the transformation engine is restricted to transduction of trees, it is computationally efficient.

Having declarative rules facilitates their reuse when migrating from one programming environment to another; if the rules are based on functions specific to a programming language, the implementation of these functions might no longer be available in a different environment. In addition, having all lexical information and all rules represented declaratively makes it relatively easy to integrate into the framework techniques for generating some of the rules automatically, for example using corpus-based methods. The declarative form of transformations makes it easier to process them, compare them, and cluster them to achieve proper classification and ordering.

[1] In this paper, we use the term *syntactic dependency (tree) structure* as defined in the Meaning-Text Theory (MTT; Mel'cuk, 1988). However, we extrapolate from this theory when we use the term conceptual dependency (tree) structure, which has no equivalent in MTT (and is unrelated to Shank's CD structures proposed in the 1970s).

Thus, the framework represents a generalized processing environment that can be reused in different types of natural language processing (NLP) applications. So far the framework has been used successfully to build a wide variety of NLG and MT applications in several limited domains (meteorology, battlefield messages, object modeling) and for different languages (English, French, Arabic, and Korean).

In the next sections, we present the design of the core tree transduction module (Section 2), describe the representations that it uses (Section 3) and the linguistic resources (Section 4). We then discuss the processing performed by the tree transduction module (Section 5) and its instantiation for different applications (Section 6). Finally, we discuss lessons learned from developing and using the framework (Section 7) and describe the history of the framework comparing it to other systems (Section 8).

2 The Framework's Tree Transduction Module

The core processing engine of the framework is a generic tree transduction module for lexico-structural processing, shown in Figure 1. The module has dependency stuctures as input and output, expressed in the same tree formalism, although not necessarily at the same level (see Section 3). This design facilitates the pipelining of modules for stratificational transformation. In fact, in an application, there are usually several instantiations of this module.

The transduction module consists of three processing steps: lexico-structural pre-processing, main lexico-structural processing, and lexico-structural post-processing. Each of these steps is driven by a separate grammar, and all three steps draw on a common feature data base and lexicon. The grammars, the lexicon and the feature data base are referred to as the *linguistic resources* (even if they sometimes apply to a conceptual representation). All linguistic resources are represented in a declarative manner. An *instantiation* of the tree transduction module consists of a specification of the linguistic resources.

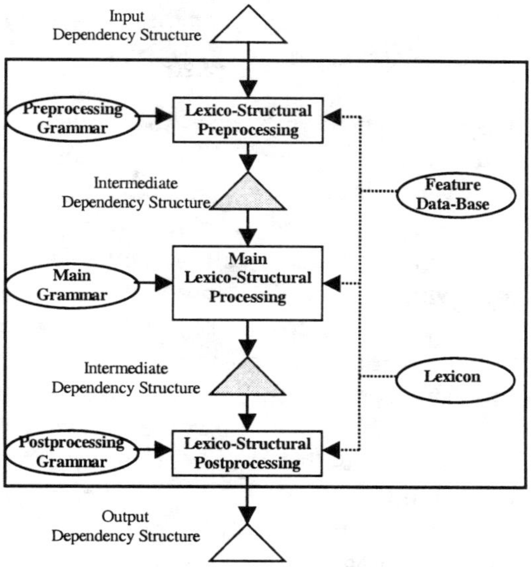

Figure 1: Design of the Tree Transduction Module

3 The Framework's Representations

The representations used by all instantiations of the tree transduction module in the framework are dependency tree structures. The main characteristics of all the dependency tree structures are:

- A dependency tree is unordered (in contrast with phrase structure trees, there is no ordering between the branches of the tree).
- All the nodes in the tree correspond to lexemes (i.e., lexical heads) or concepts depending on the level of representation. In contrast with a phrase structure representation, there are no phrase-structure nodes labeled with nonterminal symbols. Labelled arcs indicate the dependency relationships between the lexemes.

The first of these characteristics makes a dependency tree structure a very useful representation for MT and multilingual NLG, since it gives linguists a representation that allows them to abstract over numerous cross-linguistic divergences due to language specific ordering (Polguère, 1991).

We have implemented 4 different types of dependency tree structures that can be used for NLG, MT or both:

- Deep-syntactic structures (DSyntSs);
- Surface syntactic structures (SSyntSs);

- Conceptual structures (ConcSs);
- Parsed syntactic structures (PSyntSs).

The DSyntSs and SSyntSs correspond closely to the equivalent structures of the Meaning-Text Theory (MTT; Mel'cuk, 1988): both structures are unordered syntactic representations, but a DSyntS only includes full meaning-bearing lexemes while a SSyntS also contains function words such as determiners, auxiliaries, and strongly governed prepositions. In the implemented applications, the DSyntSs are the pivotal representations involved in most transformations, as this is also often the case in practice in linguistic-based MT (Hutchins and Somers, 1997). Figure 2 illustrates a DSyntS from a meteorological application, MeteoCogent (Kittredge and Lavoie, 1998), represented using the standard graphical notation and also the RealPro ASCII notation used internally in the framework (Lavoie and Rambow, 1997). As Figure 2 illustrates, there is a straightforward mapping between the graphical notation and the ASCII notation supported in the framework. This also applies for all the transformation rules in the framework which illustrates the declarative nature of our approach.

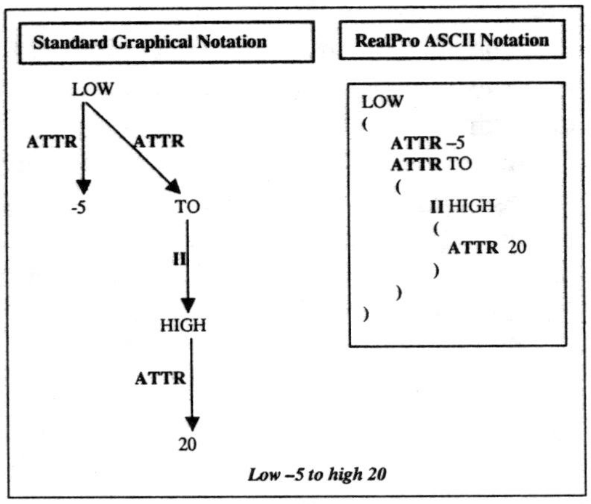

Figure 2: DSyntS (Graphical and ASCII Notation)

The ConcSs correspond to the standard frame-like structures used in knowledge representation, with labeled arcs corresponding to slots. We have used them only for a very limited meteorological domain (in MeteoCogent), and we imagine that they will typically be defined in a domain-specific manner.

Figure 3 illustrates the mapping between an interlingua defined as a ConcS and a corresponding English DSyntS. This example, also taken from MeteoCogent, illustrates that the conceptual interlingua in NLG can be closer to a database representation of domain data than to its linguistic representations.

As mentioned in (Polguère, 1991), the high level of abstraction of the ConcSs makes them a suitable interlingua for multilingual NLG since they bridge the semantic discrepancies between languages, and they can be produced easily from the domain data. However, most off-the-shelf parsers available for MT produce only syntactic structures, thus the DSyntS level is often more suitable for transfer.

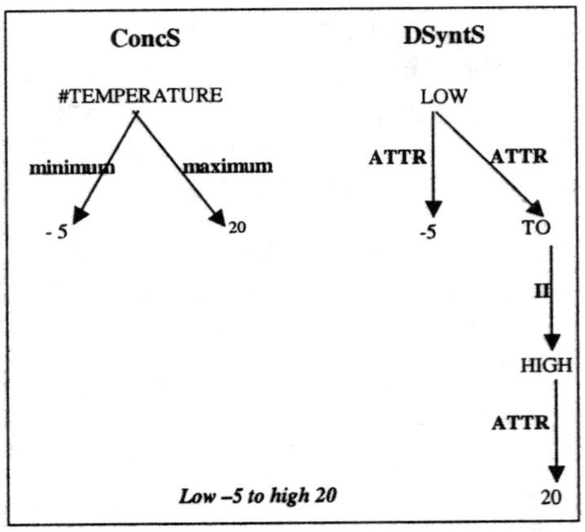

Figure 3: ConcS Interlingua and English DSyntS

Finally, the PSyntSs correspond to the parser outputs represented using RealPro's dependency structure formalism. The PSyntSs may not be valid directly for realization or transfer since they may contain unsupported features or dependency relations. However, the PSyntSs are represented in a way to allow the framework to convert them into valid DSyntS via lexico-structural processing. This conversion is done via conversion grammars customized for each parser. There is a practical need to convert one syntactic formalism to another and so far we have implemented converters for three off-the-shelf parsers (Palmer et al., 1998).

4 The Framework's Linguistic Resources

As mentioned previously, the framework is composed of instantiations of the tree transduction module shown in Figure 1. Each module has the following resources:

- *Feature Data-Base*: This consists of the feature system defining available features and their possible values in the module.
- *Lexicon*: This consists of the available lexemes or concepts, depending on whether the module works at syntactic or conceptual level. Each lexeme and concept is defined with its features, and may contain specific lexico-structural rules: transfer rules for MT, mapping rules to the next level of representation for surface realization of DSyntS or lexicalization of ConcS.
- *Main Grammar*: This consists of the lexico-structural mapping rules that apply at this level and which are not lexeme- or concept-specific (e.g. DSynt-rules for the DSynt-module, Transfer-rules for the Transfer module, etc.)
- *Preprocessing grammar*: This consists of the lexico-structural mapping rules for transforming the input structures in order to make them compliant with the main grammar, if this is necessary. Such rules are used to integrate new modules together when discrepancies in the formalism need to be fixed. This grammar can also be used for adding default features (e.g. setting the default number of nouns to singular) or for applying default transformations (e.g. replacing non meaning-bearing lexemes with features).
- *Postprocessing grammar*: This consists of lexico-structural mapping rules for transforming the output structures before they can be processed by the next module. As for the preprocessing rules, these rules can be used to fix some discrepancies between modules.

Our representation of the lexicon at the lexical level (as opposed to conceptual) is similar to the one found in RealPro. Figure 4 shows a specification for the lexeme SELL. This lexeme is defined as a verb of regular morphology with two lexical-structural mappings, the first one introducing the preposition TO for its 3rd actant, and the preposition FOR for its 4th actant: *(a seller) X1 sells (merchandise) X2 to (a buyer) X3 for (a price) X4*. What is important is that each mapping specifies a transformation between structures at different levels of representation but that are represented in one and the same representation formalism (DSyntS and SSyntS in this case). As we will see below, grammar rules are also expressed in a similar way.

```
LEXEME:      SELL
CATEGORY:    verb
FEATURES:    [ ]
GOV-PATTERN: [
             DSYNT-RULE:
                 SELL ( III $X3 )
               <-->
                 SELL
                     ( completive2 TO
                         ( prepositional $X3 ) )

             DSYNT-RULE:
                 SELL ( IV $X4 )
               <-->
                 SELL
                     ( completive3 FOR
                           ( prepositional $X4 ) )
             ]
MORPHOLOGY:  [
               ( [ tense:past ]       sold  [ inv ]
               ( [ mood:past-part ]   sold  [ inv ]
               ( [ ]                  sell  [ reg ]
             ]
```

Figure 4: Specification of Lexeme SELL

At the conceptual level, the conceptual lexicon associates lexical-structural mapping with concepts in a similar way. Figure 5 illustrates the mapping at the deep-syntactic level associated with the concept #TEMPERATURE. Except for the slight differences in the labelling, this type of specification is similar to the one used on the lexical level. The first mapping rule corresponds to one of the lexico-structural transformations used to convert the interlingual ConcS of Figure 3 to the corresponding DSyntS.

```
CONCEPT: #TEMPERATURE
LEXICAL: [
         LEX-RULE:
            #TEMPERATURE   ( #minimum   $X
                             #maximum   $Y )
         <-->
            LOW  ( ATTR    $X
                   ATTR    TO
                   ( II HIGH
                        ( ATTR $Y ) ) )

         LEX-RULE:
            #TEMPERATURE   ( #minimum   $X )
         <-->
            LOW  ( ATTR    $X  )

         LEX-RULE:
            #TEMPERATURE   ( #maximum   $X )
         <-->
            HIGH  ( ATTR    $X  )
         ]
```

Figure 5: Specification of Concept #TEMPERATURE

Note that since each lexicon entry can have more than one lexical-structural mapping rule, the list of these rules represents a small grammar specific to this lexeme or concept.

Realization grammar rules of the main grammar include generic mapping rules (which are not lexeme-specific) such as the DSyntS-rule illustrated in Figure 6, for inserting a determiner.

```
DSYNT-RULE:

        $X [ class:noun article:def ]
<-->
        $X ( determinative THE )
```

Figure 6: Deep-Syntactic Rule for Determiner Insertion

The lexicon formalism has also been extended to implement lexeme-specific lexico-structural transfer rules. Figure 7 shows the lexico-structural transfer of the English verb lexeme MOVE to French implemented for a military and weather domain (Nasr et al., 1998):

*Cloud will **move into** the western regions.*
*→ Des nuages **envahiront** les régions ouest.*

*They **moved** the assets forward.*
*→ Ils ont **amené** les ressources vers l'avant.*

*The 79 dcg **moves** forward.*
*→ La 79 dcg **avance** vers l'avant.*

*A disturbance will **move** north of Lake Superior.*
*→ Une perturbation **se déplacera** au nord du lac supérieur.*

```
LEXEME:     MOVE
CATEGORY:   verb
FEATURES:   [ ]
TRANSFER:   [
             TRANSFER-RULE:
                   MOVE
                    ( ATTR INTO [class:preposition]
                       ( II $X1 ) )
                <-->
                   ENVAHIR  [class:verb]
                       ( II $X1 )

             TRANSFER-RULE:
                   MOVE
                    ( II $X2 )
                <-->
                   AMENER [class:verb]
                    ( II $X2 )

             TRANSFER-RULE:
                   MOVE
                    ( ATTR $X [lexeme:FORWARD class:adverb] )
                <-->
                   AVANCER
                    ( ATTR $X )

             TRANSFER-RULE:
                   MOVE
                <-->
                   DEPLACER [class:verb refl:+]
            ]
```

Figure 7: Lexico-Structural Transfer of English Lexeme MOVE to French

More general lexico-structural rules for transfer can also be implemented using our grammar rule formalism. Figure 8 gives an English-French transfer rule applied to a weather domain for the transfer of a verb modified by the adverb ALMOST:

*It **almost** rained.*
*→ Il a **failli** pleuvoir.*

```
TRANSFER-RULE:

          $X [ class:verb ]
              ( ATTR ALMOST )
<-->
          FAILLIR [ class:verb ]
              ( II $X [ mood:inf ] )
```

Figure 8: English to French Lexico-Structural Transfer Rule with Verb Modifier ALMOST

More details on how the structural divergences described in (Dorr, 1994) can be accounted for using our formalism can be found in (Nasr et al., 1998).

5 The Rule Processing

Before being processed, the rules are first compiled and indexed for optimisation. Each module applies the following processing.

The rules are assumed to be ordered from most specific to least specific. The application of the rules to the structures is top-down in a recursive way from the first rule to the last. For the main grammar, before applying a grammar rule to a given node, dictionary lookup is carried out in order to first apply the lexeme- or concept-specific rules associated with this node. These are also assumed to be ordered from the most specific to the least specific.

If a lexico-structural transformation involves switching a governor node with one of its dependents in the tree, the process is reapplied with the new node governor. When no more rules can be applied, the same process is applied to each dependent of the current governor. When all nodes have been processed, the processing is completed.

6 Using the Framework to build Applications

Figure 9 shows how different instantiations of the tree transduction module can be combined to build NLP applications. The diagram does not represent a particular system, but rather shows the kind of transformations that have been implemented using the framework, and how they interact. Each arrow represents one type of processing implemented by an instantiation of the tree transduction module. Each triangle represents a different level of representation.

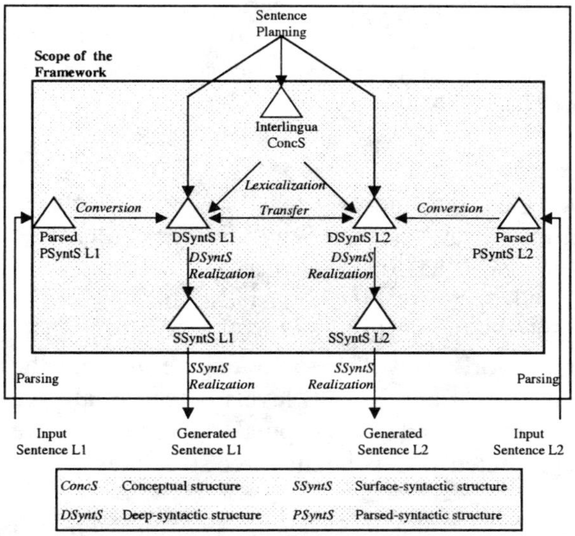

Figure 9: Scope of the Framework's Transformations

For example, in Figure 9, starting with the "Input Sentence L1" and passing through Parsing, Conversion, Transfer, DSyntS Realization and SSyntS Realization to "Generated Sentence L2" we obtain an L1-to-L2 MT system. Starting with "Sentence Planning" and passing through DSyntS Realization, and SSyntS Realization (including linearization and inflection) to "Generated Sentence L1", we obtain a monolingual NLG system for L1.

So far the framework has been used successfully for building a wide variety of applications in different domains and for different languages:

NLG:

- Realization of English DSyntSs via SSyntS level for the domains of meteorology (MeteoCogent; Kittredge and Lavoie, 1998) and object modeling (ModelExplainer; Lavoie et al., 1997).
- Generation of English text from conceptual interlingua for the meteorology domain (MeteoCogent). (The design of the interlingua can also support the generation of French but this functionality has not yet been implemented.)

MT:

- Transfer on the DSyntS level and realization via SSyntS level for English—French, English—Arabic, English—Korean and Korean—English. Translation in the meteorology and battlefield domains (Nasr et al., 1998).
- Conversion of the output structures from off-the-shelf English, French and Korean parsers to DSyntS level before their processing by the other components in the framework (Palmer et al., 1998).

7 Lessons Learned Using the Framework

Empirical results obtained from the applications listed in Section 6 have shown that the approach used in the framework is flexible enough and easily portable to new domains, new languages, and new applications. Moreover, the time spent for development was relatively short compared to that formerly required in developing similar types of applications. Finally, as intended, the limited computational power of the transduction module, as well as careful implementation, including the compilation of declarative linguistic knowledge to Java, have ensured efficient run-time behavior. For example, in the MT domain we did not originally plan for a separate conversion step from the parser output to DSyntS. However, it quickly became apparent that there was a considerable gap between the output of the parsers we were using and the DSyntS representation that was required, and furthermore, that we could use the tree transduction module to quickly bridge this gap.

Nevertheless, our tree transduction-based approach has some important limitations. In particular, the framework requires the developer of the transformation rules to maintain them and specify the order in which the rules must be applied. For a small or a stable grammar, this does not pose a problem. However, for large or rapidly changing grammar (such as a transfer grammar in MT that may need to be adjusted when switching from one parser to another), the burden of the developer's task may be quite heavy. In practice, a considerable amount of time can be spent in testing a grammar after its revision.

Another major problem is related to the maintenance of both the grammar and the lexicon. On several occasions during the development of these resources, the developer in charge of adding lexical and grammatical data must make some decisions that are domain specific. For example, in MT, writing transfer rules for terms that can have several meanings or uses, they may simplify the problem by choosing a solution based on the context found in the current corpus, which is a perfectly natural strategy. However, later, when porting the transfer resources to other domains, the chosen strategy may need to be revised because the context has changed, and other meanings or uses are found in the new corpora. Because the current approach is based on handcrafted rules, maintenance problems of this sort cannot be avoided when porting the resources to new domains.

An approach such as the one described in (Nasr et al., 1998; and Palmer and al., 1998) seems to be solving a part of the problem when it uses corpus analysis techniques for automatically creating a first draft of the lexical transfer dictionary using statistical methods. However, the remaining work is still based on handcrafting because the developer must refine the rules manually. The current framework offers no support for merging handcrafted rules with new lexical rules obtained statistically while preserving the valid handcrafted changes and deleting the invalid ones. In general, a better integration of linguistically based and statistical methods during all the development phases is greatly needed.

8 History of the Framework and Comparison with Other Systems

The framework represents a generalization of several predecessor NLG systems based on Meaning-Text Theory: FoG (Kittredge and Polguère, 1991), LFS (Iordanskaja et al., 1992), and JOYCE (Rambow and Korelsky, 1992). The framework was originally developed for the realization of deep-syntactic structures in NLG (Lavoie and Rambow, 1997). It was later extended for generation of deep-syntactic structures from conceptual interlingua (Kittredge and Lavoie, 1998). Finally, it was applied to MT for transfer between deep-syntactic structures of different languages (Palmer et al., 1998). The current framework encompasses the full spectrum of such transformations, i.e. from the processing of conceptual structures to the processing of deep-syntactic structures, either for NLG or MT.

Compared to its predecessors (Fog, LFS, JOYCE), our approach has obvious advantages in uniformity, declarativity and portability. The framework has been used in a wider variety of domains, for more languages, and for more applications (NLG as well as MT). The framework uses the same engine for all the transformations at all levels because all the syntactic and conceptual structures are represented as dependency tree structures.

In contrast, the predecessor systems were not designed to be rapidly portable. These systems used programming languages or scripts for the implementation of the transformation rules, and used different types of processing at different levels of representation. For instance, in LFS conceptual structures were represented as graphs, whereas syntactic structures were represented as trees which required different types of processing at these two levels.

Our approach also has some disadvantages compared with the systems mentioned above.

Our lexico-structural transformations are far less powerful than those expressible using an arbitrary programming language. In practice, the formalism that we are using for expressing the transformations is inadequate for long-range phenomena (inter-sentential or intra-sentential), including syntactic phenomena such as long-distance *wh*-movement and discourse phenomena such as anaphora and ellipsis. The formalism could be extended to handle intra-sentential syntactic effects, but inter-sentential discourse phenomena probably require procedural rules in order to access lexemes in other sentences. In fact, LFS and JOYCE include a specific module for elliptical structure processing.

Similarly, the limited power of the tree transformation rule formalism distinguishes the framework from other NLP frameworks based on more general processing paradigms such as unification of FUF/SURGE in the generation domain (Elhadad and Robin, 1992).

9 Status

The framework is currently being improved in order to use XML-based specifications for representing the dependency structures and the transformation rules in order to offer a more standard development environment and to facilitate the framework extension and maintenance.

Acknowledgements

A first implementation of the framework (C++ processor and ASCII formalism for expressing the lexico-structural transformation rules) applied to NLG was developed under SBIR F30602-92-C-0015 awarded by USAF Rome Laboratory. The extensions to MT were developed under SBIR DAAL01-97-C-0016 awarded by the Army Research Laboratory. The Java implementation and general improvements of the framework were developed under SBIR DAAD17-99-C-0008 awarded by the Army Research Laboratory. We are thankful to Ted Caldwell, Daryl McCullough, Alexis Nasr and Mike White for their comments and criticism on the work reported in this paper.

References

Dorr, B. J. (1994) Machine translation divergences: A formal description and proposed solution. In *Computational Linguistics*, vol. 20, no. 4, pp. 597–635.

Elhadad, M. and Robin, J. (1992) Controlling Content Realization with Functional Unification Grammars. In *Aspects of Automated Natural Language Generation*, Dale, R., Hovy, E., Rosner, D. and Stock, O. Eds., Springer Verlag, pp. 89–104.

Hutchins, W. J. and Somers, H. L. (1997) *An Introduction to Machine Translation.* Academic Press, second edition.

Iordanskaja, L., Kim, M., Kittredge, R., Lavoie, B. and Polguère, A. (1992) Generation of Extended Bilingual Statistical Reports. In *Proceedings of the 15th International Conference on Computational Linguistics*, Nantes, France, pp. 1019–1023.

Kittredge, R. and Lavoie, B. (1998) MeteoCogent: A Knowledge-Based Tool For Generating Weather Forecast Texts. In *Proceedings of the American Meteorological Society AI Conference (AMS-98),* Phoenix, Arizona, pp. 80–83.

Kittredge, R. and Polguère, A. (1991) Dependency Grammars for Bilingual Text Generation: Inside FoG's Stratificational Models. In *Proceedings of the International Conference on Current Issues in Computational Linguistics*, Penang, Malaysia, pp. 318–330.

Lavoie, B. (1995) Interlingua for Bilingual Statistical Reports. In *Notes of IJCAI-95 Workshop on Multilingual Text Generation*, Montréal, Canada, pp. 84–94.

Lavoie, B. and Rambow, O. (1997) A Fast and Portable Realizer for Text Generation Systems. In *Proceedings of the Fifth Conference on Applied Natural Language Processing*, Washington, DC., pp. 265–268.

Lavoie, B., Rambow, O. and Reiter, E. (1997) Customizable Descriptions of Object-Oriented Models. In *Proceedings of the Fifth Conference on Applied Natural Language Processing*, Washington, DC., pp. 253–256.

Mel'cuk, I. (1988) Dependency Syntax. State University of New York Press, Albany, NY.

Nasr, A., Rambow, O., Palmer, M. and Rosenzweig, J. (1998) Enriching lexical transfer with cross-linguistic semantic features. In *Proceedings of the Interlingua Workshop at the MT Summit*, San Diego, California.

Palmer, M., Rambow, O. and Nasr, A. (1998) Rapid Prototyping of Domain-Specific Machine Translation Systems. *In Proceedings of the Third Conference on Machine Translation in the Americas (AMTA-98),* PA, USA, pp. 95–102.

Polguère, A. (1991) Everything has not been said about interlinguae: the case of multi-lingual text generation system. In *Proc. of Natural Language Processing Pacific Rim Symposium*, Singapore.

Rambow, O. and Korelsky, T. (1992) Applied Text Generation. In *Proceedings of the 6th International Workshop on Natural Language Generation,* Trento, Italy, pp. 40–47.

Vauquois, B. and Boitet C. (1985) Automated translation at Grenoble University. In *Computational Linguistics*, Vol. 11, pp. 28–36.

TALK'N'TRAVEL: A CONVERSATIONAL SYSTEM FOR AIR TRAVEL PLANNING

David Stallard
BBN Technologies, GTE
70 Fawcett St.
Cambridge, MA, USA, 02238
Stallard@bbn.com

Abstract

We describe Talk'n'Travel, a spoken dialogue language system for making air travel plans over the telephone. Talk'n'Travel is a fully conversational, mixed-initiative system that allows the user to specify the constraints on his travel plan in arbitrary order, ask questions, etc., in general spoken English. The system operates according to a plan-based agenda mechanism, rather than a finite state network, and attempts to negotiate with the user when not all of his constraints can be met.

Introduction

This paper describes Talk'n'Travel, a spoken language dialogue system for making complex air travel plans over the telephone. Talk'n'Travel is a research prototype system sponsored under the DARPA Communicator program (MITRE, 1999). Some other systems in the program are Ward and Pellom (1999), Seneff and Polifroni (2000) and Rudnicky et al (1999). The common task of this program is a mixed-initiative dialogue over the telephone, in which the user plans a multi-city trip by air, including all flights, hotels, and rental cars, all in conversational English over the telephone.

The Communicator common task presents special challenges. It is a complex task with many subtasks, including the booking of each flight, hotel, and car reservation. Because the number of legs of the trip may be arbitrary, the number of such subtasks is not known in advance. Furthermore, the user has complete freedom to say anything at any time. His utterances can affect just the current subtask, or multiple subtasks at once ("I want to go from Denver to Chicago and then to San Diego"). He can go back and change the specifications for completed subtasks. And there are important constraints, such as temporal relationships between flights, that must be maintained for the solution to the whole task to be coherent.

In order to meet this challenge, we have sought to develop dialogue techniques for Talk'n'Travel that go beyond the rigid system-directed style of familiar IVR systems. Talk'n'Travel is instead a mixed initiative system that allows the user to specify constraints on his travel plan in arbitrary order. At any point in the dialogue, the user can supply information other than what the system is currently prompting for, change his mind about information he has previously given and even ask questions himself. The system also tries to be helpful, eliciting constraints from the user when necessary. Furthermore, if at any point the constraints the user has specified cannot all be met, the system steps in and offers a relaxation of them in an attempt to negotiate a partial solution with the user.

The next section gives a brief overview of the system. Relevant components are discussed in subsequent sections.

1 System Overview

The system consists of the following modules: speech recognizer, language understander, dialogue manager, state manager, language generator, and speech synthesizer. The modules interact with each other via the central hub module of the Communicator Common Architecture.

The speech recognizer is the Byblos system (Nguyen, 1995). It uses an acoustic model trained from the Macrophone telephone corpus, and a bigram/trigram language model trained from ~40K utterances derived from various sources, including data collected under the previous ATIS program (Dahl et al, 1994).

The speech synthesizer is Lucent's commercial system. Synthesizer and recognizer both interface to the telephone via Dialogics telephony board. The database is currently a frozen snapshot of actual flights between 40 different US cities (we are currently engaged in interfacing to a commercial air travel website). The various language components are written in Java. The complete system runs on Windows NT, and is compliant with the DARPA Communicator Common architecture.

The present paper is concerned with the dialogue and discourse management, language generation and language understanding components. In the remainder of the paper, we present more detailed discussion of these components, beginning with the language understander in Section 2. Section 3 discusses the discourse and dialogue components, and Section 4, the language generator.

2 Language Understanding

2.1 Meaning Representation

Semantic frames have proven useful as a meaning representation for many applications. Their simplicity and useful computational properties have often been seen as more important than their limitations in expressive power, especially in simpler domains.

Even in such domains, however, frames still have some shortcomings. While most naturally representing equalities between slot and filler, frames have a harder time with inequalities, such as 'the departure time is *before* 10 AM', or 'the airline is *not* Delta'. These require the slot-filler to be some sort of predicate, interval, or set object, at a cost to simplicity uniformity. Other problematic cases include n-ary relations ('3 miles from Denver'), and disjunctions of properties on different slots.

In our Talk'n'Travel work, we have developed a meaning representation formalism called path constraints, which overcomes these problems, while retaining the computational advantages that made frames attractive in the first place. A path constraint is an expression of the form :

(<path> <relation> <arguments>*)

The path is a compositional chain of one or more attributes, and relations are 1-place or higher predicates, whose first argument is implicitly the path. The relation is followed by zero or more other arguments. In the simplest case, path constraints can be thought of as flattenings of a tree of frames. The following represents the constraint that the departure time of the first leg of the itinerary is the city Boston :

LEGS.0.ORIG_CITY EQ BOSTON

Because this syntax generalizes to any relation, however, the constraint "departing before 10 AM" can be represented in a syntactically equivalent way:

LEGS.0.DEPART_TIME LT 1000

Because the number of arguments is arbitrary, it is equally straightforward to represent a one-place property like "x is nonstop" and a three place predicate like "x is 10 miles from Denver".

Like frames, path constraints have a fixed format that is indexed in a computationally useful way, and are simpler than logical forms. Unlike frames, however, path constraints can be combined in arbitrary conjunctions, disjunctions, and negations, even across different paths. Path constraint meaning representations are also flat lists of constraints rather than trees, making matching rules, etc, easier to write for them.

2.2 The GEM Understanding System

Language understanding in Talk'n'Travel is carried out using a system called GEM (for Generative Extraction Model). GEM (Miller, 1998) is a probabilistic semantic grammar that is an outgrowth of the work on the HUM system (Miller, 1996), but uses hand-specified knowledge in addition to probability. The hand-specified knowledge is quite simple, and is expressed by a two-level semantic dictionary. In the first level, the entries map alternative word strings to a single word class. For example, the following entry maps several alternative forms to the word class DEPART:

Leave, depart, get out of => DEPART

In the second level, entries map sequences of word classes to constraints:

Name: DepartCity1
Head: DEPART
Classes: [DEPART FROM CITY]
Meaning: (DEST_CITY EQ <CITY>)

The "head" feature allows the entry to pass one of its constituent word classes up to a higher level pattern, allowing the given pattern to be a constituent of others.

The dictionary entries generate a probabilistic recursive transition network (PRTN), whose specific structure is determined by dictionary entries. Paths through this network correspond one-to-one with parse trees, so that given a path, there is exactly one corresponding tree. The probabilities for the arcs in this network can be estimated from training data using the EM (Expectation-Maximization) procedure.

GEM also includes a noise state to which arbitrary input between patterns can be mapped, making the system quite robust to ill-formed input. There is no separate phase for handling ungrammatical input, nor any distinction between grammatical and ungrammatical input.

3 Discourse and Dialogue Processing

A key feature of the Communicator task is that the user can say anything at any time, adding or changing information at will. He may add new subtasks (e.g. trip legs) or modifying existing ones. A conventional dialogue state network approach would be therefore infeasible, as the network would be almost unboundedly large and complex.

A signifigant additional problem is that changes need not be monotonic. In particular, when changing his mind, or correcting the system's misinterpretations, the user may delete subtask structures altogether, as in the subdialog:

S: What day are you returning to Chicago?
U: No, I don't want a return flight.

Because they take information away rather than add it, scenarios like this one make it problematic to view discourse processing as producing a contextualized, or "thick frame", version of the user's utterance. In our system, therefore, we have chosen a somewhat different approach.

The discourse processor, called the state manager, computes the most likely new task state, based on the user's input and the current task state. It also computes a discourse event, representing its interpretation of what happened in the conversation as a result of the user's utterance.

The dialogue manager is a separate module, as has no state managing responsibilities at all. Rather, it simply computes the next action to take, based on its current goal agenda, the discourse event returned by the state manager, and the new state. This design has the advantage of making the dialogue manager considerably simpler. The discourse event also becomes available to convey to the user as confirmation.

We discuss these two modules in more detail below.

3.1 State Manager

The state manager is responsible for computing and maintaining the current task state. The task state is simply the set of path constraints which currently constrain the user's itinerary. Also included in the task state are the history of user and system utterances, and the current subtask and object in focus, if any.

The state manager takes the N-best list of recognition hypotheses as input. It invokes the understanding module on a hypothesis to obtain a semantic interpretation. The semantic interpretation so obtained is subjected to the following steps:

1. Resolve ellipses if any
2. Match input meaning to subtask(s)
3. Expand local ambiguities
4. Apply inference and coherency rules
5. Compute database satisfiers
6. Relax constraints if neccesary
7. Determine the most likely alternative and compute the discourse event

At any of these steps, zero or more alternative new states can result, and are fed to the next step. If zero states result at any step, the new meaning representation is rejected, and another one requested from the understander. If no more hypotheses are available, the entire utterance is rejected, and a DONT_UNDERSTAND event is returned to the dialogue manager.

Step 1 resolves ellipses. Ellipses include both short responses like "Boston" and yes/no responses. In this step, a complete meaning representation such as '(ORIG_CITY EQ BOSTON)' is generated based on the system's prompt and the input meaning. The hypothesis is rejected if this cannot be done.

Step 2 matches the input meaning to one or more of the subtasks of the problem. For the Communicator problem, the subtasks are legs of the user's itinerary, and matching is done based on cities mentioned in the input meaning. The default is the subtask currently in focus in the dialogue.

A match to a subtask is represented by adding the prefix for the subtask to the path of the constraint. For example, "I want to arrive in Denver by 4 PM" and then continue on to Chicago would be :

LEGS.0.DEST_CITY EQ DENVER
LEGS.0.ARRIVE_TIME LE 1600
LEGS.1.ORIG_CITY EQ DENVER
LEGS.1.DEST_CITY EQ CHICAGO

In Step 3, local ambiguities are expanded into their different possibilities. These include partially specified times such as "2 o'clock ".

Step 4 applies inference and coherency rules. These rules will vary from application to application. They are written in the path constraint formalism, augmented with variables that can range over attributes and other values. The following is an example, representing the constraint a flight leg cannot be scheduled to depart until after the preceding flight arrives:

LEGS.$N.ARRIVE
LT
LEGS.$N+1.DEPART

States that violate coherency constraints are discarded.

Step 5 computes the set of objects in the database that satisfy the constraints on the current subtask. This set will be empty when the constraints are not all satisfiable, in which case the relaxation of Step 6 is invoked. This relaxation is a best-first search for the satisfiable subset of the constraints that are deemed closest to what the user originally wanted. Alternative relaxations are scored according to a sum of penalty scores for each relaxed constraint, derived from earlier work by Stallard (1995). The penalty score is the sum of two terms: one for the relative importance of the attribute concerned (e.g. relaxations of DEPART_DATE are penalised more than relaxations of AIRLINE) and the other for the nearness of the satisfiers to the original constraint (relevant for number-like attributes like departure time).

The latter allows the system to give credit to solutions that are near fits to the user's goals, even if they relax strongly desired constraints. For example, suppose the user has expressed a desire to fly on Delta and arrive by 3 PM, while the system is only able to find a flight on Delta that arrives at 3:15 PM. In this case, this flight, which meets one constraint and almost meets the other, may well satisfy the user more than a flight on a different airline that happens to meet the time constraint exactly.

In the final step, the alternative new states are rank-ordered according to a pragmatic score, and the highest-scoring alternative is chosen. The pragmatic score is computed based on a number of factors, including the plausibility of disambiguated times and whether or not the state interpreted the user as responding to the system prompt.

The appropriate discourse event is then deterministically computed and returned. There are several types of discourse event. The most common is UPDATE, which specifies the constraints that have been added, removed, or relaxed. Another type is REPEAT, which is generated when the user has simply repeated constraints the system already knows. Other types include QUESTION, TIMEOUT, and DONT_UNDERSTAND.

3.1 Dialogue Manager

Upon receiving the new discourse event from the state manager, the dialogue manager determines what next action to take. Actions can be external, such as speaking to the user or asking him a question, or internal, such as querying the database or other elements of the system state. The current action is determined by consulting a stack-based agenda of goals and actions.

The agenda stack is in turn determined by an application-dependent library of plans. Plans are tree structures whose root is the name of the goal the plan is designed to solve, and whose leaves are either other goal names or actions. An example of a plan is the following:

```
CompleteItinerary =>
    (Prompt "How can I help you?")
    (forall legs $n
        GetRouteInfo
        GetSpecificFlight
        GetHotelAndCar
        GetNextLeg))
```

This is a plan for achieving the goal CompleteItinerary. It begins with a open-ended prompt and then iterates over values of the variable $N for which constraints on the prefix LEGS.$N exist, working on high-level subgoals, such as getting the route and booking a flight, for each leg. The last goal determines whether there is another leg to the itinerary, in which case the itera

The system begins the interaction with the high-level goal START on its stack. At each step, the system examines the top of its goal stack and either executes it if it is an action suitable for execution, or replaces it on the stack with its plan steps if it is a goal.

Actions are objects with success and relevancy predicates and an execute method, somewhat similar to the "handlers" of Rudnicky and Xu (1999). An action has an underlying goal, such as finding out the user's constraints on some attribute. The action's success predicate will return true if this underlying goal has been achieved, and its relevancy predicate will return true if it is still relevant to the current situation. Before carrying out an action, the dialogue manager first checks to see if its success predicate returns false and its relevancy predicate returns true. If either condition is not met, the action is popped off the stack and disposed of without being executed. Otherwise, the action's execute method is invoked.

The system includes a set of actions that are built in, and may be parameterized for each each domain. For example, the action type ELICIT is parameterized by an attribute A, a path prefix P, and verbalization string S. Its success predicate returns true if the path 'P.A' is constrained in the current state. Its execute method generates a meaning frame that is passed to the language generator, ultimately prompting the user with a question such as "What city are you flying to?"

Once an action's execute method is invoked, it remains on the stack for the next cycle, where it is tested again for success and relevancy. In this case, if the success condition is met – that is, if the user did indeed reply with a specification of his destination city – the action is popped off the stack. If the system did not receive this information, either because the user made a stipulation about some different attribute, asked a question, or simply was not understood, the action remains on the stack to be executed again. Of course, the user may have already specified the destination city in a previous utterance. In this case, the action is already satisfied, and is not executed. In this way, the user has flexibility in how he actually carries out the dialogue.

In certain situations, other goals and actions may be pushed onto the stack, temporarily interrupting the execution of the current plan. For example, the user himself may ask a question. In this case, an action to answer the question is created, and pushed onto the stack. The dialogue manager then executes this action to answer the user's question before continuing on with the plan. Or the state manager may generate a clarification question, which the dialogue manager seeks to have the user answer.

Actions can also have a set of conditional branchings that are tested after the action is executed. If present, these determine the next action to execute or goal to work on. For example, the action that asks the user "Do you want a return flight to X?" specifies the branch to be taken when the user replies in the negative. This branch includes an action that asks the user "Is Y your final destination?", an action that is executed if the user did not specify an additional destination along with his negative reply.

Unlike the approach taken by Ward and Pellom (1999), which seeks to avoid scripting entirely by driving the dialogue off the current status of the itinerary, the Talk'n'Travel dialogue manager thus seeks to allow partially scripted dialogue where appropriate to the situation.

4 Language Generation

The language generator takes a meaning frame from the dialogue manager, and generates a text string in English for it. It uses a set of pattern-based rules that map constraints into alternative syntactic realisations. For example, the following rule allows a constraint on departure time to be realized as "leave at 3 PM" or "3 PM flight":

```
LEG.$N.DEPART_TIME EQ $X
  ⇨ [leave at $X],
     [nom-comp $X]
```

Different realization rules can be selected for depending upon whether the constraint is to be realized as an assertion or as a description. The generation algorithm assembles the selected realizations for each constraint into a simplified syntax tree, selecting appropriate inflections of verb and noun heads as it does so. Terminal values in constraints are realized as type-specific nominals, such as "3 PM" or "Delta".

A crucial feature of the generation process is that it adds to each prompt a paraphrase of the most recent discourse event, corresponding to what the system thinks the user just said. This helps keep the conversation grounded in terms of mutual understanding between the participants.

5 Example Scenario

The following is an example dialog with the system:

S: Welcome to Talk'n'Travel. How can I help you?
U: I need a flight from Boston to Denver tomorrow.
S: On Thursday, November 18, flying from Boston to Denver. What time do you want to leave?
U: I want to leave before 10 AM.
S: Leaving before 10 AM. Do you have an airline preference?
U: Continental.

S: Continental. I'm sorry, there are no flights on Continental leaving before 10 AM. I can get you a flight on Continental leaving at 10:10 AM instead. Would that be OK?
U: Yes.
S: OK, I've got you on Continental flight 429, departing Boston at 10:10 AM, arriving at Denver at 3:44 PM. Do you want to book a return flight from Denver to Boston?
U: Yes, on Monday.
S: Alright, we'll add a flight on Monday, November 22, from Boston to Denver to your itinerary. I have a Continental flight at 7 AM. Is that OK?
U. Anything later?
S: Leaving after 7 AM. There are no flights on Continental after 7 AM. I can get you a flight after 7 AM on Frontier, Northwest, and United instead. Would that be OK?
U: How about United.
S: United. I have a United flight at 8:01 AM. Is that flight OK?
U: Yes.
S: OK, I've got you on United flight 1762, departing Denver at 8:01 AM, arriving at Boston at 1:42 PM.

6 Current Status and Conclusions

The Talk'n'Travel system described here was successfully demonstrated at the DARPA Communicator Compare and Contrast Workshop in June 1999. We are currently collecting data with test subjects and are using the results to improve the system's performance in all areas, in preparation for the forthcoming common evaluation of Communicator systems in June 2000.

To determine the performance of the system, we ran an informal experiment in which 11 different subjects called into the system and attempted to use it to solve a travel problem. None of the subjects were system developers. Each subject had a single session in which he was given a three-city trip to plan, including dates of travel, constraints on departure and arrival times, airline preferences.

8 of the subjects were successful. Of successful sessions, the average duration was 387 seconds, with a minimum of 272 and a maximum of 578. The average number of user utterances was 25, with a minimum of 18 and a maximum of 37. The word error rate of the recognizer was 11.8%.

The primary cause of failure to complete the scenario, as well as excessive time spent on completing it, was corruption of the discourse state due to recognition or interpretation errors. While the system informs the user of the change in state after every utterance, the user was not always successful in correcting it when it made errors, and sometimes the user did not even notice when the system had made an error. If the user is not attentive at the time, or happens not to understand what the synthesizer said, there is no implicit way for him to find out afterwards what the system thinks his constraints are.

While preliminary, these results point to two directions for future work. One is that the system needs to be better able to recognize and deal with problem situations in which the dialogue is not advancing. The other is that the system needs to be more communicative about its current understanding of the user's goals, even at points in the dialogue at which it might be assumed that user and system were in agreement.

Acknowledgements

This work was sponsored by DARPA and monitored by SPAWAR Systems Center under Contract No. N66001-99-D-8615.

The author wishes to thank Scott Miller for the use of his GEM system.

References

MITRE (1999) DARPA Communicator homepage http://fofoca.mitre.org/

Ward W., and Pellom, B. (1999) The CU Communicator System. In *1999 IEEE Workshop on Automatic Speech Recognition and Understanding*, Keystone, Colorado.

Miller S. (1998) The Generative Extraction Model. Unpublished manuscript.

Dahl D., Bates M., Brown M., Fisher, W. Hunicke-Smith K., Pallet D., Pao C., Rudnicky A., and Shriberg E. (1994) Expanding the scope of the ATIS task. In *Proceedings of the ARPA Spoken Language Technology Workshop*, Plainsboro, NJ., pp 3-8.

Constantinides P., Hansma S., Tchou C. and Rudnicky, A. (1999) A schema-based approach to dialog control. *Proceedings of ICSLP*, Paper 637.

Rudnicky A., Thayer, E., Constantinides P., Tchou C., Shern, R., Lenzo K., Xu W., Oh A. (1999) Creating natural dialogs in the Carnegie Mellon Communicator system. *Proceedings of Eurospeech, 1999*, Vol 4, pp. 1531-1534

Rudnicky A., and Xu W. (1999) An agenda-based dialog management architecture for soken language systems. In *1999 IEEE Workshop on Automatic Speech Recognition and Understanding*, Keystone, Colorado.

Seneff S., and Polifroni, J. (2000) Dialogue Management in the Mercury Flight Reservation System. *ANLP Conversational Systems Workshop.*

Nguyen L., Anastasakos T., Kubala F., LaPre C., Makhoul J., Schwartz R., Yuan N., Zavaliagkos G., and Zhao Y. (1995) The 1994 BBN/BYBLOS Speech Recognition System, In *Proc of ARPA Spoken Language Systems Technology Workshop*, Austin, Texas, pp. 77-81.

Stallard D. (1995) The Initial Implementation of the BBN ATIS4 Dialog System, In *Proc of ARPA Spoken Language Systems Technology Workshop*, Austin, Texas, pp. 208-211.

Miller S. and Stallard D. (1996) A Fully Statistical Approach to Natural Language Interfaces, In *Proc of the 34th Annual Meeting of the Association for Computational Linguistics*, Santa Cruz, California.

REES: A Large-Scale Relation and Event Extraction System

Chinatsu Aone
SRA International, Inc.
4300 Fair Lakes Court
Fairfax, VA 22033
aonec@verdi.sra.com

Mila Ramos-Santacruz
SRA International, Inc.
4300 Fair Lakes Court
Fairfax, VA 22033
mila@verdi.sra.com

Abstract

This paper reports on a large-scale, end-to-end relation and event extraction system. At present, the system extracts a total of 100 types of relations and events, which represents a much wider coverage than is typical of extraction systems. The system consists of three specialized pattern-based tagging modules, a high-precision co-reference resolution module, and a configurable template generation module. We report quantitative evaluation results, analyze the results in detail, and discuss future directions.

Introduction

One major goal of information extraction (IE) technology is to help users quickly identify a variety of relations and events and their key players in a large volume of documents. In contrast with this goal, state-of-the-art information extraction systems, as shown in the various Message Understanding Conferences (MUCs), extract a small number of relations and events. For instance, the most recent MUC, MUC-7, called for the extraction of 3 relations (person-employer, maker-product, and organization-location) and 1 event (spacecraft launches). Our goal is to develop an IE system which scales up to extract as many types of relations and events as possible with a minimum amount of porting effort combined with high accuracy. Currently, REES handles 100 types of relations and events, and it does so in a modular, configurable, and scalable manner.

Below, Section 1 presents the ontologies of relations and events that we have developed. Section 2 describes REES' system architecture. Section 3 evaluates the system's performance, and offers a qualitative analysis of system errors. Section 4 discusses future directions.

1 Relation and Event Ontologies

As the first step in building a large-scale relation and event extraction system, we developed ontologies of the relations and events to be extracted. These ontologies represent a wide variety of domains: political, financial, business, military, and life-related events and relations. "Relations" covers what in MUC-7 are called Template Elements (TEs) and Template Relations (TRs). There are 39 types of relations. While MUC TE's only dealt with singular entities, REES extracts both singular and plural entities (e.g., "five executives"). The TR relations are shown in italic in the table below.

Relations	
Place Relations	**Artifact Relations**
Place-Name&Aliases	Artifact-Name&Aliases
Place-Type	Artifact-Type
Place-Subtype	Artifact-Subtype
Place-Descriptor	Artifact-Descriptor
Place-Country	*Artifact-Maker*
	Artifact-Owner
Organization Relations	**Person Relations**
Org-Name&Aliases	Person-Name&Aliases
Org-Descriptor	Person-Type
Org-FoundationDate	Person-Subtype
Org-Nationality	Person-Descriptor
Org-TickerSymbol	Person-Honorific
Org-Location	Person-Age
Org-ParentOrg	Person-PhoneNumber
Org-Owner	Person-Nationality
Org-Founder	*Person-Affiliation*
Org-StockMarket	*Person-Sibling*
	Person-Spouse
	Person-Parent
	Person-Grandparent

	Person-OtherRelative *Person-BirthPlace* *Person-BirthDate*

Table 1: Relation Ontology

"Events" are extracted along with their event participants, e.g., "who did what to whom when and where?" For example, for a BUYING event, REES extracts the buyer, the artifact, the seller, and the time and location of the BUYING event. REES currently covers 61 types of events, as shown below.

Events	
Vehicle	**Transaction**
Vehicle departs Vehicle arrives Spacecraft launch Vehicle crash	Buy artifact Sell artifact Import artifact Export artifact Give money
Personnel Change	**Business**
Hire Terminate contract Promote Succeed Start office	Start business Close business Make artifact Acquire company Sell company Sue organization Merge company
Crime	**Financial**
Sexual assault Steal money Seize drug Indict Arrest Try Convict Sentence Jail	Currency moves up Currency moves down Stock moves up Stock moves down Stock market moves up Stock market moves down Stock index moves up Stock index moves down
Political	**Conflict**
Nominate Appoint Elect Expel person Reach agreement Hold meeting Impose embargo Topple **Family** Die Marry	Kill Injure Hijack vehicle Hold hostages Attack target Fire weapon Weapon hit Invade land Move forces Retreat Surrender Evacuate

Table 2: Event Ontology

Figures 1 and 2 show sample relation and event templates. Figure 1 shows a Person-Affiliation relation template for *"Frank Ashley, a spokesman for Occidental Petroleum Corp."*

```
<PERSON_AFFILIATION-AP8802230207-54> :=
  TYPE:     PERSON_AFFILIATION
  PERSON:   [TE for "Frank Ashley"]
  ORG:      [TE for "Occidental Petroleum"]
```

Figure 1: Example of Relation Template

Figure 2 shows an Attack Target event template for the sentence *"an Iraqi warplane attacked the frigate Stark with missiles May 17, 1987."*

```
<ATTACK_TARGET-AP8804160078-12>:=
   TYPE:       CONFLICT
   SUBTYPE:    ATTACK_TARGET
   ATTACKER:   [TE for "an Iraqi warplane"]
   TARGET:     [TE for "the frigate Stark"]
   WEAPON:     [TE for "missiles"]
   TIME:       "May 17, 1987"
   PLACE:      [TE for "the gulf"]
   COMMENT:    "attacked"
```

Figure 2: Example of Event Template

2 System Architecture and Components

Figure 3 illustrates the REES system architecture. REES consists of three main components: a tagging component (cf. Section 2.1), a co-reference resolution module (cf. Section 2.2), and a template generation module (cf. Section 2.3). Figure 3 also illustrates that the user may run REES from a Graphical User Interface (GUI) called TemplateTool (cf. Section 2.4).

2.1 Tagging Modules

The tagging component consists of three modules as shown in Figure 3: NameTagger, NPTagger and EventTagger. Each module relies on the same pattern-based extraction engine, but uses different sets of patterns. The NameTagger recognizes names of people, organizations, places, and artifacts (currently only vehicles).

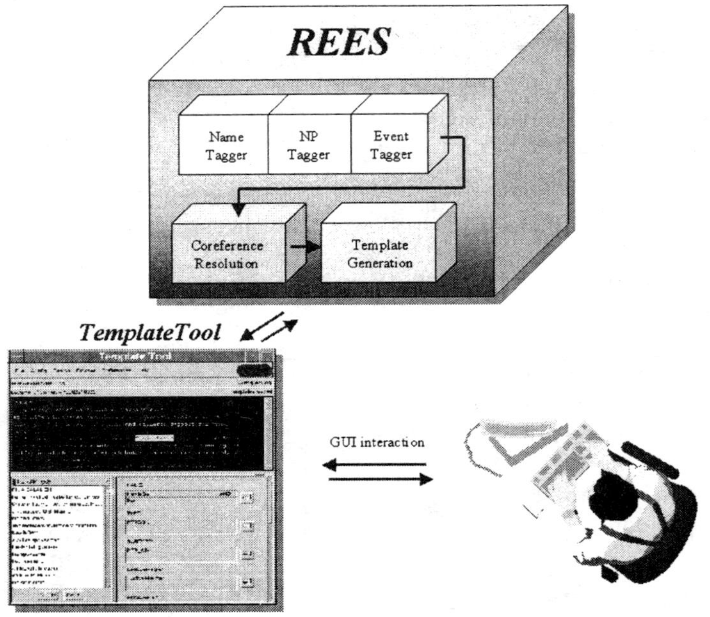

Figure 3: The REES System Architecture

The NPTagger then takes the XML-tagged output of the NameTagger through two phases. First, it recognizes non-recursive Base Noun Phrase (BNP) (our specifications for BNP resemble those in Ramshaw and Marcus 1995). Second, it recognizes complex NPs for only the four main semantic types of NPs, i.e., Person, Organization, Location, and Artifact (vehicle, drug and weapon). It makes post-modifier attachment decisions only for those NPs that are crucial to the extraction at hand. During this second phase, relations which can be recognized locally (e.g., Age, Affiliation, Maker) are also recognized and stored using the XML attributes for the NPs. For instance, the XML tag for "*President of XYZ Corp.*" below holds an AFFILIATION attribute with the ID for "*XYZ Corp.*"

<PNP ID="03" AFFILIATION="04">*President of* <ENTITY ID="04">*XYZ Corp.*</ENTITY> </PNP>

Building upon the XML output of the NPTagger, the EventTagger recognizes events applying its lexicon-driven, syntactically-based generic patterns. These patterns tag events in the presence of at least one of the arguments specified in the lexical entry for a predicate. Subsequent patterns try to find additional arguments as well as place and time adjunct information for the tagged event. As an example of the EventTagger's generic patterns, consider the simplified pattern below. This pattern matches on an event-denoting verb that requires a direct object of type weapon (e.g., "*fire a gun*")

```
(&
  {AND $VP {ARG2_SYN=DO}
        {ARG2_SEM=WEAPON}}
  {AND $ARTIFACT {SUBTYPE=WEAPON}})1
```

The important aspect of REES is its declarative, lexicon-driven approach. This approach requires a lexicon entry for each event-denoting word, which is generally a

[1] &=concatenation, AND=Boolean operator, $VP and $ARTIFACT are macro references for complex phrases.

verb. The lexicon entry specifies the syntactic and semantic restrictions on the verb's arguments. For instance, the following lexicon entry is for the verb "*attack*." It indicates that the verb "*attack*" belongs to the CONFLICT ontology and to the ATTACK_TARGET type. The first argument for the verb "*attack*" is semantically an organization, location, person, or artifact (ARG1_SEM), and syntactically a subject (ARG1_SYN). The second argument is semantically an organization, location, person or artifact, and syntactically a direct object. The third argument is semantically a weapon and syntactically a prepositional phrase introduced by the preposition "*with*".

```
ATTACK {{{CATEGORY VERB}
   {ONTOLOGY CONFLICT}
   {TYPE ATTACK_TARGET}
   {ARG1_SEM {ORGANIZATION LOCATION
                    PERSON ARTIFACT}}
   {ARG1_SYN {SUBJECT}}
   {ARG2_SEM {ORGANIZATION LOCATION
                    PERSON ARTIFACT}}
   {ARG2_SYN {DO}}
   {ARG3_SEM{WEAPON}}
   {ARG3_SYN {WITH}}}}
```

About 50 generic event extraction patterns, supported by lexical information as shown above, allow extraction of events and their arguments in cases like:

An Iraqi warplane ***attacked*** *the frigate Stark with missiles May 17, 1987.*

This generic, lexicon-driven event extraction approach makes REES easily portable because new types of events can be extracted by just adding new verb entries to the lexicon. No new patterns are required. Moreover, this approach allows for easy customization capability: a person with no knowledge of the pattern language would be able to configure the system to extract new events.

While the tagging component is similar to other pattern-based IE systems (e.g., Appelt *et al.* 1995; Aone *et al.* 1998, Yangarber and Grishman 1998), our EventTagger is more portable through a lexicon-driven approach.

2.2 Co-reference Resolution

After the tagging phase, REES sends the XML output through a rule-based co-reference resolution module that resolves:

- definite noun phrases of Organization, Person, and Location types, and
- singular person pronouns: *he* and *she*.

Only "high-precision" rules are currently applied to selected types of anaphora. That is, we resolve only those cases of anaphora whose antecedents the module can identify with high confidence. For example, the pronoun rules look for the antecedents only within 3 sentences, and the definite NP rules rely heavily on the head noun matches. Our high-precision approach results from our observation that unless the module is very accurate (above 80% precision), the co-reference module can hurt the overall extraction results by over-merging templates.

2.3 Template Generation Module

A typical template generation module is a hard-coded post-processing module which has to be written for each type of template. By contrast, our Template Generation module is unique as it uses declarative rules to generate and merge templates automatically so as to achieve portability.

2.3.1 Declarative Template Generation

REES outputs the extracted information in the form of either MUC-style templates, as illustrated in Figure 1 and 2, or XML. A crucial part of a portable, scalable system is to be able to output different types of relations and events without changing the template generation code. REES maps XML-tagged output of the co-reference module to templates using declarative template definitions, which specifies the template label (e.g., ATTACK_TARGET), XML attribute names (e.g., ARGUMENT1), corresponding template slot names (e.g., ATTACKER), and the type restrictions on slot values (e.g., string).

2.3.2 Event Merging

One of the challenges of event extraction is to be able to recognize and merge those event descriptions which refer to the same event. The Template Generation module uses a set of declarative, customizable rules to merge co-referring events into a single event. Often, the rules reflect pragmatic knowledge of the world. For example, consider the rule below for the DYING event type. This rule establishes that if two *die* events have the same subject, then they refer to the same event (i.e., a person cannot die more than once).

```
{merge
  {EVENT 1 {AND {SUBTYPE DIE} {PERSON
                  $foo}}
  {EVENT 2 {AND {SUBTYPE DIE} {PERSON
                  $foo}}}
```

2.4 Graphical User Interface (GUI)

For some applications such as database population, the user may want to validate the system output. REES is provided with a Java-based Graphical User Interface that allows the user to run REES and display, delete, or modify the system output. As illustrated in Figure 4, the tool displays the templates on the bottom half of the screen, and the user can choose which template to display. The top half of the screen displays the input document with extracted phrases in different colors. The user can select any slot value, and the tool will highlight the portion of the input text responsible for the slot value. This feature is very useful in efficiently verifying system output. Once the system's output has been verified, the resulting templates can be saved and used to populate a database.

3 System Evaluation

The table below shows the system's recall, precision, and F-Measure scores for the training set (200 texts) and the blind set (208 texts) from about a dozen news sources. Each set contains at least 3 examples of each type of relations and events. As we mentioned earlier, "relations" includes MUC-style TEs and TRs.

Text Set	Task	Templates in keys	R	P	F-M
Train	Rel.	9955	76	74	75.35
	Events	2525	57	74	64.57
	Rel. & Events	10707	74	74	73.95
Blind	Rel.	8938	74	74	73.74
	Events	2020	42	75	53.75
	Rel. & Events	9526	69	74	71.39

Table 3: Evaluation Results

The blind set F-Measure for 31 types of relations (73.95%) exceeded our initial goal of 70%. While the blind set F-Measure for 61 types of events was 53.75%, it is significant to note that 26 types of events achieved an F-Measure over 70%, and 37 types over 60% (cf. Table 4). For reference, though not exactly comparable, the best-performing MUC-7 system achieved 87% in TE, 76% in TR, and 51% in event extraction.

F-M in blind set	Event types
90-100	2 : Buy artifact. Marry
80-89	9 : Succeed, Merge company, Kill, Surrender, Arrest, Convict, Sentence, Nominate, Expel.
70-79	15 : Die, Sell artifact, Export Artifact, Hire, Start office, Make artifact, Acquire company, Sue organization, Stock Index moves down, Steal money, Indict, Jail, Vehicle crash, Elect, Hold meeting.

Table 4: Top-performing Event Types

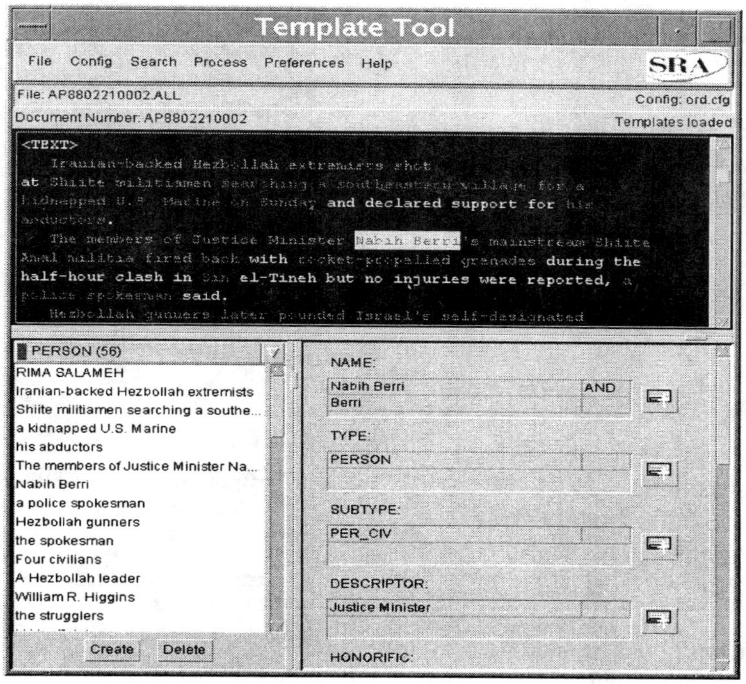

Figure 4: TemplateTool

Regarding relation extraction, the difference in the score between the training and blind sets was very small. In fact, the total F-Measure on the blind set is less than 2 points lower than that of the training set. It is also interesting to note that for 8 of the 12 relation types where the F-Measure dropped more than 10 points, the training set includes less than 20 instances. In other words, there seems to be a natural correlation between low number of instances in the training set and low performance in the blind set.

There was a significant drop between the training and blind sets in event extraction: 11 points. We believe that the main reason is that the total number of events in the training set is fairly low: 801 instances of 61 types of events (an average of 13/event), where 35 of the event types had fewer than 10 instances. In fact, 9 out of the 14 event types which scored lower than 40% F-Measure had fewer than 10 examples. In comparison, there were 34,000 instances of 39 types of relations in the training set.

The contribution of the co-reference module is illustrated in the table below. Co-reference resolution consistently improves F-Measures both in training and blind sets. Its impact is larger in relation than event extraction.

Text set	Task	Co-reference rules	No co-reference rules
Training	Relations	75.35	72.54
	Events	64.57	63.62
	Relations & Events	73.95	71.34
Blind	Relations	73.74	72.03
	Events	53.75	53.22
	Relations & Events	71.39	69.86

Table 5: Comparative results with and without co-reference rules

In the next two sections, we analyze both false positives and false negatives.

3.1 False Positives (or Precision Errors)

REES produced precision errors in the following cases:

- Most of the errors were due to over-generation of templates. These are mostly cases of co-referring noun phrases that the system failed to resolve. For example: *"Panama ... the nation ...this country...his country"*
  Rules for the co-reference module are still under development, and at present REES handles only limited types of plural noun phrase anaphora.
- Spurious events resulted from verbs in conditional constructions (e.g., "if ... then...") or from ambiguous predicates. For instance, "appoint" as a POLITICAL event vs. a PERSONNEL_CHANGE event.
- The subject of a verb was misidentified. This is particularly frequent in reduced relative clauses.
  Kabul radio said the latest deaths brought to 38 the number of people killed in the three car bomb explosions.
  (Wrong subject: *"the number of people"* as the KILLER instead of the victim)

3.2 False Negatives (or Recall Errors)

Below, we list the most frequent recall errors in the training set.

- Some event arguments are mentioned with event nouns instead of event verbs. The current system does not handle noun-based event extraction.
  India's acquisition last month of the nuclear submarine from the Soviet Union...
  (SELLER="*Soviet Union*" and TIME="*last month*" come with the noun-based event "*acquisition.*")
- Pronouns "*it*" and "*they,*" which carry little semantic information, are currently not resolved by the co-reference module.
  It also has bought three late-1970s vintage Kilo class Soviet submarines and two West German HDW 209 subs
  (Missed BUYER=*India* because of unresolved *it.)*
- Verb arguments are a conjunction of noun phrases. The current system does not handle coordination of verb arguments.
  Hezbollah killed 21 Israelis and 43 of Lahad's soldiers
  (The system gets only the first object: *21 Israelis.*)
- Ellipsis cases. The current system does not handle ellipsis.
  The two were sentenced to five-year prison terms with hard labor by the state security court...
  (Missed PERSON_SENTENCED fill because of unresolved *the two.*)
- The subject of the event is relatively far from the event-denoting verb:
  Vladislav Listyev, 38, who brought television interview shows in the style of Phil Donahue or Larry King to Russian viewers and pioneered hard-hitting television journalism in the 1980s, was shot in the heart by unknown assailants and died immediately...
  (The system missed subject *Vladislav Listyev* for attack event *shot*)
- Missed ORG_LOCATION relations for locations that are part of the organization's name.
  Larnaca General Hospital
  (Missed ORG_LOCATION TR for this and *Larnaca.*)

We asked a person who is not involved in the development of REES to review the event extraction output for the blind set. This person reported that:

- In 35% of the cases where the REES system completely missed an event, it was because the lexicon was missing the predicate. REES's event predicate lexicon is rather small at present (a total of 140 verbs for 61 event types) and is mostly based on the examples found in the training set.
- In 30% of the cases, the subject or object was elliptical. The system does not currently handle ellipsis.

- In 25% of the cases, syntactic/semantic argument structures were missing from existing lexical entries.

It is quite encouraging that simply adding additional predicates and predicate argument structures to the lexicon could significantly increase the blind set performance.

4 Future Directions

We believe that improving co-reference resolution and adding noun-based event extraction capability are critical to achieving our ultimate goal of at least 80% F-Measure for relations and 70% for events.

4.1 Co-reference Resolution

As discussed in Section 3.1 and 3.2, accurate co-reference resolution is crucial to improving the accuracy of extraction, both in terms of recall and precision. In particular, we identified two types of high-payoff co-reference resolution:

- definite noun phrase resolution, especially plural noun phrases
- 3rd person neutral pronouns "it" and "they."

4.2 Noun-based Event Extraction

REES currently handles only verb-based events. Noun-based event extraction adds more complexity because:

- Nouns are often used in a generic, non-referential manner (e.g., "We see a **merger** as being in the consumer's interest"), and

- When referential, nouns often refer to verb-based events, thus requiring noun-verb co-reference resolution ("An F-14 crashed shortly after takeoff...The crash").

However, noun-based events are crucial because they often introduce additional key information, as the underlined phrases below indicate:

*While **Bush's meetings** with prominent anti-apartheid leaders such as Archbishop Desmond Tutu and Albertina Sisulu are important...*

We plan to develop a generic set of patterns for noun-based event extraction to complement the set of generic verb-based extraction patterns.

5 Conclusions

In this paper, we reported on a fast, portable, large-scale event and relation extraction system REES. To the best of our knowledge, this is the first attempt to develop an IE system which can extract such a wide range of relations and events with high accuracy. It performs particularly well on relation extraction, and it achieves 70% or higher F-Measure for 26 types of events already. In addition, the design of REES is highly portable for future addition of new relations and events.

Acknowledgements

This project would have not been possible without the contributions of Arcel Castillo, Lauren Halverson, and Sandy Shinn. Our thanks also to Brandon Kennedy, who prepared the hand-tagged data.

References

Aone, Chinatsu, Lauren Halverson, Tom Hampton, and Mila Ramos-Santacruz. 1998. *"SRA: Description of the IE² System Used for MUC-7."* In Proceedings of the 7th Message Understanding Conference (MUC-7).

Appelt, Douglas E., Jerry R Hobbs, John Bear, David Israel, Megumi Kameyama, Andy Kehler, David Martin, Karen Myers, and Mabry Tyson. 1995. *"SRI International FASTUS System: MUC-6 Test Results and Analysis."* In Proceedings of the 6th Message Understanding Conference (MUC-6).

Ramshaw, Lance A., and Mitchell P. Marcus. 1995. *"Text Chunking Using Transformation-Based Learning"*. In Proceedings of the 3rd ACL Workshop on Very Large Corpora (WVLC95).

Yangarber, Roman and Ralph Grishman. 1998. *"NYU: Description of the Proteus/PET System as Used for MUC-7 ST."* In Proceedings of the 6th Message Understanding Conference (MUC-7).

Experiments on Sentence Boundary Detection

Mark Stevenson and Robert Gaizauskas
Department of Computer Science,
University of Sheffield
Regent Court, 211 Portobello Street,
Sheffield
S1 4DP United Kingdom
{marks, robertg}@dcs.shef.ac.uk

Abstract

This paper explores the problem of identifying sentence boundaries in the transcriptions produced by automatic speech recognition systems. An experiment which determines the level of human performance for this task is described as well as a memory-based computational approach to the problem.

1 The Problem

This paper addresses the problem of identifying sentence boundaries in the transcriptions produced by automatic speech recognition (ASR) systems. This is unusual in the field of text processing which has generally dealt with well-punctuated text: some of the most commonly used texts in NLP are machine readable versions of highly edited documents such as newspaper articles or novels. However, there are many types of text which are not so-edited and the example which we concentrate on in this paper is the output from ASR systems. These differ from the sort of texts normally used in NLP in a number of ways; the text is generally in single case (usually upper), unpunctuated and may contain transcription errors.[1] Figure 1 compares a short text in the format which would be produced by an ASR system with a fully punctuated version which includes case information. For the remainder of this paper error-free texts such as newspaper articles or novels shall be referred to as "standard text" and the output from a speech recognition system as "ASR text".

There are many possible situations in which an NLP system may be required to process ASR text. The most obvious examples are NLP systems which take speech input (eg. Moore et al. (1997)). Also, dictation software programs do not punctuate or capitalise their output but, if this information could be added to ASR text, the results would be far more usable. One of the most important pieces of information which is not available in ASR output is sentence boundary information. However, knowledge of sentence boundaries is required by many NLP technologies. Part of speech taggers typically require input in the format of a single sentence per line (for example Brill's tagger (Brill, 1992)) and parsers generally aim to produce a tree spanning each sentence. Only the most trivial linguistic analysis can be carried out on text which is not split into sentences.

```
GOOD EVENING GIANNI VERSACE ONE OF THE
WORLDS LEADING FASHION DESIGNERS HAS
BEEN MURDERED IN MIAMI POLICE SAY IT WAS
A PLANNED KILLING CARRIED OUT LIKE AN
EXECUTION SCHOOLS INSPECTIONS ARE GOING
TO BE TOUGHER TO FORCE BAD TEACHERS OUT
AND THE FOUR THOUSAND COUPLES WHO SHARED
THE QUEENS GOLDEN DAY
```

```
Good evening.  Gianni Versace, one of
the world's leading fashion designers,
has been murdered in Miami.  Police say
it was a planned killing carried out
like an execution.  Schools inspections
are going to be tougher to force bad
teachers out.  And the four thousand
couples who shared the Queen's golden
day.
```

Figure 1: Example text shown in standard and ASR format

It is worth mentioning that not all transcribed speech can be sensibly divided into sentences. It has been argued by Gotoh and Renals (2000) that the main unit in spoken language is the phrase rather than the sentence. However, there are situations in which it is appropriate to consider spoken language to be made up from sentences. One example is broadcast news: radio and television news programs. The DARPA HUB4 broadcast news evaluation (Chinchor et al., 1998) focussed on information extraction from ASR text from news programs. Although news programs are scripted there are often deviations from the script and they cannot be relied upon as accurate transcriptions of the news

[1] Speech recognition systems are often evaluated in terms of word error rate (WER), the percentage of tokens which are wrongly transcribed. For large vocabulary tasks and speaker-independent systems, WER varies between 7% and 50%, depending upon the quality of the recording being recognised. See, e.g., Cole (1996).

program. The spoken portion of the British National Corpus (Burnard, 1995) contains 10 million words and was manually marked with sentence boundaries. A technology which identifies sentence boundaries could be used to speed up the process of creating any future corpus of this type.

It is important to distinguish the problem just mentioned and another problem sometimes called "sentence splitting". This problem aims to identify sentence boundaries in standard text but since this includes punctuation the problem is effectively reduced to deciding which of the symbols which potentially denote sentence boundaries (`.,!,?`) actually do. This problem is not trivial since these punctuation symbols do not always occur at the end of sentences. For example in the sentence "`Dr. Jones lectures at U.C.L.A.`" only the final full stop denotes the end of a sentence. For the sake of clarity we shall refer to the process of discovering sentence boundaries in standard punctuated text as "punctuation disambiguation" and that of finding them in unpunctuated ASR text as "sentence boundary detection".

2 Related Work

Despite the potential application of technology which can carry out the sentence boundary detection task, there has been little research into the area. However, there has been work in the related field of punctuation disambiguation. Palmer and Hearst (1994) applied a neural network to the problem. They used the Brown Corpus for training and evaluation, noting that 90% of the full stops in this text indicate sentence boundaries. They used the part of speech information for the words surrounding a punctuation symbol as the input to a feed-forward neural network. But, as we mentioned, most part of speech taggers require sentence boundaries to be pre-determined and this potential circularity is avoided by using the prior probabilities for each token, determined from the Brown corpus markup. The network was trained on 573 potential sentence ending marks from the Wall Street Journal and tested on 27,294 items from the same corpus. 98.5% of punctuation marks were correctly disambiguated.

Reynar and Ratnaparkhi (1997) applied a maximum entropy approach to the problem. Their system considered only the first word to the left and right of any potential sentence boundary and claimed that examining wider context did not help. For both these words the prefix, suffix, presence of particular characters in the prefix or suffix, whether the candidate is honorific (Mr., Dr. etc.) and whether the candidate is a corporate designator (eg. Corp.) are features that are considered. This system was tested on the same corpus as Palmer and Hearst's system and correctly identified 98.8% of sentence boundaries. Mikheev (1998) optimised this approach and evaluated it on the same test corpus. An accuracy of 99.2477% was reported, to our knowledge this is the highest quoted result for this test set.

These three systems achieve very high results for the punctuation disambiguation task. It would seem, then, that this problem has largely been solved. However, it is not clear that these techniques will be as successful for ASR text. We now go on to describe a system which attempts a task similar to sentence boundary detection of ASR text.

Beeferman et al. (1998) produced a system, "CYBERPUNC", which added intra-sentence punctuation (i.e. commas) to the output of an ASR system. They mention that the comma is the most frequently used punctuation symbol and its correct insertion can make a text far more legible. CYBERPUNC operated by augmenting a standard trigram speech recognition model with information about commas; it accesses only lexical information. CYBERPUNC was tested by separating the trigram model from the ASR system and applying it to 2,317 sentences from the Wall Street Journal. The system achieved a precision of 75.6% and recall of 65.6% compared against the original punctuation in the text.[2] A further qualitative evaluation was carried out using 100 randomly-drawn output sentences from the system and 100 from the Wall Street Journal. Six human judges blindly marked each sentence as either acceptable or unacceptable. It was found that the Penn TreeBank sentences were 86% correct and the system output 66% correct. It is interesting that the human judges do not agree completely on the acceptability of many sentences from the Wall Street Journal.

In the next section we go on to describe experiments which quantify the level of agreement that can be expected when humans carry out sentence boundary detection. Section 4 goes on to describe a computational approach to the problem.

3 Determining Human Ability

Beeferman et. al.'s experiments demonstrated that humans do not always agree on the acceptability of comma insertion and therefore it may be useful to determine how often they agree on the placing of sentence boundaries. To do this we carried out experiments using transcriptions of news programmes, specifically the transcriptions of two editions of the

[2]Precision and recall are complementary evaluation metrics commonly used in Information Retrieval (van Rijsbergen, 1979). In this case precision is the percentage of commas proposed by the system which are correct while recall is the percentage of the commas occurring in the test corpus which the system identified.

BBC television program "The Nine O'Clock News".[3] The transcriptions consisted of punctuated mixed case text with sentences boundaries marked using a reserved character (";"). These texts were produced by trained transcribers listening to the original program broadcast.

Six experimental subjects were recruited. All subjects were educated to at least Bachelor's degree level and are either native English speakers or fluent second language speakers. Each subject was presented with the same text from which the sentence boundaries had been removed. The texts were transcriptions of two editions of the news program from 1997, containing 534 sentences and represented around 50 minutes of broadcast news. The subjects were randomly split into two groups. The subjects in the first group (subjects 1-3) were presented with the text stripped of punctuation and converted to upper case. This text simulated ASR text with no errors in the transcription. The remaining three subjects (4-6) were presented with the same text with punctuation removed but case information retained (i.e. mixed case text). This simulated unpunctuated standard text. All subjects were asked to add sentence boundaries to the text whenever they thought they occurred.

The process of determining human ability at some linguistic task is generally made difficult by the lack of an appropriate reference. Often all we have to compare one person's judgement with is that of another. For example, there have been attempts to determine the level of performance which can be expected when humans perform word sense disambiguation (Fellbaum et al., 1998) but these have simply compared some human judgements against others with one being chosen as the "expert". We have already seen, in Section 2, that there is a significant degree of human disagreement over the acceptability of intra-sentential punctuation. The human transcribers of the "Nine O'Clock News" have access to the original news story which contains more information than just the transcription. Under these conditions it is reasonable to consider their opinion as expert.

Table 1 shows the performance of the human subjects compared to the reference transcripts.[4]

An algorithm was implemented to provide a baseline tagging of the text. The average length of sentences in our text is 19 words and the baseline algorithm randomly assigns a sentence break at each word boundary with a probability of $\frac{1}{19}$. The two annotators labelled "random" show the results when this algorithm is applied. This method produced a very low result in comparison to the expert annotation.

Annotator	Text	P	R	F
1	Upper	84	68	76
2	Upper	93	78	85
3	Upper	90	76	82
4	Mixed	97	90	94
5	Mixed	96	89	92
6	Mixed	97	67	79
Random	Upper	5	5	5
Random	Mixed	5	5	5

Table 1: Results from Human Annotation Experiment

The performance of the human annotators on the upper case text is quite significantly lower than the reported performance of the algorithms which performed punctuation disambiguation on standard text as described in Section 2. This suggests that the performance which may be obtained for this task may be lower than has been achieved for standard text.

Further insight into the task can be gained from determining the degree to which the subjects agreed. Carletta (1996) argues that the kappa statistic (κ) should be adopted to judge annotator consistency for classification tasks in the area of discourse and dialogue analysis. It is worth noting that the problem of sentence boundary detection presented so far in this paper has been formulated as a classification task in which each token boundary has to be classified as either being a sentence boundary or not. Carletta argues that several incompatible measures of annotator agreement have been used in discourse analysis, making comparison impossible. Her solution is to look to the field of content analysis, which has already experienced these problems, and adopt their solution of using the kappa statistic. This determines the difference between the observed agreement for a linguistic task and that which would be expected by chance. It is calculated according to formula 1, where $\Pr(A)$ is the proportion of times the annotators agree and $\Pr(E)$ the proportion which would be expected by chance. Detailed instructions on calculating these probabilities are described by Siegel and Castellan (1988).

$$\kappa = \frac{\Pr(A) - \Pr(E)}{1 - \Pr(E)} \qquad (1)$$

The value of the kappa statistic ranges between 1 (perfect agreement) and 0 (the level which would be expected by chance). It has been claimed that content analysis researchers usually regard $\kappa > .8$ to demonstrate good reliability and $.67 < \kappa < .8$ al-

[3]This is a 25 minute long television news program broadcast in the United Kingdom on Monday to Friday evenings.

[4]F-measure (F) is a weighted harmonic combining precision (P) and recall (R) via the formula $\frac{2PR}{P+R}$.

lows tentative conclusions to be drawn (see Carletta (1996)).

We began to analyse the data by computing the kappa statistic for both sets of annotators. Among the two annotators who marked the mixed case (subjects 4 and 5) there was an observed kappa value of 0.98, while there was a measure of 0.91 for the three subjects who annotated the single case text. These values are high and suggest a strong level of agreement between the annotators. However, manual analysis of the annotated texts suggested that the subjects did not agree on many cases. We then added the texts annotated by the "random" annotation algorithm and calculated the new κ values. It was found that the mixed case test produced a kappa value of 0.92 and the upper case text 0.91. These values would still suggest a high level of agreement although the sentences produced by our random algorithm were nonsensical.

The problem seems to be that most word boundaries in a text are not sentence boundaries. Therefore we could compare the subjects' annotations who had not agreed on any sentence boundaries but find that they agreed most word boundaries were not sentence boundaries. The same problem will effect other standard measures of inter-annotator agreement such as the Cramer, Phi and Kendall coefficients (see Siegel and Castellan (1988)). Carletta mentions this problem, asking what the difference would be if the kappa statistic were computed across "clause boundaries, transcribed word boundaries, and transcribed phoneme boundaries" (Carletta, 1996, p. 252) rather than the sentence boundaries she suggested. It seems likely that more meaningful κ values would be obtained if we restricted to the boundaries between clauses rather than all token boundaries. However, it is difficult to imagine how clauses could be identified without parsing and most parsers require part of speech tagged input text. But, as we already mentioned, part of speech taggers often require input text split into sentences. Consequently, there is a lack of available systems for splitting ASR text into grammatical clauses.

4 A Computational Approach to Sentence Boundary Detection

The remainder of this paper describes an implemented program which attempts sentence boundary detection. The approach is based around the `Timbl` memory-based learning algorithm (Daelemans et al., 1999) which we previously found to be very successful when applied to the word sense disambiguation problem (Stevenson and Wilks, 1999).

Memory-based learning, also known as case-based and lazy learning, operates by memorising a set of training examples and categorising new cases by assigning them the class of the most similar learned example. We apply this methodology to the sentence boundary detection task by presenting `Timbl` with examples of word boundaries from a training text, each of which is categorised as either `sentence_boundary` or `no_boundary`. Unseen examples are then compared and categorised with the class of the most similar example. We shall not discuss the method by which `Timbl` determines the most similar training example which is described by Daelemans et al. (1999).

Following the work done on punctuation disambiguation and that of Beeferman et. al. on comma insertion (Section 2), we used the Wall Street Journal text for this experiment. These texts are reliably part of speech tagged[5] and sentence boundaries can be easily derived from the corpus. This text was initially altered so as to remove all punctuation and map all characters into upper case. 90% of the corpus, containing 965 sentence breaks, was used as a training corpus with the remainder, which contained 107 sentence breaks, being held-back as unseen test data. The first stage was to extract some statistics from the training corpus. We examined the training corpus and computed, for each word in the text, the probability that it started a sentence and the probability that it ended a sentence. In addition, for each part of speech tag we also computed the probability that it is assigned to the first word in a sentence and the probability that it is assigned to the last word.[6] Each word boundary in the corpus was translated to a feature-vector representation consisting of 13 elements, shown in Table 2. Vectors in the test corpus are in a similar format, the difference being that the classification (feature 13) is not included.

The results obtained are shown in the top row of Table 3. Both precision and recall are quite promising under these conditions. However, this text is different from ASR text in one important way: the text is mixed case. The experimented was repeated with capitalisation information removed; that is, features 6 and 12 were removed from the feature-vectors. The results form this experiment are shown in the bottom row of Table 3. It can be seen that the recorded performance is far lower when capitalisation information is not used, indicating that this is an important feature for the task.

These experiments have shown that it is much easier to add sentence boundary information to mixed case test, which is essentially standard text with punctuation removed, than ASR text, even as-

[5]Applying a priori tag probability distributions could have been used rather than the tagging in the corpus as such reliable annotations may not be available for the output of an ASR system. Thus, the current experiments should be viewed as making an optimistic assumption.

[6]We attempted to smooth these probabilities using Good-Turing frequency estimation (Gale and Sampson, 1996) but found that it had no effect on the final results.

Position	Feature
1	Preceding word
2	Probability preceding word ends a sentence
3	Part of speech tag assigned to preceding word
4	Probability that part of speech tag (feature 3) is assigned to last word in a sentence
5	Flag indicating whether preceding word is a stop word
6	Flag indicating whether preceding word is capitalised
7	Following word
8	Probability following word begins a sentence
9	Part of speech tag assigned to following word
10	Probability that part of speech (feature 9) is assigned to first word in a sentence
11	Flag indicating whether following word is a stop word
12	Flag indicating whether following word is capitalised word
13	`sentence_boundary` or `no_boundary`

Table 2: Features used in `Timbl` representation

Case information	P	R	F
Applied	78	75	76
Not applied	36	35	35

Table 3: Results of the sentence boundary detection program

suming a zero word error rate. This result is in agreement with the results from the human annotation experiments described in Section 3. However, there is a far greater difference between the automatic system's performance on standard and ASR text than the human annotators.

Reynar and Ratnaparkhi (1997) (Section 2) argued that a context of one word either side is sufficient for the punctuation disambiguation problem. However, the results of our system suggest that this may be insufficient for the sentence boundary detection problem even assuming reliable part of speech tags (cf note 5).

These experiments do not make use of prosodic information which may be included as part of the ASR output. Such information includes pause length, pre-pausal lengthening and pitch declination. If this information was made available in the form of extra features to a machine learning algorithm then it is possible that the results will improve.

5 Conclusion

This paper has introduced the problem of sentence boundary detection on the text produced by an ASR system as an area of application for NLP technology.

An attempt was made to determine the level of human performance which could be expected for the task. It was found that there was a noticeable difference between the observed performance for mixed and upper case text. It was found that the kappa statistic, a commonly used method for calculating inter-annotator agreement, could not be applied directly in this situation.

A memory-based system for identifying sentence boundaries in ASR text was implemented. There was a noticeable difference when the same system was applied to text which included case information demonstrating that this is an important feature for the problem.

This paper does not propose to offer a solution to the sentence boundary detection problem for ASR transcripts. However, our aim has been to highlight the problem as one worthy of further exploration within the field of NLP and to establish some baselines (human and algorithmic) against which further work may be compared.

Acknowledgements

The authors would like to thank Steve Renals and Yoshihiko Gotoh for providing the data for human annotation experiments and for several useful conversations. They are also grateful to the following people who took part in the annotation experiment: Paul Clough, George Demetriou, Lisa Ferry, Michael Oakes and Andrea Setzer.

References

D. Beeferman, A. Berger, and J. Lafferty. 1998. CYBERPUNC: A lightweight punctuation annotation system for speech. In *Proceedings of the IEEE International Conference on Acoustics, Speech and Signal Processing*, pages 689–692, Seattle, WA.

E. Brill. 1992. A simple rule-based part of speech tagger. In *Proceeding of the Third Conference on Applied Natural Language Processing (ANLP-92)*, pages 152–155, Trento, Italy.

L. Burnard, 1995. *Users Reference Guide for the British National Corpus.* Oxford University Computing Services.

J. Carletta. 1996. Assessing agreement on classification tasks: the kappa statistic. *Computational Linguistics*, 22(2):249–254.

N. Chinchor, P. Robinson, and E. Brown. 1998. HUB-4 Named Entity Task Definition (version 4.8). Technical report, SAIC. `http://www.nist.gov/speech/hub4_98`.

R. Cole, editor. 1996. *Survey of the State of the Art in Human Language Technology.* Available at: http://cslu.cse.ogi.edu/HLTsurvey/HLTsurvey.html. Site visited 17/11/99.

W. Daelemans, J. Zavrel, K. van der Sloot, and A. van den Bosch. 1999. TiMBL: Tilburg memory based learner version 2.0, reference guide. Technical report, ILK Technical Report 98-03. ILK Reference Report 99-01, Available from `http://ilk.kub.nl/~ilk/papers/ilk9901.ps.gz`.

C. Fellbaum, J. Grabowski, S. Landes, and A. Baumann. 1998. Matching words to senses in WordNet: Naive vs. expert differentiation of senses. In C. Fellbaum, editor, *WordNet: An electronic lexical database and some applications.* MIT Press, Cambridge, MA.

W. Gale and G. Sampson. 1996. Good-Turing frequency estimation without tears. *Journal of Quantitave Linguistics*, 2(3):217–37.

Y. Gotoh and S. Renals. 2000. Information extraction from broadcast news. *Philosophical Transactions of the Royal Society of London, series A: Mathematical, Physical and Engineering Sciences.* (to appear).

A. Mikheev. 1998. Feature lattices for maximum entropy modelling. In *Proceedings of the 36th Meeting of the Association for Computational Linguistics (COLING-ACL-98)*, pages 848–854, Montreal, Canada.

R. Moore, J. Dowding, H. Bratt, J. Gawron, Y. Gorfu, and A. Cheyer. 1997. CommandTalk: A Spoken-Language Interface to Battlefield Simulations. In *Proceedings of the Fifth Conference on Applied Natural Language Processing*, pages 1–7, Washington, DC.

D. Palmer and M. Hearst. 1994. Adaptive sentence boundary disambiguation. In *Proceedings of the 1994 Conference on Applied Natural Language Processing*, pages 78–83, Stutgart, Germany.

J. Reynar and A. Ratnaparkhi. 1997. A maximum entropy approach to identifying sentence boundries. In *Proceedings of the Fifth Conference on Applied Natural Language Processing*, pages 16–19, Washington, D.C.

S. Siegel and N. Castellan. 1988. *Nonparametric Statistics for the Behavioural Sciences.* McGraw-Hill, second edition.

M. Stevenson and Y. Wilks. 1999. Combining weak knowledge sources for sense disambiguation. In *Proceedings of the Sixteenth International Joint Conference on Artificial Intelligence*, pages 884–889. Stockholm, Sweden.

C. van Rijsbergen. 1979. *Information Retrieval.* Butterworths, London.

DP: A Detector for Presuppositions in survey questions

Katja WIEMER-HASTINGS
Psychology Department / Institute for Intelligent Systems
University of Memphis
Memphis, TN 38152
kwiemer@latte.memphis.edu

Peter WIEMER-HASTINGS
Human Communication Research Centre
University of Edinburgh
2 Buccleuch Place
Edinburgh EH8 9LW, UK
peterwh@cogsci.ed.ac.uk

Sonya RAJAN, Art GRAESSER, Roger KREUZ, & Ashish KARNAVAT
Institute for Intelligent Systems, University of Memphis, Memphis, TN 38152
sonyarajan@hotmail.com, graesser@memphis.edu, rkreuz@memphis.edu, akarnavat@hotmail.com

Abstract

This paper describes and evaluates a detector of presuppositions (DP) for survey questions. Incorrect presuppositions can make it difficult to answer a question correctly. Since they can be difficult to detect, DP is a useful tool for questionnaire designer. DP performs well using local characteristics of presuppositions. It reports the presupposition to the survey methodologist who can determine whether the presupposition is valid.

Introduction

Presuppositions are propositions that take some information as given, or as "the logical assumptions underlying utterances" (Dijkstra & de Smedt , 1996, p. 255; for a general overview, see McCawley, 1981). Presupposed information includes state of affairs, such as being married; events, such as a graduation; possessions, such as a house, children, knowledge about something; and others. For example, the question, "when did you graduate from college", presupposes the event that the respondent did in fact graduate from college. The answer options may be ranges of years, such as "between 1970 and 1980". Someone who has never attended college can either not respond at all, or give a random (and false) reply. Thus, incorrect presuppositions cause two problems. First, the question is difficult to answer. Second, assuming that people feel obliged to answer them anyway, their answers present false information. This biases survey statistics, or, in an extreme case, makes them useless.

The detector for presuppositions (DP) is part of the computer tool QUAID (Graesser, Wiemer-Hastings, Kreuz, Wiemer-Hastings & Marquis, in press), which helps survey methodologists design questions that are easy to process. DP detects a presupposition and reports it to the survey methodologist, who can examine if the presupposition is correct. QUAID is a computerized QUEST questionnaire evaluation aid. It is based on QUEST (Graesser & Franklin, 1990), a computational model of the cognitive processes underlying human question answering. QUAID critiques questions with respect to unfamiliar technical terms, vague terms, working memory overload, complex syntax, incorrect presuppositions, and unclear question purpose or category. These problems are a subset of potential problems that have been identified by Graesser, Bommareddy, Swamer, and Golding (1996; see also Graesser, Kennedy, Wiemer-Hastings & Ottati, 1999).

QUAID performs reliably on the first five problem categories. In comparison to these five problems, presupposition detection is even more challenging. For unfamiliar technical terms, for example, QUAID reports words with frequencies below a certain threshold. Such an elegant solution is impossible for presuppositions. Their forms vary widely across presupposition types. Therefore, their detection requires a complex set of rules, carefully tuned to identify a variety of presupposition problems. DP prints out the presuppositions of a question, and relies on the survey methodologist to make the final decision whether the presuppositions are valid.

1 How to detect presuppositions

We conducted a content analysis of questions with presupposition problems to construct a list of indicators for presuppositions. 22 questions containing problematic presuppositions were selected from a corpus of 550 questions, taken from questionnaires provided by the U.S. Census Bureau. The 22 questions were identified based on ratings by three human expert raters. It may seem that this problem is infrequent, but then, these questions are part of commonly used questionnaires that have been designed and revised very thoughtfully.

Additionally, we randomly selected a contrast question sample of 22 questions rated unproblematic with regard to incorrect presuppositions by all three raters. Examples (1) and (2) are questions rated as problematic by at least two raters; examples (3) and (4) present questions that do not contain presuppositions.

(1) Is that the same place you USUALLY go when you need routine or preventive care, such as a physical examination or check up?

(2) How much do your parents or parent know about your close friends' parents?

(3) From date to December 31, did you take one or more trips or outings in the United States, of at least one mile, for the PRIMARY purpose of observing, photographing, or feeding wildlife?

(4) Are you now on full-time active duty with the armed forces?

Example (1) presupposes the habit of making use of routine / preventive care; (2) presupposes that the respondent has close friends.

As stated above, incorrect presuppositions are infrequent in well-designed questionnaires. For example, questions about details of somebody's marriage are usually preceded by a question establishing the person's marital status.

In spite of this, providing feedback about presuppositions to the survey methodologist is useful. Importantly, QUAID is designed to aid in the design process. Consider a survey on health-related issues. In the context of this topic, a survey methodologist may be interested in how many days of work a person missed because of illness, but not think about whether the person actually has a job. Upon entering the question "how many days of work did you miss last year because of illness" into the QUAID tool, DP would report that the question presupposes employment. The survey methodologist could then insert a question about employment.

Second, there are subtle presuppositions that may go undetected even by a skilled survey designer. These are presuppositions about things that are likely (but not necessarily) true. For example, a question may inquire about a person's close friends (presupposing close friends) or someone's standard place for preventive care (presupposing the habit of making use of preventive care). DP does not know which presuppositions are likely to be valid or invalid, and is therefore more likely to detect such subtle incorrect presuppositions than a human expert.

1.1 The presupposition detector (DP)

We constructed a set of presupposition detection rules based on the content analysis. The rules use a wide range of linguistic information about the input sentences, including particular words (such as "why"), part of speech categories (e.g., wh-pronoun), and complex syntactic subtrees (such as a quantification clause, followed by a noun phrase).

1.1.1 The syntactic analysis component

We used Eric Brill's rule-based word tagger (1992, 1994a, 1994b), the *de facto* state of the art tagging system, to break the questions down into part-of-speech categories. Brill's tagger produces a single lexical category for each word in a sentence by first assigning tags based on the frequency of occurrence of the word in that category, and then applying a set of context-based re-tagging rules. The tagged text was then passed on to Abney's SCOL/CASS system (1996a, 1996b), an extreme bottom-up parser. It is designed to avoid ambiguity problems by applying grammar rules on a level-by-level basis. Each level contains rules that will only fire if they are correct with high probability. Once the parse moves on to a higher level, it will not attempt to apply lower-level rules. In this way, the parser identifies chunks of information, which it can be reasonably certain are connected, even when it cannot create a complete parse of a sentence.

1.1.2 The presupposition indicators

The indicators for presuppositions were tested against questions rated as "unproblematic" to eliminate items that failed to discriminate questions with versus without presuppositions. We constructed a second list of indicators that detect questions containing no presuppositions. All indicators are listed in Table 1. These lists are certainly far from complete, but they present a good basis for evaluating of how well presuppositions can be detected by an NLP system. These rules were integrated into a decision tree structure, as illustrated in Figure 1.

Table 1: Indicators of absence or presence of presuppositions

	Presupposition	No presupposition
First word(s)	When VP What time Who VP Why How much How many How often etc. How VP Where V NP	Initial or following comma: - is there - are there Does / do NP have ... Will NP have ... Has / Have NP ... Is / are NP ...
Keywords	usually Possessives: mine, yours, NP's while Indexicals: this, these, such	ever any anybody anything whether if could, would
Specific constructions	V infinitive when NP	

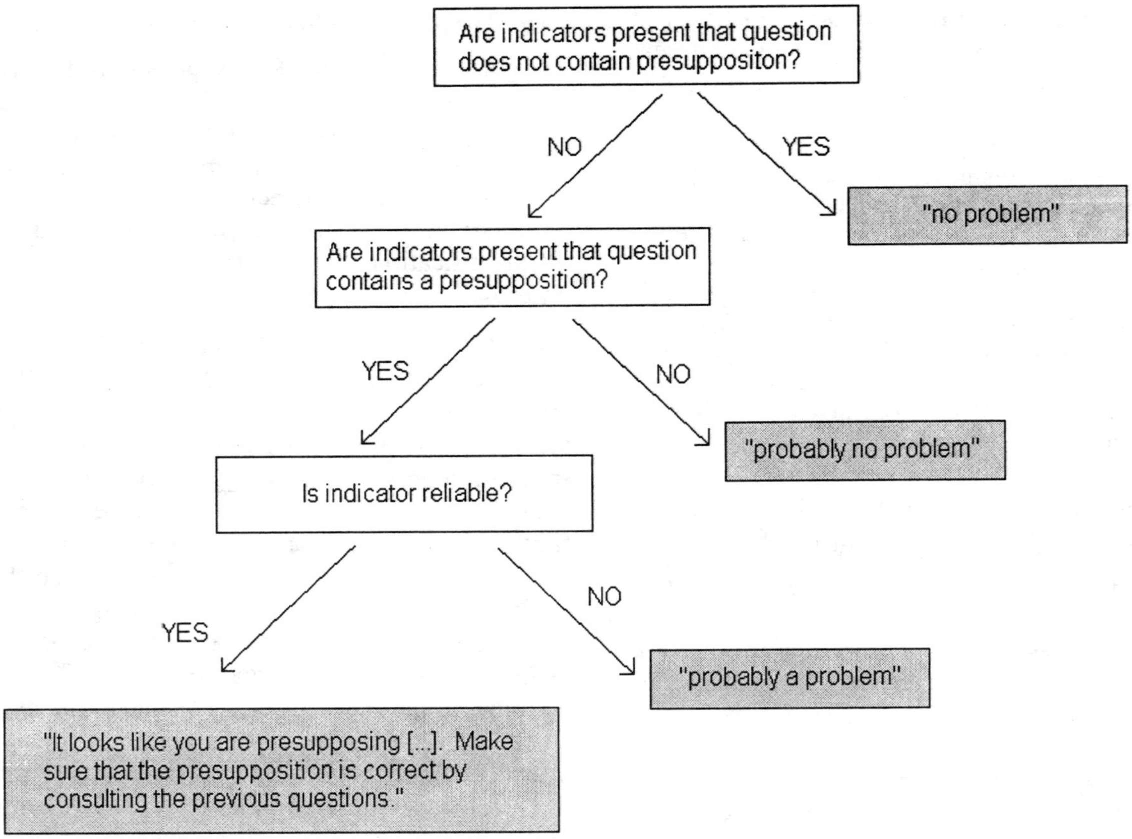

Figure 1 : The DP decision structure tree

1.2 Classifying presuppositions

Different types of presuppositions can be distinguished based on particular indicators. Examples for presupposition types, such as events or possessions, were mentioned above. Table 2 presents an exhaustive overview of presupposition types identified in our analysis. Note that some indicators can point to more than one type of presupposition.

Table 2 : Classification of presupposition based on indicators. In the right column, expressions in parentheses identify the presupposed unit.

Indicator	Presupposition type: The question presupposes…
"how often" …VP "how" aux NP VP "while" … VP "where" … VP "why" … VP	an action (V)
"usually" … VP "how often", "frequently", etc.	a habit (V)
"how many" NP "where is" NP	an entity: object, state, or person (NP)
Indexicals: "this" / "that" NP "these" / "those" NP "such a(n)" NP	a shared referent or common ground (NP)
"how much" NP … "how much does" NP "know" "how many" NP … Possessive pronouns Apostrophe 's': NP's	a possession (NP); exception list: NP's that can be presupposed (name, age, etc.)
"why" S	a state of affairs, fact, or assertion (S)
VP infinitive "why" VP NP	an intention / a goal (infinitive / NP VP)
"who" VP	an agent (A person who VP)
"When" VP …"when" NP VP	an event (VP)

DP reports when a presupposition is present, and it also indicates the type of presupposition that is made (e.g., a common ground presupposition or the presupposition of a habit) in order to point the question designer to the potential presupposition error. DP uses the expressions in the right column in Table 2, selected in accordance with the indicators, and fills them into the brackets in its output (see Figure 1). For example, given the question "How old is your child?", DP would detect the possessive pronoun "your", and accordingly respond: "It looks like you are presupposing a possession (child). Make sure that the presupposition is correct by consulting the previous questions."

2 Evaluation

In this section, we report summary statistics for the human ratings of our test questions and the measures we computed based on these ratings to evaluate DP's performance.

2.1 Human ratings

We used human ratings as the standard against which to evaluate the performance of DP. Three raters rated about 90 questions from 12 questionnaires provided by the Census Bureau. DP currently does not use context. To have a fair test of its performance, the questions were presented to the human raters out of context, and they were instructed to rate them as isolated questions. Ratings were made on a four-point scale, indicating whether the question contained no presupposition (1), probably contained no presupposition (2), probably contained a presupposition (3), or definitely contained a presupposition (4). We transformed the ratings into Boolean ratings by combining ratings of 1 and 2 ("no problem") versus ratings of 3 and 4 ("problem"). We obtained very similar results for analyses of the ratings based on the four-point and the Boolean scale. For simplicity, we just report the results for the Boolean scale.

2.2 Agreement among the raters

We evaluated the agreement among the raters with three measures: correlations, Cohen's kappa, and percent agreement. Correlations were significant only between two raters ($\underline{r}$ = 0. 41); the correlations of these two with the third rater produced non-significant correlations, indicating that the third rater may have used a different strategy. The kappa scores, similarly, were significant only for two raters ($\underline{k}$ = 0.36). In terms of percent agreement, the raters with correlated ratings agreed in 67% of the cases. The percentages of agreement with rater 3 were 57% and 56%, respectively.

DP ratings were significantly correlated with the ratings provided by the two human raters who agreed well ($\underline{r}$ = 0.32 and 0.31), resulting in agreement of ratings in 63% and 66% of the questions. In other words, the agreement of ratings provided by the system and by two human raters is comparable to the highest agreement rate achieved between the human raters.

Some of the human ratings diverged substantially. Therefore, we computed two restrictive measures based on the ratings to evaluate the performance of DP. Both scores are Boolean. The first score is "lenient"; it reports a presupposition only if at least two raters report a presupposition for the question (rating of 3 or 4). We call this measure P_{maj}, a majority-based presupposition count. The second score is strict. It reports a presupposition only if all three raters report a presupposition. This measure is called P_{comp}, a presupposition count based on complete agreement. It results in fewer detected presuppositions overall: P_{comp} reports presuppositions for 29 of the questions (33%), whereas P_{maj} reports 57 (64%).

2.3 Evaluation of the DP

DP ratings were significantly correlated only with P_{comp} (0.35). DP and P_{comp} ratings were in agreement for 67% of the questions. Table 3 lists hit and false alarm rates for DP, separately for P_{maj} and P_{comp}. The hit rate indicates how many of the presuppositions identified by the human ratings were detected by DP. The false alarm rate indicates how often DP reported a presupposition when the human raters did not. The measures look better with respect to the complete agreement criterion, P_{comp}.

Table 3 further lists recall and precision scores. The recall rate indicates how many presuppositions DP detects out of the presuppositions reported by the human rating criterion (computed as hits, divided by the sum of hits and misses). The precision score (computed as hits, divided by the sum of hits and false alarms) measures how many presuppositions reported by DP are actually present, as reported by the human ratings.

Table 3: Performance measures for DP with respect to hits, false alarms, and misses.

	Hit rate	False alarm rate	Recall	Precision	d'
P_{maj}	0.54	0.34	0.66	0.74	0.50
P_{comp}	0.72	0.35	0.72	0.50	0.95

All measures, except for precision, look comparable or better in relation to P_{comp}, including d', which measures the actual power of DP to discriminate questions with and without presuppositions. Of course, picking a criterion with better matches does not improve the system's performance in itself.

3 An updated version of DP

Based on the first results, we made a few modifications and then reevaluated DP. In particular, we added items to the possession exception list based on the new corpus and made some of the no-presupposition rules more specific. As a more drastic change, we updated the decision tree structure so that presupposition indicators overrule indicators against presuppositions, increasing the number of reported presuppositions for cases of conflicting indicators:

If there is evidence for a problem, report "Problem"
Else
  if evidence against problem, report "No problem"
  else, report "Probably not a problem"

Separate analyses show that the modification of the decision tree accounts for most of the performance improvement.

3.1 Results

Table 4 lists the performance measures for the updated DP. Hit and recall rate increased, but so did the false alarm rate, resulting in a lower precision score. The d' score of the updated system with respect to P_{comp} (1.3) is substantially better. The recall rate for this setting is perfect, i.e., DP did not miss any presuppositions. Since survey methodologists will decide whether the presupposition is really a problem, a higher false alarm rate is preferable to missing out presupposition cases. Thus, the updated DP is an improvement over the first version.

Table 4: Performance measures for the updated DP with respect to hits, false alarms, and misses.

	Hit rate	False alarm rate	Recall	Precision	d'
P_{maj}	0.75	0.44	0.84	0.75	0.8
P_{comp}	0.90	0.52	1.00	0.46	1.3

Conclusion

DP can detect presuppositions, and can thereby reliably help a survey methodologist to eliminate incorrect presuppositions. The results for DP with respect to P_{comp} are comparable to, and in some cases even better than, the results for the other five categories. This is a very good result, since most of the five problems allow for "easy" and "elegant" solutions, whereas DP needs to be adjusted to a variety of problems.

It is interesting that the performance of DP looks so much better when compared to the complete agreement score, P_{comp} than when compared to P_{maj}. Recall that P_{comp} only reports a presupposition if all the raters report one. The high agreement of the raters in these cases can presumably be explained by the salience of the presupposition problem. This indicates that DP makes use of reliable indicators for its performance. Good agreement with the other measure, P_{maj}, would suggest that DP additionally reports presuppositions in cases where humans do not agree that a presupposition is present. The higher agreement with the stricter measure is thus a good result.

DP currently works like the other modules of QUAID: it reports potential problems, but leaves it to the survey methodologist to decide whether to act upon the feedback. As such, DP is a substantial addition to QUAID. A future challenge is to turn DP into a DIP (detector of incorrect presuppositions), that is, to reduce the number of reported presuppositions to those likely to be incorrect. DP currently evaluates all questions independent of context, resulting in frequent detections. For example, 20 questions about "this person" may follow one question that establishes the referent. High-frequency repetitive presupposition reports could easily get annoying.

Is a DIP system feasible? At present, it is difficult for NLP systems to use information from context in the evaluation of a statement. What is required to solve this problem is a mechanism that determines whether a presupposed entity (an object, an activity, an assertion, etc.) has been established as applicable in the previous discourse (e.g., in preceding questions).

The Construction Integration (CI) model by Kintsch (1998) provides a good example for how such reference ambiguity can be resolved. CI uses a semantic network that represents an entity in the discourse focus (such as "this person") through higher activations of its links to other concept nodes. Perhaps models such as the CI model can be integrated into the QUAID model to perform context analyses, in combination with tools like Latent Semantic Analysis (LSA, Landauer & Dumais, 1997), which represents text units as vectors in a high-dimensional semantic space. LSA measures the semantic similarity of text units (such as questions) by computing vector cosines. This feature may make LSA a useful tool in the detection of a previous question that establishes a presupposed entity in a later question.

However, questionnaires differ from connected discourse, such as coherent stories, in aspects that make the present problem rather more difficult. Most importantly, the referent for "this person" may have been established in question number 1, and the current question containing the presupposition "this person" is question number 52. A DIP system would have to handle a flexible amount of context, because the distance between questions establishing the correctness of a presupposition and a question building up on it can vary. On the one hand, one could limit the considered context to, say, three questions and risk missing the critical question. On the other hand, it is computationally expensive to keep the complete previous context in the systems "working memory" to evaluate the few presuppositions which may refer back over a large number of questions. Solving this problem will likely require comparing a variety of different settings.

Acknowledgements

This work was partially supported by the Census Bureau (43-YA-BC-802930) and by a grant from the National Science Foundation (SBR 9720314 and SBR 9977969). We wish to acknowledge three colleagues for rating the questions in our evaluation text corpus, and our collaborator Susan Goldman as well as two anonymous reviewers for helpful comments.

References

Abney, S. (1996a). Partial parsing via finite-state cascades. In *Proceedings of the ESSLLI '96 Robust Parsing Workshop*.

Abney, S. (1996b). Methods and statistical linguistics. In J. Klavans & P. Resnik (Eds.), *The Balancing Act*. Cambridge, MA: MIT Press

Brill, E. (1992). A simple rule-based part of speech tagger. In *Proceedings of the Third Conference on Applied Natural Language Processing*. ACL.

Brill, E. (1993). *A corpus-based approach to language learning*. Ph.D. thesis, University of Pennsylvania, Philadelphia, PA.

Brill, E. (1994). Some advances in rule-based part of speech tagging. In *Proceedings of the Twelfth National Conference on Articial Intelligence*. AAAI Press.

Dijkstra, T., & de Smedt, K. (1996). Computational psycholinguistics. *AI and connectionist models of human language processing*. London: Taylor & Francis.

Graesser, A. C., Bommareddy, S., Swamer, S., & Golding, J. (1996). Integrating questionnaire design with a cognitive computational model of human question answering. In N. Schwarz & S. Sudman (Eds.), *Answering questions: Methods of determining cognitive and communicative processes in survey research* (pp. 343-175). San Francisco, CA: Jossey-Bass.

Graesser, A.C., & Franklin, S.P. (1990). QUEST: A cognitive model of question answering. *Discourse Processes, 13*, 279-304.

Graesser, A.C., Kennedy, T., Wiemer-Hastings, P., & Ottati, V. (1999). The use of computational cognitive models to improve questions on surveys and questionnaires. In M. Sirken, D. Herrmann, S. Schechter, N. Schwarz, J. Tanur, & R. Tourangeau (Eds.), *Cognition and Survey Research* (pp. 199-216). New York: John Wiley & Sons.

Graesser, A.C., Wiemer-Hastings, K., Kreuz, R., Wiemer-Hastings, P., & Marquis, K. (in press). QUAID: A questionnaire evaluation aid for survey methodologists. *Behavior Research Methods, Instruments, & Computers.*

Kintsch, W. (1998). *Comprehension. A paradigm for cognition.* Cambridge, UK: Cambridge University Press.

Landauer, T.K., & Dumais, S.T. (1997). A solution to Plato's problem: The latent semantic analysis theory of acquisition, induction, and representation of knowledge. *Psychological Review, 104,* 211-240.

McCawley, J.D. (1981). *Everything that linguists have always wanted to know about logic.* Chicago: University of Chicago Press.

MIMIC: An Adaptive Mixed Initiative Spoken Dialogue System for Information Queries

Jennifer Chu-Carroll
Lucent Technologies Bell Laboratories
600 Mountain Avenue
Murray Hill, NJ 07974, U.S.A.
jencc@research.bell-labs.com

Abstract

This paper describes MIMIC, an adaptive mixed initiative spoken dialogue system that provides movie showtime information. MIMIC improves upon previous dialogue systems in two respects. First, it employs initiative-oriented strategy adaptation to automatically adapt response generation strategies based on the cumulative effect of information dynamically extracted from user utterances during the dialogue. Second, MIMIC's dialogue management architecture decouples its initiative module from the goal and response strategy selection processes, providing a general framework for developing spoken dialogue systems with different adaptation behavior.

1 Introduction

In recent years, speech and natural language technologies have matured enough to enable the development of spoken dialogue systems in limited domains. Most existing systems employ dialogue strategies pre-specified during the design phase of the dialogue manager without taking into account characteristics of actual dialogue interactions. More specifically, mixed initiative systems typically employ rules that specify conditions (generally based on local dialogue context) under which initiative may shift from one agent to the other. Previous research, on the other hand, has shown that changes in initiative strategies in human-human dialogues can be dynamically modeled in terms of characteristics of the user and of the on-going dialogue (Chu-Carroll and Brown, 1998) and that adaptability of initiative strategies in dialogue systems leads to better system performance (Litman and Pan, 1999). However, no previous dialogue system takes into account these dialogue characteristics or allows for initiative-oriented adaptation of dialogue strategies.

In this paper, we describe MIMIC, a voice-enabled telephone-based dialogue system that provides movie showtime information, emphasizing its dialogue management aspects. MIMIC improves upon previous systems along two dimensions. First, MIMIC automatically adapts dialogue strategies based on participant roles, characteristics of the current utterance, and dialogue history. This automatic adaptation allows appropriate dialogue strategies to be employed based on both local dialogue context and dialogue history, and has been shown to result in significantly better performance than non-adaptive systems. Second, MIMIC employs an initiative module that is decoupled from the goal selection process in the dialogue manager, while allowing the outcome of both components to jointly determine the strategies chosen for response generation. As a result, MIMIC can exhibit drastically different dialogue behavior with very minor adjustments to parameters in the initiative module, allowing for rapid development and comparison of experimental prototypes and resulting in general and portable dialogue systems.

2 Adaptive Mixed Initiative Dialogue Management

2.1 Motivation

In naturally occurring human-human dialogues, speakers often adopt different dialogue strategies based on hearer characteristics, dialogue history, etc. For instance, the speaker may provide more guidance if the hearer is having difficulty making progress toward task completion, while taking a more passive approach when the hearer is an expert in the domain. Our main goal is to enable a spoken dialogue system to simulate such human behavior by dynamically adapting dialogue strategies during an interaction based on information that can be automatically detected from the dialogue. Figure 1 shows an excerpt from a dialogue between MIMIC and an actual user where the user is attempting to find the times at which the movie *Analyze This* playing at theaters in Montclair. S and U indicate system and user utterances, respectively, and the italicized utterances are the output of our automatic speech recognizer. In addition, each system turn is annotated with its *task* and *dialogue* initiative holders, where *task initiative* tracks the lead in the process toward achieving the dialogue participants' domain goal, while *dialogue initiative* models the lead in determining the current discourse focus (Chu-Carroll and Brown, 1998). In our information query application domain, the system has task (and thus dialogue) initiative if its utterances provide helpful guidance toward achieving the user's domain goal, as in utterances (6) and (7) where MIMIC provided valid response choices to its query intending to solicit a theater name, while the system has dialogue but not task initiative if its utterances only specify the current discourse goal, as in utterance (4).[1]

This dialogue illustrates several features of our adaptive mixed initiative dialogue manager. First, MIMIC automatically adapted the initiative distribution based on information extracted from user utterances and dialogue history. More specifically, MIMIC took over task initiative in utterance (6), after failing to obtain a valid answer to its query soliciting a missing theater name in (4). It retained task initiative until utterance (12), after the user implicitly indicated her intention to take over task initiative by providing a fully-specified query (utterance (11)) to a limited prompt (utterance (10)). Second, initiative distribution may affect the strategies MIMIC selects to achieve its goals. For instance, in the context of soliciting missing information, when MIMIC did not have task initiative, a simple information-seeking query was generated (utterance (4)). On the other hand, when MIMIC had task initiative, additional guidance was provided (in the form of valid response choices in utterance (6)), which helped the user successfully respond to the system's query. In the context of prompting the user for a new query, when MIMIC had task initiative, a limited prompt was selected to better constrain the user's response (utterance (10)), while an open-ended prompt was generated to allow the user to take control of the problem-solving process otherwise (utterances (1) and (13)).

In the next section, we briefly review a framework for dynamic initiative modeling. In Section 3, we discuss how this framework was incorporated into the dialogue management component of a spoken dialogue system to allow for automatic adaptation of dialogue strategies. Finally, we outline experiments evaluating the resulting system and show that MIMIC's automatic adaptation capabilities resulted in better system performance.

2.2 An Evidential Framework for Modeling Initiative

In previous work, we proposed a framework for modeling initiative during dialogue interaction (Chu-Carroll and Brown, 1998). This framework predicts task and dialogue initiative holders on a turn-by-turn basis in human-human dialogues based on participant roles (such as each dialogue agent's level of expertise and the role that she plays in the application domain), cues observed in the current dialogue turn, and dialogue history. More specifically, we utilize the Dempster-Shafer theory (Shafer, 1976; Gordon and Shortliffe, 1984), and represent the current initiative distribution as two *basic probability assignments (bpas)* which indicate the amount of support for each dialogue participant having the task and dialogue initiatives. For instance, the bpa $m_{t-cur}(\{S\}) = 0.3, m_{t-cur}(\{U\}) = 0.7$ indicates that, with all evidence taken into account, there is more support (to the degree 0.7) for the user having task initiative in the current turn than for the system. At the end of each turn, the bpas are updated based on the effects that cues observed during that turn have on changing them, and the new bpas are used to predict the next task and dialogue initiative holders.

In this framework, cues that affect initiative distribution include *NoNewInfo*, triggered when the speaker simply repeats or rephrases an earlier utterance, implicitly suggesting that the speaker may want to give up initiative, *AmbiguousActions*, triggered when the speaker proposes an action that is ambiguous in the application domain, potentially prompting the hearer to take over initiative to resolve the detected ambiguity, etc. The effects that each cue has on changing the current bpas are also represented as bpas, which were determined by an iterative training procedure using a corpus of transcribed dialogues where each turn was annotated with the task/dialogue initiative holders and the observed cues.

The bpas for the next turn are computed by combining the bpas representing the current initiative distribution and the bpas representing the effects of cues observed during the current turn, using Dempster's combination rule (Gordon and Shortliffe, 1984). The task and dialogue initiative holders are then predicted based on the new bpas. This framework was evaluated using annotated dialogues from four task-oriented domains, achieving, on average, a correct prediction rate of 97% and 88% for task and dialogue initiative holders, respectively. In Section 3.2, we discuss how this predictive model is converted into a generative model by enabling the system to automatically detect cues that were previously labelled manually. We further discuss how the model is used by the dialogue manager for dynamic dialogue strategy adaptation.

3 MIMIC: Mixed Initiative Movie Information Consultant

MIMIC is a telephone-based dialogue system that provides movie showtime information. It consists of the following main components, implemented on a distributed, client-server architecture (Zhou et al., 1997):

1. **Telephony server**: this component detects rings and hang-ups, and enables streaming of audio data on channels of a telephony board.
2. **Speech recognizer**: the recognizer receives audio data from the telephony server and generates the word string hypothesis that best matches the audio input. We used the Lucent Automatic Speech Recognizer (Reichl and Chou, 1998; Ortmanns et al., 1999), configured to use class-based probabilistic n-gram language models to allow for rapid updates of movie/theater/town names.

[1]Although the dialogues we collected in our experiments (Section 5) include cases in which MIMIC has neither initiative, such cases are rare in this application domain, and will not be discussed further in this paper.

		Utterance	Task Initiative	Dialogue Initiative
(1)	S:	Hello, this is MIMIC, the movie information system.	User	System
(2)		How can I help you?		
(3)	U:	What time is Analyze This playing in Montclair?		
		[what time is analyze this playing in montclair]		
(4)	S:	What theater would you like?	User	System
(5)	U:	Montclair.		
		[montclair]		
(6)	S:	Choices for theater are Wellmont Theater and Clearviews Screening Zone.	System	System
(7)		What theater would you like?		
(8)	U:	Clearviews Screening Zone.		
		[um movie screening zone]		
(9)	S:	Analyze This is playing at Clearviews Screening Zone in Montclair at 1:15pm, 4:10pm, and 6:30pm.	System	System
(10)		Please say the name of the movie or theater or town you would like information about.		
(11)	U:	What time is Analyze This playing at the Wellmont Theater?		
		[what time is analyze this playing at the wellmont theater]		
(12)	S:	Analyze This is playing at Wellmont Theater in Montclair at 3:15pm, 5:45pm, 8:20pm, and 10:10pm.	User	System
(13)		Can I help you with anything else?		

Figure 1: Excerpt of an Adaptive Mixed Initiative Dialogue

3. **NLP/Dialogue component**: this main application-dependent component receives a user utterance hypothesis from the speech recognizer, and generates system utterance(s) in response. Three major tasks are carried out by this component: 1) semantic interpretation, which constructs frame-based semantic representations from user utterances, 2) dialogue management, where response strategies are selected based on the semantic representation of the user's utterance, system's domain knowledge, and initiative distribution, and 3) utterance generation, where utterance templates are chosen and instantiated to realize the selected response strategies. These three tasks will be discussed in further detail in the rest of this section.

4. **Text-to-speech engine**: the TTS system receives the word string comprising the system's response from the dialogue component and converts the text into speech for output over the telephone. We used the Bell Labs TTS system (Sproat, 1998), which in addition to converting plain text into speech, accepts text strings annotated to override default pitch height, accent placement, speaking rate, etc.[2]

3.1 Semantic Interpretation

MIMIC utilizes a non-recursive frame-based semantic representation commonly used in spoken dialogue systems (e.g. (Seneff et al., 1991; Lamel, 1998)), which represents an utterance as a set of attribute-value pairs. Figure 2(a) shows the frame-based semantic representation for the utterance *"What time is Analyze This playing in Montclair?"*

Question-Type:	When
Movie:	Analyze This
Theater:	null
Town:	Montclair

(a) Semantic Representation

Question-Type:	When
Movie:	mandatory
Theater:	mandatory
Town:	optional

(b) Task Specification

Figure 2: Semantic Representation and Task Specification

MIMIC's semantic representation is constructed by first extracting, for each attribute, a set of keywords from the user utterance. Using a vector-based topic identification process (Salton, 1971; Chu-Carroll and Carpenter, 1999), these keywords are used to determine a set of likely values (including *null*) for that attribute. Next, the utterance is interpreted with respect to the dialogue history and the system's domain knowledge. This allows MIMIC to handle elliptical sentences and anaphoric references, as well as automatically infer missing values and detect inconsistencies in the current representation.

This semantic representation allows for decoupling of domain-dependent task specifications and domain-

[2] See (Nakatani and Chu-Carroll, 2000) for how MIMIC's dialogue-level knowledge is used to override default prosodic assignments for concept-to-speech generation.

independent dialogue management strategies. Each query type is specified by a template indicating, for each attribute, whether a value must, must not, or can optionally be provided in order for a query to be considered well-formed. Figure 2(b) shows that to solicit movie showtime information (question type *when*), a movie name and a theater name must be provided, whereas a town may optionally be provided. These specifications are determined based on domain semantics, and must be reconstructed when porting the system to a new domain.

3.2 Dialogue Management

Given a semantic representation, the dialogue history and the system's domain knowledge, the dialogue manager selects a set of strategies that guides MIMIC's response generation process. This task is carried out by three subprocesses: 1) *initiative modeling*, which determines the initiative distribution for the system's dialogue turn, 2) *goal selection*, which identifies a goal that MIMIC's response attempts to achieve, and 3) *strategy selection*, which chooses, based on the initiative distribution, a set of dialogue acts that MIMIC will adopt in its attempt to realize the selected goal.

3.2.1 Initiative Modeling

MIMIC's initiative module determines the task and dialogue initiative holders for each system turn in order to enable dynamic strategy adaptation. It automatically detects cues triggered during the current user turn, and combines the effects of these cues with the current initiative distribution to determine the initiative holders for the system's turn.

Cue Detection The cues and the bpas representing their effects are largely based on a subset of those described in (Chu-Carroll and Brown, 1998),[3] as shown in Figures 3(a) and 3(b). Figure 3(a) shows that observation of *TakeOverTask* supports a task initiative shift to the speaker to the degree .35. The remaining support is assigned to Θ, the set of all possible conclusions (i.e., {speaker,hearer}), indicating that to the degree .65, observation of this cue does not commit to identifying which dialogue participant should have task initiative in the next dialogue turn.

The cues used in MIMIC are classified into two categories, *discourse cues* and *analytical cues*, based on the types of knowledge needed to detect them:

1. Discourse cues, which can be detected by considering the semantic representation of the current utterance and dialogue history:
   - *TakeOverTask*, an implicit indication that the user wants to take control of the problem-solving process, triggered when the user provides more information than the discourse expectation.
   - *NoNewInfo*, an indication that the user is unable to make progress toward task completion, triggered when the semantic representations of two consecutive user turns are identical (a result of the user not knowing what to say or the speech recognizer failing to recognize the user utterances).
2. Analytical cues, which can only be detected by taking into account MIMIC's domain knowledge:
   - *InvalidAction*, an indication that the user made an invalid assumption about the domain, triggered when the system database lookup based on the user's query returns null.
   - *InvalidActionResolved*, triggered when the previous invalid assumption is corrected.
   - *AmbiguousAction*, an indication that the user query is not well-formed, triggered when a mandatory attribute is unspecified or when more than one value is specified for an attribute.
   - *AmbiguousActionResolved*, triggered when the attribute in question is uniquely instantiated.

Computing Initiative Distribution To determine the initiative distribution, the bpas representing the effects of cues detected in the current user utterance are instantiated (i.e., *speaker/hearer* in Figure 3 are instantiated as *system/user* accordingly). These effects are then interpreted with respect to the current initiative distribution by applying Dempster's combination rule (Gordon and Shortliffe, 1984) to the bpas representing the current initiative distribution and the instantiated bpas. This results in two new bpas representing the task and dialogue initiative distributions for the system's turn. The dialogue participant with the greater degree of support for having the task/dialogue initiative in these bpas is the task/dialogue initiative holder for the system's turn[4] (see Section 4 for an example).

3.2.2 Goal Selection

The goal selection module selects a goal that MIMIC attempts to achieve in its response by utilizing information from analytical cue detection as shown in Figure 4. MIMIC's goals focus on two aspects of cooperative dialogue interaction: 1) initiating subdialogues to resolve anomalies that occur during the dialogue by attempting to instantiate an unspecified attribute, constraining an attribute for which multiple values have been specified, or correcting an invalid assumption in the case of invalid

[3] We selected only those cues that can be automatically detected in a spoken dialogue system with speech recognition errors and limited semantic interpretation capabilities.

[4] In practice, this is the *preferred* initiative holder since practical reasons may prevent the dialogue participant from actually holding the initiative. For instance, if having task initiative dictates inclusion of additional helpful information, this can only be realized if MIMIC's knowledge base provides such information.

Cue Class	Cue	BPA
Discourse	TakeOverTask	$m_{t-tot}(\{speaker\}) = 0.35; m_{t-tot}(\Theta) = 0.65$
	NoNewInfo	$m_{t-nni}(\{hearer\}) = 0.35; m_{t-nni}(\Theta) = 0.65$
Analytical	InvalidAction	$m_{t-ia}(\{hearer\}) = 0.35; m_{t-ia}(\Theta) = 0.65$
	InvalidActionResolved	$m_{t-iar}(\{hearer\}) = 0.35; m_{t-iar}(\Theta) = 0.65$
	AmbiguousAction	$m_{t-aa}(\{hearer\}) = 0.35; m_{t-aa}(\Theta) = 0.65$
	AmbiguousActionResolved	$m_{t-aar}(\{speaker\}) = 0.35; m_{t-aar}(\Theta) = 0.65$

(a) Task Initiative

Cue Class	Cue	BPA
Discourse	TakeOverTask	$m_{d-tot}(\{speaker\}) = 0.35; m_{d-tot}(\Theta) = 0.65$
	NoNewInfo	$m_{d-nni}(\{hearer\}) = 0.35; m_{d-nni}(\Theta) = 0.65$
Analytical	InvalidAction	$m_{d-ia}(\{hearer\}) = 0.7; m_{d-ia}(\Theta) = 0.3$
	InvalidActionResolved	$m_{d-iar}(\{hearer\}) = 0.7; m_{d-iar}(\Theta) = 0.3$
	AmbiguousAction	$m_{d-aa}(\{hearer\}) = 0.7; m_{d-aa}(\Theta) = 0.3$
	AmbiguousActionResolved	$m_{d-aar}(\{speaker\}) = 0.7; m_{d-aar}(\Theta) = 0.3$

(b) Dialogue Initiative

Figure 3: Cues and BPAs for Modeling Initiative in MIMIC

Select-Goal(SemRep):
(1) If *AmbiguousAction* detected
(2) ambiguous-attr ← get-ambiguous(SemRep)
/* *get name of ambiguous attribute* */
(3) If (number-values(ambiguous-attr) == 0)
/* *attribute unspecified* */
(4) **Instantiate**(ambiguous-attr)
(5) Else /* *more than one value specified* */
(6) **Constrain**(ambiguous-attr)
(7) Else if *InvalidAction* detected
(8) **ProvideNegativeAnswer**(SemRep)
(9) Else /* *well-formed query* */
(10) answer ← database-query(SemRep)
(11) **ProvideAnswer**(answer)

Figure 4: Goal Selection Algorithm

user queries (steps 1-8)[5] (van Beek et al., 1993; Raskutti and Zukerman, 1993; Qu and Beale, 1999), and 2) providing answers to well-formed queries (steps 9-11).

3.2.3 Strategy Selection

Previous work has argued that initiative affects the degree of control an agent has in the dialogue interaction (Whittaker and Stenton, 1988; Walker and Whittaker, 1990; Chu-Carroll and Brown, 1998). Thus, a cooperative system may adopt different strategies to achieve the same goal depending on the initiative distribution. Since task initiative models contribution to domain/problem-solving goals, while dialogue initiative affects the current discourse goal, we developed alternative strategies for achieving the goals in Figure 4 based on initiative distribution, as shown in Table 1.

The strategies employed when MIMIC has only dialogue initiative are similar to the mixed initiative dialogue strategies employed by many existing spoken dialogue systems (e.g., (Bennacef et al., 1996; Stent et al., 1999)). To instantiate an attribute, MIMIC adopts the *InfoSeek* dialogue act to solicit the missing information. In contrast, when MIMIC has both initiatives, it plays a more active role by presenting the user with additional information comprising valid instantiations of the attribute (*GiveOptions*). Given an invalid query, MIMIC notifies the user of the failed query and provides an open-ended prompt when it only has dialogue initiative. When MIMIC has both initiatives, however, in addition to *NotifyFailure*, it suggests an alternative close to the user's original query and provides a limited prompt. Finally, when MIMIC has neither initiative, it simply adopts *NotifyFailure*, allowing the user to determine the next discourse goal.

3.3 Utterance Generation

MIMIC employs a simple template-driven utterance generation approach. Templates are associated with dialogue acts as shown in Table 2.[6] The generation component receives from the dialogue manager the selected dialogue acts and the parameters needed to instantiate the templates. It then generates the system response, which is sent to the TTS module for spoken output synthesis.

[5] An alternative strategy to step (4) is to perform a database lookup based on the ambiguous query and summarize the results (Litman et al., 1998), which we leave for future work.

[6] In most cases, there is a one-to-one-mapping between dialogue acts and templates. The exceptions are Answer, NotifyFailure, and SuggestAlternative, whose templates vary based on the question type.

	Task + Dialogue	Dialogue	None
Constrain	Clarify	Clarify	Acknowledge
Instantiate	GiveOptions InfoSeek	InfoSeek	Acknowledge
ProvideAnswer	Answer LimitedPrompt	Answer OpenPrompt	Answer
ProvideNegativeAnswer	NotifyFailure SuggestAlternative LimitedPrompt	NotifyFailure OpenPrompt	NotifyFailure

Table 1: Strategy Selection Based on Goal and Initiative Distribution

Dialogue Act	**Template**
Clarify	"Did you say $< value_1 > \ldots$, or $< value_n >$?"
Acknowledge	"Uh-huh."
GiveOptions	"Choices for $< attribute >$ are $< value_1 > \ldots < value_n >$."
InfoSeek	"What $< attribute >$ would you like?"
Answer	E.g., "$< movie >$ is playing at $< theater >$ at $< time_1 > \ldots < time_n >$."
OpenPrompt	"Can I help you with anything else?"
LimitedPrompt	"Please say the name of the movie or theater or town you would like information about."
NotifyFailure	E.g., "$< movie >$ is not playing at $< theater >$.
SuggestAlternative	E.g., "$< movie >$ is playing at $< alternativetheater >$ at $< time_1 > \ldots < time_n >$."

Table 2: Mappings Between Dialogue Acts and Utterance Templates

4 Examples

To illustrate MIMIC's adaptation capabilities, we return to the dialogue in Figure 1, which is repeated in Figure 5 and annotated with the cues detected in each user turn (in boldfaced italics) and the dialogue acts employed for response generation in each system turn (in boldface).

The bpas representing the initiative distribution for utterance (3) are the initial bpas, which, based on MIMIC's role as an information provider, are

$$m_{t-(3)}(\{S\}) = 0.3, \qquad m_{t-(3)}(\{U\}) = 0.7;$$
$$m_{d-(3)}(\{S\}) = 0.6, \qquad m_{d-(3)}(\{U\}) = 0.4.$$

The cue *AmbiguousAction* is detected in utterance (3) because the mandatory attribute *theater* was not specified and cannot be inferred (since the town of Montclair has multiple theaters). The bpas representing its effect are instantiated as follows (Figure 3):

$$m_{t-aa}(\{S\}) = 0.35, \qquad m_{t-aa}(\Theta) = 0.65;$$
$$m_{d-aa}(\{S\}) = 0.7, \qquad m_{d-aa}(\Theta) = 0.3.$$

Combining the current bpas with the effects of the observed cue, we obtain the following new bpas:

$$m_{t-(4)}(\{S\}) = 0.4, \qquad m_{t-(4)}(\{U\}) = 0.6;$$
$$m_{d-(4)}(\{S\}) = 0.83, \qquad m_{d-(4)}(\{U\}) = 0.17.$$

The updated bpas indicate that MIMIC should have dialogue but not task initiative when attempting to resolve the detected ambiguity in utterance (4).

MIMIC selects *Instantiate* as its goal to be achieved (Figure 4), which, based on the initiative distribution, leads it to select the *InfoSeek* action (Table 1) and generate the query *"What theater would you like?"*

The user's response in (5) again triggers *AmbiguousAction*, as well as *NoNewInfo* since the semantic representations of (3) and (5) are identical, given the dialogue context. When the effects of these cues are taken into account, we have the following initiative distribution for utterance (6):

$$m_{t-(6)}(\{S\}) = 0.62, \qquad m_{t-(6)}(\{U\}) = 0.38;$$
$$m_{d-(6)}(\{S\}) = 0.96, \qquad m_{d-(6)}(\{U\}) = 0.04.$$

Although *Instantiate* is again selected as the goal, MIMIC now has both task and dialogue initiatives; thus it selects both *GiveOptions* and *InfoSeek* to achieve this goal and generates utterances (6) and (7). The additional information, in the form of valid theater choices, helps the user provide the missing value in (8), allowing MIMIC to answer the query in (9) and prompt for the next query. However, despite the limited prompt, the user provides a well-formed query in (11), triggering *TakeOverTask*. Thus, MIMIC answers the query and switches to an open-ended prompt in (13), relinquishing task initiative to the user.

In addition to its automatic adaptation capabilities, another advantage of MIMIC is the ease of modifying its adaptation behavior, enabled by the decoupling of the initiative module from the goal and strategy selection processes. For instance, a system-initiative version of MIMIC can be achieved by setting the initial bpas as follows:

$$m_{t-initial}(\{S\}) = 1;$$
$$m_{d-initial}(\{S\}) = 1.$$

(1)	S:	Hello, this is MIMIC, the movie information system.	
(2)		How can I help you?	
(3)	U:	What time is Analyze This playing in Montclair?	
		[what time is analyze this playing in montclair]	***[AmbiguousAction]***
(4)	S:	What theater would you like?	**[InfoSeek]**
(5)	U:	Montclair.	
		[montclair]	***[AmbiguousAction,NoNewInfo]***
(6)	S:	Choices for theater are Wellmont theater and Clearviews Screening Zone	**[GiveOptions]**
(7)		What theater would you like?	**[InfoSeek]**
(8)	U:	Clearviews Screening Zone.	
		[um movie screening zone]	***[AmbiguousActionResolved]***
(9)	S:	Analyze This is playing at Clearviews Screening Zone in Montclair at 1:15pm, 4:10pm, and 6:30pm.	**[Answer]**
(10)		Please say the name of the movie or theater or town you would like information about.	**[LimitedPrompt]**
(11)	U:	What time is Analyze This playing at the Wellmont theater?	
		[what time is analyze this playing at the wellmont theater]	***[TakeOverTask]***
(12)	S:	Analyze this is playing at Wellmont theater in Montclair at 3:15pm, 5:45pm, 8:20pm, and 10:10pm.	**[Answer]**
(13)		Can I help you with anything else?	**[OpenPrompt]**

Figure 5: Annotated Dialogue Shown in Figure 1

This is because in the Dempster-Shafer theory, if the initial bpas or the bpas for a cue provide definite evidence for drawing a certain conclusion, then no subsequent cue has any effect on changing that conclusion. Thus, MIMIC will retain both initiatives throughout the dialogue. Alternatively, versions of MIMIC with different adaptation behavior can be achieved by tailoring the initial bpas and/or the bpas for each cue based on the application. For instance, for an electronic sales agent, the effect of *InvalidAction* can be increased so that when the user orders an out-of-stock item, the system will always take over task initiative and suggest an alternative item.

5 System Evaluation

We conducted two experiments to evaluate MIMIC's automatic adaptation capabilities. We compared MIMIC with two control systems: MIMIC-SI, a system-initiative version of MIMIC in which the system retains both initiatives throughout the dialogue, and MIMIC-MI, a non-adaptive mixed-initiative version of MIMIC that resembles the behavior of many existing dialogue systems. In this section we summarize these experiments and their results. A companion paper describes the evaluation process and results in further detail (Chu-Carroll and Nickerson, 2000).

Each experiment involved eight users interacting with MIMIC and MIMIC-SI or MIMIC-MI to perform a set of tasks, each requiring the user to obtain specific movie information. User satisfaction was assessed by asking the subjects to fill out a questionnaire after interacting with each version of the system. Furthermore, a number of performance features, largely based on the PARADISE dialogue evaluation scheme (Walker et al., 1997), were automatically logged, derived, or manually annotated. In addition, we logged the cues automatically detected in each user utterance, as well as the initiative distribution for each turn and the dialogue acts selected to generate each system response.

The features gathered from the dialogue interactions were analyzed along three dimensions: *system performance*, *discourse features* (in terms of characteristics of the resulting dialogues, such as the cues detected in user utterances), and *initiative distribution*. Our results show that MIMIC's adaptation capabilities 1) led to better system performance in terms of user satisfaction, dialogue efficiency (shorter dialogues), and dialogue quality (fewer ASR timeouts), and 2) better matched user expectations (by giving up task initiative when the user intends to have control of the dialogue interaction) and more efficiently resolved dialogue anomalies (by taking over task initiative to provide guidance when no progress is made in the dialogue, or to constrain user utterances when ASR performance is poor).

6 Conclusions

In this paper, we discussed MIMIC, an adaptive mixed-initiative spoken dialogue system. MIMIC's automatic adaptation capabilities allow it to employ appropriate strategies based on the cumulative effect of information dynamically extracted from user utterances during dialogue interactions, enabling MIMIC to provide more cooperative and satisfactory responses than existing non-adaptive systems. Furthermore, MIMIC was implemented as a general framework for information query systems by decoupling its initiative module from the goal selection process, while allowing the outcome of both processes to jointly determine the response strategies employed. This feature enables easy modification to MIMIC's adaptation behavior, thus allowing the framework to be used for rapid development and comparisons of experimental prototypes of spoken dialogue systems.

Acknowledgments

The author would like to thank Egbert Ammicht, Antoine Saad, Qiru Zhou, Wolfgang Reichl, and Stefan Ortmanns for their help on system integration and on ASR/telephony server development, Jill Nickerson for conducting the evaluation experiments, and Bob Carpenter, Diane Litman, Christine Nakatani, and Jill Nickerson for their comments on an earlier draft of this paper.

References

S. Bennacef, L. Devillers, S. Rosset, and L. Lamel. 1996. Dialog in the RAILTEL telephone-based system. In *Proceedings of the 4th International Conference on Spoken Language Processing*.

Jennifer Chu-Carroll and Michael K. Brown. 1998. An evidential model for tracking initiative in collaborative dialogue interactions. *User Modeling and User-Adapted Interaction*, 8(3-4):215–253.

Jennifer Chu-Carroll and Bob Carpenter. 1999. Vector-based natural language call routing. *Computational Linguistics*, 25(3):361–388.

Jennifer Chu-Carroll and Jill S. Nickerson. 2000. Evaluating automatic dialogue strategy adaptation for a spoken dialogue system. In *Proceedings of the 1st Conference of the North American Chapter of the Association for Computational Linguistics*. To appear.

Jean Gordon and Edward H. Shortliffe. 1984. The Dempster-Shafer theory of evidence. In Bruce Buchanan and Edward Shortliffe, editors, *Rule-Based Expert Systems: The MYCIN Experiments of the Stanford Heuristic Programming Project*, chapter 13, pages 272–292. Addison-Wesley.

Lori Lamel. 1998. Spoken language dialog system development and evaluation at LIMSI. In *Proceedings of the International Symposium on Spoken Dialogue*, pages 9–17.

Diane J. Litman and Shimei Pan. 1999. Empirically evaluating an adaptable spoken dialogue system. In *Proceedings of the 7th International Conference on User Modeling*, pages 55–64.

Diane J. Litman, Shimei Pan, and Marilyn A. Walker. 1998. Evaluating response strategies in a web-based spoken dialogue agent. In *Proceedings of the 36th Annual Meeting of the Association for Computational Linguistics*, pages 780–786.

Christine H. Nakatani and Jennifer Chu-Carroll. 2000. Using dialogue representations for concept-to-speech generation. In *Proceedings of the ANLP-NAACL Workshop on Conversational Systems*.

Stefan Ortmanns, Wolfgang Reichl, and Wu Chou. 1999. An efficient decoding method for real time speech recognition. In *Proceedings of the 5th European Conference on Speech Communication and Technology*.

Yan Qu and Steve Beale. 1999. A constraint-based model for cooperative response generation in information dialogues. In *Proceedings of the Sixteenth National Conference on Artificial Intelligence*.

Bhavani Raskutti and Ingrid Zukerman. 1993. Eliciting additional information during cooperative consultations. In *Proceedings of the 15th Annual Meeting of the Cognitive Science Society*.

Wolfgang Reichl and Wu Chou. 1998. Decision tree state tying based on segmental clustering for acoustic modeling. In *Proceedings of the International Conference on Acoustics, Speech, and Signal Processing*.

Gerald Salton. 1971. *The SMART Retrieval System*. Prentice Hall, Inc.

Stephanie Seneff, James Glass, David Goddeau, David Goodine, Lynette Hirschman, Hong Leung, Michael Phillips, Joseph Polifroni, and Victor Zue. 1991. Development and preliminary evaluation of the MIT ATIS system. In *Proceedings of the DARPA Speech and Natural Language Workshop*, pages 88–93.

Glenn Shafer. 1976. *A Mathematical Theory of Evidence*. Princeton University Press.

Richard Sproat, editor. 1998. *Multilingual Text-to-Speech Synthesis: The Bell Labs Approach*. Kluwer, Boston, MA.

Amanda Stent, John Dowding, Jean Mark Gawron, Elizabeth Owen Bratt, and Robert Moore. 1999. The CommandTalk spoken dialogue system. In *Proceedings of the 37th Annual Meeting of the Association for Computational Linguistics*, pages 183–190.

Peter van Beek, Robin Cohen, and Ken Schmidt. 1993. From plan critiquing to clarification dialogue for cooperative response generation. *Computational Intelligence*, 9(2):132–154.

Marilyn Walker and Steve Whittaker. 1990. Mixed initiative in dialogue: An investigation into discourse segmentation. In *Proceedings of the 28th Annual Meeting of the Association for Computational Linguistics*, pages 70–78.

Marilyn A. Walker, Diane J. Litman, Candance A. Kamm, and Alicia Abella. 1997. PARADISE: A framework for evaluating spoken dialogue agents. In *Proceedings of the 35th Annual Meeting of the Association for Computational Linguistics*, pages 271–280.

Steve Whittaker and Phil Stenton. 1988. Cues and control in expert-client dialogues. In *Proceedings of the 26th Annual Meeting of the Association for Computational Linguistics*, pages 123–130.

Qiru Zhou, Chin-Hui Lee, Wu Chou, and Andrew Pargellis. 1997. Speech technology integration and research platform: A system study. In *Proceedings of the 5th European Conference on Speech Communication and Technology*.

Javox: A Toolkit for Building Speech-Enabled Applications

Michael S. Fulkerson and **Alan W. Biermann**
Department of Computer Science
Duke University
Durham, North Carolina 27708, USA
{msf, awb}@cs.duke.edu

Abstract

JAVOX provides a mechanism for the development of spoken-language systems from existing desktop applications. We present an architecture that allows existing Java[1] programs to be speech-enabled with no source-code modification, through the use of reflection and automatic modification to the application's compiled code. The grammars used in JAVOX are based on the Java Speech Grammar Format (JSGF); JAVOX grammars have an additional semantic component based on our JAVOX Scripting Language (JSL). JAVOX has been successfully demonstrated on real-world applications.

1 Overview

JAVOX is an implemented set of tools that allows software developers to *speech-enable* existing applications. The process requires no changes to the program's source code: Speech capacity is *plugged-in* to the existing code by modifying the compiled program as it loads. JAVOX is intended to provide similar functionality to that usually associated with menus and mouse actions in graphical user interfaces (GUIs). It is completely programmable – developers can provide a speech interface to whatever functionality they desire. JAVOX has been successfully demonstrated with several GUI-based applications.

Previous systems to assist in the development of spoken-language systems (SLSs) have focused on building stand-alone, customized applications, such as (Sutton et al., 1996) and (Pargellis et al., 1999). The goal of the JAVOX toolkit is to speech-enable traditional desktop applications – this is similar to the goals of the MELISSA project (Schmidt et al., 1998). It is intended to both speed the development of SLSs and to localize the speech-specific code within the application. JAVOX allows developers to add speech interfaces to applications at the end of the development process; SLSs no longer need to be built from the ground up.

We will briefly present an overview of how JAVOX works, including its major modules. First, we will examine TRANSLATOR, the implemented JAVOX natural language processing (NLP) component; its role is to translate from natural language utterances to the JAVOX Scripting Language (JSL). Next, we will discuss JSL in conjunction with a discussion of EXECUTER, the interface between JAVOX and the application. We will explain the JAVOX infrastructure and its current implementation in Java. In conclusion, we will discuss the current state of the project and where it is going.

2 Basic Operation

JAVOX can be used as the sole location of NLP for an application; the application is written as a non-speech-enabled program and JAVOX adds the speech capability. The current implementation is written in Java and works with Java programs. The linkage between the application program and JAVOX is created by modifying – at load time – all constructors in the application to *register* new objects with JAVOX. For this reason, the application's source code does not need any modification to enable JAVOX. A thorough discussion of this technique is presented in Section 4. The schematic in Figure 1 shows a high-level overview of the JAVOX architecture.

Issuing a voice command begins with a user utterance, which the speech recognizer processes and passes to the NLP component, TRANSLATOR. We are using the IBM implementation of Sun's Java Speech application program interface (API) (Sun Microsystems, Inc., 1998) in conjunction with IBM's VIAVOICE. The job of TRANSLATOR – or a different module conforming to its API – is to translate the utterance into a form that represents the corresponding program actions. The current implementation of TRANSLATOR uses a context-free grammar, with each rule carrying an optional JSL fragment. A typical bottom-up parser processes utterances and a complete JSL program results. The resulting JSL is forwarded to EXECUTER, where the JSL code is executed. For example, in a hypothetical banking application, the utterance *add $100 to the account* might be translated into the JSL command:

```
myBalance = myBalance + 100;
```

[1] Java and Java Speech are registered trademarks of Sun Microsystems, Inc.

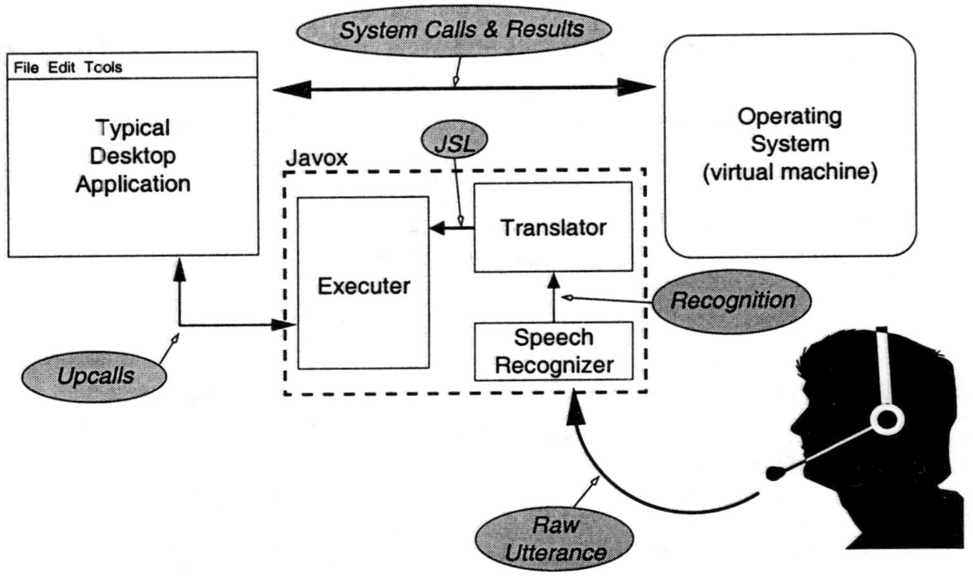

Figure 1: Schematic of the JAVOX architecture.

The job of EXECUTER – or a different module that conforms to EXECUTER's API – is to execute and monitor upcalls into the running application. The upcalls are the actual functions that would be made by the appropriate mouse clicks or menu selections had the user not used speech. For this reason, we are currently concentrating our efforts on event-driven programs, the class of most GUI applications. Their structure is usually amenable to this approach. Our implementation of EXECUTER performs the upcalls by interpreting and executing JSL, though the technology could be used with systems other than JSL. In the banking example, EXECUTER would identify the `myBalance` variable and increment it by $100.

The main JAVOX components, TRANSLATOR and EXECUTER, are written to flexible APIs. Developers may choose to use their own custom components instead of these two. Those who want a different NLP scheme can implement a different version of TRANSLATOR and – as long as it outputs JSL – still use EXECUTER. Conversely, those who want a different scripting system can replace JSL and still use TRANSLATOR and even EXECUTER's low-level infrastructure.

3 Javox Grammars

The JAVOX infrastructure is not tied to any particular NLP method; in fact, the JAVOX grammar system is the second NLP implementation we have used. It is presented here because it is straightforward, easy to implement, and surprisingly powerful. JAVOX grammars are based on Sun's Java Speech Grammar Format (JSGF) (Sun Microsystems, Inc., 1998). JSGF is a rule-based, speech-recognition grammar, designed to specify acceptable input to a recognizer. In JAVOX grammars, each JSGF rule may be augmented with a fragment of JAVOX Scripting Language code – we refer to JAVOX grammars as *scriptable* grammars. The result of parsing an utterance with a JAVOX grammar is a complete piece of JSL code, which is then interpreted to perform the action specified by the user.

The process of speech-enabling an application in JAVOX consists of writing a grammar that contains the language to be used and the corresponding actions to be performed. Building on top of JSGF means – in many cases – only one file is needed to contain all application-specific information. JSL-specific code is automatically stripped from the grammar at runtime, leaving an ordinary JSGF grammar. This JSGF grammar is sent to a Java-Speech-compliant recognizer as its input grammar. In the current Java implementation, each Java source file (`Foo.java`) can have an associated JAVOX grammar file (`Foo.gram`) that contains all the information needed to *speak* to the application. Encapsulating all natural language information in one file also means that porting the application to different languages is far easier than in most SLSs.

3.1 Scriptable Grammars

Since JSGF grammars are primarily speech-recognition grammars, they lack the ability to encode semantic information. They only possess a limited *tag* mechanism. Tags allow the recognizer to output a canonical representation of the utterance instead of the recognition verbatim. For example,

```
public <ACTION> = move [the] <PART> <DIR>;
public <PART> = eyes;
public <PART> = ( cap | hat );
public <DIR> = up;
public <DIR> = down;
```

Grammar 1: A JSGF fragment from the Mr. Potato Head domain.

the tag `rm` may be the output from both *delete the file* and *remove it*.

Tags are not implemented in Javox grammars; instead, we augment the rules of JSGF with fragments of a scripting language, which contains much richer semantic information than is possible with tags. Translator receives the raw utterance from the recognizer and translates it into the appropriate semantic representation. Javox grammars do not mandate the syntax of the additional semantic portion. Though JSL is presented here, Translator has been used to form Prolog predicates and Visual Basic fragments.

JSGF rules can be explicitly made *public* or are implicitly *private*. Public rules can be imported by other grammars and can serve as the result of a recognition; a private rule can be used in a recognition, but cannot be the sole result. The five rules in Grammar 1 are from a JSGF-only grammar fragment from the Mr. Potato Head[2] domain (discussed later). Grammar 1 allows eight sentences, such as *move the eyes up*, *move the eyes down*, *move the cap up*, *move the cap down*, and *move cap up*. Rule names are valid Java identifiers enclosed within angle brackets; the left-hand side (LHS) is everything to the left of the equality sign and the right-hand side (RHS) is everything to the right. Javox grammars include the standard constructs available in JSGF, these include:

Imports Any grammar file can be imported into other grammar files, though only public rules are exported. This allows for the creation of grammar libraries. When using JSL, Java classes can also be imported.

Comments Grammars can be documented using Java comments: single-line comments (//) and delimited ones (/* until */).

Parenthesis Precedence can be modified with parentheses.

Alternatives A vertical bar (|) can be used to separate alternative elements, as in the `<PART>` rule of Grammar 1.

Optionals Optional elements are enclosed within brackets ([and]), such as `the` in Grammar 1's `<ACTION>` rule.

Kleene Star Operator A postfix Kleene star (*) operator can be used to indicate that the preceding element may occur zero or more times.

Plus Operator A similar operator to indicate that an element may appear one or more times.

A grammar's rules may be organized however the developer wishes. Some may choose to have one rule per utterance, while others may divide rules to the parts-of-speech level or group them by semantic value. In practice, we tend to write rules grouped by semantic value for nouns and verbs and at the parts-of-speech level for function words. Grammar 2 shows the Mr. Potato Head grammar augmented with JSL fragments.

The semantic component of each rule is separated from the RHS by a colon and delimited with a brace and colon ({: until :}). Using Grammar 2, the parse and translation for *Move the cap up* is shown in Figure 2.

Each rule may have either *one* semantic fragment or *any number* of named fields. A single fragment is sufficient when there is a one-to-one correlation between a lexical item and its representation in the program. Occasionally, a single lexical item may require several components to adequately express its meaning within a program. In Grammar 2, there is a one-to-one correlation between the direction of movement and the `slideUp` and `slideDown` functions in the `<DIR>` rules. These functions can also written as a single `slide` function, with the direction of the movement given by two parametric variables (`cos` and `sin`). In this situation, the direction rule (`<DIR_NF>`) needs to be expressed with two values, each known as a named field. The word *up* may be represented by the named fields `cos` and `sin`, with the values 0 and 1 respectively.

Another issue in JSL – which does not arise in the syntax-only JSGF – is the need to uniquely identify multiple sub-rules of the same type, when they occur in the same rule. For example, in a geometry grammar, two `<POINT>`s may be needed in a rule to declare a `<LINE>`, as in:

```
public <LINE> = make a line from
<POINT> to <POINT> :  ...
```

Uniquely numbering the sub-rules eliminates the ambiguity as to which `<POINT>` is which. Numbering

[2] Mr. Potato Head is a registered trademark of Hasbro, Inc.

```
public <ACTION> = move [the] <PART> <DIR> : {: <PART>.<DIR>(); :};
public <PART> = eyes : {: Canvas.eyesObj :};
public <PART> = ( cap | hat ): {: Canvas.capObj :};
public <DIR> = up : {: slideUp :};
public <DIR> = down : {: slideDown :};
public <ACTION_NF> = slide [the] <PART> <DIR> : {: <PART>.slide(<DIR:cos>,<DIR:sin>); :};
public <DIR_NF> = up : cos {: 0 :}
                       sin {: 1 :};
public <DIR_NF> = down : cos {: 0 :}
                         sin {: -1 :};
```

Grammar 2: A JAVOX grammar fragment for the Mr. Potato Head domain.

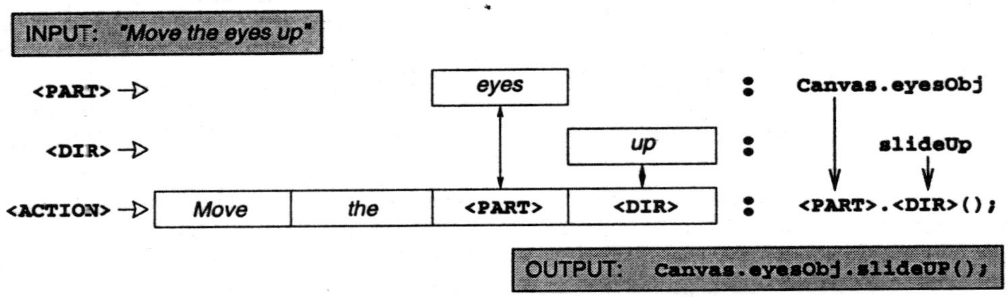

Figure 2: The JAVOX translation process – NL to JSL – for *Move the cap up.*

can be used in both the RHS and the semantic portion of a rule; numbering is not allowed in the LHS of a rule. Syntactically, sub-rules are numbered with a series of single quotes[3]:

```
public <LINE> = make a line from
<POINT'> to <POINT''> :  ...
```

3.2 Javox Scripting Language (JSL)

The JAVOX Scripting Language (JSL) is a stand-alone programming language, developed for use with the JAVOX infrastructure. JSL can be used to manipulate a running Java program and can be thought of as an application-independent macro language. The EXECUTER module interprets JSL and performs the specified actions. The specifics of JSL are not important to understanding JAVOX; for this reason, only a brief summary is presented here.

JSL can read of modify the contents of an object's fields (data members) and can execute methods (member functions) on objects. Unlike Java, JSL is loosely-typed: Type checking is not done until a given method is executed. JSL has its own variables, which can hold objects from the host application; a JSL variable can store an object of any type and no casting is required. JSL supports Java's primitive types, Java's reference types (objects), and Lisp-like lists. Though JSL does support Java's primitive types, they are converted into their reference-type equivalent. For example, an `integer` is stored as a `java.lang.Integer` and is converted back to an `integer` when needed.

JSL has the standard control flow mechanisms found in most conventional programming languages, including `if-else`, `for` and `while` loops. With the exception of the evaluation of their boolean expressions, these constructs follow the syntax and behavior of their Java counterparts. Java requires that `if-else` conditions and loop termination criteria be a boolean value. JSL conditionals are more flexible; in addition to booleans, it evaluates non-empty strings as true, empty strings as false, non-zero values as true, zero as false, non-`null` objects as true, and `null` as false.

In addition to Java's control flow mechanisms, JSL also supports `foreach` loops, similar to those found in Perl. These loops iterate over both JSL lists and members of `java.util.List`, executing the associated code block on each item. JSL lists are often constructed by recursive rules in order to handle conjunctions, as seen in Section 5.

4 Infrastructure

The JAVOX infrastructure has been designed to completely separate NLP code from the application's code. The application still can be run without JAVOX, as a typical, non-speech-enabled program – it is only speech-enabled when run with JAVOX.

[3]This representation is motivated by the grammars of (Hipp, 1992).

From the application's perspective, JAVOX operates at the *systems-level* and sits between the application and the operating system (virtual machine), as shown in Figure 1. TRANSLATOR interfaces with the speech recognizer and performs all necessary NLP. EXECUTER interfaces directly with the application and performs upcalls into the running program.

Java has two key features that make it an ideal test platform for our experimental implementation: reflection and a redefineable loading scheme. Reflection provides a running program the ability to inspect itself, sometimes called *introspection.* Objects can determine their parent classes; every class is itself an object in Java (an instance of `java.lang.Class`). Methods, fields, constructors, and all class attributes can be obtained from a `Class` object. So, given an object, reflection can determine its class; given a class, reflection can find its methods and fields. JAVOX uses reflection to (1) map from the JSL-textual representation of an object to the actual instance in the running program; (2) find the appropriate `java.lang.reflect.Methods` for an object/method-name combination; and (3) actually invoke the method, once all of its arguments are known.

Reflection is very helpful in examining the application program's structure; however, prior to using reflection, EXECUTER needs access to the objects in the running program. To obtain pointers to the objects, JAVOX uses JOIE, a load-time transformation tool (Cohen et al., 1998). JOIE allows us to modify each application class as it is loaded into the virtual machine. The JAVOX transform adds code to every constructor in the application that registers the new object with `Executer`. Conceptually, the following line is added to every constructor:

```
Executer.register(this).
```

This modification is done as the class is loaded, the compiled copy – on disk – is not changed. This allows the program to still be run without JAVOX, as a non-speech application. EXECUTER can – once it has the registered objects – use reflection to obtain everything else it needs to perform the actions specified by the JSL.

5 Example

Our longest running test application has been a Mr. Potato Head program; that allows users to manipulates a graphical representation of the classic children's toy. Its operations include those typically found in drawing programs, to include moving, recoloring and hiding various pieces of Mr. Potato Head. Grammar 3 shows a portion of application's grammar needed to process the utterance *Move the eyes and glasses up.* The result of parsing this utterance is shown in Figure 3.

Once TRANSLATOR has processed an utterance, it forwards the resulting JSL fragment to EXECUTER. Figure 4 provides a reduced class diagram for the Mr. Potato Head application; the arrows correspond to the first iteration in the following trace. The following steps are performed as the JSL fragment from Figure 3 is interpreted:

1. A new variable – local to EXECUTER – named `$iter` is created. Any previously-declared variable with the same name is destroyed.
2. The `foreach` loop starts by initializing the loop variable to the first item in the list: `Canvas.eyesObj`. This object's name consists of two parts; the steps to locate the actual instance in the application are:
   (a) The first part of the name, `Canvas`, is mapped to the only instance of the `Canvas` class in the context of this application. JAVOX has a reference to the instance because it *registered* with EXECUTER when it was created, thanks to a JOIE transformation.
   (b) The second part of the name, `eyesObj`, is found through reflection. Every instance of `Canvas` has a field named `eyesObj` of type `BodyPart`. This field is the `eyesObj` for which we are looking.
3. Once `eyesObj` is located, the appropriate method must be found. We determine – through reflection – that there are two methods in the `BodyPart` class with the name `move`, as seen in Figure 4.
4. We next examine the two arguments and determine them to be both integers. Had the arguments been objects, fields, or other method calls, this entire procedure would be done recursively on each.
5. We examine each possible method and determine that we need the one with two integer arguments, not the one taking a single `Point` argument.
6. Now that we have the object, the method, and the arguments, the upcall is made and the method is executed in the application. The result is that Mr. Potato Head's eyes move up on the screen.
7. This process is repeated for `glassObj` and the loop terminates.

After this process, both the eyes and glasses have moved up 20 units and `Executer` waits for additional input. The application continues to accept mouse and keyboard commands, just as it would without speech.

```
public <modPOS> = move <PARTS> <DIR> : {:
                dim $iter;
                foreach $iter (<PARTS>)
                  $iter.move(<DIR:X>,<DIR:Y>);
           :};
public <PARTS> = [<ART>] <PART> : {: [<PART>] :};
public <PARTS> = <PARTS> [<CONJ>] [<ART>] <PART> : {: [<PARTS> , <PART>] :};
public <DIR> = up : X {: 0 :} : Y {: -20 :};
public <DIR> = left : X {: -20 :} : Y {: 0 :};
public <ART> = (the | a | an);
public <CONJ> = ( and | plus );
public <PART> = eyes          : {: Canvas.eyesObj :};
public <PART> = glasses       : {: Canvas.glassObj :};
```

Grammar 3: A detailed JAVOX grammar for the Mr. Potato Head domain.

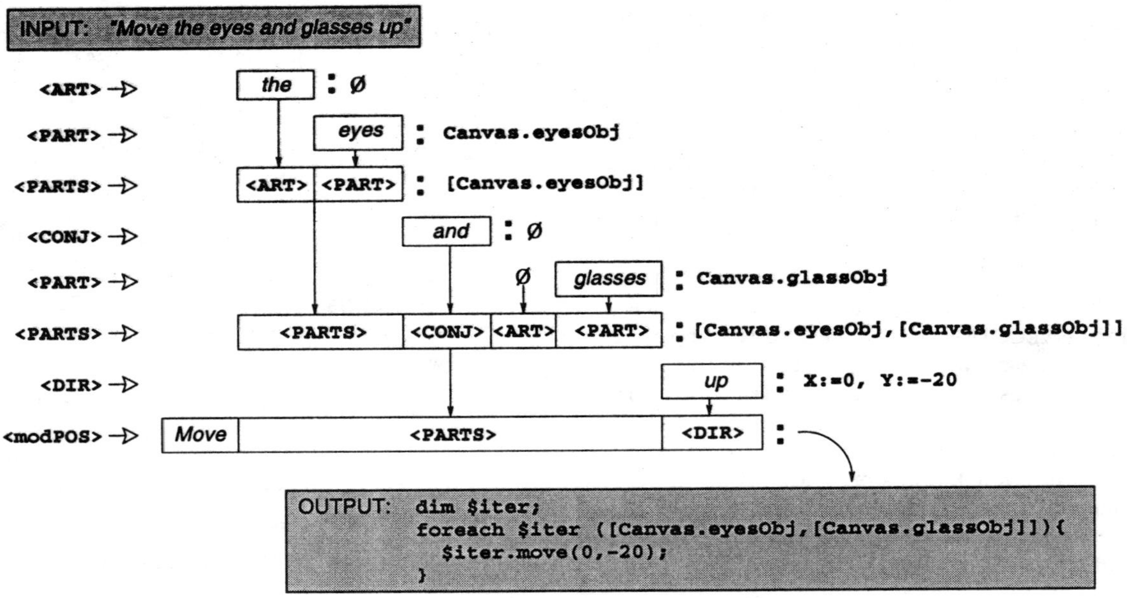

Figure 3: The translation process for the utterance *Move the eyes and glasses up.*

6 Discussion and Future Work

In practice, building a JAVOX-based, speech interface – for limited-functionality applications – is straightforward and reasonably quick. To date, we have used three diverse applications as our test platforms. Speech-enabling the last of these, an image manipulation program, took little more than one person-day. Though these applications have been small; we are beginning to explore JAVOX's scalability to larger applications. We are also developing a library of JAVOX grammars for use with the standard Java classes. This resource will shorten development times even more; especially compared to building a SLS from the ground up.

One of the existing challenges is to work with applications consisting entirely of dynamic objects, those that cannot be identified at load time. Some typical dynamic-object applications are drawing programs or presentation software; in both cases, the user creates the interesting objects during runtime. We have implemented a system in JSL which allows objects to be filtered based on an attribute, such as color in the utterance: *Move the blue square.*

In situations where there is a one-to-one correlation between a lexical item in the grammar and an object in the program, it is often the case that the lexical item is very similar to the element's identifier. It is quite often the same word or a direct synonym. Since JAVOX is primarily performing upcalls based on existing functions within the program, it also can be predicted what type of objects will co-occur in utterances. In the Mr. Potato Head appli-

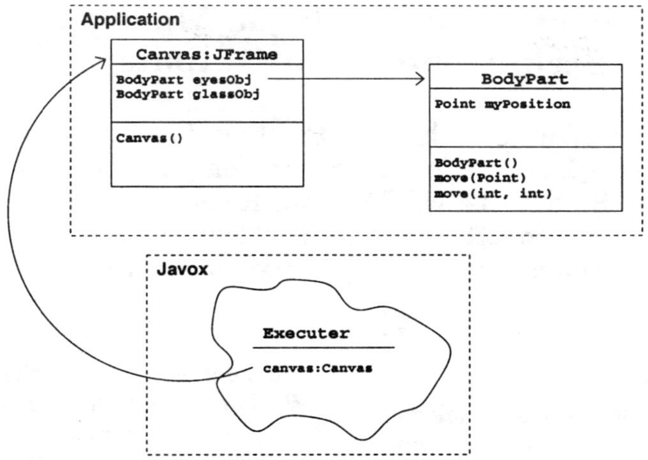

Figure 4: A simplified class diagram for the Mr. Potato Head application.

cation, we can assume that objects representing a `Point` or `integers` will occur when the user speaks of moving a `BodyPart`. We are developing a system to exploit these characteristics to automatically generate JAVOX grammars from an application's compiled code. The automatically-generated grammars are intended to serve as a starting point for developers – though they may certainly require some hand crafting. Our current, grammar-generation tool assumes the program is written with Java's standard naming conventions. It is imaginable that additional data sources – such as a sample corpus – will allow us to more accurately generate grammars for an application. Though in its infancy, we believe this approach holds vast potential for SLS development.

7 Conclusion

JAVOX provides a fast and flexible method to add a speech-interface to existing Java applications. The application program requires no source-code modification: The JAVOX infrastructure provides all NLP capabilities. We have implemented a grammar and scripting system that is straightforward enough that inexperienced developers and those unfamiliar with NLP can learn it quickly. We have demonstrated the technology on several programs and are commencing work on more ambitious applications. The current implementation of JAVOX is available for download at:

`http://www.cs.duke.edu/~msf/javox`

8 Acknowledgments

This work has been partially supported by the Defense Advanced Research Projects Agency under contract F30602-99-C-0060.

References

Geoff A. Cohen, Jeffrey S. Chase, and David L. Kaminsky. 1998. Automatic program transformation with JOIE. In *USENIX Annual Technical Conference (NO98)*, New Orleans, LA.

D. Richard Hipp. 1992. *A New Technique for Parsing Ill-formed Spoken Natural-language Dialog.* Ph.D. thesis, Duke University.

Andrew Pargellis, Jeff Kuo, and Chin-Hui Lee. 1999. Automatic dialogue generator creates user defined applications. In *6th European Conference on Speech Communication and Technology*, volume 3, pages 1175—1178, Budapest, Hungary.

Paul Schmidt, Sibylle Rieder, Axel Theofilidis, Marius Groenendijk, Peter Phelan, Henrik Schulz, Thierry Declerck, and Andrew Brenenkamp. 1998. Natural language access to software applications. In *Proceedings of COLING-ACL-98*, pages 1193–1197, Montreal, Quebec.

Sun Microsystems, Inc. 1998. Java speech API specification 1.0.

Stephen Sutton, David G. Novick, Ronald A. Cole, Pieter Vermeulen, Jacques de Villiers, Johan Schalkwyk, and Mark Fanty. 1996. Building 10,000 spoken-dialogue systems. In *Proceedings of the International Conference on Spoken Language Processing (ICSLP)*, pages 709—712, Philadelphia, PA.

A Compact Architecture for Dialogue Management Based on Scripts and Meta-Outputs

Manny Rayner, Beth Ann Hockey, Frankie James
Research Institute for Advanced Computer Science
Mail Stop 19-39, NASA Ames Research Center
Moffett Field, CA 94035-1000
{manny,bahockey,fjames}@riacs.edu

Abstract

We describe an architecture for spoken dialogue interfaces to semi-autonomous systems that transforms speech signals through successive representations of linguistic, dialogue, and domain knowledge. Each step produces an output, and a meta-output describing the transformation, with an executable program in a simple scripting language as the final result. The output/meta-output distinction permits perspicuous treatment of diverse tasks such as resolving pronouns, correcting user misconceptions, and optimizing scripts.

1 Introduction

The basic task we consider in this paper is that of using spoken language to give commands to a semi-autonomous robot or other similar system. As evidence of the importance of this task in the NLP community note that the early, influential system SHRDLU (Winograd, 1973) was intended to address just this type of problem. More recent work on spoken language interfaces to semi-autonomous robots include SRI's Flakey robot (Konolige et al., 1993) and NCARAI's InterBOT project (Perzanowski et al., 1998; Perzanowski et al., 1999). A number of other systems have addressed part of the task. CommandTalk (Moore et al., 1997), Circuit Fix-It Shop (Smith, 1997) and TRAINS-96 (Traum and Allen, 1994; Traum and Andersen, 1999) are spoken language systems but they interface to simulation or help facilities rather than semi-autonomous agents. Jack's MOOse Lodge (Badler et al., 1999) takes text rather than speech as natural language input and the avatars being controlled are not semi-autonomous. Other researchers have considered particular aspects of the problem such as accounting for various aspects of actions (Webber, 1995; Pym et al., 1995). In most of this and other related work the treatment is some variant of the following. If there is a speech interface, the input speech signal is converted into text. Text either from the recognizer or directly input by the user is then converted into some kind of logical formula, which abstractly represents the user's intended command; this formula is then fed into a command interpreter, which executes the command.

We do not think the standard treatment outlined above is in essence incorrect, but we do believe that, as it stands, it is in need of some modification. This paper will in particular make three points. First, we suggest that the output representation should not be regarded as a logical expression, but rather as a program in some kind of scripting language. Second, we argue that it is not merely the case that the process of converting the input signal to the final representation can sometimes go wrong; rather, this is the normal course of events, and the interpretation process should be organized with that assumption in mind. Third, we claim, perhaps surprisingly, that the first and second points are related. These claims are elaborated in Section 2.

The remainder of the paper describes an architecture which addresses the issues outlined above, and which has been used to implement a prototype speech interface to a simulated semi-autonomous robot intended for deployment on the International Space Station. Sections 3 and 4 present an overview of the implemented interface, focussing on representational issues relevant to dialogue management. Illustrative examples of interactions with the system are provided in Section 5. Section 6 concludes.

2 Theoretical Ideas

2.1 Scripts vs Logical Forms

Let's first look in a little more detail at the question of what the output representation of a spoken language interface to a semi-autonomous robot/agent should be. In practice, there seem to be two main choices: atheoretical representations, or some kind of logic.

Logic is indeed an excellent way to think about representing static relationships like database queries, but it is much less clear that it is a good way to represent *commands*. In real life, when people wish to give a command to a computer, they usually do so via its operating system; a complex command is an expression in a scripting language like CSHELL, Perl, or VBScript. These languages are related to logical formalisms, but cannot be mapped onto them in a simple way. Here are some of the obvious differences:

- A scripting language is essentially imperative, rather than relational.
- The notion of temporal sequence is fundamental to the language. "Do P and then Q" is not the same as "Make the goals P and Q true"; it is explicitly stated that P is to be done first. Similarly, "For each X in the list $(A\ B\ C)$, do $P(X)$" is not the same as "For all X, make $P(X)$ true"; once again, the scripting language defines an order, but not the logical language[1].
- Scripting languages assume that commands do not always succeed. For example, UNIX-based scripting languages like CSHELL provide each script with the three predefined streams `stdin`, `stdout` and `stderr`. Input is read from `stdin` and written to `stdout`; error messages, warnings and other comments are sent to `stderr`.

We do not think that these properties of scripting language are accidental. They have evolved as the result of strong selectional pressure from real users with real-world tasks that need to be carried out, and represent a competitive way to meet said users' needs. We consequently think it is worth taking seriously the idea that a target representation produced by a spoken language interface should share many of these properties.

2.2 Fallible Interpretation: Outputs and Meta-outputs

We now move on to the question of modelling the interpretation process, that is to say the process that converts the input (speech) signal to the output (executable) representation. As already indicated, we think it is important to realize that interpretation is a process which, like any other process, may succeed more or less well in achieving its intended goals. Users may express themselves unclearly or incompletely, or the system may more or less seriously fail to understand exactly what they mean. A good interpretation architecture will keep these considerations in mind.

Taking our lead from the description of scripting languages sketched above, we adapt the notion of the "error stream" to the interpretation process. In the course of interpreting an utterance, the system translates it into successively "deeper" levels of representation. Each translation step has not only an input (the representation consumed) and an output (the representation produced), but also something we will refer to as a "meta-output": this provides information about how the translation was performed.

At a high level of abstraction, our architecture will be as follows. Interpretation proceeds as a series of non-deterministic translation steps, each producing a set of possible outputs and associated meta-outputs. The final translation step produces an executable script. The interface attempts to simulate execution of each possible script produced, in order to determine what would happen if that script were selected; simulated execution can itself produce further meta-outputs. Finally, the system uses the meta-output information to decide what to do with the various possible interpretations it has produced. Possible actions include selection and execution of an output script, paraphrasing meta-output information back to the user, or some combination of the two.

In the following section, we present a more detailed description showing how the output/meta-output distinction works in a practical system.

3 A Prototype Implementation

The ideas sketched out above have been realized as a prototype spoken language dialogue interface to a simulated version of the Personal Satellite Assistant (PSA; (PSA, 2000)). This section gives an overview of the implementation; in the following section, we focus on the specific aspects of dialogue management which are facilitated by the output/meta-output architecture.

3.1 Levels of Representation

The real PSA is a miniature robot currently being developed at NASA Ames Research Center, which is intended for deployment on the Space Shuttle and/or International Space Station. It will be capable of free navigation in an indoor micro-gravity environment, and will provide mobile sensory capacity as a backup to a network of fixed sensors. The PSA will primarily be controlled by voice commands through a hand-held or head-mounted microphone, with speech and language processing being handled by an offboard processor. Since the speech processing units are not in fact physically connected to the PSA we envisage that they could also be used to control or monitor other environmental functions. In particular, our simulation allows voice access to the current and past values of the fixed sensor readings.

The initial PSA speech interface demo consists of a simple simulation of the Shuttle. State parameters include the PSA's current position, some environmental variables such as local temperature, pressure and carbon dioxide levels, and the status of the Shuttle's doors (open/closed). A visual display gives direct feedback on some of these parameters.

[1] In cases like these, the theorem prover or logic programming interpreter used to evaluate the logical formula typically assigns a conventional order to the conjuncts; note however that this is part of the *procedural* semantics of the theorem prover/interpreter, and does not follow from the declarative semantics of the logical formalism.

The speech and language processing architecture is based on that of the SRI CommandTalk system (Moore et al., 1997; Stent et al., 1999). The system comprises a suite of about 20 agents, connected together using the SRI Open Agent Architecture (OAA; (Martin et al., 1998)). Speech recognition is performed using a version of the Nuance recognizer (Nuance, 2000). Initial language processing is carried out using the SRI Gemini system (Dowding et al., 1993), using a domain-independent unification grammar and a domain-specific lexicon. The language processing grammar is compiled into a recognition grammar using the methods of (Moore et al., 1997); the net result is that only grammatically well-formed utterances can be recognized. Output from the initial language-processing step is represented in a version of Quasi Logical Form (van Eijck and Moore, 1992), and passed in that form to the dialogue manager. We refer to these as *linguistic level* representations.

The aspects of the system which are of primary interest here concern the dialogue manager (DM) and related modules. Once a linguistic level representation has been produced, the following processing steps occur:

- The linguistic level representation is converted into a *discourse level representation*. This primarily involves regularizing differences in surface form: so, for example, "measure the pressure" and "what is the pressure?" have different representations at the linguistic level, but the same representation at the discourse level.
- If necessary, the system attempts to resolve instances of ellipsis and anaphoric reference. For example, if the previous command was "measure temperature at flight deck", then the new command "lower deck" will be resolved to an expression meaning "measure temperature at lower deck". Similarly, if the previous command was "move to the crew hatch", then the command "open it" will be resolved to "open the crew hatch". We call the output of this step a *resolved discourse level representation*.
- The resolved discourse level representation is converted into an executable script in a language essentially equivalent to a subset of CSHELL. This involves two sub-steps. First, quantified variables are given *scope*: for example, "go to the flight deck and lower deck and measure pressure" becomes something approximately equivalent to the script

  ```
  foreach x (flight_deck lower_deck)
    go_to $x
    measure pressure
  end
  ```

  The point to note here is that the **foreach** has scope over both the **go_to** and the **measure** actions; an alternate (incorrect) scoping would be

  ```
  foreach x (flight_deck lower_deck)
    go_to $x
  end
  measure pressure
  ```

  The second sub-step is to attempt to optimize the plan. In the current example, this can be done by reordering the list (flight_deck lower_deck). For instance, if the PSA is already at the lower deck, reversing the list will mean that the robot only makes one trip, instead of two.
- The final step in the interpretation process is *plan evaluation*: the system tries to work out what will happen if it actually executes the plan. (The relationship between plan evaluation and plan execution is described in more detail in Section 4.1). Among other things, this gives the dialogue manager the possibility of comparing different interpretations of the original command, and picking the one which is most efficient.

3.2 How Meta-outputs Participate in the Translation

The above sketch shows how context-dependent interpretation is arranged as a series of non-deterministic translation steps; in each case, we have described the input and the output for the step in question. We now go back to the concerns of Section 2. First, note that each translation step is in general fallible. We give several examples:

- One of the most obvious cases arises when the user simply issues an invalid command, such as requesting the PSA to open a door D which is already open. Here, one of the meta-outputs issued by the plan evaluation step will be the term

  ```
  presupposition_failure(already_open(D));
  ```

  the DM can decide to paraphrase this back to the user as a surface string of the form "D is already open". Note that plan evaluation does not involve actually executing the final script, which can be important. For instance, if the command is "go to the crew hatch and open it" and the crew hatch is already open, the interface has the option of informing the user that there is a problem without first carrying out the "go to" action.
- The resolution step can give rise to similar kinds of meta-output. For example, a command may

include a referring expression that has no denotation, or an ambiguous denotation; for example, the user might say "both decks", presumably being unaware that there are in fact three of them. This time, the meta-output produced is

```
presupposition_failure(
    incorrect_size_of_set(2,3))
```

representing the user's incorrect belief about the number of decks. The DM then has the possibility of informing the user of this misconception by realizing the meta-output term as the surface string "in fact there are three of them".

Ambiguous denotation occurs when a description is under-specified. For instance, the user might say "the deck" in a situation where there is no clearly salient deck, either in the discourse situation or in the simulated world: here, the meta-output will be

```
presupposition_failure(
    underspecified_definite(deck))
```

which can be realized as the clarification question "which deck do you mean?"

- A slightly more complex case involves plan costs. During plan evaluation, the system simulates execution of the output script while keeping track of execution cost. (Currently, the cost is just an estimate of the time required to execute the script). Execution costs are treated as meta-outputs of the form

  ```
  cost(C)
  ```

  and passed back through the interpreter so that the plan optimization step can make use of them.

- Finally, we consider what happens when the system receives incorrect input from the speech recognizer. Although the recognizer's language model is constrained so that it can only produce grammatical utterances, it can still misrecognize one grammatical string as another one. Many of these cases fall into one of a small number of syntactic patterns, which function as fairly reliable indicators of bad recognition. A typical example is conjunction involving a pronoun: if the system hears "it and flight deck", this is most likely a misrecognition of something like "go to flight deck".

  During the processing phase which translates linguistic level representations into discourse level representations, the system attempts to match each misrecognition pattern against the input linguistic form, and if successful produces a meta-output of the form

  ```
  presupposition_failure(
      dubious_lf(<Type>))
  ```

  These meta-outputs are passed down to the DM, which in the absence of sufficiently compelling contrary evidence will normally issue a response of the form "I'm sorry, I think I misheard you".

4 A Compact Architecture for Dialogue Management Based on Scripts and Meta-Outputs

None of the individual functionalities outlined above are particularly novel in themselves. What we find new and interesting is the fact that they can all be expressed in a uniform way in terms of the script output/meta-output architecture. This section presents three examples illustrating how the architecture can be used to simplify the overall organization of the system.

4.1 Integration of plan evaluation, plan execution and dialogue management

Recall that the DM simulates evaluation of the plan before running it, in order to obtain relevant meta-information. At plan execution time, plan actions result in changes to the world; at plan evaluation time, they result in *simulated* changes to the world and/or produce meta-outputs.

Conceptualizing plans as scripts rather than logical formulas permits an elegant treatment of the execution/evaluation dichotomy. There is one script interpreter, which functions both as a script executive and a script evaluator, and one set of rules which defines the procedural semantics of script actions. Rules are parameterized by execution type which is either "execute" or "evaluate". In "evaluate" mode, primitive actions modify a state vector which is threaded through the interpreter; in "execute" mode, they result in commands being sent to (real or simulated) effector agents. Conversely, "meta-information" actions, such as presupposition failures, result in output being sent to the meta-output stream in "evaluate" mode, and in a null action in "execute" mode. The upshot is that a simple semantics can be assigned to rules like the following one, which defines the action of attempting to open a door which may already be open:

```
procedure(
 open_door(D),
 if_then_else(status(D, open_closed, open),
   presupposition_failure(already_open(D)),
   change_status(D, open_closed, open)))
```

4.2 Using meta-outputs to choose between interpretations

As described in the preceding section, the resolution step is in general non-deterministic and gives rise to meta-outputs which describe the type of resolution carried out. For example, consider a command involving a definite description, like "open the door". Depending on the preceding context, resolution will produce a number of possible interpretations; "the door" may be resolved to one or more contextually available doors, or the expression may be left unresolved. In each case, the type of resolution used appears as a meta-output, and is available to the dialogue manager when it decides which interpretation is most felicitous. By default, the DM's strategy is to attempt to supply antecedents for referring expressions, preferring the most recently occurring sortally appropriate candidate. In some cases, however, it is desirable to allow the default strategy to be overridden: for instance, it may result in a script which produces a presupposition failure during plan evaluation. Treating resolution choices and plan evaluation problems as similar types of objects makes it easy to implement this kind of idea.

4.3 Using meta-outputs to choose between dialogue management moves

Perhaps the key advantage of our architecture is that collecting together several types of information as a bag of meta-outputs simplifies the top-level structure of the dialogue manager. In our application, the critical choice of dialogue move comes after the dialogue manager has selected the most plausible interpretation. It now has to make two choices. First, it must decide whether or not to paraphrase any of the meta-outputs back to the user; for example, if resolution was unable to fill some argument position or find an antecedent for a pronoun, it may be appropriate to paraphrase the corresponding meta-output as a question, e.g. "where do you mean?", or "what do you mean by 'it'?". Having all the meta-outputs available together means that the DM is able to plan a coherent response: so if there are several meta-outputs which could potentially be worth paraphrasing, it typically realizes only the most important one.

Second, if interpretation was able to produce a well-formed plan, the DM currently has the three options of executing it, paraphrasing it back to the user as a confirmation question, or doing nothing. Once again, this decision often requires global information about what has happened during the interpretation process. For example, knowing that plan evaluation showed that the plan would take significant time to execute makes it more plausible that the user would prefer to receive a confirmation.

5 Examples

This section presents a commented sample dialogue with the implemented PSA interface demo chosen to illustrate the points discussed in the previous sections. We focus in particular on the role that meta-outputs play in interpretation. Text preceded by USER represents spoken utterances from the user. Text preceded by PSA represents synthesized spoken responses from the PSA. Text inside square brackets describes the actions carried out by the PSA.

1. The PSA can move to various locations and measure environmental factors. In the first exchange, reference resolution is used to interpret the phrase "all three decks" as referring to the lower deck, mid deck and flight deck. Plan optimization finds the most efficient way to order the locations, and paraphrases the resulting plan back to the user.

   USER: Go to all three decks and measure carbon dioxide.

   PSA: I will move to flight deck, mid deck and then lower deck and I will measure carbon dioxide level, okay?

   USER: Okay. *[PSA moves to flight deck]*

   PSA: The carbon dioxide level at the flight deck is one percent. *[PSA moves to mid deck]*

   PSA: The carbon dioxide level at the mid deck is one percent. *[PSA moves to lower deck]*

   PSA: The carbon dioxide level at the lower deck is one percent.

2. The next example involves resolution of ellipsis. The relevant context is recovered from the preceding dialogue.

   USER: Do the same for the pilot's seat.

   PSA: I will move to the pilot's seat and I will measure carbon dioxide level, okay?

   USER: Right. *[PSA moves to pilot's seat]*

   PSA: The carbon dioxide level at the pilot's seat is one percent.

3. Resolution of ellipsis can involve filling in unspecified semantic parameters to a syntactically complete command. It is not meaningful to talk about a sensor reading without reference to the place at which that reading was carried out; in the following example, resolution assumes that the location in question is the one most recently mentioned in the dialogue.

   Note also that since the PSA does not have to move in order to carry out the command, and hence can execute it immediately, the DM reasonably decides to skip the confirmation question. This decision is made based on the meta-output encoding the estimated cost of executing the script.

USER: What was the carbon dioxide level at fifteen oh five according to the fixed sensors?

PSA: According to the fixed sensors, at fifteen oh five the carbon dioxide level at the pilot's seat was one percent.

4. The system encounters a user misconception, which results in a "presupposition failure" meta-output being produced during reference resolution. It consequently decides to alert the user to this, rather than attempt to carry out the command.

   USER: Close both doors.

   PSA: There are in fact three of them.

5. The user utterance includes a pronoun, "it". The system resolves "it" to "the crew hatch", and issues an appropriate paraphrase in order to confirm that this is what the user meant.

   USER: Go to crew hatch and close it.

   PSA: I will go to crew hatch and I will close crew hatch, okay?

   USER: Yeah. *[PSA moves to crew hatch and closes it]*

6. The user asks the system to close the door, but it is unclear which door they are referring to. An "ambiguous reference" meta-output is produced by reference resolution, resulting in the DM issuing a clarification question.

   USER: Close the door.

   PSA: Which door do you mean?

7. The user response is successfully interpreted by reference resolution as an instance of ellipsis. Trying to close the crew hatch a second time however causes a presupposition failure meta-output to be generated during plan evaluation. The system informs the user of this and takes no action.

   USER: The crew hatch.

   PSA: The crew hatch is already closed.

8. The user presents three locations in a suboptimal order. Plan evaluation finds a more efficient ordering.

   USER: Move to storage lockers, commander's seat and flight deck and measure temperature.

   PSA: I will move to flight deck, commander's seat and then storage lockers and I will measure temperature, okay?

   USER: Sure.
   [PSA moves to flight deck, commander's seat and storage lockers in that order and reports temperature at each location]

9. The user asks the system to repeat the previous command. Since the PSA is now starting from a different position, its most efficient plan is no longer the same, and it informs the user of this.

   USER: Do that again.

   PSA: I will move to storage lockers, commander's seat and then flight deck and I will measure temperature, okay?

   USER: Yes. *[PSA moves to storage lockers]*

   PSA: The temperature at the storage lockers is 19.9 degrees Celsius. *[PSA starts moving to commander's seat]*

10. The user interrupts the PSA in the middle of the plan, and asks it to go back to its last stopping place. Since "stop" may involve a potentially hazardous condition, the interface obeys immediately, without attempting to confirm first.

    USER: Stop. *[PSA stops]*

    USER: Go back. *[PSA returns to storage lockers]*

6 Summary

We have described a generic architecture for spoken language dialogue interfaces to semi-autonomous agents, based on the standard notion of translating to successively deeper levels of representation. The novel aspects of our scheme center around two ideas: first, that the final output representations are best conceptualized not as logical expressions but rather as programs in a scripting language; second, that steps in the translation process should produce not only a simple output, but also meta-information describing how the output was produced. We have presented examples suggesting how several apparently diverse types of dialogue behavior can be captured simply within our framework, and outlined a prototype implementation of the scheme.

References

N. Badler, R. Bindiganavale, J. Bourne, J. Allbeck, J. Shi, and M. Palmer. 1999. Real time virtual humans. In *International Conference on Digital Media Futures.*

J. Dowding, M. Gawron, D. Appelt, L. Cherny, R. Moore, and D. Moran. 1993. Gemini: A natural language system for spoken language understanding. In *Proceedings of the Thirty-First Annual Meeting of the Association for Computational Linguistics.*

K. Konolige, K. Myers, E. Ruspini, and A. Saffiotti. 1993. Flakey in action: The 1992 AAAI robot competition. Technical Report SRI Technical Note 528, SRI, AI Center, SRI International, 333 Ravenswood Ave., Menlo Park, CA 94025.

D. Martin, A. Cheyer, and D. Moran. 1998. Building distributed software systems with the open agent architecture. In *Proceedings of the Third International Conference on the Practical Application of Intelligent Agents and Multi-Agent Technology*.

R. Moore, J. Dowding, H. Bratt, J. Gawron, Y. Gorfu, and A. Cheyer. 1997. CommandTalk: A spoken-language interface for battlefield simulations. In *Proceedings of the Fifth Conference on Applied Natural Language Processing*, pages 1–7.

Nuance, 2000. *Nuance Communications, Inc.* http://www.nuance.com. As of 9 March 2000.

D. Perzanowski, A. Schultz, and W. Adams. 1998. Integrating natural language and gesture in a robotics domain. In *IEEE International Symposium on Intelligent Control: ISIC/CIRA/ISAS Joint Conference*, pages 247–252, Gaithersburg, MD: National Institute of Standards and Technology.

D. Perzanowski, A. Schultz, W. Adams, and E. Marsh. 1999. Goal tracking in a natural language interface: Towards achieving adjustable autonomy. In *ISIS/CIRA99 Conference*, Monterey, CA. IEEE.

PSA, 2000. *Personal Satellite Assistant (PSA) Project.* http://ic.arc.nasa.gov/ic/psa/. As of 9 March 2000.

D. Pym, L. Pryor, and D. Murphy. 1995. Actions as processes: a position on planning. In *Working Notes, AAAI Symposium on Extending Theories of Action*, pages 169–173.

R. W. Smith. 1997. An evaluation of strategies for selective utterance verification for spoken natural language dialog. In *Proceedings of the Fifth Conference on Applied Natural Language Processing*, pages 41–48.

A. Stent, J. Dowding, J. Gawron, E. Bratt, and R. Moore. 1999. The CommandTalk spoken dialogue system. In *Proceedings of the Thirty-Seventh Annual Meeting of the Association for Computational Linguistics*, pages 183–190.

D. R. Traum and J. Allen. 1994. Discourse obligations in dialogue processing. In *Proceedings of the Thirty-Second Annual Meeting of the Association for Computational Linguistics*, pages 1–8.

D. R. Traum and C. F. Andersen. 1999. Representations of dialogue state for domain and task independent meta-dialogue. In *Proceedings of the IJCAI'99 Workshop on Knowledge and Reasoning in Practical Dialogue Systems*, pages 113–120.

J. van Eijck and R. Moore. 1992. Semantic rules for English. In H. Alshawi, editor, *The Core Language Engine.* MIT Press.

B. Webber. 1995. Instructing animated agents: Viewing language in behavioral terms. In *Proceedings of the International Conference on Cooperative Multi-modal Communication.*

T. A. Winograd. 1973. A procedural model of language understanding. In R. C. Shank and K. M. Colby, editors, *Computer Models of Thought and Language.* Freeman, San Francisco, CA.

A Representation for Complex and Evolving Data Dependencies in Generation

C Mellish[‡], R Evans[†], L Cahill[†], C Doran[†*], D Paiva[†], M Reape[‡], D Scott[†], N Tipper[†]
[†]Information Technology Research Institute, University of Brighton, Lewes Rd, Brighton, UK
[‡]Division of Informatics, University of Edinburgh, 80 South Bridge, Edinburgh, UK
rags@itri.brighton.ac.uk
http:/www.itri.brighton.ac.uk/projects/rags

Abstract

This paper introduces an approach to representing the kinds of information that components in a natural language generation (NLG) system will need to communicate to one another. This information may be partial, may involve more than one level of analysis and may need to include information about the history of a derivation. We present a general representation scheme capable of handling these cases. In addition, we make a proposal for organising intermodule communication in an NLG system by having a central server for this information. We have validated the approach by a reanalysis of an existing NLG system and through a full implementation of a runnable specification.

1 Introduction

One of the distinctive properties of natural language generation when compared with other language engineering applications is that it has to take seriously the full range of linguistic representation, from concepts to morphology, or even phonetics. Any processing system is only as sophisticated as its input allows, so while a natural language understanding system might be judged primarily by its syntactic prowess, even if its attention to semantics, pragmatics and underlying conceptual analysis is minimal, a generation system is only as good as its *deepest* linguistic representations. Moreover, any attempt to abstract away from individual generation systems to a more generic architectural specification faces an even greater challenge: not only are complex linguistic representations required, able to support the dynamic evolutionary development of data during the generation process, but they must do so in a generic and flexible fashion.

This paper describes a representation developed to meet these requirements. It offers a formally well-defined declarative representation language, which provides a framework for expressing the complex and dynamic data requirements of NLG systems. The approach supports different levels of representation, mixed representations that cut across levels, partial and shared structures and 'canned' representations, as well as dynamic relationships between data at different stages in processing. We are using the approach to develop a high level data model for NLG systems as part of a generic generation architecture called RAGS[1].

The framework has been implemented in the form of a database server for modular generation systems. As proof of concept of the framework, we have reimplemented an existing NLG system. The system we chose was the Caption Generation System (CGS) (Mittal et al., 1995; Mittal et al., 1998). The reimplementation involved defining the interfaces to the modules of CGS in terms of the RAGS representations and then implementing modules that had the requisite input and output representations.

Generation systems, especially end-to-end, applied generation systems, have, unsurprisingly, many things in common. Reiter (1994) proposed an analysis of such systems in terms of a simple three stage pipeline. More recently, the RAGS project attempted to repeat the anal-

* Now at the MITRE Corporation, Bedford, MA, USA, cdoran@mitre.org.

[1]This work is supported by ESPRC grants GR/L77041 (Edinburgh) and GR/L77102 (Brighton), *RAGS: Reference Architecture for Generation Systems.* We would also like to acknowledge the contribution of Jo Calder to the ideas and formalisation described in this paper. In particular, parts of this paper are based on (Calder et al., 1999).

ysis (Cahill et al., 1999a), but found that while most systems did implement a pipeline, they did not implement the *same* pipeline – different functionalities occurred in different places and different orders in different systems. In order to accommodate this result, we sought to develop an architecture that is more general than a simple pipeline, and thus supports the range of pipelines observed, as well as other more complex control regimes (see (Cahill et al., 1999a; Cahill et al., 1999b)). In this paper, we argue that supporting such an architecture requires careful consideration of the way data representations interact and develop. Any formal framework for expressing the architecture must take account of this.

2 The representational requirements of generation systems

We noted in the introduction that generation systems have to deal with a range of linguistic information. It is natural, especially in the context of a generic architecture proposal, to model this breadth in terms of discrete layers of representation: (1999a) introduce layers such as conceptual, semantic, rhetorical, syntactic and document structure, but the precise demarcation is not as important here as the principle. The different kinds of information are typically represented differently, and built up separately. However the layers are far from independent: objects at one layer are directly related to those at others, forming chains of dependency from conceptual through rhetorical and semantic structure to final syntactic and document realisation. This means that data resources, such as grammars and lexicons, and processing modules in the system, are often defined in terms of **mixed** data: structures that include information in more than one representation layer. So the ability to represent such mixed structures in a single formal framework is an important property of a generic data proposal.

In addition, it is largely standard in generation as elsewhere in language applications, to make extensive use of **partial** representations, often using a type system to capture grades of underspecification. An immediate corollary of providing support for partial structures is the notion that they may become further specified over time, that data structures **evolve**. If the framework seeks to avoid over-commitment to particular processing strategies it needs to provide a way of representing such evolution explicitly if required, rather than relying on destructive modification of a structure. Related to this, it should provide explicit support for representing **alternative** specifications at any point. Finally, to fully support efficient processing across the range of applications, from the simple to the most complex, the representation must allow for compact sharing of information in **tangled** structures (two structures which share components).

In addition to these direct requirements of the generation task itself, additional requirements arise from more general methodological considerations: we desire a representation that is formally **well defined**, allows for theoretical **reasoning** about the data and performance of systems, and supports control regimes from simple deterministic pipelines to complex parallel architectures.

3 The Representation Scheme

In this section, we present our proposal for a general representation scheme capable of covering the above requirements. Our formulation is layered: the foundation is a simple, flexible, rigorously defined graph representation formalism, on top of which we introduce notions of complex types and larger data structures and relationships between them. This much is sufficient to capture the requirements just discussed. We suppose a yet higher level of specification could capture a more constraining data model but make no specific proposals about this here, however the following sections use examples that do conform to such a higher level data model.

The lowest level of the representation scheme is:

- **relational:** the basic data entity is $x \rightarrow y$, an *arrow* representing a relation from object x to object y;
- **typed:** objects and arrows have an associated type system, so it is possible to define classes and subclasses of objects and arrows.

At the most fundamental level, this is more or less the whole definition. There is no commitment to what object or arrow types there are or how they relate to each other. So a representation allowed by the scheme consists of:

- a set of objects, organised into types;
- a set of binary relations, organised into types;
- a set of arrows, each indicating that a relation holds between one object and another object.

Sets, sequences and functions

For the next level, we introduce more structure in the type system to support sets, sequences and functions. Objects are always atomic (though they can be of type set, sequence or function) – it is not possible to make an object which actually is a set of two other objects (as you might with data structures in a computer program). To create a set, we introduce a set *type* for the object, and a set membership arrow type (*el*), that links the set's elements to the set. Similarly, for a sequence, we introduce a sequence type and sequence member arrow types (*1-el, 2-el, 3-el, ...*), and for a function, we have a complex type which specifies the types of the arrows that make up the domain and the range of the function.

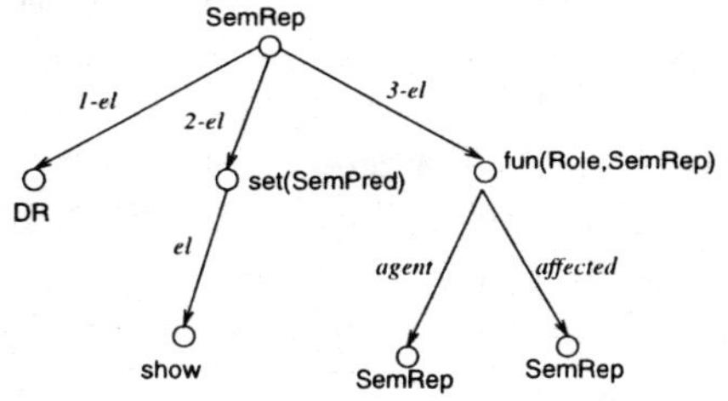

Figure 1: The partial semantic representation of "The second chart shows the number of days on the market"

As an example, consider Figure 1, which shows a semantic representation (SemRep) from the CGS reimplementation. Here, the tree nodes correspond to objects, each labelled with its type. The root node is of type SemRep, and although it is not an explicit sequence type, we can see that it is a triple, as it has three sequence member arrows (with types *1-el, 2-el* and *3-el*). Its first arrow's target is an object of type DR (Discourse Referent). Its second represents a set of SemPred (Semantic Predicate) objects, and in this case there's just one, of type show. Its third element is a (partial) function, from Role arrow types (*agent* and *affected* are both subtypes of Role) to SemReps. (In this case, the SemReps have not yet been fully specified.)

Local and non-local arrows

The second extension to the basic representation scheme is to distinguish two different abstract kinds of arrows – local and non-local. Fundamentally we are representing just a homogeneous network of objects and relationships. In the example above we saw a network of arrows that we might want to view as a single data structure, and other major data types might similarly appear as networks. Additionally, we want to be able to express relationships *between* these larger 'structures' – between structures of the same type (alternative solutions, or revised versions) or of different types (semantic and syntactic for example). To capture these distinctions among arrows, we classify our arrow types as local or non-local (we could do this in the type system itself, or leave it as an informal distinction). Local arrows are used to build up networks that we think of as single data structures. Non-local arrows express relationships between such data structures.

All the arrow types we saw above were local. Examples of non-local arrows might include:

realises These arrows link something more abstract to something less abstract that realises it. Chains of realises arrows might lead from the original conceptual input to the generator through rhetorical, semantic and syntactic structures to the actual words that express the input.

revises These arrows link a structure to another one of the same type, which is considered to be a 'better' solution – perhaps because it is more instantiated. It is important to note that parts of larger structures can be revised without revising the entire structure.

coreference These arrows link structures which are somehow "parallel" and which perhaps share some substructure, i.e., tangled structures. For instance, document representations may be linked to rhetorical representations, either as whole isomorphic structures or at the level of individual constituents.

Notice that the representation scheme does not enforce any kind of well-formedness with respect to local and non-local arrows. In fact, although it is natural to think of a 'structure' as being a maximal network of local arrows with a single root object, there's no reason why this should be so – networks with multiple roots represent tangled structures (structures that share content), networks that include non-local links might be *mixed* representations, containing information of more than one sort. Such techniques might be useful for improving generator efficiency, or representing canned text or templates, cf. (Calder et al., 1999).

Partial and Opaque structures

Partial structures are essential when a module needs to produce a skeleton of a representation that it does not have the competence to completely fill out. For instance, lexical choice brings with it certain syntactic commitments, but in most NLG systems lexical choice occurs some time before a grammar is consulted to flesh out syntactic structure in detail.

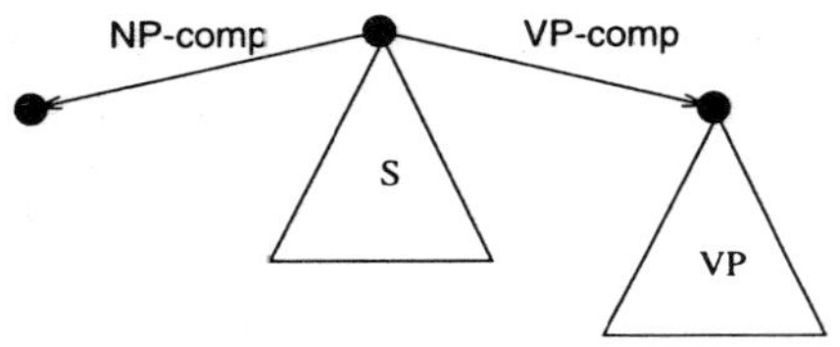

Figure 2: A partial structure

By simply leaving out local arrows, we can represent a range of partial structures. Consider Fig. 2, where the triangles represent local structure, representing a sentence object and its component verb phrase. There is a link to a subject noun phrase object, but none of the local arrows of the actual noun phrase are present. In subsequent processing this local structure might be filled in. This is possible as long as the noun phrase object has been declared to be of the right type.

An opaque structure is one which has an incomplete derivational history – for example part of a syntactic structure without any corresponding semantic structure. Three possible reasons for having such structures are (a) to allow structure to be introduced that the generator is not capable of producing directly, (b) to prevent the generator from interfering with the structure thus built (for example, by trying to modify an idiom in an inappropriate way), or (c) to improve generator efficiency by hiding detail that may lead to wasteful processing. An opaque structure is represented simply by the failure to include a `realises` arrow to that structure. Such structures provide the basis for a generalised approach to "canning".

4 Implementation

There are many ways that modules in an NLG system could communicate information using the representation scheme just outlined. Here we describe a particularly general model of inter-module communication, based around modules communicating with a single centralised repository of data called the *whiteboard* (Calder et al., 1999). A whiteboard is a *cumulative typed relational blackboard*:

- **typed and relational:** because it is based on using the above representation scheme;
- **a blackboard:** a control architecture and data store shared between processing modules; typically, modules add/change/remove objects in the data store, examine its contents, and/or ask to be notified of changes;
- **cumulative:** unlike standard blackboards, once data is added, it can't be changed or removed. So a structure is built incrementally by making successive copies of it (or of constituents of it) linked by `revises` links (although actually, there's no constraint on the order in which they are built).

A whiteboard allows modules to add arrows (typically forming networks through arrows sharing source or target objects), to inspect the set of arrows looking for particular configurations of types, or to be informed when a particular type of arrow (or group of arrows) is added.

The whiteboard is an active database server. This means that it runs as an independent process that other modules connect to by appropriate means. There are essentially three kinds of interaction that a module might have with the whiteboard server:

- **publish** – add an arrow or arrows to the whiteboard;

- **query** – look for an arrow or arrows in the whiteboard;
- **wait** – register interest in an arrow or arrows appearing in the whiteboard.

In both `query` and `wait`, arrows are specified by type, and with a hierarchical type system on objects and relations, this amounts to a pattern that matches arrows of subtypes as well. The `wait` function allows the whiteboard to take the initiative in processing – if a module `waits` on a query then the whiteboard waits until the query is satisfied, and then tells the module about it. So the module does not have to continuously scan the whiteboard for work to do, but can let the whiteboard tell it as soon as anything interesting happens.

Typically a module will start up and register interest in the kind of arrow that represents the module's input data. It will then wait for the whiteboard to notify it of instances of that data (produced by other modules), and whenever anything turns up, it processes it, adding its own results to the whiteboard. All the modules do this asynchronously, and processing continues until no module has any more work to do. This may sound like a recipe for confusion, but more standard pipelined behaviour is not much different. In fact, pipelining is exactly a data-based constraint – the second module in a pipeline does not start until the first one produces its output.

However, to be a strict pipeline, the first module must produce *all* of its output before the second one starts. This can be achieved simply by making the first module produce all its output at once, but sometimes that is not ideal – for example if the module is recursive and wishes to react to its own output. Alternative strategies include the use of markers in the whiteboard, so that modules can tell each other that they've finished processing (by adding a marker), or extending the whiteboard architecture itself so that modules can tell the whiteboard that they have finished processing, and other modules can wait for that to occur.

5 Reconstruction of the Caption Generation System

In order to prove this representation scheme in practice, we have implemented the whiteboard in Sicstus Prolog and used it to support data communications between modules in a reconstruction of the Caption Generation System (Mittal et al., 1995). CGS is a system developed at the University of Pittsburgh, which takes input from the SAGE graphics presentation system (Roth et al., 1994) and generates captions for the graphics SAGE produces. We selected it for this effort because it appeared to be a fairly simple pipelined system, with modules performing clearly defined linguistic tasks. As such, we thought it would be a good test case for our whiteboard specification.

Although the CGS is organised as a pipeline, shown in Figure 3, the representations communicated between the modules do not correspond to complete, separate instances of RAGS datatype representations. Instead, the representations at the various levels accumulate along the pipeline or are revised in a way that does not correspond exactly to module boundaries. Figure 3 gives a simple picture of how the different levels of representation build up. The labels for the RAGS representations refer to the following:

- I = conceptual;
- II = semantic;
- III = rhetorical;
- IV = document;
- V = syntactic.

For instance, some semantic (II) information is produced by the Text Planning module, and more work is done on this by Aggregation, but the semantic level of representation is not complete and final until the Referring Expression module has run. Also, for instance, at the point where the Ordering module has run, there are partially finished versions of three different types of representation. It is clear from this that the interfaces between the modules are more complex than could be accounted for by just referring to the individual levels of representation of RAGS. The ability to express combinations of structures and partial structures was fundamental to the reimplementation of CGS. We highlight below a few of the interesting places where these features were used.

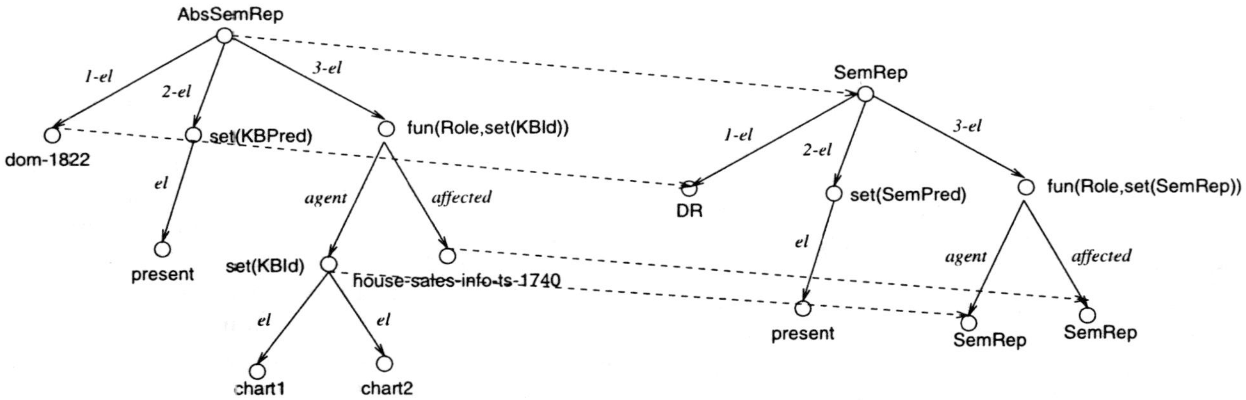

Figure 4: Combined Abstract Semantic Representation and Concrete Semantic Representation for the output: "These two charts present information about house sales from data-set ts-1740"

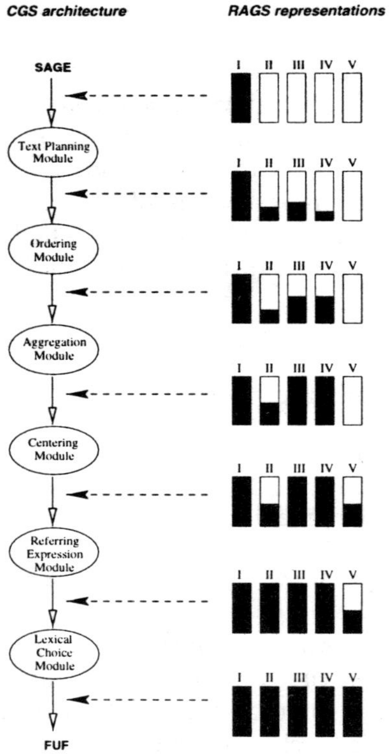

Figure 3: A RAGS view of the CGS system

5.1 Referring Expression Generation

In many NLG systems, (nominal) referring expression generation is an operation that is invoked at a relatively late stage, after the structure of individual sentences is fairly well specified (at least semantically). However, referring expression generation needs to go right back to the original world model/knowledge base to select appropriate semantic content to realise a particular conceptual item as an NP (whereas all other content has been determined much earlier). In fact, there seems to be no place to put referring expression generation in a pipeline without there being some resulting awkwardness.

In RAGS, pointers to conceptual items can be included inside the first, "abstract", level of semantic representation (AbsSemRep), which is intended to correspond to an initial bundling of conceptual material under semantic predicates. On the other hand, the final, "concrete", level of semantic representation (SemRep) is more like a fully-fledged logical form and it is no longer appropriate for conceptual material to be included there. In the CGS reimplementation, it is necessary for the Aggregation module to reason about the final high-level semantic representation of sentences, which means that this module must have access to "concrete" semantic representations. The Referring Expression generation module does not run until later, which means that these representations cannot be complete.

Our way around this was to ensure that the initial computation of concrete semantics from abstract semantics (done as part of Aggregation here) left a record of the relationship by including **realises** arrows between corresponding structures. That computation could not be completed whenever it reached conceptual material – at that point it left a "hole" (an object with no further specification) in the concrete semantic representation linked back to the conceptual material. When referring expression was later invoked, by following the arrows in the resulting mixed structure, it could tell exactly which conceptual entity needed to be referred to and where in the semantic structure the resulting semantic expression should be placed. Figure 4 shows the resulting arrangement for one example CGS sentence. The dashed lines indicate **realises**, i.e. non-local, arrows.

5.2 Handling Centering Information

The CGS Centering module reasons about the entities that will be referred to in each sentence and produces a representation which records the forward and backward-looking centers (Grosz et al., 1995). This representation is later used by the Referring Expression generation module in making pronominalisation decisions. This information could potentially also be used in the Realisation module.

Since Centering is not directly producing referring expressions, its results have to sit around until they can actually be used. This posed a possible problem for us, because the RAGS framework does not provide a specific level of representation for Centering information and therefore seems on first sight unable to account for this information being communicated between modules. The solution to the problem came when we realised that Centering information is in fact a kind of abstract syntactic information. Although one might not expect abstract syntactic structure to be determined until the Realisation module (or perhaps slightly earlier), the CGS system starts this computation in the Centering module.

Thus in the reimplementation, the Centering module computes (very partial) abstract syntactic representations for the entities that will eventually be realised as NPs. These representations basically just indicate the relevant Centering statuses using syntactic features. Figure 5 shows an example of the semantics for a typical output sentence and the two partial abstract syntactic representations computed by the Centering module for what will be the two NPs in that sentence[2]. As before, dashed lines indicate **realises** arrows. Of course, given the discussion of the last section, the semantic representation objects that are the source of these arrows are in fact themselves linked back to conceptual entities by being the destination of **realises** arrows from them.

When the Referring Expression generation module runs, it can recover the Centering information by inspecting the partial syntactic representations for the phrases it is supposed to generate. These partial representations are then further instantiated by, e.g., Lexical Choice at later stages of the pipeline.

[2]FVM = Feature Value Matrix.

6 Conclusion

The representation scheme we have proposed here is designed specifically to support the requirements of the current state-of-the-art NLG systems, and our pilot implementation demonstrates the practical applicability of the proposal. Tangled, partial and mixed structures are of obvious utility to any system with a flexible control strategy and we have shown here how the proposed representation scheme supports them. By recording the derivational history of computations, it also supports decisions which partly depend on earlier stages of the generation process (e.g., possibly, lexical choice) and revision-based architectures which typically make use of such information. We have shown how the representation scheme might be the basis for an inter-module communication model, the *whiteboard*, which supports a wide range of processing strategies that require the representation of complex and evolving data dependencies. The fact that the whiteboard is *cumulative*, or *monotonic* in a logical sense, means that the whiteboard also supports reasoning about the behaviour of NLG systems implemented in terms of it. This is something that we would like to exploit directly in the future.

The reimplementation of the CGS system in the RAGS framework was a challenge to the framework because it was a system that had already been developed completely independently. Even though we did not always understand the detailed motivation for the structure of CGS being as it was, within a short time we reconstructed a working system with modules that corresponded closely to the original CGS modules. The representation scheme we have proposed here was a key ingredient in giving us the flexibility to achieve the particular processing scheme used by CGS whilst remaining faithful to the (relatively simple) RAGS data model.

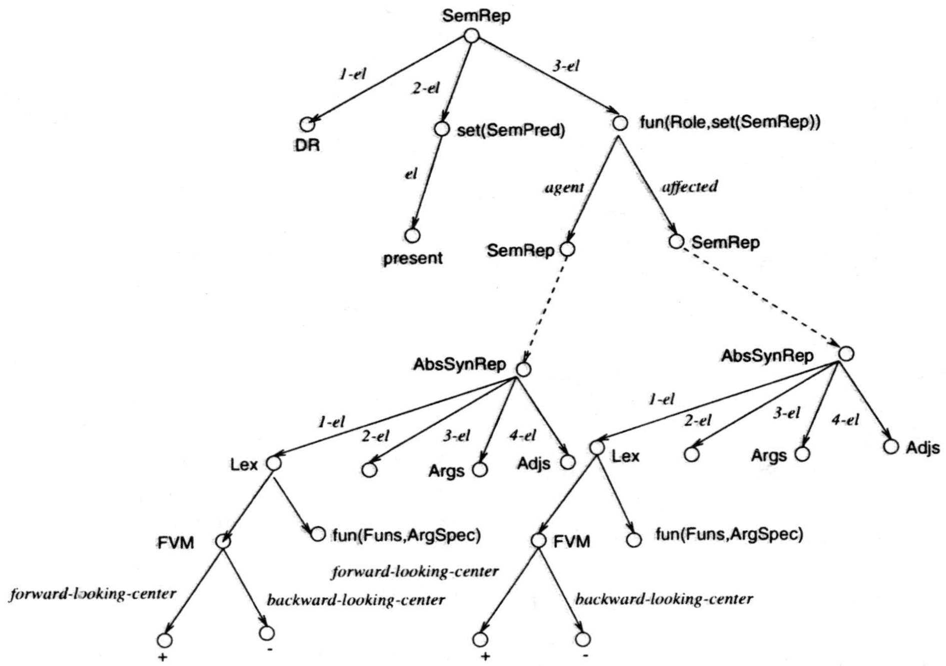

Figure 5: Arrangement of centering information for the output sentence above

The representation scheme is useful in situations where modules need to be defined and implemented to work with other modules, possibly developed by different people. In such cases, the representation scheme we propose permits precise definition of the interfaces of the modules, even where they are not restricted to a single 'level' of representation. Even though the control structure of CGS is quite simple, we found that the use of a centralised whiteboard was useful in helping us to agree on interfaces and on the exact contribution that each module should be making. Ultimately, it is hoped that the use of a scheme of this type will permit much more widespread 'plug-and-play' among members of the NLG community.

References

Lynne Cahill, Christy Doran, Roger Evans, Chris Mellish, Daniel Paiva, Mike Reape, Donia Scott, and Neil Tipper. 1999a. In Search of a Reference Architecture for NLG Systems. In *Proceedings of the 7th European Workshop on Natural Language Generation*, pages 77–85, Toulouse.

Lynne Cahill, Christy Doran, Roger Evans, Chris Mellish, Daniel Paiva, Mike Reape, Donia Scott, and Neil Tipper. 1999b. Towards a Reference Architecture for Natural Language Generation Systems. Technical Report ITRI-99-14, Information Technology Research Institute (ITRI), University of Brighton. Available at `http://www.itri.brighton.ac.uk/projects/rags`.

Jo Calder, Roger Evans, Chris Mellish, and Mike Reape. 1999. "Free choice" and templates: how to get both at the same time. In *"May I speak freely?" Between templates and free choice in natural language generation*, number D-99-01, pages 19–24. Saarbrücken.

B.J. Grosz, A.K. Joshi, and S. Weinstein. 1995. Centering: a framework for modelling the local coherence of discourse. *Computational Linguistics*, 21(2):203–226.

V. O. Mittal, S. Roth, J. D. Moore, J. Mattis, and G. Carenini. 1995. Generating explanatory captions for information graphics. In *Proceedings of the 15th International Joint Conference on Artificial Intelligence (IJCAI'95)*, pages 1276–1283, Montreal, Canada, August.

V. O. Mittal, J. D. Moore, G. Carenini, and S. Roth. 1998. Describing complex charts in natural language: A caption generation system. *Computational Linguistics*, 24(3):431–468.

Ehud Reiter. 1994. Has a consensus NL generation architecture appeared and is it psycholinguistically plausible? In *Proceedings of the Seventh International Workshop on Natural Language Generation*, pages 163–170, Kennebunkport, Maine.

Steven F. Roth, John Kolojejchick, Joe Mattis, and Jade Goldstein. 1994. Interactive graphic design using automatic presentation knowledge. In *Proceedings of CHI'94: Human Factors in Computing Systems*, Boston, MA.

An Automatic Reviser: The TransCheck System

Jean-Marc Jutras
RALI, Université de Montréal
C.P. 6128, succ. Centre-ville, Montréal (QC), Canada
jutras@iro.umontreal.ca

Abstract

Over the past decade or so, a lot of work in computational linguistics has been directed at finding ways to exploit the ever increasing volume of electronic bilingual corpora. These efforts have allowed for substantial expansion of the computational toolbox. We describe a system, TransCheck, which makes intensive use of these new tools in order to detect potential translation errors in preliminary or non-revised translations.

Introduction

For the sake of argument, let's consider a translator to be a black box with source text in and target text out. We feed that box with texts and, to be really tricky, we input the same text a couple of times. Looking at the results, the first thing we notice is that though the different translations are quite similar, they're not exactly the same. Nothing to worry about, this may simply exemplify the potential for synonymy and paraphrase. But let's further suppose the text to translate is too big for one individual to translate in the given time frame. In realistic conditions, such a text would be split among perhaps half a dozen translators, each with his own vocabulary, experience and stylistic preferences, which would normally lead to the well known problem of non-uniformity of the translation.

It is therefore part of the normal translation process to have a reviser look at a translator's output. His job will be to spot any typos (taken in a very broad sense to include missing chapters!). Usually, at this point the translator probably has submitted the preliminary version to a spell checker, so what could be done automatically at that level has already been done. No automatic detection of typical translation mistakes has been attempted though. That's the gap TransCheck is designed to fill. The concept of a "translation checker" was initially proposed in Isabelle and al. [8] and eventually led to a demonstration prototype concerned with the detection of a very restricted type of mistake: *deceptive cognates*. In comparison, the system described in this paper goes much further toward a "real " usable translation checker by allowing for the detection of errors of omission, the comparison of diverse numerical expressions and the flagging of inconsistent terminology.

On the interface side, it allows for the automatic alignment of the source and target texts, the flagging of potential mistakes and the possibility of saving any modifications made to the target text.

1 Error detection

Complete automatic modelling of the translation process is still far beyond our technical ability. The same is true of our ability to detect all types of translation mistakes. We can however, for certain well-defined sub-types of mistake, devise specific mechanisms. And if a program capable of detecting all mistakes of translation would undoubtedly be extremely useful, so would one capable of detecting frequent mistakes, especially when time is short and a thorough revision isn't possible. Errors are then bound to escape the reviser's attention from time to time. This will not necessary be the case of an "automatic reviser", though. In that respect, we can compare TransCheck's behaviour to the familiar "find and replace" now common to every text editors. Who would know consider doing that particular task by hand? We now give a short description of those sub-problems TransCheck is addressing.

1.1 Errors of omission

The ability to automatically detect unintended errors of omission would be much valued, as they can prove quite embarrassing to the translator. Yet a diversity of situations can lead to such errors among which translator's fatigue and the accidental pressing of a key in a text editor, as was pointed out by Melamed [12]. Unfortunately, detecting an omission is far from being simple when taken in all its generality (from omission of single words to whole chapters). This is due in part to the fact that one language may express some ideas with a greater economy of means than another, so length difference alone isn't sufficient to identify omitted text. Consider:

- French: Quant à la section 5, elle fournit les résultats de nos simulations, que suit notre conclusion, à la sixième et dernière section.
- English: Section 5 describes our simulation results and the final section concludes.

Excluding punctuation, the French sentence in the example above has twice as many words as its English counterpart. Yet there's nothing wrong with the French translation. The task is therefore to determine whether or not correspondence at the word level is scattered throughout the whole aligned segment. Word alignment in general tends to be rather fuzzy though, as the following example shows:

- French: Voici le plan du document.
  Literal translation: (Here's) (the) (plan) (of the) (document)
- English: The paper is organized as follows.
  Literal translation: (Le) (papier) (est) (organisé) (comme) (suit)

Independently of the exact method used, alignment at the word level for this pair of sentences would prove to be rather weak. It should be noted however that the above examples are extreme cases and, without being extremely rare, they aren't exactly typical either. They're still a reminder that small omissions are unlikely to be detected with sufficient precision considering the methods available to TransCheck.

1.2 Normative usage of words

Entire repositories of usage mistakes and other linguistic difficulties of translation from English to French have been written to help language professionals become aware of them (Colpron [3], Dagenais [5], De Villiers [6], Rey [14], Van Roey and al. [17]). Unfortunately, those books are only useful to confirm existing suspicions. To warn the unsuspecting translator, TransCheck incorporates a repository of that nature.

What's particular about some of these words, and of interest for an *automatic reviser*, is that they cannot be detected by a simple dictionary lookup, for they do appear in a monolingual dictionary. What's wrong isn't the words themselves but the context in which they are used. Consider, for example, the English word *definitely* (en effet) together with the French *définitivement* (for good, once and for all). Though very similar in form, and both acceptable adverbs in their respective languages, they simply do not mean the same thing. TransCheck, therefore, looks through aligned pairs of sentences for such forbidden word pairs. It also looks for other types of mistakes, for example calques, which could potentially be detected by a complex dictionary lookup. Calques consist of sequences of legitimate words that incorrectly mimic the structure of the other language by being sort of literal translations.

1.3 Numerical expressions

A variety of phenomena can be found under this heading (telephone numbers, percentages, fractions, etc.). One important point these otherwise very diverse types of constructions have in common is that, being open sets, they cannot be listed in repositories. Therefore, their detection will require the use of grammatical tools of some sort. But identification is not enough in most cases. Having simply identified "2" in one text and "two" in the other will not alone permit their comparison. Conversion toward a common form is required. Part of this normalised form must also indicate the type of phenomenon observed. This is so because, though there is a *6* underlying the ordinal *sixth*, only alignment with an other ordinal of the same value could be considered an appropriate match. In TransCheck, recognition, normalisation and phenomenon identification of numerical expressions are done through appropriate transducers as will be shown in the next section.

1.4 Terminological coherence

It's not rare for two or more terms to refer to the same concept. However, all things being equal, it's generally taken to be bad practice to use more than one of the synonyms for technical terms in a given translation. Failure to follow this is referred to as terminological inconsistency. To try and minimise this problem, each translator working on a project is given specific instructions that involve standardising terminology. Unfortunately, it's not rare for some translators to ignore these instructions or even for these instructions never to reach the translator. Inadequacies are therefore to be expected, and the bigger the project the more so. As an example, given the term *air bag* and possible translations *sac gonflable* and *coussin gonflable* (literally, inflatable bag/cushion), it shouldn't be allowed for both forms to appear in a given translation, though either one of the two could actually appear.

2 Tracking mistakes

We have presented briefly the type of errors detection TransCheck seeks to accomplish automatically. We will now see in more details how they are currently being implemented.

2.1 Prerequisites

In order for TransCheck to detect potential translation errors, a relatively impressive set of mechanisms is required. These include:

1. An aligner. After identification of word and sentence boundaries the text is processed into a bi-text by an alignment program. This alignment is done on the basis of both length (Gale and Church [7]) and a notion of cognateness (Simard [16]).
2. Transducers. In order to compare numerical expressions, which often diverge in format between given pairs of languages, normalisation toward a common format is required. This is done with transducers (Kaplan and Kay, [10]).
3. Part-of-speech tagger. Misleading similarities in graphical form can sometime induce translation mistakes (deceptive cognates).[1] These forbidden pairs normally involve only one of several possible parts of speech, hence the need to disambiguate them. We do this with a first-order HMM part-of-speech tagger (Merialdo [13]).

---

[1] In the rest of the paper, we will use *deceptive cognate* very losely often to refer to *normative usage of word* in general.

4. Translation models. Being robust, the alignment program will align a pair of texts regardless of possible omissions in the target text. To detect such omissions of text, a probabilistic bilingual dictionary is called upon. This dictionary was estimated along the line of Brown and al.'s first translation model [2]. It is used to align (coarsely) at the word level.

In what follows, we assume the reader to be at least remotely familiar with most of these mechanisms. We will however go into more technical details concerning the transducers considering the central role they play in TransCheck.

2.2 Identifying omissions

Grammatical correctors greatly relies on complex grammars to identify "typical" mistakes. We could imagine doing something similar for omission detection trying to construct the meaning of every sentences in a text and then "flag" those where semantic discontinuity were found, not unlike what a human would do. This is, of course, in our wildest dreams as, semantic analyses still remain to this day extremely elusive. Not only that, but unlike grammatical errors, we cannot anticipate something like a "typical" omission as they will appear randomly and span over any possible length of text. We must therefore recast what appears as a semantic problem in terms of more readily accessible data. The basic idea here is to assimilate an omission to a particular type of alignment where an important contiguous set of words present in the source text cannot be aligned at the word level with the target text. For this we rely on mechanisms similar to those described in Russell [15].

We can distinguish between small (a couple of sentences) and big omissions (any thing bigger than a few paragraphs). One might expect the detection of whole missing pages and chapters not to be difficult, but that's not necessarily true, as the burden of the problem then falls on the aligning program instead of the checker *per se*. Robustness here is the key-word since an alignment program that couldn't fall back on its feet after seeing big chunks of missing text would cause TransCheck to output only noise thereafter. The alignment program we use is one such robust program which, as a first step, seeks to approximate the real alignment by drawing lines in regions with high densities of cognate words. Since the distribution of cognates is *a priori* uniform throughout the text, omitted sections, when big enough, will show up on the appropriate graph as an important discontinuity in those approximation lines. As the omissions become smaller and smaller, however, the cognate's uniform distribution hypothesis becomes increasingly questionable.[2]

Still, we are interested in detecting missing sentences with acceptable precision. Ideally, this should be reflected as an X to zero alignment, but alignment programs tend to associate a high penalty to these cases, preferring to distribute extra text on adjacent regions. In order to recover from these mergings, TransCheck takes a closer look at pairs of aligned texts whenever the length ratio between source and target text falls under a certain threshold. It then attempts to aligned those pairs at the word level using a probabilistic bilingual dictionary that was estimated on the Canadian Hansard.

The "Art" of omission detection can be seen as one of trial and error in adjusting precision and recall by choosing appropriate values for what will constitute a significant difference in length ratio, a significant span of words that can't be aligned, and the penalty to be imposed if some words

[2] The probability for there to be only a few cognates between say two paragraphs is very low for French and English, but not that low for two sentences.

accidentally align due to the imprecision of the word to word alignment algorithm.

As we have just seen, the problem of detecting a missing portion of text is, in TransCheck, closely related to that of alignment, as it can be reduced to a misalignment at the word level. All the other types of errors TransCheck is concerned with are different in that respect. Correct alignment is presupposed, and when given specific pairs of aligned "tokens" the task will be to decide whether they represent valid translations. We now present the steps involved in this evaluation.

2.3 Identification

In order for TransCheck to evaluate a translation pair, their constitutive elements must first be identified. In some cases, this process requires morphological analysis and, in other, a limited type of syntactical analysis. Both type of analysis serve, to a certain extend, a single purpose: that of expressing compactly what would otherwise be a big list of tokens (in some cases, involving numerical expressions, an infinite one). This identification step is done through appropriate transducers. Basically, there are two things to keep in mind when dealing with transducers. One is that, like finite-state-automaton, they behave like recognisers; that is, when applied to an input string, if it can parse it from start to finish, the string is accepted and otherwise rejected. The second is that when doing so, it will produce an output as a result. TransCheck relies on that last property of transducers to produce a unique representation for tokens that are different in form, but semantically identical, as we will now see.

2.4 Normalisation

Though we will normally be interested in the identification of every morphological form for a given "interesting" token, once identified, these differences will be discarded by TranCheck. Compare the examples below.

- Air bag / air bags
- $2,000,000 / two million dollars / $2 million
- June 1st , 2000 / the first of June, 2000

The examples above are all in English, but the same type of diversity can be found in French too. In Figure 1 we can see an example showing the result of both the process of identification (underlined) and normalisation (=>).

It			Ce
will			sera
definitely	=> (FAC) 74		fait
be			avant
done			le
by			1er
January		(DAT) <=	janvier
first	=> (DAT) 01012001	01012001	2001
2001			,
.		(FAC) <= 74	définitivement
			.

Fig. 1: Token identification and normalisation.[3]

Notice that the central part of figure 1 acts somewhat like a partial transfer[4] component (in a word to word translation model) between the French and the English texts. Though we haven't implemented it yet, this could be used to present the user with proper translation suggestions.[5]

The normalisation process depicted in figure 1, can be slightly complicated by two factors. One is the need to disambiguate the part of speech of the identified token. Consider:

[3] FAC stands for "faux-amis complets" (deceptive cognates in all contexts)

[4] In the case of deceptive congnates, we could talk of a forbidden transfer.

[5] Transducers can be inverted to create new transducers that will recognise what was previously outputted and output what was recognised.

- French and English: Local → **(POS)NomC**(FAC)22

Here, the *condition* field ((POS)NomC)) state that only when nouns are involved will we be in presence of deceptive cognates (but not, say, when adjectives are involved).
Consider now:

- from May 19th to 24th, 1999

Here, the dates are intermingled. The transducers we use to analyse such constructs will produced two distinct normalised forms that will both be involved in the comparison process that follows.

2.5 Comparison

The identification and normalisation process described in the previous two sections are common to deceptive cognates, technical terms and numerical expressions altogether. However, the comparison of the resulting normalised forms as well as the processing they should further undergo is of a rather case specific nature.

During the comparison process, TransCheck will only be concerned with the normalised forms resulting from the previous transduction process (the two central columns in figure 1). Each of these two columns will be considered as a set in the mathematical sense. As a consequence, the English sentence in figure 1 and the one given below are indistinguishable from TransCheck's point of view.

- It will definitely, and I mean definitely, be done by January first, 2001.

Of course, both occurrences of the word *definitely* will be flagged if the decision to flag either one is eventually taken. Each of these two sets will then be split into up to three subsets depending on whether they correspond to numerical expressions, deceptive cognates or technical terms. At this point the comparison process will be very simple. Given these subsets, the matching conditions will simply amount to the following:

- If a numeral expression appears in one language but not in the other, flag it.
- If a deceptive cognate appears in both languages, flag it.
- If a term was requested to be flagged, flag it.

2.6 Putting it all together

To recapitulate, the transducers we use in TransCheck all have the general form:

***String of interest* →**
(condition)(type)identifier

If a transducer identifies a *string of interest* and if boundary conditions are met, information about the nature of the string will be outputted. In a second step, the information from one language will have to be matched against the information from the other in accordance with the *condition* imposed by the specific nature of the identified strings.

3 The TransCheck Prototype

In the previous section, we have described what happens when a bi-text is submitted to TransCheck. We now turn to the steps that will lead to a request.

Currently, TransCheck's interface is implemented in Tcl/Tk. This has allowed us to develop a *proof of concept* without preoccupying ourselves with word processing particularities. The down side to this is a limitation to ascii characters that will eventually have to be overcome by making TransCheck part of a text editor not unlike a spell checker.

But for the time being, a TransCheck session would look something like this: The user selects through an interface a French and an English text specifying with a radio-button which of the two is the source text.[6]

[6] The system was initialy developed having in mind

Then the name of an alignment file is supplied (it will be created if it doesn't already exist). These are the minimal steps that must be taken before any analysis can take place. If, at this point, the bi-text is submitted for analysis, TransCheck will use all of it's default values and, after some window pop-up and progress report, a window containing the target text will appear on screen together with the source text facing it. All the potential errors will appear highlighted. At this point, the user can modify the target text to correct any found errors. When the session ends, the modified text will be saved (together with the appropriately modified alignment file).

We've just seen TransCheck's default behaviour. The user is also offered some customisation possibilities. This includes highlighting only those type of errors of interest to the user and setting the alignment parameters. The omission detection parameters can also be modified through an interface. Also, since as with any normative judgement, what is and what isn't a "correct" form will always be subject to debate, TransCheck allows the user to silence those alleged mistakes causing too much noise on a given text. Finally, the human reviser is allowed, any time during a session, to modify TransCheck's behaviour so that newly identified incorrect terms will be flagged thereafter, this to ensure that none of subsequent occurrences of these errors will escape his attention. This list of forbidden terms can be saved in order to constitute client specific databases so that identified problems will not be lost between projects.

4 Further development and discussion

At present, TransCheck allows for only limited customisation. However, we are well aware that the repositories available for say deceptive cognates are costly to develop and tend to include only those mistakes having a certain "history" (stability over time). That suggests the user should be allowed to add new pairs of prohibited translations on the fly. In most cases, however, adding new behaviour is a complex process available only to the system's designer because of morphology and part-of-speech considerations. Added flexibility in this regard seems mandatory. Since we cannot expect the human reviser to concern himself with such technical details, these would have to be hidden from him through adequate input interfaces. This flexibility seems to be desired independently from the now emerging problem of *localisation*.[7] We are currently addressing these issues one at a time.

So far, we have described the types of errors TransCheck is concerned with, the way they are handled and how some aspects of the processing can be customised. No figures as to precision and recall have been given though. This is in part due to the difficulty of finding preliminary translations and in part to TransCheck's customisability. For example, performance on omission detection will ultimately depend on the user's selected values. It seems to us that the best way to address both of these problems should be to actually put the system in the hands of human revisers and monitor the changes they would actually choose to make. Efforts in that direction are currently being made.

Conclusion

To our knowledge, TransCheck is still unique among *text checkers* in addressing the problem of translation errors. For a long time, only a concept without form, TransCheck, as presented in this paper, has shown the concept of a *translation checker*

English as the source text. Currently, this is still reflected only in the deceptive cognate database.

[7] Adaptation of a text for use in a different region. For example, Canadian postal code (A1B 2C3) compared to American Zip Code (12345).

to be sound and realistic. Admittedly, a lot of work, especially on the specific grammars, still has to be done. But all this now seems like a worthwhile effort considering that the resulting program could help translators considerably in their efforts to meet the quality requirements and tight deadlines they are frequently facing. We have also stressed TransCheck's adaptability to be somewhat limited. The problem seems more one of ergonomics than of principle, though. Interfaces would have to be devised to guide users through the sometime complicated steps associated with adding new restrictions. We are now considering the possibility of integrating TransCheck in an off-the-shelf text editor to cross the *ascii barrier*.

Acknowledgements

I would like to thank Elliott Macklovich, Claude Bédard, Michèle Lamarche and Guy Lapalme for their invaluable comments on drafts of this paper.

References

[1] Brown P., Cocke J., Della Pietra S., Della Pietra V., Jelinek F., Lafferty J., Mercer R., Roosin P., A. (1990) *Statistical Approach to Machine Translation.* Computational Linguistics, 16, pp. 79-85.

[2] Brown P., Della Pietra S., Della Pietra V., Mercer R. (1993) *The Mathematics of Machine Translation: Parameter Estimation tatistical Approach to Machine Translation.* Computational Linguistics, 19, pp. 263-311.

[3] Colpron, G. (1982) *Dictionnaire d'anglicismes.* Laval (Québec), Éditions Beauchemin.

[4] Dagan, I and Church K. (1997) *Termight: Coordinating Humans and Machines in Bilingual Terminology Acquisition.* Machine Translation, 12, pp. 89-107.

[5] Dagenais, G. (1984) *Dictionnaire des difficultés de la langue française au Canada.* Boucherville, Les Éditions françaises.

[6] De Villiers, J.-É. (1988) *Multidictionnaire des difficultés de la langue française.* Montréal, Éditions Québec/Amérique.

[7] Gale, W., Church K. (1991) *A Program for Aligning Sentences in Bilingual Corpora.* Proceedings of the 29th Annual Meeting of the Association for Computational Linguistics, Berkeley, pp. 177-184.

[8] Isabelle P. and al. (1993) *Translation Analysis and Translation Automation.* Proceedings of the Fifth International Conference on Theoretical and Methodological Issues in Machine Translation (TMI-93), Kyoto, pp. 201-217.

[9] Justeson, J. and Slava K. (1995) *Technical Terminology: some linguistic properties and an algorithm for identification in text.* Natural Language Engineering, 1, pp. 9-28.

[10] Kaplan, R. M., Kay, M. (1994) *Regular Models of Phonological Rule Systems,* Computational Linguistics, 20, pp. 331-378.

[11] Macklovitch, E. (1996) *Peut-on vérifier automatiquement la cohérence terminologique?* Meta, 41, pp. 299-316.

[12] Melamed, I. D. (1996) *Automatic Detection of Omissions in Translations.* In the 16th International Conference on Computational Linguistics. Copenhagen, pp. 764-769.

[13] Merialdo, B. (1994) *Tagging English Text with a Probabilistic Model.* Computational Linguistics, 20, pp. 155-168.

[14] Rey J. (1984) *Dictionnaire sélectif et commenté des difficultés de la version anglaise.* Paris, Éditions Ophrys.

[15] Russell, G. (1999) *Errors of omission in translation.* Proceedings of the Eighth International Conference on Theoretical and Methodological Issues in Machine Translation (TMI-99), Chester, 1999, pp. 128-138.

[16] Simard M., Foster G. and Isabelle P. (1992) *Using Cognates to Align Sentences in Parallel Corpora.* Proceedings of the Fourth International Conference on Theoretical and Methodological Issues in Machine Translation (TMI-92), Montréal, pp. 67-81.

[17] Van Roey, J., Granger S. and Swallow J. (1988) *Dictionnaire des faux amis français-anglais.* Paris, Duculot.

Unit Completion for a Computer-aided Translation Typing System

Philippe Langlais, George Foster and Guy Lapalme
RALI / DIRO
Université de Montréal
C.P. 6128, succursale Centre-ville
Montral (Qubec), Canada, H3C 3J7
{*felipe,foster,lapalme*} *@iro.umontreal.ca*

Abstract

This work is in the context of TRANSTYPE, a system that observes its user as he or she types a translation and repeatedly suggests *completions* for the text already entered. The user may either accept, modify, or ignore these suggestions. We describe the design, implementation, and performance of a prototype which suggests completions of units of texts that are longer than one word.

1 Introduction

TRANSTYPE is part of a project set up to explore an appealing solution to *Interactive Machine Translation* (IMT). In constrast to classical IMT systems, where the user's role consists mainly of assisting the computer to analyse the source text (by answering questions about word sense, ellipses, phrasal attachments, etc), in TRANSTYPE the interaction is directly concerned with establishing the target text.

Our interactive translation system works as follows: a translator selects a sentence and begins typing its translation. After each character typed by the translator, the system displays a proposed completion, which may either be accepted using a special key or rejected by continuing to type. Thus the translator remains in control of the translation process and the machine must continually adapt its suggestions in response to his or her input. We are currently undertaking a study to measure the extent to which our word-completion prototype can improve translator productivity. The conclusions of this study will be presented elsewhere.

The first version of TRANSTYPE (Foster et al., 1997) only proposed completions for the current word. This paper deals with predictions which extend to the next several words in the text. The potential gain from multiple-word predictions can be appreciated in the one-sentence translation task reported in table 1, where a hypothetical user saves over 60% of the keystrokes needed to produce a translation in a word completion scenario, and about 85% in a "unit" completion scenario.

In all the figures that follow, we use different fonts to differentiate the various input and output: *italics* are used for the source text, sans-serif for characters typed by the user and `typewriter-like` for characters completed by the system.

The first few lines of the table 1 give an idea of how TransType functions. Let us assume the unit scenario (see column 2 of the table) and suppose that the user wants to produce the sentence "Ce projet de loi est examiné à la chambre des communes" as a translation for the source sentence "***This bill is examined in the house of commons***". The first hypothesis that the system produces before the user enters a character is `loi` (*law*). As this is not a good guess from TRANSTYPE the user types the first character (c) of the words he or she wants as a translation. Taking this new input into account, TRANSTYPE then modifies its proposal so that it is compatible whith what the translator has typed. It suggests the desired sequence ce projet de loi, which the user can simply validate by typing a dedicated key. Continuing in this way, the user and TRANSTYPE alternately contribute to the final translation. A screen copy of this prototype is provided in figure 1.

2 The Core Engine

The core of TRANSTYPE is a completion engine which comprises two main parts: an *evaluator* which assigns probabilistic scores to completion hypotheses and a *generator* which uses the evaluation function to select the best candidate for completion.

2.1 The Evaluator

The evaluator is a function $p(t|t', s)$ which assigns to each target-text unit t an estimate of its probability given a source text s and the tokens t' which precede t in the current translation of s.[1] Our approach to modeling this distribution is based to a large extent on that of the IBM group (Brown et al., 1993), but it differs in one significant aspect: whereas the IBM model involves a "noisy channel" decomposition, we use a linear combination of separate predictions from a language model $p(t|t')$ and a translation model $p(t|s)$. Although the noisy channel technique

[1] We assume the existence of a deterministic procedure for tokenizing the target text.

This bill is examined in the house of commons				
	word-completion task		unit-completion task	
	pref.	completions	pref.	completions
ce	ce+	/loi · c/'	c+	/loi · c/e projet de loi
projet	p+	/est · p/rojet	-	
de	d+	/très · d/e	-	
loi	l+	/très · l/oi	-	
est	e+	/de · e/st	e+	/de · e/st
examiné	e+	/en · e/xaminé	ex+	/à la chambre des communes · e/n · ex/aminé
à la	à+	/par · à/ la	+	/à la chambre des communes
chambre	+	/chambre	-	
des	de+	/communes · d/e · de/s	-	
communes	+	/communes	-	
54 char.	10 + 10 accept. → **20 keystrokes**		4 + 4 accept. → **8 keystrokes**	

Table 1: A one-sentence session illustrating the word- and unit-completion tasks. The first column indicates the target words the user is expected to produce. The next two columns indicate respectively the prefixes typed by the user and the completions proposed by the system in a word-completion task. The last two columns provide the same information for the unit-completion task. The total number of keystrokes for both tasks is reported in the last line. + indicates the acceptance key typed by the user. A completion is denoted by α/β where α is the typed prefix and β the completed part. Completions for different prefixes are separated by · .

is powerful, it has the disadvantage that $p(s|t', t)$ is more expensive to compute than $p(t|s)$ when using IBM-style translation models. Since speed is crucial for our application, we chose to forego the noisy channel approach in the work described here. Our linear combination model is described as follows:

$$p(t|t', s) = \underbrace{p(t|t')\,\alpha(t', s)}_{\text{language}} + \underbrace{p(t|s)\,[1 - \alpha(t', s)]}_{\text{translation}} \quad (1)$$

where $\alpha(t', s) \in [0, 1]$ are context-dependent interpolation coefficients. For example, the translation model could have a higher weight at the start of a sentence but the contribution of the language model might become more important in the middle or the end of the sentence. A study of the weightings for these two models is described elsewhere. In the work described here we did not use the contribution of the language model (that is, $\alpha(t', s) = 0, \forall t', s$).

Techniques for weakening the independence assumptions made by the IBM models 1 and 2 have been proposed in recent work (Brown et al., 1993; Berger et al., 1996; Och and Weber, 98; Wang and Waibel, 98; Wu and Wong, 98). These studies report improvements on some specific tasks (task-oriented limited vocabulary) which by nature are very different from the task TRANSTYPE is devoted to. Furthermore, the underlying decoding strategies are too time consuming for our application. We therefore use a translation model based on the simple linear interpolation given in equation 2 which combines predictions of two translation models — M_s and M_u — both based on IBM-like model 2(Brown et al., 1993). M_s was trained on single words and M_u, described in section 3, was trained on both words and units.

$$p(t|s) = \underbrace{\beta p_s(t|s)}_{\text{word}} + \underbrace{(1 - \beta)p_u(t|\mathcal{G}(s))}_{\text{unit}} \quad (2)$$

where p_s and p_u stand for the probabilities given respectively by M_s and M_u. $\mathcal{G}(s)$ represents the new sequence of tokens obtained after grouping the tokens of s into units. The grouping operator $\mathcal{G}$ is illustrated in table 2 and is described in section 3.

2.2 The Generator

The task of the generator is to identify units that match the current prefix typed by the user, and pick the best candidate according to the evaluator. Due to time considerations, the generator introduces a division of the target vocabulary into two parts: a small *active* component whose contents are always searched for a match to the current prefix, and a much larger *passive* part over (380,000 word forms) which comes into play only when no candidates are found in the active vocabulary. The active part is computed dynamically when a new sentence is selected by the translator. It is composed of a few entities (tokens and units) that are likely to appear in the translation. It is a union of the best candidates provided by each model M_s and M_u over the set of all possible target tokens (resp. units) that have a non-null translation probability of being translated by any of the current source tokens (resp. units). Table 2 shows the 10 most likely tokens and units in the active vocabulary for an example source sentence.

s	*that · is · what · the · prime · minister · said · , · and · i · have · outlined · what · has · happened · since · then · .*	
t	c' · est · ce · que · le · premier · ministre · a · dit · , · et · j' · ai · résumé · ce · qui · s' · est · produit · depuis · .	
$\mathcal{G}(s)$	*that is what · the prime minister said · , and i · have · outlined · what has happened · since then · .*	
A_s	, · . · est · ce · ministre · que · et · a · premier · le	
A_u	ce qui s' est produit · et je · c' est ce que · voilà ce que · qu' est · c' est · , et · le premier ministre disait	

Table 2: Role of the generator for a sample pair of sentences (t is the translation of s in our corpus). $\mathcal{G}(s)$ is the sequence of source tokens recasted by the grouping operator $\mathcal{G}$. A_s indicates the 10 best tokens according to the word model, A_u the 10 best units according to the unit model.

3 Modeling Unit Associations

Automatically identifying which source words or groups of words will give rise to which target words or groups of words is a fundamental problem which remains open. In this work, we decided to proceed in two steps: a) monolingually identifying groups of words that would be better handled as units in a given context, and b) mapping the resulting source and target units. To train our unit models, we used a segment of the Hansard corpus consisting of 15,377 pairs of sentences, totaling 278,127 english tokens (13,543 forms) and 292,865 french tokens (16,399 forms).

3.1 Finding Monolingual Units

Finding relevant units in a text has been explored in many areas of natural language processing. Our approach relies on distributional and frequency statistics computed on each sequence of words found in a training corpus. For sake of efficiency, we used the suffix array technique to get a compact representation of our training corpus. This method allows the efficient retrieval of arbitrary length n-grams (Nagao and Mori, 94; Haruno et al., 96; Ikehara et al., 96; Shimohata et al., 1997; Russell, 1998).

The literature abounds in measures that can help to decide whether words that co-occur are linguistically significant or not. In this work, the strength of association of a sequence of words $w_1^n = w_1, \ldots, w_n$ is computed by two measures: a likelihood-based one $\rho(w_1^n)$ (where ℓ is the likelihood ratio given in (Dunning, 93)) and an entropy-based one $e(w_1^n)$ (Shimohata et al., 1997). Letting T stand for the training text and m a token:

$$\rho(w_1^n) = \operatorname*{argmin}_{i \in]1,n[} \ell(w_1^i, w_{i+1}^n) \quad (3)$$

$$e(w_1^n) = 0.5 \times \left(\begin{array}{c} \sum_{m|mw_1^n \in T} h\left(\frac{freq(mw_1^n)}{freq(w_1^n)}\right) \\ + \\ \sum_{m|w_1^n m \in T} h\left(\frac{freq(w_1^n m)}{freq(w_1^n)}\right) \end{array} \right)$$

Intuitively, the first measurement accounts for the fact that parts of a sequence of words that should be considered as a whole should not appear often by themselves. The second one reflects the fact that a salient unit should appear in various contexts (i.e. should have a high entropy score).

We implemented a cascade filtering strategy based on the likelihood score ρ, the frequency f, the length l and the entropy value e of the sequences. A first filter ($\mathcal{F}_1(l_{min}, f_{min}, \rho_{min}, e_{min})$) removes any sequence s for which $l(s) < l_{min}$ or $\rho(s) < \rho_{min}$ or $e(s) < e_{min}$ or $f(s) < f_{min}$. A second filter ($\mathcal{F}_2$) removes sequences that are included in preferred ones. In terms of sequence reduction, applying $\mathcal{F}_1(2, 2, 5.0, 0.2)$ on the 81,974 English sequences of at least two tokens seen at least twice in our training corpus, less than 50% of them (39,093) were filtered: 17,063 (21%) were removed because of their low entropy value, 25,818 (31%) because of their low likelihood value.

3.2 Mapping

Mapping the identified units (tokens or sequences) to their equivalents in the other language was achieved by training a new translation model (IBM 2) using the EM algorithm as described in (Brown et al., 1993). This required grouping the tokens in our training corpus into sequences, on the basis of the unit lexicons identified in the previous step (we will refer to the results of this grouping as the *sequence-based corpus*). To deal with overlapping possibilities, we used a dynamic programming scheme which optimized a criterion $\mathcal{C}$ given by equation 4 over a set $\mathcal{S}$ of all units collected for a given language plus all single words. $\mathcal{G}(w_1^n)$ is obtained by returning the path that maximized $B(n)$. We investigated several $\mathcal{C}$-criteria and we found $\mathcal{C}_l$—a length-based measure—to be the most satisfactory. Table 2 shows an output of the grouping function.

$$B(i) = \begin{cases} 0 \ if \ \ i = 0 \\ \operatorname*{argmax}_{I \in [1,i[\, , \, w_{i-I}^i \in \mathcal{S}} \left(\begin{array}{c} \mathcal{C}(w_{i-I}^i) \\ + \\ B(i-I-1) \end{array} \right) \end{cases} \quad (4)$$

$$\text{with: } \mathcal{C}_l(w_i^j) = \begin{cases} 0 & if \ j <= i \\ j - i + 1 & else \end{cases}$$

source unit (s)	$f(s)$	target units ($[\alpha, p]$)
we have	1748	[nous,0.49] [avons,0.41] [, nous avons,0.07]
we must	720	[nous devons,0.61] [il faut,0.19] [nous,0.14]
this bill	640	[ce projet de loi,0.35] [projet de loi .,0.21] [projet de loi,0.18]
people of canada	282	[les canadiens,0.26] [des canadiens,0.21] [la population,0.07]
mr. speaker :	269	[m. le président :,0.80] [a,0.07] [à la,0.06]
what is happening	190	[ce qui se passe,0.21] [ce qui se,0.16] [et,0.15]
of course ,	178	[évidemment ,,0.26] [naturellement,0.08] [bien sûr,0.08]
is it the pleasure of the house to adopt the	14	[plaît-il à la chambre d' adopter,0.49] [la motion ?,0.42] [motion ?,0.04]
the world	201	[le monde,0.46] [du monde,0.33] [le monde entier,0.19]
child care	86	[les garderies,0.59] [la garde d' enfants,0.23] [des services de garde d' enfants,0.13]
the free trade agreement	75	[l' accord de libre-échange,0.96] [la décision du gatt,0.04]
post-secondary education	66	[l' enseignement postsecondaire,0.75] [l' éducation postsecondaire,0.15] [des fonds,0.06]
the first time	62	[la première fois,1.00]
the canadian aviation safety board	36	[le bureau canadien de la sécurité aérienne,0.55] [du bureau canadien de la sécurité aérienne,0.31] [l' un,0.14]
the next five years	26	[au cours des cinq prochaines années,0.53] [cinq prochaines années,0.27] [25 milliards de d ollars,0.10]
the people of china	17	[le peuple chinois,0.38] [la population chinoise,0.25] [les chinois,0.13]

Table 3: Bilingual associations. The first column indicates a source unit, the second one its frequency in the training corpus. The third column reports its 3-best ranked target associations (α being a token or a unit, p being the translation probability). The second half of the table reports NP-associations obtained after the filter described in the text.

We investigated three ways of estimating the parameters of the unit model. In the first one, $\mathcal{E}_1$, the translation parameters are estimated by applying the EM algorithm in a straightforward fashion over all entities (tokens and units) present at least twice in the sequence-based corpus [2]. The two next methods filter the probabilities obtained with the $\mathcal{E}_1$ method. In $\mathcal{E}_2$, all probabilities $p(t|s)$ are set to 0 whenever s is a token (not a unit), thus forcing the model to contain only associations between source units and target entities (tokens or units). In $\mathcal{E}_3$ any parameter of the model that involves a token is removed (that is, $p(t|s) = 0$ if t or s is a token). The resulting model will thus contain only unit associations. In both cases, the final probabilities are renormalized. Table 3 shows a few entries from a unit model (M_u) obtained after 15 iterations of the EM-algorithm on a sequence corpus resulting from the application of the length-grouping criterion ($\mathcal{C}_l$) over a lexicon of units whose likelihood score is above 5.0. The probabilities have been obtained by application of the method $\mathcal{E}_2$.

We found many partially correct associations (*over the years/au fils des*, *we have/nous*, etc) that illustrate the weakness of decoupling the unit identification from the mapping problem. In most cases however, these associations have a lower probability than the good ones. We also found few erratic associations (*the first time/ c'était*, *some hon. members/!*, etc) due to distributional artifacts. It is also interesting to note that the good associations we found are not necessary compositional in nature (*we must/il faut*, *people of canada/les canadiens*, *of course/évidemment*, etc).

[2] The entities seen only once are mapped to a special "unknown" word

3.3 Filtering

One way to increase the precision of the mapping process is to impose some linguistic constraints on the sequences such as simple noun-phrase contraints (Gaussier, 1995; Kupiec, 1993; hua Chen and Chen, 94; Fung, 1995; Evans and Zhai, 1996). It is also possible to focus on non-compositional compounds, a key point in bilingual applications (Su et al., 1994; Melamed, 1997; Lin, 99). Another interesting approach is to restrict sequences to those that do not cross constituent boundary patterns (Wu, 1995; Furuse and Iida, 96). In this study, we filtered for potential sequences that are likely to be noun phrases, using simple regular expressions over the associated part-of-speech tags. An excerpt of the association probabilities of a unit model trained considering only the NP-sequences is given in table 3. Applying this filter (referred to as $\mathcal{F}_{NP}$ in the following) to the 39,093 english sequences still surviving after previous filters $\mathcal{F}_1$ and $\mathcal{F}_2$ removes 35,939 of them (92%).

	model	*spared*	*ok*	*good*	*nu*	*u*
1	*baseline* – model 1	*48.98*	*0*	*0*	*747*	*0*
2	**baseline** – model 2	**51.83**	**0**	**0**	**747**	**0**
3	$\mathcal{E}_1 + \mathcal{F}_1(2,2,0,0.2)$	50.98	527	1702	5	626
4	$\mathcal{E}_1 + \mathcal{F}_1(2,2,5,0.2)$	51.61	596	2149	5	658
5	$\mathcal{E}_1 + \mathcal{F}_1(2,2,5,0.2) + \mathcal{F}_2$	51.72	633	2265	5	657
6	$\mathcal{E}_2 + \mathcal{F}_1(2,2,0,0.2)$	51.39	514	1551	43	578
7	$\mathcal{E}_2 + \mathcal{F}_1(2,2,5,0.2)$	51.99	470	1889	46	614
8	$\mathcal{E}_2 + \mathcal{F}_1(2,2,5,0.2) + \mathcal{F}_2$	52.12	493	1951	46	606
9	$\mathcal{E}_3 + \mathcal{F}_1(2,2,0,0.2)$	51.07	577	1699	43	588
10	$\mathcal{E}_3 + \mathcal{F}_1(2,2,5,0.2)$	51.47	629	2124	46	618
11	$\mathcal{E}_3 + \mathcal{F}_1(2,2,5,0.2) + \mathcal{F}_2$	51.68	665	2209	46	615
12	$\mathcal{E}_1 + \mathcal{F}_1(2,2,5,0.2) + \mathcal{F}_2 + \mathcal{F}_{NP}$	52.83	416	1302	4	564
13	$\mathcal{E}_3 + \mathcal{F}_1(2,2,5,0.2) + \mathcal{F}_{NP}$	53.12	439	1031	228	425
14	$\mathcal{E}_3 + \mathcal{F}_1(2,2,5,0.2) + \mathcal{F}_2 + \mathcal{F}_{NP}$	53.16	458	1052	199	439
15	$\mathcal{E}_3 + \beta = 0.4 + \mathcal{F}_1(2,2,5,0.2) + \mathcal{F}_{NP}$	53.22	495	1031	228	425

Table 4: Completion results of several translation models. *spared*: theoretical proportion of characters saved; *ok*: number of target units accepted by the user; *good*: number of target units that matched the expected whether they were proposed or not; *nu*: number of sentences for which no target unit was found by the translation model; *u*: number of sentences for which at least one helpful unit has been found by the model, but not necessarily proposed.

More than half of the 3,154 remaining NP-sequences contain only two words.

4 Results

We collected completion results on a test corpus of 747 sentences (13,386 english tokens and 14,506 french ones) taken from the Hansard corpus. These sentences have been selected randomly among sentences that have not been used for the training. Around 18% of the source and target words are not known by the translation model.

The baseline models (line 1 and 2) are obtained without any unit model (*i.e.* $\beta = 1$ in equation 2). The first one is obtained with an IBM-like model 1 while the second is an IBM-like model 2. We observe that for the pair of languages we considered, model 2 improves the amount of saved keystrokes of almost 3% compared to model 1. Therefore we made use of alignment probabilities for the other models.

The three next blocks in table 4 show how the parameter estimation method affects performance. Training models under the $\mathcal{E}_1$ method gives the worst results. This results from the fact that the word-to-word probabilities trained on the sequence based corpus (predicted by M_u in equation 2) are less accurate than the ones learned from the token based corpus. The reason is simply that there are less occurrences of each token, especially if many units are identified by the grouping operator.

In methods $\mathcal{E}_2$ and $\mathcal{E}_3$, the unit model of equation 2 only makes predictions $p_u(t|s)$ when s is a source unit, thus lowering the noise compared to method $\mathcal{E}_1$. We also observe in these three blocks the influence of sequence filtering: the more we filter, the better the results. This holds true for all estimation methods tried. In the fifth block of table 4 we observe the positive influence of the NP-filtering, especially when using the third estimation method.

The best combination we found is reported in line 15. It outperforms the baseline by around 1.5%. This model has been obtained by retaining all sequences seen at least two times in the training corpus for which the likelihood test value was above 5 and the entropy score above 0.2 ($\mathcal{F}_1(2,2,5,0.2)$). In terms of the coverage of this unit model, it is interesting to note that among the 747 sentences of the test session, there were 228 for which the model did not propose any units at all. For 425 of the remaining sentences, the model proposed at least one helpful (good or partially good) unit. The active vocabulary for these sentences contained an average of around 2.5 good units per sentence, of which only half (495) were proposed during the session. The fact that this model outperforms others despite its relatively poor coverage (compared to the others) may be explained by the fact that it also removes part of the noise introduced by decoupling the identification of the salient units from the training procedure. Furthermore, as we mentionned earlier, the more we filter, the less the grouping scheeme presented in equation 4 remains necessary, thus reducing a possible source of noise.

The fact that this model outperforms others, despite its relatively poor coverage, is due to the fact

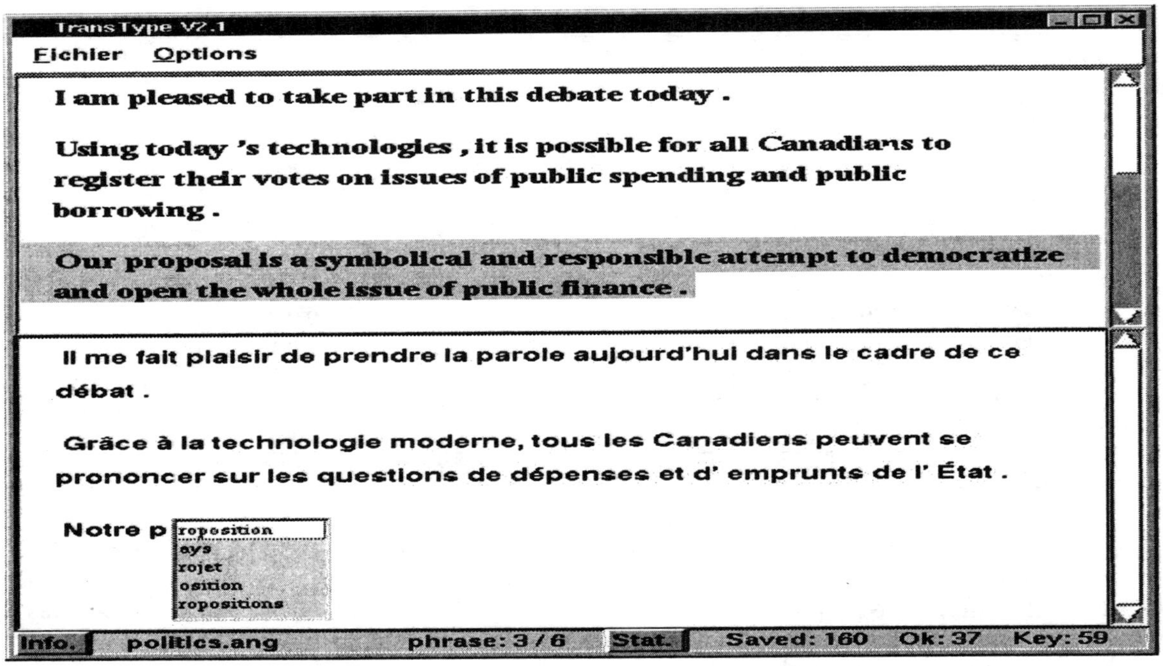

Figure 1: Example of an interaction in TRANSTYPE with the source text in the top half of the screen. The target text is typed in the bottom half with suggestions given by the menu at the insertion point.

that it also removes part of the noise that is introduced by dissociating the identification of the salient units from the training procedure. Furthermore, as we mentioned earlier, the more we filter, the less the grouping scheme presented in equation 4 remains necessary, thus further reducing an other possible source of noise.

5 Conclusion

We have described a prototype system called TRANSTYPE which embodies an innovative approach to interactive machine translation in which the interaction is directly concerned with establishing the target text. We proposed and tested a mechanism to enhance TRANSTYPE by having it predict sequences of words rather than just completions for the current word. The results show a modest improvement in prediction performance which will serve as a baseline for our future investigations. One obvious direction for future research is to revise our current strategy of decoupling the selection of units from their bilingual context.

Acknowlegments

TRANSTYPE is a project funded by the Natural Sciences and Engineering Research Council of Canada. We are undebted to Elliott Macklovitch and Pierre Isabelle for the fruitful orientations they gave to this work.

References

Adam L. Berger, Stephen A. Della Pietra, and Vincent J. Della Pietra. 1996. A maximum entropy approach to natural language processing. *Computational Linguistics*, 22(1):39–71.

Peter F. Brown, Stephen A. Della Pietra, Vincent Della J. Pietra, and Robert L. Mercer. 1993. The mathematics of machine translation: Parameter estimation. *Computational Linguistics*, 19(2):263–312, June.

Ted Dunning. 93. Accurate methods for the statistics of surprise and coincidence. *Computational Linguistics*, 19(1):61–74.

David A. Evans and Chengxiang Zhai. 1996. Noun-phrase analysis in unrestricted text for information retrieval. In *Proceedings of the 34th Annual Meeting of the Association for Computational Linguistics*, pages 17–24, Santa Cruz, California.

George Foster, Pierre Isabelle, and Pierre Plamondon. 1997. Target-text Mediated Interactive Machine Translation. *Machine Translation*, 12:175–194.

Pascale Fung. 1995. A pattern matching method for finding noun and proper noun translations from noisy parallel corpora. In *Proceedings of the 33rd Annual Meeting of the Association for Computational Linguistics*, pages 236–243, Cambridge, Massachusetts.

Osamu Furuse and Hitoshi Iida. 96. Incremental translation utilizing constituent boundray patterns. In *Proceedings of the 16th International Conference On Computational Linguistics*, pages 412–417 Copenhagen, Denmark.

Éric Gaussier. 1995. *Modles statistiques et patrons morphosyntaxiques pour l'extraction de lexiques bilingues*. Ph.D. thesis, Universit de Paris 7, janvier.

Masahiko Haruno, Satoru Ikehara, and Takefumi Yamazaki. 96. Learning bilingual collocations by word-level sorting. In *Proceedings of the 16th International Conference On Computational Linguistics*, pages 525–530, Copenhagen, Denmark.

Kuang hua Chen and Hsin-Hsi Chen. 94. Extracting noun phrases from large-scale texts: A hybrid approach and its automatic evaluation. In *Proceedings of the 32nd Annual Meeting of the Association for Computational Linguistics*, pages 234–241, Las Cruces, New Mexico.

Satoru Ikehara, Satoshi Shirai, and Hajine Uchino. 96. A statistical method for extracting uinterupted and interrupted collocations from very large corpora. In *Proceedings of the 16th International Conference On Computational Linguistics*, pages 574–579, Copenhagen, Denmark.

Julian Kupiec. 1993. An algorithm for finding noun phrase correspondences in bilingual corpora. In *Proceedings of the 31st Annual Meeting of the Association for Computational Linguistics*, pages 17–22, Colombus, Ohio.

Dekang Lin. 99. Automatic identification of non-compositional phrases. In *Proceedings of the 37th Annual Meeting of the Association for Computational Linguistics*, pages 317–324, College Park, Maryland.

I. Dan Melamed. 1997. Automatic discovery of non-compositional coumpounds in parallel data. In *Proceedings of the 2nd Conference on Empirical Methods in Natural Language Processing*, pages 97–108, Providence, RI, August, 1st-2nd.

Makoto Nagao and Shinsuke Mori. 94. A new method of n-gram statistics for large number of n and automatic extraction of words and phrases from large text data of japanese. In *Proceedings of the 16th International Conference On Computational Linguistics*, volume 1, pages 611–615, Copenhagen, Denmark.

Franz Josef Och and Hans Weber. 98. Improving statistical natural language translation with categories and rules. In *Proceedings of the 36th Annual Meeting of the Association for Computational Linguistics*, pages 985–989, Montréal, Canada.

Graham Russell. 1998. Identification of salient token sequences. Internal report, RALI, University of Montreal, Canada.

Sayori Shimohata, Toshiyuki Sugio, and Junji Nagata. 1997. Retrieving collocations by co-occurrences and word order constraints. In *Proceedings of the 35th Annual Meeting of the Association for Computational Linguistics*, pages 476–481, Madrid Spain.

Keh-Yih Su, Ming-Wen Wu, and Jing-Shin Chang. 1994. A corpus-based approach to automatic compound extraction. In *Proceedings of the 32nd Annual Meeting of the Association for Computational Linguistics*, pages 242–247, Las Cruces, New Mexico.

Ye-Yi Wang and Alex Waibel. 98. Modeling with structures in statistical machine translation. In *Proceedings of the 36th Annual Meeting of the Association for Computational Linguistics*, volume 2, pages 1357–1363, Montréal, Canada.

Dekai Wu and Hongsing Wong. 98. Machine translation with a stochastic grammatical channel. In *Proceedings of the 36th Annual Meeting of the Association for Computational Linguistics*, pages 1408–1414, Montréal, Canada.

Dekai Wu. 1995. Stochastic inversion transduction grammars, with application to segmentation, bracketing, and alignment of parallel corpora. In *Proceedings of the International Joint Conference on Artificial Intelligence*, volume 2, pages 1328–1335, Montréal, Canada.

Multilingual Coreference Resolution

Sanda M. Harabagiu
Southern Methodist University
Dallas, TX 75275-0122
sanda@seas.smu.edu

Steven J. Maiorano
IPO
Washington, D.C. 20505
maiorano@cais.com

Abstract

In this paper we present a new, multilingual data-driven method for coreference resolution as implemented in the SWIZZLE system. The results obtained after training this system on a bilingual corpus of English and Romanian tagged texts, outperformed coreference resolution in each of the individual languages.

1 Introduction

The recent availability of large bilingual corpora has spawned interest in several areas of multilingual text processing. Most of the research has focused on bilingual terminology identification, either as parallel multiwords forms (e.g. the *Champollion* system (Smadja et al.1996)), technical terminology (e.g. the *Termight* system (Dagan and Church, 1994) or broad-coverage translation lexicons (e.g. the *SABLE* system (Resnik and Melamed, 1997)). In addition, the Multilingual Entity Task (MET) from the TIPSTER program[1] (*http://www-nlpir.nist.gov/related-projects/tipster/met.htm*) challenged the participants in the Message Understanding Conference (MUC) to extract named entities across several foreign language corpora, such as Chinese, Japanese and Spanish.

In this paper we present a new application of aligned multilingual texts. Since coreference resolution is a pervasive discourse phenomenon causing performance impediments in current IE systems, we considered a corpus of aligned English and Romanian texts to identify coreferring expressions. Our task focused on the same kind of coreference as considered in the past MUC competitions, namely the *identity* coreference. Identity coreference links nouns, pronouns and noun phrases (including proper names) to their corresponding antecedents.

We created our bilingual collection by translating the MUC-6 and MUC-7 coreference training texts into Romanian using native speakers. The training data set for Romanian coreference used, wherever possible, the same coreference identifiers as the English data and incorporated additional tags as needed. Our claim is that by adding the wealth of coreferential features provided by multilingual data, new powerful heuristics for coreference resolution can be developed that outperform monolingual coreference resolution systems.

For both languages, we resolved coreference by using `SWIZZLE`, our implementation of a bilingual coreference resolver. `SWIZZLE` is a multilingual enhancement of `COCKTAIL` (Harabagiu and Maiorano, 1999), a coreference resolution system that operates on a mixture of heuristics that combine semantic and textual cohesive information[2]. When `COCKTAIL` was applied separately on the English and the Romanian texts, coreferring links were identified for each English and Romanian document respectively. When aligned referential expressions corefer with non-aligned anaphors, `SWIZZLE` derived new heuristics for coreference. Our experiments show that `SWIZZLE` outperformed `COCKTAIL` on both English and Romanian test documents.

The rest of the paper is organized as follows. Section 2 presents `COCKTAIL`, a monolingual coreference resolution system used separately on both the English and Romanian texts. Section 3 details the data-driven approach used in `SWIZZLE` and presents some of its resources. Section 4 reports and discusses the experimental results. Section 5 summarizes the

[1] The TIPSTER Text Program was a DARPA-led government effort to advance the state of the art in text processing technologies.

[2] The name of `COCKTAIL` is a pun on `CogNIAC` because `COCKTAIL` combines a larger number of heuristics than those reported in (Baldwin, 1997). `SWIZZLE`, moreover, adds new heuristics, discovered from the bilingual aligned corpus.

conclusions.

2 COCKTAIL

Currently, some of the best-performing and most robust coreference resolution systems employ knowledge-based techniques. Traditionally, these techniques have combined extensive syntactic, semantic, and discourse knowledge. The acquisition of such knowledge is time-consuming, difficult, and error-prone. Nevertheless, recent results show that knowledge-poor methods perform with amazing accuracy (cf. (Mitkov, 1998), (Kennedy and Boguraev, 1996) (Kameyama, 1997)). For example, CogNIAC (Baldwin, 1997), a system based on seven ordered heuristics, generates high-precision resolution (over 90%) for some cases of pronominal reference. For this research, we used a coreference resolution system ((Harabagiu and Maiorano, 1999)) that implements different sets of heuristics corresponding to various forms of coreference. This system, called COCKTAIL, resolves coreference by exploiting several textual cohesion constraints (e.g. term repetition) combined with lexical and textual coherence cues (e.g. subjects of communication verbs are more likely to refer to the last person mentioned in the text). These constraints are implemented as a set of heuristics ordered by their priority. Moreover, the COCKTAIL framework uniformly addresses the problem of interaction between different forms of coreference, thus making the extension to multilingual coreference very natural.

2.1 Data-Driven Coreference Resolution

In general, we define a data-driven methodology as a sequence of actions that captures the data patterns capable of resolving a problem with both a high degree of precision and recall. Our data-driven methodology reported here generated *sets of heuristics* for the coreference resolution problem. *Precision* is the number of correct references out of the total number of coreferences resolved, whereas the *recall* measures the number of resolved references out of the total number of keys, i.e., the annotated coreference data.

The data-driven methodology used in COCKTAIL is centered around the notion of a *coreference chain*. Due to the *transitivity* of coreference relations, k coreference relations having at least one common argument generate $k+1$ *coreferring expressions*. The text position induces an order among coreferring expressions. A *coreference structure* is created when a set of coreferring expressions are connected in an oriented graph such that each node is related only to one of its preceding nodes. In turn, a *coreference chain* is the coreference structure in which every node is connected to its immediately preceding node. Clearly, multiple coreference structures for the same set of coreferring expressions can be mapped to a single coreference chain. As an example, both coreference structures illustrated in Figure 1(a) and (c) are cast into the coreference chain illustrated in Figure 1(b).

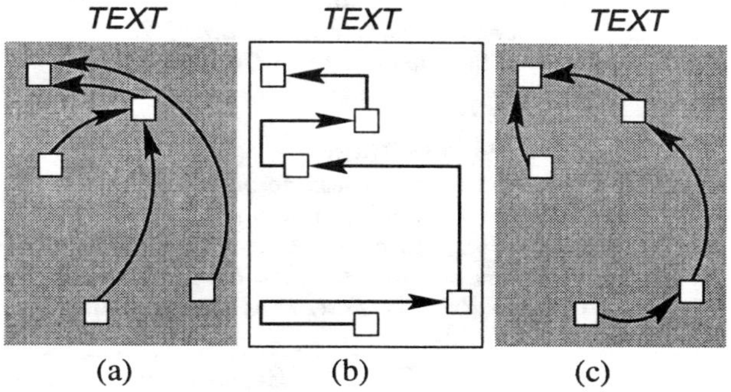

Figure 1: Three coreference structures.

Given a corpus annotated with coreference data, the data-driven methodology first generates all coreference chains in the data set and then considers all possible combinations of coreference relations that would generate the same coreference chains. For a coreference chain of length l with nodes n_1, n_2, ... n_{l+1}, each node n_k ($1 \leq k \leq l$) can be connected to any of the $l-k$ nodes preceding it. From this observation, we find that a number of $1 \times 2 \times ... \times (l-k) ... \times l = l!$ coreference structures can generate the same coreference chain. This result is very important, since it allows for the automatic generation of coreference data. For each coreference relation $\mathcal{R}$ from an annotated corpus we created a median of $(l-1)!$ new coreference relations, where l is the length of the coreference chain containing relation $\mathcal{R}$. This observation gave us the possibility of expanding the test data provided by the coreference keys available in the MUC-6 and MUC-7 competitions (MUC-6 1996), (MUC-7 1998). The MUC-6 coreference annotated corpus contains 1626 coreference relations, while the MUC-7 corpus has 2245 relations. The average length of a coreference chain is 7.21 for the MUC-6 data, and 8.57 for the MUC-7 data. We were able to expand the number of annotated coreference relations to 6,095,142 for the MUC-6 corpus and to 8,269,403 relations for the MUC-7 corpus; this represents an expansion factor of 3,710. We are not aware of any other automated way of creating coreference annotated data, and we believe that much of the COCKTAIL's impressive performance is due to the plethora of data provided by this method.

Heuristics for 3rd person pronouns	Heuristics for nominal reference
o<u>*Heuristic 1-Pronoun*</u>(H1Pron) *Search in the same sentence for the* **same** *3rd person pronoun Pron'* **if** *(Pron' belongs to coreference chain CC)* **and** *there is an element from CC which is closest to Pron in Text, Pick that element.* **else** *Pick Pron'.* o<u>*Heuristic 2-Pronoun*</u>(H2Pron) *Search for PN, the closest proper name from Pron* **if** *(PN agrees in number and gender with Pron)* **if** *(PN belongs to coreference chain CC)* **then** *Pick the element from CC which is closest to Pron in Text.* **else** *Pick PN.* o<u>*Heuristic 3-Pronoun*</u>(H3Pron) *Search for Noun, the closest noun from Pron* **if** *(Noun agrees in number and gender with Pron)* **if** *(Noun belongs to coreference chain CC)* **and** *there is an element from CC which is closest to Pron in Text, Pick that element.* **else** *Pick Noun*	o<u>*Heuristic 1-Nominal*</u>(H1Nom) **if** (*Noun* is the head of an appositive) **then** Pick the preceding NP. o<u>*Heuristic 2-Nominal*</u>(H2Nom) **if** (*Noun belongs to an NP, Search for NP' such that Noun'=same_name(head(NP),head(NP'))* **or** *Noun'=same_name(adjunct(NP),adjunct(NP')))* **then if** *(Noun' belongs to coreference chain CC)* **then** *Pick the element from CC which is closest to Noun in Text.* **else** *Pick Noun'.* o<u>*Heuristic 3-Nominal*</u>(H3Nom) **if** *Noun is the head of an NP* **then** *Search for proper name PN such that head(PN)=Noun* **if** *(PN belongs to coreference chain CC)* **and** *there is an element from CC which is closest to Noun in Text, Pick that element.* **else** *Pick PN.*

Table 1: Best performing heuristics implemented in COCKTAIL

2.2 Knowledge-Poor Coreference Resolution

The result of our data-driven methodology is the set of heuristics implemented in COCKTAIL which cover both nominal and pronoun coreference. Each heuristic represents a pattern of coreference that was mined from the large set of coreference data. COCKTAIL uses knowledge-poor methods because (a) it is based only on a limited number of heuristics and (b) text processing is limited to part-of-speech tagging, named-entity recognition, and approximate phrasal parsing. The heuristics from COCKTAIL can be classified along two directions. First of all, they can be grouped according to the type of coreference they resolve, e.g., heuristics that resolve the anaphors of reflexive pronouns operate differently than those resolving bare nominals. Currently, in COCKTAIL there are heuristics that resolve five types of pronouns (personal, possessive, reflexive, demonstrative and relative) and three forms of nominals (definite, bare and indefinite).

Secondly, for each type of coreference, there are three classes of heuristics categorized according to their suitability to resolve coreference. The first class is comprised of strong indicators of coreference. This class resulted from the analysis of the distribution of the antecedents in the MUC annotated data. For example, repetitions of named entities and appositives account for the majority of the nominal coreferences, and, therefore, represent anchors for the first class of heuristics.

The second class of coreference covers cases in which the arguments are recognized to be semantically consistent. COCKTAIL's test of semantic consistency blends together information available from WordNet and statistics gathered from Treebank. Different consistency checks are modeled for each of the heuristics.

Example of the application of heuristic H2Pron
Mr. Adams$_1$, 69 years old, is the retired chairman of Canadian-based Emco Ltd., a maker of plumbing and petroleum equipment; *he*$_1$ has served on the Woolworth board since 1981.
Example of the application of heuristic H3Pron
"We have got to stop pointing our fingers at *these kids*$_2$ who have no future," he said, "and reach our hands out to *them*$_2$.
Example of the application of heuristic H2Nom
The chairman and *the chief executive officer*$_3$ of Woolworth Corp. have temporarily relinquished their posts while the retailer conducts its investigation into *alleged accounting irregularities*$_4$. Woolworth's board named John W. Adams, an outsider, to serve as interim chairman and *executive officer*$_3$, while a special committee, appointed by the board last week and led by Mr. Adams, investigates *the alleged irregularities*$_4$.

Table 2: Examples of coreference resolution. The same annotated index indicates coreference.

The third class of heuristics resolves coreference by coercing nominals. Sometimes coercions involve only derivational morphology - linking verbs with their nominalizations. On other occasions, coercions are obtained as paths of meronyms (e.g. is-part relations) and hypernyms (e.g. is-a relations). Consistency checks implemented for this class of coreference are conservative: either the adjuncts must be identical or the adjunct of the referent must be less specific than the antecedent. Table 1 lists the top performing heuristics of COCKTAIL for pronominal and nominal coreference. Examples of the heuristics operation on the MUC data are presented presented in Table 2. Details of the top performing heuristics of COCKTAIL were reported in (Harabagiu and Maiorano, 1999).

2.3 Bootstrapping for Coreference Resolution

One of the major drawbacks of existing coreference resolution systems is their inability to recognize many forms of coreference displayed by many real-world texts. Recall measures of current systems range between 36% and 59% for both knowledge-based and statistical techniques. Knowledge based-systems would perform better if more coreference constraints were available whereas statistical methods would be improved if more annotated data were available. Since knowledge-based techniques outperform inductive methods, we used high-precision coreference heuristics as knowledge seeds for machine learning techniques that operate on large amounts of unlabeled data. One such technique is *bootstrapping*, which was recently presented in (Riloff and Jones 1999), (Jones et al.1999) as an ideal framework for text learning tasks that have knowledge seeds. The method does not require large training sets. We extended COCKTAIL by using *meta-bootstrapping* of both new heuristics and clusters of nouns that display semantic consistency for coreference.

The coreference heuristics are the seeds of our bootstrapping framework for coreference resolution. When applied to large collections of texts, the heuristics determine classes of coreferring expressions. By generating coreference chains out of all these coreferring expressions, often new heuristics are uncovered. For example, Figure 2 illustrates the application of three heuristics and the generation of data for a new heuristic rule. In COCKTAIL, after a heuristic is applied, a new coreference chain is calculated. For the example illustrated in Figure 2, if the reference of expression A is sought, heuristic H1 indicates expression B to be the antecedent. When the coreference chain is built, expression A is directly linked to expression D, thus uncovering a new heuristic H0.

As a rule of thumb, we do not consider a new heuristic unless there is massive evidence of its coverage in the data. To measure the coverage we use the *FOIL_Gain measure*, as introduced by the FOIL inductive algorithm (Cameron-Jones and Quinlan 1993). Let H_0 be the new heuristic and H_1 a heuristic that is already in the seed set. Let p_0 be the number of positive coreference examples of H_{new} (i.e. the number of coreference relations produced by the heuristic that can be found in the test data) and n_0 the number of negative examples of H_{new} (i.e. the number of relations generated by the heuristic which cannot be found in the test data). Similarly, p_1 and n_1 are the positive and negative examples of H_1. The new heuristics are scored by their *FOIL_Gain* distance to the existing set of heuristics, and the best scoring one is added to the COCKTAIL system. The *FOIL_Gain* formula is:

$$FOIL\_Gain(H_1, H_0) = k(log_2 \frac{p_1}{p_1 + n_1} - log_2 \frac{p_0}{p_0 + n_0})$$

where k is the number of positive examples covered by both H_1 and H_0. Heuristic H_0 is added to the seed set if there is no other heuristic providing larger *FOIL_Gain* to any of the seed heuristics.

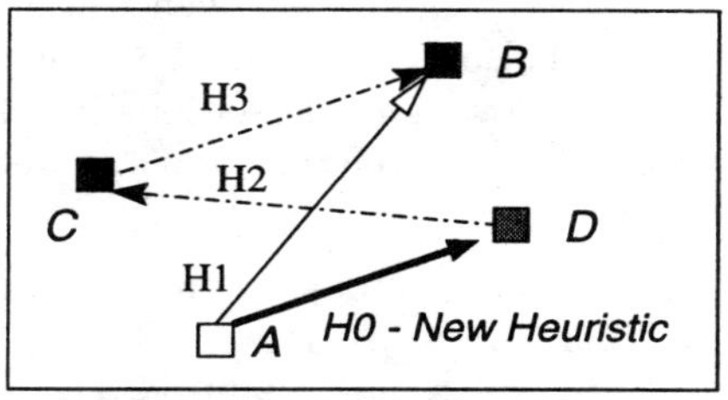

Figure 2: Bootstrapping new heuristics.

Since in COCKTAIL, semantic consistency of coreferring expressions is checked by comparing the similarity of noun classes, each new heuristic determines the adjustment of the similarity threshold of all known coreferring noun classes. The steps of the bootstrapping algorithm that learns both new heuristics and adjusts the similarity threshold of coreferential expressions is:

MUTUAL BOOTSTRAPPING LOOP

1. *Score all candidate heuristics with FOIL_Gain*
2. *Best_h=closest candidate to heuristics(COCKTAIL)*
3. *Add Best_h to heuristics(COCKTAIL)*
4. *Adjust semantic similarity threshold for semantic consistency of coreferring nouns*
5. *Goto step 1 if the precision and recall did not degrade under minimal performance.*

(Riloff and Jones 1999) note that the bootstrapping algorithm works well but its performance can deteriorate rapidly when non-coreferring data enter as candidate heuristics. To make the algorithm more robust, a second level of bootstrapping can be introduced. The outer bootstrapping mechanism, called *meta-bootstrapping* compiles the results of the inner (mutual) bootstrapping process and identifies the k most reliable heuristics, where k is a number determined experimentally. These k heuristics are retained and the rest of them are discarded.

3 SWIZZLE

3.1 Multilingual Coreference Data

To study the performance of a data-driven multilingual coreference resolution system, we prepared a corpus of Romanian texts by translating the MUC-6 and MUC-7 coreference training texts. The translations were performed by a group of four Romanian native speakers, and were checked for style by a certified translator from Romania. In addition, the Romanian texts were annotated with coreference keys. Two rules were followed when the annotations were done:

∘*1:* Whenever an expression E_R represents a translation of an expression E_E from the corresponding English text, if E_E is tagged as a coreference key with identification number *ID*, then the Romanian expression E_R is also tagged with the same *ID* number. This rule allows for translations in which the textual position of the referent and the antecedent have been swapped.

∘*2:* Since the translations often introduce new coreferring expressions in the same chain, the new expressions are given new, unused *ID* numbers. For example, Table 3 lists corresponding English and Romanian fragments of coreference chains from the original MUC-6 Wall Street Journal document DOCNO: 930729-0143.

Table 3 also shows the original MUC coreference SGML annotations. Whenever present, the *REF* tag indicates the *ID* of the antecedent, whereas the *MIN* tag indicates the minimal reference expression.

3.2 Lexical Resources

The multilingual coreference resolution method implemented in `SWIZZLE` incorporates the heuristics derived from `COKCTAIL`'s monolingual coreference resolution processing in both languages. To this end, `COCKTAIL` required both sets of texts to be tagged for part-of-speech and to recognize the noun phrases. The English texts were parsed with Brill's part-of-speech tagger (Brill 1992) and the noun phrases were identified by the grammar rules implemented in the phrasal parser of `FASTUS` (Appelt et al., 1993). Corresponding resources are not available in Romanian.

To minimize `COCKTAIL`'s configuration for processing Romanian texts, we implemented a Romanian part-of-speech rule-based tagger that used the same

Economic adviser Gene Sperling described <COREF ID="29" TYPE="IDENT" REF="30"> **it**< /COREF> as "a true full-court press" to pass <COREF ID="31" TYPE="IDENT" REF="26" MIN="bill">**the** <COREF ID="32" TYPE="IDENT" REF="10" MIN="reduction"> <COREF ID="33" TYPE="IDENT" REF="12"> **deficit**< /COREF>**-reduction**< /COREF> bill, the final version of which is now being hammered out by <COREF ID="43">**House** < /COREF> and <COREF ID="41">**Senate** < /COREF>**negotiators**< /COREF>.

....

<COREF ID="34" TYPE="IDENT" REF="2"> The executives< /COREF>' backing – however tepid – gives the administration a way to counter <COREF ID="35" TYPE="IDENT" REF="36"> **business**< /COREF> critics of <COREF ID="500" TYPE="IDENT" REF="31" MIN="package" STATUS="OPT">**the overall package** < /COREF>,...

Consilierul cu probleme economice Gene Sperling a descris-<COREF ID="29" TYPE="IDENT" REF="30">**o**< /COREF> ca pe un efort de avengură menit să promoveze <COREF ID="1125" TYPE="IDENT" REF="26" MIN="legea">**legea** < /COREF> pentru <COREF TYPE="IDENT" REF="10" MIN="reducerea"> reducerea < /COREF><COREF ID="33" TYPE="IDENT" REF="12"> deficitului in bugetul SUA< /COREF>. Versiunea finala a acestei <COREF ID="1126" TYPE="IDENT" REF="1125" MIN="legi">**legi** < /COREF> este desfiinţată chiar în aceste zile în cadrul dezbaterilor ce au loc în <COREF ID="43">**Camera Reprezentativilor** < /COREF> şi în <COREF ID="41"> **Senat**< /COREF>< /COREF>.

....

Sprijinirea <COREF ID="127" TYPE="IDENT" REF="1126" MIN="legii">**legii**> /COREF> de către specialişti în economie – deşi în manieră moderată – oferă administraţiei o modalitate de a contrabalansa criticile aduse <COREF ID="500" TYPE="IDENT" REF="31" MIN="legii" STATUS="OPT">**legii**< /COREF> de către companiile americane,...

Table 3: Example of parallel English and Romanian text annotated for coreference. The elements from a coreference chain in the respective texts are underlined. The English text has only two elements in the coreference chain, whereas the Romanian text contains four different elements. The two additional elements of the Romanian coreference chain are derived due to (1) the need to translate the relative clause from the English fragment into a separate sentence in Romanian; and (2) the reordering of words in the second sentence.

tags as generated by the Brill tagger. In addition, we implemented rules that identify noun phrases in Romanian.

To take advantage of the aligned corpus, SWIZZLE also relied on bilingual lexical resources that help translate the referential expressions. For this purpose, we used a core Romanian WordNet (Harabagiu, 1999) which encoded, wherever possible, links between the English synsets and their Romanian counterparts. This resource also incorporated knowledge derived from several bilingual dictionaries (e.g. (Bantaş, 1969)).

Having the parallel coreference annotations, we can easily identify their translations because they have the same identification coreference key. Looking at the example given in Table 3, the expression *"legii"*, with *ID=500* is the translation of the expression *"package"*, having the same *ID* in the English text. However, in the test set, the *REF* fields are intentionally voided, entrusting COCKTAIL to identify the antecedents. The bilingual coreference resolution performed in SWIZZLE, however, requires the translations of the English and Romanian antecedents. The principles guiding the translations of the English and Romanian antecedents (A^{E-R} and A^{R-E}, respectively) are:

• *Circularity:* Given an English antecedent, due to semantic ambiguity, it can belong to several English WordNet sysnsets. For each such sysnset S_i^E we consider the Romanian corresponding sysnet(s) S_j^R. We filter out all S_j^R that do not contain A^{E-R}. If only one Romanian sysnset is left, then we identified a translation. Otherwise, we start from the Romanian antecedent, find all synsets S_k^R to which it belongs, and obtain the corresponding English sysnets S_l^E. Similarly, all English synsets not containing the English antecedent are filtered out. If only one synset remains, we have again identified a translation. Finally, in the last case, the intersection of the multiple synsets in either language generates a legal translation. For example, the English synset S^E ={*bill, measure*} translates into the Romanian synset S^R ={*lege*}. First, none of the dictionary translations of *bill* into Romanian (e.g. *poliţă, bacnotă, afiş*) translate back into any of the elements of S^E. However the translation of *measure* into the Romanian *lege* translates back into *bill*, its synonym.

• *Semantic density:* Given an English and a Romanian antecedent, to establish whether they are translations of one another, we disambiguate them by first collapsing all sysnsets that have common elements. Then we apply the circularity principle, relying on the semantic alignment encoded in the Romanian WordNet. When this core lexical database was first implemented, several other principles were applied. In our experiment, we were satisfied with the quality of the translations recognized by following only these two principles.

3.3 Multilingual Coreference Resolution

The SWIZZLE system was run on a corpus of 2335 referential expressions in English (927 from MUC-6 and 1408 from MUC-7) and 2851 Romanian expressions (1219 from MUC-6 and 1632 from MUC-7). Initially, the heuristics implemented in COCKTAIL were applied separately to the two textual collections. Several special cases arose.

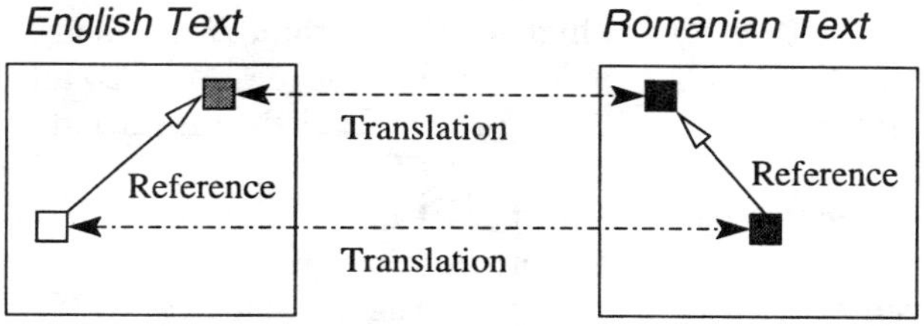

Figure 3: Case 1 of multilingual coreference

Case 1, which is the ideal case, is shown in Figure 3. It occurs when two referential expressions have antecedents that are translations of one another. This situation occurred in 63.3% of the referential expressions from MUC-6 and in 58.7% of the MUC-7 references. Over 50% of these are pronouns or named entities. However, all the non-ideal cases are more interesting for SWIZZLE, since they port knowledge that enhances system performance.

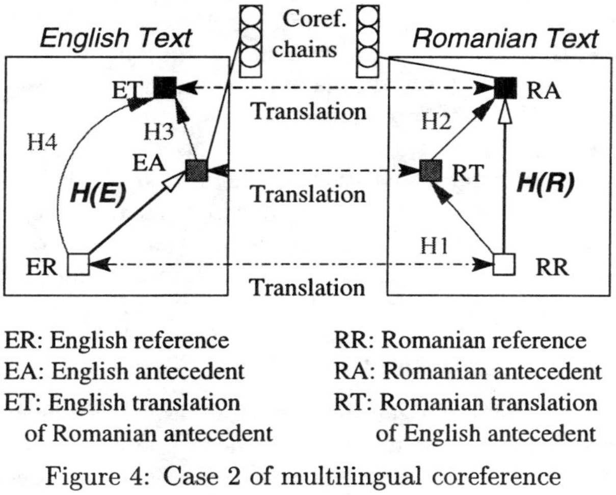

Figure 4: Case 2 of multilingual coreference

Case 2 occurs when the antecedents are not translations, but belong to or corefer with elements of some coreference chains that were already established. Moreover, one of the antecedents is textually closer to its referent. Figure 4 illustrates the case when the English antecedent is closer to the referent than the Romanian one.

SWIZZLE Solutions: (1) If the heuristic *H(E)* used to resolve the reference in the English text has higher priority than *H(R)*, which was used to resolve the reference from the Romanian text, then we first search for *RT*, the Romanian translation of *EA*, the English antecedent. In the next step, we add heuristic *H1* that resolves *RR* into *RT*, and give it a higher priority than *H(R)*. Finally, we also add heuristic *H2* that links *RT* to *RA* when there is at least one translation between the elements of the coreference chains containing *EA* and *ET* respectively.

(2) If *H(R)* has higher priority than *H(E)*, heuristic *H3* is added while *H(E)* is removed. We also add *H4* that relates *ER* to *ET*, the English translation of *RA*.

Case 3 occurs when at least one of the antecedents starts a new coreference chain (i.e., no coreferring antecedent can be found in the current chains).

SWIZZLE Solution: If one of the antecedents corefers with an element from a coreference chain, then the antecedent in the opposite language is its translation. Otherwise, SWIZZLE chooses the antecedent returned by the heuristic with highest priority.

4 Results

The foremost contribution of SWIZZLE was that it improved coreference resolution over both English and Romanian texts when compared to monolingual coreference resolution performance in terms of precision and recall. Also relevant was the contribution of SWIZZLE to the process of understanding the cultural differences expressed in language and the way these differences influence coreference resolution. Because we do not have sufficient space to discuss this issue in detail here, let us state, in short, that English is more economical than Romanian in terms of referential expressions. However the referential expressions in Romanian contribute to the resolution of some of the most difficult forms of coreference in English.

4.1 Precision and Recall

Table 4 summarizes the precision results for both English and Romanian coreference. The results indicate that the English coreference is more precise than the Romanian coreference, but SWIZZLE improves coreference resolution in both languages. There were 64% cases when the English coreference was resolved by a heuristic with higher priority than the corresponding heuristic for the Romanian counterpart. This result explains why there is better precision enhancement for the English coreference.

	Nominal	Pronominal	Total
English	73%	89%	84%
Romanian	66%	78%	72%
SWIZZLE on English	76%	93%	87%
SWIZZLE on Romanian	71%	82%	76%

Table 4: Coreference precision

	Nominal	Pronominal	Total
English	69%	89%	78%
Romanian	63%	83%	72%
SWIZZLE on English	66%	87%	77%
SWIZZLE on Romanian	61%	80%	70%

Table 5: Coreference recall

Table 5 also illustrates the recall results. The advantage of the data-driven coreference resolution over other methods is based on its better recall performance. This is explained by the fact that this method captures a larger variety of coreference patterns. Even though other coreference resolution systems perform better for some specific forms of reference, their recall results are surpassed by the data-driven approach. Multilingual coreference in turn improves more the precision than the recall of the monolingual data-driven coreference systems.

In addition, Table 5 shows that the English coreference results in better recall than Romanian coreference. However, the recall shows a decrease for both languages for SWIZZLE because imprecise coreference links are deleted. As is usually the case, deleting data lowers the *recall.* All results were obtained by using the automatic scorer program developed for the MUC evaluations.

5 Conclusions

We have introduced a new data-driven method for multilingual coreference resolution, implemented in the SWIZZLE system. The results of this method are encouraging since they show clear improvements over monolingual coreference resolution. Currently, we are also considering the effects of a bootstrapping algorithm for multilingual coreference resolution. Through this procedure we would learn concurrently semantic consistency knowledge and better performing heuristic rules. To be able to develop such a learning approach, we must first develop a method for automatic recognition of multilingual referential expressions.

We also believe that a better performance evaluation of SWIZZLE can be achieved by measuring its impact on several complex applications. We intend to analyze the performance of SWIZZLE when it is used as a module in an IE system, and separately in a Question/Answering system.

Acknowledgements This paper is dedicated to the memory of our friend Megumi Kameyama, who inspired this work.

References

Douglas E. Appelt, Jerry R. Hobbs, John Bear, David Israel, Megumi Kameyama and Mabry Tyson. 1993. The SRI MUC-5 JV-FASTUS Information Extraction System. In *Proceedings of the Fifth Message Understanding Conference (MUC-5)*.

Brack Baldwin. 1997. CogNIAC: high precision coreference with limited knowledge and linguistic resources. In *Proceedings of the ACL'97/EACL'97 Workshop on Operational factors in practical, robust anaphora resolution*, pages 38–45, Madrid, Spain.

Andrei Bantaş. 1969. Dicţionar Român-Englez, Enlgez-Român. Editura Ştiinţifică, Bucureşti.

David Bean and Ellen Riloff. 1999. Corpus-Based Identification of Non-Anaphoric Noun Phrases. In *Proceedings of the 37th Conference of the Assosiation for Computatioanl Linguistics (ACL-99)*, pages 373–380.

Eric Brill. A simple rule-based part of speech tagger. In *Proceedings of the Third Conference on Applied Natural Language Processing*, pages 152–155, 1992.

Joseph F. Cameron-Jones and Ross Quinlan. 1993. Avoiding Pitfalls When Learning Recursive Theories. In *Proceedings of the 13th International Joint Conference on Artificial Intelligence (IJCAI-93)*, pages 1050-1055.

Claire Cardie and Kiri Wagstaff. 1999. Noun phrase coreference as clustering. In *Proceedings of the Joint Conference on Empirical Methods in NLP and Very Large Corpora*, pages 82–89.

Niyu Ge, John Gale and Eugene Charniak. 1998. Anaphora Resolution: A Multi-Strategy Approach. In *Proceedings of the 6th Workshop on Very Large Corpora, (COLING/ACL'98)*.

Ido Dagan and Ken W. Church. 1994. TERMIGHT: Identifying and translating technical terminology. In *Proceedings of the 4th ACL Conference on Applied Natural Language Processing (ANLP-94)*.

Sanda M. Harabagiu. 1999. Lexical Acquisition for a Romanian WordNet. *Proceeding of the 3rd European Summer School on Computational Linguistics.*

Sanda M. Harabagiu and Steve J. Maiorano. 1999. Knowledge-Lean Coreference Resolution and its Relation to Textual Cohesion and Coherence. In *Proceedings of the Workshop on the Relation of Discourse/Dialogue Structure and Reference, ACL'98*, pages 29–38.

Jerry R. Hobbs. Resolving pronoun references. *Lingua*, 44:311–338.

Andrew Kehler. 1997. Probabilistic Coreference in Information Extraction. In *Proceedings of the Second Conference on Empirical Methods in Natural Language Processing (SIGDAT)*, pages 163–173.

Shalom Lappin and Herbert Leass. 1994. An algorithm for pronominal anaphora resolution. *Computational Linguistics*, 20(4):535–562.

Rosie Jones, Andrew McCallum, Kevin Nigam and Ellen Riloff. 1999. Bootstrapping for Text Learning Tasks. In *Proceedings of the IJCAI-99 Workshop on Text Mining: Foundations, Techniques, and Applications.*

Megumi Kameyama. 1997. Recognizing Referential Links: An Information Extraction Perspective. In *Proceedings of the Workshop on Operational Factors in Practical, Robust Anaphora Resolution for Unrestricted Texts, (ACL-97/EACL-97)*, pages 46–53, Madrid, Spain.

Christopher Kennedy and Branimir Bogureav. 1996. Anaphora for everyone: Pronominal anaphora resolution without a parser. In *Proceedings of the 16th International Conference on Computational Linguistics (COLING-96)*.

George A. Miller. 1995. WordNet: A Lexical Database. *Communication of the ACM*, 38(11):39–41.

Ruslan Mitkov. 1998. Robust pronoun resolution with limited knowledge. In *Proceedings of COLING-ACL'98*, pages 869–875.

1996. *Proceedings of the Sixth Message Understanding Conference (MUC-6)*,Morgan Kaufmann, San Mateo, CA.

1998. *Proceedings of the Seventh Message Understanding Conference (MUC-7)* ,Morgan Kaufmann, San Mateo, CA.

Philip Resnik and I. Dan Melamed. 1997. Semi-Automatic Acquisition of Domain-Specific Translation Lexicons. In *Proceedings of the 5th ACL Conference on Applied Natural Language Processing (ANLP-97)*.

Ellen Riloff and Rosie Jones. 1999. Learning Dictionaries for Information Extraction by Multi-Level Bootstrapping. In *Proceedings of the Sixteenth National Conference on Artificial Intelligence (AAAI-99)*.

Frank Smadja, Katheleen R. McKeown and Vasileios Hatzivassiloglou. 1996. Translating collocations for bilingual lexicons: A statistical approach. *Computational Linguistics* , 21(1):1–38.

Ranking suspected answers to natural language questions using predictive annotation

Dragomir R. Radev*
School of Information
University of Michigan
Ann Arbor, MI 48103
radev@umich.edu

John Prager
TJ Watson Research Center
IBM Research Division
Hawthorne, NY 10532
jprager@us.ibm.com

Valerie Samn*
Teachers College
Columbia University
New York, NY 10027
vs115@columbia.edu

Abstract

In this paper, we describe a system to rank suspected answers to natural language questions. We process both corpus and query using a new technique, predictive annotation, which augments phrases in texts with labels anticipating their being targets of certain kinds of questions. Given a natural language question, our IR system returns a set of matching passages, which we then rank using a linear function of seven predictor variables. We provide an evaluation of the techniques based on results from the TREC Q&A evaluation in which our system participated.

1 Introduction

Question Answering is a task that calls for a combination of techniques from Information Retrieval and Natural Language Processing. The former has the advantage of years of development of efficient techniques for indexing and searching large collections of data, but lacks of any meaningful treatment of the semantics of the query or the texts indexed. NLP tackles the semantics, but tends to be computationally expensive.

We have attempted to carve out a middle ground, whereby we use a modified IR system augmented by shallow NL parsing. Our approach was motivated by the following problem with traditional IR systems. Suppose the user asks "Where did <some event> happen?". If the system does no pre-processing of the query, then "where" will be included in the bag of words submitted to the search engine, but this will not be helpful since the target text will be unlikely to contain the word "where". If the word is stripped out as a stop-word, then the search engine will have no idea that a location is sought. Our approach, called *predictive annotation*, is to augment the query with semantic category markers (which we call *QA-Tokens*), in this case with the PLACE$ token, and also to label with QA-Tokens all occurrences in text that are recognized entities, (for example, places). Then traditional bag-of-words matching proceeds successfully, and will return matching passages. The answer-selection process then looks for and ranks in these passages occurrences of phrases containing the particular QA-Token(s) from the augmented query. This classification of questions is conceptually similar to the query expansion in (Voorhees, 1994) but is expected to achieve much better performance since potentially matching phrases in text are classified in a similar and synergistic way.

Our system participated in the official TREC Q&A evaluation. For 200 questions in the evaluation set, we were asked to provide a list of 50-byte and 250-byte extracts from a 2-GB corpus. The results are shown in Section 7.

Some techniques used by other participants in the TREC evaluation are paragraph indexing, followed by abductive inference (Harabagiu and Maiorano, 1999) and knowledge-representation combined with information retrieval (Breck et al., 1999). Some earlier systems related to our work are FaqFinder (Kulyukin et al., 1998), MURAX (Kupiec, 1993), which uses an encyclopedia as a knowledge base from which to extract answers, and PROFILE (Radev and McKeown, 1997) which identifies named entities and noun phrases that describe them in text.

2 System description

Our system (Figure 1) consists of two pieces: an IR component (GuruQA) that which returns matching texts, and an answer selection compo-

* The work presented in this paper was performed while the first and third authors were at IBM Research.

nent (AnSel/Werlect) that extracts and ranks potential answers from these texts.

This paper focuses on the process of *ranking potential answers* selected by the IR engine, which is itself described in (Prager et al., 1999).

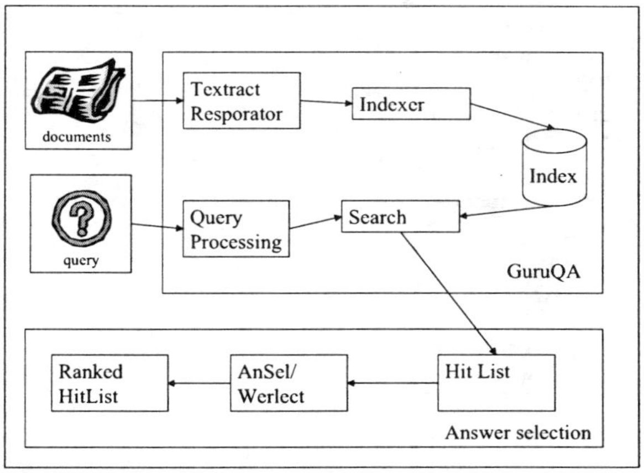

Figure 1: System Architecture.

2.1 The Information Retrieval component

In the context of fact-seeking questions, we made the following observations:

- In documents that contain the answers, the query terms tend to occur in close proximity to each other.
- The answers to fact-seeking questions are usually phrases: "President Clinton", "in the Rocky Mountains", and "today").
- These phrases can be categorized by a set of a dozen or so labels (Figure 2) corresponding to question types.
- The phrases can be identified in text by pattern matching techniques (without full NLP).

As a result, we defined a set of about 20 categories, each labeled with its own QA-Token, and built an IR system which deviates from the traditional model in three important aspects.

- We process the query against a set of approximately 200 question templates which, may replace some of the query words with a set of QA-Tokens, called a **SYN-class**. Thus "Where" gets mapped to "PLACE$", but "How long " goes to "@SYN(LENGTH$, DURATION$)". Some templates do not cause complete replacement of the matched string. For example, the pattern "What is the population" gets replaced by "NUMBER$ population".
- Before indexing the text, we process it with Textract (Byrd and Ravin, 1998; Wacholder et al., 1997), which performs lemmatization, and discovers proper names and technical terms. We added a new module (Resporator) which annotates text segments with QA-Tokens using pattern matching. Thus the text "for 5 centuries" matches the DURATION$ pattern "for :CARDINAL _timeperiod", where :CARDINAL is the label for cardinal numbers, and _timeperiod marks a time expression.
- GuruQA scores text passages instead of documents. We use a simple document- and collection-independent weighting scheme: QA-Tokens get a weight of 400, proper nouns get 200 and any other word - 100 (stop words are removed in query processing after the pattern template matching operation). The density of matching query tokens within a passage is contributes a score of 1 to 99 (the highest scores occur when all matched terms are consecutive).

Predictive Annotation works best for *Where, When, What, Which* and *How+adjective* questions than for *How+verb* and *Why* questions, since the latter are typically not answered by phrases. However, we observed that "by" + the present participle would usually indicate the description of a procedure, so we instantiate a METHOD$ QA-Token for such occurrences. We have no such QA-Token for Why questions, but we do replace the word "why" with "@SYN(result, cause, because)", since the occurrence of any of these words usually betokens an explanation.

3 Answer selection

So far, we have described how we retrieve relevant passages that may contain the answer to a query. The output of GuruQA is a list of 10 short passages containing altogether a large

QA-Token	Question type	Example
PLACE$	Where	In the Rocky Mountains
COUNTRY$	Where/What country	United Kingdom
STATE$	Where/What state	Massachusetts
PERSON$	Who	Albert Einstein
ROLE$	Who	Doctor
NAME$	Who/What/Which	The Shakespeare Festival
ORG$	Who/What	The US Post Office
DURATION$	How long	For 5 centuries
AGE$	How old	30 years old
YEAR$	When/What year	1999
TIME$	When	In the afternoon
DATE$	When/What date	July 4th, 1776
VOLUME$	How big	3 gallons
AREA$	How big	4 square inches
LENGTH$	How big/long/high	3 miles
WEIGHT$	How big/heavy	25 tons
NUMBER$	How many	1,234.5
METHOD$	How	By rubbing
RATE$	How much	50 per cent
MONEY$	How much	4 million dollars

Figure 2: Sample QA-Tokens.

number (often more than 30 or 40) of potential answers in the form of phrases annotated with QA-Tokens.

3.1 Answer ranking

We now describe two algorithms, AnSel and Werlect, which rank the spans returned by GuruQA. AnSel and Werlect[1] use different approaches, which we describe, evaluate and compare and contrast. The output of either system consists of five text extracts per question that contain the likeliest answers to the questions.

3.2 Sample Input to AnSel/Werlect

The role of answer selection is to decide which among the spans extracted by GuruQA are most likely to contain the precise answer to the questions. Figure 3 contains an example of the data structure passed from GuruQA to our answer selection module.

The input consists of four items:

- a query (marked with <QUERY> tokens in the example),
- a list of 10 passages (one of which is shown above),
- a list of annotated text spans within the passages, annotated with QA-Tokens, and
- the SYN-class corresponding to the type of question (e.g., "PERSON$ NAME$").

[1]from ANswer SELect and ansWER seLECT, respectively

The text in Figure 3 contains five spans (potential answers), of which three ("Biography of Margaret Thatcher", "Hugo Young", and "Margaret Thatcher") are of types included in the SYN-class for the question (PERSON NAME). The full output of GuruQA for this question includes a total of 14 potential spans (5 PERSONs and 9 NAMEs).

3.3 Sample Output of AnSel/Werlect

The answer selection module has two outputs: internal (phrase) and external (text passage).

Internal output: The internal output is a ranked list of spans as shown in Table 1. It represents a ranked list of the spans (potential answers) sent by GuruQA.

External output: The external output is a ranked list of 50-byte and 250-byte extracts. These extracts are selected in a way to cover the highest-ranked spans in the list of potential answers. Examples are given later in the paper.

The external output was required for the TREC evaluation while system's internal output can be used in a variety of applications, e.g., to highlight the actual span that we believe is the answer to the question within the context of the passage in which it appears.

```
<p><NUMBER>1</NUMBER></p>

<p><QUERY>Who is the author of the book, "The Iron Lady: A Biography of Margaret Thatcher"?
</QUERY></p>

<p><PROCESSED_QUERY>@excwin(*dynamic* @weight(200 *Iron_Lady) @weight(200
Biography_of_Margaret_Thatcher) @weight(200 Margaret) @weight(100 author)
@weight(100 book) @weight(100 iron) @weight(100 lady) @weight(100 :) @weight(100 biography)
@weight(100 thatcher) @weight(400 @syn(PERSON$ NAME$)))</PROCESSED_QUERY></p>

<p><DOC>LA090290-0118</DOC></p> <p><SCORE>1020.8114</SCORE></p>

<TEXT><p>THE IRON LADY; A <span class="NAME">Biography of Margaret Thatcher </span>
by <span class="PERSON">Hugo Young</span> (<span class="ORG">Farrar , Straus
& Giroux</span>) The central riddle revealed here is why, as a woman <span class="PLACEDEF">in a
man</span>'s world, <span class="PERSON">Margaret Thatcher</span> evinces such an exclusionary
attitude toward women.</p></TEXT>
```

Figure 3: Input sent from GuruQA to AnSel/Werlect.

Score	Span
5.06	Hugo Young
-8.14	Biography of Margaret Thatcher
-13.60	David Williams
-18.00	Williams
-19.38	Sir Ronald Millar
-26.06	Santiago
-31.75	Oxford
-32.38	Maggie
-36.78	Seriously Rich
-42.68	FT
-198.34	Margaret Thatcher
-217.80	Thatcher
-234.55	Iron Lady

Table 1: Ranked potential answers to Quest. 1.

4 Analysis of corpus and question sets

In this section we describe the corpora used for training and evaluation as well as the questions contained in the training and evaluation question sets.

4.1 Corpus analysis

For both training and evaluation, we used the TREC corpus, consisting of approximately 2 GB of articles from four news agencies.

4.2 Training set TR38

To train our system, we used 38 questions (see Figure 4) for which the answers were provided by NIST.

4.3 Test set T200

The majority of the 200 questions (see Figure 5) in the evaluation set (T200) were not substantially different from these in TR38, although the introduction of "why" and "how" questions as well as the wording of questions in the format "Name X" made the task slightly harder.

Question/Answer (TR38)
Q: Who was Johnny Mathis' high school track coach? A: Lou Vasquez
Q: What year was the Magna Carta signed? A: 1215
Q: What two companies produce bovine somatotropin? A: Monsanto and Eli Lilly

Figure 4: Sample questions from TR38.

Question/Answer (T200)
Q: Why did David Koresh ask the FBI for a word processor? A: to record his revelations.
Q: How tall is the Matterhorn? A: 14,776 feet 9 inches
Q: How tall is the replica of the Matterhorn at Disneyland? A: 147-foot

Figure 5: Sample questions from T200.

Some examples of problematic questions are shown in Figure 6.

Q: Why did David Koresh ask the FBI for a word processor?
Q: Name the first private citizen to fly in space.
Q: What is considered the costliest disaster the insurance industry has ever faced?
Q: What did John Hinckley do to impress Jodie Foster?
Q: How did Socrates die?

Figure 6: Sample harder questions from T200.

5 AnSel

AnSel uses an optimization algorithm with 7 predictive variables to describe how likely a given span is to be the correct answer to a question. The variables are illustrated with examples related to the sample question number 10001 from TR38 "Who was Johnny Mathis' high school track coach?". The potential answers (extracted by GuruQA) are shown in Table 2.

5.1 Feature selection

The seven span features described below were found to correlate with the correct answers.

Number: position of the span among all spans returned from the hit-list.

Rspanno: position of the span among all spans returned within the current passage.

Count: number of spans of any span class retrieved within the current passage.

Notinq: the number of words in the span that do not appear in the query.

Type: the position of the span type in the list of potential span types. Example: Type ("Lou Vasquez") = 1, because the span type of "Lou Vasquez", namely "PERSON" appears first in the SYN-class "PERSON ORG NAME ROLE".

Avgdst: the average distance in words between the beginning of the span and query words that also appear in the passage. Example: given the passage "Tim O'Donohue, Woodbridge High School's varsity baseball coach, resigned Monday and will be replaced by assistant Johnny Ceballos, Athletic Director Dave Cowen said." and the span "Tim O'Donohue", the value of avgdst is equal to 8.

Sscore: passage relevance as computed by GuruQA.

Number: the position of the span among all retrieved spans.

5.2 AnSel algorithm

The TOTAL score for a given potential answer is computed as a linear combination of the features described in the previous subsection:

$$TOTAL = \sum_i w_i * f_i$$

The algorithm that the training component of AnSel uses to learn the weights used in the formula is shown in Figure 7.

```
For each <question,span> tuple in training
set:
1. Compute features for each span
2. Compute TOTAL score for each span
   using current set of weights
Repeat
   3. Compute performance on training
      set
   4. Adjust weights wi through
      logistic regression
Until performance > threshold
```

Figure 7: Training algorithm used by AnSel.

Training discovered the following weights: $w_{number} = -0.3; w_{rspanno} = -0.5; w_{count} = 3.0; w_{notinq} = 2.0; w_{types} = 15.0; w_{avgdst} = -1.0; w_{sscore} = 1.5$

At runtime, the weights are used to rank potential answers. Each span is assigned a TOTAL score and the top 5 distinct extracts of 50 (or 250) bytes centered around the span are output. The 50-byte extracts for question 10001 are shown in Figure 8. For lack of space, we are omitting the 250-byte extracts.

6 Werlect

The Werlect algorithm used many of the same features of phrases used by AnSel, but employed a different ranking scheme.

6.1 Approach

Unlike AnSel, Werlect is based on a two-step, rule-based process approximating a function with interaction between variables. In the first stage of this algorithm, we assign a rank to

Span	Type	Number	Rspanno	Count	Notinq	Type	Avgdst	Sscore	TOTAL
Ollie Matson	PERSON	3	3	6	2	1	12	0.02507	-7.53
Lou Vasquez	PERSON	1	1	6	2	1	16	0.02507	-9.93
Tim O'Donohue	PERSON	17	1	4	2	1	8	0.02257	-12.57
Athletic Director Dave Cowen	PERSON	23	6	4	4	1	11	0.02257	-15.87
Johnny Ceballos	PERSON	22	5	4	1	1	9	0.02257	-19.07
Civic Center Director Martin Durham	PERSON	13	1	2	5	1	16	0.02505	-19.36
Johnny Hodges	PERSON	25	2	4	1	1	15	0.02256	-25.22
Derric Evans	PERSON	33	4	4	2	1	14	0.02256	-25.37
NEWSWIRE Johnny Majors	PERSON	30	1	4	2	1	17	0.02256	-25.47
Woodbridge High School	ORG	18	2	4	1	2	6	0.02257	-28.37
Evan	PERSON	37	6	4	1	1	14	0.02256	-29.57
Gary Edwards	PERSON	38	7	4	2	1	17	0.02256	-30.87
O.J. Simpson	NAME	2	2	6	2	3	12	0.02507	-37.40
South Lake Tahoe	NAME	7	5	6	3	3	14	0.02507	-40.06
Washington High	NAME	10	6	6	1	3	18	0.02507	-49.80
Morgan	NAME	26	3	4	1	3	12	0.02256	-52.52
Tennesseefootball	NAME	31	2	4	1	3	15	0.02256	-56.27
Ellington	NAME	24	1	4	1	3	20	0.02256	-59.42
assistant	ROLE	21	4	4	1	4	8	0.02257	-62.77
the Volunteers	ROLE	34	5	4	2	4	14	0.02256	-71.17
Johnny Mathis	PERSON	4	4	6	-100	1	11	0.02507	-211.33
Mathis	NAME	14	2	2	-100	3	10	0.02505	-254.16
coach	ROLE	19	3	4	-100	4	4	0.02257	-259.67

Table 2: Feature set and span rankings for training question 10001.

Document ID	Score	Extract
LA053189-0069	892.5	of O.J. Simpson , Ollie Matson and Johnny Mathis
LA053189-0069	890.1	Lou Vasquez , track coach of O.J. Simpson , Ollie
LA060889-0181	887.4	Tim O'Donohue , Woodbridge High School 's varsity
LA060889-0181	884.1	nny Ceballos , Athletic Director Dave Cowen said.
LA060889-0181	880.9	aced by assistant Johnny Ceballos , Athletic Direc

Figure 8: Fifty-byte extracts.

every relevant phrase within each sentence according to how likely it is to be the target answer. Next, we generate and rank each N-byte fragment based on the sentence score given by GuruQA, measures of the fragment's relevance, and the ranks of its component phrases. Unlike AnSel, Werlect was optimized through manual trial-and-error using the TR38 questions.

6.2 Step One: Feature Selection

The features considered in Werlect that were also used by AnSel, were Type, Avgdst and Sscore. Two additional features were also taken into account:

NotinqW: a modified version of Notinq. As in AnSel, spans that are contained in the query are given a rank of 0. However, partial matches are weighted favorably in some cases. For example, if the question asks, "Who was Lincoln's Secretary of State?" a noun phrase that contains "Secretary of State" is more likely to be the answer than one that does not. In this example, the phrase, "Secretary of State William Seward" is the most likely candidate. This criterion also seems to play a role in the event that Resporator fails to identify relevant phrase types. For example, in the training question, "What shape is a porpoise's tooth?" the phrase "spade-shaped" is correctly selected from among all nouns and adjectives of the sentences returned by Guru-QA.

Frequency: how often the span occurs across different passages. For example, the test question, "How many lives were lost in the Pan Am crash in Lockerbie, Scotland?" resulted in four potential answers in the first two sentences returned by Guru-QA. Table 3 shows the frequencies of each term, and their eventual influence on the span rank. The repeated occurrence of "270", helps promote it to first place.

6.3 Step two: ranking the sentence spans

After each relevant span is assigned a rank, we rank all possible text segments of 50 (or 250) bytes from the hit list based on the sum of the phrase ranks plus additional points for other words in the segment that match the query.

The algorithm used by Werlect is shown in Figure 9.

Initial Sentence Rank	Phrase	Frequency	Span Rank
1	Two	5	2
1	365 million	1	3
1	11	1	4
2	270	7	1 (ranked highest)

Table 3: Influence of frequency on span rank.

```
1. Let candidate_set = all potential
   answers, ranked and sorted.
2. For each hit-list passage, extract
   all spans of 50 (or 250) bytes, on
   word boundaries.
3. Rank and sort all segments based
   on phrase ranks, matching terms,
   and sentence ranks.
4. For each candidate in sorted
   candidate_set
     - Let highest_ranked_span
       = highest-ranked span
       containing candidate
     - Let answer_set[i++] =
       highest_ranked_span
     - Remove every candidate from
       candidate_set that is found in
       highest_ranked_span
     - Exit if i > 5
5. Output answer_set
```

Figure 9: Algorithm used by Werlect.

7 Evaluation

In this section, we describe the performance of our system using results from our four official runs.

7.1 Evaluation scheme

For each question, the performance is computed as the reciprocal value of the rank (RAR) of the highest-ranked correct answer given by the system. For example, if the system has given the correct answer in three positions: second, third, and fifth, RAR for that question is $\frac{1}{2}$.

The Mean Reciprocal Answer Rank (MRAR) is used to compute the overall performance of systems participating in the TREC evaluation:

$$RAR = \frac{1}{rank_i}, MRAR = \frac{1}{n}(\sum_i^n \frac{1}{rank_i})$$

7.2 Performance on the official evaluation data

Overall, Ansel (runs A50 and A25) performed marginally better than Werlect. However, we noted that on the 14 questions we were unable to classify with a QA-Token, Werlect (runs W50 and W250) achieved an MRAR of 3.5 to Ansel's 2.0.

The cumulative RAR of A50 on T200 (Table 4) is 63.22 (i.e., we got 49 questions among the 198 right from our first try and 39 others within the first five answers).

The performance of A250 on T200 is shown in Table 5. We were able to answer 71 questions with our first answer and 38 others within our first five answers (cumulative RAR = 85.17).

To better characterize the performance of our system, we split the 198 questions into 20 groups of 10 questions. Our performance on groups of questions ranged from 0.87 to 5.50 MRAR for A50 and from 1.98 to 7.5 MRAR for A250 (Table 6).

	50 bytes	250 bytes
n	20	20
Avg	3.19	4.30
Min	0.87	1.98
Max	5.50	7.50
Std Dev	1.17	1.27

Table 6: Performance on groups of ten questions

Finally, Table 7 shows how our official runs compare to the rest of the 25 official submissions. Our performance using AnSel and 50-byte output was 0.430. The performance of Werlect was 0.395. On 250 bytes, AnSel scored 0.319 and Werlect - 0.280.

8 Conclusion

We presented a new technique, **predictive annotation**, for finding answers to natural language questions in text corpora. We showed that a system based on predictive annotation can deliver very good results compared to other competing systems.

We described a set of features that correlate with the plausibility of a given text span being a good answer to a question. We experi-

	First	Second	Third	Fourth	Fifth	TOTAL
nb of cases	49	15	11	9	4	88
Points	49.00	7.50	3.67	2.25	0.80	63.22

Table 4: Performance of A50 on T200

	First	Second	Third	Fourth	Fifth	TOTAL
nb of cases	71	16	11	6	5	109
Points	71.00	8.00	3.67	1.50	1.00	85.17

Table 5: Performance of A250 on T200

Run	Median Average	Our Average	Nb Times > Median	Nb Times = Median	Nb Times < Median
W50	0.12	0.280	56	126	16
A50	0.12	0.319	72	112	14
W250	0.29	0.395	60	106	32
A250	0.29	0.430	66	110	22

Table 7: Comparison of our system with the other participants

mented with two algorithms for ranking potential answers based on these features. We discovered that a linear combination of these features performs better overall, while a non-linear algorithm performs better on unclassified questions.

9 Acknowledgments

We would like to thank Eric Brown, Anni Coden, and Wlodek Zadrozny from IBM Research for useful comments and collaboration. We would also like to thank the organizers of the TREC Q&A evaluation for initiating such a wonderful research initiative.

References

Eric Breck, John Burger, David House, Marc Light, and Inderjeet Mani. 1999. Question answering from large document collections. In *Proceedings of AAAI Fall Symposium on Question Answering Systems*, North Falmouth, Massachusetts.

Roy Byrd and Yael Ravin. 1998. Identifying and extracting relations in text. In *Proceedings of NLDB*, Klagenfurt, Austria.

Sanda Harabagiu and Steven J. Maiorano. 1999. Finding answers in large collections of texts : Paragraph indexing + abductive inference. In *Proceedings of AAAI Fall Symposium on Question Answering Systems*, North Falmouth, Massachusetts.

Vladimir Kulyukin, Kristian Hammond, and Robin Burke. 1998. Answering questions for an organization online. In *Proceedings of AAAI*, Madison, Wisconsin.

Julian M. Kupiec. 1993. MURAX: A robust linguistic approach for question answering using an on-line encyclopedia. In *Proceedings, 16th Annual International ACM SIGIR Conference on Research and Development in Information Retrieval.*

John Prager, Dragomir R. Radev, Eric Brown, Anni Coden, and Valerie Samn. 1999. The use of predictive annotation for question answering in TREC8. In *Proceedings of TREC-8*, Gaithersburg, Maryland.

Dragomir R. Radev and Kathleen R. McKeown. 1997. Building a generation knowledge source using internet-accessible newswire. In *Proceedings of the 5th Conference on Applied Natural Language Processing*, pages 221–228, Washington, DC, April.

Ellen Voorhees. 1994. Query expansion using lexical-semantic relations. In *Proceedings of ACM SIGIR*, Dublin, Ireland.

Nina Wacholder, Yael Ravin, and Misook Choi. 1997. Disambiguation of proper names in text. In *Proceedings of the Fifth Applied Natural Language Processing Conference*, Washington, D.C. Association for Computational Linguistics.

Message Classification in the Call Center

Stephan Busemann, Sven Schmeier, Roman G. Arens
DFKI GmbH
Stuhlsatzenhausweg 3, D-66123 Saarbrücken, Germany
e-mail: {busemann, schmeier, arens}@dfki.de

Abstract

Customer care in technical domains is increasingly based on e-mail communication, allowing for the reproduction of approved solutions. Identifying the customer's problem is often time-consuming, as the problem space changes if new products are launched. This paper describes a new approach to the classification of e-mail requests based on shallow text processing and machine learning techniques. It is implemented within an assistance system for call center agents that is used in a commercial setting.

1 Introduction

Customer care in technical domains is increasingly based on e-mail communication, allowing for the reproduction of approved solutions. For a call center agent, identifying the customer's problem is often time-consuming, as the problem space changes if new products are launched or existing regulations are modified. The typical task of a call center agent processing e-mail requests consists of the following steps:

Recognize the problem(s): read and understand the e-mail request;

Search a solution: identify and select predefined text blocks;

Provide the solution: if necessary, customize text blocks to meet the current request, and send the text.

This task can partly be automated by a system suggesting relevant solutions for an incoming e-mail. This would cover the first two steps. The last step can be delicate, as its primary goal is to keep the customer satisfied. Thus human intervention seems mandatory to allow for individual, customized answers. Such a system will

- reduce the training effort required since agents don't have to know every possible solution for every possible problem;
- increase the agents' performance since agents can more quickly select a solution among several offered than searching one;
- improve the quality of responses since agents will behave more homogeneously – both as a group and over time – and commit fewer errors.

Given that free text about arbitrary topics must be processed, in-depth approaches to language understanding are not feasible. Given further that the topics may change over time, a top-down approach to knowledge modeling is out of the question. Rather a combination of shallow text processing (STP) with statistics-based machine learning techniques (SML) is called for. STP gathers partial information about text such as part of speech, word stems, negations, or sentence type. These types of information can be used to identify the linguistic properties of a large training set of categorized e-mails. SML techniques are used to build a classifier that is used for new, incoming messages. Obviously, the change of topics can be accommodated by adding new categories and e-mails and producing a new classifier on the basis of old and new data. We call this replacement of a classifier "relearning".

This paper describes a new approach to the classification of e-mail requests along these lines. It is implemented within the ICC-MAIL system, which is an assistance system for call center agents that is currently used in a commercial setting. Section 2 describes important properties of the input data, i.e. the e-mail texts on the one hand, and the categories on the other. These properties influenced the system architecture, which is presented in Section 3. Various publicly available SML systems have been tested with different methods of STP-based preprocessing. Section 4 describes the results. The implementation and usage of the system including the graphical user interface is presented in Section 5. We conclude by giving an outlook to further expected improvements (Section 6).

2 Data Characteristics

A closer look at the data the ICC-MAIL system is processing will clarify the task further. We carried out experiments with unmodified e-mail data accumulated over a period of three months in the call center database. The total amount was 4777 e-mails.

We used 47 categories, which contained at least 30 documents. This minimum amount of documents turned out to render the category sufficiently distinguishable for the SML tools. The database contained 74 categories with at least 10 documents, but the selected ones covered 94% of all e-mails, i.e. 4490 documents.

It has not yet generally been investigated how the type of data influences the learning result (Yang, 1999), or under which circumstances which kind of preprocessing and which learning algorithm is most appropriate. Several aspects must be considered: Length of the documents, morphological and syntactic well-formedness, the degree to which a document can be uniquely classified, and, of course, the language of the documents.

In our application domain the documents differ very much from documents generally used in benchmark tests, for example the Reuters corpus[1]. First of all, we have to deal with German, whereas the Reuters data are in English. The average length of our e-mails is 60 words, whereas for documents of Reuters-21578 it is 129 words. The number of categories we used compares to the top 47 categories of the Reuters *TOPICS* category set. While we have 5008 documents, *TOPICS* consists of 13321 instances[2]. The Reuters documents usually are morphologically and syntactically well-formed. As emails are a more spontaneously created and informal type of document, they require us to cope with a large amount of jargon, misspellings and grammatical inaccuracy. A drastic example is shown in Figure 2. The bad conformance to linguistic standards was a major argument in favor of STP instead of in-depth syntactic and semantic analysis.

The degree to which a document can be uniquely classified is hard to verify and can only be inferred from the results in general terms.[3] It is, however, dependent on the ability to uniquely distinguish the classes. In our application we encounter overlapping and non-exhaustive categories as the category system develops over time.

3 Integrating Language Technology With Machine Learning

STP and SML correspond to two different paradigms. STP tools used for classification tasks promise very high recall/precision or accuracy values. Usually human experts define one or several template structures to be filled automatically by extracting information from the documents (cf. e.g. (Ciravegna et al., 1999)). Afterwards, the partially filled templates are classified by hand-made rules. The whole process brings about high costs in analyzing and modeling the application domain, especially if it is to take into account the problem of changing categories in the present application.

SML promises low costs both in analyzing and modeling the application at the expense of a lower accuracy. It is independent of the domain on the one hand, but does not consider any domain specific knowledge on the other.

By combining both methodologies in ICC-MAIL, we achieve high accuracy and can still preserve a useful degree of domain-independence. STP may use both general linguistic knowledge and linguistic algorithms or heuristics adapted to the application in order to extract information from texts that is relevant for classification. The input to the SML tool is enriched with that information. The tool builds one or several categorizers[4] that will classify new texts.

In general, SML tools work with a vector representation of data. First, a *relevancy vector* of relevant features for each class is computed (Yang and Pedersen, 1997). In our case the relevant features consist of the user-defined output of the linguistic preprocessor. Then each single document is translated into a vector of numbers isomorphic to the defining vector. Each entry represents the occurrence of the corresponding feature. More details will be given in Section 4

The ICC-MAIL architecture is shown in Figure 1. The workflow of the system consists of a learning step carried out off-line (the light gray box) and an online categorization step (the dark gray box). In the off-line part, categorizers are built by processing classified data first by an STP and then by an SML tool. In this way, categorizers can be replaced by the system administrator as she wants to include new or remove expired categories. The categorizers are used on-line in order to classify new documents after they have passed the linguistic preprocessing. The resulting category is in our application associated with a standard text that the call center agent uses in her answer. The on-line step provides new classified data that is stored in a dedicated ICC-MAIL database (not shown in Figure 1). The relearning step is based on data from this database.

3.1 Shallow Text Processing

Linguistic preprocessing of text documents is carried out by re-using smes, an information extraction core system for real-world German text processing (Neumann et al., 1997). The fundamental design criterion of smes is to provide a set of basic, powerful, robust, and efficient STP components and

[1] `http://www.research.att.com/~lewis/reuters21578.html`

[2] We took only uniquely classified documents into account.

[3] Documents containing multiple requests can at present only be treated manually, as described in Section 5.

[4] Almost all tools we examined build a single multi-categorizer except for SVM_Light, which builds multiple binary classifiers.

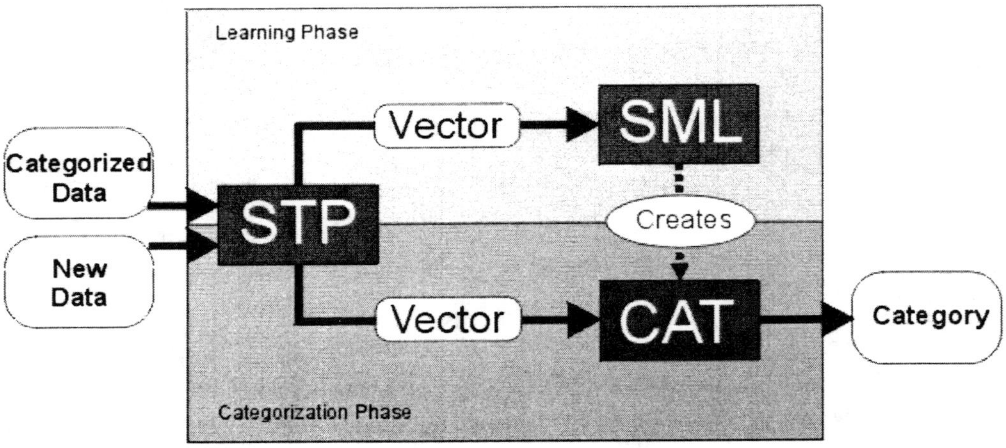

Figure 1: Architecture of the ICC-MAIL System.

generic linguistic knowledge sources that can easily be customized to deal with different tasks in a flexible manner. smes includes a text tokenizer, a lexical processor and a chunk parser. The chunk parser itself is subdivided into three components. In the first step, phrasal fragments like general nominal expressions and verb groups are recognized. Next, the dependency-based structure of the fragments of each sentence is computed using a set of specific sentence patterns. Third, the grammatical functions are determined for each dependency-based structure on the basis of a large subcategorization lexicon. The present application benefits from the high modularity of the usage of the components. Thus, it is possible to run only a subset of the components and to tailor their output. The experiments described in Section 4 make use of this feature.

3.2 Statistics-Based Machine Learning

Several SML tools representing different learning paradigms have been selected and evaluated in different settings of our domain:

Lazy Learning: Lazy Learners are also known as memory-based, instance-based, exemplar-based, case-based, experience-based, or k-nearest neighbor algorithms. They store all documents as vectors during the learning phase. In the categorization phase, the new document vector is compared to the stored ones and is categorized to same class as the k-nearest neighbors. The distance is measured by computing e.g. the Euclidean distance between the vectors. By changing the number of neighbors k or the kind of distance measure, the amount of generalization can be controlled.

We used IB (Aha, 1992), which is part of the MLC++ library (Kohavi and Sommerfield, 1996).

Symbolic Eager Learning: This type of learners constructs a representation for document vectors belonging to a certain class during the learning phase, e.g. decision trees, decision rules or probability weightings. During the categorization phase, the representation is used to assign the appropriate class to a new document vector. Several pruning or specialization heuristics can be used to control the amount of generalization.

We used ID3 (Quinlan, 1986), C4.5 (Quinlan, 1992) and C5.0, RIPPER (Cohen, 1995), and the Naive Bayes inducer (Good, 1965) contained in the MLC++ library. ID3, C4.5 and C5.0 produce decision trees, RIPPER is a rule-based learner and the Naive Bayes algorithm computes conditional probabilities of the classes from the instances.

Support Vector Machines (SVMs): SVMs are described in (Vapnik, 1995). SVMs are binary learners in that they distinguish positive and negative examples for each class. Like eager learners, they construct a representation during the learning phase, namely a hyper plane supported by vectors of positive and negative examples. For each class, a categorizer is built by computing such a hyper plane. During the categorization phase, each categorizer is applied to the new document vector, yielding the probabilities of the document belonging to a class. The probability increases with the distance of thevector from the hyper plane. A document is said to belong to the class with the highest probability.

We chose SVM_Light (Joachims, 1998).

Neural Networks: Neural Networks are a special kind of "non-symbolic" eager learning algorithm. The neural network links the vector elements to the document categories The learning phase defines thresholds for the activation of neurons. In the categorization phase, a new document vector leads to the activation of a single category. For details we refer to (Wiener et al., 1995).

In our application, we tried out the Learning Vector Quantization (LVQ) (Kohonen et al., 1996). LVQ has been used in its default configuration only. No adaptation to the application domain has been made.

4 Experiments and Results

We describe the experiments and results we achieved with different linguistic preprocessing and learning algorithms and provide some interpretations.

We start out from the corpus of categorized e-mails described in Section 2. In order to normalize the vectors representing the preprocessing results of texts of different length, and to concentrate on relevant material (cf. (Yang and Pedersen, 1997)), we define the relevancy vector as follows. First, all documents are preprocessed, yielding a list of results for each category. From each of these lists, the 100 most frequent results – according to a TF/IDF measure – are selected. The relevancy vector consists of all selected results, where doubles are eliminated. Its length was about 2500 for the 47 categories; it slightly varied with the kind of preprocessing used.

During the learning phase, each document is preprocessed. The result is mapped onto a vector of the same length as the relevancy vector. For every position in the relevancy vector, it is determined whether the corresponding result has been found. In that case, the value of the result vector element is 1, otherwise it is 0.

In the categorization phase, the new document is preprocessed, and a result vector is built as described above and handed over to the categorizer (cf. Figure 1).

While we tried various kinds of linguistic preprocessing, systematic experiments have been carried out with morphological analysis (*MorphAna*), shallow parsing heuristics (*STP-Heuristics*), and a combination of both (*Combined*).

MorphAna: Morphological Analysis provided by smes yields the word stems of nouns, verbs and adjectives, as well as the full forms of unknown words. We are using a lexicon of approx. 100000 word stems of German (Neumann et al., 1997).

STP-Heuristics: Shallow parsing techniques are used to heuristically identify sentences containing relevant information. The e-mails usually contain questions and/or descriptions of problems. The manual analysis of a sample of the data suggested some linguistic constructions frequently used to express the problem. We expected that content words in these constructions should be particularly influential to the categorization. Words in these constructions are extracted and processed as in *MorphAna*, and all other words are ignored.[5] The heuristics were implemented in ICC-MAIL using smes.

The constructions of interest include negations at the sentence and the phrasal level, yes-no and wh-questions, and declaratives immediately preceding questions. Negations were found to describe a state to be changed or to refer to missing objects, as in *I cannot read my email* or *There is no correct date.* We identified them through negation particles.[6] Questions most often refer to the problem in hand, either directly, e.g. *How can I start my email program?* or indirectly, e.g. *Why is this the case?*. The latter most likely refers to the preceding sentence, e.g. *My system drops my e-mails.* Questions are identified by their word order, i.e. yes-no questions start with a verb and wh-questions with a wh-particle.

Combined: In order to emphasize words found relevant by the STP heuristics without losing other information retrieved by *MorphAna*, the previous two techniques are combined. Emphasis is represented here by doubling the number of occurrences of the tokens in the normalization phase, thus increasing their TF/IDF value.

Call center agents judge the performance of ICC-MAIL most easily in terms of accuracy: In what percentage of cases does the classifier suggest the correct text block? In Table 1, detailed information about the accuracy achieved is presented. All experiments were carried out using 10-fold cross-validation on the data described in Section 2.

In all experiments the SVM_Light system outperformed other learning algorithms, which confirms Yang's (Yang and Liu, 1999) results for SVMs fed with Reuters data. The k-nearest neighbor algorithm IB performed surprisingly badly although different values of k were used. For IB, ID3, C4.5, C5.0, Naive Bayes, RIPPER and SVM_Light, linguistic preprocessing increased the overall performance. In fact, the method performing best, SVM_Light, gained 3.5% by including the task-oriented heuristics. However, the boosted RIPPER and LVQ scored a decreased accuracy value there. For LVQ the decrease may be due to the fact that no adaptations to

[5] If no results were found this way, *MorphAna* was applied instead.

[6] We certainly would have benefited from lexical semantic information, e.g. *The correct date is missing* would not be captured by our approach.

	SML algorithm	MorphAna Best	Best5	STP-Heuristics Best	Best5	Combined Best	Best5
Neural Nets	**LVQ**	35.66		22.29		25.97	
Lazy Learner	**IB**	33.81		33.01		35.14	
Symbolic Eager Learners	**Naive Bayes**	33.83		33.76		34.01	
	ID3	38.53		38.11		40.02	
	RIPPER	47.08		49.38		50.54	
	Boosted Ripper	52.73		49.96		50.78	
	C4.5	52.00		52.90		53.40	
	C5.0	52.60		53.20		54.20	
Support Vectors	**SVM_Light**	53.85	74.91	54.84	78.05	56.23	78.17

Table 1: Results of Experiments. Most SML tools deliver the best result only. SVM_Light produces ranked results, allowing to measure the accuracy of the top five alternatives (Best5).

the domain were made, such as adapting the number of codebook vectors, the initial learning parameters or the number of iterations during training (cf. (Kohonen et al., 1996)). Neural networks are rather sensitive to misconfigurations. The boosting for RIPPER seems to run into problems of overfitting. We noted that in six trials the accuracy could be improved in *Combined* compared to *MorphAna*, but in four trials, boosting led to deterioration. This effect is also mentioned in (Quinlan, 1996).

These figures are slightly lower than the ones reported by (Neumann and Schmeier, 1999) that were obtained from a different data set. Moreover, these data did not contain multiple queries in one e-mail.

It would be desirable to provide explanations for the behavior of the SML algorithms on our data. As we have emphasized in Section 2, general methods of explanation do not exist yet. In the application in hand, we found it difficult to account for the effects of e.g. ungrammatical text or redundant categories. For the time being, we can only offer some speculative and inconclusive assumptions: Some of the tools performing badly – IB, ID3, and the Naive Bayes inducer of the MLC++ library – have no or little pruning ability. With rarely occurring data, this leads to very low generalization rates, which again is a problem of overfitting. This suggests that a more canonical representation for the many ways of expressing a technical problem should be sought for. Would more extensive linguistic preprocessing help?

Other tests not reported in Table 1 looked at improvements through more general and sophisticated STP such as chunk parsing. The results were very discouraging, leading to a significant decrease compared to *MorphAna*. We explain this with the bad compliance of e-mail texts to grammatical standards (cf. the example in Figure 2).

However, the practical usefulness of chunk parsing or even deeper language understanding such as semantic analysis may be questioned in general: In a moving domain, the coverage of linguistic knowledge will always be incomplete, as it would be too expensive for a call center to have language technology experts keep pace with the occurrence of new topics. Thus the preprocessing results will often differ for e-mails expressing the same problem and hence not be useful for SML.

As a result of the tests in our application domain, we identified a favorite statistical tool and found that task-specific linguistic preprocessing is encouraging, while general STP is not.

5 Implementation and Use

In this section we describe the integration of the ICC-MAIL system into the workflow of the call center of AOL Bertelsmann Online GmbH & Co. KG, which answers requests about the German version of AOL software. A client/server solution was built that allows the call center agents to connect as clients to the ICC-MAIL server, which implements the system described in Section 3. For this purpose, it was necessary to

- connect the server module to AOL's own Sybase database that delivers the incoming mail and dispatches the outgoing answers, and to ICC-MAIL's own database that stores the classified e-mail texts;
- design the GUI of the client module in a self-explanatory and easy to use way (cf. Figure 2).

The agent reads in an e-mail and starts ICC-MAIL using GUI buttons. She verifies the correctness of the suggested answer, displaying and perhaps selecting alternative solutions. If the agent finds the appropriate answer within these proposals, the associated text is filled in at the correct position of the answer e-mail. If, on the other hand, no proposed solution is found to be adequate, the ICC-MAIL tool can still be used to manually select any text block

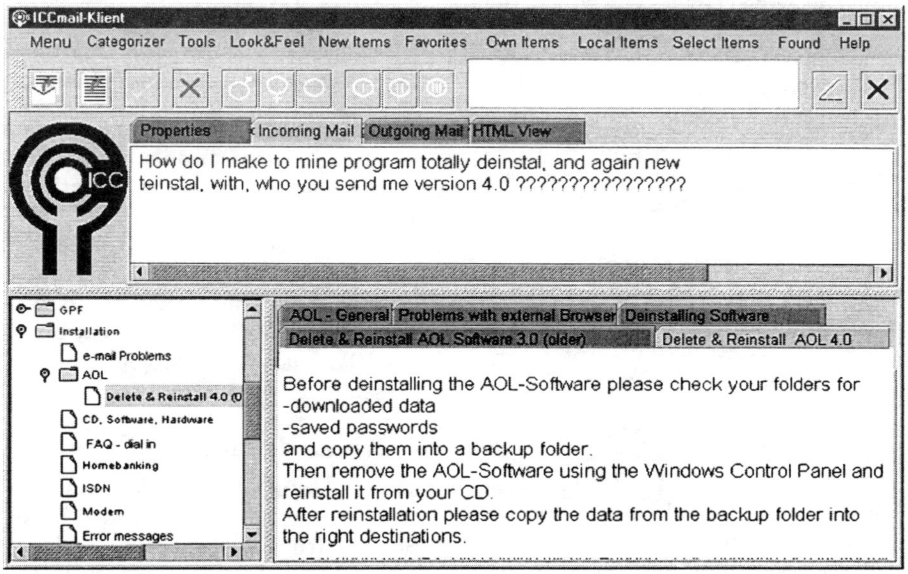

Figure 2: The GUI of the ICC-MAIL Client. All labels and texts were translated by the authors. The English input is based on the following original text, which is similarly awkward though understandable: *Wie mache ich zum mein Programm total deinstalieren, und wieder neu instalierem, mit, wen Sie mir senden Version 4.0 ??????????????.* The suggested answer text is associated with the category named "Delete & Reinstall AOL 4.0". Four alternative answers can be selected using the tabs. The left-hand side window displays the active category in context.

from the database. The ICC-MAIL client had to provide the functionality of the tool already in use since an additional tool was not acceptable to the agents, who are working under time pressure.

In the answer e-mail window, the original e-mail is automatically added as a quote. If an e-mail contains several questions, the classification process can be repeated by marking each question and iteratively applying the process to the marked part. The agent can edit the suggested texts before sending them off. In each case, the classified text together with the selected category is stored in the ICC-MAIL database for use in future learning steps.

Other features of the ICC-MAIL client module include a spell checker and a history view. The latter displays not only the previous e-mails of the same author but also the solutions that have been proposed and the elapsed time before an answer was sent.

The assumed average time for an agent to answer an e-mail is a bit more than two minutes with AOL's own mail processing system.[7] With the ICC-MAIL system the complete cycle of fetching the mail, checking the proposed solutions, choosing the appropriate solutions, inserting additional text fragments and sending the answer back can probably be achieved in half the time. Systematic tests supporting this claim are not completed yet,[8] but the following preliminary results are encouraging:

- A test under real-time conditions at the call-center envisaged the use of the ICC-MAIL system as a mail tool only, i.e. without taking advantage of the system's intelligence. It showed that the surface and the look-and-feel is accepted and the functionality corresponds to the real-time needs of the call center agents, as users were slightly faster than within their usual environment.
- A preliminary test of the throughput achieved by using the STP and SML technology in ICC-MAIL showed that experienced users take about 50-70 seconds on average for one cycle, as described above. This figure was gained through experiments with three users over a duration of about one hour each.

Using the system with a constant set of categories will improve its accuracy after repeating the off-line learning step. If a new category is introduced, the accuracy will slightly decline until 30 documents are manually classified and the category is automatically included into a new classifier. Relearning may take place at regular intervals. The definition of new categories must be fed into ICC-MAIL by a "knowledge

[7]This system does not include automatic analysis of mails.

[8]As of end of February 2000.

engineer", who maintains the system. The effects of new categories and new data have not been tested yet.

The optimum performance of ICC-MAIL can be achieved only with a well-maintained category system. For a call center, this may be a difficult task to achieve, espescially under severe time pressure, but it will pay off. In particular, all new categories should be added, outdated ones should be removed, and redundant ones merged. Agents should only use these categories and no others. The organizational structure of the team should reflect this by defining the tasks of the "knowledge engineer" and her interactions with the agents.

6 Conclusions and Future Work

We have presented new combinations of STP and SML methods to classify unrestricted e-mail text according to a changing set of categories. The current accuracy of the ICC-MAIL system is 78% (correct solution among the top five proposals), corresponding to an overall performance of 73% since ICC-MAIL processes only 94% of the incoming e-mails. The accuracy improves with usage, since each relearning step will yield better classifiers. The accuracy is expected to approximate that of the agents, but not improve on it. With ICC-MAIL, the performance of an experienced agent can approximately be doubled.

The system is currently undergoing extensive tests at the call center of AOL Bertelsmann Online. Details about the development of the performance depending on the throughput and change of categories are expected to be available by mid 2000.

Technically, we expect improvements from the following areas of future work.

- Further task-specific heuristics aiming at general structural linguistic properties should be defined. This includes heuristics for the identification of multiple requests in a single e-mail that could be based on key words and key phrases as well as on the analysis of the document structure.

- Our initial experiments with the integration of GermaNet (Hamp and Feldweg, 1997), the evolving German version of WordNet, seem to confirm the positive results described for WordNet (de Buenaga Rodriguez et al., 1997) and will thus be extended.

- A reorganization of the existing three-level category system into a semantically consistent tree structure would allow us to explore the nonterminal nodes of the tree for multi-layered SML. This places additional requirements on the knowledge engineering task and thus needs to be thoroughly investigated for pay-off.

- Where system-generated answers are acceptable to customers, a straightforward extension of ICC-MAIL can provide this functionality. For the application in hand, this was not the case.

The potential of the technology presented extends beyond call center applications. We intend to explore its use within an information broking assistant in document classification. In a further industrial project with German Telekom, the ICC-MAIL technology will be extended to process multi-lingual press releases. The nature of these documents will allow us to explore the application of more sophisticated language technologies during linguistic preprocessing.

Acknowledgments

We are grateful to our colleagues Günter Neumann, Matthias Fischmann, Volker Morbach, and Matthias Rinck for fruitful discussions and for support with smes modules. This work was partially supported by a grant of the Minister of Economy and Commerce of the Saarland, Germany, to the project ICC.

References

David W. Aha. 1992. Tolerating noisy, irrelevant and novel attributes in instance based learning algorithms. *International Journal of Man-Machine Studies, 36(1)*, pages 267–287.

Fabio Ciravegna, Alberto Lavelli, Nadia Mana, Johannes Matiasek, Luca Gilardoni, Silvia Mazza, Massimo Ferraro, William J.Black, Fabio Rinaldi, and David Mowatt. 1999. Facile: Classifying texts integrating pattern matching and information extraction. In *Proceedings of IJCAI'99, Stockholm*, pages 890–895.

William W. Cohen. 1995. Fast effective rule induction. In *Proceedings of the Twelfth International Conference on Machine Learning, Lake Tahoe, California.*

Manuel de Buenaga Rodriguez, Jose Maria Gomez-Hidalgo, and Belen Diaz-Agudo. 1997. Using WordNet to complement training information in text categorization. In *Proceedings of the Second International Conference on Recent Advances in Natural Language Processing, Montreal, Canada.*

I.J. Good. 1965. *The Estimation of Probabilities. An Essay on Modern Bayesian Methods.* MIT-Press.

Birgit Hamp and Helmut Feldweg. 1997. GermaNet - a lexical-semantic net for German. In *Proceedings of ACL workshop Automatic Information Extraction and Building of Lexical Semantic Resources for NLP Applications, Madrid, Spain*

Thorsten Joachims. 1998. Text categorization with support vector machines - learning with meany relevant features. In *Proceedings of the Euro-*

pean Conference on Machine Learning (ECML), Chemnitz, Germany, pages 137–142.

Ronny Kohavi and Dan Sommerfield, 1996. *MLC++ Machine Learning library in C++*. http://www.sgi.com/Technology/mlc.

Teuvo Kohonen, Jussi Hynninen, Jari Kangas, Jorma Laaksonen, and Kari Torkkola. 1996. LVQ-PAK the learning vector quantization program package. Technical Report A30, Helsinki University of Technology.

Günter Neumann, Rolf Backofen, Judith Baur, Markus Becker, and Christian Braun. 1997. An information extraction core system for real world German text processing. In *Proceedings of 5th ANLP, Washington*, pages 209–216.

Günter Neumann and Sven Schmeier. 1999. Combining shallow text processing and macine learning in real world applications. In *Proceedings of IJCAI workshop on Machine Learning for Information Filtering, Stockholm*, pages 55–60.

J.R. Quinlan. 1986. *Induction of Decision Trees.* Reprinted in Shavlik, Jude W. and Dietterich, Thomas G, *Readings in machine learning.* Machine learning series. Morgan Kaufmann (1990)

J.R. Quinlan. 1992. *C4.5: Programs for Machine Learning.* Morgan Kaufmann, San Mateo, California.

J.R. Quinlan. 1996. Bagging, Boosting and C4.5. In *Proceedings of AAAI'96, Portland*, pages 725–730.

Vladimir N. Vapnik. 1995. *The Nature of Statistical Learning Theory.* Springer.

E.D. Wiener, J. Pedersen, and A.S. Weigend. 1995. A neural network approach to topic spotting. In *Proceedings of the SDAIR.*

Y. Yang and Xin Liu. 1999. A re-examination of text categorization methods. In *Proceedings of ACMSIGIR Conference on Research and Development in Information Retrieval, Berkley, Calfornia.*

Y. Yang and J.P. Pedersen. 1997. A comparative study on feature selection. In *Proceedings of the Fourteenth International Conference on Machine Learning (ICML'97).*

Y. Yang. 1999. An evaluation of statistical approaches to text categorization. *Information Retrieval Journal (May 1999).*

A Question Answering System Supported by Information Extraction*

Rohini Srihari
Cymfony Inc.
5500 Main Street
Williamsville, NY14221
rohini@cymfony.com

Wei Li
Cymfony Inc.
5500 Main Street
Williamsville, NY14221
wei@cymfony.com

Abstract

This paper discusses an information extraction (IE) system, *Textract*, in natural language (NL) question answering (QA) and examines the role of IE in QA application. It shows: (i) Named Entity tagging is an important component for QA, (ii) an NL shallow parser provides a structural basis for questions, and (iii) high-level domain independent IE can result in a QA breakthrough.

Introduction

With the explosion of information in Internet, Natural language QA is recognized as a capability with great potential. Traditionally, QA has attracted many AI researchers, but most QA systems developed are toy systems or games confined to lab and a very restricted domain. More recently, Text Retrieval Conference (TREC-8) designed a QA track to stimulate the research for real world application.

Due to little linguistic support from text analysis, conventional IR systems or search engines do not really perform the task of *information* retrieval; they in fact aim at only *document* retrieval. The following quote from the QA Track Specifications (www.research.att.com/~singhal/qa-track-spec.txt) in the TREC community illustrates this point.

> *Current information retrieval systems allow us to locate documents that might contain the pertinent information, but most of them leave it to the user to extract the useful information from a ranked list. This leaves the (often unwilling) user with a relatively large amount of text to consume. There is an urgent need for tools that would reduce the amount of text one might have to read in order to obtain the desired information. This track aims at doing exactly that for a special (and popular) class of information seeking behavior: QUESTION ANSWERING. People have questions and they need answers, not documents. Automatic question answering will definitely be a significant advance in the state-of-art information retrieval technology.*

Kupiec (1993) presented a QA system MURAX using an on-line encyclopedia. This system used the technology of robust shallow parsing but suffered from the lack of basic information extraction support. In fact, the most siginifcant IE advance, namely the NE (Named Entity) technology, occured after Kupiec (1993), thanks to the MUC program (MUC-7 1998). High-level IE technology beyond NE has not been in the stage of possible application until recently.

AskJeeves launched a QA portal (www.askjeeves.com). It is equipped with a fairly sophisticated natural language question parser, but it does not provide direct answers to the asked questions. Instead, it directs the user to the relevant web pages, just as the traditional search engine does. In this sense, AskJeeves has only done half of the job for QA.

We believe that QA is an ideal test bed for demonstrating the power of IE. There is a natural co-operation between IE and IR; we regard QA as one major intelligence which IE can offer IR.

* This work was supported in part by the SBIR grants F30602-98-C-0043 and F30602-99-C-0102 from Air Force Research Laboratory (AFRL)/IFED.

An important question then is, what type of IE can support IR in QA and how well does it support it? This forms the major topic of this paper. We structure the remaining part of the paper as follows. In Section 1, we first give an overview of the underlying IE technology which our organization has been developing. Section 2 discusses the QA system. Section 3 describes the limitation of the current system. Finally, in Section 4, we propose a more sophisticated QA system supported by three levels of IE.

1 Overview of Textract IE

The last decade has seen great advance and interest in the area of IE. In the US, the DARPA sponsored Tipster Text Program [Grishman 1997] and the Message Understanding Conferences (MUC) [MUC-7 1998] have been the driving force for developing this technology. In fact, the MUC specifications for various IE tasks have become *de facto* standards in the IE research community. It is therefore necessary to present our IE effort in the context of the MUC program.

MUC divides IE into distinct tasks, namely, NE (Named Entity), TE (Template Element), TR (Template Relation), CO (Co-reference), and ST (Scenario Templates) [Chinchor & Marsh 1998]. Our proposal for three levels of IE is modelled after the MUC standards using MUC-style representation. However, we have modified the MUC IE task definitions in order to make them more useful and more practical. More precisely, we propose a hierarchical, 3-level architecture for developing a kernel IE system which is domain-independent throughout.

The core of this system is a state-of-the-art NE tagger [Srihari 1998], named *Textract 1.0*. The *Textract* NE tagger has achieved speed and accuracy comparable to that of the few deployed NE systems, such as *NetOwl* [Krupka & Hausman 1998] and *Nymble* [Bikel et al 1997].

It is to be noted that in our definition of NE, we significantly expanded the type of information to be extracted. In addition to all the MUC defined NE types (person, organization, location, time, date, money and percent), the following types/sub-types of information are also identified by the *TextractNE* module:

- duration, frequency, age
- number, fraction, decimal, ordinal, math equation
- weight, length, temperature, angle, area, capacity, speed, rate
- product, software
- address, email, phone, fax, telex, www
- name (default proper name)

Sub-type information like *company*, *government agency*, *school* (belonging to the type *organization*) and *military person*, *religious person* (belonging to person) are also identified. These new sub-types provide a better foundation for defining multiple relationships between the identified entities and for supporting question answering functionality. For example, the key to a question processor is to identify the asking point (*who, what, when, where*, etc.). In many cases, the asking point corresponds to an NE beyond the MUC definition, e.g. the *how*+adjective questions: *how long* (*duration* or *length*), *how far* (*length*), *how often* (*frequency*), *how old* (*age*), etc.

Level-2 IE, or CE (Correlated Entity), is concerned with extracting pre-defined multiple relationships between the entities. Consider the person entity as an example; the *TextractCE* prototype is capable of extracting the key relationships such as *age, gender, affiliation, position, birth_time, birth_place, spouse, parents, children, where_from, address, phone, fax, email, descriptors*. As seen, the information in the CE represents a mini-CV or profile of the entity. In general, the CE template integrates and greatly enriches the information contained in MUC TE and TR.

The final goal of our IE effort is to further extract open-ended general events (GE, or level 3 IE) for information like *who* did *what* (to *whom*) *when* (or *how* often) and *where*. By general events, we refer to argument structures centering around verb notions plus the associated information of time/frequency and location. We show an example of our defined GE extracted from the text below:

Julian Hill, a research chemist whose accidental discovery of a tough, taffylike compound revolutionized everyday life after it proved its worth in warfare and courtship, died on Sunday in Hockessin, Del.

[1] <GE_TEMPLATE> :=
PREDICATE: die
ARGUMENT1: Julian Hill
TIME: Sunday
LOCATION: Hockessin, Del

Figure 1 is the overall system architecture for the IE system *Textract* that our organization has been developing.

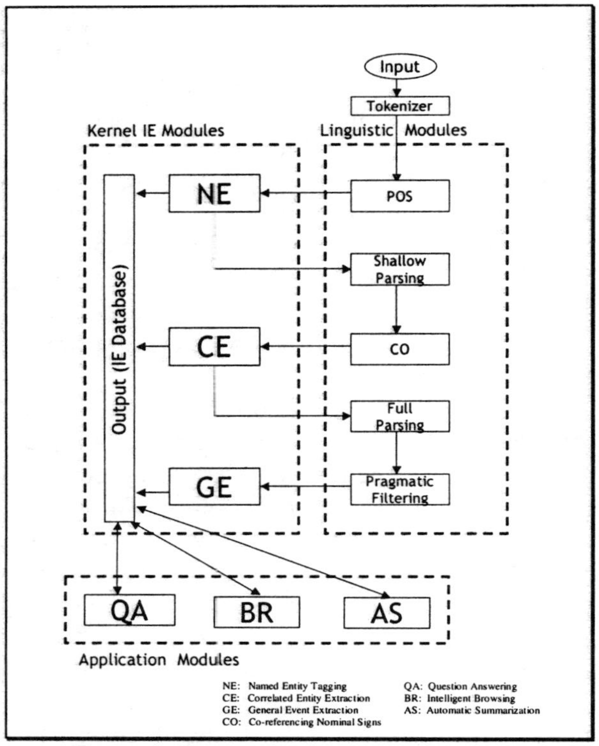

Figure 1: Textract IE System Architecture

The core of the system consists of three kernel IE modules and six linguistic modules. The multi-level linguistic modules serve as an underlying support system for different levels of IE. The IE results are stored in a database which is the basis for IE-related applications like QA, BR (Browsing, threading and visualization) and AS (Automatic Summarization). The approach to IE taken here, consists of a unique blend of machine learning and FST (finite state transducer) rule-based system [Roche & Schabes 1997]. By combining machine learning with an FST rule-based system, we are able to exploit the best of both paradigms while overcoming their respective weaknesses [Srihari 1998, Li & Srihari 2000].

2 NE-Supported QA

This section presents the QA system based on Named Entity tagging. Out of the 200 questions that comprised the TREC-8 QA track competition, over 80% asked for an NE, e.g. *who* (PERSON), *when* (TIME | DATE), *where* (LOCATION), *how far* (LENGTH). Therefore, the NE tagger has been proven to be very helpful. Of course, the NE of the targeted type is only necessary but not complete in answering such questions because NE by nature only extracts isolated individual entities from the text. Nevertheless, using even crude methods like "the nearest NE to the queried key words" or "the NE and its related key words within the same line (or same paragraph, etc.)", in most cases, the QA system was able to extract text portions which contained answers in the top five list.

Figure 2 illustrates the system design of *TextractQA* Prototype. There are two components for the QA prototype: Question Processor and Text Processor. The Text Matcher module links the two processing results and tries to find answers to the processed question. Matching is based on keywords, plus the NE type and their common location within a same sentence.

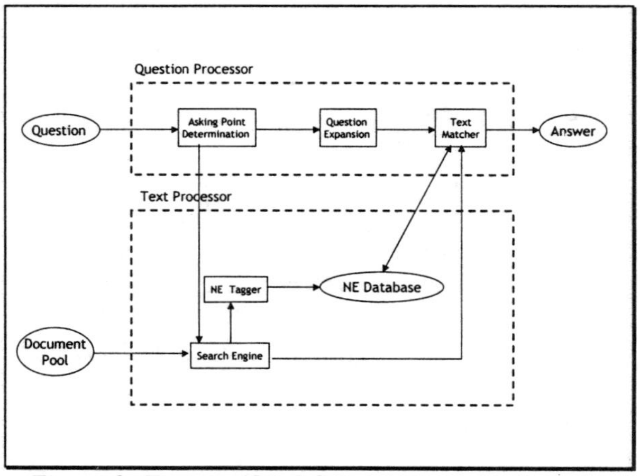

Figure 2: Textract/QA 1.0 Prototype Architecture

The general algorithm for question answering is as follows:

Process Question
    Shallow parse question
    Determine Asking Point
    Question expansion (using word lists)
Process Documents
    Tokenization, POS tagging, NE Indexing
    Shallow Parsing (not yet utilized)
Text Matcher
    Intersect search engine results with NE
    rank answers

2.1 Question Processing

The Question Processing results are a list of keywords plus the information for asking point. For example, the question:

[2] *Who won the 1998 Nobel Peace Prize?*

contains the following keywords: *won, 1998, Nobel, Peace, Prize*. The asking point *Who* refers to the NE type *person*. The output before question expansion is a simple 2-feature template as shown below:

[3] asking_point: PERSON
    key_word: {won, 1998, Nobel, Peace, Prize}

The following is an example where the asking point does not correspond to any type of NE in our definition.

[3] *Why did David Koresh ask the FBI for a word processor?*

The system then maps it to the following question template :

[4] asking_point: REASON
    key_word: {ask, David, Koresh, FBI, word, processor }

The question processor scans the question to search for question words (wh-words) and maps them into corresponding NE types/sub-types or pre-defined notions like REASON.

We adopt two sets of pattern matching rules for this purpose: (i) structure based pattern matching rules; (ii) simple key word based pattern matching rules (regarded as default rules). It is fairly easy to exhaust the second set of rules as interrogative question words/phrases form a closed set. In comparison, the development of the first set of rules are continuously being fine-tuned and expanded. This strategy of using two set of rules leads to the robustness of the question processor.

The first set of rules are based on shallow parsing results of the questions, using Cymfony FST based Shallow Parser. This parser identifies basic syntactic constructions like *BaseNP* (Basic Noun Phrase), *BasePP* (Basic Prepositional Phrase) and *VG* (Verb Group).

The following is a sample of the first set of rules:

[6] Name NP (city | country | company) --> CITY|COUNTRY|COMPANY
[7] Name NP(person_w) --> PERSON
[8] Name NP(org_w) --> ORGANIZATION
[9] Name NP(NOT person_w, NOT org_w) --> NAME

Rule [6] checks the head word of the NP. It covers cases like *VG[Name] NP[a country] that VG[is developing] NP[a magnetic levitation railway system]*. Rule [7] works for cases like *VG[Name] NP[the first private citizen] VG[to fly] PP[in space]* as *citizen* belongs to the word class *person_w*. Rule [9] is a catch-all rule: if the NP is not of class person (*person_w*) or organization (*org_w*), then the asking point is a proper name (default NE), often realized in English in capitalized string of words. Examples include *Name a film that has won the Golden Bear in the Berlin Film Festival.*

The word lists *org_w* and *person_w* are currently manually maintained based on inspection of large volumes of text. An effort is underway to automate the learning of such word lists by utilizing machine learning techniques.

We used the following pattern transformations to expand our ruleset:

(Please) name NP[X]
--> what/which Aux(be) (the name of) NP[X]
--> NP(what/which...X)

In other words, the four rules are expanded to 12 rules. For example, Rule [10] below corresponds to Rule [6]; Rule [11] is derived from Rule [7].

[10] what/which Aux(be) NP (city | country | company) -->
CITY | COUNTRY | COMPANY
[11] NP(what/which ... person_w) -->
PERSON

Rule [10] extracts the asking point from cases like *NP[What] Aux[is] NP[the largest country] PP[in the world]*. Rule [11] covers the following questions: *NP[What costume designer] VG[decided] that NP[Michael Jackson] VG[should only wear] NP[one glove], NP[Which former Ku Klux Klan member] VG[won] NP[an elected office] PP[in the U.S.], NP[What Nobel laureate] VG[was expelled] PP[from the Philippines] PP[before the conference] PP[on East Timor], NP[What famous communist leader] VG[died] PP[in Mexico City]*, etc.

As seen, shallow parsing helps us to capture a variety of natural language question expressions. However, there are cases where some simple key word based pattern matching would be enough to capture the asking point. That is our second set of rules. These rules are used when the first set of rules has failed to produce results. The following is a sample of such rules:

[12] who/whom --> PERSON
[13] when --> TIME/DATE
[14] where/what place --> LOCATION
[15] what time (of day) --> TIME
[16] what day (of the week) --> DAY
[17] what/which month --> MONTH
[18] what age/how old --> AGE
[19] what brand --> PRODUCT
[20] what --> NAME
[21] how far/tall/high --> LENGTH
[22] how large/big/small --> AREA
[23] how heavy --> WEIGHT
[24] how rich --> MONEY
[25] how often --> FREQUENCY
[26] how many --> NUMBER
[27] how long --> LENGTH/DURATION
[28] why/for what --> REASON

In the stage of question expansion, the template in [4] would be expanded to the template shown in [29]:

[29] asking_point: {because|because of|due to|thanks to|since|in order|to VB}
key_word: {ask|asks|asked|asking, David,Koresh,FBI, word, processor}

The last item in the *asking_point* list attempts to find an infinitive by checking the word *to* followed by a verb (with the part-of-speech tag VB). As we know, infinitive verb phrases are often used in English to explain a reason for some action.

2.2 Text Processing

On the text processing side, we first send the question directly to a search engine in order to narrow down the document pool to the first *n*, say 200, documents for IE processing. Currently, this includes tokenization, POS tagging and NE tagging. Future plans include several levels of parsing as well; these are required to support CE and GE extraction. It should be noted that all these operations are extremely robust and fast, features necessary for large volume text indexing. Parsing is accomplished through cascaded finite state transducer grammars.

2.3 Text Matching

The Text Matcher attempts to match the question template with the processed documents for both the asking point and the key words. There is a preliminary ranking standard built-in the matcher in order to find the most probable answers. The primary rank is a count of how many unique keywords are contained within a sentence. The secondary ranking is based on the order that the keywords appear in the sentence compared to their order in the question. The third ranking is based on whether there is an exact match or a variant match for the key verb.

In the TREC-8 QA track competition, Cymfony QA accuracy was 66.0%. Considering we have only used NE technology to support QA in this run, 66.0% is a very encouraging result.

3 Limitation

The first limitation comes from the types of questions. Currently only wh-questions are handled although it is planned that yes-no questions will be handled once we introduce CE and GE templates to support QA. Among the wh-questions, the *why*-question and *how*-question[1] are more challenging because the asking point cannot be simply mapped to the NE types/sub-types.

The second limitation is from the nature of the questions. Questions like *Where can I find the homepage for Oscar winners* or *Where can I find info on Shakespeare's works* might be answerable easily by a system based on a well-maintained data base of home pages. Since our system is based on the processing of the underlying documents, no correct answer can be provided if there is no such an answer (explicitly expressed in English) in the processed documents. In TREC-8 QA, this is not a problem since every question is guaranteed to have at least one answer in the given document pool. However, in the real world scenario such as a QA portal, it is conceived that the IE results based on the processing of the documents should be complemented by other knowledge sources such as e-copy of yellow pages or other manually maintained and updated data bases.

The third limitation is the lack of linguistic processing such as sentence-level parsing and cross-sentential co-reference (CO). This problem will be gradually solved when high-level IE technology is introduced into the system.

4 Future Work: Multi-level IE Supported QA

A new QA architecture is under development; it will exploit all levels of the IE system, including CE and GE.

The first issue is how much CE can contribute to a better support of QA. It is found that there are some frequently seen questions which can be better answered once the CE information is provided. These questions are of two types: (i) *what/who* questions about an NE; (ii) relationship questions.

Questions of the following format require CE templates as best answers: *who/what* is NE? For example, *Who is Julian Hill? Who is Bill Clinton? What is Du Pont? What is Cymfony?* To answer these questions, the system can simply retrieve the corresponding CE template to provide an "assembled" answer, as shown below.

Q: Who is Julian Hill?
A: name: Julian Werner Hill
type: PERSON
age: 91
gender: MALE
position: research chemist
affiliation: Du Pont Co.
education: Washington University; MIT

Q: What is Du Pont?
A: name: Du Pont Co.
type: COMPANY
staff: Julian Hill; Wallace Carothers.

Questions specifically about a CE relationship include: *For which company did Julian Hill work?* (affiliation relationship) *Who are employees of Du Pont Co.?* (staff relationship) *What does Julian Hill do?* (position/profession relationship) *Which university did Julian Hill graduate from?* (education relationship), etc.[2]

The next issue is the relationships between GE and QA. It is our belief that the GE technology will result in a breakthrough for QA.

In order to extract GE templates, the text goes through a series of linguistic processing as shown in Figure 1. It should be noted that the question processing is designed to go through parallel processes and share the same NLP resources until the point of matching and ranking.

The merging of question templates and GE templates in Template Matcher are fairly straightforward. As they both undergo the same NLP processing, the resulting semantic templates are of the same form. Both question templates and GE templates correspond to fairly standard/predictable patterns (the PREDICATE value is open-ended, but the structure remains stable). More precisely, a user can ask questions on general events themselves (*did what*) and/or on the participants of the event (*who, whom, what*) and/or the time, frequency and place of events (*when, how often, where*). This addresses

[1] For example, *How did one make a chocolate cake? How*+Adjective questions (e.g. *how long, how big, how old,* etc.) are handled fairly well.

[2] An alpha version of *TextractQA* supported by both NE and CE has been implemented and is being tested.

by far the most types of general questions of a potential user.

For example, if a user is interested in company acquisition events, he can ask questions like: *Which companies ware acquired by Microsoft in 1999? Which companies did Microsoft acquire in 1999?* Our system will then parse these questions into the templates as shown below:

[31] <Q_TEMPLATE> :=
PREDICATE: acquire
ARGUMENT1: Microsoft
ARGUMENT2: WHAT(COMPANY)
TIME: 1999

If the user wants to know *when* some acquisition happened, he can ask: *When was Netscape acquired?* Our system will then translate it into the pattern below:

[32] <Q_TEMPLATE> :=
PREDICATE: acquire
ARGUMENT1: WHO
ARGUMENT2: Netscape
TIME: WHEN

Note that WHO, WHAT, WHEN above are variable to be instantiated. Such question templates serve as search constraints to filter the events in our extracted GE template database. Because the question templates and the extracted GE template share the same structure, a simple merging operation would suffice. Nevertheless, there are two important questions to be answered: (i) what if a different verb with the same meaning is used in the question from the one used in the processed text? (ii) what if the question asks about something beyond the GE (or CE) information? These are issues that we are currently researching.

References

Bikel D.M. et al. (1997) *Nymble: a High-Performance Learning Name-finder*. "Proceedings of the Fifth Conference on Applied Natural Language Processing", Morgan Kaufmann Publishers, pp. 194-201

Chinchor N. and Marsh E. (1998) *MUC-7 Information Extraction Task Definition* (version 5.1), "Proceedings of MUC-7".

Grishman R. (1997) *TIPSTER Architecture Design Document Version 2.3*. Technical report, DARPA

Krupka G.R. and Hausman K. (1998) *IsoQuest Inc.: Description of the NetOwl (TM) Extractor System as Used for MUC-7*, "Proceedings of MUC-7".

Kupiec J. (1993) *MURAX: A Robust Linguistic Approach For Question Answering Using An On-Line Encyclopaedia,* "Proceedings of SIGIR-93 93" Pittsburgh, Penna.

Li, W & Srihari, R. 2000. *Flexible Information Extraction Learning Algorithm*, Final Technical Report, Air Force Research Laboratory, Rome Research Site, New York

MUC-7 (1998) *Proceedings of the Seventh Message Understanding Conference* (MUC-7), published on the website http://www.muc.saic.com/

Roche E. and Schabes Y. (1997) *Finite-State Language Processing*, MIT Press, Cambridge, MA

Srihari R. (1998) *A Domain Independent Event Extraction Toolkit*, AFRL-IF-RS-TR-1998-152 Final Technical Report, Air Force Research Laboratory, Rome Research Site, New York

Categorizing Unknown Words: Using Decision Trees to Identify Names and Misspellings

Janine Toole
Natural Language Laboratory
Department of Computing Science
Simon Fraser University
Burnaby, BC, Canada V5A 1S6
toole@cs.sfu.ca

Abstract

This paper introduces a system for categorizing unknown words. The system is based on a multi-component architecture where each component is responsible for identifying one class of unknown words. The focus of this paper is the components that identify names and spelling errors. Each component uses a decision tree architecture to combine multiple types of evidence about the unknown word. The system is evaluated using data from live closed captions - a genre replete with a wide variety of unknown words.

1 Introduction

In any real world use, a Natural Language Processing (NLP) system will encounter words that are not in its lexicon, what we term 'unknown words'. Unknown words are problematic because a NLP system will perform well only if it recognizes the words that it is meant to analyze or translate: the more words a system does not recognize the more the system's performance will degrade. Even when unknown words are infrequent, they can have a disproportionate effect on system quality. For example, Min (1996) found that while only 0.6% of words in 300 e-mails were misspelled, this meant that 12% of the sentences contained an error (discussed in (Min and Wilson, 1998)).

Words may be unknown for many reasons: the word may be a proper name, a misspelling, an abbreviation, a number, a morphological variant of a known word (e.g. *recleared*), or missing from the dictionary. The first step in dealing with unknown words is to identify the class of the unknown word; whether it is a misspelling, a proper name, an abbreviation etc. Once this is known, the proper action can be taken, misspellings can be corrected, abbreviations can be expanded and so on, as deemed necessary by the particular text processing application. In this paper we introduce a system for categorizing unknown words. The system is based on a multi- component architecture where each component is responsible for identifying one category of unknown words. The main focus of this paper is the components that identify names and spelling errors. Both components use a decision tree architecture to combine multiple types of evidence about the unknown word. Results from the two components are combined using a weighted voting procedure. The system is evaluated using data from live closed captions - a genre replete with a wide variety of unknown words.

This paper is organized as follows. In section 2 we outline the overall architecture of the unknown word categorizer. The name identifier and the misspelling identifier are introduced in section 3. Performance and evaluation issues are discussed in section 4. Section 5 considers portability issues. Section 6 compares the current system with relevant preceding research. Concluding comments can be found in section 6.

2 System Architecture

The goal of our research is to develop a system that automatically categorizes unknown words. According to our definition, an unknown word is a word that is not contained in the lexicon of an NLP system. As defined, 'unknown-ness' is a relative concept: a word that is known to one system may be unknown to another system.

Our research is motivated by the problems that we have experienced in translating live closed captions: live captions are produced under tight time constraints and contain many unknown words. Typically, the caption transcriber has a five second window to transcribe the broadcast dialogue. Because of the live nature of the broadcast, there is no opportunity to post-edit the transcript in any way. Although motivated by our specific requirements, the unknown word categorizer would benefit any NLP system that encounters unknown words of differing categories. Some immediately obvious domains where unknown words are frequent include e-mail messages, internet chat rooms, data typed in by call centre operators, etc.

To deal with these issues we propose a multi-component architecture where individual components specialize in identifying one particular type of unknown word. For example, the misspelling identifier will specialize in identifying misspellings, the abbreviation component will specialize in identifying abbreviations, etc. Each component will return a confidence measure of the reliability of its prediction, c.f. (Elworthy, 1998). The results from each component are evaluated to determine the final category of the word.

There are several advantages to this approach. Firstly, the system can take advantage of existing research. For example, the name recognition module can make use of the considerable research that exists on name recognition, e.g. (McDonald, 1996), (Mani et al., 1996). Secondly, individual components can be replaced when improved models are available, without affecting other parts of the system. Thirdly, this approach is compatible with incorporating multiple components of the same type to improve performance (cf. (van Halteren et al., 1998) who found that combining the results of several part of speech taggers increased performance).

3 The Current System

In this paper we introduce a simplified version of the unknown word categorizer: one that contains just two components: misspelling identification and name identification. In this section we introduce these components and the 'decision' component which combines the results from the individual modules.

3.1 The Name Identifier

The goal of the name identifier is to differentiate between those unknown words which are proper names, and those which are not. We define a name as word identifying a person, place, or concept that would typically require capitalization in English.

One of the motivations for the modular architecture introduced above, was to be able to leverage existing research. For example, ideally, we should be able to plug in an existing proper name recognizer and avoid the problem of creating our own. However, the domain in which we are currently operating - live closed captions - makes this approach difficult. Closed captions do not contain any case information, all captions are in upper case. Existing proper name recognizers rely heavily on case to identify names, hence they perform poorly on our data.

A second disadvantage of currently available name recognizers is that they do not generally return a confidence measure with their prediction. Some indication of confidence is required in the multi-component architecture we have implemented. However, while currently existing name recognizers are inappropriate for the needs of our domain, future name recognizers may well meet these requirements and be able to be incorporated into the architecture we propose.

For these reasons we develop our own name identifier. We utilize a decision tree to model the characteristics of proper names. The advantage of decision trees is that they are highly explainable: one can readily understand the features that are affecting the analysis (Weiss and Indurkhya, 1998). Furthermore, decision trees are well-suited for combining a wide variety of information.

For this project, we made use of the decision tree that is part of IBM's Intelligent Miner suite for data mining. Since the point of this paper is to describe an application of decision trees rather than to argue for a particular decision tree algorithm, we omit further details of the decision tree software. Similar results should be obtained by using other decision tree software. Indeed, the results we obtain could perhaps be improved by using more sophisticated decision-tree approaches such as the adaptive-resampling described in (Weiss et al, 1999).

The features that we use to train the decision tree are intended to capture the characteristics of names. We specify a total of ten features for each unknown word. These identify two features of the unknown word itself as well as two features for each of the two preceding and two following words.

The first feature represents the part of speech of the word. We use an in-house statistical tagger (based on (Church, 1988)) to tag the text in which the unknown word occurs. The tag set used is a simplified version of the tags used in the machine-readable version of the Oxford Advanced Learners Dictionary (OALD). The tag set contains just one tag to identify nouns.

The second feature provides more informative tagging for specific parts of speech (these are referred to as 'detailed tags' (DETAG)). This tagset consists of the nine tags listed in Table 1. All parts of speech apart from noun and punctuation tags are assigned the tag 'OTHER'. All punctuation tags are assigned the tag 'BOUNDARY'. Words identified as nouns are assigned one of the remaining tags depending on the information provided in the OALD (although the unknown word, by definition, will not appear in the OALD, the preceding and following words may well appear in the dictionary). If the word is identified in the OALD as a common noun it is assigned the tag 'COM'. If it is identified in the OALD as a proper name it is assigned the tag 'NAME'. If the word is specified as both a name and a common noun (e.g. 'bill'), then it is assigned the tag 'NCOM'. Pronouns are assigned the tag 'PRON'. If the word is in a list of titles that we have compiled, then the tag 'TITLE' is assigned. Similarly, if the word is a member of the class of words that can follow a name (e.g. 'jr'), then the tag 'POST' is assigned. A simple rule-based sys-

COM	common noun
NAME	name
NCOM	name and common noun
PRONOUN	pronoun
TITLE	title
POST	post-name word
BOUNDARY	boundary marker
OTHER	not noun or boundary
UNKNOWN	unknown noun

Table 1: List of Detailed Tags (DETAG)

Corpus frequency
Word length
Edit distance
Ispell information
Character sequence frequency
Non-English characters

Table 2: Features used in misspelling decision tree

tem is used to assign these tags.

If we were dealing with data that contains case information, we would also include fields representing the existence/non-existence of initial upper case for the five words. However, since our current data does not include case information we do not include these features.

3.2 The Misspelling Identifier

The goal of the misspelling identifier is to differentiate between those unknown words which are spelling errors and those which are not. We define a misspelling as an unintended, orthographically incorrect representation (with respect to the NLP system) of a word. A misspelling differs from the intended known word through one or more additions, deletions, substitutions, or reversals of letters, or the exclusion of punctuation such as hyphenation or spacing. Like the definition of 'unknown word', the definition of a misspelling is also relative to a particular NLP system.

Like the name identifier, we make use of a decision tree to capture the characteristics of misspellings. The features we use are derived from previous research, including our own previous research on misspelling identification. An abridged list of the features that are used in the training data is listed in Table 2 and discussed below.

Corpus frequency: (Vosse, 1992) differentiates between misspellings and neologisms (new words) in terms of their frequency. His algorithm classifies unknown words that appear infrequently as misspellings, and those that appear more frequently as neologisms. Our corpus frequency variable specifies the frequency of each unknown word in a 2.6 million word corpus of business news closed captions.

Word Length: (Agirre et al., 1998) note that their predictions for the correct spelling of misspelled words are more accurate for words longer than four characters, and much less accurate for shorter words. This observation can also be found in (Kukich, 1992). Our word length variables measures the number of characters in each word.

Edit distance: Edit-distance is a metric for identifying the orthographic similarity of two words. Typically, one edit-distance corresponds to one substitution, deletion, reversal or addition of a character. (Damerau, 1964) observed that 80% of spelling errors in his data were just one edit-distance from the intended word. Similarly, (Mitton, 1987) found that 70% of his data was within one edit-distance from the intended word. Our edit distance feature represents the edit distance from the unknown word to the closest suggestion produced by the unix spell checker, ispell. If ispell does not produce any suggestions, an edit distance of thirty is assigned. In previous work we have experimented with more sophisticated distance measures. However, simple edit distance proved to be the most effective (Toole, 1999).

Character sequence frequency: A characteristic of some misspellings is that they contain character sequences which are not typical of the language, e.g.*tlted, wful*. Exploiting this information is a standard way of identifying spelling errors when using a dictionary is not desired or appropriate, e.g. (Hull and Srihari, 1982), (Zamora et al., 1981).

To calculate our character sequence feature, we firstly determine the frequencies of the two least frequent character tri-gram sequences in the word in each of a selection of corpora. In previous work we included each of these values as individual features. However, the resulting trees were quite unstable as one feature would be relevant to one tree, whereas a different character sequence feature would be relevant to another tree. To avoid this problem, we developed a composite feature that is the sum of all individual character sequence frequencies.

Non-English characters: This binary feature specifies whether a word contains a character that is not typical of English words, such as accented characters, etc. Such characters are indicative of foreign names or transmission noise (in the case of captions) rather than misspellings.

3.3 Decision Making Component

The misspelling identifier and the name identifier will each return a prediction for an unknown word. In cases where the predictions are compatible, e.g. where the name identifier predicts that it is a name and the spelling identifier predicts that it is not a misspelling, then the decision is straightforward. Similarly, if both decision trees make negative predictions, then we can assume that the unknown word is neither a misspelling nor a name, but some other category of unknown word.

However, it is also possible that both the spelling identifier and the name identifier will make positive predictions. In these cases we need a mechanism to decide which assignment is upheld. For the purposes of this paper, we make use of a simple heuristic where in the case of two positive predictions the one with the highest confidence measure is accepted. The decision trees return a confidence measure for each leaf of the tree. The confidence measure for a particular leaf is calculated from the training data and corresponds to the proportion of correct predictions over the total number of predictions at this leaf.

4 Evaluation

In this section we evaluate the unknown word categorizer introduced above. We begin by describing the training and test data. Following this, we evaluate the individual components and finally, we evaluate the decision making component.

The training and test data for the decision tree consists of 7000 cases of unknown words extracted from a 2.6 million word corpus of live business news captions. Of the 7000 cases, 70.4% were manually identified as names and 21.3% were identified as misspellings.The remaining cases were other types of unknown words such as abbreviations, morphological variants, etc. Seventy percent of the data was randomly selected to serve as the training corpus. The remaining thirty percent, or 2100 records, was reserved as the test corpus. The test data consists of ten samples of 2100 records selected randomly with replacement from the test corpus.

We now consider the results of training a decision tree to identify misspellings using those features we introduced in the section on the misspelling identifier. The tree was trained on the training data described above. The tree was evaluated using each of the ten test data sets. The average precision and recall data for the ten test sets are given in Table 3, together with the base-line case of assuming that we categorize all unknown words as names (the most common category). With the baseline case we achieve 70.4% precision but with 0% recall. In contrast, the decision tree approach obtains 77.1% precision and 73.8% recall.

We also trained a decision tree using not only the features identified in our discussion on misspellings but also those features that we introduced in our discussion of name identification. The results for this tree can be found in the second line of Table 3. The inclusion of the additional features has increased precision by approximately 5%. However, it has also decreased recall by about the same amount. The overall F-score is quite similar. It appears that the name features are not predictive for identifying misspellings in this domain. This is not surprising considering that eight of the ten features specified for name identification are concerned with features of the two preceding and two following words. Such word-external information is of little use in identifying a misspelling.

An analysis of the cases where the misspelling decision tree failed to identify a misspelling revealed two major classes of omissions. The first class contains a collection of words which have typical characteristics of English words, but differ from the intended word by the addition or deletion of a syllable. Words in this class include *creditability* for *credibility*, *coordinatored* for *coordinated*, and *representives* for *representatives*. The second class contains misspellings that differ from known words by the deletion of a blank. Examples in this class include *webpage*, *crewmembers*, and *rainshower*. The second class of misspellings can be addressed by adding a feature that specifies whether the unknown word can be split up into two component known words. Such a feature should provide strong predictability for the second class of words. The first class of words are more of a challenge. These words have a close homophonic relationship with the intended word rather than a close homographic relationship (as captured by edit distance). Perhaps this class of words would benefit from a feature representing phonetic distance rather than edit distance.

Among those words which were incorrectly identified as misspellings, it is also possible to identify common causes for the misidentification. Among these words are many foreign words which have character sequences which are not common in English. Examples include *khanchanalak*, *phytoplankton*, *bryceen*.

The results for our name identifier are given in Table 4. Again, the decision tree approach is a significant improvement over the baseline case. If we take the baseline approach and assume that all unknown words are names, then we would achieve a precision of 70.4%. However, using the decision tree approach, we obtain 86.5% precision and 92.9% recall.

We also trained a tree using both the name and misspelling features. The results can be found in the second line of Table 4. Unlike the case when we trained the misspelling identifier on all the features, the extended tree for the name identifier provides increased recall as well as increased precision. Unlike the case with the misspelling decision-tree, the misspelling-identification features do provide predictive information for name identification. If we review the features, this result seems quite reasonable: features such as corpus frequency and non-English characters can provide evidence for/against name iden-

	Baseline Precision/Recall	Precision	Recall	F-score
Misspelling features only	70.4%/0%	73.8%	77.1%	75.4
All features		82.8%	68.9%	75.2

Table 3: Precision and recall for misspelling identification

tification as well as for/against misspelling identification. For example, an unknown word that occurs quite frequently (such as *clinton*) is likely to be a name, whereas an unknown word that occurs infrequently (such as *wful*) is likely to be a misspelling.

A review of the errors made by the name identifier again provides insight for future development. Among those unknown words that are names but which were not identified as such are predominantly names that can (and did) appear with determiners. Examples of this class include *steelers* in *the steelers*, and *pathfinder* in *the pathfinder*. Hence, the name identifier seems adept at finding the names of individual people and places, which typically cannot be combined with determiners. But, the name identifier has more problems with names that have similar distributions to common nouns.

The cases where the name identifier incorrectly identifies unknown words as names also have identifiable characteristics. These examples mostly include words with unusual character sequences such as the misspellings *sxetion* and *fwlamg*. No doubt these have similar characteristics to foreign names. As the misidentified words are also correctly identified as misspellings by the misspelling identifier, these are less problematic. It is the task of the decision-making component to resolve issues such as these.

The final results we include are for the unknown word categorizer itself using the voting procedure outlined in previous discussion. As introduced previously, confidence measure is used as a tie-breaker in cases where the two components make positive decision. We evaluate the categorizer using precision and recall metrics. The precision metric identifies the number of correct misspelling or name categorizations over the total number of times a word was identified as a misspelling or a name. The recall metric identifies the number of times the system correctly identifies a misspelling or name over the number of misspellings and names existing in the data. As illustrated in Table 5, the unknown word categorizer achieves 86% precision and 89.9% recall on the task of identifying names and misspellings.

An examination of the confusion matrix of the tie-breaker decisions is also revealing. We include the confusion matrix for one test data set in Table 6. Firstly, in only about 5% of the cases was it necessary to revert to confidence measure to determine the category of the unknown word. In all other cases the predictions were compatible. Secondly, in the majority of cases the decision-maker rules in favour of the name prediction. In hindsight this is not surprising since the name decision tree has higher results and hence is likely to have higher confidence measures.

A review of the largest error category in this confusion matrix is also insightful. These are cases where the decision-maker classifies the unknown word as a name when it should be a misspelling (37 cases). The words in this category are typically examples where the misspelled word has a phonetic relationship with the intended word. For example, *temt* for *tempt*, *floyda* for *florida*, and *dimow* part of the intended word *democrat*. Not surprisingly, it was these types of words which were identified as problematic for the current misspelling identifier. Augmenting the misspelling identifier with features to identify these types of misspellings should also lead to improvement in the decision-maker.

We find these results encouraging: they indicate that the approach we are taking is productive. Our future work will focus on three fronts. Firstly, we will improve our existing components by developing further features which are sensitive to the distinction between names and misspellings. The discussion in this section has indicated several promising directions. Secondly, we will develop components to identify the remaining types of unknown words, such as abbreviations, morphological variants, etc. Thirdly, we will experiment with alternative decision-making processes.

5 Examining Portability

In this paper we have introduced a means for identifying names and misspellings from among other types of unknown words and have illustrated the process using the domain of closed captions. Although not explicitly specified, one of the goals of the research has been to develop an approach that will be portable to new domains and languages.

We are optimistic that the approach we have developed is portable. The system that we have developed requires very little in terms of linguistic resources. Apart from a corpus of the new domain and language, the only other requirements are some means of generating spelling suggestions (ispell is available for many languages) and a part-of-speech tagger. For this reason, the unknown word categorizer should be portable to new languages, even where extensive language resources do not exist. If

	Baseline Precision	Precision	Recall	F-score
Name features only	70.4%	86.5%	92.9%	89.6
All Features		91.8%	94.5%	93.1

Table 4: Precision and recall for name identification

	Precision	Recall	F-score
Predicting Names and Misspellings	86.6%	89.9%	88.2

Table 5: Precision and recall for decision-making component

more information sources are available, then these can be readily included in the information provided to the decision tree training algorithm.

For many languages, the features used in the unknown word categorizer may well be sufficient. However, the features used do make some assumptions about the nature of the writing system used. For example, the edit distance feature in the misspelling identifier assumes that words consist of alphabetic characters which have undergone substitution/addition/deletion. However, this feature will be less useful in a language such as Japanese or Chinese which use ideographic characters. However, while the exact features used in this paper may be inappropriate for a given language, we believe the general approach is transferable. In the case of a language such as Japanese, one would consider the means by which misspellings differ from their intended word and identify features to capture these differences.

6 Related Research

There is little research that has focused on differentiating the different types of unknown words. For example, research on spelling error detection and correction for the most part assumes that all unknown words are misspellings and makes no attempt to identify other types of unknown words, e.g. (Elmi and Evens, 1998). Naturally, these are not appropriate comparisons for the work reported here. However, as is evident from the discussion above, previous spelling research does provide an important role in suggesting productive features to include in the decision tree.

Research that is more similar in goal to that outlined in this paper is Vosse (Vosse, 1992). Vosse uses a simple algorithm to identify three classes of unknown words: misspellings, neologisms, and names. Capitalization is his sole means of identifying names. However, capitalization information is not available in closed captions. Hence, his system would be ineffective on the closed caption domain with which we are working. (Granger, 1983) uses expectations generated by scripts to analyze unknown words. The drawback of his system is that it lacks portability since it incorporates scripts that make use of world knowledge of the situation being described; in this case, naval ship-to-shore messages.

Research that is similar in technique to that reported here is (Baluja et al., 1999). Baluja and his colleagues use a decision tree classifier to identify proper names in text. They incorporate three types of features: word level (essentially utilizes case information), dictionary-level (comparable to our ispell feature), and POS information (comparable to our POS tagging). Their highest F-score for name identification is 95.2, slightly higher than our name identifier. However, it is difficult to compare the two sets of results since our tasks are slightly different. The goal of Baluja's research, and all other proper name identification research, is to identify all those words and phrases in the text which are proper names. Our research, on the other hand, is not concerned with all text, but only those words which are unknown. Also preventing comparison is the type of data that we deal with. Baluja's data contains case information whereas ours does not- the lack of case information makes name identification significantly more difficult. Indeed, Baluja's results when they exclude their word-level (case) features are significantly lower: a maximum F-score of 79.7.

7 Conclusion

In this paper we have introduced an unknown word categorizer that can identify misspellings and names. The unknown word categorizer consists of individual components, each of which specialize in identifying a particular class of unknown word. The two existing components are implemented as decision trees. The system provides encouraging results when evaluated against a particularly challenging domain: transcripts from live closed captions.

References

E. Agirre, K. Gojenola, K. Sarasola, , and A. Voutilainen. 1998. Towards a single proposal in spelling correction. In *Proceedings of the 36th Annual Meeting of the ACL and the 17th International*

	Predicted Spelling	Predicted Name
Neither name nor misspelling	0	6
Misspelling	10	37
Name	4	43

Table 6: Confusion matrix for decision maker: includes only those examples where both components made a positive prediction.

Conference on Computational Linguistics, pages 22–28.

S. Baluja, V. Mittal, and R.. Sukthankar. 1999. Applying machine learning for high performance named-entity extraction. In *Proceedings of the Conference of the Pacific Association for Computational Linguistics*, pages 365–378.

K. Church 1988. A stochastic parts program and noun phrase parser for unrestricted text. In *Proceedings of the Second Conference on Applied Natural Language Processing*, pages 136–143.

F. Damerau. 1964. A technique for computer detection and correction of spelling errors. *Communications of the ACM*, 7:171–176.

M. Elmi and M. Evens. 1998. Spelling correction using context. In *Proceedings of the 36th Annual Meeting of the ACL and the 17th International Conference on Computational Linguistics*, pages 360–364.

D. Elworthy. 1998. Language identification with confidence limits. In *Proceedings of the 6th Workshop on Very large Corpora*.

R. Granger. 1983. The nomad system: expectation-based detection and correction of errors during understanding of syntactically and semantically ill-formed text. *American Journal of Computational Linguistics*, 9:188–198.

J. Hull and S. Srihari. 1982. Experiments in text recognition with binary n-gram and viterbi algorithms. *IEEE Trans. Patt. Anal. Machine Intell. PAMI-4*, 5:520–530.

K.. Kukich. 1992. Techniques for automatically correcting words in text. *ACM Computing Surveys*, 24:377–439.

I. Mani, R. McMillan, S. Luperfoy, E. Lusher, and S. Laskowski, 1996. *Corpus Processing for Lexical Acquisition*, chapter Identifying unknown proper names in newswire text. MIT Press, Cambridge.

D. McDonald, 1996. *Corpus Processing for Lexical Acquisition*, chapter Internal and external evidence in the identification and semantic categorization of proper names. MIT Press, Cambridge.

K. Min and W. Wilson. 1998. Integrated control of chart items for error repair. In *Proceedings of the 36th Annual Meeting of the Association for Computational Linguistics and the 17th International Conference on Computational Linguistics*.

K. Min. 1996. *Hierarchical Error Recovery Based on Bidirectional Chart Parsing Techniques*. Ph.D. thesis, University of NSW, Sydney, Australia.

R. Mitton. 1987. Spelling checkers, spelling correctors, and the misspellings of poor spellers. *Inf. Process. Manage*, 23:495–505.

J. Toole 1999 Categorizing Unknown Words: A decision tree-based misspelling identifier In Foo, N (ed.) *Advanced Topics in Artificial Intelligence*, pages 122-133.

H. van Halteren, J. Zavrel, and W. Daelemans. 1998. Improving data driven word class tagging by system combination. In *Proceedings of the 36th Annual Meeting of the ACL and the 17th International Conference on Computational Linguistics*, pages 491–497.

T. Vosse. 1992. Detecting and correcting morpho-syntactic errors in real texts. In *Proceedings of the 3rd Conference on Applied Natural Language Processing*, pages 111–118.

S. Weiss and N. Indurkhya. 1998. *Predictive Data Mining*. Morgan Kauffman Publishers.

S. Weiss, and C. Apte, and F. Damerau, and D. Johnson, and F. Oles and T. Goetz, and T. Hampp. 1999 Maximizing text-mining performance. *IEEE Intelligent Systems and their Applications*,14(4):63-69

E. Zamora, J. Pollock, and A. Zamora. 1981. The use of tri-gram analysis for spelling error detection. *Inf. Process. Manage.*, 17:305–316.

Examining the Role of Statistical and Linguistic Knowledge Sources in a General-Knowledge Question-Answering System

Claire Cardie[1] and **Vincent Ng**[1] and **David Pierce**[1] and **Chris Buckley**[2]
Department of Computer Science, Cornell University, Ithaca, NY 14853[1]
SaBIR Research[2]
E-mail: cardie,yung,pierce@cs.cornell.edu, chrisb@sabir.com

Abstract

We describe and evaluate an implemented system for general-knowledge question answering. The system combines techniques for standard ad-hoc information retrieval (IR), query-dependent text summarization, and shallow syntactic and semantic sentence analysis. In a series of experiments we examine the role of each statistical and linguistic knowledge source in the question-answering system. In contrast to previous results, we find first that statistical knowledge of word co-occurrences as computed by IR vector space methods can be used to quickly and accurately locate the relevant documents for each question. The use of query-dependent text summarization techniques, however, provides only small increases in performance and severely limits recall levels when inaccurate. Nevertheless, it is the text summarization component that allows subsequent linguistic filters to focus on relevant passages. We find that even very weak linguistic knowledge can offer substantial improvements over purely IR-based techniques for question answering, especially when smoothly integrated with statistical preferences computed by the IR subsystems.

1 Introduction

In this paper, we describe and evaluate an implemented system for general-knowledge question answering. Open-ended question-answering systems that allow users to pose a question of any type, in any language, without domain restrictions, remain beyond the scope of today's text-processing systems. We investigate instead a restricted, but nevertheless useful variation of the problem (TREC-8, 2000):

> Given a large text collection and a set of questions specified in English, find answers to the questions in the collection.

In addition, the restricted task guarantees that:

- the answer exists in the collection,
- all supporting information for the answer lies in a single document, and
- the answer is short — less than 50 bytes in length.

Consider, for example, the question *Which country has the largest part of the Amazon rain forest?*, taken from the TREC8 Question Answering development corpus. The answer (in document LA032590-0089) is *Brazil*.

Previous research has addressed similar question-answering (QA) scenarios using a variety of natural language processing (NLP) and information retrieval (IR) techniques. Lehnert (1978) tackles the difficult task of answering questions in the context of story understanding. Unlike our restricted QA task, questions to Lehnert's system often require answers that are not explicitly mentioned in the story. Her goal then is to answer questions by making inferences about actions and actors in the story using world knowledge in the form of scripts, plans, and goals (Schank and Abelson, 1977). More recently, Burke et al. (1995; 1997) describe a system that answers natural language questions using a database of question-answer pairs built from existing frequently-asked question (FAQ) files. Their FAQFinder system uses IR techniques to match the given question to questions in the database. It then uses the WordNet lexical semantic knowledge base (Miller et al., 1990; Fellbaum, 1998) to improve the quality of the match.

Kupiec (1993) investigates a closed-class QA task that is similar in many respects to the TREC8 QA task that we address here: the system answers general-knowledge questions using an encyclopedia. In addition, Kupiec assumes that all answers are noun phrases. Although our task does not explicitly include a "noun phrase" constraint, the answer length restriction effectively imposes the same bias toward noun phrase answers. Kupiec's MURAX system applies a combination of statistical (IR) and linguistic (NLP) techniques. A series of secondary boolean search queries with proximity constraints is combined with shallow parsing methods to find relevant sections of the encyclopedia, to extract answer hypotheses, and to confirm phrase relations specified in the question. In an evaluation on 70 "Trivial

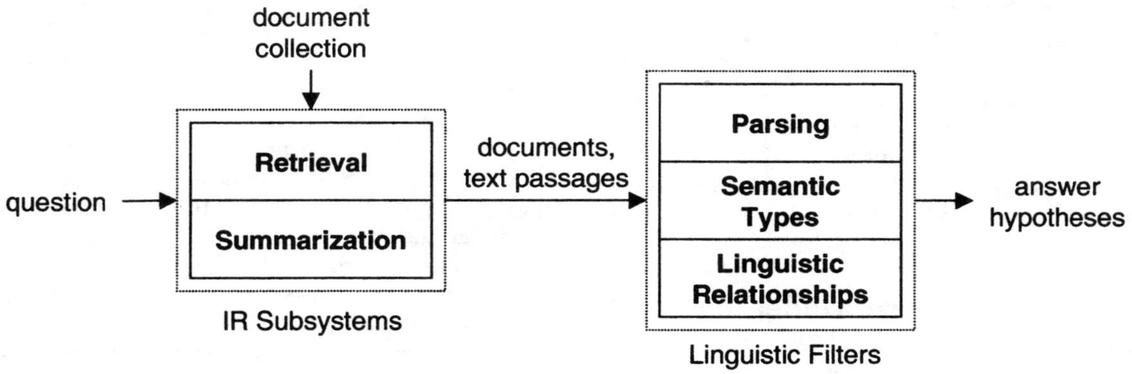

Figure 1: General Architecture of the Question-Answering System

Pursuit" *who* and *what* questions, Kupiec concludes that robust natural language analysis can add to the quality of the information retrieval process. In addition, he claims that, for their closed-class QA task, vector space IR methods (Salton et al., 1975) appear inadequate.

We present here a new approach to the restricted question-answering task described above. Like MURAX, our system draws from both statistical and linguistic sources to find answers to general-knowledge questions. The underlying architecture of the system, however, is very different: it combines vector space IR techniques for document retrieval, a vector space approach to query-dependent text summarization, shallow corpus-based syntactic analysis, and knowledge-based semantic analysis. We evaluate the system on the TREC8 QA development corpus as well as the TREC8 QA test corpus. In particular, all parameters for the final QA system are determined using the development corpus. Our current results are encouraging but not outstanding: the system is able to correctly answer 22 out of 38 of the development questions and 91 out of 200 of the test questions given five guesses for each question. Furthermore, the first guess is correct for 16 out of the 22 development questions and 53 out of 91 of the test questions.

More importantly, we investigate the relative role of each statistical and linguistic knowledge source in the proposed IR/NLP question-answering system. In contrast to previous results, we find that statistical knowledge of word co-occurrences as computed by vector space models of IR can be used to quickly and accurately locate relevant documents in the restricted QA task. When used in isolation, vector space methods for query-dependent text summarization, however, provide relatively small increases in performance. In addition, we find that the text summarization component can severely limit recall levels. Nevertheless, it is the summarization component that allows the linguistic filters to focus on relevant passages. In particular, we find that very weak linguistic knowledge can offer substantial improvements over purely IR-based techniques for question answering, especially when smoothly integrated with the statistical preferences computed by the IR subsystems.

In the next section, we describe the general architecture of the question-answering system. Section 3 describes the baseline system and its information retrieval component. Sections 4–7 describe and evaluate a series of variations to the baseline system that incorporate, in turn, query-dependent text summarization, a syntactic filter, a semantic filter, and an algorithm that allows syntactic knowledge to influence the initial ordering of summary extracts. Section 8 compares our approach to some of those in the recent TREC8 QA evaluation (TREC-8, 2000) and describes directions for future work.

2 System Architecture

The basic architecture of the question-answering system is depicted in Figure 1. It contains two main components: the IR subsystems and the linguistic filters. As a preliminary, offline step, the **IR subsystem** first indexes the text collection from which answers are to be extracted. Given a question, the goal of the IR component is then to return a ranked list of those text chunks (e.g. documents, sentences, or paragraphs) from the indexed collection that are most relevant to the query and from which answer hypotheses can be extracted. Next, the QA system optionally applies one or more **linguistic filters** to the text chunks to extract an ordered list of answer hypotheses. The top hypotheses are concatenated to form five 50-byte guesses as allowed by the TREC8 guidelines. Note that many of these guesses may be difficult to read and judged as incorrect by the

TREC8 assessors: we will also describe the results of generating single phrases as guesses wherever this is possible.

In the sections below, we present and evaluate a series of instantiations of this general architecture, each of which makes different assumptions regarding the type of information that will best support the QA task. The next section begins by describing the baseline QA system.

3 The Vector Space Model for Document Retrieval

It is clear that a successful QA system will need some way to find the documents that are most relevant to the user's question. In a baseline system, we assume that standard IR techniques can be used for this task. In contrast to MURAX, however, we hypothesize that the vector space retrieval model will suffice. In the vector space model, both the question and the documents are represented as vectors with one entry for every unique word that appears in the collection. Each entry is the *term weight*, a real number that indicates the presence or absence of the word in the text. The similarity between a question vector, $Q = q_1, q_2, \ldots, q_n$, and a document vector, $D = d_1, d_2, \ldots, d_n$, is traditionally computed using a cosine similarity measure:

$$Sim(Q, D) = \sum_{i=1}^{n} d_i \cdot q_i$$

Using this measure, the IR system returns a ranked list of those documents most similar to the question.

The Baseline QA System: The Smart Vector Space Model. For the IR component of the baseline QA system, we use Smart (Salton, 1971), a sophisticated text-processing system based on the vector space model and employed as the retrieval engine for a number of the top-performing systems at recent Text REtrieval Conferences (e.g. Buckley et al., 1998a, 1998b). Given a question, Smart returns a ranked list of the documents most relevant to the question. For the baseline QA system and all subsequent variations, we use Smart with standard term-weighting strategies[1] and do not use automatic relevance feedback (Buckley, 1995). In addition, the baseline system applies no linguistic filters. To generate answers for a particular question, the system starts at the beginning of the top-ranked document returned by Smart for the question and constructs five 50-byte chunks consisting of document text with stopwords removed.

[1]We use *Lnu* term weighting for documents and *ltu* term weighting for the question (Singhal et al., 1996).

Evaluation. As noted above, we evaluate each variation of our QA system on 38 TREC8 development questions and 200 TREC8 test questions. The indexed collection is TREC disks 4 and 5 (without Congressional Records). Results for the baseline Smart IR QA system are shown in the first row of Table 1. The system gets 3 out of 38 development questions and 29 out of 200 test questions correct. We judge the system correct if any of the five guesses contains each word of one of the answers. The final column of results shows the mean answer rank across all questions correctly answered.

Smart is actually performing much better than its scores would suggest. For 18 of the 38 development questions, the answer appears in the top-ranked document; for 33 questions, the answer appears in one of the top seven documents. For only two questions does Smart fail to retrieve a good document in the top 25 documents. For the test corpus, over half of the 200 questions are answered in the top-ranked document (110); over 75% of the questions (155) are answered in top five documents. Only 19 questions were not answered in the top 20 documents.

4 Query-Dependent Text Summarization for Question Answering

We next hypothesize that query-dependent text summarization algorithms will improve the performance of the QA system by focusing the system on the most relevant portions of the retrieved documents. The goal for query-dependent summarization algorithms is to provide a short summary of a document *with respect to a specific query*. Although a number of methods for query-dependent text summarization are beginning to be developed and evaluated in a variety of realistic settings (Mani et al., 1999), we again propose the use of vector space methods from IR, which can be easily extended to the summarization task (Salton et al., 1994):

1. Given a question and a document, divide the document into chunks (e.g. sentences, paragraphs, 200-word passages).
2. Generate the vector representation for the question and for each document chunk.
3. Use the cosine similarity measure to determine the similarity of each chunk to the question.
4. Return as the query-dependent summary the most similar chunks up to a predetermined summary length (e.g. 10% or 20% of the original document).

This approach to text summarization was shown to be quite successful in the recent SUMMAC evaluation of text summarization systems (Mani et al., 1999; Buckley et al., 1999). Our general assumption here is that IR approaches can be used to quickly and accurately find both relevant documents and relevant document portions. In related work, Chali *et al.* (1999) also propose text summarization techniques as a primary component for their QA system. They employ a combination of vector-space methods and lexical chaining to derive their sentence-based summaries. We hypothesize that deeper analysis of the summary extracts is better accomplished by methods from NLP that can determine syntactic and semantic relationships between relevant constituents. There is a risk in using query-dependent summaries to focus the search for answer hypotheses, however: if the summarization algorithm is inaccurate, the desired answers will occur outside of the summaries and will not be accessible to subsequent components of the QA system.

The Query-Dependent Text Summarization QA System. In the next version of the QA system, we augment the baseline system to perform query-dependent text summarization for the top k retrieved documents. More specifically, the IR subsystem returns the summary extracts (sentences or paragraphs) for the top k documents after sorting them according to their cosine similarity scores w.r.t. the question. As before, no linguistic filters are applied, and answers are generated by constructing 50-byte chunks from the ordered extracts after removing stopwords. In the experiments below, $k = 7$ for the development questions and $k = 6$ for the test questions.[2]

Evaluation. Results for the Text Summarization QA system using sentence-based summaries are shown in the second row of Table 1. Here we see a relatively small improvement: the system now answers four development and 45 test questions correctly. The mean answer rank, however, improves noticeably from 3.33 to 2.25 for the development corpus and from 3.07 to 2.67 for the test corpus. Paragraph-based summaries yield similar but slightly smaller improvements; as a result, sentence summaries are used exclusively in subsequent sections. Unfortunately, the system's reliance on query-dependent text summarization actually limits its potential: in only 23 of the 38 development questions (61%), for example, does the correct answer appear in the summary for one of the top $k = 7$ documents. The QA system cannot hope to answer correctly any of the remaining 15 questions. For only 135 of the 200 questions in the test corpus (67.5%) does the correct answer appear in the summary for one of the top $k = 6$ documents.[3] It is possible that automatic relevance feedback or coreference resolution would improve performance. We are investigating these options in current work.

The decision of whether or not to incorporate text summarization in the QA system depends, in part, on the ability of subsequent processing components (i.e. the linguistic filters) to locate answer hypotheses. If subsequent components are very good at discarding implausible answers, then summarization methods may limit system performance. Therefore, we investigate next the use of two linguistic filters in conjunction with the query-dependent text summarization methods evaluated here.

5 Incorporating the Noun Phrase Filter

The restricted QA task that we investigate requires answers to be short — no more than 50 bytes in length. This effectively eliminates *how* or *why* questions from consideration. Almost all of the remaining question types are likely to have noun phrases as answers. In the TREC8 development corpus, for example, 36 of 38 questions have noun phrase answers.

As a result, we next investigate the use of a very simple linguistic filter that considers only noun phrases as answer hypotheses. The filter operates on the ordered list of summary extracts for a particular question and produces a list of answer hypotheses, one for each noun phrase (NP) in the extracts in the left-to-right order in which they appeared.

The NP-based QA System. Our implementation of the NP-based QA system uses the Empire noun phrase finder, which is described in detail in Cardie and Pierce (1998). Empire identifies *base NPs* — non-recursive noun phrases — using a very simple algorithm that matches part-of-speech tag sequences based on a learned noun phrase grammar. The approach is able to achieve 94% precision and recall for base NPs derived from the Penn Treebank Wall Street Journal (Marcus et al., 1993). In the experiments below, the NP filter follows the application of the document retrieval and text summarization components. Pronoun answer hypotheses are discarded, and the NPs are assembled into 50-byte chunks.

Evaluation. Results for the NP-based QA system are shown in the third row of Table 1. The noun phrase filter markedly improves system performance for the development corpus, nearly dou-

[2]The value for k was chosen so that at least 80% of the questions in the set had answers appearing in the retrieved documents ranked 1–k. We have not experimented extensively with many values of k and expect that better performance can be obtained by tuning k for each text collection.

[3]Paragraph-based summaries provide better coverage on the test corpus than sentence-based summaries: for 151 questions, the correct answer appears in the summary for one of the top k documents. This suggests that paragraph summaries might be better suited for use with more sophisticated linguistic filters that are capable of discerning the answer in the larger summary.

Question-Answering System Variation	Development Corpus Correct (%)		Development Corpus MAR	Test Corpus Correct (%)		Test Corpus MAR
Smart Vector Space Model	3/38	0.079	3.33	29/200	0.145	3.07
Query-Dependent Text Summarization	4/38	0.105	2.25	45/200	0.225	2.67
Text Summarization + NPs	7/38	0.184	2.29	50/200	0.250	2.66
Text Summarization + NPs + Semantic Type	21/38	0.553	1.38	86/200	0.430	1.90
Text Summarization with Syntactic Ordering + NPs + Semantic Type	22/38	0.579	1.32	91/200	0.455	1.82

Table 1: Evaluation of the Role of Statistical and Limited Linguistic Knowledge for the TREC8 Question Answering Task. Results for 38 development and 200 test questions are shown. The mean answer rank (MAR) is computed w.r.t. all questions correctly answered.

bling the number of questions answered correctly. We found these results somewhat surprising since this linguistic filter is rather weak: we expected it to work well only in combination with the semantic filter described below. The noun phrase filter has much less of an effect on the test corpus, improving performance on questions answered from 45 to 50.

In a separate experiment, we applied the NP filter to the baseline system that includes no text summarization component. Here the NP filter does not improve performance — the system gets only two questions correct. This indicates that the NP filter depends critically on the text summarization component. As a result, we will continue to use query-dependent text summarization in the experiments below.

The NP filter provides the first opportunity to look at single-phrase answers. The preceding QA systems produced answers that were rather unnaturally chunked into 50-byte strings. When such chunking is disabled, only one development and 20 test questions are answered. The difference in performance between the NP filter with chunking and the NP filter alone clearly indicates that the NP filter is extracting good guesses, but that subsequent linguistic processing is needed to promote the best guesses to the top of the ranked guess list.

6 Incorporating Semantic Type Information

The NP filter does not explicitly consider the question in its search for noun phrase answers. It is clear, however, that a QA system must pay greater attention to the syntactic and semantic constraints specified in the question. For example, a question like *Who was president of the US in 1995?* indicates that the answer is likely to be a person. In addition, there should be supporting evidence from the answer document that the person was *president*, and, more specifically, held this office *in the US* and *in 1995*.

We introduce here a second linguistic filter that considers the primary semantic constraint from the question. The filter begins by determining the *question type*, i.e. the semantic type requested in the question. It then takes the ordered set of summary extracts supplied by the IR subsytem, uses the syntactic filter from Section 5 to extract NPs, and generates an answer hypothesis for every noun phrase that is semantically compatible with the question type. Our implementation of this semantic class filter is described below. The filter currently makes no attempt to confirm other linguistic relations mentioned in the question.

The Semantic Type Checking QA System. For most questions, the question word itself determines the semantic type of the answer. This is true for *who*, *where*, and *when* questions, for example, which request a *person*, *place*, and *time* expression as an answer. For many *which* and *what* questions, however, determining the question type requires additional syntactic analysis. For these, we currently extract the head noun in the question as the question type. For example, in *Which country has the largest part of the Amazon rain forest?* we identify *country* as the question type. Our heuristics for determining question type were based on the development corpus and were designed to be general, but have not yet been directly evaluated on a separate question corpus.

Given the question type and an answer hypothesis, the Semantic Type Checking QA System then uses WordNet to check that an appropriate ancestor-descendent relationship holds. Given *Brazil* as an answer hypothesis for the above question, for example, Wordnet's type hierarchy confirms that *Brazil* is a subtype of *country*, allowing the system to conclude that the semantic type of the answer hypothesis matches the question type.

For words (mostly proper nouns) that do not appear in WordNet, heuristics are used to determine semantic type. There are heuristics to recognize 13 basic question types: Person, Location, Date, Month, Year, Time, Age, Weight, Area, Volume, Length, Amount, and Number. For Person questions, for example, the system relies primarily on a rule that checks for capitalization and abbreviations in order to identify phrases that correspond to people. There are approximately 20 such rules that together cover all 13 question types listed above. The rules effectively operate as a very simple named entity identifier.

Evaluation. Results for the Semantic Type Checking variation of the QA system are shown in the fourth row of Table 1. Here we see a dramatic increase in performance: the system answers three times as many development questions (21) correctly over the previous variation. This is especially encouraging given that the IR and text summarization components limit the maximum number correct to 23. In addition, the mean answer rank improves from 2.29 to 1.38. A closer look at Table 1, however, indicates problems with the semantic type checking linguistic filter. While performance on the development corpus increases by 37 percentage points (from 18.4% correct to 55.3% correct), relative gains for the test corpus are much smaller. There is only an improvement of 18 percentage points, from 25.0% correct (50/200) to 43.0% correct (86/200). This is a clear indication that the heuristics used in the semantic type checking component, which were designed based on the development corpus, do not generalize well to different question sets. Replacing the current heuristics with a Named Entity identification component or learning the heuristics using standard inductive learning techniques should help with the scalability of this linguistic filter.

Nevertheless, it is somewhat surprising that very weak syntactic information (the NP filter) and weak semantic class information (question type checking) can produce such improvements. In particular, it appears that it is reasonable to rely implicitly on the IR subsystems to enforce the other linguistic relationships specified in the query (e.g. that *Clinton* is *president*, that this office was held *in the US* and *in 1995*).

Finally, when 50-byte chunking is disabled for the semantic type checking QA variation, there is a decrease in the number of questions correctly answered, to 19 and 57 for the development and test corpus, respectively.

7 Syntactic Preferences for Ordering Summary Extracts

Syntactic and semantic linguistic knowledge has been used thus far as post-processing filters that locate and confirm answer hypotheses from the statistically specified summary extracts. We hypothesized that further improvements might be made by allowing this linguistic knowledge to influence the initial ordering of text chunks for the linguistic filters. In a final system, we begin to investigate this claim. Our general approach is to define a new scoring measure that operates on the summary extracts and can be used to reorder the extracts based on linguistic knowledge.

The QA System with Linguistic Reordering of Summary Extracts. As described above, our final version of the QA system ranks summary extracts according to both their vector space similarity to the question as well as linguistic evidence that the answer lies within the extract. In particular, each summary extract E for question q is ranked according to a new score, s_q:

$$s_q(E) = w(E) \cdot LR_q(E)$$

The intuition behind the new score is to prefer summary extracts that exhibit the same linguistic relationships as the question (as indicated by LR_q) and to give more weight (as indicated by w) to linguistic relationship matches in extracts from higher-ranked documents. More specifically, $LR_q(E)$ is the number of linguistic relationships from the question that appear in E. In the experiments below, $LR_q(E)$ is just the number of base NPs from the question that appear in the summary extract. In future work, we plan to include other pairwise linguistic relationships (e.g. subject-verb relationships, verb-object relationships, pp-attachment relationships). The weight $w(E)$ is a number between 0 and 1 that is based on the retrieval rank r of the document that contains E:

$$w(E) = max(m, 1 - p \cdot r)$$

In our experiments, $m = 0.5$ and $p = 0.1$. Both values were selected manually based on the development corpus; an extensive search for the best such values was not done.

The summary extracts are sorted according to the new scoring measure and the ranked list of sentences is provided to the linguistic filters as before.

Evaluation. Results for this final variation of the QA system are shown in the bottom row of Table 1. Here we see a fairly minor increase in performance over the use of linguistic filters alone: the system answers only one more question correctly than the previous variation for the development corpus and answers five additional questions for the test corpus. The mean answer rank improves only negligibly. Sixteen of the 22 correct answers (73%) appear as the top-ranked guess for the development corpus; only 53 out of 91 correct answers (58%) appear as the top-ranked guess for the test corpus. Unfortunately, when 50-byte chunking is disabled, system performance drops precipitously, by 5% (to 20 out of 38) for the development corpus and by 13% (to 65 out of 200) for the test corpus. As noted above, this indicates that the filters are finding the answers, but more sophisticated linguistic sorting is needed to promote the best answers to the top. Through its LR_q term, the new scoring measure does provide a mechanism for allowing other linguistic relationships to influence the initial ordering of summary extracts. The current results, however, indicate that with only very weak syntactic information (i.e. base noun phrases), the new scoring measure is only marginally successful in reordering the summary extracts based on syntactic information.

As noted above, the final system (with the liberal 50-byte answer chunker) correctly answers 22 out of 38 questions for the development corpus. Of the 16 errors, the text retrieval component is responsible for five (31.2%), the text summarization component for ten (62.5%), and the linguistic filters for one (6.3%). In this analysis we consider the linguistic filters responsible for an error if they were unable to promote an available answer hypothesis to one of the top five guesses. A slightly different situation arises for the test corpus: of the 109 errors, the text retrieval component is responsible for 39 (35.8%), the text summarization component for 26 (23.9%), and the linguistic filters for 44 (40.4%). As discussed in Section 6, the heuristics that comprise the semantic type checking filter do not scale to the test corpus and are the primary reason for the larger percentage of errors attributed to the linguistic filters for that corpus.

8 Related Work and Conclusions

We have described and evaluated a series of question-answering systems, each of which incorporates a different combination of statistical and linguistic knowledge sources. We find that even very weak linguistic knowledge can offer substantial improvements over purely IR-based techniques especially when smoothly integrated with the text passage preferences computed by the IR subsystems. Although our primary goal was to investigate the use of statistical and linguistic knowledge sources, it is possible to compare our approach and our results to those for systems in the recent TREC8 QA evaluation. Scores on the TREC8 test corpus for systems participating in the QA evaluation ranged between 3 and 146 correct. Discarding the top three scores and the worst three scores, the remaining eight systems achieved between 52 and 91 correct. Using the liberal answer chunker, our final QA system equals the best of these systems (91 correct); without it, our score of 65 correct places our QA system near the middle of this group of eight.

Like the work described here, virtually all of the top-ranked TREC8 systems use a combination of IR and shallow NLP for their QA systems. IBM's AnSel system (Prager et al., 2000), for example, employs finite-state patterns as its primary shallow NLP component. These are used to recognize a fairly broad set of about 20 named entities. The IR component indexes only text passages associated with these entities. The AT&T QA system (Singhal et al., 2000), the Qanda system (Breck et al., 2000), and the SyncMatcher system (Oard et al., 2000) all employ vector-space methods from IR, named entity identifiers, and a fairly simple question type determiner. In addition, SyncMatcher uses a broad-coverage dependency parser to enforce phrase relationship constraints. Instead of the vector space model, the LASSO system (Moldovan et al., 2000) uses boolean search operators for paragraph retrieval. Recognition of answer hypotheses in their system relies on identifying named entities. Finally, the Cymphony QA system (Srihari and Li, 2000) relies heavily on named entity identification; it also employs standard IR techniques and a shallow parser.

In terms of statistical and linguistic knowledge sources employed, the primary difference between these systems and ours is our lack of an adequate named entity tagger. Incorporation of such a tagger will be a focus of future work. In addition, we believe that the retrieval and summarization components can be improved by incorporating automatic relevance feedback (Buckley, 1995) and coreference resolution. Morton (1999), for example, shows that coreference resolution improves passage retrieval for their question-answering system. We also plan to reconsider paragraph-based summaries given their coverage on the test corpus. The most critical area for improvement, however, is the linguistic filters. The semantic type filter will be greatly improved by the addition of a named entity tagger, but we believe that additional gains can be attained by augmenting named entity identification with information from WordNet. Finally, we currently make no attempt to confirm any phrase relations from the query. Without this, system performance will remain severely limited.

9 Acknowledgments

This work was supported in part by NSF Grants IRI-9624639 and GER-9454149.

References

E. Breck, J. Burger, L. Ferro, D. House, M. Light, and I. Mani. 2000. A Sys Called Qanda. In E. Voorhees, editor, *Proceedings of the Eighth Text REtrieval Conference TREC 8*. NIST Special Publication. In press.

C. Buckley, M. Mitra, J. Walz, and C. Cardie. 1998a. SMART high precision: TREC 7. In E. Voorhees, editor, *Proceedings of the Seventh Text REtrieval Conference TREC 7*, pages 285–298. NIST Special Publication 500-242.

C. Buckley, M. Mitra, J. Walz, and C. Cardie. 1998b. Using clustering and superconcepts within

SMART : TREC 6. In E. Voorhees, editor, *Proceedings of the Sixth Text REtrieval Conference TREC 6*, pages 107–124. NIST Special Publication 500–240.

C. Buckley, C. Cardie, S. Mardis, M. Mitra, D. Pierce, K. Wagstaff, and J. Walz. 1999. The Smart/Empire TIPSTER IR System. In *Proceedings, TIPSTER Text Program (Phase III)*. Morgan Kaufmann. To appear.

Chris Buckley. 1995. *Massive Query Expansion for Relevance Feedback*. Cornell University, Ph.D. Thesis, Ithaca, New York.

R. Burke, K. Hammond, and J. Kozlovsky. 1995. Knowledge-Based Information Retrieval from Semi-Structured Text. In *Working Notes of the AAAI Fall Symposium on AI Applications in Knowledge Navigation and Retrieval*, pages 19–24. AAAI Press.

R. Burke, K. Hammond, V. Kulyukin, S. Lytinen, N. Tomuro, and S. Schoenberg. 1997. question answering from Frequently-Asked Question Files. Technical Report TR–97–05, University of Chicago.

C. Cardie and D. Pierce. 1998. Error-Driven Pruning of Treebank Grammars for Base Noun Phrase Identification. In *Proceedings of the 36th Annual Meeting of the Association for Computational Linguistics and COLING-98*, pages 218–224, University of Montreal, Montreal, Canada. Association for Computational Linguistics.

Y. Chali, S. Matwin, and S. Szpakowicz. 1999. Query-Biased Text Summarization as a Question-Answering Technique. In *Proceedings of the AAAI Fall Symposium on Question Answering Systems*, pages 52–56. AAAI Press. AAAI TR FS–99–02.

C. Fellbaum. 1998. *WordNet: An Electronical Lexical Database*. MIT Press, Cambridge, MA.

J. Kupiec. 1993. MURAX: A Robust Linguistic approach For Question Answering Using An On-Line Encyclopedia. In *Proceedings of ACM SIGIR*, pages 181–190.

W. Lehnert. 1978. *The Process of Question Answering*. Lawrence Erlbaum Associates, Hillsdale, NJ.

I. Mani, T. Firmin, D. House, G. Klein, B. Sundheim, and L. Hirschman. 1999. The TIPSTER SUMMAC Text Summarization Evaluation. In *Ninth Annual Meeting of the EACL*, University of Bergen, Bergen, Norway.

M. Marcus, M. Marcinkiewicz, and B. Santorini. 1993. Building a Large Annotated Corpus of English: The Penn Treebank. *Computational Linguistics*, 19(2):313–330.

G. A. Miller, R. Beckwith, C. Fellbaum, D. Gross, and K. J. Miller. 1990. WordNet: an on-line lexical database. *International Journal of Lexicography*, 3(4):235–245.

D. Moldovan, S. Harabagiu, M. Paşca, R. Mihalcea, R. Goodrum, R. Gîrju, and V. Rus. 2000. LASSO: A Tool for Surfing the Answer Net. In E. Voorhees, editor, *Proceedings of the Eighth Text REtrieval Conference TREC 8*. NIST Special Publication. In press.

T. S. Morton. 1999. Using Coreference to Improve Passage Retrieval for Question Answering. In *Proceedings of the AAAI Fall Symposium on Question Answering Systems*, pages 72–74. AAAI Press. AAAI TR FS–99–02.

D. W. Oard, J. Wang, D. Lin, and I. Soboroff. 2000. TREC-8 Experiments at Maryland: CLIR, QA and Routing. In E. Voorhees, editor, *Proceedings of the Eighth Text REtrieval Conference TREC 8*. NIST Special Publication. In press.

J. Prager, D. Radev, E. Brown, A. Coden, and V. Samn. 2000. The Use of Predictive Annotation for Question Answering in TREC8. In E. Voorhees, editor, *Proceedings of the Eighth Text REtrieval Conference TREC 8*. NIST Special Publication. In press.

G. Salton, A. Wong, and C.S. Yang. 1975. A vector space model for information retrieval. *Communications of the ACM*, 18(11):613–620.

G. Salton, J. Allan, C. Buckley, and M. Mitra. 1994. Automatic analysis, theme generation and summarization of machine-readable texts. *Science*, 264:1421–1426, June.

Gerard Salton, editor. 1971. *The SMART Retrieval System—Experiments in Automatic Document Processing*. Prentice Hall Inc., Englewood Cliffs, NJ.

R. C. Schank and R. P. Abelson. 1977. *Scripts, plans, goals, and understanding*. Lawrence Erlbaum Associates, Hillsdale, NJ.

Amit Singhal, Chris Buckley, and Mandar Mitra. 1996. Pivoted document length normalization. In H. Frei, D. Harman, P. Schauble, and R. Wilkinson, editors, *Proceedings of the Nineteenth Annual International ACM SIGIR Conference on Research and Development in Information Retrieval*, pages 21–29. Association for Computing Machinery.

A. Singhal, S. Abney, M. Bacchiani, M. Collins, D. Hindle, and F. Pereira. 2000. AT&T at TREC-8. In E. Voorhees, editor, *Proceedings of the Eighth Text REtrieval Conference TREC 8*. NIST Special Publication. In press.

R. Srihari and W. Li. 2000. Question Answering Supported by Information Extraction. In E. Voorhees, editor, *Proceedings of the Eighth Text REtrieval Conference TREC 8*. NIST Special Publication. In press.

TREC-8. 2000. *Proceedings of the Eighth Text REtrieval Conference TREC 8*. NIST. In press.

Extracting Molecular Binding Relationships from Biomedical Text

Thomas C. RINDFLESCH
National Library of Medicine
8600 Rockville Pike
Bethesda, MD, 20894
tcr@nlm.nih.gov

Jayant V. RAJAN
University of Rochester
Rochester, NY, 14620
Jayant.Rajan@mc.rochester.edu

Lawrence HUNTER
National Cancer Institute
7550 Wisconsin Avenue
Bethesda, MD, 20894
lhunter@nih.gov

Abstract

ARBITER is a Prolog program that extracts assertions about macromolecular binding relationships from biomedical text. We describe the domain knowledge and the underspecified linguistic analyses that support the identification of these predications. After discussing a formal evaluation of ARBITER, we report on its application to 491,000 MEDLINE® abstracts, during which almost 25,000 binding relationships suitable for entry into a database of macromolecular function were extracted.

Introduction

Far more scientific information exists in the literature than in any structured database. Convenient access to this information could significantly benefit research activities in various fields. The emerging technology of information extraction (Appelt and Israel 1997, Hearst 1999) provides a means of gaining access to this information. In this paper we report on a project to extract biomolecular data from biomedical text. We concentrate on molecular binding affinity, which provides a strong indication of macromolecular function and is a core phenomenon in molecular biology. Our ultimate goal is to automatically construct a database of binding relationships asserted in MEDLINE citations.

The National Library of Medicine's MEDLINE textual database is an online repository of more than 10 million citations from the biomedical literature. All citations contain the title of the corresponding article along with other bibliographic information. In addition, a large number of citations contain author-supplied abstracts. Initial studies indicate that there are approximately 500,000 MEDLINE citations relevant to molecular binding affinity.

Our decision to apply information extraction technology to binding relationships was guided not only by the biological importance of this phenomenon but also by the relatively straightforward syntactic cuing of binding predications in text. The inflectional forms of a single verb, *bind,* indicate this relationship in the vast majority of cases, and our initial work is limited to these instances. For example, our goal in this project is to extract the binding predications in (2) from the text in (1).

(1) CC chemokine receptor 1 (CCR1) is expressed in neutrophils, monocytes, lymphocytes, and eosinophils, and binds the leukocyte chemoattractant and hematopoiesis regulator macrophage inflammatory protein (MIP)- 1alpha, as well as several related CC chemokines.

(2) <CC chemokine receptor 1>
BINDS
<leukocyte chemoattractant>
<CC chemokine receptor 1>
BINDS
<hematopoiesis regulator macrophage inflammatory protein-1alpha>
<CC chemokine receptor 1>
BINDS
<related CC chemokine>

Considerable interest in information extraction has concentrated on identifying named entities in text pertaining to current events (for example, Wacholder et al. 1997, Voorhees and Harman 1998, and MUC-7); however, several recent efforts have been directed at biomolecular data (Blaschke et al. 1999, Craven and Kumlien 1999, and Rindflesch et al. 2000, for example). The overall goal is to transform the information encoded in text into a more readily accessible format, typically a template with slots named for the participants in the scenario of interest. The template for molecular binding can be thought of as a simple predication with predicate "bind" and two arguments which participate (symmetrically) in the relationship: BINDS(<X>, <Y>).

Various strategies, both linguistic and statistical, have been used in information extraction efforts. We introduce a Prolog program called ARBITER (Assess and Retrieve Binding Terminology) that takes advantage of an existing domain knowledge source and relies on syntactic cues provided by a partial parser in order to identify and extract binding relations from text. We discuss the syntactic processing used and then report on a formal evaluation of ARBITER against a test collection of 116 MEDLINE citations in which the binding relations were marked by hand. Finally, we provide a brief overview of the results of applying ARBITER to the 500,000 MEDLINE citations discussing molecular binding affinity.

1 Extracting Binding Relationships from Text

Our strategy for extracting binding relationships from text divides the task into two phases: During the first phase we identify all potential binding arguments, and then in the second phase we extract just those binding terms which are asserted in the text as participating in a particular binding predication. In support of this processing, we rely on the linguistic and domain knowledge contained in the National Library of Medicine's Unified Medical Language System® (UMLS®) as well an existing tool, the SPECIALIST minimal commitment parser (Aronson et al. 1994).

The UMLS (Humphreys et al. 1998) consists of several knowledge sources applicable in the biomedical domain: the Metathesaurus, Semantic Network, and SPECIALIST Lexicon (McCray et al. 1994). The Metathesaurus was constructed from more than forty controlled vocabularies and contains more than 620,000 biomedical concepts. The characteristic of the Metathesaurus most relevant for this project is that each concept is associated with a semantic type that categorizes the concept into subareas of biology or medicine. Examples pertinent to binding terminology include the semantic types 'Amino Acid, Peptide, or Protein' and 'Nucleotide Sequence'. The SPECIALIST Lexicon (with associated lexical access tools) supplies syntactic information for a large compilation of biomedical and general English terms.

The SPECIALIST minimal commitment parser relies on the SPECIALIST Lexicon as well as the Xerox stochastic tagger (Cutting et al. 1992). The output produced is in the tradition of partial parsing (Hindle 1983, McDonald 1992, Weischedel et al. 1993) and concentrates on the simple noun phrase, what Weischedel et al. (1993) call the "core noun phrase," that is a noun phrase with no modification to the right of the head. Several approaches provide similar output based on statistics (Church 1988, Zhai 1997, for example), a finite-state machine (Ait-Mokhtar and Chanod 1997), or a hybrid approach combining statistics and linguistic rules (Voutilainen and Padro 1997).

The SPECIALIST parser is based on the notion of barrier words (Tersmette et al. 1988), which indicate boundaries between phrases. After lexical look-up and resolution of category label ambiguity by the Xerox tagger, complementizers, conjunctions, modals, prepositions, and verbs are marked as boundaries. Subsequently, boundaries are considered to open a new phrase (and close the preceding phrase). Any phrase containing a noun is considered to be a (simple) noun phrase, and in such a phrase, the right-most noun is labeled as the head, and all other items (other than determiners) are labeled as modifiers. An example of the output from the SPECIALIST parser is given below in (4). The partial parse produced serves as the basis for the first phase of extraction of binding relationships, namely the identification of those simple noun phrases acting as potential binding arguments (referred to as "binding terms").

1.1 Identifying binding terminology

In order to identify binding terminology in text we rely on the approach discussed in (Rindflesch et al. 1999). Text with locally-defined acronyms expanded is submitted to the Xerox tagger and the SPECIALIST parser. Subsequent processing concentrates on the heads of simple noun phrases and proceeds in a series of cascaded steps that depend on existing domain knowledge as well as several small, special-purpose resources in order to determine whether each noun phrase encountered is to be considered a binding term.

As the first step in the process, an existing program, MetaMap, (Aronson et al. 1994) attempts to map each simple noun phrase to a concept in the UMLS Metathesaurus. The semantic type for concepts corresponding to successfully mapped noun phrases is then checked against a small subset of UMLS semantic types referring to bindable entities, such as 'Amino Acid, Peptide, or Protein', 'Nucleotide Sequence', 'Carbohydrate', 'Cell', and 'Virus'. For concepts with a semantic type in this set, the corresponding noun phrase is considered to be a binding term.

The heads of noun phrases that do not map to a concept in the Metathesaurus are tested against a small set of general "binding words," which often indicate that the noun phrase in which they appear is a binding term. The set of binding words includes such nouns as *cleft, groove, membrane, ligand, motif, receptor, domain, element,* and *molecule.*

The head of a noun phrase that did not submit to the preceding steps is examined to see whether it adheres to the morphologic shape of a normal English word. In this context such a word is often an acronym not defined locally and indicates the presence of a binding term (Fukuda et al. 1998). A normal English word has at least one vowel and no digits, and a text token that contains at least one letter and is not a normal English word functions as a binding word in this context.

The final step in identifying binding terms is to join contiguous simple noun phrases qualifying as binding terms into a single macro-noun phrase. Rindflesch et al. (1999) use the term "macro-noun phrase" to refer to structures that include reduced relative clauses (commonly introduced by prepositions or participles) as well as appositives. Two binding terms joined by a form of *be* are also treated as though they formed a macro-noun phrase, as in <u>*Jel42 is an IgG*</u> *which binds ...*

The results of identifying binding terms (and thus potential binding arguments) are given in (4) for the sentence in (3). In (4) evidence supporting identification as a binding term is given in braces. Note that in the underspecified syntactic analysis, prepositional phrases are treated as (simple) noun phrases that have a preposition as their first member.

(3) Jel42 is an IgG which binds to the small bacterial protein, HPr and the structure of the complex is known at high resolution.

(4) [**binding_term(**[head(Jel42)],
{Morphology Shape Rule}
[aux(is)] ,
[det(an), head(IgG)] {Metathesaurus}
),
[pron(which)],
[verb(binds)],
binding_term([prep(to), det(the),
mod(small), mod(bacterial), head(protein),
punc(,)], {Metathesaurus}
[head(HPr)] {Morphology Shape Rule}
),
[conj(and)],
[det(the), head(structure)],
binding_term([prep(of), det(the),
head(complex)] {General Binding Word}
),
[aux(is)],
[verb(known)],
[prep(at), mod(high), head(resolution),
punc(.)]]

1.2 Identifying binding terms as arguments of relationships

Before addressing the strategy for determining the arguments of binding predications, we discuss the general treatment of macro-noun phrases during the second part of the processing. Although ARBITER attempts to recover complete macro-noun phrases during the first phase, only the most specific (and biologically useful) part of a macro-noun phrase is recovered during the extraction of binding predications. Terms referring to specific molecules are more useful than those referring to general classes of bindable entities, such as *receptor, ligand, protein,* or *molecule.* The syntactic head of a macro-noun phrase (the first simple noun phrase in the list) is not always the most specific or most useful term in the construction.

The Specificity Rule for determining the most specific part of the list of simple binding terms constituting a macro-noun phrase chooses the first simple term in the list which has either of the following two characteristics: a) The head was identified by the Morphology Shape Rule. b) The noun phrase maps to a UMLS concept having one of the following semantic types: 'Amino Acid, Peptide, or Protein', 'Nucleic Acid, Nucleoside, or Nucleotide', 'Nucleotide Sequence', 'Immunologic Factor', or 'Gene or Genome'. For example, in (5), the second simple term, *TNF-alpha promoter*, maps to the Metathesaurus with semantic type 'Nucleotide Sequence' and is thus considered to be the most specific term in this complex-noun phrase.

(5) binding_term(
  [transcriptionally active kappaB motifs],
  [in the TNF-alpha promoter],
  [in normal cells])

In identifying binding terms as arguments of a complete binding predication, as indicated above, we examine only those binding relations cued by some form of the verb *bind* (*bind, binds, bound,* and *binding*). The list of minimal syntactic phrases constituting the partial parse of the input sentence is examined from left to right; for each occurrence of a form of *binds,* the two binding terms serving as arguments are then sought. (During the tagging process, we force *bind, binds,* and *bound* to be labeled as "verb," and *binding* as "noun.")

A partial analysis of negation and coordination is undertaken by ARBITER, but anaphora resolution and a syntactic treatment of relativization are not attempted. With the added constraint that a binding argument must have been identified as a binding term based on the domain knowledge resources used, the partial syntactic analysis available to ARBITER supports the accurate identification of a large number of binding predications asserted in the research literature.

1.2.1 Arguments of binding

It is convenient to categorize binding predications into two classes depending on which form of *bind* cues the predication: a) *binding* and b) *bind, binds,* and *bound*. In our test collection (discussed below), about half of the binding relationships asserted in the text are cued by the gerundive or participial form *binding*. In this syntactic predication, the resources available from the underspecified syntactic parse serve quite well as the basis for correctly identifying the arguments of the binding relationship.

The most common argument configuration associated with *binding* is for both arguments to occur to the right, cued by prepositions, most commonly *of* and *to*; however, other frequent patterns are *of-by* and *to-by*. Another method of argument cuing for *binding* is for the subject of the predication to function syntactically as a modifier of the head *binding* in the same simple noun phrase. The object in this instance is then cued by either *of* or *to* (to the right). A few other patterns are seen and some occurrences of *binding* do not cue a complete predication; either the subject is missing or neither argument is explicitly mentioned. However, the examples in (6) fairly represent the interpretation of *binding*.

(6) These results suggest that 2 amino acids, Thr-340 and Ser-343, play important but distinct roles in promoting the **binding** of arrestin to rhodopsin.

  <arrestin>
   BINDS
  <rhodopsin>

  Surprisingly, arrestin **binding** to phosphorylated T340E did not increase to the level observed for wild-type rhodopsin.

  <arrestin>
   BINDS
  <phosphorylated t340e>

1.2.2 Arguments of bind

The arguments of forms of *bind* other than *binding* invariably occur on either side of the cuing verb form. The default strategy for identifying both arguments in these instances is to choose the closest binding term on either side of the verb. In the cases we have investigated, this strategy works often enough to be useful for the surface object. However, due to predicate coordination as well as relativization, such a strategy often fails to identify correctly the surface subject of *bind* (*binds* or *bound*) when more than one binding term precedes the verb. We therefore use the strategy summarized in (7) for recovering the surface subject in such instances.

(7) When more than one binding term precedes a form of *bind* other than *binding*, choose the most specific of these binding terms as the surface subject of the predication.

"Most specific" is determined (recursively) for a series of binding terms in the same way that the most specific part of a complex binding term is determined.

The input text (8) provides an example of a binding predication cued by *binds* in which the arguments appear (immediately) on either side of the cuing verb. The two macro-noun phrases serving as potential arguments are underlined.

(8) A transcription factor, Auxin Response Factor 1, that **binds** to the sequence TGTCTC in auxin response elements was cloned from Arabidopsis by using a yeast one-hybrid system.

(9) <auxin response factor 1>
BINDS
<sequence tgtctc>

In the extracted binding relationship in (9), the Specificity Rule chooses *Auxin Response Factor 1* from the first macro-noun phrase because it maps to the UMLS Metathesaurus with semantic type 'Amino Acid, Peptide, or Protein'. In the second argument, *the sequence TGTCTC* has a head that submits to the Morphology Shape Rule and hence is considered to be more specific than *auxin response elements*.

In (10), the Specificity Rule applies correctly to select the surface subject of the binding predication when multiple binding terms appear to the left of the verb.

(10) Phosphatidylinositol transfer protein has a single lipid-binding site that can reversibly **bind** phosphatidylinositol and phosphatidylcholine and transfer these lipids between membrane compartments in vitro.

<phosphatidylinositol transfer protein>
BINDS
<phosphatidylcholine>
<phosphatidylinositol transfer protein>
BINDS
<phosphatidylinositol>

Both *Phosphatidylinositol transfer protein* and *a single lipid-binding site* occur to the left of *bind* and have been identified as binding terms by the first phase of processing. However, *Phosphatidylinositol transfer protein* maps to the corresponding Metathesaurus concept with semantic type 'Amino Acid, Peptide, or Protein, thus causing it to be more specific than *a single lipid-binding site*. The second predication listed in (10) was correctly extracted due to coordination processing.

ARBITER pursues limited coordination identification in the spirit of Agarwal and Boggess (1992) and Rindflesch (1995). Only binding terms are considered as candidates for coordination. For each conjunction encountered, the phrase immediately to the right is examined; if it is a binding term, all contiguous binding terms occurring immediately to the left of the conjunct are considered to be coordinate with the right conjunct. Coordination inside the simple noun phrase is not considered, and therefore structures such as *The TCR alpha beta or -gamma delta chains* are not recognized. Nonetheless, as indicated in (11), this limited approach to noun phrase coordination is often effective.

(11) Purified recombinant NC1, **like** authentic NC1, also bound specifically to fibronectin, collagen type I, **and** a laminin 5/6 complex.

<authentic nc1>
BINDS
<laminin 5 / 6 complex>
<authentic nc1>
BINDS
<collagen type i>
<authentic nc1>
BINDS
<fibronectin>
<purified recombinant nc1>
BINDS
<laminin 5 / 6 complex>
<purified recombinant nc1>
BINDS
<collagen type i>
<purified recombinant nc1>
BINDS
<fibronectin>

Although the particular underspecified syntactic analysis used in the identification of binding predications in the biomedical research literature is limited in several important ways, it appears adequate to enable this project with a useful level of effectiveness, and this is supported by evaluation.

2 Evaluation

In order to determine ARBITER's effectiveness, the program was formally evaluated against a gold standard of MEDLINE citations in which the binding predications asserted were marked by hand. A search of MEDLINE limited to one month (June 1997) and based on the text words ((*bind, binds, binding,* or *bound*) and (*protein* or *proteins*)) retrieved 116 citations with 1,141 sentences; of these, 346 contained some form of the verb *bind*. 260 binding predications were identified in the binding sentences. (The binding sentences also contained 2,025 simple noun phrases, 1,179 of which were marked as being binding terms.)

In processing this test collection, ARBITER extracted 181 binding predications, 132 of which were correct. Since ARBITER missed 128 marked binding predications (false negatives) and incorrectly identified 49 such relationships, recall and precision as measures of effectiveness are 51% and 73%, respectively.

In comparing ARBITER's output against that marked in the gold standard, fairly stringent matching criteria were used. A binding predication extracted from a particular sentence by ARBITER had to appear in that same sentence in the gold standard (not just the same citation) in order to be counted as correct. Further, in the gold standard, only the most specific component of a macro-noun phrase was marked as being the correct argument for a particular binding predication. If ARBITER retrieved any other part of a macro-noun phrase in identifying the arguments of that predication, it was assessed as an error.

A large number of ARBITER errors are due to two phenomena: difficulties in correctly identifying binding terms during the first phase of processing and syntactic complexity confounding argument identification during the second phase. An example of the first error type is seen in (12), where the failure to identify *ran* as a binding term caused ARBITER to miss the correct binding predication asserted in this sentence (indicated by "-FN->").

(12) Requirement of guanosine triphosphate-bound ran for signal-mediated nuclear protein export.
-FN-> <guanosine triphosphate>
BINDS
<Ran>
-FP-> < guanosine triphosphate>
BINDS
<signal - mediate nuclear protein export>

This error then led to the false positive error ("-FP->") when the program wrongly interpreted the next noun phrase in the sentence (*signal-mediated nuclear protein export*) as the second argument in this predication.

The interaction of coordination and negation in (13) caused ARBITER to partially misinterpret the binding predications in this sentence.

(13) The nonvisual arrestins, beta-arrestin and arrestin3, but not visual arrestin, bind specifically to a glutathione S-transferase- clathrin terminal domain fusion protein.

<arrestin3>
BINDS
<glutathione s-transferase-clathrin terminal domain fusion protein>
<beta arrestin>
BINDS
<glutathione s-transferase-clathrin terminal domain fusion protein>
<nonvisual arrestin>
BINDS
<glutathione s-transferase-clathrin terminal domain fusion protein>
-FN-> <visual arrestin>
DOES_NOT_BIND
<glutathione s-transferase-clathrin terminal domain fusion protein>

Although some of the coordination in (13) was processed properly, resulting in the relationships listed, the negated coordination associated with the noun phrase *visual arrestin* was not interpreted correctly, and thus ARBITER failed to identify the predication marked as a false negative.

3 Application

As an initial application of ARBITER we ran the program on 491,356 MEDLINE citations, which were retrieved using the same search strategy responsible for the gold standard. During this run, 331,777 sentences in 192,997 citations produced 419,782 total binding assertions. Extrapolating from the gold standard evaluation, we assume that this is about half of the total binding predications asserted in the citations processed and that somewhat less than three quarters of those extracted are correct.

The initial list of 419,982 binding triples represents what ARBITER determined was asserted in the text being processed. Many of these assertions, such as those in (14), while correct, are too general to be useful.

(14) <receptors>
BINDS
<Peptides>
<Erythrocytes>
BINDS
<Antibodies>

Further processing on ARBITER raw output extracted specific protein names and genomic structures and reduced the number of such binding predications to 345,706. From these more specific binding predication, we began the construction of a database containing binding relations asserted in the literature. More detailed discussion of this database can be found in (Rajan et al. in prep); however, here we give an initial description of its characteristics.

We submitted the 345,706 more specific ARBITER binding predications to a search in GenBank (Benson et al. 1998) and determined that 106,193 referred to a GenBank entry. The number of Genbank entries with at least one binding assertion is 11,617. Preliminary results indicate that the database we are constructing will have some of the following characteristics:

- 10,769 bindings between two distinct Genbank entries (5,569 unique)
- 875 more binding assertions found between an entry and a specific DNA sequence
- 27,345 bindings between a Genbank entry and a UMLS Metathesaurus concept
- 5,569 unique relationships among pairs of entries (involving 11,617 unique entries)

Conclusion

The cooperation of structured domain knowledge and underspecified syntactic analysis enables the extraction of macromolecular binding relationships from the research literature. Although our implementation is domain-specific, the underlying principles are amenable to broader applicability.

ARBITER makes a distinction between first labeling binding terms and then identifying certain of these terms as arguments in a binding predication. The first phase of this processing is dependent on biomedical domain knowledge accessible from the UMLS. Applying the techniques we propose in other areas would require at least a minimum of semantic classification of the concepts involved. General, automated techniques that could supply this requirement are becoming increasingly available (Morin and Jacquemin 1999, for example).

Although we concentrated on the inflectional forms of a single verb, the principles we invoke to support argument identification during the second phase of processing apply generally to English predication encoding strategies (with a minimum of effort necessary to address prepositional cuing of gerundive arguments for specific verbs). The approach to noun phrase coordination also applies generally, so long as hypernymic classification is available for the heads of the potential conjuncts.

Acknowledgements

We are grateful to John Wilbur for assistance with accessing GenBank, to Alan Aronson for modifications to MetaMap, and to James Mork for providing the distributed system that supported the processing of MEDLINE citations.

References

Agarwal R. and Boggess L. (1992) *A simple but useful approach to conjunct identification.* Proceedings of the 30th Annual Meeting of the Association for Computational Linguistics, pp. 15-21.

Ait-Mokhtar S. and Chanod J.-P. (1997) *Incremental finite-state parsing*. Proceedings of the Fifth Conference on Applied Natural Language Processing, pp. 72-9.

Appelt D. E. and Israel D. (1997) *Tutorial on building information extraction systems*. Fifth Conference on Applied Natural Language Processing.

Aronson A. R., Rindflesch T. C., and Browne A. C. (1994) *Exploiting a large thesaurus for information retrieval*. Proceedings of RIAO 94, pp. 197-216.

Benson D. A., Boguski M. S., Lipman D. J., Ostell J., and Ouelette B. F. (1998) *GenBank*. Nucleic Acids Research, 26/1, pp. 1-7.

Blaschke C., Andrade M. A., Ouzounis C., and Valencia A. (1999) *Automatic extraction of biological information from scientific text: protein-protein interactions*. Intelligent Systems for Molecular Biology (ISMB), 7, pp. 60-7.

Church K. W. (1988) *A stochastic parts program and noun phrase parser for unrestricted text*. Proceedings of the Second Conference on Applied Natural Language Processing, pp. 136-143.

Craven M. and Kumlien J. (1999) *Constructing biological knowledge bases by extracting information from text sources*. Intelligent Systems for Molecular Biology (ISMB), 7, pp. 77-86.

Cutting D. R., Kupiec J., Pedersen J. O., and Sibun P. (1992) *A practical part-of-speech tagger*. Proceedings of the Third Conference on Applied Natural Language Processing.

Fukuda F., Tsunoda T., Tamura A., and Takagi T. (1998) *Toward information extraction: Identifying protein names from biological papers*. Pacific Symposium on Biocomputing (PSB), 3, pp. 705-16.

Hearst M. A. (1999) *Untangling text data mining*. Proceedings of the 37th Annual Meeting of the Association for Computational Linguistics, pp. 3-10.

Hindle D. (1983) *Deterministic parsing of syntactic non-fluencies*. Proceedings of the 21st Annual Meeting of the Association for Computational Linguistics, pp. 123-8.

Humphreys B. L., Lindberg D. A. B., Schoolman H. M., and Barnett G. O. (1998) *The Unified Medical language System: An informatics research collaboration*. Journal of the American Medical Informatics Association, 5/1, pp. 1-13.

McCray A. T., Srinivasan S., and Browne A. C. (1994) *Lexical methods for managing variation in biomedical terminologies*. Proceedings of the 18th Annual Symposium on Computer Applications in Medical Care, pp. 235-9.

McDonald D. D. (1992) *Robust partial parsing through incremental, multi-algorithm processing*. In "Text-Based Intelligent Systems," P. S. Jacobs, ed., pp. 83-99.

Morin E. and Jacquemin C. *Projecting corpus-based semantic links on a thesaurus*. Proceedings of the 37th Annual Meeting of the Association for Computational Linguistics, pp. 389-96.

MUC-7. *Message Understanding Conference Proceedings*. http://www.muc.saic.com.

Rajan J. V., Hunter L., and Rindflesch T. C. (In prep.) *Mining MEDLINE*.

Rindflesch T. C. (1995) *Integrating natural language processing and biomedical domain knowledge for increased information retrieval effectiveness*. Proceedings of the 5th Annual Dual-Use Technologies and Applications Conference, pp. 260-5.

Rindflesch T. C., Hunter L., and Aronson A. R. (1999) *Mining molecular binding terminology from biomedical text*. Proceedings of the AMIA Annual Symposium, pp. 127-131.

Rindflesch T. C., Tanabe L., Weinstein J. N., and Hunter L. (2000) *EDGAR: Extraction of drugs, genes and relations from the biomedical literature*. Pacific Symposium on Biocomputing (PSB), 5, pp. 514-25.

Tersmette K. W. F., Scott A. F., Moore G.W., Matheson N. W., and Miller R. E. (1988) *Barrier word method for detecting molecular biology multiple word terms*. Proceedings of the 12th Annual Symposium on Computer Applications in Medical Care, pp. 207- 11.

Voorhees E. M. and Harman D. K. (1998) *The Seventh Text Retrieval Conference*.

Vourtilainen A. and Padro L. (1997) *Developing a hybrid NP parser*. Proceedings of the Fifth Conference on Applied Natural Language Processing, pp. 80-7.

Wacholder N., Ravin Y., and Choi M. (1997) *Disambiguation of proper names in text*. Proceedings of the Fifth Conference on Applied Natural Language Processing, pp. 202-208.

Weischedel R., Meteer M., Schwartz R., Ramshaw L., and Palmucci J. (1993) *Coping with ambiguity and unknown words through probabilistic models*. Computational Linguistics, 19/2, pp. 359-382.

Zhai C. (1997) *Fast statistical parsing of noun phrases for document indexing*. Proceedings of the Fifth Conference on Applied Natural Language Processing, pp. 312-31.

Compound Noun Segmentation Based on Lexical Data Extracted from Corpus*

Juntae Yoon
jtyoon@linc.cis.upenn.edu
IRCS, University of Pennsylvania,
3401 Walnut St., Suite 400A,
Philadelphia, PA 19104-6228, USA

Abstract

Compound noun analysis is one of the crucial problems in Korean language processing because a series of nouns in Korean may appear without white space in real texts, which makes it difficult to identify the morphological constituents. This paper presents an effective method of Korean compound noun segmentation based on lexical data extracted from corpus. The segmentation is done by two steps: First, it is based on manually constructed built-in dictionary for segmentation whose data were extracted from 30 million word corpus. Second, a segmentation algorithm using statistical data is proposed, where simple nouns and their frequencies are also extracted from corpus. The analysis is executed based on CYK tabular parsing and min-max operation. By experiments, its accuracy is about 97.29%, which turns out to be very effective.

1 Introduction

Morphological analysis is crucial for processing the agglutinative language like Korean since words in such languages have lots of morphological variants. A sentence is represented by a sequence of eojeols which are the syntactic unit delimited by spacing characters in Korean. Unlike in English, an eojeol is not one word but composed of a series of words (content words and functional words). In particular, since an eojeol can often contain more than one noun, we cannot get proper interpretation of the sentence or phrase without its accurate segmentation.

The problem in compound noun segmentation is that it is not possible to register all compound nouns in the dictionary since nouns are in the open set of words as well as the number of them is very large. Thus, they must be treated as unseen words without a segmentation process. Furthermore, accurate compound noun segmentation plays an important role in the application system. Compound noun segmentation is necessarily required for improving recall and precision in Korean information retrieval, and obtaining better translation in machine translation. For example, suppose that a compound noun '*seol'agsan-gugrib-gongwon*(Seol'ag Mountain National Park)' appear in documents. A user might want to retrieve documents about '*seol'agsan*(Seol'ag Mountain)', and then it is likely that the documents with *seol'agsan-gugrib-gongwon'* are also the ones in his interest. Therefore, it should be exactly segmented before indexing in order for the documents to be retrieved with the query '*seol'agsan*'. Also, to translate '*seol'agsan-gugrib-gongwon*' to Seol'ag Mountain National Park, the constituents should be identified first through the process of segmentation.

This paper presents two methods for segmentation of compound nouns. First, we extract compound nouns from a large size of corpus, manually divide them into simple nouns and construct the hand built segmentation dictionary with them. The dictionary includes compound nouns which are frequently used and need exceptional process. The number of data are about 100,000.

Second, the segmentation algorithm is applied if the compound noun does not exist in the built-in dictionary. Basically, the segmenter is based on frequency of individual nouns extracted from corpus. However, the problem is that it is difficult to distinguish proper noun and common noun since there is no clue like capital letters in Korean. Thus, just a large amount of lexical knowledge does not make good results if it contains incorrect data and also it is not appropriate to use frequencies obtained by automatically tagging large corpus. Moreover, sufficient lexical data cannot be acquired from small amounts of tagged corpus.

In this paper, we propose a method to get simple nouns and their frequencies from frequently occurring eojeols using repetitiveness of natural language. The amount of eojeols investigated is manually tractable and frequently used nouns extracted from them are crucial for compound noun segmentation. Furthermore, we propose *min-max* composition to divide a sequence of syllables, which would be proven to be an effective method by experiments.

* This work was supported by a KOSEF's postdoctoral fellowship grant.

To briefly show the reason that we select the operation, let us consider the following example. Suppose that a compound noun be composed of four syllables '$s_1 s_2 s_3 s_4$'. There are several possibilities of segmentation in the sequence of syllables, where we consider the following possibilities ($s_1/s_2 s_3 s_4$) and ($s_1 s_2/s_3 s_4$). Assume that 's_1' is a frequently appearing word in texts whereas '$s_2 s_3 s_4$' is a rarely occurring sequence of syllables as a word. On the other hand '$s_1 s_2$' and '$s_3 s_4$' occurs frequently but although they don't occur as frequently as 's_1'. In this case, the more likely segmentation would be ($s_1 s_2/s_3 s_4$). It means that a sequence of syllables should not be divided into frequently occurring one and rarely occurring one. In this sense, min-max is the appropriate operation for the selection. In other words, min value is selected between two sequences of syllables, and then max is taken from min values selected. To apply the operation repetitively, we use the CYK tabular parsing style algorithm.

2 Lexical Data Acquisition

Since the compound noun consists of a series of nouns, the probability model using transition among parts of speech is not helpful, and rather lexical information is required for the compound noun segmentation. Our segmentation algorithm is based on a large collection of lexical information that consists of two kinds of data: One is the hand built segmentation dictionary (**HBSD**) and the other is the simple noun dictionary for segmentation (**SND**).

2.1 Hand-Built Segmentation Dictionary

The first phase of compound noun segmentation uses the built-in dictionary (HBSD). The advantage of using the built-in dictionary is that the segmentation could (1) be very accurate by hand-made data and (2) become more efficient. In Korean compound noun, one syllable noun is sometimes highly ambiguous between suffix and noun, but human can easily identify them using semantic knowledge. For example, one syllable noun '*ssi*' in Korean might be used either as a suffix or as a noun which means 'Mr/Ms' or 'seed' respectively. Without any semantic information, the best way to distinguish them is to record all the compound noun examples containing the meaning of seed in the dictionary since the number of compound nouns containing a meaning of 'seed' is even smaller. Besides, we can treat general spacing errors using the dictionary. By the spacing rule for Korean, there should be one content word except noun in an eojeol, but it turns out that one or more content words of short length sometimes appear without space in real texts, which causes the lexical ambiguities. It makes the system inefficient to deal with all these words on the phase of basic morphological analysis.

compound nouns	analysis information
gajuggudu(leather shoes)	gajug(leather)+gudu(shoes)
gajugggeun(leather string)	gajug(leather)+ggeun(string)
gaguyong(used for furniture)	gagu(furniture)+*x*yong(used for)
sagwassi(apple seed)	sagwa(apple)+*n*ssi(seed)
podossi(graph seed)	podo(grape)+*n*ssi(seed)
chuggutim(football team)	chuggu(football)+tim(team)

Table 1: Examples of compound noun and analysis information in built-in dictionary

To construct the dictionary, compound nouns are extracted from corpus and manually elaborated. First, the morphological analyzer analyzes 30 million eojeol corpus using only simple noun dictionary, and the failed results are candidates for compound noun. After postpositions, if any, are removed from the compound noun candidates of the failure eojeols, the candidates are modified and analyzed by hand. In addition, a collection of compound nouns of KAIST (Korea Advanced Institute of Science & Technology) is added to the dictionary in order to supplement them. The number of entries contained in the built-in dictionary is about 100,000. Table 1 shows some examples in the built-in dictionary. The italic characters such as '*n*' or '*x*' in analysis information (right column) of the table is used to make distinction between noun and suffix.

2.2 Extraction of Lexical Information for Segmentation from Corpus

As we said earlier, it is impossible for all compound nouns to be registered in the dictionary, and thus the built-in dictionary cannot cover all compound nouns even though it gives more accurate results. We need some good segmentation model for compound noun, therefore.

In compound noun segmentation, the thing that we pay attention to was that lexical information is crucial for segmenting noun compounds. Since a compound noun consists only of a sequence of nouns i.e. $\{noun\}+$, the transition probability of parts of speech is no use. Namely, the frequency of each noun plays highly important role in compound noun segmentation. Besides, since the parameter space is huge, we cannot extract enough lexical information from hundreds of thousands of POS tagged corpus[1] even if accurate lexical information can be extracted from annotated corpus. Thus, a large size of corpus should be used to extract proper frequencies of nouns. However, it is difficult to look at a large size of corpus and to assign analyses to it, which makes it difficult to estimate the frequency distribution of words. Therefore, we need another approach for obtaining frequencies of nouns.

[1] It is the size of POS tagged corpus currently publicized by ETRI (Electronics and Telecommunications Research Institute) project.

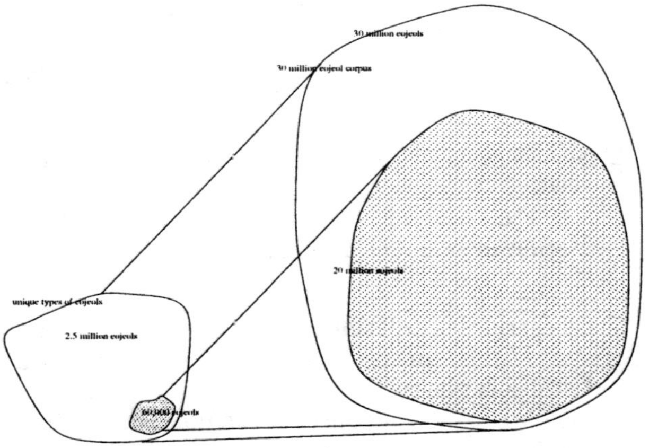

Figure 1: Distribution of eojeols in Korean corpus

It must be noted here that each noun in compound nouns could be easily segmented by human in many cases because it has a prominent figure in the sense that it is a frequently used word and so familiar with him. In other words, nouns prominent in documents can be defined as frequently occurred ones, which we call *distinct nouns*. Compound nouns contains these distinct nouns in many cases, which makes it easier to segment them and to identify their constituents. Empirically, it is well-known that too many words in the dictionary have a bad influence on morphological analysis in Korean. It is because rarely used nouns result in oversegmentation if they are included in compound noun segmentation dictionary. Therefore, it is necessary to select distinct nouns, which leads us to use a part of corpus instead of entire corpus that consists of frequently used ones in the corpus.

First, we examined distribution of eojeols in corpus in order to make the subset of corpus to extract lexical frequencies of nouns. The notable thing in our experiment is that the number of eojeols in corpus is increased in proportion to the size of corpus, but a small portion of eojeols takes most parts of the whole corpus. For instance, 70% of the corpus consists of just 60 thousand types of eojeols which take 7.5 million of frequency from 10 million eojeol corpus and 20.5 million from 30 million eojeols. The lowest frequency of the 60,000 eojeols is 49 in 30 million eojeol corpus. We decided to take 60,000 eojeols which are manually tractable and compose most parts of corpus (Figure 1).

Second, we made morphological analyses for the 60,000 eojeols by hand. Since Korean is an agglutinative language, an eojeol is represented by a sequence of content words and functional words as mentioned before. Especially, content words and functional words often have different distribution of syllables. In addition, inflectional endings for predicate and postpositions for nominals also have quite different distribution for syllables. Hence we can distinguish the constituents of eojeols in many cases. Of course, there are also many cases in which the result of morphological analysis has ambiguities. For example, an eojeol '*na-neun*' in Korean has ambiguity of '*na*/N+*neun*/P', '*na*/PN+*neun*/P' and '*nal*/V+*neun*/E'. In this example, the parts of speech N, PN, P, V and E mean noun, pronoun, postposition, verb and ending, respectively. On the other hand, many eojeols which are analyzed as having ambiguities by a morphological analyzer are actually not ambiguous. For instance, '*ga-geora*' (go/imperative) has ambiguities by most morphological analyzer among '*ga*/V+*geora*/E' and '*ga*/N+*i*/C+*geora*/E' (C is copula), but it is actually not ambiguous. Such morphological ambiguity is caused by overgeneration of the morphological analyzer since the analyzer uses less detailed rules for robustness of the system. Therefore, if we examine and correct the results scrupulously, many ambiguities can be removed through the process.

As the result of the manual process, only 15% of 60,000 eojeols remain ambiguous at the mid-level of part of speech classification[2]. Then, we extracted simple nouns and their frequencies from the data. Despite of manual correction, there must be ambiguities left for the reason mentioned above. There may be some methods to distribute frequencies in case of ambiguous words, but we simply assign the equal distribution to them. For instance, *gage* has two possibilities of analysis i.e. '*gage*/N' and '*ga*/V+*ge*/E', and its frequency is 2263, in which the noun '*gage*' is assigned 1132 as its frequency. Table 2 shows examples of manually corrected morphological analyses of eojeols containing a noun '*gage*' and their frequencies. We call the nouns extracted in such a way *a set of distinct nouns.*

In addition, we supplement the dictionary with other nouns not appeared in the words obtained by the method mentioned above. First, nouns of more than three syllables are rare in real texts in Korean, as shown in Lee and Ahn (1996). Their experiments proved that syllable based bigram indexing model makes much better result than other n-gram model such as trigram and quadragram in Korean IR. It follows that two syllable nouns take an overwhelming majority in nouns. Thus, there are not many such nouns in the simple nouns extracted by the manually corrected nouns (a set of distinct nouns). In particular, since many nouns of more

[2] At the mid-level of part of speech classification, for example, endings and postpositions are represented just by one tag e.g. E and P. To identify the sentential or clausal type (subordinate or declarative) in Korean, the ending should be subclassified for syntactic analysis more detail which can be done by statistical process. It is beyond the subject of this paper.

eojeols	constituents	meaning	frequencies
gage	gage/N@ga/V+ge/E	store@go	2263
gage-ga	gage/N+ga/P	store/SUBJ	165
gage-neun	gage/N+neun/P@ga/V+geneun/E	store/TOP@go	113
gage-ro	gage/N+ro/P	to the store	166
gage-reul	gage/N+reul/P	store/OBJ	535
gage-e	gage/N+e/P	in the store	312
gage-eseo	gage/N+eseo/P	in the store	299
gage-yi	gage/N+yi/P	of the store	132
extracted noun			frequency
gage		store	2797

Table 2: Example of extraction of distinct nouns. Here N, V, P and E mean tag for noun, verb, postposition and ending and '@' is marked for representation of ambiguous analysis

than three syllables are derived by a word and suffixes and have some syllable features, they are useful for distinguishing the boundaries of constituents in compound nouns. We select nouns of more than three syllables from morphological dictionary which is used for basic morphological analysis and consists of 89,000 words (noun, verb, adverb etc). Second, simple nouns are extracted from hand-built segmentation dictionary. We selected nouns which do not exist in a set of distinct nouns.

The frequency is assigned equally with some value fq. Since the model is based on min-max composition and the nouns extracted in the first phase are most important, the value does not take an effect on the system performance.

The nouns extracted in this way are referred to as *a set of supplementary nouns*. And the SND for compound noun segmentation is composed of a set of distinct nouns and a set of supplementary nouns. The number of simple nouns for compound noun segmentation is about 50,000.

3 Compound Word Segmentation Algorithm

3.1 Basic Idea

To simply describe the basic idea of our compound noun segmentation, we first consider a compound noun to be segmented into only two nouns. Given a compound noun, it is segmented by the possibility that a sequence of syllables inside it forms a word. The possibility that a sequence of syllables forms a word is measured by the following formula.

$$Word(s_i, \ldots s_j) = \frac{fq(s_i, \ldots s_j)}{fq_N} \qquad (1)$$

In the formula, $fq(s_i, \ldots s_j)$ is the frequency of the syllable $s_i \ldots s_j$, which is obtained from SND constructed on the stages of lexical data extraction. And, fq_N is the total sum of frequencies of simple nouns. Colloquially, the equation (1) estimates how much the given sequence of syllables are likely to be word. If a sequence of syllables in the set of distinct nouns is included in a compound noun, it is more probable that it is divided around the syllables. If a compound noun consists of, for any combination of syllables, sequences of syllables in the set of supplementary nouns, the boundary of segmentation is somewhat fuzzy. Besides, if a given sequence of syllables is not found in SND, it is not probable that it is a noun.

Consider a compound noun '*hag-gyo-saeng-hwal*(school life)'. In case that segmentation of syllables is made into two, there would be four possibilities of segmentation for the example as follows:

1.	*hag*	*gyo-saeng-hwal*
2.	*hag-gyo*	*saeng-hwal*
3.	*hag-gyo-saeng*	*hwal*
4.	*hag-gyo-saeng-hwal*	ϕ

As we mentioned earlier, it is desirable that the eojeol is segmented in the position where each sequence of syllables to be divided occurs frequently enough in training data. As the length of a sequence of syllables is shorter in Korean, it occurs more frequently. That is, the shorter part usually have higher frequency than the other (longer) part when we divide syllables into two. Moreover, if the other part is the syllables that we rarely see in texts, then the part would not be a word. In the first of the above example, *hag* is a sequence of syllable appearing frequently, but *gyo-saeng-hwal* is not. Actually, *gyo-saeng-hwal* is not a word. On the other hand, both *hag-gyo* and *saeng-hwal* are frequently occurring syllables, and actually they are all words. Put another way, if it is unlikely that one sequence of syllables is a word, then it is more likely that the entire syllables are not segmented. The min-max composition is a suitable operation for this case. Therefore, we first take the minimum value from the function $Word$ for each possibility of segmentation, and then we choose the maximum from the selected minimums. Also, the argument taking the maximum is selected as the most likely segmentation result.

Here, $Word(s_i \dots s_j)$ is assigned the frequency of the syllables $s_i \dots s_j$ from the dictionary SND. Besides, if two minimums are equal, the entire syllable such as *hag-gyo-saeng-hwal*, if compared, is preferred, the values of the other sequence of syllables are compared or the dominant pattern has the priority.

3.2 Segmentation Algorithm

In this section, we generalize the word segmentation algorithm based on data obtained by the training method described in the previous section. The basic idea is to apply min-max operation to each syllable in a compound noun by the bottom-up strategy. That is, if the minimum between $Words$ of two sequences of syllables is greater than $Word$ of the combination of them, the syllables should be segmented. For instance, let us suppose a compound noun consist of two syllable s_1 and s_2. If $\min(Word(s_1), Word(s_2)) > Word(s_1 s_2)$, then the compound noun is segmented into s_1 and s_2. It is not segmented, otherwise. That is, we take the maximum among minimums. For example, '*hag*' is a frequently occurring word, but '*gyo*' is not in Korean. In this case, we can hardly regard the sequence of syllable '*hag-gyo*' as the combination of two words '*hag*' and '*gyo*'. The algorithm can be applied recursively from individual syllable to the entire syllable of the compound noun.

The segmentation algorithm is effectively implemented by borrowing the CYK parsing method. Since we use the bottom-up strategy, the execution looks like composition rather than segmentation. After all possible segmentation of syllables being checked, the final result is put in the top of the table. When a compound noun is composed of n syllables, i.e. $s_1 s_2 \dots s_n$, the composition is started from each s_i $(i = 1 \dots n)$. Thus, the possibility that the individual syllable forms a word is recorded in the cell of the first row.

Here, $C_{i,j}$ is an element of CYK table where the segment result of the syllables $s_{j,\dots,j+i-1}$ is stored (Figure 2). For instance, the segmentation result such that $arg \max(\min(Word(s_1), Word(s_2)), Word(s_1 s_2))$ is stored in $C_{1,2}$. What is interesting here is that the procedure follows the dynamic programming. Thus, each cell $C_{i,j}$ has the most probable segmentation result for a series of syllables $s_{j,\dots,j+i-1}$. Namely, $C_{1,2}$ and $C_{2,3}$ have the most likely segmentation of $s_1 s_2$ and $s_2 s_3$ respectively. When the segmentation of $s_1 s_2 s_3$ is about to be checked, $\min(value(C_{2,1}), value(C_{1,3}))$,

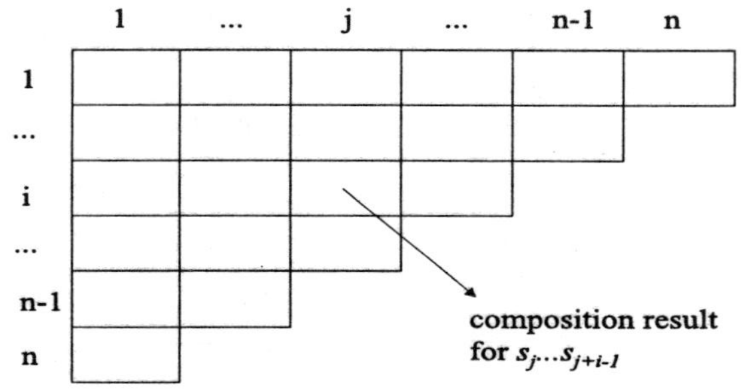

Figure 2: Composition Table

$\min(value(C_{1,1}), value(C_{2,2}))$ and $Word(s_1 s_2 s_3)$ are compared to determine the segmentation for the syllables, because all $C_{i,j}$ have the most likely segmentation. Here, $value(C_{i,j})$ represents the possibility value of $C_{i,j}$.

Then, we can describe the segmentation algorithm as follows:

When it is about to make the segmentation of syllables $s_i \dots s_j$, the segmentation results of less length of syllables like $s_i \dots s_{j-1}$, $s_{i+1} \dots s_j$ and so forth would be already stored in the table. In order to make analysis of $s_i \dots s_j$, we combine two shorter length of analyses and the word generation possibilities are computed and checked.

To make it easy to explain the algorithm, let us take an example compound noun '*hag-gyo-saeng-hwal*' (school life) which is segmented with '*haggyo*' (school) and '*saenghwal*' (life) (Figure 3). When it comes up to cell $C_{4,1}$, we have to make the most probable segmentation for '*hag-gyo-saeng-hwal*' i.e. $s_1 s_2 s_3 s_4$. There are three kinds of sequences of syllables, i.e. s_1 in $C_{1,1}$, $s_1 s_2$ in $C_{2,1}$ and $s_1 s_2 s_3$ in $C_{3,1}$ that can construct the word consisting of $s_1 s_2 s_3 s_4$ which would be put in $C_{4,1}$. For instance, the word $s_1 s_2 s_3 s_4$ (*hag-gyo-saeng-hwal*) is made with s_1 (*hag*) combined with $s_2 s_3 s_4$ (*gyo-saeng-hwal*). Likewise, it might be made by $s_1 s_2$ combined with $s_3 s_4$ and $s_1 s_2 s_3$ combined with s_4. Since each cell has the most probable result and its value, it is simple to find the best segmentation for each syllables. In addition, four cases, including the whole sequences of syllables, are compared to make segmentation of $s_1 s_2 s_3 s_4$ as follows:

1. $\min(value(C_{3,1}), value(C_{3,4}))$
2. $\min(value(C_{2,1}), value(C_{2,3}))$
3. $\min(value(C_{1,1}), value(C_{3,2}))$
4. $Word(s_1 s_2 s_3 s_4) = Word(hag\text{-}gyo\text{-}saeng\text{-}hwal)$

Again, the most probable segmentation result is put in $C_{4,1}$ with the likelihood value for its segmentation. We call it MLS (Most Likely Segmentation)

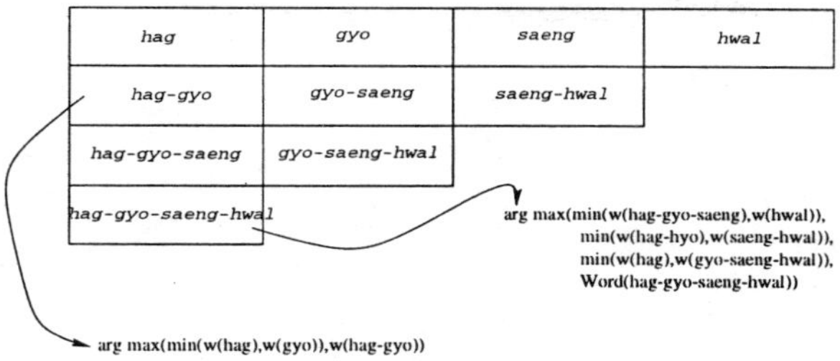

Figure 3: State of table when analyzing 'hag-gyo-saeng-hwal'. Here, $w(s_i \dots s_j) = value(C_{i,j})$

which is found in the following way:

$$
\begin{aligned}
MLS(C_{4,1}) = \\
arg \max(&\min(value(C_{3,1}), value(C_{3,4})),\\
&\min(value(C_{2,1}), value(C_{2,3})),\\
&\min(value(C_{1,1}), value(C_{3,2})),\\
&Word(s_1 s_2 s_3 s_4))
\end{aligned}
$$

From the four cases, the maximum value and the segmentation result are selected and recorded in $C_{4,1}$. To generalize it, the algorithm is described as shown in Figure 4.

The algorithm is straightforward. Let $Word$ and MLS be the likelihood of being a noun and the most likely segmentation for a sequence of syllables. In the initialization step, each cell of the table is assigned $Word$ value for a sequence of syllables $s_j \dots s_{j+i+1}$ using its frequency if it is found in SND. In other words, if the value of $Word$ for the sequence in each cell is greater than zero, the syllables might be as a noun a part of a compound noun and so the value is recorded as MLS. It could be substituted by more likely one in the segmentation process.

In order to make it efficient, the segmentation result is put as MLS instead of the syllables in case the sequence of syllables exists in the HBND. The minimum of each $Word$ for constituents of the result as $Word$ is recorded.

Then, the segmenter compares possible analyses to make a larger one as shown in Figure 4. Whenever $Word$ of the entire syllables is less than that of segmented one, the syllables and value are replaced with the segmented result and its value. For instance, $s_1 + s_2$ and its likelihood substitutes $C_{2,1}$ if $\min(Word(s_1), Word(s_2)) > Word(s_1 s_2)$. When the entire syllables from the first to nth syllable are processed, $C_{n,1}$ has the segmentation result.

The overall complexity of the algorithm follows that of CYK parsing, $O(n^3)$.

3.3 Default Analysis and Tuning

For the final result, we should take into consideration several issues which are related with the syllables that left unsegmented. There are several reasons that the given string remains unsegmented:

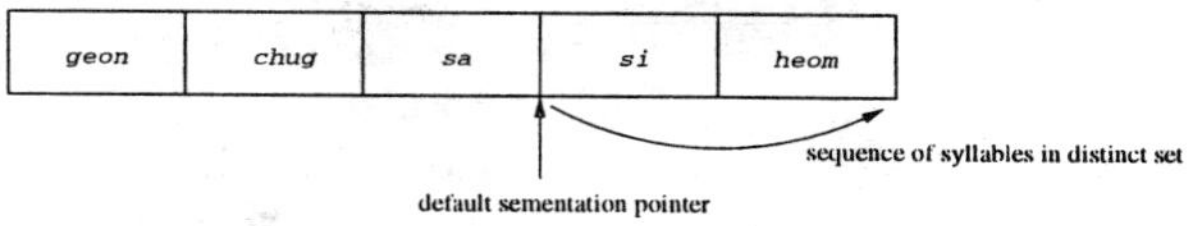

Figure 5: Default segmentation pointer for '*geon-chug-sa-si-heom*' where '*si-heom*' is a very frequently used noun.

1. The first one is a case where the string consists of several nouns but one of them is a unregistered word. A compound noun '*geon-chug-sa-si-heom*' is composed of '*geon-chug-sa*' and '*si-heom*', which have the meanings of *authorized architect* and *examination*. In this case, the unknown noun is caused by the suffix such as '*sa*' because the suffix derives many words. However, it is known that it is very difficult to treat the kinds of suffixes since the suffix like '*sa*' is a very frequently used character in Korean and thus prone to make oversegmentation if included in basic morphological analysis.

2. The string might consist of a proper noun and a noun representing a position or geometric information. For instance, a compound noun '*kim-dae-jung-dae-tong-ryeong*' is composed of '*kim-dae-jung*' and '*dae-tong-ryeong*' where the former is personal name and the latter means president respectively.

3. The string might be a proper noun itself. For example, '*willi'amseu*' is a transliterated word for foreign name 'Williams' and '*hong-gil-dong*' is a personal name in Korean. Generally, since it has a different sequence of syllables from in a general Korean word, it often remains unsegmented.

If the basic segmentation is failed, three procedures would be executed for solving three problems above. For the first issue, we use the *set of distinct nouns*. That is, the offset pointer is stored in the initialization step as well as frequency of each noun in compound noun is recorded in the table. Attention should be paid to non-frequent sequence of syllables (ones in the set of supplementary nouns) in the default segmentation because it could be found in any proper noun such as personal names, place names, etc or transliterated words. It is known that the performance drops if all nouns in the compound noun segmentation dictionary are considered for default segmentation. We save the pointer to the boundary only when a noun in distinct set appears. For the above example '*geon-chug-sa-si-heom*', the default segmentation would be '*geon-chug-sa*' and '*si-heom*' since '*si-heom*' is in the set of distinct nouns and the pointer is set before '*si-heom*' (Figure 5).

/* initialization step */
for i=1 to n do
  for j=1 to n-i+1 do
    $value(C_{i,j}) = Word(s_j \ldots s_{j+i-1});$
    $MLS(C_{i,j}) = s_j \ldots s_{j+i-1};$ if $value(C_{i,j}) > 0$
    $\phi;$ otherwise

for i=2 to n do
  for j=1 to i do

$$\begin{aligned} value(C_{i,j}) = \max(&\min(value(C_{i-1,j}), value(C_{1,j+i-1})),\\ &\min(value(C_{i-2,j}), value(C_{2,j-2})),\\ &\ldots\\ &\min(value(C_{1,j}), value(C_{i-1,j+1})),\\ &Word(s_j \ldots s_{i+j})) \end{aligned}$$

$$\begin{aligned} MLS(C_{i,j}) = arg\max(&\min(value(C_{i-1,j}), value(C_{1,j+i-1})),\\ &\min(value(C_{i-2,j}), value(C_{2,j-2})),\\ &\ldots\\ &\min(value(C_{1,j}), value(C_{i-1,j+1})),\\ &Word(s_j \ldots s_{i+j})) \end{aligned}$$

Figure 4: The segmentation algorithm

If this procedure is failed, the sequence of syllables is checked whether it might be proper noun or not. Since proper noun in Korean could have a kind of nominal suffix such as '*daetongryeong*(president)' or '*ssi*(Mr/Ms)' as mentioned above, we can identify it by detaching the nominal suffixes. If there does not exist any nominal suffix, then the entire syllables would be regarded just as the transliterated foreign word or a proper noun like personal or place name.

4 Experimental Results

For the test of compound noun segmentation, we first extracted compound noun from ETRI POS tagged corpus[3]. By the processing, 1774 types of compound nouns were extracted, which was used as a gold standard test set.

We evaluated our system by two methods: (1) the precision and recall rate, and (2) segmentation accuracy per compound noun which we refer to as SA. They are defined respectively as follows:

Precision =
$$\frac{number\ of\ correct\ constituents\ in\ proposed\ segment\ results}{total\ number\ of\ constituents\ in\ proposed\ segment\ results}$$

Recall =
$$\frac{number\ of\ correct\ constituents\ in\ proposed\ segment\ results}{total\ number\ of\ constituents\ in\ compoundnouns}$$

SA =
$$\frac{number\ of\ correctly\ segmented\ compound\ nouns}{total\ number\ of\ compoundnouns}$$

[3]The corpus was constructed by the ETRI (Electronics and Telecommunications Research Institute) project for standardization of natural language processing technology and the corpus presented consists of about 270,000 eojeols at present.

What influences on the Korean IR system is whether words are appropriately segmented or not. The precision and recall estimate how appropriate the segmentation results are. They are 98.04% and 97.80% respectively, which shows that our algorithm is very effective (Table 3).

SA reflects how accurate the segmentation is for a compound noun at all. We compared two methods: (1) using only the segmentation algorithm with default analysis which is a baseline of our system and so is needed to estimate the accuracy of the algorithm. (2) using both the built-in dictionary and the segmentation algorithm which reflects system accuracy as a whole. As shown in Table 4, the baseline performance using only distinct nouns and the algorithm is about 94.3% and fairly good. From the results, we can find that the distinct nouns has great impact on compound noun segmentation. Also, the overall segmentation accuracy for the gold standard is about 97.29% which is a very good result for the application system. In addition, it shows that the built-in dictionary supplements the algorithm which results in better segmentation.

Lastly, we compare our system with the previous work by (Yun *et al.* , 1997). It is impossible that we directly compare our result with theirs, since the test set is different. It was reported that the accuracy given in the paper is about 95.6%. When comparing the performance only in terms of the accuracy, our system outperforms theirs.

Embeded in the morphological analyzer, the compound noun segmentater is currently being used for some projects on MT and IE which are worked in several institutes and it turns out that the system is very effective.

	Precision	Recall
Number of correct constituents	3553/3628	3553/3637
Rate	98.04	97.80

Table 3: Result 1: Precision and recall rate

	SA	
	Whole System	Baseline
Number of correct constituents	1726/1774	1673/1774
Rate	97.29	94.30

Table 4: Result 2: Segmentation accuracy for Compound Noun

5 Conclusions

In this paper, we presented the new method for Korean compound noun segmentation. First, we proposed the lexical acquisition for compound noun analysis, which consists of the manually constructed segmentation dictionary (HBSD) and the dictionary for applying the segmentation algorithm (SND). The hand-built segmentation dictionary was made manually for compound nouns extracted from corpus. The simple noun dictionary is based on very frequently occurring nouns which are called distinct nouns because they are clues for identifying constituents of compound nouns. Second, the compound noun was segmented based on the modification of CYK tabular parsing and min-max composition, which was proven to be the very effective method by experiments. The bottom up approach using min-max operation guarantees the most likely segmentation, being applied in the same way as dynamic programming.

With our new method, the result for segmentation is as accurate as 97.29%. Especially, the algorithm made results good enough and the built-in dictionary supplemented the algorithm. Consequently, the methodology is promising and the segmentation system would be helpful for the application system such as machine translation and information retrieval.

6 Acknowledgement

We thank Prof. Mansuk Song at Yonsei Univ. and Prof. Key-Sun Choi at KAIST to provide data for experiments.

References

Cha, J., Lee, G. and Lee, J. 1998. Generalized Unknown Morpheme Guessing for Hybrid POS Tagging of Korean. In *Proceedings of the 6th Workshop on Very Large Corpora.*

Choi, K. S., Han, Y. S., Han, Y. G., and Kwon, O. W. 1994. KAIST Tree Bank Project for Korean: Present and Future Development. In *Proceedings of the International Workshop on Sharable Natural Language Resources.*

Elmi, M. A. and Evens, M. 1998. Spelling Correction Using Context. In *Proceedings of COLING/ACL 98*

Hopcroft, J. E. and Ullman, J. D. 1979. Introduction to Automata Theory, Languages, and Computation.

Jin, W. and Chen, L. 1995. Identifying Unknown Words in Chinese Corpora In *Proceedings of NLPRS 95*

Lee, J. H. and Ahn, J. S. 1996. Using n-grams for Korean Text Retrieval. In *Proceedings of 19th Annual International ACM SIGIR Conference on Research and Development in Information Retrieval*

Li, J. and Wang, K. 1995. Study and Implementation of Nondictionary Chinese Segmentation. In *Proceedings of NLPRS 95*

Nagao, M. and Mori, S. 1994. A New Method of N-gram Statistics for Large Number of N and Automatic Extraction of Words and Phrases from Large Text Data of Japanese. In *Proceedings of COLING 94*

Park, B, R., Hwang, Y. S. and Rim, H. C. 1997. Recognizing Korean Unknown Words by Comparatively Analyzing Example Words. In *Proceedings of ICCPOL 97*

Sproat, R. W., Shih, W., Gale, W. and Chang, N. 1994. A Stochastic Finite-State Word-segmentation Algorithm for Chinese. In *Proceedings of the 32nd Annual Meeting of ACL*

Yoon, J., Kang, B. and Choi, K. S. 1999. Information Retrieval Based on Compound Noun Analysis for Exact Term Extraction. Submitted in Journal of Computer Processing of Orientla Language.

Yoon, J., Lee, W. and Choi, K. S. 1999. Word Segmentation Based on Estimation of Words from Examples. Technical Report.

Yun, B. H., Cho, M. C. and Rim, H. C. 1997. Segmenting Korean Compound Nouns Using Statistical Information and a Preference Rules. In *Proceedings of PACLING.*

Experiments with Corpus-based LFG Specialization

Nicola Cancedda and Christer Samuelsson
Xerox Research Centre Europe,
6, chemin de Maupertuis
38240 Meylan, France
{cancedda|samuelsson}@xrce.xerox.com

Abstract

Sophisticated grammar formalisms, such as LFG, allow concisely capturing complex linguistic phenomena. The powerful operators provided by such formalisms can however introduce spurious ambiguity, making parsing inefficient. A simple form of corpus-based grammar pruning is evaluated experimentally on two wide-coverage grammars, one English and one French. Speedups of up to a factor 6 were obtained, at a cost in grammatical coverage of about 13%. A two-stage architecture allows achieving significant speedups without introducing additional parse failures.

1 Introduction

Expressive grammar formalisms allow grammar developers to capture complex linguistic generalizations concisely and elegantly, thus greatly facilitating grammar development and maintenance. (Carrol, 1994) found that the empirical performance when parsing with unification-based grammars is nowhere near the theoretical worst-case complexity. Nonetheless, directly parsing with such grammars, in the form they were developed, can be very inefficient. For this reason, grammars are typically compiled into representations that allow faster parsing. This does however not solve the potential problem of the grammars overgenerating considerably, thus allowing large amounts of spurious ambiguity. Indeed, a current trend in high-coverage parsing, especially when employing a statistical model of language, see, e.g., (Collins 97), is to allow the grammar to massively overgenerate and instead disambiguate by statistical means during or after parsing. If the benefits resulting from more concise grammatical descriptions are to outweigh the costs of spurious ambiguity, the latter must be brought down.

In such a situation, corpus-based compilation techniques can drastically improve parsing performance without burdening the grammar developer. The initial, and much seminal work in this area was been carried out by Rayner and coworkers, see (Rayner 1988), (Samuelsson and Rayner 91) and (Rayner and Carter 1996). In the current article, we apply similar ideas to Lexical Functional Grammar (LFG) in the incarnation of the Xerox Linguistic Environment (XLE). The goal is to investigate to what extent corpus-based compilation techniques can reduce overgeneration and spurious ambiguity, and increase parsing efficiency, without jeopardizing coverage. The rest of the article is organized as follows: Section 2 presents the relevant aspects of the LFG formalism and the pruning strategy employed, Section 3 describes the experimental setup, Section 4 reports the experimental results and Section 5 relates this to other work.

2 LFG and Grammar Pruning

The LFG formalism (Kaplan and Bresnan, 1982) allows the right-hand sides (RHS) of grammar rules to consist of a regular expression over grammar symbols. This makes it more appropriate to refer to the grammar rules as *rule schemata*, since each RHS can potentially be expanded into a (possibly infinite) number of distinct sequences of grammar symbols, each corresponding to a traditional phrase-structure rule. As can easily be imagined, the use of regular-expression operators such as *Kleene-star* and *complementation* may introduce a considerable amount of spurious ambiguity. Moreover, the LFG formalism provides operators which — although not increasing its theoretical expressive power — allow rules to be written more concisely. Examples of such operators are the *ignore* operator, which allows skipping any sequence of grammar symbols that matches a given pattern; the *shuffle* operator, which allows a set of grammar symbols to occur in any order; and the *linear precedence* operator, which allows partially specifying the order of grammar symbols.

The pruning method we propose consists in eliminating complex operators from the grammar description by considering how they were actually instantiated when parsing a corpus. In LFGs, each rule scheme corresponds to a particular grammar symbol, since different expansions of the same symbol are expressed as alternatives in the regular expression on its RHS. We can define a specific path through the RHS of a rule scheme by the choices made when matching it against some sequence of grammar symbols. Our training data allows us to derive, for each training example, the choices made at each rule expansion. By applying these choices to the rule scheme in isolation, we can derive a phrase-structure rule from it.

The grammar is specialized, or *pruned*, by retaining all and only those phrase-structure rules that correspond to a path taken through a rule scheme when expanding some node in some training example. Since the grammar formalism requires that each LHS occur only in one rule scheme in the grammar, extracted rules with the same LHS symbol are merged into a single rule scheme with a disjunction operator at its top level. For instance, if a rule scheme with the structure

$$A \rightarrow B^{*}\{C \mid D\}$$

is expanded in the training data only in the following ways

$$\begin{aligned} A &\rightarrow C \\ A &\rightarrow BC \\ A &\rightarrow BD \end{aligned}$$

then it will be replaced by a rule scheme with the following structure

$$A \rightarrow \{C \mid BC \mid BD\}$$

The same approach is taken to replace all regular-expression operators, other than concatenation, with the actual sequences of grammar symbols that are matched against them. A more realistic example, taken from the actual data, is shown in Figure 1: none of the optional alternative portions following the V is ever used in any correct parse in the corpus. Moreover, the $ADVP$ preceding the V occurs only 0 or 1 times in correct parses.

Like other unification-based formalisms, lexical functional grammars allow grammar rules to be annotated with sets of feature-based constraints, here called "functional descriptions", whose purpose is both to enforce additional constraints on rule applicability and to build an enriched predicate-argument structure called "f-structure", which, together with the parse tree, constitutes the output of the parsing process. As these constraints are maintained verbatim in the specialized version of the rule scheme, this poses no problem for this form of grammar pruning.

3 Experimental Setup

The experiments carried out to determine the effectiveness of corpus-based specialization were performed as illustrated in Figure 2. Two broad-coverage LFG grammars were used, one for French and one for English, both of which were developed within the Pargram project (Butt et al., 1999) during several years time. The French grammar consists of 133 rule schemata, the English grammar of 85 rule schemata.

Each grammar is equipped with a treebank, which was developed for other purposes than grammar specialization. Each treebank was produced by letting the system parse a corpus of technical documentation. Any sentence that did not obtain any parse was discarded. At this point, the French corpus was reduced to 960 sentences, and the English corpus to 970. The average sentence length was 9 for French and 8 for English. For each sentence, a human expert then selected the most appropriate analysis among those returned by the parser.

In the current experiments, each treebank was used to specialize the grammar it had been developed with. A set of 10-fold cross-validation experiments was carried out to measure several interesting quantities under different conditions. This means that, for each language, the corpus was randomly split into ten equal parts, and one tenth at a time was held out for testing while the remaining nine tenths were used to specialize the grammar, and the results were averaged over the ten runs. For each grammar the average number of parses per sentence, the fraction of sentences which still received at least one parse (*anyparse*) and the fraction of sentences for which the parse selected by the expert was still derived (*coverage*) were measured[1]. The average CPU time required by parsing was also measured, and this was used to compute the *speedup* with respect to the original grammar.

The thus established results constitute one data point in the trade-off between ambiguity reduction on one side, which is in turn related to parsing speed, and loss in coverage on the other. In order to determine other points of this trade-off, the same set of experiments was performed where specialization was inhibited for certain rule schemata. In particular, for each grammar, the two rule schemata that received the largest number of distinct expansions in the corpora were determined. These proved to be those associated with the LHS symbols 'VPverb[main]' and 'NP' for the French grammar, and 'VPv' and 'NPadj' for the English one.[2] The experiments were repeated while inhibiting specialization of first the scheme with the most expansions, and then the two most expanded schemata.

Measures of coverage and speedup are important

[1] As long as we are interested in preserving the f-structure assigned to sentences, this notion of coverage is stricter than necessary. The same f-structure can in fact be assigned by more than one parse, so that in some cases a sentence is considered out of coverage even if the specialized grammar assigns to it the correct f-structure.

[2] 'VPv' and 'VPverb[main]' cover VPs headed by a main verb. 'NPadj' covers NPs with adjectives attached.

The original rule:

$$VPperfp \;\rightarrow\; \begin{array}{l} ADVP* \\ \downarrow\in (\uparrow ADJUNCT) \\ (\downarrow ADV\_TYPE) = vpadv \end{array} \quad \begin{array}{l} V \\ \{@M\_Head\_Perfp \;|@M\_Head\_Passp\} \\ @(Anaph\_Ctrl \uparrow) \end{array}$$

$$\left(\left\{ \begin{array}{l} ADVP+ \\ \downarrow\in (\uparrow ADJUNCT) \\ (\downarrow ADV\_TYPE) = vpadv \end{array} \;\middle|\; \begin{array}{l} PP \\ @PPadjunct \end{array} \;\middle|\; \begin{array}{l} PPcase \\ @PPcase\_obl \end{array} \right\}\right)$$

is replaced by the following:

$$VPperfp \;\rightarrow\; \left\{ \begin{array}{l} \begin{array}{l} ADVP \\ \downarrow\in (\uparrow ADJUNCT) \\ (\downarrow ADV\_TYPE) = vpadv \end{array} \quad \begin{array}{l} V \\ \{@M\_Head\_Perfp \;|@M\_Head\_Passp\} \\ @(Anaph\_Ctrl \uparrow) \end{array} \\ \\ \;\middle|\; \begin{array}{l} V \\ \{@M\_Head\_Perfp \;|@M\_Head\_Passp\} \\ @(Anaph\_Ctrl \uparrow) \end{array} \end{array} \right\}$$

Figure 1: The pruning of a rule from the actual French grammar. The "*" and the "+" signs have the usual interpretation as in regular expressions. A sub-expression enclosed in parenthesis is optional. Alternative sub-expressions are enclosed in curly brackets and separated by the "|" sign. An "@" followed by an identifier is a macro expansion operator, and is eventually replaced by further functional descriptions.

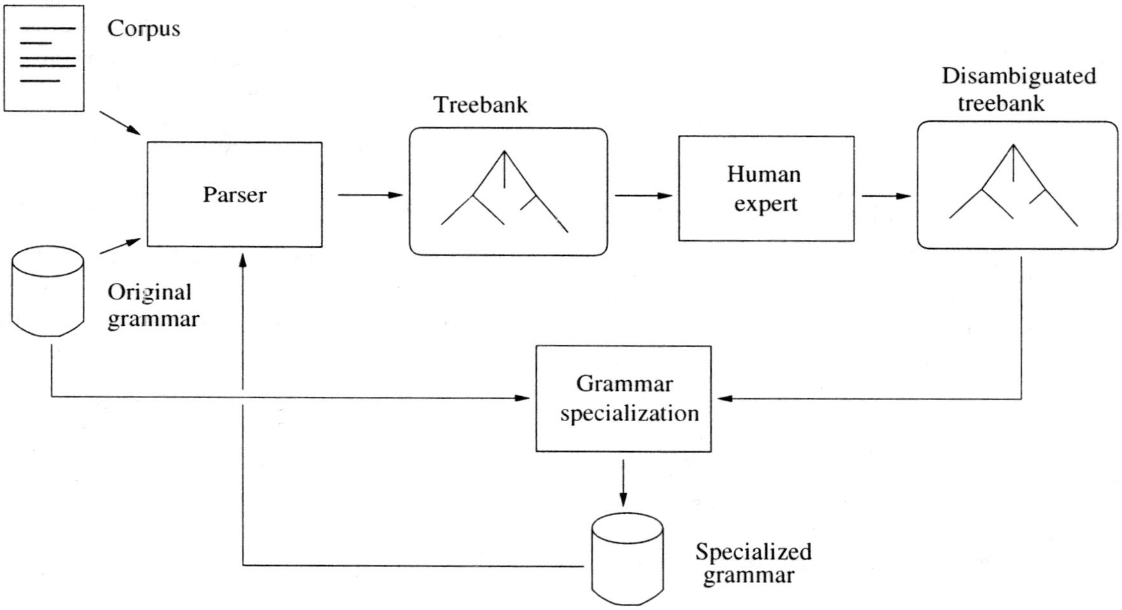

Figure 2: The setting for our experiments on grammar specialization.

indicators of what can be achieved with this form of grammar pruning. However, they could potentially be misleading, since failure times for uncovered sentences might be considerably lower than their parsing times, had they not been out of coverage. If the pruned grammar fails more frequently on sentences which take longer to parse, the measured speedup might be artificially high. This is easily realized, as simply removing the hardest sentences from the corpus would cause a decrease in the average parsing time, and thus result in a speedup, without any pruning at all. To factor out the contribution of uncovered sentences from the results, the performance of a two-stage architecture analogous to that of (Samuelsson and Rayner, 1991) was simulated, in which the pruned grammar is attempted

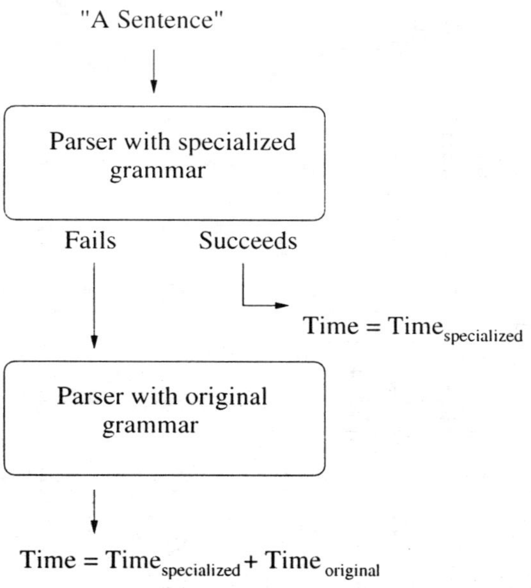

Figure 3: A schematic representation of the simulated two-stage coverage-preserving architecture.

first, and the sentence is passed on to the original unpruned grammar whenever the pruned grammar fails to return a parse (see Figure 3). The measured speedup of this simulated architecture, which preserves the *anyparse* measure of the original grammar, takes into account the contribution of uncovered sentences, as it penalizes sweeping difficult sentences under the carpet.

4 Experimental Results

The results of the experiments described in the section above are summarized in the table in Figure 4. The upper part of the table refers to experiments with the French grammar, the lower part to experiments with the English grammar. For each language, the first line presents data gathered for the original grammar for comparison with the pruned grammars. The figures in the second line were collected by pruning the grammar based on the whole corpus, and then testing on the corpus itself. The grammars obtained in this way contain 516 and 388 disjuncts — corresponding to purely concatenative rules — for French and English respectively. *Anyparse* and *coverage* are not, of course, relevant in this case, but the statistics on parsing time are, especially the one on the maximum parsing time. For each iteration in the 10-fold cross-validation experiment, the maximum parsing time was retained, and those ten times were eventually averaged. If pruning tended to leave sentences which take long to parse uncovered, then we would observe a significant difference between the average over maximum times on the grammar trained and tested on the same corpus (which parses all sentences, including the hardest), and the average over maximum times for grammars trained and tested on different sets. The fact that this does not seem to be the case indicates that pruning does not penalize difficult sentences. Note also that the average number of parses per sentence is significantly smaller than with the full grammar, of almost a factor of 9 in the case of the French grammar.

The third line contains results for the fully pruned grammar. In the case of the French grammar a speedup of about 6 is obtained with a loss in coverage of 13%. The smaller speedup gained with the English grammar can be explained by the fact that here, the parsing times are lower in general, and that a non-negligible part of this time, especially that needed for morphological analysis, is unaffected by pruning. Even in the case of the English grammar, though, speedup is substantial (2.67). For both grammars, the reduction in the average maximum parsing time is particularly good, confirming our hypothesis that trimming the grammar by removing heavy constructs makes it considerably more efficient. A partially negative note comes from the average number of disjuncts in the pruned grammars, which is 501 for French and 374 for English. Comparing this figures to the number of disjuncts in grammars pruned on the full corpus (516 and 388), we find that after training on nine tenths of the corpus, adding the last tenth still leads to an increase of 3-4% in the size of the resulting grammars. In other words, the marginal gain of further training examples is still significant after considering about 900 sentences, indicating that the training corpora are somewhat too small.

The last two lines for each language show figures for grammars with pruning inhibited on the most variable and the two most variable symbols respectively. For both languages, inhibiting pruning on the most variable symbol has the expected effect of increasing both parsing time and coverage. Inhibiting pruning also on the second most variable symbol has almost no effect for French, and only a small effect for English.

The table in Figure 5 summarizes the measures on the simulated two-stage architecture. For both languages the best trade-off, once the distribution of uncovered sentences has been taken into account, is achieved by the fully pruned grammars.

5 Related Work

The work presented in the current article is related to previous work on corpus-based grammar specialization as presented in (Rayner, 1988; Samuelsson and Rayner, 1991; Rayner and Carter, 1996; Samuelsson, 1994; Srinivas and Joshi, 1995; Neumann, 1997).

	Parses/sentence	Anyparse	Coverage	Avg. time (secs.)	Max. time (secs.)	Speedup
French						
original grammar	1941	1.00	1.00	1.52	78.5	1
test = training	219	1.00	1.00	0.28	5.62	5.43
First-order pruning	164	0.91	0.87	0.25	5.69	6.08
no pruning on 'VPverb[main]'	1000	0.94	0.91	0.42	8.70	3.62
no pruning on 'Vpverb[main]' and 'NP'	1279	0.94	0.92	0.42	8.42	3.62
English						
original grammar	58	1.00	1.00	0.56	31.73	1
test = training	24	1.00	1.00	0.23	3.92	2.43
First-order pruning	21	0.94	0.88	0.21	3.92	2.67
no pruning on 'VPv'	25	0.96	0.91	0.32	11.06	1.75
no pruning on 'Vpv' and 'NPadj'	31	0.96	0.93	0.35	11.16	1.60

Figure 4: The results of the experiments on LFG specialization.

	Avg. CPU time (secs.)	Speedup
French		
First-order pruning	0.570	2.67
no pruning on 'VPverb[main]'	0.616	2.47
no pruning on 'VPverb[main]' and 'NP'	0.614	2.48
English		
First-order pruning	0.311	1.81
no pruning on 'VPv'	0.380	1.47
no pruning on 'VPv' and 'NPadj'	0.397	1.40

Figure 5: Results for the simulated two-stage architecture.

The line of work described in (Rayner, 1988; Samuelsson and Rayner, 1991; Rayner and Carter, 1996; Samuelsson, 1994) deals with unification-based grammars that already have a purely-concatenative context-free backbone, and is more concerned with a different form of specialization, consisting in the application of explanation-based learning (EBL). Here, the central idea is to collect the most frequently occurring subtrees in a treebank and use them as atomic units for parsing. The cited works differ mainly in the criteria adopted for selecting subtrees from the treebank. In (Rayner, 1988; Samuelsson and Rayner, 1991; Rayner and Carter, 1996) these criteria are handcoded: all subtrees satisfying some properties are selected, and a new grammar rule is created by flattening each such subtree, i.e., by taking the root as left-hand side and the yield as right-hand side, and in the process performing all unifications corresponding to the thus removed internal nodes. Experiments carried out on a corpus of 15,000 trees from the ATIS domain using a version of the SRI Core Language Engine resulted in a speedup of about 3.4 at a cost of 5% in grammatical coverage, which however was compensated by an increase in parsing accuracy.

Finding suitable tree-cutting criteria requires a considerable amount of work, and must be repeated for each new grammar and for each new domain to which the grammar is to be specialized. Samuelsson (Samuelsson, 1994) proposes a technique to automatically selects what subtrees to retain. The selection of appropriate subtrees is done by choosing a subset of nodes at which to cut trees. Cutnodes are determined by computing the *entropy* of each node, and selecting only those nodes whose entropy exceeds a given threshold. Intuitively, nodes with low entropy indicate locations in the trees where a given symbol was expanded using a predictable set of rules, at least most of the times, so that the loss of coverage that derives from ignoring the remaining cases is low. Nodes with high entropy, on the other hand, indicate positions in which there is a high uncertainty in what rule was used to expand the symbol, so that it is better to preserve all alternatives. Several schemas are proposed to compute entropies, each leading to a different trade-off between coverage reduction and speedup. In general, results are not quite as good as those obtained using handcoded criteria, though of course the specialized grammar is obtained fully automatically, and thus with much less effort.

When ignoring issues related to the elimination of complex operators from the RHS of rule schemata, the grammar-pruning strategy described in the current article is equivalent to explanation-based learning where all nodes have been selected as cutnodes. Conversely, EBL can be viewed as higher-order grammar pruning, removing not grammar rules, but grammar-rule combinations.

Some of the work done on data-oriented parsing (DOP) (Bod, 1993; Bod and Scha, 1996; Bod and Kaplan, 1998; Sima'an, 1999) can also be considered related to our work, as it can be seen as a way to specialize in an EBL-like way the (initially unknown) grammar implicitly underlying a treebank.

(Srinivas and Joshi, 1995) and (Neumann, 1997) apply EBL to speed up parsing with tree-adjoining grammars and sentence generation with HPSGs respectively, though they do so by introducing new components in their systems rather then by modifying the grammars they use.

6 Conclusions

Sophisticated grammar formalisms are very useful and convenient when designing high-coverage grammars for natural languages. Very expressive grammatical constructs can make the task of developing and maintaining such a large resource considerably easier. On the other hand, their use can result in a considerable increase in grammatical ambiguity. Grammar-compilation techniques based on grammar structure alone are insufficient remedies in those cases, as they cannot access the information required to determine which alternatives to retain and which alternatives to discard.

The current article demonstrates that a relatively simple pruning technique, employing the kind of reference corpus that is typically used for grammar development and thus often already available, can significantly improve parsing performance. On large lexical functional grammars, speedups of up to a factor 6 were observed, at the price of a reduction in grammatical coverage of about 13%. A simple two-stage architecture was also proposed that preserves the *anyparse* measure of the original grammar, demonstrating that significant speedups can be obtained without increasing the number of parsing failures.

Future work includes extending the study of corpus-based grammar specialization from first-order grammar pruning to higher-order grammar pruning, thus extending previous work on explanation-based learning for parsing, and applying it to the LFG formalism.

References

Rens Bod and Ronald Kaplan. 1998. A probabilistic corpus-driven model for lexical-functional analysis. In *Proceedings of Coling-ACL-98*, Montreal, Canada.

R. Bod and R. Scha. 1996. Data-oriented language processing: An overview. Technical report, ILLC, University of Amsterdam, Amsterdam, The Netherlands.

Rens Bod. 1993. Using an annotated corpus as a stochastic grammar. In *Proceedings of EACL-93*, Utrecht, The Netherlands.

M. Butt, T.H. King, M.E. Niño, and F. Segond. 1999. *A Grammar Writer's Cookbook*. CSLI Publications, Stanford, CA.

John Carrol. 1994. Relating complexity to practical performance in parsing with wide-coverage unification grammars. In *Proceedings of (ACL'94)*, Las Cruces, New Mexico, June.

Ronald Kaplan and Joan Bresnan. 1982. Lexical-functional grammar: A formal system for grammatical representation. In Joan Bresnan, editor, *The Mental Representation of Grammatical Relations*, pages 173–281. MIT Press.

Günter Neumann. 1997. Applying explanation-based learning to control and speeding-up natural language generation. In *Proceedings of ACL-EACL-97*, Madrid, Spain.

Manny Rayner and David Carter. 1996. Fast parsing using pruning and grammar specialization. In *Proceedings of the ACL-96*, Santa Cruz, CA.

Manny Rayner. 1988. Applying explanation-based generalization to natural-language processing. In *Proceedings of the International Conference on Fifth Generation Computer Systems*, Tokyo, Japan.

Christer Samuelsson and Manny Rayner. 1991. Quantitative evaluation of explanation-based learning as an optimization tool for a large-scale natural language system. In *Proceedings of the IJCAI-91*, Sydney, Oz.

Christer Samuelsson. 1994. Grammar specialization through entropy thresholds. In *Proceedings of the ACL-94*, Las Cruces, New Mexico. Available as cmp-lg/9405022.

Khalil Sima'an. 1999. *Learning Efficient Disambiguation*. Ph.D. thesis, Institute for Logic, Language and Computation, Amsterdam, The Netherlands.

B. Srinivas and A. Joshi. 1995. Some novel applications of explanation-based learning to parsing lexicalized tree-adjoining grammars. In *Proceedings of the ACL-95*, Cambridge, MA.

A Tool for Automated Revision of Grammars for NLP Systems

Nanda Kambhatla and Wlodek Zadrozny
IBM T.J. Watson Research Center
30 Saw Mill River Road,
Hawthorne, NY, 10532
{*nanda,wlodz*}@us.ibm.com

Abstract

We present an algorithm and a tool for automatically revising grammars for natural language processing (NLP) systems to disallow specifically identified sentences or sets of sentences. We also outline an approach for automatically revising attribute value grammars using counter-examples. Developing grammars for NLP systems that are both general enough to accept most sentences about a domain, but constrained enough to disallow other sentences is very tedious. Our approach of revising grammars automatically using counter-examples greatly simplifies the development and revision of tightly constrained grammars. We have successfully used our tool to constrain over-generalizing grammars of speech understanding systems and obtained higher recognition accuracy.

1 Introduction

Natural language processing systems often constrain the set of "utterances" from a user (spoken, typed in, etc.) to narrow down the possible syntactic and semantic resolutions of the utterance and reduce the number of misrecognitions and/or misunderstandings by the system. Such constraints on the allowed syntax and the inferred semantics are often expressed in the form of a "grammar"[1], a set of rules specifying the set of allowed utterances and possibly also specifying the semantics associated with these utterances. For instance, grammars are commonly used in speech understanding systems to specify both the set of allowed sentences and to specify "tags" to extract semantic entities (e.g. the "amount" of money).

Constraining the number of sentences accepted by a grammar is essential for reducing misinterpretations of user queries by an NLP system. For instance, for speech understanding systems, if the grammar accepts a large number of sentences, then the likelihood of recognizing uttered sentences as random, irrelevant, or undesirable sentences is increased. For transaction processing systems, misrecognized words can lead to unintended transactions being processed. An effective constraining grammar can reduce transactional errors by limiting the number of sentence level errors. The problem of over-generalization of speech grammars and related issues is well discussed by Seneff (1992).

Thus, speech grammars must often balance the conflicting requirements of

- accepting a wide variety of sentences to increase flexibility, and
- accepting a small number of sentences to increase system accuracy and robustness.

Developing tight grammars which trade-off these conflicting constraints is a tedious and

[1] Throughout this document, by using the word "grammar", we refer to a Context-Free Grammar that consists of a finite set of *non-terminals*, a finite set of *terminals*, a unique non-terminal called the *start symbol*, and a set of *production rules* of the form ***A*-> *a***, where ***A*** is a non-terminal and ***a*** is a string of terminal or non-terminal symbols. The 'language' accepted by a grammar is the set of all terminal strings that can be generated from the start symbol by successive application of the production rules. The grammar may optionally have semantic interpretation rules associated with each production rule (e.g. see (Allen 95)).

difficult process. Typically, grammars overgeneralize and accept too many sentences that are irrelevant or undesirable for a given application. We call such sentences "counter-examples". The problem is usually handled by revising the grammar manually to disallow such counter-examples. For instance, the sentence "give me my last eighteen transactions" may need to be excluded from a grammar for a speech understanding system, since the words "eighteen" and "ATM" are easily confused by the speech recogniser. However, "five" and "ten" should remain as possible modifiers of "transactions". Counter-examples can also be sets of sentences that need to be excluded from a grammar (specified by allowing the inclusion of non-terminals in counter-examples). For example, for a banking application that disallows money transfers to online accounts, we might wish to exclude the set of sentences "transfer <AMOUNT> dollars to my online account" from the grammar, where <AMOUNT> is a non-terminal in the grammar that maps to all possible ways of specifying amounts.

In this paper, we are proposing techniques for automatically revising grammars using counter-examples. The grammar developer identifies counter-examples from among sentences (or sets of sentences) mis-recognized by the speech recognizer or from sentences randomly generated by a sentence generator using the original grammar. The grammar reviser modifies

Figure 1

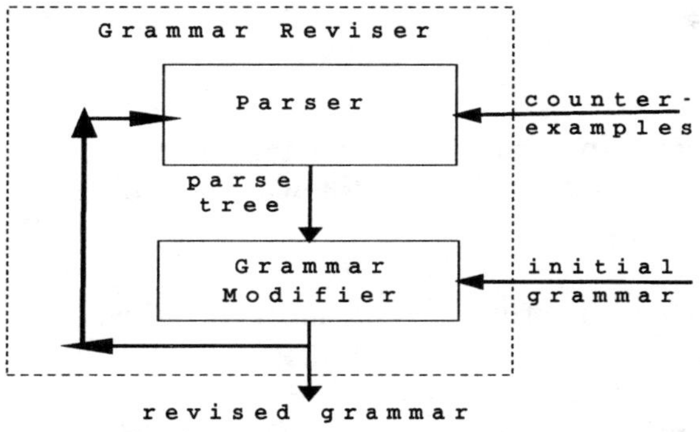

the original grammar to invalidate the counter-examples. The revised grammar can be fed back to the grammar reviser and whole process can be iterated several times until the resulting grammar is deemed satisfactory.

In the next sections, we first describe our algorithm for revising grammars to disallow counter-examples. We also discuss algorithms to make the revised grammar compact using minimum description length (MDL) based grammar compaction techniques and extensions to our basic algorithm to handle grammars with recursion. We then present some results of applying our grammar reviser tool to constrain speech grammars of speech understanding systems. Finally, we present an approach for revising attribute value grammars using our technique and present our conclusions.

2 Automated Grammar Revision by rule modification

In this section, we describe an algorithm (see Figure 1) for revising grammars that directly modifies the rules of the grammar to disallow counter-examples. For each counter-example[2], we generate the parse tree (representation of all the grammar rules needed to generate the sentence or set of sentences) and the grammar modifier modifies the production rules of the grammar to invalidate the counter-example. This process is repeated for each counter-example using the revised grammar from the previous iteration for generating the parse tree for the current counter-example. If a counter-example generates multiple parse trees, the above algorithm is repeated for each parse tree in turn.

2.1 Grammar modification algorithm

We present the grammar modification algorithm below. For, we assume that the parse-tree(s) of the counter-example contain no recursion (i.e. the same production rule does not occur twice in any of the parse trees). In section 2.4, we present an approach for using the algorithm even when the parse-trees contain recursion. Thus, the algorithm is applicable for any context-free grammar. The grammar modification algorithm

[2] Note that a counter-example can be a sentence such as "move to operator" or a set of sentences such as "transfer <AMOUNT> to online account". The latter is specified using non-terminals interspersed with words.

for modifying the rules of a grammar to disallow a counter-example **c** (identified by a grammar developer) using a parse-tree for **c** proceeds as follows :

1. For each non-terminal <N> in the parse tree, except the <<START>> symbol,
    a. Add a rule to define a new non-terminal <N'> such that <N'> generates all phrases that <N> generates except for the phrase in the counter-example that <N> generates.
    b. Add a rule to define a new non-terminal <No> such that <No> generates only the phrase(s) in the counter-example that <N> generates.
2. Modify the rule that contains the <<START>> symbol in the parse tree, such that the <<START>> symbol no longer generates the given counter-example.

Figure 2

(a) Original grammar:

```
<<START>> ::= <V> <N> <PP> |
              <V> <PP> .
     <PP> ::= "to" <N> .
  <V> ::= "move" | "transfer" .
  <N> ::= "checking" | "savings" |
          "money" | "operator" .
```

(b) Parse Tree for "move to operator"

```
<<START>> ::= <V> <PP> .
      <V> ::= "move" .
     <PP> ::= "to" <N> .
      <N> ::= "operator".
```

We illustrate the algorithm with an example. Figure 2(a) shows a simple grammar. Suppose the sentence "move to operator" is a counter-example for an application. Figure 2(b) shows the parse-tree for "move to operator". Since the parse tree contains the rule: <V> ::= "move", new rules are added to define non-terminals <V'> and <Vo>, where <V'> does not generate "move" and <Vo> generates only "move". Similarly, since the parse tree contains the rule: <N>::= "operator", the new rules: <N'>::= "checking" | "savings" | "money"; and <No>::= "operator", are added. For the non-terminal <PP>, the new rules: <PP'>::= "to" <N'>; and <PPo>::= "to" <No>, are added. Note that since <No> only generates the phrase "operator" which is part of the counter-example, <PPo> only generates the phrase "to operator" which is part of the counter-example. Also, <PP'> generates all phrases that <PP> generates except for the phrase "to operator". Finally, the rule: <<START>>::= <V> <PP> is modified using the newly created non-terminals <V'>, <Vo>, <PP'> and <PPo> such that the only sentences which are accepted by the grammar and begin with the phrase "move" do not end with the phrase "to operator", and also, the only sentences which are accepted by the grammar and end with the phrase "to operator" do not begin with the phrase "move". Figure 3 shows the final modified grammar that accepts all the sentences that the grammar in Figure 2(a) accepts except for the sentence "move to operator". In Figure 3, all the grammar rules that are new or modified are shown in bold and italics.

Figure 3

```
<<START>> ::= <V> <N> <PP> |
              <V'> <PPo> /
              <Vo> <PP'> /
              <V'> <PP'> .
     <PP> ::= "to" <N> .
    <PP'> ::= "to" <N'> .
    <PPo> ::= "to" <No> .
      <V> ::= "move" | "transfer" .
     <V'> ::= "transfer" .
     <Vo> ::= "move" .
      <N> ::= "checking" | "savings" |
              "money" | "operator" .
     <N'> ::= "checking" / "savings" /
              "money" .
     <No> ::= "operator" .
```

The above algorithm for grammar modification has a time complexity of $O(m*2^k)$ rule creation (or modification) steps for removing a counter-example, where m is the number of production rules in the parse tree of the counter-example and k is the largest number of non-terminals on the right hand side of any of these production rules. Since grammars used for real applications rarely have more than a handful of non-terminals on the right hand side of production rules, this complexity is quite manageable.

2.2 Automated grammar compaction using MDL based grammar induction

As seen in the example described above, the size of the grammar (number of production rules) can increase greatly by applying our algorithm successively for a number of counter-examples. However, we can remedy this by applying grammar induction algorithms based on minimum description length (MDL) (e.g. Grunwald (1996) and Zadrozny (1997)) to combine rules and create a compact grammar that accepts the same language.

The MDL principle (Rissanen (1982)) selects that description (theory) of data, which minimizes the sum of the length, in bits, of the description of the theory, and the length, in bits, of data when encoded using the theory. In our case, the data is the set of possible word combinations and the theory is the grammar that specifies it. We are primarily interested in using the MDL principle to obtain (select) a compact grammar (the theory) from among a set of equivalent grammars. Since the set of possible word combinations (data) is the same for all grammars in consideration, we focus on the description length of the grammars itself, which we approximate by using a set of heuristics described in step 1 below.

We use the following modified version of Zadrozny's (1997) algorithm to generate a more compact grammar from the revised grammar using the MDL principle:

1. Compute the description length of the grammar, i.e. the total number of symbols needed to specify the grammar, where each non-terminal, "::=", and " | " are counted as one symbol.
2. Modify the current grammar by concatenating all possible pairs of non-terminals, and compute the description length of each such resultant grammar. For concatenating <N1> and <N2>, introduce the rule <N3>::= <N1> <N2>, search all other rules for consecutive occurrences of <N1> and <N2>, and replace such occurrences with <N3>. Note that this change results in an equivalent grammar (that accepts the same set of sentences as the original grammar).
3. Modify the current grammar by merging all possible pairs of non-terminals, and compute the description length of each such resultant grammar. For merging <N4> and <N5>, introduce the rule: <N6>::= <N4> | <N5>, search for pairs of rules which differ only in one position such that for one of the rules, <N4> occurs in that position and the other rule, the <N5> occurs in the same position. Replace the pair of rules with a new rule that is exactly the same as either of the pairs of rules, except for the use of <N6> instead of <N3> or <N4>. Note that this change results in an equivalent grammar (that accepts the same set of sentences as the original grammar).
4. Compute a table of description lengths of the grammars obtained by concatenating or merging all possible pairs of non- terminals of the initial grammar, as described above. Select the pair of non-terminals (if any) together with the action (concatenate or merge) that results in the least description length and execute the corresponding action.
5. Iterate steps 2, 3, and 4 until the description length does not decrease. No further modification is performed if the base description length of the grammar is lower than that resulting from merging or concatenating any pair of non- terminals.

In variations of this algorithm, the selection of the pairs of non-terminals to concatenate or merge, can be based on; the syntactic categories of the corresponding terminals, the semantic categories of the corresponding terminals, and the frequency of occurrence of the non-terminals.

Using the algorithm described above in conjunction with the algorithm in section 2.1, we can obtain a compact grammar that is guaranteed to disallow the counter-examples.

2.3 Results for grammar revision for speech understanding systems

We have built a graphical tool for revising grammars for NLP systems based on the algorithm described in sections 2.1 and 2.2 above. The tool takes as input an existing grammar and can randomly generate sentences accepted by the grammar including non-terminal strings and strings containing terminals and non-terminals (e.g. both "move to operator" and "transfer <AMOUNT> to online account" would be generated if they were accepted by the grammar). A grammar developer (a human) interacts with the tool and either inputs counter-examples selected from speech recognition error logs or selects counter-examples like the ones listed above. The grammar developer can then revise the grammar to disallow the counter-examples by pressing a button and then reduce the size of the resulting grammar using the algorithm in section 2.2 by pressing another button to obtain a compact grammar that does not accept any of the identified counter-examples. Typically, the grammar developer repeats the above cycle several times to obtain a tightly constrained grammar.

We have successfully used the tool described above to greatly constrain overgeneralizing grammars for speech understanding systems that we built for telephony banking, stock trading and directory assistance (Zadrozny *et al*, 1998). The speech recognition grammars for these systems accepted around fifty million sentences each. We successfully used the reviser tool to constrain these grammars by eliminating thousands of sentences and obtained around 20-30% improvement in sentence recognition accuracy. We conducted two user studies of our telephony banking system at different stages of development. The user studies were conducted eight months apart. During these eight months, we used a multi-pronged strategy of constraining grammars using the grammar revision algorithms described in this paper, improving the pronunciation models of some words and redesigning the prompts of the system to enable fast and easy error recovery by users. The combination of all these techniques resulted in improving the 'successful transaction in first try'[3] from 43% to 71%, an improvement of 65%. The average number of wrong tries (turns of conversation) to get a successful answer was reduced from 2.1 to 0.5 tries. We did not conduct experiments to isolate the contribution of each factor towards this improvement in system performance.

It is important to note here that we would probably have obtained this improvement in recognition accuracy even with a manual revision of the grammars. However, the main advantage in using our tool is the tremendous simplification of the whole process of revision for a grammar developer who now selects counter-examples with an interactive tool instead of manually revising the grammars.

2.4 Handling recursion in grammars

We now describe an extension of the algorithm in section 2.1 that can modify grammars with recursion to disallow a finite set of counter-examples. The example grammars shown above are regular grammars (i.e. equivalent finite state automatons exist). For regular grammars (and only for regular grammars), an alternative approach for eliminating counter-examples using standard automata theory is:

- Compute the finite state automaton (FSA) G corresponding to the original grammar.
- Compute the FSA C corresponding to the set of counter-examples.
- Compute C', the complement of C with respect to the given alphabet.
- Compute G', the intersection of G and C'. The FSA G' is equivalent to a revised grammar which disallows the counter-examples.

[3] We measured the number of times the user's transactional intent (e.g. checking balance, last five transactions etc.) was recognized and acted upon correctly by the system in the first try, even when the actual utterance may not have been recognized correctly word for word.

The time complexity of the algorithm is O(n*m), where n and m are the number of states in the finite state automatons G and C respectively. This is comparable to the quadratic time complexity of our grammar revision algorithm presented in Section 3.1.

However, the above algorithm for eliminating counter-examples only works for regular grammars. This is because context-free grammars are not closed under complementation and intersection. However we can use our algorithm for grammar modification (section 2.1) to handle any context-free grammar as follows:

1) As before, generate parse tree p for counter-example c for an initial grammar G.
2) If p contains a recursion (two or more repetitions of any production rule in the same parse tree), rewrite the initial grammar G as the equivalent grammar G', where the recursion is "unrolled" sufficiently many times (at least one more time than the number of repetitions of the recursive production rule in the parse tree). We explain the unrolling of recursion in greater detail below. If p does not contain any recursion, go to step 4.
3) Generate parse tree p' for the counter-example c for the rewritten grammar G'. Note that p' will no longer contain a recursive application of any production rules, though G' itself will still have recursion.
4) Use the algorithm described in section 2.1 to modify the grammar G' to eliminate the counter-example c using the parse tree p'.

We illustrate the above algorithm with an example. Figure 4(a) shows a context free grammar which accepts all strings of the form $a^n b^n$, for any ***n*** greater than 0. Note that this is not a regular language. Suppose we wish to eliminate the counter-example ***aaabbb*** from the initial grammar. The parse tree ***p*** for the counter-example ***aaabbb*** is shown in Figure 4(b). The grammar in 4(a) can be rewritten as the equivalent grammar 4(c), where the recursion of (***S->aSb***) is unrolled three times. The parse tree ***p'*** for the counter-example aaabbb with respect to grammar in 4(c) is shown in Figure 4(d). Note that ***p'*** does not contain any recursion, though the rewritten grammar does. We revised the grammar in 4(c) to eliminate the counter-example ***aaabbb*** using the parse tree in Figure 4(d). The revised grammar is shown in Figure 4(e). Note that here we are assuming that a mechanism exists for rewriting the rules of a grammar with recursion to unroll the recursion (if it exists) a finite number of times. Such an unrolling is readily accomplished by introducing a set of new non-terminal's, one for each iteration of unrolling as shown in Figure 4(c).

FIGURE 4

(a) ORIGINAL GRAMMAR G

```
<S> ::= "a" <S> "b" | "a" "b" .
```

(b) PARSE TREE p

```
<S> ::= "a" <S> "b" .
<S> ::= "a" <S> "b" .
<S> ::= "a" "b" .
```

(c) REWRITTEN GRAMMAR G'

```
<S>  ::= "a" <S1> "b" | "a" "b" .
<S1> ::= "a" <S2> "b" | "a" "b" .
<S2> ::= "a" <S3> "b" | "a" "b" .
<S3> ::= "a" <S3> "b" | "a" "b" .
```

(d) PARSE TREE p'

```
<S>  ::= "a" <S1> "b" .
<S1> ::= "a" <S2> "b" .
<S2> ::= "a" "b" .
```

(e) REVISED GRAMMAR Gr

```
<S>  ::= "a" <S1> "b" | "a" "b" .
<S1> ::= "a" <S2> "b" | "a" "b" .
<S2> ::= "a" <S3> "b" .
<S3> ::= "a" <S3> "b" | "a" "b" .
```

3 Automated revision of attribute-value grammars

In this section, we delineate an approach for automatically modifying attribute value grammars using counter-examples. We first convert an attribute value grammar into an equivalent non-attributed grammar by creating new non-terminals and encoding the attributes in the names of the new non-terminals (see Manaster Ramer and Zadrozny (1990) and Pollard and Sag (1994)).

For example, suppose the grammar in Figure 2(a) is an attribute value grammar with an

Figure 5

```
<<START>> ::= <V> <N> <PP> |
              <V> <PP> .
     <PP> ::= "to" <N> .
      <V> ::= "move" | "transfer" .
      <N> ::= <N_account_checking> |
              <N_account_savings> |
              <N_account_unspecified> .

  <N_account_checking> ::= "checking" .
   <N_account_savings> ::= "savings".
<N_account_unspecified> ::= "money" |
                            "operator" .
```

attribute 'account', which encodes information about the type of account specified, e.g. 'account' might have the values, SAVINGS, CHECKING and UNSPECIFIED. Figure 5 shows an equivalent non-attributed grammar, where the value of the attribute 'account' has been encoded in the names of the non-terminals. Note that such an encoding can potentially create a very large number of non-terminals. Also, the specific coding used needs to be such that the attributes can be easily recovered from the non-terminal names later on.

Figure 6

```
             <<START>> ::= <V> <N> <PP> | <V'> <PPo> |
                           <Vo> <PP'> | <V'> <PP'> .
                  <PP> ::= "to" <N> .
                 <PP'> ::= "to" <N'> .
                 <PPo> ::= "to" <No> .
                   <V> ::= "move" | "transfer" .
                  <V'> ::= "transfer" .
                  <Vo> ::= "move" .
                   <N> ::= <N_account_checking> |
                           <N_account_savings> |
                           <N_account_unspecified> .
                  <N'> ::= <N_account_checking> |
                           <N_account_savings> |
                           <N'_account_unspecified> .
                  <No> ::= <No_account_unspecified> .
  <N_account_checking> ::= "checking" .
   <N_account_savings> ::= "savings".
<N_account_unspecified> ::= "money" |
                           "operator" .
<N'_account_unspecified> ::= "money" .
<No_account_unspecified> ::= "operator" .
```

We can now use our modification algorithms (Section 2.1 and 2.2) to eliminate counter-examples from the non-attributed grammar. For instance, suppose we wish to eliminate 'move to operator' from the attributed grammar based on Figure 2(a), as discussed above. We apply our algorithm (Section 2.1) to the grammar in Figure 5 and obtain the grammar shown in Figure 6. Note that we name any new non-terminals created during the grammar modification in such a way as to leave the encoding of the attribute values in the non-terminal names intact.

After applying the grammar revision algorithm, we can extract the attribute values from the encoding in the non-terminal names. For instance, in the example outlined above, we might systematically check for suffixes of a certain type and recover the attributes and their values. Also, as described earlier, we can use the algorithm described in section 2.2 to make the resulting grammar compact again by using MDL based grammar induction algorithms.

4 Conclusions

We have presented a set of algorithms and an interactive tool for automatically revising grammars of NLP systems to disallow identified counter-examples (sentences or sets of sentences accepted by the current grammar but deemed to be irrelevant for a given application). We have successfully used the tool to constrain overgeneralizing grammars of speech understanding systems and obtained 20-30% higher recognition accuracy. However, we believe the primary benefit of using our tool is the tremendously reduced effort for the grammar developer. Our technique relieves the grammar developer from the burden of going through the tedious and time consuming task of revising grammars by manually modifying production rules one at a time. Instead, the grammar developer simply identifies counter-examples to an interactive tool that revises the grammar to invalidate the identified sentences.

We also discussed an MDL based algorithm for grammar compaction to reduce the size of the revised grammar. Thus, using a combination of the algorithms presented in this paper, one can obtain a compact grammar that is guaranteed to disallow the counter-examples.

Although our discussion here was focussed on speech understanding applications, the algorithms and the tool described here are applicable for any domain where grammars are used. We are currently implementing an extension of the grammar modifier to handle attribute-value grammars. We outlined an approach for automated modification of attribute-value grammars in Section 3.

We conclude that algorithms for automatically constraining grammars based on counter-examples can be highly effective in reducing the burden on grammar developers to develop constrained, domain specific grammars. Moreover, these algorithms can be used in any applications, which deal with grammars.

Acknowledgements

We thank all of our colleagues in the conversation machines group at IBM T.J. Watson Research Center for several helpful comments and suggestions through the course of this work.

References

Zadrozny W., Wolf C., Kambhatla N., and Ye Y. (1998). *Conversation machines for transaction processing*. In proceedings of AAAI'98/IAAI'98, AAAI Press/MIT Press, pp 1160-1166.

Allen J. (1995). *Natural Language Understanding.* The Benjamin/Cummings Publishing Company, Redwood City, CA 94065.

Grunwald P. (1996). *A minimum description length approach to grammar inference.* In S. Wemter et al., editors, Symbolic, Connectionist and Statistical Approach to Learning for Natural Language Processing, Springer, Berlin, p 203-216.

Manaster-Ramer and Zadrozny W. (1990), *Expressive Power of Grammatical Formalisms*, Proceedings of Coling-90. Universitas Helsingiensis. Helsinki, Finland", pp.195-200.

Pollard, C. and Sag I A. (1994). *Head-Driven Phrase Structure Grammar.* The U. of Chicago Press.

Rissanen J. (1982). *A universal prior for integers and estimation by minimum description length.* Annals of Statistics, 11:416-431.

Seneff S. (1992). TINA: *A natural language system for spoken language applications*, Computational Linguistics, 18:p61-86.

Zadrozny W. (1997). *Minimum description length and compositionality.* Proceedings of Second International Workshop for Computational Semantics, Tilburg. Recently re-published as a book chapter in: H.Bunt and R.Muskens (eds.) *Computing Meaning.* Kluwer Academic Publishers, Dordrecht/Boston,1999.

Aggressive Morphology for Robust Lexical Coverage

William A. Woods
Sun Microsystems Laboratories
1 Network Drive
Burlington, MA 01803
William.Woods@east.sun.com

Abstract

This paper describes an approach to providing lexical information for natural language processing in unrestricted domains. A system of approximately 1200 morphological rules is used to extend a core lexicon of 39,000 words to provide lexical coverage that exceeds that of a lexicon of 80,000 words or 150,000 word forms. The morphological system is described, and lexical coverage is evaluated for random words chosen from a previously unanalyzed corpus.

1 Motivation

Many applications of natural language processing have a need for a large vocabulary lexicon. However, no matter how large a lexicon one starts with, most applications will encounter terms that are not covered. This paper describes an approach to the lexicon problem that emphasizes recognition of morphological structure in unknown words in order to extend a relatively small core lexicon to allow robust natural language processing in unrestricted domains. This technique, which extends functionality originally developed for the Lunar system (Woods et al., 1972), has been most recently applied in a conceptual indexing and retrieval system (Woods, 1997; Ambroziak and Woods, 1998; Woods et al., 2000).

The system described here uses a collection of approximately 1200 knowledge-based morphological rules to extend a core lexicon of approximately 39,000 words to give coverage that exceeds that of an English lexicon of more than 80,000 base forms (or 150,000 base plus inflected forms). To illustrate the need for a robust extensible lexicon, a random sample of 100 words from the vocabulary of the million-word Brown corpus (Kucera and Francis, 1967), contained 24 words that were not included in a 300,000-word list of English word forms. This suggests that approximately 25% of the words in the Brown corpus would not be covered by an independent lexicon of even 300,000 words.

In a recent experiment, 54% of approximately 34,000 word types (numbers and hyphenated words excluded) from a 3.1-million-word corpus of technical literature would not be covered by our hypothetical 300,000-word lexicon. Many of these are special forms (e.g., *Nb2O3* and *Ti/tin*), and some are apparent misspellings (e.g., *auniprocessor* and *sychronized*), but the following are a sampling of fairly normal words that were not in the 300,000-word list:

busmaster
copyline
hereabove
preprocessing
uniprocessors
unreacted

2 Integrated, Preferential, Heuristic Morphology

There are a number of systems that have been used to describe natural language morphology for computational use. The most popular of these is perhaps the finite-state Kimmo system (Koskenniemi, 1983). Other approaches are described in (Sproat, 1992). The system described here differs from other systems in a number of dimensions. First, it is integrated with an extensive lexicon, a semantic ontology, and a syntactic analysis system, which it both consults and augments. For example, subsumption relationships in the semantic ontology enable the system to determine whether a proposed root is a container or a mental attitude, so that *cupful* is interpreted as a unit of measure (a kind of noun), while *hopeful* is interpreted as an adjective.

Second, it uses ordered preferential rules that attempt to choose a small number of correct analyses of a word (usually 1–3) from the many potential analyses that might be found. Finally, it uses rules that are heuristic in that they are not guaranteed to give correct analyses, but rather are designed to deal with various states of lack of knowledge and to make plausible inferences in the face of uncertainty. The focus is to use what it knows (or can infer) to determine a usable set of part-of-speech classifications for the word and to determine any root-plus-affix or internal compound structure that is apparent. If possible, it also assigns a semantic categorization to the word. It deals with unknown as well as known roots, and it indicates relative confidences in its classifications when its rules indicate uncertainty in the result.

The role of the morphological analysis component in this system is to construct lexical entries for words that do not already have entries, so that subsequent encounters with the same word will find an already existing lexical entry. Thus, morphological analysis happens only once for each encountered word type that is not already in the core lexicon. The resulting lexical entries can be saved in a supplementary lexicon that is constructed as a side-effect of analyzing text. The rules of the morphological analysis system can ask syntactic and semantic questions about potential base forms. The system handles prefixes, suffixes, and lexical compounds (e.g., *bitmap* and *replybuffer*). It also handles multiword lexical items and many special forms, including Roman numerals, dates, and apparent phone numbers.

2.1 Morphological rules and the lexicon

The morphological analysis system makes use of a number of different kinds of morphological rules, applied in the following preferential order to words that are not already in the lexicon:

1. Morph-precheck for special forms
2. Phase one pass with suffix rules (allow only "known" roots in phase one)
3. Prefix rules
4. Lexical compound rules
5. Check of name lists and city lists for words not yet recognized
6. Phase two pass with suffix rules (allow unknown roots and default rules)

Generally, the rules are ordered in decreasing order of specificity, confidence and likelihood. Very specific tests are applied in Step 1 to identify and deal with "words" that are not ordinary sequences of alphabetic characters. These include numbers, alphanumeric sequences, and expressions involving special characters. Failing this, an ordered sequence of suffix rules is applied in Step 2 in a first pass that will allow a match only if the proposed root word is "known." The same list of rules will be applied later in a second pass without this known-root condition if an earlier analysis does not succeed. This issue of "known" roots is a subtle one that can involve consulting external lists of known words as well as words already in the lexicon, and can also consider certain derived forms of known roots to be "known," even when they have not been previously encountered. For example, if *fish* is a known word, then *fishing* is as good as known, so is considered a "known" root for this purpose. In general, suffix rules applied to "known" roots are more reliable than applications of rules to unknown roots or to words with no identifiable root.

If no phase-one suffix rules apply, prefix rules are tried in Step 3 to see if an interpretation of this word as a prefix combined with some other "known" word is possible. Failing this, a set of lexical compound rules is tried, in Step 4, to see if the word is interpretable as a compound of two or more words, and failing that, lists of first and last names of people and names of cities are checked in Step 5. All of steps 3–5 are considered more reliable if they succeed than the phase-two pass of the suffix rules that comes in Step 6. This ordering allows prefixes and compounding to be tried before less confident suffix analyses are attempted, and avoids applying weak suffix analyses to known names. Various other ways to order these rules have been tried, but this order has been found to be the most effective.

2.2 Special form tests

Before trying pattern-based rules for suffixes, prefixes, and lexical compounds, the morphological analyzer makes a number of tests for special forms that require idiosyncratic treatment. These tests include the following:

- number (including integer, floating, and exponential notations, including numbers too large to be represented internally as numbers in the machine),
- Roman numeral (*vii*, *mcm*),
- ordinal (*1st*, *2nd*, *twenty-third*),
- alphanum (*Al2O3*, *79D*),
- letter (*b*, *x*),
- initial (*B.*),
- phone number (*123-4567*),
- hyphenated adjective (*all-volunteer*),
- ratio (*3/4*, *V/R*),
- multiword lexical item (*snake_in_the_grass*),
- special proper nouns (*gls@mit.edu*, */usr/bin*, *http://www.sun.com*, *C++*)

2.3 Pattern-action rules

Suffix rules in this system are pattern-action rules that specify:

1. a pattern of characters to match at the end of the word to be analyzed,
2. possibly a number of characters to remove and/or a sequence of characters to add to form a root (or base form),
3. a sequence of tests and action clauses indicating possible interpretations of a word matching this pattern.

These rules are organized into blocks that are typically indexed by a shared final letter, and are applied in order within a block until a rule is encountered that generates one or more interpretations. At that point, no further rules are tried, and the interpretations generated by that rule are used to construct a lexical entry for the analyzed word.

The following is an example of a fairly specific, but productive, knowledge-rich morphological suffix rule:

```
((f i s h) (kill 4)
   (test (plausible-root root))
   (cat nmsp
        (is-root-of-cat root '(adj n))
        eval (progn (mark-dict lex
                               'false-root
                               root t t)
                    (mark-dict lex
                               'kindof
                               'fish t t)
                    (mark-dict lex
                               'has-prefix
                               root t t)
                    (mark-dict lex
                               'root
                               'fish t t)
                    '-es)))
```

This rule matches a word that ends in *fish* and removes four letters from the end (the *fish* part) to produce a root word which it then tests to see if it is a plausible root (e.g., does it at least have a vowel in it?). If it gets this far, the rule will construct a category **nmsp** interpretation (a kind of noun), if the condition `(is-root-of-cat root '(adj n))` is true (i.e., if the root is a known adjective or noun). This rule deals with words like *hagfish* and *goatfish* and comes before the rules that handle words with *ish* as a suffix, like *doltish* and *oafish*. Incidentally, this rule doesn't apply to *oafish* because the hypothesized root *oa*, which would result from removing four letters, is not known to be an adjective or noun. When this rule succeeds, it specifies that the word will be assigned the category **nmsp**, a category indicating a word that has a mass sense, a singular count sense, and can also be used as a plural (e.g., *Goatfish are funny-looking.*). (The category **nmsp** comes from a collection of 91 syntactic categories, organized in a hierarchy based on generality, so that, for example, **nm** subsumes **nmsp**.) The action part of this rule specifies that (contrary to the usual case) the "root" obtained by removing characters from the end of the word (e.g., *goat*) is in this case a false root. The real root is *fish*, and the false root (*goat*) is actually a prefix. The rule also specifies that the word refers to a kind of fish and that the inflectional paradigm for this word is *-es* (thus allowing *goatfishes* as an alternative plural).

The rules within a block are ordered in decreasing order of confidence and specificity. Thus, rules with conditions that check explicit inflectional paradigms of known roots are ordered before rules that guess the inflectional paradigm from the spelling of the root, and rules with more specific conditions are ordered before rules with less specific conditions so that the latter can assume that the former will already have been tested and rejected. The rules within a block of suffix rules will typically try for interpretations in roughly the following order:

1. inflected form of a known root satisfying a named inflectional paradigm (paradigmatic)
2. inflected form of a known word in right category with unknown inflectional paradigm
3. apparent inflected form of a known word of some other category
4. apparent inflected form of an unknown word
5. apparent derived form of a known root of the right category
6. apparent derived form of a known root regardless of category
7. apparent derived form of an unknown root
8. word with apparent syntactic category and perhaps suffix, without identifiable root
9. guessed noun (and perhaps verb also, if core vocabulary is not comprehensive)

The last rule in this sequence is a default guessing rule that depends on a flag that tells it whether it is running with a core lexicon that is believed to contain most nonobvious verbs. If so, then only the noun part-of-speech is assigned, but with a smaller core lexicon, the guessing rules would also assign a less likely interpretation as a verb, in order to provide a way for unknown verbs to be parsed correctly in sentences.

Prefix rules are similar in structure to suffix rules, except that the pattern is matched at the beginning of the word, and the rule blocks are indexed by the initial letter of the word. Lexical compound rules have a slightly different format and are called by a specialized interpreter that looks for places to divide a word into two pieces of sufficient size. The points of potential decomposition are searched from right to left, and the first such point that has an interpretation is taken, with the following exception: The morph compound analyzer checks for special cases where, for example, the first word is plural and ends in an *s*, but there is an alternative segmentation in which the singular of the first word is followed by a word starting with the *s*. In such cases, the decomposition using the singular first word is preferred over the one using the plural. For example, the word *minesweeper* will be analyzed as *mine+sweeper* rather than *mines+weeper*. This preference heuristic is specific to English and might be different for other languages.

2.4 Recursive application of rules

When attempting to apply a rule to a word, the morphological analyzer can be applied recursively to analyze the hypothesized root. A simple caching technique is used to control the potential for combinatoric explosion and to block looping. This is sufficiently effective that the time required for morphological analysis is a negligible part of the time required for processing large amounts of natural language text. Protection against looping is especially important for a kind of morphological rule that derives one word from another without either of them being a root of the other in the usual sense (e.g., deriving *communist* from *communism* or *external* from *internal*). Operating in a loop-safe environment allows rules like these to identify the relationship between a new word and a known word in either direction, whichever of the two forms is encountered first.

3 Evaluation

Since analyzing a word is done once per unknown word type and consumes a negligible fraction of the overall text-processing time, speed of operation is not considered a factor for evaluation. The interesting dimension of evaluation deals with the coverage of the rules and the kinds of errors that are made. This was tested by applying the system to two word lists randomly selected from the Brown corpus and provided to me by Philip Resnik, using some sampling tools that he developed. The first of these (the token sample) consists of 100 word tokens selected randomly, without eliminating duplicates, and the second (the type sample) consists of 100 distinct word types selected randomly from the vocabulary of the Brown corpus. Prior to a single test run on each of these samples, neither the lexicon nor the morphological rule system had any exposure to the Brown corpus, nor had either of these word lists been looked at by the experimenter. Consequently, the results are a fair evaluation of the expected performance of this system on an unknown domain.

3.1 Grading rule performance

Since different syntactic category errors have different consequences for parsing text, it is useful to grade the syntactic category assignments of the analyzer on an A-B-C-D-F scale according to the severity of any mistakes. Grades are assigned to a lexical entry as follows:

A if all appropriate syntactic categories are assigned and no incorrect categories are assigned

B if all categories are correct, allowing for categorizing an adjective or a name as a noun or a noun as a name

C if an entry has at least one correct category and is correct except for missing a noun category or having a single extra category

D if there is more than one extra category or if there is a missing category other than one of the above cases, provided that there is at least one correct category

F if there are no correct categories

Both A and B grades are considered acceptable assignments for the sake of evaluation, since category B errors would allow a reasonable parse to be found. This is because the grammar used for parsing sentences and phrases allows a noun to be used as an adjective modifier and a proper noun to be used in place of a noun. One parser/grammar that uses this lexicon also allows any other category to be used as a noun, at the expense of a penalty, so that a C grade will still enable a parse, although with a penalty and a substantial likelihood that other false parses might score better. Similarly, a D grade increases the likelihood that a false parse might score better.

Separately, we measure whether count/mass distinctions are made correctly (for nouns only), and whether roots of derived and inflected forms are identified correctly. We are interested in the count/mass distinction because, like the common/proper noun distinction, it affects the grammaticality and likelihood of a noun phrase interpretation for a singular noun in absence of an explicit determiner.

3.2 Sampling rule performance

The morphological analyzer has been applied to the words from the two sample word lists that were not already in its core lexicon. There were 17 such words from the token sample and 72 such words from the type sample. Of the 17 unknown token-sample words, 100% were graded B or better (88% A and 12% B); 85% of the roots were identified correctly (all but one); 85% of the count noun senses were found (all but one); and 100% of the mass noun senses were found. Token-sample performance is not a very challenging test for a morphological analyzer because it is biased toward a relatively small number of frequently occurring word types. Token-sample performance is used to assess the per-token error rate that one would expect in analyzing large amounts of running text. In contrast, type-sample performance

Table 1: Syntactic category performance of the analyzer.

Category Grade	A	B	C	D	F	B or better
Number	62	8	1	0	1	70
Percent	86%	11%	1.5%	0%	1.5%	97%

Table 2: Count/mass distinction performance of the analyzer.

Count/mass	Good count	Extra count	Good mass	Missing mass
Number	39	1	14	1
Percent	100%	2.6%	93%	6.7%

Table 3: Root identification performance of the analyzer.

Detect root	Good	Wrong	Debatable	Missing	Extra
Number	57	1	1	0	1
Percent	95%	1.7%	1.7%	0	1.7%

gives a measure of the expected performance on new words the analyzer is likely to encounter.

For the 72 words in the type sample that are not covered by the lexicon, Tables 1–3 show the syntactic category performance of the analyzer and its abilities to make count/mass distinctions and identify roots.

Notes on incorrect or debatable analyses:

1. One N (noun) for a probable name (*Tonio*), counted as B.
2. Two NPR(proper name) for abbreviations; (*A.V.* may be ADJ, *W.B.* is correct), counted as one B and one A.
3. One wrong root when suffix *ism* was identified as root of *hooliganism* in a hypothesized compound *hooligan+ism* (arguably justifiable as a kind of *ism*, which is known in the lexicon, but counted as an error anyway). Reanalyzing this word after *hooligan* is a known word gets the correct interpretation.
4. One debatable root in the hyphenated phrase *reference-points* whose root was listed as *points* rather than *reference-point.* This is due to a bug that caused the hyphenated word rules to incorrectly identify this as a verb, rather than a noun (counted as F for syntax).
5. One extra root for *embouchure* from *embouche* (but a correct form of the French root?).
6. One missing category N for *bobbles*, which was given category V but not N because the core lexicon incorrectly listed *bobble* only as a verb (counted as C for syntax). This is corrected by adding the missing category to the lexical entry for *bobble.*

4 Conclusions

We have described an approach to robust lexical coverage for unrestricted text applications that makes use of an aggressive set of morphological rules to supplement a core lexicon of approximately 39,000 words to give lexical coverage that exceeds that of a much larger lexicon. This morphological analyzer is integrated with an extensive lexicon, an ontology, and a syntactic analysis system, which it both consults and augments. It uses ordered preferential rules that attempt to choose a small number of correct analyses of a word and are designed to deal with various states of lack of knowledge. When applied to 72 unknown words from a random sample of 100 distinct word types from the Brown corpus, its syntactic category assignments received a grade of B or better (using a grading system explained herein) for 97% of the words, and it correctly identified 95% of the root words. This performance demonstrates that one can obtain robust lexical coverage for natural language processing applications in unrestricted domains, using a relatively small core lexicon and an aggressive collection of morphological rules.

References

Jacek Ambroziak and William A. Woods. 1998. Natural language technology in precision content retrieval. In *International Conference on Natural Language Processing and Industrial Applications*, Moncton, New Brunswick, Canada, August. www.sun.com/research/techrep/1998/abstract-69.html.

Kimmo Koskenniemi. 1983. Two-level model for morphological analysis. In *Proceedings of the International Joint Conference on Artificial Intelligence*, pages 683–685, Los Angelos, CA. Morgan Kauffmann.

H. Kucera and W. Francis. 1967. *Computational Analysis of Present-Day American English.* Brown University Press.

Richard Sproat. 1992. *Morphology and Computation.* MIT Press, Cambridge, MA.

William A. Woods, Ronald M. Kaplan, and Bonnie L. Nash-Webber. 1972. The lunar sciences natural language information system: Final report. Technical Report BBN Report No. 2378, Bolt Beranek and Newman Inc, Cambridge, MA, June. (available from NTIS as N72-28984).

William A. Woods, Lawrence A. Bookman, Ann C. Houston, Robert J. Kuhns, Paul A. Martin, and Stephen Green. 2000. Linguistic knowledge can improve information retrieval. In *(these proceedings).*

William A. Woods. 1997. Conceptual indexing: A better way to organize knowledge. Technical Report SMLI TR-97-61, Sun Microsystems Laboratories, Mountain View, CA, April. www.sun.com/research/techrep/1997/abstract-61.html.

TnT — A Statistical Part-of-Speech Tagger

Thorsten Brants
Saarland University
Computational Linguistics
D-66041 Saarbrücken, Germany
thorsten@coli.uni-sb.de

Abstract

Trigrams'n'Tags (TnT) is an efficient statistical part-of-speech tagger. Contrary to claims found elsewhere in the literature, we argue that a tagger based on Markov models performs at least as well as other current approaches, including the Maximum Entropy framework. A recent comparison has even shown that TnT performs significantly better for the tested corpora. We describe the basic model of TnT, the techniques used for smoothing and for handling unknown words. Furthermore, we present evaluations on two corpora.

1 Introduction

A large number of current language processing systems use a part-of-speech tagger for pre-processing. The tagger assigns a (unique or ambiguous) part-of-speech tag to each token in the input and passes its output to the next processing level, usually a parser. Furthermore, there is a large interest in part-of-speech tagging for corpus annotation projects, who create valuable linguistic resources by a combination of automatic processing and human correction.

For both applications, a tagger with the highest possible accuracy is required. The debate about which paradigm solves the part-of-speech tagging problem best is not finished. Recent comparisons of approaches that can be trained on corpora (van Halteren et al., 1998; Volk and Schneider, 1998) have shown that in most cases statistical aproaches (Cutting et al., 1992; Schmid, 1995; Ratnaparkhi, 1996) yield better results than finite-state, rule-based, or memory-based taggers (Brill, 1993; Daelemans et al., 1996). They are only surpassed by combinations of different systems, forming a "voting tagger".

Among the statistical approaches, the Maximum Entropy framework has a very strong position. Nevertheless, a recent independent comparison of 7 taggers (Zavrel and Daelemans, 1999) has shown that another approach even works better: Markov models combined with a good smoothing technique and with handling of unknown words. This tagger, TnT, not only yielded the highest accuracy, it also was the fastest both in training and tagging.

The tagger comparison was organized as a "black-box test": set the same task to every tagger and compare the outcomes. This paper describes the models and techniques used by TnT together with the implementation.

The reader will be surprised how simple the underlying model is. The result of the tagger comparison seems to support the maxime "the simplest is the best". However, in this paper we clarify a number of details that are omitted in major previous publications concerning tagging with Markov models. As two examples, (Rabiner, 1989) and (Charniak et al., 1993) give good overviews of the techniques and equations used for Markov models and part-of-speech tagging, but they are not very explicit in the details that are needed for their application. We argue that it is not only the choice of the general model that determines the result of the tagger but also the various "small" decisions on alternatives.

The aim of this paper is to give a detailed account of the techniques used in TnT. Additionally, we present results of the tagger on the NEGRA corpus (Brants et al., 1999) and the Penn Treebank (Marcus et al., 1993). The Penn Treebank results reported here for the Markov model approach are at least equivalent to those reported for the Maximum Entropy approach in (Ratnaparkhi, 1996). For a comparison to other taggers, the reader is referred to (Zavrel and Daelemans, 1999).

2 Architecture

2.1 The Underlying Model

TnT uses second order Markov models for part-of-speech tagging. The states of the model represent tags, outputs represent the words. Transition probabilities depend on the states, thus pairs of tags. Output probabilities only depend on the most recent category. To be explicit, we calculate

$$\operatorname*{argmax}_{t_1 \ldots t_T} \left[\prod_{i=1}^{T} P(t_i | t_{i-1}, t_{i-2}) P(w_i | t_i) \right] P(t_{T+1} | t_T) \quad (1)$$

for a given sequence of words $w_1 \ldots w_T$ of length T. $t_1 \ldots t_T$ are elements of the tagset, the additional tags t_{-1}, t_0, and t_{T+1} are beginning-of-sequence and end-of-sequence markers. Using these additional tags, even if they stem from rudimentary processing of punctuation marks, slightly improves tagging results. This is different from formulas presented in other publications, which just stop with a "loose end" at the last word. If sentence boundaries are not marked in the input, TnT adds these tags if it encounters one of [.!?;] as a token.

Transition and output probabilities are estimated from a tagged corpus. As a first step, we use the maximum likelihood probabilities $\hat{P}$ which are derived from the relative frequencies:

$$\text{Unigrams:} \quad \hat{P}(t_3) = \frac{f(t_3)}{N} \tag{2}$$

$$\text{Bigrams:} \quad \hat{P}(t_3|t_2) = \frac{f(t_2,t_3)}{f(t_2)} \tag{3}$$

$$\text{Trigrams:} \quad \hat{P}(t_3|t_1,t_2) = \frac{f(t_1,t_2,t_3)}{f(t_1,t_2)} \tag{4}$$

$$\text{Lexical:} \quad \hat{P}(w_3|t_3) = \frac{f(w_3,t_3)}{f(t_3)} \tag{5}$$

for all t_1, t_2, t_3 in the tagset and w_3 in the lexicon. N is the total number of tokens in the training corpus. We define a maximum likelihood probability to be zero if the corresponding nominators and denominators are zero. As a second step, contextual frequencies are smoothed and lexical frequences are completed by handling words that are not in the lexicon (see below).

2.2 Smoothing

Trigram probabilities generated from a corpus usually cannot directly be used because of the sparse-data problem. This means that there are not enough instances for each trigram to reliably estimate the probability. Furthermore, setting a probability to zero because the corresponding trigram never occured in the corpus has an undesired effect. It causes the probability of a complete sequence to be set to zero if its use is necessary for a new text sequence, thus makes it impossible to rank different sequences containing a zero probability.

The smoothing paradigm that delivers the best results in TnT is linear interpolation of unigrams, bigrams, and trigrams. Therefore, we estimate a trigram probability as follows:

$$P(t_3|t_1,t_2) = \lambda_1 \hat{P}(t_3) + \lambda_2 \hat{P}(t_3|t_2) + \lambda_3 \hat{P}(t_3|t_1,t_2) \tag{6}$$

$\hat{P}$ are maximum likelihood estimates of the probabilities, and $\lambda_1 + \lambda_2 + \lambda_3 = 1$, so P again represent probability distributions.

We use the context-independent variant of linear interpolation, i.e., the values of the λs do not depend on the particular trigram. Contrary to intuition, this yields better results than the context-dependent variant. Due to sparse-data problems, one cannot estimate a different set of λs for each trigram. Therefore, it is common practice to group trigrams by frequency and estimate tied sets of λs. However, we are not aware of any publication that has investigated frequency groupings for linear interpolation in part-of-speech tagging. All groupings that we have tested yielded at most equivalent results to context-independent linear interpolation. Some groupings even yielded worse results. The tested groupings included a) one set of λs for each frequency value and b) two classes (low and high frequency) on the two ends of the scale, as well as several groupings in between and several settings for partitioning the classes.

The values of λ_1, λ_2, and λ_3 are estimated by deleted interpolation. This technique successively removes each trigram from the training corpus and estimates best values for the λs from all other n-grams in the corpus. Given the frequency counts for uni-, bi-, and trigrams, the weights can be very efficiently determined with a processing time linear in the number of different trigrams. The algorithm is given in figure 1. Note that subtracting 1 means taking unseen data into account. Without this subtraction the model would overfit the training data and would generally yield worse results.

2.3 Handling of Unknown Words

Currently, the method of handling unknown words that seems to work best for inflected languages is a suffix analysis as proposed in (Samuelsson, 1993). Tag probabilities are set according to the word's ending. The suffix is a strong predictor for word classes, e.g., words in the Wall Street Journal part of the Penn Treebank ending in *able* are adjectives (JJ) in 98% of the cases (e.g. fashionable, variable) , the rest of 2% are nouns (e.g. cable, variable).

The probability distribution for a particular suffix is generated from all words in the training set that share the same suffix of some predefined maximum length. The term suffix as used here means "final sequence of characters of a word" which is not necessarily a linguistically meaningful suffix.

Probabilities are smoothed by successive abstraction. This calculates the probability of a tag t given the last m letters l_i of an n letter word: $P(t|l_{n-m+1}, \ldots l_n)$. The sequence of increasingly more general contexts omits more and more characters of the suffix, such that $P(t|l_{n-m+2}, \ldots, l_n)$, $P(t|l_{n-m+3}, \ldots, l_n)$, $\ldots$, $P(t)$ are used for smoothing. The recursion formula is

$$P(t|l_{n-i+1}, \ldots l_n) = \frac{\hat{P}(t|l_{n-i+1}, \ldots l_n) + \theta_i P(t|l_{n-i}, \ldots, l_n)}{1 + \theta_i} \tag{7}$$

```
set λ1 = λ2 = λ3 = 0
foreach trigram t1, t2, t3 with f(t1, t2, t3) > 0
    depending on the maximum of the following three values:
        case (f(t1,t2,t3) − 1)/(f(t1,t2) − 1):  increment λ3 by f(t1, t2, t3)
        case (f(t2,t3) − 1)/(f(t2) − 1):  increment λ2 by f(t1, t2, t3)
        case (f(t3) − 1)/(N − 1):  increment λ1 by f(t1, t2, t3)
    end
end
normalize λ1, λ2, λ3
```

Figure 1: Algorithm for calculting the weights for context-independent linear interpolation $\lambda_1, \lambda_2, \lambda_3$ when the n-gram frequencies are known. N is the size of the corpus. If the denominator in one of the expressions is 0, we define the result of that expression to be 0.

for $i = m \ldots 0$, using the maximum likelihood estimates $\hat{P}$ from frequencies in the lexicon, weights θ_i and the initialization

$$P(t) = \hat{P}(t). \tag{8}$$

The maximum likelihood estimate for a suffix of length i is derived from corpus frequencies by

$$\hat{P}(t|l_{n-i+1}, \ldots l_n) = \frac{f(t, l_{n-i+1}, \ldots l_n)}{f(l_{n-i+1}, \ldots l_n)} \tag{9}$$

For the Markov model, we need the inverse conditional probabilities $P(l_{n-i+1}, \ldots l_n|t)$ which are obtained by Bayesian inversion.

A theoretical motivated argumentation uses the standard deviation of the maximum likelihood probabilities for the weights θ_i (Samuelsson, 1993).

This leaves room for interpretation.

1) One has to identify a good value for m, the longest suffix used. The approach taken for TnT is the following: m depends on the word in question. We use the longest suffix that we can find in the training set (i.e., for which the frequency is greater than or equal to 1), but at most 10 characters. This is an empirically determined choice.

2) We use a context-independent approach for θ_i, as we did for the contextual weights λ_i. It turned out to be a good choice to set all θ_i to the standard deviation of the unconditioned maximum likelihood probabilities of the tags in the training corpus, i.e., we set

$$\theta_i = \frac{1}{s-1} \sum_{j=1}^{s} (\hat{P}(t_j) - \bar{P})^2 \tag{10}$$

for all $i = 0 \ldots m-1$, using a tagset of s tags and the average

$$\bar{P} = \frac{1}{s} \sum_{j=1}^{s} \hat{P}(t_j) \tag{11}$$

This usually yields values in the range $0.03 \ldots 0.10$.

3) We use different estimates for uppercase and lowercase words, i.e., we maintain two different suffix tries depending on the capitalization of the word. This information improves the tagging results.

4) Another freedom concerns the choice of the words in the lexicon that should be used for suffix handling. Should we use all words, or are some of them better suited than others? Accepting that unknown words are most probably infrequent, one can argue that using suffixes of infrequent words in the lexicon is a better approximation for unknown words than using suffixes of frequent words. Therefore, we restrict the procedure of suffix handling to words with a frequency smaller than or equal to some threshold value. Empirically, 10 turned out to be a good choice for this threshold.

2.4 Capitalization

Additional information that turned out to be useful for the disambiguation process for several corpora and tagsets is capitalization information. Tags are usually not informative about capitalization, but probability distributions of tags around capitalized words are different from those not capitalized. The effect is larger for English, which only capitalizes proper names, and smaller for German, which capitalizes all nouns.

We use flags c_i that are true if w_i is a capitalized word and false otherwise. These flags are added to the contextual probability distributions. Instead of

$$P(t_3|t_1, t_2) \tag{12}$$

we use

$$P(t_3, c_3|t_1, c_1, t_2, c_2) \tag{13}$$

and equations (3) to (5) are updated accordingly. This is equivalent to doubling the size of the tagset and using different tags depending on capitalization.

2.5 Beam Search

The processing time of the Viterbi algorithm (Rabiner, 1989) can be reduced by introducing a beam search. Each state that receives a δ value smaller than the largest δ divided by some threshold value θ is excluded from further processing. While the Viterbi algorithm is guaranteed to find the sequence of states with the highest probability, this is no longer true when beam search is added. Nevertheless, for practical purposes and the right choice of θ, there is virtually no difference between the algorithm with and without a beam. Empirically, a value of $\theta = 1000$ turned out to approximately double the speed of the tagger without affecting the accuracy.

The tagger currently tags between 30,000 and 60,000 tokens per second (including file I/O) on a Pentium 500 running Linux. The speed mainly depends on the percentage of unknown words and on the average ambiguity rate.

3 Evaluation

We evaluate the tagger's performance under several aspects. First of all, we determine the tagging accuracy averaged over ten iterations. The overall accuracy, as well as separate accuracies for known and unknown words are measured.

Second, learning curves are presented, that indicate the performance when using training corpora of different sizes, starting with as few as 1,000 tokens and ranging to the size of the entire corpus (minus the test set).

An important characteristic of statistical taggers is that they not only assign tags to words but also probabilities in order to rank different assignments. We distinguish reliable from unreliable assignments by the quotient of the best and second best assignments[1]. All assignments for which this quotient is larger than some threshold are regarded as reliable, the others as unreliable. As we will see below, accuracies for reliable assignments are much higher.

The tests are performed on partitions of the corpora that use 90% as training set and 10% as test set, so that the test data is guaranteed to be unseen during training. Each result is obtained by repeating the experiment 10 times with different partitions and averaging the single outcomes.

In all experiments, contiguous test sets are used. The alternative is a round-robin procedure that puts every 10th sentence into the test set. We argue that contiguous test sets yield more realistic results because completely unseen articles are tagged. Using the round-robin procedure, parts of an article are already seen, which significantly reduces the percentage of unknown words. Therefore, we expect even higher results when testing on every 10th sentence instead of a contiguous set of 10%.

In the following, accuracy denotes the number of correctly assigned tags divided by the number of tokens in the corpus processed. The tagger is allowed to assign exactly one tag to each token.

We distinguish the overall accuracy, taking into account all tokens in the test corpus, and separate accuracies for known and unknown tokens. The latter are interesting, since usually unknown tokens are much more difficult to process than known tokens, for which a list of valid tags can be found in the lexicon.

3.1 Tagging the NEGRA corpus

The German NEGRA corpus consists of 20,000 sentences (355,000 tokens) of newspaper texts (Frankfurter Rundschau) that are annotated with parts-of-speech and predicate-argument structures (Skut et al., 1997). It was developed at the Saarland University in Saarbrücken[2]. Part of it was tagged at the IMS Stuttgart. This evaluation only uses the part-of-speech annotation and ignores structural annotations.

Tagging accuracies for the NEGRA corpus are shown in table 2.

Figure 3 shows the learning curve of the tagger, i.e., the accuracy depending on the amount of training data. Training length is the number of tokens used for training. Each training length was tested ten times, training and test sets were randomly chosen and disjoint, results were averaged. The training length is given on a logarithmic scale.

It is remarkable that tagging accuracy for known words is very high even for very small training corpora. This means that we have a good chance of getting the right tag if a word is seen at least once during training. Average percentages of unknown tokens are shown in the bottom line of each diagram.

We exploit the fact that the tagger not only determines tags, but also assigns probabilities. If there is an alternative that has a probability "close to" that of the best assignment, this alternative can be viewed as almost equally well suited. The notion of "close to" is expressed by the distance of probabilities, and this in turn is expressed by the quotient of probabilities. So, the distance of the probabilities of a best tag t_{best} and an alternative tag t_{alt} is expressed by $p(t_{best})/p(t_{alt})$, which is some value greater or equal to 1 since the best tag assignment has the highest probability.

Figure 4 shows the accuracy when separating assignments with quotients larger and smaller than the threshold (hence reliable and unreliable assignments). As expected, we find that accuracies for

[1] By definition, this quotient is ∞ if there is only one possible tag for a given word.

[2] For availability, please check
`http://www.coli.uni-sb.de/sfb378/negra-corpus`

Table 2: Part-of-speech tagging accuracy for the NEGRA corpus, averaged over 10 test runs, training and test set are disjoint. The table shows the percentage of unknown tokens, separate accuracies and standard deviations for known and unknown tokens, as well as the overall accuracy.

	percentage unknowns	known acc.	known σ	unknown acc.	unknown σ	overall acc.	overall σ
NEGRA corpus	11.9%	97.7%	0.23	89.0%	0.72	96.7%	0.29

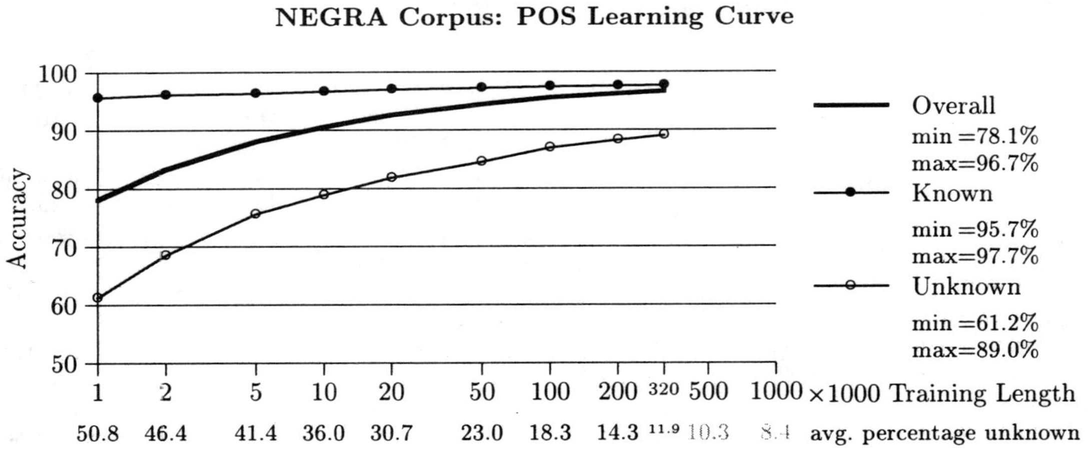

Figure 3: Learning curve for tagging the NEGRA corpus. The training sets of variable sizes as well as test sets of 30,000 tokens were randomly chosen. Training and test sets were disjoint, the procedure was repeated 10 times and results were averaged. Percentages of unknowns for 500k and 1000k training are determined from an untagged extension.

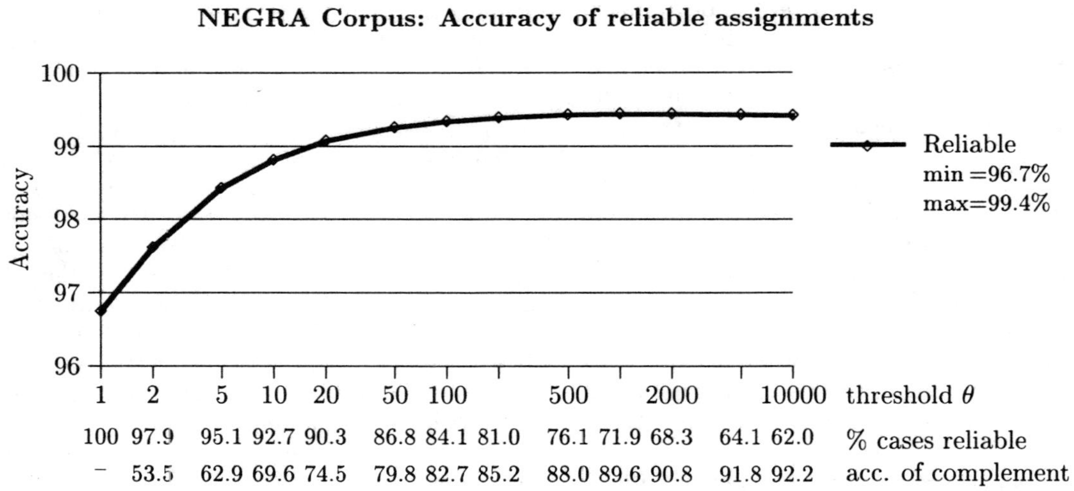

Figure 4: Tagging accuracy for the NEGRA corpus when separating reliable and unreliable assignments. The curve shows accuracies for reliable assignments. The numbers at the bottom line indicate the percentage of reliable assignments and the accuracy of the complement set (i.e., unreliable assignments).

Table 5: Part-of-speech tagging accuracy for the Penn Treebank. The table shows the percentage of unknown tokens, separate accuracies and standard deviations for known and unknown tokens, as well as the overall accuracy.

	percentage unknowns	known acc.	known σ	unknown acc.	unknown σ	overall acc.	overall σ
Penn Treebank	2.9%	97.0%	0.15	85.5%	0.69	96.7%	0.15

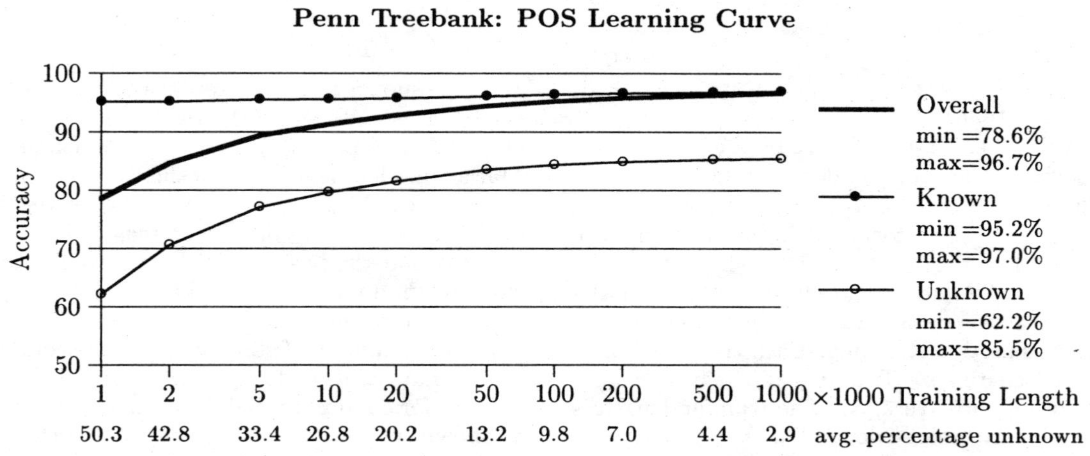

Figure 6: Learning curve for tagging the Penn Treebank. The training sets of variable sizes as well as test sets of 100,000 tokens were randomly chosen. Training and test sets were disjoint, the procedure was repeated 10 times and results were averaged.

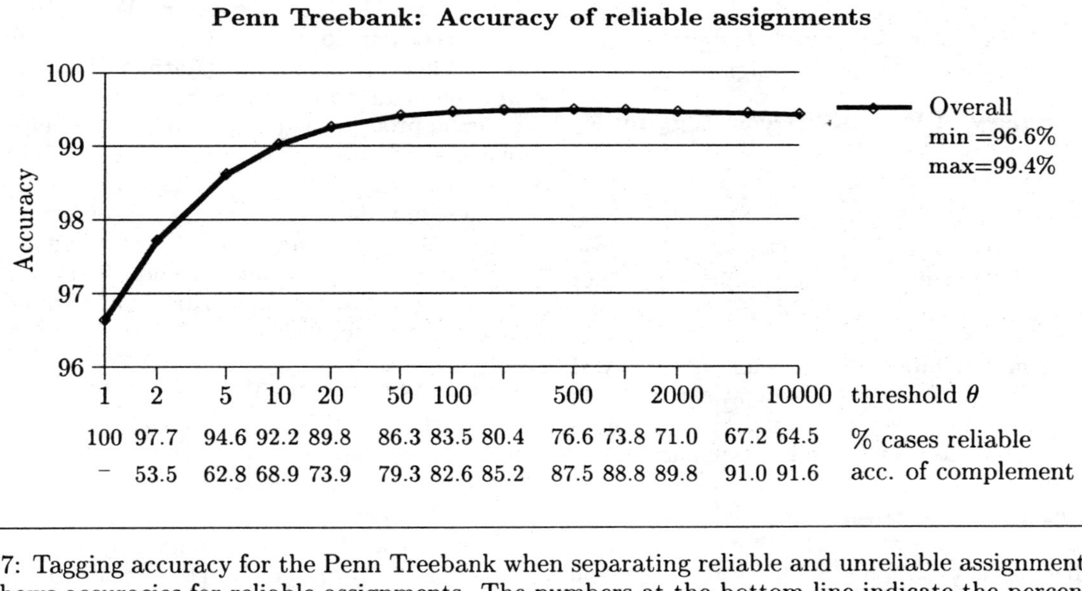

Figure 7: Tagging accuracy for the Penn Treebank when separating reliable and unreliable assignments. The curve shows accuracies for reliable assignments. The numbers at the bottom line indicate the percentage of reliable assignments and the accuracy of the complement set.

reliable assignments are much higher than for unreliable assignments. This distinction is, e.g., useful for annotation projects during the cleaning process, or during pre-processing, so the tagger can emit multiple tags if the best tag is classified as unreliable.

3.2 Tagging the Penn Treebank

We use the Wall Street Journal as contained in the Penn Treebank for our experiments. The annotation consists of four parts: 1) a context-free structure augmented with traces to mark movement and discontinuous constituents, 2) phrasal categories that are annotated as node labels, 3) a small set of grammatical functions that are annotated as extensions to the node labels, and 4) part-of-speech tags (Marcus et al., 1993). This evaluation only uses the part-of-speech annotation.

The Wall Street Journal part of the Penn Treebank consists of approx. 50,000 sentences (1.2 million tokens).

Tagging accuracies for the Penn Treebank are shown in table 5. Figure 6 shows the learning curve of the tagger, i.e., the accuracy depending on the amount of training data. Training length is the number of tokens used for training. Each training length was tested ten times. Training and test sets were disjoint, results are averaged. The training length is given on a logarithmic scale. As for the NEGRA corpus, tagging accuracy is very high for known tokens even with small amounts of training data.

We exploit the fact that the tagger not only determines tags, but also assigns probabilities. Figure 7 shows the accuracy when separating assignments with quotients larger and smaller than the threshold (hence reliable and unreliable assignments). Again, we find that accuracies for reliable assignments are much higher than for unreliable assignments.

3.3 Summary of Part-of-Speech Tagging Results

Average part-of-speech tagging accuracy is between 96% and 97%, depending on language and tagset, which is at least on a par with state-of-the-art results found in the literature, possibly better. For the Penn Treebank, (Ratnaparkhi, 1996) reports an accuracy of 96.6% using the Maximum Entropy approach, our much simpler and therefore faster HMM approach delivers 96.7%. This comparison needs to be re-examined, since we use a ten-fold crossvalidation and averaging of results while Ratnaparkhi only makes one test run.

The accuracy for known tokens is significantly higher than for unknown tokens. For the German newspaper data, results are 8.7% better when the word was seen before and therefore is in the lexicon, than when it was not seen before (97.7% vs. 89.0%). Accuracy for known tokens is high even with very small amounts of training data. As few as 1000 tokens are sufficient to achieve 95%–96% accuracy for them. It is important for the tagger to have seen a word at least once during training.

Stochastic taggers assign probabilities to tags. We exploit the probabilities to determine reliability of assignments. For a subset that is determined during processing by the tagger we achieve accuracy rates of over 99%. The accuracy of the complement set is much lower. This information can, e.g., be exploited in an annotation project to give an additional treatment to the unreliable assignments, or to pass selected ambiguities to a subsequent processing step.

4 Conclusion

We have shown that a tagger based on Markov models yields state-of-the-art results, despite contrary claims found in the literature. For example, the Markov model tagger used in the comparison of (van Halteren et al., 1998) yielded worse results than all other taggers. In our opinion, a reason for the wrong claim is that the basic algorithms leave several decisions to the implementor. The rather large amount of freedom was not handled in detail in previous publications: handling of start- and end-of-sequence, the exact smoothing technique, how to determine the weights for context probabilities, details on handling unknown words, and how to determine the weights for unknown words. Note that the decisions we made yield good results for both the German and the English Corpus. They do so for several other corpora as well. The architecture remains applicable to a large variety of languages.

According to current tagger comparisons (van Halteren et al., 1998; Zavrel and Daelemans, 1999), and according to a comparsion of the results presented here with those in (Ratnaparkhi, 1996), the Maximum Entropy framework seems to be the only other approach yielding comparable results to the one presented here. It is a very interesting future research topic to determine the advantages of either of these approaches, to find the reason for their high accuracies, and to find a good combination of both.

TnT is freely available to universities and related organizations for research purposes (see `http://www.coli.uni-sb.de/~thorsten/tnt`).

Acknowledgements

Many thanks go to Hans Uszkoreit for his support during the development of TnT. Most of the work on TnT was carried out while the author received a grant of the Deutsche Forschungsgemeinschaft in the Graduiertenkolleg Kognitionswissenschaft Saarbrücken. Large annotated corpora are the pre-requisite for developing and testing part-of-speech taggers, and they enable the generation of high-quality language models. Therefore, I would like to thank all the people who took the effort to annotate the Penn Treebank, the Susanne Corpus, the Stuttgarter Referenzkorpus, the NEGRA Corpus, the Verbmobil Corpora, and several others. And, last but not least, I would like to thank the users of TnT who provided me with bug reports and valuable suggestions for improvements.

References

Thorsten Brants, Wojciech Skut, and Hans Uszkoreit. 1999. Syntactic annotation of a German newspaper corpus. In *Proceedings of the ATALA Treebank Workshop*, pages 69–76, Paris, France.

Eric Brill. 1993. *A Corpus-Based Approach to Language Learning.* Ph.D. Dissertation, Department of Computer and Information Science, University of Pennsylvania.

Eugene Charniak, Curtis Hendrickson, Neil Jacobson, and Mike Perkowitz. 1993. Equations for part-of-speech tagging. In *Proceedings of the Eleventh National Conference on Artificial Intelligence*, pages 784–789, Menlo Park: AAAI Press/MIT Press.

Doug Cutting, Julian Kupiec, Jan Pedersen, and Penelope Sibun. 1992. A practical part-of-speech tagger. In *Proceedings of the 3rd Conference on Applied Natural Language Processing (ACL)*, pages 133–140.

Walter Daelemans, Jakub Zavrel, Peter Berck, and Steven Gillis. 1996. Mbt: A memory-based part of speech tagger-generator. In *Proceedings of the Workshop on Very Large Corpora*, Copenhagen, Denmark.

Mitchell Marcus, Beatrice Santorini, and Mary Ann Marcinkiewicz. 1993. Building a large annotated corpus of English: The Penn Treebank. *Computational Linguistics*, 19(2):313–330.

Lawrence R. Rabiner. 1989. A tutorial on Hidden Markov Models and selected applications in speech recognition. In *Proceedings of the IEEE*, volume 77(2), pages 257–285.

Adwait Ratnaparkhi. 1996. A maximum entropy model for part-of-speech tagging. In *Proceedings of the Conference on Empirical Methods in Natural Language Processing EMNLP-96*, Philadelphia, PA.

Christer Samuelsson. 1993. Morphological tagging based entirely on Bayesian inference. In *9th Nordic Conference on Computational Linguistics NODALIDA-93*, Stockholm University, Stockholm, Sweden.

Helmut Schmid. 1995. Improvements in part-of-speech tagging with an application to German. In Helmut Feldweg and Erhard Hinrichts, editors, *Lexikon und Text.* Niemeyer, Tübingen.

Wojciech Skut, Brigitte Krenn, Thorsten Brants, and Hans Uszkoreit. 1997. An annotation scheme for free word order languages. In *Proceedings of the Fifth Conference on Applied Natural Language Processing ANLP-97*, Washington, DC.

Hans van Halteren, Jakub Zavrel, and Walter Daelemans. 1998. Improving data driven wordclass tagging by system combination. In *Proceedings of the International Conference on Computational Linguistics COLING-98*, pages 491–497, Montreal, Canada.

Martin Volk and Gerold Schneider. 1998. Comparing a statistical and a rule-based tagger for german. In *Proceedings of KONVENS-98*, pages 125–137, Bonn.

Jakub Zavrel and Walter Daelemans. 1999. Evaluatie van part-of-speech taggers voor het corpus gesproken nederlands. CGN technical report, Katholieke Universiteit Brabant, Tilburg.

Language Independent Morphological Analysis

Yamashita, Tatsuo and Matsumoto, Yuji
Graduate School of Information Science
Nara Institute of Science and Technology
{tatuo-y,matsu}@is.aist-nara.ac.jp

Abstract

This paper proposes a framework of language independent morphological analysis and mainly concentrate on tokenization, the first process of morphological analysis. Although tokenization is usually not regarded as a difficult task in most segmented languages such as English, there are a number of problems in achieving precise treatment of lexical entries. We first introduce the concept of morpho-fragments, which are intermediate units between characters and lexical entries. We describe our approach to resolve problems arising in tokenization so as to attain a language independent morphological analyzer.

1 Introduction

The first step in natural language processing is to identify words in a sentence. We call this process a morphological analysis. Various languages exist in the world, and strategies for morphological analysis differ by types of language. Conventionally, morphological analyzers have been developed in *one analyzer for each language* approach. This is a language dependent approach. In contrast, We propose a framework of language independent morphological analysis system. We employ *one analyzer for any language* approach. This approach enables a rapid implementation of morphological analysis systems for new languages.

We define two types of written languages: one is a *segmented language*, and the other is a *non-segmented language*. In non-segmented languages such as Chinese and Japanese, since words are not separated by delimiters such as white spaces, tokenization is a important and difficult task. In segmented languages such as English, since words are seemingly separated by white spaces or punctuation marks, tokenization is regarded as a relatively easy task and little attention has been paid to. Therefore, each language dependent morphological analyzer has its own strategy for tokenization. We call a string defined in the dictionary *lexeme*. From an algorithmic point of view, *tokenization* is regarded as the process of converting an input stream of characters into a stream of lexemes.

We assume that a morphological analysis consists of three processes: tokenization, dictionary look-up, and disambiguation. Dictionary look-up gets a string and returns a set of lexemes with part-of-speech information. This implicitly contains lemmatization. Disambiguation selects the most plausible sequence of lexemes by a use of a rule-base model or a hidden Markov model (HMM)(Manning and Schütze, 1999). Disambiguation is already language independent, since it does not process strings directly and therefore will not be taken up. On the other hand, tokenization and dictionary look-up are language dependent and shall be explained more in this paper.

We consider problems concerning tokenization of segmented languages in Section 2. To resolve these problem, we first apply the method of non-segmented languages processing to segmented languages (Section 3). However, we do not obtain a satisfactory result. Then, we introduce the concept of morpho-fragments to generalize the method of non-segmented language processing (Section 4). The proposed framework resolves most problems in tokenization, and an efficient language independent part-of-speech tagging becomes possible.

2 Problems of Tokenization in Segmented Languages

In segmented languages such as English, tokenization is regarded as a relatively easy task and little attention has been paid to. When a sentence has clear word boundaries, the analyzer just consults the dictionary look-up component whether strings between delimiters exist in the dictionary. If any string exists, the dictionary look-up component returns the set of possible parts-of-speech. This string is known as *graphic word* which is defined as "a string of contiguous alphanumeric characters with space on either side; may include hyphens and apostrophes, but no other punctuation marks" (Kučera and Francis, 1967).

Conventionally, in segmented languages, an analyzer converts a stream of characters into graphic words (see the rows labeled "Characters" and

Sentence	Dr. Lee and John's son go to the McDonald's in New York.
Characters	|D|r|.| |L|e|e| |a|n|d| |J|o|h|n|'|s| |s|o|n| |g|o| |t|o| |t|h|e| |M|c|D|o|n|a|l|d|'|s| |i|n| |N|e|w| |Y|o|r|k|.|
Graphic Words	|Dr|.| |Lee| |and| |John's| |son| |go| |to| |the| |McDonald's| |in| |New| |York|.|
Lexemes	|Dr.| |Lee| |and| |John|'s| |son| |go| |to| |the| |McDonald's| |in| |New York|.|
Morpho-fragments	|Dr|.| |Lee| |and| |John|'|s| |son| |go| |to| |the| |McDonald|'|s| |in| |New| |York|.|

Figure 1: Decomposition of Sentence in English

Sentence	彼は休暇で帰省している。 (He is home for holiday.)
Characters	|彼|は|休|暇|で|帰|省|し|て|い|る|。
Lexemes	|彼|は|休暇|で|帰省|して|いる|。
Morpho-fragments	|彼|は|休|暇|で|帰|省|し|て|い|る|。

Figure 2: Decomposition of Sentence in Japanese

"Graphic Words" in Figure 1) and searches the dictionary for these graphic words. However, in practice, we want a sequence of lexemes (see the line labeled "Lexemes" in Figure 1). We list two major problems of tokenization in segmented languages below (examples in English). We use the term *segment* to refer to a string separated by white spaces.

1. Segmentation(one segment into several lexemes):

   Segments with a period at the end (e.g, "Calif." and "etc.") suffer from segmentation ambiguity. The period can denote an abbreviation, the end of a sentence, or both. The problem of sentence boundary ambiguity is not easy to solve (Palmer and Hearst, 1997). A segment with an apostrophe also has segmentation ambiguity. For example, "McDonald's" is ambiguous since this string can be segmented into either "McDonald / Proper noun" + " 's / Possessive ending" or "McDonald's / Proper noun (company name)". In addition, "boys' " in a sentence "... the boys' toys ..." is ambiguous. The string can be segmented into either "boys' / Plural possessive" or "boys / Plural Noun" + " ' / Punctuation (the end of a quotation)" (Manning and Schütze, 1999). If a hyphenated segment such as "data-base," "F-16," or "MS-DOS" exists in the dictionary, it should be an independent lexeme. However, if a hyphenated segment such as "55-years-old" does not exist in the dictionary, hyphens should be treated as independent tokens(Fox, 1992). Other punctuation marks such as "/" or "_" have the same problem in "OS/2" or "`max_size`"(in programming languages).

2. Round-up(several segments into one lexeme):

   If a lexeme consisting of a sequence of segments such as a proper noun (e.g., "New York") or a phrasal verb (e.g., "look at" and "get up") exists in the dictionary, it should be a lexeme. To handle such lexemes, we need to store multi-segment lexemes in the dictionary. Webster and Kit handle idioms and fixed expressions in this way(Webster and Kit, 1992). In Penn Treebank(Santorini, 1990), a proper noun like "New York" is defined as two individual proper nouns "New / NNP" + "York / NNP," disregarding round-up of several segments into a lexeme.

The definition of lexemes in a dictionary depends on the requirement of application. Therefore, a simple pattern matcher is not enough to deal with language independent tokenization.

Non-segmented languages do not have a delimiter between lexemes (Figure 2). Therefore, a treatment of further segmentation and rounding up has been well considered. In a non-segmented language, the analyzer considers all prefixes from each position in the sentence, checks whether each prefix matches the lexeme in the dictionary, stores these lexemes in a graph structure, and finds the most plausible sequence of lexemes in the graph structure. To find the sequence, Nagata proposed a probabilistic language model for non-segmented languages(Nagata, 1994)(Nagata, 1999).

The crucial difference between segmented and

non-segmented languages in the process of morphological analysis appears in the way of the dictionary look-up. The standard technique for looking up lexemes in Japanese dictionaries is to use a trie structure(Fredkin, 1960)(Knuth, 1998). A trie structured dictionary gives all possible lexemes that start at a given position in a sentence effectively(Morimoto and Aoe, 1993). We call this method of word looking-up as "common prefix search" (hereafter CPS). Figure 3 shows a part of the trie for Japanese lexeme dictionary. The results of CPS for "海老名へ行く。"(I go to Ebina.) are "海老" and "海老名." To get all possible lexemes in the sentence, the analyzer has to slide the start position for CPS to the right by character by character.

3 A Naive Approach

A simple method that directly applies the morphological analysis method for non-segmented languages can handle the problems of segmented languages. For instance, to analyze the sentence, "They've gone to school together," we first delete all white spaces in the sentence and get "They'vegonetoschooltogether." Then we pass it to the analyzer for non-segmented languages. However, the analyzer may return the result as "They / 've / gone / to / school / to / get / her / ." inducing a spurious ambiguity. Mills applied this method and tokenized the medieval manuscript in Cornish(Mills, 1998).

We carried out experiments to examine the influence of delimiter deletion. We use Penn Treebank(Santorini, 1990) part-of-speech tagged corpus (1.3M lexemes) to train an HMM and analyze sentences by HMM-based morphological analyzer MOZ(Yamashita, 1999)(Ymashita et al., 1999). We use a bigram model for training it from the corpus. Test data is the same as the training corpus. Table 1 shows accuracy of segmentation and part-of-speech tagging. The accuracy is expressed in terms of recall and precision(Nagata, 1999). Let the number of lexemes in the tagged corpus be Std, the number of lexemes in the output of the analyze be Sys, and the number of matched lexemes be M. *Recall* is defined as M/Std, *precision* is defined as M/Sys. The following are the labels in Table 1 (sentence formats and methods we use):

LXS We isolate all the lexemes in sentences and apply the method for segmented languages to the sentences. This situation is ideal, since the problems we discussed in Section 2 do not exist. In other words, all the sentences do not have segmentation ambiguity. We use the results as the baseline. Example sentence: "`It␣'s␣Mr.␣Lee␣'s␣pen␣.`"

NSP We remove all the spaces in sentences and apply the method for non-segmented languages to the sentences. Example sentence: "`It'sMr.Lee'spen.`"

NOR Sentences are in the original normal format. We apply the method for non-segmented languages to the sentences. Example sentence: "`It's␣Mr.␣Lee's␣pen.`"

Because of no segmentation ambiguity, "LXS" performs better than "NSP" and "NOR." The following are typical example of segmentation errors. The errors originate from conjunctive ambiguity and disjunctive ambiguity(Guo, 1997).

conjunctive ambiguity The analyzer recognized "away," "ahead," "anymore," and "workforce" as "a way," "a head," "any more," and "work force," respectively. In the results of "NSP," the number of this type of error is 11,267.

disjunctive ambiguity The analyzer recognized "a tour," "a ton," and "Alaskan or" as "at our," "at on," and "Alaska nor," respectively. In the results of "NSP," the number of this type of error is 233.

Since only "NSP" has disjunctive ambiguity, "NOR" performs better than "NSP." This shows that white spaces between segments help to decrease segmentation ambiguity.

Though the proportional difference in accuracy looks slight between these models, there is a considerable influence in the analysis efficiency. In the cases of "NSP" and "NOR," the analyzer may look up the dictionary from any position in a given sentence, therefore candidates for lexemes increase, and the analysis time also increase. The results of our experiments show that the run time of analyses of "NSP" or "NOR" takes about 4 times more than that of "LXS."

4 Morpho-fragments: The Building Blocks

Although segmented languages seemingly have clear word boundaries, there are problems of further segmentation and rounding up as introduced in Section 2. The naive approach in Section 3 does not work well. In this section, we propose an efficient and sophisticated method to solve the problems by introducing the concept of *morpho-fragments*. We also show that a uniform treatment of segmented and non-segmented languages is possible without inducing the spurious ambiguity.

4.1 Definition

The *morpho-fragments* (MFs) of a language is defined as the smallest set of strings of the alphabet which can compose all lexemes in the dictionary. In other words, MFs are intermediate units between

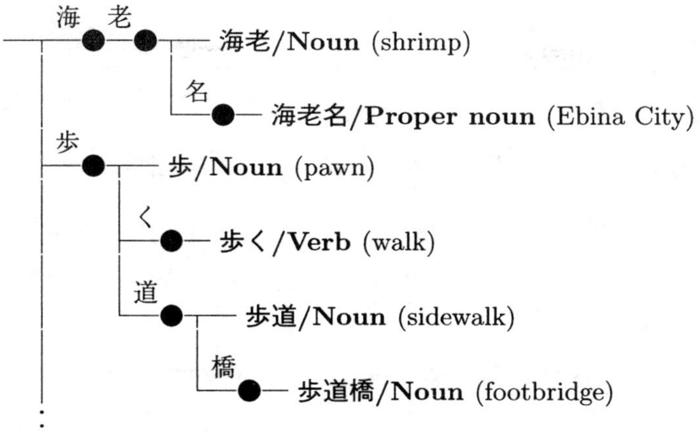

Figure 3: Japanese Trie Structured Dictionary

	Segmentation (Recall / Precision)	POS Tagging (Recall / Precision)	Analysis Time (Ratio)
LXS	100	96.98	1.0
NSP	99.52 / 99.67	96.52 / 96.69	4.3
NOR	99.87 / 99.91	96.84 / 96.88	4.2
MF	99.88 / 99.93	96.85 / 96.91	1.4

Table 1: Results of Experiments

characters and lexemes (see Figure 1 and Figure 2). MFs are well defined tokens which are specialized for language independent morphological analysis.

For example, in English, all punctuation marks are MFs. Parts of a token separated by a punctuation mark such as "He," "s," and the punctuation mark itself, " ' " in "He's" are MFs. The tokens in a compound lexeme such as "New" and "York" in "New York" are also MFs. In non-segmented languages such as Chinese and Japanese, every single character is a MF. Figure 4 shows decomposition of sentences into MFs (enclosed by "[" and "]") for several languages. *Delimiters* (denoted "␣") are treated as special MFs that cannot start nor end a lexeme.

Once the set of MFs is determined, the dictionary is compiled into a trie structure in which the edges are labeled by MFs, as shown in Figure 5 for English and in Figure 3 for Japanese. A trie structure ensures to return all and only possible lexemes starting at a particular position in a sentence by a one-time consultation to the dictionary, resulting in an efficient dictionary look-up with no spurious ambiguity.

When we analyze a sentence of a non-segmented language, to get all possible lexemes in the sentence, the analyzer slides the position one character by one character from the beginning to the end of the sentence and consults the trie structured dictionary (Section 2). Note that every character is a MF in non-segmented languages. In the same way, to analyze a sentence of a segmented language, the analyzer slides the position one MF by one MF and consults the trie structured dictionary, then, all possible lexemes are obtained. For example, in Figure 5, the results of CPS for "'m in ..." are "' " and "'m," and the results for "New York is ..." are "New" and "New York."

Therefore, a morphological analyzer with CPS-based dictionary look-up for non-segmented languages can be used for the analysis of segmented languages. In other words, MFs make possible language independent morphological analysis. We can also say MFs specify the positions to start as well as to end the dictionary look-up.

Language	Sentence		Recognized Morpho-fragments
English	`I'm in New York.`	→	[I][']\[m]␣[in]␣[New]␣[York][.]
Chinese	他是我弟弟. (He is my little brother.)	→	[他][是][我][弟][弟][.]
Korean	나는 학교에 간다. (I go to school.)	→	[나][는]␣[학][교][에]␣[간][다][.]
Japanese	学校へ行きましょう。 (Let's go to school.)	→	[学][校][へ][行][き][ま][し][ょ][う][。]

Figure 4: Recognition of Morpho-fragments

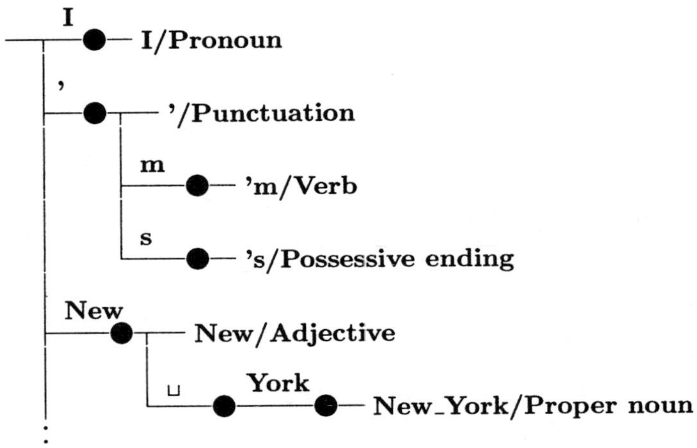

Figure 5: English Trie Structured Dictionary

4.2 How to Recognize Morpho-fragments

The problem is that it is not easy to identify the complete set of MFs for a segmented language. We do not make effort to find out the minimum and complete set of MFs. Instead, we decide to specify all the possible delimiters and punctuation marks appearing in the dictionary, these may separate MFs or become themselves as MFs. By specifying the following three kinds of information for the language under consideration, we attain a pseudo-complete MF definition. The following setting not only simplifies the identification of MFs but also achieves a uniform framework of language dependent morphological analysis system.

1. The language type:

   The languages are classified into two groups: segmented and non-segmented languages. "Language type" decides if every character in the language can be an MF. In non-segmented language every character can be an MF. In segmented language, punctuation marks and sequences of characters except for delimiters can be an MF.

2. The set of the delimiters acting as boundaries:

   These act as boundaries of MFs. However, these can not be independent MFs (can not start nor end a lexeme). For example, white spaces are delimiters in segmented languages.

3. The set of the punctuation marks and other symbols:

   These act as a boundary of MFs as well as an MF. Examples are an apostrophe in "It's," a period in "Mr.," and a hyphen in "F-16."

Using these information, the process of recognizing MFs becomes simple and easy. The process can be implemented by a finite state machine or a simple pattern matcher.

The following is the example of the definition for English:

1. Language type: segmented language
2. Delimiters: white spaces, tabs, and carriage-returns
3. Punctuation marks: [.][,][:][;]['][\"][-]···[0][1][2]···

As is clear from the definition, "punctuation marks" are not necessary for non-segmented language, since every character is an MF. The following is the example for Japanese and Chinese.

1. Language type: non-segmented language
2. Delimiters: not required
3. Punctuation marks: not required

Though Korean sentences are separated by spaces into phrasal segments, Korean is a non-segmented language essentially, since each phrasal segment does not have lexeme boundaries. We call this type of languages incompletely-segmented languages. German is also categorized as this type. The following is the example for Korean.

1. Language type: non-segmented language
2. Delimiters: spaces, tabs, and carriage-returns
3. Punctuation marks: not required

In incompletely-segmented languages, such as Korean, we have to consider two types of connection of lexemes, one is "over a delimiter" and the other is "inside a segment" (Hirano and Matsumoto, 1996). If we regard delimiters as lexemes, a trigram model can make it possible to treat both types.

The definition gives possible starting positions of MFs in sentences of the language and the same morphological analysis system is usable for any language.

We examined an effect of applying the morpho-fragments to analysis. Conditions of the experiment are almost the same as "NOR." The difference is that we use the morpho-fragments definition for English. The row labeled "MF" in Table 1 shows the results of the analysis. Using the morpho-fragments decreases the analysis time drastically. The accuracy is also better than those of the naive approaches.

Well studied language such as English may have a hand tuned tokenizer which is superior to ours. However, to tune a tokenizer by hand is not suitable to implement many minor languages.

4.3 Implementation

We implement a language independent morphological analysis system based on the concept of morpho-fragments(Yamashita, 1999). With an existence of tagged corpus, it is straightforward to implement part-of-speech taggers. We have implemented several of such taggers. The system uses an HMM. This is trained by a part-of-speech tagged corpus. We overview the setting and performance of tagging for several languages.

English

An HMM is trained by the part-of-speech tagged corpus part of Penn Treebank(Santorini, 1990) (1.3 million morphemes). We use a trigram model. The lexemes in the dictionary are taken from the corpus as well as from the entry words in Oxford Advanced Learner's Dictionary(Mitton, 1992). The system achieves 97% precision and recall for training data, 95% precision and recall for test data.

Japanese

An HMM is trained by Japanese part-of-speech tagged corpus(Rea, 1998) (0.9 million morphemes). We use a trigram model. The lexemes in the dictionary are taken from the corpus as well as from the dictionary of ChaSen(Matsumoto et al., 1999), a freely available Japanese morphological analyzer. The system achieves 97% precision and recall for training and test data.

Chinese

An HMM is trained by the Chinese part-of-speech tagged corpus released by CKIP(Chinese Knowledge Information Processing Group, 1995) (2.1 million morphemes). We use a bigram model. The lexemes in the dictionary are taken only from the corpus. The system achieves 95% precision and recall for training data, 91% precision and recall for test data.

5 Related Work and Remarks

We address two problems of tokenization in segmented languages: further segmentation and round-up. These problems are discussed by several authors including Mills(Mills, 1998) Webster & Kit(Webster and Kit, 1992). However, their proposed solutions are not language independent.

To resolve the problems of tokenization, we first apply the method of non-segmented languages processing. However, this causes spurious segmentation ambiguity and a considerable influence in the analysis times. Therefore, we propose the concept of morpho-fragments that minimally comprises the lexemes in a language. Although the idea is quite simple, our approach avoids spurious ambiguity and attains an efficient look-up of a trie structured dictionary. In conclusion, the concept of morpho-fragments makes it easy to implemented language independent morphological analysis.

References

Chinese Knowledge Information Processing Group, 1995. 中央研究院平衡語料庫的內容與說明. Academia Sinica Institute of Information Science. in Chinese.

Christopher Fox, 1992. *Lexical Analysis and Stoplists*, chapter 7, pages 102–130. In Frakes and Baeza-Yates (Frakes and Baeza-Yates, 1992).

William B. Frakes and Ricardo A. Baeza-Yates, editors. 1992. *Information Retrieval: Data Structures & Algorithms*. Prentice-Hall.

Edward Fredkin. 1960. Trie memory. *Communications of the ACM*, 3(9):490–500, September.

Jin Guo. 1997. Critical tokenization and its properties. *Computational Linguistics*, 23(4):569–596, December.

Yoshitaka Hirano and Yuji Matsumoto. 1996. A proposal of korean conjugation system and its application to morphological analysis. In *Proceedings of the 11th Pacific Asia Conference on Language, Information and Computation (PACLIC 11)*, pages 229–236, December.

Donald E. Knuth. 1998. *The Art of Computer Programming : Sorting and Searching*, volume 3. Addison-Wesley, second edition, May.

Henry Kučera and W. Nelson Francis. 1967. *Computational Analysis of Present-Day American English.* Brown University Press.

Christopher D. Manning and Hinrich Schütze. 1999. *Foundations of Statistical Natural Language Processing.* The MIT Press.

Yuji Matsumoto, Akira Kitauchi, Tatsuo Yamashita, and Yoshitaka Hirano, 1999. *Japanese Morphological Analysis System ChaSen version 2.0 Manual.* NAIST Technical Report NAIST-IS-TR99009, April.

Jon Mills. 1998. Lexicon based critical tokenization: An algorithm. In *Euralex'98*, pages 213–220, August.

Roger Mitton, 1992. *A Description of A Computer-Usable Dictionary File Based on The Oxford Advanced Learner's Dictionary of Current English.*

K. Morimoto and J. Aoe. 1993. Two trie structures for natural language dictionaries. In *Proceedings of Natural Language Processing Pacific Rim Symposium*, pages 302–311.

Masaaki Nagata. 1994. A stochastic japanese morphological analyzer using a forward-dp backward-a* n-best search algorithm. In *COLING-94*, volume 1, pages 201–207, August.

Masaaki Nagata. 1999. A part of speech estimation method for japanese unknown words using a statistical model of morphology and context. In *37th Annual Meeting of the Association for Computational Linguistics, Proceedings of the Conference*, pages 277–284, June.

David D. Palmer and Marti A. Hearst. 1997. Adaptive multilingual sentence boundary disambiguation. *Computational Linguistics*, 23(2):241–267, June.

Real World Computing Partnership, 1998. *RWC Text Database Report.* in Japanese.

Beatrice Santorini, 1990. *Part-of-Speech Tagging Guidelines for the Penn Treebank Project (3rd Revision, 2nd printing)*, June.

Jonathan J. Webster and Chunyu Kit. 1992. Tokenization as the initial phase in nlp. In *COLING-92*, volume 4, pages 1106–1110, August.

Tatsuo Yamashita, 1999. *MOZ and LimaTK Manual.* NAIST Computational Linguistics Laboratory, <http://cl.aist-nara.ac.jp/~tatuo-y/ma/>, August. in Japanese.

Tatsuo Ymashita, Msakazu Fujio, and Yuji Matsumoto. 1999. Language independent tools for natural language processing. In *Proceedings of the Eighteenth International Conference on Computer Processing*, pages 237–240, March.

A Divide-and-Conquer Strategy for Shallow Parsing of German Free Texts

Günter Neumann* **Christian Braun†** **Jakub Piskorski‡**

Abstract

We present a divide-and-conquer strategy based on finite state technology for shallow parsing of real-world German texts. In a first phase only the topological structure of a sentence (i.e., verb groups, subclauses) are determined. In a second phase the phrasal grammars are applied to the contents of the different fields of the main and sub-clauses. Shallow parsing is supported by suitably configured preprocessing, including: morphological and on-line compound analysis, efficient POS-filtering, and named entity recognition. The whole approach proved to be very useful for processing of free word order languages like German. Especially for the divide-and-conquer parsing strategy we obtained an f-measure of 87.14% on unseen data.

1 Introduction

Current information extraction (IE) systems are quite successful in efficient processing of large free text collections due to the fact that they can provide a partial understanding of specific types of text with a certain degree of partial accuracy using fast and robust language processing strategies (basically finite state technology). They have been "made sensitive" to certain key pieces of information and thereby provide an easy means to skip text without deep analysis. The majority of existing IE systems are applied to English text, but there are now a number of systems which process other languages as well (e.g., German (Neumann et al., 1997), Italian (Ciravegna et al., 1999) or Japanese (Sekine and Nobata, 1998)). The majority of current systems perform a partial parsing approach using only very few general syntactic knowledge for the identification of nominal and prepositional phrases and verb groups. The combination of such units is then performed by means of domain-specific templates. Usually, these templates are triggered by domain-specific predicates attached only to a relevant subset of verbs which express domain-specific selectional restrictions for possible argument fillers.

In most of the well-known shallow text processing systems (cf. (Sundheim, 1995) and (SAIC, 1998)) cascaded chunk parsers are used which perform clause recognition after fragment recognition following a bottom-up style as described in (Abney, 1996). We have also developed a similar bottom-up strategy for the processing of German texts, cf. (Neumann et al., 1997). However, the main problem we experienced using the bottom-up strategy was insufficient robustness: because the parser depends on the lower phrasal recognizers, its performance is heavily influenced by their respective performance. As a consequence, the parser frequently wasn't able to process structurally simple sentences, because they contained, for example, highly complex nominal phrases, as in the following example:

> "[Die vom Bundesgerichtshof und den Wettbewerbshütern als Verstoß gegen das Kartellverbot gegeißelte zentrale TV-Vermarktung] ist gängige Praxis."
>
> *Central television marketing, censured by the German Federal High Court and the guards against unfair competition as an infringement of anti-cartel legislation, is common practice.*

During free text processing it might be not possible (or even desirable) to recognize such a phrase completely. However, if we assume that domain-specific templates are associated with certain verbs or verb groups which trigger template filling, then it will be very difficult to find the appropriate fillers without knowing the correct clause structure. Furthermore in a sole bottom-up approach some ambiguities – for example relative pronouns – can't be resolved without introducing much underspecification into the intermediate structures.

Therefore we propose the following *divide-and-conquer* parsing strategy: In a first phase only the verb groups and the topological structure of a sentence according to the linguistic *field the-*

* DFKI GmbH, Stuhlsatzenhausweg 3, 66123 Saarbrücken, Germany, neumann@dfki.de

† DFKI GmbH, Stuhlsatzenhausweg 3, 66123 Saarbrücken, Germany, cbraun@dfki.de

‡ DFKI GmbH, Stuhlsatzenhausweg 3, 66123 Saarbrücken, Germany, piskorsk@dfki.de

"[$_{CoordS}$ [$_{SSent}$ Diese Angaben konnte der Bundesgrenzschutz aber nicht bestätigen], [$_{SSent}$ Kinkel sprach von Horrorzahlen, [$_{relcl}$ denen er keinen Glauben schenke]]]."
This information couldn't be verified by the Border Police, Kinkel spoke of horrible figures that he didn't believe.

Figure 1: An example of a topological structure.

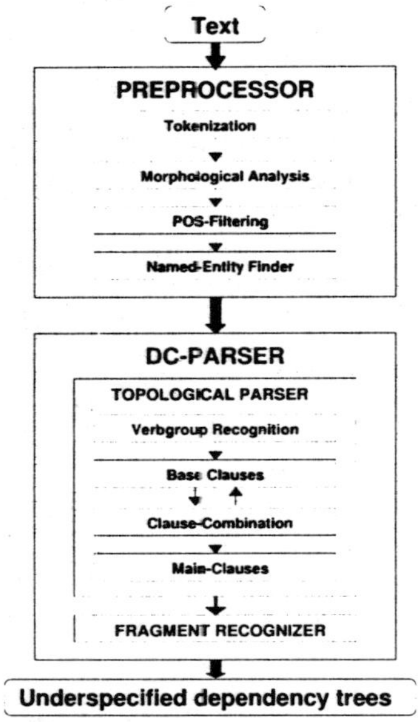

Figure 2: Overview of the system's architecture.

ory (cf. (Engel, 1988)) are determined domain-independently. In a second phase, general (as well as domain-specific) phrasal grammars (nominal and prepositional phrases) are applied to the contents of the different fields of the main and sub-clauses (see fig. 1)
This approach offers several advantages:

- improved robustness, because parsing of the sentence topology is based only on simple indicators like verbgroups and conjunctions and their interplay,
- the resolution of some ambiguities, including relative pronouns vs. determiner, subjunction vs. preposition and sentence coordination vs. NP coordination, and
- a high degree of modularity (easy integration of domain-dependent subcomponents).

The shallow divide-and-conquer parser (DC-PARSER) is supported by means of powerful morphological processing (including on-line compound analysis), efficient POS-filtering and named entity recognition. Thus the architecture of the complete shallow text processing approach consists basically of two main components: the preprocessor and the DC-PARSER itself (see fig. 2).

2 Preprocessor

The DC-PARSER relies on a suitably configured preprocessing strategy in order to achieve the desired simplicity and performance. It consists of the following main steps:

Tokenization The tokenizer maps sequences of consecutive characters into larger units called tokens and identifies their types. Currently we use more than 50 domain-independent token classes including generic classes for semantically ambiguous tokens (e.g., "10:15" could be a time expression or volleyball result, hence we classify this token as number-dot compound) and complex classes like abbreviations or complex compounds (e.g., "AT&T-Chief"). It proved that such variety of token classes simplifies the processing of subsequent submodules significantly.

Morphology Each token identified as a potential wordform is submitted to the morphological analysis including on-line recognition of compounds (which is crucial since compounding is a very productive process of the German language) and hyphen coordination (e.g., in "An- und Verkauf" (*purchase and sale*) "An-" is resolved to "Ankauf" (*purchase*)). Each token recognized as a valid word form is associated with the list of its possible readings, characterized by stem, inflection information and part of speech category.

POS-filtering Since a high amount of German word forms is ambiguous, especially word forms with a verb reading[1] and due to the fact that the quality of the results of the DC-PARSER relies essentially on the proper recognition of verb groups, efficient disambiguation strategies are needed. Using case-sensitive rules is straightforward since generally only nouns (and proper names) are written in standard German with a capitalized initial letter (e.g., "das Unternehmen" - *the enterprise* vs. "wir unternehmen" - *we undertake*). However for disambiguation of word forms appearing at the beginning of the sentence local contextual filtering rules are applied. For instance, the rule which forbids the verb written with a capitalized initial letter to be followed by a finite verb would filter out the verb reading of the word "unternehmen" in the sentence

[1]30% of the wordforms in the test corpus "Wirtschaftswoche" (business news journal), which have a verb reading, turned to have at least one other non-verb reading.

"Unternehmen sind an Gewinnmaximierung interessiert." (*Enterprises are interested in maximizing their profits*). A major subclass of ambiguous wordforms are those which have an adjective or attributivly used participle reading beside the verb reading. For instance, in the sentence "Sie bekannten, die bekannten Bilder gestohlen zu haben." (*They confessed they have stolen the famous paintings.*) the wordform "bekannten" is firstly used as a verb (confessed) and secondly as an adjective (famous). Since adjectives and attributively used participles are in most cases part of a nominal phrase a convenient rule would reject the verb reading if the previous word form is a determiner or the next word form is a noun. It is important to notice that such rules are based on some regularities, but they may yield false results, like for instance the rule for filtering out the verb reading of some word forms extremely rarely used as verbs (e.g., "recht" - *right, to rake* (3rd person,sg)). All rules are compiled into a single finite-state transducer according to the approach described in (Roche and Schabes, 1995).[2]

Named entity finder Named entities such as organizations, persons, locations and time expressions are identified using finite-state grammars. Since some named entities (e.g. company names) may appear in the text either with or without a designator, we use a dynamic lexicon to store recognized named entities without their designators (e.g., "Braun AG" vs. "Braun") in order to identify subsequent occurrences correctly. However a named entity, consisting solely of one word, may be also a valid word form (e.g., "Braun" – brown). Hence we classify such words as candidates for named entities since generally such ambiguities cannot be resolved at this level. Recognition of named entities could be postponed and integrated into the fragment recognizer, but performing this task at this stage of processing seems to be more appropriate. Firstly because the results of POS-filtering could be partially verified and improved and secondly the amount of the word forms to be processed by subsequent modules could be considerably reduced. For instance the verb reading of the word form "achten" (watch vs. eight) in the time expression "am achten Oktober 1995" (at the eight of the October 1995) could be filtered out if not done yet.

3 A Shallow Divide-and-Conquer Strategy

The DC-PARSER consists of two major domain-independent modules based on finite state technology: 1) construction of the topological sentence structure, and 2) application of phrasal grammars on each determined subclause (see also fig. 3). In this paper we will concentrate on the first step, because it is the more novel part of the DC-PARSER, and will only briefly describe the second step in section 3.2.

3.1 Topological structure

The DC-PARSER applies cascades of finite-state grammars to the stream of tokens and named entities delivered by the preprocessor in order to determine the topological structure of the sentence according to the linguistic field theory (Engel, 1988).[3]

Based on the fact that in German a verb group (like "hätte überredet werden müssen" — **have convinced been should* meaning *should have been convinced*) can be split into a left and a right verb part ("hätte" and "überredet werden müssen'") these parts (abbreviated as LVP and RVP) are used for the segmentation of a main sentence into several parts: the front field (VF), the left verb part, middle field (MF), right verb part, and rest field (RF). Subclauses can also be expressed in that way such that the left verb part is either empty or occupied by a relative pronoun or a subjunction element, and the complete verb group is placed in the right verb part, cf. figure 3. Note that each separated field can be arbitrarily complex with very few restrictions on the ordering of the phrases inside a field.

Recognition of the topological structure of a sentence can be described by the following four phases realized as cascade of finite state grammars (see also fig. 2; fig. 4 shows the different steps in action).[4] Initially, the stream of tokens and named entities is separated into a list of sentences based on punctuation signs.[5]

Verb groups A verb grammar recognizes all single occurrences of verbforms (in most cases corresponding to LVP) and all closed verbgroups (i.e., sequences of verbforms, corresponding to RVP). The parts of discontinuous verb groups (e.g., separated LVP and RVP or separated verbs and verb-prefixes) cannot be put together at that step of processing because one needs contextual information which will only be available in the next steps. The major problem at this phase is not a structural one but the

[2]The manually constructed rules proved to be a useful means for disambiguation, however not sufficient enough to filter out all unplausible readings. Hence supplementary rules determined by Brill's tagger were used in order to achieve broader coverage.

[3]Details concerning the implementation of the topological parsing strategy can be found in (Braun, 1999). Details concerning the representation and compilation of the used finite state machinery can be found in (Neumann et al., 1997)

[4]In this paper we can give only a brief overview of the current coverage of the individual steps. An exhaustive description of the covered phenomena can be found in (Braun, 1999).

[5] Performing this step after preprocessing has the advantage that the tokenizer and named entity finder already have determined abbreviation signs, so that this sort of disambiguation is resolved.

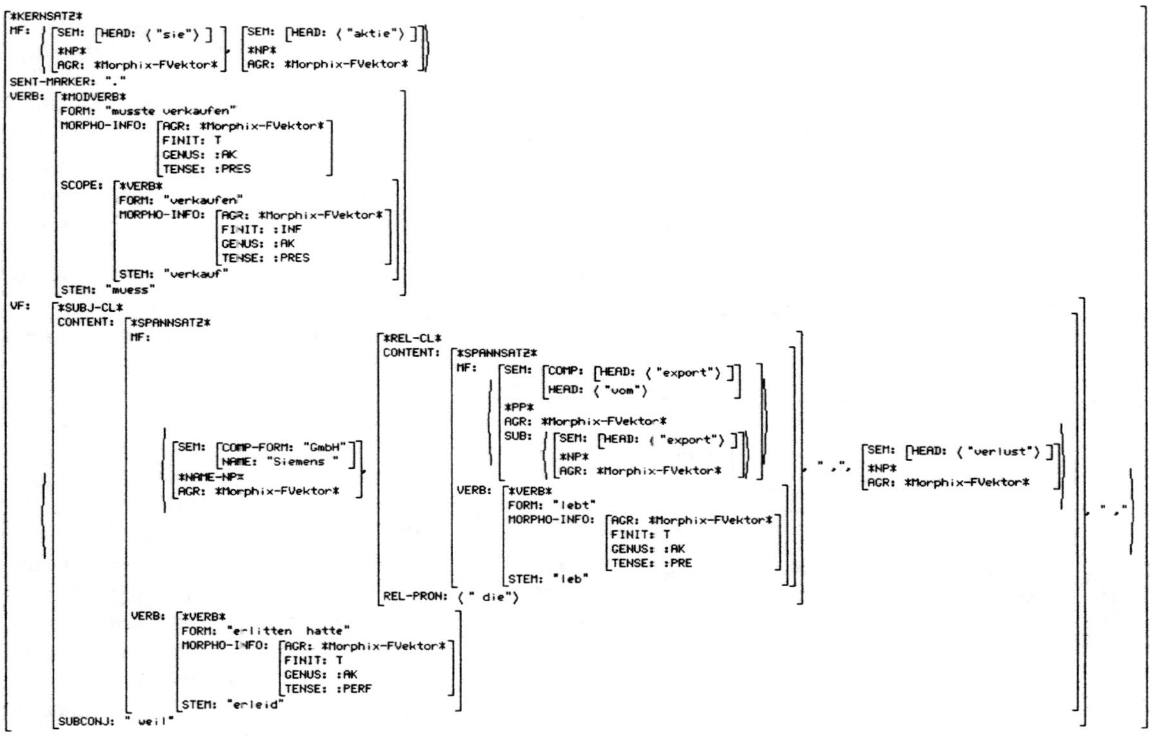

Figure 3: The result of the DC-PARSER for the sentence "Weil die Siemens GmbH, die vom Export lebt, Verluste erlitten hat, musste sie Aktien verkaufen." (*Because the Siemens GmbH which strongly depends on exports suffered from losses they had to sell some of the shares.*) abbreviated where convenient. It shows the separation of a sentence into the front field (VF), the verb group (VERB), and the middle field (MF). The elements of different fields have been computed by means of fragment recognition which takes place after the (possibly recursive) topological structure has been computed. Note that the front field consists only of one but complex subclause which itself has an internal field structure.

```
Weil die Siemens GmbH, die vom Export lebt, Verluste erlitt, musste sie Aktien verkaufen.
⇓
Weil die Siemens GmbH, die ...[Verb-Fin], Verl.  [Verb-Fin], [Modv-Fin] sie Akt.  [FV-Inf].
⇓
Weil die Siemens GmbH [Rel-Cl], Verluste [Verb-Fin], [Modv-Fin] sie Aktien [FV-Inf].
⇓
[Subconj-CL], [Modv-Fin] sie Aktien [FV-Inf].
⇓
[Subconj-CL], [Modv-Fin] sie Aktien [FV-Inf].
⇓
[clause]
```

Figure 4: The different steps of the DC-PARSER for the sentence of figure 3.

massive morphosyntactic ambiguity of verbs (for example, most plural verb forms can also be non-finite or imperative forms). This kind of ambiguity cannot be resolved without taking into account a wider context. Therefore these verb forms are assigned disjunctive types, similar to the underspecified chunk categories proposed by (Federici et al., 1996). These types, like for example Fin-Inf-PP or Fin-PP, reflect the different readings of the verbform and enable following modules to use these verb forms according to the wider context, thereby removing the ambiguity. In addition to a type each recognized verb form is assigned a set of features which represent various properties of the form like tense and mode information. (cf. figure 5).

Base clauses (BC) are subclauses of type subjunctive and subordinate. Although they are embedded into a larger structure they can independently

Type	VG-final
Subtype	Mod-Perf-Ak
Modal-stem	könn
Stem	lob
Form	nicht gelobt haben kann
Neg	T
Agr	...

Figure 5: The structure of the verb fragment "nicht gelobt haben kann" – **not praised have could-been* meaning *could not have been praised*

and simply be recognized on the basis of commas, initial elements (like complementizer, interrogative or relative item – see also fig. 4, where SUBCONJ-CL and REL-CL are tags for subclauses) and verb fragments. The different types of subclauses are described very compactly as finite state expressions. Figure 6 shows a (simplified) BC-structure in feature matrix notation.

```
[Type  Subj-Cl
 Subj  wenn
 Cont  [Type  Spannsatz
        Verb  [Type  Verb
               Form  stellten
               ...]
        MF    (die Arbeitgeber Forderungen)
        NF    ([Type  Inf-Cl
                Subj  ohne
                Cont  [Type  Simple-Inf
                       Verb  [Type  Verb
                              Form  zu schaffen
                              ...]
                       MF    (als Gegenleistung
                              neue Stellen)]])]]
```

Figure 6: Simplified feature matrix of the base clause "..., wenn die Arbeitgeber Forderungen stellten, ohne als Gegenleistung neue Stellen zu schaffen." ... *if the employers make new demands, without compensating by creating new jobs.*

Clause combination It is very often the case that base clauses are recursively embedded as in the following example:

> ... weil der Hund den Braten gefressen hatte, den die Frau, nachdem sie ihn zubereitet hatte, auf die Fensterbank gestellt hatte.
> *Because the dog ate the beef which was put on the window sill after it had been prepared by the woman.*

Two sorts of recursion can be distinguished: 1) *middle field* (MF) recursion, where the embedded base clause is framed by the left and right verb parts of the embedding sentence, and 2) the *rest field* (RF) recursion, where the embedded clause follows the right verb part of the embedding sentence. In order to express and handle this sort of recursion using a finite state approach, both recursions are treated as iterations such that they destructively substitute recognized embedded base clauses with their type. Hence, the complexity of the recognized structure of the sentence is reduced successively. However, because subclauses of MF-recursion may have their own embedded RF-recursion the CLAUSE COMBINATION (CC) is used for bundling subsequent base clauses before they would be combined with subclauses identified by the outer MF-recursion. The BC and CC module are called until no more base clauses can be reduced. If the CC module would not be used, then the following incorrect segmentation could not be avoided:

> ... *[daß das Glück [, das Jochen Kroehne empfunden haben sollte `Rel-Cl`] [, als ihm jüngst sein Großaktionär die Übertragungsrechte bescherte `Subj-Cl`], nicht mehr so recht erwärmt `Subj-Cl`]

In the correct reading the second subclause "... als ihm jüngst sein ..." is embedded into the first one "... das Jochen Kroehne ...".

Main clauses (MC) Finally the MC module builds the complete topological structure of the input sentence on the basis of the recognized (remaining) verb groups and base clauses, as well as on the word form information not yet consumed. The latter includes basically punctuations and coordinations. The following figure schematically describes the current coverage of the implemented MC-module (see figure 1 for an example structure):

CSent	::=	...LVP ...[RVP] ...
SSent	::=	LVP ...[RVP] ...
CoordS	::=	CSent (, CSent)* Coord CSent |
	::=	CSent (, SSent)* Coord SSent
AsyndSent	::=	CSent , CSent
CmpCSent	::=	CSent , SSent | CSent , CSent
AsyndCond	::=	SSent , SSent

3.2 Phrase recognition

After the topological structure of a sentence has been identified, each substring is passed to the FRAGMENT RECOGNIZER in order to determine the internal phrasal structure. Note that processing of a substring might still be partial in the sense that no complete structure need be found (e.g., if we cannot combine sequences of phrases to one larger unit). The FRAGMENT RECOGNIZER uses finite state grammars in order to extract nominal and prepositional phrases, where the named entities recognized by the preprocessor are integrated into appropriate places (unplausible phrases are rejected by agreement checking; see (Neumann et al., 1997) for more details)). The phrasal recognizer currently only considers processing of simple, non-recursive structures (see fig. 3; here, *NP* and *PP* are used for denoting phrasal types). Note that because of the high degree of modularity of our shallow parsing architecture, it is very easy to exchange the currently domain-independent fragment recognizer with a domain-specific one, without effecting the domain-independent DC-PARSER.

The final output of the parser for a sentence is an underspecified dependence structure UDS. An UDS is a flat dependency-based structure of a sentence, where only upper bounds for attachment and scoping of modifiers are expressed. This is achieved by collecting all NPs and PPs of a clause into separate sets as long as they are not part of some subclauses. This means that although the exact attachment point of each individual PP is not known it is guaranteed that a PP can only be attached to phrases which are dominated by the main verb of the sentence (which is the root node of the clause's tree). However, the exact point of attachment is a matter of domain-specific knowledge and hence should be defined as part of the domain knowledge of an application.

4 Evaluation

Due to the limited space, we concentrate on the evaluation of the topological structure. An evaluation of the other components (based on a subset of 20.000 tokens of the mentioned corpus from the "Wirtschaftswoche", see below) yields: From the 93,89% of the tokens which were identified by the morphological component as valid word forms, 95,23% got a unique POS-assignment with an accuracy of 97,9%. An initial evaluation on the same subset yielded a precision of 95.77% and a recall of 85% (90.1% F-measure) for our current named entity finder. Evaluation of the compound analysis of nouns, i.e. how often a morphosyntactical correct segmentation was found yield: Based on the 20.000 tokens, 1427 compounds are found, where 1417 have the correct segmentation (0.9929% precision). On a smaller subset of 1000 tokens containing 102 compounds, 101 correct segmentations where found (0.9901% recall), which is a quite promising result. An evaluation of simple NPs yielded a recall of 0.7611% and precision of 0.9194%. The low recall was mainly because of unknown words.

During the 2nd and 5th of July 1999 a test corpus of 43 messages from different press releases (viz. DEUTSCHE PREESSEAGENTUR (dpa), ASSOCIATED PRESS (ap) and REUTERS) and different domains (equal distribution of politics, business, sensations) was collected.[6] The corpus contains 400 sentences with a total of 6306 words. Note that it also was created after the DC-PARSER and all grammars were finally implemented. Table 1 shows the result of the evaluations (the F-measure was computed with β=1). We used the correctness criteria as defined in figure 7.

The evaluation of each component was measured on the basis of the result of all previous components. For the BC and MC module we also measured the performance by manually correcting the errors of the previous components (denoted as "isolated evaluation"). In most cases the difference between the precision and recall values is quite small, meaning that the modules keep a good balance between coverage and correctness. Only in the case of the MC-module the difference is about 5%. However, the result for the isolated evaluation of the MC-module suggests that this is mainly due to errors caused by previous components.

A more detailed analysis showed that the majority of errors were caused by mistakes in the preprocessing phase. For example ten errors were caused by an ambiguity between different verb stems (only the first reading is chosen) and ten errors because of wrong POS-filtering. Seven errors were caused by unknown verb forms, and in eight cases the parser failed because it could not properly handle the ambiguities of some word forms being either a separated verb prefix or adverb.

The evaluation has been performed with the Lisp-based version of SMES (cf. (Neumann et al., 1997)) by replacing the original bidirectional shallow buttom-up parsing module with the DC-PARSER. The average run-time per sentence (average length 26 words) is 0.57 sec. A C++-version is nearly finished missing only the re-implementation of the base and main clause recognition phases, cf. (Piskorski and Neumann, 2000). The run-time behavior is already encouraging: processing of a German text document (a collection of business news articles from the "Wirtschaftswoche") of 197118 tokens (1.26 MB) needs 45 seconds on a PentiumII, 266 MHz, 128 RAM, which corresponds to 4380 tokens per second. Since this is an increase in speed-up by a factor > 20 compared to the Lisp-version, we expect to be able to process 75-100 sentences per second.

5 Related Work

To our knowledge, there are only very few other systems described which process free German texts. The new shallow text processor is a direct successor of the one used in the SMES-system, an IE-core system for real world German text processing (Neumann et al., 1997). Here, a bidirectional verb-driven bottom-up parser was used, where the problems described in this paper concerning parsing of longer sentences were encountered. Another similar divide-

[6] This data collection and evaluation was carried out by (Braun, 1999).

Criterium	Matching of annotated data and results	Used by module
`Borders`	start and end points	verbforms, BC
`Type`	start and end points, type	verbforms, BC, MC
`Partial`	start or end point, type	BC
`Top`	start and end points, type for the largest tag	MC
`Struct1`	see `Top`, plus test of substructures using `Partial`	MC
`Struct2`	see `Top`, plus test of substructures using `Type`	MC

Figure 7: Correctness criteria used during evaluation.

Verb-Module						
correctness	*Verbfragments*			*Recall*	*Precision*	*F-measure*
criterium	total	found	correct	in %	in %	in %
`Borders`	897	894	883	98.43	98.77	98.59
`Type`	897	894	880	98.10	98.43	98.26
Base-Clause-Module						
correctness	*BC-Fragments*			*Recall*	*Precision*	*F-measure*
criterium	total	found	correct	in %	in %	in %
`Type`	130	129	121	93.08	93.80	93.43
`Partial`	130	129	125	96.15	96.89	96.51
Base-Clause-Module (isolated evaluation)						
correctness	*Base-Clauses*			*Recall*	*Precision*	*F-measure*
criterium	total	found	correct	in %	in %	in %
`Type`	130	131	123	94.61	93.89	94.24
`Partial`	130	131	127	97.69	96.94	97.31
Main-Clause-Module						
correctness	*Main-Clauses*			*Recall*	*Precision*	*F-measure*
criterium	total	found	correct	in %	in %	in %
`Top`	400	377	361	90.25	95.75	92.91
`Struct1`	400	377	361	90.25	95.75	92.91
`Struct2`	400	377	356	89.00	94.42	91.62
Main-Clause-Module (isolated evaluation)						
correctness	*Main-Clauses*			*Recall*	*Precision*	*F-measure*
criterium	total	found	correct	in %	in %	in %
`Top`	400	389	376	94.00	96.65	95.30
`Struct1`	400	389	376	94.00	96.65	95.30
`Struct2`	400	389	372	93.00	95.62	94.29
complete analysis						
correctness	*all components*			*Recall*	*Precision*	*F-measure*
criterium	total	found	correct	in %	in %	in %
`Struct2`	400	377	339	84.75	89.68	87.14

Table 1: Results of the evaluation of the topological structure

and-conquer approach using a chart-based parser for analysis of German text documents was presented by (Wauschkuhn, 1996). Nevertheless, comparing its performance with our approach seems to be rather difficult since he only measures for an unannotated test corpus how often his parser finds at least one result (where he reports 85.7% "coverage" of a test corpus of 72.000 sentences) disregarding to measure the accuracy of the parser. In this sense, our parser achieved a "coverage" of 94.25% (computing $found/total$), almost certainly because we use more advanced lexical and phrasal components, e.g., pos-filter, compound and named entity processing. (Peh and Ting, 1996) also describe a divide-and-conquer approach based on statistical methods, where the segmentation of the sentence is done by identifying so called link words (solely punctuations, conjunctions and prepositions) and disambiguating their specific role in the sentence. On an annotated test corpus of 600 English sentences they report an accuracy of 85.1% based on the correct recognition of part-of-speech, comma and conjunction disambiguation, and exact noun phrase recognition.

6 Conclusion and future work

We have presented a divide-and-conquer strategy for shallow analysis of German texts which is supported by means of powerful morphological processing, efficient POS-filtering and named entity recognition. Especially for the divide-and-conquer parsing strategy we obtained an F-measure of 87.14% on unseen data. Our shallow parsing strategy has a high degree of modularity which allows the integration of the domain-independent sentence recognition part with arbitrary domain-dependent subcomponents (e.g., specific named entity finders and fragment recognizers).

Considered from an application-oriented point of view, our main experience is that even if we are only interested in some parts of a text (e.g., only in those linguistic entities which verbalize certain aspects of a domain-concept) we have to unfold the structural relationship between all elements of a large enough area (a paragraph or more) up to a certain level of depth in which the relevant information is embedded. Beside continuing the improvement of the whole approach we also started investigations towards the integration of deep processing into the DC-PARSER. The core idea is to call a deep parser only to the separated field elements which contain sequences of simple NPs and PPs (already determined by the shallow parser). Thus seen the shallow parser is used as an efficient preprocessor for dividing a sentence into syntactically valid smaller units, where the deep parser's task would be to identify the exact constituent structure only on demand.

Acknowledgments

The research underlying this paper was supported by a research grant from the German Bundesministerium für Bildung, Wissenschaft, Forschung und Technologie (BMBF) to the DFKI project PARADIME, FKZ ITW 9704. Many thanks to Thierry Declerck and Milena Valkova for their support during the evaluation of the system.

References

S. Abney. 1996. Partial parsing via finite-state cascades. Proceedings of the ESSLLI 96 Robust Parsing Workshop.

C. Braun. 1999. Flaches und robustes Parsen Deutscher Satzgefüge. Master's thesis, University of the Saarland.

F. Ciravegna, A. Lavelli, N. Mana, L. Gilardoni, S. Mazza, M. Ferraro, J. Matiasek, W. Black, F. Rinaldi, and D. Mowatt. 1999. Facile: Classifying texts integrating pattern matching and information extraction. In *Proceedings of IJCAI-99*, Stockholm.

Ulrich Engel. 1988. *Deutsche Grammatik.* Julius Groos Verlag, Heidelberg, 2., improved edition.

S. Federici, S. Monyemagni, and V. Pirrelli. 1996. Shallow parsing and text chunking: A view on underspecification in syntax. In *Workshop on Robust Parsing, 8th ESSLLI*, pages 35–44.

G. Neumann, R. Backofen, J. Baur, M. Becker, and C. Braun. 1997. An information extraction core system for real world german text processing. In *5th International Conference of Applied Natural Language*, pages 208–215, Washington, USA, March.

L. Peh and Christopher H. Ting. 1996. A divide-and-conquer strategy for parsing. In *Proceedings of the ACL/SIGPARSE 5th International Workshop on Parsing Technologies*, pages 57–66.

J. Piskorski and G. Neumann. 2000. An intelligent text extraction and navigation system. In *6th International Conference on Computer-Assisted Information Retrieval (RIAO-2000)*. Paris, April. 18 pages.

E. Roche and Y. Schabes. 1995. Deterministic part-of-speech tagging with finite state transducers. *Computational Linguistics*, 21(2):227–253.

SAIC, editor. 1998. *Seventh Message Understanding Conference (MUC-7)*, http://www.muc.saic.com/. SAIC Information Extraction.

S. Sekine and C. Nobata. 1998. An information extraction system and a customization tool. In *Proceedings of Hitachi workshop-98*, http://cs.nyu.edu/cs/projects/proteus/sekine/.

B. Sundheim, editor. 1995. *Sixth Message Understanding Conference (MUC-6)*, Washington. Distributed by Morgan Kaufmann Publishers, Inc.,San Mateo, California.

O. Wauschkuhn. 1996. Ein Werkzeug zur partiellen syntaktischen Analyse deutscher Textkorpora. In Dafydd Gibbon, editor, *Natural Language Processing and Speech Technology. Results of the Third KONVENS Conference*, pages 356–368. Mouton de Gruyter, Berlin.

A Hybrid Approach for Named Entity and Sub-Type Tagging*

Rohini Srihari
Cymfony Net, Inc.
5500 Main Street
Williamsville, NY 14260
rohini@cymfony.com

Cheng Niu and Wei Li
Cymfony Net, Inc.
5500 Main Street
Williamsville, NY 14260
chengniu@cymfony.com
wei@cymfony.com

Abstract

This paper presents a hybrid approach for named entity (NE) tagging which combines Maximum Entropy Model (MaxEnt), Hidden Markov Model (HMM) and handcrafted grammatical rules. Each has innate strengths and weaknesses; the combination results in a very high precision tagger. MaxEnt includes external gazetteers in the system. Sub-category generation is also discussed.

Introduction

Named entity (NE) tagging is a task in which location names, person names, organization names, monetary amounts, time and percentage expressions are recognized and classified in unformatted text documents. This task provides important semantic information, and is a critical first step in any information extraction system.

Intense research has been focused on improving NE tagging accuracy using several different techniques. These include rule-based systems [Krupka 1998], Hidden Markov Models (HMM) [Bikel et al. 1997] and Maximum Entropy Models (MaxEnt) [Borthwick 1998]. A system based on manual rules may provide the best performance; however these require painstaking intense skilled labor. Furthermore, shifting domains involves significant effort and may result in performance degradation. The strength of HMM models lie in their capacity for modeling local contextual information. HMMs have been widely used in continuous speech recognition, part-of-speech tagging, OCR, etc., and are generally regarded as the most successful statistical modelling paradigm in these domains. MaxEnt is a powerful tool to be used in situations where several ambiguous information sources need to be combined. Since statistical techniques such as HMM are only as good as the data they are trained on, they are required to use back-off models to compensate for unreliable statistics. In contrast to empirical back-off models used in HMMs, MaxEnt provides a systematic method by which a statistical model consistent with all obtained knowledge can be trained. [Borthwick et al. 1998] discuss a technique for combining the output of several NE taggers in a black box fashion by using MaxEnt. They demonstrate the superior performance of this system; however, the system is computationally inefficient since many taggers need to be run.

In this paper we propose a hybrid method for NE tagging which combines all the modelling techniques mentioned above. NE tagging is a complex task and high-performance systems are required in order to be practically usable. Furthermore, the task demonstrates characteristics that can be exploited by all three techniques. For example, time and monetary expressions are fairly predictable and hence processed most efficiently with handcrafted grammar rules. Name, location and organization entities are highly variable and thus lend themselves to statistical training algorithms such as HMMs. Finally, many conflicting pieces of information regarding the class of a tag are

* This work was supported in part by the SBIR grant F30602-98-C-0043 from Air Force Research Laboratory (AFRL)/IFED.

frequently present. This includes information from less than perfect gazetteers. For this, a MaxEnt approach works well in utilizing diverse sources of information in determining the final tag. The structure of our system is shown in Figure 1.

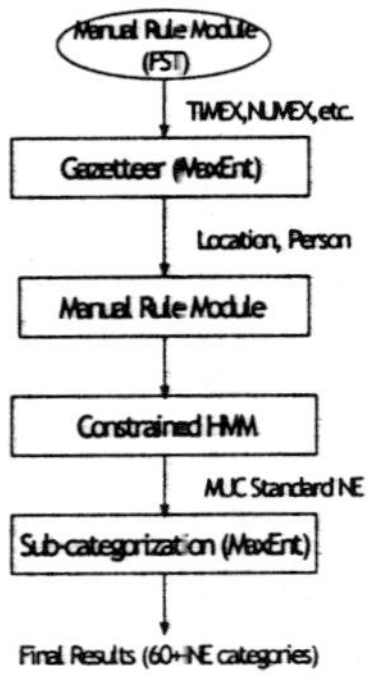

Fig.1 Structure of NE Tagger

The first module is a rule-based tagger containing pattern match rules, or templates, for time, date, percentage, and monetary expressions. These tags include the standard MUC tags [Chinchor 1998], as well as several other sub-categories defined by our organization. More details concerning the sub-categories are presented later. The pattern matcher is based on Finite State Transducer (FST) technology [Roches & Schabes 1997] that has been implemented in-house. The subsequent modules are focused on location, person and organization names. The second module assigns tentative person and location tags based on external person and location gazetteers. Rather than relying on simple lookup of the gazetteer which is very error prone, this module employs MaxEnt to build a statistical model that incorporates gazetteers with common contextual information. The core module of the system is a bigram-based HMM [Bikel et al.1997]. Rules designed to correct errors in NE segmentation are incorporated into a constrained HMM network. These rules serve as constraints on the HMM model and enable it to utilize information beyond bigrams and remove obvious errors due to the limitation of the training corpus. HMM generates the standard MUC tags, person, location and organization. Based on MaxEnt, the last module derives sub-categories such as city, airport, government, etc. from the basic tags.

Section 1 describes the FST rule module. Section 2 discusses combining gazetteer information using MaxEnt. The constrained HMM is described in Section 3. Section 4 discusses sub-type generation by MaxEnt. The experimental results and conclusion are presented finally.

1 FST-based Pattern Matching Rules for Textract NE

The most attractive feature of the FST (Finite State Transducer) formalism lies in its superior time and space efficiency [Mohri 1997] [Roche & Schabes 1997]. Applying a deterministic FST depends linearly only on the input size of the text. Our experiments also show that an FST rule system is extraordinarily robust. In addition, it has been verified by many research programs [Krupka & Hausman 1998] [Hobbs 1993] [Silberztein 1998] [Srihari 1998] [Li & Srihari 2000], that FST is also a convenient tool for capturing linguistic phenomena, especially for idioms and semi-productive expressions like time NEs and numerical NEs.

The rules which we have currently implemented include a grammar for temporal expressions (time, date, duration, frequency, age, etc.), a grammar for numerical expressions (money, percentage, length, weight, etc.), and a grammar for other non-MUC NEs (e.g. contact information like address, email).

The following sample pattern rules give an idea of what our NE grammars look like. These rules capture typical US addresses, like: *5500 Main St., Williamsville, NY14221; 12345 Xyz Avenue, Apt. 678, Los Angeles, CA98765-4321.* The following notation is used: @ for macro; | for logical OR; + for one or more; (...) for optionality.

```
0_9 =         0|1|2|3|4|5|6|7|8|9
number =      @0_9+
uppercase =   A|B|C|D|E|F|G|H|I|J|
              K|L|M|N|O|P|Q|R|S|T
              U|V|W|X|Y|Z
```

```
lowercase =     a | b | c | d | e | f | g | h | i | j | k | l |
                m | n | o | p | q | r | s | t | u |v | w |
                x | y | z
letter =        @uppercase | @lowercase
word =          @letter+
delimiter =     (",") " "+
zip =   @0_9 @0_9 @0_9 @0_9 @0_9
        ("-" @0_9 @0_9 @0_9 @0_9)
street =        [[St | ST | Rd | RD | Dr | DR |
                Ave | AVE ] (".")] | Street |
                Road | Drive | Avenue
city =  @word (@word)
state = @uppercase (".") @uppercase (".")
us =    USA | U.S.A | US | U.S. |
        (The) United States (of America)
street_addr =   @number @word @street
apt_addr =      [APT (".") | Apt (".") |
                Apartment] @number
local_addr =    @street_addr
                (@delimiter @apt_addr)
address =       @local_addr
                @delimiter @city
                @delimiter @state  @zip
                (@delimiter @us)
```

Our work is similar to the research on FST local grammars at LADL/University Paris VII [Silberztein 1998][1], but that research was not turned into a functional rule based NE system.

The rules in our NE grammars cover expressions with very predictable patterns. They were designed to address the weaknesses of our statistical NE tagger. For example, the following missings (underlined) and mistagging originally made by our statistical NE tagger have all been correctly identified by our temporal NE grammar.

began <TIMEX TYPE="DATE">Dec. 15, the</TIMEX> space agency
on Jan. 28, <TIMEX TYPE="DATE">1986</TIMEX>,
in September <TIMEX TYPE="DATE">1994</TIMEX>on <TIMEX TYPE="TIME">Saturday at</TIMEX> 2:42 a.m. ES<ENAMEX TYPE="PERSON">T.</ENAMEX>
He left the United States in <TIMEX TYPE="DATE">1984 and</TIMEX> moved
in early <TIMEX TYPE="DATE">1962 and</TIMEX>
in <TIMEX TYPE="DATE">1987 the Bonn</TIMEX> government ruled

[1] They have made public their research results at their website (http://www.ladl.jussieu.fr/index.html), including a grammar for certain temporal expressions and a grammar for stock exchange sub-language.

2 Incorporating Gazetteers with the Maximum Entropy Model

We use two gazetteers in our system, one for person and one for location. The person gazetteer consists of 3,000 male names, 5,000 female names and 14,000 family names. The location gazetteer consists of 250,000 location names with their categories such as CITY, PROVINCE, COUNTRY, AIRPORT, etc. The containing and being-contained relationship among locations is also provided.

The following is a sample line in the location gazetteer, which denotes "Aberdeen" as a city in "California", and "California" as a province of "United States".

Aberdeen (CITY) California (PROVINCE) United States (COUNTRY)

Although gazetteers obviously contain useful name entity information, a straightforward word match approach may even degrade the system performance since the information from gazetteers is too ambiguous. There are a lot of common words that exist in the gazetteers, such as "I", "A", "Friday", "June", "Friendship", etc. Also, there is large overlap between person names and location names, such as "Clinton", "Jordan", etc.

Here we propose a machine learning approach to incorporate the gazetteer information with other common contextual information based on MaxEnt. Using MaxEnt, the system may learn under what situation the occurrence in gazetteers is a reliable evidence for a name entity.

We first define "LFEATURE" based on occurrence in the location gazetteer as follows:

COUNTRY (country name)
USSTATE (US state name)
MULTITOKEN (a location name consisting of multiple tokens)
BIGCITY (a location name occurring in OXFD dictionary)
COEXIST (where COEXIST(A,B) is true iff A and B are in the same US state, or in the same foreign country)
OTHER

There is precedence from the first LFEATURE to the last one. Each token in the input document is assigned a unique "LFEATURE". We also define "NFEATURE" based on occurrence in the name gazetteer as follows:

FAMILY (family name)
MALE (male name)
FEMALE (female name)
FAMILYANDMALE (family and male name)
FAMILYANDFEMALE (family and female name)
OTHER

With these two extra features, every token in the document is regarded as a three-component vector (word, LFEATURE, NFEATURE). We can build a statistical model to evaluate the conditional probability based on these contextual and gazetteer features. Here "tag" represents one of the three possible tags (Person, Location, Other), and history represents any possible contextual history. Generally, we have:

$$p(tag \mid history) = \frac{p(tag, history)}{\sum_{tag'} p(tag', history)} \qquad (1)$$

A maximum entropy solution for probability has the form [Rosenfeld 1994] [Ratnaparkhi 1998]

$$p(tag, history) = \frac{\prod_i \alpha_i^{f_i(history,tag)}}{Z(history)} \qquad (2)$$

$$Z(history) = \sum_{tag'} \prod_i \alpha_i^{f_i(history,tag')} \qquad (3)$$

where $f_i(history, tag)$ are binary-valued feature functions that are dependent on whether the feature is applicable to the current contextual history. Here is an example of our feature function:

$$f(history, tag) = \begin{cases} 1 & \text{if current token is a country name, and tag is location} \\ 0 & \text{otherwise} \end{cases}$$

(4)

In (2) and (3) α_i are weights associated to feature functions.

The weight evaluation scheme is as follows: We first compute the average value of each feature function according to a specific training corpus. The obtained average observations are set as constraints, and the Improved Iterative Scaling (IIS) algorithm [Pietra et al. 1995] is employed to evaluate the weights. The resulting probability distribution (2) possesses the maximum entropy among all the probability distributions consistent with the constraints imposed by feature function average values.

In the training stage, our gazetteer module contains two sub-modules: feature function induction and weight evaluation [Pietra et al. 1995]. The structure is shown in Figure 2.

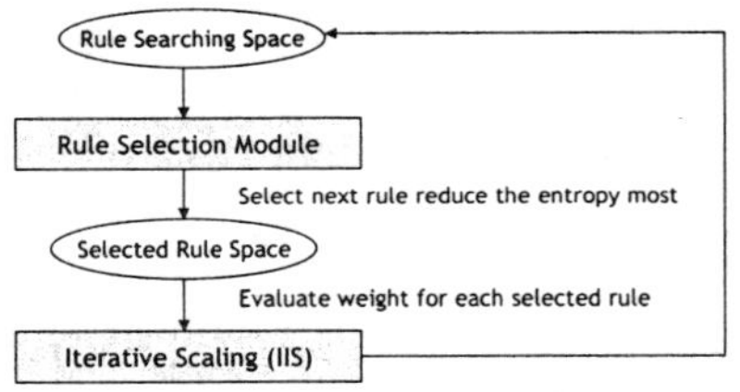

Fig.2, Structure of MaxEnt learning Process

We predefine twenty-four feature function templates. The following are some examples and others have similar structures:

$$f(history, tag) = \begin{cases} 1 & \text{if LFEATURE = \_, and tag = \_} \\ 0 & \text{else} \end{cases}$$

$$f(history, tag) = \begin{cases} 1 & \text{if NFEATURE = \_, and tag = \_} \\ 0 & \text{else} \end{cases}$$

$$f(history, tag) = \begin{cases} 1 & \text{if current word = \_, and tag = \_} \\ 0 & \text{else} \end{cases}$$

$$f(history, tag) = \begin{cases} 1 & \text{if previous word = \_, and tag = \_} \\ 0 & \text{else} \end{cases}$$

$$f(history, tag) = \begin{cases} 1 & \text{if following word = \_, and tag = \_} \\ 0 & \text{else} \end{cases}$$

where the symbol "_" denotes any possible values which may be inserted into that field. Different fields will be filled different values.

Then, using a training corpus containing 230,000 tokens, we set up a feature function candidate space based on the feature function templates. The "Feature Function Induction Module" can select next feature function that reduces the Kullback-Leibler divergence the most [Pietra et al. 1995]. To make the weight evaluation computation tractable at the feature function induction stage, when trying a new feature function, all previous computed weights are held constant, and we only fit one new constraint that is imposed by the candidate feature function. Once the next feature function is selected, we recalculate the weights by IIS to satisfy all the constraints, and thus obtain the next tentative probability. The feature function induction module will stop when the Log-likelihood gain is less than a pre-set threshold.

The gazetteer module recognizes the person and location names in the document despite the fact that some of them may be embedded in an organization name. For example, "New York Fire Department" may be tagged as <LOCATION> New York </NE> Fire Department. In the input stream for HMM, each token being tagged as location is accordingly transformed into one of the built-in tokens "CITY","PROVINCE", "COUNTRY". The HMM may group "CITY Fire Department" into an organization name. A similar technique is applied for person names.

Since the tagged tokens from the gazetteer module are regarded by later modules as either person or location names, we require that the current module generates results with the highest possible precision. For each tagged token we will compute the entropy of the answer. If the entropy is higher than a pre-set threshold, the system will not be certain enough about the answer, and the word will be untagged. The missed location or person names may be recognized by the following HMM module.

3 Improving NE Segmentation through constrained HMM

Our original HMM is similar to the Nymble [Bikel et al. 1997] system that is based on bigram statistics. To correct some of the leading errors, we incorporate manual segmentation rules with HMM. These syntactic rules may provide information beyond bigram and balance the limitation of the training corpus.

Our manual rules focus on improving the NE segmentation. For example, in the token sequence "College of William and Mary", we have rules based on global sequence checking to determine if the words "and" or "of" are common words or parts of organization name.

The output of the rules are some constraints on the HMM transition network, such as "same tags for tokens A, B", or "common word for token A". The Viterbi algorithm will select the optimized path that is consistent with such constraints.

The manual rules are divided into three categories: (i) preposition disambiguation, (ii) spurious capitalized word disambiguation, and (iii) spurious NE sequence disambiguation.

The rules of preposition disambiguation are responsible for determination of boundaries involving prepositions ("of", "and", "'s", etc.). For example, for the sequence "A of B", we have the following rule: A and B have same tags if the lowercase of A and B both occur in OXFD dictionary. A "global word sequence checking" [Mikheev, 1999] is also employed. For the sequence "Sprint and MCI", we search the document globally. If the word "Sprint" or

"MCI" occurs individually somewhere else, we mark "and" as a common word.

The rules of spurious capitalized word disambiguation are designed to recognize the first word in the sentence. If the first word is unknown in the training corpus, but occurs in OXFD as a common word in lowercase, HHM's unknown word model may be not accurate enough. The rules in the following paragraph are designed to treat such a situation.

If the second word of the same sentence is in lowercase, the first word is tagged as a common word since it never occurs as an isolated NE token in the training corpus unless it has been recognized as a NE elsewhere in the document. If the second word is capitalized, we will check globally if the same sequence occurs somewhere else. If so, the HMM is constrained to assign the same tag to the two tokens. Otherwise, the capitalized token is tagged as a common word.

The rules of spurious NE sequence disambiguation are responsible for finding spurious NE output from HMM, adding constraints, and re-computing NE by HMM. For example, in a sequence "Person Organization", we will require the same output tag for these two tokens and run HMM again.

4 NE Sub-Type Tagging using Maximum Entropy Model

The output document from constrained HMM contains MUC-standard NE tags such as person, location and organization. However, for a real information extraction system, the MUC-standard NE tag may not be enough and further detailed NE information might be necessary. We have predefined the following sub-types for person, location and organization:

Person: Military Person
Religious Person
Man
Woman
Location: City
Province
Country
Continent
Lake
River
Mountain
Road
Region
District
Airport
Organization: Company
Government
Army
School
Association
Mass Medium

If a NE is not covered by any of the above sub-categories, it should remain a MUC-standard tag. Obviously, the sub-categorization requires much more information beyond bigram than MUC-standard tagging. For example, it is hard to recognize CNN as a Mass Media company by bigram if the token "CNN" never occurs in the training corpus. External gazetteer information is critical for some sub-category recognition, and trigger word models may also play an important role.

With such considerations, we use the Maximum entropy model for sub-categorization, since MaxEnt is powerful enough to incorporate into the system gazetteer or other information sources which might become available at some later time.

Similar to the gazetteer module in Section 2, the sub-categorization module in the training stage contains two sub-modules, (i) feature function induction and (ii) weight evaluation. We have the following seven feature function templates:

$$f(history, tag) = \begin{cases} 1 & \text{if MUC\_tag = \_, and tag = \_} \\ 0 & \text{else} \end{cases}$$

$$f(history, tag) = \begin{cases} 1 & \text{if MUC\_tag = \_, LFEATURE = \_, and tag = \_} \\ 0 & \text{else} \end{cases}$$

$$f(history, tag) = \begin{cases} 1 & \text{if contain\_word(\_), MUC\_tag(history) = \_, and tag = \_} \\ 0 & \text{else} \end{cases}$$

$$f(history, tag) = \begin{cases} 1 & \text{if Previous\_Word = \_, MUC\_tag = \_, and tag = \_} \\ 0 & \text{else} \end{cases}$$

$$f(history, tag) = \begin{cases} 1 & \text{if following\_Word = \_, MUC\_tag = \_, and tag = \_} \\ 0 & \text{else} \end{cases}$$

$$f(history, tag) = \begin{cases} 1 & \text{if MUC\_tag = \_, contain\_male\_name, and tag = \_} \\ 0 & \text{else} \end{cases}$$

$$f(history, tag) = \begin{cases} 1 & \text{if MUC\_tag = \_, contain\_female\_name, and tag = \_} \\ 0 & \text{else} \end{cases}$$

We have trained 1,000 feature functions by the feature function induction module according to the above templates.

Because much more external gazetteer information is necessary for the sub-categorization and there is an overlap between male and female name gazetteers, the result from the current MaxEnt module is not sufficiently accurate. Therefore, a conservative strategy has been applied. If the entropy of the output answer is higher than a threshold, we will back-off to the MUC-standard tags. Unlike MUC NE categories, local contextual information is not sufficient for sub-categorization. In the future more external gazetteers focusing on recognition of government, company, army, etc. will be incorporated into our system. And we are considering using trigger words [Rosenfeld, 1994] to recognize some sub-categories. For example, "psalms" may be a trigger word for "religious person", and "Navy" may be a trigger word for "military person".

Experiment and Conclusion

We have tested our system on MUC-7 dry run data; this data consists of 22,000 words and represents articles from The New York Times. Since a key was provided with the data, it is possible to properly evaluate the performance of our NE tagger. The scoring program computes both the precision and recall, and combines these two measures into f-measure as the weighted harmonic mean [Chinchor, 1998]. The formulas are as follows:

$$\text{Precision} = \frac{\text{number of correct responses}}{\text{number responses}}$$

$$\text{Recall} = \frac{\text{number of correct responses}}{\text{number correct in key}}$$

$$\text{F} = \frac{(\beta^2 + 1)\text{Precision} * \text{Recall}}{(\beta^2 \text{Recall}) + \text{Precision}}$$

The score of our system is as follows:

	Recall	Precision
Organization	95	95
Person	96	93
Location	96	94
Date	92	91
Time	92	91
Money	100	86
Percentage	100	75

F-measure =93.39

If the gazetteer module is removed from our system, and the constrained HMM is restored to the standard HMM, the f-measures for person, location, and organization are as follows:

	Recall	Precision
Organization	94	92
Person	95	91
Location	95	92

Obviously, our gazetteer model and constrained HMM have greatly increased the system accuracy on the recognition of persons, locations, and organizations. Currently, there are some errors in our gazetteers. Some common words such as "Changes", "USER", "Administrator", etc. are mistakenly included in the person name gazetteer. Also, too many person names are included into the location gazetteer. By cleaning up the gazetteers, we can continue improving the precision on person name and locations.

We also ran our NE tagger on the formal test files of MUC-7. The following are the results:

	Recall	Precision
Person	92	95
Organization	85	86
Location	90	92
Date	95	85

Time	79	72
Money	95	82
Percentage	97	80
Overall F-measure	89	

There is some performance degradation in the formal test. This decrease is because that the formal test is focused on satellite and rocket domains in which our system has not been trained. There are some person/location names used as spacecraft or robot names (ex. Mir, Alvin, Columbia...), and there are many high-tech company names which do not occur in our HMM training corpus. Since the finding of organization names totally relies on the HMM model, it suffers most from domain shift (10% degradation). This difference implies that gazetteer information may be useful in overcoming the domain dependency.

This paper has demonstrated improved performance in an NE tagger by combining symbolic and statistical approaches. MaxEnt has been demonstrated to be a viable technique for integrating diverse sources of information and has been used in NE sub-categorization.

References

G. R Krupka and K. Hausman, "IsoQuest Inc: Description of the NetOwl Text Extraction System as used for MUC-7" in Proceedings of Seventh Machine Understanding Conference (MUC-7) (1998)

D. M. Bikel, "Nymble: a high-performance learning name-finder" in Proceedings of the Fifth Conference on Applied Natural Language Processing, 1997, pp. 194-201, Morgan Kaufmann Publishers.

A. Borthwick, et al., Description of the MENE named Entity System, In Proceedings of the Seventh Machine Understanding Conference (MUC-7) (1998)

R. Rosenfeld, Adaptive Statistical language Modeling, PHD thesis, Carnegie Mellon University, (1994)

A. Ratnaparkhi, Maximum Entropy Models for Natural Language Ambiguity resolution, PHD thesis, Univ. of Pennsylvania, (1998)

S. D. Pietra, Vincent Della Pietra, and John Lafferty, Inducing Features of Random Fields, Tech Report, Carnegie Mellon University, (1995)

A. Mikheev, A Knowledge-free Method for Capitalized Word Disambiguation, in *Proceedings of the 37th Annual Meeting of the Association for Computational Linguistics*, (1999), pp. 159-166

J. R. Hobbs, 1993. FASTUS: A System for Extracting Information from Text, Proceedings of the DARPA workshop on Human Language Technology", Princeton, NJ, pp. 133-137.

Emmanuel Roche & Yves Schabes, 1997. Finite-State Language Processing, The MIT Press, Cambridge, MA.

Li, W & Srihari, R. 2000. *Flexible Information Extraction Learning Algorithm*, Final Technical Report, Air Force Research Laboratory, Rome Research Site, New York

M. Silberztein, 1998. Tutorial Notes: Finite State Processing with INTEX, COLING-ACL'98, Montreal (also available at http://www.ladl.jussieu.fr)

M. Mohri,. 1997. Finite-State Transducers in Language and Speech Processing, Computational Linguistics, Vol. 23, No. 2, pp. 269-311.

R. Srihari, 1998. A Domain Independent Event Extraction Toolkit, AFRL-IF-RS-TR-1998-152 Final Technical Report, Air Force Research Laboratory, Rome Research Site, New York

Spelling and Grammar Correction for Danish in SCARRIE

Patrizia Paggio
Center for Sprogteknologi
Copenhagen (DK)
patrizia@cst.ku.dk

Abstract

This paper reports on work carried out to develop a spelling and grammar corrector for Danish, addressing in particular the issue of how a form of shallow parsing is combined with error detection and correction for the treatment of context-dependent spelling errors. The syntactic grammar for Danish used by the system has been developed with the aim of dealing with the most frequent error types found in a parallel corpus of unedited and proofread texts specifically collected by the project's end users. By focussing on certain grammatical constructions and certain error types, it has been possible to exploit the linguistic 'intelligence' provided by syntactic parsing and yet keep the system robust and efficient. The system described is thus superior to other existing spelling checkers for Danish in its ability to deal with context-dependent errors.

1 Introduction

In her much-quoted and still relevant review of technologies for automatic word correction (Kukich, 1992), Kukich observes that "research in context-dependent spelling correction is in its infancy" (p. 429), and that the task of treating context-dependent errors is still an elusive one due to the complexity of the linguistic knowledge often necessary to analyse the context in sufficient depth to find and correct such errors. But progress in parsing technology and the growing speed of computers seem to have made the task less of a chimera. The '90s have in fact seen a renewed interest in grammar checking, and proposals have been made for systems covering English (Bernth, 1997) and other languages such as Italian (Bolioli et al., 1992), Spanish and Greek (Bustamante and Léon, 1996), Czech (Holan et al., 1997) and Swedish (Hein, 1998).

This paper describes the prototype of a spelling and grammar corrector for Danish which combines traditional spelling checking functionalities with the ability to carry out compound analysis and to detect and correct certain types of context-dependent spelling errors (hereafter simply "grammar errors"). Grammar correction is carried out by parsing the text, making use of feature overriding and error weights to accommodate the errors. Although a full parse of each sentence is attempted, the grammar has been developed with the aim of dealing only with the most frequent error types found in a parallel corpus of unedited and proofread texts specifically collected by the project's end users. By focussing on certain grammatical constructions and certain error types, it has been possible to exploit the linguistic 'intelligence' provided by syntactic parsing and yet keep the system robust and efficient. The system described is thus superior to other existing spelling checkers for Danish in its ability to deal with certain types of grammar errors.

We begin by giving an overview of the system's components in Section 2. In Section 3 we describe the error types we want to deal with. Section 4 gives an overview of the grammar: in particular, the methods adopted for treating feature mismatches and structural errors are explained. Finally, in Section 5 evaluation results are presented and a conclusion is drawn.

2 The prototype

The prototype is a system for high-quality proofreading for Danish which has been developed in the context of a collaborative EU-project[1]. Together with the Danish prototype,

[1] Main contractors in the consortium were: WordFinder Software AB (Sweden), Center for

the project has also produced similar systems for Swedish and Norwegian, all of them tailored to meet the specific needs of the Scandinavian publishing industry. They all provide writing support in the form of word and grammar checking.

The Danish version of the system[2] constitutes a further development of the CORRie prototype (Vosse, 1992) (Vosse, 1994), adapted to deal with the Danish language, and to the needs of the project's end users. The system processes text in batch mode and produces an annotated output text where errors are flagged and replacements suggested where possible. Text correction is performed in two steps: first the system deals with spelling errors and typos resulting in invalid words, and then with grammar errors.

Invalid words are identified on the basis of dictionary lookup. The dictionary presently consists of 251,000 domain-relevant word forms extracted from a collection of 68,000 newspaper articles. A separate idiom list allowing for the identification of multi-word expressions is also available. Among the words not found in the dictionary or the idiom list, those occurring most frequently in the text (where frequency is assessed relative to the length of the text) are taken to be new words or proper names[3]. The remaining unknown words are passed on to the compound analysis grammar, which is a set of regular expressions covering the most common types of compound nominals in Danish. This is an important feature, as in Danish compounding is very productive, and compounds are written as single words.

Words still unknown at this point are taken to be spelling errors. The system flags them as such and tries to suggest a replacement. The algorithm used is based on *trigram and triphone analysis* (van Berkel and Smedt, 1988), and takes into account the orthographic strings corresponding to the invalid word under consideration and its possible replacement, as well as the phonetic representations of the same two words. Phonetic representations are generated by a set of grapheme-to-phoneme rules (Hansen, 1999) the aim of which is to assign phonetically motivated misspellings and their correct counterparts identical or similar phonetic representations.

Then the system tries to identify context-dependent spelling errors. This is done by parsing the text. Parsing results are passed on to a corrector to find replacements for the errors found. The parser is an implementation of the Tomita algorithm with a component for error recognition whose job is to keep track of error weights and feature mismatches as described in (Vosse, 1991). Each input sentence is assigned the analysis with the lowest error weight. If the error is due to a feature mismatch, the offending feature is overridden, and if a dictionary entry satisfying the grammar constraints expressed by the context is found in the dictionary, it is offered as a replacement. If the structure is incomplete, on the other hand, an error message is generated. Finally, if the system identifies an error as a split-up or a run-on, it will suggest either a possible concatenation, or a sequence of valid words into which the misspelt word can be split up.

3 The errors

To ensure the coverage of relevant error types, a set of parallel unedited and proofread texts provided by the Danish end users has been collected. This text collection consists of newspaper and magazine articles published in 1997 for a total of 270,805 running words. The articles have been collected in their raw version, as well as in the edited version provided by the publisher's own proofreaders. Although not very large in number of words, the corpus consists of excerpts from 450 different articles to ensure a good spread of lexical domains and error types. The corpus has been used to construct test suites for progress evaluation, and also to guide grammar development. The aim set for

Sprogteknologi (Denmark), Department of Linguistics at Uppsala University (Sweden), Institutt for lingvistikk og litteraturvitenskab at the University of Bergen (Norway), and Svenska Dagbladet (Sweden). A number of subcontractors also contributed to the project. Subcontractors in Denmark were: Munksgaard International Publishers, Berlingske Tidende, Det Danske Sprog- og Litteraturselskab, and Institut for Almen og Anvendt Sprogvidenskab at the University of Copenhagen.

[2]In addition to the author of the present paper, the Danish SCARRIE team at CST consisted of Claus Povlsen, Bart Kongejan and Bradley Music.

[3]The system also checks whether a closely matching alternative can be found in the dictionary, to avoid mistaking a consistently misspelt word for a new word.

Error type	No.	%
Context independent errors	386	38
Context dependent errors	308	30
Punctuation problems	212	21
Style problems	89	9
Graphical problems	24	2
Total	1019	100

Figure 1: Error distribution in the Danish corpus

grammar development was then to enable the system to identify and analyse the grammatical constructions in which errors typically occur, whilst to some extent disregarding the remainder of the text.

The errors occurring in the corpus have been analysed according to the taxonomy in (Rambell, 1997). Figure 1 shows the distribution of the various error types into the five top-level categories of the taxonomy. As can be seen, grammar errors account for 30% of the errors. Of these, 70% fall into one of the following categories (Povlsen, 1998):

- Too many finite verbal forms or missing finite verb
- Errors in nominal phrases:
  - agreement errors,
  - wrong determination,
  - genitive errors,
  - errors concerning pronouns;
- Split-ups and run-ons.

Another way of grouping the errors is by the kind of parsing failure they generate: they can then be viewed as either feature mismatches, or as structural errors. Agreement errors are typical examples of feature mismatches. In the following nominal phrase, for example:

(1) de *interessant projekter
(the interesting projects)

the error can be formalised as a mismatch between the definiteness of the determiner *de* (the) and the indefiniteness of the adjective *interessant* (interesting). Adjectives have in fact both an indefinite and a definite form in Danish.

The sentence below, on the other hand, is an example of structural error.

(2) i sin tid *skabet han skulpturer over atomkraften
(during his time wardrobe/created he sculptures about nuclear power)

Since the finite verb *skabte* (created) has been misspelt as *skabet* (the wardrobe), the syntactic structure corresponding to the sentence is missing a verbal head.

Run-ons and split-ups are structural errors of a particular kind, having to do with leaves in the syntactic tree. In some cases they can only be detected on the basis of the context, because the misspelt word has the wrong category or bears some other grammatical feature that is incorrect in the context. Examples are given in (3) and (4) below, which like the preceding examples are taken from the project's corpus. In both cases, the error would be a valid word in a different context. More specifically, *rigtignok* (indeed) is an adverb, whilst *rigtig nok* (actually correct) is a modified adjective; and *inden for* (inside) is a preposition, whilst *indenfor* (indoors) is an adverb. In both examples the correct alternative is indicated in parentheses.

(3) ... studerede min gruppe *rigtig nok (rigtignok) under temaoverskrifter
(studied my group indeed on the basis of topic headings)

(4) *indenfor (inden for) de gule mure
(inside the yellow walls)

Although the system has a facility for identifying and correcting split-ups and run-ons based on a complex interaction between the dictionary, the idiom list, the compound grammar and the syntactic grammar, this facility has not been fully developed yet, and will therefore not be described any further here. More details can be found in (Paggio, 1999).

4 The grammar

The grammar is an augmented context-free grammar consisting of rewrite rules where symbols are associated with features. Error weights and error messages can also be attached to either rules or single features. The rules are applied by unification, but in cases where one or more features do not unify, the offending features will be overridden.

In the current version of the grammar, only the structures relevant to the error types we want the system to deal with – in other words nominal phrases and verbal groups – are accounted for in detail. The analysis produced is thus a kind of shallow syntactic analysis where the various sentence constituents are attached under the topmost S node as fragments.

For example, adjective phrases can be analysed as fragments, as shown in the following rule:

```
Fragment ->
  AP "?Fragment AP rule":2
```

To indicate that the fragment analysis is not optimal, it is associated with an error weight, as well as an error message to be used for debugging purposes (the message is not visible to the end user). The weight penalises parse trees built by applying the rule. The rule is used e.g. to analyse an AP following a copula verb as in:

(5) De projekter er ikke interessante.
(Those projects are not interesting)

The main motivation for implementing a grammar based on the idea of fragments was efficiency. Furthermore, the fragment strategy could be implemented very quickly. However, as will be clarified in Section 5, this strategy is sometimes responsible for bad flags.

4.1 Feature mismatches

As an alternative to the fragment analysis, APs can be attached as daughters in NPs. This is of course necessary for the treatment of agreement in NPs, one of the error types targeted in our application. This is shown in the following rule:

```
NP(def Gender PersNumber) ->
        Det(def Gender PersNumber)
        AP(def _ _)
        N(indef Gender:2 PersNumber)
```

The rule will parse a correct definite NP such as:

(6) de interessante projekter
(the interesting projects)

but also

(7) de *interessant projekter
(8) de interessante *projekterne

The feature overriding mechanism makes it possible for the system to suggest *interessante* as the correct replacement in (7), and *projekter* in (8). Let us see how this is done in more detail for example (7). The parser tries to apply the NP rule to the input string. The rule states that the adjective phrase must be definite (AP (def _ _)). But the dictionary entry corresponding to *interessant* bears the feature 'indef'. The parser will override this feature and build an NP according to the constraints expressed by the rule. At this point, a new dictionary lookup is performed, and the definite form of the adjective can be suggested as a replacement.

Weights are used to control rule interaction as well as to establish priorities among features that may have to be overridden. For example in our NP rule, a weight has been attached to the Gender feature in the N node. The weight expresses the fact that it costs more to override gender on the head noun than on the determiner or adjective. The rationale behind this is the fact that if there is a gender mismatch, the parser should not try to find an alternative form of the noun (which does not exist), but if necessary override the gender feature either on the adjective or the determiner.

4.2 Capturing structural errors in grammar rules

To capture structural errors, the formalism allows the grammar writer to write so-called error rules. The syntax of error rules is very similar to that used in 'normal' rules, the only difference being that an error rule must have an error weight and an error message attached to it. The purpose of the weight is to ensure that error rules are applied only if 'normal' rules are not applicable. The error message can serve two purposes. Depending on whether it is stated as an implicit or an explicit message (i.e. whether it is preceded by a question mark or not), it will appear in the log file where it can be used for debugging purposes, or in the output text as a message to the end user.

The following is an error rule example.

```
VGroup(_ finite Tense) ->
  V(_ finite:4 Tense)
  V(_ finite:4 _)
"Sequence of two finite verbs":4
```

Error type	*Total*	*Flagged*		*Hits*		*Misses*		*No suggs*	
Errors in single words	81	69	(85.2%)	35	(50.8%)	11	(15.9%)	23	(33.3%)
Errors in compounds	42	28	(66.7%)	8	(28.6%)	8	(28.6%)	12	(42.8%)
NP agreement errors	18	15	(83.3%)	15	(100.0%)	0	(0.0%)	0	(0.0%)
VP errors	13	8	(61.6%)	8	(100.0%)	0	(0.0%)	0	(0.0%)
Total	154	120	(78.0%)	66	(55.0%)	19	(15.8%)	35	(29.2%)

Figure 2: Error coverage and suggestion adequacy evaluated on test suites

A weight of 4 is attached to the rule as a whole, but there are also weights attached to the 'finiteness' feature on the daughters: their function is to make it costly for the system to apply the rule to non-finite forms. In other words, the feature specification 'finite' is made difficult to override to ensure that it is indeed a sequence of *finite* verbal forms the rule applies to and flags.

The rule will for example parse the verbal sequence in the following sentence:

(9) Jeg vil *bevarer (bevare) min frihed.
(*I want keep my freedom)

As a result of parsing, the system in this case will not attempt to correct the wrong verbal form, but issue the error message "Sequence of two finite verbs".

Error rules can thus be used to explicitly describe an error and to issue error messages. However, so far we have made very limited use of them, as controlling their interaction with 'normal' rules and with the feature overriding mechanism is not entirely easy. In fact, they are consistently used only to identify incorrect sequences of finite verbal forms or sentences missing a finite verb. To this sparse use of error rules corresponds, on the other hand, an extensive exploitation of the feature overriding mechanism. This strategy allows us to keep the number of rules in the grammar relatively low, but relies on a careful manual adjustment of the weights attached to the various features in the rules.

5 Evaluation and Conclusion

The project's access to a set of parallel unedited and proofread texts has made it possible to automate the evaluation of the system's linguistic functionality. A tool has been implemented to compare the results obtained by the system with the corrections suggested by the publisher's human proofreaders in order to derive measures telling us how well the system performed on *recall* (lexical coverage as well as coverage of errors), *precision* (percentage of correct flaggings), as well as *suggestion adequacy* (hits, misses and no suggestions offered). The reader is referred to (Paggio and Music, 1998) for more details on the evaluation methodology. The automatic procedure was used to evaluate the system during development, and in connection with the user validation. Testing was done on constructed test suites displaying examples of the errors targeted in the project and with text excerpts from the parallel corpora.

Figure 2 shows error recall and suggestion adequacy figures for the various error types represented in the test suites. These figures are very positive, especially with regard to the treatment of grammar errors. To make a comparison with a commercial product, the Danish version of the spelling and grammar checker provided by Microsoft Word does not flag any of the grammar errors.

Figure 3 shows how the system performed on one of the test corpora. The corpus was assembled by mixing short excerpts containing relevant grammar errors and randomly chosen text. Since unlike test suites, the corpus also contains correct text, the figure this time also shows lexical coverage and precision figures. The corpus consists of 278 sentences, with an average length of 15.18 words per sentence. It may be surprising to see that it contains a limited number of errors, but it must be remembered that the texts targeted in the project are written by experienced journalists.

The corpus was processed in 58 cpu-seconds on an HP 9000/B160. As expected, the system performs less well than on the test suites, and in general precision is clearly too low. However, we still consider these results encouraging given the relatively small resources the project has been able to spend on grammar development, and we

Recall
    4220 total words
    4157 valid words
        3996 (96.1%) valid words accepted
        161 (3.9%) valid words rejected
    63 invalid words (real errors)
        36 (57.1%) real errors spotted (good flags)
        27 (42.9%) real errors missed
Precision
    175 flaggings
        36 (20.6%) good flags
        139 (79.4%) bad flags (false positives)
Suggestion adequacy
    36 good flags
        15 (41.7%) hits (initial suggestion correct)
        8 (22.2%) misses (suggestions offered, none correct)
        13 (36.1%) with no suggestions offered

Figure 3: Test corpus evaluation

believe they can be improved.

We regard error coverage as quite satisfactory for a research prototype. In a comparative test made on a similar (slightly smaller) corpus, SCARRIE obtained 58.1% error coverage, and Word 53.5%. To quote a figure from another recently published test (Martins et al., 1998), the ReGra system is reported to miss 48.1% real errors. It is worth noting that ReGra has much more extensive linguistic resources available than SCARRIE, i.e. a dictionary of 1.5 million words and a grammar of 600 production rules. Most of the errors not found by SCARRIE in the test have to do with punctuation and other stylistic matters not treated in the project. There are also, however, agreement errors which go unnoticed. These failures are due to one of two reasons: either that no parse has been produced for the sentence in question, or that the grammar has produced a wrong analysis.

The precision obtained is at least at first sight much too low. On the same test corpus, however, Word only reached 15.9% precision. On closer inspection, 72 of the bad flags produced by SCARRIE turned out to be due to unrecognised proper names. Disregarding those, precision goes up to 34.9%. As was mentioned early, SCARRIE has a facility for guessing unknown proper names on the basis of their frequency of occurrence in the text. But since the test corpus consists of short unrelated excerpts, a large number of proper names only occur once or twice. To get an impression of how the system would perform in a situation where the same proper names and unknown words had a higher frequency of occurrence, we doubled the test corpus by simply repeating the same text twice. As expected, precision increased. The system produced 178 flags, 60 of which were correct (39.7%). This compares well with the 40% precision reported for instance for ReGra.

In addition to the problem of unkown proper names, false flags are related to unrecognised acronyms and compounds (typically forms containing acronyms or dashes), and a not very precise treatment of capitalisation. Only 13 false flags are due to wrong grammar analyses caused either by the fragment approach or by the grammar's limited coverage. In particular, genitive phrases, which are not treated at the moment, are responsible for most of these false alarms.

In conclusion, we consider the results obtained so far promising, and the problems revealed by the evaluation tractable within the current system design. In particular, future development should focus on treating stylistic matters such as capitalisation and punctuation which have not been in focus in the current prototype. The coverage of the grammar, in particular the treatment of genitive phrases, should also be further developed. The data provided by the evaluation reported on in this paper, however, are much too limited to base further development on. Therefore, more extensive testing and debugging should also be carried out.

In addition, two aspects of the system that have only be touched on in this paper would be worth further attention: one is the mechanism for the treatment of split-ups and run-ons, which as mentioned earlier is not well-integrated at the moment; the other is the weight adjustment process, which is done manually at the moment, and for which the adoption of a semi-automatic tool could be considered.

References

A. Bernth. 1997. EasyEnglish: a tool for improving document quality. In *Proceedings of the Fifth Conference on Applied Natural Language Processing.*

A. Bolioli, L. Dini, and G. Malnati. 1992. JDII: Parsing Italian with a robust constraint grammar. In *Proceedings of COLING-92*, pages 1003–1007.

Flora Ramírez Bustamante and Fernando Sánchez Léon. 1996. GramCheck: A grammar and style checker. In *Proceedings of COLING-96*, pages 175–181, Copenhagen, Denmark.

Peter Molbæk Hansen. 1999. Grapheme-to-phoneme rules for the Danish component of the SCARRIE project. In Hanne E. Thomsen and Sabine Kirchmeier-Andersen, editors, *Datalingvistisk Forenings årsmøde 1998 i København, Proceedings*, number 25 in LAMBDA, pages 79-91. Institut for datalingvistik, Handelshøjskolen i København.

Anna Sågvall Hein. 1998. A chart-based framework for grammar checking: Initial studies. In *Proceedings of Nodalida-98.*

Tomáš Holan, Vladislav Kuboň, and Martin Plátek. 1997. A prototype of a grammar checker for Czech. In *Proceedings of ANLP'97.*

Karen Kukich. 1992. Techniques for automatically correcting words in text. *ACM Computing Surveys*, 24(4):377–439.

Ronaldo Teixeira Martins, Ricardo Hasegawa, Maria Volpe Nunes, Gisele Monthila, and Osvaldo Novais De Oliveira Jr. 1998. Linguistic issues in the development ofReGra: a grammar checker for Brazilian Portuguese. *Natural Language Engineering*, 4(4):287–307, December.

Patrizia Paggio and Bradley Music. 1998. Evaluation in the SCARRIE project. In *Proceedings of the First International Conference on Language Resources & Evaluation*, pages 277–282. Granada, Spain.

Patrizia Paggio. 1999. Treatment of grammatical errors and evaluation in SCARRIE. In Hanne E. Thomsen and Sabine Kirchmeier-Andersen, editors, *Datalingvistisk Forenings årsmøde 1998 i København, Proceedings*, number 25 in LAMBDA, pages 65–78. Institut for datalingvistik, Handelshøjskolen i København.

Claus Povlsen. 1998. Three types of grammatical errors in Danish. Technical report, Copenhagen: Center for Sprogteknologi.

Olga Rambell. 1997. Error typology for automatic proof-reading purposes. Technical report, Uppsala: Uppsala University.

Brigitte van Berkel and Koenraad De Smedt. 1988. Triphone analysis: a combined method for the correction of orthographical and typographical errors. In *Proceedings of the 2nd conference on Applied Natural Language Processing*, pages 77–83. ACL, Austin.

Theo Vosse. 1991. Detection and correction of morpho-syntactic errors in shift-reduce parsing. In R. Heemels, A. Nijholt, and K. Sikkel, editors, *Tomita's Algorithm: Extensions and Applications*, number 91-68 in Memoranda Informatica, pages 69–78. University of Twente.

Theo Vosse. 1992. Detecting and correcting morpho-syntactic errors in real texts. In *Proceedings of the Third Conference on Applied Natural Language Processing*, pages 111–118, Trento, Italy.

Theo G. Vosse. 1994. *The Word Connection - Grammar-based Spelling Error Correction in Dutch.* Ph.D. thesis, Rijksuniversiteit at Leiden: the Netherlands. ISBN 90-75296-01-0.

Linguistic Knowledge can Improve Information Retrieval

William A. Woods and **Lawrence A. Bookman*** and **Ann Houston** and **Robert J. Kuhns** and **Paul Martin** and **Stephen Green**
Sun Microsystems Laboratories
1 Network Drive
Burlington, MA 01803
{William.Woods,Ann.Houston,Robert.Kuhns,Paul.Martin,Stephen.Green}@east.sun.com

Abstract

This paper describes the results of some experiments using a new approach to information access that combines techniques from natural language processing and knowledge representation with a penalty-based technique for relevance estimation and passage retrieval. Unlike many attempts to combine natural language processing with information retrieval, these results show substantial benefit from using linguistic knowledge.

1 Introduction

An online information seeker often fails to find what is wanted because the words used in the request are different from the words used in the relevant material. Moreover, the searcher usually spends a significant amount of time reading retrieved material in order to determine whether it contains the information sought. To address these problems, a system has been developed at Sun Microsystems Laboratories (Ambroziak and Woods, 1998) that uses techniques from natural language processing and knowledge representation, with a technique for dynamic passage selection and scoring, to significantly improve retrieval performance. This system is able to locate specific passages in the indexed material where the requested information appears to be, and to score those passages with a penalty-based score that is highly correlated with the likelihood that they contain relevant information. This ability, which we call "Precision Content Retrieval" is achieved by combining a system for Conceptual Indexing with an algorithm for Relaxation-Ranking Specific Passage Retrieval.

In this paper, we show how linguistic knowledge is used to improve search effectiveness in this system. This is of particular interest, since many previous attempts to use linguistic knowledge to improve information retrieval have met with little or mixed success (Fagan, 1989; Lewis and Sparck Jones, 1996; Sparck Jones, 1998; Varile and Zampolli, 1997; Voorhees, 1993; Mandala et al., 1999) (but see the latter for some successes as well).

* Lawrence Bookman is now at Torrent Systems, Inc.

2 Conceptual Indexing

The conceptual indexing and retrieval system used for these experiments automatically extracts words and phrases from unrestricted text and organizes them into a semantic network that integrates syntactic, semantic, and morphological relationships. The resulting conceptual taxonomy (Woods, 1997) is used by a specific passage-retrieval algorithm to deal with many paraphrase relationships and to find specific passages of text where the information sought is likely to occur. It uses a lexicon containing syntactic, semantic, and morphological information about words, word senses, and phrases to provide a base source of semantic and morphological relationships that are used to organize the taxonomy. In addition, it uses an extensive system of knowledge-based morphological rules and functions to analyze words that are not already in its lexicon, in order to construct new lexical entries for previously unknown words (Woods, 2000). In addition to rules for handling derived and inflected forms of known words, the system includes rules for lexical compounds and rules that are capable of making reasonable guesses for totally unknown words.

A pilot version of this indexing and retrieval system, implemented in Lisp, uses a collection of approximately 1200 knowledge-based morphological rules to extend a core lexicon of approximately 39,000 words to give coverage that exceeds that of an English lexicon of more than 80,000 base forms (or 150,000 base plus inflected forms). Later versions of the conceptual indexing and retrieval system, implemented in C++, use a lexicon of approximately 150,000 word forms that is automatically generated by the Lisp-based morphological analysis from its core lexicon and an input word list. The base lexicon is extended further by an extensive name dictionary and by further morphological analysis of unknown words at indexing time. This paper will describe some experiments using several versions of this system. In particular, it will focus on the role that the linguistic knowledge sources play in its operation.

The lexicon used by the conceptual indexing system contains syntactic information that can be used for the analysis of phrases, as well as morphological and semantic information that is used to relate more specific concepts to more general concepts in the conceptual taxonomy. This information is integrated into the conceptual taxonomy by considering base forms of words to subsume their derived and inflected forms ("root subsumption") and more general terms to subsume more specific terms. The system uses these relationships as the basis for inferring subsumption relationships between more general phrases and more specific phrases according to the intensional subsumption logic of Woods (Woods, 1991).

The largest base lexicon used by this system currently contains semantic subsumption information for something in excess of 15,000 words. This information consists of basic "kind of" and "instance of" information such as the fact that *book* is a kind of *document* and *washing* is a kind of *cleaning*. The lexicon also records morphological roots and affixes for words that are derived or inflected forms of other words, and information about different word senses and their interrelationships. For example, the conceptual indexing system is able to categorize *becomes black* as a kind of *color change* because *becomes* is an inflected form of *become*, *become* is a kind of *change*, and *black* is a *color*. Similarly, *color disruption* is recognized as a kind of *color change*, because the system recognizes *disruption* as a derived form of *disrupt*, which is known in the lexicon to be a kind of *damage*, which is known to be a kind of *change*.

When using root subsumption as a technique for information retrieval, it is important to have a core lexicon that knows correct morphological analyses for words that the rules would otherwise analyze incorrectly. For example, the following are some examples of words that could be analyzed incorrectly if the correct interpretations were not specified in the lexicon:

delegate (de+leg+ate) take the legs from

caress (car + ess) female car

cashier (cashy + er) more wealthy

daredevil (dared + evil) serious risk

lacerate (lace + rate) speed of tatting

pantry (pant + ry) heavy breathing

pigeon (pig + eon) the age of peccaries

ratify (rat + ify) infest with rodents

infantry (infant + ry) childish behavior

Although they are not always as humorous as the above examples, there are over 3,000 words in the core lexicon of 39,000 English words that would receive false morphological analyses like the above examples, if the words were not already in the lexicon.

3 Relaxation Ranking and Specific Passage Retrieval

The system we are evaluating uses a technique called "relaxation ranking" to find specific passages where as many as possible of the different elements of a query occur near each other, preferably in the same form and word order and preferably closer together. Such passages are ranked by a penalty score that measures the degree of deviation from an exact match of the requested phrase, with smaller penalties being preferred. Differences in morphological form and formal subsumption of index terms by query terms introduce small penalties, while intervening words, unexplained permutations of word order, and crossing sentence boundaries introduce more significant penalties. Elements of a query that cannot be found nearby introduce substantial penalties that depend on the syntactic categories of the missing words.

When the conceptual indexing system is presented with a query, the relaxation-ranking retrieval algorithm searches through the conceptual taxonomy for appropriately related concepts and uses the positions of those concepts in the indexed material to find specific passages that are likely to address the information needs of the request. This search can find relationships from base forms of words to derived forms and from more general terms to more specific terms, by following paths in the conceptual taxonomy.

For example, the following is a passage retrieved by this system, when applied to the UNIX® operating system online documentation (the "man pages"):

> Query: print a message from the mail tool

6\. -2.84 **print mail mail mailtool**

> Print sends copies of all the selected mail items to your default printer. If there are no selected items, mailtool sends copies of those items you are currently...

The indicated passage is ranked 6th in a returned list of found passages, indicated by the 6 in the above display. The number -2.84 is the penalty score assigned to the passage, and the subsequent words *print*, *mail*, *mail*, and *mailtool* indicate the words in the text that are matched to the corresponding content words in the input query. In this case, *print* is matched to *print*, *message* to *mail*, *mail* to *mail*, and *tool* to *mailtool*, respectively. This is followed by the content of the actual passage located. The information provided in these hit displays gives the information seeker a clear idea of why the passage was retrieved and enables the searcher to quickly skip down the hit list with little time spent looking at irrelevant passages. In this case, it was easy to identify that the 6th ranked hit was the best one and contained the relevant information.

The retrieval of this passage involved use of a semantic subsumption relationship to match *message* to *mail*, because the lexical entry for *mail* recorded that it was a kind of *message*. It used a morphological root subsumption to match *tool* to *mailtool* because the morphological analyzer analyzed the unknown word *mailtool* as a compound of *mail* and *tool* and recorded that its root was *tool* and that it was a kind of *tool* modified by *mail*. Taking away the ability to morphologically analyze unknown words would have blocked the retrieval of this passage, as would eliminating the lexical subsumption entry that recorded *mail* as a kind of *message*.

Like other approaches to passage retrieval (Kaszkiel and Zobel, 1997; Salton et al., 1993; Callan, 1994), the relaxation-ranking retrieval algorithm identifies relevant passages rather than simply identifying whole documents. However, unlike approaches that involve segmenting the material into paragraphs or other small passages before indexing, this algorithm dynamically constructs relevant passages in response to requests. When responding to a request, it uses information in the index about positions of concepts in the text to identify relevant passages. In response to a single request, identified passages may range in size from a single word or phrase to several sentences or paragraphs, depending on how much context is required to capture the various elements of the request.

In a user interface to the specific passage retrieval system, retrieved passages are reported to the user in increasing order of penalty, together with the rank number, penalty score, information about which target terms match the corresponding query terms, and the content of the identified passage with some surrounding context as illustrated above. In one version of this technology, results are presented in a hypertext interface that allows the user to click on any of the presented items to see that passage in its entire context in the source document. In addition, the user can be presented with a display of portions of the conceptual taxonomy related to the terms in the request. This frequently reveals useful generalizations of the request that would find additional relevant information, and it also conveys an understanding of what concepts have been found in the material that will be matched by the query terms. For example, in one experiment, searching the online documentation for the Emacs text editor, the request *jump to end of file* resulted in feedback showing that *jump* was classified as a kind of *move* in the conceptual taxonomy. This led to a reformulated request, *move to end of file*, which successfully retrieved the passage *go to end of buffer*.

4 Experimental Evaluation

In order to evaluate the effectiveness of the above techniques, a set of 90 queries was collected from a naive user of the UNIX operating system, 84 of which could be answered from the online documentation known as the man pages. A set of "correct" answers for each of these 84 queries was manually determined by an independent UNIX operating system expert, and a snapshot of the man pages collection was captured and indexed for retrieval. In order to compare this methodology with classical document retrieval techniques, we assign a ranking score to each document equal to the ranking score of the best ranked passage that it contains.

In rating the performance of a given method, we compute average recall and precision values at 10 retrieved documents, and we also compute a "success rate" which is simply the percentage of queries for which an acceptable answer occurs in the top ten hits. The success rate is the principal factor on which we base our evaluations, since for this application, the user is not interested in subsequent answers once an acceptable answer has been found, and finding one answer for each of two requests is a substantially better result than finding two answers to one request and none for another.

These experiments were conducted using an experimental retrieval system that combined a Lisp-based language processing stage with a C++ implementation of a conceptual indexer. The linguistic knowledge sources used in these experiments included a core lexicon of approximately 18,000 words, a substantial set of morphological rules, and specialized morphological algorithms covering inflections, prefixes, suffixes, lexical compounding, and a variety of special forms, including numbers, ordinals, Roman numerals, dates, phone numbers, and acronyms. In addition, they made use of a lexical subsumption taxonomy of approximately 3000 lexical subsumption relations, and a small set of semantic entailment axioms (e.g., *display* entails *see*, but is not a kind of *see*). This system is described in (Woods, 1997). The database was a snapshot of the local man pages (frozen at the time of the experiment so that it wouldn't change during the experiment), consisting of approximately 1800 files of varying lengths and constituting a total of approximately 10 megabytes of text.

Table 1 shows the results of comparing three versions of this technology with a textbook implementation of the standard *tf·idf* algorithm (Salton, 1989) and with the SearchIt™search application developed at Sun Microsystems, Inc., which combines a

Table 1: A comparison of different retrieval techniques.

System	Success Rate	Recall (10 docs)	Precision (10 docs)
tf·idf	28.6%	14.8%	2.9%
SearchIt system	44.0%	28.5%	7.4%
Recall II	60.7%	38.6%	7.3%
w/o morph	50.0%	not measured	not measured
w/o knowledge	42.9%	not measured	not measured

simple morphological query expansion with a state-of-the-art commercial search engine. In the table, Recall II refers to the full conceptual indexing and search system with all of its knowledge sources and rules. The line labeled "w/o morph" refers to this system with its dynamic morphological rules turned off, and the line labeled "w/o knowledge" refers to this system with all of its knowledge sources and rules turned off. The table presents the success rate and the measured recall and precision values for 10 retrieved documents. We measured recall and precision at the 10 document level because internal studies of searching behavior had shown that users tended to give up if an answer was not found in the first ten ranked hits. We measured success rate, rather than recall and precision, for our ablation studies, because standard recall and precision measures are not sensitive to the distinction between finding multiple answers to a single request versus finding at least one answer for more requests.

5 Discussion

Table 1 shows that for this task, the relaxation-ranking passage retrieval algorithm without its supplementary knowledge sources (Recall II w/o knowledge) is roughly comparable in performance (42.9% versus 44.0% success rate) to a state-of-the-art commercial search engine (SearchIt) at the pure document retrieval task (neglecting the added benefit of locating the specific passages). Adding the knowledge in the core lexicon (which includes morphological relationships, semantic subsumption axioms, and entailment relationships), but without morphological analysis of unknown words (Recall II w/o morph), significantly improves these results (from 42.9% to 50.0%). Further adding the morphological analysis capability that automatically analyzes unknown words (deriving additional morphological relationships and some semantic subsumption relationships) significantly improves that result (from 50.0% to 60.7%). In contrast, we found that adding the same semantic subsumption relationships to the commercial search engine, using its provided thesaurus capability degraded its results, and results were still degraded when we added only those facts that we knew would help find relevant documents. It turned out that the additional relevant documents found were more than offset by additional irrelevant documents that were also ranked more highly.

6 Anecdotal Evaluation of Specific Passage Retrieval Benefits

As mentioned above, comparing the relaxation-ranking algorithm with document retrieval systems measures only a part of the benefit of the specific passage retrieval methodology. Fully evaluating the quality and ranking of the retrieved passages involves a great many subtleties. However, two informal evaluations have been conducted that shed some light on the benefits.

The first of these was a pilot study of the technology at a telecommunications company. In that study, one user found that she could use a single query to the conceptual indexing system to find both of the items of information necessary to complete a task that formerly required searching two separate databases. The conclusion of that study was that the concept retrieval technology performs well enough to be useful to a person talking live with a customer. It was observed that the returned hits can be compared with one another easily and quickly by eye, and attention is taken directly to the relevant content of a large document. The automatic indexing was considered a plus compared with manual methods of content indexing. It was observed that an area of great potential may be in a form of knowledge management that involves organizing and providing intelligent access to small, unrelated "nuggets" of textual knowledge that are not amenable to conventional database archival or categorization.

A second experiment was conducted by the Human Resources Webmaster of a high-tech company, an experienced user of search engines who used this technology to index his company's internal HR web site. He then measured the time it took him to process 15 typical HR requests, first using conventional search tools that he had available, and then using the Conceptual Indexing technology. In both cases, he measured the time it took him to either find the answer or to conclude that the answer wasn't in the indexed material. His measured times for the total suite were 55 minutes using the conventional tools and 11 minutes using the conceptual indexing technology. Of course, this was an uncontrolled experiment, and there is some potential that information learned from searching with the traditional tools (which were apparently used first) might have provided some benefit when using the conceptual indexing technology. However, the fact that he found things with the latter that he did not find with the former and the magnitude of the time difference suggests that there is an effect, albeit perhaps not as great as the measurements. As a result of this experience, he concluded that he would expect many users to take much longer to find materials or give up, when using the traditional tools. He anticipated that after finding some initial materials, more time would be required, as users would end up having to call people for additional information. He estimated that users could spend up to an hour trying to get the information they needed...having to call someone, wait to make contact and finally get the information they needed. Using the conceptual indexing search engine, he expected that these times would be at least halved.

7 Conclusion

We have described some experiments using linguistic knowledge in an information retrieval system in which passages within texts are dynamically found in response to a query and are scored and ranked based on a relaxation of constraints. This is a different approach from previous methods of passage retrieval and from previous attempts to use linguistic knowledge in information retrieval. These experiments show that linguistic knowledge can significantly improve information retrieval performance when incorporated into a knowledge-based relaxation-ranking algorithm for specific passage retrieval.

The linguistic knowledge considered here includes the use of morphological relationships between words, taxonomic relationships between concepts, and general semantic entailment relationships between words and concepts. We have shown that the combination of these three knowledge sources can significantly improve performance in finding appropriate answers to specific queries when incorporated into a relaxation-ranking algorithm. It appears that the penalty-based relaxation-ranking algorithm figures crucially in this success, since the addition of such linguistic knowledge to traditional information retrieval models typically degrades retrieval performance rather than improving it, a pattern that was borne out in our own experiments.

Acknowledgments

Many other people have been involved in creating the conceptual indexing and retrieval system described here. These include: Gary Adams, Jacek Ambroziak, Cookie Callahan, Chris Colby, Jim Flowers, Ellen Hays, Patrick Martin, Peter Norvig, Tony Passera, Philip Resnik, Robert Sproull, and Mark Torrance.

References

Jacek Ambroziak and William A. Woods. 1998. Natural language technology in precision content retrieval. In *International Conference on Natural Language Processing and Industrial Applications*, Moncton, New Brunswick, Canada, August. www.sun.com/research/techrep/1998/abstract-69.html.

Jamie P. Callan. 1994. Passage-level evidence in document retrieval. *SIGIR*, pages 302–309.

J. L. Fagan. 1989. The effectiveness of a nonsyntactic approach to automatic phrase indexing for document retrieval. *Journal of the American Society for Information Science*, 40(2):115–132, March.

Marcin Kaszkiel and Justin Zobel. 1997. Passage retrieval revisited. *SIGIR*, pages 302–309.

David D. Lewis and Karen Sparck Jones. 1996. Natural language processing for information retrieval. *CACM*, 39(1):92–101.

Rila Mandala, Takenobu Tokunaga, and Hozumi Tanaka. 1999. Combining multiple evidence from different types of thesaurus for query expansion. In *Proceedings on the 22nd annual international ACM SIGIR conference on Research and development in information retrieval.* ACM-SIGIR.

Gerald Salton, James Allan, and Chris Buckley. 1993. Approaches to passage retrieval in full text information systems. *SIGIR*, pages 49–58.

Gerard Salton. 1989. *Automatic Text Processing.* Addison Wesley, Reading, MA.

Karen Sparck Jones. 1998. A look back and a look forward. *SIGIR*, pages 13–29.

Giovanni Varile and Antonio Zampolli, editors. 1997. *Survey of the State of the Art in Human Language Technology.* Cambridge Univ. Press.

Ellen M. Voorhees. 1993. Using wordnet to disambiguate word senses for text retrieval. In *Proceedings of 16th ACM SIGIR Conference.* ACM-SIGIR.

William A. Woods. 1991. Understanding subsumption and taxonomy: A framework for progress. In John Sowa, editor, *Principles of Semantic*

Networks: Explorations in the Representation of Knowledge, pages 45–94. Morgan Kaufmann, San Mateo, CA.

William A. Woods. 1997. Conceptual indexing: A better way to organize knowledge. Technical Report SMLI TR-97-61, Sun Microsystems Laboratories, Mountain View, CA, April. www.sun.com/research/techrep/1997/abstract-61.html.

William A. Woods. 2000. Aggressive morphology for robust lexical coverage. In *(these proceedings)*.

Domain-Specific Knowledge Acquisition from Text

Dan Moldovan, Roxana Girju and Vasile Rus
Department of Computer Science and Engineering
University of Southern Methodist University
Dallas, Texas, 75275-0122
{*moldovan, roxana, rus*}*@seas.smu.edu*

Abstract

In many knowledge intensive applications, it is necessary to have extensive domain-specific knowledge in addition to general-purpose knowledge bases. This paper presents a methodology for discovering domain-specific concepts and relationships in an attempt to extend WordNet. The method was tested on five seed concepts selected from the financial domain: *interest rate*, *stock market*, *inflation*, *economic growth*, and *employment*.

1 Desiderata for Automated Knowledge Acquisition

The need for knowledge

The knowledge is infinite and no matter how large a knowledge base is, it is not possible to store all the concepts and procedures for all domains. Even if that were possible, the knowledge is generative and there are no guarantees that a system will have the latest information all the time. And yet, if we are to build common-sense knowledge processing systems in the future, it is necessary to have general-purpose and domain-specific knowledge that is up to date. Our inability to build large knowledge bases without much effort has impeded many ANLP developments.

The most successful current Information Extraction systems rely on hand coded linguistic rules representing lexico-syntactic patterns capable of matching natural language expressions of events. Since the rules are hand-coded it is difficult to port systems across domains. Question answering, inference, summarization, and other applications can benefit from large linguistic knowledge bases.

The basic idea

A possible solution to the problem of rapid development of flexible knowledge bases is to design an automatic knowledge acquisition system that extracts knowledge from texts for the purpose of merging it with a core ontological knowledge base. The attempt to create a knowledge base manually is time consuming and error prone, even for small application domains, and we believe that automatic knowledge acquisition and classification is the only viable solution to large-scale, knowledge intensive applications.

This paper presents an interactive method that acquires new concepts and connections associated with user-selected *seed* concepts, and adds them to the WordNet linguistic knowledge structure (Fellbaum 1998). The sources of the new knowledge are texts acquired from the Internet or other corpora. At the present time, our system works in a semi-automatic mode, in the sense that it acquires concepts and relations automatically, but their validation is done by the user.

We believe that domain knowledge should not be acquired in a vacuum; it should expand an existent ontology with a skeletal structure built on consistent and acceptable principles. The method presented in this paper is applicable to any Machine Readable Dictionary. However, we chose WordNet because it is freely available and widely used.

Related work

This work was inspired in part by Marti Hearst's paper (Hearst 1998) where she discovers manually lexico-syntactic patterns for the HYPERNYMY relation in WordNet.

Much of the work in pattern extraction from texts was done for improving the performance of Information Extraction systems. Research in this area was done by (Kim and Moldovan 1995) (Riloff 1996), (Soderland 1997) and others.

The MindNet (Richardson 1998) project at Microsoft is an attempt to transform the Longman Dictionary of Contemporary English (LDOCE) into a form of knowledge base for text processing.

Woods studied knowledge representation and classification for long time (Woods 1991), and more recently is trying to automate the construction of taxonomies by extracting concepts directly from texts (Woods 1997).

The Knowledge Acquisition from Text (KAT) system is presented next. It consists of four parts: (1) discovery of new concepts, (2) discovery of new lexical patterns, (3) discovery of new relationships reflected by the lexical patterns, and (4) the classification and integration of the knowledge discovered with a WordNet - like knowledge base.

2 KAT System

2.1 Discover new concepts

Select seed concepts. New domain knowledge can be acquired around some seed concepts that a user considers important. In this paper we focus on the financial domain, and use: *interest rate*, *stock market*, *inflation*, *economic growth*, and *employment* as seed concepts. The knowledge we seek to acquire relates to one or more of these concepts, and consists of new concepts not defined in WordNet and new relations that link these concepts with other concepts, some of which are in WordNet.

For example, from the sentence: *When the US economy enters a boom, mortgage interest rates rise,* the system discovers: (1) the new concept *mortgage interest rate* not defined in WordNet but related to the seed concept *interest rate*, and (2) the state of the *US economy* and the value of *mortgage interest rate* are in a DIRECT RELATIONSHIP.

In WordNet, a concept is represented as a synset that contains words sharing the same meaning. In our experiments, we extend the seed words to their corresponding synset. For example, *stock market* is synonym with *stock exchange* and *securities market*, and we aim to learn concepts related to all these terms, not only to *stock market*.

Extract sentences. Queries are formed with each seed concept to extract documents from the Internet and other possible sources. The documents retrieved are further processed such that only the sentences that contain the seed concepts are retained. This way, an arbitrarily large corpus $\mathcal{A}$ is formed of sentences containing the seed concepts. We limit the size of this corpus to 1000 sentences per seed concept.

Parse sentences. Each sentence in this corpus is first part-of-speech (POS) tagged then parsed. We use Brill's POS tagger and our own parser. The output of the POS tagger for the example above is: *When*/WRB *the*/DT *U.S.*/NNP *economy*/NN *enters*/VBZ *a*/DT *boom*/NN ,/, *mortgage*/NN *interest_rates*/NNS *rise*/VBP ./.

The syntactic parser output is:
TOP (S (SBAR (WHADVP (WRB *When*)) (S (NP (DT *the*) (NNP *U.S.*) (NN *economy*)) (VP (VBZ *enters*) (NP (DT *a*) (NN *boom*) (, ,))))) (NP (NN *mortgage*) (NNS *interest_rates*)) (VP (VBP *rise*)))

Extract new concepts. In this paper only noun concepts are considered. Since, most likely, one-word nouns are already defined in WordNet, the focus here is on *compound nouns* and *nouns with modifiers* that have meaning but are not in WordNet.

The new concepts directly related to the seeds are extracted from the noun phrases (NPs) that contain the seeds. In the example above, we see that the seed belongs to the NP: *mortgage interest rate.*

This way, a list of NPs containing the seeds is assembled automatically from the parsed texts. Every such NP is considered a potential new concept. This is only the "raw material" from which actual concepts are discovered.

In some noun phrases the seed is the head noun, i.e. [*word, word,..seed*], where *word* can be a noun or an adjective. For example, [*interest rate*] is in WordNet, but [*short term nominal interest rate*] is not in WordNet. Most of the new concepts related to a seed are generated this way. In other cases the seed is not the head noun i.e. [*word, word,..seed, word, word*]. For example [*interest rate peg*], or [*international interest rate differential*].

The following procedures are used to discover concepts, and are applicable in both cases:

Procedure 1.1. *WordNet reduction.* Search NP for words collocations that are defined in WordNet as concepts. Thus [*long term interest rate*] becomes [*long_term interest_rate*], [*prime interest rate*] becomes [*prime_interest_rate*], as all hyphenated concepts are in WordNet.

Procedure 1.2. *Dictionary reduction.* For each NP, search further in other on-line dictionaries for more compound concepts, and if found, hyphenate the words. Many domain-specific dictionaries are available on-line. For example, [*mortgage interest_rate*] becomes *[mortgage_interest_rate]*, since it is defined in the on-line dictionary *OneLook Dictionaries* (http://www.onelook.com).

Procedure 1.3. *User validation.* Since currently we lack a formal definition of a concept, it is not possible to completely automate the discovery of concepts. The human inspects the list of noun phrases and decides whether to accept or decline each concept.

2.2 Discover lexico-syntactic patterns

Texts represent a rich source of information from which in addition to concepts we can also discover relations between concepts. We are interested in discovering semantic relationships that link the concepts extracted above with other concepts, some of which may be in WordNet. The approach is to search for lexico-syntactic patterns comprising the concepts of interest. The semantic relations from WordNet are the first we search for, as it is only natural to add more of these relations to enhance the WordNet knowledge base. However, since the focus is on the acquisition of domain-specific knowledge, there are semantic relations between concepts other than the WordNet relations that are important. These new relations can be discovered automatically from the clauses and sentences in which the seeds occur.

Pick a semantic relation R. These can be WordNet semantic relations or any other relations defined by the user. So far, we have experimented with the WordNet HYPERNYMY (or so-called IS-A) relation, and three other relations. By inspecting a few sentences containing *interest rate* one can notice that INFLUENCE is a frequently used relation. The two other relations are CAUSE and EQUIVALENT.

Pick a pair of concepts C_i, C_j among which R holds. These may be any noun concepts. In the context of finance domain, some examples of concepts linked by the INFLUENCE relation are:
interest rate INFLUENCES *earnings*, or
credit worthiness INFLUENCES *interest rate*.

Extract lexico-syntactic patterns C_i $\mathcal{P}$ C_j. Search any corpus $\mathcal{B}$, different from $\mathcal{A}$ for all instances where C_i and C_j occur in the same sentence. Extract the lexico-syntactic patterns that link the two concepts. For example, from the sentence : *The graph indicates the impact on earnings from several different interest rate scenarios*, the generally applicable pattern extracted is:
impact on NP2 from NP1
This pattern corresponds unambiguously to the relation R we started with, namely INFLUENCE. Thus we conclude: INFLUENCE(NP1, NP2).

Another example is: *As the credit worthiness decreases, the interest rate increases.* From this sentence we extract another lexical pattern that expresses the INFLUENCE relation:
[as NP1 vb1, NP2 vb2] & *[vb1 and vb2 are antonyms]*
This pattern is rather complex since it contains not only the lexical part but also the verb condition that needs to be satisfied.

This procedure repeats for all relations R.

2.3 Discover new relationships between concepts

Let us denote with C_s the seed-related concepts found with Procedures 1.1 through 1.3. We search now corpus $\mathcal{A}$ for the occurrence of patterns $\mathcal{P}$ discovered above such that one of their two concepts is a concept C_s.

Search corpus $\mathcal{A}$ for a pattern $\mathcal{P}$. Using a lexico-syntactic pattern $\mathcal{P}$, one at a time, search corpus $\mathcal{A}$ for its occurrence. If found, search further whether or not one of the NPs is a seed-related concept C_s.

Identify new concepts C_n. Part of the pattern $\mathcal{P}$ are two noun phrases, one of which is C_s. The head noun from the other noun phrase is a concept C_n we are looking for. This may be a WordNet concept, and if it is not it will be added to the list of concepts discovered.

Form relation $R(C_s, C_n)$. Since each pattern $\mathcal{P}$ is a linguistic expression of its corresponding semantic relation R, we conclude $R(C_s, C_n)$ (this is interpreted "C_s is relation R C_n)"). These steps are repeated for all patterns.

User intervention to accept or reject relationships is necessary mainly due to our system inability of handling coreference resolution and other complex linguistic phenomena.

2.4 Knowledge classification and integration

Next, a taxonomy needs to be created that is consistent with WordNet. In addition to creating a taxonomy, this step is also useful for validating the concepts acquired above. The classification is based on the *subsumption* principle (Schmolze and Lipkis 1983), (Woods 1991).

This algorithm provides the overall steps for the classification of concepts within the context of WordNet. Figure 1 shows the inputs of the Classification Algorithm and suggests that the classification is an iterative process. In addition to WordNet, the inputs consist of the corpus $\mathcal{A}$, the sets of concepts $\mathbf{C}_s$ and $\mathbf{C}_n$, and the relationships $\mathcal{R}$. Let's denote with $\mathbf{C} = \mathbf{C}_s \cup \mathbf{C}_n$ the union of the seed related concepts with the new concepts. All these concepts need to be classified.

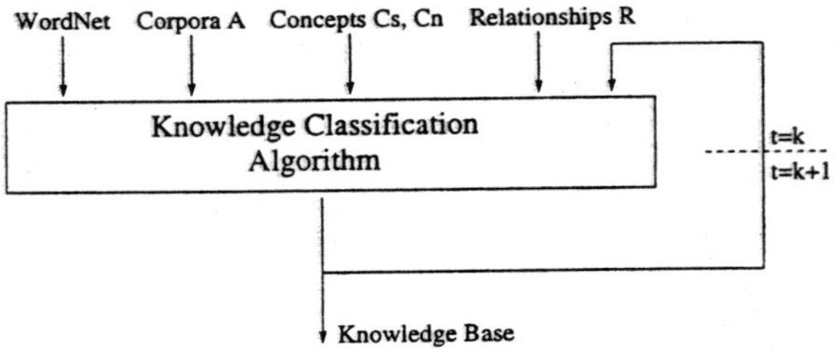

Figure 1: The knowledge classification diagram

Step 1. From the set of relationships $\mathcal{R}$ discovered in Part 3, pick all the HYPERNYMY relations. From the way these relations were developed, there are two possibilities:
(1) A HYPERNYMY relation links a WordNet concept C_w with another concept from the set $\mathbf{C}$ denoted with C^1_{hw}, or
(2) A HYPERNYMY relation links a concept $\mathbf{C}_s$ with a concept $\mathbf{C}_n$.

Concepts C^1_{hw} are immediately linked to WordNet and added to the knowledge base. The concepts from case (2) are also added to the knowledge base but they form at this point only some isolated islands since are not yet linked to the rest of the knowledge base.

Step 2. Search corpus $\mathcal{A}$ for all the patterns associated with the HYPERNYMY relation that may link

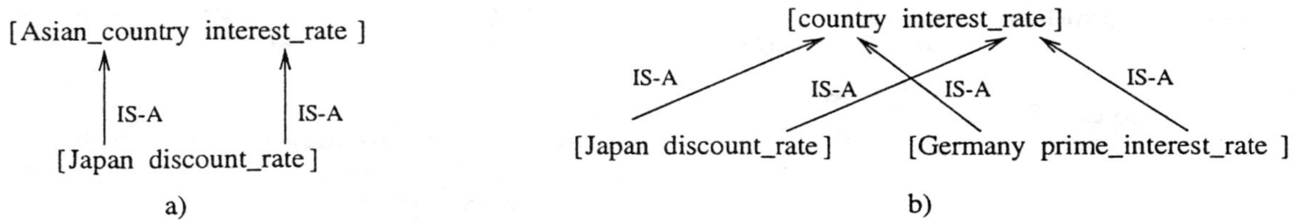

Figure 2: Relative classification of two concepts

concepts in the set $\mathbf{C}_n$ with any WordNet concepts. Altough concepts $\mathbf{C}_n$ are not seed-based concepts, they are related to at least one $\mathbf{C}_s$ concept via a relationship (as found in Task 3). Here we seek to find HYPERNYMY links between them and WordNet concepts. If such $\mathbf{C}_n$ concepts exist, denote them with $\mathbf{C}^2_{hw}$. The union $\mathbf{C}_{hw} = \mathbf{C}^1_{hw} \cup \mathbf{C}^2_{hw}$ represents all concepts from the set $\mathbf{C}$ that are linked to WordNet without any further effort. We focus now on the rest of concepts, $\mathbf{C}_c = \mathbf{C} \cap \overline{\mathbf{C}}_{hw}$, that are not yet linked to any WordNet concepts.

Step 3. Classify all concepts in set $\mathbf{C}_c$ using Procedures 4.1 through 4.5 below.

Step 4. Repeat Step 3 for all the concepts in set $\mathbf{C}_c$ several times till no more changes occur. This reclassification is necessary since the insertion of a concept into the knowledge base may perturb the ordering of other surrounding concepts in the hierarchy.

Step 5. Add the rest of relationships $\mathcal{R}$ other than the HYPERNYMY to the new knowledge base. The HYPERNYMY relations have already been used in the Classification Algorithm, but the other relations, i.e. INFLUENCE, CAUSE and EQUIVALENT need to be added to the knowledge base.

Concept classification procedures

Procedure 4.1. *Classify a concept of the form [word, head] with respect to concept [head].*
It is assumed here that the [head] concept exists in WordNet simply because in many instances the "head" is the "seed" concept, and because frequently the head is a single word common noun usually defined in WordNet. In this procedure we consider only those head nouns that do not have any hyponyms since the other case when the head has other concepts under it is more complex and is treated by Procedure 4.4. Here "word" is a noun or an adjective.

The classification is based on the simple idea that a compound concept [word, head] is ontologically subsumed by concept [head]. For example, *mortgage_interest_rate* is a kind of *interest_rate*, thus linked by a relation HYPERNYMY(interest_rate, mortgage_interest_rate).

Procedure 4.2. *Classify a concept [$word_1$, $head_1$] with respect to another concept [$word_2$, $head_2$].*
For a relative classification of two such concepts, the ontological relations between $head_1$ and $head_2$ and between $word_1$ and $word_2$, if exist, are extended to the two concepts. We distinguish here three possibilities:

1. $head_1$ subsumes $head_2$ and $word_1$ subsumes $word_2$. In this case [$word_1$, $head_1$] subsumes [$word_2$, $head_2$]. The subsumption may not always be a direct connection; sometimes it may consist of a chain of subsumption relations since subsumption is (usually) a transitive relation (Woods 1991). An example is shown in Figure 2a; in WordNet, *Asian_country* subsumes *Japan* and *interest_rate* subsumes *discount_rate*. A particular case of this is when $head_1$ is identical with $head_2$.
2. Another case is when there is no direct subsumption relation in WordNet between $word_1$ and $word_2$, and/or $head_1$ and $head_2$, but there are a common subsuming concepts, for each pair. When such concepts are found, pick the most specific common subsumer (MSCS) concepts of $word_1$ and $word_2$, and of $head_1$ and $head_2$, respectively. Then form a concept [MSCS($word_1$, $word_2$), MSCS($head_1$, $head_2$)] and place [$word_1$ $head_1$] and [$word_2$ $head_2$] under it. This is exemplified in Figure 2b. In WordNet, *country* subsumes *Japan* and *Germany*, and *interest_rate* subsumes *discount_rate* and *prime_interest_rate*.
3. In all other cases, no subsumption relation is established between the two concepts. For example, we cannot say whether *Asian_country discount_rate* is more or less abstract then *Japan interest_rate*.

Procedure 4.3. *Classify concept [$word_1$ $word_2$ head].*
Several possibilities exist:

1. When there is already a concept [$word_2$ head] in the knowledge base under the [head], then place [$word_1$ $word_2$ head] under concept [$word_2$ head].
2. When there is already a concept [$word_1$ head] in the knowledge base under the [head], then place [$word_1$ $word_2$ head] under concept [$word_1$ head].
3. When both cases 1 and 2 are true then place [$word_1$ $word_2$ head] under both concepts.

4. When neither [word_1 head] nor [word_2 head] are in the knowledge base, then place [word_1 word_2 head] under the [head]. The example in Figure 3 corresponds to case 3.

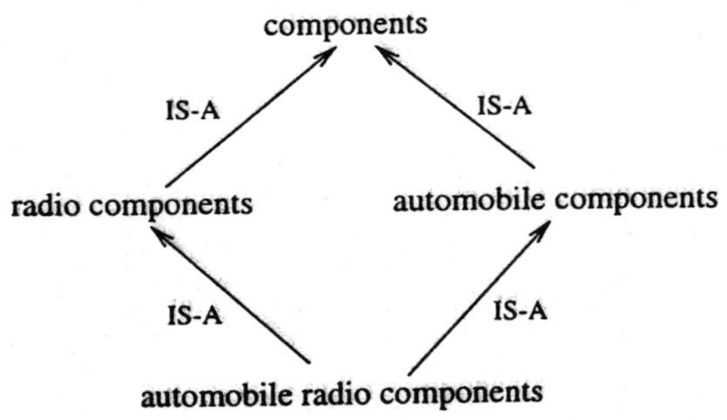

Figure 3: **Classification of a compound concept with respect to its HYPERNYM concepts**

Since we do not deal here with the sentence semantics, it is not possible to completely determine the meaning of [word_1 word_2 head], as it may be either [((word_1 word_2) head)] or [(word_1 (word_2 head))] often depending on the sentence context.

In the example of Figure 3 there is only one meaning, i.e. [*(automobile radio) components*]. However, in the case of [*performance skiing equipment*] there are two valid interpretations, namely [*(performance skiing) equipment*] and [*performance (skiing equipment)*].

Procedure 4.4 *Classify a concept [word_1, head] with respect to a concept hierarchy under the [head].*
The task here is to identify the most specific subsumer (MSS) from all the concepts under the head that subsumes [word_1, head]. By default, [word_1 head] is placed under [head], however, since it may be more specific than other hyponyms of [head], a more complex classification analysis needs to be implemented.

In the previous work on knowledge classification it was assumed that the concepts were accompanied by rolesets and values (Schmolze and Lipkis 1983), (Woods 1991), and others. Knowledge classifiers are part of almost any knowledge representation system.

However, the problem we face here is more difficult. While in build-by-hand knowledge representation systems, the relations and values defining concepts are readily available, here we have to extract them from text. Fortunately, one can take advantage of the glossary definitions that are associated with concepts in WordNet and other dictionaries. One approach is to identify a set of semantic relations into which the verbs used in the gloss definitions are mapped into for the purpose of working with a manageable set of relations that may describe the concepts restrictions. In WordNet these basic relations are already identified and it is easy to map every verb into such a semantic relation.

As far as the newly discovered concepts are concerned, their defining relations need to be retrieved from texts. Human assistance is required, at least for now, to pinpoint the most characteristic relations that define a concept.

Below is a two step algorithm that we envision for the relative classification of two concepts A and B. Let's us denote with AR_aC_a and BR_bC_b the relationships that define concepts A and B respectively. These are similar to rolesets and values.

1. Extract relations (denoted by verbs) between concept and other gloss concepts.
   $AR_{a1}C_{a1}$ $\quad BR_{b1}C_{b1}$
   $AR_{a2}C_{a2}$ $\quad BR_{b2}C_{b2}$
   ...
   $AR_{am}C_{am}$ $\quad BR_{bn}C_{bn}$
2. A subsumes B if and only if
   (a) Relations R_{ai} subsume R_{bi}, for $1 \leq i \leq m$.
   (b) C_{ai} subsumes or is a meronym of C_{bi}.
   (c) Concept B has more relations than concept A, i.e. $m \leq n$.

Example: In Figure 4 it is shown the classification of concept *monetary policy* that has been discovered. By default this concept is placed under *policy*. However in WordNet there is a hierarchy *fiscal policy* - IS-A - *economic policy* - IS-A - *policy*. The question is where exactly to place *monetary policy* in this hierarchy.

The gloss of *economic policy* indicates that it is MADE BY *Government*, and that it CONTROLS *economic growth* - (here we simplified the explanation and used *economy* instead of *economic growth*). The gloss of *fiscal policy* leads to relations MADE BY *Government*, CONTROLS *budget*, and CONTROLS *taxation*. The concept *money supply* was found by Procedure 1.2 in several dictionaries, and its dictionary definition leads to relations MADE BY *Federal Government*, and CONTROLS *money supply*. In WordNet *Government* subsumes *Federal Government*, and *economy* HAS PART *money*. All necessary conditions are satisfied for *economic policy* to subsume *monetary policy*. However, *fiscal policy* does not subsume *monetary policy* since *monetary policy* does not control *budget* or *taxation*, or any of their hyponyms.

Procedure 4.5 *Merge a structure of concepts with the rest of the knowledge base.*
It is possible that structures consisting of several inter-connected concepts are formed in isolation of the main knowledge base as a result of some procedures. The task here is to merge such structures with the main knowledge base such that the new knowledge base will be consistent with both the structure and the main knowledge base. This is done by

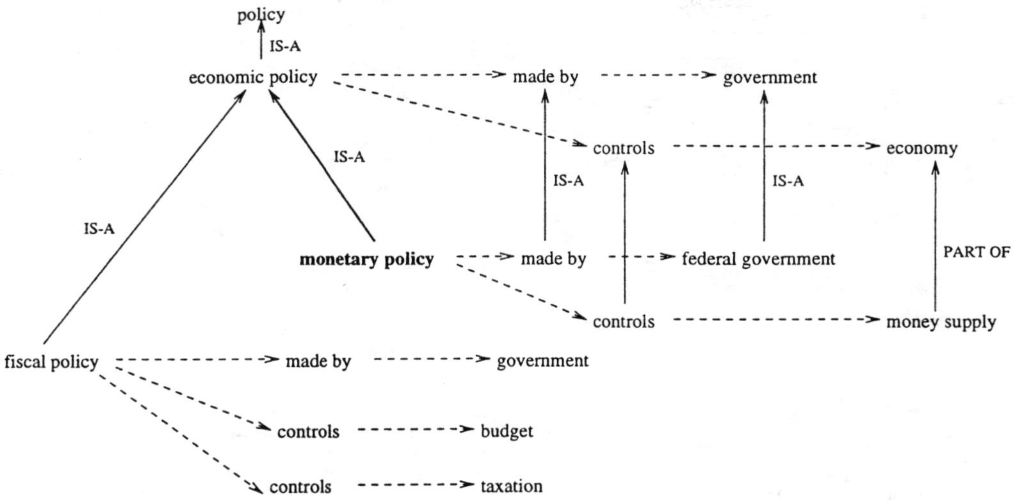

Figure 4: Classification of the new concept *monetary policy*

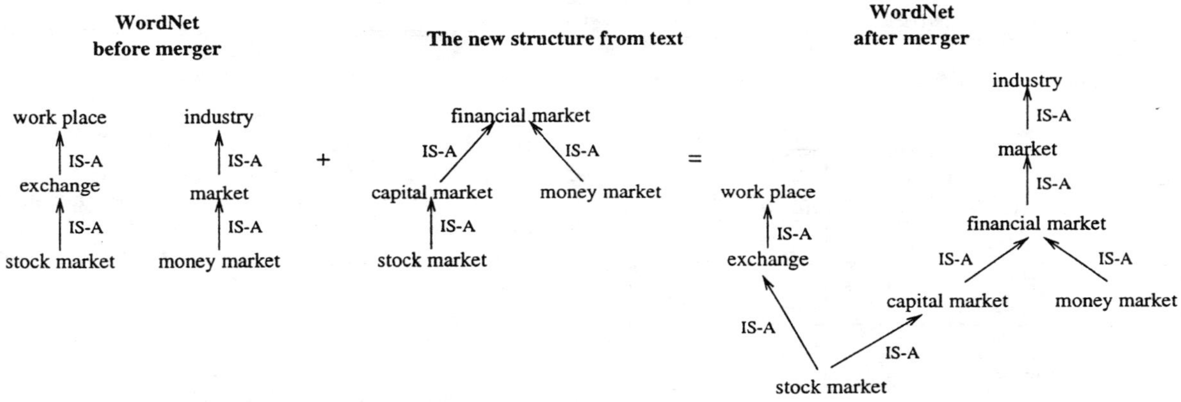

Figure 5: Merging a structure of concepts with WordNet

bridging whenever possible the structure concepts and the main knowledge base concepts. It is possible that as a result of this merging procedure, some HYPERNYMY relations either from the structure or the main knowledge base will be destroyed to keep the consistency. An example is shown in Figure 5.

Example : The following HYPERNYMY relationships were discovered in Part 3:
HYPERNYMY(financial market,capital market)
HYPERNYMY(financial market,money market)
HYPERNYMY(capital market,stock market)
The structure obtained from these relationships along with a part of WordNet hierarchy is shown in Figure 5. An attempt is made to merge the new structure with WordNet. To these relations it corresponds a structure as shown in Figure 5. An attempt is made to merge this structure with WordNet. Searching WordNet for all concepts in the structure we find *money market* and *stock market* in WordNet where as *capital market* and *financial market* are not. Figure 5 shows how the structure merges with WordNet and moreover how concepts that were unrelated in WordNet (i.e. *stock market* and *money market*) become connected through the new structure. It is also interesting to notice that the IS-A link in WordNet from *money market* to *market* is interrupted by the insertion of *financial market* in-between them.

3 Implementation and Results

The KAT Algorithm has been implemented, and when given some seed concepts, it produces new concepts, patterns and relationships between concepts in an interactive mode. Table 1 shows the number of concepts extracted from a 5000 sentence corpus, in which each sentence contains at least one of the five seed concepts.

The NPs were automatically searched in WordNet and other on-line dictionaries. There were 3745 distinct noun phrases of interest extracted; the rest contained only the seeds or repetitions. Most of the

Relations	Lexico-syntactic Patterns	Examples
		WordNet Relations
HYPERNYMY	NP1 [<be>] a kind of NP2 ⇒ HYPERNYMY(NP1,NP2)	Thus, *LIBOR* is a kind of *interest rate*, as it is charged on deposits between banks in the Eurodolar market.
		New Relations
CAUSE	NP1 [<be>] cause NP2 ⇒ CAUSE(NP1,NP2)	Phillips, a British economist, stated in 1958 that high *inflation* causes low *unemployment rates*.
INFLUENCE	NP1 impact on NP2 ⇒ INFLUENCE(NP1,NP2)	The Bank of Israel governor said that the *tight economic policy* would have an immediate impact on *inflation* this year.
	As NP1 vb, so <do> NP2 ⇒ INFLUENCE(NP1,NP2)	As the *economy* picks up steam, so does *inflation*.
	NP1 <be> associated with NP2 ⇒ INFLUENCE(NP1,NP2) INFLUENCE(NP2,NP1)	Higher *interest rates* are normally associated with weaker *bond markets*.
	As/if/when NP1 vb1, NP2 vb2. + vb1, vb2 = antonyms / go in opposite directions ⇒ INFLUENCE(NP1,NP2)	On the other hand, if *interest rates* go down, *bonds* go up, and your bond becomes more valuable.
	the effect(s) of NP1 on/upon NP2 ⇒ INFLUENCE(NP1,NP2)	The effects of *inflation* on *debtors* and *creditors* varies as the actual inflation is compared to the expected one.
	inverse relationship between NP1 and NP2 ⇒ INFLUENCE(NP1,NP2) ⇒ INFLUENCE(NP2,NP1)	There exists an inverse relationship between *unemployment rates* and *inflation*, best illustrated by the Phillips Curve.
	NP2 <be> function of NP1 ⇒ INFLUENCE(NP1,NP2)	*Irish employment* is also largely a function of the past high *birth rate*.
	NP1 (and thus NP2) ⇒ INFLUENCE(NP1,NP2)	We believe that the *Treasury bonds* (and thus *interest rates*) are in a downward cycle.

Table 2: Examples of lexico-syntactic patterns and semantic relations derived from the 5000 sentence corpus

		a	b	c	d	e
Total potential concepts (NPs)		773	382	833	921	836
Total concepts extracted with Procedure1						
Concepts found in WordNet		2	0	1	0	2
Concepts found in on-line dictionaries, but not in WordNet	Concepts with seed head	6	0	3	0	0
	Concepts with seed not head	7	0	1	1	1
Concepts accepted by human		78	62	58	60	37

Table 1: Results showing the number of new concepts learned from the corpus related to (a) *interest rate*, (b) *stock market*, (c) *inflation*, (d) *economic growth*, and (e) *employment*.

processing in Part 1 is taken by the parser. The human intervention to accept or decline concepts takes about 4 min./seed.

The next step was to search for lexico-syntactic patterns. We considered one WordNet semantic relation, HYPERNYMY and three other relations that we found relevant for the domain, namely INFLUENCE, CAUSE and EQUIVALENT. For each relation, a pair of related words was selected and searched for on the Internet. The first 500 sentences/relation were retained. A human selected and validated semi-automatically the patterns for each sentence. A sample of the results is shown in Table 2. A total of 22 patterns were obtained and their selection and validation took approximately 35 minutes/relation.

Next, the patterns are searched for on the 5000 sentence corpus (Part 3). The procedure provided a total of 43 new concepts and 166 relationships in which at least one of the seeds occurred. From these relationships, by inspection, we have accepted 63 and rejected 102, procedure which took about 7 minutes. Table 3 lists some of the 63 relationships discovered.

Relationships Examples
HYPERNYMY(interest rate, LIBOR)
HYPERNYMY(leading stock market, New York Stock Exchange)
HYPERNYMY(market risks, interest rate risk)
HYPERNYMY(capital markets, stock markets)
CAUSE(inflation, unemployment)
CAUSE(labour shortage, wage inflation)
CAUSE(excessive demand, inflation)
INFLUENCE_DIRECT_PROPORTIONALY(economy, inflation)
INFLUENCE_DIRECT_PROPORTIONALY(settlements, interest rate)
INFLUENCE_DIRECT_PROPORTIONALY(U.S. interest rates, dollars)
INFLUENCE_DIRECT_PROPORTIONALY(oil prices, inflation)
INFLUENCE_DIRECT_PROPORTIONALY(inflation, nominal interest rates)
INFLUENCE_DIRECT_PROPORTIONALY(deflation, real interest rates)
INFLUENCE_DIRECT_PROPORTIONALY(currencies,inflation)
INFLUENCE_INVERSE_PROPORTIONALY(unemployment rates, inflation)
INFLUENCE_INVERSE_PROPORTIONALY(monetary policies, inflation)
INFLUENCE_INVERSE_PROPORTIONALY(economy, interest rates)
INFLUENCE_INVERSE_PROPORTIONALY(inflation, unemployment rates)
INFLUENCE_INVERSE_PROPORTIONALY(credit worthiness, interest rate)
INFLUENCE_INVERSE_PROPORTIONALY(interest rates, bonds)
INFLUENCE(Internal Revenue Service, interest rates)
INFLUENCE(economic growth, share prices)
EQUIVALENT(big mistakes, high inflation rates of 1970s)
EQUIVALENT(fixed interest rate, coupon)

Table 3: A part of the relationships derived from the 5000 sentence corpus

4 Applications

An application in need of domain-specific knowledge is Question Answering. The concepts and the relationships acquired can be useful in answering difficult questions that normally cannot be easily answered just by using the information from WordNet. Consider the processing of the following questions after the new domain knowledge has been acquired:

Q1: What factors have an impact on the *interest rate*?

Q2: What happens with the *employment* when the *economic growth* rises?

Q3: How does *deflation* influence *prices*?

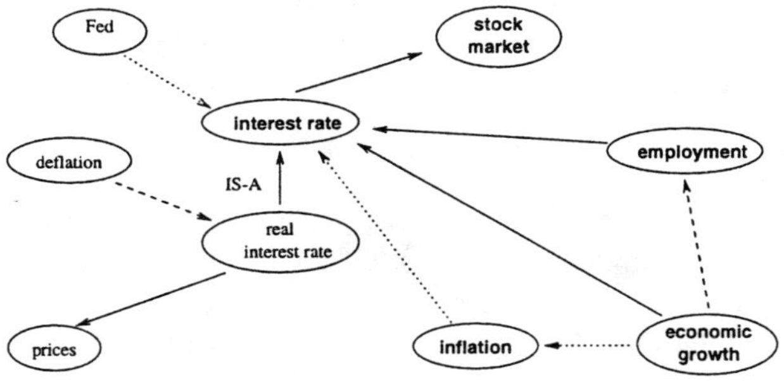

Figure 6: A sample of concepts and relations acquired from the 5000 sentence corpus. Legend: continue lines represent *influence inverse proportionally*, dashed lines represent *influence direct proportionally*, and dotted lines represent *influence* (the direction of the relationship was not specified in the text).

Figure 6 shows a portion of the new domain knowledge that is relevant to these questions. The first question can be easily answered by extracting the relationships that point to the concept *interest rate*. The factors that influence the *interest rate* are *Fed, inflation, economic growth*, and *employment*.

The last two questions ask for more detailed information about the complex relationship among these concepts. Following the path from the *deflation* concept up to *prices*, the system learns that *deflation* influences direct proportionally *real interest rate*, and *real interest rate* has an inverse proportional impact on *prices*. Both these relationships came from the sentence: *Thus, the deflation and the real interest rate are positively correlated, and so a higher real interest rate leads to falling prices.*

This method may be adapted to acquire information when the question concepts are not in the knowledge base. Procedures may be invoked to discover these concepts and the relations in which they may be used.

5 Conclusions

The knowledge acquisition technology described above is applicable to any domain, by simply selecting appropriate seed concepts. We started with five concepts *interest rate*, *stock market*, *inflation*, *economic growth*, and *employment* and from a corpus of 5000 sentences we acquired a total of 362 concepts of which 319 contain the seeds and 43 relate to these via selected relations. There were 22 distinct lexico-syntactic patterns discovered used in 63 instances. Most importantly, the new concepts can be integrated with an existing ontology.

The method works in an interactive mode where the user accepts or declines concepts, patterns and relationships. The manual operation took on average 40 minutes per seed for the 5000 sentence corpus. KAT is useful considering that most of the knowledge base construction today is done manually.

Complex linguistic phenomena such as coreference resolution, word sense disambiguation, and others have to be dealt with in order to increase the automation of the knowledge acquisition system. Without a good handling of these problems the results are not always accurate and human intervention is necessary.

References

Christiane Fellbaum. WordNet - *An Electronic Lexical Database*, MIT Press, Cambridge, MA, 1998.

Marti Hearst. Automated Discovery of WordNet Relations. In *WordNet: An Electronic Lexical Database and Some of its Applications*, editor Fellbaum, C., MIT Press, Cambridge, MA, 1998.

J. Kim and D. Moldovan. Acquisition of Linguistic Patterns for knowledge-based information extraction. *IEEE Transactions on Knowledge and Data Engineering 7(5): pages 713-724.*

R. MacGregor. A Description Classifier for the Predicate Calculus. *Proceedings of the 12th National Conference on Artificial Intelligence* (AAAI94), pp. 213-220, 1994.

Stephen D. Richardson, William B. Dolan, Lucy Vanderwende. MindNet: acquiring and structuring semantic information from text. Proceedings of ACL-Coling 1998, pages 1098-1102.

Ellen Riloff. Automatically Generating Extraction Patterns from Untagged Text. In *Proceedings of the Thirteenth National Conference on Artificial Intelligence*, 1044-1049. The AAAI Press/MIT Press.

J.G. Schmolze and T. Lipkis. Classification in the KL-ONE knowledge representation system. *Proceedings of 8th Int'l Joint Conference on Artificial Intelligence* (IJCAI83), 1983.

S. Soderland. Learning to extract text-based information from the world wide web. In the *Proceedings of the Third International Conference on Knowledge Discovery and Data Mining (KDD-97).*

Text REtrieval Conference. http://trec.nist.gov 1999

W.A. Woods. Understanding Subsumption and Taxonomy: A Framework for Progress. In the *Principles of Semantic Networks: Explorations in the Representation of Knowledge*, Morgan Kaufmann, San Mateo, Calif. 1991, pages 45-94.

W.A. Woods. *A Better way to Organize Knowledge.* Technical Report of Sun Microsystems Inc., 1997.

Large-scale Controlled Vocabulary Indexing for Named Entities

Mark Wasson
LEXIS-NEXIS, a Division of Reed Elsevier plc
9443 Springboro Pike
Miamisburg, Ohio 45342 USA
mark.wasson@lexis-nexis.com

Abstract

A large-scale controlled vocabulary indexing system is described. The system currently covers almost 70,000 named entity topics, and applies to documents from thousands of news publications. Topic definitions are built through substantially automated knowledge engineering.

1 Introduction

The goal of the Entity Indexing R&D program at LEXIS-NEXIS is to add controlled vocabulary indexing for named entities to searchable fields in appropriate news documents across thousands of news publications, where documents include both incoming news articles as well as news articles already in the LEXIS-NEXIS archives. A *controlled vocabulary term* (*CVT*) is a consistently specified topic indicator that users can incorporate into their queries in order to retrieve documents about the corresponding topic. When a CVT is added to an appropriate field in a document, it can be included in a Boolean query using

field-name(controlled vocabulary term)

The initial Entity Indexing release focused on companies as topics. For company indexing, the *primary CVT* is a standard form of the company name. When we add a company CVT to a document, we often also want to add *secondary CVTs* to the document that specify attributes of that company. Attributes may include the ticker symbol, SIC product codes, industry codes and company headquarters information. Secondary CVTs allow customers to easily search on groups of companies that have one or more attributes in common, such as searching for documents about banks in our set of companies that are headquartered in Utah.

It is generally easy to get high recall with Boolean queries when searching for documents about named entities. Typically the query will only need a short form of the entity's name. For example, the query

American

will retrieve virtually every document that mentions American Airlines. Of course, this query results in poor precision due to the ambiguity of *American*. The problem we wanted to address with controlled vocabulary indexing is to help online customers limit their search results to only those documents that contain a *major reference* to the topic, that is, to documents that are substantially about the topic.

Because of the volume of news data we have, it is necessary that we fully automate the document categorization and indexing step in our data preparation process. LEXIS-NEXIS adds 100,000 news articles daily to its collection of over 2 billion documents.

For marketing and product positioning reasons, we want to provide indexing for tens of thousands of companies, where companies are targeted based on their presence on the New York, American and NASDAQ exchanges or on revenue-based criteria. Although such selection criteria help us explain the product feature to customers, it does not ensure that the targeted companies actually appear all that often in the news. In fact, for many targeted companies there is little training and test data available.

Our company indexing system should address the following business product requirements:

- Assign primary and corresponding secondary CVTs to appropriate documents

- Add CVTs only to those documents that contain major references to the topic(s)
- Process documents fast; target 30,000 characters per CPU second
- Apply tens of thousands of topics to the data in a single pass
- Minimize the cost of developing and maintaining topic definitions

Also, we target 90% recall and 95% precision when using the CVTs to retrieve major reference documents about the corresponding companies.

2 Related Work

The Carnegie Group's Text Categorization Shell (TCS) (Hayes, 1992) uses shallow knowledge engineering techniques to categorize documents with respect to large sets of predefined topics. Each topic requires the development of a rule set that includes terms, contextual information, weighting, if-then rules and other pattern matching operations. This initially involved a manual, iterative approach to rule development, although Hayes (1992) discusses their intent to explore ways to automate this. TCS accuracy is quite good. One application deployed at Reuters achieved 94% recall and 84% precision. Other reported tests achieved recall and precision rates of 90% or better.

SRA's NameTag (Krupka, 1995) uses a pattern recognition process that combines a rule base with lexicons to identify and extract targeted token classes in text, such as company, people and place names. It achieved 96% recall and 97% precision when tested on Wall Street Journal news articles at MUC-6. Aone et al. (1997) describes a NameTag-based application for indexing English and Japanese language texts. NameTag addresses a key weakness of approaches that use predefined topic sets. Predefined topic sets are inherently limited in their coverage to those topics that have been explicitly defined. NameTag can recognize any number of companies or entities of other domains whose names have structure that the rules can recognize. (Not all entity domains have structure that pattern recognition processes can exploit, e.g., product names).

A problem for pattern recognition approaches has to do with our requirement to assign CVTs. Pattern recognition approaches extract patterns such as company names as they appear in the text. Limited coreference resolution may link variant forms of names with one another to support choosing the best variant as a "semi-controlled" vocabulary term, but this does not allow for the assignment of true primary and secondary CVTs. SRA has attempted to address this through its Name Resolver function, which reconciles extracted names with an authority file, but the authority file also limits scope of coverage for CVTs to those that are defined and maintained in the authority file. The system must also go beyond straight recognition in order to make a distinction between documents with major references to the targeted entities and documents with lesser or passing references. SRA's NameTag addresses this with the calculation of relevance scores for each set of linked variant forms.

Preliminary research suggests that recognizing named entities in data and queries may lead to a significant improvement in retrieval quality (Thompson & Dozier, 1999). Such an approach may complement Entity Indexing, but it does not yet meet the controlled vocabulary indexing and accuracy requirements for Entity Indexing.

Our own Term-based Topic Identification (TTI) system (Leigh, 1991) combines knowledge engineering with limited learning in support of document categorization and indexing by CVTs. We have used TTI since 1990 to support a number of topically-related news or legal document collections. Categories are defined through *topic definitions*. A definition includes terms to look up, term weights, term frequency thresholds, document selection scoring thresholds, one or more CVTs, and source-specific document structure information. Although creating TTI topic definitions is primarily an iterative, manual task, limited regression-based supervised learning tools are available to help identify functionally redundant terms, and to suggest term weights, frequency thresholds and scoring thresholds. When these tools have been used in building topic definitions, recall and precision have topped 90% in almost all tests.

3 Approach

TTI was originally proposed as a tool to support controlled vocabulary indexing, and most early tests focused on narrowly defined legal and news topics such as *insurable interest* and *earthquakes*. TTI was also tested on a number of companies, people, organizations and places as topics. TTI was first put into production to categorize documents by broadly-defined topics such as *Europe political and business news* and *federal tax law*.

When we began investigating the possibility of creating Entity Indexing, TTI was a natural starting point. It had demonstrated high accuracy and flexibility across a variety of topics and data types. Three problems were also apparent. First, TTI would not scale to support several thousand topics. Second, it took a long time to build a topic definition, about one staff day each. Third, topics were defined on a publication-specific basis. With then-700 publications in our news archives in combination with our scale goals and the time needed to build topic definitions, the definition building costs were too high. We needed to scale the technology, and we needed to substantially automate the topic definition-building process.

For Entity Indexing, we addressed scale concerns through software tuning, substantially improved memory management, a more efficient hash function in the lookup algorithm, and moving domain-specific functionality from topic definitions into the software. The rest of this paper focuses on the cost of building the definitions.

3.1 Analyzing Companies in the News

In order to reduce definition building costs, we originally believed that we would focus on increasing our reliance on TTI's training tools. Training data would have to include documents from a variety of publications if we were to be able to limit definitions to one per topic regardless of the publications covered.

Unfortunately the data did not cooperate. Using a list of all companies on the major U.S. stock exchanges, we randomly selected 89 companies for investigation. Boolean searches were used to retrieve documents that mentioned those companies. We found that several of these companies were rarely mentioned in the news. One company was not mentioned at all in our news archives, a second one was mentioned only once, and twelve were mentioned only in passing. Several appeared as major references in only a few documents. In a second investigation involving 40,000 companies from various sources, fully half appeared in zero or only one news document in one two-year window. We questioned whether we even wanted to create topic definitions for such rarely occurring companies. Again, marketing and product positioning reasons dictated that we do so: it is easier to tell customers that the product feature covers *all* companies that meet one of a few criteria than it is to give customers a list of the individual companies covered. It is also reasonable to assume that public and larger companies may appear in the news at some future point.

3.2 Company Name Usage

While analyzing news articles about these companies, we noted how company names and their variants were used. For most companies discussed in documents that contained major references to the company, some form of the full company name typically appears in the leading text. Shorter variants typically are used for subsequent mentions as well as in the headline. Corresponding ticker symbols often appear in the headline or leading text, but only after a variant of the company name appears. In some publications, ticker symbols are used as shorter variants throughout the document. Acronyms are somewhat rare; when they are used, they behave like other shorter variants of the name.

Shorter variants typically are substrings of the full company name beginning with the leftmost words in the name. For a company named

Samson Computing Supply Inc.

shorter variants might include

Samson Computing Supply
Samson Computing
Samson

Acronyms typically exist only for companies whose names consist of at least two words in addition to company designators such as *Inc.* or *Corp.* There is no consistency as to whether the company designators contribute to acronyms. Thus for the above example

SCSI
SCS

are both potential acronyms.

Generating such variants from a full form of a company name is straightforward. Similarly, rules working with a table of equivalences can handle common abbreviations, so the variant

Samson Computing Supply Incorporated

can be generated from

Samson Computing Supply Inc.

We assign weights to term variants based on term length and the presence or absence of company designators. Longer variants with designators are regarded as less ambiguous than shorter variants without designators, and thus have higher weights. A table of particularly problematic one-word variants, such as *American*, *National* and *General*, is used to make a weighting distinction between these and other one-word variants. One-word variants are also marked so they do not match lower case strings during lookup. A label is assigned to each variant to indicate its function and relative strength in the document categorization process.

3.3 Generating Topic Definitions

Our company controlled vocabulary indexing process requires definition builders to provide a primary CVT and zero or more secondary CVTs for each targeted company. The CVTs are the primary input to the automatic topic definition generation process. If the definition builder provides the company name and ticker symbol to be used as CVTs for some company, as in

#CO = Samson Computing Supply Inc.
#TS = SMCS (NYSE)

the following definition can be generated automatically:

#NAME1 = Samson Computing Supply Inc.
#NAME1 = Samson Computing Supply Incorporated
#NAME2 = Samson Computing Supply
#NAME3 = Samson Computing
#NAME4 = Samson
#TS @= SMCS {upper case only}
#ACRONYM @= SCSI {upper case only}
#ACRONYM @= SCS {upper case only}
#BLOCK @= samson {do not match lower case}

That two acronyms were generated points out a potential problem with using robust variant generation as a means to automatically build topic definitions. Overgeneration will produce some name variants that have nothing to do with the company. However, although overgeneration of variants routinely occurs, testing showed that such overgeneration has little adverse effect.

This approach to automatically generating topic definitions is successful for most companies, including those that appear rarely in our data, because most company names and their variants have consistent structure and use patterns. There are exceptions. Some companies are so well-known that they often appear in news articles without the corresponding full company name. Large companies and companies with high visibility (e.g., Microsoft, AT&T, NBC and Kmart) are among these. Other companies simply have unusual names. Our authority file is an editable text file where definition builders not only store and maintain the primary and secondary CVTs for each company, but it also allows builders to specify exception information that can be used to override any or all of the results of the automatic definition generation process. In addition, builders can use two additional labels to identify especially strong name variants (e.g., *IBM* for International Business Machines) and related terms whose presence in a document provide disambiguating context (e.g., *Delta*, *airport* and *flights* for American Airlines, often referred to only as *American*). For our initial release of 15,000 companies, 17% of the definitions had some manual intervention beyond providing primary and secondary CVTs. Entity definitions built entirely manually usually took less than thirty minutes apiece. Overall, on average less than five minutes were spent per topic on definition building. This includes the time used to identify the targeted companies and add their primary and secondary CVTs to the authority file. Populating the authority file is required regardless of the technical approach used.

3.4 Applying Definitions to Documents

All topic definitions contain a set of labeled terms to look up. The document categorization process combines these into a large lookup table. A lookup step applies the table to a document and records term frequency information. If a match occurs in the headline or leading text, extra "frequency" is recorded in order to place extra emphasis on lookup matches in those parts of the document. If the same term is in several definitions (e.g., *American* is a short name variant in hundreds of definitions), frequency information is recorded for each definition.

Once the end of the document is reached, frequency and term label-based weights are used to calculate a score for each topic. If the score exceeds some threshold, corresponding CVTs are added to the document. Typically a few matches of high-weight terms or a variety of lower-weighted terms are necessary to produce scores above the threshold. A document may be about more than one targeted topic.

3.5 System Implementation

The tools used to build and maintain topic definitions were implemented in C/C++ on UNIX-based workstations. The document categorization process was implemented in PL1 and a proprietary lexical scanner, and operates in a mainframe MVS environment.

4 Evaluation

In the final pre-release test, Entity Indexing was applied to more than 13,500 documents from 250 publications. Each document in the test was reviewed by a data analyst. Several of these were also reviewed by a researcher to verify the analysts' consistency with the formal evaluation criteria. Recall was 92.0% and precision was 96.5% when targeting documents with major references. Additional spot tests were done after the process was applied in production to archived documents and to incoming documents. These tests routinely showed recall and precision to be in the 90% to 96% range on over 100,000 documents examined.

Some recall errors were due to company names with unusual structure. Many such problems can be addressed through manual intervention in the topic definitions. Some publication styles also led to recall errors. One publisher introduces a variety of unanticipated abbreviations, such as *Intnl* for *International*. Trade publications tend to use only short forms of company names even for lesser known companies. Those companies may be well-known only within an industry and thus to the audience of the trade publication. These types of problems can be addressed through manual intervention in the topic definitions, although for the abbreviations problem this is little more than patching.

Capitalized and all upper case text in headlines and section headings was a routine source of precision errors. These often led to unwanted term matching, particularly affecting acronyms and one-word company name variants. Different companies with similar names also led to precision problems. This was particularly true for subsidiaries of the same company whose names differed only by geographically-distinct company designators.

5 Discussion

Entity Indexing applies in production to tens of thousands of documents daily from thousands of news publications. Further tests have shown that we can reach comparably high levels of accuracy for company topics when Entity Indexing is applied to financial, patents and public records sources. Accuracy rates dropped about 10% in tests applied to case law parties.

Since the initial completion of the company indexing work, Entity Indexing has been extended to cover more companies and other named entities, including people, organizations and places. Topic definitions have been built for almost 70,000 entities, including over 30,000 companies. Entity Indexing applies these definitions during a single pass of the data, processing more than 86,000 characters (approximately 16 news documents) per CPU second.

The approach used for the other named entity types is similar to that for companies. However, because most of the place names we targeted lacked useful internal structure, manual intervention was a part of creating all 800 definitions for places. Accuracy rates for people, organization and geographic indexing are comparable to those for company indexing.

Knowledge engineering can be a bottleneck in building large-scale applications, which is why machine learning-based approaches are often preferred, but there has been little work in quantifying the difference between the two approaches in linguistic tasks (Brill & Ngai, 1999). In our case, adopting a machine learning-based approach was a problem not just because we lacked annotated training data, but for many of the topics we were required to target we had little or no available data at all. However, because of the regularity we observed in company name variants and their use across a variety of news sources, we determined that the knowledge engineering task would be quite repetitive and thus could be automated for most companies.

Our Entity Indexing system meets all of our business requirements for accuracy, scale and performance. We have also substantially automated the definition building process. Even if a number of documents were available for each targeted entity, it is unlikely that we would see the time needed to populate the authority file and to create and annotate appropriate training data in a machine learning-based approach fall much below the under five minutes we average per definition with our chosen approach.

Acknowledgments

I would like to thank colleagues Mary Jane Battle, Ellen Hamilton, Tom Kresin, Sharon Leigh, Mark Shewhart, Chris White, Christi Wilson and others for their roles in the research, development and ongoing production support of Entity Indexing.

References

Aone, C., Charocopos, N., & Gorlinsky, J. (1997). *An Intelligent Multilingual Information Browsing and Retrieval System Using Information Extraction*. Proceedings of the Fifth Conference on Applied Natural Language Processing.

Brill, E., & Ngai, G. (1999). *Man vs. Machine: A Case Study in Base Noun Phrase Learning*. Proceedings of the 37th Annual Meeting of the Association for Computational Linguistics.

Hayes, P. (1992). *Intelligent High-volume Text Processing Using Shallow, Domain-specific Techniques*. In P. Jacobs (ed.), Text-based Intelligent Systems. Lawrence Erlbaum.

Krupka, G. (1995). *SRA: Description of the SRA System as Used for MUC-6*. Proceedings of the Sixth Message Understanding Conference (MUC-6).

Leigh, S. (1991). *The Use of Natural Language Processing in the Development of Topic Specific Databases*. Proceedings of the Twelfth National Online Meeting.

Thompson, P., & Dozier, C. (1999). *Name Recognition and Retrieval Performance*. In T. Strzalkowski (ed.), Natural Language Information Retrieval. Kluwer Academic.

Unsupervised Discovery of Scenario-Level Patterns for Information Extraction

Roman Yangarber
roman@cs.nyu.edu
Courant Institute of Mathematical Sciences
New York University

Ralph Grishman
grishman@cs.nyu.edu
Courant Institute of Mathematical Sciences
New York University

Pasi Tapanainen †
tapanain@conexor.fi
† Conexor Oy
Helsinki, Finland

Silja Huttunen ‡
sihuttun@ling.helsinki.fi
‡ University of Helsinki
Finland

Abstract

Information Extraction (IE) systems are commonly based on pattern matching. Adapting an IE system to a new scenario entails the construction of a new pattern base—a time-consuming and expensive process. We have implemented a system for finding patterns automatically from *un-annotated* text. Starting with a small initial set of *seed* patterns proposed by the user, the system applies an incremental discovery procedure to identify new patterns. We present experiments with evaluations which show that the resulting patterns exhibit high precision and recall.

0 Introduction

The task of Information Extraction (IE) is the selective extraction of meaning from free natural language text.[1] "Meaning" is understood here in terms of a fixed set of semantic objects—*entities*, *relationships* among entities, and *events* in which entities participate. The semantic objects belong to a small number of *types*, all having fixed regular structure, within a fixed and closely circumscribed subject domain. The extracted objects are then stored in a relational database. In this paper, we use the nomenclature accepted in current IE literature; the term *subject domain* denotes a class of textual documents to be processed, e.g., "business news," and *scenario* denotes the specific topic of interest within the domain, i.e., the set of facts to be extracted. One example of a scenario is "management succession," the topic of MUC-6 (the Sixth Message Understanding Conference); in this scenario the system seeks to identify events in which corporate managers left their posts or assumed new ones. We will consider this scenario in detail in a later section describing experiments.

IE systems today are commonly based on pattern matching. The patterns are regular expressions, stored in a "pattern base" containing a general-purpose component and a substantial domain- and scenario-specific component.

Portability and performance are two major problem areas which are recognized as impeding widespread use of IE. This paper presents a novel approach, which addresses *both* of these problems by automatically discovering good patterns for a new scenario. The viability of our approach is tested and evaluated with an actual IE system.

In the next section we describe the problem in more detail in the context of our IE system; sections 2 and 3 describe our algorithm for pattern discovery; section 4 describes our experimental results, followed by comparison with prior work and discussion, in section 5.

1 The IE System

Our IE system, among others, contains a a back-end core engine, at the heart of which is a regular-expression pattern matcher. The engine draws on attendant knowledge bases (KBs) of varying degrees of domain-specificity. The KB components are commonly factored out to make the systems portable to new scenarios. There are four customizable knowledge bases in our IE system: the *Lexicon* contains general dictionaries and scenario-specific terms; the *concept base* groups terms into classes; the *predicate base* describes the logical structure of events to be extracted, and the *pattern base* contains patterns that catch the events in text.

Each KB has a substantial domain-specific component, which must be modified when mov-

[1] For general references on IE, cf., e.g., (Pazienza, 1997; muc, 1995; muc, 1993).

ing to new domains and scenarios. The system allows the *user* (i.e. scenario developer) to start with example sentences in text which contain events of interest, the *candidates*, and generalize them into patterns. However, the user is ultimately responsible for *finding* all the candidates, which amounts to manually processing example sentences in a very large training corpus. Should s/he fail to provide an example of a particular class of syntactic/semantic construction, the system has no hope of recovering the corresponding events. Our experience has shown that (1) the process of discovering candidates is highly expensive, and (2) gaps in patterns directly translate into gaps in coverage.

How can the system help automate the process of *discovering* new good candidates? The system should find examples of all common linguistic constructs relevant to a scenario. While there has been prior research on identifying the primary lexical patterns of a sub-language or corpus (Grishman et al., 1986; Riloff, 1996), the task here is more complex, since we are typically not provided in advance with a sub-corpus of relevant passages; these passages must themselves be found as part of the discovery process. The difficulty is that one of the best indications of the relevance of the passages is precisely the presence of these constructs. Because of this circularity, we propose to acquire the constructs and passages *in tandem*.

2 Solution

We outline our procedure for automatic acquisition of patterns; details are elaborated in later sections. The procedure is *unsupervised* in that it does not require the training corpus to be manually annotated with events of interest, nor a *pre-classified corpus* with relevance judgements, nor any feedback or intervention from the user[2]. The idea is to combine IR-style document selection with an *iterative relaxation* process; this is similar to techniques used elsewhere in NLP, and is inspired in large part, if remotely, by the work of (Kay and Röscheisen, 1993) on automatic alignment of sentences and words in a bilingual corpus. There, the reasoning was: sentences that are translations of each other are good indicators that words they contain are translation pairs; conversely, words that are translation pairs indicate that the sentences which contain them correspond to one another.

In our context, we observe that documents that are relevant to the scenario will necessarily contain good patterns; conversely, good patterns are strong indicators of relevant documents. The outline of our approach is as follows.

0. Given: (1) a large corpus of *un-annotated and un-classified* documents in the domain; (2) an initial set of trusted scenario patterns, as chosen *ad hoc* by the user—the *seed*; as will be seen, the seed can be quite small—two or three patterns seem to suffice. (3) an initial (possibly empty) set of concept classes

1. The pattern set induces a binary partition (a *split*) on the corpus: on any document, either zero or more than zero patterns will match. Thus the universe of documents, U, is partitioned into the relevant sub-corpus, R, vs. the non-relevant sub-corpus, $\overline{R} = U - R$, with respect to the given pattern set. Actually, the documents are assigned weights which are 1 for documents matched by the trusted seed, and 0 otherwise.[3]

2. Search for new candidate patterns:

   (a) Automatically convert each sentence in the corpus into a set of candidate patterns.[4]

   (b) Generalize each pattern by replacing each lexical item which is a member of a concept class by the class name.

   (c) Working from the relevant documents, select those patterns whose distribution is strongly correlated with other relevant documents (i.e., much more

[2]however, it may be supervised after each iteration, where the user can answer yes/no questions to improve the quality of the results

[3]R represents the trusted truth through the discovery iterations, since it was induced by the manually-selected seed.

[4]Here, for each clause in the sentence we extract a tuple of its major roles: the head of the subject, the verb group, the object, object complement, as described below. This tuple is considered to be a pattern for the present purposes of discovery; it is a skeleton for the rich, syntactically transformed patterns our system uses in the extraction phase.

densely distributed among the relevant documents than among the non-relevant ones). The idea is to consider those candidate patterns, p, which meet the *density* criterion:

$$\frac{|H \cap R|}{|H \cap U|} \gg \frac{|R|}{|U|}$$

where $H = H(p)$ is the set of documents where p hits.

(d) Based on co-occurrence with the chosen patterns, extend the concept classes.

3. *Optional:* Present the new candidates and classes to the user for review, retaining those relevant to the scenario.

4. The new pattern set induces a new partition on the corpus. With this pattern set, return to step 1. Repeat the procedure until no more patterns can be added.

3 Methodology

3.1 Pre-processing: Normalization

Before applying the discovery procedure, we subject the corpus to several stages of pre-processing. First, we apply a name recognition module, and replace each name with a token describing its class, e.g. *C-Person*, *C-Company*, etc. We collapse together all numeric expressions, currency values, dates, etc., using a single token to designate each of these classes.

3.2 Syntactic Analysis

We then apply a parser to perform syntactic normalization to transform each clause into a common predicate-argument structure. We use the general-purpose dependency parser of English, based on the FDG formalism (Tapanainen and Järvinen, 1997) and developed by the Research Unit for Multilingual Language Technology at the University of Helsinki, and Conexor Oy. The parser (modified to understand the name labels attached in the previous step) is used for reducing such variants as passive and relative clauses to a tuple, consisting of several elements.

1. For each claus, the first element is the subject, a "semantic" subject of a non-finite sentence or agent of the passive.[5]

2. The second element is the verb.

3. The third element is the object, certain object-like adverbs, subject of the passive or subject complement[6]

4. The fourth element is a phrase which refers to the object or the subject. A typical example of such an argument is an object complement, such as *Company named John Smith* **president**. Another instance is the so-called *copredicative* (Nichols, 1978), in the parsing system (Järvinen and Tapanainen, 1997). A copredicative refers to a subject or an object, though this distinction is typically difficult to resolve automatically.[7]

Clausal tuples also contain a locative modifier, and a temporal modifier. We used a corpus of 5,963 articles from the Wall Street Journal, randomly chosen. The parsed articles yielded a total of 250,000 clausal tuples, of which 135,000 were distinct.

3.3 Generalization and Concept Classes

Because tuples may not repeat with sufficient frequency to obtain reliable statistics, each tuple is reduced to a set of pairs: e.g., a verb-object pair, a subject-object pair, etc. Each pair is used as a generalized pattern during the candidate selection stage. Once we have identified pairs which are relevant to the scenario, we use them to construct or augment concept classes, by grouping together the missing roles, (for example, a class of verbs which occur with a relevant subject-object pair: "*company* {hire/fire/expel...} *person*"). This is similar to work by several other groups which aims to induce semantic classes through syntactic co-occurrence analysis (Riloff and Jones, 1999; Pereira et al., 1993; Dagan et al., 1993; Hirschman et al., 1975), although in our case the contexts are limited to selected patterns, relevant to the scenario.

[5] E.g., "**John** sleeps", "John is appointed by **Company**", "I saw a **dog** which sleeps", "She asked **John** to buy a car".

[6] E.g., "**John** is appointed by Company", "John is the **president** of Company", "I saw a **dog** which sleeps", The **dog** which I saw sleeps.

[7] For example, "She gave us our coffee **black**", "Company appointed John Smith as **president**".

3.4 Pattern Discovery

Here we present the results from experiments we conducted on the MUC-6 scenario, "management succession". The discovery procedure was seeded with a small pattern set, namely:

Subject	*Verb*	*Direct Object*
C-Company	C-Appoint	C-Person
C-Person	C-Resign	—

Here *C-Company* and *C-Person* denote semantic classes containing named entities of the corresponding semantic types. *C-Appoint* denotes a class of verbs, containing four verbs { *appoint, elect, promote, name*}; *C-Resign* = { *resign, depart, quit, step-down* }.

During a single iteration, we compute the score[8], $L(p)$, for each candidate pattern p:

$$L(p) = P_c(p) \cdot \log |H \cap R| \qquad (1)$$

where R denotes the relevant subset, and $H = H(p)$ the documents matching p, as above, and $P_c(p) = \frac{|H \cap R|}{|H|}$ is the conditional probability of relevance. We further impose two *support* criteria: we distrust such frequent patterns where $|H \cap U| > \alpha |U|$ as uninformative, and rare patterns for which $|H \cap R| < \beta$ as noise.[9] At the end of each iteration, the system selects the pattern with the highest score, $L(p)$, and adds it to the seed set. The documents which the winning pattern hits are added to the relevant set. The pattern search is then restarted.

3.5 Re-computation of Document Relevance

The above is a simplification of the actual procedure, in several important respects.

Only generalized patterns are considered for candidacy, with one or more slots filled with wild-cards. In computing the score of the generalized pattern, we do not take into consideration *all* possible values of the wild-card role. We instead constrain the wild-card to those values which themselves in turn produce patterns with high scores. These values then become members of a new class, which is output in tandem with the winning pattern[10]

[8]similarly to (Riloff, 1996)

[9]U denotes the universe of documents. We used $\alpha = 0.1$ and $\beta = 2$.

[10]The classes are currently unused by subsequent iterations; this important issue is considered in future work.

Documents are assigned relevance scores on a scale between 0 and 1. The seed patterns are accepted as ground truth; thus the documents they match have relevance 1. On subsequent iterations, the newly accepted patterns are not trusted as absolutely. On iteration number $i + 1$, each pattern p is assigned a precision measure, based on the relevance of the documents it matches:

$$Prec^{i+1}(p) = \frac{1}{|H(p)|} \cdot \sum_{d \in H(p)} Rel^i(d) \qquad (2)$$

where $Rel^i(d)$ is the relevance of the document from the previous iteration, and $H(p)$ is the set of documents where p matched. More generally, if K is a classifier consisting of a *set* of patterns, we can define $H(K)$ as the set of documents where *all* of patterns $p \in K$ match, and the "cumulative" precision[11] of K as

$$Prec^{i+1}(K) = \frac{1}{|H(K)|} \cdot \sum_{d \in H(K)} Rel^i(d) \qquad (3)$$

Once the new winning pattern is accepted, the relevance scores of the documents are re-adjusted as follows. For each document d which is matched by some (non-empty) subset of the currently accepted patterns, we can view that subset of patterns as a classifier $K_d = \{p_j\}$. These patterns determine the new relevance score of the document as

$$Rel^{i+1}(d) = \max\left(Rel^i(d), Prec^{i+1}(K_d)\right) \qquad (4)$$

This ensures that the relevance score grows monotonically, and only when there is sufficient positive evidence, as the patterns in effect vote "conjunctively" on the documents. The results which follow use this measure.

Thus in the formulas above, R is not simply the count of the relevant documents, but is rather their *cumulative relevance.* The two formulas, (3) and (4), capture the mutual dependency of patterns and documents; this re-computation and growing of precision and relevance scores is at the heart of the procedure.

[11]Of course, this measure is defined only when $H(K) \neq \emptyset$.

4 Results

An objective measure of goodness of a pattern is not trivial to establish since the patterns cannot be used for extraction directly, without being properly incorporated into the knowledge base. Thus, the discovery procedure does not lend itself easily to MUC-style evaluations, since a pattern lacks information about which events it induces and which slots its arguments should fill.

However, it is possible to apply some objective measures of performance. One way we evaluated the system is by noting that in addition to growing the pattern set, the procedure also grows the relevance of documents. The latter *can* be objectively evaluated.

We used a test corpus of 100 MUC-6 formal-training documents (which were included in the main development corpus of about 6000 documents) plus another 150 documents picked at random from the main corpus and judged by hand. These judgements constituted the ground truth and were used only for evaluation, (not in the discovery procedure).

4.1 Text Filtering

Figure 1 shows the recall/precision measures with respect to the test corpus of 250 documents, over a span of 60 generations, starting with the seed set in table 3.4. The seed patterns matched 184 of the 5963 documents, yielding an initial recall of .11 and precision of .93; by the last generation it searched through 982 documents with non-zero relevance, and ended with .80 precision and .78 recall. This facet of the discovery procedure is closely related to the MUC "text-filtering" sub-task, where the systems are judged at the level of *documents* rather than event slots. It is interesting to compare the results with other MUC-6 participants, shown anonymously in figure 2. Considering recall and precision separately, the discovery procedure attains values comparable to those achieved by some of the participants, all of which were either heavily-supervised or manually coded systems. It is important to bear in mind that the discovery procedure had no benefit of training material, or any information beyond the seed pattern set.

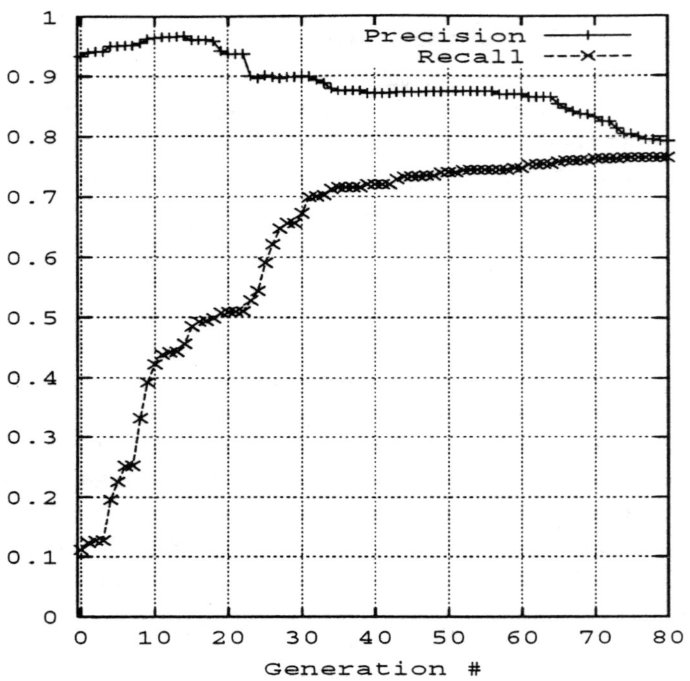

Figure 1: Recall/Precision curves for Management Succession

4.2 Choice of Test Corpus

Figure 2 shows two evaluations of our discovery procedure, tested against the original MUC-6 corpus of 100 documents, and against our test corpus, which consists of an additional 150 documents judged manually. The two plots in the figure show a slight difference in results, indicating that in some sense, the MUC corpus was more "random", or that our expanded corpus was somewhat skewed in favor of more common patterns that the system is able to find more easily.

4.3 Choice of Evaluation Metric

The graphs shown in Figures 1 and 2 are based on an "objective" measure we adopted during the experiments. This is the same measure of relevance used internally by the discovery procedure on each iteration (relative to the "truth" of relevance scores of the previous iteration), and is not quite the standard measure used for text filtering in IR. According to this measure, the system gets a score for each document based on the relevance which it assigned to the document. Thus if the system assigned relevance of X percent to a relevant document, it only received X

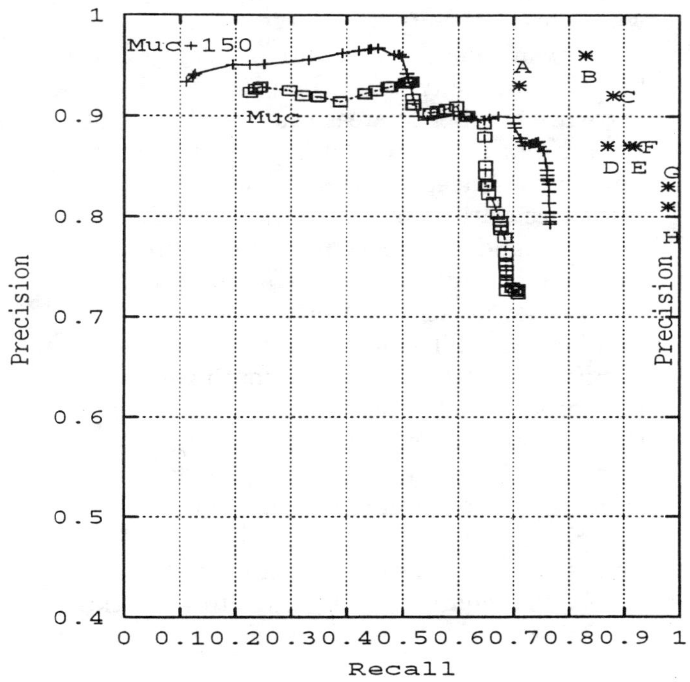

Figure 2: Precision vs. Recall

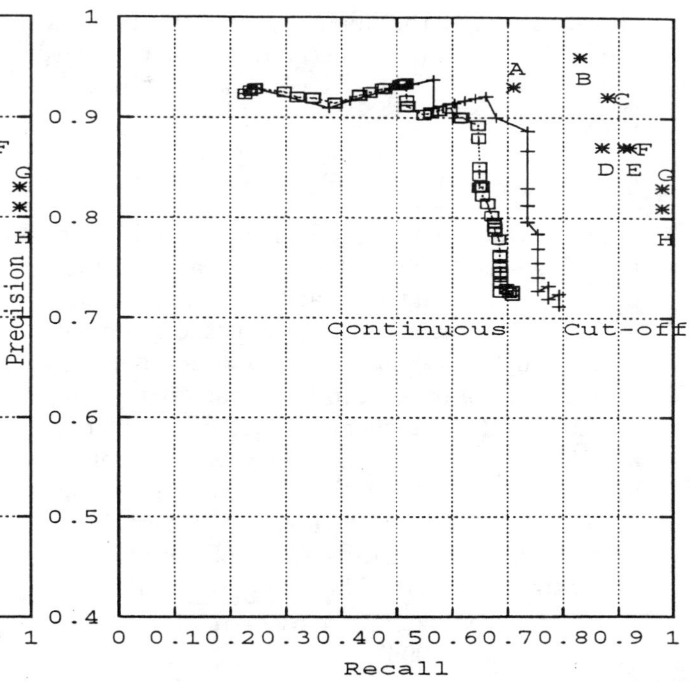

Figure 3: Results on the MUC corpus

percent on the recall score for classifying that document correctly. Similarly, if the system assigned relevance Y to an irrelevant document, it was penalized only for the mis-classified Y percent on the precision score. To make our results more comparable to those of other MUC competitors, we chose a cut-off point and force the system to make a binary relevance decision on each document. The cut-off of 0.5 seemed optimal from empirical observations. Figure 3 shows a noticeable improvement in scores, when using our continuous, "objective" measure, vs. the cut-off measure, with the entire graph essentially translated to the right for a gain of almost 10 percentage points of recall.

4.4 Evaluating Patterns

Another effective, if simple, measure of performance is how many of the patterns the procedure found, and comparing them with those used by an extraction engine which was manually constructed for the same task. Our MUC-6 system used approximately 75 clause level patterns, with 30 distinct verbal heads. In one conservative experiment, we observed that the discovery procedure found 17 of these verbs, or 57%. However, it also found at least 8 verbs the manual system lacked, which seemed relevant to the scenario:

company-bring-person-[as+officer][12]
person-come-[to+company]-[as+officer]
person-rejoin-company-[as+officer]
person-{return, continue, remain, stay}-[as+officer]
person-pursue-interest

At the risk of igniting a philosophical debate over what is or is not relevant to a scenario, we note that the first four of these verbs are evidently essential to the scenario in the strictest definition, since they imply changes of post. The next three are "staying" verbs, and are actually also needed, since higher-level inferences required in *tracking* events for long-range merging over documents, require knowledge of persons *occupying* posts, rather than only assuming or leaving them. The most curious one is *"person-pursue-interest"*; surprisingly, it too is useful, even in the strictest MUC sense, cf., (muc, 1995). Systems are judged on filling a slot called *"other-organization"*, indicating from or to which company the person came or went. This pattern is consistently used in text to indi-

[12]bracketed constituents are outside of the central SVO triplet, included here for clarity.

cate that the person left to pursue other, undisclosed interests, the knowledge of which would relieve the system from seeking other information in order to fill this slot. This is to say that here strict evaluation is elusive.

5 Discussion and Current Work

Some of the prior research has emphasized interactive tools to convert examples to extraction patterns, cf. (Yangarber and Grishman, 1997), while others have focused on methods for automatically converting a corpus annotated with extraction examples into such patterns (Lehnert et al., 1992; Fisher et al., 1995; Miller et al., 1998). These methods, however, do not reduce the burden of *finding* the examples to annotate. With either approach, the portability bottleneck is shifted from the problem of building patterns to that of finding good candidates.

The prior work most closely related to this study is (Riloff, 1996), which, along with (Riloff, 1993), seeks automatic methods for filling slots in event templates. However, the prior work differs from that presented here in several crucial respects; firstly, the prior work does not attempt to find entire events, after the fashion of MUC's highest-level scenario-template task. Rather the patterns produced by those systems identify NPs that fill *individual* slots, without specifying how these slots may be combined at a later stage into complete event templates. The present work focuses on directly discovering *event-level*, multi-slot relational patterns. Secondly, the prior work either relies on a set of documents with relevance judgements to find slot fillers where they are relevant to events, (Riloff, 1996), or utilizes an un-classified corpus containing a very high proportion of relevant documents to find all instances of a semantic class, (Riloff and Jones, 1999). By contrast, our procedure requires no relevance judgements, and works on the assumption that the corpus is balanced and the proportion of relevant documents is small. Classifying documents by hand, although admittedly easier than tagging *event* instances in text for automatic training, is still a formidable task. When we prepared the test corpus, it took 5 hours to mark 150 short documents.

The presented results indicate that our method of corpus analysis can be used to rapidly identify a large number of relevant patterns without pre-classifying a large training corpus. We are at the early stages of understanding how to optimally tune these techniques, and there are number of areas that need refinement. We are working on capturing the rich information about concept classes which is currently returned as part of our pattern discovery procedure, to build up a concept dictionary in tandem with the pattern base. We are also considering the proper selection of weights and thresholds for controlling the rankings of patterns and documents, criteria for terminating the iteration process, and for dynamic adjustments of these weights. We feel that the generalization technique in pattern discovery offers a great opportunity for combating sparseness of data, though this requires further research. Lastly, we are studying these algorithms under several unrelated scenarios to determine to what extent scenario-specific phenomena affect their performance.

References

Ido Dagan, Shaul Marcus, and Shaul Markovitch. 1993. Contextual word similarity and estimation from sparse data. In *Proceedings of the 31st Annual Meeting of the Assn. for Computational Linguistics*, pages 31–37, Columbus, OH, June.

David Fisher, Stephen Soderland, Joseph McCarthy, Fangfang Feng, and Wendy Lehnert. 1995. Description of the UMass system as used for MUC-6. In *Proc. Sixth Message Understanding Conf. (MUC-6)*, Columbia, MD, November. Morgan Kaufmann.

R. Grishman, L. Hirschman, and N.T. Nhan. 1986. Discovery procedures for sublanguage selectional patterns: Initial experiments. *Computational Linguistics*, 12(3):205–16.

Lynette Hirschman, Ralph Grishman, and Naomi Sager. 1975. Grammatically-based automatic word class formation. *Information Processing and Management*, 11(1/2):39–57.

Timo Järvinen and Pasi Tapanainen. 1997. A dependency parser for English. Technical Report TR-1, Department of General Linguistics, University of Helsinki, Finland, February.

Martin Kay and Martin Röscheisen. 1993.

Text-translation alignment. *Computational Linguistics*, 19(1).

W. Lehnert, C. Cardie, D. Fisher, J. McCarthy, E. Riloff, and S. Soderland. 1992. University of massachusetts: MUC-4 test results and analysis. In *Proc. Fourth Message Understanding Conf.*, McLean, VA, June. Morgan Kaufmann.

Scott Miller, Michael Crystal, Heidi Fox, Lance Ramshaw, Richard Schwartz, Rebecca Stone, Ralph Weischedel, and the Annotation Group. 1998. Algorithms that learn to extract information; BBN: Description of the SIFT system as used for MUC-7. In *Proc. of the Seventh Message Understanding Conference*, Fairfax, VA.

1993. *Proceedings of the Fifth Message Understanding Conference (MUC-5)*, Baltimore, MD, August. Morgan Kaufmann.

1995. *Proceedings of the Sixth Message Understanding Conference (MUC-6)*, Columbia, MD, November. Morgan Kaufmann.

Johanna Nichols. 1978. Secondary predicates. *Proceedings of the 4th Annual Meeting of Berkeley Linguistics Society*, pages 114–127.

Maria Teresa Pazienza, editor. 1997. *Information Extraction.* Springer-Verlag, Lecture Notes in Artificial Intelligence, Rome.

Fernando Pereira, Naftali Tishby, and Lillian Lee. 1993. Distributional clustering of English words. In *Proceedings of the 31st Annual Meeting of the Assn. for Computational Linguistics*, pages 183–190, Columbus, OH, June.

Ellen Riloff and Rosie Jones. 1999. Learning dictionaries for information extraction by multi-level bootstrapping. In *Proceedings of Sixteenth National Conference on Artificial Intelligence (AAAI-99)*, Orlando, Florida.

Ellen Riloff. 1993. Automatically constructing a dictionary for information extraction tasks. In *Proceedings of Eleventh National Conference on Artificial Intelligence (AAAI-93)*, pages 811–816. The AAAI Press/MIT Press.

Ellen Riloff. 1996. Automatically generating extraction patterns from untagged text. In *Proceedings of Thirteenth National Conference on Artificial Intelligence (AAAI-96)*, pages 1044–1049. The AAAI Press/MIT Press.

Pasi Tapanainen and Timo Järvinen. 1997. A non-projective dependency parser. In *Proceedings of the 5th Conference on Applied Natural Language Processing*, pages 64–71, Washington, D.C., April. ACL.

Roman Yangarber and Ralph Grishman. 1997. Customization of information extraction systems. In Paola Velardi, editor, *International Workshop on Lexically Driven Information Extraction*, pages 1–11, Frascati, Italy, July. Università di Roma.

Using Corpus-derived Name Lists for Named Entity Recognition

Mark Stevenson and Robert Gaizauskas
Department of Computer Science,
University of Sheffield
Regent Court, 211 Portobello Street,
Sheffield
S1 4DP United Kingdom
{marks, robertg}@dcs.shef.ac.uk

Abstract

This paper describes experiments to establish the performance of a named entity recognition system which builds categorized lists of names from manually annotated training data. Names in text are then identified using only these lists. This approach does not perform as well as state-of-the-art named entity recognition systems. However, we then show that by using simple filtering techniques for improving the automatically acquired lists, substantial performance benefits can be achieved, with resulting F-measure scores of 87% on a standard test set. These results provide a baseline against which the contribution of more sophisticated supervised learning techniques for NE recognition should be measured.

1 Introduction

Named entity (NE) recognition is the process of identifying and categorising names in text. Systems which have attempted the NE task have, in general, made use of lists of common names to provide clues. Name lists provide an extremely efficient way of recognising names, as the only processing required is to match the name pattern in the list against the text and no expensive advanced processing such as full text parsing is required. However, name lists are a naive method for recognising names. McDonald (1996) defines internal and external evidence in the NE task. The first is found within the name string itself, while the second is gathered from its context. For example, in the sentence "President Washington chopped the tree" the word "President" is clear external evidence that "Washington" denotes a person. In this case internal evidence from the name cannot conclusively tell us whether "Washington" is a person or a location ("Washington, DC"). A NE system based solely on lists of names makes use of only internal evidence and examples such as this demonstrate the limitations of this knowledge source.

Despite these limitations, many NE systems use extensive lists of names. Krupke and Hausman (1998) made extensive use of name lists in their system. They found that reducing their size by more than 90% had little effect on performance, conversely adding just 42 entries led to improved results. This implies that the quality of list entries is a more important factor in their effectiveness than the total number of entries. Mikheev et al. (1999) experimented with different types of lists in an NE system entered for MUC7 (MUC, 1998). They concluded that small lists of carefully selected names are as effective as more complete lists, a result consistent with Krupke and Hausman. However, both studies altered name lists within a larger NE system and it is difficult to tell whether the consistency of performance is due to the changes in lists or extra, external, evidence being used to balance against the loss of internal evidence.

In this paper a NE system which uses only the internal evidence contained in lists of names is presented. Section 3 explains how such lists can be automatically generated from annotated text. Sections 4 and 5 describe experiments in which these corpus-generated lists are applied and their performance compared against hand-crafted lists. In the next section the NE task is described in further detail.

2 NE background

2.1 NE Recognition of Broadcast News

The NE task itself was first introduced as part of the MUC6 (MUC, 1995) evaluation exercise and was continued in MUC7 (MUC, 1998). This formulation of the NE task defines seven types of NE: `PERSON`, `ORGANIZATION`, `LOCATION`, `DATE`, `TIME`, `MONEY` and `PERCENT`. Figure 1 shows a short text marked up in SGML with NEs in the MUC style.

The task was duplicated for the DARPA/NIST HUB4 evaluation exercise (Chinchor et al., 1998) but this time the corpus to be processed consisted of single case transcribed speech, rather than mixed case newswire text. Participants were asked to carry out NE recognition on North American broadcast news stories recorded from radio and television and processed by automatic speech recognition (ASR) software. The participants were provided with a training corpus consisting of around 32,000 words of transcribed broadcast news stories from 1997 annotated with NEs. Participants used these text to

```
"It's a chance to think about first-level questions," said Ms. <enamex
type="PERSON">Cohn<enamex>, a partner in the <enamex type="ORGANIZATION">McGlashan
& Sarrail<enamex> firm in <enamex type="LOCATION">San Mateo<enamex>, <enamex
type="LOCATION">Calif.<enamex>
```

Figure 1: Text with MUC-style NE's marked

develop their systems and were then provided with new, unannotated texts, consisting of transcribed broadcast news from 1998 which they were given a short time to annotate using their systems and return. Participants are not given access to the evaluation data while developing their systems.

After the evaluation, BBN, one of the participants, released a corpus of 1 million words which they had manually annotated to provide their system with more training data. Through the remainder of this paper we refer to the HUB4 training data provided by DARPA/NIST as the `SHORT_TRAIN` corpus and the union of this with the BBN data as the `LONG_TRAIN` corpus. The data used for the 1998 HUB4 evaluation was kept blind, we did not examine the text themselves, and shall be referred to as the `TEST` corpus.

The systems were evaluated in terms of the complementary precision (P) and recall (R) metrics. Briefly, precision is the proportion of names proposed by a system which are true names while recall is the proportion of the true names which are actually identified. These metrics are often combined using a weighted harmonic called the F-measure (F) calculated according to formula 1 where β is a weighting constant often set to 1. A full explanation of these metrics is provided by van Rijsbergen (1979).

$$F = \frac{(\beta + 1) \times P \times R}{(\beta \times P) + R} \quad (1)$$

The best performing system in the MUC7 exercise was produced by the Language Technology Group of Edinburgh University (Mikheev et al., 1999). This achieved an F-measure of 93.39% (broken down as a precision of 95% and 92% recall). In HUB4 BBN (Miller et al., 1999) produced the best scoring system which achieved an F-measure of 90.56% (precision 91%, recall 90%) on the manually transcribed test data.

2.2 A Full NE system

The NE system used in this paper is based on Sheffield's LaSIE system (Wakao et al., 1996), versions of which have participated in MUC and HUB4 evaluation exercises (Renals et al., 1999). The system identifies names using a process consisting of four main modules:

List Lookup This module consults several lists of likely names and name cues, marking each occurrence in the input text. The name lists include lists of organisations, locations and person first names and the name cue lists of titles (eg. "Mister", "Lord"), which are likely to precede person names, and company designators (eg. "Limited" or "Incorporated"), which are likely to follow company names.

Part of speech tagger The text is the part of speech tagged using the Brill tagger (Brill, 1992). This tags some tokens as "proper name" but does not attempt to assign them to a NE class (eg. `PERSON`, `LOCATION`).

Name parsing Next the text is parsed using a collection of specialised NE grammars. The grammar rules identify sequences of part of speech tags as added by the **List Lookup** and **Part of speech tagger** modules. For example, there is a rule which says that a phrase consisting of a person first name followed by a word part of speech tagged as a proper noun is a person name.

Namematching The names identified so far in the text are compared against all unidentified sequences of proper nouns produced by the part of speech tagger. Such sequences form candidate NEs and a set of heuristics is used to determine whether any such candidate names match any of those already identified. For example one such heuristics says that if a person is identified with a title (eg. "President Clinton") then any occurrences without the title are also likely to be person names (so "Clinton" on it own would also be tagged as a person name).

For the experiments described in this paper a restricted version of the system which used only the **List Lookup** module was constructed. The list lookup mechanism marks all words contained in any of the name lists and each is proposed as a NE. Any string occurring in more than one list is assigned the category form the first list in which it was found, although this did not occur in any of the sets of lists used in the experiments described here.

3 List Generation

The **List Lookup** module uses a set of handcrafted lists originally created for the MUC6 evaluation. They consisted of lists of names from the gazetteers provided for that competition, supplemented by manually added entries. These lists evolved for the MUC7 competition with new entries and lists being added. For HUB4 we used a selection of these lists, again manually supplementing them where necessary. These lists included lists of companies, organisations (such as government departments), countries and continents, cities, regions (such as US states) and person first names as well as company designators and person titles. We speculate that this ad hoc, evolutionary, approach to creating name lists is quite common amongst systems which perform the NE task.

In order to compare this approach against a simple system which gathers together all the names occurring in NE annotated training text, a program was implemented to analyse text annotated in the MUC SGML style (see Figure 1) and create lists for each NE type found. For example, given the NE `<enamex type="LOCATION">SAN MATEO<enamex>` an entry `SAN MATEO` would be added a list of locations.

This simple approach is certainly acceptable for the `LOCATION`, `ORGANIZATION` and, to a more limited extent, `PERSON` classes. It is less applicable to the remaining classes of names (`DATE`, `TIME`, `MONEY` and `PERCENT`) because these are most easily recognised by their grammatical structure. For example, there is a rule in the NE grammar which says a number followed by a currency unit is as instance of the `MONEY` name class – eg. `FIFTY THREE DOLLARS`, `FIVE MILLION ECU`. According to Przbocki et al. (1999) 88% of names occurring in broadcast news text fall into one of the `LOCATION`, `ORGANIZATION` and `PERSON` categories.

Two sets of lists were derived, one from the `SHORT_TRAIN` corpus and a second from the `LONG_TRAIN` texts. The lengths of the lists produced are shown in Table 1.

	Corpus	
Category	SHORT_TRAIN	LONG_TRAIN
ORGANIZATION	245	2,157
PERSON	252	3,947
LOCATION	230	1,489

Table 1: Lengths of lists derived from `SHORT_TRAIN` and `LONG_TRAIN` corpora

4 List Application

The `SHORT_TRAIN` and `LONG_TRAIN` lists were each applied in two ways, alone and appended to the original, manually-created, lists. In addition, we computed the performance obtained using only the original lists for comparison. Although both sets of lists were derived using the `SHORT_TRAIN` data (since the `LONG_TRAIN` corpus includes `SHORT_TRAIN`), we still compute the performance of the `SHORT_TRAIN` lists on that corpus since this provides some insight into the best possible performance which can be expected from NE recognition using a simple list lookup mechanism. No scores were computed for the `LONG_TRAIN` lists against the `SHORT_TRAIN` corpus since this is unlikely to provide more information.

Table 2 shows the results obtained when the `SHORT_TRAIN` lists were applied to that corpus. This first experiment was designed to determine how well the list lookup approach would perform given lists compiled directly from the corpus to which they are being applied. Only `PERSON`, `LOCATION` and `ORGANIZATION` name classes are considered since they form the majority of names occurring in the HUB4 text. As was mentioned previously, the remaining categories of name are more easily recognised using the NE parser. For each configuration of lists the precision, recall and F-measure are calculated for the each name class both individually and together.

We can see that the original lists performed reasonably well, scoring an F-measure of 79% overall. However, the corpus-based lists performed far better achieving high precision and perfect recall. We would expect the system to recognise every name in the text, since they are all in the lists, but perfect precision is unlikely as this would require that no word appeared as both a name and non-name or in more than one name class. Even bearing this in mind the calculated precision for the `ORGANIZATION` class of names is quite low. Analysis of the output showed that several words occurred as names a few times in the text but also as non-names more frequently. For example, "police" appeared 35 times but only once as an organisation; similarly "finance" and "republican" occur frequently but only as a name a few times. In fact, these three list entries account for 61 spuriously generated names, from a total of 86 for the `ORGANIZATION` class. The original lists do not include words which are likely to generate spurious entries and names like "police" would only be recognised when there was further evidence.

The `SHORT_TRAIN` lists contain all the names occurring in that text. When these lists are combined with the original system lists the observed recall remains 100% while the precision drops. The original system lists introduce more spurious entries, leading to a drop of 3% F-measure.

The results of applying the corpus-derived lists to the texts from which they were obtained show that, even under these circumstances, perfect results cannot be obtained. Table 3 shows a more meaningful evaluation; the `SHORT_TRAIN` lists are applied to the `TEST` corpus, an unseen text. The original system lists achieve an F-measure of 83% on this text and the corpus-derived lists perform 8% worse. However, the configuration of lists which performs best is the union of the original lists with those derived from the

Lists	Original			SHORT_TRAIN			Combination		
Name Type	P	R	F	P	R	F	P	R	F
ALL	86	73	79	94	100	97	88	100	94
ORGANIZATION	84	49	62	83	100	90	79	100	88
PERSON	78	71	74	99	100	99	88	100	94
LOCATION	92	88	90	98	100	99	95	100	97

Table 2: SHORT_TRAIN lists applied to SHORT_TRAIN corpus

corpus. This out-performs each set of lists taken in isolation both overall and for each name category individually. This is clear evidence that the lists used by the system described could be improved with the addition of lists derived from annotated text.

It is worth commenting on some of the results for individual classes of names in this experiment. We can see that the performance for the ORGANIZATION class actually increases when the corpus-based lists are used. This is partially because names which are made up from initials (eg. "C.N.N." and "B.B.C.") are not generally recognised by the list lookup mechanism in our system, but are captured by the parser and so were not included in the original lists. However, it is also likely that the organisation list is lacking, at least to some level. More interestingly, there is a very noticeable drop in the performance for the PERSON class. The SHORT_TRAIN lists achieved an F-measure of 99% on that text but only 48% on the TEST text. In Section 2.1 we mentioned that the HUB4 training data consists of news stories from 1997, while the test data contains stories from 1998. We therefore suggest that the decrease in performance for the PERSON category demonstrates a general property of broadcast news: many person names mentioned are specific to a particular time period (eg. "Monica Lewinksi" and "Rodney King"). In contrast, the locations and organisations mentioned are more stable over time.

Table 4 shows the performance obtained when the lists derived from LONG_TRAIN were applied to the TEST corpus. The corpus-derived lists perform significantly worse than the original system lists, showing a large drop in precision. This is to be expected since the lists derived from LONG_TRAIN contain all the names occurring in a large body of text and therefore contain many words and phrases which are not names in this text, but spuriously match non-names. Although the F-measure result is worse than when the SHORT_TRAIN lists were used, the recall is higher showing that a higher proportion of the true names can be found by analysing a larger body of text. Combining the original and corpus-derived lists leads to a 1% improvement. Recall is noticeably improved compared with the original lists, however precision is lowered and this shows that the corpus-derived lists introduce a large number of spurious names.

From this first set of experiments it can be seen that perfect results will not be obtained even using lists contain all and only the names in a particular text, thus demonstrating the limitations of this naive approach to named entity recognition. We have also demonstrated that it is possible for the addition of corpus-derived lists to improve the performance of a NE recognition system based on gazetteers. However, this is not guaranteed and it appears that adding too many names without any restriction may actually lead to poorer results, as happened when the LONG_TRAIN lists were applied.

5 Filtering Lists

The results from our first set of experiments led us to question whether it is possible to restrict the entries being added to the lists in order to avoid those likely to generate spurious names. We now go on to describe some methods which can be used to identify and remove list entries which may generate spurious names.

Method 1: Dictionary Filtering The derived lists can be improved by removing items in the list which also occur as entries in a dictionary.

We began by taking the *Longman Dictionary of Contemporary English* (LDOCE)(Procter, 1978) and extracting a list of words it contained including all derived forms, for example pluralisation of nouns and different verb forms. This produced a list of 52,576 tokens which could be used to filter name lists.

Method 2: Probability Filtering The lists can be improved by removing names which occur more frequently in the corpus as non-names than names.

Another method for filtering lists was implemented, this time using the relative frequencies of phrases occurring as names and non-names. We can extract the probability that a phrase occurs as a name in the training corpus by dividing the number of times it occurs as a name by the total number of corpus occurrences. If this probability estimate is an accurate reflection of the name's behaviour in a

Lists	Original			SHORT_TRAIN			Combination		
Name Type	P	R	F	P	R	F	P	R	F
ALL	86	79	83	90	65	75	83	86	84
ORGANIZATION	82	57	67	76	66	71	79	81	80
PERSON	77	80	78	93	32	48	79	83	81
LOCATION	93	89	91	97	81	88	92	94	93

Table 3: SHORT_TRAIN lists applied to TEST corpus

Lists	Original			LONG_TRAIN			Combination		
Name Type	P	R	F	P	R	F	P	R	F
ALL	86	79	83	64	86	73	62	91	74
ORGANIZATION	82	57	67	44	85	58	43	88	58
PERSON	77	80	78	55	75	63	53	86	66
LOCATION	93	89	91	87	92	89	84	94	89

Table 4: LONG_TRAIN lists applied to TEST corpus

new text we can use it to estimate the accuracy of adding that name to the list. Adding a name to a list will lead to a recall score of 1 for that name and a precision of Pr (where Pr is the probability value estimated from the training corpus) which implies an F-measure of $\frac{2Pr}{1+Pr}$.[1] Therefore the probabilities can be used to filter out candidate list items which imply low F-measure scores. We chose names whose corpus probabilities produced an F-measure lower than the overall score for the list. The LONG_TRAIN lists scored an F-measure of 73% on the unseen, TEST, data (see Table 4). Hence a filtering probability of 73% was used for these lists, with the corpus statistics gathered from LONG_TRAIN.

Method 3: Combining Filters These filtering strategies can be improved by combining them.

We also combined these two filtering strategies in two ways. Firstly, all names which appeared in the lexicon *or* whose corpus probability is below the filtering probability are removed from the lists. This is dubbed the "or combination". The second combination strategy removes any names which appear in the lexicon *and* occur with a corpus frequency below the filtering probability are removed. This second strategy is called the "and combination".

These filtering strategies were applied to the LONG_TRAIN lists. The lengths of the lists produced are shown in Table 5.

The strategies were evaluated by applying the filtered LONG_TRAIN lists to the TEST corpus, the results of which are shown in Table 6. There is an improvement in performance of 4% F-measure when lists filtered using the "and" combination are used compared to the original, hand-crafted, lists. Although this approach removes only 108 items from all the lists there is a 14% F-measure improvement over the un-filtered lists. Each filtering strategy used individually demonstrates a lower level of improvement: the dictionary filtered lists 12% and the probability filtered 10%.

The "and" combination is more successful because filtering lists using the dictionary alone removes many names we would like to keep (eg. country names are listed in LDOCE) but many of these are retained since both filters must agree. These experiments demonstrate that appropriately filtered corpus-derived lists can be more effective for NE recognition than hand-crafted lists. The difference between the observed performance of our simple method and those reported for the best-performing HUB4 system is perhaps lower that one may expect. The BBN system achieved 90.56% overall, and about 92% when only the PERSON, LOCATION and ORGANIZATION name classes are considered, 5% more than the method reported here. This difference is perhaps lower than we might expect given that name lists use only internal evidence (in the sense of Section 1). This indicates that simple application of the information contained in manually annotated NE training data can contribute massively to the overall performance of a system. They also provide a baseline against which the contribution of more sophisticated supervised learning techniques for NE recognition should be measured.

[1] Analysis of the behaviour of the function $f(Pr) = \frac{2Pr}{1+Pr}$ shows that it does not deviate too far from the value of Pr (ie. $f(Pr) \approx Pr$) and so there is an argument for simply filtering the lists using the raw probabilities.

NE Category	Un-Filtered List	Dictionary Filtered	Probability Filtered	Or Combined	And Combined
ORGANIZATION	2,157	1,978	2,000	1,964	2,049
PERSON	3,947	3,769	3,235	3,522	3,809
LOCATION	1,489	1,412	1,364	1,382	1,449

Table 5: Lengths of corpus-derived lists

	Original Lists			Un-Filtered Lists			Dictionary Filtered			Probability Filtered			Or Combination			And Combination		
Name Type	P	R	F	P	R	F	P	R	F	P	R	F	P	R	F	P	R	F
ALL	86	79	83	64	86	73	95	79	85	96	73	83	95	73	83	93	81	87
ORGANIZATION	82	57	67	44	85	58	86	72	78	85	74	79	84	60	70	84	76	80
PERSON	77	80	78	55	75	63	96	66	78	96	40	56	100	49	66	94	66	78
LOCATION	93	89	91	87	92	89	98	89	93	97	90	93	98	90	94	97	92	94

Table 6: Filtered and un-filtered LONG_TRAIN lists applied to TEST corpus

6 Conclusion

This paper explored the role of lists of names in NE recognition, comparing hand-crafted and corpus-derived lists. It was shown that, under certain conditions, corpus-derived lists outperform hand-crafted ones. Also, supplementing hand-crafted lists with corpus-based ones often improves their performance. The reported method was more effective for the ORGANIZATION and LOCATION classes of names than for PERSON, which was attributed to the fact that reportage of these names does not change as much over time in broadcast news.

The method reported here achieves 87% F-measure, 5% less than the best performing system in the HUB4 evaluation. However, it should be remembered that this technique uses only a simple application of internal evidence.

References

E. Brill. 1992. A simple rule-based part of speech tagger. In *Proceeding of the Third Conference on Applied Natural Language Processing (ANLP-92)*, pages 152–155, Trento, Italy.

N. Chinchor, P. Robinson, and E. Brown. 1998. Hub-4 named entity task definition (version 4.8). Technical report, SAIC. http://www.nist.gov/speech/hub4_98.

G. Krupke and K. Hausman. 1998. Isoquest Inc: description of the NetOwl(TM) extractor system as used for MUC-7. In *Message Understanding Conference Proceedings: MUC 7*. Available from http://www.muc.saic.com.

D. McDonald. 1996. Internal and external evidence in the identification and semantic categorization of proper names. In B. Boguraev and J. Pustejovsky, editors, *Corpus Processing for Lexical Aquisition*, chapter 2, pages 21–39. MIT Press, Cambridge, MA.

A. Mikheev, M. Moens, and C. Grover. 1999. Named entity recognition without gazeteers. In *Proceedings of the Ninth Conference of the European Chapter of the Association for Computational Linguistics*, pages 1–8, Bergen, Norway.

D. Miller, R. Schwartz, R. Weischedel, and R. Stone. 1999. Named entity extraction from broadcast news. In *Proceedings of the DARPA Broadcast News Workshop*, pages 37–40, Herndon, Virginia.

MUC. 1995. *Proceedings of the Sixth Message Understanding Conference (MUC-6)*, San Mateo, CA. Morgan Kaufmann.

1998. Message Understanding Conference Proceedings: MUC7. http://www.muc.saic.com.

P. Procter, editor. 1978. *Longman Dictionary of Contemporary English.* Longman Group, Essex, UK.

M. Przbocki, J. Fiscus, J. Garofolo, and D. Pallett. 1999. 1998 HUB4 Information Extraction Evaluation. In *Proceedings of the DARPA Broadcast News Workshop*, pages 13–18, Herndon, Virginia.

S. Renals, Y. Gotoh, R. Gaizausaks, and M. Stevenson. 1999. Baseline IE-NE Experimants Using the SPRACH/LASIE System. In *Proceedings of the DAPRA Broadcast News Workshop*, pages 47–50, Herndon, Virginia.

C. van Rijsbergen. 1979. *Information Retrieval.* Butterworths, London.

T. Wakao, R. Gaizauskas, and K. Humphreys. 1996. Evaluation of an algorithm for the recognition and classification of proper names. In *Proceedings of the 16th International Conference on Computational Linguistics (COLING-96)*, pages 418–423, Copenhagen, Denmark.

Answer Extraction

Steven Abney Michael Collins Amit Singhal
AT&T Shannon Laboratory
180 Park Ave.
Florham Park, NJ 07932
{abney,mcollins,singhal}@research.att.com

Abstract

Information retrieval systems have typically concentrated on retrieving a set of *documents* which are relevant to a user's query. This paper describes a system that attempts to retrieve a much smaller section of text, namely, a direct *answer* to a user's question. The SMART IR system is used to extract a ranked set of passages that are relevant to the query. Entities are extracted from these passages as potential answers to the question, and ranked for plausibility according to how well their type matches the query, and according to their frequency and position in the passages. The system was evaluated at the TREC-8 question answering track: we give results and error analysis on these queries.

1 Introduction

In this paper, we describe and evaluate a question-answering system based on passage retrieval and entity-extraction technology.

There has long been a concensus in the Information Retrieval (IR) community that natural language processing has little to offer for retrieval systems. Plausibly, this is creditable to the preeminence of ad hoc document retrieval as the task of interest in IR. However, there is a growing recognition of the limitations of ad hoc retrieval, both in the sense that current systems have reached the limit of achievable performance, and in the sense that users' information needs are often not well characterized by document retrieval.

In many cases, a user has a question with a specific answer, such as *What city is it where the European Parliament meets?* or *Who discovered Pluto?* In such cases, ranked answers with links to supporting documentation are much more useful than the ranked list of documents that standard retrieval engines produce.

The ability to answer specific questions also provides a foundation for addressing quantitative inquiries such as *How many times has the Fed raised interest rates this year?* which can be interpreted as the cardinality of the set of answers to a specific question that happens to have multiple correct answers, like *On what date did the Fed raise interest rates this year?*

We describe a system that extracts specific answers from a document collection. The system's performance was evaluated in the question-answering track that has been introduced this year at the TREC information-retrieval conference. The major points of interest are the following.

- Comparison of the system's performance to a system that uses the same passage retrieval component, but no natural language processing, shows that NLP provides significant performance improvements on the question-answering task.
- The system is designed to build on the strengths of both IR and NLP technologies. This makes for much more robustness than a pure NLP system would have, while affording much greater precision than a pure IR system would have.
- The task is broken into subtasks that admit of independent development and evaluation. Passage retrieval and entity extraction are both recognized independent tasks. Other subtasks are entity classification and query classification—both being classification tasks that use features obtained by parsing—and entity ranking.

In the following section, we describe the question-answering system, and in section 3, we quantify its performance and give an error analysis.

2 The Question-Answering System

The system takes a natural-language query as input and produces a list of answers ranked in order of confidence. The top five answers were submitted to the TREC evaluation.

Queries are processed in two stages. In the information retrieval stage, the most promising passages of the most promising documents are retrieved. In the linguistic processing stage, potential answers are extracted from these passages and ranked.

The system can be divided into five main components. The information retrieval stage consists of a single component, passage retrieval, and the linguistic processing stage circumscribes four components: entity extraction, entity classification, query classification, and entity ranking.

Passage Retrieval Identify relevant documents, and within relevant documents, identify the passages most likely to contain the answer to the question.

Entity Extraction Extract a candidate set of possible answers from the passages.

Entity Classification The candidate set is a list of entities falling into a number of categories, including people, locations, organizations, quantities, dates, and linear measures. In some cases (dates, quantities, linear measures), entity classification is a side effect of entity extraction, but in other cases (proper nouns, which may be people, locations, or organizations), there is a separate classification step after extraction.

Query Classification Determine what category of entity the question is asking for. For example, if the query is

> Who is the author of the book, The Iron Lady: A Biography of Margaret Thatcher?

the answer should be an entity of type `Person`.

Entity Ranking Assign scores to entities, representing roughly belief that the entity is the correct answer. There are two components of the score. The most-significant bit is whether or not the category of the entity (as determined by entity classification) matches the category that the question is seeking (as determined by query classification). A finer-grained ranking is imposed on entities with the correct category, through the use of frequency and other information.

The following sections describe these five components in detail.

2.1 Passage Retrieval

The first step is to find passages likely to contain the answer to the query. We use a modified version of the SMART information retrieval system (Buckley and Lewit, 1985; Salton, 1971) to recover a set of documents which are relevant to the question. We define passages as overlapping sets consisting of a sentence and its two immediate neighbors. (Passages are in one-one correspondence with with sentences, and adjacent passages have two sentences in common.) The score for passage i was calculated as

$$\tfrac{1}{4}S_{i-1} + \tfrac{1}{2}S_i + \tfrac{1}{4}S_{i+1} \qquad (1)$$

where S_j, the score for sentence j, is the sum of IDF weights of non-stop terms that it shares with the query, plus an additional bonus for pairs of words (bigrams) that the sentence and query have in common.

The top 50 passages are passed on as input to linguistic processing.

2.2 Entity Extraction

Entity extraction is done using the Cass partial parser (Abney, 1996). From the Cass output, we take dates, durations, linear measures, and quantities.

In addition, we constructed specialized code for extracting proper names. The proper-name extractor essentially classifies capitalized words as intrinsically capitalized or not, where the alternatives to intrinsic capitalization are sentence-initial capitalization or capitalization in titles and headings. The extractor uses various heuristics, including whether the words under consideration appear unambiguously capitalized elsewhere in the document.

2.3 Entity Classification

The following types of entities were extracted as potential answers to queries.

Person, Location, Organization, Other Proper names were classified into these categories using a classifier built using the method described in (Collins and Singer, 1999).[1] This is the only place where entity classification was actually done as a separate step from entity extraction.

Dates Four-digit numbers starting with `1...` or `20..` were taken to be years. Cass was used to extract more complex date expressions (such as *Saturday, January 1st, 2000*).

Quantities Quantities include bare numbers and numeric expressions like *The Three Stooges*, *4 1/2 quarts*, *27%*. The head word of complex numeric expressions was identified (*stooges*, *quarts* or *percent*); these entities could then be later identified as good answers to *How many* questions such as *How many stooges were there?*

Durations, Linear Measures Durations and linear measures are essentially special cases of quantities, in which the head word is a time unit or a unit of linear measure. Examples of durations are *three years*, *6 1/2 hours*. Examples of linear measures are *140 million miles*, *about 12 feet*.

We should note that this list does not exhaust the space of useful categories. Monetary amounts (e.g.,

[1]The classifier makes a three way distinction between `Person`, `Location` and `Organization`; names where the classifier makes no decision were classified as `Other Named Entity`.

\$25 million) were added to the system shortly after the Trec run, but other gaps in coverage remain. We discuss this further in section 3.

2.4 Query Classification

This step involves processing the query to identify the category of answer the user is seeking. We parse the query, then use the following rules to determine the category of the desired answer:

- *Who, Whom* → `Person`.
- *Where, Whence, Whither* → `Location`.
- *When* → `Date`.
- *How few, great, little, many, much* → `Quantity`. We also extract the head word of the *How* expression (e.g., *stooges* in *how many stooges*) for later comparison to the head word of candidate answers.
- *How long* → `Duration` or `Linear Measure`. *How tall, wide, high, big, far* → `Linear Measure`.
- The wh-words *Which* or *What* typically appear with a head noun that describes the category of entity involved. These questions fall into two formats: *What X* where *X* is the noun involved, and *What is the ... X*. Here are a couple of examples:

  What company is the largest Japanese ship builder?

  What is the largest city in Germany?

  For these queries the head noun (e.g., *company* or *city*) is extracted, and a lexicon mapping nouns to categories is used to identify the category of the query. The lexicon was partly hand-built (including some common cases such as *number* → `Quantity` or *year* → `Date`). A large list of nouns indicating `Person`, `Location` or `Organization` categories was automatically taken from the contextual (appositive) cues learned in the named entity classifier described in (Collins and Singer, 1999).
- In queries containing no wh-word (e.g., *Name the largest city in Germany*), the first noun phrase that is an immediate constituent of the matrix sentence is extracted, and its head is used to determine query category, as for *What X* questions.
- Otherwise, the category is the wildcard `Any`.

2.5 Entity Ranking

Entity scores have two components. The first, most-significant, component is whether or not the entity's category matches the query's category. (If the query category is `Any`, all entities match it.)

In most cases, the matching is boolean: either an entity has the correct category or not. However, there are a couple of special cases where finer distinctions are made. If a question is of the `Date` type, and the query contains one of the words *day* or *month*, then "full" dates are ranked above years. Conversely, if the query contains the word *year*, then years are ranked above full dates. In *How many X* questions (where *X* is a noun), quantified phrases whose head noun is also *X* are ranked above bare numbers or other quantified phrases: for example, in the query *How many lives were lost in the Lockerbie air crash*, entities such as *270 lives* or *almost 300 lives* would be ranked above entities such as *200 pumpkins* or *150*.[2]

The second component of the entity score is based on the frequency and position of occurrences of a given entity within the retrieved passages. Each occurrence of an entity in a top-ranked passage counts 10 points, and each occurrence of an entity in any other passage counts 1 point. ("Top-ranked passage" means the passage or passages that received the maximal score from the passage retrieval component.) This score component is used as a secondary sort key, to impose a ranking on entities that are not distinguished by the first score component.

In counting occurrences of entities, it is necessary to decide whether or not two occurrences are tokens of the same entity or different entities. To this end, we do some normalization of entities. Dates are mapped to the format year-month-day: that is, *last Tuesday, November 9, 1999* and *11/9/99* are both mapped to the normal form *1999 Nov 9* before frequencies are counted. Person names are aliased based on the final word they contain. For example, *Jackson* and *Michael Jackson* are both mapped to the normal form *Jackson*.[3]

3 Evaluation

3.1 Results on the TREC-8 Evaluation

The system was evaluated in the TREC-8 question-answering track. TREC provided 198 questions as a blind test set: systems were required to provide five potential answers for each question, ranked in order of plausibility. The output from each system was then scored by hand by evaluators at NIST, each answer being marked as either correct or incorrect. The system's score on a particular question is a function of whether it got a correct answer in the five ranked answers, with higher scores for the answer appearing higher in the ranking. The system receives a score of 1, 1/2, 1/3, 1/4, 1/5, or 0, re-

[2]Perhaps less desirably, *people* would not be recognized as a synonym of *lives* in this example: *200 people* would be indistinguishable from *200 pumpkins*.

[3]This does introduce occasional errors, when two people with the same last name appear in retrieved passages.

System	Mean Ans Len	Answer in Top 5	Mean Score
Entity	10.5 B	46%	0.356
Passage 50	50 B	38.9%	0.261
Passage 250	250 B	68%	0.545

Figure 1: Results on the TREC-8 Evaluation

spectively, according as the correct answer is ranked 1st, 2nd, 3rd, 4th, 5th, or lower in the system output. The final score for a system is calculated as its mean score on the 198 questions.

The TREC evaluation considered two question-answering scenarios: one where answers were limited to be less than 250 bytes in length, the other where the limit was 50 bytes. The output from the passage retrieval component (section 2.1), with some trimming of passages to ensure they were less than 250 bytes, was submitted to the 250 byte scenario. The output of the full entity-based system was submitted to the 50 byte track. For comparison, we also submitted the output of a 50-byte system based on IR techniques alone. In this system single-sentence passages were retrieved as potential answers, their score being calculated using conventional IR methods. Some trimming of sentences so that they were less than 50 bytes in length was performed.

Figure 1 shows results on the TREC-8 evaluation. The 250-byte passage-based system found a correct answer somewhere in the top five answers on 68% of the questions, with a final score of 0.545. The 50-byte passage-based system found a correct answer on 38.9% of all questions, with an average score of 0.261. The reduction in accuracy when moving from the 250-byte limit to the 50-byte limit is expected, because much higher precision is required; the 50-byte limit allows much less extraneous material to be included with the answer. The benefit of the including less extraneous material is that the user can interpret the output with much less effort.

Our entity-based system found a correct answer in the top five answers on 46% of the questions, with a final score of 0.356. The performance is not as good as that of the 250-byte passage-based system. But when less extraneous material is permitted, the entity-based system outperforms the passage-based approach. The accuracy of the entity-based system is significantly better than that of the 50-byte passage-based system, and it returns virtually no extraneous material, as reflected in the average answer length of only 10.5 bytes. The implication is that NLP techniques become increasingly useful when short answers are required.

3.2 Error Analysis of the Entity-Based System

3.2.1 Ranking of Answers

As a first point, we looked at the performance of the entity-based system, considering the queries where the correct answer was found somewhere in the top 5 answers (46% of the 198 questions). We found that on these questions, the percentage of answers ranked 1, 2, 3, 4, and 5 was 66%, 14%, 11%, 4%, and 4% respectively. This distribution is by no means uniform; it is clear that when the answer is somewhere in the top five, it is very likely to be ranked 1st or 2nd. The system's performance is quite bimodal: it either completely fails to get the answer, or else recovers it with a high ranking.

3.2.2 Accuracy on Different Categories

Figure 2 shows the distribution of question types in the TREC-8 test set ("Percentage of Q's"), and the performance of the entity-based system by question type ("System Accuracy"). We categorized the questions by hand, using the eight categories described in section 2.3, plus two categories that essentially represent types that were not handled by the system at the time of the TREC competition: `Monetary Amount` and `Miscellaneous`.

"System Accuracy" means the percentage of questions for which the correct answer was in the top five returned by the system. There is a sharp division in the performance on different question types. The categories `Person`, `Location`, `Date` and `Quantity` are handled fairly well, with the correct answer appearing in the top five 60% of the time. These four categories make up 67% of all questions. In contrast, the other question types, accounting for 33% of the questions, are handled with only 15% accuracy.

Unsurprisingly, the `Miscellaneous` and `Other Named Entity` categories are problematic; unfortunately, they are also rather frequent. Figure 3 shows some examples of these queries. They include a large tail of questions seeking other entity types (mountain ranges, growth rates, films, etc.) and questions whose answer is not even an entity (e.g., "Why did David Koresh ask the FBI for a word processor?")

For reference, figure 4 gives an impression of the sorts of questions that the system does well on (correct answer in top five).

3.2.3 Errors by Component

Finally, we performed an analysis to gauge which components represent performance bottlenecks in the current system. We examined system logs for a 50-question sample, and made a judgment of what caused the error, when there was an error. Figure 5 gives the breakdown. Each question was assigned to exactly one line of the table.

The largest body of errors, accounting for 18% of the questions, are those that are due to unhandled

Question	Rank	Output from System
Who is the author of the book, The Iron Lady: A Biography of Margaret Thatcher?	2	Hugo Young
What is the name of the managing director of Apricot Computer?	1	Dr Peter Horne
What country is the biggest producer of tungsten?	1	China
Who was the first Taiwanese President?	1	Taiwanese President Li Teng hui
When did Nixon visit China?	1	1972
How many calories are there in a Big Mac?	4	562 calories
What is the acronym for the rating system for air conditioner efficiency?	1	EER

Figure 4: A few TREC questions answered correctly by the system.

Type	Percent of Q's	System Accuracy
Person	28	62.5
Location	18.5	67.6
Date	11	45.5
Quantity	9.5	52.7
TOTAL	67	60
Other Named Ent	14.5	31
Miscellaneous	8.5	5.9
Linear Measure	3.5	0
Monetary Amt	3	0
Organization	2	0
Duration	1.5	0
TOTAL	33	15

Figure 2: Performance of the entity-based system on different question types. "System Accuracy" means percent of questions for which the correct answer was in the top five returned by the system. "Good" types are in the upper block, "Bad" types are in the lower block.

What does the Peugeot company manufacture?
Why did David Koresh ask the FBI for a word processor?
What are the Valdez Principles?
What was the target rate for M3 growth in 1992?
What does El Nino mean in spanish?

Figure 3: Examples of "Other Named Entity" and "Miscellaneous" questions.

types, of which half are monetary amounts. (Questions with non-entity answers account for another 4%.) Another large block (16%) is due to the passage retrieval component: the correct answer was not present in the retrieved passages. The linguistic components together account for the remaining 14% of error, spread evenly among them.

The cases in which the correct answer is in the top five, but not at rank one, are almost all due to failures of entity ranking.[4] Various factors contributing to misrankings are the heavy weighting assigned to answers in the top-ranked passage, the failure to adjust frequencies by "complexity" (e.g., it is significant if *22.5 million* occurs several times, but not if *3* occurs several times), and the failure of the system to consider the linguistic context in which entities appear.

Errors	
Passage retrieval failed	16%
Answer is not an entity	4%
Answer of unhandled type: money	10%
Answer of unhandled type: misc	8%
Entity extraction failed	2%
Entity classification failed	4%
Query classification failed	4%
Entity ranking failed	4%
Successes	
Answer at Rank 2-5	16%
Answer at Rank 1	32%
TOTAL	100%

Figure 5: Breakdown of questions by error type, in particular, by component responsible. Numbers are percent of questions in a 50-question sample.

4 Conclusions and Future Work

We have described a system that handles arbitrary questions, producing a candidate list of answers ranked by their plausibility. Evaluation on the TREC question-answering track showed that the correct answer to queries appeared in the top five answers 46% of the time, with a mean score of 0.356. The average length of answers produced by the system was 10.5 bytes.

[4]The sole exception was a query misclassification caused by a parse failure—miraculously, the correct answer made it to rank five despite being of the "wrong" type.

There are several possible areas for future work. There may be potential for improved performance through more sophisticated use of NLP techniques. In particular, the syntactic context in which a particular entity appears may provide important information, but it is not currently used by the system.

Another area of future work is to extend the entity-extraction component of the system to handle arbitrary types (mountain ranges, films etc.). The error analysis in section 3.2.2 showed that these question types cause particular difficulties for the system.

The system is largely hand-built. It is likely that as more features are added a trainable statistical or machine learning approach to the problem will become increasingly desirable. This entails developing a training set of question-answer pairs, raising the question of how a relatively large corpus of questions can be gathered and annotated.

References

Steven Abney. 1996. Partial parsing via finite-state cascades. *J. Natural Language Engineering*, 2(4):337–344, December.

C. Buckley and A.F. Lewit. 1985. Optimization of inverted vector searches. In *Proc. Eighth International ACM SIGIR Conference*, pages 97–110.

Michael Collins and Yoram Singer. 1999. Unsupervised models for named entity classification. In *EMNLP*.

G. Salton, editor. 1971. *The Smart Retrieval System – Experiments in Automatic Document Processing.* Prentice-Hall, Inc., Englewood Cliffs, NJ.

Evaluation of Automatically Identified Index Terms for Browsing Electronic Documents[1]

Nina Wacholder, Judith L. Klavans and David K. Evans
Columbia University
Department of Computer Science and
Center for Research on Information Access

1. Abstract

We present an evaluation of domain-independent natural language tools for use in the identification of significant concepts in documents. Using qualitative evaluation, we compare three shallow processing methods for extracting index terms, i.e., terms that can be used to model the content of documents. We focus on two criteria: quality and coverage. In terms of quality alone, our results show that technical term (TT) extraction [Justeson and Katz 1995] receives the highest rating. However, in terms of a combined quality and coverage metric, the Head Sorting (HS) method, described in [Wacholder 1998], outperforms both other methods, keyword (KW) and TT.

2. Introduction

In this paper, we consider the problem of how to evaluate the automatic identification of index terms that have been derived without recourse to lexicons or to other kinds of domain-specific information. By index terms, we mean natural language expressions that constitute a meaningful representation of a document for humans. The premise of this research is that if significant topics coherently represent information in a document, these topics can be used as index terms that approximate the content of individual documents in large collections of electronic documents.

We compare three shallow processing methods for identifying index terms:

- **Keywords (KW)** are terms identified by counting frequency of stemmed words in a document;
- **Technical terms (TT)** are noun phrases (NPs) or subparts of NPs repeated more than twice in a document [Justeson and Katz 1995];
- **Head sorted terms (HS)** are identified by a method in which simplex noun phrases (as defined below) are sorted by head and then ranked in decreasing order of frequency [Wacholder 1998].

The three methods that we evaluated are domain-independent in that they use statistical and/or linguistic properties that apply to any natural language document in any field. These methods are also corpus-independent, in that the ranking of terms for an individual document is not dependent on properties of the corpus.

2.1 Overview of methods and results

Subjects were drawn from two groups: professionals and students. Professionals included librarians and publishing professionals familiar with both manual and automatic text indexing. Students included undergraduate and graduate students with a variety of academic interests.

To assess terms, we used a standard qualitative ranking technique. We presented subjects with an article and a list of terms identified by one of the three methods. Subjects were asked to answer the following general question: "Would this term be useful in an electronic index for this article?" Terms were rated on a scale of 1 to 5, where 1 indicates a high quality term that should definitely be included in the index and 5 indicates a junk term that definitely should not be included. For ex-

[1] This research was partly funded by NSF IRI 97-12069, "Automatic identification of significant topics in domain independent full text documents" and NSF IRI 97-53054, "Computationally tractable methods for document analysis".

ample, the phrase *court-approved affirmative action plans* received an average rating of 1 from the professionals, meaning that it was ranked as useful for the article; the KW *affirmative* received an average rating of 3.75, meaning that it was less useful; and the KW *action* received an average ranking of 4.5, meaning that it was not useful.

The goal of our research is to determine which method, or combination of methods, provides the best results. We measure results in terms of two criteria: **quality** and **coverage**. By quality, we mean that evaluators ranked terms high on the 1 to 5 scale from highest to lowest. By coverage, we mean the thoroughness with which the terms cover the significant topics in the document. Our methodology permits us to measure both criteria, as shown in Figure 4.

Our results from both the professionals and students show that TTs are superior with respect to quality; however, there are only a small number of TTs per document, so they do not provide adequate coverage in that they are not fully representative of the document as a whole. In contrast, KWs provide good coverage but relatively poor quality in that KWs are vague, and not well filtered. SNPs, which have been sorted using HS and filtered, provide a better balance of quality and coverage.

From our study, we draw the following conclusions:

- The KW approach identifies some useful index terms, but they are mixed in with a large number of low-ranked terms.
- The TT approach identifies high quality terms, but with low coverage, i.e., relatively few indexing terms.
- The HS approach achieves a balance between quality and coverage.

3. Domain-independent metrics for identifying significant topics

In order to identify significant topics in a document, a significance measure is needed, i.e., a method for determining which concepts in the document are relatively important for a given task. The need to determine the importance of a particular concept within a document is motivated by a range of applications, including information retrieval [Salton 1989], automatic determination of authorship [Mosteller and Wallace 1963], similarity metrics for cross-document clustering [Hatzivassiloglou et al. 1999], automatic indexing [Hodges et al. 1996] and input to summarization [Paice 1990].

For example, one of the earlier applications using frequency for identifying significant topics in a document was proposed by [Luhn 1958] for use in creating automatic abstracts. For each document, a list of stoplisted stems was created, and ranked by frequency; the most frequent keywords were used to identify significant sentences in the original document. Luhn's premise was that emphasis, as indicated by repetition of words and collocation is an indicator of significance. Namely, "the more often certain words are found in each other's company within a sentence, the more significance may be attributed to each of these words." This basic observation, although refined extensively by later summarization techniques (as reviewed in [Paice 1990]), relies on the capability of identifying significant concepts.

The standard IR technique known as tf*idf [Salton 1989] seeks to identify documents relevant to a particular query by relativizing keyword frequency in a document as compared to frequency in a corpus. This method can be used to locate at least some important concepts in full text. Although it has been effective for information retrieval, for other applications, such as human-oriented indexing, this technique is impractical. Ambiguity of stems (*trad* might refer to *trader* or *tradition*) and of isolated words (*state* might be a political entity or a mode of being) means that lists of keywords have not usually been used to represent the content of a document to human beings. Furthermore, humans have a difficult time processing stems and parts of words out of phrasal context.

The technical term (TT) method, another technique for identification of significant terms in text that can be used as index terms was introduced by [Justeson and Katz 1995], who developed an algorithm for identifying repeated multi-word phrases such as *central processing unit* in the computer domain or *word sense* in the lexical semantic domain.

This algorithm identifies candidate TTs in a corpus by locating NPs consisting of nouns, adjectives, and sometimes prepositional phrases. TTs are defined as those NPs, or their subparts, which occur above some frequency threshold in a corpus. However, as [Boguraev and Kennedy 1998] observe, the TT technique may not characterize the full content of documents. Indeed, even in a technical document, TTs do not provide adequate coverage of the NPs in a document that contribute to its content, especially since TTs are by definition multi-word. A truly domain-general method should apply to both technical and non-technical documents. The relevant difference between technical and non-technical documents is that in technical documents, many of the topics which are significant to the document as a whole may be also TTs.

[Wacholder 1998] proposed the method of Head Sorting for identifying significant topics that can be used to represent a source document. HS also uses a frequency measure to provide an approximation of topic significance. However, instead of counting frequency of stems or repetition of word sequences, this method counts frequency of a relatively easily identified grammatical element, heads of simplex noun phrases (SNPs). For common NPs (NPs whose head is a common noun), an SNP is a maximal NP that includes premodifiers such as determiners and possessives but not post-nominal constituents such as prepositions or relativizers. For example, *the well-known book* is an SNP but *the well-known book on asteroids* includes two SNPs, *well-known book* and *asteroids*. For proper names, an SNP is a name that refers to a single entity. For example, *Museum of the City of New York*, the name of an organization, is an SNP even though the organizational name incorporates a city name. Others, such as [Church 1988], have discussed a similar concept, sometimes called simple or base NPs.

The HS approach is based on the assumption that nominal elements can be used to convey the gist of a document. SNPs, which are semantically and syntactically coherent, appear to be at a good level of detail for content representation of the document. '

SNPs are identified by a system [Evans 1998; Evans et al. 2000] which sequentially parses text that has been tagged with part of speech using a finite state machine. Next, the complete list of SNPs identified in a document is sorted by the head of the phrase, which, at least for English-language common SNPs, is almost always the last word. The intuitive justification for sorting SNPs by head is based on the fundamental linguistic distinction between head and modifier: in general, a head makes a greater contribution to the syntax and semantics of a phrase than does a modifier. This linguistic insight can be extended to the document level. If, as a practical matter, it is necessary to rank the contribution to a whole document made by the sequence of words constituting an NP, the head should be ranked more highly than other words in the phrase. This distinction is important in linguistic theory; for example, [Jackendoff 1977] discusses the relationship of heads and modifiers in phrase structure. It is also important in NLP, where, for example, [Strzalkowski 1997] and [Evans and Zhai 1996] have used the distinction between heads and modifiers to add query terms to information retrieval systems.

Powerful corpus processing techniques have been developed to measure deviance from an average occurrence or co-occurrence in the corpus. In this paper we chose to evaluate methods that depend only on document-internal data, independent of corpus, domain or genre. We therefore did not use, for example, tf*idf, the purely statistical technique that is the used by most information retrieval systems, or [Smadja 1993], a hybrid statistical and symbolic technique for identifying collocations.

4. Experimental Method

To evaluate techniques, we performed a qualitative user evaluation in which the terms identified by each method were compared for usefulness as index terms.

4.1 Subjects

We performed our study with librarians, publishing professionals and undergraduate and graduate students at our university. 29 subjects participated in the study: 7 librarians and publishing professionals and 22 students.

4.2 Data

For this experiment, we selected three articles from the 1990 *Wall Street Journal* contained in the Tipster collection of documents. The articles were about 500 words in length.

To compare methods, each article was processed three times: 1) with SMART to identify stemmed keywords [Salton 1989]; 2) with an implementation of the TT algorithm based on [Justeson and Katz 1995]; and 3) with our implementation of the HS method. Output for one article is shown in Appendix A. Figure 1 shows the articles selected, their length in words and the number of index terms from each method for each article presented to the subjects.

DOC	words	KW	TT	HS
415-0109	509	63	4	49
516-0043	594	51	9	54
517-0062	514	52	8	57

Figure 1: Word and term count, by type, per article

The number of TTs is much lower than the number of KWs or HSs. This presented us with a problem: on the one hand, we were concerned about preserving the integrity of the three methods, each of which has their own logic, and at the same time, we were concerned to present lists that were balanced relative to each other. Toward this end, we made several decisions about presentation of the data:

1. **Threshold:** So that no bias would be unintentionally introduced, we presented subjects with all terms output by each method, up to a specified cut-off poin- However, using lists of equal length for each method would have necessitated either omitting HSs and KWs or changing the definition of TTs. Therefore we made the following decisions:
   - For TTs, we included all identified terms;
   - For HSs, we included all terms whose head occurred more than once in the document;
   - For KWs, we included all terms in order of decreasing frequency, up to the point where we observed diminishing quality and where the number of KWs approximated the number of HSs.
2. **Order:** For the KW and TT approach, order is not significant. However, for the HS approach, the grouping together of phrases with common heads is, we claim, one of the advantages of the method. We therefore alphabetized the KWs and TTs in standard left to right order and alphabetized the HSs by head, e.g., *trust account* precedes *money market fund.*
3. **Morphological expansion:** The KW approach identifies stems which represent a set of one or more morphological variants of the stem. Since in some cases the stem is not an English word, we expanded each stem to include the morphological variants that actually occurred in the article. For example, for the stem *reject*, we listed *rejected* and *rejecting* but did not list *rejects*, which did not occur in the article.

4.3 Presentation to subjects

Each subject was presented with three articles. For one article, the subject received a head sorted list of HSs; for another article, the subject received a list of technical terms, and for the third article, the subject saw a list of keywords. No time limit was placed on the task.

5. Results

Our results for the three types of terms, by document, are shown in Figure 2. Although we asked subjects to rate three articles, some volunteers rated only two. All results were included.

Doc	**Avg KW rating**	**Avg TT rating**	**Avg HS rating**
900405-0109	3.08	1.45	2.71
900516-0043	3.73	2.19	2.71
900517-0062	2.98	1.7	3.25
Avg of Avgs	**3.27**	**1.79**	**2.89**

Figure 2: Average ratings of 3 types of index terms

5.1 Quality

For the three lists of index terms, TTs received the highest ratings for all three documents—an average of 1.79 on the scale of 1 to 5, with 1 being the best rating. HS came in second, with an average of 2.89, and KW came in last with an average of 3.27. It should be noted that averaging the average conceals the fact that the number of TTs is much lower than the other two types of terms, as shown in Figure 1.

Figure 3 (included before Appendix A) shows cumulative rankings of terms by method. The X axis represents ratings awarded by subjects. The Y axis reflects the percentage of terms receiving a given rank or better. All data series must reach 100% since every term has been assigned a rating by the evaluators. At any given data point, a larger value indicates that a larger percentage of that series' data has that particular rating or better. For example, 100% of the TTs have a rating of 3 or better; while only about 30% of the terms of the lowest-scoring KW document received a score of 3 or better. In two out of the three documents, HS terms fall between TTs and KWs.

5.2 Coverage

The graph in Figure 3 shows results for quality, not coverage. In contrast, Figure 4, which shows the total number of terms rated at or below specified rankings, allows us to measure quality and coverage. (1 is the highest rating; 5 is the lowest.) This figure shows that the HS method identifies more high quality terms than the TT method does.

	Number of terms ranked at or better than			
Method	**2**	**3**	**4**	**5**
KW	27	75	124	166
HS	41	96	132	160
TT	15	21	21	21

Figure 4: Running total of terms identified at or below a specified rank

TT clearly identifies the highest quality terms: 100% of TTs receive a rating of 2 or better. However, only 8 TTs received a rating of 2 or better (38% of the total), while 41 HSs received a rating of 2 or better (26% of the total). This indicates that the TT method misses many high quality terms. KW, the least discriminating method in terms of quality, also provides better coverage than does TT.

This result is consistent with our observation that TT identifies the highest quality terms, but there are very few of them: an average of 7 per 500 words compared to over 50 for HS and KW. Therefore there is a need for additional high quality terms. The list of HSs received a higher average rating than did the list of KWs, as shown in Figure 2. This is consistent with our expectation that phrases containing more content-bearing modifiers would be perceived as more useful index terms than would single word phrases consisting only of heads.

5.3 Ranking variability

The difference in the average ratings for the list of KWs and the list of head-sorted SNPs was less than expected. The small difference in average ratings for the HS list and the KW list can be explained, at least in part, by two factors: 1) Differences among professionals and students in inter-subject agreement and reliability; 2) A discrepancy in the rating of single word terms across term types.

22 students and 7 professionals participated in the study. Figure 5 shows differences in the ratings of professionals and of students.

	Professionals	Students
KW	2.64	3.30
HS	2.3	3.03
TT	1.49	2.1

Figure 5: Average ratings, by term type, of professionals and students

When variation in the scores for terms was calculated using standard deviation, the standard deviation for the professionals was 0.78, while for the students it was 1.02. Because of the relatively low number of professionals, the standard deviation was calculated only over terms that were rated by more than one professional. A review of the students' results showed that they appeared not to be as careful as the professionals. For example, the phrase 'Wall

Street Journal' was included on the HS list only because it is specified as the document source. However, four of the eight students assigned this term a high rating (1 or 2); this is puzzling because the document is about asbestos-related disease. The other four students assigned a 4 or 5 to 'Wall Street Journal', as we expected. But the average score for this term was 3, due to the anomalous ratings. We therefore have more confidence in the reliability of the professional ratings, even though there are relatively few of them.

We examined some of the differences in rating for term types. Single word index terms are rated more highly by professionals when they appear in the context of other single word index terms, but are downrated in the context of phrasal expansions that make the meaning of the one-word term more specific. The KW list and HS list overlap when the SNP consists only of a single word (the head) or only of a head modified by determiners. When the same word appears in both lists in identical form, the token in the KW list tends to receive a better rating than the token does when it appears in the HS list, where it is often followed by expansions of the head. For example, the word *exposure* received an average rating of 2.2 when it appeared on the KW list, but a rating of only 2.75 on the HS list. However, the more specific phrase *racial quotas*, which immediately followed *quota* on the HS list received a rating of 1.

To better understand these differences, we selected 40 multi-word phrases and examined the average score that the phrase received in the TT and HS lists, and compared it to the average ratings that individual words received in the KW list. We found that in about half of the cases (21 of 40), the phrase as a whole and the individual words in the phrase received similar scores, as in Example 1 in Figure 6. In just over one-fourth of the cases (12 of 40), the phrase scored well, but scores from the individual words were rated from good to poor, as in Example 2. In about one-eighth of the cases (6 of 40), the phrase scored well, but the individual words scored poorly, as in Example 3. Finally, in only one case, shown in Example 4 of Figure 6, the phrase scored poorly but the individual words scored well.

	Phrase	Word 1	Word 2
1	Supreme Court (1.5)	Supreme (1)	Court (1.25)
2	reverse discrimination (1)	reverse (3.25)	discrimination (3.25)
3	lymph system (1)	lymph (1)	system (5)
4	employment decisions (2.75)	employment (1.25)	decisions (1.25)

Figure 6: Comparison of scores of phrases and single words

This shows that single words in isolation are judged differently than the same word when presented in the context of a larger phrase. These results have important implications in the design of indexing tools.

6. Conclusion

Our results show that the head sorting technique outperforms two other indexing methods, technical terms and keywords, as measured by balance of quality and coverage. We have performed a qualitative evaluation of three techniques for identifying significant terms in a document, driven by an indexing task. Such an application can be used to create a profile or thumbnail of a document by presenting to users a set of terms which can be considered to be a representation of the content of the document. We have used human judges to evaluate the effectiveness of each method. This research is a contribution to the overall evaluation of computational linguistic tools in terms of their usefulness for human-oriented computational applications.

8. References

Boguraev, Branimir and Kennedy, Christopher (1998) "Applications of term identification terminology: domain description and content characterisation", *Natural Language Engineering* 1(1):1-28.

Church, Kenneth Ward (1988) "A stochastic parts program and noun phrase parser for unrestricted text", in *Proceedings of the Second*

Conference on Applied Natural Language Processing, pp.136-143.

Evans, David A. and Chengxiang Zhai (1996) "Noun-phrase analysis in unrestricted text for information retrieval", *Proceedings of the 34th Annual Meeting of the Association for Computational Linguistics*, pp.17-24. 24-27 June 1996, University of California, Santa Cruz, California, Morgan Kaufmann Publishers.

Evans, David K. (1998) LinkIT Documentation, Columbia University Department of Computer Science Report.

Evans, David K., Klavans, Judith, and Wacholder, Nina (2000) "Document processing with LinkIT", RIAO Conference, Paris, France, to appear.

Hatzivassiloglou, Vasileios, Judith L. Klavans and Eleazar Eskin (1999) "Detecting text similarity over short passages: exploring linguistic feature combinations via machine learning", *Proceedings of the EMNLP/VLC-99 Joint SIGDAT Conference on Empirical Methods in NLP and Very Large Corpora*, June 21-22, 1999, University of Maryland, College Park, MD.

Hodges, Julia, Shiyun Yie, Ray Reighart and Lois Boggess (1996) "An automated system that assists in the generation of document indexes", *Natural Language Engineering* 2(2):137-160.

Jackendoff, Ray (1977) *X-bar Syntax: A Study of Phrase Structure*, MIT Press, Cambridge, MA.

Justeson, John S. and Slava M. Katz (1995) "Technical terminology: some linguistic properties and an algorithm for identification in text", *Natural Language Engineering* 1(1):9-27.

Luhn, Hans P. (1958) "The automatic creation of literature abstracts", *IBM Journal*, 159-165.

Mosteller, Frederick and David L. Wallace (1963) "Inference in an authorship problem", *Journal of the American Statistical Association* 58(302):275-309. Available at http://www.jstor.org/.

Paice, Chris D. (1990) "Constructing literature abstracts by computer: techniques and prospects". *Information Processing & Management* 26(1):171-186.

Salton, Gerald (1989) *Automatic Text Processing: The Transformation, Analysis and Retrieval of Information by Computer*. Addison-Wesley, Reading, MA.

Smadja, Frank (1993) "Retrieving collocations from text", *Computational Linguistics* 19(1):143-177.

Strzalkowski, Thomas (1997) "Building effective queries in natural language information retrieval", *Proceedings of the ANLP*, ACL, Washington, DC., pp.299-306.

Wacholder, Nina (1998) "Simplex NPS sorted by head: a method for identifying significant topics within a document", *Proceedings of the Workshop on the Computational Treatment of Nominals*, pp.70-79. COLING-ACL '98, Montreal, Canada, August 16, 1998.

Figure 3: Cumulative ranking of terms, by method

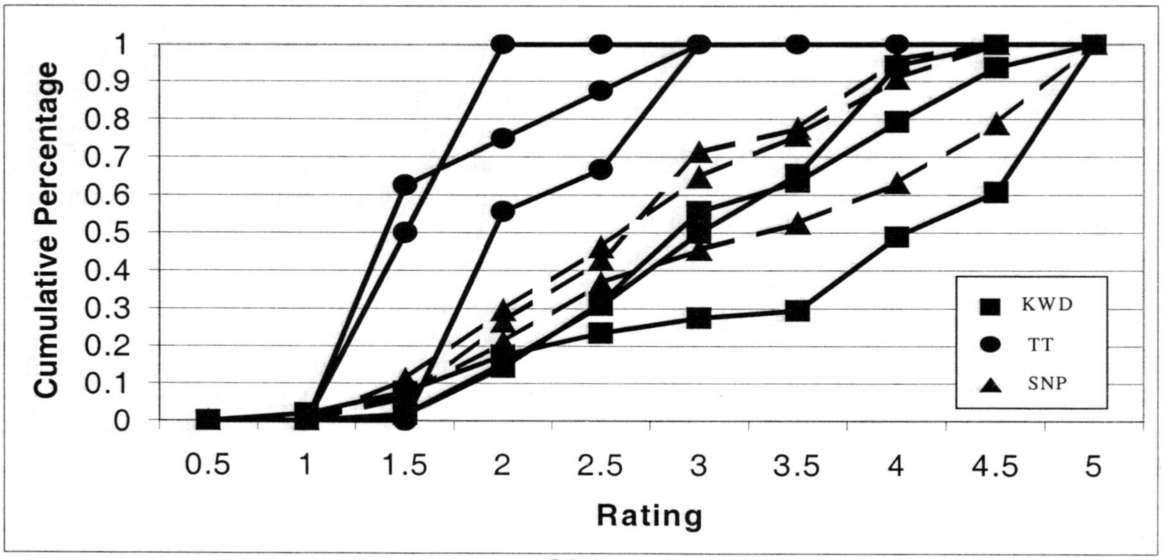

Appendix A: Terms identified in WSJ900405-0109

HSs
amendments
Hatch amendment
other amendments
attempts
bias
job bias
intentional bias
bill
committee
Senate labor Committee
court
Supreme Court
co-workers
decisions
Supreme Court decisions
employment decisions
Democrats
discrimination
reverse discrimination
employees
women employees
employers
groups
civil-rights groups
conservative policy groups
Orrin Hatch
health
discriminatory impact
Job-Bias Measure
basic employment anti-discrimination law
1866 civil-rights law
lawsuits
lawmakers
legislation
comprehensive legislation
more modest measure
minority/minorities
panel
plans
court-approved affirmative action plans
discriminatory seniority plans
practices
employment practices
quotas
racial quotas
right/rights
equal rights
year

Keywords
action
address/addressing
adopt/adopted
affirmative
agree
aimed
alleged/alleging
amend
approved
attempt/attempts
bias
bill
Bush
challenge
circumstances
civil
clears
committee
court/Court
decision
Democrats
discrimination
employment/employers/employees
force/Force
give/giving
GOP
groups
Hatch
health
high
impact
job
justify
labor/Labor
law
lawmakers
lawsuits
legislative/legislation
make
measure
minority/minorities
Mr.
overturning
panel
plans
policy
practices
quotas
racial
rejected/rejecting
reverse
rights
rules/ruling
safety
Sen./Sens.
Senate
shown
street
Supreme; vote/voted
women
workers
year

Technical terms
discriminatory impact
employment practice
Senator Hatch
Supreme Court

Sentence Reduction for Automatic Text Summarization

Hongyan Jing
Department of Computer Science
Columbia University
New York, NY 10027, USA
hjing@cs.columbia.edu

Abstract

We present a novel sentence reduction system for automatically removing extraneous phrases from sentences that are extracted from a document for summarization purpose. The system uses multiple sources of knowledge to decide which phrases in an extracted sentence can be removed, including syntactic knowledge, context information, and statistics computed from a corpus which consists of examples written by human professionals. Reduction can significantly improve the conciseness of automatic summaries.

1 Motivation

Current automatic summarizers usually rely on sentence extraction to produce summaries. Human professionals also often reuse the input documents to generate summaries; however, rather than simply extracting sentences and stringing them together, as most current summarizers do, humans often "edit" the extracted sentences in some way so that the resulting summary is concise and coherent. We analyzed a set of articles and identified six major operations that can be used for editing the extracted sentences, including removing extraneous phrases from an extracted sentence, combining a reduced sentence with other sentences, syntactic transformation, substituting phrases in an extracted sentence with their paraphrases, substituting phrases with more general or specific descriptions, and reordering the extracted sentences (Jing and McKeown, 1999; Jing and McKeown, 2000).

We call the operation of removing extraneous phrases from an extracted sentence *sentence reduction*. It is one of the most effective operations that can be used to edit the extracted sentences. Reduction can remove material at any granularity: a word, a prepositional phrase, a gerund, a to-infinitive or a clause. We use the term "phrase" here to refer to any of the above components that can be removed in reduction. The following example shows an original sentence and its reduced form written by a human professional:

Original sentence:
When it arrives sometime next year in new TV sets, the V-chip will give parents a *new and potentially revolutionary* device to block out programs they don't want their children to see.

Reduced sentence by humans:
The V-chip will give parents a device to block out programs they don't want their children to see.

We implemented an automatic sentence reduction system. Input to the reduction system includes extracted sentences, as well as the original document. Output of reduction are reduced forms of the extracted sentences, which can either be used to produce summaries directly, or be merged with other sentences. The reduction system uses multiple sources of knowledge to make reduction decisions, including syntactic knowledge, context, and statistics computed from a training corpus. We evaluated the system against the output of human professionals. The program achieved a success rate of 81.3%, meaning that 81.3% of reduction decisions made by the system agreed with those of humans.

Sentence reduction improves the conciseness of automatically generated summaries, making it concise and on target. It can also improve the coherence of generated summaries, since extraneous phrases that can potentially introduce incoherece are removed. We collected 500 sentences and their corresponding reduced forms written by humans, and found that humans reduced the length of these 500 sentences by 44.2% on average. This indicates that a good sentence reduction system can improve the conciseness of generated summaries significantly.

In the next section, we describe the sentence reduction algorithm in details. In Section 3, we introduce the evaluation scheme used to access the performance of the system and present evaluation results. In Section 4, we discuss other applications of sentence reduction, the interaction between reduction and other modules in a summarization system, and related work on sentence simplication. Finally, we conclude with future work.

2 Sentence reduction based on multiple sources of knowledge

The goal of sentence reduction is to "reduce without major loss"; that is, we want to remove as many extraneous phrases as possible from an extracted sentence so that it can be concise, but without detracting from the main idea the sentence conveys. Ideally, we want to remove a phrase from an extracted sentence *only if it is irrelevant to the main topic.* To achieve this, the system relies on multiple sources of knowledge to make reduction decisions. We first introduce the resources in the system and then describe the reduction algorithm.

2.1 The resources

(1) The corpus. One of the key features of the system is that it uses a corpus consisting of original sentences and their corresponding reduced forms written by humans for training and testing purpose. This corpus was created using an automatic program we have developed to automatically analyze human-written abstracts. The program, called the decomposition program, matches phrases in a human-written summary sentence to phrases in the original document (Jing and McKeown, 1999). The human-written abstracts were collected from the free daily news service "Communications-related headlines", provided by the Benton Foundation (http://www.benton.org). The articles in the corpus are news reports on telecommunication related issues, but they cover a wide range of topics, such as law, labor, and company mergers.

(2) The lexicon. The system also uses a large-scale, reusable lexicon we combined from multiple resources (Jing and McKeown, 1998). The resources that were combined include COMLEX syntactic dictionary (Macleod and Grishman, 1995), English Verb Classes and Alternations (Levin, 1993), the WordNet lexical database (Miller et al., 1990), the Brown Corpus tagged with WordNet senses (Miller et al., 1993). The lexicon includes subcategorizations for over 5,000 verbs. This information is used to identify the obligatory arguments of verb phrases.

(3) The WordNet lexical database. WordNet (Miller et al., 1990) is the largest lexical database to date. It provides lexical relations between words, including synonymy, antonymy, meronymy, entailment (e.g., *eat* $\rightarrow$ *chew*), or causation (e.g., *kill* $\rightarrow$ *die*). These lexical links are used to identify the focus in the local context.

(4) The syntactic parser. We use the English Slot Grammar(ESG) parser developed at IBM (McCord, 1990) to analyze the syntactic structure of an input sentence and produce a sentence parse tree. The ESG parser not only annotates the syntactic category of a phrase (e.g., "np" or "vp"), it also annotates the thematic role of a phrase (e.g., "subject" or "object").

2.2 The algorithm

There are five steps in the reduction program:

Step 1: Syntactic parsing.

We first parse the input sentence using the ESG parser and produce the sentence parse tree. The operations in all other steps are performed based on this parse tree. Each following step annotates each node in the parse tree with additional information, such as syntactic or context importance, which are used later to determine which phrases (they are represented as subtrees in a parse tree) can be considered extraneous and thus removed.

Step 2: Grammar checking.

In this step, we determine which components of a sentence *must not* be deleted to keep the sentence grammatical. To do this, we traverse the parse tree produced in the first step in top-down order and mark, for each node in the parse tree, which of its children are grammatically obligatory. We use two sources of knowledge for this purpose. One source includes simple, linguistic-based rules that use the thematic role structure produced by the ESG parser. For instance, for a sentence, the main verb, the subject, and the object(s) are essential if they exist, but a prepositional phrase is not; for a noun phrase, the head noun is essential, but an adjective modifier of the head noun is not. The other source we rely on is the large-scale lexicon we described earlier. The information in the lexicon is used to mark the obligatory arguments of verb phrases. For example, for the verb "convince", the lexicon has the following entry:

```
convince
   sense 1:
      NP-PP :PVAL (''of'')
      NP-TO-INF-OC
   sense 2:
      NP
```

This entry indicates that the verb "convince" can be followed by a noun phrase and a prepositional phrase starting with the preposition "of" (e.g., he convinced me of his innocence). It can also be followed by a noun phrase and a to-infinitive phrase (e.g., he convinced me to go to the party). This information prevents the system from deleting the "of" prepositional phrase or the to-infinitive that is part of the verb phrase.

At the end of this step, each node in the parse tree — including both leaf nodes and intermediate nodes — is annotated with a value indicating whether it is grammatically obligatory. Note that whether a node is obligatory is relative to its parent node only. For example, whether a determiner is obligatory is relative to the noun phrase it is in; whether a prepositional phrase is obligatory is relative to the sentence or the phrase it is in.

Step 3: Context information.
In this step, the system decides which components in the sentence are most related to the main topic being discussed. To measure the importance of a phrase in the local context, the system relies on lexical links between words. The hypothesis is that the more connected a word is with other words in the local context, the more likely it is to be the focus of the local context. We link the words in the extracted sentence with words in its local context, if they are repetitions, morphologically related, or linked in WordNet through one of the lexical relations. The system then computes an importance score for each word in the extracted sentence, based on the number of links it has with other words and the types of links. The formula for computing the context importance score for a word w is as follows:

$$ContextWeight(w) = \sum_{i=1}^{9}(L_i \times NUM_i(w))$$

Here, i represents the different types of lexical relations the system considered, including repetition, inflectional relation, derivational relation, and the lexical relations from WordNet. We assigned a weight to each type of lexical relation, represented by L_i in the formula. Relations such as repetition or inflectional relation are considered more important and are assigned higher weights, while relations such as hypernym are considered less important and assigned lower weights. $NUM_i(w)$ in the formula represents the number of a particular type of lexical links the word w has with words in the local context.

After an importance score is computed for each word, each phrase in the sentence gets a score by adding up the scores of its children nodes in the parse tree. This score indicates how important the phrase is in the local context.

Step 4: Corpus evidence.
The program uses a corpus consisting of sentences reduced by human professionals and their corresponding original sentences to compute how likely humans remove a certain phrase. The system first parsed the sentences in the corpus using ESG parser. It then marked which subtrees in these parse trees (i.e., phrases in the sentences) were removed by humans. Using this corpus of marked parse trees, we can compute how likely a subtree is removed from its parent node. For example, we can compute the probability that the "when" temporal clause is removed when the main verb is "give", represented as *Prob*("when-clause is removed"|"v=give"), or the probability that the to-infinitive modifier of the head noun "device" is removed, represented as *Prob*("to-infinitive modifier is removed"|"n=device"). These probabilities are computed using Bayes's rule. For example, the probability that the "when" temporal clause is removed when the main verb is "give", *Prob*("when-clause is removed"|"v=give"), is computed as the product of *Prob*("v=give"|"when-clause is removed") (i.e., the probability that the main verb is "give" when the "when" clause is removed) and *Prob*("when-clause is removed") (i.e., the probability that the "when" clause is removed), divided by *Prob*("v=give") (i.e., the probability that the main verb is "give").

Besides computing the probability that a phrase is removed, we also compute two other types of probabilities: the probability that a phrase is reduced (i.e., the phrase is not removed as a whole, but some components in the phrase are removed), and the probability that a phrase is unchanged at all (i.e., neither removed nor reduced).

These corpus probabilities help us capture human practice. For example, for sentences like "The agency reported that ...", "The other source says that ...", "The new study suggests that ...", the that-clause following the say-verb (i.e., report, say, and suggest) in each sentence is very rarely changed at all by professionals. The system can capture this human practice, since the probability that *that-clause* of the verb *say* or *report* being unchanged at all will be relatively high, which will help the system to avoid removing components in the that-clause.

These corpus probabilities are computed beforehand using a training corpus. They are then stored in a table and loaded at running time.

Step 5: Final Decision.
The final reduction decisions are based on the results from all the earlier steps. To decide which phrases to remove, the system traverses the sentence parse tree, which now have been annotated with different types of information from earlier steps, in the top-down order and decides which subtrees should be removed, reduced or unchanged. A subtree (i.e., a phrase) is removed only if it is not grammatically obligatory, not the focus of the local context (indicated by a low importance score), and has a reasonable probability of being removed by humans.

Figure 1 shows sample output of the reduction program. The reduced sentences produced by humans are also provided for comparison.

3 Evaluation

3.1 The evaluation scheme

We define a measure called *success rate* to evaluate the performance of our sentence reduction program.

Example 1:
Original sentence : *When it arrives sometime next year in new TV sets,* **the V-chip will give parents a new and potentially revolutionary device to block out programs they don't want their children to see.**
Reduction program: The V-chip will give parents a new and potentially revolutionary device to block out programs they don't want their children to see.
Professionals : The V-chip will give parents a device to block out programs they don't want their children to see.

Example 2:
Original sentence : **Som and Hoffman's creation would allow broadcasters to insert multiple ratings into a show,** *enabling the V-chip to filter out racy or violent material but leave unexceptional portions of a show alone.*
Reduction Program: Som and Hoffman's creation would allow broadcasters to insert multiple ratings into a show.
Professionals : *(the same)*

Figure 1: Sample output of sentence reduction program

The success rate computes the percentage of system's reduction decisions that agree with those of humans.

We compute the *success rate* in the following way. The reduction process can be considered as a series of decision-making process along the edges of a sentence parse tree. At each node of the parse tree, both the human and the program make a decision whether to remove the node or to keep it. If a node is removed, the subtree with that node as the root is removed as a whole, thus no decisions are needed for the descendants of the removed node. If the node is kept, we consider that node as the root and repeat this process.

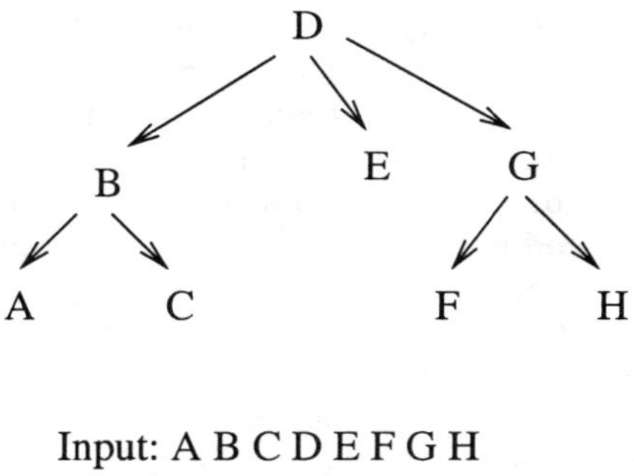

Figure 2: Sample sentence and parse tree

Suppose we have an input sentence *(ABCDEFGH)*, which has a parse tree shown in Figure 2. Suppose a human reduces the sentence to *(ABDGH)*, which can be translated to a series of decisions made along edges in the sentence parse tree as shown in Figure 3. The symbol "y" along an edge means the node it points to will be kept, and "n" means the node will be removed. Suppose the program reduces the sentence to *(BCD)*, which can be translated similarly to the annotated tree shown in Figure 4.

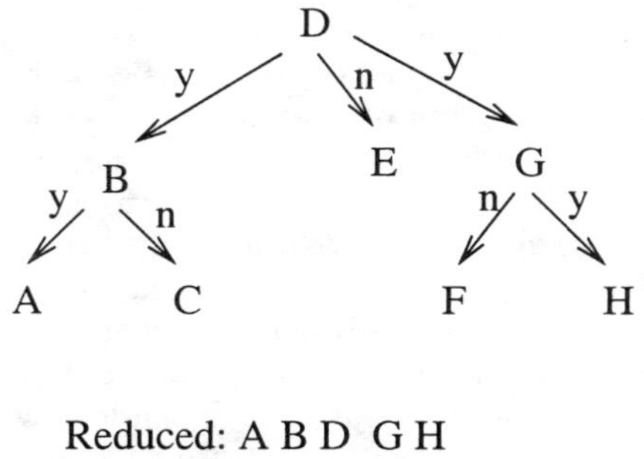

Figure 3: Reduced form by a human

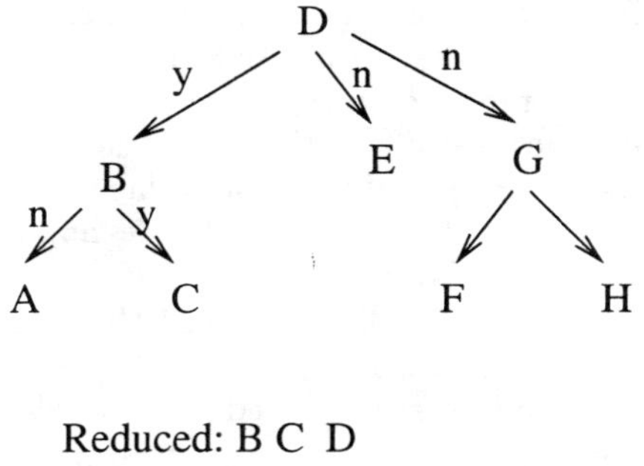

Figure 4: Reduced form by the program

We can see that along five edges (they are D→B, D→E, D→G, B→A, B→C), both the human and the program made decisions. Two out of the five decisions agree (they are D→B and D→E), so the success rate is 2/5 (40%). The *success rate* is defined as:

$$\text{success rate} = \frac{\text{\# of edges along which the human and the program have made the same decision}}{\text{the total \# of edges along which both the human and the progam have made decisions}}$$

Note that the edges along which only the human or the program has made a decision (e.g., G→F and G→F in Figure 3 and Figure 4) are not considered in the computation of success rate, since there is no agreement issue in such cases.

3.2 Evaluation result

In the evaluation, we used 400 sentences in the corpus to compute the probabilities that a phrase is removed, reduced, or unchanged. We tested the program on the rest 100 sentences.

Using five-fold validation (i.e., chose different 100 sentences for testing each time and repeating the experiment five times), The program achieved an average success rate of 81.3%. If we consider the baseline as removing all the prepositional phrases, clauses, to-infinitives and gerunds, the baseline performance is 43.2%.

We also computed the success rate of program's decisions on particular types of phrases. For the decisions on removing or keeping a clause, the system has a success rate of 78.1%; for the decisions on removing or keeping a to-infinitive, the system has a success rate of 85.2%. We found out that the system has a low success rate on removing adjectives of noun phrases or removing adverbs of a sentence or a verb phrase. One reason for this is that our probability model can hardly capture the dependencies between a particular adjective and the head noun since the training corpus is not large enough, while the other sources of information, including grammar or context information, provide little evidence on whether an adjective or an adverb should be removed. Given that whether or not an adjective or an adverb is removed does not affect the conciseness of the sentence significantly and the system lacks of reliability in making such decisions, we decide not to remove adjectives and adverbs.

On average, the system reduced the length of the 500 sentence by 32.7% (based on the number of words), while humans reduced it by 41.8%.

The probabilities we computed from the training corpus covered 58% of instances in the test corpus. When the corpus probability is absent for a case, the system makes decisions based on the other two sources of knowledge.

Some of the errors made by the system result from the errors by the syntactic parser. We randomly checked 50 sentences, and found that 8% of the errors made by the system are due to parsing errors. There are two main reasons responsible for this relative low percentage of errors resulted from mistakes in parsing. One reason is that we have taken some special measures to avoid errors introduced by mistakes in parsing. For example, PP attachment is a difficult problem in parsing and it is not rare that a PP is wrongly attached. Therefore, we take this into account when marking the obligatory components using subcategorization knowledge from the lexicon (step 2) – we not only look at the PPs that are attached to a verb phrase, but also PPs that are next to the verb phrase but not attached, in case it is part of the verb phrase. We also wrote a preprocessor to deal with particular structures that the parser often has problems with, such as appositions. The other reason is that parsing errors do not always result in reduction errors. For example, given a sentence "The spokesperson of the University said that ...", although that-clause in the sentence may have a complicated structure and the parser gets it wrong, the reduction system is not necessarily affected since it may decide in this case to keep that-clause as it is, as humans often do, so the parsing errors will not matter in this example.

4 Discussion and related work

The reduction algorithm we present assumes generic summarization; that is, we want to generate a summary that includes the most important information in an article. We can tailor the reduction system to queries-based summarization. In that case, the task of the reduction is not to remove phrases that are extraneous in terms of the main topic of an article, but phrases that are not very relevant to users' queries. We extended our sentence reduction program to query-based summarization by adding another step in the algorithm to measure the relevance of users' queries to phrases in the sentence. In the last step of reduction when the system makes the final decision, the relevance of a phrase to the query is taken into account, together with syntactic, context, and corpus information.

Ideally, the sentence reduction module should interact with other modules in a summarization system. It should be able to send feedback to the extraction module if it finds that a sentence selected by the extraction module may be inappropriate (for example, having a very low context importance score). It should also be able to interact with the modules that run after it, such as the sentence combination module, so that it can revise reduction decisions according to the feedback from these modules.

Some researchers suggested removing phrases or clauses from sentences for certain applications. (Grefenstette, 1998) proposed to remove phrases in sentences to produce a telegraphic text that can be used to provide audio scanning service for the blind. (Corston-Oliver and Dolan, 1999) proposed to remove clauses in sentences before indexing documents for Information Retrieval. Both studies removed phrases based only on their syntactic categories, while the focus of our system is on deciding *when it is appropriate to remove a phrase.*

Other researchers worked on the text simplification problem, which usually involves in simplifying text but not removing any phrases. For example, (Carroll et al., 1998) discussed simplifying newspaper text by replacing uncommon words with common words, or replacing complicated syntactic structures with simpler structures to assist people with reading disabilities. (Chandrasekar et al., 1996) discussed text simplification in general. The difference between these studies on text simplification and our system is that a text simplification system usually does not *remove* anything from an original sentence, although it may change its structure or words, but our system removes extraneous phrases from the extracted sentences.

5 Conclusions and future work

We present a novel sentence reduction system which removes extraneous phrases from sentences that are extracted from an article in text summarization. The deleted phrases can be prepositional phrases, clauses, to-infinitives, or gerunds, and multiple phrases can be removed form a single sentence. The focus of this work is on determining, for a sentence in a particular context, which phrases in the sentence are less important and can be removed. Our system makes intelligent reduction decisions based on multiple sources of knowledge, including syntactic knowledge, context, and probabilities computed from corpus analysis. We also created a corpus consisting of 500 sentences and their reduced forms produced by human professionals, and used this corpus for training and testing the system. The evaluation shows that 81.3% of reduction decisions made by the system agreed with those of humans.

In the future, we would like to integrate our sentence reduction system with extraction-based summarization systems other than the one we have developed, improve the performance of the system further by introducing other sources of knowledge necessary for reduction, and explore other interesting applications of the reduction system.

Acknowledgment

This material is based upon work supported by the National Science Foundation under Grant No. IRI 96-19124 and IRI 96-18797. Any opinions, findings, and conclusions or recommendations expressed in this material are those of the authors and do not necessarily reflect the views of the National Science Foundation.

References

John Carroll, Guido Minnen, Yvonne Canning, Siobhan Devlin, and John Tait. 1998. Practical simplification of English newspaper text to assist aphasic readers. In *Proceedings of AAAI-98 Workshop on Integrating Artificial Intelligence and Assistive Technology*, Madison, Wisconsin, July.

R. Chandrasekar, C. Doran, and B. Srinivas. 1996. Motivations and methods for text simplification. In *Proceedings of the 16th International Conference on Computational Linguistics (COLING'96)*, Copenhagen, Denmark, August.

Simon H. Corston-Oliver and William B. Dolan. 1999. Less is more: Eliminating index terms from subordinate clauses. In *Proceedings of the 37th Annual Meeting of the Association for Computational Linguistics(ACL'99)*, pages 349–356, University of Maryland, Maryland, June.

Gregory Grefenstette. 1998. Producing intelligent telegraphic text reduction to provide an audio scanning service for the blind. In *Working Notes of AAAI 1998 Spring Symposium on Intelligent Text Summarization*, Stanford University, Standford, California, March.

Hongyan Jing and Kathleen R. McKeown. 1998. Combining multiple, large-scale resources in a reusable lexicon for natural language generation. In *Proceedings of the 36th Annual Meeting of the Association for Computational Linguistics and the 17th International Conference on Computational Linguistics*, volume *1*, pages 607–613, Université de Montréal, Quebec, Canada, August.

Hongyan Jing and Kathleen R. McKeown. 1999. The decomposition of human-written summary sentences. In *Proceedings of the 22nd International ACM SIGIR Conference on Research and Development in Information Retrieval*, pages 129–136, University of Berkeley, CA, August.

Hongyan Jing and Kathleen R. McKeown. 2000. Cut and paste based text summarization. In *Proceedings of NAACL 2000.*

Beth Levin. 1993. *English Verb Classes and Alternations: A Preliminary Investigation.* University of Chicago Press, Chicago, Illinois.

Catherine Macleod and Ralph Grishman, 1995. *COMLEX Syntax Reference Manual.* Proteus Project, New York University.

Michael McCord, 1990. *English Slot Grammar.* IBM.

George A. Miller, Richard Beckwith, Christiane Fellbaum, Derek Gross, and Katherine J. Miller. 1990. Introduction to WordNet: An on-line lexical database. *International Journal of Lexicography (special issue)*, **3**(4):235–312.

George A. Miller, Claudia Leacock, Randee Tengi, and Ross T. Bunker. 1993. A semantic concordance. Cognitive Science Laboratory, Princeton University.

Named Entity Extraction from Noisy Input: Speech and OCR

David Miller, Sean Boisen, Richard Schwartz, Rebecca Stone, Ralph Weischedel
BBN Technologies
70 Fawcett Street
Cambridge, MA 02138
dmiller@bbn.com, boisen@bbn.com, schwartz@bbn.com, rwstone@bbn.com, weischedel@bbn.com

Abstract

In this paper, we analyze the performance of name finding in the context of a variety of automatic speech recognition (ASR) systems and in the context of one optical character recognition (OCR) system. We explore the effects of word error rate from ASR and OCR, performance as a function of the amount of training data, and for speech, the effect of out-of-vocabulary errors and the loss of punctuation and mixed case

1 Introduction

Information extraction systems have traditionally been evaluated on online text with relatively few errors in the input. For example, this description of the Nominator system (Wacholder et al. 1997) would apply to several other systems: "We chose The Wall Street Journal corpus because it follows standard stylistic conventions, especially capitalization, which is essential for Nominator to work." The real-world challenge, however, is pointed out in Palmer and Day (1997): "It is also unknown how the existing high-scoring systems would perform on less well-behaved texts, such as single-case texts, non-newswire texts, or text obtained via optical character recognition (OCR)."

In this paper we explore how performance degrades on noisy input, in particular on broadcast news (speech) and on newspaper (printed matter). Error rates of automatic speech recognizers (ASR) on broadcast news are still very high, e.g., 14-28% word error. Though character error can be very low for laser printer output, word error rates of 20% are possible for OCR systems applied to newsprint or low-quality printed matter.

In this paper, we evaluate a learning algorithm, a hidden Markov model (HMM), for named entity extraction applied to human transcripts of news, to transcripts without case or punctuation (perfect speech output), to errorful ASR output and to OCR output. Extracting information from noisy sources poses the following challenges, which are addressed in the paper.

- Since speech recognizers do not generate mixed case nor punctuation, how much do case and punctuation contribute to recognizing names in English? (Section 3.) Note that these challenges also arise in languages without case to signal proper nouns (e.g., Chinese, German, Japanese), in mono-case English or informal English (e.g., emails).
- How much will performance degrade with increasing error in the input? (Section 4.)
- How does closed vocabulary recognition affect information extraction performance? (Section 5)
- For the learning algorithm employed, how much training and effort are required? (Section 6)
- How much do lists of names contribute to performance? (Section 7)

2 Algorithms and Data

2.1 Task Definition and Data

The named entity (NE) task used for this evaluation requires the system to identify all named locations, named persons, named organizations, dates, times, monetary amounts, and percentages. The task definition is given in Chinchor, et al. (1998).

For speech recognition, roughly 175 hours of news broadcasts (roughly 1.2m words of audio) were available from the National Institute for Science and Technology (NIST) for training. All of that data includes both the audio and a manual transcription. The test set consisted of 3 hours of news (roughly 25k words).

For the combined OCR/NE system, the OCR component was trained on the University of Washington English Image Database, which is comprised primarily of technical journal articles. The NE system was trained separately on 690K words of 1993 Wall Street Journal (WSJ) data (roughly 1250 articles), including development data from the Sixth Message Understanding Conference (MUC-6) Named Entity evaluation. The test set was approximately 20K words of separate WSJ data (roughly 45 articles), also taken from the MUC-6 data set. Both test and training texts were original text (no OCR errors) in mixed case with normal punctuation. Printing the on-line text, rather than using the original newsprint, produced the images for OCR, which were all scanned at 600 DPI.

2.2 Algorithms

The information extraction system tested is IdentiFinder(TM), which has previously been detailed in Bikel et al. (1997, 1999). In that system, an HMM labels each word either with one of the desired classes (e.g., person, organization, etc.) or with the label NOT-A-NAME (to represent "none of the desired classes"). The states of the HMM fall into regions, one region for each desired class plus one for NOT-A-NAME. (See Figure 2-1.) The HMM thus has a model of each desired class and of the other text. Note that the implementation is not confined to the seven name classes used in the NE task; the particular classes to be recognized can be easily changed via a parameter.

Within each of the regions, we use a statistical bigram language model, and emit exactly one word upon entering each state. Therefore, the number of states in each of the name-class regions is equal to the vocabulary size. Additionally, there are two special states, the START-OF-SENTENCE and END-OF-SENTENCE states. In addition to generating the word, states may also generate features of that word.

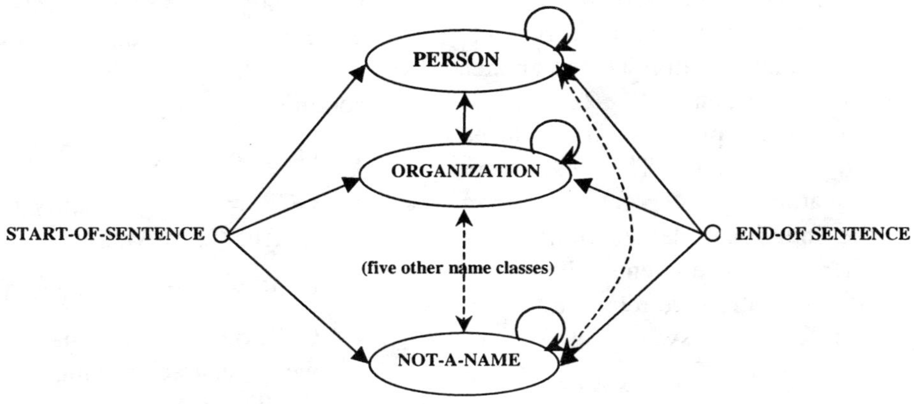

Figure 2-1: Pictorial representation of conceptual model

3 Effect of Textual Clues

The output of each of the speech recognizers is in SNOR (speech normalized orthographic representation) format, a format which is largely unpunctuated and in all capital letters (apostrophes and periods after spoken letters are preserved). When a typical NE extraction system runs on ordinary English text, it uses punctuation and capitalization as features that contribute to its decisions. In order to learn how much degradation in performance is caused by the absence of these features from SNOR format, we performed the following experiment. We took a corpus that had full punctuation and mixed case and preprocessed it to make three new versions: one with all upper case letters but punctuation preserved, one with original case but punctuation marks removed, and one with both case and punctuation removed. We then partitioned all four versions of the corpus into a training set and a held-out test set, using the same partition in all four versions, and measured IdentiFinder's performance.

The corpus we used for this experiment was the transcriptions of the second 100 hours of the Broadcast News acoustic modelling data, comprising 114 episodes. We partitioned this data to form a training set of 98 episodes (640,000 words) and a test set of 16 episodes (130,000 words). Because the test transcriptions were created by humans, they have a 0% word error rate. The results are shown in Table 3-1. The removal of case information has the greater effect, reducing performance by 2.3 points, while the loss of punctuation reduces performance by 1.4 points. The loss from removing both features is 3.4 points, less than the sum of the individual degradations. This suggests that there are some events where both mixed case and punctuation are required to lead IdentiFinder to the correct answer.

	Mixed Case	Upper Case
With punctuation	92.4	90.1
Without punctuation	91.0	89.0

Table 3-1: Effect of case and punctuation on performance(F-measure) on Broadcast News data

It should be noted that because the data are transcriptions of speech, no version of the corpus contains all the textual clues that would appear in newspaper text like the MUC-7 New York Times data. In particular, numbers are written out in words as they would be spoken, not represented using digits, and abbreviations such as "Dr.", "Jr." or "Sept." are expanded out to their full spoken word. We conclude that the degradation in performance going from newspaper text to SNOR recognizer output is at least 3.4 points in the 0% WER case, and probably more due to these other missing text clues.

4 Effect of Word Errors

4.1 Optical Character Recognition (OCR)

The OCR experiments were performed using the system described in Makhoul et al. (1998). Recognition was performed at the character level, rather than the word level, so the vocabulary is not closed (unlike the ASR results discussed in subsequent sections). Figure 4-1 shows IdentiFinder's performance under 4 conditions of varying word error rate (WER):

1. Original text (no OCR, 0% WER)
2. OCR from high-quality (laser-printed) text images (2.7% WER)
3. OCR on degraded images (13.7% WER).
4. OCR on degraded images, processed with a weak character language model (19.1% WER)

For the second and third conditions, 1.3M characters of Wall Street Journal were used for

OCR language model training: the fourth condition used a much weaker character language model, which accounts for the poorer performance.[1]

The interpolated line has been fit to the performance of the OCR-based systems, with a slope indicating 0.6 points of F-measure lost for each percentage point increase in word error. The line has been extrapolated to 0% WER: the actual 0% WER condition is 95.4, which only slightly exceeds the projected value.

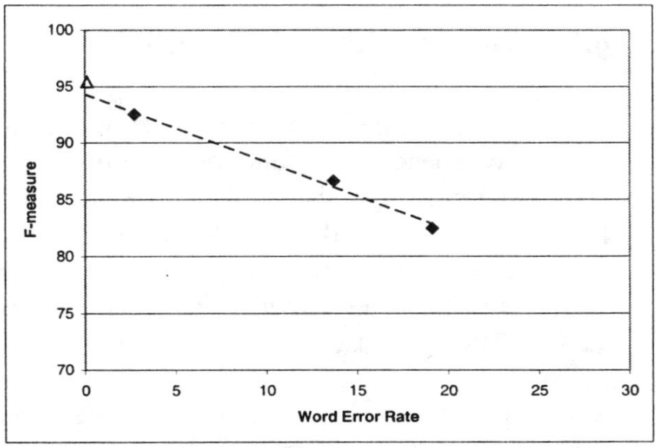

Figure 4-1: IdentiFinder Named Entity performance as a function of OCR word error rate

4.2 Automatic Speech Recognition (ASR)

Figure 5-1 shows IdentiFinder's performance on all speech systems in the 1998 Hub-4 evaluations (Przybocki, et al., 1999). These experiments were run in co-operation with NIST. The interpolated line has been fit to the errorful transcripts, and then extrapolated out to 0% WER speech. As can be seen, the line fits the data extremely well, and has a slope of 0.7 points of F-measure lost for each additional 1% of word error rate. The fact that the extrapolated line slightly overestimates the actual performance at 0% WER (given by a Δ) indicates that the degradation may be sub-linear in the range 0-15% WER.

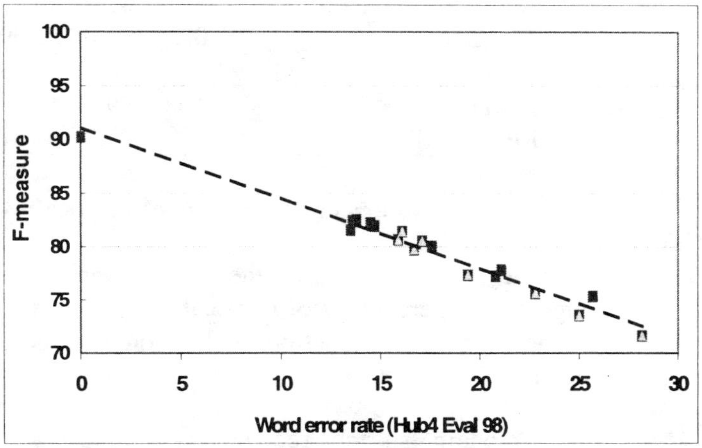

Figure 4-2: IdentiFinder named-entity performance as a function of word error rate (in cooperation with NIST)

5 Out of Vocabulary Rates for Names

It is generally agreed that out-of-vocabulary (OOV) words do not have a major impact on the word error rate achieved by large vocabulary speech recognizers doing transcription. The reason is that speech lexicons are designed to include the most frequent words, thus ensuring that OOV words will represent only a small fraction of the words in any test set. However, we have seen that the OOV rate for words that are part of named-entities can be as much as a factor of ten greater than the baseline OOV for non-name words. This could make OOV a major problem for NE extraction from speech.

To explore this, we measured the percentage of names in the Broadcast News data that contain at least one OOV word as a function of lexicon size. For this purpose, we built lexicons simply by ordering the words of the 1998 Hub-4 Language Modeling data according to

[1] These figures do not reflect the best possible performance of the OCR system: for example, when testing on degraded data, it would be usual to include representative data in training. This was not a concern for this experiment, however, which focussed on name finding performance.

Name Category	Lexicon Size							
	5K	10K	20K	40K	60K	80K	100K	120K
PERSON	34.7	52.7	69.9	85.1	89.4	91.1	91.9	93.9
ORGANIZATION	73.2	90.2	94.2	97.5	98.2	98.5	98.7	98.8
LOCATION	76.6	87.1	92.2	96.2	97.5	98.0	98.8	99.1
TIME	97.0	97.0	99.0	100	100	100	100	100
MONEY	94.4	98.2	98.8	100	100	100	100	100
DATE	96.1	99.3	99.8	100	100	100	100	100
PERCENT	98.9	99.3	100	100	100	100	100	100

Table 5-1: Percentage of in-vocabulary events as a function of lexicon size.

frequency, and truncating the list at various lengths. The percentage of in-vocabulary events of each type as a function of lexicon size is shown in Table 5-1.

Most modern speech recognizers employ a vocabulary of roughly 60,000 words; using a larger lexicon introduces more errors from acoustic perplexity than it fixes through enlarged vocabulary. It is clear from the table that the only name category that might suffer a significant OOV problem with a 60K vocabulary is PERSONs. One might imagine that a more carefully constructed lexicon could reduce the OOV rate for PERSONs while still staying within the 60,000 word limit. However, even if a cleverly designed 60K lexicon succeeded in having the name coverage of the frequency-ordered 120K word lexicon (which contains roughly 40,000 more proper names than the 60K lexicon), it would reduce the PERSON OOV rate by only 4% absolute.

Given that PERSONs account for roughly 50% of the named-entities in broadcast news, the maximum gain in F measure available for doubling the lexicon size is 2 points. Moreover, this gain would require that every PERSON name added to the vocabulary be recognized properly -- an unlikely prospect, since most of these words will not appear in the acoustic training for the recognizer. For these reasons, we conclude that the OOV problem is not a major factor in determining NE performance from speech.

6 Effect of training set size

6.1 Automatic Speech Recognition

We have measured NE performance in the context of speech as a function of training set size and found that the performance increases logarithmically with the amount of training data for 15% WER test data as well as for 0% WER input. However the growth rate is slower for 15% WER test data. We constructed small training sets of various size by randomly selecting sets of 6, 12, 25, and 49 episodes from the second 100 hours of annotated Broadcast News training data. We also defined a training set of 98 episodes from the second 100 hours, as well as sets containing the full 98 episodes plus some or all of the first 100 hours of Broadcast News training. Our largest training set contained 1.2 million words, and our smallest a mere 30,000 words. All training data were converted to SNOR format.

For each training set, we trained a separate IdentiFinder model and evaluated it on two versions of the 1998 Hub4-IE data -- the 0% WER transcription created by a human, and an ASR transcript with 15%. The results are plotted in Figure 6-1. The slopes of the interpolated lines predict that IdentiFinder's performance on 15% WER speech will increase by 1.5 points for each additional doubling of the training data, while performance goes up 1.8 points per doubling of the training for perfect speech input.

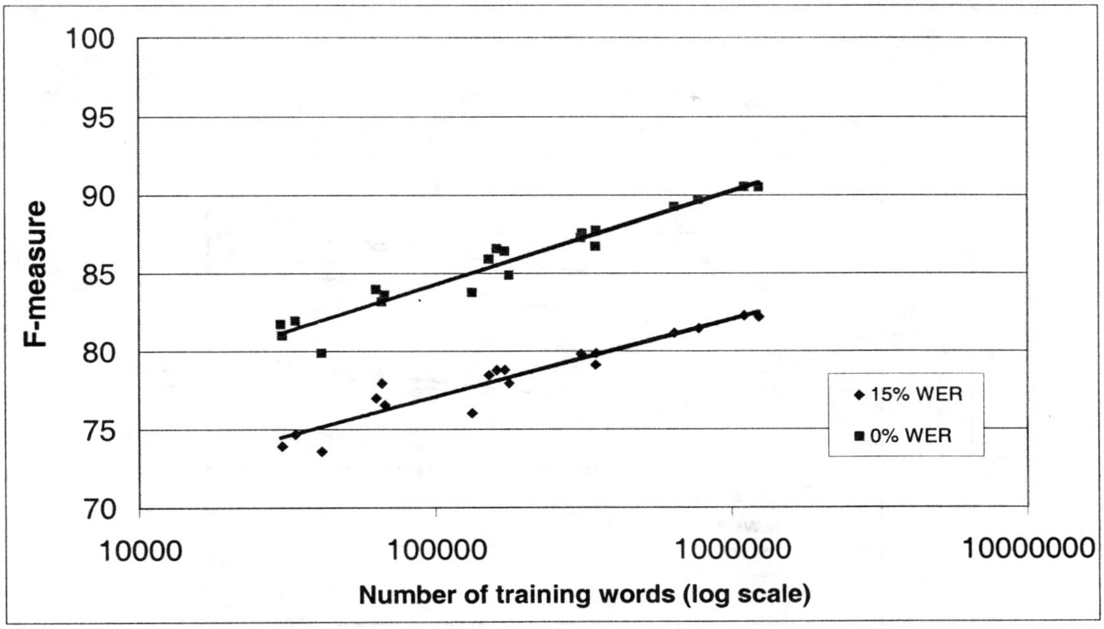

Figure 6-1: Performance as a function of training data for speech.

Possibly, the difference in slope of the two lines is that the real value of increasing the training set lies in increasing the number of distinct rare names that appear. Once an example is in the training, IdentiFinder is able to extract it and use it in test. However, when the test data is recognizer output, the rare names are less likely to appear in the test, either because they don't appear in the speech lexicon or they are poorly trained in the speech model and misrecognized. If they don't appear in the test, IdentiFinder can't make full use of the additional training, and thus performance on errorful input increases more slowly than it does on error-free input text.

6.2 Optical Character Recognition

A similar relationship between training size and performance is seen for the OCR test condition.

The training was partitioned by documents into equal sized sets:

Partition size	Training Size
Eighth	77.5 K words
Quarter	155 K words
Half	310 K words
Whole	620 K words

Using the same test set, each partition was used to train a separate model, which was then evaluated on the different word error conditions: performance was then averaged across each partition size to produce the data points below.

Input Word Error Rate (WER)	Eighth	Quarter	Half	Whole
0% WER (Original text)	92.4	93.7	94.3	95.3
2.7% WER	90.0	90.8	91.6	92.5
13.7% WER	84.3	85.2	86.0	86.6
19.1% WER	79.6	80.4	80.8	82.5

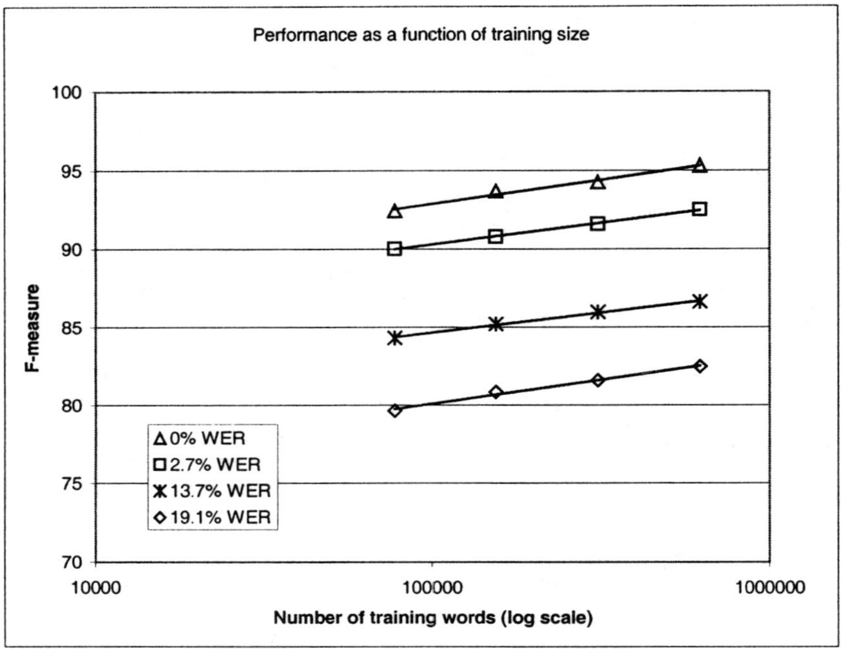

Figure 6–2: Performance as a function of training data for OCR.

While this graph of this data in Figure 6-2 shows a logarithmic improvement, as with the ASR experiments, the rate of improvement is substantially less, roughly 0.9 increase in F-measure for doubling the training data. This may be explained by the difference in difficulty between the two tests: even with only 77.5k words of training, the 0% WER performance exceeds the ASR system trained on 1.2M words.

7 Effect of Lists

Like most NE extraction systems, IdentiFinder can use lists of strings of known to be names to estimate the probability that a word will be a name, given that it appears on a particular list. We trained two models on 1.2 million words of SNOR data, one with lists and one without. We tested on the human transcription (0% WER) and the ASR (15% WER) versions of the 1998 evaluation transcripts. Table 7-1 shows the results. We see that on human constructed transcripts, lists improve the performance by a full point, while on recognizer produced output, performance goes up by only 0.3 points.

	0% WER	15% WER
Without lists	89.5	81.9
With lists	90.5	82.2

Table 7-1: Effect of lists in the presence of speech errors.

8 Related Work and Future Work

To our knowledge, no other information extraction technology has been applied to OCR material.

For audio materials, three related efforts were benchmarked on NE extraction from broadcast news. Palmer, et al. (1999) employs an HMM very similar to that reported for IdentifFinder (Bikel et al., 1997,1999). Renals et al. (1999) reports on a rule-based system and an HMM integrated with a speech recognizer. Appelt and Martin (1999) report on the TEXTPRO system, which recognises names using manually written finite state sales.

Of these, the Palmer system and TEXTPRO report results on five different word error rates. Both degrade linearly, about .7F, with each 1% increase in WER from ASR. None report the effect of training set size, capitalization, punctuation, or out-of-vocabulary items.

Of the four systems, IdentiFinder represents state-of-the-art performance. Of all the systems evaluated, those with the simple architecture of ASR followed by information extraction performed markedly better than the system where extraction was more integrated with ASR.

In general, these results compare favorably with results reported in the Message Understanding Conference (Chinchor, et al., 1998). The highest NE score in MUC-7 was 93.39; for 0% WER, our best score was 90.5 without case and punctuation which costs about 3.4 points.

9 Conclusions

First and foremost, the hidden Markov model is quite robust in the face of errorful input. Performance on both speech and OCR input degrades linearly as a function of word error. Even, without case information or punctuation in the input, the performance on the broadcast news task is above 90%, with only a 3.4 point degradation in performance due to missing textual clues. Performance even with 15% word error degrades by only about 8 points of F for both OCR and ASR systems.

Second, because annotation can be performed quickly and inexpensively by non-experts, training-based systems like IdentiFinder offer a powerful advantage in moving to new languages and new domains. In our experience, annotation of English typically proceeds at 5k words per hour or more. This means interesting performance can be achieved with as little as 20 hours of student annotation (i.e., at least 100k words). Increasing training continually improves performance, generally as the logarithm of the training set size. On transcribed speech, performance is already good (89.3 on 0% WER) with only 100 hours or 643K words of training data.

Third, though errors due to words out of the vocabulary of the speech recognizer are a problem, they represent only about 15% of the errors made by the combined speech recognition and named entity system.

Fourth, we used exactly the same training data, modeling, and search algorithm for errorful input as we do for error-free input. For OCR, we trained on correct newswire once only for both correct text input 0% (WER) and for a variety of errorful text input conditions. For speech, we simply transformed text training data into SNOR format and retrained. Using this approach, the only cost of handling errorful input from OCR or ASR was a small amount of computing time. There were no rules to rewrite, no lists to change, and no vocabulary adjustments. Even so, the degradation in performance on errorful input is no worse than the word error rate of the OCR/ASR system.

Acknowledgments

The work reported here was supported in part by the Defense Advanced Research Projects Agency. Technical agent for part of this work was NRaD under contract number N66001-97-D-8501. The views and conclusions contained in this document are those of the authors and should not be interpreted as necessarily representing the official policies, either expressed or implied, of the Defense Advanced Research Projects Agency or the United States Government.

References

D. E. Appelt, D. Martin, "Named Entity Extraction from Speech: Approach and Results Using the TextPro System," *Proceedings Of The DARPA Broadcast News Workshop, February 28-March 3,* Morgan Kaufmann Publishers, pp 51-54 (1999).

D. Bikel, S. Miller, R. Schwartz, and R. Weischedel, 'Nymble: a High-Performance Learning Name-finder". In *Fifth Conference on Applied Natural Language Processing*, (published by ACL) pp 194-201 (1997).

D. Bikel, R. Schwartz, and R. Weischedel, "An Algorithm that Learns What's in a Name," *Machine Learning 34*, pp 211-231, (1999).

N. Chinchor, "MUC-7 Named Entity Task Definition Version 3.5". Available by ftp from ftp.muc.saic.com/pub/MUC/MUC7-guidelines. (1997).

N. Chincor, P. Robinson, E. Brown, "HUB-4 Named Entity Task Definition Version 4.8". Available by ftp from www.nist.gov/speech/hub4_98. (1998).

J. Makhoul, R. Schwartz, C. Lapre, and I. Bazzi, "A Script-Independent Methodology for Optical Character Recognition,", *Pattern Recognition,* pp 1285-1294 (1998).

Z. Lu, R. Schwartz, P. Natarajan, I. Bazzi, J. Makhoul, "Advances in the BBN BYBLOS OCR System," *Proceedings of the International Conference on Document Analysis and Recognition*, (1999).

D. D. Palmer, J. D. Burger, M. Ostendorf, "Information Extraction from Broadcast News Speech Data," *Proceedings Of The DARPA Broadcast News Workshop, February 28-March 3,* Morgan Kaufmann Publishers, pp 41-46 (1999).

M. A. Przybocki, J. G. Fiscus, J. S. Garofolo, D. S. Pallett, "1998 Hub-4 Information Extraction Evaluation," *Proceedings Of The DARPA Broadcast News Workshop, February 28-March 3,* Morgan Kaufmann Publishers, pp 13-18 (1999).

S. Renals, Y. Gotoh, R. Gaizauskas, M. Stevenson, "Baseline IE-NE Experiments Using the SPRACH/LASIE System," *Proceedings Of The DARPA Broadcast News Workshop, February 28-March 3,* Morgan Kaufmann Publishers, pp 47-50 (1999).

Improving Testsuites via Instrumentation

Norbert Bröker
Eschenweg 3
69231 Rauenberg
Germany
norbert.broeker@sap.com

Abstract

This paper explores the usefulness of a technique from software engineering, namely code instrumentation, for the development of large-scale natural language grammars. Information about the usage of grammar rules in test sentences is used to detect untested rules, redundant test sentences, and likely causes of overgeneration. Results show that less than half of a large-coverage grammar for German is actually tested by two large testsuites, and that 10–30% of testing time is redundant. The methodology applied can be seen as a re-use of grammar writing knowledge for testsuite compilation.

1 Introduction

Computational Linguistics (CL) has moved towards the marketplace: One finds programs employing CL-techniques in every software shop: Speech Recognition, Grammar and Style Checking, and even Machine Translation are available as products. While this demonstrates the applicability of the research done, it also calls for a rigorous development methodology of such CL application products.

In this paper,[1] I describe the adaptation of a technique from Software Engineering, namely code instrumentation, to grammar development. Instrumentation is based on the simple idea of marking any piece of code used in processing, and evaluating this usage information afterwards. The application I present here is the evaluation and improvement of grammar and testsuites; other applications are possible.

1.1 Software Engineering vs. Grammar Engineering

Both software and grammar development are similar processes: They result in a system transforming some input into some output, based on a functional specification (e.g., cf. (Ciravegna et al., 1998) for the application of a particular software design methodology to linguistic engineering). Although Grammar Engineering usually is not based on concrete specifications, research from linguistics provides an informal specification.

Software Engineering developed many methods to assess the quality of a program, ranging from static analysis of the program code to dynamic testing of the program's behavior. Here, we adapt dynamic testing, which means running the implemented program against a set of test cases. The test cases are designed to maximize the probability of detecting errors in the program, i.e., incorrect conditions, incompatible assumptions on subsequent branches, etc. (for overviews, cf. (Hetzel, 1988; Liggesmeyer, 1990)).

1.2 Instrumentation in Grammar Engineering

How can we fruitfully apply the idea of measuring the coverage of a set of test cases to grammar development? I argue that by exploring the relation between grammar and testsuite, one can improve both of them. Even the traditional usage of testsuites to indicate grammar gaps or overgeneration can profit from a precise indication of the grammar rules used to parse the sentences (cf. Sec.4). Conversely, one may use the grammar to improve the testsuite, both in terms of its coverage (cf. Sec.3.1) and its economy (cf. Sec.3.2).

Viewed this way, testsuite writing can benefit from grammar development because both describe the syntactic constructions of a natural language. Testsuites systematically list these constructions, while grammars give generative procedures to construct them. Since there are currently many more grammars than testsuites, we may re-use the work that has gone into the grammars for the improvement of testsuites.

The work reported here is situated in a large cooperative project aiming at the development of large-coverage grammars for three languages. The grammars have been developed over years by different people, which makes the existence of tools for navigation, testing, and documentation mandatory. Although the sample rules given below are in the format of LFG, nothing of the methodology relies on

[1] The work reported here was conducted during my time at the Institut für Maschinelle Sprachverarbeitung (IMS), Stuttgart University, Germany.

$$\begin{aligned} \text{VP} \Rightarrow \text{V} \quad & \downarrow = \uparrow; \\ \text{NP?} & \downarrow = (\uparrow \text{OBJ}); \\ \text{PP*} & \{ \downarrow = (\uparrow \text{OBL}); \\ & \mid \downarrow \in (\uparrow \text{ADJUNCT}); \}. \end{aligned}$$

Figure 1: Sample Rule

the choice of linguistic or computational paradigm.

2 Grammar Instrumentation

Measures from Software Engineering cannot be simply transferred to Grammar Engineering, because the structure of programs is different from that of unification grammars. Nevertheless, the *structure* of a grammar allows the derivation of suitable measures, similar to the structure of programs; this is discussed in Sec.2.1. The actual instrumentation of the grammar depends on the formalism used, and is discussed in Sec.2.2.

2.1 Coverage Criteria

Consider the LFG grammar rule in Fig. 1.[2] On first view, one could require of a testsuite that each such rule is exercised at least once. Further thought will indicate that there are hidden alternatives, namely the optionality of the NP and the PP. The rule can only be said to be thoroughly tested if test cases exist which test both presence and absence of optional constituents (requiring 4 test cases for this rule).

In addition to context-free rules, unification grammars contain equations of various sorts, as illustrated in Fig.1. Since these annotations may also contain disjunctions, a testsuite with complete rule coverage is not guaranteed to exercise all equation alternatives. The phrase-structure-based criterion defined above must be refined to cover all equation alternatives in the rule (requiring two test cases for the PP annotation). Even if we assume that (as, e.g., in LFG) there is at least one equation associated with each constituent, equation coverage does not subsume rule coverage: Optional constituents introduce a rule disjunct (without the constituent) that is not characterizable by an equation. A measure might thus be defined as follows:

disjunct coverage The disjunct coverage of a testsuite is the quotient

$$T_{\text{dis}} = \frac{\text{number of disjuncts tested}}{\text{number of disjuncts in grammar}}$$

where a disjunct is either a phrase-structure alternative, or an annotation alternative. Optional constituents (and equations, if the formalism allows them) have to be treated as a disjunction of the constituent and an empty category (cf. the instrumented rule in Fig.2 for an example).

Instead of considering disjuncts in isolation, one might take their interaction into account. The most complete test criterion, doing this to the fullest extent possible, can be defined as follows:

interaction coverage The interaction coverage of a testsuite is the quotient

$$T_{\text{inter}} = \frac{\text{number of disjunct combinations tested}}{\text{number of legal disjunct combinations}}$$

There are methodological problems in this criterion, however. First, the set of legal combinations may not be easily definable, due to far-reaching dependencies between disjuncts in different rules, and second, recursion leads to infinitely many legal disjunct combinations as soon as we take the number of usages of a disjunct into account. Requiring complete interaction coverage is infeasible in practice, similar to the path coverage criterion in Software Engineering.

We will say that an analysis (and the sentence receiving this analysis) *relies on* a grammar disjunct if this disjunct was used in constructing the analysis.

2.2 Instrumentation

Basically, grammar instrumentation is identical to program instrumentation: For each disjunct in a given source grammar, we add grammar code that will identify this disjunct in the solution produced, iff that disjunct has been used in constructing the solution.

Assuming a unique numbering of disjuncts, an annotation of the form `DISJUNCT-nn = +` can be used for marking. To determine whether a certain disjunct was used in constructing a solution, one only needs to check whether the associated feature occurs (at some level of embedding) in the solution. Alternatively, if set-valued features are available, one can use a set-valued feature `DISJUNCTS` to collect atomic symbols representing one disjunct each: `DISJUNCT-nn` ∈ `DISJUNCTS`.

One restriction is imposed by using the unification formalism, though: One occurrence of the mark cannot be distinguished from two occurrences, since the second application of the equation introduces no new information. The markers merely unify, and there is no way of counting.

[2]Notation: ?/*/+ represent optionality/iteration including/excluding zero occurrences on categories. Annotations to a category specify equality (=) or set membership (∈) of feature values, or non-existence of features (¬); they are terminated by a semicolon (;). Disjunctions are given in braces ({...|...}). ↑ (↓) are metavariables representing the feature structure corresponding to the mother (daughter) of the rule. Comments are enclosed in quotation marks ("..."). Cf. (Kaplan and Bresnan, 1982) for an introduction to LFG notation.

```
VP⇒V     ↓=↑;
    { e     DISJUNCT-001 ∈ o*;
    | NP   ↓= (↑ OBJ)
            DISJUNCT-002 ∈ o*;
    }
    { e     DISJUNCT-003 ∈ o*;
    | PP+ { ↓= (↑ OBL)
              DISJUNCT-004 ∈ o*;
            | ↓∈ (↑ ADJUNCT)
              DISJUNCT-005 ∈ o*;}.
    }
```

Figure 2: Instrumented rule

Therefore, we have used a special feature of our grammar development environment: Following the LFG spirit of different representation levels associated with each solution (so-called *projections*), it provides for a multiset of symbols associated with the complete solution, where structural embedding plays no role (so-called *optimality projection*; see (Frank et al., 1998)). In this way, from the root node of each solution the set of all disjuncts used can be collected, together with a usage count.

Fig. 2 shows the rule from Fig.1 with such an instrumentation; equations of the form `DISJUNCT-nn`∈ $o*$ express membership of the disjunct-specific atom `DISJUNCT-nn` in the sentence's multiset of disjunct markers.

2.3 Processing Tools

Tool support is mandatory for a scenario such as instrumentation: Nobody will manually add equations such as those in Fig. 2 to several hundred rules. Based on the format of the grammar rules, an algorithm instrumenting a grammar can be written down easily.

Given a grammar and a testsuite or corpus to compare, first an instrumented grammar must be constructed using such an algorithm. This instrumented grammar is then used to parse the testsuite, yielding a set of solutions associated with information about usage of grammar disjuncts. Up to this point, the process is completely automatic. The following two sections discuss two possibilities to evaluate this information.

3 Quality of Testsuites

This section addresses the aspects of completeness ("does the testsuite exercise all disjuncts in the grammar?") and economy of a testsuite ("is it minimal?").

Complementing other work on testsuite construction (cf. Sec.5), we will assume that a grammar is already available, and that a testsuite has to be constructed or extended. While one may argue that grammar and testsuite should be developed in parallel, such that the coding of a new grammar disjunct is accompanied by the addition of suitable test cases, and vice versa, this is seldom the case. Apart from the existence of grammars which lack a testsuite, and to which this procedure could be usefully applied, there is the more principled obstacle of the evolution of the grammar, leading to states where previously necessary rules silently loose their usefulness, because their function is taken over by some other rules, structured differently. This is detectable by instrumentation, as discussed in Sec.3.1.

On the other hand, once there is a testsuite, you want to use it in the most economic way, avoiding redundant tests. Sec.3.2 shows that there are different levels of redundancy in a testsuite, dependent on the specific grammar used. Reduction of this redundancy can speed up the test activity, and give a clearer picture of the grammar's performance.

3.1 Testsuite Completeness

If the disjunct coverage of a testsuite is 1 for some grammar, the testsuite is *complete* w.r.t. this grammar. Such a testsuite can reliably be used to monitor changes in the grammar: Any reduction in the grammar's coverage will show up in the failure of some test case (for negative test cases, cf. Sec.4).

If there is no complete testsuite, one can – via instrumentation – identify disjuncts in the grammar for which no test case exists. There might be either (i) appropriate, but untested, disjuncts calling for the addition of a test case, or (ii) inappropriate disjuncts, for which one cannot construct a grammatical test case relying on them (e.g., left-overs from rearranging the grammar). Grammar instrumentation singles out all untested disjuncts automatically, but cases (i) and (ii) have to be distinguished manually.

Checking completeness of our local testsuite of 1787 items, we found that only 1456 out of 3730 grammar disjuncts in our German grammar were tested, yielding $T_{dis} = 0.39$ (the TSNLP testsuite containing 1093 items tests only 1081 disjuncts, yielding $T_{dis} = 0.28$).[3] Fig.3 shows an example of a gap in our testsuite (there are no examples of circumpositions), while Fig.4 shows an inapproppriate disjunct thus discovered (the category ADVadj has been eliminated in the lexicon, but not in all rules). Another error class is illustrated by Fig.5, which shows a rule that can never be used due to an LFG coherence violation; the grammar is inconsistent here.[4]

[3]There are, of course, unparsed but grammatical test cases in both testsuites, which have not been taken into account in these figures. This explains the difference to the overall number of 1582 items in the German TSNLP testsuite.

[4]Test cases using a free dative pronoun may be in the testsuite, but receive no analysis since the grammatical function FREEDAT is not defined as such in the configuration section.

```
PPstd⇒ Pprae      ↓=↑;
       NPstd      ↓= (↑ OBJ);
       { e        DISJUNCT-011 ∈ o*;
       | Pcircum ↓=↑;
                  DISJUNCT-012 ∈ o*
                  "unused disjunct";
       }
```

Figure 3: Appropriate untested disjunct

```
ADVP⇒ { { e        DISJUNCT-021 ∈ o*;
        | ADVadj ↓=↑
                   DISJUNCT-022 ∈ o*
                   "unused disjunct";
        }
        ADVstd  ↓=↑
                   DISJUNCT-023 ∈ o*
                   "unused disjunct";
        }
      | ...
      }.
```

Figure 4: Inappropriate disjunct

```
VPargs ⇒ { ...
         | PRONstd ↓= (↑ FREEDAT)
                   (↓ CASE) = dat
                   (↓ PRON-TYPE) = pers
                   ¬(↑ OBJ2)
                   DISJUNCT-041 ∈ o*
                   "unused disjunct";

         | ...
         }.
```

Figure 5: Inconsistent disjunct

1 ein guter alter Wein
ein guter alter trockener Wein
'*a good old (dry) wine*'
2 Er ißt das Schnitzel roh.
Er ißt das Schnitzel nackt.
Er ißt das Schnitzel schnell.
'*He eats the schnitzel naked/raw/quickly.*'
3 Otto versucht oft zu lachen.
Otto versucht zu lachen.
'*Otto (often) tries to laugh.*'

Figure 6: Sets of equivalent test cases

3.2 Testsuite Economy

Besides being complete, a testsuite must be economical, i.e., contain as few items as possible without sacrificing its diagnostic capabilities. Instrumentation can identify redundant test cases. Three criteria can be applied in determining whether a test case is redundant:

similarity There is a set of other test cases which jointly rely on all disjunct on which the test case under consideration relies.

equivalence There is a single test case which relies on exactly the same combination(s) of disjuncts.

strict equivalence There is a single test case which is equivalent to and, additionally, relies on the disjuncts exactly as often as, the test case under consideration.

For all criteria, lexical and structural ambiguities must be taken into account. Fig.6 shows some equivalent test cases derived from our testsuite: Example 1 illustrates the distinction between equivalence and strict equivalence; the test cases contain different numbers of attributive adjectives, but are nevertheless considered equivalent. Example 2 shows that our grammar does not make any distinction between adverbial usage and secondary (subject or object) predication. Example 3 shows test cases which should not be considered equivalent, and is discussed below.

The reduction we achieved in size and processing time is shown in Table 1, which contains measurements for a test run containing only the parseable test cases, one without equivalent test cases (for every set of equivalent test cases, one was arbitrarily selected), and one without similar test cases. The last was constructed using a simple heuristic: Starting with the sentence relying on the most disjuncts, working towards sentences relying on fewer disjuncts, a sentence was selected only if it relied on a disjunct on which no previously selected sentence relied. Assuming that a disjunct working correctly once will work correctly more than once, we did not consider strict equivalence.

We envisage the following use of this redundancy detection: There clearly are linguistic reasons to distinguish all test cases in example 2, so they cannot simply be deleted from the testsuite. Rather, their equivalence indicates that the grammar is not yet perfect (or never will be, if it remains purely syntactic). Such equivalences could be interpreted as

	# test cases	relative size	total runtime (sec)	relative runtime	# disjuncts in grammar
TSNLP testsuite					
parseable	1093	100%	1537	100%	3561
no equivalents	783	71%	665.3	43%	
no similar cases	214	19%	128.5	8%	
local testsuite					
parseable	1787	100%	1213	100%	5480
no equivalents	1600	89%	899.5	74%	
no similar cases	331	18%	175.0	14%	

Table 1: Reduction of Testsuites

a reminder which linguistic distinctions need to be incorporated into the grammar. Thus, this level of redundancy may drive your grammar development agenda. The level of equivalence can be taken as a limited interaction test: These test cases represent one complete selection of grammar disjuncts, and (given the grammar) there is nothing we can gain by checking a test case if an equivalent one was tested. Thus, this level of redundancy may be used for ensuring the quality of grammar changes prior to their incorporation into the production version of the grammar. The level of similarity contains much less test cases, and does not test any (systematic) interaction between disjuncts. Thus, it may be used during development as a quick rule-of-thumb procedure detecting serious errors only.

Coming back to example 3 in Fig.6, building equivalence classes also helps in detecting grammar errors: If, according to the grammar, two cases are equivalent which actually aren't, the grammar is incorrect. Example 3 shows two test cases which are syntactically different in that the first contains the adverbial *oft*, while the other doesn't. The reason why they are equivalent is an incorrect rule that assigns an incorrect reading to the second test case, where the infinitival particle "*zu*" functions as an adverbial.

4 Negative Test Cases

To control overgeneration, appropriately marked ungrammatical sentences are important in every testsuite. Instrumentation as proposed here only looks at successful parses, but can still be applied in this context: If an ungrammatical test case receives an analysis, instrumentation informs us about the disjuncts used in the incorrect analysis. One (or more) of these disjuncts must be incorrect, or the sentence would not have received a solution. We exploit this information by accumulation across the entire test suite, looking for disjuncts that appear in unusually high proportion in parseable ungrammatical test cases.

In this manner, six grammar disjuncts are singled out by the parseable ungrammatical test cases in the TSNLP testsuite. The most prominent disjunct appears in 26 sentences (listed in Fig.7), of which group 1 is really grammatical and the rest fall into two groups: A partial VP with object NP, interpreted as an imperative sentence (group 2), and a weird interaction with the tokenizer incorrectly handling capitalization (group 3).

Far from being conclusive, the similarity of these sentences derived from a suspicious grammar disjunct, and the clear relation of the sentences to only two exactly specifiable grammar errors make it plausible that this approach is very promising in reducing overgeneration.

1 Der Test fällt leicht .
Die schlafen .

3 Man schlafen .
Dieser schlafen .
Ich schlafen .
Der schlafen .
Jeder schlafen .
Derjenige schlafen .
Jener schlafen .
Keiner schlafen .
Derselbe schlafen .
Er schlafen .
Irgendjemand schlafen .

2 Dieselbe schlafen .
Das schlafen .
Eines schlafen .
Jede schlafen .
Dieses schlafen .
Eine schlafen .
Meins schlafen .
Dasjenige schlafen .
Jedes schlafen .
Diejenige schlafen .
Jenes schlafen .
Keines schlafen .
Dasselbe schlafen .

Figure 7: Sentences relying on a suspicious disjunct

5 Other Approaches to Testsuite Construction

Although there are a number of efforts to construct reusable large-coverage testsuites, none has to my knowledge explored how existing grammars could be used for this purpose.

Starting with (Flickinger et al., 1987), testsuites have been drawn up from a linguistic viewpoint, *"informed by [the] study of linguistics and [reflecting] the grammatical issues that linguists have concerned themselves with"* (Flickinger et al., 1987, , p.4). Although the question is not explicitly addressed in (Balkan et al., 1994), all the testsuites reviewed there also seem to follow the same methodology. The TSNLP project (Lehmann and Oepen, 1996) and its successor DiET (Netter et al., 1998), which built large multilingual testsuites, likewise fall into this category.

The use of corpora (with various levels of annotation) has been studied, but even here the recommendations are that much manual work is required to turn corpus examples into test cases (e.g., (Balkan and Fouvry, 1995)). The reason given is that corpus sentences neither contain linguistic phenomena in isolation, nor do they contain systematic variation. Corpora thus are used only as an inspiration.

(Oepen and Flickinger, 1998) stress the interdependence between application and testsuite, but don't comment on the relation between grammar and testsuite.

6 Conclusion

The approach presented tries to make available the linguistic knowledge that went into the grammar for development of testsuites. Grammar development and testsuite compilation are seen as complementary and interacting processes, not as isolated modules. We have seen that even large testsuites cover only a fraction of existing large-coverage grammars, and presented evidence that there is a considerable amount of redundancy within existing testsuites.

To empirically validate that the procedures outlined above improve grammar and testsuite, careful grammar development is required. Based on the information derived from parsing with instrumented grammars, the changes and their effects need to be evaluated. In addition to this empirical work, instrumentation can be applied to other areas in Grammar Engineering, e.g., to detect sources of spurious ambiguities, to select sample sentences relying on a disjunct for documentation, or to assist in the construction of additional test cases. Methodological work is also required for the definition of a practical and intuitive criterion to measure limited interaction coverage.

Each existing grammar development environment undoubtely offers at least some basic tools for comparing the grammar's coverage with a testsuite. Regrettably, these tools are seldomly presented publicly (which accounts for the short list of such references). It is my belief that the thorough discussion of such infrastructure items (tools and methods) is of more immediate importance to the quality of the lingware than the discussion of open linguistic problems.

References

L. Balkan and F. Fouvry. 1995. *Corpus-based test suite generation.* TSNLP-WP 2.2, University of Essex.

L. Balkan, S. Meijer, D. Arnold, D. Estival, and K. Falkedal. 1994. *Test Suite Design Annotation Scheme.* TSNLP-WP2.2, University of Essex.

F. Ciravegna, A. Lavelli, D. Petrelli, and F. Pianesi. 1998. Developing language reesources and applications with geppetto. In *Proc. 1st Int'l Conf. on Language Resources and Evaluation*, pages 619–625. Granada/Spain, 28-30 May 1998.

D. Flickinger, J. Nerbonne, I. Sag, and T. Wasow. 1987. *Toward Evaluation of NLP Systems.* Hewlett-Packard Laboratories, Palo Alto/CA.

A. Frank, T.H. King, J. Kuhn, and J. Maxwell. 1998. Optimality theory style constraint ranking in large-scale lfg gramma. In *Proc. of the LFG98 Conference.* Brisbane/AUS, Aug 1998, CSLI Online Publications.

W.C. Hetzel. 1988. *The complete guide to software testing.* QED Information Sciences, Inc. Wellesley/MA 02181.

R.M. Kaplan and J. Bresnan. 1982. Lexical-functional grammar: A formal system for grammatical representation. In J. Bresnan and R.M. Kaplan, editors, *The Mental Representation of Grammatical Relations*, pages 173–281. Cambridge, MA: MIT Press.

S. Lehmann and S. Oepen. 1996. TSNLP - Test Suites for Natural Language Processing. In *Proc. 16th Int'l Conf. on Computational Linguistics*, pages 711–716. Copenhagen/DK.

P. Liggesmeyer. 1990. *Modultest und Modulverifikation.* Angewandte Informatik 4. Mannheim: BI Wissenschaftsverlag.

K. Netter, S. Armstrong, T. Kiss, J. Klein, and S. Lehman. 1998. Diet - diagnostic and evaluation tools for nlp applications. In *Proc. 1st Int'l Conf. on Language Resources and Evaluation*, pages 573–579. Granada/Spain, 28-30 May 1998.

S. Oepen and D.P. Flickinger. 1998. Towards systematic grammar profiling:test suite techn. 10 years afte. *Journal of Computer Speech and Language*, 12:411–435.

The Efficiency of Multimodal Interaction for a Map-based Task

Philip COHEN, David McGEE, Josh CLOW
Center for Human-Computer Communication
Oregon Graduate Institute of Science & Technology
20000 N.W. Walker Road
Beaverton, Oregon 97006
{pcohen, dmcgee}@cse.ogi.edu

Abstract

This paper compares the efficiency of using a standard direct-manipulation graphical user interface (GUI) with that of using the QuickSet pen/voice multimodal interface for supporting a military task. In this task, a user places military units and control measures (e.g., various types of lines, obstacles, objectives) on a map. Four military personnel designed and entered their own simulation scenarios via both interfaces. Analyses revealed that the multimodal interface led to an average 3.5-fold speed improvement in the average entity creation time, including all error handling. The mean time to repair errors also was 4.3 times faster when interacting multimodally. Finally, all subjects reported a strong preference for multimodal interaction. These results indicate a substantial efficiency advantage for multimodal over GUI-based interaction during map-based tasks.

Introduction

Nearly two decades ago at ACL'80, Professor Ben Shneiderman challenged the field of natural language processing as follows:

In constructing computer systems which mimic rather than serve people, the developer may miss opportunities for applying the unique and powerful features of a computer: extreme speed, capacity to repeat tedious operations accurately, virtually unlimited storage for data, and distinctive input/output devices. Although the slow rate of human speech makes menu selection impractical, high-speed computer displays make menu selection an appealing alternative. Joysticks, light pens or the "mouse" are extremely rapid and accurate ways of selecting and moving graphic symbols or text on a display screen. Taking advantage of these and other computer-specific techniques will enable designers to create powerful tools without natural language commands. [20, p. 139]

He also challenged us to go beyond mere claims, but to demonstrate the benefits of natural language processing technologies empirically. Since then, not only has there been a long period of unprecedented innovation in hardware, software architectures, speech processing, and natural language processing, but NLP research has also embraced empirical methods as one of its foundations. Still, we have yet to defend claims empirically that technologies for processing natural human communication are more efficient, effective, and/or preferred, than interfaces that are best viewed as "tools," especially interfaces involving a direct manipulation style of interaction. The present research attempts to take a small step in this direction.

In fact, it has often been claimed that spoken language-based human-computer interaction will not only be more natural but also more efficient than keyboard-based interaction. Many of these claims derive from early modality comparison studies [1], which found a 2-3 fold speedup in task performance when people communicated with each other by telephone vs. by keyboard. Studies of the use of some of the initial commercial speech recognition systems have reported efficiency gains of approximately 20% - 40% on a variety of interactive hands-busy tasks [10] compared with keyboard input. Although these results were promising, once the time needed for error correction was included, the speed advantage of speech often evaporated [18][1]. A recent study of speech-based dictation systems [9] reported that dictation resulted in a slower and more errorful method of text creation than typing. From such results, it is often concluded that the age of spoken human-computer interaction is not yet upon us.

Most of these studies have compared speech with typing. However, in order to affect mainstream computing, spoken interaction would at a minimum need to be found to be superior to graphical user interfaces (GUIs) for a variety of tasks. In an early study of one component of GUIs, Rudnicky [18] compared spoken interaction with use of a scroll bar, finding that error correction wiped out the speed advantages of speech, but users still preferred to speak. Pausch and Leatherby [17] examined the use of simple speaker-dependent discrete speech commands with a graphical editor, as compared with the standard menu-based interface. With a 19-word vocabulary, subjects were found to create drawings 21% faster using speech and mouse than with the menu-based system. They conjectured that reduction in mouse-movement was the source of the advantage. In general, more research comparing speech and spoken-language-based interfaces with graphical user interfaces still is needed.

We hypothesize that one reason for the equivocal nature of these results is that speech is often being asked to perform an unnatural act — the interface design requires people to speak when other modalities of communication would be more appropriate. In the past, strengths and weaknesses of various communication modalities have been described [2, 6, 13], and a strategy of developing *multimodal* user interfaces has been developed using the strengths of one mode to overcome weaknesses in another. Interface simulation studies

[1] See also [6, 10] for a survey of results.

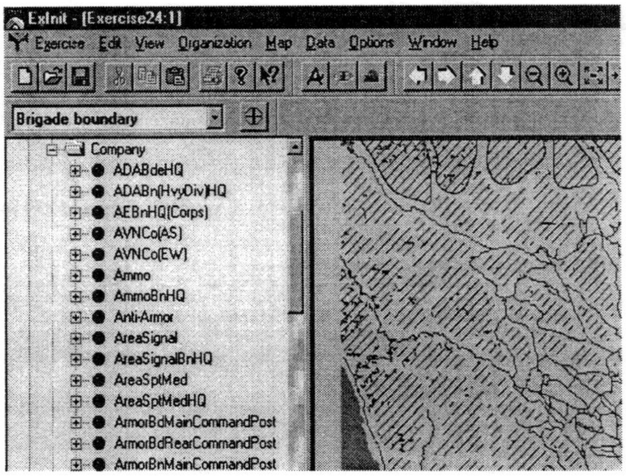

Figure 1. The ExInit GUI

comparing multimodal (speech/pen) interaction with speech-only have found a 35% reduction in user errors, a 30% reduction in spoken dysfluencies (which lead to recognition errors), a 10% increase in speed, and a 100% user preference for multimodal interaction over speech-only in a map-based task [14]. These results suggest that multimodal interaction may well offer advantages over GUI's for map-based tasks, and may also offer advantages for supporting error correction during dictation [16, 19].

In order to investigate these issues, we undertook a study comparing a multimodal and a graphical user interface that were built for the same map-based task[2].

1 Study[3]

This study compares a direct-manipulation graphical user interface with the QuickSet pen/voice multimodal interface [4] for supporting a common military planning/simulation task. In this task, a user arrays forces on a map by placing icons representing military units (e.g., the 82nd Airborne Division) and "control measures,"

[2] A high-performance spoken language system was also developed for a similar task [12] but to our knowledge it was not formally evaluated against the relevant GUI.

[3] A case study of one user was reported in [3]. This paper reports a fuller study, with different users, statistical analyses, and an expanded set of dependent measures (including error correction).

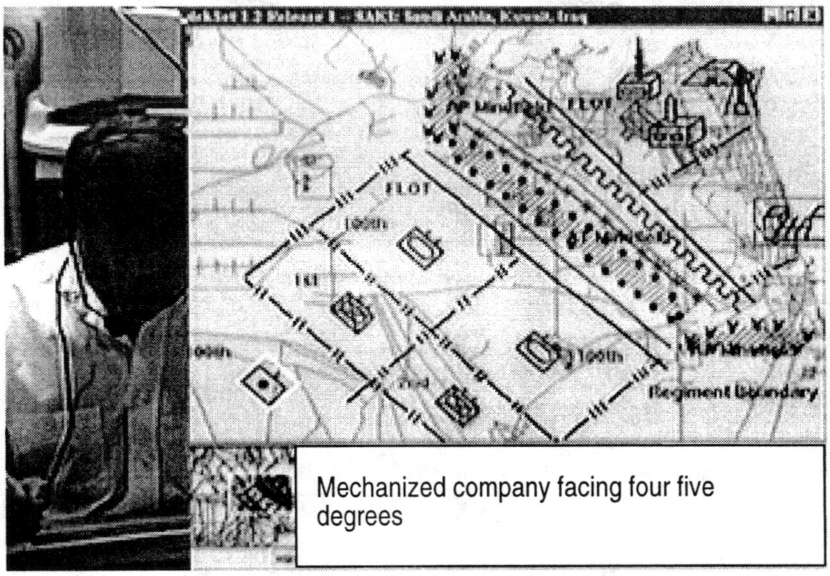

Figure 2. QuickSet

(e.g., various types of lines, obstacles, and objectives). A shared backend application subsystem, called ExInit, takes the user specifications and attempts to decompose the higher echelon units into their constituents. It then positions the constituent units on the map, subject to the control measures and features of the terrain.

1.2 ExInit's GUI

ExInit provides a direct manipulation GUI (built by MRJ Corp.) based on the Microsoft Windows suite of interface tools, including a tree-browser, drop-down scrolling lists, buttons (see Figure 1). Many military systems incorporate similar user interface tools for accomplishing these types of tasks (e.g., ModSAF [7]). The tree-browser is used to represent and access the collection of military units. The user employs the unit browser to explore the echelon hierarchy until the desired unit is located. The user then selects that unit, and drags it onto the map in order to position it on the terrain. The system then asks for confirmation of the unit's placement. Once confirmed, ExInit invokes its deployment server to decompose the unit into its constituents and position them on the terrain. Because this is a time-consuming process depending on the echelon of the unit, only companies and smaller units were considered.

To create a linear or area control measure, the user pulls down a list of all control measure types, then scrolls and selects the desired type.[4] Then the user pushes a button to start entering points, selects the desired locations, and finally clicks the button to exit the point creation mode. The user is asked to confirm that the selected points are correct, after which the system connects them and creates a control measure object of the appropriate type.

Finally, there are many more features to this GUI, but they were not considered for the present comparison. The system and its GUI were well-received by the client, and were used to develop the largest known distributed simulation (60,000 entities) for the US Government's Synthetic Theater of War program (STOW).

[4] There were 45 entries, viewable in a window of size 9. The entries consisted of linear features (boundaries, obstacles, etc.), then areas.

1.3 QuickSet's Multimodal Interface

QuickSet is a multimodal (pen/voice) interface for map-based tasks. With this system, a user can create entities on a map by simultaneously speaking and drawing [4]. With pen-based, spoken, or multimodal input, the user can annotate the map, creating points, lines, and areas of various types (see Figure 2). In virtue of its distributed multiagent architecture, QuickSet operates in various heterogeneous hardware configurations, including wearable, handheld, desktop, and wall-sized. Moreover, it controls numerous backend applications, including 3D terrain visualization [5] military simulation, disaster management [15] and medical informatics.

The system operates as follows: When the pen is placed on the screen, the speech recognizer is activated, thereby allowing users to speak and gesture simultaneously. For this task, the user either selects a spot on the map and speaks the name of a unit to be placed there (e.g, "mechanized company"), or draws a control measure while speaking its name (e.g., "phase line green"). In response, QuickSet creates the appropriate military icon on its map and asks for confirmation. Speech and gesture are recognized in parallel, with the speech interpreted by a definite-clause natural language parser. For this study, IBM's Voice Type Application Factory, a continuous, speaker-independent speech recognition system, was used with a bigram grammar and 662-word vocabulary. In general, analyses of spoken language and of gesture each produce a list of interpretations represented as typed feature structures [8]. The language supported by the system essentially consists of complex noun phrases, including attached prepositional phrases and gerunds, and a small collection of sentence forms. Utterances can be just spoken, or coupled with pen-based gestures. Multimodal integration searches among the set of interpretations for the best joint interpretation [8, 22], which often disambiguates both speech and gesture simultaneously [15]. Typed feature structure unification provides the basic information fusion operation. Taking advantage of the system's mutual disambiguation capability, QuickSet confirms its interpretation of the user input after multimodal integration [11], thereby allowing the system to correct recognition and interpretation errors. If the result is acceptable, the user needs only to proceed; only unacceptable results require explicit disconfirmation. Finally, the multimodal interpretation is sent directly to the ExInit deployment server, effectively bypassing the ExInit GUI.

2 Procedure

The study involved four subjects who were retired US military domain experts, including a US Army National Guard Brigadier General, a US Army Reserve Major, a US Marine Corps Captain, and a US Army communications specialist. Each of the subjects was a frequent computer user, and all had familiarity both with GUIs built around the Microsoft user interface tools as well as with pen-and-paper based drawing of unit symbology and diagrams on maps. Not having used either system before, the subjects were given 30 minutes to learn the ExInit GUI, and the same amount of time to learn QuickSet. The subjects created scenarios of their own design, using entities common to both systems, first on paper, then with each of the two systems. The scenarios had 8-21 units, and 9-33 control measures. The order of interface styles was counterbalanced across subjects in this within-subject design. The systems were run on a Pentium Pro 200MHz computer with an Input Technologies 14" color flat-panel display. Stylus input was used for QuickSet, and keyboard and mouse were employed with the GUI.

The mean time needed for each expert subject to create and position a unit or control measure was calculated for each interface. The time to create an entity began when the mouse entered the relevant interface tool or the time when the microphone was engaged by placing the pen on the map. Mouse "travel" time to the desired interface tool was not included because the pen could not be tracked when it was out of the sensitivity range of the digitizer. Timing ended when the system asked for confirmation of its impending action. Separate creation time calculations were made for units and control measures because the GUI employed different user interface tools for each. Also, whereas the set of QuickSet units was a subset of the units available to the GUI, the set of control measures was identical for QuickSet and the GUI.

The entity creation times reported in this study include correction of all errors needed for both QuickSet and the GUI. Error correction time was accumulated for each attempt until a user confirmation (explicit or implicit) was achieved, or until the entire entity creation attempt was aborted. Only 4 multimodal interactions (total = 20.7 secs.) and 1 GUI interaction (total = 43.2 secs.) were aborted. Errors for QuickSet included out-of-vocabulary or grammar, procedural errors (e.g., not clicking on the map), disfluencies, and recognition errors. For the GUI, errors involved failure to enter or leave drawing mode, selecting the wrong unit in the browser, disconfirming, etc. Overall, QuickSet provided an 88.5% successful understanding rate.

By saying "multiple Xs," the QuickSet user could enter a "mode" in which he was creating an entity of type X (e.g., a mechanized company). To support this process, the system stored a discourse referent that was then unified with subsequent input. The user needed only to say "here" and touch the screen in order to create another entity of that type at that location.[5] In these cases, the time taken to enter the mode was amortized over the entities created. Likewise, the time taken to open the unit browser to show the desired unit was amortized over the units of that type created before the browser was again scrolled.

3 Results

Analyses revealed that multimodal interaction resulted in a 3.7-fold speed increase in creating units compared to the GUI, paired t-test, $t(3) = 5.791$, $p < 0.005$, one-tailed. In addition, it provided a 3.3-fold increase in creating control measures paired t-test $t(3) = 8.298$, $p < 0.002$, one-tailed (see Table I).[6] Much of this speed differential can be traced to the need to browse the echelons of the US military, scrolling long lists of units with the GUI (e.g., 126 units are in the list of US Army companies), followed by a separate dragging operation to position the selected unit. In contrast, QuickSet users specified the type of entity directly, and supplied its location in parallel. Likewise, the speed differential for the control measures may be attributed to the user's ability to both draw and speak in parallel, where the GUI required separate actions for going into and out of drawing mode, for selecting the type of control measure, and for selecting appropriate points on the map.

Although there were fewer errors on average when using the direct manipulation GUI, they were not significantly fewer than when interacting multimodally. In contrast, the time needed to repair an error was significantly lower when interacting multimodally than with the GUI, paired t-test, $t(3) = 4.703$, $p<0.009$, one-tailed. On balance, the same users completing the same tasks spent 26% more total time correcting errors with the GUI than with the multimodal interface.

[5] In general, the user could at that point say anything that would unify with the type of entity being created, such as "facing two two five degrees in defensive posture." This would add additional data to the type of entity being created. Similar data could be added via the GUI, but it required interacting with a dialogue box that was only created after the unit's constituents were loaded (a time-consuming operation). Since QuickSet users could supply the data before the constituents were loaded, it was deemed more fair to ignore this QuickSet capability even though it speeds up multimodal interaction considerably, and employs more extensive natural language processing.

[6] It should be pointed out that the paired t-test takes into consideration the number of subjects. Thus, these findings at these significance levels are particularly strong. A second set of nonparametric tests (Wilcox on signed ranks) were also performed, indicating that multimodal interaction was significantly faster ($p < 0.034$, one-tailed), in creating units and control measures, and also in correcting errors.

Expert Subject	Create Units		Create Contrôl Measures		Repair Errors	
	MM	GUI	MM	GUI	MM	GUI
S1	8.4	25.6	6.5	27.5	12.9	49.3
S2	6.0	14.4	5.2	19.0	7.7	30
S3	6.3	27.2	11.0	24.3	11.6	56.1
S4	4.0	18.5	4.0	17.7	6.3	23.0
Means	6.2	21.4	6.7	22.1	9.6	39.6

Table I: Mean time in seconds required to create various types of entities and to repair errors when interacting multimodally versus with the ExInit GUI

The expert users were interviewed after the study regarding which interface they preferred and why. Multimodal interaction was strongly preferred by all users. Reasons cited included its efficiency and its support of precise drawing of linear and area features.

Conclusions

This study indicates that when the user knows what s/he wants, there can be substantial efficiency advantages of multimodal interaction over direct manipulation GUIs for a map-based taste. Despite having only four subjects, the results exhibited extremely strong statistical significance. These results stand in contrast to prior research [6, 9, 10, 18] in which speed advantages of spoken input were washed out by the cost of correcting recognition errors.

In the present study, not only was multimodal interaction substantially faster than GUI-based interaction, even including error correction times, error correction itself was four times more costly with a GUI than with multimodal interaction. These findings do not support those of Karat et al. [9] who found that for correcting errors in a dictation task, keyboard-mouse input led to a 2.3-fold speed increase over speech. Both sets of findings might be reconciled by noting that advantages of any type of user interface, especially spoken and multimodal interaction, may be task dependent.

We attribute the findings here to the ability of multimodal interfaces to support parallel specification of complementary parts of a communicative act, as well as direct rather than hierarchical or scrolled access to types of entities. Moreover, because the user can employ each mode for its strengths s/he can offload different aspects of the communication to different human cognitive systems, leading to greater efficiency [21] and fewer user errors [13].

It might be claimed that these results apply only to this GUI, and that a different GUI might offer superior performance. First, it is worth noting that the same pattern of results were found for the two GUI elements (drop-down list and hierarchical browser). Thus, the results cannot simply be attributed to the misuse of a hierarchical tool. Second, we point out that this GUI was developed as a product, and that many military systems use very similar user interface tools for the same purposes (selecting units).[7] Thus, these results may have substantial practical impact for users performing this task. More generally, one study cannot establish results for all possible user interfaces. There will certainly be occasions in which a menu-based GUI will be superior to a multimodal interface – e.g., when the user does not in fact know what s/he wants and needs to browse. Other GUI interface tools, such as a search field with command completion, can be envisioned that would provide direct access. However, it is arguable that such an interface element belongs squarely to *graphical* user interfaces, but draws more on features of language. Also, it would require the user to type, even in circumstances (such as mobile usage) where typing would be infeasible. Given our philosophy of using each modality for its strengths, we believe multimodal and graphical user interfaces should be integrated, rather than cast as opposites. Finally, we would expect that these advantages of multimodal interaction may generalize to other tasks and other user interfaces in which

[7] In fact, a recent experiment by the US Marines had mobile combatants using small portable computers with a similar direct manipulation interface as they participated in field exercises. The user interface was generally regarded as the weakest aspect of the experiment.

selection among many possible options is required.

Obviously, a small experiment only illuminates a small space. But it should be clear that when current technologies are blended into a synergistic multimodal interface the result may provide substantial improvements on some types of tasks heretofore performed with graphical user interface technologies. We conjecture that the more we can take advantage of the strengths of spoken language technology, the larger this advantage will become. Future research should be searching for more such tasks, and developing more general toolkits that support rapid adaptation of multimodal technologies to support them.

Acknowledgements

This work was supported in part by the Information Technology and Information Systems offices of DARPA under multiple contract numbers DABT63-95-C-007 and N66001-99-D-8503, and in part by ONR grant N00014-95-1-1164. Many thanks to Jay Pittman for the ExInit integration, Michael Johnston for ExInit vocabulary and grammar development, Liang Chen for graphics and military symbology, Sharon Oviatt for advice in experimental analysis, and to our test subjects.

References

1. Chapanis, A., Ochsman, R.B., Parrish, R.N., Weeks, G. D., Studies in interactive communication: I. The effects of four communication modes on the behavior of teams during cooperative problem solving. *Human Factors*, 1972. 14: pp. 487-509.

2. Cohen, P.R., Dalrymple, M., Moran, D.B., Pereira, F., Sullivan, J., Gargan, R., Schlossberg, J., and Tyler, S., Synergistic use of natural language and direct manipulation, in *Proc. of the Human-Factors in Computing Systems Con-ference (CHI'89)*. 1989, ACM Press: New York, pp. 227-234.

3. Cohen, P.R., Johnston, M., McGee, D., Oviatt, S., Clow, J., and Smith, I., The efficiency of multimodal interaction: A case study, in the *Proceedings of the 5th International Conference on Spoken Language Processing,* Sydney, Australia, 1998, 2: pp. 249-252.

4. Cohen, P.R., Johnston, M., McGee, D., Oviatt, S., Pittman, J., Smith, I., Chen, L., Clow, J., QuickSet: Multimodal interaction for distributed applications, in *Proc. of the Fifth ACM International Multmedia Conference*, E. Glinert, Editor. 1997, ACM Press: New York. pp. 31-40.

5. Cohen, P.R., McGee, D., Oviatt, S., Wu, L., Clow, J., King, R., Julier, S., Rosenblum, L., Multimodal Interaction for 2D and 3D Environments. *IEEE Computer Graphics and Applications*, 1999. 19(4): pp. 10-13.

6. Cohen, P.R. and Oviatt, S.L., The Role of Voice Input for Human-Machine Communication. *Proc. of the National Academy of Sciences*, 1995. 92: pp. 9921-9927.

7. Courtemanche, A.J., Ceranowicz, A., ModSAF Development Status., in the *Proc. of the Fifth Con-ference on Computer Generated Forces and Behavioral Rep-resentation,* Orlando, 1995, Univ. of Central Florida, pp. 3-13.

8. Johnston, M., Cohen, P. R., McGee, D., Oviatt, S. L., Pittman, J. A., Smith., I. Unification-based multimodal integration., in the *Proc. of the 35th Annual Meeting of the Association for Computational Linguistics (ACL) and 8th Conference of the European Chapter of the ACL,* 1997, pp. 281-288.

9. Karat, C., Halverson, C., Horn, D., and Karat, J., Patterns of entry and correction in large vocabulary continuous speech recognition systems, in the *Proc. of Human Factors in Com-puting Systems,* New York, 1999, ACM Press, pp. 568-575.

10. Martin, G.L., The utility of speech input in user-computer interfaces. *International Journal of Man-machine Studies*, 1989. 30(4): pp. 355-375.

11. McGee, D., Cohen, P.R., and Oviatt, S.L., Confirmation in Multimodal Systems, in *Proc. of the 17th International Conference on Computational Linguistics (COLING '98) and 36th Annual Meeting of the Association for Computational Linguistics (ACL'98)*. 1998: Montreal, Canada. pp. 823-829.

12. Moore, R., Dowding, J., Bratt, H., Gawron, J., Gorfu, Y., Cheyer, A., CommandTalk: A Spoken-Language Interface for Battlefield Simulations, *Proc. of the 5th Conference on Applied Natural Language Processing*, Association for Computational Linguistics, 1997: Washington, DC. pp. 1-7.

13. Oviatt, S. L., Pen/Voice: Complementary multimodal communication, Proc. of Speech Tech'92, New York, 238-241

14. Oviatt, S.L., Multimodal interactive maps: Designing for human performance. *Human Computer Interaction*, 1997. 12: pp. 93-129.

15. Oviatt, S.L., Mutual disambiguation of recognition errors in a multimodal architecture, in the *Proc. of the Conference on Human Factors in Computing System,* New York, 1999, ACM Press, pp. 576-583.

16. Oviatt, S.L., Cohen, P. R., Wu, L., Vergo, J., Duncan, L., Suhm, B., Bers, J., Holzman, T., Winograd, T., Landay, J., Larson, J., Ferro, D., Designing the user interface for multimodal speech and gesture applications: State-of-the-art systems and research directions for 2000 and beyond. In submission.

17. Pausch, R. and Leatherby, J. H., A study comparing mouse-only vs. mouse-plus-voice input for a graphical editor, *Journal of the American Voice Input/Output Society, 9:2*, July, 1991, pp 55-66

18. Rudnicky, A.I., Mode Preference in a simple data-retrieval task, in *ARPA Human Language Technology Workshop*. March 1993: Princeton, New Jersey.

19. Suhm, B., Myers, B., and Waibel, A., Model-based and empirical evaluation of multimodal interactive error correction, in the *Proc. of the Conf. on Human Factors in Computing Systems,* New York, 1999, ACM Press, 584-591.

20. Shneiderman, B., Natural vs. precise concise languages for human operation of computers: Research issues and experimental approaches. Proceedings of the 18th Annual Meeting of the Association for Computational Linguistics, and Parasession on Topics in Interactive Discourse, Univ. of Pennsylvania, June, 1980, pp. 139-141.

21. Wickens, C., Sandry, D., and Vidulich, M., Compatibility and resource competition between modalities of input, central processing, and output. *Human Factors*, 1983. 25(2): pp. 227-248.

22. Wu, L., Oviatt, S., L. and Cohen, P. R., Statistical multimodal integration for intelligent HCI, in *Neural Networks for Signal Processing*, Y.H. Hu, Larsen, J., Wilson, E., and Douglas, S., Editors. 1999, IEEE Press: New York. pp. 487-496.

Association for Computational Linguistics

1st Meeting of the North American Chapter of the Association for Computational Linguistics

Proceedings of the Conference

April 29—May 4, 2000
Seattle, Washington, USA

NAACL 2000–PREFACE

On behalf of the Program Committee for NAACL 2000, I am pleased to present you with the papers accepted for presentation at the First Meeting of the North American Chapter of the Association for Computational Linguistics, held in Seattle, Washington, April 29-May 4, 2000.

NAACL received a gratifyingly large number of papers from around the world. Submissions were received from 28 countries. Reviewing was blind to all reviewers and area chairs. It was also highly selective. Out of 166 submissions, 43 were selected for presentation at NAACL 2000.

Selecting the papers was not an easy task. In total, over 110 reviewers, representing 20 different countries, reported to a senior program committee consisting of eight area chairs. The senior program committee spent an intensive day at a meeting in Virginia reaching the final decisions. The area chairs and reviewers cannot be thanked enough for the conscientious and painstaking jobs they performed. All those who contributed are named on the following page, but I would particularly like to express my thanks here to the area chairs: Michael Collins (AT&T Labs - Research), Nancy Green (University of North Carolina at Greensboro), Graeme Hirst (University of Toronto), Kevin Knight (USC/Information Sciences Institute), Dekang Lin (University of Manitoba), Diane Litman (AT&T Labs - Research), Philip Resnik (University of Maryland), and Andreas Stolcke (SRI International).

In its first year, it was advantageous to co-locate NAACL with ANLP, an established conference. To coordinate the two conferences, submissions focusing on end-applications were invited to ANLP 2000, while submissions focusing on methodology were invited to NAACL 2000. Future NAACL conferences will encourage both types of submissions.

Many thanks to Marie Meteer for her outstanding service and support in her role as General Chair.

We are extremely grateful to Linda Fresques for her work on all aspects of the process, from managing the submissions to preparing the proceedings, and to Eli Kane for developing and maintaining the review assignment and submission software. We also thank Lori Allen, Jacob Feddersen, and Nayana Datta for help with the submission process. In addition, we thank the Computing Research Laboratory at New Mexico State University for providing significant internal administrative and technical support.

Finally, we would like to express our gratitude to Kathy McCoy and Priscilla Rasmussen for their consistent support and guidance, and to the ACL and NAACL Executive Committees.

Welcome to NAACL 2000!

Janyce Wiebe
Program Chair
April 2000

NAACL Program Committee

Program Committee Chair:
Janyce Wiebe, New Mexico State University

Area Chairs:
Michael Collins, AT&T Labs - Research
Nancy Green, University of North Carolina at Greensboro
Graeme Hirst, University of Toronto
Kevin Knight, USC/Information Sciences Institute
Dekang Lin, University of Manitoba
Diane Litman, AT&T Labs - Research
Philip Resnik, University of Maryland
Andreas Stolcke, SRI International

Reviewers:
Steve Abney, AT&T Labs-Research
Chinatsu Aone, SRA Corporation
Steven Bird, University of Pennsylvania
Francis Bond, NTT
Eric Brill, Microsoft
Ted Briscoe, University of Cambridge
Rebecca Bruce, University of North Carolina at Asheville
Sandra Carberry, University of Delaware
Claire Cardie, Cornell University
Jean Carletta, University of Edinburgh
Bob Carpenter, SpeechWorks International
John Carroll, University of Sussex
Patrick Caudal, Université Paris
Justine Cassell, Massachusetts Institute of Technology
Eugene Charniak, Brown University
Ciprian Chelba, Johns Hopkins University
Jennifer Chu-Carroll, Bell Labs, Lucent Technologies
Kenneth W. Church , AT&T Labs - Research
Phil Cohen, Oregon Graduate Institute of Science and Technology
Walter Daelemans, University of Antwerp
Ido Dagan , Bar-Ilan University
Mary Dalrymple, Xerox PARC
Barbara DiEugenio, University of Illinois at Chicago
Bonnie J. Dorr, University of Maryland
Michael Elhadad, Ben-Gurion University of the Negev
Thierry Fontenelle, Luxembourg
Robert Gaizauskas, University of Sheffield
Claire Gardent, University of the Saarland
Oren Glickman, Bar-Ilan University
Joshua Goodman, Microsoft Research
Gregory Grefenstette, Xerox Research Centre Europe
Udo Hahn, University of Freiburg
Jan Hajič, Charles University
Eva Hajičova, Charles University
Christine Halverson, SRI International
Mary Harper, Purdue University
Peter Heeman, Oregon Graduate Institute of Science and Technology
Jamie Henderson, University of Exeter
Ulf Hermjakob, USC/Information Sciences Institute
Vasileios Hatzivassiloglou, Columbia University
Julia Hirschberg, AT&T Labs - Research
Beth-Ann Hockey, NASA/RIACS
Rukmini Iyer, BBN Technologies
Mark Johnson, Brown University
Doug Jones, Department of Defense
Arne Jonsson, Linköping University
Sanjeev Khudanpur, Johns Hopkins University
Adam Kilgarriff, University of Brighton
George Kiraz, Bell Labs, Lucent Technologies
Judith Klavans, Columbia University
Alistair Knott, University of Otago
Yuval Krymolowski, Bar-Ilan University
Sadao Kurohashi, Kyoto University
John Lafferty, Carnegie Mellon University
Alon Lavie, Carnegie Mellon University
Claudia Leacock, Educational Testing Service
Lilian Lee, Cornell University
James Lester, North Carolina State University
Lori Levin, Carnegie Mellon University
Hang Li, NEC

Ken Litkowski, CL Research
Mike Macon, Oregon Graduate Institute of Science and Technology
Inderjeet Mani, Mitre Corporation
Chris Manning, Stanford University
Daniel Marcu, USC/Information Sciences Institute
Zvi Marx, Bar-Ilan University
Yuji Matsumoto, Nara Institute of Science and Technology
Susan McRoy, University of Wisconsin-Milwaukee
Dan Melamed, West Group
Paola Merlo, University of Geneva
Vibhu Mittal, JPRC
Mehryar Mohri, AT&T Labs-Research
Johanna Moore, University of Edinburgh
Hwee Tou Ng, DSO National Laboratories, Singapore
Christine Nakatani, Bell Labs, Lucent Technologies
Doug Oard, University of Maryland
Martha Palmer, University of Pennsylvania
Cecile Paris, CSIRO Australia
Dragomir Radev, University of Michigan
Adwait Rathnaparkhi, IBM
Manny Rayner, NASA/RIACS
Jeff Reynar, Microsoft
Klaus Ries, Carnegie Mellon University
Ellen Riloff, University of Utah
Dan Roth, University of Illinois at Urbana-Champaign
Anoop Saakar, University of Pennsylvania
Mark Sanderson, University of Sheffield
Antonio Sanfilippo, European Commission, DG Information Society
Giorgio Satta, University of Padua
Stuart Shieber, Harvard University
Lenhart Schubert, University of Rochester
Donia Scott, Information Technology Research Institute
Satoshi Sekine, New York University
Kristie Seymore, Carnegie Mellon University
Liz Shriberg, SRI International
Karen Sparck-Jones, Cambridge University
Srinivas Bangalore, AT&T Labs-Research
Manfred Stede, Technische Universitat Berlin
Mark Steedman, University of Edinburgh
Suzanne Stevenson, Rutgers University
Richard Sproat, AT&T Labs-Research
Matthew Stone, Rutgers University
Michael Strube, University of Edinburgh
Keh-Yih Su, Behavior Design Corporation
Marc Swerts, IPO Eindhoven
Paul Taylor, University of Edinburgh
David Traum, University of Maryland
Lucy Vanderwende, Microsoft Research
Piek Vossen, Sail Labs
Bonnie Webber, University of Edinburgh
David Weir, University of Sussex
Steve Whittaker, AT&T Labs - Research
David Yarowsky, Johns Hopkins University

NAACL Table of Contents

Section 2: North American Chapter of the Association for Computational Linguistics (NAACL)

Modelling Grounding and Discourse Obligations Using Update Rules

Colin Matheson
University of Edinburgh
Edinburgh, Scotland
colin.matheson@ed.ac.uk

Massimo Poesio
University of Edinburgh
Edinburgh, Scotland
massimo.poesio@ed.ac.uk

David Traum
University of Maryland
Maryland, USA
traum@cs.umd.edu

Abstract

This paper describes an implementation of some key aspects of a theory of dialogue processing whose main concerns are to provide models of GROUNDING and of the role of DISCOURSE OBLIGATIONS in an agent's deliberation processes. Our system uses the TrindiKit dialogue move engine toolkit, which assumes a model of dialogue in which a participant's knowledge is characterised in terms of INFORMATION STATES which are subject to various kinds of updating mechanisms.

1 Introduction

In this paper we describe a preliminary implementation of a 'middle-level' dialogue management system. The key tasks of a dialogue manager are to *update* the representation of dialogue on the basis of processed input (generally, but not exclusively, language utterances), and to *decide* what (if anything) the system should do next. There is a wide range of opinions concerning how these tasks should be performed, and in particular, how the ongoing dialogue state should be represented: e.g., as something very specific to a particular domain, or according to some more general theory of (human or human inspired) dialogue processing. At one extreme, some systems represent only the (typically very rigid) transitions possible in a perceived dialogue for the given task, often using finite states in a transition network to represent the dialogue: examples of this are systems built using Nuance's DialogueBuilder or the CSLU's Rapid Application Prototyper. The other extreme is to build the dialogue processing theory on top of a full model of rational agency (e.g., (Bretier and Sadek, 1996)). The approach we take here lies in between these two extremes: we use rich representations of information states, but simpler, more dialogue-specific deliberation methods, rather than a deductive reasoner working on the basis of an axiomatic theory of rational agency. We show in this paper that the theory of information states we propose can, nevertheless, be used to give a characterisation of dialogue acts such as those proposed by the Discourse Resource Initiative precise enough to formalise the deliberation process of a dialogue manager in a completely declarative fashion.

Our implementation is based on the approach to dialogue developed in (Traum, 1994; Poesio and Traum, 1997; Poesio and Traum, 1998; Traum et al., 1999). This theory, like other action-based theories of dialogue, views dialogue participation in terms of agents performing dialogue acts, the effects of which are to update the information state of the participants in a dialogue. However, our view of dialogue act effects is closer in some respects to that of (Allwood, 1976; Allwood, 1994) and (Singh, 1998) than to the belief and intention model of (Sadek, 1991; Grosz and Sidner, 1990; Cohen and Levesque, 1990). Particular emphasis is placed on the *social* commitments of the dialogue participants (obligations to act and commitments to propositions) without making explicit claims about the actual beliefs and intentions of the participants. Also, heavy emphasis is placed on how dialogue participants socially GROUND (Clark and Wilkes-Gibbs, 1986) the information expressed in dialogue: the information state assumed in this theory specifies which information is assumed to be already part of the common ground at a given point, and which part has been introduced, but not yet been established.

The rest of this paper is structured as follows. The theory of dialogue underlying the implementation is described in more detail in Section 2. Section 3 describes the implementation itself. Section 4 shows how the system updates its information state while participating in a fairly simple dialogue.

2 Theoretical Background

One basic assumption underlying this work is that it is useful to analyse dialogues by describing the relevant 'information' that is available to each participant. The notion of INFORMATION STATE (IS) is therefore employed in deciding what the next action should be, and the effects of utterances are described in terms of the changes they bring about in ISs. A particular instantiation of a dialogue manager, from this point of view, consists of a definition of the contents of ISs plus a description of the update processes which map from IS to IS. Updates are typically triggered by 'full' dialogue acts such as assertions or directives,[1] of course, but the theory allows parts of utterances, including individual words and even subparts of words, to be the trigger. The update rules for dialogue acts that we assume here are a simplified version of the formalisations proposed in (Poesio and Traum, 1998; Traum et al., 1999) (henceforth, PTT).

The main aspects of PTT which have been implemented concern the way discourse obligations are handled and the manner in which dialogue participants interact to add information to the common ground. Obligations are essentially social in nature, and directly characterise spoken dialogue; a typical example of a discourse obligation concerns the relationship between questions and answers. Poesio and Traum follow (Traum and Allen, 1994) in suggesting that the utterance of a question imposes an obligation on the hearer to address the question (e.g., by providing an answer), irrespective of intentions.

As for the process by which common ground is established, or GROUNDING (Clark and Schaefer, 1989; Traum, 1994), the assumption in PTT is that classical speech act theory is inherently too simplistic in that it ignores the fact that co-operative interaction is essential in discourse; thus, for instance, simply asserting something does not make it become mutually 'known' (part of the common ground). It is actually necessary for the hearer to provide some kind of acknowledgement that the assertion has been received, understood or not understood, accepted or rejected, and so on. Poesio and Traum view the public information state as including both material that has already been grounded, indicated by GND here, and material that hasn't been grounded yet. These components of the information state are updated when GROUNDING ACTS such as acknowledgement are performed. Each new contribution results in a new DISCOURSE UNIT (DU) being added to the information state (Traum, 1994) and recorded in a list of 'ungrounded discourse units' (UDUS); these DUs can then be subsequently grounded as the result, e.g., of (implicit or explicit) acknowledgements.

3 Implementing PTT

In this section, we describe the details of the implementation. First, in Section 3.1, we describe the TrindiKit tool for building dialogue managers that we used to build our system. In Section 3.2, we describe the information states used in the implementation, an extension and simplification of the ideas from PTT discussed in the previous section. Then, in Section 3.3, we discuss how the information state is updated when dialogue acts are observed. Finally, in Section 3.4, we describe the rules used by the system to adopt intentions and perform its own actions. An extended example of how these mechanisms are used to track and participate in a dialogue is presented in Section 4.

[1] We assume here the DRI classification of dialogue acts (Discourse Resource Initiative, 1997).

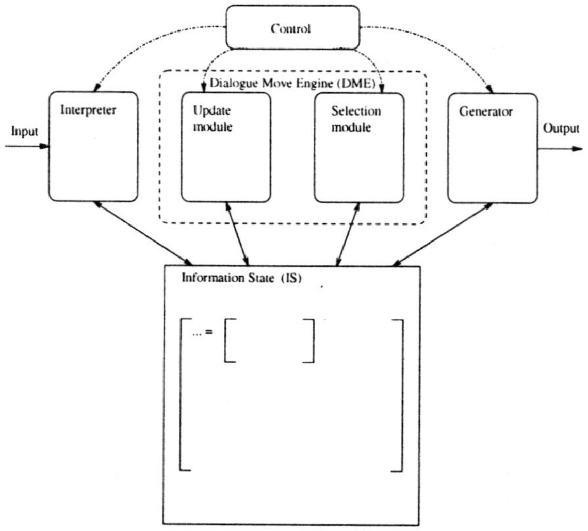

Figure 1: TrindiKit Architecture

3.1 TrindiKit

The basis for our implementation is the TrindiKit dialogue move engine toolkit implemented as part of the TRINDI project (Larsson et al., 1999). The toolkit provides support for developing dialogue systems, focusing on the central dialogue management components.

The system architecture assumed by the TrindiKit is shown in Figure 1. A prominent feature of this architecture is the information state, which serves as a central 'blackboard' that processing modules can examine (by means of defined CONDITIONS) or change (by means of defined OPERATIONS). The structure of the IS for a particular dialogue system is defined by the developer who uses the TrindiKit to build that system, on the basis of his/her own theory of dialogue processing; no predefined notion of information state is provided.[2]. The toolkit provides a number of abstract data-types such as lists, stacks, and records, along with associated conditions and operations, that can be used to implement the user's theory of information states; other abstract types can also be defined. In addition to this customisable notion of information state, TrindiKit provides a few system variables that can also used for intermodule communication. These include `input` for the raw observed (language) input, `latest_moves` which

[2] In TRINDI we are experimenting with multiple instantiations of three different theories of information state (Traum et al., 1999).

contains the dialogue moves observed in the most recent turn, `latest_speaker`, and `next_moves`, containing the dialogue moves to be performed by the system in the next turn.

A complete system is assumed to consist of several modules interacting via the IS. (See Figure 1 again.) The central component is called the DIALOGUE MOVE ENGINE (DME). The DME performs the processing needed to integrate the observed dialogue moves with the IS, and to select new moves for the system to perform. These two functions are encapsulated in the UPDATE and SELECTION submodules of the DME. The update and select modules are specified by means of typed rules, as well as sequencing procedures to determine when to apply the rules. We are here mainly concerned with UPDATE RULES (**urules**), which consist of four parts: a name, a type, a list of conditions to check in the information state, and a list of operations to perform on the information state. **urules** are described in more detail below, in Section 3.3. There are also two modules outside the DME proper, but still crucial to a complete system: INTERPRETATION, which consumes the input and produces a list of dialogue acts in the `latest_moves` variable (potentially making reference to the current information state), and GENERATION, which produces NL output from the dialogue acts in the `next_moves` variable. Finally, there is a CONTROL module, that governs the sequencing (or parallel invocation) of the other modules. In this paper we focus on the IS and the DME; our current implementation only uses very simple interpretation and generation components.

3.2 Information States in PTT

In this section we discuss the information state used in the current implementation. The main difference between the implemented IS and the theoretical proposal in (Poesio and Traum, 1998) is that in the implementation the information state is partitioned in fields, each containing information of different types, whereas in the theoretical version the information state is a single repository of facts (a DISCOURSE REPRESENTATION STRUCTURE). Other differences are discussed below. An example IS with some fields filled is shown in Figure 2; this is the IS which results from the second utterance in the example dialogue discussed in Section 4, *A route please.*[3]

The IS in Figure 2 is a record with two main parts, W and C. The first of these represents the system's (Wizard) view of his own mental state and of the (semi-)public information discussed in the dialogue; the second, his view of the user's (Caller) information state. This second part is needed to

[3]All diagrams in this paper are automatically generated from TrindiKit system internal representations and displayed using the Thistle dialogue editor (Calder, 1998). Some have been subsequently edited for brevity and clarity.

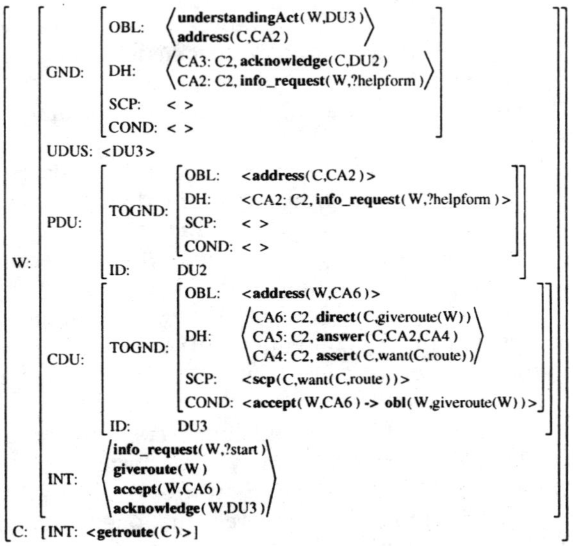

Figure 2: Structure of Information States

model misunderstandings arising from the dialogue participants having differing views on what has been grounded; as we are not concerned with this problem here, we will ignore C in what follows.

W contains information on the grounded material (GND), on the ungrounded information (UDUS, PDU and CDU), and on W's intentions (INT). GND contains the information that has already been grounded; the other fields contain information about the contributions still to be grounded. As noticed above, in PTT it is assumed that for each new utterance, a new DU is created and added to the IS. The current implementation differs from the full theory in that only two DUs are retained at each point; the current DU (CDU) and the previous DU (PDU). The CDU contains the information in the latest contribution, while the PDU contains information from the penultimate contribution. Information is moved from PDU to GND as a result of an **ack** (acknowledgement) dialogue act (see below.)

The DUs and the GND field contain four fields, representing obligations (OBL), the dialogue history (DH), propositions to which agents are socially committed (SCP) , and conditional updates (COND). The value of OBL is a list of action types: actions that agents are obliged to perform. An action type is specified by a PREDICATE, a DIALOGUE PARTICIPANT, and a list of ARGUMENTS. The value of SCP is a list of a particular type of mental states, social commitments of agents to propositions.[4] These are specified by a DIALOGUE PARTICIPANT, and a PROPOSITION. Finally, the elements in DH are dia-

[4]SCPs play much the same role in PTT as do beliefs in many BDI accounts of speech acts.

logue actions, which are instances of dialogue action types. A dialogue action is specified by an action type, a dialogue act id, and a confidence level CONF (the confidence that an agent has that that dialogue act has been observed).

The situation in Figure 2 is the result of updates to the IS caused by utterance [2] in the dialogue in (6), which is assumed to generate a **direct** act as well as an **assert** act and an **answer** act.[5] That utterance is also assumed to contain an implicit acknowledgement of the original question; this understanding act has resulted in the contents of DU2 being grounded (and subsequently merged with GND), as discussed below.

GND.OBL in Figure 2 includes two obligations. The first is an obligation on W to perform an understanding act (the predicate is **understandingAct**, the participant is W, and there is just one argument, DU3, which identifies the DU in CDU by referring to its ID). The second obligation is an obligation on C to **address** conversational act CA2; this ID points to the appropriate **info_request** in the DH list by means of the ID number. Obligations are specified in CDU and PDU, as well. Those in PDU are simply a subset of those in GND, since at point in the update process shown in Figure 2 this field contains information that has already been grounded (note that DU2 is not in UDUS anymore); but CDU contains obligations that have not been grounded yet – in particular, the obligation on W to **address** CA6.

GND.DH in this IS contains a list of dialogue actions whose occurrence has already been grounded: the **info_request** performed by utterance 1, with argument a question,[6] and the implicit **acknowledge** performed by utterance 2.[7] The DH field in CDU contains dialogue acts performed by utterance 2 that *do* need to be grounded: a directive by C to W to perform an action of type **giveroute**, and an **assert** by C of the proposition **want**(C, route), by which C provides an **answer** to the previous **info_request** CA2.

The COND field in CDU contains a conditional update resulting from the directive performed by that utterance. The idea is that directives do not immediately lead to obligations to perform the mentioned action: instead (in addition to an obligation to address the action with some sort of response), their effect is to add to the common ground the information that *if* the directive is **accepted** by the addressee, *then* he or she has the obligation to perform the action type requested. (In this case, to give a route to C.)

[5]The fact that the utterance of *a route please* constitutes an answer is explicitly assumed; however, it should be possible to derive this information automatically (perhaps along the lines suggested by Kreutel (Kreutel, 1998)).

[6]We use the notation ?p to indicate a question of the form ?([x],**p**(x)) .

[7]We assume here, as in (Traum, 1994) and (Poesio and Traum, 1998), that understanding acts do not have to be grounded themselves, which would result in a infinite regress.

3.3 Update Rules in PTT

We are now in a position to examine the update mechanisms which are performed when new dialogue acts are recognised. When a dialogue participant takes a turn and produces an utterance, the interpretation module sets the system variable `latest_moves` to contain a representation of the dialogue acts performed with the utterance. The updating procedure then uses update rules to modify the IS on the basis of the contents of `latest_moves` and of the previous IS. The basic procedure is described in (1) below.[8]

(1)
1. Create a new DU and push it on top of UDUs.
2. Perform updates on the basis of backwards grounding acts.
3. If any other type of act is observed, record it in the dialogue history in CDU and apply the update rules for this kind of act
4. Apply update rules to all parts of the IS which contain newly added acts.

The first step involves moving the contents of CDU to PDU (losing direct access to the former PDU contents) and putting in CDU a new empty DU with a new identifier. The second and third steps deal explicitly with the contents of `latest_moves`, applying one urule (of possibly a larger set) for each act in `latest_moves`. The relevant effects for each act are summarised in (2), where the variables have the following types:

IDx	Dialogue Act Identification Number
DUx	DU Identification Number
DP	Dialogue Participant (i.e., the speaker)
Q	A Question
PROP	A Proposition
Act	An Action
o(DP)	The other dialogue participant
P(ID)	The content of the ID, a proposition
Q(ID)	The content of the ID, a question

[8]See (Poesio et al., 1999; Traum et al., 1999) for different versions of this update procedure used for slightly different versions of the theory.

(2)

act	ID:2, **accept**(DP,ID2)
effect	*accomplished via rule resolution*
act	ID:2, **ack**(DP,DU1)
effect	peRec(w.Gnd,w.pdu.tognd)
effect	remove(DU1,UDUS)
act	ID:2, **agree**(DP,ID2)
effect	push(SCP,**scp**(DP,**P**(ID2)))
act	ID:2, **answer**(DP,ID2,ID3)
effect	push(SCP,**ans**(DP,**Q**(ID2),**P**(ID2)))
act	ID:2, **assert**(DP,PROP)
effect	push(SCP,**scp**(DP,PROP))
effect	push(COND,**accept**(**o**(DP),ID)→ **scp**(**o**(DP),PROP))
act	ID:1, **assert**(DP,PROP)
effect	push(COND,**accept**(**o**(DP),ID)→ **scp**(**o**(DP),PROP))
act	ID:2, **check**(DP,PROP)
effect	push(OBL,**address**(**o**(DP),ID))
effect	push(COND,**agree**(**o**(DP),ID) → **scp**(DP,PROP))
act	ID:2, **direct**(DP,Act)
effect	push(OBL,**address**(**o**(DP),ID))
effect	push(COND,**accept**(**o**(DP),ID) → **obl**(**o**(DP),Act))
act	ID:2, **info_request**(DP,Q)
effect	push(OBL,**address**(**o**(DP),ID))

The **ack** act is the only backward grounding act implemented at the moment. The main effect of an **ack** is to merge the information in the acknowledged DU (assumed to be PDU) into GND, also removing this DU from UDUS. Unlike the other acts described below, **ack** acts are recorded directly into GND.DH, rather than into CDU.TOGND.DH.

All of the other updates are performed in the third step of the procedure in (1). The only effect of **accept** acts is to enable the conditional rules which are part of the effect of **assert** and **direct**, leading to social commitments and obligations, respectively. **agree** acts also trigger conditional rules introduced by **check**; in addition, they result in the agent being socially committed to the proposition introduced by the act with which the agent agrees. Performing an **answer** to question ID2 by asserting proposition P(ID3) commits the dialogue participant to the proposition that P(ID3) is indeed an answer to Q(ID2).

The two rules for **assert** are where the confidence levels are actually used, to implement a simple verification strategy. The idea is that the system only assumes that the user is committed to the asserted proposition when a confidence level of 2 is observed, while some asserts are assumed not to have been sufficiently well understood, and are only assigned a confidence level 1. This leads the system to perform a check, as we will see shortly.

The next three update rules, for **check**, **direct**, and **info_req**, all impose an obligation on the other dialogue participant to address the dialogue act. In addition, the **direct** rule introduces a conditional act: acceptance of the directive will impose an obligation on the hearer to act on its contents.

In addition, all FORWARD ACTS[9] in the DRI scheme (Discourse Resource Initiative, 1997) impose an obligation to perform an understanding act (e.g., an acknowledgement):

(3)

act	ID:c, **forward-looking-act**(DP)
effect	push(OBL,**u-act**(**o**(DP),CDU.id))

The internal urules implementing the updates in (2) have the format shown in (4), which is the urule for **info_request**.

(4)
```
urule( doInfoReq, ruletype3,
  [ hearer(DP),
    latest_moves: in(Move),
    Move:valRec(pred,inforeq) ],
  [ incr_set(update_cycles,_),
    incr_set(next_dh_id,HID),
    next_du_name(ID),
    pushRec(w^cdu^tognd^dh,
          record([atype=Move,clevel=2,id=HID ])),
    pushRec(w^cdu^tognd^obl,
          record([pred=address,dp=DP,
                  args=stackset(
                    [record([item=HID])])])),
    pushRec(w^gnd^obl,
          record([pred=uact,dp=P,
                  args=stackset(
                    [record([item=ID])])])) ]).
```

As noted above, these rules have four parts; a name, a type, a list of conditions, and a list of effects. The conditions in (4) state that there must be a move in `latest_moves` whose predicate is `inforeq`. The effects[10] state that the move should be recorded in the dialogue history in CDU, that an obligation to address the request should be pushed into OBL in CDU, and that the requirement for an understanding act by W should be pushed directly into the list in W.GND.

The fourth and final step of the algorithm cycles through the updating process in case recently added facts have further implications. For instance, when an action has been performed that matches the antecedent of a rule in COND, the consequent is established. Likewise, when an action is performed it releases any obligations to perform that action. Thus, **accept**, **answer**, and **agree** are all ways of releasing an obligation to **address**, since these are all appropriate backward looking actions. Similarly, an agent will drop intentions to perform actions it has already (successfully) performed.

3.4 Deliberation

We assume, in common with BDI-approaches to agency (e.g., (Bratman et al., 1988)) that intentions

[9] Forward acts include **assert**, **check**, **direct**, and **info_request**.

[10] The ID and HID values simply contain numbers identifying the discourse units and conversational acts.

are the primary mental attitude leading to an agent's actions. The main issues to explain then become how such intentions are adopted given the rest of the information state, and how an agent gets from intentions to actual performance.

For the latter question, we take a fairly simplistic approach here: all the intentions to perform dialogue acts are simply transferred to the `next_moves` system variable, with the assumption that the generation module can realise all of them as a single utterance. A more sophisticated approach would be to weight the importance of (immediate) realisation of sets of intentions and compare this to the likelihood that particular utterances will achieve these effects at minimal cost, and choose accordingly. We leave this for future work (see (Traum and Dillenbourg, 1998) for some preliminary ideas along these lines), concentrating here on the first issue – how the system adopts intentions to perform dialogue acts from other aspects of the mental state.

The current system takes the following factors into account:

- obligations (to perform understanding acts, to address previous dialogue acts, to perform other actions)
- potential obligations (that would result if another act were performed, as represented in the COND field)
- insufficiently understood dialogue acts (with a 1 confidence level in CDU.DH)
- intentions to perform complex acts

The current deliberation process assumes maximal cooperativity, in that the system always chooses to meet its obligations whenever possible, and also chooses to provide a maximally helpful response when possible. Thus, when obliged to **address** a previous dialogue act such as a question or directive, it will choose to actually return the answer or perform the action, if possible, rather than reject or negotiate such a performance, which would also be acting in accordance with the obligations (see (Kreutel, 1998) on how acts might be rejected).

In the current implementation, the following rules are used to adopt new intentions (i.e., to update the INT field):

(5)
1. add an intention to **acknowledge**(W,CDU), given an obligation to perform a **u-act**, if everything in CDU is sufficiently understood (i.e., to level 2);
2. add an intention to accept a directive or answer a question as the result of an obligation to address a dialogue act;
3. add an intention to perform an action if COND contains a conditional that will establish an obligation to perform the action, and the antecedent of this conditional is another action that is already intended. (This *anticipatory* planning allows the obligation to be discharged at the same time it is invoked, e.g., without giving an intermediate acceptance of an directive.)
4. add an intention to perform a (dialogue) action motivated by the intention to perform the current task. In the case of the Autoroute domain, we have two cases: the system may decide
   (a) to **check** any dialogue acts in CDU at confidence level 1, which contain information needed to discharge the intention to give a route; or
   (b) to perform a question asking about a new piece of information that has not been established (this is decided by inspecting GND.SCP and CDU.SCP). For example, it may decide to ask about the starting point, the time of departure, etc.

4 Extended Example

In this section, we discuss more examples of how the information state changes as a result of processing and performing dialogue acts. It is useful to do this by looking briefly at a typical Autoroute dialogue, shown in (6).[11] Our implementation can process this sort of dialogue using very simple interpretation and generation routines that provide the dialogue acts in `latest_moves` from the text strings, and produce W's output text from the dialogue acts which the system places in `next_moves`.

(6)

W	[1]:	How can I help?
C	[2]:	A route please
W	[3]:	Where would you like to start?
C	[4]:	Malvern
W	[5]:	Great Malvern?
C	[6]:	Yes
W	[7]:	Where do you want to go?
C	[8]:	Edwinstowe
W	[9]:	Edwinstowe in Nottingham?
C	[10]:	Yes
W	[11]:	When do you want to leave?
C	[12]:	Six pm
W	[13]:	Leaving at 6 p.m.?
C	[14]:	Yes
W	[15]:	Do you want the quickest or the shortest route?
C	[16]:	Quickest
W	[17]:	Please wait while your route is calculated.

We assume that before the dialogue starts, W has the intention to ask C what kind of help is required,

[11]The interchanges have been cleaned up to some extent here, mainly by removing pauses and hesitations.

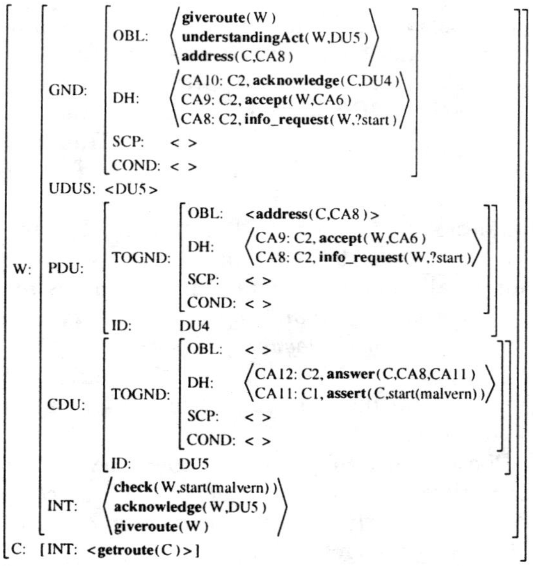

Figure 3: Information State Prompting Check in [5]

and that C has the intention to find a route. We also assume that W has the turn, and that the presence of the *how can I help* intention triggers an utterance directly. Figure 2, presented above, shows the information state after utterance [2]. The intentions in that figure lead directly to the system producing utterance [3].

Looking a little further ahead in the dialogue, Figure 3 shows the information state after utterance [4].[12] Here we can see in CDU.TOGND.DH (along with the **ack** act CA10, in GND.DH) the dialogue moves that this utterance has generated. Note that the assert, CA11, is only at confidence level 1, indicating lack of sufficient certainty in this interpretation as the town 'Great Malvern'. This lack of certainty and the resulting lack of a relevant SCP in CDU.TOGND lead the deliberation routines to produce an intention to check this proposition rather than to move directly on to another information request. This intention leads to utterance [5], which, after interpretation and updating on the new dialogue acts, leads to the information state in Figure 4. The interesting thing here is the condition which appears in CDU.TOGND.COND as a result of the check; the interpretation of this is that, if C agrees with the check, then W will be committed to the proposition that the starting place is Malvern (C would also be committed to this by way of the direct effects of an agree act).

[12]The actual information state contains all the previously established dialogue acts, SCPs and Obligations in GND, from Figure 2 and intermediate utterances. Here we have deleted these aspects from the figures for brevity and clarity.

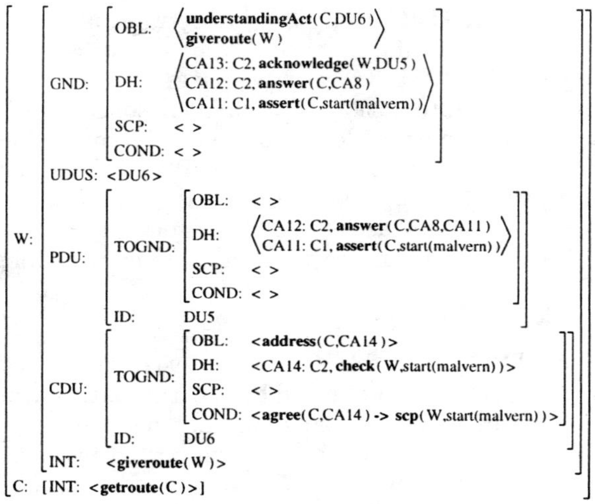

Figure 4: Information State Following Check in [5]

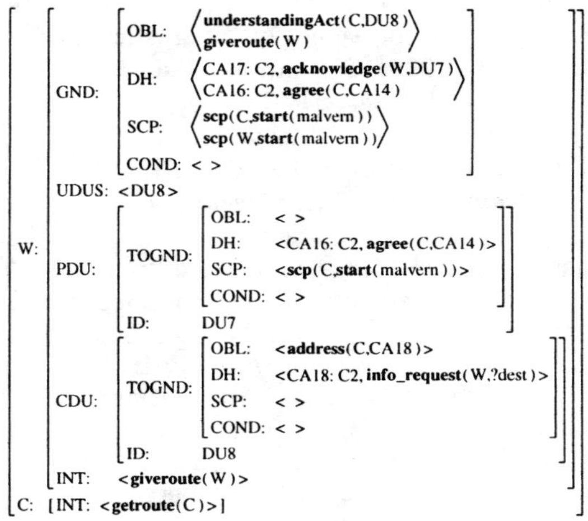

Figure 5: Information state following [7]

After C's agreement in [6], the deliberation routine is able to move past discussion of the starting point, and add an intention to ask about the next piece of information, the destination. This leads to producing utterance [7], which also implicitly acknowledges [6], after which C's agreement is grounded, leading to the IS shown in Figure 5. Note that the list in W.GND.SCP in Figure 5 indicates that both C *and* W are committed to the proposition that the starting place is Malvern.

5 Conclusions

It has only been possible here to introduce the basic concerns of the PTT account of dialogue modelling and to pick out one or two illustrative examples to highlight the implementational approach which has been assumed. Current and future work is directed towards measuring the theory against more challenging data to test its validity; cases where grounding is less automatic are an obvious source of such tests, and we have identified a few relevant problem cases in the Autoroute dialogues. We do claim, however, that the implementation as it stands validates a number of key aspects of the theory and provides a good basis for future work in dialogue modelling.

Acknowledgments

The TRINDI (Task Oriented Instructional Dialogue) project is supported by the Telematics Applications Programme, Language Engineering Project LE4-8314. Massimo Poesio is supported by an EPSRC Advanced Research Fellowship.

References

J. Allwood. 1976. *Linguistic Communication as Action and Cooperation.* Ph.D. thesis, Göteborg University, Department of Linguistics.

J. Allwood. 1994. Obligations and options in dialogue. *Think Quarterly*, 3:9–18.

M. E. Bratman, D. J. Israel and M. E. Pollack. 1988. Plans and Resource-Bounded Practical Reasoning. *Computational Intelligence*, 4(4).

P. Bretier and M. D. Sadek. 1996. A rational agent as the kernel of a cooperative spoken dialogue system: Implementing a logical theory of interaction. In J. P. Müller, M. J. Wooldridge, and N. R. Jennings, editors, *Intelligent Agents III — Proceedings of the Third International Workshop on Agent Theories, Architectures, and Languages (ATAL-96)*, Lecture Notes in Artificial Intelligence. Springer-Verlag, Heidelberg.

J. Calder. 1998. Thistle: diagram display engines and editors. Technical Report HCRC/TR-97, HCRC, University of Edinburgh, Edinburgh.

H. H. Clark and E. F. Schaefer. 1989. Contributing to discourse. *Cognitive Science*, 13:259–294.

H. H. Clark and D. Wilkes-Gibbs. 1986. Referring as a collaborative process. *Cognition*, 22:1–39. Also appears as Chapter 4 in (Clark, 1992).

H. H. Clark. 1992. *Arenas of Language Use.* University of Chicago Press.

P. R. Cohen and H. J. Levesque. 1990. Rational interaction as the basis for communication. In P. R. Cohen, J. Morgan, and M. E. Pollack, editors, *Intentions in Communication.* MIT Press.

Discourse Resource Initiative. 1997. Standards for dialogue coding in natural language processing. Report no. 167, Dagstuhl-Seminar.

B. J. Grosz and C. L. Sidner. 1990. Plans for discourse. In P. R. Cohen, J. Morgan, and M. E. Pollack, editors, *Intentions in Communication.* MIT Press.

J. Kreutel. 1998. An obligation-driven computational model for questions and assertions in dialogue. Master's thesis, Department of Linguistics, University of Edinburgh, Edinburgh.

S. Larsson, P. Bohlin, J. Bos, and D. Traum. 1999. Trindikit manual. Technical Report Deliverable D2.2 - Manual, Trindi.

M. Poesio, R. Cooper, S. Larsson, D. Traum, and C. Matheson. 1999. Annotating conversations for information state update. In *Proceedings of Amstelogue 99, 3rd Workshop on the Semantics and Pragmatics of Dialogues.*

M. Poesio and D. R. Traum. 1997. Conversational actions and discourse situations. *Computational Intelligence*, 13(3).

M. Poesio and D. R. Traum. 1998. Towards an axiomatization of dialogue acts. In *Proceedings of Twendial'98, 13th Twente Workshop on Language Technology*, pages 207–222.

M. D. Sadek. 1991. Dialogue acts are rational plans. In *Proceedings of the ESCA/ETR workshop on multi-modal dialogue.*

M. P. Singh. 1998. Agent communication languages: Rethinking the principles. *IEEE Computer*, 31(12):40–47.

D. R. Traum and J. F. Allen. 1992. A speech acts approach to grounding in conversation. In *Proceedings 2nd International Conference on Spoken Language Processing (ICSLP-92)*, pages 137–40, October.

D. R. Traum and J. F. Allen. 1994. Discourse obligations in dialogue processing. In *Proceedings of the 32nd Annual meeting of the Association for Computational Linguistics*, pages 1–8, June.

D. R. Traum, J. Bos, R. Cooper, S. Larsson, I. Lewin, C. Matheson, and M. Poesio. 1999. A model of dialogue moves and information state revision. Technical Report Deliverable D2.1, Trindi.

D. R. Traum and P. Dillenbourg. 1998. Towards a Normative Model of Grounding in Collaboration. In *Proceedings of the ESSLLI98 workshop on Mutual Knowledge, Common Ground and Public Information.*

D. R. Traum. 1994. *A computational theory of grounding in natural language conversation.* Ph.D. thesis, Computer Science, University of Rochester, New York, December.

The Automatic Translation of Discourse Structures

Daniel Marcu
Information Sciences Institute and
Department of Computer Science
University of Southern California
4676 Admiralty Way, Suite 1001
Marina del Rey, CA 90292
marcu@isi.edu

Lynn Carlson
U.S. Department of Defense
Ft. Meade, MD 20755
lmcarls@afterlife.ncsc.mil

Maki Watanabe
Department of Linguistics
University of Southern California
Los Angeles, CA 90089
mwatanab@usc.edu

Abstract

We empirically show that there are significant differences between the discourse structure of Japanese texts and the discourse structure of their corresponding English translations. To improve translation quality, we propose a computational model for rewriting discourse structures. When we train our model on a parallel corpus of manually built Japanese and English discourse structure trees, we learn to rewrite Japanese trees as trees that are closer to the natural English rendering than the original ones.

1 Motivation

Almost all current MT systems process text one sentence at a time. Because of this limited focus, MT systems cannot re-group and re-order the clauses and sentences of an input text to achieve the most natural rendering in a target language. Yet, even between languages as close as English and French, there is a 10% mismatch in number of sentences — what is said in two sentences in one language is said in only one, or in three, in the other (Gale and Church, 1993). For distant language pairs, such as Japanese and English, the differences are more significant.

Consider, for example, Japanese sentence (1), a word-by-word "gloss" of it (2), and a two-sentence translation of it that was produced by a professional translator (3).

[厚生省が昨年公表した[1]] [人口の将来推計では、[2]] [将来、一・四九九人を最低に、[3]] [その後は上昇に転ずると[4]] [推計していたが、[5]] [早くも予想がはずれる[6]] [見通しとなった。[7]] (1)

[The Ministry of Health and Welfare last year revealed[1]] [population of future estimate according to[2]] [in future 1.499 persons as the lowest[3]] [that after *SAB* rising to turn that[4]] [*they* estimated but[5]] [already the estimate misses a point[6]] [prediction became.[7]] (2)

[In its future population estimates[1]] [made public last year,[2]] [the Ministry of Health and Welfare predicted that the SAB would drop to a new low of 1.499 in the future,[3]] [but would make a comeback after that,[4]] [increasing once again.[5]] [However, it looks as if that prediction will be quickly shattered.[6]] (3)

The labeled spans of text represent elementary discourse units (*edus*), i.e., minimal text spans that have an unambiguous discourse function (Mann and Thompson, 1988). If we analyze the text fragments closely, we will notice that in translating sentence (1), a professional translator chose to realize the information in Japanese unit 2 first (unit 2 in text (1) corresponds roughly to unit 1 in text (3)); to realize then some of the information in Japanese unit 1 (part of unit 1 in text (1) corresponds to unit 2 in text (3)); to fuse then information given in units 1, 3, and 5 in text (1) and realize it in English as unit 3; and so on. Also, the translator chose to repackage the information in the original Japanese sentence into two English sentences.

At the elementary unit level, the correspondence between Japanese sentence (1) and its English translation (3) can be represented as in (4), where $j \subset e$ denotes the fact that the semantic content of unit j is realized fully in unit e; $j \supset e$ denotes the fact that the semantic content of unit e is realized fully in unit j; $j = e$ denotes the fact that units j and e are semantically equivalent; and $j \cong e$ denotes the fact that there is a semantic overlap between units j and e, but neither proper inclusion nor proper equivalence.

$$
\begin{aligned}
& j_1 \supset e_2; j_1 \cong e_3; \\
& j_2 = e_1; \\
& j_3 \subset e_3; \\
& j_4 \cong e_4; j_4 \cong e_5; \\
& j_5 \cong e_3; \\
& j_6 \subset e_6; \\
& j_7 \subset e_6
\end{aligned} \tag{4}
$$

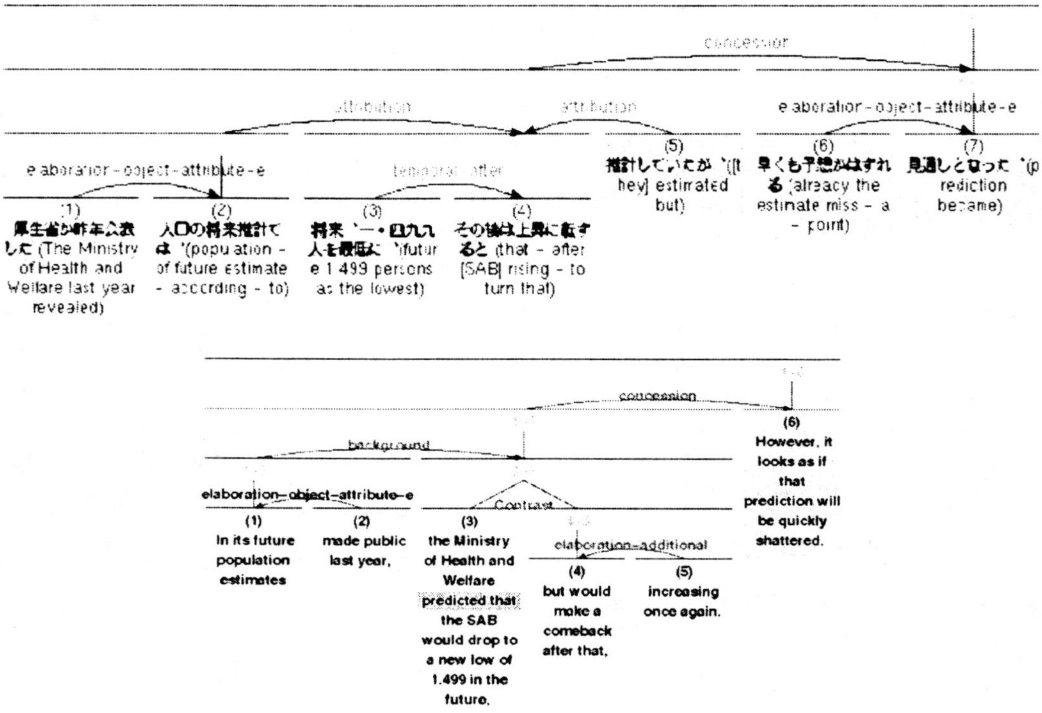

Figure 1: The discourse structures of texts (1) and (3).

Hence, the mappings in (4) provide an explicit representation of the way information is re-ordered and re-packaged when translated from Japanese into English. However, when translating text, it is also the case that the rhetorical rendering changes. What is realized in Japanese using an CONTRAST relation can be realized in English using, for example, a COMPARISON or a CONCESSION relation.

Figure 1 presents in the style of Mann and Thompson (1988) the discourse structures of text fragments (1) and (3). Each discourse structure is a tree whose leaves correspond to the *edus* and whose internal nodes correspond to contiguous text spans. Each node is characterized by a *status* (NUCLEUS or SATELLITE) and a *rhetorical relation*, which is a relation that holds between two non-overlapping text spans. The distinction between nuclei and satellites comes from the empirical observation that the nucleus expresses what is more essential to the writer's intention than the satellite; and that the nucleus of a rhetorical relation is comprehensible independent of the satellite, but not vice versa. When spans are equally important, the relation is multinuclear; for example, the CONTRAST relation that holds between unit [3] and span [4,5] in the rhetorical structure of the English text in figure 1 is multinuclear. Rhetorical relations that end in the suffix "-e" denote relations that correspond to embedded syntactic constituents. For example, the ELABORATION-OBJECT-ATTRIBUTE-E relation that holds between units 2 and 1 in the English discourse structure corresponds to a restrictive relative.

If one knows the mappings at the *edu* level, one can determine the mappings at the span (discourse constituent) level as well. For example, using the elementary mappings in (4), one can determine that Japanese span [1,2] corresponds to English span [1,2], Japanese unit [4] to English span [4,5], Japanese span [6,7] to English unit [6], Japanese span [1,5] to English span [1,5], and so on. As Figure 1 shows, the CONCESSION relation that holds between spans [1,5] and [6,7] in the Japanese tree corresponds to a similar relation that holds between span [1,5] and unit [6] in the English tree (modulo the fact that, in Japanese, the relation holds between sentence fragments, while in English it holds between full sentences). However, the TEMPORAL-AFTER relation that holds between units [3] and [4] in the Japanese tree is realized as a CONTRAST relation between unit [3] and span [4,5] in the English tree. And because Japanese units [6] and [7] are fused into unit [6] in English, the relation ELABORATION-OBJECT-ATTRIBUTE-E is no longer made explicit in the English text.

Some of the differences between the two discourse trees in Figure 1 have been traditionally addressed

Corpus	k_u (#)	k_s (#)	k_n (#)	k_r (#)
Japanese	0.856 (80)	0.785 (3377)	0.724 (3377)	0.650 (3377)
English	0.925 (60)	0.866 (1826)	0.839 (1826)	0.748 (1826)

Table 1: Tagging reliability

in MT systems at the syntactic level. For example, the re-ordering of units 1 and 2, can be dealt with using only syntactic models. However, as we will see in Section 2, there are significant differences between Japanese and English with respect to the way information is packaged and organized rhetorically not only at the sentence level, but also, at the paragraph and text levels. More specifically, as humans translate Japanese into English, they *re-order* the clauses, sentences, and paragraphs of Japanese texts, they *re-package* the information into clauses, sentences, and paragraphs that *are not* a one-to-one mapping of the original Japanese units, and they *rhetorically re-organize* the structure of the translated text so as to reflect rhetorical constraints specific to English. If a translation system is to produce text that is not only grammatical but also coherent, it will have to ensure that the discourse structure of the target text reflects the natural renderings of the target language, and not that of the source language.

In Section 2, we empirically show that there are significant differences between the rhetorical structure of Japanese texts and their corresponding English translations. These differences justify our investigation into developing computational models for discourse structure rewriting. In Section 3, we present such a rewriting model, which re-orders the *edus* of the original text, determines English-specific clause, sentence, and paragraph boundaries, and rebuilds the Japanese discourse structure of a text using English-specific rhetorical renderings. In Section 4, we evaluate the performance of an implementation of this model. We end with a discussion.

2 Experiment

In order to assess the role of discourse structure in MT, we built manually a corpus of discourse trees for 40 Japanese texts and their corresponding translations. The texts were selected randomly from the ARPA corpus (White and O'Connell, 1994). On average, each text had about 460 words. The Japanese texts had a total of 335 paragraphs and 773 sentences. The English texts had a total of 337 paragraphs and 827 sentences.

We developed a discourse annotation protocol for Japanese and English along the lines followed by Marcu et al. (1999). We used Marcu's discourse annotation tool (1999) in order to manually construct the discourse structure of all Japanese and English texts in the corpus. 10% of the Japanese and English texts were rhetorically labeled by two of us. The tool and the annotation protocol are available at *http://www.isi.edu/~marcu/software/*. The annotation procedure yielded over the entire corpus 2641 Japanese *edus* and 2363 English *edus*.

We computed the reliability of the annotation using Marcu et al. (1999)'s method for computing kappa statistics (Siegel and Castellan, 1988) over hierarchical structures. Table 1 displays average kappa statistics that reflect the reliability of the annotation of elementary discourse units, k_u, hierarchical discourse spans, k_s, hierarchical nuclearity assignments, k_n, and hierarchical rhetorical relation assignments, k_r. Kappa figures higher than 0.8 correspond to good agreement; kappa figures higher than 0.6 correspond to acceptable agreement. All kappa statistics were statistically significant at levels higher than $\alpha = 0.01$. In addition to the kappa statistics, table 1 also displays in parentheses the average number of data points per document, over which the kappa statistics were computed.

For each pair of Japanese-English discourse structures, we also built manually an alignment file, which specified in the notation discussed on page 1 the correspondence between the *edus* of the Japanese text and the *edus* of its English translation.

We computed the similarity between English and Japanese discourse trees using labeled recall and precision figures that reflected the resemblance of the Japanese and English discourse structures with respect to their assignment of *edu* boundaries, hierarchical spans, nuclearity, and rhetorical relations.

Because the trees we compared differ from one language to the other in the number of elementary units, the order of these units, and the way the units are grouped recursively into discourse spans, we computed two types of recall and precision figures. In computing *Position-Dependent* (P-D) recall and precision figures, a Japanese span was considered to match an English span when the Japanese span contained all the Japanese *edus* that corresponded to the *edus* in the English span, and when the Japanese and English spans appeared in the same position with respect to the overall structure. For example, the English tree in figure 1 is characterized by 10 subsentential spans: [1], [2], [3], [4], [5], [6], [1,2], [4,5], [3,5], and [1,5]. (Span [1,6] subsumes 2 sentences, so it is not sub-sentential.) The Japanese discourse tree has only 4 spans that could be matched in the same positions with English spans, namely spans [1,2], [4], [5], and [1,5]. Hence the similarity between the Japanese tree and the English tree with respect

Level	Units		Spans		Status/Nuclearity		Relations	
	P-D R	P-D P	P-D R	P-D P	P-D R	P-D P	P-D R	P-D P
Sentence	29.1	25.0	27.2	22.7	21.3	17.7	14.9	12.4
Paragraph	53.9	53.4	46.8	47.3	38.6	39.0	31.9	32.3
Text	41.3	42.6	31.5	32.6	28.8	29.9	26.1	27.1
Weighted Average	36.0	32.5	31.8	28.4	26.0	23.1	20.1	17.9
All	8.2	7.4	5.9	5.3	4.4	3.9	3.3	3.0
	P-I R	P-I P	P-I R	P-I P	P-I R	P-I P	P-I R	P-I P
Sentence	71.0	61.0	56.0	46.6	44.3	36.9	30.5	25.4
Paragraph	62.1	61.6	53.2	53.8	43.3	43.8	35.1	35.5
Text	74.1	76.5	54.4	56.5	48.5	50.4	41.1	42.7
Weighted Average	69.6	63.0	55.2	49.2	44.8	39.9	33.1	29.5
All	74.5	66.8	50.6	45.8	39.4	35.7	26.8	24.3

Table 2: Similarity of the Japanese and English discourse structures

to their discourse structure below the sentence level has a recall of 4/10 and a precision of 4/11 (in Figure 1, there are 11 sub-sentential Japanese spans).

In computing *Position-Independent* (P-I) recall and precision figures, even when a Japanese span "floated" during the translation to a position in the English tree that was different from the position in the initial tree, the P-I recall and precision figures were not affected. The Position-Independent figures reflect the intuition that if two trees t_1 and t_2 both have a subtree t, t_1 and t_2 are more similar than if they were if they didn't share any tree. At the sentence level, we hence assume that if, for example, the syntactic structure of a relative clause is translated appropriately (even though it is not appropriately attached), this is better than translating wrongly that clause. The Position-Independent figures offer a more optimistic metric for comparing discourse trees. They span a wider range of values than the Position-Dependent figures, which enable a finer grained comparison, which in turn enables a better characterization of the differences between Japanese and English discourse structures. When one takes an optimistic stance, for the spans at the sub-sentential level in the trees in Table 1 the recall is 6/10 and the precision is 6/11 because in addition to spans [1,2], [4], [5], and [1,5], one can also match Japanese span [1] to English span [2] and Japanese span [2] to Japanese span [1].

In order to provide a better estimate of how close two discourse trees were, we computed Position-Dependent and -Independent recall and precision figures for the sentential level (where units are given by *edus* and spans are given by sets of *edus* or single sentences); paragraph level (where units are given by sentences and spans are given by sets of sentences or single paragraphs); and text level (where units are given by paragraphs and spans are given by sets of paragraphs). These figures offer a detailed picture of how discourse structures and relations are mapped from one language to the other across all discourse levels, from sentence to text. The differences at the sentence level can be explained by differences between the syntactic structures of Japanese and English. The differences at the paragraph and text levels have a purely rhetorical explanation.

As expected, when we computed the recall and precision figures with respect to the nuclearity and relation assignments, we also factored in the statuses and the rhetorical relations that labeled each pair of spans.

Table 2 summarizes the results (P-D and P-I (R)ecall and (P)recision figures) for each level (Sentence, Paragraph, and Text). The numbers in the "Weighted Average" line report averages of the Sentence-, Paragraph-, and Text-specific figures, weighted according to the number of units at each level. The numbers in the "All" line reflect recall and precision figures computed across the entire trees, with no attention paid to sentence and paragraph boundaries.

Given the significantly different syntactic structures of Japanese and English, we were not surprised by the low recall and precision results that reflect the similarity between discourse trees built below the sentence level. However, as Table 2 shows, there are significant differences between discourse trees at the paragraph and text levels as well. For example, the Position-Independent figures show that only about 62% of the sentences and only about 53% of the hierarchical spans built across sentences could be matched between the two corpora. When one looks at the status and rhetorical relations associated with the spans built across sentences at the paragraph level, the P-I recall and precision figures drop to about 43% and 35% respectively.

The differences in recall and precision are explained both by differences in the way information is packaged into paragraphs in the two languages and the way it is structured rhetorically both within and above the paragraph level.

These results strongly suggest that if one attempts

to translate Japanese into English on a sentence-by-sentence basis, it is likely that the resulting text will be unnatural from a discourse perspective. For example, if some information rendered using a CONTRAST relation in Japanese is rendered using an ELABORATION relation in English, it would be inappropriate to use a discourse marker like "but" in the English translation, although that would be consistent with the Japanese discourse structure.

An inspection of the rhetorical mappings between Japanese and English revealed that some Japanese rhetorical renderings are consistently mapped into one or a few preferred renderings in English. For example, 34 of 115 CONTRAST relations in the Japanese texts are mapped into CONTRAST relations in English; 27 become nuclei of relations such as ANTITHESIS and CONCESSION, 14 are translated as COMPARISON relations, 6 as satellites of CONCESSION relations, 5 as LIST relations, etc. Our goal is to learn these systematic discourse mapping rules and exploit them in a machine translation context.

3 Towards a discourse-based machine translation system

3.1 Overall architecture

We are currently working towards building the modules of a Discourse-Based Machine Translation system that works along the following lines.

1. A discourse parser, such as those described by Sumita et al. (1992), Kurohashi (1994), and Marcu (1999), initially derives the discourse structure of the text given as input.
2. A discourse-structure transfer module rewrites the discourse structure of the input text so as to reflect a discourse rendering that is natural to the target language.
3. A statistical module maps the input text into the target language using translation and language models that incorporate discourse-specific features, which are extracted from the outputs of the discourse parser and discourse transfer modules.

In this paper, we focus only on the discourse-structure transfer module. That is, we investigate the feasibility of building such a module.

3.2 The discourse-based transfer model

In order to learn to rewrite discourse structure trees, we first address a related problem, which we define below:

Definition 3.1 *Given two trees T_s and T_t and a correspondence Table C defined between T_s and T_t at the leaf level in terms of $=, \subset, \supset$, and $\cong$ relations, find a sequence of actions that rewrites the tree T_s into T_t.*

If for any tuple $\langle T_s, T_t, C\rangle$ such a sequence of actions can be derived, it is then possible to use a corpus of $\langle T_s, T_t, C\rangle$ tuples in order to automatically learn to derive from an unseen tree T_{s_i}, which has the same structural properties as the trees T_s, a tree T_{t_j}, which has structural properties similar to those of the trees T_t.

In order to solve the problem in definition 3.1, we extend the shift-reduce parsing paradigm applied by Magerman (1995), Hermjakob and Mooney (1997), and Marcu (1999). In this extended paradigm, the transfer process starts with an empty Stack and an Input List that contains a sequence of elementary discourse trees *edts*, one *edt* for each *edu* in the tree T_s given as input. The status and rhetorical relation associated with each *edt* is undefined. At each step, the transfer module applies an operation that is aimed at building from the units in T_s the discourse tree T_t. In the context of our discourse-transfer module, we need 7 types of operations:

- SHIFT operations transfer the first *edt* from the input list into the stack;
- REDUCE operations pop the two discourse trees located at the top of the stack; combine them into a new tree updating the statuses and rhetorical relation names of the trees involved in the operation; and push the new tree on the top of the stack. These operations are used to build the structure of the discourse tree in the target language.
- BREAK operations are used in order to break the *edt* at the beginning of the input list into a predetermined number of units. These operations are used to ensure that the resulting tree has the same number of *edts* as T_t. A BREAK operation is necessary whenever a Japanese *edu* is mapped into multiple English units.
- CREATE-NEXT operations are used in order to create English discourse constituents that have no correspondent in the Japanese tree.
- FUSE operations are used in order to fuse the *edt* at the top of the stack into the tree that immediately precedes it. These operations are used whenever multiple Japanese *edus* are mapped into one English *edu*.
- SWAP operations swap the *edt* at the beginning of the input list with an *edt* found one or more positions to the right. These operations are necessary for re-ordering discourse constituents.
- ASSIGNTYPE operations assign one or more of the following types to the tree at the top of the stack: Unit, MultiUnit, Sentence, Paragraph, MultiParagraph, and Text. These op-

erations are necessary in order to ensure sentence and paragraph boundaries that are specific to the target language.

For example, the first sentence of the English tree in Figure 1 can be obtained from the original Japanese sequence by following the sequence of actions (5), whose effects are shown in Figure 2. For the purpose of compactness, the figure does not illustrate the effect of ASSIGNTYPE actions. For the same purpose, some lines correspond to more than one action.

BREAK 2; SWAP 2; SHIFT; ASSIGNTYPE UNIT; SHIFT; REDUCE-NS-ELABORATION-OBJECT-ATTRIBUTE-E; ASSIGNTYPE MULTIUNIT; SHIFT; ASSIGNTYPE UNIT; SHIFT; ASSIGNTYPE UNIT; FUSE; ASSIGNTYPE UNIT; SWAP 2; SHIFT; ASSIGNTYPE UNIT; FUSE; BREAK 2; SHIFT; ASSIGNTYPE UNIT; SHIFT; ASSIGNTYPE UNIT; REDUCE-NS-ELABORATION-ADDITIONAL; ASSIGNTYPE MULTIUNIT; REDUCE-NS-CONTRAST; ASSIGNTYPE MULTIUNIT; REDUCE-SN-BACKGROUND; ASSIGNTYPE SENTENCE. (5)

For our corpus, in order to enable a discourse-based transfer module to derive any English discourse tree starting from any Japanese discourse tree, it is sufficient to implement:

- one SHIFT operation;
- $3 \times 2 \times 85$ REDUCE operations; (For each of the three possible pairs of nuclearity assignments NUCLEUS-SATELLITE (NS), SATELLITE-NUCLEUS (SN), AND NUCLEUS-NUCLEUS (NN), there are two possible ways to reduce two adjacent trees (one results in a binary tree, the other in a non-binary tree (Marcu, 1999)), and 85 relation names.)
- three types of BREAK operations; (In our corpus, a Japanese unit is broken into two, three, or at most four units.)
- one type of CREATE-NEXT operation;
- one type of FUSE operation;
- eleven types of SWAP operations; (In our corpus, Japanese units are at most 11 positions away from their location in an English-specific rendering.)
- seven types of ASSIGNTYPE operations: Unit, MultiUnit, Sentence, MultiSentence, Paragraph, MultiParagraph, and Text.

These actions are sufficient for rewriting any tree T_s into any tree T_t, where T_t may have a different number of *edus*, where the *edus* of T_t may have a different ordering than the *edus* of T_s, and where the hierarchical structures of the two trees may be different as well.

3.3 Learning the parameters of the discourse-transfer model

We associate with each configuration of our transfer model a learning case. The cases were generated by a program that automatically derived the sequence of actions that mapped the Japanese trees in our corpus into the sibling English trees, using the correspondences at the elementary unit level that were constructed manually. Overall, the 40 pairs of Japanese and English discourse trees yielded 14108 cases.

To each learning example, we associated a set of features from the following classes:

Operational and discourse features reflect the number of trees in the stack, the input list, and the types of the last five operations. They encode information pertaining to the types of the partial trees built up to a certain time and the rhetorical relations that hold between these trees.

Correspondence-based features reflect the nuclearity, rhetorical relations, and types of the Japanese trees that correspond to the English-like partial trees derived up to a given time.

Lexical features specify whether the Japanese spans that correspond to the structures derived up to a given time use potential discourse markers, such as *dakara (because)* and *no ni (although)*.

The discourse transfer module uses the C4.5 program (Quinlan, 1993) in order to learn decision trees and rules that specify how Japanese discourse trees should be mapped into English-like trees. A ten-fold cross-validation evaluation of the classifier yielded an accuracy of 70.2% ($\pm$ 0.21).

In order to better understand the strengths and weaknesses of the classifier, we also attempted to break the problem into smaller components. Hence, instead of learning all actions at once, we attempted to learn first whether the rewriting procedure should choose a SHIFT, REDUCE, BREAK, FUSE, SWAP, or ASSIGNTYPE operation (the "Main Action Type" classifier in table 3), and only then to refine this decision by determining what type of reduce operation to perform, how many units to break a Japanese units into, how big the distance to the SWAP-ed unit should be, and what type of ASSIGNTYPE operation one should perform. Table 3 shows the sizes of each

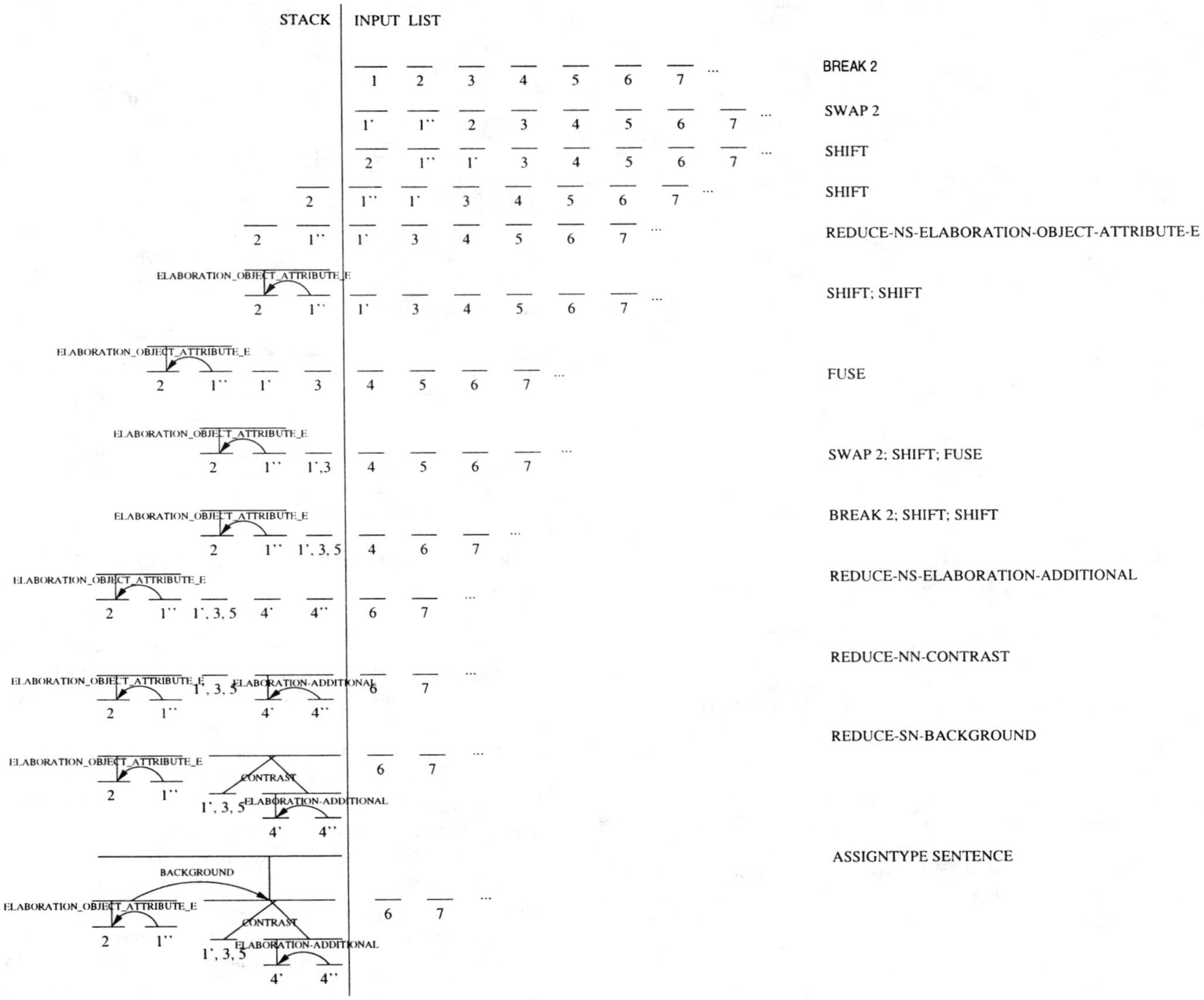

Figure 2: Example of incremental tree reconstruction.

data set and the performance of each of these classifiers, as determined using a ten-fold cross-validation procedure. For the purpose of comparison, each classifier is paired with a majority baseline.

The results in Table 3 show that the most difficult subtasks to learn are that of determining the number of units a Japanese unit should be broken into and that of determining the distance to the unit that is to be swapped. The features we used are not able to refine the baseline classifiers for these action types. The confusion matrix for the "Main Action Type" classifier (see Table 5) shows that the system has trouble mostly identifying BREAK and CREATE-NEXT actions. The system has difficulty learning what type of nuclearity ordering to prefer (the "Nuclearity-Reduce" classifier) and what relation to choose for the English-like structure (the "Relation-Reduce" classifier).

Figure 3 shows a typical learning curve, the one that corresponds to the "Reduce Relation" classifier. Our learning curves suggest that more training data may improve performance. However, they also suggest that better features may be needed in order to improve performance significantly.

Table 4 displays some learned rules. The first rule accounts for rhetorical mappings in which the order of the nucleus and satellite of an ATTRIBUTION relation is changed when translated from Japanese into English. The second rule was learned in order to map EXAMPLE Japanese satellites into EVIDENCE English satellites.

Classifier	# cases	Accuracy (10-fold cross validation)	Majority baseline accuracy
General (Learns all classes at once)	14108	70.20% (±0.21)	22.05% (on ASSIGNTYPE UNIT)
Main Action Type	14108	82.53% (±0.25)	45.47% (on ASSIGNTYPE)
AssignType	6416	90.46% (±0.39)	57.30% (on ASSIGNTYPE Unit)
Break	394	82.91% (±1.40)	82.91% (on BREAK 2)
Nuclearity-Reduce	2388	67.43% (±1.03)	50.92% (on NS)
Relation-Reduce	2388	48.20% (±1.01)	17.18% (on ELABORATION-OBJECT-ATTRIBUTE-E)
Swap	842	62.98% (±1.62)	62.98% (on SWAP 1)

Table 3: Performance of the classifiers

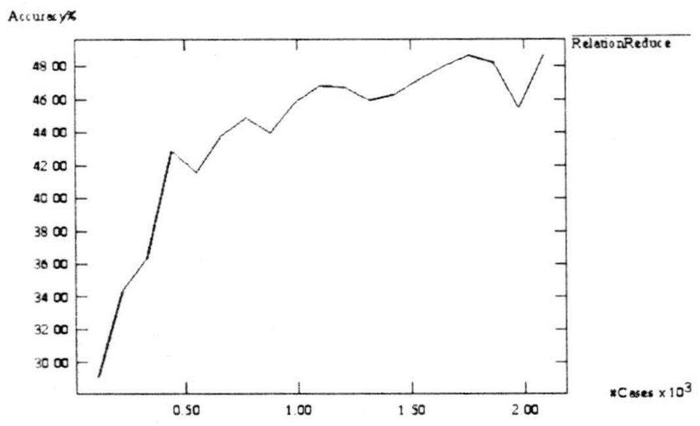

Figure 3: Learning curve for the Relation-Reduce classifier.

if rhetRelOfStack-1InJapTree = ATTRIBUTION
then rhetRelOfTopStackInEngTree ← ATTRIBUTION

if rhetRelOfTopStackInJapTree = EXAMPLE ∧
isSentenceTheLastUnitInJapTreeOfTopStack = false
then rhetRelOfTopStackInEngTree ← EVIDENCE

Table 4: Rule examples for the Relation-Reduce classifier.

4 Evaluation of the discourse-based transfer module

By applying the General classifier or the other six classifiers successively, one can map any Japanese discourse tree into a tree whose structure comes closer to the natural rendering of English. To evaluate the discourse-based transfer module, we carried out a ten-fold cross-validation experiment. That is, we trained the classifiers on 36 pairs of manually built and aligned discourse structures, and we then used the learned classifiers in order to map 4 unseen Japanese discourse trees into English-like trees. We measured the similarity of the derived trees with the English trees built manually, using the metrics discussed in Section 2. We repeated the procedure ten times, each time training and testing on different subsets of tree pairs.

Action	(a)	(b)	(c)	(d)	(e)	(f)	(g)
ASSIGNTYPE (a)	660						
BREAK (b)		1			2	28	1
CREATE-NEXT (c)					1	8	
FUSE (d)				69	8	3	
REDUCE (e)		4		18	193	30	3
SHIFT (f)	1	4		15	44	243	25
SWAP (g)		3		4	14	43	25

Table 5: Confusion matrix for the Main Action Type classifier.

We take the results reported in Table 2 as a baseline for our model. The baseline corresponds to applying no knowledge of discourse. Table 6 displays the absolute improvement (in percentage points) in recall and precision figures obtained when the General classifier was used to map Japanese trees into English-looking trees. The General classifier yielded the best results. The results in Table 6 are averaged over a ten-fold cross-validation experiment.

The results in Table 6 show that our model outperforms the baseline with respect to building English-like discourse structures for sentences, but it under-performs the baseline with respect to building English-like structures at the paragraph and text levels. The main shortcoming of our model seems to come from its low performance in assigning paragraph boundaries. Because our classifier does not learn correctly which spans to consider paragraphs and which spans not, the recall and precision results at the paragraph and text levels are negatively affected. The poorer results at the paragraph and text levels can be also explained by errors whose effect cumulates during the step-by-step tree-reconstruction procedure; and by the fact that, for these levels, there is less data to learn from.

However, if one ignores the sentence and paragraph boundaries and evaluates the discourse structures overall, one can see that our model outperforms the baseline on all accounts according to the Position-Dependent evaluation; outperforms the baseline with respect to the assignment of elementary units, hierarchical spans, and nuclearity statuses according to the Position-Independent evaluation and under-performs the baseline only slightly

Level	Units		Spans		Status/Nuclearity		Relations	
	P-D R	P-D P	P-D R	P-D P	P-D R	P-D P	P-D R	P-D P
Sentence	+9.1	+25.5	+2.0	+19.9	+0.4	+13.4	−0.01	+8.4
Paragraph	−14.7	+1.4	−12.5	−1.7	−11.0	−2.4	−9.9	−3.3
Text	−9.6	−13.5	−7.1	−11.1	−6.3	−10.0	−5.2	−8.8
Weighted Average	+1.5	+14.1	−2.1	+9.9	−3.1	+6.4	−3.0	+3.9
All	−1.2	+2.5	−0.1	+2.9	+0.6	+3.5	+0.7	+2.6
	P-I R	P-I P	P-I R	P-I P	P-I R	P-I P	P-I R	P-I P
Sentence	+13.4	+30.4	+3.1	+36.1	−6.3	+18.6	−10.1	+3.9
Paragraph	−15.6	+0.6	−13.5	−0.8	−11.7	−1.8	−10.3	−2.8
Text	−15.4	−23.3	−13.0	−20.4	−13.2	−19.5	−11.5	−17.0
Weighted Average	+3.6	+15.5	−2.7	+17.1	−8.5	+7.3	−10.5	-0.4
All	+12.7	+29.6	+2.0	+28.8	−5.1	+13.0	−7.9	+2.2

Table 6: Relative evaluation of the discourse-based transfer module with respect to the figures in Table 2.

with respect to the rhetorical relation assignment according to the Position-Independent evaluation. More sophisticated discourse features, such as those discussed by Maynard (1998), for example, and a tighter integration with the lexicogrammar of the two languages may yield better cues for learning discourse-based translation models.

5 Conclusion

We presented a systematic empirical study of the role of discourse structure in MT. Our study strongly supports the need for enriching MT systems with a discourse module, capable of re-ordering and re-packaging the information in a source text in a way that is consistent with the discourse rendering of a target language. We presented an extended shift-reduce parsing model that can be used to map discourse trees specific to a source language into discourse trees specific to a target language. Our model outperforms a baseline with respect to its ability to predict the discourse structure of sentences. Our model also outperforms the baseline with respect to its ability to derive discourse structures that are closer to the natural, rhetorical rendering in a target language than the original discourse structures in the source language. Our model is still unable to determine correctly how to re-package sentences into paragraphs; a better understanding of the notion of "paragraph" is required in order to improve this.

References

William A. Gale and Kenneth W. Church. 1993. A program for aligning sentences in bilingual corpora. *Computational Linguistics*, 19(1):75–102.

Ulf Hermjakob and Raymond J. Mooney. 1997. Learning parse and translation decisions from examples with rich context. In *Proc. of ACL'97*, pages 482–489, Madrid, Spain. .

Sadao Kurohashi and Makoto Nagao. 1994. Automatic detection of discourse structure by checking surface information in sentences. In *Proc. of COLING'94*, volume 2, pages 1123–1127, Kyoto, Japan.

David M. Magerman. 1995. Statistical decision-tree models for parsing. In *Proc. of ACL'95*, pages 276–283, Cambridge, Massachusetts.

William C. Mann and Sandra A. Thompson. 1988. Rhetorical structure theory: Toward a functional theory of text organization. *Text*, 8(3):243–281.

Daniel Marcu. 1999. A decision-based approach to rhetorical parsing. In *Proc. of ACL'99*, pages 365–372, Maryland.

Daniel Marcu, Estibaliz Amorrortu, and Magdalena Romera. 1999. Experiments in constructing a corpus of discourse trees. In *Proc. of the ACL'99 Workshop on Standards and Tools for Discourse Tagging*, pages 48–57, Maryland.

Senko K. Maynard. 1998. *Principles of Japanese Discourse: A Handbook*. Cambridge Univ. Press.

J. Ross Quinlan. 1993. *C4.5: Programs for Machine Learning*. Morgan Kaufmann Publishers.

Sidney Siegel and N.J. Castellan. 1988. *Non-parametric Statistics for the Behavioral Sciences*. McGraw-Hill, Second edition.

Kazuo Sumita, Kenji Ono, T. Chino, Teruhiko Ukita, and Shin'ya Amano. 1992. A discourse structure analyzer for Japanese text. In *Proceedings of the International Conference on Fifth Generation Computer Systems*, v 2, pages 1133–1140.

J. White and T. O'Connell. 1994. Evaluation in the ARPA machine-translation program: 1993 methodology. In *Proceedings of the ARPA Human Language Technology Workshop*, pages 135–140, Washington, D.C.

A Probabilistic Genre-Independent Model of Pronominalization

Michael Strube
European Media Laboratory GmbH
Villa Bosch
Schloß-Wolfsbrunnenweg 33
69118 Heidelberg, Germany
Michael.Strube@eml.villa-bosch.de

Maria Wolters
Inst. f. Kommunikationsforschung u. Phonetik
Universität Bonn
Poppelsdorfer Allee 47
53115 Bonn, Germany
wolters@ikp.uni-bonn.de

Abstract

Our aim in this paper is to identify genre-independent factors that influence the decision to pronominalize. Results based on the annotation of twelve texts from four genres show that only a few factors have a *strong* influence on pronominalization across genres, i.e. distance from last mention, agreement, and form of the antecedent. Finally, we describe a probabilistic model of pronominalization derived from our data.

1 Introduction

Generating adequate referring expressions is an active research topic in Natural Language Generation. Adequate referring expressions are those that enable the user to quickly and unambiguously identify the discourse entity that the expression co-specifies with. In this paper, we concentrate on an important aspect of that question, which has received less attention than the question of anaphora resolution in discourse interpretation, i.e., when is it feasible to pronominalize?

Our aim is to identify the central factors that influence pronominalization across genres. Section 2 motivates and presents the factors that were investigated in this study: distance from last mention, parallelism, ambiguity, syntactic function, agreement, sortal class, syntactic function of the antecedent and form of the antecedent. Our analyses are based on a corpus of twelve texts from four different genres with a total of more than 24,000 words and 7126 referring expressions (Section 3). The results of the statistical analyses are summarized in Section 4. There are strong statistical associations between each of the factors and pronominalization. Only when we combine them into a probabilistic model we can identify those factors whose contribution is really important, i.e. distance from last mention, agreement, and to a certain degree form of the antecedent. Since these factors can be annotated relatively cheaply, we conclude that it is possible to develop reasonable statistical pronominalization algorithms.

2 Factors in Pronoun Generation

2.1 Previous Work

Lately, a number of researchers have done corpus-based work on NP generation and pronoun resolution, and a number of studies have found differences in the frequency of both personal and demonstrative pronouns across genres. However, none of these studies compares the influence of different factors on pronoun *generation* across genres.

Recently, Poesio et al. (1999) have described a corpus-based approach to statistical NP generation. While they ask the same question as previous researchers (e.g. Dale (1992)), their methods differ from traditional work on NP generation. Poesio et al. (1999) use two kinds of factors: (1) factors related to the NP under consideration such as agreement information, semantic factors, and discourse factors, and (2) factors related to the antecedent, such as animacy, clause type, thematic role, proximity, etc. Poesio et al. (1999) report that they were not able to annotate many of these factors reliably. On the basis of these annotations, they constructed decision trees for predicting surface forms of referring expressions based on these factors - with good results: all 28 personal pronouns in their corpus were generated correctly. Unfortunately, they do not evaluate the contribution of each of these factors, so we do not know which ones are important.

Work on corpus-based approaches to anaphora resolution is more numerous. Ge et al. (1998) describe a supervised probabilistic pronoun resolution algorithm which is based on complete syntactic information. The factors they use include distance from last mention, syntactic function and context, agreement information, animacy of the referent, a simplified notion of selectional restrictions,

Agree	Agreement in person, gender, and number
Syn	Syntactic function
Class	Sortal Class (cf. Tab. 2)
SynAnte	Syntactic function of antecedent. "F" for first mention, "N" for deadend
FormAnte	Form of antecedent (pers. pron., poss. pron., def. NP, indef. NP, proper name)
Dist	Distance to last mention in units
Dist4	Dist reduced to 4 values (deadend, Dist=0, Dist=1, Dist>=2)
Par	Parallelism (Syn=SynAnte)
Ambig	Number of competing discourse entities

Table 1: Overview of factors

and the length of the coreference chain. Cardie & Wagstaff (1999) describe an unsupervised algorithm for noun phrase coreference resolution. Their factors are taken from Ge et al. (1998), with two exceptions. First, they replace complete syntactic information with information about NP bracketing. Second, they use the sortal class of the referent which they determine on the basis of WordNet (Fellbaum, 1998).

There has been no comparison between corpus-based approaches for anaphora resolution and more traditional algorithms based on focusing (Sidner, 1983) or centering (Grosz et al., 1995) except for Azzam et al. (1998). However, their comparison is flawed by evaluating a syntax-based focus algorithm on the basis of insufficient syntactic information. For pronoun generation, the original centering model (Grosz et al., 1995) provides a rule which is supposed to decide whether a referring expression has to be realized as a pronoun. However, this rule applies only to the referring expression which is the backward-looking center (*Cb*) of the current utterance. With respect to all other referring expression in this utterance centering is underspecified.

Yeh & Mellish (1997) propose a set of handcrafted rules for the generation of anaphora (zero and personal pronouns, full NPs) in Chinese. However, the factors which appear to be important in their evaluation are similar to factors described by authors mentioned above: distance, syntactic constraints on zero pronouns, discourse structure, salience and animacy of discourse entities.

2.2 Our Factors

The factors we investigate in this paper only rely on annotations of NPs and their co-specification relations. We did not add any discourse structural annotation, because (1) the texts are extracts from larger texts which are not available to us, and (2) we have not yet found a labelling scheme for discourse structure that has an inter-coder reliability comparable to the MUC coreference annotation scheme.

Based on our review of the literature and relevant work in linguistics (for sortal class, mainly Fraurud (1996) and Fellbaum (1998)), we have chosen the nine factors listed in Table 1. Methodologically, we distinguish two kinds of factors:

NP-level factors are independent from co-specification relations. They depend on the semantics of the discourse entity or on discourse information supplied for the NP generation algorithm by the NLG system. Typical examples are NP agreement by gender, number, person and case, the syntactic function of the NP (subject, object, PP adjunct, other), the sortal class of the discourse entity to which an NP refers, discourse structure, or topicality of the discourse entities. In this paper, we focus on the first three factors, agreement (Agree), syntactic function (Syn), and sortal class (Class).

Since we are using syntactically annotated data in the Penn Treebank-II format, the syntactic function of an NP was derived from these annotations. Agreement for gender, number, and person was labelled by hand. Since English has almost no nominal case morphemes, case was not annotated.

Sortal classes provide information about the discourse entity that a referring expression evokes or accesses. The classes, summarized in Table 2, were derived from EuroWordNet BaseTypes (Vossen, 1998) and are defined extensionally on the basis of WordNet synsets. Their selection was motivated by two main considerations: all classes should occur in all genres, and the number of classes should be as small as possible in order to avoid problems with sparse data. Four classes, State, Event, Action, and Property, cover different types of situations, two cover spatiotemporal characteristics of situations (Loc/Time). The four remaining classes cover the two dimensions "concrete vs. abstract (Concept)" and "human (Pers) vs. non-human (PhysObj) vs. institutionalised groups of humans (Group)".

Since we are only interested in the decision whether to employ pronouns rather than full NPs and less in the form of the NP itself, and since our methodology is based on corpus annotation, we did not take into account more formal semantic categories such as kinds vs. individuals.

Co-specification-level factors depend on information about sequences of referring expressions

Person	one or more human beings
Group	institutionalized group of human beings
PhysObj	physical object
Concept	abstract concept
Loc	geographical location
Time	date, time span
Event	sth. which takes place in space and time
Action	sth. which is done
State	state of affairs, feeling, ...
Property	characteristic or attribute of sth.

Table 2: Overview of Sortal Classes with rough characterizations of relevant synsets

which co-specify with each other. Such a sequence consists of all referring expressions that evoke or access the same discourse entity. In this paper, we use the following factors from the literature: distance to last mention (Dist and Dist4), ambiguity (Ambig), parallelism (Par), form of the antecedent (FormAnte), and syntactic function of the antecedent (SynAnte). We also distinguish between discourse entities that are only evoked once, *deadend* entities, and entities that are accessed repeatedly.

Parallelism is defined on the basis of syntactic function: a referring expression and its antecedent are parallel if they have the same syntactic function.

For calculating distance and ambiguity, we segmented the texts into major clause units (MCUs). Each MCU consists of a major clause C plus any subordinate clauses and any coordinated major clauses whose subject is the same as that of C and where that subject has been elided.

Dist provides the number of MCUs between the current and the last previous mention of a discourse entity. When an entity is evoked for the first time, Dist is set to "D". Dist4 is derived from Dist by assigning the fixed distance 2 to all referring expressions whose antecedent is more than 1 MCU away. Ambiguity is defined as the number of all discourse entities with the same agreement features that occur in the previous unit or in the same unit before the current referring expression.

3 Data

Our data consisted of twelve (plus two) texts from the Brown corpus and the corresponding part-of-speech and syntactic annotations from the Penn Treebank (LDC, 1995). The texts were selected because they contained relatively little or no direct speech; segments of direct speech pose problems for both pronoun resolution and generation because of the change in point of view. Morpho-syntactic information such as markables, part-of-speech labels, grammatical role labels, and form of referring expression were automatically extracted from the existing Treebank annotations.

The texts come from four different genres: Popular Lore (CF), Belles Lettres (CG), Fiction/General (CK), and Fiction/Mystery (CL). The choice of genres was dictated by the availability of detailed Treebank-II parses. Table 3 shows that the distribution of referring expressions differs considerably between genres.

The texts from the two non-narrative types, CF and CG, contain far more discourse entities and far less pronouns than the narrative genres CK and CL. The high number of pronouns in CK and CL is partly due to the fact that in one text from each genre, we have a first person singular narrator. CK patterns with CF and CG in the average number of MCUs; the sentences in the sample from mystery fiction are shorter and arguably less complex. CL also has disproportionally few deadend referents. The high percentage of deadend referents in CK is due to the fact that two of the texts deal with relationship between two people. These four discourse referents account for the 4 longest coreference chains in CK (85, 96, 109, and 127 mentions).

Two annotators (the authors, both trained linguists), hand-labeled the texts with co-specification information based on the specifications for the Message Understanding Coreference task (Hirschman & Chinchor (1997); for theoretical reasons, we did not mark reflexive pronouns and appositives as co-specifying). The MCUs were labelled by the second author. All referring expressions were annotated with agreement and sortal class information. Labels were placed using the GUI-based annotation tool REFEREE (DeCristofaro et al., 1999).

The annotators developed the Sortal Class annotation guidelines on the basis of two training texts. Then, both labellers annotated two texts from each genre independently (eight in total). These eight texts were used to determine the reliability of the sortal class coding scheme. Since sortal class annotation is intrinsically hard, the annotators looked up the senses of the head noun of each referring NP that was not a pronoun or a proper name in WordNet. Each sense was mapped directly to one or more of the ten classes given in Table 2. The annotators then chose the adequate sense.

The reliability of the annotations were measured

Genre	words	ref. expr.	entities	sequ.	MCUs	% pron.	% deadend	med. len.
CF	6097	1725	1223	125	304	19.59% (1.8%, 0.3%, 58.3%)	89.78%	3
CG	6103	1707	1290	120	269	16.17% (9.8%, 1.1%, 4%)	90.70%	2
CK	6020	1848	1071	113	386	36.15% (19.5%, 1.2%, 56.1%)	89.45%	2
CL	6018	1846	954	170	477	35.64% (14.0%, 1.5%, 53.6%)	80.09%	4

Table 3: Relevant quantitative characteristics of the texts. Average length: 2020 words, 120 MCUs. *sequ.:* number of sequences of co-specifying referring expressions. *% deadend:* percentage of discourse entities mentioned only once. *% pronouns:* percentage of all referring expressions realized as pronouns, in brackets: perc. of first person singular pronouns, perc. of second person singular pronouns, perc. of third person singular masculine and feminine pronouns. *med. len.:* median length of sequences of co-specifying referring expressions

with Cohen's κ (Cohen, 1960; Carletta, 1996). Cohen (1960) shows that a κ between 0.68 and 0.80 allows tentative conclusions, while $\kappa > 0.80$ indicates reliable annotations. For genres CF ($\kappa = 0.83$), CK ($\kappa = 0.84$) and CL ($\kappa = 0.83$), the sortal class annotations were indeed reliable, but not for genre CG ($\kappa = 0.63$). Nevertheless, overall, the sortal class annotations were reliable ($\kappa = 0.8$). Problems are mainly due to the abstract classes Concept, Action, Event, State, and Property. Abstract head nouns sometimes have several senses that fit the context almost equally well, but that lead to different sortal classes. Another problem is metaphorical usage. This explains the bad results for CG, which features many abstract discourse entities.

4 Towards a Probabilistic Genre-Independent Model

In this section, we investigate to what extent the factors proposed in section 2.2 influence the decision to prominalize. For the purpose of the statistical analysis, pronominalization is modelled by a feature Pro. For a given referring expression, that feature has the value "P" if the referring expression is a personal or a possessive pronoun, else "N". We model this variable with a binomial distribution. [1]

4.1 How do the Factors Affect Pronominalization?

First, we examine for all nine factors if there is a statistical association between these factors and Pro. Standard non-parametric tests show a strong association between all nine factors and Pro.[2] This holds both for all referring expressions and for those that occur in sequences of co-specifying referring expressions. All of the tests were significant at the $p < 0.001$-level, with the exception of Par: for expressions that are part of co-specification sequences the effect of that factor is not significant.

In the next analysis step, we determine which of the feature values are associated disproportionally often with pronouns, and which values tend to be associated with full NPs. More specifically, we test for each feature-value pair if the pronominalization probability is significantly higher or lower than that computed over (a) the complete data set, (b) all referring expressions in sequences of co-specifying referring expressions, (c) all third person referring expressions in sequences. Almost all feature values show highly significant effects for (a) and (b), but some of these effects vanish in condition (c). Below, we report on associations which are significant at $p < 0.001$ under all three conditions.

Unsurprisingly, there is a strong effect of agreement values: NPs referring to the first and second person are always pronominalized, and third person masculine or feminine NPs, which can refer to persons, are pronominalized more frequently than third person neuter and third person plural. Pronouns are strongly preferred if the distance to the antecedent is 0 or 1 MCUs. Referring expressions are more likely to be pronominalized in subject position than as a PP adjunct, and referring expressions with adjuncts as antecedents are also pronominalized less often than those with antecedents in subject or object position. There is a clear preference for pronouns as possessive determiners, and referring expressions that co-specify with an antecedent possessive pronoun are highly likely to be pronominalised. We

[1] For all statistical calculations and for the logistic regression analyses reported below, we used R (Ihaka & Gentleman, 1996).

[2] We used the Kruskal-Wallis test for the ordinal Ambig variable and the χ^2-test for the other, nominal, variables. Since first mentions and deadends are coded by the character "D" in both Dist and Dist4, both are treated as a categorical variable by R. For more on these tests, see (Agresti, 1990).

also notice strong genre-independent effects of parallelism. Although at first glance, Ambig appears to have a significant effect as well, (median ambiguity for nouns is 3, median ambiguity for pronouns 0), closer inspection reveals that this is mainly due to first and second person and third person masculine and feminine pronouns.

The sortal classes show a number of interesting patterns (cf. Table 4). Not only do the classes differ in the percentage of deadend entities, there are also marked differences in pronominalizability. There appear to be three groups of sortal classes: Person/Group, with the lowest rate of deadend entities and the highest percentage of pronouns – not only due to the first and second person personal pronouns – , Location/PhysObj, with roughly two thirds of all entities not in sequences and a significantly lower pronominalization rate, and Concept/Action/Event/Property/State/Concept, with over 80% deadend entities. Within this group, Action, Event, and Concept are pronominalized more frequently than State and Property. Time is the least frequently pronominalized class. An important reason for the difference between Loc and Time might be that Times are almost always referred back to by temporal adverbs, while locations, especially towns and countries, can also be accessed via third person neuter personal pronouns.

Interactions between the factors and genre were examined by an analysis of deviance run on a fitted logistic regression model; significance was calculated using the F-test. All factors except for Par show strong ($p < 0.001$) interactions with Genre. In other words, the influence of all factors but parallelism on pronominalization is mediated by Genre. There are two main reasons for this effect: first, some genres contain far more first and second person personal pronouns, which adds to the weight of Agree, and second, texts which are about persons and the actions of persons, such as the texts in CK and CL, tend to use more pronouns than texts which are mainly argumentative or expository.

4.2 Which Factors are Important?

To separate the important from the unimportant factors, many researchers use decision and regression trees, mostly the binary CART variant (Breiman et al., 1984). We use a different kind of model here, logistic regression, which is especially well suited for categorical data analysis (cf. eg. Agresti (1990) or Kessler et al. (1997)). In this model, the value of the binary target variable is predicted by a linear combination of the predictor variables. Variable weights indicate the importance of a variable for classification: the higher the absolute value of the weight, the more important it is.

Logistic regression models are not only evaluated by their performance on training and test data. We could easily construct a perfect model of any training data set with n variables, where n is the size of the data set. But we need models that are small, yet predict the target values well. A suitable criterion is the Akaike Information Criterion (AIC, Akaike (1974)), which punishes both models that do not fit the data well and models that have too many parameters. The quality of a factor is judged by the amount of variation in the target variable that it explains. Note that increased prediction accuracy does not necessarily mean an increase in the amount of variation explained. As the model itself is a *continuous* approximation of the *categorical* distinctions to be modelled, it may occur that the numerical variation in the predictions decreases, but that this decrease is lost when re-translating numerical predictions into categorical ones.

The factors for our model were selected based on the following procedure: We start with a model that always predicts the most frequent class. We then determine which factor provides the greatest reduction in the AIC, add that factor to the model and retrain. This step is repeated until all factors have been used or adding another factor does not yield any significant improvements anymore.[3]

This procedure invariably yields the sequence Dist4, Agree, Class, FormAnte, Syn, SynAnte, Ambig, Par, both when training models on the complete data set and when training on a single genre. Inspection of the AIC values suggests that parallelism is the least important factor, and does not improve the AIC significantly. Therefore, we will discard it from the outset. All other factors are maintained in the initial full model. This model is purely additive; it does not include interactions between factors. This approach allows us to filter out factors which only mediate the influence of other factors, but do not exert any significant influence of their own. Note that this probabilistic model only provides a numerical description of how its factors affect pronominalization in our corpus. As such, it is not equivalent to a theoretical model, but rather provides data for fur-

[3]We excluded Dist from this stepwise procedure, since the relevant information is covered already by Dist4, which furthermore has much fewer values.

Class	Act	Concept	Event	Group	Loc	Pers	PhysObj	Prop	State	Time
% deadend	84.1	80.0	88.0	46.1	63.3	17.3	65.5	88.5	87.8	92.9
% pronouns	6.2	8,5	6.0	28.4	5.7	63.4	10.2	2.5	3.2	0.3
% pron. (sequences)	32.5	29.6	33.3	51.6	15.4	73.8	27.2	21.4	23,7	4.5

Table 4: Results for Sortal Classes. % deadend: percentage of deadend entities; % pronouns: percent pronominalised, % pron. (sequences: percent pronominalised relative to all occurrences in co-specification sequences

	CF	CG	CK	CL	all
% correct	**97.1**	93.5	93.6	91.5	93.1
AIC	**324.7**	654.8	786.1	904.0	2685.8
% variation	**83.0**	65.4	70.1	65.4	68.7

Table 5: Quality of models fitted to each of the genre-specific corpora (CF, CG, CK, CL) and the complete data set (all). % correct: correctly predicted pronominalization decition, AIC: Akaike Information Criterion, % variation: percentage of original variation in the data (as measured by deviance) accounted for by the model

ther theoretical interpretation.

Results of a first evaluation of the full model are summarized in Table 5. The model can explain more than two thirds of the variation in the complete data set and can predict pronominalization quite well on the data it was fitted on. The matter becomes more interesting when we examine the genre-specific results. Although overall prediction performance remains stable, the model is obviously suited better to some genres than to others. The best results are obtained on CF, the worst on CL (mystery fiction). In the CL texts, MCUs are short, a third of all referring expressions are pronouns, there is no first person singular narrator, and most paragraphs which mention persons are about the interaction between two persons.

The Relative Importance of Factors. All values of Dist4 have very strong weights in all models; this is clearly the most important factor. The same goes for Agree, where the first and second person are strong signs of pronominalization, and, to a lesser degree, masculine and feminine third person singular. The most important distinction provided by Class appears to be that between Persons, non-Persons, and Times. This holds as well when the model is only trained on third person referring expressions. For singular referring expressions, Personhood information is reflected in gender, but not for plural referring expressions. Another important influence is the form of the antecedent. The syntactic function of the referring expression and of its antecedent are less important, as is ambiguity.

In order to examine the importance of the factors in more detail, we refitted the models on the complete data set while omitting one or more of the three central features Dist4, Agree, and Class. The results are summarized in Table 6. The most interesting finding is that even if we exclude all three factors, prediction accuracy only drops by 3.2%. This means that the remaining 4 factors also contain most of the relevant information, but that this information is coded more "efficiently", so to speak, in the first three. Speaking of these factors, questions concerning the effect of sortal class remains. Remarkably enough, when sortal class is omitted, accuracy *increases* by 0.7%. The increase in AIC can be explained by a decrease in the amount of explained variation. A third result is that information about the *form of the antecedent* can substitute for distance information, if that information is missing. Both variables code the crucial distinctions between expressions that evoke entities and those that access evoked entities. Furthermore, a pronominal antecedent tends to occur at a distance of less than 2 MCUs. The contribution of syntactic function remains stable and significant, albeit comparatively unimportant.

Predictive Power: To evaluate the predictive power of the models computed so far, we determine the percentage of correctly predicted pronouns and NPs. The performance of the trained models was compared to two very simple algorithms:

Algorithm A: Always choose the most frequent option (i.e. noun).

Algorithm B: If the antecedent is in the same MCU, or if it is in the previous MCU and there is no ambiguity, choose a pronoun; else choose a noun.

Table 7 summarises the results of the comparison. To determine the overall predictive power of

excluded	fit		% explained variation						
	AIC	%correct	Dist4	Agree	Class	PForm	Syn	PSyn	Ambig
none	2686	92.6	54.4	21.1	5.7	3.8	2.3	*0.5*	1.1
Class	2785	**93.3**	54.4	21.1	n.a.	4.7	2.8	0.5	1.1
Agree	2984	**92.6**	54.4	n.a.	**14.3**	6.2	2.7	0.6	1.1
Dist4	3346	90.2	n.a.	35.8	6.1	**32**	3	0.8	*0.1*
Dist4 + Class	3443	90.2	n.a.	35.8	n.a.	**33.7**	3.4	0.8	*0.1*
Dist4 + Agree	3597	89.6	n.a.	n.a.	**31.4**	**35.4**	3.1	0.8	*0.2*
Agree + Class	3098	**92.6**	54.4	n.a.	n.a.	13.11	3.5	*0.5*	3.6
Dist4 + Agree + Class	3739	89.4	n.a.	n.a.	n.a.	**52.62**	4	0.7	1.7

Table 6: Effect of leaving out any one of the three most important factors on model fit. *italics:* significance is $p < 0.05$, for all other factors, $p < 0.005$ or better.

	test data set				
	CF	CG	CK	CL	all
Alg. A	80.4	83.8	63.8	65.4	72.8
Alg. B	91.1	**93.0**	88.6	84.7	89.4
Model	96.5	92.2	**91.8**	**90.9**	92.6 ± 0.02
w/o Class	**96.8**	92.4	91.7	90.7	$\mathbf{93.0 \pm 0.01}$

Table 7: Results of algorithms vs. models on test data in % correct prediction if referring expression is to be pronominalised or not. Setup for genres: model is trained on three genres, tested on the remaining one

the model, we used 10-fold cross-validation. Algorithm A always fares worst, while algorithm B, which is based mainly on distance, the strongest factor in the model, performs quite well. Its overall performance is 3.2% below that of the full model, and 3.6% below that of the full model without sortal class information. It even outperforms the models on CG, which has the lowest percentage of Persons (12.9% vs. 35% for CF and 43.4% and 43.5% for CL and CK). For all other genres, the statistical models outperform the simple heuristics. Excluding sortal class information can boost prediction performance on unseen data by as much as 0.4% for the complete corpus. The apparent contradiction between this finding and the results reported in the previous section can be explained if we consider that not only were some sortal classes comparatively rare in the data (Property, Event), but that our sortal class definition may still be too fine-grained.

We evaluated the genre-independence of the model by training on three genres and testing on the fourth. The results show that the model fares quite well for genre CF, which is also the genre where the overall fit was best (see Table 5). We therefore hypothesize that the decrease in performance is mainly due to the model itself, not to the training data. The results presented in both Table 5 and 7 show that although the model we have found is not quite as genre-independent as we would want it to be, it provides a reasonable fit to all the genres we examined.

5 Future Work

We have described a probabilistic model of pronominalization that is able to correctly predict 93% of all pronouns in a corpus that consists of twelve texts from four different genres. Since the model was derived from a limited corpus and a limited number of genres, we cannot guarantee that our results are applicable to all texts without modifications. But since its performance on our sample is consistently above 90% correct, we are reasonably confident that our main findings will hold for a wide variety of texts and text types. In particular, we isolated several factors which are robust predictors of pronominalization across genres: distance from last mention and agreement, and to a certain extent the form of the antecedent, which appears to be a good substitute if the other two factors are not available. All three features can be computed on the basis of a chunk parse, a rough morphosyntactic analysis of the resulting NPs, and co-specification sequences. In computational terms, they are comparatively cheap. Large corpora can be annotated relatively quickly with this information, which can then be used for statistical pronoun generation.

The comparatively expensive sortal class annotation, on the other hand, was not very important in the final model; in fact, prediction accuracy decreased when sortal class was included. There are two main reasons for this: first, the proposed sortal class annotation scheme needs further work, second, the relationship between sortal class and pronominalization may well be too intricate to be modelled by the factor Class alone.

We set out to find a genre-independent model of pronominalization. The model we found performs quite well, but genre still considerably affects its performance. Where does the remaining, unexplained variation come from? The variation might be just that – stylistic variation. It might stem from one of the traditional factors that we did not take into account here, such as thematic role. However, we suspect that the crucial factor at play here is discourse structure (McCoy & Strube, 1999).

Acknowledgements Work on this paper was begun while Michael Strube was a postdoctoral fellow at the Institute for Research in Cognitive Science, University of Pennsylvania, and Maria Wolters visited the Institute for a week in summer 1999. We would like to thank Kathleen McCoy, Jonathan DeCristofaro, and the three anonymous reviewers for their comments on earlier stages of this work.

References

Agresti, Alan (1990). *Categorical Data Analysis.* New York, N.Y.: Wiley.

Akaike, H. (1974). A new look at statistical model identification. *IEEE Transactions Automatic Control*, 19:716–722.

Azzam, Saliha, Kevin Humphreys & Robert Gaizauskas (1998). Evaluating a focus-based approach to anaphora resolution. In *Proceedings of the 17th International Conference on Computational Linguistics and 36th Annual Meeting of the Association for Computational Linguistics,* Montréal, Québec, Canada, 10–14 August 1998, pp. 74–78.

Breiman, Leo, Jerome H. Friedman, Charles J. Stone & R.A. Olshen (1984). *Classification and Regression Trees.* Belmont, Cal.: Wadsworth and Brooks/Cole.

Cardie, Claire & Kiri Wagstaff (1999). Noun phrase coreference as clustering. In *Proceedings of the 1999 SIGDAT Conference on Empirical Methods in Natural Language Processing and Very Large Corpora,* College Park, Md., 21–22 June 1999, pp. 82–89.

Carletta, Jean (1996). Assessing agreement on classification tasks: The kappa statistic. *Computational Linguistics*, 22(2):249–254.

Cohen, Jacob (1960). A coefficient of agreement for nominal scales. *Educational and Psychological Measurement*, 20:37–46.

Dale, Robert (1992). *Generating Referring Expressions: Constructing Descriptions in a Domain of Objects and Processes.* Cambridge, Mass.: MIT Press.

DeCristofaro, Jonathan, Michael Strube & Kathleen F. McCoy (1999). Building a tool for annotating reference in discourse. In *ACL '99 Workshop on the Relationship between Discourse/Dialogue Structure and Reference, University of Maryland, Maryland, 21 June, 1999*, pp. 54–62.

Fellbaum, Christiane (Ed.) (1998). *WordNet: An Electronic Lexical Database.* Cambridge, Mass.: MIT Press.

Fraurud, Kari (1996). Cognitive ontology and NP form. In T. Fretheim & J. Gundel (Eds.), *Reference and Referent Accessibility*, pp. 65–87. Amsterdam, The Netherlands: Benjamins.

Ge, Niyu, John Hale & Eugene Charniak (1998). A statistical approach to anaphora resolution. In *Proceedings of the Sixth Workshop on Very Large Corpora,* Montréal, Canada, pp. 161–170.

Grosz, Barbara J., Aravind K. Joshi & Scott Weinstein (1995). Centering: A framework for modeling the local coherence of discourse. *Computational Linguistics*, 21(2):203–225.

Hirschman, Lynette & Nancy Chinchor (1997). *MUC-7 Coreference Task Definition,* `http://www.muc.sais.com/proceedings/`.

Ihaka, Ross & Ross Gentleman (1996). R: A language for data analysis and graphics. *Journal of Computational and Graphical Statistics*, 5:299–314.

Kessler, Brett, Geoffrey Nunberg & Hinrich Schütze (1997). Automatic detection of text genre. In *Proceedings of the 35th Annual Meeting of the Association for Computational Linguistics and of the 8th Conference of the European Chapter of the Association for Computational Linguistics,* Madrid, Spain, 7–12 July 1997, pp. 32–38.

LDC (1995). *Penn Treebank-II.* Linguistic Data Consortium. University of Pennsylvania, Philadelphia, Penn.

McCoy, Kathleen F. & Michael Strube (1999). Generating anaphoric expressions: Pronoun or definite description? In *ACL '99 Workshop on the Relationship between Discourse/Dialogue Structure and Reference, University of Maryland, Maryland, 21 June, 1999*, pp. 63–71.

Poesio, Massimo, Renate Henschel, Janet Hitzeman & Rodger Kibble (1999). Statistical NP generation: A first report. In R. Kibble & K. van Deemter (Eds.), *Proceedings of the Workshop on The Generation of Nominal Expressions, 11th European Summer School on Logic, Language, and Information, Utrecht, 9-13 August 1999.*

Sidner, Candace L. (1983). Focusing in the comprehension of definite anaphora. In M. Brady & R.C. Berwick (Eds.), *Computational Models of Discourse*, pp. 267–330. Cambridge, Mass.: MIT Press.

Vossen, Piek (Ed.) (1998). *EuroWordNet: A Multilingual Database with Lexical Semantic Networks.* Dordrecht, The Netherlands: Kluwer.

Yeh, Ching-Long & Chris Mellish (1997). An empirical study on the generation of anaphora in Chinese. *Computational Linguistics*, 23(1):169–190.

Advances in domain independent linear text segmentation

Freddy Y. Y. Choi
Artificial Intelligence Group
Department of Computer Science
University of Manchester
Manchester, England
choif@cs.man.ac.uk

Abstract

This paper describes a method for linear text segmentation which is twice as accurate and over seven times as fast as the state-of-the-art (Reynar, 1998). Inter-sentence similarity is replaced by rank in the local context. Boundary locations are discovered by divisive clustering.

1 Introduction

Even moderately long documents typically address several topics or different aspects of the same topic. The aim of linear text segmentation is to discover the topic boundaries. The uses of this procedure include information retrieval (Hearst and Plaunt, 1993; Hearst, 1994; Yaari, 1997; Reynar, 1999), summarization (Reynar, 1998), text understanding, anaphora resolution (Kozima, 1993), language modelling (Morris and Hirst, 1991; Beeferman et al., 1997b) and improving document navigation for the visually disabled (Choi, 2000).

This paper focuses on domain independent methods for segmenting written text. We present a new algorithm that builds on previous work by Reynar (Reynar, 1998; Reynar, 1994). The primary distinction of our method is the use of a ranking scheme and the cosine similarity measure (van Rijsbergen, 1979) in formulating the similarity matrix. We propose that the similarity values of short text segments is statistically insignificant. Thus, one can only rely on their order, or rank, for clustering.

2 Background

Existing work falls into one of two categories, lexical cohesion methods and multi-source methods (Yaari, 1997). The former stem from the work of Halliday and Hasan (Halliday and Hasan, 1976). They proposed that text segments with similar vocabulary are likely to be part of a coherent topic segment. Implementations of this idea use word stem repetition (Youmans, 1991; Reynar, 1994; Ponte and Croft, 1997), context vectors (Hearst, 1994; Yaari, 1997; Kaufmann, 1999; Eichmann et al., 1999), entity repetition (Kan et al., 1998), semantic similarity (Morris and Hirst, 1991; Kozima, 1993), word distance model (Beeferman et al., 1997a) and word frequency model (Reynar, 1999) to detect cohesion. Methods for finding the topic boundaries include sliding window (Hearst, 1994), lexical chains (Morris, 1988; Kan et al., 1998), dynamic programming (Ponte and Croft, 1997; Heinonen, 1998), agglomerative clustering (Yaari, 1997) and divisive clustering (Reynar, 1994). Lexical cohesion methods are typically used for segmenting written text in a collection to improve information retrieval (Hearst, 1994; Reynar, 1998).

Multi-source methods combine lexical cohesion with other indicators of topic shift such as cue phrases, prosodic features, reference, syntax and lexical attraction (Beeferman et al., 1997a) using decision trees (Miike et al., 1994; Kurohashi and Nagao, 1994; Litman and Passonneau, 1995) and probabilistic models (Beeferman et al., 1997b; Hajime et al., 1998; Reynar, 1998). Work in this area is largely motivated by the topic detection and tracking (TDT) initiative (Allan et al., 1998). The focus is on the segmentation of transcribed spoken text and broadcast news stories where the presentation format and regular cues can be exploited to improve accuracy.

3 Algorithm

Our segmentation algorithm takes a list of tokenized sentences as input. A tokenizer (Grefenstette and Tapanainen, 1994) and a sentence boundary disambiguation algorithm (Palmer and Hearst, 1994; Reynar and Ratnaparkhi, 1997) or EAGLE (Reynar et al., 1997) may be used to convert a plain text document into the acceptable input format.

3.1 Similarity measure

Punctuation and uninformative words are removed from each sentence using a simple regular expression pattern matcher and a stopword list. A stemming algorithm (Porter, 1980) is then applied to the remaining tokens to obtain the word stems. A dictionary of word stem frequencies is constructed for each sentence. This is represented as a vector of frequency counts.

Let $f_{i,j}$ denote the frequency of word j in sentence i. The similarity between a pair of sentences x, y

is computed using the cosine measure as shown in equation 1. This is applied to all sentence pairs to generate a similarity matrix.

$$sim(x,y) = \frac{\sum_j f_{x,j} \times f_{y,j}}{\sqrt{\sum_j f_{x,j}^2 \times \sum_j f_{y,j}^2}} \quad (1)$$

Figure 1 shows an example of a similarity matrix[1]. High similarity values are represented by bright pixels. The bottom-left and top-right pixel show the self-similarity for the first and last sentence, respectively. Notice the matrix is symmetric and contains bright square regions along the diagonal. These regions represent cohesive text segments.

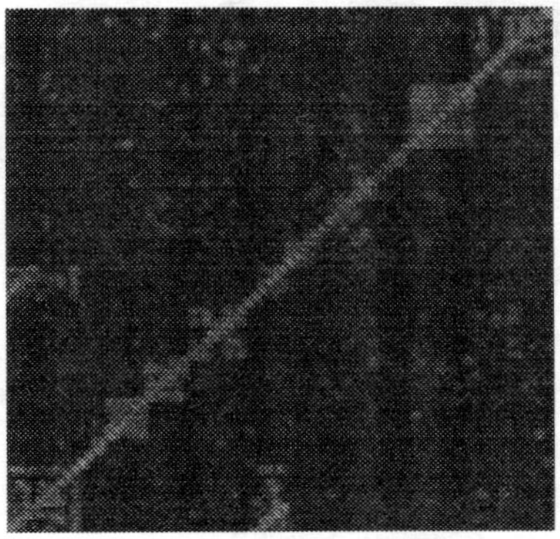

Figure 1: An example similarity matrix.

3.2 Ranking

For short text segments, the absolute value of $sim(x,y)$ is unreliable. An additional occurrence of a common word (reflected in the numerator) causes a disproportionate increase in $sim(x,y)$ unless the denominator (related to segment length) is large. Thus, in the context of text segmentation where a segment has typically < 100 informative tokens, one can only use the metric to estimate the order of similarity between sentences, e.g. a is more similar to b than c.

Furthermore, language usage varies throughout a document. For instance, the introduction section of a document is less cohesive than a section which is about a particular topic. Consequently, it is inappropriate to directly compare the similarity values from different regions of the similarity matrix.

In non-parametric statistical analysis, one compares the rank of data sets when the qualitative behaviour is similar but the absolute quantities are unreliable. We present a ranking scheme which is an adaptation of that described in (O'Neil and Denos, 1992).

[1]The contrast of the image has been adjusted to highlight the image features.

Each value in the similarity matrix is replaced by its rank in the local region. The rank is the number of neighbouring elements with a lower similarity value. Figure 2 shows an example of image ranking using a 3×3 rank mask with output range $\{0, 8\}$. For segmentation, we used a 11×11 rank mask. The output is expressed as a ratio r (equation 2) to circumvent normalisation problems (consider the cases when the rank mask is not contained in the image).

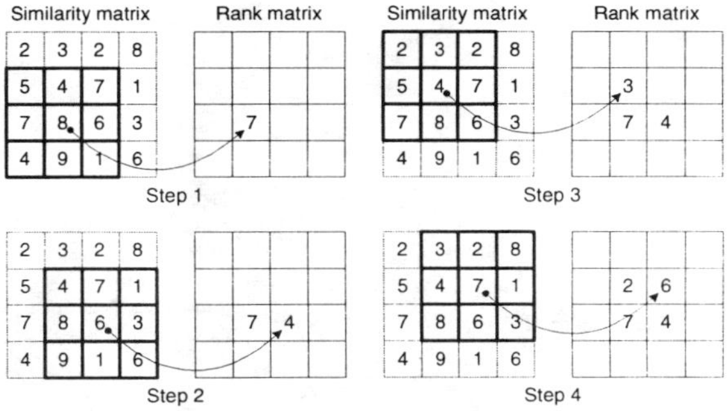

Figure 2: A working example of image ranking.

$$r = \frac{\#\text{ of elements with a lower value}}{\#\text{ of elements examined}} \quad (2)$$

To demonstrate the effect of image ranking, the process was applied to the matrix shown in figure 1 to produce figure 3[2]. Notice the contrast has been improved significantly. Figure 4 illustrates the more subtle effects of our ranking scheme. $r(x)$ is the rank (1×11 mask) of $f(x)$ which is a sine wave with decaying mean, amplitude and frequency (equation 3).

Figure 3: The matrix in figure 1 after ranking.

[2]The process was applied to the original matrix, prior to contrast enhancement. The output image has not been enhanced.

$$f(x) = g(x \times \frac{2\pi}{200})$$
$$g(z) = \frac{1}{2}(e^{-z/2} + \frac{1}{2}e^{-z/2}(1 + \sin(10z^{0.7}))) \quad (3)$$

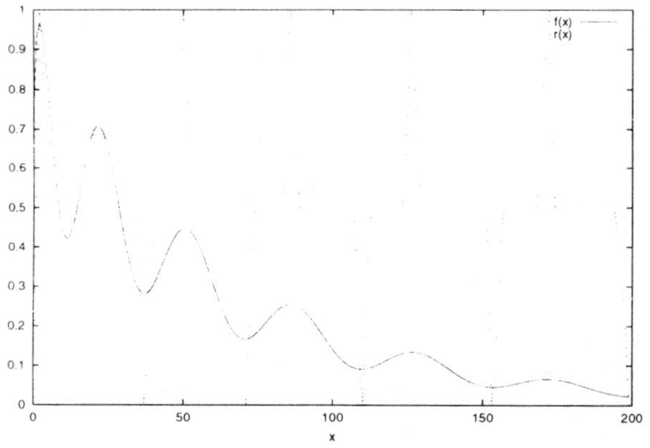

Figure 4: An illustration of the more subtle effects of our ranking scheme.

3.3 Clustering

The final process determines the location of the topic boundaries. The method is based on Reynar's maximisation algorithm (Reynar, 1998; Helfman, 1996; Church, 1993; Church and Helfman, 1993). A text segment is defined by two sentences i, j (inclusive). This is represented as a square region along the diagonal of the rank matrix. Let $s_{i,j}$ denote the sum of the rank values in a segment and $a_{i,j} = (j - i + 1)^2$ be the inside area. $B = \{b_1, ..., b_m\}$ is a list of m coherent text segments. s_k and a_k refers to the sum of rank and area of segment k in B. D is the inside density of B (see equation 4).

$$D = \frac{\sum_{k=1}^{m} s_k}{\sum_{k=1}^{m} a_k} \quad (4)$$

To initialise the process, the entire document is placed in B as one coherent text segment. Each step of the process splits one of the segments in B. The split point is a potential boundary which maximises D. Figure 5 shows a working example.

The number of segments to generate, m, is determined automatically. $D^{(n)}$ is the inside density of n segments and $\delta D^{(n)} = D^{(n)} - D^{(n-1)}$ is the gradient. For a document with b potential boundaries, b steps of divisive clustering generates $\{D^{(1)}, ..., D^{(b+1)}\}$ and $\{\delta D^{(2)}, ..., \delta D^{(b+1)}\}$ (see figure 6 and 7). An unusually large reduction in δD suggests the optimal clustering has been obtained[3] (see $n = 10$ in

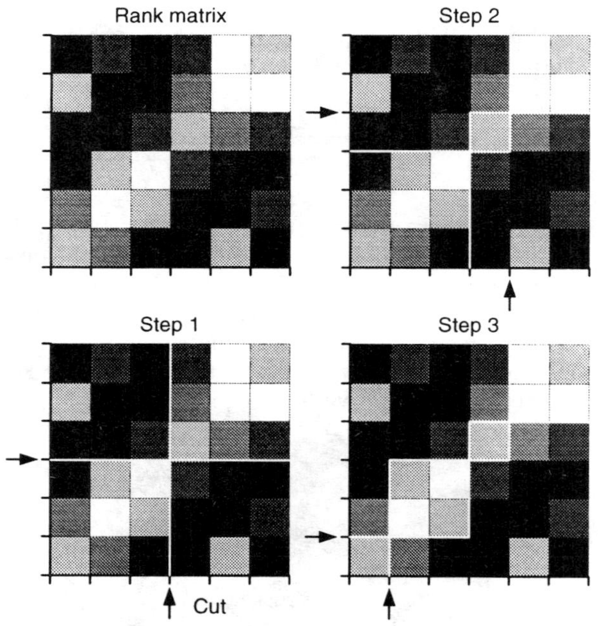

Figure 5: A working example of the divisive clustering algorithm.

figure 7). Let μ and ν be the mean and variance of $\delta D^{(n)}, n \in \{2, ..., b+1\}$. m is obtained by applying the threshold, $\mu + c \times \sqrt{\nu}$, to δD ($c = 1.2$ works well in practice).

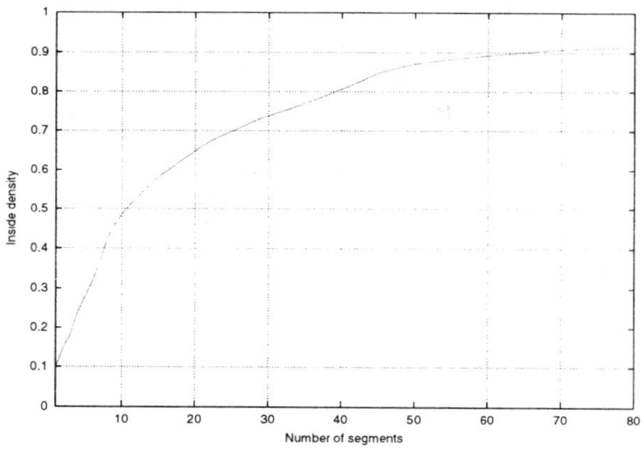

Figure 6: The inside density of all levels of segmentation.

3.4 Speed optimisation

The running time of each step is dominated by the computation of s_k. Given $s_{i,j}$ is constant, our algorithm pre-computes all the values to improve speed performance. The procedure computes the values along diagonals, starting from the main diagonal and

[3]In practice, convolution (mask $\{1, 2, 4, 8, 4, 2, 1\}$) is first applied to δD to smooth out sharp local changes

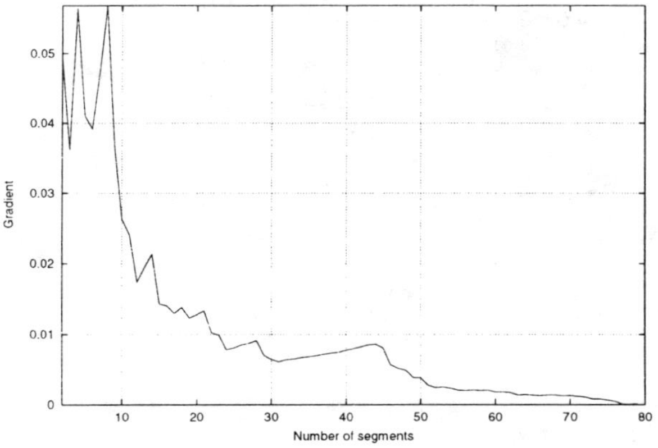

Figure 7: Finding the optimal segmentation using the gradient.

works towards the corner. The method has a complexity of order $1\frac{1}{2}n^2$. Let $r_{i,j}$ refer to the rank value in the rank matrix R and S to the sum of rank matrix. Given R of size $n \times n$, S is computed in three steps (see equation 5). Figure 8 shows the result of applying this procedure to the rank matrix in figure 5.

$$
\begin{array}{lllll}
1. & s_{i,i} & = & r_{i,i} & \\
 & & \text{for} & i \in \{1, ..., n\} & \\
2. & s_{i+1,i} & = & 2r_{i+1,i} + s_{i,i} + s_{i+1,i+1} & \\
 & s_{i,i+1} & = & s_{i+1,i} & \\
 & & \text{for} & i \in \{1, ..., n-1\} & \\
3. & s_{i+j,i} & = & 2r_{i+j,i} + s_{i+j-1,i} + & \\
 & & & s_{i+j,i+1} - s_{i+j-1,i+1} & \\
 & s_{i,i+j} & = & s_{i+j,i} & \\
 & & \text{for} & j \in \{2, ..., n-1\} & \\
 & & & i \in \{1, ..., n-j\} &
\end{array} \quad (5)
$$

Rank matrix

1	2	1	2	5	4
4	1	1	3	5	5
1	1	2	4	3	2
1	4	5	2	1	1
3	5	4	1	1	2
4	3	1	1	4	1

Sum of rank matrix

91	67	46	33	19	4
65	43	26	15	5	19
42	28	13	4	15	33
30	18	5	13	26	46
15	5	18	28	43	67
4	15	30	42	65	91

Figure 8: Improving speed performance by pre-computing $s_{i,j}$.

4 Evaluation

The definition of a topic segment ranges from complete stories (Allan et al., 1998) to summaries (Ponte and Croft, 1997). Given the quality of an algorithm is task dependent, the following experiments focus on the relative performance. Our evaluation strategy is a variant of that described in (Reynar, 1998, 71-73) and the TDT segmentation task (Allan et al., 1998). We assume a good algorithm is one that finds the most prominent topic boundaries.

4.1 Experiment procedure

An artificial test corpus of 700 samples is used to assess the accuracy and speed performance of segmentation algorithms. A sample is a concatenation of ten text segments. A segment is the first n sentences of a randomly selected document from the Brown corpus[4]. A sample is characterised by the range of n. The corpus was generated by an automatic procedure[5]. Table 1 presents the corpus statistics.

Range of n	$3-11$	$3-5$	$6-8$	$9-11$
# samples	400	100	100	100

Table 1: Test corpus statistics.

$$
\begin{aligned}
& p(\text{error}|\text{ref}, \text{hyp}, k) = \\
& \quad p(\text{miss}|\text{ref}, \text{hyp}, \text{diff}, k)p(\text{diff}|\text{ref}, k) + \\
& \quad p(\text{fa}|\text{ref}, \text{hyp}, \text{same}, k)p(\text{same}|\text{ref}, k)
\end{aligned} \quad (6)
$$

Speed performance is measured by the average number of CPU seconds required to process a test sample[6]. Segmentation accuracy is measured by the error metric (equation 6, fa → false alarms) proposed in (Beeferman et al., 1999). Low error probability indicates high accuracy. Other performance measures include the popular precision and recall metric (PR) (Hearst, 1994), fuzzy PR (Reynar, 1998) and edit distance (Ponte and Croft, 1997). The problems associated with these metrics are discussed in (Beeferman et al., 1999).

4.2 Experiment 1 - Baseline

Five degenerate algorithms define the baseline for the experiments. B_n does not propose any boundaries. B_a reports all potential boundaries as real boundaries. B_e partitions the sample into regular segments. $B_{(r,?)}$ randomly selects any number of

[4] Only the news articles `ca**.pos` and informative text `cj**.pos` were used in the experiment.

[5] All experiment data, algorithms, scripts and detailed results are available from the author.

[6] All experiments were conducted on a Pentium II 266MHz PC with 128Mb RAM running RedHat Linux 6.0 and the Blackdown Linux port of JDK1.1.7 v3.

boundaries as real boundaries. $B_{(r,b)}$ randomly selects b boundaries as real boundaries.

The accuracy of the last two algorithms are computed analytically. We consider the status of m potential boundaries as a bit string ($1 \rightarrow$ topic boundary). The terms $p(\text{miss})$ and $p(\text{fa})$ in equation 6 corresponds to $p(\text{same}|k)$ and $p(\text{diff}|k) = 1 - p(\text{same}|k)$. Equation 7, 8 and 9 gives the general form of $p(\text{same}|k)$, $B_{(r,?)}$ and $B_{(r,b)}$, respectively[7].

Table 2 presents the experimental results. The values in row two and three, four and five are not actually the same. However, their differences are insignificant according to the Kolmogorov-Smirnov, or KS-test (Press et al., 1992).

$$p(\text{same}|k) = \frac{\#\text{ valid segmentations}}{\#\text{ possible segmentations}} \quad (7)$$

$$p(\text{same}|k, B_{(r,?)}) = \frac{2^{m-k}}{2^m} = 2^{-k} \quad (8)$$

$$\begin{aligned} p(\text{same}|k, m, B_{(r,b)}) &= \frac{{}_{(m-k)}C_b}{{}_mC_b} \\ {}_xC_y &= \frac{x!}{y!(x-y)!} \end{aligned} \quad (9)$$

	3-11	3-5	6-8	9-11
B_e	45%	38%	39%	36%
B_n	47%	47%	47%	46%
$B_{(r,b)}$	47%	47%	47%	46%
B_a	53%	53%	53%	54%
$B_{(r,?)}$	53%	53%	53%	54%

Table 2: The error rate of the baseline algorithms.

4.3 Experiment 2 - TextTiling

We compare three versions of the TextTiling algorithm (Hearst, 1994). $H94_{(c,d)}$ is Hearst's C implementation with default parameters. $H94_{(c,r)}$ uses the recommended parameters $k = 6$, $w = 20$. $H94_{(j,r)}$ is my implementation of the algorithm. Experimental result (table 3) shows $H94_{(c,d)}$ and $H94_{(c,r)}$ are more accurate than $H94_{(j,r)}$. We suspect this is due to the use of a different stopword list and stemming algorithm.

4.4 Experiment 3 - DotPlot

Five versions of Reynar's optimisation algorithm (Reynar, 1998) were evaluated. $R98$ and $R98_{(min)}$ are exact implementations of his maximisation and minimisation algorithm. $R98_{(s,cos)}$ is my version of the maximisation algorithm which uses the cosine coefficient instead of dot density for measuring similarity. It incorporates the optimisations described

[7]The full derivation of our method is available from the author.

	3-11	3-5	6-8	9-11
$H94_{(c,d)}$	46%	44%	43%	48%
$H94_{(c,r)}$	46%	44%	44%	49%
$H94_{(j,r)}$	54%	45%	52%	53%
$H94_{(c,d)}$	0.67s	0.52s	0.66s	0.88s
$H94_{(c,r)}$	0.68s	0.52s	0.67s	0.92s
$H94_{(j,r)}$	3.77s	2.21s	3.69s	5.07s

Table 3: The error rate and speed performance of TextTiling.

in section 3.4. $R98_{(m,dot)}$ is the modularised version of $R98$ for experimenting with different similarity measures.

$R98_{(m,sa)}$ uses a variant of Kozima's semantic similarity measure (Kozima, 1993) to compute block similarity. Word similarity is a function of word co-occurrence statistics in the given document. Words that belong to the same sentence are considered to be related. Given the co-occurrence frequencies $f(w_i, w_j)$, the transition probability matrix t is computed by equation 10. Equation 11 defines our spread activation scheme. s denotes the word similarity matrix, x is the number of activation steps and $\text{norm}(y)$ converts a matrix y into a transition matrix. $x = 5$ was used in the experiment.

$$t_{i,j} = p(w_j|w_i) = \frac{f(w_i, w_j)}{\sum_j f(w_i, w_j)} \quad (10)$$

$$s = \text{norm}\left(\sum_{i=1}^{x} t^i\right) \quad (11)$$

Experimental result (table 4) shows the cosine coefficient and our spread activation method improved segmentation accuracy. The speed optimisations significantly reduced the execution time.

	3-11	3-5	6-8	9-11
$R98_{(m,sa)}$	18%	20%	15%	12%
$R98_{(s,cos)}$	21%	18%	19%	18%
$R98_{(m,dot)}$	22%	21%	18%	16%
$R98$	22%	21%	18%	16%
$R98_{(min)}$	n/a	34%	37%	37%
$R98_{(s,cos)}$	4.54s	2.24s	4.36s	6.99s
$R98$	29.58s	9.29s	28.09s	55.03s
$R98_{(m,sa)}$	41.02s	7.34s	40.05s	113.5s
$R98_{(m,dot)}$	46.58s	9.24s	42.72s	115.4s
$R98_{(min)}$	n/a	19.62s	58.77s	122.6s

Table 4: The error rate and speed performance of Reynar's optimisation algorithm.

4.5 Experiment 4 - Segmenter

We compare three versions of Segmenter (Kan et al., 1998). $K98_{(p)}$ is the original Perl implementation of the algorithm (version 1.6). $K98_{(j)}$ is my implementation of the algorithm. $K98_{(j,a)}$ is a version of $K98_{(j)}$ which uses a document specific chain breaking strategy. The distribution of link distances are used to identify unusually long links. The threshold is a function $\mu + c \times \sqrt{\nu}$ of the mean μ and variance ν. We found $c = 1$ works well in practice.

Table 5 summarises the experimental results. $K98_{(p)}$ performed significantly better than $K98_{(j,*)}$. This is due to the use of a different part-of-speech tagger and shallow parser. The difference in speed is largely due to the programming languages and term clustering strategies. Our chain breaking strategy improved accuracy (compare $K98_{(j)}$ with $K98_{(j,a)}$).

	3-11	3-5	6-8	9-11
$K98_{(p)}$	36%	23%	33%	43%
$K98_{(j,a)}$	n/a	41%	46%	50%
$K98_{(j)}$	n/a	44%	48%	51%
$K98_{(p)}$	4.24s	2.57s	4.21s	6.00s
$K98_{(j)}$	n/a	21.43s	65.54s	129.3s
$K98_{(j,a)}$	n/a	21.44s	65.49s	129.7s

Table 5: The error rate and speed performance of Segmenter.

4.6 Experiment 5 - Our algorithm, $C99$

Two versions of our algorithm were developed, $C99$ and $C99_{(b)}$. The former is an exact implementation of the algorithm described in this paper. The latter is given the expected number of topic segments for fair comparison with $R98$. Both algorithms used a 11×11 ranking mask.

The first experiment focuses on the impact of our automatic termination strategy on $C99_{(b)}$ (table 6). $C99_{(b)}$ is marginally more accurate than $C99$. This indicates our automatic termination strategy is effective but not optimal. The minor reduction in speed performance is acceptable.

	3-11	3-5	6-8	9-11
$C99_{(b)}$	12%	12%	9%	9%
$C99$	13%	18%	10%	10%
$C99_{(b)}$	4.00s	1.91s	3.73s	5.99s
$C99$	4.04s	2.12s	4.04s	6.31s

Table 6: The error rate and speed performance of our algorithm, $C99$.

The second experiment investigates the effect of different ranking mask size on the performance of $C99$ (table 7). Execution time increases with mask size. A 1×1 ranking mask reduces all the elements in the rank matrix to zero. Interestingly, the increase in ranking mask size beyond 3×3 has insignificant effect on segmentation accuracy. This suggests the use of extrema for clustering has a greater impact on accuracy than linearising the similarity scores (figure 4).

	3-11	3-5	6-8	9-11
1×1	48%	48%	50%	49%
3×3	12%	11%	10%	8%
5×5	12%	11%	10%	8%
7×7	12%	11%	10%	8%
9×9	12%	11%	10%	9%
11×11	12%	11%	10%	9%
13×13	12%	11%	10%	9%
15×15	12%	11%	10%	9%
17×17	12%	10%	10%	8%
1×1	3.92s	2.06s	3.84s	5.91s
3×3	3.83s	2.03s	3.79s	5.85s
5×5	3.86s	2.04s	3.84s	5.92s
7×7	3.90s	2.06s	3.88s	6.00s
9×9	3.96s	2.07s	3.92s	6.12s
11×11	4.02s	2.09s	3.98s	6.26s
13×13	4.11s	2.11s	4.07s	6.41s
15×15	4.20s	2.14s	4.14s	6.60s
17×17	4.29s	2.17s	4.25s	6.79s

Table 7: The impact of mask size on the performance of $C99$.

4.7 Summary

Experimental result (table 8) shows our algorithm $C99$ is more accurate than existing algorithms. A two-fold increase in accuracy and seven-fold increase in speed was achieved (compare $C99_{(b)}$ with $R98$). If one disregards segmentation accuracy, $H94$ has the best algorithmic performance (linear). $C99$, $K98$ and $R98$ are all polynomial time algorithms. The significance of our results has been confirmed by both t-test and KS-test.

	3-11	3-5	6-8	9-11
$C99_{(b)}$	12%	12%	9%	9%
$C99$	13%	18%	10%	10%
$R98$	22%	21%	18%	16%
$K98_{(p)}$	36%	23%	33%	43%
$H94_{(c,d)}$	46%	44%	43%	48%
$H94_{(j,r)}$	3.77s	2.21s	3.69s	5.07s
$C99_{(b)}$	4.00s	1.91s	3.73s	5.99s
$C99$	4.04s	2.12s	4.04s	6.31s
$R98$	29.58s	9.29s	28.09s	55.03s
$K98_{(j)}$	n/a	21.43s	65.54s	129.3s

Table 8: A summary of our experimental results.

5 Conclusions and future work

A segmentation algorithm has two key elements, a clustering strategy and a similarity measure. Our results show divisive clustering ($R98$) is more precise than sliding window ($H94$) and lexical chains ($K98$) for locating topic boundaries.

Four similarity measures were examined. The cosine coefficient ($R98_{(s,cos)}$) and dot density measure ($R98_{(m,dot)}$) yield similar results. Our spread activation based semantic measure ($R98_{(m,sa)}$) improved accuracy. This confirms that although Kozima's approach (Kozima, 1993) is computationally expensive, it does produce more precise segmentation.

The most significant improvement was due to our ranking scheme which linearises the cosine coefficient. Our experiments demonstrate that given insufficient data, the qualitative behaviour of the cosine measure is indeed more reliable than the actual values.

Although our evaluation scheme is sufficient for this comparative study, further research requires a large scale, task independent benchmark. It would be interesting to compare $C99$ with the multi-source method described in (Beeferman et al., 1999) using the TDT corpus. We would also like to develop a linear time and multi-source version of the algorithm.

Acknowledgements

This paper has benefitted from the comments of Mary McGee Wood and the anonymous reviewers. Thanks are due to my parents and department for making this work possible; Jeffrey Reynar for discussions and guidance on the segmentation problem; Hideki Kozima for help on the spread activation measure; Min-Yen Kan and Marti Hearst for their segmentation algorithms; Daniel Oram for references to image processing techniques; Magnus Rattray and Stephen Marsland for help on statistics and mathematics.

References

James Allan, Jaime Carbonell, George Doddington, Jonathan Yamron, and Yiming Yang. 1998. Topic detection and tracking pilot study final report. In *Proceedings of the DARPA Broadcast News Transcription and Understanding Workshop.*

Doug Beeferman, Adam Berger, and John Lafferty. 1997a. A model of lexical attraction and repulsion. In *Proceedings of the 35th Annual Meeting of the ACL.*

Doug Beeferman, Adam Berger, and John Lafferty. 1997b. Text segmentation using exponential models. In *Proceedings of EMNLP-2.*

Doug Beeferman, Adam Berger, and John Lafferty. 1999. Statistical models for text segmentation. *Machine learning, special issue on Natural Language Processing*, 34(1-3):177–210. C. Cardie and R. Mooney (editors).

Freddy Y. Y. Choi. 2000. A speech interface for rapid reading. In *Proceedings of IEE colloquium: Speech and Language Processing for Disabled and Elderly People*, London, England, April. IEE.

Kenneth W. Church and Jonathan I. Helfman. 1993. Dotplot: A program for exploring self-similarity in millions of lines of text and code. *The Journal of Computational and Graphical Statistics.*

Kenneth W. Church. 1993. Char_align: A program for aligning parallel texts at the character level. In *Proceedings of the 31st Annual Meeting of the ACL.*

David Eichmann, Miguel Ruiz, and Padmini Srinivasan. 1999. A cluster-based approach to tracking, detection and segmentation of broadcast news. In *Proceedings of the 1999 DARPA Broadcast News Workshop (TDT-2).*

Gregory Grefenstette and Pasi Tapanainen. 1994. What is a word, what is a sentence? problems of tokenization. In *Proceedings of the 3rd Conference on Computational Lexicography and Text Research (COMPLEX'94)*, Budapest, July.

Mochizuki Hajime, Honda Takeo, and Okumura Manabu. 1998. Text segmentation with multiple surface linguistic cues. In *Proceedings of COLING-ACL'98*, pages 881–885.

Michael Halliday and Ruqaiya Hasan. 1976. *Cohesion in English.* Longman Group, New York.

Marti Hearst and Christian Plaunt. 1993. Subtopic structuring for full-length document access. In *Proceedings of the 16th Annual International ACM/SIGIR Conference*, Pittsburgh, PA.

Marti A. Hearst. 1994. Multi-paragraph segmentation of expository text. In *Proceedings of the ACL'94.* Las Crces, NM.

Oskari Heinonen. 1998. Optimal multi-paragraph text segmentation by dynamic programming. In *Proceedings of COLING-ACL'98.*

Jonathan I. Helfman. 1996. Dotplot patterns: A literal look at pattern languages. *Theory and Practice of Object Systems*, 2(1):31–41.

Min-Yen Kan, Judith L. Klavans, and Kathleen R. McKeown. 1998. Linear segmentation and segment significance. In *Proceedings of the 6th International Workshop of Very Large Corpora (WVLC-6)*, pages 197–205, Montreal, Quebec, Canada, August.

Stefan Kaufmann. 1999. Cohesion and collocation: Using context vectors in text segmentation. In *Proceedings of the 37th Annual Meeting of the Association of for Computational Linguistics (Student Session)*, pages 591–595, College Park, USA, June. ACL.

Hideki Kozima. 1993. Text segmentation based on similarity between words. In *Proceedings of ACL'93*, pages 286–288, Ohio.

Sadao Kurohashi and Makoto Nagao. 1994. Automatic detection of discourse structure by checking surface information in sentences. In *Processings of COLING'94*, volume 2, pages 1123–1127.

Diane J. Litman and Rebecca J. Passonneau. 1995. Combining multiple knowledge sources for discourse segmentation. In *Proceedings of the 33rd Annual Meeting of the ACL*.

S. Miike, E. Itoh, K. Ono, and K. Sumita. 1994. A full text retrieval system. In *Proceedings of SIGIR'94*, Dublin, Ireland.

J. Morris and G. Hirst. 1991. Lexical cohesion computed by thesaural relations as an indicator of the structure of text. *Computational Linguistics*, (17):21–48.

Jane Morris. 1988. Lexical cohesion, the thesaurus, and the structure of text. Technical Report CSRI 219, Computer Systems Research Institute, University of Toronto.

M. A. O'Neil and M. I. Denos. 1992. Practical approach to the stereo-matching of urban imagery. *Image and Vision Computing*, 10(2):89–98.

David D. Palmer and Marti A. Hearst. 1994. Adaptive sentence boundary disambiguation. In *Proceedings of the 4th Conference on Applied Natural Language Processing*, Stuttgart, Germany, October. ACL.

Jay M. Ponte and Bruce W. Croft. 1997. Text segmentation by topic. In *Proceedings of the first European Conference on research and advanced technology for digital libraries*. U.Mass. Computer Science Technical Report TR97-18.

M. Porter. 1980. An algorithm for suffix stripping. *Program*, 14(3):130–137, July.

William H. Press, Saul A. Teukolsky, William T. Vettering, and Brian P. Flannery, 1992. *Numerical recipes in C: The Art of Scientific Computing*, chapter 14, pages 623–628. Cambridge University Press, second edition.

Jeffrey Reynar and Adwait Ratnaparkhi. 1997. A maximum entropy approach to identifying sentence boundaries. In *Proceedings of the fifth conference on Applied NLP*, Washington D.C.

Jeffrey Reynar, Breck Baldwin, Christine Doran, Michael Niv, B. Srinivas, and Mark Wasson. 1997. Eagle: An extensible architecture for general linguistic engineering. In *Proceedings of RIAO '97*, Montreal, June.

Jeffrey C. Reynar. 1994. An automatic method of finding topic boundaries. In *Proceedings of ACL'94 (Student session)*.

Jeffrey C. Reynar. 1998. *Topic segmentation: Algorithms and applications*. Ph.D. thesis, Computer and Information Science, University of Pennsylvania.

Jeffrey C. Reynar. 1999. Statistical models for topic segmentation. In *Proceedings of the 37th Annual Meeting of the ACL*, pages 357–364. 20-26th June, Maryland, USA.

C. J. van Rijsbergen. 1979. *Information Retrieval*. Buttersworth.

Yaakov Yaari. 1997. Segmentation of expository texts by hierarchical agglomerative clustering. In *Proceedings of RANLP'97*. Bulgaria.

Gilbert Youmans. 1991. A new tool for discourse analysis: The vocabulary-management profile. *Language*, pages 763–789.

Bagging and Boosting a Treebank Parser

John C. Henderson
The MITRE Corporation
202 Burlington Road
Bedford, MA 01730
jhndrsn@mitre.org

Eric Brill
Microsoft Research
1 Microsoft Way
Redmond, WA 98052
brill@microsoft.com

Abstract

Bagging and boosting, two effective machine learning techniques, are applied to natural language parsing. Experiments using these techniques with a trainable statistical parser are described. The best resulting system provides roughly as large of a gain in F-measure as doubling the corpus size. Error analysis of the result of the boosting technique reveals some inconsistent annotations in the Penn Treebank, suggesting a semi-automatic method for finding inconsistent treebank annotations.

1 Introduction

Henderson and Brill (1999) showed that independent human research efforts produce parsers that can be combined for an overall boost in accuracy. Finding an ensemble of parsers designed to complement each other is clearly desirable. The parsers would need to be the result of a unified research effort, though, in which the errors made by one parser are targeted with priority by the developer of another parser.

A set of five parsers which each achieve only 40% exact sentence accuracy would be extremely valuable if they made errors in such a way that at least two of the five were correct on any given sentence (and the others abstained or were wrong in different ways). 100% sentence accuracy could be achieved by selecting the hypothesis that was proposed by the two parsers that agreed completely.

In this paper, the task of automatically creating complementary parsers is separated from the task of creating a single parser. This facilitates study of the ensemble creation techniques in isolation. The result is a method for increasing parsing performance by creating an ensemble of parsers, each produced from data using the same parser induction algorithm.

2 Bagging and Parsing

2.1 Background

The work of Efron and Tibshirani (1993) enabled Breiman's refinement and application of their techniques for machine learning (Breiman, 1996). His technique is called *bagging*, short for "bootstrap aggregating". In brief, bootstrap techniques and bagging in particular reduce the systematic biases many estimation techniques introduce by aggregating estimates made from randomly drawn representative resamplings of those datasets.

Bagging attempts to find a set of classifiers which are consistent with the training data, different from each other, and distributed such that the aggregate sample distribution approaches the distribution of samples in the training set.

Algorithm: Bagging Predictors (Breiman, 1996) (1)
Given: training set $\mathcal{L} = \{(y_i, x_i), i \in \{1 \dots m\}\}$ drawn from the set Λ of possible training sets where y_i is the label for example x_i, classification induction algorithm $\Psi : \Lambda \rightarrow \Phi$ with classification algorithm $\phi \in \Phi$ and $\phi : X \rightarrow Y$.

1. Create k bootstrap replicates of $\mathcal{L}$ by sampling m items from $\mathcal{L}$ *with replacement*. Call them $L_1 \dots L_k$.
2. For each $j \in \{1 \dots k\}$, Let $\phi_j = \Psi(\mathcal{L}_j)$ be the classifier induced using L_j as the training set.
3. If Y is a discrete set, then for each x_i observed in the test set, $y_i = \text{mode}\langle\phi_j(x_i) \dots \phi_j(x_i)\rangle$. y_i is the value predicted by the most predictors, the majority vote.

2.2 Bagging for Parsing

An algorithm that applies the technique of bagging to parsing is given in Algorithm 2. Previous work on combining independent parsers is leveraged to produce the combined parser. The rest of the algorithm is a straightforward transformation of bagging for classifiers. Exploratory work in this vein was described by Hajič et al. (1999).

Algorithm: Bagging A Parser (2)
Given: A corpus (again as a function) $\mathcal{C} : S \times T \rightarrow N$, S is the set of possible sentences, and T is the set of trees, with size $m = |\mathcal{C}| = \sum_{s,t} \mathcal{C}(s,t)$ and parser induction algorithm g.

1. Draw k bootstrap replicates $C_1 \dots C_k$ of $\mathcal{C}$ each containing m samples of (s,t) pairs randomly

picked from the domain of $\mathcal{C}$ according to the distribution $D(s,t) = \mathcal{C}(s,t)/|\mathcal{C}|$. Each bootstrap replicate is a bag of samples, where each sample in a bag is drawn randomly with replacement from the bag corresponding to $\mathcal{C}$.

2. Create parser $f_i = g(C_i)$ for each i.

3. Given a novel sentence $s_{test} \in C_{test}$, combine the collection of hypotheses $t_i = f_i(s_{test})$ using the unweighted constituent voting scheme of Henderson and Brill (1999).

2.3 Experiment

The training set for these experiments was sections 01-21 of the Penn Treebank (Marcus et al., 1993). The test set was section 23. The parser induction algorithm used in all of the experiments in this paper was a distribution of Collins's model 2 parser (Collins, 1997). All comparisons made below refer to results we obtained using Collins's parser.

The results for bagging are shown in Figure 2 and Table 1. The row of figures are (from left-to-right) training set F-measure[1], test set F-measure, percent perfectly parsed sentences in training set, and percent perfectly parsed sentences in test set. An ensemble of bags was produced one bag at a time. In the table, the `Initial` row shows the performance achieved when the ensemble contained only one bag, `Final(X)` shows the performance when the ensemble contained X bags, `BestF` gives the performance of the ensemble size that gave the best F-measure score. `TrainBestF` and `TestBestF` give the test set performance for the ensemble size that performed the best on the training and test sets, respectively.

On the training set all of the accuracy measures are improved over the original parser, and on the test set there is clear improvement in precision and recall. The improvement on exact sentence accuracy for the test set is significant, but only marginally so.

The overall gain achieved on the test set by bagging was 0.8 units of F-measure, but because the entire corpus is not used in each bag the initial performance is approximately 0.2 units below the best previously reported result. The net gain using this technique is 0.6 units of F-measure.

3 Boosting

3.1 Background

The AdaBoost algorithm was presented by Freund and Schapire in 1996 (Freund and Schapire, 1996; Freund and Schapire, 1997) and has become a widely-known successful method in machine learning. The AdaBoost algorithm imposes one constraint on its underlying learner: it may abstain from making predictions about labels of some samples, but it must consistently be able to get more than 50% accuracy on the samples for which it commits to a decision. That accuracy is measured according to the distribution describing the importance of samples that it is given. The learner must be able to get more correct samples than incorrect samples *by mass of importance* on those that it labels. This statement of the restriction comes from Schapire and Singer's study (1998). It is called the *weak learning criterion.*

Schapire and Singer (1998) extended AdaBoost by describing how to choose the hypothesis mixing coefficients in certain circumstances and how to incorporate a general notion of confidence scores. They also provided a better characterization of its theoretical performance. The version of AdaBoost used in their work is shown in Algorithm 3, as it is the version that most amenable to parsing.

Algorithm: AdaBoost
(Freund and Schapire, 1997) (3)
Given: Training set $\mathcal{L}$ as in bagging, except $y_i \in \{-1, 1\}$ is the label for example x_i. Initial uniform distribution $D_1(i) = 1/m$. Number of iterations, T. Counter $t = 1$. Ψ, Φ, and ϕ are as in Bagging.

1. Create L_t by randomly choosing with replacement m samples from $\mathcal{L}$ using distribution D_t.

2. Classifier induction: $\phi_t \leftarrow \Psi(L_t)$

3. Choose $\alpha_t \in \mathbb{R}$.

4. Adjust and normalize the distribution. Z_t is a normalization coefficient.
$$D_{t+1}(i) = \frac{1}{Z_t} D_t(i) \exp(-\alpha_t y_i \phi_t(x_i))$$

5. Increment t. Quit if $t > T$.

6. Repeat from step 1.

7. The final hypothesis is
$$\phi_{boost}(x) = \text{sign} \sum_t \alpha_t \phi_t(x)$$

The value of α_t should generally be chosen to minimize
$$\sum_i D_t(i) \exp(-\alpha_t y_i \phi_t(x_i))$$
in order to minimize the expected per-sample training error of the ensemble, which Schapire and Singer show can be concisely expressed by $\prod_t Z_t$. They also give several examples for how to pick an appropriate α, and selection generally depends on the possible outputs of the underlying learner.

Boosting has been used in a few NLP systems. Haruno et al. (1998) used boosting to produce more accurate classifiers which were embedded as control

[1] This is the balanced version of F-measure, where precision and recall are weighted equally.

Set	Instance	P	R	F	Gain	Exact	Gain
Training	Original Parser	96.25	96.31	96.28	NA	64.7	NA
	Initial	93.61	93.63	93.62	0.00	55.5	0.0
	BestF(15)	96.16	95.86	96.01	2.39	62.1	6.6
	Final(15)	96.16	95.86	96.01	2.39	62.1	6.6
Test	Original Parser	88.73	88.54	88.63	NA	34.9	NA
	Initial	88.43	88.34	88.38	0.00	33.3	0.0
	TrainBestF(15)	89.54	88.80	89.17	0.79	34.6	1.3
	TestBestF(13)	89.55	88.84	89.19	0.81	34.7	1.4
	Final(15)	89.54	88.80	89.17	0.79	34.6	1.3

Table 1: Bagging the Treebank

mechanisms of a parser for Japanese. The creators of AdaBoost used it to perform text classification (Schapire and Singer, 2000). Abney et al. (1999) performed part-of-speech tagging and prepositional phrase attachment using AdaBoost as a core component. They found they could achieve accuracies on both tasks that were competitive with the state of the art. As a side effect, they found that inspecting the samples that were consistently given the most weight during boosting revealed some faulty annotations in the corpus. In all of these systems, AdaBoost has been used as a traditional classification system.

3.2 Boosting for Parsing

Our goal is to recast boosting for parsing while considering a parsing system as the embedded learner. The formulation is given in Algorithm 4. The intuition behind the additive form is that the weight placed on a sentence should be the sum of the weight we would like to place on its constituents. The weight on constituents that are predicted incorrectly are adjusted by a factor of 1 in contrast to a factor of α for those that are predicted incorrectly.

Algorithm: Boosting A Parser (4)
Given corpus $\mathcal{C}$ with size $m = |\mathcal{C}| = \sum_{s,\tau} \mathcal{C}(s,t)$ and parser induction algorithm g. Initial uniform distribution $D_1(i) = 1/m$. Number of iterations, T. Counter $t = 1$.

1. Create C_t by randomly choosing with replacement m samples from $\mathcal{C}$ using distribution D_t.
2. Create parser $f_t \leftarrow g(C_t)$.
3. Choose $\alpha_t \in \mathbb{R}$ (described below).
4. Adjust and normalize the distribution. Z_t is a normalization coefficient. For all i, let parse tree $\tau_i' \leftarrow f_t(s_i)$. Let $\delta(\tau, c)$ be a function indicating that c is in parse tree τ, and $|\tau|$ is the number of constituents in tree τ. $T(s)$ is the set of constituents that are found in the reference or hypothesized annotation for s.

$$D_{t+1}(i) = \frac{1}{Z_t} D_t(i) \sum_{c \in T(s_i)} (\alpha + (1-\alpha)|\delta(\tau_i', c) - \delta(\tau_i, c)|)$$

5. Increment t. Quit if $t > T$.
6. Repeat from step 1.
7. The final hypothesis is computed by combining the individual constituents. Each parser ϕ_t in the ensemble gets a vote with weight α_t for the constituents they predict. Precisely those constituents with weight strictly larger than $\frac{1}{2}\sum_t \alpha_t$ are put into the final hypothesis.

A potential constituent can be considered correct if it is predicted in the hypothesis and it exists in the reference, or it is not predicted and it is not in the reference. Potential constituents that do not appear in the hypothesis or the reference should not make a big contribution to the accuracy computation. There are many such potential constituents, and if we were maximizing a function that treated getting them incorrect the same as getting a constituent that appears in the reference correct, we would most likely decide not to predict any constituents.

Our model of constituent accuracy is thus simple. Each prediction correctly made over $T(s)$ will be given equal weight. That is, correctly hypothesizing a constituent in the reference will give us one point, but a precision or recall error will cause us to miss one point. Constituent accuracy is then $a/(a+b+c)$, where a is the number of constituents correctly hypothesized, b is the number of precision errors and c is the number of recall errors.

In Equation 1, a computation of α_{ca} as described is shown.

$$\alpha_{ca} = \frac{\sum_i \frac{D(i)}{|T(s_i)|} \sum_{c \in T(s_i)} \delta(\tau_i, c) + \delta(\tau_i', c) - 2\delta(\tau_i, c)\delta(\tau_i', c)}{\sum_i \frac{D(i)}{|T(s_i)|} \sum_{c \in T(s_i)} \delta(\tau_i, c)\delta(\tau_i', c)} \quad (1)$$

Boosting algorithms were developed that attempted to maximize F-measure, precision, and recall by varying the computation of α, giving results too numerous to include here. The algorithm given here performed the best of the lot, but was only marginally better for some metrics.

Set	Instance	P	R	F	Gain	Exact	Gain
Training	Original Parser	96.25	96.31	96.28	NA	64.7	NA
	Initial	93.54	93.61	93.58	0.00	54.8	0.0
	BestF(15)	96.21	95.79	96.00	2.42	57.3	2.5
	Final(15)	96.21	95.79	96.00	2.42	57.3	2.5
Test	Original Parser	88.73	88.54	88.63	NA	34.9	NA
	Initial	88.05	88.09	88.07	0.00	33.3	0.0
	TrainBestF(15)	89.37	88.32	88.84	0.77	33.0	-0.3
	TestBestF(14)	89.39	88.41	88.90	0.83	33.4	0.1
	Final(15)	89.37	88.32	88.84	0.77	33.0	-0.3

Table 2: Boosting the Treebank

3.3 Experiment

The experimental results for boosting are shown in Figure 3 and Table 2. There is a large plateau in performance from iterations 5 through 12. Because of their low accuracy and high degree of specialization, the parsers produced in these iterations had little weight during voting and had little effect on the cumulative decision making.

As in the bagging experiment, it appears that there would be more precision and recall gain to be had by creating a larger ensemble. In both the bagging and boosting experiments time and resource constraints dictated our ensemble size.

In the table we see that the boosting algorithm equaled bagging's test set gains in precision and recall. The `Initial` performance for boosting was lower, though. We cannot explain this, and expect it is due to unfortunate resampling of the data during the first iteration of boosting. Exact sentence accuracy, though, was not significantly improved on the test set.

Overall, we prefer bagging to boosting for this problem when raw performance is the goal. There are side effects of boosting that are useful in other respects, though, which we explore in Section 4.2.

3.3.1 Weak Learning Criterion Violations

It was hypothesized in the course of investigating the failures of the boosting algorithm that the parser induction system did not satisfy the weak learning criterion. It was noted that the distribution of boosting weights were more skewed in later iterations. Inspection of the sentences that were getting much mass placed upon them revealed that their weight was being boosted *in every iteration.* The hypothesis was that the parser was simply unable to learn them.

39832 parsers were built to test this, one for each sentence in the training set. Each of these parsers was trained on only a single sentence[2] and evaluated on the same sentence. It was discovered that a full 4764 (11.2%) of these sentences could not be parsed completely correctly by the parsing system.

[2]The sentence was replicated 10 times to avoid thresholding effects in the learner.

3.3.2 Corpus Trimming

In order to evaluate how well boosting worked with a learner that better satisfied the weak learning criterion, the boosting experiment was run again on the Treebank minus the troublesome sentences described above. The results are in Table 3. This dataset produces a larger gain in comparison to the results using the entire Treebank. The initial accuracy, however, is lower. We hypothesize that the boosting algorithm did perform better here, but the parser induction system was learning useful information in those sentences that it could not memorize (e.g. lexical information) that was successfully applied to the test set.

In this manner we managed to clean our dataset to the point that the parser could learn each sentence in isolation. The corpus-makers cannot necessarily be blamed for the sentences that could not be memorized. All that can be said about those sentences is that for better or worse, the parser's model would not accommodate them.

4 Corpus Analysis

4.1 Noisy Corpus: Empirical Investigation

To acquire experimental evidence of noisy data, distributions that were used during boosting the stable corpus were inspected. The distribution was expected to be skewed if there was noise in the data, or be uniform with slight fluctuations if it fit the data well.

We see how the boosting weight distribution changes in Figure 1. The individual curves are indexed by boosting iteration in the key of the figure. This training run used a corpus of 5000 sentences. The sentences are ranked by the weight they are given in the distribution, and sorted in decreasing order by weight along the x-axis. The distribution was smoothed by putting samples into equal weight bins, and reporting the average mass of samples in the bin as the y-coordinate. Each curve on this graph corresponds to a boosting iteration. We used 1000 bins for this graph, and a log scale on the x-axis. Since there were 5000 samples, all samples initially had a y-value of 0.0002.

Set	Instance	P	R	F	Gain	Exact	Gain
Training	Original Parser	96.25	96.31	96.28	NA	64.7	NA
	Initial	94.60	94.68	94.64	0.00	62.2	0.0
	BestF(8)	97.38	97.00	97.19	2.55	63.1	0.9
	Final(15)	97.00	96.17	96.58	1.94	55.0	-7.2
Test	Original Parser	88.73	88.54	88.63	NA	34.9	NA
	Initial	87.43	87.21	87.32	0.00	32.6	0.0
	TrainBestF(8)	89.12	87.62	88.36	1.04	32.8	0.2
	TestBestF(6)	89.07	87.77	88.42	1.10	32.9	0.4
	Final(15)	89.18	87.19	88.18	0.86	31.7	-0.8

Table 3: Boosting the Stable Corpus

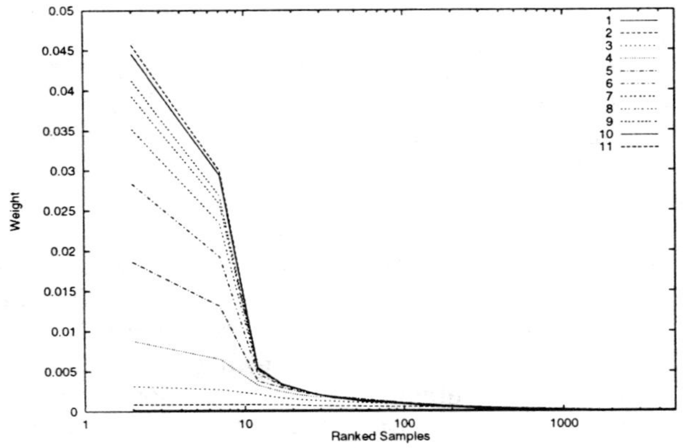

Figure 1: Weight Change During Boosting

Notice first that the left endpoints of the lines move from bottom to top in order of boosting iteration. The distribution becomes monotonically more skewed as boosting progresses. Secondly we see by the last iteration that most of the weight is concentrated on less than 100 samples. This graph shows behavior consistent with noise in the corpus on which the boosting algorithm is focusing.

4.2 Treebank Inconsistencies

There are sentences in the corpus that can be learned by the parser induction algorithm in isolation but not in concert because they contain conflicting information. Finding these sentences leads to a better understanding of the quality of our corpus, and gives an idea for where improvements in annotation quality can be made. Abney et al. (1999) showed a similar corpus analysis technique for part of speech tagging and prepositional phrase tagging, but for parsing we must remove errors introduced by the parser as we did in Section 3.3.2 before questioning the corpus quality. A particular class of errors, inconsistencies, can then be investigated. Inconsistent annotations are those that appear plausible in isolation, but which conflict with annotation decisions made elsewhere in the corpus.

In Figure 5 we show a set of trees selected from within the top 100 most heavily weighted trees at the end of 15 iterations of boosting the stable corpus. Collins's parser induction system is able to learn to produce any one of these structures in isolation, but the presence of conflicting information *in different sentences* prevents it from achieving 100% accuracy on the set.

5 Training Corpus Size Effects

We suspect our best parser diversification techniques gives performance gain approximately equal to doubling the size of the training set. While this cannot be directly tested without hiring more annotators, an expected performance bound for a larger training set can be produced by extrapolating from how well the parser performs using smaller training sets. There are two characteristics of training curves for large corpora that can provide such a bound: training curves generally increase monotonically in the absence of over-training, and their first derivatives generally decrease monotonically.

Set	Sentences	P	R	F	Exact
Training	50	67.57	32.15	43.57	5.4
	100	69.03	56.23	61.98	8.5
	500	78.12	75.46	76.77	18.2
	1000	81.36	80.70	81.03	22.9
	5000	87.28	87.09	87.19	34.1
	10000	89.74	89.56	89.65	41.0
	20000	92.42	92.40	92.41	50.3
	39832	96.25	96.31	96.28	64.7
Testing	50	68.13	32.24	43.76	4.7
	100	69.90	54.19	61.05	7.8
	500	78.72	75.33	76.99	19.1
	1000	81.61	80.68	81.14	22.2
	5000	86.03	85.43	85.73	28.6
	10000	87.29	86.81	87.05	30.8
	20000	87.99	87.87	87.93	32.7
	39832	88.73	88.54	88.63	34.9

Table 4: Effects of Varying Training Corpus Size

The training curves we present in Figure 4 and Table 4 suggest that roughly doubling the corpus size in the range of interest (between 10000 and 40000 sentences) gives a test set F-measure gain of approximately 0.70.

Bagging achieved significant gains of approximately 0.60 over the best reported previous F-measure without adding any new data. In this respect, these techniques show promise for making performance gains on large corpora without adding more data or new parsers.

6 Conclusion

We have shown two methods, bagging and boosting, for automatically creating ensembles of parsers that produce better parses than any individual in the ensemble. Neither of the algorithms exploit any specialized knowledge of the underlying parser induction algorithm, and the data used in creating the ensembles has been restricted to a single common training set to avoid issues of training data quantity affecting the outcome.

Our best bagging system performed consistently well on all metrics, including exact sentence accuracy. It resulted in a statistically significant F-measure gain of 0.6 over the performance of the baseline parser. That baseline system is the best known Treebank parser. This gain compares favorably with a bound on potential gain from increasing the corpus size.

Even though it is computationally expensive to create and evaluate a small (15-30) ensemble of parsers, the cost is far outweighed by the opportunity cost of hiring humans to annotate 40000 more sentences. The economic basis for using ensemble methods will continue to improve with the increasing value (performance per price) of modern hardware.

Our boosting system, although dominated by the bagging system, also performed significantly better than the best previously known individual parsing result. We have shown how to exploit the distribution created as a side-effect of the boosting algorithm to uncover inconsistencies in the training corpus. A semi-automated technique for doing this as well as examples from the Treebank that are inconsistently annotated were presented. Perhaps the biggest advantage of this technique is that it requires no a priori notion of how the inconsistencies can be characterized.

7 Acknowledgments

We would like to thank Michael Collins for enabling all of this research by providing us with his parser and helpful comments.

This work was funded by NSF grant IRI-9502312. The views expressed in this paper are those of the authors and do not necessarily reflect the views of the MITRE Corporation. This work was done while both authors were at Johns Hopkins University.

References

Steven Abney, Robert E. Schapire, and Yoram Singer. 1999. Boosting applied to tagging and PP attachment. In *Proceedings of the Joint SIGDAT Conference on Empirical Methods in Natural Language Processing and Very Large Corpora*, pages 38–45, College Park, Maryland.

L. Breiman. 1996. Bagging predictors. In *Machine Learning*, volume 24, pages 123–140.

Michael Collins. 1997. Three generative, lexicalised models for statistical parsing. In *Proceedings of the Annual Meeting of the Association for Computational Linguistics*, volume 35, Madrid.

B. Efron and R. Tibshirani. 1993. *An Introduction to the Bootstrap*. Chapman and Hall.

Y. Freund and R.E. Schapire. 1996. Experiments with a new boosting algorithm. In *Proceedings of the International Conference on Machine Learning*.

Y. Freund and R.E. Schapire. 1997. A decision-theoretic generalization of on-line learning and an application to boosting. *Journal of Computer and Systems Sciences*, 55(1):119–139, Aug.

Jan Hajič, E. Brill, M. Collins, B. Hladka, D. Jones, C. Kuo, L. Ramshaw, O. Schwartz, C. Tillmann, and D. Zeman. 1999. Core natural language processing technology applicable to multiple languages. *Prague Bulletin of Mathematical Linguistics*, 70.

Masahiko Haruno, Satoshi Shirai, and Yoshifumi Ooyama. 1998. Using decision trees to construct a practical parser. In *Proceedings of the 36th Annual Meeting of the Association for Computational Linguistics and 17th International Conference on Computational Linguistics*, volume 1, pages 505–511, Montreal, Canada.

John C. Henderson and Eric Brill. 1999. Exploiting diversity in natural language processing: Combining parsers. In *Proceedings of the Fourth Conference on Empirical Methods in Natural Language Processing*, College Park, Maryland.

Mitchell P. Marcus, Beatrice Santorini, and Mary Ann Marcinkiewicz. 1993. Building a large annotated corpus of english: The Penn Treebank. *Computational Linguistics*, 19(2):313–330.

Robert E. Schapire and Yoram Singer. 1998. Improved boosting algorithms using confidence-rated predictions. In *Proceedings of the Eleventh Annual Conference on Computational Learning Theory*, pages 80–91.

Robert E. Schapire and Yoram Singer. 2000. Boostexter: A boosting-based system for text categorization. *Machine Learning*, 39(2/3):1–34, May. To appear.

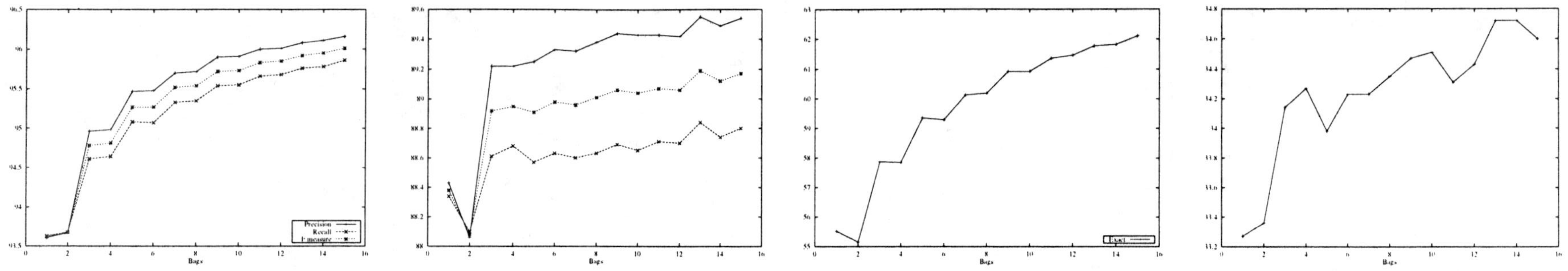

Figure 2: Bagging the Treebank

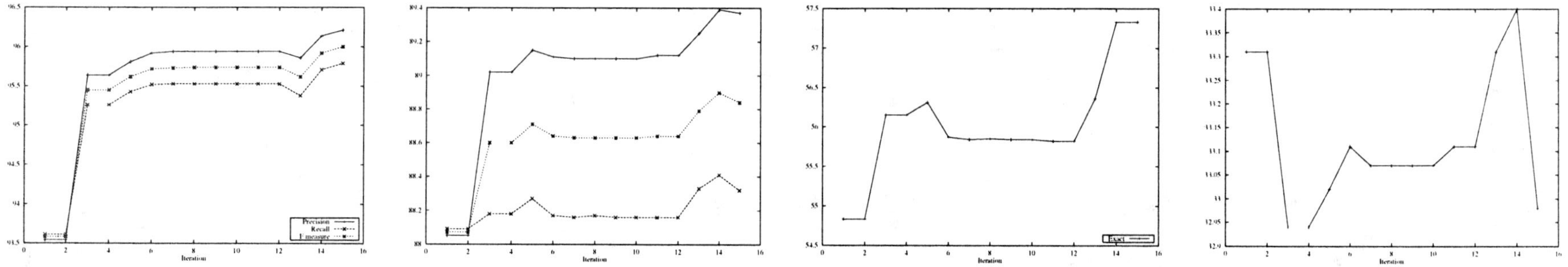

Figure 3: Boosting the Treebank

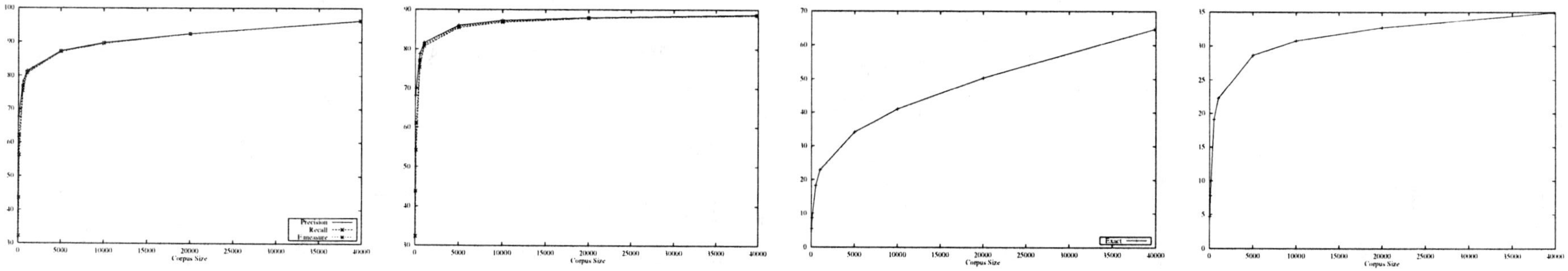

Figure 4: Effects of Varying Training Corpus Size

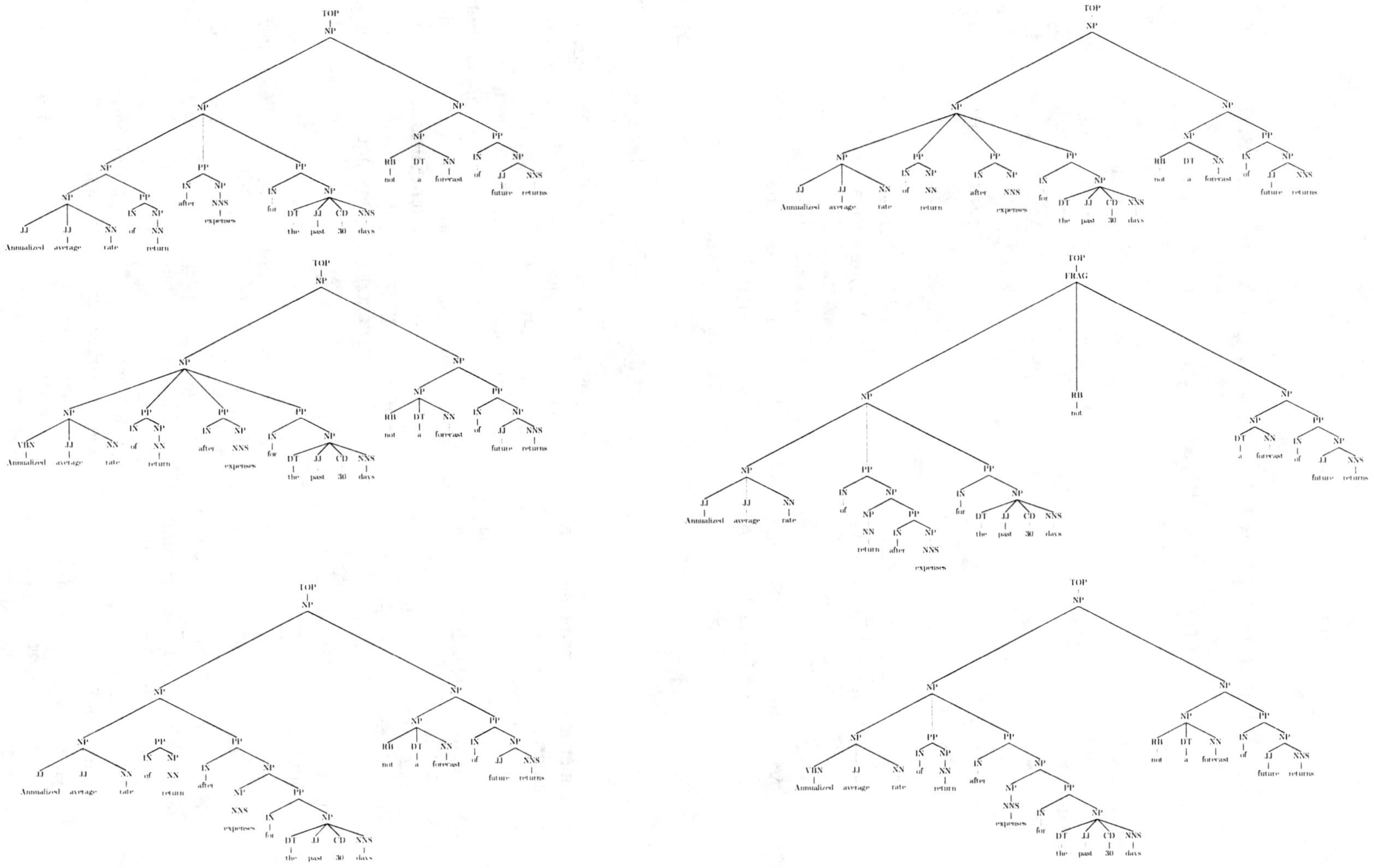

Figure 5: An inconsistent set of annotations from the Treebank

Encoding information on adjectives in a lexical-semantic net for computational applications

Antonietta ALONGE
Istituto di Linguistica
Computazionale, CNR
Area della Ricerca di Pisa
Via Alfieri 1, Loc. S. Cataldo
Ghezzano 56010 (PI) - ITALY
antoalonge@libero.it

Francesca BERTAGNA
Consorzio Pisa Ricerche
Via S. Maria 40
Pisa 56100 - ITALY
F.Bertagna@ilc.pi.cnr.it

Nicoletta CALZOLARI
Istituto di Linguistica
Computazionale, CNR
Area della Ricerca di Pisa
Via Alfieri 1, Loc. S. Cataldo
Ghezzano 56010 (PI) - ITALY
glottolo@ilc.pi.cnr.it

Adriana ROVENTINI
Istituto di Linguistica
Computazionale, CNR
Area della Ricerca di Pisa
Via Alfieri 1, Loc. S. Cataldo
Ghezzano 56010 (PI) - ITALY
adriana@ilc.pi.cnr.it

Antonio ZAMPOLLI
Istituto di Linguistica
Computazionale, CNR
Area della Ricerca di Pisa
Via Alfieri 1, Loc. S. Cataldo
Ghezzano 56010 (PI) - ITALY
pisa@ilc.pi.cnr.it

Abstract

The goal of this paper is to describe how the EuroWordNet framework for representing lexical meaning is being modified within an Italian National Project in order to include information on adjectives. The focus is on the 'new' semantic relations being encoded and on the revisions we have made to the EuroWordNet Top Ontology structure. We also briefly discuss the utility of the information which is being encoded for computational applications.

Introduction

The Princeton *WordNet* (henceforth WN) is a lexical semantic network in which the meanings of words are represented in terms of their conceptual and lexical relations to other words. The basic notion around which it is developed is that of a *synset* (synonyms set), i.e. a set of words with the same Part-of-Speech (PoS) that can be interchanged in a certain context. Various conceptual and lexical relations are then encoded between synsets of the same PoS: e.g., hyponymy, antonymy, meronymy, etc. (Miller et al. 1990; Fellbaum 1998b).

Within the *EuroWordNet* (henceforth EWN) project[1] a similar (multilingual) lexical resource was developed, retaining the basic underlying design of WN, but enriching the set of lexical-semantic relations to be encoded for nouns and verbs in various ways[2], in order to obtain a maximally re-usable resource for computational applications. Thus, a) cross-PoS (XPOS) relations were added so that different surface realizations of similar concepts within and across languages could be matched (e.g., the noun *research* and the verb *to research* could be linked as

---

[1] EWN was a project in the EC Language Engineering (LE-4003 and LE-8328) programme. In a first phase, the partners involved were the University of Amsterdam (coordinator); the Istituto di Linguistica Computazionale, CNR, Pisa; the Fundacíon Universidad Empresa (a cooperation of UNED, Madrid, Politecnica de Catalunya, Barcelona, and the University of Barcelona); the University of Sheffield; and Novell Linguistic Development (Antwerp), changed to Lernout & Hauspie during the project. In a further phase, the database was extended with German, French, Estonian and Czech. Complete information on EWN can be found at its web site: http://www.hum.uva.nl/~ewn/.

[2] Adjectives and adverbs were encoded in EWN only as targets of relations from nouns and verbs.

'XPOS_NEAR_SYNONYMS' in EWN); b) some relations were identified which provide detailed information on semantic components lexicalized within word roots (e.g., *to hammer* could be linked to the noun *hammer* by means of an 'INVOLVED_INSTRUMENT' relation); c) some labels were distinguished which could be added to relations to make their semantic entailments more explicit and precise (cf. Alonge et al. 1998). The links among the wordnets of different languages were realized by means of an Interlingual-Index (ILI), constituted by an unstructured list of the Princeton WN (version 1.5) synsets. In addition, a hierarchy of language-independent concepts, reflecting fundamental semantic distinctions (e.g., *Object* and *Substance*, *Dynamic* and *Static*, *Cause*, *Manner*, etc.), was built: the Top Ontology (TO). The TO consists of language-independent features which may (or may not) be lexicalized in various ways, or according to different patterns, in different languages (Rodriguez et al. 1998). Via the ILI, all the concepts in the monolingual wordnets are directly or indirectly linked to the TO. The following picture shows the EWN data structure (see also Vossen 1999):

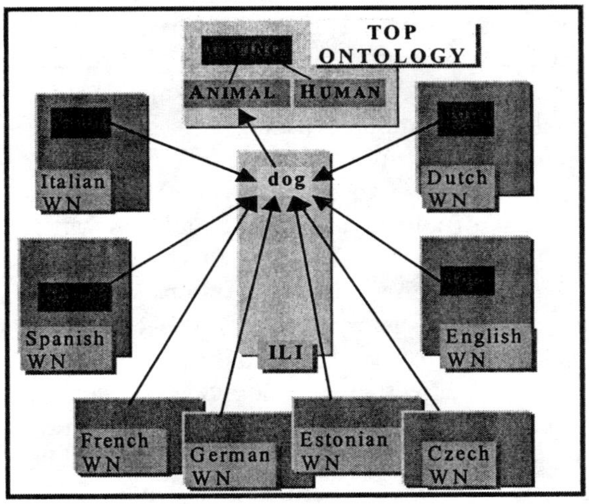

While in WN all PoSs are represented, in EWN detailed information was encoded only for nouns and verbs and no analysis was carried out with respect to lexical-semantic relations which could be used to describe the semantics of adjectives and adverbs. In an Italian National Project we are building a large wordnet, *ItalWordNet* (henceforth IWN)[3], by extending the network built for Italian in EWN. Thus, we are both increasing the coverage for nouns and verbs and adding adjectives and some adverbs[4]. To be able to encode information on adjectives we have enriched the set of the EWN lexical-semantic relations, aiming at encoding data which can be useful for computational applications. Moreover, we have revised the TO in order to account for the semantics of the new lexical categories being encoded.

In this paper we describe the main changes made to the EWN framework in order to encode information on adjectives in IWN. Firstly, we provide a brief overview of the WN treatment of adjectives. Then, we discuss the set of relations being encoded for this category in IWN. Finally, we show the integration made to the EWN TO. We then conclude the paper by adding some remarks on the utility of the data being encoded for computational applications.

1 Adjectives in WN

In WN adjectives are divided into two major classes: descriptive adjectives and relational adjectives. A descriptive adjective is "one that ascribes a value of an attribute to a noun" (Fellbaum et al. 1993:27). Descriptive adjectives combine with nouns to express some qualities of the thing, person or concept they designate. Typically, in this group we find adjectives that designate the physical dimension of an object, its weight, abstract values etc. Besides these *referent-modifying* adjectives, we also find *reference-modifying* adjectives (cf. Bolinger 1967; Chierchia & McConnel-Ginet 1990 name them *intensional adjectives*). Typical examples of the latter are *former*, *future*, *present*.

[3] *ItalWordNet* will be the reference lexical resource among various integrated language resources and software tools for the automatic treatment of the Italian written and spoken language which are being developed within the SI-TAL ('Integrated System for the Automatic Treatment of Language') National Project.

[4] Actually, we shall only encode adverbs derived from adjectives by adding the suffix *–mente*, for which a derivation relation with an adjective will be encoded.

Relational adjectives, on the other hand, mean something like "relating/pertaining to, associated with", and usually have a morphologically strong link with a noun. Typical examples are *musical, atomic, chemical*[5].

Synonymy is the basic relation encoded for all the PoSs (since it is used to build synsets). While in WN the noun and verb networks are then mainly developed around the superordinate (hyper/hyponymy) relationship, the organization of descriptive adjectives can "be visualized in terms of barbell-like structures, with a direct antonym in the centre of each disk surrounded by its semantically similar adjectives (which constitute the indirect antonyms of the adjectives in the opposed disk)" (Fellbaum 1998a: 212). The main relation encoded for these adjective synsets is antonymy, claimed to be the most prominent relation, both from a psycholinguistic point of view and from a more strictly lexical-semantic one, in the definition of the semantics of descriptive adjectives. Hyponymy is substituted by a 'similarity' relation.

Relational adjectives, on the contrary, are not organized in this way, because their semantics cannot be described by using these relations. Indeed, they only point to the noun to which they pertain (e.g. *atomic* is linked to *atom*).

Finally, information on the selectional preferences of both descriptive and relational adjectives is sometimes encoded (e.g., between *high* and *degree*), by using an 'is_attribute_of' relation.

2 The IWN relations for adjectives

As for the other lexical categories, also in IWN the basic relation encoded for adjectives is synonymy, on the basis of which synsets are built. Following EWN, we also encode a NEAR_SYNONYMY relation when two synsets are very close in meaning but their members cannot be put in the same synset (and no other relation results appropriate to link them; see Alonge et al. 1998 for a discussion of this relation, and Alonge et al., in prep., for a complete and detailed discussion of the linguistic design of IWN). Then, we encode a number of additional relations, which have been identified by taking into consideration i) theoretical works; ii) the EAGLES recommendations on semantic encoding (cf. Sanfilippo et al. 1999); iii) the data available in our sources; iv) possible use of data encoded in computational applications.

2.1 Hyponymy

Together with synonymy, the hyponymy relation constitutes the 'bone structure' of both WN and EWN. However, as we have seen, in WN the possibility of encoding hyponymy for adjectives is denied and the basic relation encoded for adjectives is antonymy, while EWN did not really deal with adjectives and a complete network for them was not built.

Within IWN we have reconsidered the possibility of encoding hyponymy for adjectives. By analysing data coming from machine-readable dictionaries we find subsets of adjectives which have a *genus* + *differentia* definition, like nouns or verbs. That is, these adjectives seem to be organised into classes sharing a superordinate. This is the case, e.g., of adjectives indicating a 'containing' property (*acquoso* - watery; *alcalino* - alkaline), or a 'suitable-for' property (*difensivo* - defensive; *educativo* - educational), etc. In IWN we have decided, therefore, to encode hyponymy also for these sets of adjectives. The taxonomies which can be built on the basis of this relation are different from those built for nouns or verbs, since they are generally very flat, consisting almost always of two levels only (an exception is the color adjectives taxonomy). However, by encoding a hyponymy relation for these adjectives, we obtain classes for which it will be possible to make various inferences. For instance, it will be possible to infer semantic preferences of certain classes: e.g., all the adjectives occurring in the taxonomy of *contenente* (containing) will occur as attributes of concrete nouns; adjectives found in the taxonomy of *affetto* (affected by an illness) will never be predicated of nouns referring to objects, etc. Furthermore, it will also be possible to infer information on syntactic characteristics

[5] Note that some adjectives have both a descriptive sense and a relational one. For example, *musicale* (musical) can modify the noun *voce* (voice) when we want to say that a voice is sweet-sounding and melodious, but can also be combined with the noun *strumento* (instrument) when we want to indicate that an instrument can be used to produce music.

of adjectives found in the same taxonomy: e.g., the hyponyms of *atto* (suitable for) are always found in predicative position (and do not accept any complements); the hyponyms of *privo* (lacking) may occur both in attributive and in predicative position (and may take certain prepositional complements), etc.
As it was done for all the relations identified in EWN, we have built substition tests or diagnostic frames based on normality judgements (cf. Cruse 1986). Inserting two words in the test sentences built evokes a 'normality'/ 'abnormality' judgement on the basis of which each relation can be determined. These tests are used by encoders both to verify the existence of relations between synsets and to encode them in a consistent way (for a complete lists of the tests built see Alonge et al., in prep.)

2.2 Antonymy

As in WN, also in IWN the antonymy relation remains an important relation to describe the semantics of various adjectives. Following theoretical work (Lyons 1977; Cruse 1986), we have further distinguished between COMPLEMENTARY_ANTONYMY and GRADABLE_ ANTONYMY[6]. The former relation links adjectives referring to opposing properties/ concepts: when one holds the other is excluded (*alive/dead*). The latter relation is used for those antonym pairs which refer to gradable properties (*long/short*). In case it is not clear if two opposing adjectives refer to complementary or gradable properties, we can still use an underspecified ANTONYMY relation. Also this information can be useful for computational applications since word pairs presenting one of the two kinds of opposition may occur in different contexts (cf. Cruse 1986).

2.3 Other relations

In WN a relation between adjectives and nouns is encoded for relational adjectives which point to a noun to which they 'pertain': *atomic/atom*, *industrial/industry*, etc. This relation will be encoded also in IWN, by using the label PERTAINS_TO.
Another relation 'inherited' from WN can be useful to distinguish both adjective senses and their semantic preferences[7]:

$alto_1$ (tall)	IS_A_VALUE_OF	statura (stature)
$alto_2$ (high)	IS_A_VALUE_OF	altezza (height).

Other relations are then being encoded which are not in WN, but are encoded for nouns and verbs in EWN. In WN each PoS forms a separate system of language-internal relations and conceptually close concepts are totally separated only because they differ in PoS. In EWN, instead of using as main classificatory criterion the traditional distinction among PoSs, drawn upon heterogeneous criteria, a purely semantic distinction was adopted (following Lyons 1977). Thus, a distinction was drawn among *1st order entities* (1oes - referred to by concrete nouns), *2nd order entities* (2oes - referred to by verbs, adjectives or nouns indicating properties, states, processes or events), and *3rd order entities* (3oes - referred to by abstract nouns indicating propositions existing independently of time and space). By drawing this distinction it was possible to relate lexical items that, either within a language or across different languages, refer to close concepts, although they belong to different PoSs. Thus, as said above, the possibility to encode 'near-synonymy' between synsets of the same order (but different PoSs) was provided. Furthermore, other cross-PoS relations were identified which allow to obtain a better description of word meanings. In IWN we maintain the same distinction among semantic orders and encode for adjectives some relations which can be encoded for the other 2oes. In particular, we encode the 'INVOLVED' and 'CAUSE' relations.
The INVOLVED relation links a 2oes with a 1oe or 3oe referring to a concept *incorporated* within

[6] A similar distinction is also made within the SIMPLE EC project (LE-8346), whose goal is adding semantic information to the set of harmonized lexicons built within the PAROLE project for twelve European languages. Of course, the sub-classification of antonymy can also be used for nouns and verbs.

[7] Furthermore, these relations being encoded between an adjectival synset and a nominal or verbal one are also useful to distinguish adjective classes as described by Dixon (1991), and reported in Sanfilippo et al. (1999). Indeed, such classes are often indicated by the nouns linked to adjectives.

the meaning of the 2oe[8]. Examples for adjectives are given in the following:

filoso (= pieno di fili) (thready, filamentous)
  HAS_HYPERONYM pieno (full)
  INVOLVED filo (thread)

imberbe (= privo di barba) (beardless)
  HAS_HYPERONYM privo (lacking)
  INVOLVED barba (beard).

Another relation which can be encoded is the CAUSE relation:

depuratorio (= atto a depurare) (depurative, purifying)
  HAS_HYPERONYM atto, adatto (suitable for)
  CAUSES *non-factive*[9] depurare (to purify)

compensativo (= che serve a compensare) (compensatory)
  HAS_HYPERONYM atto, adatto (suitable for)
  CAUSES *non-factive* compensare (to compensate)

A new relation, not present either in WN or in EWN, will be encoded for a class of adjectives indicating the possibility of some events occurring:

giudicabile (= che può essere giudicato) (triable)
  LIABLE_TO giudicare (to judge)

inaccostabile, inavvicinabile (= che non può essere avvicinato) (which cannot be approached)
  LIABLE_TO avvicinare, accostare (to approach) *negative*.

[8] E.g., *to lapidate* has as INVOLVED_INSTRUMENT *stone*; *to work* has as INVOLVED_AGENT *worker* (see Alonge et al. 1998).

[9] As said above, in EWN various features were encoded to make implications of relations explicit: *conjunction* and *disjunction* (for multiple relations of the same kind encoded for a synset); *non-factivity* (to indicate that a causal relation does not necessarily apply); *intention* (added to a cause relation to indicate intention to cause a certain result); *negation* (to explicitly encode the impossibility of a relation occurring). These features are also used in IWN.

The table below gives an overview of the main relations being encoded for adjectives in IWN (for the other relations being encoded for adjectives see Alonge et al., in prep.):

Relation	*PoS linked*	*Example*
ANTONYMY	adj/adj	happy/unhappy
GRAD_ANTONYMY	adj/adj	beautiful/ugly
COMP_ANTONYMY	adj/adj	alive/dead
HYPONYMY	adj/adj	watery/containing
PERTAINS_TO	adj/noun	chemical/chemistry
IS_A_VALUE_OF	adj/noun	tall/stature
INVOLVED	adj/noun	dental/tooth
CAUSE	adj/verb; adj/noun	depurative/ to depurate
LIABLE_TO	adj/verb; adj/noun	triable/to judge

3 The IWN Top Ontology

In the EWN TO all the entities belonging to the 2nd order have been organized into two different classification schemes, which represent the first division below 2nd Order Entity:

- *Situation Type*: the event-structure or *Aktionsart* (or lexical aspect) of a situation;
- *Situation Components*: the most salient semantic components that characterize situations.

The Situation Types provide a classification of 2oes in terms of the event-structure (or *Aktionsart*) of the situation they refer to: a basic distinction was drawn between *Static* and *Dynamic*. The Situation Components represent a more conceptual and intuitive classification of word meanings because they can be viewed like the most salient semantic components of a concept. Examples of Situation Components are: *Manner*, *Existence*, *Communication, Cause*. Situation Type represents disjoint features that cannot be combined, whereas it is possible to assign any combination of Situation Components to a word meaning. Here below the Top Concepts identified for 2oes are shown:

- 2ND ORDER ENTITY
  - SITUATION COMPONENT
    - Cause
    - Communication
    - Condition
    - Existence
    - Experience
    - Location
    - Manner
    - Mental
    - Modal
    - Physical
    - Possession
    - Purpose
    - Quantity
    - Social
    - Time
  - SITUATION TYPE
    - Dynamic
      - BoundedEvent
      - UnboundedEvent
    - Static
      - Property
      - Relation

In order to be able to draw generalizations on adjective meanings by using the TO, we partially modified this scheme. First of all, we moved the PROPERTY and RELATION nodes under the SITUATION COMPONENT node. This was done for two interconnected reasons: first of all, because this distinction is not directly linked to *Aktionsart* (lexical aspect), while the distinctions under SITUATION TYPE are *Aktionsart* distinctions, i.e. they are connected with the "the procedural characteristics (i.e. the 'phasal structure', 'time extension' and 'manner of development') ascribed to any given situation referred to by a verb phrase" (Bache 1982: 70)[10]. Secondly, adjectives may refer to PROPERTIES or RELATIONS, but they may be either stative or not (cfr. e.g. Lakoff 1966; Quirk et al. 1985; Peters et al. 1999). Thus, in our system it has to be possible to specify that an adjective expresses a PROPERTY while being DYNAMIC. In any case, since many adjectives may have both a DYNAMIC sense and a STATIC one, we have also the possibility to under-specify this information by linking adjectives directly to the SITUATION TYPE node.

Adjectives may indicate many different types of properties: temporal (*passeggiata mattutina* - morning walk), psychological (*canzone triste* - sad song), social (*uomo ricco* - rich man), physical (*superficie legnosa* - wooden surface), physiological (*bambino magro* - thin child), perceptive (*minestra calda* - hot soup), quantitative (*magra ricompensa* - poor reward) and intensity properties (*vino forte* - strong wine). In the EWN TO there are already nodes which may be used to represent these distinctions (TIME, MENTAL, SOCIAL, PHYSICAL, QUANTITY) but we needed to better specify or also add some features. For example, we have added, under the already present node PHYSICAL, the node MATERIAL, to represent, among others, some Italian adjectives ending in *–oso* (for example *legnoso* - wooden, *acquoso* - watery) which indicate the property of containing a certain material. Moreover, we added the node PHYSIOLOGICAL (to classify adjectives corresponding to *tired*, *hungry*, *sick*, etc.) under PHYSICAL. For adjectives denoting an intensity, we then added the node INTENSITY directly under the SITUATION COMPONENT node.

One of the main problem we had was that no Top Concept in the EWN TO could be used to classify the reference-modifying adjectives (cf. above). These are a very particular kind of adjectives, because they do not indicate a property of the referent of the noun they modify. So, aiming at showing the distinction between referent-modifiers and reference-modifiers, we created two new Top Concepts under the node PROPERTY: ATTRIBUTE and FUNCTIONAL, where the latter can be used for reference-modifying adjectives (according to the definition provided by Chierchia & McConnel-Ginet 1990 for the category referred to by these adjectives: "*a function from properties to properties*").

Like all descriptive adjectives, also the reference-modifiers classified under the node FUNCTIONAL can be linked to other SITUATION COMPONENTS. Functional adjectives for which the temporal aspect prevails (*ex* - former, *presente* - present) can be classified under the node TIME; adjectives referring to some 'epistemological' property (*potenziale* - potential, *necessario* - necessary) can be linked

[10] Of course, in EWN all 2oes (and therefore also nouns or adjectives) can be classified according to their *Aktionsart*.

to MODAL[11]; etc. A particular case of functional adjectives are the 'argumental' ones. They introduce a comparison between different entities (e.g., *simile* - similar, *diverso* - different, etc.). A comparison presupposes a relation between different entities so these adjectives can be linked to both PROPERTY and RELATION. Since in the EWN TO these two Top Concepts were two different kinds of SITUATION TYPE, they were mutually exclusive; now, in the IWN revised TO they can be conjoined.

Here below the IWN Top Concepts for 2nd Order Entities are shown:

```
2ND ORDER ENTITY
    SITUATION COMPONENT
            Cause
            Communication
            Condition
            Existence
            Experience
            Location
            Manner
            Mental
            Modal
            Physical
                    Material
                    Physiological
            Possession
            Purpose
            Quantity
            Social
            Time
            Intensity
            Property
                    Attribute
                    Functional
            Relation
    SITUATION TYPE
            Dynamic
                    BoundedEvent
                    UnboundedEvent
            Static
```

Concluding remarks

Although the ANTONYMY, PERTAINS_TO, and IS_ATTRIBUTE_OF relations, already encoded in the Princeton WN, are fundamental relations to describe the adjective semantics, and they can be useful for computational applications which exploit our resource, we believe that the 'new' relations being encoded may provide equally relevant information, especially because many adjectives cannot be defined by means of the WN relations. Let's take into consideration just a few examples.

The adjective *depresso* is ambiguous in that it has (at least) three readings:

1) which has been lowered, flattened (said of a land);
2) being in bad physical or moral conditions (said of an area, a country);
3) affected by depression (said of a person).

For these three senses of the adjective we would encode different relations, extractable from our sources:

$depresso_1$	IS_CAUSED_BY	deprimere (to lower)
	IS_A_VALUE_OF	terreno (land)
$depresso_2$	HAS_HYPERONYM	colpito (affected)
	IS_CAUSED_BY	$depressione_1$ (depression - economic sense)
$depresso_3$	HAS_HYPERONYM	affetto (affected, suffering from sthg.)
	IS_CAUSED_BY	$depressione_2$ (depression - medical sense)

The relations encoded could, e.g., help disambiguate the occurrences of the adjective in contexts such as: *Gianni era depresso* (Gianni was depressed) or *Quella regione è depressa* (That area is depressed). Indeed, by checking the semantic information encoded for the two senses of *depressione* linked to *depresso*, it's possible to provide the right interpretation for the sentences under analysis; on the other hand, the first sense of the adjective would be excluded because of the IS_A_VALUE_OF relation encoded. In this case, also the TO links could be helpful: actually, *depresso*$_2$ would be linked to SOCIAL and CONDITION, while *depresso*$_3$ would be linked to MENTAL and EXPERIENCE.

Many adjectives found in our sources do not seem to have (lexicalized) antonyms, nor cannot be defined by using the PERTAINS_TO or IS_A_VALUE_OF relations. These are often linked to nouns or verbs, by various relations:

[11] Since this node is used for situations involving the possibility or likelihood of other situations.

piumato = coperto di piume (plumed = covered with plumage)

HAS_HYPERONYM coperto
INVOLVED piuma

distillabile = che può essere distillato (distillable = which can be distilled)

LIABLE_TO distillare.

For these and many other adjectives the 'new' relations identified in IWN are necessary, given that we often cannot encode other relations for them. The relations encoded provide fundamental semantic information on them, which can, for instance, be used to infer semantic preferences (e.g., only certain 1oes can be modified by *piumato*, etc.). The inclusion of this information in a large database which is mainly intended for computational applications can be very useful, mainly because it may help in resolving ambiguities and may be used to draw inferences of different nature.

References

Alonge A., Calzolari N., Vossen P., Bloksma L., Castellon I., Martì T., Peters W. (1998) *The Linguistic Design of the EuroWordNet Database*. In "Special Issue on EuroWordNet. Computers and the Humanities" N. Ide, D. Greenstein, P. Vossen (eds.), 32, 2-3, pp. 91-115.

Alonge A., Bertagna F., Calzolari N., Magnini B., Roventini A. (in prep.) *ItalWordNet : a Large Semantic Database for Italian.*

Bache C. (1982) *Aspect and Aktionsart: towards a Semantic Distinction*. Journal of Linguistics, 18, 1.

Bolinger D. (1967) *Adjectives in English: Attribution and Predication.* Lingua, 18, pp. 1-34.

Chierchia G. and McConnel-Ginet S. (1990) *An Introduction to Semantics.* The MIT Press, Cambridge.

Cruse D. A. (1986) *Lexical Semantics*. Cambridge University Press, Cambridge.

Dixon R. M. W. (1991) *A new Approach to English Grammar on Semantic Principles.* Clarendon Press, Oxford.

Fellbaum C. (1998a) *A Semantic Network of English: the Mother of all WordNets.* In "Special Issue on EuroWordNet. Computers and the Humanities" N. Ide, D. Greenstein, P. Vossen (eds.), 32, 2-3, pp. 209-220.

Fellbaum C. (1998b) *WordNet, An Electronic Lexical Database*, The MIT Press, Cambridge.

Fellbaum C., Gross D., Miller K.J. (1993) *Adjectives in WordNet*, Five Papers on WordNet.

Lakoff G. (1966) *Stative Adjectives and Verbs in English.* Computation Laboratory, Harvard University Report No. NSF-17.

Lyons J. (1977) *Semantics*. Cambridge University Press, London.

Miller G., Beckwith R., Fellbaum C., Gross D., Miller K.J (1990) *Introduction to WordNet: An On-line Lexical Database.* International Journal of Lexicography, Vol 3, No.4, pp. 235-244.

Quirk R., Greenbaum S., Leech G. Svartvik J. (1985) *A Comprehensive Grammar of the English Language*. Longman, London.

Peters I., Peter W. and Gaizauskas R. (1999) *The Representation of Adjectives in SIMPLE*. Ms.

Richardson S. D., Dolan W. B., Vanderwende L. (1998) *MindNet: Acquiring and Structuring Semantic Information from Text.* In "COLING-ACL Proceedings", Montreal, pp. 1098-1102.

Rodriguez H., Climent S., Vossen P., Bloksma L., Roventini A., Bertagna F., Alonge A., Peters W. (1998) *The Top-Down Strategy for Building EuroWordNet: Vocabulary Coverage, Base Concepts and Top Ontology.* In "Special Issue on EuroWordNet. Computers and the Humanities", N. Ide, D. Greenstein, P. Vossen (eds.), 32, 2-3, pp. 117-152.

Vossen P. (ed.) (1999) *EuroWordNet General Document.* In "The EWN CD-Rom" (see also: http://www.hum.uva.nl/~ewn).

Sanfilippo A., Calzolari N., Ananiadou S., Gaizauskas R., Saint-Dizier P., Vossen P. (eds.) (1999) *Preliminary Recommendations on Lexical Semantic Encoding.* EAGLES LE3-4244 Final Report.

Noun Phrase Recognition by System Combination

Erik F. Tjong Kim Sang
Center for Dutch Language and Speech
University of Antwerp
erikt@uia.ua.ac.be

Abstract

The performance of machine learning algorithms can be improved by combining the output of different systems. In this paper we apply this idea to the recognition of noun phrases. We generate different classifiers by using different representations of the data. By combining the results with voting techniques described in (Van Halteren et al., 1998) we manage to improve the best reported performances on standard data sets for base noun phrases and arbitrary noun phrases.

1 Introduction

(Van Halteren et al., 1998) and (Brill and Wu, 1998) describe a series of successful experiments for improving the performance of part-of-speech taggers. Their results have been obtained by combining the output of different taggers with system combination techniques such as majority voting. This approach cancels errors that are made by the minority of the taggers. With the best voting technique, the combined results decrease the lowest error rate of the component taggers by as much as 19% (Van Halteren et al., 1998). The fact that combination of classifiers leads to improved performance has been reported in a large body of machine learning work.

We would like to know what improvement combination techniques would cause in noun phrase recognition. For this purpose, we apply a single memory-based learning technique to data that has been represented in different ways. We compare various combination techniques on a part of the Penn Treebank and use the best method on standard data sets for base noun phrase recognition and arbitrary noun phrase recognition.

2 Methods and experiments

In this section we start with a description of our task: recognizing noun phrases. After this we introduce the different data representations we use and our machine learning algorithms. We conclude with an outline of techniques for combining classifier results.

2.1 Task description

Noun phrase recognition can be divided in two tasks: recognizing base noun phrases and recognizing arbitrary noun phrases. Base noun phrases (baseNPs) are noun phrases which do not contain another noun phrase. For example, the sentence

> In [early trading] in [Hong Kong]
> [Monday] , [gold] was quoted at
> [$ 366.50] [an ounce] .

contains six baseNPs (marked as phrases between square brackets). The phrase *$ 366.50 an ounce* is a noun phrase as well. However, it is not a baseNP since it contains two other noun phrases. Two baseNP data sets have been put forward by (Ramshaw and Marcus, 1995). The main data set consist of four sections (15-18) of the Wall Street Journal (WSJ) part of the Penn Treebank (Marcus et al., 1993) as training material and one section (20) as test material[1]. The baseNPs in this data are slightly different from the ones that can be derived from the Treebank, most notably in the attachment of genitive markers.

The recognition task involving arbitrary noun phrases attempts to find both baseNPs and noun phrases that contain other noun phrases. A standard data set for this task was put forward at the CoNLL-99 workshop. It consist on the same parts of the Penn Treebank as the main baseNP data set: WSJ sections 15-18 as training data and section 20 as test data[2]. The noun phrases in this data set are the same as in the Treebank and therefore the baseNPs in this data set are slightly different from the ones in the (Ramshaw and Marcus, 1995) data sets.

In both tasks, performance is measured with three scores. First, with the percentage of detected noun phrases that are correct (precision). Second, with the percentage of noun phrases in the data that were found by the classifier (recall). And third,

[1]This (Ramshaw and Marcus, 1995) baseNP data set is available via ftp://ftp.cis.upenn.edu/pub/chunker/

[2]Software for generating the data is available from http://lcg-www.uia.ac.be/conll99/npb/

with the $F_{\beta=1}$ rate which is equal to (2*precision*recall)/(precision+recall). The latter rate has been used as the target for optimization.

2.2 Data representation

In our example sentence in section 2.1, noun phrases are represented by bracket structures. Both (Muñoz et al., 1999) and (Tjong Kim Sang and Veenstra, 1999) have shown how classifiers can process bracket structures. One classifier can be trained to recognize open brackets (O) while another will process close brackets (C). Their results can be converted to baseNPs by making pairs of open and close brackets with large probability scores (Muñoz et al., 1999) or by regarding only the shortest phrases between open and close brackets as baseNPs (Tjong Kim Sang and Veenstra, 1999). We have used the bracket representation (O+C) in combination with the second baseNP construction method.

An alternative representation for baseNPs has been put forward by (Ramshaw and Marcus, 1995). They have defined baseNP recognition as a tagging task: words can be inside a baseNP (I) or outside of baseNPs (O). In the case that one baseNP immediately follows another baseNP, the first word in the second baseNP receives tag B. Example:

> In_O early_I trading_I in_O Hong_I Kong_I Monday_B $,_O$ gold_I was_O quoted_O at_O $\$_I$ 366.50_I an_B ounce_I $._O$

This set of three tags is sufficient for encoding baseNP structures since these structures are nonrecursive and nonoverlapping.

(Tjong Kim Sang and Veenstra, 1999) have presented three variants of this tagging representation. First, the B tag can be used for the first word of every noun phrase (IOB2 representation). Second, instead of the B tag an E tag can be used to mark the last word of a baseNP immediately before another baseNP (IOE1). And third, the E tag can be used for every noun phrase final word (IOE2). They have used the (Ramshaw and Marcus, 1995) representation as well (IOB1). We will use these four tagging representations as well as the O+C representation.

2.3 Machine learning algorithms

We have used the memory-based learning algorithm IB1-IG which is part of TiMBL package (Daelemans et al., 1999b). In memory-based learning the training data is stored and a new item is classified by the most frequent classification among training items which are closest to this new item. Data items are represented as sets of feature-value pairs. In IB1-IG each feature receives a weight which is based on the amount of information which it provides for computing the classification of the items in the training data. These feature weights are used for computing the distance between a pair of data items (Daelemans et al., 1999b). IB1-IG has been used successfully on a large variety of natural language processing tasks.

Beside IB1-IG, we have used IGTREE in the combination experiments. IGTREE is a decision tree variant of IB1-IG (Daelemans et al., 1999b). It uses the same feature weight method as IB1-IG. Data items are stored in a tree with the most important features close to the root node. A new item is classified by traveling down from the root node until a leaf node is reached or no branch is available for the current feature value. The most frequent classification of the current node will be chosen.

2.4 Combination techniques

Our experiments will result in different classifications of the data and we need to find out how to combine these. For this purpose we have evaluated different voting mechanisms, effectively the voting methods as described in (Van Halteren et al., 1998). All combination methods assign some weight to the results of the individual classifier. For each input token, they pick the classification score with the highest total score. For example, if five classifiers have weights 0.9, 0.4, 0.8, 0.6 and 0.6 respectively and they classify some token as npstart, null, npstart, null and null, then the combination method will pick npstart since it has a higher total score (1.7) than null (1.6). The values of the weights are usually estimated by processing a part of the training data, the tuning data, which has been kept separate as training data for the combination process.

In the first voting method, each of the five classifiers receives the same weight (majority). The second method regards as the weight of each individual classification algorithm its accuracy on the tuning data (TotPrecision). The third voting method computes the precision of each assigned tag per classifier and uses this value as a weight for the classifier in those cases that it chooses the tag (TagPrecision). The fourth method uses the tag precision weights as well but it subtracts from them the recall values of the competing classifier results. Finally, the fifth method uses not only a weight for the current classification but it also computes weights for other possible classifications. The other classifications are determined by examining the tuning data and registering the correct values for every pair of classifier results (pair-wise voting).

Apart from these five voting methods we have also processed the output streams with two classifiers: IB1-IG (memory-based) and IGTREE (decision tree). This approach is called classifier stacking. Like (Van Halteren et al., 1998), we have used different input versions: one containing only the classifier output and another containing both classifier output and a compressed representation of the classifier input.

train	O	C
All correct	96.21%	96.66%
Majority correct	1.98%	1.64%
Minority correct	0.88%	0.75%
All wrong	0.93%	0.95%

Table 1: Token classification agreement between the five classifiers applied to the baseNP training data after conversion to the open bracket (O) and the close bracket representation (C).

For the latter purpose we have used the part-of-speech tag of the current word.

3 Results

Our first goal was to find out whether system combination could improve performance of baseNP recognition and, if this was the fact, to select the best combination technique. For this purpose we performed a 10-fold cross validation experiment on the baseNP training data, sections 15-18 of the WSJ part of the Penn Treebank (211727 tokens). Like the data used by (Ramshaw and Marcus, 1995), this data was retagged by the Brill tagger in order to obtain realistic part-of-speech (POS) tags[3]. The data was segmented into baseNP parts and non-baseNP parts in a similar fashion as the data used by (Ramshaw and Marcus, 1995).

The data was converted to the five data representations (IOB1, IOB2, IOE1, IOE2 and O+C) and IB1-IG was used to classify it by using 10-fold cross validation. This means that the data was divided in ten consecutive parts of about the same size after which each part was used as test data with the other nine parts as training data. The standard parameters of IB1-IG have been used except for k, the number of examined nearest neighbors, which was set to three. Each word in the data was represented by itself and its POS tag and additionally a left and right context of four word-POS tag pairs. For the first four representations, we have used a second processing stage as well. In this stage, a word was represented by itself, its POS tag, a left and right context of three word-POS tag pairs and a left and right context of two classification results of the first processing stage (see figure 1). The second processing stage improved the $F_{\beta=1}$ scores with almost 0.7 on average.

The classifications of the IOB1, IOB2, IOE1 and IOE2 representations were converted to the open bracket (O) and close bracket (C) representations.

[3]No perfect Penn Treebank POS tags will be available for novel texts. If we would have used the Treebank POS tags for NP recognition, our performance rates would have been unrealistically high.

train	O	C
Representation		
IOB1	98.01%	98.14%
IOB2	97.80%	98.08%
IOE1	97.97%	98.04%
IOE2	97.89%	98.08%
O+C	97.92%	98.13%
Simple Voting		
Majority	98.19%	98.30%
TotPrecision	98.19%	98.30%
TagPrecision	98.19%	98.30%
Precision-Recall	98.19%	98.30%
Pairwise Voting		
TagPair	98.19%	98.30%
Memory-Based		
Tags	98.19%	98.34%
Tags + POS	98.19%	98.35%
Decision Trees		
Tags	98.17%	98.34%
Tags + POS	98.17%	98.34%

Table 2: Open and close bracket accuracies for the baseNP training data (211727 tokens). Each combination performs significantly better than any of the five individual classifiers listed under Representation. The performance differences between the combination methods are not significant.

After this conversion step we had five O results and five C results. In the bracket representations, tokens can be classified as either being the first token of an NP (or the last in the C representation) or not. The results obtained with these representations have been measured with accuracy rates: the percentage of tokens that were classified correctly. Only about one in four tokens are at a baseNP boundary so guessing that a text does not contains baseNPs will already give us an accuracy of 75%. Therefore the accuracy rates obtained with these representations are high and the room for improvement is small (see table 1). However, because of the different treatment of neighboring chunks, the five classifiers disagree in about 2.5% of the classifications. It seems useful to use combination methods for finding the best classification for those ambiguous cases.

The five O results and the five C results were processed by the combination techniques described in section 2.4. The accuracies per input token for the combinations can be found in table 2. For both data representations, all combinations perform significantly better than the best individual classifier ($p<0.001$ according to a χ^2 test)[4]. Unlike in (Van

[4]We have performed significance computations on the bracket accuracy rates because we have been unable to find a satisfactory method for computing significance scores for

trading/NN in/IN Hong/NNP Kong/NNP Monday/NNP ,/, gold/NN was/VBD quoted/VBN
in/IN Hong/NNP/I Kong/NNP/I Monday/NNP ,/,/O gold/NN/I was/VBD

Figure 1: Example of the classifier input features used for classifying *Monday* in the example sentence. The first processing stage (top) contains a word and POS context of four left and four right while the second processing stage (bottom) contains a word and POS context of three and a chunk tag context of two.

section 20	accuracy	precision	recall	$F_{\beta=1}$
Majority voting	O:98.10% C:98.29%	93.63%	92.89%	93.26
(Muñoz et al., 1999)	O:98.1% C:98.2%	93.1%	92.4%	92.8
(Tjong Kim Sang and Veenstra, 1999)	97.58%	92.50%	92.25%	92.37
(Ramshaw and Marcus, 1995)	97.37%	91.80%	92.27%	92.03
(Argamon et al., 1998)	-	91.6%	91.6%	91.6

section 00	accuracy	precision	recall	$F_{\beta=1}$
Majority voting	O:98.59% C:98.65%	95.04%	94.75%	94.90
(Tjong Kim Sang and Veenstra, 1999)	98.04%	93.71%	93.90%	93.81
(Ramshaw and Marcus, 1995)	97.8%	93.1%	93.5%	93.3

Table 3: The results of majority voting of different data representations applied to the two standard data sets put forward by (Ramshaw and Marcus, 1995) compared with earlier work. The accuracy scores indicate how often a word was classified correctly with the representation used (O, C or IOB1). The training data for WSJ section 20 contained 211727 tokens while section 00 was processed with 950028 tokens of training data. Majority voting outperforms all earlier reported results for the two data sets.

Halteren et al., 1998), the best voting technique did not outperform the best stacked classifier. Furthermore the performance differences between the combination methods are not significant (p>0.05). To our surprise the five voting techniques performed the same. We assume that this has happened because the accuracies of the individual classifiers do not differ much and because the classification involves a binary choice.

Since there is no significant difference between the combination methods, we can use any of them in the remaining experiments. We have chosen to use majority voting because it does not require tuning data. We have applied it to the two data sets mentioned in (Ramshaw and Marcus, 1995). The first data set uses WSJ sections 15-18 as training data (211727 tokens) and section 20 as test data (47377 tokens). The second one uses sections 02-21 of the same corpus as training data (950028 tokens) and section 00 as test data (46451 tokens). All data sets were processed in the same way as described earlier. The results of these experiments can be found in table 3. With section 20 as test set, we managed to reduce the error of the best result known to us with 6% with the error rate dropping from 7.2% to 6.74%, and for section 00 this difference was almost 18% with the error rate dropping from 6.19% to 5.10% (see table 3).

$F_{\beta=1}$ rates.

We have also applied majority voting to the NP data set put forward on the CoNLL-99 workshop. In this task the goal is to recognize all NPs. We have approached this as repeated baseNP recognition. A first stage detects the baseNPs. The recognized NPs are replaced by their presumed head word with a special POS tag and the result is send to a second stage which recognizes NPs with one level of embedding. The output of this stage is sent to a third stage and this stage finds NPs with two levels of embedding and so on.

In the first processing stage we have used the five data representations with majority voting. This approach did not work as well for other stages. The O+C representation outperformed the other four representations by a large margin for the validation data[5]. This caused the combined output of all five representations being worse than the O+C result. Therefore we have only used the O+C representation for recognizing non-baseNPs. The overall system reached an $F_{\beta=1}$ score of 83.79 and this is slightly better than the best rate reported at the

[5]The validation data is the test set we have used for estimating the best parameters for the CoNLL experiment: WSJ section 21.

CoNLL-99 workshop (82.98 (CoNLL-99, 1999), an error reduction of 5%).

4 Related work

(Abney, 1991) has proposed to approach parsing by starting with finding correlated chunks of words. The chunks can be combined to trees by a second processing stage, the attacher. (Ramshaw and Marcus, 1995) have build a chunker by applying transformation-based learning to sections of the Penn Treebank. Rather than working with bracket structures, they have represented the chunking task as a tagging problem. POS-like tags were used to account for the fact that words were inside or outside chunks. They have applied their method to two segments of the Penn Treebank and these are still being used as benchmark data sets.

Several groups have continued working with the Ramshaw and Marcus data sets for base noun phrases. (Argamon et al., 1998) use Memory-Based Sequence Learning for recognizing both NP chunks and VP chunks. This method records POS tag sequences which contain chunk boundaries and uses these sequences to classify the test data. Its performance is somewhat worse than that of Ramshaw and Marcus ($F_{\beta=1}$=91.6 vs. 92.0) but it is the best result obtained without using lexical information[6]. (Cardie and Pierce, 1998) store POS tag sequences that make up complete chunks and use these sequences as rules for classifying unseen data. This approach performs worse than the method of Argamon et al. ($F_{\beta=1}$=90.9).

Three papers mention having used the memory-based learning method IB1-IG. (Veenstra, 1998) introduced cascaded chunking, a two-stage process in which the first stage classifications are used to improve the performance in a second processing stage. This approach reaches the same performance level as Argamon et al. but it requires lexical information. (Daelemans et al., 1999a) report a good performance for baseNP recognition but they use a different data set and do not mention precision and recall rates. (Tjong Kim Sang and Veenstra, 1999) compare different data representations for this task. Their baseNP results are slightly better than those of Ramshaw and Marcus ($F_{\beta=1}$=92.37).

(XTAG, 1998) describes a baseNP chunker built from training data by a technique called supertagging. The performance of the chunker was an improvement of the Ramshaw and Marcus results ($F_{\beta=1}$=92.4). (Muñoz et al., 1999) use SNoW, a network of linear units, for recognizing baseNP phrases and SV phrases. They compare two data representations and report that a representation with bracket structures outperforms the IOB tagging representation introduced by (Ramshaw and Marcus, 1995). SNoW reaches the best performance on this task ($F_{\beta=1}$=92.8).

There has been less work on identifying general noun phrases than on recognizing baseNPs. (Osborne, 1999) extended a definite clause grammar with rules induced by a learner that was based upon the maximum description length principle. He processed other parts of the Penn Treebank than we with an $F_{\beta=1}$ rate of about 60. Our earlier effort to process the CoNLL data set was performed in the same way as described in this paper but without using the combination method for baseNPs. We obtained an $F_{\beta=1}$ rate of 82.98 (CoNLL-99, 1999).

5 Concluding remarks

We have put forward a method for recognizing noun phrases by combining the results of a memory-based classifier applied to different representations of the data. We have examined different combination techniques and each of them performed significantly better than the best individual classifier. We have chosen to work with majority voting because it does not require tuning data and thus enables the individual classifiers to use all the training data. This approach was applied to three standard data sets for base noun phrase recognition and arbitrary noun phrase recognition. For all data sets majority voting improved the best result for that data set known to us.

Varying data representations is not the only way for generating different classifiers for combination purposes. We have also tried dividing the training data in partitions (bagging) and working with artificial training data generated by a crossover-like operator borrowed from genetic algorithm theory. With our memory-based classifier applied to this data, we have been unable to generate a combination which improved the performance of its best member. Another approach would be to use different classification algorithms and combine the results. We are working on this but we are still to overcome the practical problems which prevent us from obtaining acceptable results with the other learning algorithms.

Acknowledgements

We would like to thank the members of the CNTS group in Antwerp, Belgium, the members of the ILK group in Tilburg, The Netherlands and three anonymous reviewers for valuable discussions and comments. This research was funded by the European TMR network Learning Computational Grammars[7].

[6] We have applied majority voting of five data representations to the Ramshaw and Marcus data set without using lexical information and the results were: accuracy O: 97.60%, accuracy C: 98.10%, precision: 92.19%, recall: 91.53% and $F_{\beta=1}$: 91.86.

[7] http://lcg-www.uia.ac.be/

References

Steven Abney. 1991. Parsing by chunks. In *Principle-Based Parsing*. Kluwer Academic Publishers.

Shlomo Argamon, Ido Dagan, and Yuval Krymolowski. 1998. A memory-based approach to learning shallow natural language patterns. In *Proceedings of COLING-ACL '98*. Association for Computational Linguistics.

Eric Brill and Jun Wu. 1998. Classifier combination for improved lexical disambiguation. In *Proceedings of COLING-ACL '98*. Association for Computational Linguistics.

Claire Cardie and David Pierce. 1998. Error-driven pruning of treebank grammars for base noun phrase identification. In *Proceedings of COLING-ACL '98*. Association for Computational Linguistics.

CoNLL-99. 1999. Conll-99 home page. http://lcg-www.uia.ac.be/conll99/.

Walter Daelemans, Antal van den Bosch, and Jakub Zavrel. 1999a. Forgetting exceptions is harmful in language learning. *Machine Learning*, 34.

Walter Daelemans, Jakub Zavrel, Ko van der Sloot, and Antal van den Bosch. 1999b. *TiMBL: Tilburg Memory Based Learner, version 2.0, Reference Guide*. ILK Technical Report 99-01. http://ilk.kub.nl/~ilk/papers/ilk9901.ps.gz.

Mitchell P. Marcus, Beatrice Santorini, and Mary Ann Marcinkiewicz. 1993. Building a large annotated corpus of English: the Penn Treebank. *Computational Linguistics*, 19.

Marcia Muñoz, Vasin Punyakanok, Dan Roth, and Dav Zimak. 1999. A learning approach to shallow parsing. In *Proceedings of EMNLP-WVLC'99*. Association for Computational Linguistics.

Miles Osborne. 1999. MDL-based DCG induction for NP identification. In Miles Osborne and Erik Tjong Kim Sang, editors, *CoNLL-99 Computational Natural Language Learning*. Association for Computational Linguistics.

Lance A. Ramshaw and Mitchell P. Marcus. 1995. Text chunking using transformation-based learning. In *Proceedings of the Third ACL Workshop on Very Large Corpora*. Association for Computational Linguistics.

Erik F. Tjong Kim Sang and Jorn Veenstra. 1999. Representing text chunks. In *Proceedings of EACL'99*. Association for Computational Linguistics.

Hans van Halteren, Jakub Zavrel, and Walter Daelemans. 1998. Improving data driven wordclass tagging by system combination. In *Proceedings of COLING-ACL'98*. Association for Computational Linguistics.

Jorn Veenstra. 1998. Fast NP chunking using memory-based learning techniques. In *BENELEARN-98: Proceedings of the Eighth Belgian-Dutch Conference on Machine Learning*. ATO-DLO, Wageningen, report 352.

The XTAG Research Group. 1998. *A Lexicalized Tree Adjoining Grammar for English*. IRCS Tech Report 98-18, University of Pennsylvania. (also cs.CL/9809024).

The FrameNet tagset for frame-semantic and syntactic coding of predicate-argument structure

Christopher JOHNSON
FrameNet Project,
International Computer Science Institute
currently: Soliloquy, Inc.
255 Park Ave S
New York NY 10010
cjohnson@soliloquy.com

Charles J. FILLMORE
FrameNet Project,
International Computer Science Institute
1947 Center St., Suite 600
Berkeley, CA, USA 94704
fillmore@icsi.berkeley.edu

Abstract

This paper presents the syntactic and semantic tags used to annotate predicate-argument structure in the Berkeley FrameNet Project. It briefly explains the theory of frame semantics on which semantic annotation is based, discusses possible applications of FrameNet annotation, and compares FrameNet to other prominent lexical resources.

Introduction

This paper presents the tagset used to annotate the predicate-argument structures of English verbs, adjectives, and nouns in the Berkeley FrameNet Project (NSF IRI-9618838, "Tools for Lexicon Building"), a corpus-based computational lexicography project based on the theory of **frame semantics** (see Fillmore 1982). It briefly explains the theoretical background and shows how frame-semantic annotation creates lexicographic generalizations that are not possible with more traditional linguistic approaches to argument structure based on thematic roles.

1 The FrameNet Project

1.1 What is frame semantics?

Frame semantics characterizes the semantic and syntactic properties of predicating words by relating them to **semantic frames**. These are schematic representations of situations involving various participants, props, and other conceptual roles, each of which is a **frame element** (FE). The semantic arguments of a predicating word correspond to the FEs of the frame or frames associated with that word.

Frames are organized in a structure that can be modeled by an inheritance lattice. They range from being very general, like case frames (Fillmore 1968) or other simple event schemas underlying thematic roles, to being lexically specific. The most interesting frames are those at an intermediate level of specificity which encapsulate generalizations about the semantic and syntactic properties of word classes that are overlooked by thematic role analyses.

1.2 An example

One example is the commercial transaction frame, which includes the following FEs: **Buyer**, **Seller**, **Goods**, and **Money**. The following sentence schemas show how these FEs are expressed differently by different Commercial Transaction words:

Buyer **bought** Goods from Seller for Money

Buyer **paid** Seller Money for Goods

Buyer **paid** Money to Seller for Goods

Seller **sold** goods to Buyer for Money

Seller **sold** Buyer Goods for Money

Buyer **spent** Money on Goods
(Seller not expressed)

Goods **cost** Buyer Money
(Seller not expressed)

Different words assign the Commercial Transaction FEs to different Phrase Types (PTs) and Grammatical Functions (GFs). For example, *buy* treats the **Buyer** as an NP subject (i.e.

External Argument) and the **Seller** as a PP complement headed by *from*, while *sell* treats the **Buyer** as a direct object or a PP complement headed by *to* and the **Seller** as a subject. The purpose of FrameNet annotation is to gather information like this about the grammatical realization of FEs for various frames.

1.2 Project goals

The goals of the project are to create a database of information about English words and the frames they inherit, provide annotated corpus examples that illustrate how information about FEs is expressed by complements and modifiers of these words in attested sentences, and contribute to a suite of software tools to support annotation, database building, and database interface.

An important part of FrameNet work is the annotation of corpus sentences with frame-semantic information. We use the British National Corpus (BNC), because no equally comprehensive corpus exists for American English (though efforts are underway to create a comparable American National Corpus—see Fillmore et al. 1998). Each annotated example sentence shows argument-structure properties of one **target** verb, adjective or noun. The main task of annotation is to tag the arguments (and occasionally modifiers) of the target with the names of the FEs that they express. A secondary task is to mark other lexicographically relevant elements, such as support verbs of target nouns, and certain non-meaningful elements that indicate lexicographically relevant grammatical constructions (e.g. extraposition and the existential construction). (See Fillmore & Atkins 1998 on lexicographic relevance.)

Here is an example sentence from the BNC showing the annotation properties of the complements of the target verb *tell*:

(1) [Maltravers (Speaker, NP, Ext)] decided not to **tell**
[Stephen (Addressee, NP, Obj)]
[about the inscription in the Le Carré book
(Topic, PP*about*, Comp)].

The annotated constituents appear in brackets. Following each constituent is a set of parentheses containing the FE, PT and GF associated with that constituent (actual annotations consist of XML markup created using the Alembic Workbench software from the Mitre Corporation). PT and GF information is added by an automatic phrase labeler developed by the technical team.

2 The FrameNet tagset

2.1 Phrase Types

Below are the FrameNet Phrase Types. This is intended to be a comprehensive list of the types of syntactic constituent that can express FEs of major predicating words of English (nouns, verbs and adjectives). These constituents occur either as arguments or as lexicographically relevant modifiers. In constructing this list, we made extensive reference to the Comlex syntax (Meyers et al. 1995).

2.1.1 Noun phrase types

NP	Noun phrase (*the witness*)
N	Non-maximal nominal (personal *chat*)
Poss	Possessive NP (*the child's* decision)
There	Expletive *there* (*there* was a fight)
It	Expletive *it* (*it*'s nice that you came)

2.1.2 Prepositional phrase types

PP	Prepositional phrase (look *at me*)
Ping	PP with gerundive object (keep *from laughing*)
Part	Particle(look it *up*)

2.1.3 Verb phrase types

VPfin	Finite verb phrase (we *ate fish*)
VPbrst	Bare stem VP (let us *eat fish*)
VPto	*To*-marked infinitive VP (we want *to eat fish*)
VPwh	WH-VP (we know *how to win*)
VPing	Gerundive VP (we like *winning*)

2.1.4 Complement clause types

Sfin	Finite clause (it's nice *that you came*)
Swh	WH-clause (ask *who won*)
Sif	*If/whether* clause (ask *if we won*)
Sing	Gerundive clause (we saw *them running*)
Sto	*To*-marked clause (we want *them to win*)
Sforto	*For-to*-marked clause (we would like *for them to win*)
Sbrst	Bare stem clause (we insist *that they win*)

In certain cases FrameNet marks as two constituents what are treated as "small clauses" in some analyses. For example, in the sentence *I consider Pat a genius*, *Pat* and *a genius* would be tagged separately.

2.1.5 Other phrase types

AjP Adjective phrase (an *interesting* idea)
AdvP Adverb phrase (you put that *nicely*)
Quo Quote (*"Indeed,"* she said)

2.2 Grammatical Functions

Below is a list of the FrameNet GFs. This list is intended to characterize all the grammatical contexts relative to English verbs, adjectives and nouns that are regularly occupied by FE-expressing constituents. In this list, we do not make the traditional distinction between obliques and arguments/complements (the former are simply PP complements).

2.2.1 FrameNet grammatical functions

Ext External Argument
(Argument outside phrase headed by target verb, adjective or noun)

Comp Complement
(Argument inside phrase headed by target verb, adjective or noun)

Mod Modifier
(Non-argument expressing FE of target verb, adjective or noun)

Xtrap Extraposed
(Verbal or clausal complement extraposed to end of VP)

Obj Object
(Post-verbal argument; passivizable or does not alternate with PP)

Pred Predicate
(Secondary predicate complement of target verb or adjective)

Head Head
(Head nominal in attributive use of target adjective)

Gen Genitive Determiner
(Genitive Determiner of nominal headed by target)

2.3 Nonexpression of FEs

Besides being expressed by the PTs and GFs listed above, FEs may remain unexpressed under the different conditions discussed below (see Fillmore 1986).

2.3.1 Indefinite Null Instantiation

In sentence (1), the FEs Message, Medium and Code are not expressed. It can however be inferred that there must be a Message, Medium and Code in a communicative event of the type described by this sentence. These FEs, while conceptually present in this sentence, are optionally expressed, and there are no particular restrictions on their nonexpression. This is called **Indefinite Null Instantiation** (INI).

2.3.2 Definite Null Instantiation

With some words, an FE may be unexpressed in a sentence only if it assumed that the person to whom the sentence is addressed has specific information about the frame element in question. This kind of non-expression is called **Definite Null Instantiation** (DNI). For example, the words *tell*, *inform* and *notify* allow a Message to be omitted when it is clear what the Message is, e.g. *How did I know you won? Because Pat already* ***told*** *me*.

2.3.3 Constructionally licensed null instantiation

Certain grammatical constructions, such as Passive and Imperative, allow an External Argument FE to be unexpressed, e.g. *Harsh things were* ***said***, ***Tell*** *me about yourself*. This is **Constructionally Licensed Null Instantiation** (CNI).

FrameNet annotation marks prominent unexpressed FEs as well as FEs that are expressed overtly. In order to achieve this, we place the symbols INI, DNI and CNI immediately after the target word in every annotated sentence, and place the appropriate FE tag on the appropriate symbol. For example, the case of DNI discussed above would be annotated as follows:

(2) [Pat (Speaker)] already **told** INI [DNI (Message)] CNI [me (Addressee)].

2.4 Frame Elements

Frames are organized into the following domains: Body, Chance, Cognition, Communication, Emotion, Health, Life Stages, Motion, Perception, Society, Space, Time, Transaction, and a General domain. Each domain contains several frames that characterize different word classes. Because there are many frames, it is not possible to give the complete list of FEs. The next section discusses FEs from the Communication domain.

3 Communication frames

It is typically the case that different frames in the same domain share FEs. For that reason, each domain can be characterized by a basic frame that defines its FEs in general terms, and more specific frames, corresponding to word classes, that are based on this basic frame through inheritance or some other principled relation. Let us consider the basic frame of verbal communication.

3.1 Basic Verbal Communication frame

The following FEs consistently appear in frames relating to verbal communication:

Speaker
(A person who performs an act of verbal communication)

Addressee
(An actual or intended recipient of a verbal message)

Message
(A communicated proposition)

Topic
(The subject matter of a message)

Medium
(A physical channel of communication)

Code
(The language or other code used to communicate)

These FEs all derive their meaning from the concept of a basic communicative event. Clearly a true frame representation cannot just consist of a list of role names, but must characterize such events. Currently FrameNet frame descriptions exist only in text form, but the ultimate aim is to express them in a machine-readable format. An important component of such a representation will be feature structures that express relations between frames symbolically. These might be combined with computational event models that are able to generate inferences, such as the x-schemas developed by Bailey et al. (1997) and Narayanan (1997).

The FEs of the Basic Verbal Communication frame are relevant to sentence (1) above, in which the Speaker is expressed as an NP Ext, the Addressee is expressed as an NP Obj, and the Topic is expressed as a PP Comp headed by *about*. The other FEs are not expressed.

We will examine how the FEs above are realized in different Communication frames, and in the process, will see some of the kinds of generalizations that can be expressed through frame-semantic lexical analysis.

3.2 Other frames in the Communication domain

The Basic Verbal Communication frame characterizes events of verbal communication in the most general terms. Different Communication words represent different types of communicative event and different ways of construing such events. Generalizations over these words are captured by different frames in the domain. Some focus on, or *profile*, in Langacker's (1987) terminology, the relation between a Speaker and a propositional Message. These are grouped into frames characterizing different speech acts, e.g. asking (Questioning frame), requesting (Request frame), asserting (Statement frame), and promising (Commitment frame). A few words profile the relation between a Speaker and an act of speaking, but not the propositional Message communicated (*talk*, *speak*). Some denote events of reciprocal communication (e.g. *discuss*, *argue*, *conversation*, etc.). And so on.

The following sections summarize properties of specific frames, and discuss some assumptions about the ontology of the Communication domain that might account for these properties.

3.3 The Statement frame

Verbs and nouns in the Statement frame profile a relation between a Speaker and a propositional

Message that has the speech act status of an assertion. Because of the importance of the Message FE, these words frequently occur with Sfin Comp (finite clausal complements):

(3) [Others (Speaker, NP, Ext)] **assert** [that anthropology is the tree and sociology the branch (Message, Sfin, Comp)].

(4) [Managers (Speaker, NP, Ext)] **claim** [there was no radiological hazzard to staff or the public (Message, Sfin, Comp)].

(5) [His (Speaker, Poss, Gen)] **claims** [to have more energy (Message, VPto, Comp)] are simply laughable.

Message can be expressed with different PPs as well. For example, with the target noun *claim*, it can be expressed as a to-marked infinitive VP, as in example (5).

3.4 The Speaking frame

Verbs and nouns in the Speaking frame profile a relation between a Speaker and an act of speaking, but do no allow a Message to be expressed:

(6) [She (Speaker, NP, Ext)] never **spoke** [about her feelings (Topic, PP*about*, Comp)].

This fact can be explained if we analyze the basic meaning of Speaking words as being something like 'X say something'. The Message role can be thought of as being **incorporated** into this meaning, with incorporation in this case being equivalent to obligatory INI.

3.5 The Request frame

Like words in the Statement frame, these words frequently occur with clausal Complements. However, because these Complements express requests rather that assertions, they often occur as bare stem clauses:

(7) In all cases [the respondent (Speaker, NP, Ext)] may **request** [in writing (Medium, PP*in*, Comp)] [that the disciplinary findings be published (Message, Sbrst, Comp)].

3.6 The Conversation frame

One class of words in the Communication domain does not use the FEs Speaker and Addressee as they occur in other frames. These are nouns and verbs or reciprocal communication, which are treated in the Conversation frame. In this frame, the human interlocutors can be expressed in separate constituents, assigned the roles **Protagonist-1** (Prot-1) and **Protagonist-2** (Prot-2), or they can be expressed in a single conjoined or plural constituent, assigned the role **Protagonists** (Prots).

This class of words demonstrates the complex interaction of frames. The FEs Prot-1, Prot-2 and Prots are not equivalent to any of the Basic Verbal Communication FEs, but do relate to them in a regular way. Each of these roles must be thought of as relating to two or more Communicative subevents, and as corresponding to a Speaker in some and an Addressee in others. This basic structure is taken not from any frame in the domain of Communication, but from a Reciprocity frame, which is in the General domain. The Reciprocity frame may be thought of as an Aktionsart frame that structures events and relations from other frames in a particular way, such that there are multiple subeventualities of the same type as that of the input frame, and the bindings or fillers of the roles are reversed from one subeventuality to the another.

The complexity introduced by frames such as these points to the need to distinguish between conceptual roles and FEs in any given frame. While the Communication roles Speaker and Addressee are not FEs in the Conversation frame, they are conceptual roles, because the conceptual representation of Conversation makes reference to them. (In the Speaking frame discussed above, we can also think of the incorporated Message role as being a conceptual role rather than an FE.) FEs in any given frame should therefore be defined as those roles for which the frame specifies conventional means of syntactic expression, even if these means are not employed in all sentences.

3.6.1 Disjoint expression: Prot-1 and Prot-2

Here is a BNC example of *argue* with a disjoint expression of interlocutors:

(8) "[You (Prot-1, NP, Ext)] can't **argue** [politics (Topic, NP, Comp)] [with foreigners (Prot-2, PP*with*, Comp)]", sighed the policeman.

Prot-2, the less prominent interlocutor, is regularly expressed in this frame by a PP Comp headed by *with*. This is consistent with the general behavior of the Reciprocity frame as it occurs in combination with other frames and domains (e.g. *Pat had a collision/relationship/agreement* ***with Kim***).

3.6.2 Joint expression: Protagonists

Here are BNC examples of the joint expression of interlocuters with argue:

(9) [They (Prots, NP, Ext)] **argued** [angrily (Manner, AdvP, Mod)] [over who was the real "Prince of Sleaze" (Topic, PP*over*, Comp)].

(10) [Mr. and Mrs. Popple (Prots, NP, Ext)] always **argued** [INI (Topic)] at least once a week.

3.7 FrameNet complements existing lexical resources

FrameNet annotations provide more detail than existing lexical resources about the way in which particular semantic roles (i.e. FEs) are linked with particular means of syntactic expression. Since different senses of ambiguous words are defined relative to different frames, this linking information could potentially be used for lexical disambiguation.

For example, consider the verb *argue* as it is treated in the WordNet database (Fellbaum 1998). Below are the three WordNet senses of *argue*, and the sentence frames that are associated with each sense:

Sense 1: argue, reason — (present reasons and arguments)

EX: Sam and Sue argue

EX: Sam wants to argue with Sue

Sense 2: argue, contend, debate, fence — (have an argument about something)

EX: Sam and Sue argue

EX; Sam wants to argue with Sue

Sense 3: argue, indicate — (give evidence of; "The evidence argues for your claim"; "The results indicate the need for more work")

The three senses listed above correspond to three different frames: Sense 1 corresponds to the Statement frame, Sense 2 to the Conversation frame, and Sense 3 to the Evidence frame in the Cognition domain. However, the information about sentence frames provided in WordNet does not correspond to the generalizations that are apparent in FrameNet. For example, WordNet gives the same sentence frames for Senses 1 and 2, while in the FrameNet database, the senses of *argue* defined relative to the Statement and Conversation frames are characterized by different argument structures: only Statement *argue* allows finite clausal complements expressing Message; Conversation *argue* has the properties of other reciprocal communication words, which Statement *argue* lacks, and does not allow clausal Complements (or any other expression of Message).

COMLEX (Meyers et al. 1995) recognizes the syntactic frames in which *argue* occurs, but does not provide information about the linking of syntactic constituents with semantic roles, or about the different complementation properties of different senses of ambiguous words.

Conclusion

FrameNet semantic annotation captures human knowledge about the ways in which semantic roles (FEs) are conventionally expressed by different words in various word classes and domains. The kind of information in the FrameNet database is not expressed in the same level of depth in any existing print dictionary or computational lexical resource. While WordNet describes semantic relations between words, it does not recognize the conceptual schemas, i.e. frames, that mediate in these relations, and therefore does not have the means to link arguments of predicating words with the semantic roles they express. COMLEX and NOMLEX provide detailed information about the syntactic frames in which verbs and nouns occur, but also lack a means to link syntactic arguments with semantic roles. FrameNet therefore provides information that complements major existing lexical resources.

Acknowledgements

The authors would like to thank the National Science Foundation for supporting this project, and the International Computer Science Institute in Berkeley for giving it a home. Thanks also to Oxford University Press and Sue Atkins for making it possible for us to use the British National Corpus, and to IMS-Stuttgart and Uli Heid for providing us with the tagged version. We are also grateful to Catherine Macleod and Ralph Grishman of the NYU Proteus Project for allowing one of use to be a visitor, and various people in the Berkeley linguistics department and in the Neural Theory of Language project at ICSI for enlightening discussions.

References

Bailey, D., J. Feldman, S. Narayanan and G. Lakoff. (1997) *Modeling embodied lexical semantics.* In Proceedings of the 19th Annual Meeting of the Cognitive Science Society COGSCI-97. Stanford, CA: Stanford University Press.

Baker, Collin F., Charles J. Fillmore, and John B. Lowe. (1998) *The Berkeley FrameNet Project.* In COLING-ACL '98 Proceedings of the Conference held August 10-14, 1998, in Montreal, Canada, pp.86-90.

Fellbaum, Christiane (1987) *WordNet: An electronic lexical database.* Cambridge, MA: MIT Press.

Fillmore, Charles J. (1968) *The case for case.* In E. Bach and R. Harms (eds.), Universals in Linguistic Theory. New York: Holt, Rinehart & Winston.

Fillmore, Charles J. (1982) Frame semantics. In Linguistics in the Morning Calm, pp. 111-137. Seoul, South Korea: Hanshin Publishing Co.

Fillmore, Charles J. (1986) *Pragmatically Controlled Zero Anaphora.* In Proceedings of the 12th annual meeting of the Berkeley Linguistics Society, pp. 95-107.

Fillmore, Charles J. and B. T. S. Atkins. (1999) *Describing polysemy: the case of 'crawl'.* In Polysemy: Linguistic and Computational Approaches, (eds.) Yael Ravin and Claudia Leacock. Oxford: Oxford University Press.

Fillmore, Charles J. and B.T.S. Atkins. (1998) *FrameNet and lexicographic relevance.* In Proceedings of the First International Conference on Language Resources and Evaluation, Granada, Spain, 28-30 May 1998.

Fillmore, Charles J., Nancy Ide, Daniel Jurafsky, and Catherine Macleod (May 1998) *An American National Corpus: A Proposal.* In Proceedings of the First International Conference on Language Resources and Evaluation (LREC); Granada, Spain 28-30 May 1998.

Gahl, Susanne (1998) *Automatic extraction of Subcorpora based on Subcategorization Frames from a Part-of-Speech tagged Corpus.* In COLING-ACL '98 Proceedings of the Conference held August 10-14, 1998, at the University of Montréal, Canada, pp.428-32.

Gahl, Susanne (1998) *Automatic extraction of Subcorpora for Corpus-based Dictionary-building.* In Thierry Fontenelle et al. (eds.), EURALEX '98 Proceedings: Papers submitted to the Eighth EURALEX Conference, at the University of Liège, Belgium, pp.445-452.

J.B. Lowe, C.F. Baker, and C.J. Fillmore. (1997) *A frame-semantic approach to semantic annotation.* In Proceedings of the SIGLEX workshop "Tagging Text with Lexical Semantics: Why, What, and How?" held April 4-5, in Washington, D.C., USA in conjunction with ANLP-97.

Johnson, Christopher (1999) *Multiple frame inheritance in lexical descriptions.* Annual Meeting of the Linguistic Society of America. Los Angeles, January 9.

Johnson, Christopher. (1999) *Syntactic and semantic principles of FrameNet annotation.* TC-99-018, International Computer Science Institute, Berkeley, CA.

Langacker, Ronald. (1987) *Foundations of Cognitive Grammar, Vol. 1: Theoretical Perspectives.* Stanford, CA: Stanford University Press.

Levin, Beth. (1993) *English Verb Classes and Alternations.* Chicago: University of Chicago Press.

Meyers, Adam, Catherine Macleod, and Ralph Grishman. (1995) *Comlex syntax 2.0 manual for tagged entries.* Technical report, Proteus Project, New York University.

Narayanan, S. (1997) *KARMA: Knowledge-Based Active Representations for Metaphor and Aspect.* Ph.D. Dissertation, Computer Science Division, University of California, Berkeley.

A Simple Approach to Building Ensembles of Naive Bayesian Classifiers for Word Sense Disambiguation

Ted Pedersen
Department of Computer Science
University of Minnesota Duluth
Duluth, MN 55812 USA
tpederse@d.umn.edu

Abstract

This paper presents a corpus-based approach to word sense disambiguation that builds an ensemble of Naive Bayesian classifiers, each of which is based on lexical features that represent co–occurring words in varying sized windows of context. Despite the simplicity of this approach, empirical results disambiguating the widely studied nouns *line* and *interest* show that such an ensemble achieves accuracy rivaling the best previously published results.

1 Introduction

Word sense disambiguation is often cast as a problem in supervised learning, where a disambiguator is induced from a corpus of manually sense–tagged text using methods from statistics or machine learning. These approaches typically represent the context in which each sense–tagged instance of a word occurs with a set of linguistically motivated features. A learning algorithm induces a representative model from these features which is employed as a classifier to perform disambiguation.

This paper presents a corpus–based approach that results in high accuracy by combining a number of very simple classifiers into an ensemble that performs disambiguation via a majority vote. This is motivated by the observation that enhancing the feature set or learning algorithm used in a corpus–based approach does not usually improve disambiguation accuracy beyond what can be attained with shallow lexical features and a simple supervised learning algorithm.

For example, a Naive Bayesian classifier (Duda and Hart, 1973) is based on a blanket assumption about the interactions among features in a sense-tagged corpus and does not learn a representative model. Despite making such an assumption, this proves to be among the most accurate techniques in comparative studies of corpus–based word sense disambiguation methodologies (e.g., (Leacock et al., 1993), (Mooney, 1996), (Ng and Lee, 1996), (Pedersen and Bruce, 1997)). These studies represent the context in which an ambiguous word occurs with a wide variety of features. However, when the contribution of each type of feature to overall accuracy is analyzed (eg. (Ng and Lee, 1996)), shallow lexical features such as co–occurrences and collocations prove to be stronger contributors to accuracy than do deeper, linguistically motivated features such as part–of–speech and verb–object relationships.

It has also been shown that the combined accuracy of an ensemble of multiple classifiers is often significantly greater than that of any of the individual classifiers that make up the ensemble (e.g., (Dietterich, 1997)). In natural language processing, ensemble techniques have been successfully applied to part–of–speech tagging (e.g., (Brill and Wu, 1998)) and parsing (e.g., (Henderson and Brill, 1999)). When combined with a history of disambiguation success using shallow lexical features and Naive Bayesian classifiers, these findings suggest that word sense disambiguation might best be improved by combining the output of a number of such classifiers into an ensemble.

This paper begins with an introduction to the Naive Bayesian classifier. The features used to represent the context in which ambiguous words occur are presented, followed by the method for selecting the classifiers to include in the ensemble. Then, the *line* and *interest* data is described. Experimental results disambiguating these words with an ensemble of Naive Bayesian classifiers are shown to rival previously published results. This paper closes with a discussion of the choices made in formulating this methodology and plans for future work.

2 Naive Bayesian Classifiers

A Naive Bayesian classifier assumes that all the feature variables representing a problem are conditionally independent given the value of a classification variable. In word sense disambiguation, the context in which an ambiguous word occurs is represented by the feature variables $(F_1, F_2, \ldots, F_n)$ and the sense of the ambiguous word is represented by the classification variable (S). In this paper, all feature variables F_i are binary and represent whether or not a particular word occurs within some number of words to the left or right of an ambiguous word, i.e., a window of context. For a Naive Bayesian classifier, the joint probability of observing a certain combination of contextual features with a particular sense is expressed as:

$$p(F_1, F_2, \ldots, F_n, S) = p(S) \prod_{i=1}^{n} p(F_i|S)$$

The parameters of this model are $p(S)$ and $p(F_i|S)$. The sufficient statistics, i.e., the summaries of the data needed for parameter estimation, are the frequency counts of the events described by the interdependent variables (F_i, S). In this paper, these counts are the number of sentences in the sense–tagged text where the word represented by F_i occurs within some specified window of context of the ambiguous word when it is used in sense S.

Any parameter that has a value of zero indicates that the associated word never occurs with the specified sense value. These zero values are smoothed by assigning them a very small default probability. Once all the parameters have been estimated, the model has been trained and can be used as a classifier to perform disambiguation by determining the most probable sense for an ambiguous word, given the context in which it occurs.

2.1 Representation of Context

The contextual features used in this paper are binary and indicate if a given word occurs within some number of words to the left or right of the ambiguous word. No additional positional information is contained in these features; they simply indicate if the word occurs within some number of surrounding words.

Punctuation and capitalization are removed from the windows of context. All other lexical items are included in their original form; no stemming is performed and non–content words remain.

This representation of context is a variation on the *bag–of–words* feature set, where a single window of context includes words that occur to both the left and right of the ambiguous word. An early use of this representation is described in (Gale et al., 1992), where word sense disambiguation is performed with a Naive Bayesian classifier. The work in this paper differs in that there are two windows of context, one representing words that occur to the left of the ambiguous word and another for those to the right.

2.2 Ensembles of Naive Bayesian Classifiers

The left and right windows of context have nine different sizes; 0, 1, 2, 3, 4, 5, 10, 25, and 50 words. The first step in the ensemble approach is to train a separate Naive Bayesian classifier for each of the 81 possible combination of left and right window sizes.

Naive_Bayes (l,r) represents a classifier where the model parameters have been estimated based on frequency counts of shallow lexical features from two windows of context; one including l words to the left of the ambiguous word and the other including r words to the right. Note that Naive_Bayes (0,0) includes no words to the left or right; this classifier acts as a majority classifier that assigns every instance of an ambiguous word to the most frequent sense in the training data. Once the individual classifiers are trained they are evaluated using previously held–out test data.

The crucial step in building an ensemble is selecting the classifiers to include as members. The approach here is to group the 81 Naive Bayesian classifiers into general categories representing the sizes of the windows of context. There are three such ranges; *narrow* corresponds to windows 0, 1 and 2 words wide, *medium* to windows 3, 4, and 5 words wide, and *wide* to windows 10, 25, and 50 words wide. There are nine possible range categories since there are separate left and right windows. For example, Naive_Bayes(1,3) belongs to the range category (narrow, medium) since it is based on a one word window to the left and a three word window to the right. The most accurate classifier in each of the nine range categories is selected for inclusion in the ensemble. Each of the nine member classifiers votes for the most probable sense given the particular context represented by that classifier; the ensemble disambiguates by assigning the sense that receives a majority of the votes.

3 Experimental Data

The *line* data was created by (Leacock et al., 1993) by tagging every occurrence of *line* in the ACL/DCI Wall Street Journal corpus and the American Printing House for the Blind corpus with one of six possible WordNet senses. These senses and their frequency distribution are shown in Table 1. This data has since been used in studies by (Mooney, 1996), (Towell and Voorhees, 1998), and (Leacock et al., 1998). In that work, as well as in this paper, a subset of the corpus is utilized such that each sense is uniformly distributed; this reduces the accuracy of the majority classifier to 17%. The uniform distribution is created by randomly sampling 349 sense–tagged examples from each sense, resulting in a training corpus of 2094 sense–tagged sentences.

The *interest* data was created by (Bruce and Wiebe, 1994) by tagging all occurrences of *interest* in the ACL/DCI Wall Street Journal corpus with senses from the Longman Dictionary of Contemporary English. This data set was subsequently used for word sense disambiguation experiments by (Ng and Lee, 1996), (Pedersen et al., 1997), and (Pedersen and Bruce, 1997). The previous studies and this paper use the entire 2,368 sense–tagged sentence corpus in their experiments. The senses and their fre-

sense	count
product	2218
written or spoken text	405
telephone connection	429
formation of people or things; queue	349
an artificial division; boundary	376
a thin, flexible object; cord	371
total	4148

Table 1: Distribution of senses for *line* – the experiments in this paper and previous work use a uniformly distributed subset of this corpus, where each sense occurs 349 times.

sense	count
money paid for the use of money	1252
a share in a company or business	500
readiness to give attention	361
advantage, advancement or favor	178
activity that one gives attention to	66
causing attention to be given to	11
total	2368

Table 2: Distribution of senses for *interest* – the experiments in this paper and previous work use the entire corpus, where each sense occurs the number of times shown above.

quency distribution are shown in Table 2. Unlike *line*, the sense distribution is skewed; the majority sense occurs in 53% of the sentences, while the smallest minority sense occurs in less than 1%.

4 Experimental Results

Eighty-one Naive Bayesian classifiers were trained and tested with the *line* and *interest* data. Five-fold cross validation was employed; all of the sense-tagged examples for a word were randomly shuffled and divided into five equal folds. Four folds were used to train the Naive Bayesian classifier while the remaining fold was randomly divided into two equal sized test sets. The first, `devtest`, was used to evaluate the individual classifiers for inclusion in the ensemble. The second, `test`, was used to evaluate the accuracy of the ensemble. Thus the training data for each word consists of 80% of the available sense-tagged text, while each of the test sets contains 10%.

This process is repeated five times so that each fold serves as the source of the test data once. The average accuracy of the individual Naive Bayesian classifiers across the five folds is reported in Tables 3 and 4. The standard deviations were between .01 and .025 and are not shown given their relative consistency.

Each classifier is based upon a distinct representation of context since each employs a different combination of right and left window sizes. The size and range of the left window of context is indicated along the horizontal margin in Tables 3 and 4 while the right window size and range is shown along the vertical margin. Thus, the boxes that subdivide each table correspond to a particular range category. The classifier that achieves the highest accuracy in each range category is included as a member of the ensemble. In case of a tie, the classifier with the smallest total window of context is included in the ensemble.

The most accurate single classifier for *line* is Naive_Bayes (4,25), which attains accuracy of 84% The accuracy of the ensemble created from the most accurate classifier in each of the range categories is 88%. The single most accurate classifier for *interest* is Naive_Bayes(4,1), which attains accuracy of 86% while the ensemble approach reaches 89%. The increase in accuracy achieved by both ensembles over the best individual classifier is statistically significant, as judged by McNemar's test with $p = .01$.

4.1 Comparison to Previous Results

These experiments use the same sense-tagged corpora for *interest* and *line* as previous studies. Summaries of previous results in Tables 5 and 6 show that the accuracy of the Naive Bayesian ensemble is comparable to that of any other approach. However, due to variations in experimental methodologies, it can not be concluded that the differences among the most accurate methods are statistically significant. For example, in this work five-fold cross validation is employed to assess accuracy while (Ng and Lee, 1996) train and test using 100 randomly sampled sets of data. Similar differences in training and testing methodology exist among the other studies. Still, the results in this paper are encouraging due to the simplicity of the approach.

4.1.1 Interest

The *interest* data was first studied by (Bruce and Wiebe, 1994). They employ a representation of context that includes the part-of-speech of the two words surrounding *interest*, a morphological feature indicating whether or not *interest* is singular or plural, and the three most statistically significant co-occurring words in the sentence with *interest*, as determined by a test of independence. These features are abbreviated as *p-o-s*, *morph*, and *co-occur* in Table 5. A decomposable probabilistic model is induced from the sense-tagged corpora using a backward sequential search where candidate models are evaluated with the log-likelihood ratio test. The selected model was used as a probabilistic classifier on a held-out set of test data and achieved accuracy of 78%.

The *interest* data was included in a study by (Ng

	50	.63	.73	.80	.82	.83	.83	.83	.83	.83
wide	25	.63	.74	.80	.82	*.84*	.83	.83	.83	.83
	10	.62	.75	*.81*	.82	.83	.83	.83	.83	*.84*
	5	.61	.75	.80	.81	.82	.82	.82	.82	*.83*
medium	4	.60	.73	*.80*	.82	.82	.82	.82	.82	.82
	3	.58	.73	.79	.82	*.83*	.83	.82	.81	.82
	2	.53	.71	*.79*	.81	*.82*	.82	*.81*	.81	.81
narrow	1	.42	.68	.78	.79	.80	.79	.80	.81	.81
	0	.14	.58	.73	.77	.79	.79	.79	.79	.80
		0	1	2	3	4	5	10	25	50
			narrow			medium			wide	

Table 3: Accuracy of Naive Bayesian classifiers for *line* evaluated with the **devtest** data. The italicized accuracies are associated with the classifiers included in the ensemble, which attained accuracy of 88% when evaluated with the **test** data.

	50	.74	.80	.82	.83	.83	.83	.82	.80	.81
wide	25	.73	.80	.82	.83	.83	.83	.81	.80	.80
	10	.75	.82	*.84*	*.84*	.84	.84	*.82*	.81	.81
	5	.73	.83	.85	.86	.85	.85	.83	.81	.81
medium	4	.72	.83	.85	.85	.84	.84	.83	.81	.80
	3	.70	.84	*.86*	*.86*	.86	.85	*.83*	.81	.80
	2	.66	.83	.85	.86	.86	.84	*.83*	.80	.80
narrow	1	.63	.82	*.85*	.85	*.86*	.85	.82	.81	.80
	0	.53	.72	.77	.78	.79	.77	.77	.76	.75
		0	1	2	3	4	5	10	25	50
			narrow			medium			wide	

Table 4: Accuracy of Naive Bayesian classifiers for *interest* evaluated with the **devtest** data. The italicized accuracies are associated with the classifiers included in the ensemble, which attained accuracy of 89% when evaluated with the **test** data.

and Lee, 1996), who represent the context of an ambiguous word with the part-of-speech of three words to the left and right of *interest*, a morphological feature indicating if *interest* is singular or plural, an unordered set of frequently occurring keywords that surround *interest*, local collocations that include *interest*, and verb-object syntactic relationships. These features are abbreviated *p-o-s*, *morph*, *co-occur*, *collocates*, and *verb-obj* in Table 5. A nearest-neighbor classifier was employed and achieved an average accuracy of 87% over repeated trials using randomly drawn training and test sets.

(Pedersen et al., 1997) and (Pedersen and Bruce, 1997) present studies that utilize the original Bruce and Wiebe feature set and include the *interest* data. The first compares a range of probabilistic model selection methodologies and finds that none outperform the Naive Bayesian classifier, which attains accuracy of 74%. The second compares a range of machine learning algorithms and finds that a decision tree learner (78%) and a Naive Bayesian classifier (74%) are most accurate.

4.1.2 Line

The *line* data was first studied by (Leacock et al., 1993). They evaluate the disambiguation accuracy of a Naive Bayesian classifier, a content vector, and a neural network. The context of an ambiguous word is represented by a bag-of-words where the window of context is two sentences wide. This feature set is abbreviated as *2 sentence b-o-w* in Table 6. When the Naive Bayesian classifier is evaluated words are not stemmed and capitalization remains. However, with the content vector and the neural network words are stemmed and words from a stop-list are removed. They report no significant differences in accuracy among the three approaches; the Naive Bayesian classifier achieved 71% accuracy, the content vector 72%, and the neural network 76%.

The *line* data was studied again by (Mooney, 1996), where seven different machine learning methodologies are compared. All learning algorithms represent the context of an ambiguous word using the bag-of-words with a two sentence window of context. In these experiments words from a stop-

	accuracy	method	feature set
Naive Bayesian Ensemble	89%	ensemble of 9	varying left & right b-o-w
Ng & Lee, 1996	87%	nearest neighbor	p-o-s, morph, co-occur collocates, verb-obj
Bruce & Wiebe, 1994	78%	model selection	p-o-s, morph, co-occur
Pedersen & Bruce, 1997	78% 74%	decision tree naive bayes	p-o-s, morph, co-occur

Table 5: Comparison to previous results for *interest*

	accuracy	method	feature set
Naive Bayesian Ensemble	88%	ensemble of 9	varying left & right b-o-w
Towell & Voorhess, 1998	87%	neural net	local & topical b-o-w, p-o-s
Leacock, Chodorow, & Miller, 1998	84%	naive bayes	local & topical b-o-w, p-o-s
Leacock, Towell, & Voorhees, 1993	76% 72% 71%	neural net content vector naive bayes	2 sentence b-o-w
Mooney, 1996	72% 71%	naive bayes perceptron	2 sentence b-o-w

Table 6: Comparison to previous results for *line*

list are removed, capitalization is ignored, and words are stemmed. The two most accurate methods in this study proved to be a Naive Bayesian classifier (72%) and a perceptron (71%).

The *line* data was recently revisited by both (Towell and Voorhees, 1998) and (Leacock et al., 1998). The former take an ensemble approach where the output from two neural networks is combined; one network is based on a representation of local context while the other represents topical context. The latter utilize a Naive Bayesian classifier. In both cases context is represented by a set of topical and local features. The topical features correspond to the open-class words that occur in a two sentence window of context. The local features occur within a window of context three words to the left and right of the ambiguous word and include co-occurrence features as well as the part-of-speech of words in this window. These features are represented as *local & topical b-o-w* and *p-o-s* in Table 6. (Towell and Voorhees, 1998) report accuracy of 87% while (Leacock et al., 1998) report accuracy of 84%.

5 Discussion

The word sense disambiguation ensembles in this paper have the following characteristics:

- The members of the ensemble are Naive Bayesian classifiers,
- the context in which an ambiguous word occurs is represented by co-occurrence features extracted from varying sized windows of surrounding words,
- member classifiers are selected for the ensembles based on their performance relative to others with comparable window sizes, and
- a majority vote of the member classifiers determines the outcome of the ensemble.

Each point is discussed below.

5.1 Naive Bayesian classifiers

The Naive Bayesian classifier has emerged as a consistently strong performer in a wide range of comparative studies of machine learning methodologies. A recent survey of such results, as well as possible explanations for its success, is presented in (Domingos and Pazzani, 1997). A similar finding has emerged in word sense disambiguation, where a number of comparative studies have all reported that no method achieves significantly greater accuracy than the Naive Bayesian classifier (e.g., (Leacock et al., 1993), (Mooney, 1996), (Ng and Lee, 1996), (Pedersen and Bruce, 1997)).

In many ensemble approaches the member classifiers are learned with different algorithms that are trained with the same data. For example, an ensemble could consist of a decision tree, a neural network, and a nearest neighbor classifier, all of which are learned from exactly the same set of training data. This paper takes a different approach, where the learning algorithm is the same for all classifiers but the training data is different. This is motivated by the belief that there is more to be gained by varying the representation of context than there is from using many different learning algorithms on the same data. This is especially true in this domain since the Naive Bayesian classifier has a history of success and since there is no generally agreed upon set of features that have been shown to be optimal for word sense disambiguation.

5.2 Co–occurrence features

Shallow lexical features such as co–occurrences and collocations are recognized as potent sources of disambiguation information. While many other contextual features are often employed, it isn't clear that they offer substantial advantages. For example, (Ng and Lee, 1996) report that local collocations alone achieve 80% accuracy disambiguating *interest*, while their full set of features result in 87%. Preliminary experiments for this paper used feature sets that included collocates, co–occurrences, part–of–speech and grammatical information for surrounding words. However, it was clear that no combination of features resulted in disambiguation accuracy significantly higher than that achieved with co–occurrence features.

5.3 Selecting ensemble members

The most accurate classifier from each of nine possible category ranges is selected as a member of the ensemble. This is based on preliminary experiments that showed that member classifiers with similar sized windows of context often result in little or no overall improvement in disambiguation accuracy. This was expected since slight differences in window sizes lead to roughly equivalent representations of context and classifiers that have little opportunity for collective improvement. For example, an ensemble was created for *interest* using the nine classifiers in the range category (medium, medium). The accuracy of this ensemble was 84%, slightly less than the most accurate individual classifiers in that range which achieved accuracy of 86%.

Early experiments also revealed that an ensemble based on a majority vote of all 81 classifiers performed rather poorly. The accuracy for *interest* was approximately 81% and *line* was disambiguated with slightly less than 80% accuracy. The lesson taken from these results was that an ensemble should consist of classifiers that represent as differently sized windows of context as possible; this reduces the impact of redundant errors made by classifiers that represent very similarly sized windows of context. The ultimate success of an ensemble depends on the ability to select classifiers that make complementary errors. This is discussed in the context of combining part–of–speech taggers in (Brill and Wu, 1998). They provide a measure for assessing the complementarity of errors between two taggers that could be adapted for use with larger ensembles such as the one discussed here, which has nine members.

5.4 Disambiguation by majority vote

In this paper ensemble disambiguation is based on a simple majority vote of the nine member classifiers.

An alternative strategy is to weight each vote by the estimated joint probability found by the Naive Bayesian classifier. However, a preliminary study found that the accuracy of a Naive Bayesian ensemble using a weighted vote was poor. For *interest*, it resulted in accuracy of 83% while for *line* it was 82%. The simple majority vote resulted in accuracy of 89% for *interest* and 88% for *line*.

6 Future Work

A number of issues have arisen in the course of this work that merit further investigation.

The simplicity of the contextual representation can lead to large numbers of parameters in the Naive Bayesian model when using wide windows of context. Some combination of stop-lists and stemming could reduce the numbers of parameters and thus improve the overall quality of the parameter estimates made from the training data.

In addition to simple co–occurrence features, the use of collocation features seems promising. These are distinct from co–occurrences in that they are words that occur in close proximity to the ambiguous word and do so to a degree that is judged statistically significant.

One limitation of the majority vote in this paper is that there is no mechanism for dealing with outcomes where no sense gets a majority of the votes. This did not arise in this study but will certainly occur as Naive Bayesian ensembles are applied to larger sets of data.

Finally, further experimentation with the size of the windows of context seems warranted. The current formulation is based on a combination of intuition and empirical study. An algorithm to determine optimal windows sizes is currently under development.

7 Conclusions

This paper shows that word sense disambiguation accuracy can be improved by combining a number of simple classifiers into an ensemble. A methodology for formulating an ensemble of Naive Bayesian classifiers is presented, where each member classifier is based on co–occurrence features extracted from a different sized window of context. This approach was evaluated using the widely studied nouns *line* and *interest*, which are disambiguated with accuracy of 88% and 89%, which rivals the best previously published results.

8 Acknowledgments

This work extends ideas that began in collaboration with Rebecca Bruce and Janyce Wiebe. Claudia Leacock and Raymond Mooney provided valuable assistance with the *line* data. I am indebted to an anonymous reviewer who pointed out the importance of separate `test` and `devtest` data sets.

A preliminary version of this paper appears in (Pedersen, 2000).

References

E. Brill and J. Wu. 1998. Classifier combination for improved lexical disambiguation. In *Proceedings of the 36th Annual Meeting of the Association for Computational Linguistics*, Montreal.

R. Bruce and J. Wiebe. 1994. Word-sense disambiguation using decomposable models. In *Proceedings of the 32nd Annual Meeting of the Association for Computational Linguistics*, pages 139–146.

T. Dietterich. 1997. Machine–learning research: Four current directions. *AI magazine*, 18(4):97–136.

P. Domingos and M. Pazzani. 1997. On the optimality of the simple Bayesian classifier under zero–one loss. *Machine Learning*, 29:103–130.

R. Duda and P. Hart. 1973. *Pattern Classification and Scene Analysis*. Wiley, New York, NY.

W. Gale, K. Church, and D. Yarowsky. 1992. A method for disambiguating word senses in a large corpus. *Computers and the Humanities*, 26:415–439.

J. Henderson and E. Brill. 1999. Exploiting diversity in natural language processing: Combining parsers. In *Proceedings of the Fourth Conference on Empirical Methods in Natural Language Processing*, College Park, MD, June.

C. Leacock, G. Towell, and E. Voorhees. 1993. Corpus-based statistical sense resolution. In *Proceedings of the ARPA Workshop on Human Language Technology*, pages 260–265, March.

C. Leacock, M. Chodorow, and G. Miller. 1998. Using corpus statistics and WordNet relations for sense identification. *Computational Linguistics*, 24(1):147–165, March.

R. Mooney. 1996. Comparative experiments on disambiguating word senses: An illustration of the role of bias in machine learning. In *Proceedings of the Conference on Empirical Methods in Natural Language Processing*, pages 82–91, May.

H.T. Ng and H.B. Lee. 1996. Integrating multiple knowledge sources to disambiguate word sense: An exemplar-based approach. In *Proceedings of the 34th Annual Meeting of the Society for Computational Linguistics*, pages 40–47.

T. Pedersen and R. Bruce. 1997. A new supervised learning algorithm for word sense disambiguation. In *Proceedings of the Fourteenth National Conference on Artificial Intelligence*, pages 604–609, Providence, RI, July.

T. Pedersen, R. Bruce, and J. Wiebe. 1997. Sequential model selection for word sense disambiguation. In *Proceedings of the Fifth Conference on Applied Natural Language Processing*, pages 388–395, Washington, DC, April.

T. Pedersen. 2000. An ensemble approach to corpus–based word sense disambiguation. In *Proceedings of the Conference on Intelligent Text Processing and Computational Linguistics*, pages 205–218, Mexico City, February.

G. Towell and E. Voorhees. 1998. Disambiguating highly ambiguous words. *Computational Linguistics*, 24(1):125–146, March.

Generation in the Lambek Calculus Framework: an Approach with Semantic Proof Nets

Sylvain Pogodalla
sylvain.pogodalla@xrce.xerox.com
Xerox Research Centre Europe
6, chemin de Maupertuis
38240 Meylan — France

1 Introduction

The linear logic (Girard, 1987) provides a powerful framework to express categorial grammars (Ajdukiewicz, 1935) and Lambek calculus (Lambek, 1958), and a lot of work has presented proof nets uses for linguistic purposes, with a special look at proof nets for Lambek calculus (Roorda, 1991; Lamarche and Retoré, 1996). But they have mainly explored the syntactic capabilities of proof nets, describing parsing processes.

This paper wants to focus on the generation capabilities of proof nets thanks to their semantic readings as expressed in (de Groote and Retoré, 1996). The main features of our proposal consist in the use of proof nets for Lambek calculus, of the Curry-Howard isomorphism (Howard, 1980; Girard et al., 1988), of semantic proof nets with semantic expressions *à la* Montague (Montague, 1974; Dowty et al., 1981), and in an algorithm for proof search with a target proof net.

Unlike a previous proposal for generation in the Lambek calculus framework (Merenciano and Morrill, 1997), this point of view avoids the use of the λ-term unification to lead the generation process. And the algorithmic undecidability of this latter mechanism (from second order unification) does not occur any more.

In this work, we do not consider the choice of lexical items from a given semantic expression the syntactic realization of which we want to generate, but rather the way we can associate given lexical entries to fit the given semantic expression and generate a syntactically correct expression. For this purpose, we express our problem as a proof search one in (multiplicative) linear logic which is decidable. Moreover, we characterize the semantic recipes of lexical items that provide a polynomial solution for the generation process.

2 Multi Usage Proof Nets

2.1 Proof Nets

(Girard, 1987) introduced proof nets formalism as the natural deduction syntax for linear logic, also studied in (Retoré, 1993). They represent proofs in linear logic with more accuracy than sequential proofs: on one hand they are more compact, on the other hand they identify unessentially different sequential proofs (for instance in the order of the rules introduction).

From a one-sided sequent and a sequential proof of it, we obtain a proof net by unfolding every formula as a tree (whose nodes are the binary connectives and the leaves are formulas, e.g. atomic ones) and linking together the formulas occurring in the same axiom rule of the sequent calculus.

But proof nets have a more intrinsic definition that prevents us to come back every time to sequential proofs. They can be defined as graphs with a certain property (i.e. verifying a correctness criterion) such that every proof net with this property corresponds to a sequential proof and such that every proof net built from a sequential proof has this property. So that we do not present the sequent calculus but only the proof net calculus.

In this paper, we do not consider all the proof nets, but a part of the multiplicative ones: those of the intuitionistic implicative linear logic. In this case, sequents are made of several antecedent formulas, but only one succedent formula. To deal with the intuitionistic notion with proof nets (since we consider one-sided sequents), we use the notion of polarities with the *input* (•: *negative)* and the *output* (∘: *positive)* (Danos, 1990; Lamarche, 1995) to decorate formulas. Positive ones correspond to succedent formulas and negative ones to antecedent formulas.

Given the links of table 1, we define *proof structures* as graphs made of these links such that:

1. any premise of any link is connected to exactly one conclusion of some other link;
2. any conclusion of any link is connected to at most one premise of some other link;
3. input (resp. output) premises are connected to input (resp. output) conclusions of the same type.

Note that the two links for the negative and positive implications correspond to the two connectives of the linear logic: Tensor and Par, so that we name these links after these latter connectives. But in the following, only the graphical forms of the links play a role.

Proof nets are proof structures that respect the correctness criterion.

We mentioned the intrinsic definition of proof nets that enables the complete representation of sequential proofs. The cut elimination property of sequent calculus also appears intrinsically in the proof net formalism with a sim-

Table 1: Links

Name	*Axiom*	*Tensor*	*Par*	*Cut*
Link	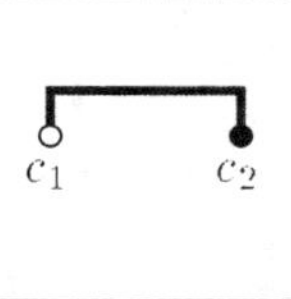	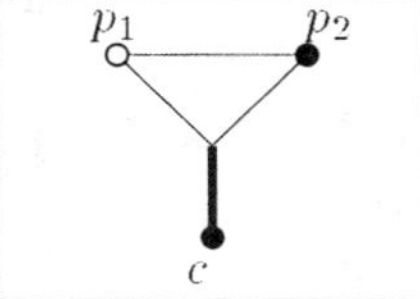	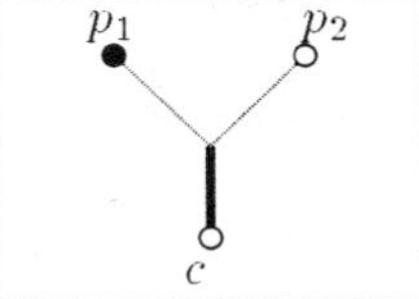	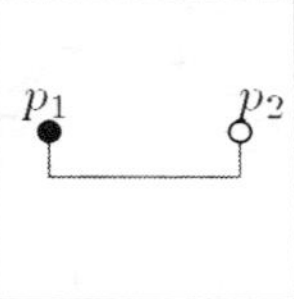
Premises	none	p_1, p_2	p_1, p_2	p_1, p_2
Conclusions	c_1, c_2	c	c	none
Types	$c_1 : A^+$ $c_2 : A^-$	$p_1 : A^+$ $p_2 : B^-$ $c : (A \multimap B)^-$	$p_1 : A^-$ $p_2 : B^+$ $c : (A \multimap B)^+$	$p_1 : A^-$ $p_2 : A^+$

Table 2: Cut-elimination rewriting rules

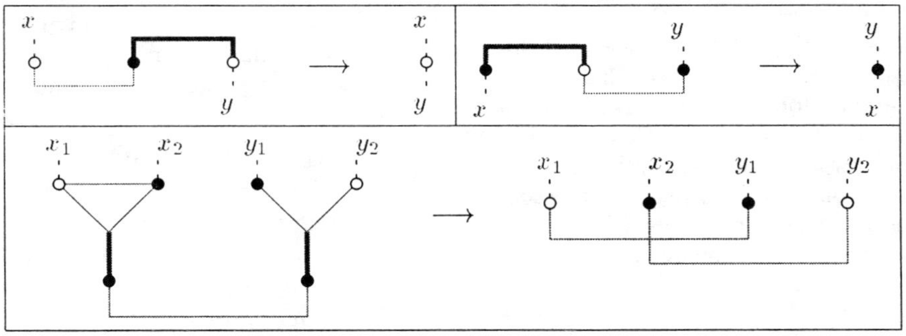

ple rewriting process described in table 2 (in case of complex formulas as in the third rewriting rule, those rules can apply again on the result and propagate until reaching atoms).

2.2 Syntactic Proof Nets

Definitions of proof nets for Lambek calculus first appeared in (Roorda, 1991). They naturally raised as Lambek calculus is an intuitionistic fragment of non commutative linar logic (with two linear implications: "\" on the left and "/" on the right), and the consequences on the proof net calculus we presented in section 2.1 are:

- we get two tensor links: one for the formulas $(B/A)^-$ (the one in table 1) and one for the formula $(B\backslash A)^-$ (just inverse the polarities of the premises). And two par links : one for the formula $(A\backslash B)^+$ and one for $(A/B)^+$ (idem);
- formulas in Lambek's sequents are ordered, so that conclusions of the proof nets are cyclically ordered and axiom links may not cross.

If T_p is the set of basic types (e.g. $S, NP \ldots$), the set T of syntactic types follows $T ::= T_p|T\backslash T|T/T$.

Note that from a syntactic category, we can unfold the formula to obtain a graph which only lacks axiom links to become a proof structure. So that the parsing process in this framework is, given the syntactic categories of the items and their order, to put non crossing axiom links such that the proof structure is a proof net. It means there is a proof of S given types in a certain order. For technical reasons, the order of the conclusions (i.e. the types used) in the proof net to prove S is the reverse order of the words associated to these types.

As an example, with the lexicon of table 3, proving that *John lives in Paris* is a correct sentence leads to find axiom links between the atoms in the figure 1(a). Figure 1(b) shows it actually happens and proves the syntactic correctness of the sentence.

Table 3: Lexicon

lexical entry	syntaxic category
John	NP
Paris	NP
lives	$NP\backslash S$
in	$(S\backslash S)/NP$

2.3 Semantic Proof Nets

In this section, we present how (de Groote and Retoré, 1996) propose to use proof nets as semantic recipes. As a slight difference with this work, we only deal in this paper with semantic recipes that correspond to *linear* λ-terms in the Montague's semantics framework.

The idea of expressing the semantics with proof nets refers to the fact that both the λ-terms (with the Curry-Howard isomorphism) and the proof nets represent proofs of intuitionistic implicative linear logic. And indeed, the linear λ-terms may be encoded as proof nets. On the other hand, given an intuitionistic implicative proof net, a simple algorithm (given in (de Groote and

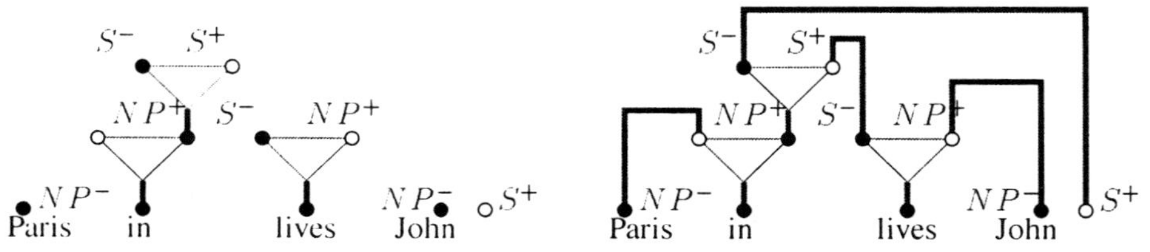

(a) Unfolding of the syntactic types

(b) Matching the dual atoms to obtain a proof net

Figure 1: Parsing of *John lives in Paris*

Retoré, 1996), based on (Lamarche, 1995)'s dependency paths), we can obtain a λ-term.

Then, instead of associating a λ-term to a lexical entry, we can associate a proof net. For instance, on the semantic side, we can use the Montagovian types ϵ and t and typed constants. Of course, we want to keep the compositionality principle of Montague's semantics that maps any syntactic association rule with a semantic association rule. We express it in a straightforward way with the following homomorphism (for as many basic categories as required):

$$\mathcal{H}(NP) = \epsilon \quad \mathcal{H}(A\backslash B) = \mathcal{H}(A) \multimap \mathcal{H}(B)$$
$$\mathcal{H}(S) = t \quad \mathcal{H}(A/B) = \mathcal{H}(B) \multimap \mathcal{H}(A)$$

And for a lexical item, given its syntactic type, we assume its semantic proof net to verify:

- the type of its unique output conclusion is the homomorphic image of the syntactic type;
- its input conclusions (if any) are decorated with typed constants.

An example of such a lexicon is given in table 4.

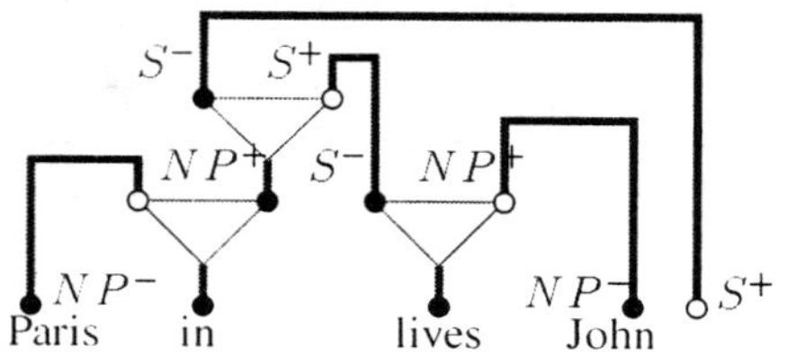

Figure 2: Syntactic proof net for *John lives in Paris*

Let us illustrate the process on a short example. We use the lexicon of table 4 to parse the sentence *John lives in Paris*. The first thing is to define with the syntactic categories of the different lexical items the syntactic proof net of figure 2. It provides the way we should compose the semantic recipes of each lexical item: we take its homomorphic image as in figure 4(a), and we substitute to every input its semantic definition with cut-links.

Then the cut-elimination on the resulting proof net gives a new proof net (on figure 4(b)) we can use as the *semantic analysis* of *John lives in Paris*. If necessary, we can come back to the λ-term expression:(**in p**)(**live j**).

3 Generation: Stating the Problem

Let us now consider the problem of generation. We have a given semantic proof net (like the one in figure 4(b)) and we want to gather syntactic entries with axiom links such that:

1. this yields a correct (syntactic) proof net;
2. the meaning of the resulting proof net matches the given semantic expression.

As we already said it, we assume that we have some lexical entries, and we try to make the generation with these entries, each one used once and only once.

Thus, if we define:

- Π_0 the semantic proof net of the expression we want to generate;
- Π_i the semantic proof nets associated to the given lexical entries i we use;
- T_i the unfolding in proof structure of the syntactic formula of the lexical item i;
- F the forest made of the syntactic trees of all the considered lexical entries plus the output (the type we want to derive).

The generation problem (see figure 5) is to find a matching M of atomic formulas of F such that:

1. F endowed with M (let us call this proof structure F') is a correct proof net;
2. when cut-linking $H(F')$ with the Π_i, and eliminating these cuts, we obtain Π_0.

This problem is not an original one: making proof search with proof nets always leads to look for matching between atomic formulas of opposite polarities. So that an answer to this problem would consist in taking F and try every possible matching. This brute-force technique would of course appear essentially inefficient, and our purpose is to use everything we know to prune the search domain.

Nevertheless, note that even with such an algorithm, we already reach the decidability (because the finitness of the number of the matchings) *without* making any assumption on the form of the semantic entries (neither on the order of the associated λ-terms, nor the presence of a free variable). And we want to keep these good properties in our algorithm.

Table 4: Lexicon

lexical entry	syntaxic category	associated λ-term	semantic proof net
John	NP	**j**	Π_{John} (cf. figure 3(a))
Mary	NP	**m**	Π_{Mary} (cf. figure 3(b))
Paris	NP	**p**	Π_{Paris} (cf. figure 3(c))
Lives	$NP\backslash S$	$\lambda x.\textbf{live}\ x$	Π_{live} (cf. figure 3(d))
In	$(S\backslash S)/NP$	$\lambda x.\lambda y.(\textbf{in}\ x)y$	Π_{in} (cf. figure 3(e))
Seeks	$(NP\backslash S)/(((NP\backslash S)/NP)\backslash(NP\backslash S))$	$\lambda x.(\textbf{try}(x\textbf{find}))$	(cf. figure 3(f))

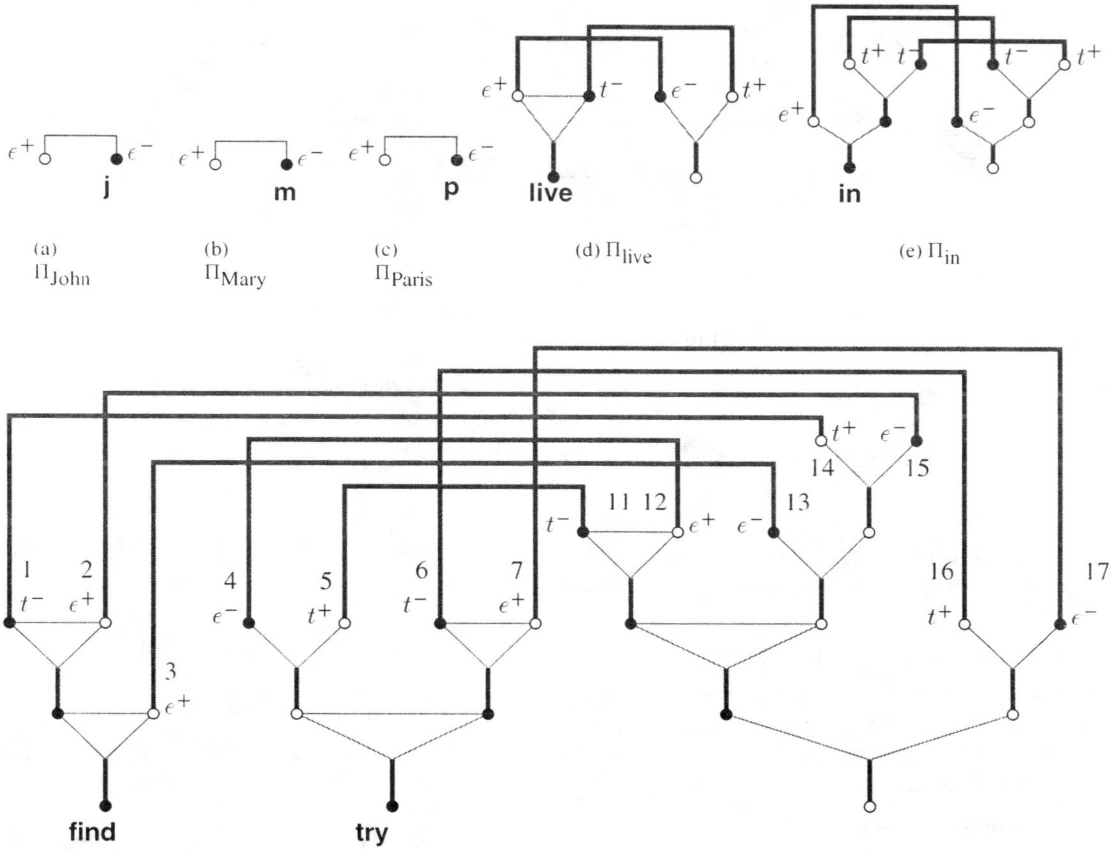

(a) Π_{John}

(b) Π_{Mary}

(c) Π_{Paris}

(d) Π_{live}

(e) Π_{in}

(f) Π_{seeks}

Figure 3: Semantic proof nets of the lexicon of table 4

4 Cut-elimination as Matrix Computation

This section first establishes some equivalent relations between cut-elimination on proof nets and matrix equations. We then show how to use these equations in the generation process and how we can solve them. It enables us to characterize the properties required by the semantic proof nets to have a polynomial resolution of the generation process.

4.1 Principles

First, as expressed in (Girard, 1989) and reformulated in (Retoré, 1990; Girard, 1993; Girard, 1995), we state the algebraic representation of cut-elimination on proof nets. Due to lack of space, we can not develop it, but the principle is to express cut-elimination between axioms with incidence matrices and paths in graphs.

Let us consider a proof net $\overline{U}$. We denote by $(\epsilon_i)_{1\leq i\leq s}$ all the vertices taking place for atoms in $\overline{U}$. We can define U the incidence matrix of *axiom links*, σ the incidence matrix of cut links (we assume without loss of generality that they happen only between axiom links), and Π the incidence matrix of axiom links of $\overline{\Pi}$ where $\overline{\Pi}$ is the proof net resulting from all the cut eliminations on $\overline{U}$.

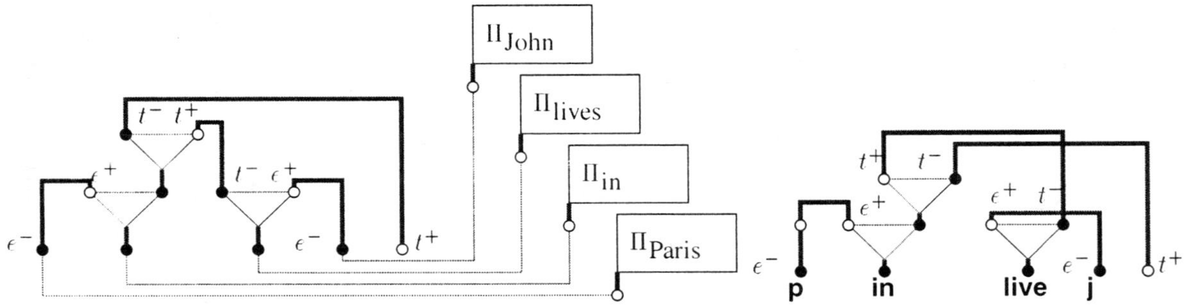

(a) Before cut-elimination

(b) After cut-elimination

Figure 4: Semantic proof nets for (**in p**)(**live j**)

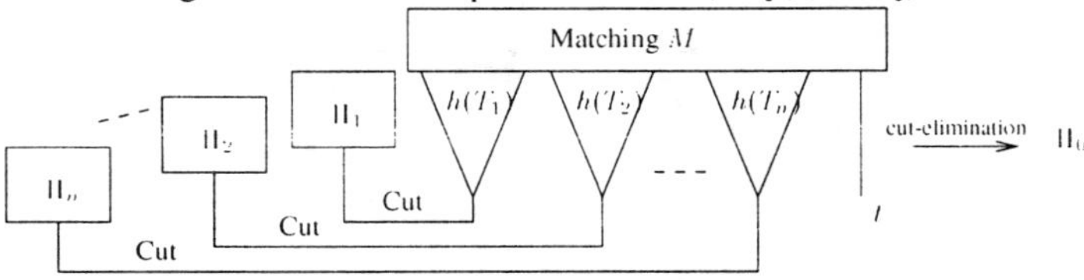

Figure 5: The generation problem

Then we have (Girard, 1989):

$$\Pi = (1 - \sigma^2)U(1 + \sum_1^{\infty}(\sigma U)^k)(1 - \sigma^2) \qquad (1)$$

Moreover, since (σU) is nilpotent, $(1+\sum_1^{\infty}(\sigma U)^k)$ is inversible, and its inverse is $(1 - \sigma U)$. The next section make explicit the relation (1) with a special choice of the base (ϵ_i).

4.2 Matrix Relation for Cut Elimination

In the problem we are dealing with, we know $\overline{\Pi}$ and some of the axiom links in $\overline{U}$. Let us assume that $\forall i \in [1, p]$, both ϵ_i and $B(\epsilon_i)$ [1] are not cut-linked in $\overline{U}$ (this assumption entails no loss of generality).

4.3 Expressing the Reduction of U into Π

In this section, we want to give a relation equivalent to (1) which focuses on some axiom links we are interested in.

As mentioned in section 4.2, we can consider the (ϵ_i) such that in $\overline{U}$:

- $\forall i \in [1, p], \epsilon_i$ is not cut-linked (then, because of the hypothesis made in section 4.2, $B(\epsilon_i)$ is cut-linked);
- $\forall i \in [p+1, p+m], \epsilon_i$ is cut-linked but $B(\epsilon_i)$ is not cut-linked;
- $\forall i \in [p+m+1, p+m+n]$, both ϵ_i and $B(\epsilon_i)$ are cut-linked.

Note: Remember we assume that there is no axiom link such that both its conclusions are not cut-linked. So $p = m$.

[1] $B(\epsilon)$ is the atom in $\overline{U}$ such that there is an axiom link between ϵ and $B(\epsilon)$.

Then in this base, we express the matrices (every axiom link of $\overline{U}$ has at least one of its conclusion involved in a cut link):

$$U = \begin{bmatrix} 0 & U_1 & 0 \\ {}^tU_1 & 0 & 0 \\ 0 & 0 & U_3 \end{bmatrix} \qquad \sigma = \begin{bmatrix} 0 & 0 & 0 \\ 0 & \sigma_1 & \sigma_2 \\ 0 & \sigma_3 & \sigma_4 \end{bmatrix}$$

$$\Pi = \begin{bmatrix} \Pi_1 & 0 & 0 \\ 0 & 0 & 0 \\ 0 & 0 & 0 \end{bmatrix}$$

If we define $A = ({}^tU_1\Pi_1 - \sigma_1 {}^tU_1)U_1$ and $X = U_3(1 - \sigma_4 U_3)^{-1}$, we can state the theorem:

Theorem 1 *Let $\overline{U}$ be a correct proof net reducing in $Res(\sigma, U)$ after cut elimination. These relations are equivalent:*

- $Res(\sigma, U) = (1 - \sigma^2)U(1 - \sigma U)^{-1}(1 - \sigma^2)$
- $({}^tU_1\Pi_1 - \sigma_1 {}^tU_1)U_1 = \sigma_2 U_3(1 - \sigma_4 U_3)^{-1}\, {}^t\sigma_2$
- $A = {}^t\sigma_2 X \sigma_2$ *and* $U_3 = X^{-1} + \sigma_4$.

Of course, all the terms are defined.

We base the proof search algorithm corresponding to the generation process we are dealing with on this third relation, as explained in the next sections.

4.4 Solving the Equations

In this section (proof search oriented), we consider that the axiom links we are looking for are those whose two conclusions are involved in cut links. That is we want to complete U_3. As in the previous section we proceeded by equivalence, solving the equation (1) correponds to solving the equation

$$A = \sigma_2 X\, {}^t\sigma_2 \qquad (2)$$

in X with X inversible. Then, we have to solve

$$U_3 = X^{-1} + \sigma_4$$

such that ${}^tU_3 = U_3$ and $U_3^2 = 1$.

Let $\sigma_2 \in \mathcal{M}_{m,n}(\mathbb{R})$, $X = (x_{i,j}) \in \mathcal{M}_n(\mathbb{R})$ and $A \in \mathcal{M}_n(\mathbb{R})$. Let the two sequences $1 \leq i_1 < \ldots < i_l \leq m$ and $1 \leq j_1 < \ldots < j_l \leq m$ be such that with $(a, b) \in [1, m] \times [1, n]$, $E_{ab} = (\delta_{ia}\delta_{jb})_{i,j \in [1,m]\times[1,n]}$ [2]

$$\sigma_2 = \sum_l E_{i_l j_l} = \sum_l (\delta_{i i_l}\delta_{j j_l})_{i,j}$$

In other words, $\sigma_{2ij} = 1 \Leftrightarrow \exists l_1 \in [1, l] \wedge i = i_{l_1} \wedge j = j_{l_1}$.

Then

$$\begin{aligned} \sigma_2 X\, {}^t\sigma_2 &= \left(\sum_{l_1=1}^{l} E_{i_{l_1} j_{l_1}}\right) * X * {}^t\left(\sum_{l_2=1}^{l} E_{i_{l_2} j_{l_2}}\right) \\ &= \sum_{l_1=1}^{l}\sum_{l_2=1}^{l} (\delta_{i i_{l_1}} x_{j_{l_1} j_{l_2}} \delta_{j i_{l_2}})_{1 \leq i,j \leq m} \end{aligned}$$

It follows that if $A = (a_{ij})_{i,j} = \sigma_2 X\, {}^t\sigma_2$ then

$$\forall (l_1, l_2) \in [1, l]^2, x_{j_{l_1} j_{l_2}} = a_{i_{l_1} i_{l_2}}. \qquad (3)$$

A consequence of this result is that if $\sigma_4 = 0$, then $l = n$ and *we determine X completely with relation* (3), *and then the same for U_3*. This configuration correspond to the fact that in the (given) semantic proof nets, no output contains the two conclusions of a same axiom link. In this latter case, the computation is not so simple and should be mixed with word order constraints.

5 Example

Let us process on an example the previous results. We still use the lexicon of table 4, and we want to generate (if possible) a sentence whose meaning is given by the proof net of figure 7: (**try**(**find j**))**m**.

We first need to associate every atom with an index (in the figures, we only indicate a number i beside the atom to express it is e_i). Of course, we have to know how to recognize the e_i that are the same in U (figure 6) and in Π (figure 7). This can be done by looking at the typed constants decorating the input conclusions (for the moment, we don't have a general procedure in the complex cases).

We also assume in this numbering that we know which of the atoms in $H(F)$ are linked to t^+ (the unique output). In our case where $\sigma_4 = 0$, it is not a problem to make such a statement. In other cases, the complexity would increase polynomially.

Then, the given matrices are:

$$U_1 = \begin{bmatrix} 0&0&0&1&0&0&0&0&0&0 \\ 0&0&0&0&1&0&0&0&0&0 \\ 0&0&1&0&0&0&0&0&0&0 \\ 0&1&0&0&0&0&0&0&0&0 \\ 1&0&0&0&0&0&0&0&0&0 \\ 0&0&0&0&0&1&0&0&0&0 \\ 0&0&0&0&0&0&1&0&0&0 \\ 0&0&0&0&0&0&0&1&0&0 \\ 0&0&0&0&0&0&0&0&1&0 \\ 0&0&0&0&0&0&0&0&0&1 \end{bmatrix} \quad \Pi_1 = \begin{bmatrix} 0&0&0&0&1&0&0&0&0&0 \\ 0&0&0&1&0&0&0&0&0&0 \\ 0&0&0&0&0&0&0&0&1&0 \\ 0&1&0&0&0&0&0&0&0&0 \\ 1&0&0&0&0&0&0&0&0&0 \\ 0&0&0&0&0&0&0&1&0&0 \\ 0&0&0&0&0&0&0&0&0&1 \\ 0&0&0&0&0&1&0&0&0&0 \\ 0&0&1&0&0&0&0&0&0&0 \\ 0&0&0&0&0&0&1&0&0&0 \end{bmatrix}$$

$$\sigma_1 = \begin{bmatrix} 0&0&0&0&0&0&0&0&0&0 \\ 0&0&0&0&0&0&0&0&0&0 \\ 0&0&0&0&0&0&0&0&0&0 \\ 0&0&0&0&0&0&0&0&0&0 \\ 0&0&0&0&0&0&0&0&0&0 \\ 0&0&0&0&0&0&0&1&0&0 \\ 0&0&0&0&0&0&0&0&0&0 \\ 0&0&0&0&0&1&0&0&0&0 \\ 0&0&0&0&0&0&0&0&0&0 \\ 0&0&0&0&0&0&0&0&0&0 \end{bmatrix} \quad \sigma_2 = \begin{bmatrix} 0&0&0&0&1&0&0&0 \\ 0&0&0&1&0&0&0&0 \\ 1&0&0&0&0&0&0&0 \\ 0&1&0&0&0&0&0&0 \\ 0&0&1&0&0&0&0&0 \\ 0&0&0&0&0&0&0&0 \\ 0&0&0&0&0&1&0&0 \\ 0&0&0&0&0&0&0&0 \\ 0&0&0&0&0&0&1&0 \\ 0&0&0&0&0&0&0&1 \end{bmatrix}$$

So

$$A = (U_1^{-1}\Pi_1 - \sigma_1\, {}^tU_1)\, {}^tU_1^{-1} = \begin{bmatrix} 0&0&0&1&0&0&0&0&0&0 \\ 0&0&0&0&1&0&0&0&0&0 \\ 0&0&0&0&0&0&0&0&1&0 \\ 1&0&0&0&0&0&0&0&0&0 \\ 0&1&0&0&0&0&0&0&0&0 \\ 0&0&0&0&0&0&0&0&0&0 \\ 0&0&0&0&0&0&0&0&0&1 \\ 0&0&0&0&0&0&0&0&0&0 \\ 0&0&1&0&0&0&0&0&0&0 \\ 0&0&0&0&0&0&1&0&0&0 \end{bmatrix}$$

According to the definition of the (i_l) and the (j_l) families such that $\sigma_2 = \sum_l E_{i_l j_l}$, we have:

i_l	3	4	5	2	1	7	9	10
j_l	1	2	3	4	5	6	7	8

Then

$$\begin{array}{lll} x_{5,2} = 1 = a_{1,4} & x_{2,5} = 1 = a_{4,1} & x_{4,3} = 1 = a_{2,5} \\ x_{3,4} = 1 = a_{5,2} & x_{1,7} = 1 = a_{3,9} & x_{7,1} = 1 = a_{9,3} \\ x_{6,8} = 1 = a_{7,10} & x_{8,6} = 1 = a_{10,7} & \end{array}$$

and in this case $\sigma_4 = 0$, so according to the preceeding notes X is completely determined and

$$X = U_3 = \begin{bmatrix} 0&0&0&0&0&0&1&0 \\ 0&0&0&0&1&0&0&0 \\ 0&0&0&1&0&0&0&0 \\ 0&0&1&0&0&0&0&0 \\ 0&1&0&0&0&0&0&0 \\ 0&0&0&0&0&0&0&1 \\ 1&0&0&0&0&0&0&0 \\ 0&0&0&0&0&1&0&0 \end{bmatrix}$$

We can add this matching to the syntactic forest of figure 8(a) (do not forget that U_3 represents the edges between e_i with $i \in [17, 22]$) and obtain on F the matching of figure 8(b).

[2] $\delta_{ij} = \begin{cases} 1 \text{ if } i = j \\ 0 \text{ if } i \neq j \end{cases}$

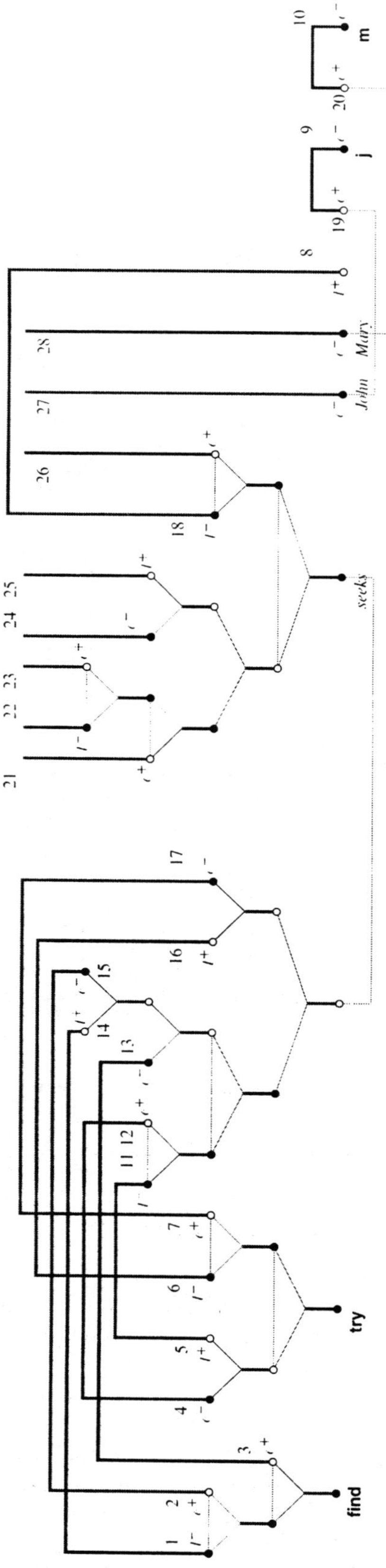

Figure 6: Marking atoms on U

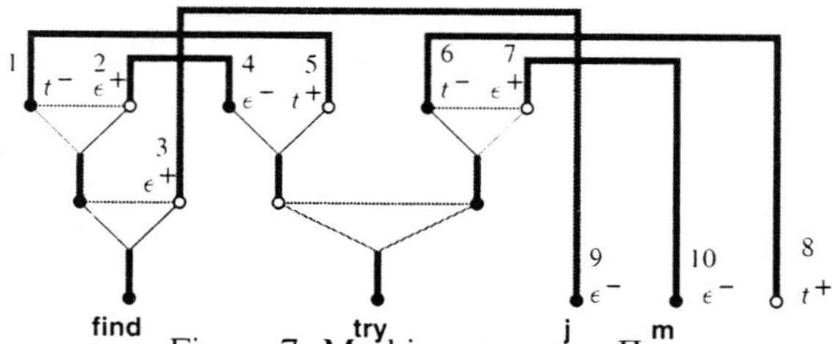

Figure 7: Marking atoms on Π

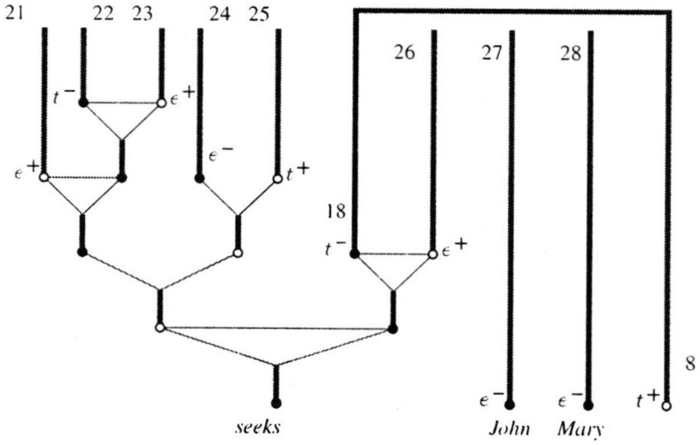

(a) The syntactic forest

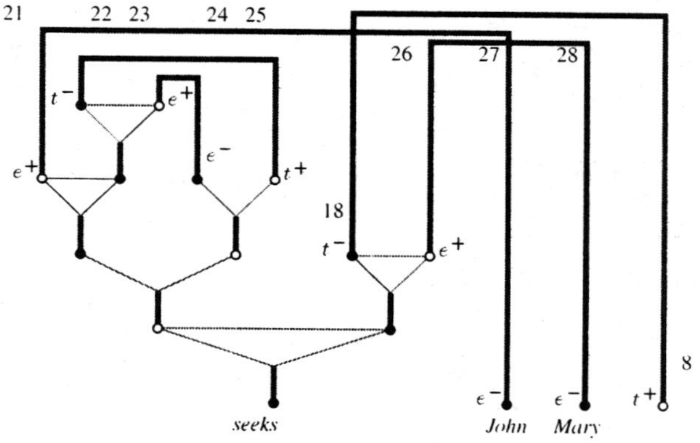

(b) The syntactic forest endowed with the matching described by U_3

Figure 8: Applying the matching on the syntactic forest

We still have to ensure the correctness of this proof net (because we add all the tensor and par links), but it has a quadratic complexity (less than the matrix computation). In this case, it is correct.

Note:

- Actually, this only gives us the axiom links. It still necessitates to compute the word order to have no crossing axiom link. This can be done from the axiom links easier than quadratic time: it is a well-bracketing check. Here, it is easy to see that putting the *John* item on the left would achieve the result of *Mary seeks John*.

- The choice of *seeks* and its high order type (for intensionnality) shows there is no limitation on the order of the λ-term.

6 Conclusion

We took advantage of proof nets on the semantic point of view and we expressed the generation process as a guided proof search. On top of keeping the decidability property of this framework, we characterized the semantic proof nets that enable a polynomial time process.

Such properties are crucial because it is the central part of the generation process (considering Lambek calculus). But there are other things left to look at. As the very next steps, we should work on the atoms numbering and the choice of the lexical items. Appropriate interactions between word order contraints and matrix resolution in the hard case should also be considered. Moreover, another point is to benefit from the power of linear logic and deal with non linear λ-terms.

Finally, since different extensions of Lambek calculus based on proof nets (Moortgat, 1996; Lecomte and Retoré, 1995) have been considered, we hope our proposal and its good properties to apply to other linguistic approaches.

Acknowledgments

I would like to thank Christian Retoré who pointed out to me Girard's algebraic interpretation of the cut elimination.

References

Kazimierz Ajdukiewicz. 1935. Die syntaktische Konnexitat. *Studia Philosophica*, 1:1–27. English translation in Storrs McCall (ed), *Polish Logic 1920-1939*, Oxford University Press, pp. 207-231.

Vincent Danos. 1990. *Une Application de la Logique Linéaire à l'Étude des Processus de Normalisation (principalement du λ-calcul)*. Ph.D. thesis, Université Paris VII, June.

Philippe de Groote and Chritian Retoré. 1996. On the semantic readings of proof-nets. In Glyn Morrill Geert-Jan Kruijff and Dick Oehrle, editors, *Formal Grammar*, pages 57–70, Prague, August. FoLLI.

David R. Dowty, Robert E. Wall, and Stanley Peters. 1981. *Introduction to Montague Semantics*. Kluwer Academic Publishers.

Jean-Yves Girard, Yves Lafont, and P. Taylor. 1988. *Proofs and Types*. Cambridge Tracts in Theoretical Computer Science 7. Cambridge University Press.

Jean-Yves Girard. 1987. Linear logic. *Theoretical Computer Science*, 50:1–102.

Jean-Yves Girard. 1989. Geometry of interaction I: Interpretation of system F. In C. Bonotto, R. Ferro, S. Valentini, and A. Zanardo, editors, *Logic Colloquium '88*, pages 221–260. North-Holland.

Jean-Yves Girard. 1993. Linear logic: Its syntax and semantics. In J.-Y. Girard NS Y. Lafont and L. Regnier, editors, *Advances in Linear Logic*, Ithaca, New York, June.

Jean-Yves Girard. 1995. Geometry of interaction III: The general case. In J.-Y. Girard, Y. Lafont, and L. Regnier, editors, *Advances in Linear Logic*, pages 329–389. Cambridge University Press. Proceedings of the Workshop on Linear Logic, Ithaca, New York, June 1993.

W. A. Howard, 1980. *To H. B. Curry: Essays on combinatory logic, Lambda Calculus and Formalism*, chapter The Formulæ-as-Types Notion of Construction, pages 479–490. Academic Press.

François Lamarche and Christian Retoré. 1996. Proofnets for the lambek calculus – an overview. In V. Michele Abrusci and Claudio Casadio, editors, *Proceedings 1996 Roma Workshop. Proofs and Linguistic Categories*, pages 241–262. Editrice CLUEB, Bologna, April.

François Lamarche. 1995. Games semantics for full propositional linear logic. In *Proceedings, Tenth Annual IEEE Symposium on Logic in Computer Science*, pages 464–473, San Diego, California, 26–29 June. IEEE Computer Society Press.

Joachim Lambek. 1958. The mathematics of sentence structure. *American Mathematical Monthly*, 65(3):154–170.

Alain Lecomte and Christian Retoré. 1995. Pomset logic as an alternative categorial grammar. In *Formal Grammar*, Barcelona.

Josep M. Merenciano and Glyn Morrill. 1997. Generation as deduction on labelled proof nets. In Christian Retoré, editor, *Proceedings of the 1st International Conference on Logical Aspects of Computational Linguistics (LACL-96)*, volume 1328 of *LNAI*, pages 310–328, Berlin, September23–25 . Springer.

Richard Montague. 1974. *Formal Philosophy: Selected Papers of Richard Montague*. Yale University Press, New Haven, CT.

Michael Moortgat. 1996. Categorial type logics. In Johan van Benthem and Alice ter Meulen, editors, *Handbook of Logic and Language*, pages 5–91. Elsevier Science Publishers, Amsterdam.

Christian Retoré. 1990. A note on turbo cut elimination. Manuscript, September.

Christian Retoré. 1993. *Réseaux et séquents ordonnés*. Ph.D. thesis, University of Paris VII.

Dirk Roorda. 1991. *Resource Logics: Proof-theoretical Investigations*. Ph.D. thesis, University of Amsterdam, September.

Word-for-Word Glossing with Contextually Similar Words

Patrick Pantel and Dekang Lin
Department of Computer Science
University of Manitoba
Winnipeg, Manitoba R3T 2N2 Canada
{ppantel, lindek}@cs.umanitoba.ca

Abstract

Many corpus-based machine translation systems require parallel corpora. In this paper, we present a word-for-word glossing algorithm that requires only a source language corpus. To gloss a word, we first identify its similar words that occurred in the same context in a large corpus. We then determine the gloss by maximizing the similarity between the set of contextually similar words and the different translations of the word in a bilingual thesaurus.

1. Introduction

Word-for-word glossing is the process of directly translating each word or term in a document without considering the word order. Automating this process would benefit many NLP applications. For example, in cross-language information retrieval, glossing a document often provides a sufficient translation for humans to comprehend the key concepts. Furthermore, a glossing algorithm can be used for lexical selection in a full-fledged machine translation (MT) system.

Many corpus-based MT systems require parallel corpora (Brown et al., 1990; Brown et al., 1991; Gale and Church, 1991; Resnik, 1999). Kikui (1999) used a word sense disambiguation algorithm and a non-parallel bilingual corpus to resolve translation ambiguity.

In this paper, we present a word-for-word glossing algorithm that requires only a source language corpus. The intuitive idea behind our algorithm is the following. Suppose *w* is a word to be translated. We first identify a set of words similar to *w* that occurred in the same context as *w* in a large corpus. We then use this set (called the **contextually similar words** of *w*) to select a translation for *w*. For example, the contextually similar words of *duty* in *fiduciary duty* include *responsibility*, *obligation*, *role*, ... This list is then used to select a translation for *duty*.

In the next section, we describe the resources required by our algorithm. In Section 3, we present an algorithm for constructing the contextually similar words of a word in a context. Section 4 presents the word-for-word glossing algorithm and Section 5 describes the group similarity metric used in our algorithm. In Section 6, we present some experimental results and finally, in Section 7, we conclude with a discussion of future work.

2. Resources

The input to our algorithm includes a collocation database (Lin, 1998b) and a corpus-based thesaurus (Lin, 1998a), which are both available on the Internet[1]. In addition, we require a bilingual thesaurus. Below, we briefly describe these resources.

2.1. Collocation database

Given a word *w* in a dependency relationship (such as *subject* or *object*), the collocation database can be used to retrieve the words that occurred in that relationship with *w*, in a large corpus, along with their frequencies[2]. Figure 1 shows excerpts of the entries in the collocation database for the words *corporate*, *duty*, and *fiduciary*. The database contains a total of 11 million unique dependency relationships.

---

[1] Available at www.cs.umanitoba.ca/~lindek/depdb.htm and www.cs.umanitoba.ca/~lindek/simdb.htm

[2] We use the term *collocation* to refer to a pair of words that occur in a dependency relationship (rather than the linear proximity of a pair of words).

Table 1. Clustered similar words of *duty* as given by (Lin, 1998a).

CLUSTER	CLUSTERED SIMILAR WORDS OF *DUTY* (WITH SIMILARITY SCORE)
1	responsibility 0.16, obligation 0.109, task 0.101, function 0.098, role 0.091, post 0.087, position 0.086, job 0.084, chore 0.08, mission 0.08, assignment 0.079, liability 0.077, ...
2	tariff 0.091, restriction 0.089, tax 0.086, regulation 0.085, requirement 0.081, procedure 0.079, penalty 0.079, quota 0.074, rule 0.07, levy 0.061, ...
3	fee 0.085, salary 0.081, pay 0.064, fine 0.058
4	personnel 0.073, staff 0.073
5	training 0.072, work 0.064, exercise 0.061
6	privilege 0.069, right 0.057, license 0.056

2.2. Corpus-based thesaurus

Using the collocation database, Lin used an unsupervised method to construct a corpus-based thesaurus (Lin, 1998a) consisting of 11839 nouns, 3639 verbs and 5658 adjectives/adverbs. Given a word *w*, the thesaurus returns a clustered list of similar words of *w* along with their similarity to *w*. For example, the clustered similar words of *duty* are shown in Table 1.

2.3. Bilingual thesaurus

Using the corpus-based thesaurus and a bilingual dictionary, we manually constructed a bilingual thesaurus. The entry for a source language word *w* is constructed by manually associating one or more clusters of similar words of *w* to each candidate translation of *w*. We refer to the assigned clusters as **Words Associated with a Translation (WAT)**. For example, Figure 2 shows an excerpt of our *English/French* bilingual thesaurus for the words *account* and *duty*.

Although the WAT assignment is a manual process, it is a considerably easier task than providing lexicographic definitions. Also, we only require entries for source language words that have multiple translations. In Section 7, we discuss a method for automatically assigning the WATs.

corporate:	
modifier-of:	client 196, debt 236, development 179, fee 6, function 16, headquarter 316, IOU 128, levy 3, liability 14, manager 203, market 195, obligation 1, personnel 7, profit 595, responsibility 27, rule 7, staff 113, tax 201, training 2, vice president 231, ...
duty:	
object-of:	assume 177, breach 111, carry out 71, do 114, have 257, impose 114, perform 151, ...
subject-of:	affect 4, apply 6, include 42, involve 8, keep 5, officer 22, protect 8, require 13, ...
adj-modifier:	active 202, additional 46, administrative 44, fiduciary 317, official 66, other 83, ...
fiduciary:	
modifier-of:	act 2, behavior 1, breach 2, claim 1, company 2, duty 317, irresponsibility 2, obligation 32, requirement 1, responsibility 89, role 2, ...

Figure 1. Excepts of entries in the collocation database for the words *corporate*, *duty*, and *fiduciary*.

account:	
1. compte:	fund, deposit, loan, asset, portfolio, investment, transaction, payment, saving, money, contract, Budget, reserve, security, contribution, debt, property, holding, interest, bond, plan, business, ...
2. rapport:	report, statement, testimony, card, story, record, document, data, information, view, check, figure, article, description, estimate, assessment, number, statistic, comment, letter, picture, note, ...
duty:	
1. devoir:	responsibility, obligation, task, function, role, post, position, job, chore, mission, assignment, liability, ...
2. taxe:	tariff, restriction, tax, regulation, requirement, procedure, penalty, quota, rule, levy, ...

WAT for *compte*

Figure 2. Bilingual thesaurus entries for *account* and *duty*.

3. Contextually Similar Words

The contextually similar words of a word *w* are words similar to the intended meaning of *w* in its context. Figure 3 gives the data flow diagram for our algorithm for identifying the contextually similar words of *w*. Data are represented by ovals, external resources by double ovals and processes by rectangles.

By parsing a sentence with *Minipar*[3], we extract the dependency relationships involving *w*. For each dependency relationship, we retrieve

[3] Available at www.cs.umanitoba.ca/~lindek/minipar.htm

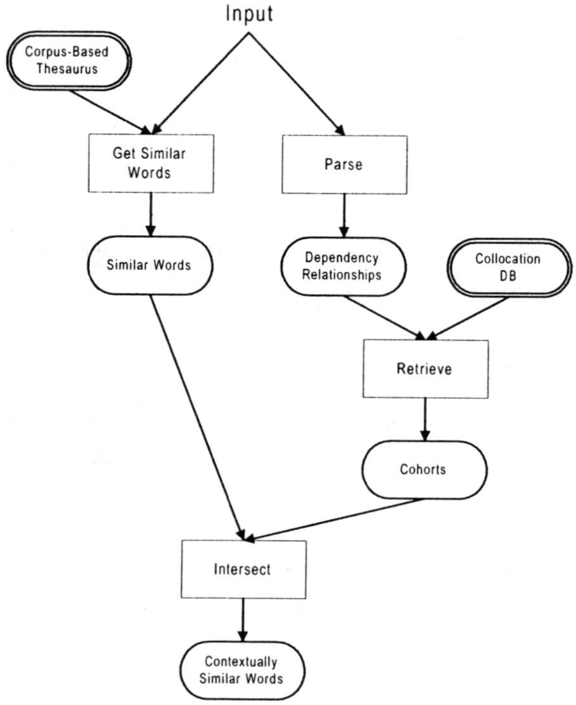

Figure 3. Data flow diagram for identifying the contextually similar words of a word in context.

from the collocation database the words that occurred in the same dependency relationship as *w*. We refer to this set of words as the **cohort** of *w* for that dependency relationship. Consider the word *duty* in the contexts *corporate duty* and *fiduciary duty*. The cohort of *duty* in *corporate duty* consists of nouns modified by *corporate* in Figure 1 (e.g. client, debt, development, ...) and the cohort of *duty* in *fiduciary duty* consists of nouns modified by *fiduciary* in Figure 1 (e.g. act, behaviour, breach, ...).

Intersecting the set of similar words and the cohort then forms the set of contextually similar words of *w*. For example, Table 2 shows the contextually similar words of *duty* in the contexts *corporate duty* and *fiduciary duty*. The words in the first row are retrieved by intersecting the words in Table 1 with the nouns modified by *corporate* in Figure 1. Similarly, the second row represents the intersection of the words in Table 1 and the nouns modified by *fiduciary* in Figure 1.

The first set of contextually similar words in Table 2 contains words that are similar to both

Table 2. The words similar to *duty* that occurred in the contexts *corporate duty* and *fiduciary duty*.

CONTEXT	CONTEXTUALLY SIMILAR WORDS OF *DUTY*
corporate duty	fee, function, levy, liability, obligation, personnel, responsibility, rule, staff, tax, training
fiduciary duty	obligation, requirement, responsibility, role

the *responsibility* and *tax* senses of *duty*, reflecting the fact that the meaning of *duty* is indeed ambiguous if *corporate duty* is its sole context. In contrast, the second row in Table 2 clearly indicates the responsibility sense of *duty*.

While previous word sense disambiguation algorithms rely on a lexicon to provide sense inventories of words, the contextually similar words provide a way of distinguishing between different senses of words without committing to any particular sense inventory.

4. Overview of the Word-for-Word Glossing Algorithm

Figure 4 illustrates the data flow of the word-for-word glossing algorithm and Figure 5 describes it.

For example, suppose we wish to translate into French the word *duty* in the context *corporate fiduciary duty*. **Step 1** retrieves the candidate translations for *duty* and its WATs from Figure 2. In **Step 2**, we construct two lists of contextually similar words, one for the dependency context *corporate duty* and one for the dependency context *fiduciary duty*, shown in Table 2. The proposed translation for the context is obtained by maximizing the group similarities between the lists of contextually similar words and the WATs.

Using the group similarity measure from Section 5, Table 3 lists the group similarity scores between each list of contextually similar words and each WAT as well as the final combined score for each candidate translation. The combined score for a candidate is the sum of the logs of all group similarity scores involving its WAT. The correct proposed translation for *duty* in this context is *devoir* since its WAT received the highest score.

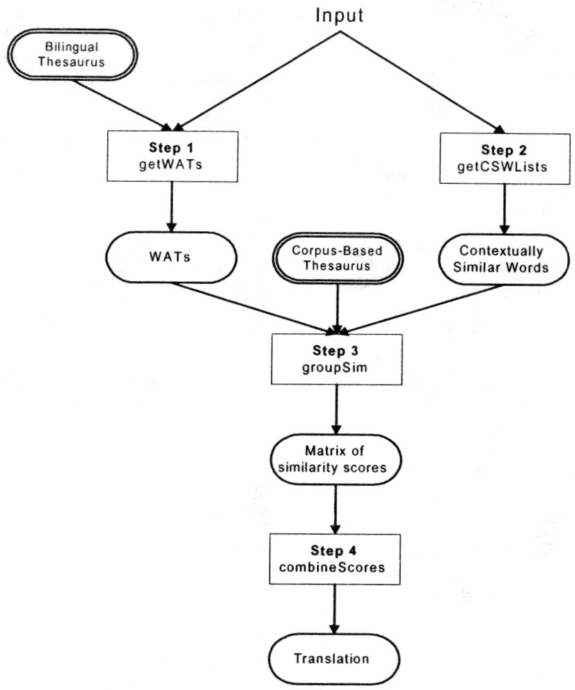

Figure 4. Data flow diagram for the word-for-word glossing algorithm.

Input:	A word w to be translated and a set of dependency contexts involving w.
Step 1:	Retrieve the candidate translations of w and the corresponding WATs from the bilingual thesaurus.
Step 2:	Find the contextually similar words of w in each dependency context using the algorithm from Section 3.
Step 3:	Compute the group similarity (see details in Section 5) between each set of contextually similar words and each WAT; the results are stored in a matrix t, where $t[i, j]$ is the group similarity between the ith list of contextually similar words and the jth WAT.
Step 4:	Add the logs of the group similarity scores in column of t to obtain a score for each WAT.
Output:	The candidate translation corresponding to the WAT with the highest score.

Figure 5. The word-for-word glossing algorithm.

5. Group Similarity

The corpus-based thesaurus contains only the similarities between individual pairs of words. In our algorithm, we require the similarity between groups of words. The group similarity measure

Table 3. Group similarity scores between the contextually similar words of *duty* in *corporate duty* and *fiduciary duty* with the WATs for candidate translations *devoir* and *taxe*.

	CANDIDATE *DEVOIR*	CANDIDATE *TAXE*
corporate duty	60.3704	16.569
fiduciary duty	51.2960	4.8325
Combined Score	8.0381	4.3829

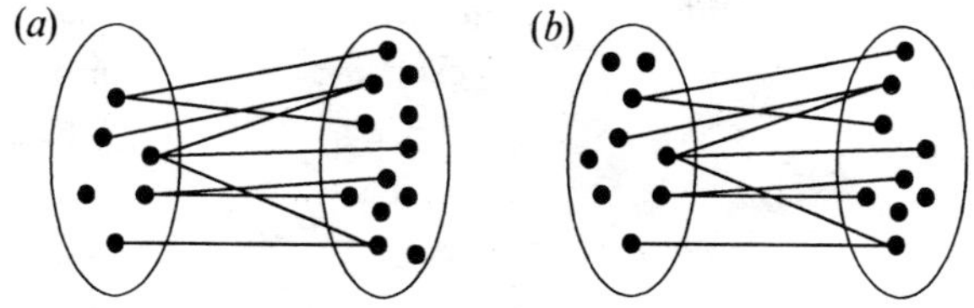

Figure 6. An example illustrating the difference between the interconnectivity and closeness measures. The interconnectivity in (*a*) and (*b*) remains constant while the closeness in (*a*) is higher than in (*b*) since there are more zero similarity pairs in (*b*).

we use is proposed by Karypis et al. (1999). It takes as input two groups of elements, G_1 and G_2, and a similarity matrix, *sim*, which specifies the similarity between individual elements. G_1 and G_2 are describable by graphs where the vertices are the words and each weighted edge between vertices w_1 and w_2 represents the similarity, $sim(w_1, w_2)$, between the words w_1 and w_2.

Karypis et al. consider both the interconnectivity and the closeness of the groups. The **absolute interconnectivity** between G_1 and G_2, $AI(G_1, G_2)$, is defined as the aggregate similarity between the two groups:

$$AI(G_1, G_2) = \sum_{x \in G_1} \sum_{y \in G_2} sim(x, y)$$

The **absolute closeness** between G_1 and G_2, $AC(G_1, G_2)$, is defined as the average similarity between a pair of elements, one from each group:

$$AC(G_1, G_2) = \frac{1}{|G_1||G_2|} AI(G_1, G_2)$$

Table 4. Candidate translations for each testing word along with their frequency of occurrence in the test corpus.

WORD	CANDIDATE TRANSLATION	ENGLISH SENSE	FREQUENCY OF OCCURRENCE
account	compte	bank account, business	245
	rapport	report, statement	55
duty	devoir	responsibility, obligation	80
	taxe	tax	30
race	course	contest	87
	race	racial group	23
suit	procès	lawsuit	281
	costume	garment	17
check	chèque	draft, bank order	105
	contrôle	evaluation, verification	25
record	record	unsurpassed statistic/performance	98
	enregistrement	recorded data or documentation	12

The difference between the absolute interconnectivity and the absolute closeness is that the latter takes zero similarity pairs into account. In Figure 6, the interconnectivity in (*a*) and (*b*) remains constant. However, the closeness in (*a*) is higher than in (*b*) since there are more zero similarity pairs in (*b*).

Karypis et al. normalized the absolute interconnectivity and closeness by the internal interconnectivity and closeness of the individual groups. The normalized measures are referred to as **relative interconnectivity**, $RI(G_1, G_2)$, and **relative closeness**, $RC(G_1, G_2)$. The internal interconnectivity and closeness are obtained by first computing a **minimal edge bisection** of each group. An even-sized partition $\{G', G''\}$ of a group G is called a minimal edge bisection of G if $AI(G', G'')$ is minimal among all such partitions. The **internal interconnectivity** of G, $II(G)$, is defined as $II(G) = AI(G', G'')$ and the **internal closeness** of G, $IC(G)$, as $IC(G) = AC(G', G'')$.

Minimal edge bisection is performed for all WATs and all sets of contextually similar words. However, the minimal edge bisection problem is *NP*-complete (Garey and Johnson, 1979). Fortunately, state of the art graph partitioning algorithms can approximate these bisections in polynomial time (Goehring and Saad, 1994; Karypis and Kumar, 1999; Kernighan and Lin, 1970). We used the same approximation methods as in (Karypis et al., 1999).

The similarity between G_1 and G_2 is then defined as follows:

$$groupSim(G_1, G_2) = RI(G_1, G_2) \times RC(G_1, G_2)$$

where

$$RI(G_1, G_2) = \frac{2AI(G_1, G_2)}{II(G_1) + II(G_2)}$$

is the relative interconnectivity and

$$RC(G_1, G_2) = \frac{AC(G_1, G_2)}{\frac{|G_1|}{|G_1| + |G_2|} IC(G_1) + \frac{|G_2|}{|G_1| + |G_2|} IC(G_2)}$$

is the relative closeness.

6. Experimental Results

The design of our glossing algorithm is applicable to any source/destination language pair as long as a source language parser is available. We considered *English-to-French* translations in our experiments.

We experimented with six English nouns that have multiple French translations: *account*, *duty*, *race*, *suit*, *check*, and *record*. Using the 1987 Wall Street Journal files on the LDC/DCI CD-

ROM, we extracted a testing corpus[4] consisting of the first 100 to 300 sentences containing the non-idiomatic usage of the six nouns[5]. Then, we manually tagged each sentence with one of the candidate translations shown in Table 4.

Each noun in Table 4 translates more frequently to one candidate translation than the other. In fact, always choosing the candidate *procès* as the translation for *suit* yields 94% accuracy. A better measure for evaluating the system's classifications considers both the algorithm's precision and recall on each candidate translation. Table 5 illustrates the precision and recall of our glossing algorithm for each candidate translation. Albeit precision and recall are used to evaluate the quality of the classifications, overall accuracy is sufficient for comparing different approaches with our system.

In Section 3, we presented an algorithm for identifying the contextually similar words of a word in a context using a corpus-based thesaurus and a collocation database. Each of the six nouns has similar words in the corpus-based thesaurus. However, in order to find contextually similar words, at least one similar word for each noun must occur in the collocation database in a given context. Thus, the algorithm for constructing contextually similar words is dependent on the coverage of the collocation database. We estimated this coverage by counting the number of times each of the six nouns, in several different contexts, has at least one contextually similar word. The result is shown in Table 6.

In Section 5, we described a group similarity metric, *groupSim*, which we use for comparing a WAT with a set of contextually similar words. In Figure 7, we compare the translation accuracy of our algorithm using other group similarity metrics. Suppose G_1 and G_2 are two groups of words and w is the word that we wish to translate. The metrics used are:

Table 5. Precision vs. Recall for each candidate translation.

WORD	CANDIDATE	PRECISION	RECALL
account	compte	0.982	0.902
	rapport	0.680	0.927
duty	devoir	0.951	0.963
	taxe	0.897	0.867
race	course	0.945	0.989
	race	0.947	0.783
suit	procès	0.996	0.993
	costume	0.889	0.941
check	chèque	0.951	0.924
	contrôle	0.714	0.800
record	record	0.968	0.918
	enregistrement	0.529	0.750

Table 6. The coverage of the collocation database, shown by the frequency with which a word in a given context has at least one contextually similar word.

WORD	NUMBER OF CONTEXTS	COVERAGE
account	1074	95.7%
duty	343	93.3%
race	294	92.5%
suit	332	91.9%
check	2519	87.5%
record	1655	92.8%

1. ***closest3:***
   sum of similarity of the three closest pairs of words from each group.

2. ***gs***:

$$\frac{\sum_{x\in G_1} sim(x,w)\times \max_{y\in G_2} sim(x,y)+\sum_{y\in G_2} sim(y,w)\times \max_{x\in G_1} sim(y,x)}{\sum_{x\in G_1} sim(x,w)+\sum_{y\in G_2} sim(y,w)}$$

3. ***AC***:
   as defined in Section 5.

4. ***AI***:
   as defined in Section 5.

5. ***RC***:
   as defined in Section 5.

6. ***RI***:
   as defined in Section 5.

[4] Available at ftp.cs.umanitoba.ca/pub/ppantel/download/wfwgtest.zip

[5] Omitted idiomatic phrases include *take into account, keep in check, check out*, …

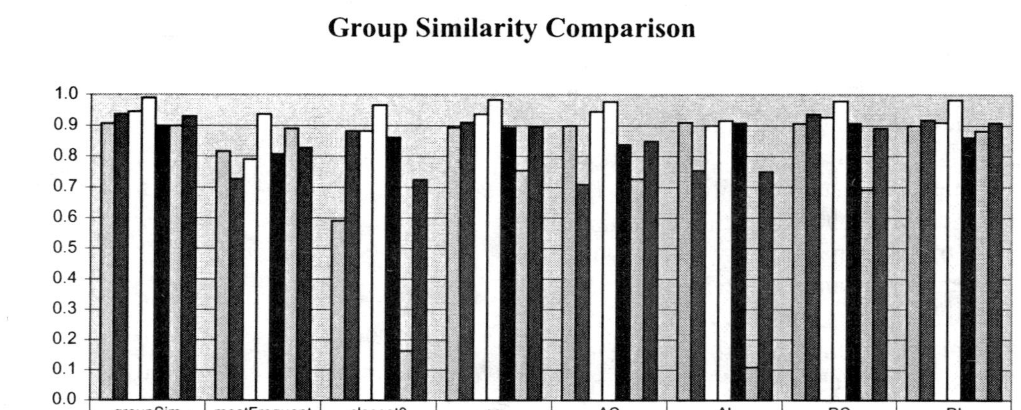

	groupSim	mostFrequent	closest3	gs	AC	AI	RC	RI
account	0.9067	0.8167	0.5900	0.8933	0.9000	0.9100	0.9067	0.9000
duty	0.9364	0.7273	0.8818	0.9091	0.7091	0.7545	0.9364	0.9182
race	0.9455	0.7909	0.8818	0.9364	0.9455	0.9000	0.9273	0.9091
suit	0.9899	0.9367	0.9664	0.9832	0.9765	0.9161	0.9799	0.9832
check	0.9000	0.8077	0.8615	0.8923	0.8385	0.9077	0.9077	0.8615
record	0.9000	0.8909	0.1636	0.7545	0.7273	0.1091	0.6909	0.8818
average	0.9297	0.8284	0.7242	0.8948	0.8495	0.7496	0.8915	0.9090

Figure 7. Performance comparison of different group similarity metrics.

In *mostFrequent*, we include the results obtained if we always choose the translation that occurs most frequently in the testing corpus.

We also compared the accuracy of our glossing algorithm with *Systran*'s translation system by feeding the testing sentences into Systran's web interface[6] and manually examining the results. Figure 8 summarizes the overall accuracy obtained by each system and the baseline on the testing corpus. Systran tended to prefer one candidate translation over the other and committed the majority of its errors on the non-preferred senses. Consequently, Systran is very accurate if its preferred sense is the frequent sense (as in *account* and *duty*) but is very inaccurate if its preferred sense is the infrequent one (as in *race*, *suit*, and *check*).

7. Conclusion and Future Work

This paper presents a word-for-word glossing algorithm. The gloss of a word is determined by maximizing the similarity between the set of contextually similar words and the different translations of the word in a bilingual thesaurus.

The algorithm presented in this paper can be improved and extended in many ways. At present, our glossing algorithm does not take the prior probabilities of translations into account. For example, in WSJ, the bank account sense of *account* is much more common than the report sense. We should thus tend to prefer this sense of *account*. This is achievable by weighting the translation scores by the prior probabilities of the translations. We are investigating an *Expectation-Maximization* (EM) (Dempster et al., 1977) algorithm to learn these prior probabilities. Initially, we assume that the candidate translations for a word are uniformly distributed. After glossing each word in a large corpus, we refine the prior probabilities using the frequency counts obtained. This process is repeated several times until the empirical prior probabilities closely approximate the true prior probabilities.

Finally, as discussed in Section 2.3, automatically constructing the bilingual thesaurus is necessary to gloss whole documents. This is attainable by adding a corpus-based destination language thesaurus to our system. The process of assigning a cluster of similar words as a WAT to a candidate translation *c* is as follows. First, we

[6] Available at babelfish.altavista.com/cgi-bin/translate

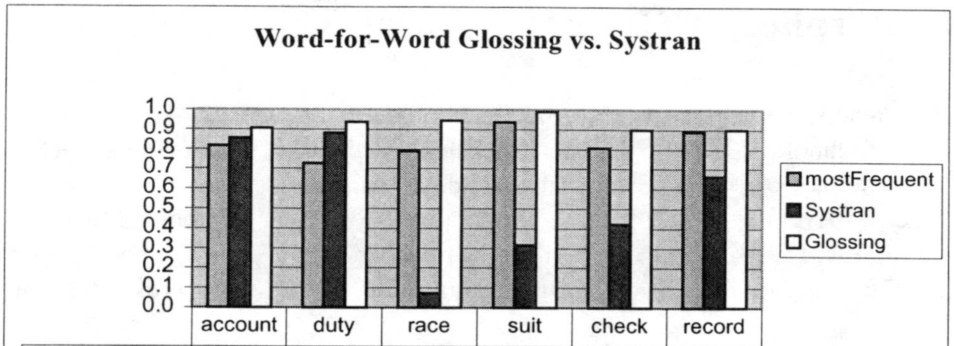

	account	duty	race	suit	check	record
mostFrequent	0.8167	0.7273	0.7909	0.9367	0.8077	0.8909
Systran	0.8567	0.8818	0.0727	0.3167	0.4231	0.6636
Glossing	0.9067	0.9364	0.9455	0.9899	0.9000	0.9000

Figure 8. Performance comparison of the word-for-word glossing algorithm and Systran.

automatically obtain the candidate translations for a word using a bilingual dictionary. With the destination language thesaurus, we obtain a list *S* of all words similar to *c*. With the bilingual dictionary, replace each word in *S* by its source language translations. Using the group similarity metric from Section 5, assign as the WAT the cluster of similar words (obtained from the source language thesaurus) most similar to *S*.

Acknowledgements

The authors wish to thank the reviewers for their helpful comments. This research was partly supported by Natural Sciences and Engineering Research Council of Canada grants OGP121338 and PGSA207797.

References

Peter F. Brown; John Cocke; Stephen A. Della Pietra; Vincent J. Della Pietra; Fredrick Jelinek; John D. Lafferty; Robert L. Mercer and Paul S. Roossin. 1990. *A Statistical Approach to Machine Translation*. Computation Linguistics, 16(2).

Peter F. Brown; Jennifer C. Lai and Robert L. Mercer. 1991. *Aligning Sentences in Parallel Corpora*. In Proceedings of ACL91. Berkeley.

A. P. Dempster; N. M. Laird; & D. B. Rubin. 1977. *Maximum likelihood from incomplete data via the EM algorithm*. Journal of the Royal Statistical Society, Series B, 39(1).

W. A. Gale and K. W. Church. 1991. *A Program for Aligning Sentences in Bilingual Corpora*. In Proceedings of ACL91. Berkeley.

M. R. Garey and D. S. Johnson. 1979. *Computers and Intractability: A Guide to the Theory of NP-Completeness*. W. H. Freeman.

T. Goehring and Y. Saad. 1994. *Heuristic Algorithms for Automatic Graph Partitioning*. Technical Report. Department of Computer Science, University of Minnesota.

George Karypis and Vipin Kumar. 1999. *A Fast and High Quality Multilevel Scheme for Partitioning Irregular Graphs*. SIAM Journal on Scientific Computing, 20(1).

George Karypis; Eui-Hong Han and Vipin Kumar. 1999. *Chameleon: A Hierarchical Clustering Algorithm Using Dynamic Modeling*. IEEE Computer: Special Issue on Data Analysis and Mining, 32(8). http://www-users.cs.umn.edu/~karypis/publications/Papers/PDF/chameleon.pdf

B. W. Kernighan and S. Lin. 1970. *An Efficient Heuristic Procedure for Partitioning Graphs*. The Bell System Technical Journal.

Genichiro Kikui. 1999. *Resolving Translation ambiguity using Non-parallel Bilingual Corpora*. In Proceedings of ACL99 Workshop on Unsupervised Learning in Natural Language Processing.

Dekang Lin. 1998a. *Automatic Retrieval and Clustering of Similar Words*. In Proceedings of COLING-ACL98. Montreal, Canada.

Dekang Lin. 1998b. *Extracting Collocations from Text Corpora*. Workshop on Computational Terminology. Montreal, Canada.

Philip Resnik. 1999. *Mining the Web for Bilingual Text*. In Proceedings of ACL99. College Park, Maryland.

Arabic Morphology Generation Using a Concatenative Strategy

Violetta Cavalli-Sforza
Carnegie Technology Education
4615 Forbes Avenue
Pittsburgh, PA, 15213
violetta@cs.cmu.edu

Abdelhadi Soudi
Computer Science Department
Ecole Nationale de L'Industrie Minerale
Rabat, Morocco
asoudi@enim.ac.ma

Teruko Mitamura
Language Technologies Institute
Carnegie Mellon University
Pittsburgh, PA 15213
teruko@cs.cmu.edu

Abstract

Arabic inflectional morphology requires infixation, prefixation and suffixation, giving rise to a large space of morphological variation. In this paper we describe an approach to reducing the complexity of Arabic morphology generation using discrimination trees and transformational rules. By decoupling the problem of stem changes from that of prefixes and suffixes, we gain a significant reduction in the number of rules required, as much as a factor of three for certain verb types. We focus on hollow verbs but discuss the wider applicability of the approach.

Introduction

Morphologically, Arabic is a non-concatenative language. The basic problem with generating Arabic verbal morphology is the large number of variants that must be generated. Verbal stems are based on triliteral or quadriliteral roots (3- or 4-radicals). Stems are formed by a derivational combination of a root morpheme and a vowel melody; the two are arranged according to canonical patterns. Roots are said to interdigitate with patterns to form stems. For example, the Arabic stem katab (he wrote) is composed of the morpheme ktb (notion of writing) and the vowel melody morpheme 'a-a'. The two are coordinated according to the pattern CVCVC (C=consonant, V=vowel).

There are 15 triliteral patterns, of which at least 9 are in common use, and 4 much rarer quadriliteral patterns. All these patterns undergo some stem changes with respect to voweling in the 2 tenses (perfect and imperfect), the 2 voices (active and passive), and the 5 moods (indicative, subjunctive, jussive, imperative and energetic).[1] The stem used in the conjugation of the verb may differ depending on the person, number, gender, tense, mood, and the presence of certain root consonants. Stem changes combine with suffixes in the perfect indicative (e.g., katab-naa 'we wrote', kutib-a 'it was written') and the imperative (e.g. uktub-uu 'write', plural), and with both prefixes and suffixes for the imperfect tense in the indicative, subjunctive, and jussive moods (e.g. ya-ktub-na 'they write, feminine plural') and in the energetic mood (e.g. ya-ktub-unna or ya-ktub-un 'he certainly writes'). There are a total of 13 person-number-gender combinations. Distinct prefixes are used in the active and passive voices in the imperfect, although in most cases this results in a change in the written form only if diacritic marks are used.[2]

Most previous computational treatments of Arabic morphology are based on linguistic models that describe Arabic in a non-concatenative way and focus primarily on analysis. Beesley (1991) describes a system that analyzes Arabic words based on Koskenniemi's

[1] The jussive is used in specific constructions, for example, negation in the past with the negative particle lam (e.g., lam aktub 'I didn't write'). The energetic expresses corroboration of an action taking place. The indicative is common to both perfect and imperfect tenses, but the subjunctive and the jussive are restricted to the imperfect tense. The imperative has a special form, and the energetic can be derived from either the imperfect or the imperative.

[2] Diacritic marks are used in Arabic language textbooks and occasionally in regular texts to resolve ambiguous words (e.g. to mark a passive verb use).

(1983) two-level morphology. In Beesley (1996) the system is reworked into a finite-state lexical transducer to perform analysis and generation. In two-level systems, the lexical level includes short vowels that are typically not realized on the the surface level. Kiraz (1994) presents an analysis of Arabic morphology based on the CV-, moraic-, and affixational models. He introduces a multi-tape two-level model and a formalism where three tapes are used for the lexical level (root, pattern, and vocalization) and one tape for the surface level.

In this paper, we propose a computational approach that applies a concatenative treatment to Arabic morphology generation by separating the issue of infixation from other inflectional variations. We are developing an Arabic morphological generator using MORPHE (Leavitt, 1994), a tool for modeling morphology based on discrimination trees and regular expressions. MORPHE is part of a suite of tools developed at the Language Technologies Institute, Carnegie Mellon University, for knowledge-based machine translation. Large systems for MT from English to Spanish, French, German, Portuguese and a prototype for Italian have already been developed. Within this framework, we are exploring English to Arabic translation and Arabic generation for pedagogical purposes. We generate Arabic words including short vowels and diacritic marks, since they are pedagogically useful and can always be stripped before display.

Our approach seeks to reduce the number of rules for generating morphological variants of Arabic verbs by breaking the problem into two parts. We observe that, with the exception of a few verb types, there is very little interaction between stem changes and the processes of prefixation and suffixation. It is therefore possible to decouple, in large part, the problem of stem changes from that of prefixes and suffixes. The gain is a significant reduction in the size number of transformational rules, as much as a factor of three for certain verb classes. This improves the space efficiency of the system and its maintainability by reducing duplication of rules, and simplifies the rules by isolating different types of changes.

To illustrate our approach, we focus on a particular type of verbs, termed *hollow* verbs, and show how we integrate their treatment with that of more regular verbs. We also discuss how the approach can be extended to other classes of verbs and other parts of speech.

1 Arabic Verbal Morphology

Verb roots in Arabic can be classified as shown in Figure 1.[3] A primary distinction is made between weak and strong verbs. Weak verbs have a weak consonant ('w' or 'y') as one or more of their radicals; strong verbs do not have any weak radicals.

Strong verbs undergo systematic changes in stem voweling from the perfect to the imperfect. The first radical vowel disappears in the imperfect. Verbs whose middle radical vowel in the perfect is 'a' can change it to 'a' (e.g., qaTa`a 'he cut' -> yaqTa`u 'he cuts'),[4] 'i' (e.g., Daraba 'he hit' -> yaDribu 'he hits'), or 'u' (e.g., kataba 'he wrote' -> yaktubu 'he writes') in the imperfect. Verbs whose middle radical vowel in the perfect is 'i' can only change it to 'a' (e.g., shariba 'he drank' -> yashrabu 'he drinks') or 'i' (e.g., Hasiba 'he supposed' -> yaHsibu 'he supposes'). Verbs with middle radical vowel 'u' in the perfect do not change it in the imperfect (e.g., Hasuna 'he was beautiful' -> yaHsunu 'he is beautiful'). For strong verbs, neither perfect nor imperfect stems change with person, gender, or number.

Hollow verbs are those with a weak middle radical. In both perfect and imperfect tenses, the underlying stem is realized by two characteristic allomorphs, one short and one long, whose use depends on the person, number and gender.

---

[3] Grammars of Arabic are not uniform in their classification of "hamzated" verbs, verbs containing the glottal stop as one of the radicals (e.g. [sa?al] 'to ask'). Wright (1968) includes them as weak verbs, but Cowan (1964) doesn't. Hamzated verbs change the written 'seat' of the hamza from 'alif' to 'waaw' or 'yaa?', depending on the phonetic context.

[4] In the Arabic transcription capital letters indicate emphatic consonants; 'H' is the voiceless pharyngeal fricative ; '`' the voiced pharyngeal fricative ; '?' is the glottal stop 'hamza'.

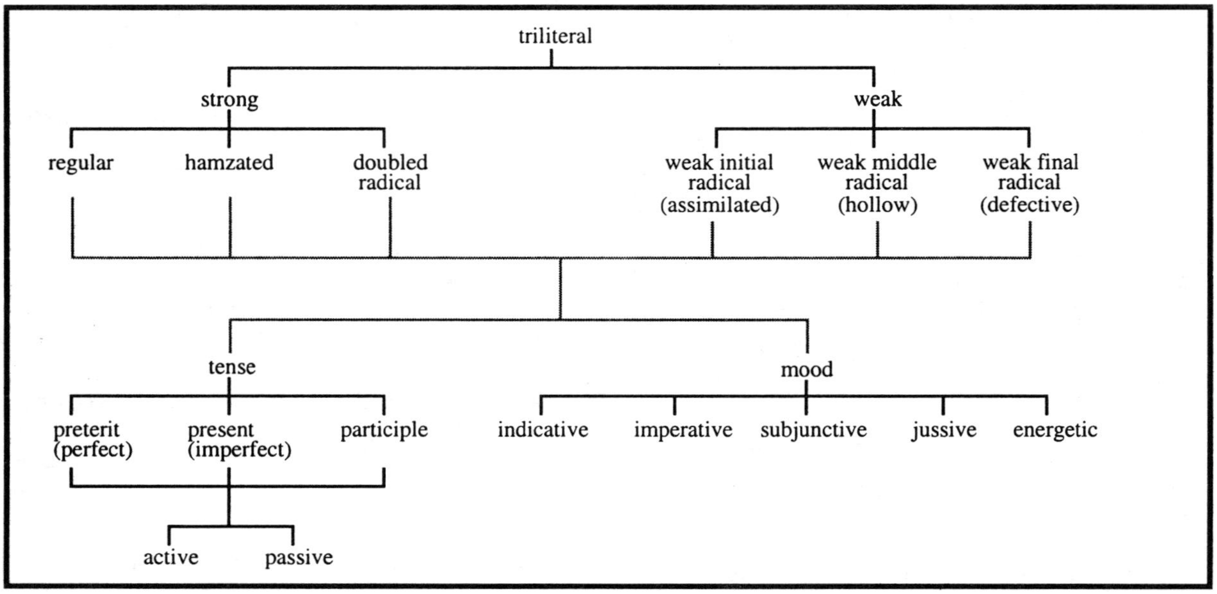

Figure 1: Classification of Arabic Verbal Roots and Mood Tense System

Hollow verbs fall into four classes:

1. Verbs of the pattern CawaC or CawuC (e.g. [Tawul] 'to be long'), where the middle radical is 'w'. Their characteristic is a long 'uu' between the first and last radical in the imperfect. E.g.,

   From the underlying root [zawar]:
   zaara 'he visited' and yazuuru 'he visits'

   Stem allomorphs:
   Perfect: -zur- and -zaar-
   Imperfect: -zur- and -zuur-

2. Verbs of the pattern CawiC, where the middle radical is 'w'. Their characteristic is a long 'aa' between the first and last radical in the imperfect. E.g.,

   From the underlying root [nawim]:
   naama 'he slept and yanaamu 'he sleeps'

   Stem allomorphs :
   Perfect: -nim- and -naam-
   Imperfect: -nam- and -naam-

3. Verbs of the pattern CayaC, where the middle radical is 'y'. Their characteristic is a long 'ii' before the first and last radical in the imperfect. E.g.,

   From the underlying root [baya`]:
   baa`a 'he sold' and yabii`u 'he sells'

   Stem allomorphs :
   Perfect: -bi`- and -baa`-
   Imperfect: and -bi`- and -bii`-

4. Verbs of the pattern CayiC, where middle radical is 'y'. E.g.,

   From the underlying root [hayib]:
   haaba 'he feared' and yahaabu 'he fears'

   Stem allomorphs :
   Perfect: -hib- and -haab-
   Imperfect: -hab- and -haab-

In the relevant literature (e.g., Beesley, 1998; Kiraz, 1994), verbs belonging to the above classes are all assumed to have the pattern CVCVC. The pattern does not show the verb conjugation class and makes it difficult to predict the type of stem allomorph to use. To avoid these problems, we keep information on the middle radical and vowel in the base form of the verb. In generation, classes 2 and 4 of the verb can be handled as one because they have the same perfect and imperfect stems.[5]

[5] The only exception is the passive participle. Verbs of classes 1 and 2 behave the same (e.g. Class 1: [zawar]: mazuwr 'visited'; Class 2 [nawil] → manuwl 'obtained'), as do verbs of classes 3 and 4 (e.g. Class 3: [baya`] → mabii` 'sold', Class 4: [hayib] → mahiib 'feared').

We describe our approach to modeling strong and hollow verbs below, following a description of the implementation framework.

2 The MORPHE System

MORPHE (Leavitt, 1994) is a tool that compiles morphological transformation rules into either a word parsing program or a word generation program.[6] In this paper we will focus on the use of MORPHE in generation.

Input and Output. MORPHE's output is simply a string. Input is a feature structure (FS) which describes the item that MORPHE must transform. A FS is implemented as a recursive Lisp list. Each element of the FS is a feature-value pair (FVP), where the value can be atomic or complex. A complex value is itself a FS. For example, the FS for generating the Arabic **zurtu** 'I visited' would be:

```
((ROOT "zawar")
 (CAT V)(PAT CVCVC)(VOW HOL)
 (TENSE PERF)(MOOD IND)
 (VOICE ACT)
 (NUMBER SG)(PERSON 1))
```

The choice of feature names and values, other than ROOT, which identifies the lexical item to be transformed, is entirely up to the user. The FVPs in a FS come from one of two sources. Static features, such as CAT (part of speech) and ROOT, come from the syntactic lexicon, which, in addition to the base form of words, can contain morphological and syntactic features. Dynamic features, such as TENSE and NUMBER, are set by MORPHE's caller.

The Morphological Form Hierarchy. MORPHE is based on the notion of a morphological form hierarchy (MFH) or tree. Each internal node of the tree specifies a piece of the FS that is common to that entire subtree. The root of the tree is a special node that simply binds all subtrees together. The leaf nodes of the tree correspond to distinct morphological forms in the language. Each node in the tree below the root is built by specifying the parent of the node and the conjunction or disjunction of FVPs that define the node. Portions of the Arabic MFH are shown in Figures 2-4.

Transformational Rules. A rule attached to each leaf node of the MFH effects the desired morphological transformations for that node. A rule consists of one or more mutually exclusive clauses. The 'if' part of a clause is a regular expression pattern, which is matched against the value of the feature ROOT (a string). The 'then' part includes one or more operators, applied in the given order. Operators include addition, deletion, and replacement of prefixes, infixes, and suffixes. The output of the transformation is the transformed ROOT string. An example of a rule attached to a node in the MFH is given in Section 3.1 below.

Process Logic. In generation, the MFH acts as a discrimination network. The specified FS is matched against the features defining each subtree until a leaf is reached. At that point, MORPHE first checks in the irregular forms lexicon for an entry indexed by the name of the leaf node (i.e., the MF) and the value of the ROOT feature in the FS. If an irregular form is not found, the transformation rule attached to the leaf node is tried. If no rule is found or none of the clauses of the applicable rule match, MORPHE returns the value of ROOT unchanged.

3 Handling Arabic Verbal Morphology in MORPHE

Figure 2 sketches the basic MFH and the division of the verb subtree into stem changes and prefix/suffix additions.[7] The inflected verb is generated in two steps. MORPHE is first called with the feature CHG set to STEM. The required stem is returned and temporarily substituted for the value of the ROOT feature.

[6] MORPHE is written in Common Lisp and the compiled MFH and transformation rules are themselves a set of Common Lisp functions.

[7] The use of two parts of the same tree for the two problems is a constraint of MORPHE's implementation, which does not permit multiple trees with separate roots.

The second call to MORPHE, with feature CHG set to PSFIX, adds the necessary prefix and/or suffix and returns the fully inflected verb.

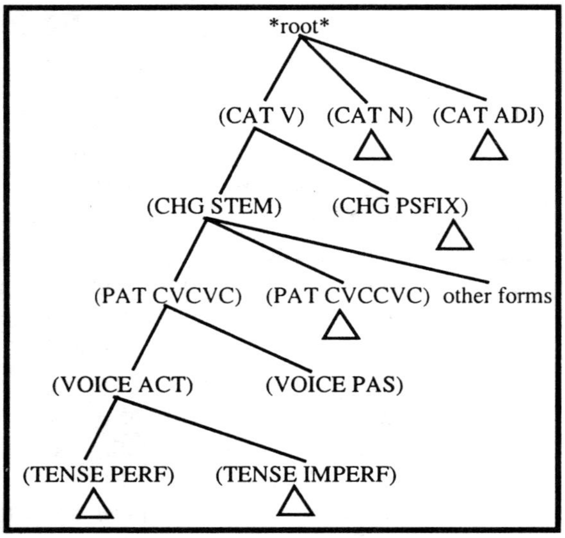

Figure 2 : The Basic Verb Hierarchy

Figure 2 also shows some of the features used to traverse the discrimination tree. The feature PAT is used in conjunction with the ROOT feature to select the appropriate affixes. Knowing the underlying root and its voweling is crucial for the determination of hollow verb stems, as described in Section 1. Knowing the pattern is also important in cases where it is unclear. For example, verbs of pattern CtVCVC insert a 't' after the first radical (e.g. ntaqal 'to move, change location', intransitive). With some consonants as first radicals, in order to facilitate pronunciation, the 't' undergoes a process of assimilation whose effects differ depending on the preceding consonant. For example, the pattern CtVCVC verb from zaHam 'to shove' instead of *ztaHam is zdaHam 'to team'. It is also difficult to determine from just the string ntaqal whether this is pattern nCVCVC of the verb *taqal (if it existed) or pattern CtVCVC of naqal 'to transport, move', transitive).

3.1 Handling Strong and Hollow Verb Morphology in MORPHE

As a demonstration of our approach, we discuss the case of hollow verbs, whose characteristics were described in Section 1. Figure 3 shows the MFH for strong and hollow verbs of pattern CVCVC in the perfect tense, active voice. We use the feature VOW to carry information about the voweling of the verb in the imperfect (discussed below) and overload it to distinguish hollow and other kinds of verbs.

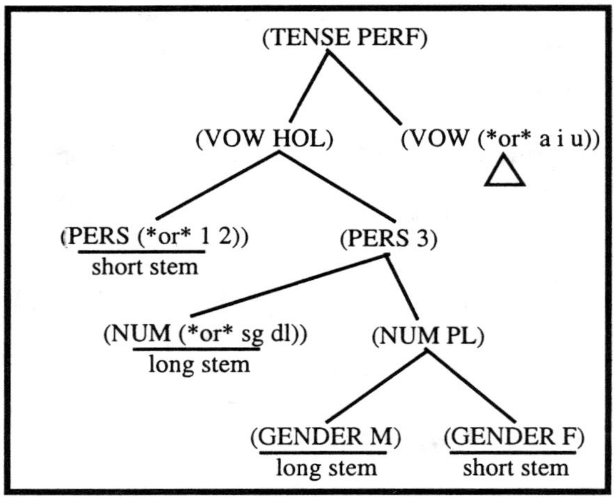

Figure 3: The Perfect Stem Change Subtree for Strong and Hollow Verbs of Pattern CVCVC

In the perfect active voice, regular strong verbs do not undergo any stem changes, but doubled radical verbs do. Rules effecting these changes are attached to the node labeled with the FVP (VOW (*or* a i u)).[8] The hollow verbs, on the other hand, use a long stem with a middle 'alif' (e.g. [daam] 'to last') for third person singular and dual (masculine and feminine) and for third person plural masculine. The remaining person-number-gender combinations take a short stem whose voweling depends on the underlying root of the verb, as specified earlier. Transformation rules attached to the leaf nodes perform the conversion of the ROOT feature value to the short and long stem.

Inside the stem change rules, the four different classes of hollow verbs are treated as three separate conditions (classes 2 and 4 can be merged, as described in Section 1) by matching on the middle radical and the adjacent vowels and replacing them with the appropriate vowel.

---

[8] Hamzated verbs changes are due to interactions with specific suffixes and are best dealt with in the prefixation and suffixation subtree.

An example of such a rule, which changes the perfect stem to a short one for persons 1 and 2 both singular and plural, follows.

```
(morph-rule v-stem-f1-act-perf-12
 ("^%{cons}(awa)%{cons}$"
    (ri *1* "u"))
 ("^%{cons}(a[wy]i)%{cons}$"
    (ri *1* "i"))
 ("^%{cons}(aya)%{cons}$"
    (ri *1* "i")))
```

The syntax `%{var}` is used to indicate variables with a given set of values. Enclosing a string in parenthesis associates it with a numbered register, so the replace infix (ri) operator can access it for substitution.

Figure 4 shows the imperfect subtree for strong and hollow verbs. Strong verbs are treated efficiently by three rules branching on the middle radical vowel, given as the value of VOW. The consonant-vowel pattern of the computed stem is shown (e.g. for kataba 'he wrote', the imperfect stem would be -ktub- in the pattern CCuC). As described in Section 1, the possible vowel in the imperfect is restricted but not always determined by the perfect vowel and so must be stored in the syntactic lexicon.[9] Separating stem changes from the addition of prefixes and suffixes significantly reduces the number of transformation rules that must be written by eliminating much repetition of prefix and suffix addition for different stem changes. For strong verbs of pattern CVCVC, there is at least a three-fold reduction in the number of rules for active voice (recall the different kinds of vowel changes for these verbs from perfect to imperfect described in Section 1). Other patterns and the passive of pattern CVCVC verbs show less variation in stem voweling but more variation in prefix and suffix voweling. Since some of the patterns share the same prefix and suffix voweling, once the stem has been determined, the prefixation and suffixation rules can be shared by pattern groups.

[9] In the presence of certain second and third radicals, the middle radical vowel is more precisely determined. This information can be incorporated into the syntactic lexicon as it is being built.

The hollow verb subtree is not as small for the imperfect as it is for the perfect, since the stem depends not only on the mood but also on the person, gender, and number. It is still advantageous to decouple stem changes from prefixation and suffixation. Suffixes differ in the indicative and subjunctive moods; if the two types of changes were merged, the stem transformations would have to be repeated in each of the two moods and for each person-number-gender combination. The same observation applies to stem changes in the passive voice as well. Significant replication of transformational rules that include stem changes makes the system bigger and harder to maintain in case of changes, particularly because each transformational rule needs to take into consideration the four different classes of hollow verbs.

3.2 An Example of Generation

Consider again the example verb form zurtu 'I visited' and the feature structure (FS) given in Section 2. During generation, the feature-value pair (CHG STEM) is added to the FS before the first call to MORPHE. Traversing the MFH shown in Figure 2, MORPHE finds the rule `v-stem-f1-act-perf-12` given in Section 3.1 above. The first clause fires, replacing the 'awa' with 'u' and MORPHE returns the stem -zur-. This stem is substituted as the value of the ROOT feature in the FS and the feature-value pair (CHG STEM) is changed to (CHG PSFIX) before the second call to MORPHE. This time MORPHE traverses a different subtree and reaches the rule:

```
(morph-rule v-psfix-perf-1-sg
  (""
     (+s "otu")))
```

This rule, currently simply appends "otu" to the string, and MORPHE returns the string "zurotu", where the 'o' denotes the diacritic "sukuun" or absence of vowel. This is the desired form for zurtu 'I visited'.

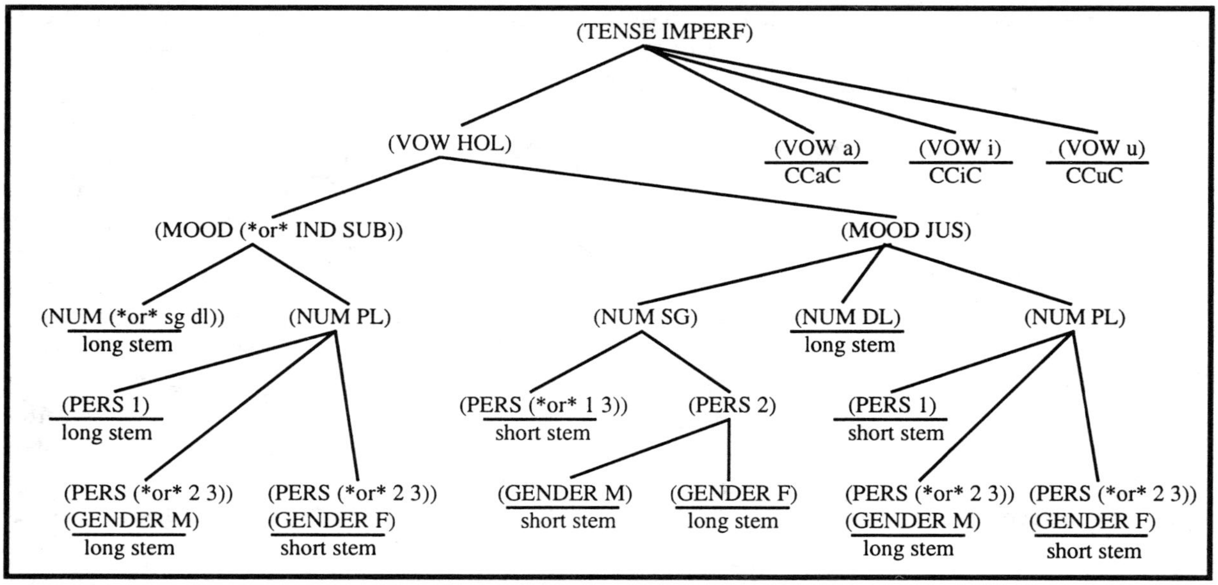

Figure 4: The Imperfect Stem Change Subtree for Strong and Hollow Verbs of Pattern CvCvC

4 Extensions

In this paper so far we have focused on regular and hollow verbs of the pattern CVCVC. Here we examine how our approach applies to other verb types and other parts of speech.

4.1 Extending the Approach to Other Verb Types

The two-step treatment of verbal inflection described in this paper is easily extended to the passive, to doubled radical and hamzated verbs, and to different patterns of strong and hollow verbs. In fact, since not all higher patterns are affected by the presence of a middle or weak radical (e.g. patterns CVCCV, CaaCVC, taCVCCVC and others), the subtrees for these patterns will be significantly less bushy than for pattern CVCVC. The two-step treatment also covers verbs with a weak first radical, especially the radical 'w', which is normally dropped in the active imperfect (e.g. perfect stem warad 'to come', imperfect stem -rid-).[10] Alternatively, it can be placed in the irregular lexicon, which MORPHE consults when it reaches a leaf node, prior to applying any of the transformational rules.

Verbs with a weak third radical, including doubly or trebly weak verbs, are the most problematic since the stem changes interact heavily with the inflectional suffixes, and less is gained by trying to modify the stem separately. We are currently investigating this issue and the best way to treat it in MORPHE.

4.2 Extending the Approach to Other Parts of Speech

The two-step approach to generating verbal morphology also presents advantages for the inflectional morphology of nouns and adjectives. In Arabic, the plural of many nouns, especially masculine nouns, is not formed regularly by suffixation. Instead, the stem itself undergoes changes according to a complex set of patterns (e.g. rajul 'man' pluralizes as rijaal 'men'), giving rise to so-called "broken plurals". The inflection of broken plurals according to case (nominative, genitive, accusative) and definiteness, however, is basically the same as the inflection

[10] Exceptions to this rule exist (e.g. the verb wajil 'to be afraid'), with imperfect stem – wjal-) but are rare and can be handled in MORPHE by placing the irregular stem in the syntactic lexicon and checking for it prior to calling MORPHE for stem changes.

The radical 'y' is largely not dropped or changed.

of most masculine or feminine singular nouns. The same holds true for adjectives.

Finally we note that our two-step approach can also be used to combine derivational and inflectional morphology for nouns and adjectives. Deverbal nouns and present and past participles can be derived regularly from each verb pattern (with the exception of deverbal nouns from pattern CVCVC). Relational or "nisba" adjectives are derived, with small variations, from nouns. Since these parts of speech are inflected as normal nouns and adjectives, we can perform derivational and inflectional morphology in two calls to MORPHE, much as we do stem change and prefix/suffix addition.

Conclusion

We have presented a computational model that handles Arabic morphology generation concatenatively by separating the infixation changes undergone by an Arabic stem from the processes of prefixation and suffixation. Our approach was motivated by practical concerns. We sought to make efficient use of a morphological generation tool that is part of our standard environment for developing machine translation systems. The two-step approach significantly reduces the number of morphological transformation rules that must be written, allowing the Arabic generator to be smaller, simpler, and easier to maintain.

The current implementation has been tested on a subset of verbal morphology including hollow verbs and various types of strong verbs. We are currently working on the other kinds of weak verbs: defective and assimilated verbs. Other categories of words can be handled in a similar manner, and we will turn our attention to them next.

References

K. Beesley. 1990. Finite-State Description of Arabic Morphology. In *Proceedings of the Second Cambridge Conference: Bilingual Computing in Arabic and English.*

K. Beesley. 1991. Computer Analysis of Arabic: A Two-Level Approach with Detours. In B. Comrie and M. Eid, editors, *Perspectives on Arabic Linguistics III: Papers from the Third Annual Symposium on Arabic Linguistics*. Benjamins, Amsterdam, pages 155-172.

K. Beesley. 1996. Arabic Finite-State Morphological Analysis and Generation. In *Proceedings COLING'96*, Vol. 1, pages 89-94.

K. Beesley. 1998. Consonant Spreading in Arabic Stems. In *Proceedings of COLING'98.*

D. Cowan. 1964. *An introduction to modern literary Arabic.* Cambridge University Press, Cambridge.

G. Hudson. 1986. Arabic Root and Pattern Morphology without Tiers. *Journal of Linguistics*, 22:85-122.

G. Kiraz. 1994. Multi-tape Two-level Morphology: A Case study in Semitic Non-Linear Morphology. In *Proceedings of COLING-94*, Vol. 1, pages 180-186.

K. Koskenniemi. 1983. *Two-level morphology: A General Computational Model for Word-Form Recognition and Production.* PhD thesis, University of Helsinki.

A. Lavie, A. Itai, U. Ornan, and M. Rimon. 1988. On the Applicability of Two Level Morphology to the Inflection of Hebrew Verbs. In *Proceedings of the Association of Literary and Linguistic Computing Conference.*

J.R. Leavitt. 1994. MORPHE: A Morphological Rule Compiler. Technical Report, CMU-CMT-94-MEMO.

J. McCarthy and A. Prince. 1990. Foot and Word in Prosodic Morphology: The Arabic Broken Plural. *Natural Language and Linguistics Theory*, 8: 209-283.

J. McCarthy and A. Prince. 1993. *Template in Prosodic Morphology.* In Stvan, L. et al., editors, *Papers from the Third Annual Formal Linguistics Society of Midamerica Conference,.* Bloomington, Indiana. Indiana University Linguistics Club, pages 187-218.

G. Ritchie. 1992. Languages Generated by Two-Level Morphological Rules. *Computational Linguistics*, 18(1), pages 41-59.

R. Sproat. 1992. *Morphology and Computation.* MIT Press, Cambridge, Mass.

H. Wehr. 1971. *A Dictionary of Modern Written Arabic*, J.M. Cowan, editor. Spoken Language Services, Ithaca, NY, fourth edition.

W. Wright. 1988. *A Grammar of the Arabic Language.* Cambridge University Press, Cambridge, third edition.

Morphological Tagging: Data vs. Dictionaries

Jan Hajič*
Department of Computer Science
Johns Hopkins University
Baltimore, MD 21218
hajic@cs.jhu.edu

Abstract

Part of Speech tagging for English seems to have reached the the human levels of error, but full morphological tagging for inflectionally rich languages, such as Romanian, Czech, or Hungarian, is still an open problem, and the results are far from being satisfactory. This paper presents results obtained by using a universalized exponential feature-based model for five such languages. It focuses on the data sparseness issue, which is especially severe for such languages (the more so that there are no extensive annotated data for those languages). In conclusion, we argue strongly that the use of an independent morphological dictionary is the preferred choice to more annotated data under such circumstances.

1 Full Morphological Tagging

English Part of Speech (POS) tagging has been widely described in the recent past, starting with the (Church, 1988) paper, followed by numerous others using various methods: neural networks (Julian Benello and Anderson, 1989), HMM tagging (Merialdo, 1992), decision trees (Schmid, 1994), transformation-based error-driven learning (Brill, 1995), and maximum entropy (Ratnaparkhi, 1996), to select just a few. However different the methods were, English dominated in these tests.

Unfortunately, English is a morphologically "impoverished" language: there are no complicated agreement relations, word order variation is minimal, and the morphological categories are either extremely simple (`-s` for plural of nouns, for example), or (almost) nonexistent (cases expressed by inflection, for example) - with not too many exceptions and irregularities. Therefore the number of tags selected for an English tagset is not that large (40-75 in the typical case). Also, the average ambiguity is low (2.32 tags per token on the manually tagged Wall Street Journal part in the Penn Treebank, for example).

Highly inflective and agglutinative languages are different. Obviously we can limit the number of tags to the major part-of-speech classes, plus some (like the Xerox Language Tools (Chanod, 1997) for such languages do), and in fact achieve similar performance, but that limits the usefulness of the results thus obtained for further analysis. These languages, obviously, do not use the rich inflection just for the amusement (or embarrassment) of their speakers (or NLP researchers): the inflectional categories carry important information which ought to be known at a later time (e.g., during parsing). Thus one wants not only to tell apart verbs from nouns, but also nominative from genitive, masculine animate from inanimate, singular from plural – all of them being often ambiguous one way or the other.

The average tagset, as found even in a moderate corpus, contains between 500 and 1,000 distinct tags – whereas the size of the set of possible and plausible tags can reach 3,000 to 5,000. Obviously, any of the statistical methods used for English (even if fully supervised) clash with (or, fall through) the data sparseness problem (see below Table 1 for details).

There have been attempts to solve this problem for some of the highly inflectional European languages ((Daelemans et al., 1996), (Erjavec et al., 1999), (Tufis, 1999), and also our own in (Hajič and Hladká, 1997), (Hajič and Hladká, 1998), see also below), but so far no method nor a tagger has been evaluated against a larger number of those languages in a similar setting, to allow for a side-by-side comparison of the difficulty (or ease) of full morphological tagging of those languages. Thanks to the Multext-East project (Véronis, 1996a), there are now five annotated corpora available (which are manually fully morphologically tagged) to perform such experiments.

2 The Languages Used and The Training Data

We use the Multext-East-annotated version of the Orwell's 1984 novel in Czech, Estonian, Hungarian,

* The work described herein has been started and largely done within author's home institution, the Institute of Formal and Applied Linguistics, Charles University, Prague, CZ, within the project VS96151 of the Ministry of Education of the Czech Republic and partially also under the grant 405/96/K214 of the Grant Agency of the Czech Republic.

Romanian and Slovene[1]. The annotation uses a single SGML-based formal scheme, and even common guidelines for tagset design and annotation, nevertheless the tagsets differ substantially since the languages differ as well: Romanian is a French-like romance language, Hungarian is agglutinative, and the other languages are more or less inflectional-type languages[2]. The annotated data contains about 100k tokens (including punctuation) for each language; out of those, the first 20k tokens has been used for testing, the rest for training. We have also extended the tag identifiers by appending a string of hyphens ('-') to suit the exponential tagger which expects the tags to be of equal length; the mapping was 1:1 for all tags in all languages, since the "long" tags are in fact the Multext-East standard.

From the tagging point of view, the language characteristics displayed in Table 1 are the most relevant[3].

3 The Methodology

The main tagger used for the comparison experiment is the probabilistic exponential-model-based, error-driven learner we described in detail in (Hajič and Hladká, 1998). Modifications had to be made, however, to make it more universal across languages.

3.1 Structure of the Model

The model described in (Hajič and Hladká, 1998) is a general exponential (specifically, a log-linear) model (such as the one used for Maximum Entropy-based models):

$$p_{AC}(y|x) = \frac{\exp(\sum_{i=1}^{n} \lambda_i f_i(y,x))}{Z(x)} \quad (1)$$

where $f_i(y,x)$ is a binary-valued *feature* of the event value being predicted and its context, λ_i is a weight of the feature f_i, and $Z(x)$ is the natural normalization factor. This model is then essentially reduced to Naive Bayes by the approximation of the λ_i parameters, which is done because there are millions of possible features in the pool and thus the full entropy maximization is prohibitively expensive, if we want to select a small number of features instead of keeping them all.

The tags are predicted separately for each morphological category (such as POS, NUMBER, CASE, DEGREE OF COMPARISON, etc.). The model makes an extensive use of so-called "ambiguity classes" (ACs). An ambiguity class is a set of values (such as genitive and accusative) of a single category (such as CASE) which arises for some word forms as a result of morphological analysis. For unambiguous word forms (unambiguous from the point of view of a certain category), the ambiguity class set contains only a single value; for ambiguous forms, there are 2 or more values in the AC. For example, let's suppose we use part-of-speech (POS), number and tense as morphological categories for English; then the word form "`borrowed`" is 2-way ambiguous in POS ({`V`,`J`} for verb and adjective, respectively), unambiguous in number (linguistic arguments apart, number is typically regarded "not applicable" to adjectives as well as to almost all forms of verbs in English), and 3-way ambiguous in tense ({`P`,`N`,`-`} for past tense, past participle, and "not applicable" in the adjective form).

The predictions of the models are always conditioned on the ambiguity class of the category (POS, NUMBER, ...) in question. In other words, there is a separate model for each category *and* an ambiguity class from that category. Naturally, there is no model for unambiguous ACs classes. However, even though the ambiguity classes bring very valuable information about the word form being tagged and a reliable information about the context (since they are fixed during tagging), using ACs causes also an unwelcome effect of partitioning the already scarce data and also effectively ignores statistics of the unambiguous cases.

The context of features uses the neighboring words (original word forms) and ambiguity classes on subtags, where their relative position in text might be either fixed (0, -1, +1) or "variable" using a value of the POS subtag as the "stop here" criterion, up to 4 text positions (words) apart.

3.2 General Subtag Features

The original model uses the ambiguity classes not only for conditioning on context in features, but also for the individual models based on category *and* an AC.

More general features have been introduced, which do not depend on the ambiguity class of the subtag being predicted any more. This allows to learn also from unambiguous tokens. However, the training time is increased dramatically by doing so since *all* events in the training data have to be taken

[1] There are more languages involved in the Multext-East project, but only these five languages have been really carefully tagged; English is unfortunately tagged using Eric Brill's tagger trained in unsupervised mode, leaving multiple output at almost every ambiguous token, and Bulgarian is totally unusable since it has been tagged automatically with only a baseline tagger. The English results reported below thus come from the Penn Treebank data, from which we have used roughly 100,000 words to match the training data sizes for the remaining languages. For Czech, Hungarian, and Slovene we use later versions of the annotated data (than those found on the Multext-East CD) which we obtained directly from the authors of the annotations after the Multext-CD had been published, since the new data contain rather substantial improvements over the originally published data.

[2] For detailed account of the lexical characteristics of these languages, see (Véronis, 1996b).

[3] We have included English here for comparison purposes, since these characteristics are independent of the annotation.

Table 1: Training data in numbers

Language	Training Size	Tagset Size	Ambiguous Tokens
English[4]	99903	139	38.65%
Czech	87071	970	45.97%
Estonian	81383	476	40.24%
Hungarian	102992	401	21.58%
Romanian	104583	486	40.00%
Slovene	94457	1033	38.01%

into consideration, as opposed to the case of training the small AC-based model, when only those training events which contain the particular AC are used.

3.3 Variable Distance Condition

The "stop" criterion for finding the appropriate relative position was originally based on hard coded choices suitable for the Czech language only, and of course it depended on the tagset as well. This dependency has been removed by selecting the appropriate conditions automatically when building the pool of possible features at the initialization phase[5] (using the relative frequency of the POS ambiguity classes, and a threshold to cut off less frequent categories to limit the size of the feature pool).

3.4 Weight Variation

Even though the full computation of the appropriate feature weight is still prohibitive (the more so when the general features are added), the learner is now allowed to vary the weights (in several discrete steps) during feature selection, as a (somewhat crude) attempt to depart from the Naive Bayes simplification to the approximation of the "correct" Maximum Entropy estimation.

3.5 Handling Unknown Words

In order to compare the effects of (not) using an independent dictionary, we have added an unknown word handling module to the code.[6] It extracts the prefix and suffix frequency information (and the combination thereof) from the training data. Then, for each of the combinations, it selects the most frequent set of tags seen in the training data and stores it for later use. When tagging, the data is first piped through a "guesser" which assigns to the unknown words such a set of possible tags which is stored with the longest matching prefix/suffix combination.

[5] Also, the use of variable-distance context may be switched off entirely.

[6] Originally, the code relied exclusively on the use of such an independent dictionary. Since the coverage of the Czech dictionary we have used is extensive, we have been simply ignoring the unknown word problem altogether in the past.

4 The Results

4.1 Reporting Error Rate: Words vs. Tokens

Since "best-only" tagging has been carried out, the error rate (i.e, 100 - accuracy in %) measure has been used throughout as the only evaluation criterion. However, since some results reported previously were apparently obtained using only the "real" words as the total for accuracy evaluation, whereas in other experiments every token counts (including punctuation[7], for example), we have computed both and report them separately[8].

4.2 Availability of Dictionary Information

We use two methods to obtain the set of possible tags for any given word form (i.e., to analyze it morphologically). Both methods include handling unknown words. First, we use only information which may be obtained automatically from the manually annotated corpus (we call this method *automatic*). This is the way the Maximum Entropy tagger (Ratnaparkhi, 1996) runs if one uses the binary version from the website (see the comparison in Section 5).

However, it is not unreasonable to assume that a larger *independent dictionary* exists which can help to obtain a list of possible tags for each word form in test data. This is what we have at our disposal for the languages in question, since the development of such a dictionary was part of the Multext-East project. We can thus assume a dictionary info is available for unknown words in the test data, i.e., even though there is no statistics available for them (since they did not appear in the training data), all possible tags for (almost[9]) every test token *are* available. This method is referred to as *independent* in the following text.

We have also used a third method of obtaining a dictionary information (called *mixed*), namely, by using only the words from the training data,

[7] And sometimes a separate token for sentence boundary

[8] Table 1 has been computed using all tokens. In fact, the languages differ significantly in the proportion of punctuation: from about 18% (English) to 30% (Estonian).

[9] Depending on the quality of the independent dictionary. Of course, the tagsets must match, which could be a problem per se. Here it is simple, since the dictionaries have been developed using the same tagsets as the tagged data.

but complementing the information about them obtained from the training data by including **all** other possible tags for such words. Therefore the net result is that during testing, we have only training words at our disposal, but with a complete dictionary information (as if coming from a full morphological dictionary)[10].

The results on the full training data set are summarized in Table 2.

The baseline error rate is computed as follows. First of all, we use the independent dictionary for obtaining the possible tags for each word. Then we extract only the lexical information from the current position[11] and counts used for smoothing (which is based on the ambiguity classes only and it does not use lexical information). The system is then trained normally, which means it uses the lexical information only if the AC-based smoothing[12] alone does not work. This baseline method is thus very close to the usual baseline method of using simple conditional distribution of tags given words.

The message of Table 2 seems to be obvious; but before we jump to conclusions, let's present another set of experiments.

In view of the recent interest in dealing with "small languages", and with regard to the questions of cost-effectiveness of using "human" resources (i.e. annotation vs. rule-writing vs. tools development etc.), we have also performed experiments with reduced training data size (but with an enriched feature pool – by lowering thresholds, adding more of the "general features" as described above, etc. – as allowed by reasonable time/space constraints).[13]

These results are summarized in Table 3 (using only the dictionary derived from the training data), Table 4 (using words from training data with morphological information complemented from a dictionary) and Table 5 (using the "independent" dictionary). In all cases, we again count only true words (no punctuation). Accordingly, the major POS error rate is reported, too (12 POS tags to be distinguished only: Noun, Verb, Adjective, ...; see Tables 6, 7, and 8).

[10]This arrangement removes the "closed vocabulary" phenomenon from the test data, since for the Multext-East data, we did not have a truly independent vocabulary available.

[11]Words from the training data which are not singletons (freq > 1) are used. Surprisingly enough, it would not hurt to use them too. We believe it is due to the smoothing method used. Even though this is valid only for the baseline experiment, we have observed in general that this form of exponential model (with error-driven training, that is) is remarkably resistant to overtraining.

[12]Using ACs linearly interpolated with global unigram subtag distribution and finally the uniform distribution.

[13]By reasonable we mean less than a day of CPU for training.

Table 9: Exponential w/feature selection vs. Maximum Entropy tagger (Words-only Error Rate, no dictionary)

Language	Tagger	
	Exp.	MaxEnt
English	9.18%	6.38%
Czech	18.83%	17.77%
Estonian	13.95%	14.92%
Hungarian	8.16%	8.55%
Romanian	7.76%	7.66%
Slovene	16.26%	17.44%

4.3 Tagger Comparison

The work (Erjavec et al., 1999) consistently compares several taggers (HMM, Brill's Transformation-based Tagger, Ratnaparkhi's Maximum Entropy tagger, and the Daelemans et al.'s Memory-based Tagger) on Slovene. We have chosen the Maximum Entropy tagger (Ratnaparkhi, 1996) for a comparison with our universal tagger, since it achieved (by a small margin) the best overall result on Slovene as reported there (86.360% on all tokens) of taggers available to us (MBT, the best overall, was not freely available to us at the time of writing). We have trained and tested the Maximum Entropy Tagger on exactly the same data, using the off-the-shelf (java binary only) version.

The results are compared in Table 9.

Since we want to show how a tagger accuracy is influenced by the amount of training data available, we have run a series of experiments comparing the results of the exponential tagger to the maximum entropy tagger when there is only a limited amount of data available. The results are summarized in Table 10. Since the public version of the MaxEnt tagger cannot be modified to take advantage of neither the *mixed* nor the *independent* dictionary, we have compared it only to the *automatic* dictionary version of the exponential tagger. To save space, the results are tabulated only for the training data sizes of 2000, 5000 and 20000 words. Again, only the "true" word error rate is reported.

As the tables show, for the languages we tested, the exponential, feature-based tagger we adapted from (Hajič and Hladká, 1998) achieves similar results as the Maximum Entropy tagger[14] [15]. (using exactly the same (**full**) training data; the "score" is 3:3, with the MaxEnt tagger being substantially better on English; probably the development lan-

[14]Otherwise the acknowledged leader in English tagging

[15]The only substantial difference we noticed was in tagging speed. The runtime speed of the MaxEnt tagger is lower, only about 10 words per second vs. almost 500 words per second; it should be noted however that we are comparing MaxEnt's java bytecode and C.

Table 2: Results (Error rate, ER) on full training data, only true words counted (no punctuation)

Dictionary:	Automatic		Mixed		Independent	
Language	Baseline	Full	Baseline	Full	Baseline	Full
English	11.42%	9.18%	11.40%	7.91%	7.07%	3.58%
Czech	23.02%	18.83%	22.61%	14.78%	19.40%	9.59%
Estonian	16.12%	13.95%	16.19%	12.98%	9.94%	5.34%
Hungarian	8.35%	8.16%	8.31%	8.00%	3.55%	2.58%
Romanian	10.87%	7.76%	10.81%	7.34%	7.49%	3.35%
Slovene	20.53%	16.26%	20.01%	13.29%	17.29%	9.00%

Table 3: Error rate on reduced training data, dictionary: automatic

Language	Training data size					
	1000	2000	5000	10000	20000	Full
English	36.20%	29.36%	23.47%	18.27%	14.46%	9.18%
Czech	48.22%	42.95%	36.54%	30.97%	27.08%	18.83%
Estonian	48.14%	42.10%	32.44%	26.81%	21.51%	13.95%
Hungarian	39.68%	32.21%	23.94%	18.04%	13.92%	8.16%
Romanian	40.61%	35.02%	25.06%	19.26%	15.16%	7.76%
Slovene	45.84%	39.58%	33.12%	28.60%	24.50%	16.26%

Table 4: Error rate on reduced training data, dictionary: mixed

Language	Training data size					
	1000	2000	5000	10000	20000	Full
English	36.15%	29.58%	22.93%	17.70%	14.00%	7.91%
Czech	48.97%	41.93%	34.37%	28.10%	23.31%	14.78%
Estonian	48.24%	42.79%	32.98%	26.60%	21.02%	12.98%
Hungarian	39.87%	32.71%	23.63%	17.98%	13.82%	8.00%
Romanian	42.85%	35.70%	25.46%	19.23%	14.81%	7.34%
Slovene	46.74%	39.88%	32.00%	26.20%	21.73%	13.29%

Table 5: Error rate on reduced training data, dictionary: "independent"

Language	Training data size					
	1000	2000	5000	10000	20000	Full
English	10.29%	7.64%	5.53%	4.54%	3.83%	3.58%
Czech	22.51%	18.07%	17.33%	15.10%	12.62%	9.59%
Estonian	13.11%	11.95%	10.70%	9.29%	8.10%	5.34%
Hungarian	6.84%	5.35%	4.29%	4.07%	3.48%	2.58%
Romanian	13.11%	9.47%	7.81%	6.18%	5.07%	3.35%
Slovene	24.63%	19.17%	16.17%	14.12%	12.62%	9.00%

guage bias shows here[16]). However, when the training data size goes down, the advantage of predicting the single morphological categories separately favors the exponential tagger (with the notable and substantial exception of English). The less data, the larger the difference (Tab 10).

The resulting accuracy (of both taggers) is still unsatisfactory not only from the point of view of results obtained on English, but also from the practical point of view: approx. 85% accuracy (Czech, Slovene) typically means that about five out of six 10-word sentences contain at least one error in it. That is bad news e.g. for parsing projects involving tagging as a preliminary step.

[16]On the other hand, the Exponential tagger has been developed on Czech originally and it lost on this language. It should be noted that the original version of the exponential tagger did contain more Czech-specific features, and thus might in fact do better.

Table 6: POS Error rate on reduced training data, dictionary: automatic

Language	Training data size					
	1000	2000	5000	10000	20000	Full
English	26.77%	20.82%	16.11%	11.86%	9.48%	5.64%
Czech	24.32%	20.20%	13.46%	9.70%	7.22%	3.72%
Estonian	35.81%	30.52%	23.02%	18.26%	14.31%	8.46%
Hungarian	30.54%	24.99%	18.09%	13.15%	10.29%	5.81%
Romanian	31.33%	27.59%	19.24%	14.51%	11.25%	5.21%
Slovene	27.16%	23.15%	17.01%	12.89%	9.74%	5.61%

Table 7: POS Error rate on reduced training data, dictionary: mixed

Language	Training data size					
	1000	2000	5000	10000	20000	Full
English	26.69%	21.09%	15.82%	11.53%	9.08%	4.94%
Czech	24.32%	20.61%	13.47%	10.19%	7.37%	3.76%
Estonian	36.48%	31.76%	23.55%	18.21%	14.32%	8.20%
Hungarian	30.28%	25.25%	17.59%	12.89%	10.15%	5.64%
Romanian	33.56%	28.34%	20.03%	14.52%	11.03%	5.04%
Slovene	27.58%	23.30%	16.85%	12.59%	9.88%	5.12%

Table 8: POS Error rate on reduced training data, dictionary: "independent"

Language	Training data size					
	1000	2000	5000	10000	20000	Full
English	6.42%	5.36%	3.63%	3.02%	2.53%	2.43%
Czech	3.21%	2.85%	2.17%	2.01%	1.65%	1.12%
Estonian	6.71%	6.32%	5.27%	4.31%	3.77%	2.36%
Hungarian	5.35%	4.42%	3.39%	3.18%	2.75%	2.04%
Romanian	9.51%	6.54%	5.36%	4.00%	3.18%	1.89%
Slovene	6.10%	5.19%	4.04%	3.59%	3.25%	2.08%

5 Conclusions

5.1 The Differences Among Languages

The following discussion abstracts from the tagset design, relying on the fact that the Multext-East project has been driven by common tagset guidelines to an unprecedented extent, given the very different languages involved. At the same time, we acknowledge that even so, their design for the individual languages might have influenced the results. Also, the quality of the annotation is an important factor; we believe though that the later data we obtained for the experiments described here are within the range of usual human error and do not suffer from negligence[17].

First of all, it is clear that these languages differ substantially just by looking at the simple training data statistics, where the number of unique tags seen in a relatively small collection of about 100k tokens is high - from 401 (Hungarian) to 1033 (Slovene); compare that to English with only 139 tags. However, it is interesting to see that the average per-token ambiguity is much more narrowly distributed, and in fact English ranks 3rd (after Hungarian and Slovene), Czech being the last with almost every other token ambiguous on average. This ambiguity does not correspond with the results obtained: Slovene, being the second least ambiguous, is the second most difficult to tag. Only Czech behaves consistently by tailing the pack in both cases.

5.2 Comparison to Previous Results

Any comparison is necessarily difficult due to different evaluation methodologies, even within the "best-only", accuracy-based reporting. Nevertheless, we will try.

For Romanian, Tufis in his recent work (Tufis, 1999) reports 98.5% accuracy (i.e. 1.5% error rate) on Romanian, using the classifier combination approach advocated by e.g. (Brill and Wu, 1998). His

[17] Specifically, we are sure that the post-release Czech, Slovene and Hungarian data we are using are without annotation defects beyond the usual occasional annotation error, as they have been double checked, and we also believe that the other two languages are reasonably clean. Bulgarian, although present on the CD, is unfortunately unusable since it has not been manually annotated; for English, see above.

Table 10: Error rate comparison on reduced training data, automatic dictionary

Language	Training data size					
	2000		5000		20000	
	ME	Exp	ME	Exp	ME	Exp
English	26.03%	29.36%	17.70%	23.47%	9.61%	14.46%
Czech	50.77%	42.95%	41.95%	36.54%	28.16%	27.08%
Estonian	51.08%	42.10%	40.09%	32.44%	25.50%	21.51%
Hungarian	41.12%	32.21%	30.68%	23.94%	17.27%	13.92%
Romanian	42.88%	35.02%	30.07%	25.06%	16.67%	15.16%
Slovene	49.46%	39.58%	39.34%	33.12%	27.77%	24.50%

results are well above the 3.29% error rate achieved here (with even a larger tagset of 1391 vs. 486 here), but the paper does not say how this number has been computed (training data size, the all-token/words-only question) thus making any conclusions difficult to make. He also argues that his method is language independent but no results are mentioned for other languages.

For Czech, previous work achieved similar results (6.20% on newspaper text using the all-tokens-based error rate computation, on 160,000 training tokens; vs. 7.04% here on approx. half that amount of training data; same handling of unknown words). This is in line with the expectations, since the same methodology (tagging as well as evaluation) has been used, except the features used in that work were specifically tuned to Czech.

The most detailed account of Slovene (Erjavec et al., 1999) reports various results, which might not be directly comparable because it is unclear whether they use the all-tokens-based or words-only computation of the error rate. They report 6.421% error rate on the full tagset on *known* words, and 13.583% on all words (tokens?) including unknown words (the exponential tagger we used achieved 13.82% on all tokens, 16.26% on words only). They use almost the same data (Orwell's 1984, but leaving out the Appendices)[18]. They also report that the original Czech-specific exponential tagger used as a basis for the work reported here achieved 7.28% error rate on Slovene on full tags on the same data, which means that by the changes to the exponential tagger aimed at its language independence we introduced in Section 3, we have not achieved any improvement (on Slovene) of the exp. tagger (the error rate stayed at 7.26% – using all-tokens-based evaluation numbers, dictionary available; but the data was not exactly the same, presumably).

5.3 Dictionary vs. Training Data

This is, according to our opinion, the most interesting result of the experiments described so far. As already Table 2 clearly suggests, even the baseline tagging results obtained with the help of an independent dictionary are comparable (if not better) than the fully-trained tagger on 100k words, but without the dictionary information. The situation is even clearer when comparing the POS-only results: here the "independent" dictionary results are better by far, with almost no training data needed.

Looking at the characteristics of the languages, it is apparent that the inflections cause the problem: the coverage of a previously unseen text is inferior to the usual coverage of English or another analytical language. Therefore, unless we can come up with a really clever way of learning rules for dealing with previously unseen words, it is clearly strongly preferable to work on a morphological dictionary[19], rather than to try to annotate more data.

6 Future Work

We would like to compare more taggers using still other methodologies, especially the MBT tagger, which achieved the best results on Slovene but which was not available to us at the time of writing this paper. Obviously, we would also like to use the classifier combination method on them, to confirm the really surprisingly good results on Romanian and test it on the other languages as well.

We would also like to enrich the best taggers available today (such as the Maximum Entropy tagger) by using the dictionary information available and compare the results with the exponential feature-based tagger we have been using in the experiments here.

For Czech and Slovene, the results are still far below what one would like to see (in absolute terms). It seems that the key lies in the initial feature set definition - including statistical tagset clustering, which might potentially lead to more reliable estimates of certain parameters while using still the same size of training data.

[18]Their tag count is lower (1021) than here (1033), but that's not really relevant. They do not report the average ambiguity or a similar measure.

[19]Not necessarily manually - apparently, even a partially supervised method would be of tremendous help.

7 Acknowledgements

The author wishes to thank many Multext-East participants for their efforts to improve the original data, especially to Niki Petkevič, Tomaz Erjavec, Heiki-Jaan Kaalep and Gábor Prószéky, and for providing the final versions of the annotated data for the experiments. Any errors and mistakes are solely to be blamed on the author, not the annotators, of course.

References

Eric Brill and Jun Wu. 1998. Classifier combination for improved lexical disambiguation. In *Proceedings of ACL/COLING'98*, pages 191–195, Montreal, Canada. ACL/ICCL.

Eric Brill. 1995. Transformation-based error-driven learning and natural language processing: A case study in part-of-speech tagging. *Computational Linguistics*, 21:543–565.

Jean-Pierre Chanod. 1997. Current developments for Central & Eastern European languages. In *Proceedings of EU Project meeting TELRI I*, Romania.

Kenneth W. Church. 1988. A stochastic parts program and noun phrase parser for unrestricted text. In *Proceedings of the Second Conference on Applied Natural Language Processing*, pages 136–143, Austin, Texas. ACL.

Walter Daelemans, Jakub Zavrel, Peter Berck, and Steven Gillis. 1996. MBT: A memory-based part of speech tagger generator. In *Proceedings of WVLC 4*, pages 14–27. ACL.

Tomaz Erjavec, Saso Dzeroski, and Jakub Zavrel. 1999. Morphosyntactic Tagging of Slovene: Evaluating PoS Taggers and Tagsets. Technical Report IJS-DP 8018, Dept. for Intelligent Systems, Jozef Stefan Institute, Ljubljana, Slovenia, April 2nd.

Jan Hajič and Barbora Hladká. 1997. Tagging of inflective languages: a comparison. In *Proceedings of ANLP'97*, pages 136–143, Washington, DC. ACL.

Jan Hajič and Barbora Hladká. 1998. Tagging inflective languages: Prediction of morphological categories for a rich, structured tagset. In *Proceedings of ACL/COLING'98*, pages 483–490, Montreal, Canada. ACL/ICCL.

Andrew W. Mackie Julian Benello and James A. Anderson. 1989. Syntactic category disambiguation with neural networks. *Computer Speech and Language*, 3:203–217.

Bernard Merialdo. 1992. Tagging text with a probabilistic model. *Computational Linguistics*, 20(2):155–171.

Adwait Ratnaparkhi. 1996. A maximum entropy model for part-of-speech tagging. In *Proceedings of EMNLP 1*, pages 133–142. ACL.

Helmut Schmid. 1994. Probabilistic part-of-speech tagging using decision trees. In *Proceedings of International Conference on New Methods in Language Processing*, pages 44–49, Manchester, England.

Dan Tufis. 1999. Tiered tagging and combined language models classifiers. In *Proceedings of Text, Speech and Dialogue'99*, Mariánské Lázně, Czech Republic, Sept. 15–18.

Jean Véronis. 1996a. Multext-East (Copernicus 106). http://www.lpl.univ-aix.fr/projects/multext-east.

Jean Véronis. 1996b. Multext-East language-specific resources (Copernicus 106). http://www.lpl.univ-aix.fr/projects/multext-east/MTE2.html.

The Effectiveness of Corpus-Induced Dependency Grammars for Post-processing Speech*

M. P. Harper, C. M. White, W. Wang, M. T. Johnson, and R. A. Helzerman
School of Electrical and Computer Engineering
Purdue University
West Lafayette, IN 47907-1285
{*harper,robot,wang28,mjohnson,helz*}*@ecn.purdue.edu*

Abstract

This paper investigates the impact of Constraint Dependency Grammars (CDG) on the accuracy of an integrated speech recognition and CDG parsing system. We compare a conventional CDG with CDGs that are induced from annotated sentences and template-expanded sentences. The grammars are evaluated on parsing speed, precision/coverage, and improvement of word and sentence accuracy of the integrated system. Sentence-derived CDGs significantly improve recognition accuracy over the conventional CDG but are less general. Expanding the sentences with templates provides us with a mechanism for increasing the coverage of the grammar with only minor reductions in recognition accuracy.

1 Background

The question of when and how to integrate language models with speech recognition systems is gaining in importance as recognition tasks investigated by the speech community become increasingly more challenging and as speech recognizers are used in human/computer interfaces and dialog systems (Block, 1997; Pieraccini and Levin, 1992; Schmid, 1994; Wright et al., 1994; Zue et al., 1991). Many systems tightly integrate N-gram stochastic language models, with a power limited to a regular grammar, into the recognizer (Jeanrenaud et al., 1995; Ney et al., 1994; Placeway et al., 1993) to build more accurate speech recognizers. However, in order to act based on the spoken interaction with the user, the speech signal must be mapped to an internal representation. Obtaining a syntactic representation for the spoken utterance has a high degree of utility for mapping to a semantic representation. Without a structural analysis of an input, it is difficult to guarantee the correctness of the mapping from a sentence to its interpretation (e.g., mathematical expressions to internal calculations). We believe that significant additional improvement in accuracy can be gained in specific domains by using a more complex language model that combines syntactic, semantic, and domain knowledge.

A language processing module that is more powerful than a regular grammar can be loosely, moderately, or tightly integrated with the spoken language system, and there are advantages and disadvantages associated with each choice (Harper et al., 1994). To tightly integrate a language model with the power of a context-free grammar with the acoustic module requires that the power of the two modules be matched, making the integrated system fairly intractable and difficult to train. By separating the language model from the acoustic model, it becomes possible to use a more powerful language model without increasing computational costs or the amount of acoustic training data required by the recognizer. Furthermore, a loosely-integrated language model can be developed independently of the speech recognition component, which is clearly an advantage. Decoupling the acoustic and language models also adds flexibility: a wide variety of language models can be tried with a single acoustic model. Systems that utilize a language model that operates as a post-processor to a speech recognizer include (Block, 1997; Seneff, 1992; Zue et al., 1991).

The goal of this research is to construct and experimentally evaluate a prototype of a spoken language system that loosely integrates a speech recognition component with an NLP component that uses syntactic, semantic, and domain-specific knowledge to more accurately select the sentence uttered by a speaker. First we describe the system we have built. Then we describe the mechanism used to rapidly develop a domain-specific grammar that improves accuracy of our speech recognizer.

2 Our System

We have developed the prototype spoken language system depicted in Figure 1 that integrates a speech recognition component based on HMMs with a powerful grammar model based on Constraint Dependency Grammar (CDG). The speech recognizer is implemented as a multiple-mixture triphone HMM with a simple integrated word co-occurrence gram-

* This research was supported by grants from Intel, Purdue Research Foundation, and National Science Foundation IRI 97-04358, CDA 96-17388, and #9980054-BCS.

mar (Ent, 1997; Young et al., 1997). Mel-scale cepstral coefficients, energy, and each of their their first and second order differences are used as the underlying feature vector for each speech frame. Model training is done using standard Baum-Welch Maximum Likelihood parameter re-estimation on diagonal covariance Gaussian Mixture Model (GMM) feature distributions. The speech recognizer employs a token-passing version of the Viterbi algorithm (Young et al., 1989) and pruning settings to produce a pruned recognition lattice. This pruned lattice contains the most likely alternative sentences that account for the sounds present in an utterance as well as their probabilities. Without any loss of information, this lattice is then compressed into a word graph (Harper et al., 1999b; Johnson and Harper, 1999), which acts as the interface between the recognizer and the CDG parser. The word graph algorithm begins with the recognition lattice and eliminates identical subgraphs by iteratively combining word nodes that have exactly the same preceding or following nodes (as well as edge probabilities), pushing excess probability to adjacent nodes whenever possible. The resulting word graph represents all possible word-level paths without eliminating or adding any paths or modifying their probabilities. Word graphs increase the bandwidth of useful acoustic information passed from the HMM to the CDG parser compared to most current speech recognition systems.

The CDG parser parses the word graph to identify the best sentence consistent with both the acoustics of the utterance and its own additional knowledge. The loose coupling of the parser with the HMM allows us to construct a more powerful combined system without increasing the amount of training data for the HMM or the computational complexity of either of the component modules. Our NLP component is implemented using a CDG parser (Harper and Helzerman, 1995; Maruyama, 1990a; Maruyama, 1990b) because of its power and flexibility, in particular:

- It supports the use of syntactic, semantic, and domain-specific knowledge in a uniform framework.
- Our CDG parser supports efficient simultaneous parsing of alternative sentence hypotheses in a word graph (Harper and Helzerman, 1995; Helzerman and Harper, 1996).
- Because CDG is a dependency grammar, it can better model free-order languages. Hence, CDG can be used in processing a wider variety of human languages than other grammar paradigms.
- It is capable of representing and using context-dependent information unlike traditional grammar approaches, thus providing a finer degree of control over the syntactic analysis of a sentence.
- A CDG can be extracted directly from sentences annotated with dependency information (i.e., feature and syntactic relationships).

We hypothesize that the accuracy of the combined HMM/CDG system should benefit from the ability to create a grammar that covers the domain as precisely as possible and that does not consider sentences that would not make sense given the domain. A corpus-based grammar is likely to have this degree of control. In the next section we describe how we construct a CDG from corpora.

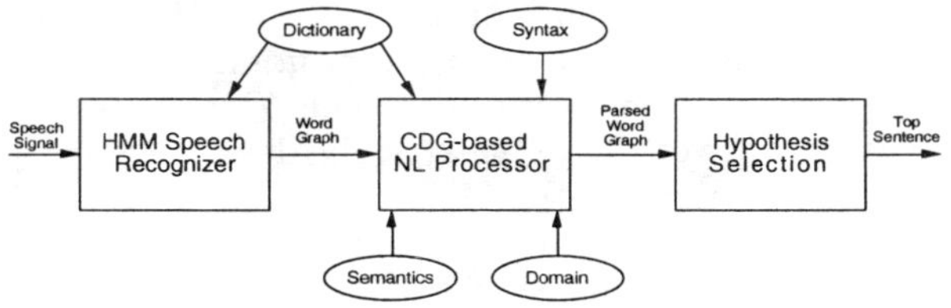

Figure 1: Block diagram of the loosely-coupled spoken language system.

3 Learning CDG Rules

In this section, we introduce CDG and then describe how CDG constraints can be learned from sentences annotated with grammatical information.

3.1 Introduction to CDG

Constraint Dependency Grammar (CDG), first introduced by Maruyama (Maruyama, 1990a; Maruyama, 1990b), uses constraints to determine the grammatical dependencies for a sentence. The parsing algorithm is framed as a constraint satisfaction problem: the rules are the constraints and the solutions are the parses. A CDG is defined as a five-tuple, $\langle \Sigma, R, L, C, T \rangle$, where $\Sigma = \{\sigma_1, \ldots, \sigma_c\}$ is a finite set of lexical categories (e.g., determiner), $R = \{r_1, \ldots, r_p\}$ is a finite set of uniquely named roles or role ids (e.g., governor, need1, need2), $L = \{l_1, \ldots, l_q\}$ is a finite set of labels (e.g., subject), C is a constraint formula, and T is a table that specifies allowable category-role-label combinations. A *sentence* $s = w_1 w_2 w_3 \ldots w_n$ has length n and is an element of Σ^*. For each word $w_i \in \Sigma$ of a sentence s, there are up to p different roles (with most words needing only one or two (Harper et al., 1999a)), yielding a maximum of $n * p$ roles for the entire sentence. A *role* is a variable that is assigned a *role value*, an element of the set $L \times \{1, 2, \ldots, n\}$. Role values are denoted as *l-m*, where $l \in L$ and $m \in \{1, 2, \ldots, n\}$ is called the *modifiee*. Maruyama originally used a modifiee of NIL to indicate that a role value does not require a modifiee, but it is more parsimonious to indicate that there is no dependent by setting the modifiee to the position of its word.

Role values are assigned to roles to record the syntactic dependencies between words in the sentence.

The governor role is assigned role values such that the modifiee of the word indicates the position of the word's governor or head (e.g., DET-3, when assigned to the governor role of a determiner, indicates its function and the position of its head). Every word in a sentence has a governor role. Need roles are used to ensure the requirements of a word are met. For example, an object is required by a verb that subcategorizes for one, unless it has passive voice. The required object is accounted for by requiring the verb's need role to be assigned a role value with a modifiee that points at the object. Words can have more than one need role, depending on the lexical category of the word. The table T indicates the roles that a word with a particular lexical category must support.

A sentence s is said to be **generated** by the grammar G if there exists an assignment **A** that maps a role value to each of the roles for s such that C is satisfied. There may be more than one assignment of role values to the roles of a sentence that satisfies C, in which case there is ambiguity. C is a first-order predicate calculus formula over all roles that requires that an assignment of role values to roles be consistent with the formula; those role values inconsistent with C can be eliminated. A subformula P_i of C is a predicate involving $=$, $<$, or $>$, or predicates joined by the logical connectives **and**, **or**, **if**, or **not**. A subformula is a *unary constraint* if it contains only a single variable (by convention, we use x_1) and a *binary constraint* if it contains two variables (by convention x_1 and x_2). An example of a unary and binary constraint appears in Figure 2. A CDG has an *arity* parameter a, which indicates the maximum number of variables in the subformulas of C, and a *degree* parameter d, which is the number of roles in the grammar. An arity of two suffices to represent a grammar at least as powerful as a context-free grammar (Maruyama, 1990a; Maruyama, 1990b). In (Harper et al., 1999a), we developed a way to write constraints concerning the category and feature values of a modifiee of a role value (or role value pair). These constraints loosely capture binary constraint information in unary constraints (or beyond binary for binary constraints) and results in more efficient parsing.

A unary constraint requiring that a role value assigned to the governor role of a determiner have the label DET and a modifiee pointing to a subsequent word.	A binary constraint requiring that a role value with the label S assigned to a need1 role of one word point at another word whose governor role is assigned a role value with the label SUBJ and a modifiee that points back at the first word.
(if (and (= (category x_1) determiner) (= (rid x_1) G)) (and (= (label x_1) DET) (> (mod x_1) (pos x_1))))	(if (and (= (label x_1) S) (= (rid x_1) N1) (= (mod x_1) (pos x_2)) (= (rid x_2) G)) (and (= (label x_2) SUBJ) (= (mod x_2) (pos x1))))

Figure 2: A Unary and binary constraint for CDG.

The white box in Figure 3 depicts a parse for the sentence *Clear the screen* from the Resource Management corpus (Price et al., 1988) (the ARV and ARVP in the gray box will be discussed later), which is a corpus we will use to evaluate our speech processing system. We have constructed a conventional CDG with around 1,500 unary and binary constraints (i.e., its arity is 2) that were designed to parse the sentences in the corpus. This CDG covers a wide variety of grammar constructs (including conjunctions and wh-movement) and has a fairly rich semantics. It uses 16 lexical categories, 4 roles (so its degree is 4), 24 labels, and 13 lexical feature types (**subcat**, **agr**, **case**, **vtype** (e.g., progressive), **mood**, **gap**, **inverted**, **voice**, **behavior** (e.g., mass), **type** (e.g., interrogative, relative), **semtype**, **takesdet**, and **conjtype**). The parse in Figure 3 is an assignment of role values to roles that is consistent with the unary and binary constraints. A role value, when assigned to a role, has access to not only the label and modifiee of its role value, but also the role name of the role to which it is assigned, information specific to the word (i.e., the word's position in the sentence, its lexical category, and feature values for each feature), and information about the lexical class and feature values of its modifiee. Our unary and binary constraints use this information to eliminate ungrammatical assignments.

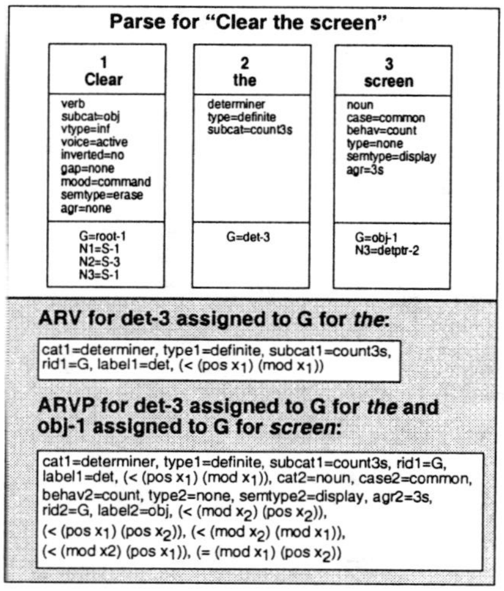

Figure 3: A CDG parse (see white box) is represented by the assignment of role values to roles associated with a word with a specific lexical category and one feature value per feature. ARVs and ARVPs (see gray box) represent grammatical relations that can be extracted from a sentence's parse.

3.2 Learning CDG Constraints

The grammaticality of a sentence in a language defined by a CDG was originally determined by applying the constraints of the grammar to the possible role value assignments. If the set of all possible role values assigned to the roles of a sentence of length n is denoted $\mathcal{S}_1 = \Sigma \times R \times POS \times L \times MOD \times F_1 \times \ldots \times F_k$, where k is the number of feature types, F_i represents the set of feature values for that type, $POS = \{1, 2, \ldots, n\}$ is the set of possible positions, $MOD = \{1, 2, \ldots, n\}$ is the set of possible modifiees, and n is sentence length (which can be any arbitrary natural number), then unary constraints partition $\mathcal{S}_1$ into grammatical and ungrammatical role values. Similarly, binary constraints partition the set $\mathcal{S}_2 = \mathcal{S}_1 \times \mathcal{S}_1 = \mathcal{S}_1^2$ into compatible and incompatible pairs. Building upon this concept of role value partitioning, it is possible to construct another way of representing unary and binary constraints because CDG constraints do not need to reference the exact position of a word or a modifiee in the sentence to parse sentences (Harper and Helzerman, 1995; Maruyama, 1990a; Maruyama, 1990b; Menzel, 1994; Menzel, 1995).

To represent the relative, rather than the absolute, position information for the role values in a grammatical sentence, it is only necessary to represent the positional relations between the modifiees and the positions of the role values. To support an arity of 2, these relations involve either equality or less-than relations over the modifiees and positions of role values assigned to the roles x_1 and x_2. Since unary constraints operate over role values assigned to a single role, the only relative position relations that can be tested are between the role value's position (denoted as $\mathrm{P}x_1$) and its modifiee (denoted as $\mathrm{M}x_1$); one and only one of the following three relations must be true: $(\mathrm{P}x_1 < \mathrm{M}x_1)$, $(\mathrm{M}x_1 < \mathrm{P}x_1)$, or $(\mathrm{P}x_1 = \mathrm{M}x_1)$. Since binary constraints operate over role values assigned to pairs of roles, x_1 and x_2, the only possible relative position relations that can be tested are between $\mathrm{P}x_1$ and $\mathrm{M}x_1$, $\mathrm{P}x_2$ and $\mathrm{M}x_2$, $\mathrm{P}x_1$ and $\mathrm{M}x_2$, $\mathrm{P}x_2$ and $\mathrm{M}x_1$, $\mathrm{P}x_1$ and $\mathrm{P}x_2$, $\mathrm{M}x_1$ and $\mathrm{M}x_2$. Note that each of the six has three positional relations (as in the case of unary relations on $\mathrm{P}x_1$ and $\mathrm{M}x_1$) such that one and only one of them is simultaneously true.

The unary and binary positional relations provide the necessary mechanism to develop an alternative view of the unary and binary constraints. First, we develop the concept of an *abstract role value* (ARV), which is a finite characterization of all possible role values using relative, rather than absolute, position relations. Formally, an ARV for a particular grammar $G = \langle \Sigma, R, L, C, T, F_1, \ldots, F_k \rangle$ is an element of the set: $\mathcal{A}_1 = \Sigma \times R \times L \times F_1 \times \ldots \times F_k \times \mathrm{UC}$, where UC encodes the three possible positional relations between Px_1 and Mx_1. The gray box of Figure 3 shows an example of an ARV obtained from the parsed sentence. Note that $\mathcal{A}_1$ is a finite set representing the space of all possible ARVs for the grammar[1]; hence, the set provides an alternative characterization of the unary constraints for the grammar, which can be partitioned into positive (grammatical) and negative (ungrammatical) ARVs. During parsing, if a role value does not match one of the elements in the positive ARV space, then it should be disallowed. Positive ARVs can be obtained directly from the parses of sentences: for each role value in a parse for a sentence, simply extract its category, feature, role, and label information, and then determine the positional relation that holds between the role value's position and modifiee.

Similarly the set of legal *abstract role value pairs* (ARVPs), $\mathcal{A}_2 = \Sigma \times R \times L \times F_1 \times \ldots \times F_k \times \Sigma \times R \times L \times F_1 \times \ldots \times F_k \times \mathrm{BC}$, where BC encodes the positional relations among Px_1, Mx_1, Px_2, and Mx_2, provides an alternative definition for the binary constraints[2]. The gray box of Figure 3 shows an example of an ARVP obtained from the parsed sentence. Positive ARVPs can be obtained directly from the parses of sentences. For each pair of role values assigned to different roles, simply extract their category, feature, role, and label information, and then determine the positional relations that hold between the positions and modifiees.

An enumeration of the positive ARV/ARVPs can be used to represent the CDG constraints, C, and ARV/ARVPs are PAC-learnable from positive examples, as can be shown using the techniques of (Natarajan, 1989; Valiant, 1984). ARV/ARVP constraints can be enforced by using a fast table lookup method to see if a role value (or role value pair) is allowed (rather than propagating thousands of constraints), thus speeding up the parser.

4 Evaluation Using the Naval Resource Management Domain

An experiment was conducted to determine the plausibility and the benefits of extracting CDG constraints from a domain-specific corpus of sentences. For our speech application, the ideal CDG should be general enough to cover sentences similar to those that appear in the corpus while being restrictive enough to eliminate sentences that are implausible given the observed sentences. Hence, we investigate whether a grammar extracted from annotated sentences in a corpus achieves this precision of coverage. We also examine whether a learned grammar has the ability to filter out incorrect sentence hypotheses produced by the HMM component of our system in Figure 1. To investigate these issues, we have performed an experiment using the standard

[1] $\mathcal{A}_1$ can also include information about the possible lexical categories and feature values of the modifiee of x_1.

[2] $\mathcal{A}_2$ can also include information about the possible lexical categories and feature values of the modifiees of x_1 and x_2.

Resource Management (RM) (Price et al., 1988) and Extended Resource Management (RM2) ((DARPA), 1990) corpora. These mid-size speech corpora have a vocabulary of 991 words and contain utterances of sentences derived from sentence templates based on interviews with naval personnel familiar with naval resource management tasks. They were chosen for several reasons: they are two existing speech corpora from the same domain; their manageable sizes make them a good platform for the development of techniques that require extensive experimentation; and the sentences have both syntactic variety and reasonably rich semantics. RM contains 5,190 separate utterances (3,990 testing, 1,200 training) of 2,845 distinct sentences (2,245 training, 600 testing). We have extracted several types of CDGs from annotations of the RM sentences and tested their generality using the 7,396 sentences in RM2 (out of the 8,173) that are in the resource management domain but are distinct from the RM sentences. We compare these CDGs to each other and to the conventional CDG described previously.

The corpus-based CDGs were created by extracting the allowable grammar relationships from the RM sentences that were annotated by language experts using the SENATOR annotation tool, a CGI (Common Gateway Interace) HTML script written in GNU C++ version 2.8.1 (White, 2000). We tested two major CDG variations: those derived directly from the RM sentences (Sentence CDGs) and those derived from simple template-expanded RM sentences (Template CDGs). For example, "List MIDPAC's deployments during ⟨date⟩" is a sentence containing a date template which allows any date representations. For these experiments, we focused on templates for dates, years, times, numbers, and latitude and longitude coordinates. Each template name identifies a sub-grammar which was produced by annotating the appropriate strings. We then annotated sentences containing the template names as if they were regular sentences. Approximately 25% of the 2,845 RM sentences were expanded with one or more templates.

Although annotating a corpus of sentences can be a labor intensive task, we used an iterative approach that is based on parsing using grammars with varying degrees of restrictiveness. A grammar can be made less restrictive by ignoring:

- lexical information associated with a role value's modifiee in the ARVPs,
- feature information of two role values in an ARVP not directly related based on their modifiee relations,
- syntactic information provided by two role values that are not directly related,
- specific feature information (e.g., semantics or subcategorization).

Initially, we bootstrapped the grammar by annotating a 200 sentence subset of the RM corpus and extracting a fairly general grammar from the annotations. Then using increasingly restrictive grammars at each iteration, we used the current grammar to identify sentences that required annotation and verified the parse information for sentences that succeeded. This iterative technique reduced the time required to build a CDG from about one year for the conventional CDG to around two months (White, 2000).

Several methods of extracting an ARV/ARVP grammar from sentences or template-extended sentences were investigated. The ARVPs are extracted differently for each method; whereas, the ARVs are extracted in the same manner regardless of the method. Recall that ARVs represent the set of observed role value assignments. In our implementation, each ARV includes: the label of the role value, the role to which the role value was assigned, the lexical category and feature values of the word containing the role, the relative position of the word and the role value's modifiee, and the modifiee's lexical category and feature values (modifiee constraints). We use modifiee constraints for ARVs regardless of extraction method because their use does not change the coverage of the extracted grammar and not using the information would significantly slow the parser (Harper et al., 1999a). Because the ARVP space is larger than the ARV space, we investigate six variations for extracting the pairs:

1. **Full Mod:** contains all grammar and feature value information for all pairs of role values from annotated sentences, as well as modifiee constraints. For a role value pair in a sentence to be considered valid during parsing with this grammar, it must match an ARVP extracted from the annotated sentences.
2. **Full:** like **Full Mod** except it does not impose modifiee constraints on a pair of role values during parsing.
3. **Feature Mod:** contains all grammar relations between all pairs of role values, but it considers feature and modifiee constraints only for pairs that are directly related by a modifiee link. During parsing, if a role value pair is related by a modifiee link, then a corresponding ARVP with full feature and modifiee information must appear in the grammar for it to be allowed. If the pair is not directly related, then an ARVP must be stored for the grammar relations, ignoring feature and modifiee constraint information.
4. **Feature:** like **Feature Mod** except it does not impose modifiee constraints on a pair of role values during parsing.
5. **Direct Mod:** stores only the grammar, feature, and modifiee information for those pairs of role

Table 1: Number of ARVs and ARVPs extracted for each RM grammar.

ARVP Variation	Sentence CDG	Template CDG	Percent Increase
Full Mod	270,034	408,912	51.43%
Full	165,480	200,792	21.34%
Feature Mod	49,468	56,758	14.74%
Feature	36,558	40,308	10.26%
Direct Mod	41,124	47,004	14.30%
Direct	28,214	30,554	8.29%
ARVs	4,424	4,648	5.06%

Table 2: Number of successfully parsed sentences in RM2 using the conventional CDG and CDGs derived from sentences only or template-expanded sentences.

ARVP Variation	# Parsed with Sentence CDG	# Parsed with Template CDG
Full Mod	3,735 (50.50%)	4,461 (60.32%)
Full	4,509 (60.97%)	5,316 (71.88%)
Feature Mod	5,365 (72.54%)	5,927 (80.14%)
Feature	5,772 (78.04%)	6,208 (83.94%)
Direct Mod	5,464 (73.88%)	5,979 (80.84%)
Direct	5,931 (80.19%)	6,275 (84.82%)
Conventional	7,144 (96.59%)	not applicable

values that are directly related by a modifiee link. During parsing, if a role value pair is related by such a link, then a corresponding ARVP must appear in the grammar for it to be allowed. Any pair of role values not related by a modifiee link is allowed (an open-world assumption).

6. **Direct:** like **Direct Mod** except it does not impose modifiee constraints on a pair of role values during parsing.

Grammar sizes for these six grammars, extracted either directly from the 2,845 sentences or from the 2,845 sentences expanded with our sub-grammar templates, appear in Table 1. The largest grammars were derived using the **Full Mod** extraction method, with a fairly dramatic growth resulting from processing template-expanded sentences. The **Feature** and **Direct** variations are more manageable in size, even those derived from template-expanded sentences.

Size is not the only important consideration for a grammar. Other important issues are grammar generality and the impact of the grammar on the accuracy of selecting the correct sentence from the recognition lattice of a spoken utterance. After extracting the CDG grammars from the RM sentences and template-expanded sentences, we tested the generality of the extracted grammars by using each grammar to parse the 7,396 RM2 sentences. See the results in Table 2. The grammar with the greatest generality was the conventional CDG for the RM corpus; however, this grammar also has the unfortunate attribute of being quite ambiguous. The most generalizable of extracted grammars uses the **Direct** method on template-expanded sentences. In all cases, the template-expanded sentence grammars gave better coverage than their corresponding sentence-only grammars.

We have also used the extracted grammars to post-process word graphs created by the word graph compression algorithm of (Johnson and Harper, 1999) for the test utterances in the RM corpus. As was reported in (Johnson and Harper, 1999), the word-error rate of our HMM recognizer with an embedded word pair language model on the RM test set of 1200 utterances was 5.0%, the 1-best sentence accuracy was 72.1%, and the word graph coverage accuracy was 95.1%. Also, the average uncompressed word graph size was 75.15 nodes, and our compression algorithm resulted in a average word graph size of 28.62 word nodes. When parsing the word graph, the probability associated with a word node can either represent its acoustic score or a combination of its acoustic and stochastic grammar score. We use the acoustic score because (Johnson and Harper, 1999) showed that by using a word node's acoustic score alone when extracting the top sentence candidate after parsing gave a 4% higher sentence accuracy.

For the parsing experiments, we processed the 1,080 word graphs produced for the RM test set that contained 50 or fewer word nodes after compression (out of 1,200 total) in order to efficiently compare the 12 ARV/ARVP CDG grammars and the conventional CDG (the larger word graphs require significant time and space to parse using the conventional CDG). These 1,080 word graphs contain 24.95 word nodes on average with a standard deviation (SD) of 10.80, and result in 1-best sentence accuracy was 75% before parsing. The number of role values prior to binary constraint propagation differ across the grammars with an average (and SD) for the conventional grammar of 504.99 (442.00), for the sentence-only grammars of 133.37 (119.48), and for the template-expanded grammars of 157.87 (145.16). Table 3 shows the word graph parsing speed and the path, node, and role value (RV) ambiguity after parsing; Table 4 shows the sentence accuracy and the accuracy and percent correct for words. Note that percent correct words is calculated using $\frac{N-D-S}{N}$ and word accuracy using $\frac{N-D-S-I}{N}$, where N is the number of words, D is the number of deletions, S is the number of substitutions, and I is the number of insertions.

The most selective RM sentence grammar, **Full Mod**, achieves the highest sentence accuracy, but at a cost of a greater average parsing time than the other RM sentence grammars. Higher accu-

ARVP Variation	Parse Time (sec.)	No. Paths	No. Nodes	No. RVs
Full Mod	33.89 (41.12)	2.21 (1.74)	10.59 (3.44)	19.51 (8.32)
Template Full Mod	41.85 (51.75)	2.78 (3.75)	10.76 (3.64)	19.93 (8.76)
Full	29.73 (36.68)	2.83 (2.92)	10.87 (3.54)	20.32 (8.86)
Template Full	36.80 (46.90)	3.40 (5.19)	11.03 (3.74)	20.77 (9.47)
Feature Mod	11.46 (14.46)	3.9 (5.97)	11.20 (3.94)	21.43 (10.49)
Template Feature Mod	13.80 (18.47)	4.22 (6.93)	11.28 (4.06)	21.81 (11.17)
Feature	11.60 (14.97)	5.19 (8.36)	11.72 (4.22)	23.41 (12.72)
Template Feature	14.24 (19.63)	6.86 (14.83)	11.94 (4.52)	24.47 (14.41)
Direct Mod	13.93 (19.73)	4.25 (6.49)	11.46 (4.27)	22.79 (13.44)
Template Direct Mod	17.28 (26.56)	4.62 (8.61)	11.45 (4.28)	22.95 (13.34)
Direct	19.95 (36.89)	8.08 (18.52)	12.81 (5.73)	32.85 (34.65)
Template Direct	28.02 (69.50)	9.98 (25.52)	12.95 (5.95)	33.36 (35.66)
Coventional	83.48 (167.51)	51.33 (132.43)	17.14 (8.02)	77.19 (76.26)

Table 3: Average parse times (SD), number of paths (SD), number of nodes (SD), and number of role values (SD) remaining after parsing the 1,080 word graphs of 50 or fewer word nodes produced for the RM test set using the 13 CDGs.

ARVP Variation	Sentence Accuracy	% Correct Words	Word Accuracy
Full Mod	91.94%	98.55%	98.19%
Template Full Mod	91.57%	98.50%	98.14%
Full	91.57%	98.49%	98.11%
Template Full	91.20%	98.45%	98.05%
Feature Mod	90.56%	98.38%	97.95%
Template Feature Mod	90.19%	98.34%	97.90%
Feature	90.28%	98.35%	97.91%
Template Feature	89.91%	98.29%	97.85%
Direct Mod	90.46%	98.37%	97.91%
Template Direct Mod	90.09%	98.32%	97.86%
Direct	89.91%	98.30%	97.82%
Template Direct	89.44%	98.25%	97.75%
Conventional	81.20%	97.11%	96.10%

Table 4: The sentence accuracy, percent correct words, and word accuracy from parsing 1,080 word graphs of 50 or fewer word nodes produced for the RM test set using the 13 CDGs.

racy appears to be correlated with the ability of the constraints to eliminate word nodes from the word graph during parsing. The least restrictive sentence grammar, **Direct**, is less accurate than the other sentence grammars and offers an intermediate speed of parsing, most likely due to the increased ambiguity in the parsing space. The fastest grammar was the **Feature-Mod** grammar, which also offers an intermediate level of accuracy. Its size (even with templates), restrictiveness, and speed make it very attractive. The template versions of each grammar showed a slight increase in average parse times (from processing a larger number of role values) and a slight decrease in parsing accuracy. The conventional grammar was the least competitive of the grammars both in speed and in accuracy.

5 Conclusion and Future Directions

The ability to extract ARV/ARVP grammars with varying degrees of specificity provides us with the ability to rapidly develop a grammar with the ability to improve sentence accuracy of our speech system. To achieve balance between precision and coverage of our corpus-induced grammars, we have expanded the RM sentences with templates for expressions like dates and times. The grammars extracted from these expanded sentences gave increased RM2 coverage without sacrificing even 1% of the sentence accuracy. We are currently expanding the number of templates in our grammar in an attempt to obtain full coverage of the RM2 corpus using only template-expanded RM sentences. We have recently added ten semantic templates to the grammar and have improved the coverage by 9.19% without losing any sentence accuracy. We are also developing a stochastic version of CDG that uses a statistical ARV, which is similar to a supertag (Srinivas, 1996).

References

H. U. Block. 1997. Language components in VERBMOBIL. In *Proc. of the Int. Conf. of Acoustics, Speech, and Signal Proc.*, pages 79–82.

Defense Advanced Research Projects Agency (DARPA). 1990. Extended resource management: Continuous speech speaker-dependent corpus (RM2). CD-ROM. NIST Speech Discs 3-1.2 and 3-2.2.

Entropic Cambridge Research Laboratory, Ltd., 1997. *HTK: Hidden Markov Model Toolkit V2.1.*

M. P. Harper and R. A. Helzerman. 1995. Extensions to constraint dependency parsing for spoken language processing. *Computer Speech and Language*, 9:187–234.

M. P. Harper, L. H. Jamieson, C. D. Mitchell, G. Ying, S. Potisuk, P. N. Srinivasan, R. Chen, C. B. Zoltowski, L. L. McPheters, B. Pellom, and R. A. Helzerman. 1994. Integrating language models with speech recognition. In *Proc. of the AAAI Workshop on the Integration of Natural Language and Speech Processing*, pages 139–146.

M. P. Harper, S. A. Hockema, and C. M. White. 1999a. Enhanced constraint dependency grammar parsers. In *Proc. of the IASTED Int. Conf. on Artificial Intelligence and Soft Computing.*

M. P. Harper, M. T. Johnson, L. H. Jamieson, and C. M. White. 1999b. Interfacing a CDG parser with an HMM word recognizer using word graphs. In *Proc. of the Int. Conf. of Acoustics, Speech, and Signal Proc.*

R. A. Helzerman and M. P. Harper. 1996. MUSE CSP: An extension to the constraint satisfaction problem. *Journal of Artificial Intelligence Research*, 5:239–288.

P. Jeanrenaud, E. Eide, U. Chaudhari, J. McDonough, K. Ng, M. Siu, and H. Gish. 1995. Reducing word error rate on conversational speech from the Switchboard corpus. In *Proc. of the Int. Conf. of Acoustics, Speech, and Signal Proc.*, pages 53–56.

M. T. Johnson and M. P. Harper. 1999. Near minimal weighted word graphs for post-processing speech. In *1999 Int. Workshop on Automatic Speech Recognition and Understanding.*

H. Maruyama. 1990a. Constraint Dependency Grammar and its weak generative capacity. *Computer Software.*

H. Maruyama. 1990b. Structural disambiguation with constraint propagation. In *Proc. of the Annual Meeting of Association for Computational Linguistics*, pages 31–38.

W. Menzel. 1994. Parsing of spoken language under time constraints. In *11th European Conf. on Artificial Intelligence*, pages 560–564.

W. Menzel. 1995. Robust processing of natural language. In *Proc. of the 19th Annual German Conf. on Artificial Intelligence.*

B. Natarajan. 1989. On learning sets and functions. *Machine Learning*, 4(1).

H. Ney, U. Essen, and R. Kneser. 1994. On structuring probabilistic dependences in stochastic language modelling. *Computer Speech and Language*, 8:1–38.

R. Pieraccini and E. Levin. 1992. Stochastic representation of semantic structure for speech understanding. *Speech Communication*, 11:283–288.

P. Placeway, R. Schwartz, P. Fung, and L. Nguyen. 1993. The estimation of powerful language models from small and large corpora. In *Proc. of the Int. Conf. of Acoustics, Speech, and Signal Proc.*, pages 33–36.

P. J. Price, W. Fischer, J. Bernstein, and D. Pallett. 1988. A database for continuous speech recognition in a 1000-word domain. In *Proc. of the Int. Conf. of Acoustics, Speech, and Signal Proc.*, pages 651–654.

L. A. Schmid. 1994. Parsing word graphs using a linguistic grammar and a statistical language model. In *Proc. of the Int. Conf. of Acoustics, Speech, and Signal Proc.*, pages 41–44.

S. Seneff. 1992. TINA: A natural language system for spoken language applications. *American Journal of Computational Linguistics*, 18:61–86.

B. Srinivas. 1996. 'Almost parsing' technique for language modeling. In *Proc. of the Int. Conf. on Spoken Language Processing*, pages 1173–1176.

L. G. Valiant. 1984. A theory of the learnable. *Communications of the ACM*, 27(11):1134–1142.

C. M. White. 2000. *Rapid Grammar Development and Parsing Using Constraint Dependency Grammars with Abstract Role Values.* Ph.D. thesis, Purdue University, School of Electrical and Computer Engineering, West Lafayette, IN.

J. H. Wright, G. J. F. Jones, and H. Lloyd-Thomas. 1994. Robust language model incorporating a substring parser and extended N-grams. In *Proc. of the Int. Conf. of Acoustics, Speech, and Signal Proc.*, pages 361–364.

S. J. Young, N. H. Russell, and J. H. S. Thornton. 1989. Token passing : a simple conceptual model for connected speech recognition systems. Technical Report TR38, Cambridge University, Cambridge, England.

S. J. Young, J. Odell, D. Ollason, V. Valtchev, and P. Woodland, 1997. *The HTK Book.* Entropic Cambridge Research Laboratory Ltd., 2.1 edition.

V. Zue, J. Glass, D. Goodine, H. Leung, M. Phillips, J. Polifroni, and S. Seneff. 1991. Integration of speech recognition and natural language processing in the MIT Voyager system. In *Proc. of the Int. Conf. of Acoustics, Speech, and Signal Proc.*, pages 713–716.

Analyzing Dependencies of Japanese Subordinate Clauses based on Statistics of Scope Embedding Preference

Takehito Utsuro, Shigeyuki Nishiokayama, Masakazu Fujio, Yuji Matsumoto
Graduate School of Information Science, Nara Institute of Science and Technology
8916-5, Takayama-cho, Ikoma-shi, Nara, 630-0101, JAPAN
E-mail: *utsuro@is.aist-nara.ac.jp*, URL: *http://cl.aist-nara.ac.jp/~utsuro/*

Abstract

This paper proposes a statistical method for learning dependency preference of Japanese subordinate clauses, in which scope embedding preference of subordinate clauses is exploited as a useful information source for disambiguating dependencies between subordinate clauses. Estimated dependencies of subordinate clauses successfully increase the precision of an existing statistical dependency analyzer.

1 Introduction

In the Japanese language, since word order in a sentence is relatively free compared with European languages, dependency analysis has been shown to be practical and effective in both rule-based and stochastic approaches to syntactic analysis. In dependency analysis of a Japanese sentence, among various source of ambiguities in a sentence, dependency ambiguities of subordinate clauses are one of the most problematic ones, partly because word order in a sentence is relatively free. In general, dependency ambiguities of subordinate clauses cause scope ambiguities of subordinate clauses, which result in enormous number of syntactic ambiguities of other types of phrases such as noun phrases.[1]

In the Japanese linguistics, a theory of Minami (1974) regarding scope embedding preference of subordinate clauses is well-known. Minami (1974) classifies Japanese subordinate clauses according to the breadths of their scopes and claim that subordinate clauses which inherently have narrower scopes are embedded within the scopes of subordinate clauses which inherently have broader scopes (details are in section 2). By manually analyzing several raw corpora, Minami (1974) classifies various types of Japanese subordinate clauses into three categories, which are totally ordered by the embedding relation of their scopes. In the Japanese computational linguistics community, Shirai et al. (1995) employed Minami (1974)'s theory on scope embedding preference of Japanese subordinate clauses and applied it to rule-based Japanese dependency analysis. However, in their approach, since categories of subordinate clauses are obtained by manually analyzing a small number of sentences, their coverage against a large corpus such as EDR bracketed corpus (EDR, 1995) is quite low.[2]

In order to realize a broad coverage and high performance dependency analysis of Japanese sentences which exploits scope embedding preference of subordinate clauses, we propose a corpus-based and statistical alternative to the rule-based manual approach (section 3).[3]

[1] In our preliminary corpus analysis using the stochastic dependency analyzer of Fujio and Matsumoto (1998), about 30% of the 210,000 sentences in EDR bracketed corpus (EDR, 1995) have dependency ambiguities of subordinate clauses, for which the precision of chunk (bunsetsu) level dependencies is about 85.3% and that of sentence level is about 25.4% (for best one) ~ 35.8% (for best five), while for the rest 70% of EDR bracketed corpus, the precision of chunk (bunsetsu) level dependencies is about 86.7% and that of sentence level is about 47.5% (for best one) ~ 60.2% (for best five). In addition to that, when assuming that those ambiguities of subordinate clause dependencies are initially resolved in some way, the chunk level precision increases to 90.4%, and the sentence level precision to 40.6% (for best one) ~ 67.7% (for best five). This result of our preliminary analysis clearly shows that dependency ambiguities of subordinate clauses are among the most problematic source of syntactic ambiguities in a Japanese sentence.

[2] In our implementation, the coverage of the categories of Shirai et al. (1995) is only 30% for all the subordinate clauses included in the whole EDR corpus.

[3] Previous works on statistical dependency analysis include Fujio and Matsumoto (1998) and Haruno et al. (1998) in Japanese analysis as well as Lafferty et al. (1992), Eisner (1996), and Collins (1996) in English analysis. In later sections, we discuss the advantages of our approach over several closely related previous works.

Table 1: Word Segmentation, POS tagging, and *Bunsetsu* Segmentation of A Japanese Sentence

Word Segmentation	Tenki	ga	yoi	kara	dekakeyou
POS (+ conjugation form) Tagging	noun	case-particle	adjective (base)	predicate-conjunctive-particle	verb (volitional)
Bunsetsu Segmentation (Chunking)	Tenki-ga		yoi-kara		dekakeyou
English Translation	*weather*	subject	*fine*	*because*	*let's go out*
	(Because the weather is fine, let's go out.)				

First, we formalize the problem of deciding scope embedding preference as a classification problem, in which various types of linguistic information of each subordinate clause are encoded as features and used for deciding which one of given two subordinate clauses has a broader scope than the other. As in the case of Shirai et al. (1995), we formalize the problem of deciding dependency preference of subordinate clauses by utilizing the correlation of scope embedding preference and dependency preference of Japanese subordinate clauses. Then, as a statistical learning method, we employ the decision list learning method of Yarowsky (1994), where optimal combination of those features are selected and sorted in the form of decision rules, according to the strength of correlation between those features and the dependency preference of the two subordinate clauses. We evaluate the proposed method through the experiment on learning dependency preference of Japanese subordinate clauses from the EDR bracketed corpus (section 4). We show that the proposed method outperforms other related methods/models. We also evaluate the estimated dependencies of subordinate clauses in Fujio and Matsumoto (1998)'s framework of the statistical dependency analysis of a whole sentence, in which we successfully increase the precisions of both chunk level and sentence level dependencies thanks to the estimated dependencies of subordinate clauses.

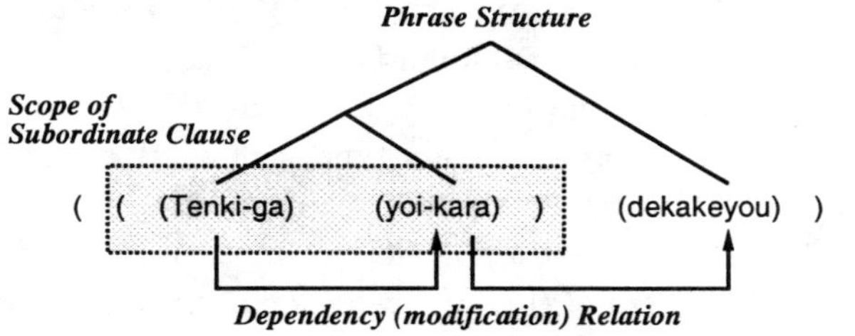

Figure 1: An Example of Japanese Subordinate Clause (taken from the Sentence of Table 1)

2 Analyzing Dependencies between Japanese Subordinate Clauses based on Scope Embedding Preference

2.1 Dependency Analysis of A Japanese Sentence

First, we overview dependency analysis of a Japanese sentence. Since words in a Japanese sentence are not segmented by explicit delimiters, input sentences are first word segmented, part-of-speech tagged, and then chunked into a sequence of segments called *bunsetsus*.[4] Each chunk (bunsetsu) generally consists of a set of content words and function words. Then, dependency relations among those chunks are estimated, where most practical dependency analyzers for the Japanese language usually assume the following two constraints:

1. Every chunk (bunsetsu) except the last one modifies only one posterior chunk (bunsetsu).

2. No modification crosses to other modifications in a sentence.

Table 1 gives an example of word segmentation, part-of-speech tagging, and *bunsetsu* segmentation (chunking) of a Japanese sentence, where the verb and the adjective are tagged with their parts-of-speech as well as conjugation forms. Figure 1 shows the phrase structure, the bracketing,[5] and the dependency (modification) relation of the chunks (bunsetsus) within the sentence.

[4] Word segmentation and part-of-speech tagging are performed by the Japanese morphological analyzer Chasen (Matsumoto et al., 1997), and chunking is done by the preprocessor used in Fujio and Matsumoto (1998).

[5] The phrase structure and the bracketing are shown just for explanation, and we do not consider them but consider only dependency relations in the analysis throughout this paper.

A Japanese *subordinate clause* is a clause whose head chunk satisfies the following properties.

1. The content words part of the chunk (bunsetsu) is one of the following types:
   (a) A predicate (i.e., a verb or an adjective).
   (b) nouns and a copula like "$Noun_1$ *dearu*" (in English, "*be* $Noun_1$").
2. The function words part of the chunk (bunsetsu) is one of the following types:
   (a) Null.
   (b) Adverb type such as "$Verb_1$ *ippou-de*" (in English, "(subject) $Verb_1$ ..., *on the other hand*,").
   (c) Adverbial noun type such as "$Verb_1$ *tame*" (in English, "*in order to* $Verb_1$").
   (d) Formal noun type such as "$Verb_1$ *koto*" (in English, gerund "$Verb_1$-ing").
   (e) Temporal noun type such as "$Verb_1$ *mae*" (in English, "*before* (subject) $Verb_1$ ...").
   (f) A predicate conjunctive particle such as "$Verb_1$ *ga*" (in English, "although (subject) $Verb_1$ ...,").
   (g) A quoting particle such as "$Verb_1$ *to (iu)*" (in English, "*(say) that* (subject) $Verb_1$ ...").
   (h) (a)~(g) followed by topic marking particles and/or sentence-final particles.

Figure 2: Definition of Japanese Subordinate Clause

2.2 Japanese Subordinate Clause

The following gives the definition of what we call a "Japanese *subordinate clause*" throughout this paper. A *clause* in a sentence is represented as a sequence of chunks. Since the Japanese language is a head-final language, the clause head is the final chunk in the sequence. A grammatical definition of a Japanese *subordinate clause* is given in Figure 2.[6] For example, the Japanese sentence in Table 1 has one subordinate clause, whose scope is indicated as the shaded rectangle in Figure 1.

2.3 Scope Embedding Preference of Subordinate Clauses

We introduce the concept of Minami (1974)'s classification of Japanese subordinate clauses by describing the more specific classification by Shirai et al. (1995). From 972 newspaper summary sentences, Shirai et al. (1995) manually extracted 54 clause final function words of Japanese subordinate clauses and classified them into the following three categories according to the embedding relation of their scopes.

Category A: Seven expressions representing simultaneous occurrences such as "$Verb_1$ *to-tomoni* ($Clause_2$)" and "$Verb_1$ *nagara* ($Clause_2$)".

Category B: 46 expressions representing cause and discontinuity such as "$Verb_1$ *te* ($Clause_2$)" (in English "$Verb_1$ *and* ($Clause_2$)") and "$Verb_1$ *node*" (in English "*because* (subject) $Verb_1$ ...,").

Category C: One expression representing independence, "$Verb_1$ *ga*" (in English, "although (subject) $Verb_1$ ...,").

The category A has the narrowest scope, while the category C has the broadest scope, i.e.,

$$\text{Category A} \prec \text{Category B} \prec \text{Category C}$$

where the relation '$\prec$' denotes the embedding relation of scopes of subordinate clauses. Then, scope embedding preference of Japanese subordinate clauses can be stated as below:

Scope Embedding Preference of Japanese Subordinate Clauses

1. A subordinate clause can be embedded within the scope of another subordinate clause which inherently has a scope of the same or a broader breadth.
2. A subordinate clause can not be embedded within the scope of another subordinate clause which inherently has a narrower scope.

For example, a subordinate clause of 'Category B' can be embedded within the scope of another subordinate clause of 'Category B' or 'Category C', but not within that of 'Category A'. Figure 3

[6] This definition includes adnominal or noun phrase modifying clauses "$Clause_1$ (NP_1)" (in English, relative clauses "(NP_1) that $Clause_1$"). Since an adnominal clause does not modify any posterior subordinate clauses, but modifies a posterior noun phrase, we regard adnominal clauses only as modifees when considering dependencies between subordinate clauses.

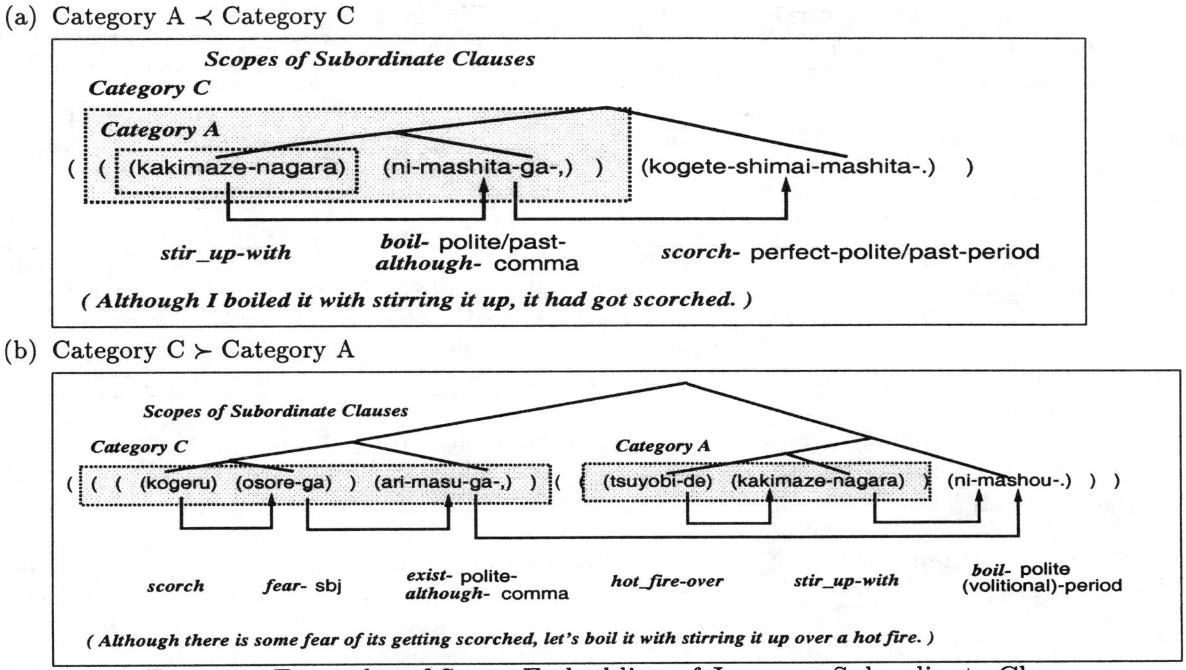

Figure 3: Examples of Scope Embedding of Japanese Subordinate Clauses

(a) gives an example of an anterior Japanese subordinate clause (*"kakimaze-nagara"*, Category A), which is embedded within the scope of a posterior one with a broader scope (*"ni-mashita-ga-,"*, Category C). Since the posterior subordinate clause inherently has a broader scope than the anterior, the anterior is embedded within the scope of the posterior. On the other hand, Figure 3 (b) gives an example of an anterior Japanese subordinate clause (*"ari-masu-ga-,"*, Category C), which is not embedded within the scope of a posterior one with a narrower scope (*"kakimaze-nagara"*, Category A). Since the posterior subordinate clause inherently has a narrower scope than the anterior, the anterior is not embedded within the scope of the posterior.

2.4 Preference of Dependencies between Subordinate Clauses based on Scope Embedding Preference

Following the scope embedding preference of Japanese subordinate clauses proposed by Minami (1974), Shirai et al. (1995) applied it to rule-based Japanese dependency analysis, and proposed the following preference of deciding dependencies between subordinate clauses. Suppose that a sentence has two subordinate clauses $Clause_1$ and $Clause_2$, where the head vp chunk of $Clause_1$ precedes that of $Clause_2$.

Dependency Preference of Japanese Subordinate Clauses

1. The head vp chunk of $Clause_1$ can modify that of $Clause_2$ if $Clause_2$ inherently has a scope of the same or a broader breadth compared with that of $Clause_1$.
2. The head vp chunk of $Clause_1$ can not modify that of $Clause_2$ if $Clause_2$ inherently has a narrower scope compared with that of $Clause_1$.

3 Learning Dependency Preference of Japanese Subordinate Clauses

As we mentioned in section 1, the rule-based approach of Shirai et al. (1995) to analyzing dependencies of subordinate clauses using scope embedding preference has serious limitation in its coverage against corpora of large size for practical use. In order to overcome the limitation of the rule-based approach, in this section, we propose a method of learning dependency preference of Japanese subordinate clauses from a bracketed corpus. We formalize the problem of deciding scope embedding preference as a classification problem, in which various types of linguistic information of each subordinate clause are encoded as features and used for deciding which one of given two subordinate clauses has a broader scope than the other. As a statistical learning method, we employ the decision list learning method of Yarowsky (1994).

Table 2: Features of Japanese Subordinate Clauses

Feature Type	# of Features	Each Binary Feature
Punctuation	2	with-comma, without-comma
Grammatical (some features have distinction of chunk-final/middle)	17	adverb, adverbial-noun, formal-noun, temporal-noun, quoting-particle, copula, predicate-conjunctive-particle, topic-marking-particle, sentence-final-particle
Conjugation form of chunk-final conjugative word	12	stem, base, mizen, ren'you, rentai, conditional, imperative, *ta*, *tari*, *te*, conjecture, volitional
Lexical (lexicalized forms of 'Grammatical' features, with more than 9 occurrences in EDR corpus)	235	adverb (e.g., *ippou-de, irai*), adverbial-noun (e.g., *tame, baai*) topic-marking-particle (e.g., *ha, mo*), quoting-particle (*to*), predicate-conjunctive-particle (e.g., *ga, kara*), temporal-noun (e.g., *ima, shunkan*), formal-noun (e.g., *koto*), copula (*dearu*), sentence-final-particle (e.g., *ka, yo*)

3.1 The Task Definition

Considering the dependency preference of Japanese subordinate clauses described in section 2.4, the following gives the definition of our task of deciding the dependency of Japanese subordinate clauses. Suppose that a sentence has two subordinate clauses $Clause_1$ and $Clause_2$, where the head vp chunk of $Clause_1$ precedes that of $Clause_2$. Then, our task of deciding the dependency of Japanese subordinate clauses is to distinguish the following two cases:

1. The head vp chunk of $Clause_1$ modifies that of $Clause_2$.
2. The head vp chunk of $Clause_1$ does not modify that of $Clause_2$, but modifies that of another subordinate clause or the matrix clause which *follows* $Clause_2$.

Roughly speaking, the first corresponds to the case where $Clause_2$ inherently has a scope of the same or a broader breadth compared with that of $Clause_1$, while the second corresponds to the case where $Clause_2$ inherently has a narrower scope compared with that of $Clause_1$.[7]

3.2 Decision List Learning

A decision list (Yarowsky, 1994) is a sorted list of the decision rules each of which decides the value of a *decision D* given some *evidence E*. Each decision rule in a decision list is sorted in descending order with respect to some preference value, and rules with higher preference values are applied first when applying the decision list to some new test data.

First, let the random variable D representing a decision varies over several possible values, and the random variable E representing some evidence varies over '1' and '0' (where '1' denotes the presence of the corresponding piece of evidence, '0' its absence). Then, given some training data in which the correct value of the decision D is annotated to each instance, the conditional probabilities $P(D=x \mid E=1)$ of observing the decision $D=x$ under the condition of the presence of the evidence E ($E=1$) are calculated and the decision list is constructed by the following procedure.

1. For each piece of evidence, calculate the *likelihood ratio* of the conditional probability of a decision $D=x_1$ (given the presence of that piece of evidence) to the conditional probability of the rest of the decisions $D=\neg x_1$:

$$\log_2 \frac{P(D=x_1 \mid E=1)}{P(D=\neg x_1 \mid E=1)}$$

   Then, a decision list is constructed with pieces of evidence sorted in descending order with respect to their likelihood ratios.[8]

2. The final line of a decision list is defined as 'a default', where the likelihood ratio is calculated as the ratio of the largest marginal probability of the decision $D=x_1$ to the marginal proba-

[7]Our modeling is slightly different from those of other standard approaches to statistical dependency analysis (Collins, 1996; Fujio and Matsumoto, 1998; Haruno et al., 1998) which simply distinguish the two cases: the case where dependency relation holds between the given two vp chunks or clauses, and the case where dependency relation does not hold. In contrast to those standard approaches, we ignore the case where the head vp chunk of $Clause_1$ modifies that of another subordinate clause which *precedes* $Clause_2$. This is because we assume that this case is more loosely related to the scope embedding preference of subordinate clauses.

[8]Yarowsky (1994) discusses several techniques for avoiding the problems which arise when an observed count is 0. Among those techniques, we employ the simplest one, i.e., adding a small constant α ($0.1 \leq \alpha \leq 0.25$) to the numerator and denominator. With this modification, more frequent evidence is preferred when there exist several evidences for each of which the conditional probability $P(D=x \mid E=1)$ equals to 1.

(a) An Example Sentence with Chunking, Bracketing, and Dependency Relations

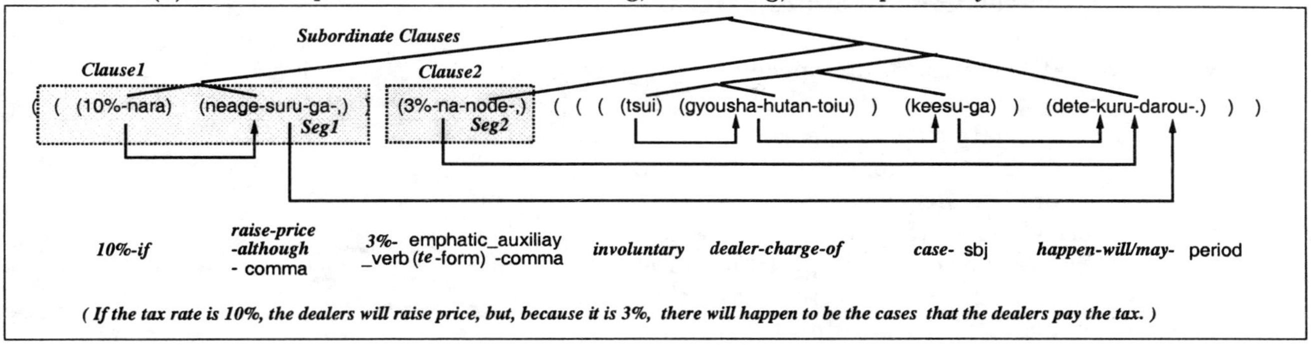

(b) Feature Expression of Head VP Chunk of Subordinate Clauses

Head VP Chunk of Subordinate Clause	Feature Set
Seg_1 : "neage-suru-ga-,"	$\mathcal{F}_1 = \{$ with-comma, predicate-conjunctive-particle(chunk-final), predicate-conjunctive-particle(chunk-final)-"*ga*" $\}$
Seg_2 : "3%-na-node-,"	$\mathcal{F}_2 = \{$ with-comma, chunk-final-conjugative-word-*te*-form $\}$

(c) Evidence-Decision Pairs for Decision List Learning

Evidence E $(E=1)$ (feature names are abbreviated)		Decision D
$\mathcal{F}_1$	$\mathcal{F}_2$	
with-comma	with-comma	"beyond"
with-comma	*te*-form	"beyond"
with-comma	with-comma, *te*-form	"beyond"
pred-conj-particle(final)	with-comma	"beyond"
...	...	...
with-comma, pred-conj-particle(final)	with-comma	"beyond"
...	...	...
pred-conj-particle(final)-"*ga*"	with-comma	"beyond"
...	...	...
with-comma, pred-conj-particle(final)-"*ga*"	with-comma	"beyond"
...	...	...

Figure 4: An Example of Evidence-Decision Pair of Japanese Subordinate Clauses

bility of the rest of the decisions $D=\neg x_1$:

$$\log_2 \frac{P(D=x_1)}{P(D=\neg x_1)}$$

The 'default' decision of this final line is $D=x_1$ with the largest marginal probability.

3.3 Feature of Subordinate Clauses

Japanese subordinate clauses defined in section 2.2 are encoded using the following four types of features: i) Punctuation: represents whether the head vp chunk of the subordinate clause is marked with a comma or not, ii) Grammatical: represents parts-of-speech of function words of the head vp chunk of the subordinate clause,[9] iii) Conjugation form of chunk-final conjugative word: used when the chunk-final word is conjugative, iv) Lexical: lexicalized forms of 'Grammatical' features which appear more than 9 times in EDR corpus. Each feature of these four types is binary and its value is '1' or '0' ('1' denotes the presence of the corresponding feature, '0' its absence). The whole feature set shown in Table 2 is designed so as to cover the 210,000 sentences of EDR corpus.

[9]Terms of parts-of-speech tags and conjugation forms are borrowed from those of the Japanese morphological analysis system Chasen (Matsumoto et al., 1997).

3.4 Decision List Learning of Dependency Preference of Subordinate Clauses

First, in the modeling of the evidence, we consider every possible correlation (i.e., dependency) of the features of the subordinate clauses listed in section 3.3. Furthermore, since it is necessary to consider the features for both of the given two subordinate clauses, we consider all the possible combination of features of the anterior and posterior head vp chunks of the given two subordinate clauses. More specifically, let Seg_1 and Seg_2 be the head vp chunks of the given two subordinate clauses (Seg_1 is the anterior and Seg_2 is the posterior). Also let $\mathcal{F}_1$ and $\mathcal{F}_2$ be the sets of features which Seg_1 and Seg_2 have, respectively (i.e., the values of these features are '1'). We consider every possible subset F_1 and F_2 of $\mathcal{F}_1$ and $\mathcal{F}_2$, respectively, and then model the evidence of the decision list learning method as any possible pair (F_1, F_2).[10]

Second, in the modeling of the decision, we distinguish the two cases of dependency relations described in section 3.1. We name the first case as the decision "modify", while the second as the decision "beyond".

3.5 Example

Figure 4 illustrates an example of transforming subordinate clauses into feature expression, and then obtaining training pairs of an evidence and a decision from a bracketed sentence. Figure 4 (a) shows an example sentence which contains two subordinate clauses $Clause_1$ and $Clause_2$, with chunking, bracketing, and dependency relations of chunks. Both of the head vp chunks Seg_1 and Seg_2 of $Clause_1$ and $Clause_2$ modify the sentence-final vp chunk. As shown in Figure 4 (b), the head vp chunks Seg_1 and Seg_2 have feature sets $\mathcal{F}_1$ and $\mathcal{F}_2$, respectively. Then, every possible subsets F_1 and F_2 of $\mathcal{F}_1$ and $\mathcal{F}_2$ are considered,[11] respectively, and training pairs of an evidence and a decision are collected as in Figure 4 (c). In this case, the value of the decision D is "beyond", because Seg_1 modifies the sentence-final vp chunk, which follows Seg_2.

[10] Our formalization of the evidence of decision list learning has an advantage over the decision tree learning (Quinlan, 1993) approach to feature selection of dependency analysis (Haruno et al., 1998). In the feature selection procedure of the decision tree learning method, the utility of each feature is evaluated independently, and thus the utility of the combination of more than one features is not evaluated directly. On the other hand, in our formalization of the evidence of decision list learning, we consider every possible pair of the subsets F_1 and F_2, and thus the utility of the combination of more than one features is evaluated directly.

[11] Since the feature 'predicate-conjunctive-particle(chunk-final)' subsumes 'predicate-conjunctive-particle(chunk-final)-"*ga*"', they are not considered together as one evidence.

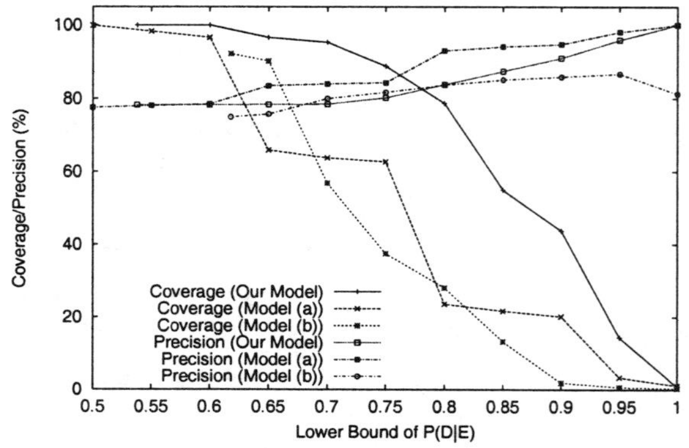

Figure 5: Precisions and Coverages of Deciding Dependency between Two Subordinate Clauses

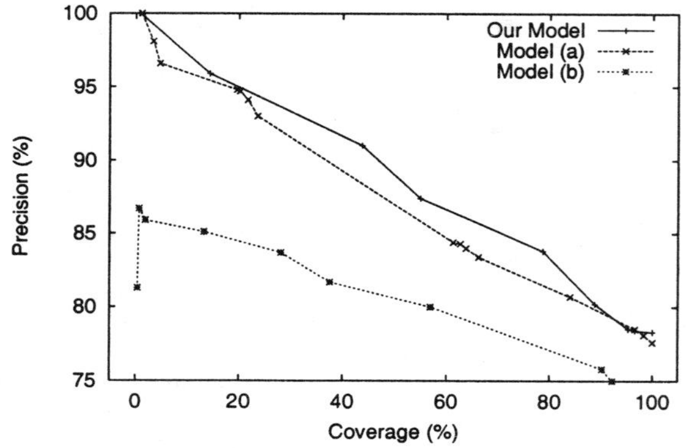

Figure 6: Correlation of Coverages and Precisions

4 Experiments and Evaluation

We divided the 210,000 sentences of the whole EDR bracketed Japanese corpus into 95% training sentences and 5% test sentences. Then, we extracted 162,443 pairs of subordinate clauses from the 199,500 training sentences, and learned a decision list for dependency preference of subordinate clauses from those pairs. The default decision in the decision list is D ="beyond", where the marginal probability $P(D = \text{"beyond"}) = 0.5378$, i.e., the baseline precision of deciding dependency between two subordinate clauses is 53.78 %. We limit the frequency of each evidence-decision pair to be more than 9. The total number of obtained evidence-decision pairs is 7,812. We evaluate the learned decision list through several experiments.[12]

First, we apply the learned decision list to deciding dependency between two subordinate clauses of the 5% test sentences. We change the threshold of the probability $P(D \mid E)$[13] in

[12] Details of the experimental evaluation will be presented in Utsuro (2000).

[13] $P(D \mid E)$ can be used equivalently to the likelihood

the decision list and plot the trade-off between coverage and precision.[14] As shown in the plot of "Our Model" in Figure 5, the precision varies from 78% to 100% according to the changes of the threshold of the probability $P(D \mid E)$.

Next, we compare our model with the other two models: (a) the model learned by applying the decision tree learning method of Haruno et al. (1998) to our task of deciding dependency between two subordinate clauses, and (b) a decision list whose decisions are the following two cases, i.e., the case where dependency relation holds between the given two vp chunks or clauses, and the case where dependency relation does not hold. The model (b) corresponds to a model in which standard approaches to statistical dependency analysis (Collins, 1996; Fujio and Matsumoto, 1998; Haruno et al., 1998) are applied to our task of deciding dependency between two subordinate clauses. Their results are also in Figures 5 and 6. Figure 5 shows that "Our Model" outperforms the other two models in coverage. Figure 6 shows that our model outperforms both of the models (a) and (b) in coverage and precision.

Finally, we examine whether the estimated dependencies of subordinate clauses improve the precision of Fujio and Matsumoto (1998)'s statistical dependency analyzer.[15] Depending on the threshold of $P(D \mid E)$, we achieve 0.8~1.8% improvement in chunk level precision, and 1.6~4.7% improvement in sentence level.[16]

5 Conclusion

This paper proposed a statistical method for learning dependency preference of Japanese subordinate clauses, in which scope embedding preference of subordinate clauses is exploited. We evaluated the estimated dependencies of subordinate clauses through several experiments and showed that our model outperformed other related models.

ratio.

[14]Coverage: the rate of the pairs of subordinate clauses whose dependencies are decided by the decision list, against the total pairs of subordinate clauses, Precision: the rate of the pairs of subordinate clauses whose dependencies are *correctly* decided by the decision list, against those *covered* pairs of subordinate clauses.

[15]Fujio and Matsumoto (1998)'s lexicalized dependency analyzer is similar to that of Collins (1996), where various features were evaluated through performance test and an optimal feature set was manually selected.

[16]The upper bounds of the improvement in chunk level and sentence level precisions, which are estimated by providing Fujio and Matsumoto (1998)'s statistical dependency analyzer with correct dependencies of subordinate clauses extracted from the bracketing of the EDR corpus, are 5.1% and 15%, respectively.

References

M. Collins. 1996. A new statistical parser based on bigram lexical dependencies. In *Proceedings of the 34th Annual Meeting of ACL*, pages 184–191.

EDR (Japan Electronic Dictionary Research Institute, Ltd.). 1995. *EDR Electronic Dictionary Technical Guide.*

J. Eisner. 1996. Three new probabilistic models for dependency parsing: An exploration. In *Proceedings of the 16th COLING*, pages 340–345.

M. Fujio and Y. Matsumoto. 1998. Japanese dependency structure analysis based on lexicalized statistics. In *Proceedings of the 3rd Conference on Empirical Methods in Natural Language Processing*, pages 88–96.

M. Haruno, S. Shirai, and Y. Oyama. 1998. Using decision trees to construct a practical parser. In *Proceedings of the 17th COLING and the 36th Annual Meeting of ACL*, pages 505–511.

J. Lafferty, D. Sleator, and D. Temperley. 1992. Grammatical trigrams: A probabilistic model of link grammar. In *Proceedings of the AAAI Fall Symposium: Probabilistic Approaches to Natural Language*, pages 89–97.

Y. Matsumoto, A. Kitauchi, T. Yamashita, O. Imaichi, and T. Imamura. 1997. Japanese morphological analyzer ChaSen 1.0 users manual. Information Science Technical Report NAIST-IS-TR97007, Nara Institute of Science and Technology. (in Japanese).

F. Minami. 1974. *Gendai Nihongo no Kouzou.* Taishuukan Shoten. (in Japanese).

J. R. Quinlan. 1993. *C4.5: Programs for Machine Learning.* Morgan Kaufmann.

S. Shirai, S. Ikehara, A. Yokoo, and J. Kimura. 1995. A new dependency analysis method based on semantically embedded sentence structures and its performance on Japanese subordinate clauses. *Transactions of Information Processing Society of Japan*, 36(10):2353–2361. (in Japanese).

T. Utsuro. 2000. Learning preference of dependency between Japanese subordinate clauses and its evaluation in parsing. In *Proceedings of the 2nd International Conference on Language Resources and Evaluation.* (to appear).

D. Yarowsky. 1994. Decision lists for lexical ambiguity resolution: Application to accent restoration in Spanish and French. In *Proceedings of the 32nd Annual Meeting of ACL*, pages 88–95.

Rapid Parser Development: A Machine Learning Approach for Korean

Ulf Hermjakob
USC Information Sciences Institute
4676 Admiralty Way #1000 · Marina del Rey, CA 90292 · USA
ulf@cs.utexas.edu

Abstract

This paper demonstrates that machine learning is a suitable approach for rapid parser development. From 1000 newly treebanked Korean sentences we generate a deterministic shift-reduce parser. The quality of the treebank, particularly crucial given its small size, is supported by a consistency checker.

1 Introduction

Given the enormous complexity of natural language, parsing is hard enough as it is, but often unforeseen events like the crises in Bosnia or East-Timor create a sudden demand for parsers and machine translation systems for languages that have not benefited from major attention of the computational linguistics community up to that point.

Good machine translation relies strongly on the context of the words to be translated, a context that often goes well beyond neighboring surface words. Often basic relationships, like that between a verb and its direct object, provide crucial support for translation. Such relationships are usually provided by parsers.

The NLP resources for a language of sudden international interest are typically quite limited. There is probably a dictionary, but most likely no treebank. Maybe basic tools for morphological analysis, but probably no semantic ontology.

This paper reports on the rapid development of a parser based on very limited resources. We show that by building a small treebank of only a thousand sentences, we could develop a good basic parser using machine learning within only three months. For the language we chose, Korean, a number of research groups have been working on parsing and/or machine translation in recent years (Yoon, 1997; Seo, 1998; Lee, 1997), but advanced resources have not been made publicly available, and we have not used any, thereby so-to-speak at least simulating a low density language scenario.

2 Korean

Like Japanese, Korean is a head-final agglutinative language. It is written in a phonetic alphabet called *hangul*, in which each two-byte character represents one syllable. While our parser operates on the original Korean hangul, this paper presents examples in a romanized transcription. In sentence (1) for example, the verb is preceded by a number of so-called *eojeols* (equivalent to *bunsetsus* in Japanese) like "chaeg-eul", which are typically composed of a content part ("chaeg" = book) and a postposition, which often corresponds to a preposition in English, but is also used as a marker of topic, subject or object ("eul").

나는	어제	그	책을	샀다.	
Na-neun	eo-je	geu	chaeg-eul	sass-da.	(1)
I$_{TOPIC}$	*yesterday*	*this*	*book*$_{OBJ}$	*bought.*	
I bought this book yesterday.					

Our parser produces a tree describing the structure of a given sentence, including syntactic and semantic roles, as well as additional information such as tense. For example, the parse tree for sentence (1) is shown below:

```
[1] na-neun eo-je geu chaeg-eul sass-da. [S]
   (SUBJ) [2] na-neun  [NP]
      (HEAD) [3] na  [REG-NOUN]
      (PARTICLE) [4] neun  [DUPLICATE-PRT]
   (TIME) [5] eo-je  [REG-ADVERB]
      (HEAD) [6] eo-je  [REG-ADVERB]
   (OBJ) [7] geu chaeg-eul  [NP]
      (MOD) [8] geu  [DEMONSTR-ADNOMINAL]
         (HEAD) [9] geu  [DEMONSTR-ADNOMINAL]
      (HEAD) [10] chaeg-eul  [NP]
         (HEAD) [11] chaeg  [REG-NOUN]
         (PARTICLE) [12] eul  [OBJ-CASE-PRT]
   (HEAD) [13] sass-da.  [VERB; PAST-TENSE]
      (HEAD) [14] sa  [VERB-STEM]
      (SUFFIX) [15] eoss  [INTERMED-SUF-VERB]
      (SUFFIX) [16] da  [CONNECTIVE-SUF-VERB]
      (DUMMY) [17] .  [PERIOD]
```

Figure 1: Parse tree for sentence 1 (simplified)

For preprocessing, we use a segmenter and morphological analyzer, KMA, and a tagger, KTAG, both provided by the research group of Prof. Rim of

Korea University. KMA, which comes with a built-in Korean lexicon, segments Korean text into *eojeols* and provides a set of possible sub-segmentations and morphological analyses. KTAG then tries to select the most likely such interpretation. Our parser is initialized with the result of KMA, preserving all interpretations, but marking KTAG's choice as the top alternative.

3 Treebanking Effort

The additional resources used to train and test a parser for Korean, which we will describe in more detail in the next section, were (1) a 1187 sentence treebank, (2) a set of 133 context features, and (3) background knowledge in form of an *'is-a'* ontology with about 1000 entries. These resources were built by a team consisting of the principal researcher and two graduate students, each contributing about 3 months.

3.1 Treebank

The treebank sentences are taken from the Korean newspaper Chosun, two-thirds from 1994 and the remainder from 1999. Sentences represent continuous articles with no sentences skipped for length or any other reason. The average sentence length is 21.0 words.

3.2 Feature Set

The feature set describes the context of a partially parsed state, including syntactic features like the part of speech of the constituent at the front/top of the input list (as sketched in figure 2) or whether the second constituent on the parse stack ends in a comma, as well as semantic features like whether or not a constituent is a time expression or contains a location particle. The feature set can accommodate any type of feature as long as it is computable, and can thus easily integrate different types of background knowledge.

3.3 Background Knowledge

The features are supported by background knowledge in the form of an ontology, which for example has a time-particle concept with nine sub-concepts (accounting for 9 of the 1000 entries mentioned above). Most of the background knowledge groups concepts like particles, suffixes, units (e.g. for lengths or currencies), temporal adverbs – semantic classes that are not covered by part of speech information of the lexicon, yet provide valuable clues for parsing.

3.4 Time Effort

The first graduate student, a native Korean and linguistics major, hired for 11 weeks, spent about 2 weeks getting trained, 6 weeks on building two-thirds of the treebank, 2 weeks providing most background knowledge entries and 1 week helping to identify useful features. The other graduate student, a native Korean and computer science major, installed Korean tools including a terminal for hangul and the above mentioned KMA and KTAG, wrote a number of scripts tying all tools together, made some tool improvements, built one-third of the treebank

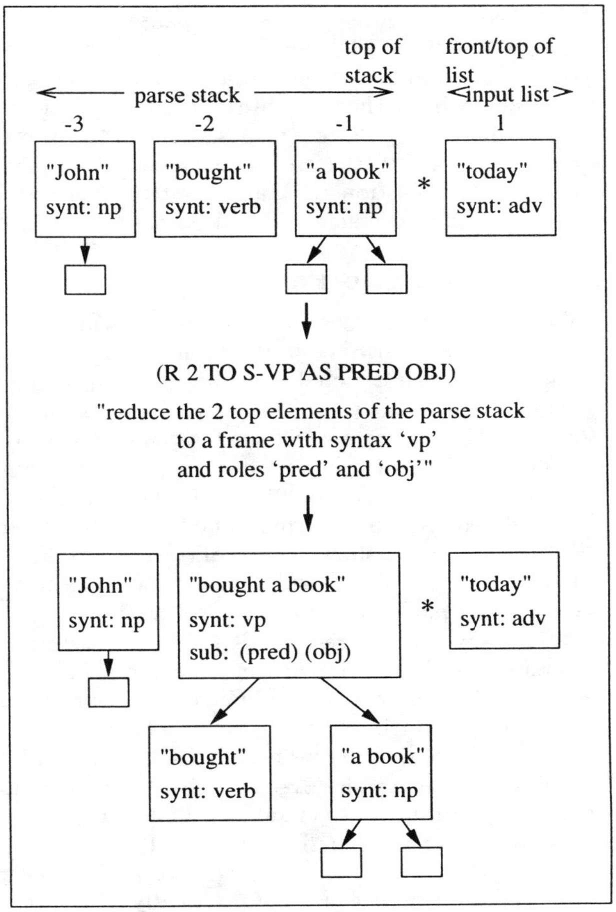

Figure 2: A typical parse action (simplified). Boxes represent *frames*. The asterisk (*) represents the current parse position. Optionally, parse actions can have additional arguments, like target syntactic or semantic classes to overwrite any default. Elements on the input list are identified by positive integers, elements on the parse stack by negative integers. The feature 'Synt of -1' for example refers to the (main) syntactic category of the top stack element. Before the reduce operation, the feature 'Synt of -1' would evaluate to *np* (for "a book"), after the operation to *vp* (for "bought a book"). The input list is initialized with the morphologically analyzed words, possibly still ambiguous. After a sequence of shift (from input list to parse stack) and reduce (on the parse stack) operations, the parser eventually ends up with a single element on the parse stack, which is then returned as the parse tree.

and also contributed to the feature set. The principal researcher, who does not speak Korean, contributed about 3 person months, coordinating the project, training the graduate students, writing treebank consistency checking rules (see section 6), making extensions to the tree-to-parse-action-sequence module (see section 4.1) and contributing to the background knowledge and feature set.

4 Learning to Parse

We base our training on the machine learning based approach of (Hermjakob & Mooney, 1997), allowing however unrestricted text and deriving the parse action sequences required for training from a treebank. The basic mechanism for parsing text into a shallow semantic representation is a shift-reduce type parser (Marcus, 1980) that breaks parsing into an ordered sequence of small and manageable parse actions. Figure 2 shows a typical reduce action. The key task of machine learning then is to learn to predict which parse action to perform next.

Two key advantages of this type of deterministic parsing are that its linear run-time complexity with respect to sentence length makes the parser very fast, and that the parser is very robust in that it produces a parse tree for every input sentence.

Figure 3 shows the overall architecture of parser training. From the treebank, we first automatically generate a parse action sequence. Then, for every step in the parse action sequence, typically several dozens per sentence, we automatically compute the value for every feature in the feature set, add on the parse action as the proper classification of the parse action example, and then feed these examples into a machine learning program, for which we use an extension of decision trees (Quinlan, 1986; Hermjakob & Mooney, 1997).

We built our parser incrementally. Starting with a small set of syntactic features that are useful across all languages, early training and testing runs reveal machine learning conflict sets and parsing errors that point to additionally required features and possibly also additional background knowledge. A conflict set is a set of training examples that have identical values for all features, yet differ in their classification (= parse action). Machine learning can therefore not possibly learn how to handle all examples correctly. This is typically resolved by adding an additional feature that differentiates between the examples in a linguistically relevant way.

Even treebanking benefits from an incremental approach. Trained on more and more sentences, and at the same time with also more and more features, parser quality improves, so that the parser as a treebanking tool has to be corrected less and less frequently, thereby accelerating the treebanking process.

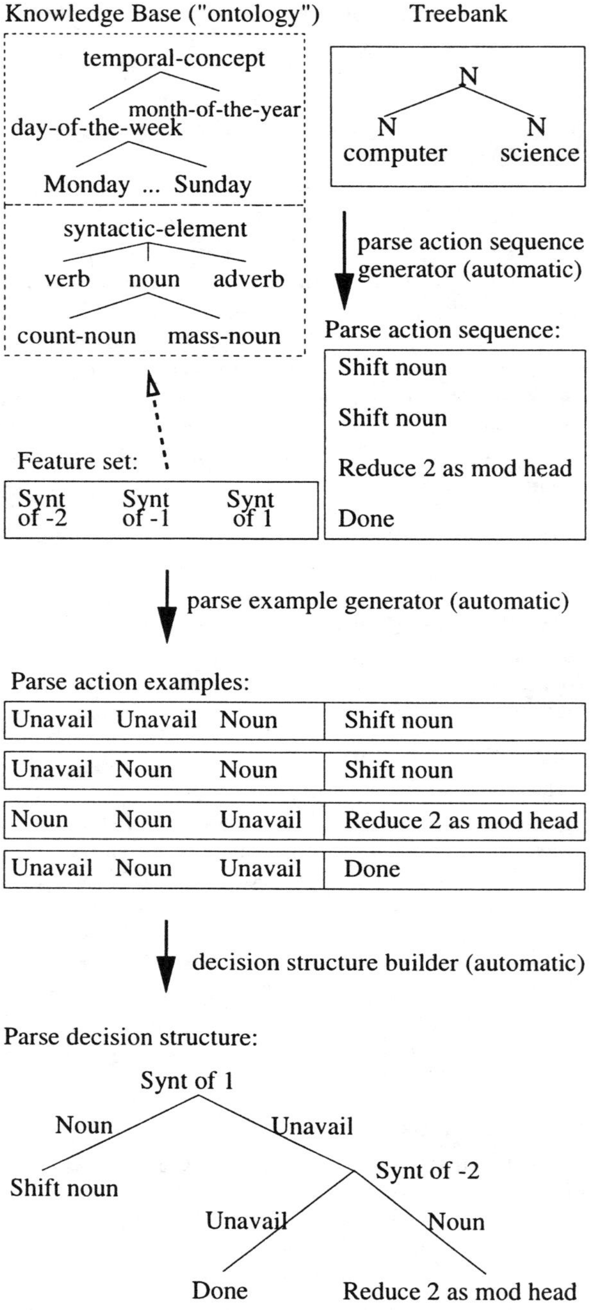

Figure 3: Derivation of the parser from a treebank and a feature set. The resulting parser has the form of a decision structure, an extension of decision trees. Given a seen or unseen sentence in form of a list of words, the decision structure keeps selecting the next parse action until a single parse tree covering the entire sentence has been built.

4.1 Special Adaptation for Korean

The segmenter and morphological analyzer KMA returns a list of alternatives for each *eojeol*. However, the alternatives are not atomic but rather two-level constituents, or mini-trees. Consider for example the following four[1] alternatives for the *eojeol* '31il' (the 31st day of a month):

```
31/NUMERAL + i/SUFFIX-NOUN + l/OBJ-CASE-PRT
31/NUMERAL + i/NUMERAL + l/OBJ-CASE-PRT
31/NUMERAL + il/UNIT-NOUN
31/NUMERAL + il/REGULAR-NOUN
```

The analyzer divides '31il' into groups with varying number of sub-components with different parts of speech. When shifting in an element, the parser has to decide which one to pick, the third one in this case, using context of course.

The module generating parse action sequences from a tree needs special split and merge operations for cases where the correct segmentation is not offered as a choice at all. To make things a little ugly, these splits can not only occur in the middle of a leaf constituent, but even in the middle of a character that might have been contracted from two characters, each with its own meaning.

5 Chosun Newspaper Experiments

Table 1 presents evaluation results with the number of training sentences varying from 32 to 1024 and with the remaining 163 sentences of the treebank used for testing.

Precision:

$$\frac{\text{number of correct constituents in system parse}}{\text{number of constituents in system parse}}$$

Recall:

$$\frac{\text{number of correct constituents in system parse}}{\text{number of constituents in logged parse}}$$

Crossing brackets: number of constituents which violate constituent boundaries with a constituent in the logged parse. **Labeled** precision/recall measures not only structural correctness, but also the correctness of the syntactic label. **Correct operations** measures the number of correct operations during a parse that is continuously corrected based on the logged sequence; it measures the core machine learning algorithm performance in isolation. A sentence has a correct **operating sequence**, if the system fully predicts the logged parse action sequence, and a correct **structure and labeling**, if the structure and syntactic labeling of the final system parse of a sentence is 100% correct, regardless of the operations leading to it.

Figures 4 and 5 plot the learning curves for two key metrics. While both curves are clearly heading in the right direction, up for precision, and down for crossing brackets, their appearance is somewhat jagged. For smaller data sets like in our case, this can often be avoided by running an n-fold cross validation test. However, we decided not to do so, because many training sentences were also used for feature set and background knowledge development

[1]KMA actually produces 10 different alternatives in this case, of which only four are shown here.

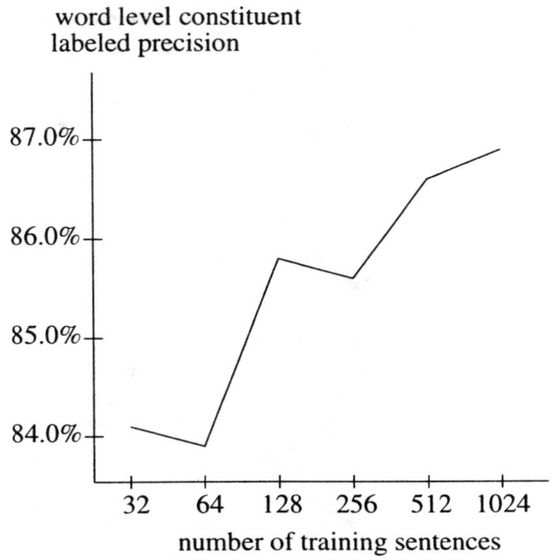

Figure 4: Learning curve for labeled precision corresponding to table 1

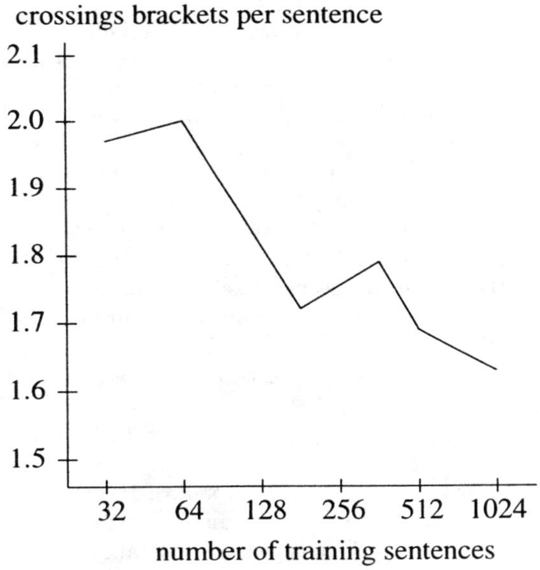

Figure 5: Learning curve for crossing brackets per sentence corresponding to table 1

Training sentences	32	64	128	256	512	1024
Precision	88.6%	88.1%	90.0%	89.6%	90.7%	91.0%
Recall	87.3%	87.4%	89.2%	89.1%	89.6%	89.8%
Labeled precision	84.1%	83.9%	85.8%	85.6%	86.7%	86.9%
Labeled recall	81.2%	81.9%	83.6%	83.6%	84.7%	85.0%
Tagging accuracy	94.3%	92.9%	93.9%	93.4%	94.0%	94.2%
Crossings/sentence	1.97	2.00	1.72	1.79	1.69	1.63
0 crossings	27.6%	35.0%	38.7%	40.5%	43.6%	42.9%
$\leq$ 1 crossing	56.4%	58.9%	63.2%	59.5%	64.4%	62.6%
$\leq$ 2 crossings	70.6%	72.4%	73.0%	71.8%	73.0%	74.2%
$\leq$ 3 crossings	81.0%	81.6%	82.2%	81.6%	82.2%	83.4%
$\leq$ 4 crossings	88.3%	84.0%	91.4%	89.0%	90.8%	89.6%
Correct operations	63.0%	68.3%	71.5%	73.4%	75.0%	76.3%
Operation Sequence	2.5%	6.1%	8.0%	8.6%	11.0%	7.4%
Structure&Label	5.5%	12.9%	11.7%	16.0%	19.0%	16.0%

Table 1: Evaluation results with varying number of training sentences

as well as for intermediate inspection, and therefore might have unduly influenced the evaluation.

5.1 Tagging accuracy

A particularly striking number is the tagging accuracy, 94.2%, which is dramatically below the equivalent 98% to 99% range for a good English or Japanese parser. In a Korean sentence, only larger constituents that typically span several words are separated by spaces, and even then not consistently, so that segmentation errors are a major source for tagging problems (as it is to some degree however also for Japanese[2]). We found that the segmentation part of KMA sometimes still struggles with relatively simple issues like punctuation, proposing for example words that contain a parenthesis in the middle of standard alphabetic characters. We have corrected some of these problems by pre- and post-processing the results of KMA, but believe that there is still a significant potential for further improvement.

In order to assess the impact of the relatively low tagging accuracy, we conducted experiments that simulated a perfect tagger by initializing the parser with the correctly segmented, morphologically analyzed and tagged sentence according to the treebank.

By construction, the tagging accuracy in table 2 rises to 100%. Since the segmenter/tagger returns not just atomic but rather two-level constituents, the precision and recall values benefit particularly strongly, possibly inflating the improvements for these metrics, but other metrics like crossing brackets per sentence show substantial gains as well. Thus we believe that refined pre-parsing tools, as they are in the process of becoming available for Korean, will greatly improve parsing accuracy.

Segmentation/ Tagging ("seg/tag")	Regular seg/tag as implemented	Simulating perfect seg/tag
Labeled precision	86.9%	93.4%
Labeled recall	85.0%	92.9%
Tagging accuracy	94.2%	100.0%
Crossings/sentence	1.63	1.13
0 crossings	42.9%	48.5%
$\leq$ 2 crossings	74.2%	85.3%
Structure&Label	16.0%	28.8%

Table 2: Impact of segmentation/tagging errors

However, for true low density languages, such high quality preprocessors are probably not available so that our experimental scenario might be more realistic for those conditions. On the other hand, some low density languages like for example Tetun, the principal indigenous language of East Timor, are based on the Latin alphabet, separate words by spaces and have relatively little inflection, and therefore make morphological analysis and segmentation relatively simple.

6 Treebank Consistency Checking

It is difficult to maintain a high treebank quality. When training on a small treebank, this is particularly important, because there is not enough data to allow generous pruning.

Treebanking is done by humans and humans err. Even with annotation guidelines there are often additional inconsistencies when there are several annotators. In the Penn Treebank (Marcus, 1993) for example, the word *ago* as in 'two years ago', is tagged

[2] While Japanese does not use spaces at all, script changes between *kanji*, *hiragana*, and *katakana* provide a lot of segmentation guidance. Modern Korean, however, almost exclusively uses only a single phonetic script.

414 times as an adverb and 150 times as a preposition.

In many treebanking efforts, basic taggers and parsers suggest parts of speech and tree structures that can be accepted or corrected, typically speeding up the treebanking effort considerably. However, incorrect defaults can easily slip through, leaving blatant inconsistencies like the one where the constituent 'that' as in 'the dog that bit her' is treebanked as a noun phrase containing a conjunction (as opposed to a pronoun).

From the very beginning of treebanking, we have therefore passed all trees to be added to the treebank through a consistency checker that looks for any suspicious patterns in the new tree. For every type of phrase, the consistency checker draws on a list of acceptable patterns in a BNF style notation. While this consistency checking certainly does not guarantee to find all errors, and can produce false alarms when encountering rare but legitimate constructions, we have found it a very useful tool to maintain treebank quality from the very beginning, easily offsetting the about three man days that it took to adapt the consistency checker to Korean.

For a number of typical errors, we extended the checker to automatically correct errors for which this could be done safely, or, alternatively, suggest a likely correction for errors and prompt for confirmation/correction by the treebanker.

7 Conclusions

Comparisons with related work are unfortunately very problematic, because the corpora are different and are sometimes not even described in other work. In most cases Korean research groups also use other evaluation metrics, particularly dependency accuracy, which is often used in dependency structure approaches. Training on about 40,000 sentences (Collins, 1997) achieves a crossing brackets rate of 1.07, a better value than our 1.63 value for regular parsing or the 1.13 value assuming perfect segmentation/tagging, but even for similar text types, comparisons across languages are of course problematic.

It is clear to us that with more training sentences, and with more features and background knowledge to better leverage the increased number of training sentences, accuracy rates can still be improved significantly. But we believe that the reduction of parser development time from two years or more down to three months is in many cases already very valuable, even if the accuracy has not 'maxed out' yet. And given the experience we have gained from this project, we hope this research to be only a first step to an even steeper development time reduction. A particularly promising research direction for this is to harness knowledge and training resources across languages.

Acknowledgments

I would like to thank Kyoosung Lee for installing, improving and conncecting Korean pre-processing tools like segmenter and tagger as well as starting the treebanking, and Mina Lee, who did most of the treebanking.

References

M. J. Collins. 1997. Three Generative, Lexicalised Models for Statistical Parsing. In *35th Proceedings of the ACL*, pages 16–23.

U. Hermjakob and R. J. Mooney. 1997. Learning Parse and Translation Decisions From Examples With Rich Context. In *35th Proceedings of the ACL*, pages 482–489.
URL: file://ftp.cs.utexas.edu/pub/mooney/papers /contex-acl-97.ps.Z

U. Hermjakob. 1997. *Learning Parse and Translation Decisions From Examples With Rich Context.* Ph.D. thesis, University of Texas at Austin, Dept. of Computer Sciences TR 97-12.
URL: file://ftp.cs.utexas.edu/pub/mooney/papers /hermjakob-dissertation-97.ps.Z

Geunbae Lee, Jong-Hyeok Lee, and Hyuncheol Rho. 1997. Natural Language Processing for Session-Based Information Retrieval Interface on the Web. In *Proceedings of IJCAI-97 workshop on AI in digital libraries*, pages 43-48.

M. P. Marcus. 1980. A Theory of Syntactic Recognition for Natural Language. MIT Press.

M. Marcus, B. Santorini, and M. A. Marcinkiewicz. 1993. Building a Large Annotated Corpus of English: The Penn Treebank. Computational Linguistics 19(2), pages 313–330.

J. R. Quinlan. 1993. C4.5 Programs for Machine Learning. Morgan Kaufmann Publishers, San Mateo, California.

K. J. Seo, K. C. Nam, and K. S. Choi. 1998. A Probabilistic Model for Dependency Parsing Considering Ascending Dependencies. Journal of Literary and Linguistic Computing, Vol 13(2).

Juntae Yoon, Seonho Kim, and Mansuk Song. 1997. New Parsing Method Using Global Association Table. In *Proc. of the International Workshop on Parsing Technology.*

A Classification Approach to Word Prediction*

Yair Even-Zohar **Dan Roth**

Department of Computer Science
University of Illinois at Urbana-Champaign
{evenzoha,danr}@uiuc.edu

Abstract

The eventual goal of a language model is to accurately predict the value of a missing word given its context. We present an approach to word prediction that is based on learning a representation for each word as a function of words and linguistics predicates in its context. This approach raises a few new questions that we address. First, in order to learn good word representations it is necessary to use an expressive representation of the context. We present a way that uses external knowledge to generate expressive context representations, along with a learning method capable of handling the large number of features generated this way that can, potentially, contribute to each prediction. Second, since the number of words "competing" for each prediction is large, there is a need to "focus the attention" on a smaller subset of these. We exhibit the contribution of a "focus of attention" mechanism to the performance of the word predictor. Finally, we describe a large scale experimental study in which the approach presented is shown to yield significant improvements in word prediction tasks.

1 Introduction

The task of predicting the most likely word based on properties of its surrounding context is the archetypical prediction problem in natural language processing (NLP). In many NLP tasks it is necessary to determine the most likely word, part-of-speech (POS) tag or any other token, given its history or context. Examples include part-of speech tagging, word-sense disambiguation, speech recognition, accent restoration, word choice selection in machine translation, context-sensitive spelling correction and identifying discourse markers. Most approaches to these problems are based on *n-gram*-like modeling. Namely, the learning methods make use of features which are conjunctions of typically (up to) three consecutive words or POS tags in order to derive the predictor.

In this paper we show that incorporating additional information into the learning process is very beneficial. In particular, we provide the learner with a rich set of features that combine the information available in the local context along with shallow parsing information. At the same time, we study a learning approach that is specifically tailored for problems in which the potential number of features is very large but only a fairly small number of them actually participates in the decision. Word prediction experiments that we perform show significant improvements in error rate relative to the use of the traditional, restricted, set of features.

* This research is supported by NSF grants IIS-9801638 and SBR-987345.

Background

The most influential problem in motivating statistical learning application in NLP tasks is that of word selection in speech recognition (Jelinek, 1998). There, word classifiers are derived from a probabilistic language model which estimates the probability of a sentence s using Bayes rule as the product of conditional probabilities,

$$\begin{aligned} Pr(s) &\doteq Pr(w_1, w_2, \ldots w_n) = \\ &\doteq \Pi_{i=1}^{n} Pr(w_i | w_1, \ldots w_{i-1}) \\ &\doteq \Pi_{i=1}^{n} Pr(w_i | h_i) \end{aligned}$$

where h_i is the relevant *history* when predicting w_i. Thus, in order to predict the most likely word in a given context, a global estimation of the sentence probability is derived which, in turn, is computed by estimating the probability of each word given its local context or history. Estimating terms of the form $Pr(w|h)$ is done by assuming some generative probabilistic model, typically using Markov or other independence assumptions, which gives rise to estimating conditional probabilities of n-grams type features (in the word or POS space). Machine learning based classifiers and maximum entropy models which, in principle, are not restricted to features of these forms have used them nevertheless, perhaps under the influence of probabilistic methods (Brill, 1995; Yarowsky, 1994; Ratnaparkhi et al., 1994).

It has been argued that the information available in the local context of each word should be augmented by global sentence information and even information external to the sentence in order to learn better classifiers and language models. Efforts in this directions consists of (1) directly adding syntactic information, as in (Chelba and Jelinek, 1998; Rosenfeld, 1996), and (2) indirectly adding syntactic and semantic information, via similarity models; in this case n-gram type features are used whenever possible, and when they cannot be used (due to data sparsity), additional information compiled into a similarity measure is used (Dagan et al., 1999). Nevertheless, the efforts in this direction so far have shown very insignificant improvements, if any (Chelba and Jelinek, 1998; Rosenfeld, 1996). We believe that the main reason for that is that incorporating information sources in NLP needs to be coupled with a learning approach that is suitable for it.

Studies have shown that both machine learning and probabilistic learning methods used in NLP make decisions using a linear decision surface over the feature space (Roth, 1998; Roth, 1999). In this view, the feature space consists of simple functions (e.g., n-grams) over the the original data so as to allow for expressive enough representations using a simple functional form (e.g., a linear function). This implies that the number of potential features that the learning stage needs to consider may be very large, and may grow rapidly when increasing the expressivity of the features. Therefore a feasible computational approach needs to be feature-efficient. It needs to tolerate a large number of potential features in the sense that the number of examples required for it to converge should depend mostly on the number features relevant to the decision, rather than on the number of potential features.

This paper addresses the two issues mentioned above. It presents a rich set of features that is constructed using information readily available in the sentence along with shallow parsing and dependency information. It then presents a learning approach that can use this expressive (and potentially large) intermediate representation and shows that it yields a significant improvement in word error rate for the task of word prediction.

The rest of the paper is organized as follows. In section 2 we formalize the problem, discuss the information sources available to the learning system and how we use those to construct features. In section 3 we present the learning approach, based on the SNoW learning architecture. Section 4 presents our experimental study and results. In section 4.4 we discuss the issue of deciding on a set of candidate words for each decision. Section 5 concludes and discusses future work.

2 Information Sources and Features

Our goal is to learn a representation for each word in terms of features which characterize the syntactic and semantic context in which the word tends to appear. Our features are defined as simple relations over a collection of predicates that capture (some of) the information available in a sentence.

2.1 Information Sources

Definition 1 *Let* $s =< w_1, w_2, ..., w_n >$ *be a sentence in which* w_i *is the i-th word. Let* $\mathcal{I}$ *be a collection of predicates over a sentence s. IS(s))*[1]*, the* ***Information source(s)*** *available for the sentence s is a representation of s as a list of predicates* $I \in \mathcal{I}$*,*

$$IS(s) = \{I_1(w_{1_1}, ...w_{1_i}), ..., I_k(w_{k_1}, ...w_{k_i})\}.$$

j_i *is the arity of the predicate* I_j*.*

Example 2 *Let s be the sentence*
< **John, X, at, the, clock, to, see, what, time, it, is** >
Let $\mathcal{I}$*={word, pos, subj-verb}, with the interpretation that* `word` *is a unary predicate that returns the value of the word in its domain;* `pos` *is a unary predicate that returns the value of the pos of the word in its domain, in the context of the sentence;* $subj - verb$ *is a binary predicate that returns the value of the two words in its domain if the second is a verb in the sentence and the first is its subject; it returns* ϕ *otherwise. Then,*

$$\begin{aligned} IS(s) &= \{word(w_1) = \texttt{John}, ..., word(w_3) = \texttt{at}, ..., \\ & word(w_{11}) = \texttt{is}, pos(w_4) = DET, ..., \\ & subj - verb(w_1, w_2) = \{\texttt{John}, \texttt{X}\} ...\}. \end{aligned}$$

The IS representation of s consists only of the predicates with non-empty values. E.g., $pos(w_6) = modal$ is not part of the IS for the sentence above. $subj - verb$ might not exist at all in the IS even if the predicate is available, e.g., in `The ball was given to Mary`.

Clearly the IS representation of s does not contain all the information available to a human reading s; it captures, however, all the input that is available to the computational process discussed in the rest of this paper. The predicates could be generated by any external mechanism, even a learned one. This issue is orthogonal to the current discussion.

2.2 Generating Features

Our goal is to learn a representation for each word of interest. Most efficient learning methods known today and, in particular, those used in NLP, make use of a linear decision surface over their feature space (Roth, 1998; Roth, 1999). Therefore, in order to learn expressive representations one needs to compose complex features as a function of the information sources available. A linear function expressed directly in terms of those will not be expressive enough. We now define a language that allows

[1] We denote IS(s) as IS wherever it is obvious what the referred sentence we is, or whenever we want to indicate Information Source in general.

one to define "types" of features[2] in terms of the information sources available to it.

Definition 3 (Basic Features) *Let $I \in \mathcal{I}$ be a k-ary predicate with range R. Denote $w^k = (w_{j_1}, \ldots, w_{j_k})$. We define two basic binary relations as follows. For $\alpha \in R$ we define:*

$$f(I(w^k), \alpha) = \begin{cases} 1 & \textit{iff } I(w^k) = \alpha \\ 0 & \textit{otherwise} \end{cases} \quad (1)$$

An existential version of the relation is defined by:

$$f(I(w^k), x) = \begin{cases} 1 & \textit{iff } \exists \alpha \in R\, s.t\, I(w^k) = \alpha \\ 0 & \textit{otherwise} \end{cases} \quad (2)$$

Features, which are defined as binary relations, can be composed to yield more complex relations in terms of the original predicates available in IS.

Definition 4 (Composing features) *Let f_1, f_2 be feature definitions. Then $f_{and}(f_1, f_2)$ $f_{or}(f_1, f_2)$ $f_{not}(f_1)$ are defined and given the usual semantic:*

$$f_{and}(f_1, f_2) = \begin{cases} 1 & \textit{if } f_1 = f_2 = 1 \\ 0 & \textit{otherwise} \end{cases}$$

$$f_{or}(f_1, f_2) = \begin{cases} 1 & \textit{if } f_1 = 1 \textit{ or } f_2 = 1 \\ 0 & \textit{otherwise} \end{cases}$$

$$f_{not}(f_1) = \begin{cases} 1 & \textit{if } f_1 = 0 \\ 0 & \textit{otherwise} \end{cases}$$

In order to learn with features generated using these definitions as input, it is important that features generated when applying the definitions on different ISs are given the same identification. In this presentation we assume that the composition operator along with the appropriate IS element (e.g., Ex. 2, Ex. 9) are written explicitly as the identification of the features. Some of the subtleties in defining the output representation are addressed in (Cumby and Roth, 2000).

2.3 Structured Features

So far we have presented features as relations over $IS(s)$ and allowed for Boolean composition operators. In most cases more information than just a list of active predicates is available. We abstract this using the notion of a *structural information source* ($SIS(s)$) defined below. This allows richer class of feature types to be defined.

[2]We note that we do not define the features will be used in the learning process. These are going to be defined in a data driven way given the definitions discussed here and the input ISs. The importance of formally defining the "types" is due to the fact that some of these are quantified. Evaluating them on a given sentence might be computationally intractable and a formal definition would help to flesh out the difficulties and aid in designing the language (Cumby and Roth, 2000).

2.4 Structured Instances

Definition 5 (Structural Information Source) *Let $s = < w_1, w_2, ..., w_n >$. SIS(s)), the* **Structural Information source(s)** *available for the sentence s, is a tuple $(s, E_1, \ldots, E_k)$ of directed acyclic graphs with s as the set of vertices and E_i's, a set of edges in s.*

Example 6 (Linear Structure) *The simplest SIS is the one corresponding to the linear structure of the sentence. That is, $SIS(s) = (s, E)$ where $(w_i, w_j) \in E$ iff the word w_i occurs immediately before w_j in the sentence (Figure 1 bottom left part).*

In a linear structure ($s = < w_1, w_2, ..., w_n >, E$), where $E = \{(w_i, w_{i+1}); i = 1, \ldots n-1\}$, we define the chain

$$C(w_j, [l, r]) = \{w_{j-l}, \ldots, w_j, \ldots w_{j+r}\} \cap s.$$

We can now define a new set of features that makes use of the structural information. Structural features are defined using the SIS. When defining a feature, the naming of nodes in s is done relative to a distinguished node, denoted w_p, which we call the *focus word* of the feature. Regardless of the arity of the features we sometimes denote the feature f defined with respect to w_p as $f(w_p)$.

Definition 7 (Proximity) *Let $SIS(s) = (s, E)$ be the linear structure and let $I \in \mathcal{I}$ be a k-ary predicate with range R. Let w_p be a focus word and $C = C(w_p, [l, r])$ the chain around it. Then, the proximity features for I with respect to the chain C are defined as:*

$$f_C(I(w), \alpha) = \begin{cases} 1 & \textit{if } I(w) = \alpha, \alpha \in R, w \in C \\ 0 & \textit{otherwise} \end{cases} \quad (3)$$

The second type of feature composition defined using the structure is a collocation operator.

Definition 8 (Collocation) *Let $f_1, \ldots f_k$ be feature definitions. $colloc_C(f_1, f_2, \ldots f_k)$ is a restricted conjunctive operator that is evaluated on a chain C of length k in a graph. Specifically, let $C = \{w_{j_1}, w_{j_2}, \ldots, w_{j_k}\}$ be a chain of length k in $SIS(s)$. Then, the collocation feature for $f_1, \ldots f_k$ with respect to the chain C is defined as*

$$colloc_C(f_1, \ldots, f_k) = \begin{cases} 1 & \textit{if } \forall i = 1, \ldots k, f_i(w_{j_i}) = 1 \\ 0 & \textit{otherwise} \end{cases} \quad (4)$$

The following example defines features that are used in the experiments described in Sec. 4.

Example 9 *Let s be the sentence in Example 2. We define some of the features with respect to the linear structure of the sentence. The word X is used as the focus word and a chain* $[-10, 10]$ *is defined with respect to it. The proximity features are defined with respect to the predicate* `word`. *We get, for example:* $\texttt{f}_\texttt{C}(\texttt{word}) = \texttt{John}; \texttt{f}_\texttt{C}(\texttt{word}) = \texttt{at}; \texttt{f}_\texttt{C}(\texttt{word}) = \texttt{clock}$.

Collocation features are defined with respect to a chain $[-2, 2]$ *centered at the focus word X. They are defined with respect to two basic features* f_1, f_2 *each of which can be either* $f(word, \alpha)$ *or* $f(pos, \alpha)$. *The resulting features include, for example:*

$$\begin{aligned} colloc_C(word, word) &= \{John - X\}; \\ colloc_C(word, word) &= \{X - at\}; \\ colloc_C(word, pos) &= \{at - DET\}. \end{aligned}$$

2.5 Non-Linear Structure

So far we have described feature definitions which make use of the linear structure of the sentence and yield features which are not too different from standard features used in the literature e.g., *n*-grams with respect to *pos* or *word* can be defined as *colloc* for the appropriate chain. Consider now that we are given a general directed acyclic graph $G = (s, E)$ on the the sentence s as its nodes. Given a distinguished *focus word* $w_p \in s$ we can define a chain in the graph as we did above for the linear structure of the sentence. Since the definitions given above, Def. 7 and Def. 8, were given for chains they would apply for any chain in any graph. This generalization becomes interesting if we are given a graph that represents a more involved structure of the sentence.

Consider, for example the graph $DG(s)$ in Figure 1. $DG(s)$ described the dependency graph of the sentence s. An edge (w_i, w_j) in $DG(s)$ represent a dependency between the two words. In our feature generation language we separate the information provided by the dependency grammar[3] to two parts. The structural information, provided in the left side of Figure 1, is used to generate $SIS(s)$. The labels on the edges are used as predicates and are part of $IS(s)$. Notice that some authors (Yuret, 1998; Berger and Printz, 1998) have used the structural information, but have not used the information given by the labels on the edges as we do.

The following example defines features that are used in the experiments described in Sec. 4.

Example 10 *Let s be the sentence in Figure 1 along with its IS that is defined using the predicates* `word, pos, subj, obj, aux_vrb`. *A* `subj-verb` *feature,* $f_{subj-verb}$, *can be defined as a collocation over chains constructed with respect to the focus word* `join`. *Moreover, we can define* $f_{subj-verb}$ *to be active also when there is an* `aux_vrb` *between the* `subj` *and* `verb`, *by defining it as a disjunction of two collocation features, the* `subj-verb` *and the* `subj-aux_vrb-verb`. *Other features that we use are conjunctions of words that occur before the focus verb (here:* `join`*) along all the chains it occurs in (here:* `will, board, as`*) and collocations of* `obj` *and* `verb`.

As a final comment on feature generation, we note that the language presented is used to define "types" of features. These are instantiated in a data driven way given input sentences. A large number of features is created in this way, most of which might not be relevant to the decision at hand; thus, this process needs to be followed by a learning process that can learn in the presence of these many features.

3 The Learning Approach

Our experimental investigation is done using the *SNoW* learning system (Roth, 1998). Earlier versions of *SNoW* (Roth, 1998; Golding and Roth, 1999; Roth and Zelenko, 1998; Munoz et al., 1999) have been applied successfully to several natural language related tasks. Here we use *SNoW* for the task of word prediction; a representation is learned for each word of interest, and these compete at evaluation time to determine the prediction.

3.1 The *SNOW* Architecture

The *SNoW* architecture is a sparse network of linear units over a common pre-defined or incrementally learned feature space. It is specifically tailored for learning in domains in which the potential number of features might be very large but only a small subset of them is actually relevant to the decision made.

Nodes in the input layer of the network represent simple relations on the input sentence and are being used as the input features. Target nodes represent words that are of interest; in the case studied here, each of the word candidates for prediction is represented as a target node. An input sentence, along with a designated word of interest in it, is mapped into a set of features which are active in it; this representation is presented to the input layer of SNoW and propagates to the target nodes. Target nodes are linked via weighted edges to (some of) the input features. Let $\mathcal{A}_t = \{i_1, \ldots, i_m\}$ be the set of features that are active in an example and are linked to the target node t. Then the linear unit corresponding to t is *active* iff

$$\sum_{i \in \mathcal{A}_t} w_i^t > \theta_t,$$

where w_i^t is the weight on the edge connecting the ith feature to the target node t, and θ_t is the threshold

[3]This information can be produced by a functional dependency grammar (FDG), which assigns each word a specific function, and then structures the sentence hierarchically based on it, as we do here (Tapanainen and Jrvinen, 1997), but can also be generated by an external rule-based parser or a learned one.

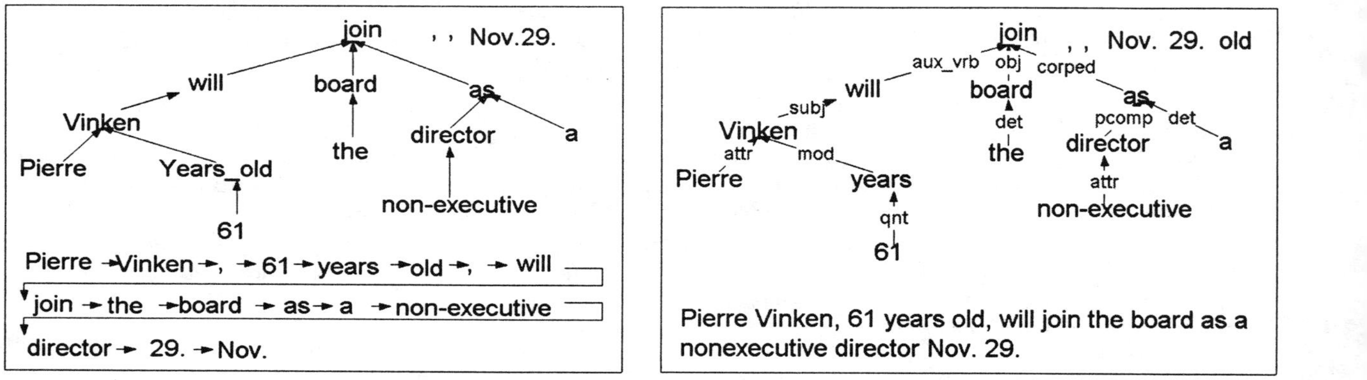

Figure 1: **A sentence with a linear and a dependency grammar structure**

for the target node t. In this way, *SNoW* provides a collection of *word representations* rather than just discriminators.

A given example is treated autonomously by each target subnetwork; an example labeled t may be treated as a positive example by the subnetwork for t and as a negative example by the rest of the target nodes. The learning policy is on-line and mistake-driven; several update rules can be used within SNoW. The most successful update rule is a variant of Littlestone's Winnow update rule (Littlestone, 1988), a multiplicative update rule that is tailored to the situation in which the set of input features is not known a priori, as in the infinite attribute model (Blum, 1992). This mechanism is implemented via the sparse architecture of SNoW. That is, (1) input features are allocated in a data driven way – an input node for the feature i is allocated only if the feature i was active in any input sentence and (2) a link (i.e., a non-zero weight) exists between a target node t and a feature i if and only if i was active in an example labeled t.

One of the important properties of the sparse architecture is that the complexity of processing an example depends only on the number of features active in it, n_a, and is independent of the total number of features, n_t, observed over the life time of the system. This is important in domains in which the total number of features is very large, but only a small number of them is active in each example.

Once target subnetworks have been learned and the network is being evaluated, a decision support mechanism is employed, which selects the dominant active target node in the SNoW unit via a winner-take-all mechanism to produce a final prediction. SNoW is available publicly at `http://L2R.cs.uiuc.edu/~cogcomp.html`.

4 Experimental Study

4.1 Task definition

The experiments were conducted with four goals in mind:

1. To compare mistake driven algorithms with naive Bayes, trigram with backoff and a simple maximum likelihood estimation (MLE) baseline.
2. To create a set of experiments which is comparable with similar experiments that were previously conducted by other researchers.
3. To build a baseline for two types of extensions of the simple use of linear features: (i) Non-Linear features (ii) Automatic focus of attention.
4. To evaluate word prediction as a simple language model.

We chose the verb prediction task which is similar to other word prediction tasks (e.g.,(Golding and Roth, 1999)) and, in particular, follows the paradigm in (Lee and Pereira, 1999; Dagan et al., 1999; Lee, 1999). There, a list of the confusion sets is constructed first, each consists of two different verbs. The verb v_1 is coupled with v_2 provided that they occur equally likely in the corpus. In the test set, every occurrence of v_1 or v_2 was replaced by a set $\{v_1, v_2\}$ and the classification task was to predict the correct verb. For example, if a confusion set is created for the verbs "make" and "sell", then the data is altered as follows:

make the paper	→	{make,sell}	the paper
sell sensitive data	→	{make,sell}	sensitive data

The evaluated predictor chooses which of the two verbs is more likely to occur in the current sentence.

In choosing the prediction task in this way, we make sure the task in difficult by choosing between competing words that have the same prior probabilities and have the same part of speech. A further advantage of this paradigm is that in future experiments we may choose the candidate verbs so that they have the same sub-categorization, phonetic transcription, etc. in order to imitate the first phase of language modeling used in creating candidates for the prediction task. Moreover, the pre-transformed data provides the correct answer so that (i) it is easy to generate training data; no supervision is required, and (ii) it is easy to evaluate the results assuming that the most appropriate word is provided in the original text.

Results are evaluated using word-error rate (WER). Namely, every time we predict the wrong word it is counted as a mistake.

4.2 Data

We used the Wall Street Journal (WSJ) of the years 88-89. The size of our corpus is about 1,000,000 words. The corpus was divided into 80% training and 20% test. The training and the test data were processed by the FDG parser (Tapanainen and Jrvinen, 1997). Only verbs that occur at least 50 times in the corpus were chosen. This resulted in 278 verbs that we split into 139 confusion sets as above. After filtering the examples of verbs which were not in any of the sets we use 73,184 training examples and 19,852 test examples.

4.3 Results

4.3.1 Features

In order to test the advantages of different feature sets we conducted experiments using the following features sets:

1. Linear features: proximity of window size ± 10 words, conjunction of size 2 using window size ± 2. The conjunction combines words and parts of speech.
2. Linear + Non linear features: using the linear features defined in (1) along with non linear features that use the predicates `subj`, `obj`, `word`, `pos`, the collocations `subj-verb`, `verb-obj` linked to the focus verb via the graph structure and conjunction of 2 linked words.

The over all number of features we have generated for all 278 target verbs was around 400,000. In all tables below the NB columns represent results of the naive Bayes algorithm as implemented within SNoW and the SNoW column represents the results of the sparse Winnow algorithm within SNoW.

Table 1 summarizes the results of the experiments with the features sets (1), (2) above. The baseline experiment uses MLE, the majority predictor. In addition, we conducted the same experiment using trigram with backoff and the WER is 29.3%. From these results we conclude that using more expressive features helps significantly in reducing the WER. However, one can use those types of features only if the learning method handles large number of possible features. This emphasizes the importance of the new learning method.

	Bline	NB	SNoW
Linear	49.6	13.54	11.56
Non Linear	49.6	12.25	9.84

Table 1: **Word Error Rate results for linear and non-linear features**

	Similarity	NB	SNoW
WSJ data		54.6%	59.1%
AP news	47.6%		

Table 2: **Comparison of the improvement achieved using similarity methods (Dagan et al., 1999) and using the methods presented in this paper. Results are shown in percentage of improvement in accuracy over the baseline.**

Table 2 compares our method to methods that use similarity measures (Dagan et al., 1999; Lee, 1999). Since we could not use the same corpus as in those experiments, we compare the ratio of improvement and not the WER. The baseline in this studies is different, but other than that the experiments are identical. We show an improvement over the best similarity method. Furthermore, we train using only 73,184 examples while (Dagan et al., 1999) train using 587,833 examples. Given our experience with our approach on other data sets we conjecture that we could have improved the results further had we used that many training examples.

4.4 Focus of attention

SNoW is used in our experiments as a multi-class predictor - a representation is learned for each word in a given set and, at evaluation time, one of these is selected as the prediction. The set of candidate words is called the *confusion set* (Golding and Roth, 1999). Let C be the set of all target words. In previous experiments we generated artificially subsets of size 2 of C in order to evaluate the performance of our methods. In general, however, the question of determining a good set of candidates is interesting in it own right. In the absence of a good method, one might end up choosing a verb from among a larger set of candidates. We would like to study the effects this issue has on the performance of our method.

In principle, instead of working with a single large confusion set C, it might be possible to split C into subsets of smaller size. This process, which we call the *focus of attention (FOA)* would be beneficial only if we can guarantee that, with high probability, given a prediction task, we know which confusion set to use, so that the true target belongs to it. In fact, the FOA problem can be discussed separately for the training and test stages.

1. Training: Given our training policy (Sec. 3) every positive example serves as a negative example to all other targets in its confusion set. For a large set C training might become computationally infeasible.
2. Testing: considering only a small set of words as candidates at evaluation time increases the baseline and might be significant from the point of view of accuracy and efficiency.

To evaluate the advantage of reducing the size of the confusion set in the training and test phases, we conducted the following experiments using the same features set (linear features as in Table 1).

	Bline	NB	SNoW
Train All Test All	87.44	65.22	65.05
Train All Test 2	49.6	13.54	13.15
Train 2 Test 2	49.6	13.54	11.55

Table 3: **Evaluating Focus of Attention: Word Error Rate for Training and testing using all the words together against using pairs of words.**

"Train All" means training on all 278 targets together. "Test all" means that the confusion set is of size 278 and includes all the targets. The results shown in Table 3 suggest that, in terms of accuracy, the significant factor is the confusion set size in the test stage. The effect of the confusion set size on training is minimal (although it does affect training time). We note that for the naive Bayes algorithm the notion of negative examples does not exist, and therefore regardless of the size of confusion set in training, it learns exactly the same representations. Thus, in the NB column, the confusion set size in training makes no difference.

The application in which a word predictor is used might give a partial solution to the FOA problem. For example, given a prediction task in the context of speech recognition the phonemes that constitute the word might be known and thus suggest a way to generate a small confusion set to be used when evaluating the predictors.

Tables 4,5 present the results of using artificially simulated speech recognizer using a method of general phonetic classes. That is, instead of transcribing a word by the phoneme, the word is transcribed by the phoneme *classes*(Jurafsky and Martin, 200). Specifically, these experiments deviate from the task definition given above. The confusion sets used are of different sizes and they consist of verbs with different prior probabilities in the corpus. Two sets of experiments were conducted that use the phonetic transcription of the words to generate confusion sets.

	Bline	NB	SNoW
Train All Test PC	19.84	11.6	12.3
Train PC Test PC	19.84	11.6	11.3

Table 4: **Simulating Speech Recognizer: Word Error Rate for Training and testing with confusion sets determined based on phonetic classes (PC) from a simulated speech recognizer.**

In the first experiment (Table 4), the transcription of each word is given by the broad phonetic groups to which the phonemes belong i.e., nasals, fricative, etc.[4]. For example, the word "b_u_y" is transcribed using phonemes as "b_Y" and here we transcribe it as "P_V1" which stands for "Plosive_Vowel1". This partition results in a partition of the set of verbs into several confusions sets. A few of these confusion sets consist of a single word and therefore have 100% baseline, which explains the high baseline.

	Bline	NB	SNoW
Train All Test PC	45.63	26.36	27.54
Train PC Test PC	45.63	26.36	25.55

Table 5: **Simulating Speech Recognizer: Word Error Rate for Training and testing with confusion sets determined based on phonetic classes (PC) from a simulated speech recognizer. In this case only confusion sets that have less than 98% baseline are used, which explains the overall lower baseline.**

Table 5 presents the results of a similar experiment in which only confusion sets with multiple words were used, resulting in a lower baseline.

As before, Train All means that training is done with all 278 targets together while Train PC means that the PC confusion sets were used also in training. We note that for the case of SNoW, used here with the sparse Winnow algorithm, that size of the confusion set in training has some, although small, effect. The reason is that when the training is done with all the target words, each target word representation with all the examples in which it does not occur are used as negative examples. When a smaller confusion set is used the negative examples are more likely to be "true" negative.

5 Conclusion

This paper presents a new approach to word prediction tasks. For each word of interest, a word representation is learned as a function of a common, but

[4]In this experiment, the vowels phonemes were divided into two different groups to account for different sounds.

potentially very large set of expressive (relational) features. Given a prediction task (a sentence with a missing word) the word representations are evaluated on it and compete for the most likely word to complete the sentence.

We have described a language that allows one to define expressive feature types and have exhibited experimentally the advantage of using those on word prediction task. We have argued that the success of this approach hinges on the combination of using a large set of expressive features along with a learning approach that can tolerate it and converges quickly despite the large dimensionality of the data. We believe that this approach would be useful for other disambiguation tasks in NLP.

We have also presented a preliminary study of a reduction in the confusion set size and its effects on the prediction performance. In future work we intend to study ways that determine the appropriate confusion set in a way to makes use of the current task properties.

Acknowledgments

We gratefully acknowledge helpful comments and programming help from Chad Cumby.

References

A. Berger and H. Printz. 1998. Recognition performance of a large-scale dependency-grammar language model. In *Int'l Conference on Spoken Language Processing (ICSLP'98)*, Sydney, Australia.

A. Blum. 1992. Learning boolean functions in an infinite attribute space. *Machine Learning*, 9(4):373–386.

E. Brill. 1995. Transformation-based error-driven learning and natural language processing: A case study in part of speech tagging. *Computational Linguistics*, 21(4):543–565.

C. Chelba and F. Jelinek. 1998. Exploiting syntactic structure for language modeling. In *COLING-ACL'98.*

C. Cumby and D. Roth. 2000. Relational representations that facilitate learning. In *Proc. of the International Conference on the Principles of Knowledge Representation and Reasoning.* To appear.

I. Dagan, L. Lee, and F. Pereira. 1999. Similarity-based models of word cooccurrence probabilities. *Machine Learning*, 34(1-3):43–69.

A. R. Golding and D. Roth. 1999. A Winnow based approach to context-sensitive spelling correction. *Machine Learning*, 34(1-3):107–130. Special Issue on Machine Learning and Natural Language.

F. Jelinek. 1998. *Statistical Methods for Speech Recognition.* MIT Press.

D. Jurafsky and J. H. Martin. 200. *Speech and Language Processing.* Prentice Hall.

L. Lee and F. Pereira. 1999. Distributional similarity models: Clustering vs. nearest neighbors. In *ACL 99*, pages 33–40.

L. Lee. 1999. Measure of distributional similarity. In *ACL 99*, pages 25–32.

N. Littlestone. 1988. Learning quickly when irrelevant attributes abound: A new linear-threshold algorithm. *Machine Learning*, 2:285–318.

M. Munoz, V. Punyakanok, D. Roth, and D. Zimak. 1999. A learning approach to shallow parsing. In *EMNLP-VLC'99, the Joint SIGDAT Conference on Empirical Methods in Natural Language Processing and Very Large Corpora*, June.

A. Ratnaparkhi, J. Reynar, and S. Roukos. 1994. A maximum entropy model for prepositional phrase attachment. In *ARPA*, Plainsboro, NJ, March.

R. Rosenfeld. 1996. A maximum entropy approach to adaptive statistical language modeling. *Computer, Speech and Language*, 10.

D. Roth and D. Zelenko. 1998. Part of speech tagging using a network of linear separators. In *COLING-ACL 98, The 17th International Conference on Computational Linguistics*, pages 1136–1142.

D. Roth. 1998. Learning to resolve natural language ambiguities: A unified approach. In *Proc. National Conference on Artificial Intelligence*, pages 806–813.

D. Roth. 1999. Learning in natural language. In *Proc. of the International Joint Conference of Artificial Intelligence*, pages 898–904.

P. Tapanainen and T. Jrvinen. 1997. A non-projective dependency parser. In *In Proceedings of the 5th Conference on Applied Natural Language Processing*, Washington DC.

D. Yarowsky. 1994. Decision lists for lexical ambiguity resolution: application to accent restoration in Spanish and French. In *Proc. of the Annual Meeting of the ACL*, pages 88–95.

D. Yuret. 1998. *Discovery of Linguistic Relations Using Lexical Attraction.* Ph.D. thesis, MIT.

A Maximum-Entropy-Inspired Parser *

Eugene Charniak
Brown Laboratory for Linguistic Information Processing
Department of Computer Science
Brown University, Box 1910, Providence, RI 02912
ec@cs.brown.edu

Abstract

We present a new parser for parsing down to Penn tree-bank style parse trees that achieves 90.1% average precision/recall for sentences of length 40 and less, and 89.5% for sentences of length 100 and less when trained and tested on the previously established [5,9,10,15,17] "standard" sections of the Wall Street Journal tree-bank. This represents a 13% decrease in error rate over the best single-parser results on this corpus [9]. The major technical innovation is the use of a "maximum-entropy-inspired" model for conditioning and smoothing that let us successfully to test and combine many different conditioning events. We also present some partial results showing the effects of different conditioning information, including a surprising 2% improvement due to guessing the lexical head's pre-terminal before guessing the lexical head.

1 Introduction

We present a new parser for parsing down to Penn tree-bank style parse trees [16] that achieves 90.1% average precision/recall for sentences of length ≤ 40, and 89.5% for sentences of length ≤ 100, when trained and tested on the previously established [5,9,10,15,17] "standard" sections of the Wall Street Journal tree-bank. This represents a 13% decrease in error rate over the best single-parser results on this corpus [9].

Following [5,10], our parser is based upon a probabilistic generative model. That is, for all sentences s and all parses π, the parser assigns a probability $p(s, \pi) = p(\pi)$, the equality holding when we restrict consideration to π whose yield is s. Then for any s the parser returns the parse π that maximizes this probability. That is, the parser implements the function

$$\begin{aligned} \arg max_{\pi} p(\pi \mid s) &= \arg max_{\pi} p(\pi, s) \\ &= \arg max_{\pi} p(\pi). \end{aligned}$$

What fundamentally distinguishes probabilistic generative parsers is how they compute $p(\pi)$, and it is to that topic we turn next.

2 The Generative Model

The model assigns a probability to a parse by a top-down process of considering each constituent c in π and for each c first guessing the pre-terminal of c, $t(c)$ (t for "tag"), then the lexical head of c, $h(c)$, and then the expansion of c into further constituents $e(c)$. Thus the probability of a parse is given by the equation

$$\begin{aligned} p(\pi) = \prod_{c \in \pi} & p(t(c) \mid l(c), H(c)) \\ & \cdot p(h(c) \mid t(c), l(c), H(c)) \\ & \cdot p(e(c) \mid l(c), t(c), h(c), H(c)) \end{aligned}$$

where $l(c)$ is the label of c (e.g., whether it is a noun phrase (np), verb-phrase, etc.) and $H(c)$ is the relevant history of c — information outside c that our probability model deems important in determining the probability in question. Much of the interesting work is determining what goes into $H(c)$. Whenever it is clear to which constituent we are referring we omit the (c) in, e.g., $h(c)$. In this notation the above equation takes the following form:

$$p(\pi) = \prod_{c \in \pi} p(t \mid l, H) \cdot p(h \mid t, l, H) \cdot p(e \mid l, t, h, H). \tag{1}$$

* This research was supported in part by NSF grant LIS SBR 9720368. The author would like to thank Mark Johnson and all the rest of the Brown Laboratory for Linguistic Information Processing.

Next we describe how we assign a probability to the expansion e of a constituent. In Section 5 we present some results in which the possible expansions of a constituent are fixed in advanced by extracting a tree-bank grammar [3] from the training corpus. The method that gives the best results, however, uses a Markov grammar — a method for assigning probabilities to any possible expansion using statistics gathered from the training corpus [6,10,15]. The method we use follows that of [10]. In this scheme a traditional probabilistic context-free grammar (PCFG) rule can be thought of as consisting of a left-hand side with a label $l(c)$ drawn from the non-terminal symbols of our grammar, and a right-hand side that is a sequence of one or more such symbols. (We assume that all terminal symbols are generated by rules of the form "*preterm* $\rightarrow$ *word*" and we treat these as a special case.) For us the non-terminal symbols are those of the tree-bank, augmented by the symbols aux and auxg, which have been assigned deterministically to certain auxiliary verbs such as "have" or "having". For each expansion we distinguish one of the right-hand side labels as the "middle" or "head" symbol $M(c)$. $M(c)$ is the constituent from which the head lexical item h is obtained according to deterministic rules that pick the head of a constituent from among the heads of its children. To the left of M is a sequence of one or more left labels $L_i(c)$ including the special termination symbol Δ, which indicates that there are no more symbols to the left, and similarly for the labels to the right, $R_i(c)$. Thus an expansion $e(c)$ looks like:

$$l \rightarrow \Delta L_m ... L_1 M R_1 ... R_n \Delta. \qquad (2)$$

The expansion is generated by guessing first M, then in order L_1 through L_{m+1} $(= \Delta)$, and similarly for R_1 through R_{n+1}.

In a pure Markov PCFG we are given the left-hand side label l and then probabilistically generate the right-hand side conditioning on no information other than l and (possibly) previously generated pieces of the right-hand side itself. In the simplest of such models, a zero-order Markov grammar, each label on the right-hand side is generated conditioned only on l — that is, according to the distributions $p(L_i \mid l)$, $p(M \mid l)$, and $p(R_i \mid l)$.

More generally, one can condition on the m previously generated labels, thereby obtaining an mth-order Markov grammar. So, for example, in a second-order Markov PCFG, L_2 would be conditioned on L_1 and M. In our complete model, of course, the probability of each label in the expansions is also conditioned on other material as specified in Equation 1, e.g., $p(e \mid l, t, h, H)$. Thus we would use $p(L_2 \mid L_1, M, l, t, h, H)$. Note that the Δs on both ends of the expansion in Expression 2 are conditioned just like any other label in the expansion.

3 Maximum-Entropy-Inspired Parsing

The major problem confronting the author of a generative parser is what information to use to condition the probabilities required in the model, and how to smooth the empirically obtained probabilities to take the sting out of the sparse data problems that are inevitable with even the most modest conditioning. For example, in a second-order Markov grammar we conditioned the L_2 label according to the distribution $p(L_2 \mid L_1, M, l, t, h, H)$. Also, remember that H is a placeholder for any other information beyond the constituent c that may be useful in assigning c a probability.

In the past few years the maximum entropy, or log-linear, approach has recommended itself to probabilistic model builders for its flexibility and its novel approach to smoothing [1,17]. A complete review of log-linear models is beyond the scope of this paper. Rather, we concentrate on the aspects of these models that most directly influenced the model presented here.

To compute a probability in a log-linear model one first defines a set of "features", functions from the space of configurations over which one is trying to compute probabilities to integers that denote the number of times some pattern occurs in the input. In our work we assume that any feature can occur at most once, so features are boolean-valued: 0 if the pattern does not occur, 1 if it does.

In the parser we further assume that features are chosen from certain feature schemata and that every feature is a boolean conjunction of sub-features. For example, in computing the probability of the head's pre-terminal t we might want a feature schema $f(t, l)$ that returns 1 if the observed pre-terminal of $c = t$ and the label of $c = l$, and zero otherwise. This feature is obviously composed of two sub-features, one recognizing t, the other l. If both return 1, then the feature returns 1.

Now consider computing a conditional probability $p(a \mid H)$ with a set of features $f_1 \dots f_j$ that connect a to the history H. In a log-linear model the probability function takes the following form:

$$p(a \mid H) = \frac{1}{Z(H)} e^{\lambda_1(a,H)f_1(a,H)+\dots+\lambda_m(a,H)f_m(a,H)} \quad (3)$$

Here the λ_i are weights between negative and positive infinity that indicate the relative importance of a feature: the more relevant the feature to the value of the probability, the higher the absolute value of the associated λ. The function $Z(H)$, called the partition function, is a normalizing constant (for fixed H), so the probabilities over all a sum to one.

Now for our purposes it is useful to rewrite this as a sequence of multiplicative functions $g_i(a, H)$ for $0 \le i \le j$:

$$p(a \mid H) = g_0(a, H) g_1(a, H) \dots g_j(a, H). \quad (4)$$

Here $g_0(a, H) = 1/Z(H)$ and $g_i(a, H) = e^{\lambda_i(a,H)f_i(a,H)}$. The intuitive idea is that each factor g_i is larger than one if the feature in question makes the probability more likely, one if the feature has no effect, and smaller than one if it makes the probability less likely.

Maximum-entropy models have two benefits for a parser builder. First, as already implicit in our discussion, factoring the probability computation into a sequence of values corresponding to various "features" suggests that the probability model should be easily changeable — just change the set of features used. This point is emphasized by Ratnaparkhi in discussing his parser [17]. Second, and this is a point we have not yet mentioned, the features used in these models need have no particular independence of one another. This is useful if one is using a log-linear model for smoothing. That is, suppose we want to compute a conditional probability $p(a \mid b, c)$, but we are not sure that we have enough examples of the conditioning event b, c in the training corpus to ensure that the empirically obtained probability $\hat{p}(a \mid b, c)$ is accurate. The traditional way to handle this is also to compute $\hat{p}(a \mid b)$, and perhaps $\hat{p}(a \mid c)$ as well, and take some combination of these values as one's best estimate for $p(a \mid b, c)$. This method is known as "deleted interpolation" smoothing. In max-entropy models one can simply include features for all three events $f_1(a, b, c)$, $f_2(a, b)$, and $f_3(a, c)$ and combine them in the model according to Equation 3, or equivalently, Equation 4. The fact that the features are very far from independent is not a concern.

Now let us note that we can get an equation of exactly the same form as Equation 4 in the following fashion:

$$p(a \mid b, c, d) = p(a \mid b) \frac{p(a \mid b, c)}{p(a \mid b)} \frac{p(a \mid b, c, d)}{p(a \mid b, c)}. \quad (5)$$

Note that the first term of the equation gives a probability based upon little conditioning information and that each subsequent term is a number from zero to positive infinity that is greater or smaller than one if the new information being considered makes the probability greater or smaller than the previous estimate.

As it stands, this last equation is pretty much content-free. But let us look at how it works for a particular case in our parsing scheme. Consider the probability distribution for choosing the pre-terminal for the head of a constituent. In Equation 1 we wrote this as $p(t \mid l, H)$. As we discuss in more detail in Section 5, several different features in the context surrounding c are useful to include in H: the label, head pre-terminal and head of the parent of c (denoted as l_p, t_p, h_p), the label of c's left sibling (l_b for "before"), and the label of the grandparent of c (l_g). That is, we wish to compute $p(t \mid l, l_p, t_p, l_b, l_g, h_p)$. We can now rewrite this in the form of Equation 5 as follows:

$$p(t \mid l, l_p, t_p, l_b, l_g, h_p) = p(t \mid l) \frac{p(t \mid l, l_p)}{p(t \mid l)} \frac{p(t \mid l, l_p, t_p)}{p(t \mid l, l_p)} \frac{p(t \mid l, l_p, t_p, l_b)}{p(t \mid l, l_p, t_p)} \frac{p(t \mid l, l_p, t_p, l_b, l_g)}{p(t \mid l, l_p, t_p, l_b)} \frac{p(t \mid l, l_p, t_p, l_b, l_g, h_p)}{p(t \mid l, l_p, t_p, l_b, l_g)}. \quad (6)$$

Here we have sequentially conditioned on steadily increasing portions of c's history. In many cases this is clearly warranted. For example, it does not seem to make much sense to condition on, say, h_p without first conditioning on t_p. In other cases, however, we seem to be conditioning on apples and oranges, so to speak. For example, one can well imagine that one might want to condition on the parent's lexical head without conditioning on the left sibling, or the grandparent label. One way to do this is to modify the simple version shown in Equation 6 to allow this:

$$p(t \mid l, l_p, t_p, b, l_g, h_p) = \\ p(t \mid l) \frac{p(t \mid l, l_p)}{p(t \mid l)} \frac{p(t \mid l, l_p, t_p)}{p(t \mid l, l_p)} \frac{p(t \mid l, l_p, t_p, l_b)}{p(t \mid l, l_p, t_p)} \\ \frac{p(t \mid l, l_p, t_p, l_g)}{p(t \mid l, l_p, t_p)} \frac{p(t \mid l, l_p, t_p, h_p)}{p(t \mid l, l_p, t_p)}. \quad (7)$$

Note the changes to the last three terms in Equation 7. Rather than conditioning each term on the previous ones, they are now conditioned only on those aspects of the history that seem most relevant. The hope is that by doing this we will have less difficulty with the splitting of conditioning events, and thus somewhat less difficulty with sparse data.

We make one more point on the connection of Equation 7 to a maximum entropy formulation. Suppose we were, in fact, going to compute a true maximum entropy model based upon the features used in Equation 7, $f_1(t, l), f_2(t, l, l_p), f_3(t, l, l_p) \ldots$ This requires finding the appropriate λ_is for Equation 3, which is accomplished using an algorithm such as iterative scaling [11] in which values for the λ_i are initially "guessed" and then modified until they converge on stable values. With no prior knowledge of values for the λ_i one traditionally starts with $\lambda_i = 0$, this being a neutral assumption that the feature has neither a positive nor negative impact on the probability in question. With some prior knowledge, non-zero values can greatly speed up this process because fewer iterations are required for convergence. We comment on this because in our example we can substantially speed up the process by choosing values picked so that, when the maximum-entropy equation is expressed in the form of Equation 4, the g_i have as their initial values the values of the corresponding terms in Equation 7. (Our experience is that rather than requiring 50 or so iterations, three suffice.) Now we observe that if we were to use a maximum-entropy approach but run iterative scaling zero times, we would, in fact, just have Equation 7.

The major advantage of using Equation 7 is that one can generally get away without computing the partition function $Z(H)$. In the simple (content-free) form (Equation 6), it is clear that $Z(H) = 1$. In the more interesting version, Equation 7, this is not true in general, but one would not expect it to differ much from one, and we assume that as long as we are not publishing the raw probabilities (as we would be doing, for example, in publishing perplexity results) the difference from one should be unimportant. As partition-function calculation is typically the major on-line computational problem for maximum-entropy models, this simplifies the model significantly.

Naturally, the distributions required by Equation 7 cannot be used without smoothing. In a pure maximum-entropy model this is done by feature selection, as in Ratnaparkhi's maximum-entropy parser [17]. While we could have smoothed in the same fashion, we choose instead to use standard deleted interpolation. (Actually, we use a minor variant described in [4].)

4 The Experiment

We created a parser based upon the maximum-entropy-inspired model of the last section, smoothed using standard deleted interpolation. As the generative model is top-down and we use a standard bottom-up best-first probabilistic chart parser [2,7], we use the chart parser as a first pass to generate candidate possible parses to be evaluated in the second pass by our probabilistic model. For runs with the generative model based upon Markov grammar statistics, the first pass uses the same statistics, but conditioned only on standard PCFG information. This allows the second pass to see expansions not present in the training corpus.

We use the gathered statistics for all observed words, even those with very low counts, though obviously our deleted interpolation smoothing gives less emphasis to observed probabilities for rare words. We guess the preterminals of words that are not observed in the training data using statistics on capitalization, hyphenation, word endings (the last two letters), and the probability that a given pre-terminal is realized using a previously unobserved word.

As noted above, the probability model uses

Parser	LR	LP	CB	0CB	2CB
	$\leq$ 40 words (2245 sentences)				
Char97	87.5	87.4	1.00	62.1	86.1
Coll99	88.5	88.7	0.92	66.7	87.1
Char00	90.1	90.1	0.74	70.1	89.6
	$\leq$ 100 words (2416 sentences)				
Char97	86.7	86.6	1.20	59.9	83.2
Coll99	88.1	88.3	1.06	64.0	85.1
Ratna99	86.3	87.5			
Char00	89.6	89.5	0.88	67.6	87.7

Figure 1: Parsing results compared with previous work

five smoothed probability distributions, one each for L_i, M, R_i, t, and h. The equation for the (unsmoothed) conditional probability distribution for t is given in Equation 7. The other four equations can be found in a longer version of this paper available on the author's website (www.cs.brown.edu/~ec). L and R are conditioned on three previous labels so we are using a third-order Markov grammar. Also, the label of the parent constituent l_p is conditioned upon even when it is not obviously related to the further conditioning events. This is due to the importance of this factor in parsing, as noted in, e.g., [14].

In keeping with the standard methodology [5, 9,10,15,17], we used the Penn Wall Street Journal tree-bank [16] with sections 2-21 for training, section 23 for testing, and section 24 for development (debugging and tuning).

Performance on the test corpus is measured using the standard measures from [5,9,10,17]. In particular, we measure labeled precision (LP) and recall (LR), average number of cross-brackets per sentence (CB), percentage of sentences with zero cross brackets (0CB), and percentage of sentences with $\leq$ 2 cross brackets (2CB). Again as standard, we take separate measurements for all sentences of length $\leq$ 40 and all sentences of length $\leq$ 100. Note that the definitions of labeled precision and recall are those given in [9] and used in all of the previous work. As noted in [5], these definitions typically give results about 0.4% higher than the more obvious ones. The results for the new parser as well as for the previous top-three individual parsers on this corpus are given in Figure 1.

As is typical, all of the standard measures tell pretty much the same story, with the new parser outperforming the other three parsers. Looking in particular at the precision and recall figures, the new parser's give us a 13% error reduction over the best of the previous work, Coll99 [9].

5 Discussion

In the previous sections we have concentrated on the relation of the parser to a maximum-entropy approach, the aspect of the parser that is most novel. However, we do not think this aspect is the sole or even the most important reason for its comparative success. Here we list what we believe to be the most significant contributions and give some experimental results on how well the program behaves without them.

We take as our starting point the parser labled Char97 in Figure 1 [5], as that is the program from which our current parser derives. That parser, as stated in Figure 1, achieves an average precision/recall of 87.5. As noted in [5], that system is based upon a "tree-bank grammar" — a grammar read directly off the training corpus. This is as opposed to the "Markov-grammar" approach used in the current parser. Also, the earlier parser uses two techniques not employed in the current parser. First, it uses a clustering scheme on words to give the system a "soft" clustering of heads and sub-heads. (It is "soft" clustering in that a word can belong to more than one cluster with different weights — the weights express the probability of producing the word given that one is going to produce a word from that cluster.) Second, Char97 uses unsupervised learning in that the original system was run on about thirty million words of unparsed text, the output was taken as "correct", and statistics were collected on the resulting parses. Without these enhancements Char97 performs at the 86.6% level for sentences of length $\leq$ 40.

In this section we evaluate the effects of the various changes we have made by running various versions of our current program. To avoid repeated evaluations based upon the testing corpus, here our evaluation is based upon sentences of length $\leq$ 40 from the development corpus. We note here that this corpus is somewhat more difficult than the "official" test corpus. For example, the final version of our system

System	Precision	Recall
Old	86.3	86.1
Explicit Pre-Term	88.0	88.1
Marked Coordination	88.6	88.7
Standard Interpolation	88.2	88.3
MaxEnt-Inspired	89.0	89.2
First-order Markov	88.6	87.4
Second-order Markov	89.5	89.3
Best	89.8	89.6

Figure 2: Labeled precision/recall for length $\leq$ 40, development corpus

achieves an average precision/recall of 90.1% on the test corpus but an average precision/recall of only 89.7% on the development corpus. This is indicated in Figure 2, where the model labeled "Best" has precision of 89.8% and recall of 89.6% for an average of 89.7%, 0.4% lower than the results on the official test corpus. This is in accord with our experience that development-corpus results are from 0.3% to 0.5% lower than those obtained on the test corpus.

The model labeled "Old" attempts to recreate the Char97 system using the current program. It makes no use of special maximum-entropy-inspired features (though their presence made it much easier to perform these experiments), it does not guess the pre-terminal before guessing the lexical head, and it uses a tree-bank grammar rather than a Markov grammar. This parser achieves an average precision/recall of 86.2%. This is consistent with the average precision/recall of 86.6% for [5] mentioned above, as the latter was on the test corpus and the former on the development corpus.

Between the Old model and the Best model, Figure 2 gives precision/recall measurements for several different versions of our parser. One of the first and without doubt the most significant change we made in the current parser is to move from two stages of probabilistic decisions at each node to three. As already noted, Char97 first guesses the lexical head of a constituent and then, given the head, guesses the PCFG rule used to expand the constituent in question. In contrast, the current parser first guesses the head's pre-terminal, then the head, and then the expansion. It turns out that usefulness of this process had already been discovered by Collins [10], who in turn notes (personal communication) that it was previously used by Eisner [12]. However, Collins in [10] does not stress the decision to guess the head's pre-terminal first, and it might be lost on the casual reader. Indeed, it was lost on the present author until he went back after the fact and found it there. In Figure 2 we show that this one factor improves performance by nearly 2%.

It may not be obvious why this should make so great a difference, since most words are effectively unambiguous. (For example, part-of-speech tagging using the most probable pre-terminal for each word is 90% accurate [8].) We believe that two factors contribute to this performance gain. The first is simply that if we first guess the pre-terminal, when we go to guess the head the first thing we can condition upon is the pre-terminal, i.e., we compute $p(h \mid t)$. This quantity is a relatively intuitive one (as, for example, it is the quantity used in a PCFG to relate words to their pre-terminals) and it seems particularly good to condition upon here since we use it, in effect, as the unsmoothed probability upon which all smoothing of $p(h)$ is based. This one "fix" makes slightly over a percent difference in the results.

The second major reason why first guessing the pre-terminal makes so much difference is that it can be used when backing off the lexical head in computing the probability of the rule expansion. For example, when we first guess the lexical head we can move from computing $p(r \mid l, l_p, h)$ to $p(r \mid l, t, l_p, h)$. So, e.g., even if the word "conflating" does not appear in the training corpus (and it does not), the "ng" ending allows our program to guess with relative security that the word has the **vbg** pre-terminal, and thus the probability of various rule expansions can be considerable sharpened. For example, the tree-bank PCFG probability of the rule "**vp** $\rightarrow$ **vbg np**" is 0.0145, whereas once we condition on the fact that the lexical head is a **vbg** we get a probability of 0.214.

The second modification is the explicit marking of noun and verb-phrase coordination. We have already noted the importance of conditioning on the parent label l_p. So, for example, information about an **np** is conditioned on the parent — e.g., an **s**, **vp**, **pp**, etc. Note that when an **np** is part of an **np** coordinate structure the

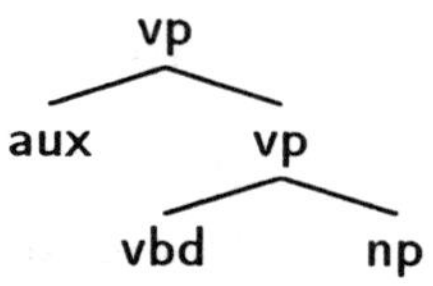

Figure 3: Verb phrase with both main and auxiliary verbs

parent will itself be an np, and similarly for a vp. But nps and vps can occur with np and vp parents in non-coordinate structures as well. For example, in the Penn Treebank a vp with both main and auxiliary verbs has the structure shown in Figure 3. Note that the subordinate vp has a vp parent.

Thus np and vp parents of constituents are marked to indicate if the parents are a coordinate structure. A vp coordinate structure is defined here as a constituent with two or more vp children, one or more of the constituents comma, cc, conjp (conjunctive phrase), and nothing else; coordinate np phrases are defined similarly. Something very much like this is done in [15]. As shown in Figure 2, conditioning on this information gives a 0.6% improvement. We believe that this is mostly due to improvements in guessing the sub-constituent's pre-terminal and head. Given we are already at the 88% level of accuracy, we judge a 0.6% improvement to be very much worth while.

Next we add the less obvious conditioning events noted in our previous discussion of the final model — grandparent label l_g and left sibling label l_b. When we do so using our maximum-entropy-inspired conditioning, we get another 0.45% improvement in average precision/recall, as indicated in Figure 2 on the line labeled "MaxEnt-Inspired'. Note that we also tried including this information using a standard deleted-interpolation model. The results here are shown in the line "Standard Interpolation". Including this information within a standard deleted-interpolation model causes a 0.6% decrease from the results using the less conventional model. Indeed, the resulting performance is worse than not using this information at all.

Up to this point all the models considered in this section are tree-bank grammar models. That is, the PCFG grammar rules are read directly off the training corpus. As already noted, our best model uses a Markov-grammar approach. As one can see in Figure 2, a first-order Markov grammar (with all the aforementioned improvements) performs slightly worse than the equivalent tree-bank-grammar parser. However, a second-order grammar does slightly better and a third-order grammar does significantly better than the tree-bank parser.

6 Conclusion

We have presented a lexicalized Markov grammar parsing model that achieves (using the now standard training/testing/development sections of the Penn treebank) an average precision/recall of 91.1% on sentences of length $\leq$ 40 and 89.5% on sentences of length $\leq$ 100. This corresponds to an error reduction of 13% over the best previously published single parser results on this test set, those of Collins [9]. That the previous three best parsers on this test [5,9,17] all perform within a percentage point of each other, despite quite different basic mechanisms, led some researchers to wonder if there might be some maximum level of parsing performance that could be obtained using the treebank for training, and to conjecture that perhaps we were at it. The results reported here disprove this conjecture. The results of [13] achieved by combining the aforementioned three-best parsers also suggest that the limit on tree-bank trained parsers is much higher than previously thought. Indeed, it may be that adding this new parser to the mix may yield still higher results.

From our perspective, perhaps the two most important numbers to come out of this research are the overall error reduction of 13% over the results in [9] and the intermediate-result improvement of nearly 2% on labeled precision/recall due to the simple idea of guessing the head's pre-terminal before guessing the head. Neither of these results were anticipated at the start of this research.

As noted above, the main methodological innovation presented here is our "maximum-entropy-inspired" model for conditioning and smoothing. Two aspects of this model deserve some comment. The first is the slight, but important, improvement achieved by using this model over conventional deleted interpolation, as indicated in Figure 2. We expect that as we experiment with other, more semantic conditioning information, the importance of this aspect of the model will increase.

More important in our eyes, though, is the flexibility of the maximum-entropy-inspired model. Though in some respects not quite as flexible as true maximum entropy, it is much simpler and, in our estimation, has benefits when it comes to smoothing. Ultimately it is this flexibility that let us try the various conditioning events, to move on to a Markov grammar approach, and to try several Markov grammars of different orders, without significant programming. Indeed, we initiated this line of work in an attempt to create a parser that would be flexible enough to allow modifications for parsing down to more semantic levels of detail. It is to this project that our future parsing work will be devoted.

References

1. Berger, A. L., Pietra, S. A. D. and Pietra, V. J. D. A maximum entropy approach to natural language processing. *Computational Linguistics 22* 1 (1996), 39–71.
2. Caraballo, S. and Charniak, E. New figures of merit for best-first probabilistic chart parsing. *Computational Linguistics 24* (1998), 275–298.
3. Charniak, E. *Tree-bank grammars*. In *Proceedings of the Thirteenth National Conference on Artificial Intelligence*. AAAI Press/MIT Press, Menlo Park, 1996, 1031–1036.
4. Charniak, E. Expected-frequency interpolation. Department of Computer Science, Brown University, Technical Report CS96-37, 1996.
5. Charniak, E. *Statistical parsing with a context-free grammar and word statistics*. In *Proceedings of the Fourteenth National Conference on Artificial Intelligence*. AAAI Press/MIT Press, Menlo Park, CA, 1997, 598–603.
6. Charniak, E. Statistical techniques for natural language parsing. *AI Magazine 18* 4 (1997), 33–43.
7. Charniak, E., Goldwater, S. and Johnson, M. *Edge-based best-first chart parsing*. In *Proceedings of the Sixth Workshop on Very Large Corpora*. 1998, 127–133.
8. Charniak, E., Hendrickson, C., Jacobson, N. and Perkowitz, M. *Equations for part-of-speech tagging*. In *Proceedings of the Eleventh National Conference on Artificial Intelligence*. AAAI Press/MIT Press, Menlo Park, 1993, 784–789.
9. Collins, M. Head-Driven Statistical Models for Natural Language Parsing. University of Pennsylvania, Ph.D. Disseration, 1999.
10. Collins, M. J. *Three generative lexicalised models for statistical parsing*. In *Proceedings of the 35th Annual Meeting of the ACL*. 1997, 16–23.
11. Darroch, J. N. and Ratcliff, D. Generalized iterative scaling for log-linear models. *Annals of Mathematical Statistics* 33 (1972), 1470–1480.
12. Eisner, J. M. An empirical comparison of probability models for dependency grammar. Institute for Research in Cognitive Science, University of Pennsylvania, Technical Report IRCS-96-11, 1996.
13. Henderson, J. C. and Brill, E. *Exploiting diversity in natural language processing: combining parsers*. In *1999 Joint Sigdat Conference on Empirical Methods in Natural Language Processing and Very Large Corpora*. ACL, New Brunswick NJ, 1999, 187–194.
14. Johnson, M. PCFG models of linguistic tree representations. *Computational Linguistics 24* 4 (1998), 613–632.
15. Magerman, D. M. *Statistical decision-tree models for parsing*. In *Proceedings of the 33rd Annual Meeting of the Association for Computational Linguistics*. 1995, 276–283.
16. Marcus, M. P., Santorini, B. and Marcinkiewicz, M. A. Building a large annotated corpus of English: the Penn treebank. *Computational Linguistics 19* (1993), 313–330.
17. Ratnaparkhi, A. Learning to parse natural language with maximum entropy models. *Machine Learning 34*1/2/3 (1999), 151–176.

An Unsupervised Method for Detecting Grammatical Errors

Martin Chodorow
Hunter College of CUNY
695 Park Avenue
New York, NY
martin.chodorow @.hunter.cuny.edu

Claudia Leacock
Educational Testing Service
Rosedale Road
Princeton, NJ
cleacock@ets.org

Abstract

We present an unsupervised method for detecting grammatical errors by inferring negative evidence from edited textual corpora. The system was developed and tested using essay-length responses to prompts on the Test of English as a Foreign Language (TOEFL). The error-recognition system, ALEK, performs with about 80% precision and 20% recall.

Introduction

A good indicator of whether a person knows the meaning of a word is the ability to use it appropriately in a sentence (Miller and Gildea, 1987). Much information about usage can be obtained from quite a limited context: Choueka and Lusignan (1985) found that people can typically recognize the intended sense of a polysemous word by looking at a narrow window of one or two words around it. Statistically-based computer programs have been able to do the same with a high level of accuracy (Kilgarriff and Palmer, 2000). The goal of our work is to automatically identify *inappropriate usage* of specific vocabulary words in essays by looking at the local contextual cues around a target word. We have developed a statistical system, ALEK (Assessing Lexical Knowledge), that uses statistical analysis for this purpose.

A major objective of this research is to avoid the laborious and costly process of collecting errors (or negative evidence) for each word that we wish to evaluate. Instead, we train ALEK on a general corpus of English and on edited text containing example uses of the target word. The system identifies inappropriate usage based on differences between the word's local context cues in an essay and the models of context it has derived from the corpora of well-formed sentences.

A requirement for ALEK has been that all steps in the process be automated, beyond choosing the words to be tested and assessing the results. Once a target word is chosen, preprocessing, building a model of the word's appropriate usage, and identifying usage errors in essays is performed without manual intervention.

ALEK has been developed using the Test of English as a Foreign Language (TOEFL) administered by the Educational Testing Service. TOEFL is taken by foreign students who are applying to US undergraduate and graduate-level programs.

1 Background

Approaches to detecting errors by non-native writers typically produce grammars that look for specific expected error types (Schneider and McCoy, 1998; Park, Palmer and Washburn, 1997). Under this approach, essays written by ESL students are collected and examined for errors. Parsers are then adapted to identify those error types that were found in the essay collection.

We take a different approach, initially viewing error detection as an extension of the word sense disambiguation (WSD) problem. Corpus-based WSD systems identify the intended sense of a polysemous word by (1) collecting a set of example sentences for each of its various senses and (2) extracting salient contextual cues from these sets to (3) build a statistical model for each sense. They identify the intended sense of a word in a novel sentence by extracting its contextual cues and selecting the most similar word sense model (e.g., Leacock, Chodorow and Miller (1998), Yarowsky (1993)).

Golding (1995) showed how methods used for WSD (decision lists and Bayesian classifiers) could be adapted to detect errors resulting from common spelling confusions among sets such as *there*, *their*, and *they're*. He extracted contexts from correct usage of each confusable word in a training corpus and then identified a new occurrence as an error when it matched the wrong context.

However, most grammatical errors are not the result of simple word confusions. This complicates the task of building a model of incorrect usage. One approach we considered was to proceed without such a model: represent appropriate word usage (across senses) in a single model and compare a novel example to that model. The most appealing part of this formulation was that we could bypass the knowledge acquisition bottleneck. All occurrences of the word in a collection of edited text could be automatically assigned to a single training set representing appropriate usage. Inappropriate usage would be signaled by contextual cues that do not occur in training.

Unfortunately, this approach was not effective for error detection. An example of a word usage error is often very similar to the model of appropriate usage. An incorrect usage can contain two or three salient contextual elements as well as a single anomalous element. The problem of error detection does not entail finding similarities to appropriate usage, rather it requires identifying one element among the contextual cues that simply does not fit.

2 ALEK Architecture

What kinds of anomalous elements does ALEK identify? Writers sometimes produce errors that violate basic principles of English syntax (e.g., *a desks*), while other mistakes show a lack of information about a specific vocabulary item (e.g., *a knowledge*). In order to detect these two types of problems, ALEK uses a 30-million word general corpus of English from the San Jose Mercury News (hereafter referred to as the *general corpus*) and, for each target word, a set of 10,000 example sentences from North American newspaper text[1] (hereafter referred to as the *word-specific corpus*).

ALEK infers negative evidence from the contextual cues that *do not* co-occur with the target word – either in the word specific corpus or in the general English one. It uses two kinds of contextual cues in a ±2 word window around the target word: function words (closed-class items) and part-of-speech tags (Brill, 1994). The Brill tagger output is post-processed to "enrich" some closed class categories of its tag set, such as subject versus object pronoun and definite versus indefinite determiner. The enriched tags were adapted from Francis and Kučera (1982).

After the sentences have been preprocessed, ALEK counts sequences of adjacent part-of-speech tags and function words (such as determiners, prepositions, and conjunctions). For example, the sequence *a/AT full-time/JJ job/NN* contributes one occurrence each to the bigrams AT+JJ, JJ+NN, a+JJ, and to the part-of-speech tag trigram AT+JJ+NN. Each individual tag and function word also contributes to its own unigram count. These frequencies form the basis for the error detection measures.

From the general corpus, ALEK computes a mutual information measure to determine which sequences of part-of-speech tags and function words are unusually rare and are, therefore, likely to be ungrammatical in English (e.g., singular determiner preceding plural noun, as in **a desks*). Mutual information has often been used to detect combinations of words that occur more frequently than we would expect based on the assumption that the words are independent. Here we use this measure for the opposite purpose – to find combinations that occur less often than expected. ALEK also looks for sequences that are common in general but unusual in the word specific corpus (e.g., the singular determiner *a* preceding a singular noun is common in English but rare when the noun is

[1] The corpora are extracted from the ACL-DCI corpora. In selecting the sentences for the word specific corpora, we tried to minimize the mismatch between the domains of newspapers and TOEFL essays. For example, in the newspaper domain, *concentrate* is usually used as a noun, as in *orange juice concentrate* but in TOEFL essays it is a verb 91% of the time. Sentence selection for the word specific corpora was constrained to reflect the distribution of part-of-speech tags for the target word in a random sample of TOEFL essays.

knowledge). These divergences between the two corpora reflect syntactic properties that are peculiar to the target word.

2.1 Measures based on the general corpus:

The system computes mutual information comparing the proportion of observed occurrences of bigrams in the general corpus to the proportion expected based on the assumption of independence, as shown below:

$$MI = \log_2\left(\frac{P(AB)}{P(A) \times P(B)}\right)$$

Here, P(AB) is the probability of the occurrence of the AB bigram, estimated from its frequency in the general corpus, and P(A) and P(B) are the probabilities of the first and second elements of the bigram, also estimated from the general corpus. Ungrammatical sequences should produce bigram probabilities that are much smaller than the product of the unigram probabilities (the value of MI will be negative). Trigram sequences are also used, but in this case the mutual information computation compares the co-occurrence of ABC to a model in which A and C are assumed to be conditionally independent given B (see Lin, 1998).

$$MI = \log_2\left(\frac{P(ABC)}{P(B) \times P(A \mid B) \times P(C \mid B)}\right)$$

Once again, a negative value is often indicative of a sequence that violates a rule of English.

2.2 Comparing the word-specific corpus to the general corpus:

ALEK also uses mutual information to compare the distributions of tags and function words in the word-specific corpus to the distributions that are expected based on the general corpus. The measures for bigrams and trigrams are similar to those given above except that the probability in the numerator is estimated from the word-specific corpus and the probabilities in the denominator come from the general corpus. To return to a previous example, the phrase *a knowledge* contains the tag bigram for singular determiner followed by singular noun (AT NN). This sequence is much less common in the word-specific corpus for *knowledge* than would be expected from the general corpus unigram probabilities of AT and NN.

In addition to bigram and trigram measures, ALEK compares the target word's part-of-speech tag in the word-specific corpus and in the general corpus. Specifically, it looks at the conditional probability of the part-of-speech tag given the major syntactic category (e.g., plural noun given noun) in both distributions, by computing the following value.

$$\log_2\left(\frac{P_{specific\_corpus}(tag \mid category)}{P_{general\_corpus}(tag \mid category)}\right)$$

For example, in the general corpus, about half of all noun tokens are plural, but in the training set for the noun *knowledge*, the plural *knowledges* occurs rarely, if at all.

The mutual information measures provide candidate errors, but this approach overgenerates – it finds rare, but still quite grammatical, sequences. To reduce the number of false positives, no candidate found by the MI measures is considered an error if it appears in the word-specific corpus at least two times. This increases ALEK's precision at the price of reduced recall. For example, *a knowledge* will not be treated as an error because it appears in the training corpus as part of the longer *a knowledge of* sequence (as in *a knowledge of mathematics*).

ALEK also uses another statistical technique for finding rare and possibly ungrammatical tag and function word bigrams by computing the χ^2 (*chi square*) statistic for the difference between the bigram proportions found in the word-specific and in the general corpus:

$$\chi^2 = \left(\frac{(P_{word\_specific} - P_{general\_corpus})^2}{P_{general\_corpus}(1 - P_{gerneral\_corpus}) / N_{word\_specific}}\right)$$

The χ^2 measure faces the same problem of overgenerating errors. Due to the large sample sizes, extreme values can be obtained even though effect size may be minuscule. To reduce false positives, ALEK requires that effect sizes be at least in the moderate-to-small range (Cohen and Cohen, 1983).

Direct evidence from the word specific corpus can also be used to control the overgeneration of errors. For each candidate error, ALEK compares the larger context in which the bigram appears to the contexts that have been analyzed in the word-specific corpus. From the word-specific corpus, ALEK forms *templates*, sequences of words and tags that represent the local context of the target. If a test sentence contains a low probability bigram (as measured by the χ^2 test), the local context of the target is compared to all the templates of which it is a part. Exceptions to the error, that is longer grammatical sequences that contain rare sub-sequences, are found by examining conditional probabilities. To illustrate this, consider the example of *a knowledge* and *a knowledge of*. The conditional probability of *of* given *a knowledge* is high, as it accounts for almost all of the occurrences of *a knowledge* in the word-specific corpus. Based on this high conditional probability, the system will use the template for *a knowledge of* to keep it from being marked as an error. Other function words and tags in the +1 position have much lower conditional probability, so for example, *a knowledge is* will not be treated as an exception to the error.

2.3 Validity of the n-gram measures

TOEFL essays are graded on a 6 point scale, where 6 demonstrates "clear competence" in writing on rhetorical and syntactic levels and 1 demonstrates "incompetence in writing". If low probability n-grams signal grammatical errors, then we would expect TOEFL essays that received lower scores to have more of these n-grams. To test this prediction, we randomly selected from the TOEFL pool 50 essays for each of the 6 score values from 1.0 to 6.0. For each score value, all 50 essays were concatenated to form a super-essay. In every super-essay, for each adjacent pair and triple of tags containing a noun, verb, or adjective, the bigram and trigram mutual information values were computed based on the general corpus.

Score	% of bigrams	% of trigrams
1.0	3.6	1.4
2.0	3.4	0.8
3.0	2.6	0.6
4.0	1.9	0.3
5.0	1.3	0.4
6.0	1.5	0.3

Table 1: Percent of n-grams with mutual information < -3.60, by score point

Table 1 shows the proportions of bigrams and trigrams with mutual information less than –3.60. As predicted, there is a significant negative correlation between the score and the proportion of low probability bigrams (r_s= -.94, n=6, p<.01, two-tailed) and trigrams (r_s= -.84, n=6, p<.05, two-tailed).

2.4 System development

ALEK was developed using three target words that were extracted from TOEFL essays: *concentrate*, *interest*, and *knowledge*. These words were chosen because they represent different parts of speech and varying degrees of polysemy. Each also occurred in at least 150 sentences in what was then a small pool of TOEFL essays. Before development began, each occurrence of these words was manually labeled as an appropriate or inappropriate usage – without taking into account grammatical errors that might have been present elsewhere in the sentence but which were not within the target word's scope.

Critical values for the statistical measures were set during this development phase. The settings were based empirically on ALEK's performance so as to optimize precision and recall on the three development words. Candidate errors were those local context sequences that produced a mutual information value of less than –3.60 based on the general corpus; mutual information of less than –5.00 for the specific/general comparisons; or a χ^2 value greater than 12.82 with an effect size greater than 0.30. Precision and recall for the three words are shown below.

Target word	n	Precision	Recall
Concentrate	169	.875	.280
Interest	416	.840	.330
Knowledge	761	.918	.570

Table 2: Development Words

Test Word	Precision	Recall	Total Recall (estimated)	Test Word	Precision	Recall	Total Recall (estimated)
Affect	.848	.762	.343	Energy	.768	.666	.104
Area	.752	.846	.205	Function	.800	.714	.168
Aspect	.792	.717	.217	Individual	.576	.742	.302
Benefit	.744	.709	.276	Job	.728	.679	.103
Career	.736	.671	.110	Period	.832	.670	.102
Communicate	.784	.867	.274	Pollution	.912	.780	.310
Concentrate	.848	.791	.415	Positive	.784	.700	.091
Conclusion	.944	.756	.119	Role	.728	.674	.098
Culture	.704	.656	.083	Stress	.768	.578	.162
Economy	.816	.666	.235	Technology	.728	.674	.093
				Mean	**.779**	**.716**	**.190**

Table 3: Precision and recall for 20 test words

3 Experimental Design and Results

ALEK was tested on 20 words. These words were randomly selected from those which met two criteria: (1) They appear in a university word list (Nation, 1990) as words that a student in a US university will be expected to encounter and (2) there were at least 1,000 sentences containing the word in the TOEFL essay pool.

To build the usage model for each target word, 10,000 sentences containing it were extracted from the North American News Corpus. Preprocessing included detecting sentence boundaries and part-of-speech tagging. As in the development system, the model of general English was based on bigram and trigram frequencies of function words and part-of-speech tags from 30-million words of the San Jose Mercury News.

For each test word, all of the test sentences were marked by ALEK as either containing an error or not containing an error. The size of the test set for each word ranged from 1,400 to 20,000 with a mean of 8,000 sentences.

3.1 Results

To evaluate the system, for each test word we randomly extracted 125 sentences that ALEK classified as containing no error (C-set) and 125 sentences which it labeled as containing an error (E-set). These 250 sentences were presented to a linguist in a random order for blind evaluation. The linguist, who had no part in ALEK's development, marked each usage of the target word as incorrect or correct and in the case of incorrect usage indicated how far from the target one would have to look in order to recognise that there was an error. For example, in the case of "an period" the error occurs at a distance of one word from *period*. When the error is an omission, as in "lived in Victorian period", the distance is where the missing word should have appeared. In this case, the missing determiner is 2 positions away from the target. When more than one error occurred, the distance of the one closest to the target was marked.

Table 3 lists the precision and recall for the 20 test words. The column labelled "Recall" is the proportion of human-judged errors in the 250-sentence sample that were detected by ALEK. "Total Recall" is an estimate that extrapolates from the human judgements of the sample to the entire test set. We illustrate this with the results for *pollution*. The human judge marked as incorrect usage 91.2% of the sample from ALEK's E-set and 18.4% of the sample from its C-set. To estimate overall incorrect usage, we computed a weighted mean of these two rates, where the weights reflected the proportion of sentences that were in the E-set and C-set. The E-set contained 8.3% of the *pollution* sentences and the C-set had the remaining 91.7%. With the human judgements as the gold standard, the estimated overall rate of incorrect usage is $(.083 \times .912 + .917 \times .184) = .245$. ALEK's estimated recall is the proportion of sentences in the E-set times its precision, divided by the overall estimated error rate $(.083 \times .912) / .245 = .310$.

The precision results vary from word to word. *Conclusion* and *pollution* have precision in the low to middle 90's while *individual*'s precision is 57%. Overall, ALEK's predictions are about 78% accurate. The recall is limited in part by the fact that the system only looks at syntactic information, while many of the errors are semantic.

3.2 Analysis of Hits and Misses

Nicholls (1999) identifies four error types: an unnecessary word (*affect *to* their emotions), a missing word (*opportunity of job.), a word or phrase that needs replacing (**every jobs*), a word used in the wrong form (**pollutions*). ALEK recognizes all of these types of errors. For closed class words, ALEK identified whether a word was *missing*, the wrong word was used (*choice*), and when an *extra* word was used. Open class words have a fourth error category, *form*, including inappropriate compounding and verb agreement. During the development stage, we found it useful to add additional error categories. Since TEOFL graders are not supposed to take punctuation into account, *punctuation* errors were only marked when they caused the judge to "garden path" or initially misinterpret the sentence. *Spelling* was marked either when a function word was misspelled, causing part-of-speech tagging errors, or when the writer's intent was unclear.

The distributions of categories for hits and misses, shown in Table 4, are not strikingly different. However, the hits are primarily syntactic in nature while the misses are both semantic (as in open-class:choice) and syntactic (as in closed-class:missing).

ALEK is sensitive to open-class word confusions (*affect* vs *effect*) where the part of speech differs or where the target word is confused with another word (**In this aspect,...* instead of *In this respect,...*). In both cases, the system recognizes that the target is in the wrong syntactic environment. Misses can also be syntactic – when the target word is confused with another word but the syntactic environment fails to trigger an error. In addition, ALEK does not recognize semantic errors when the error involves the misuse of an open-class word in combination with the target (for example, *make* in "*they *make* benefits").

Category	% Hits	% Misses
Closed-class – choice	22.5	15.5
–extra	15.5	13.0
–missing	8.0	8.5
Open-class – choice	12.0	19.0
– extra	.5	1.0
– missing	.5	1.5
– form	28.0	28.5
Punctuation	5.5	1.5
Sentence fragment	1.5	2.0
Spelling/typing error	5.5	8.5
Word order	.5	1.0

Table 4: Hits and misses based on a random sample of 200 hits and 200 misses

Closed class words typically are either selected by or agree with a head word. So why are there so many misses, especially with prepositions? The problem is caused in part by polysemy – when one sense of the word selects a preposition that another sense does not. When *concentrate* is used spatially, it selects the preposition *in*, as "the stores were concentrated *in* the downtown area". When it denotes mental activity, it selects the preposition *on*, as in "Susan concentrated *on* her studies". Since ALEK trains on all senses of *concentrate*, it does not detect the error in "*Susan concentrated *in* her studies". Another cause is that adjuncts, especially temporal and locative adverbials, distribute freely in the word-specific corpora, as in "Susan concentrated *in* her room." This second problem is more tractable than the polysemy problem – and would involve training the system to recognize certain types of adjuncts.

3.3 Analysis of False Positives

False positives, when ALEK "identifies" an error where none exists, fall into six major categories. The percentage of each false positive type in a random sample of 200 false positives is shown in Table 5.
Domain mismatch: Mismatch of the newspaper-domain word-specific corpora and essay-domain test corpus. One notable difference is that some TOEFL essay prompts call for the writer's opinion. Consequently,

Error Type	% Occurrence
Domain mismatch	12.5
Tagger	17.0
Syntactic	14.5
Free distribution	16.5
Punctuation	12.0
Infrequent tags	9.0
Other	18.5

Table 5. Distribution of false positive types

TOEFL essays often contain first person references, whereas newspaper articles are written in the third person. We need to supplement the word-specific corpora with material that more closely resembles the test corpus.

Tagger: Incorrect analysis by the part-of-speech tagger. When the part-of-speech tag is wrong, ALEK often recognizes the resulting *n*-gram as anomalous. Many of these errors are caused by training on the Brown corpus instead of a corpus of essays.

Syntactic analysis: Errors resulting from using part-of-speech tags instead of supertags or a full parse, which would give syntactic relations between constituents. For example, ALEK false alarms on arguments of ditransitive verbs such as *offer* and flags as an error "*you benefits*" in "*offers you benefits*".

Free distribution: Elements that distribute freely, such as adverbs and conjunctions, as well as temporal and locative adverbial phrases, tend to be identified as errors when they occur in some positions.

Punctuation: Most notably omission of periods and commas. Since these errors are not indicative of one's ability to use the target word, they were not considered as errors unless they caused the judge to misanalyze the sentence.

Infrequent tags. An undesirable result of our "enriched" tag set is that some tags, e.g., the post-determiner *last*, occur too infrequently in the corpora to provide reliable statistics.

Solutions to some of these problems will clearly be more tractable than to others.

4 Comparison of Results

Comparison of these results to those of other systems is difficult because there is no generally accepted test set or performance baseline. Given this limitation, we compared ALEK's performance to a widely used grammar checker, the one incorporated in Microsoft's Word97. We created files of sentences used for the three development words *concentrate*, *interest*, and *knowledge*, and manually corrected any errors outside the local context around the target before checking them with Word97. The performance for *concentrate* showed overall precision of 0.89 and recall of 0.07. For *interest*, precision was 0.85 with recall of 0.11. In sentences containing *knowledge*, precision was 0.99 and recall was 0.30. Word97 correctly detected the ungrammaticality of *knowledges* as well as *a knowledge*, while it avoided flagging *a knowledge of*.

In summary, Word97's precision in error detection is impressive, but the lower recall values indicate that it is responding to fewer error types than does ALEK. In particular, Word97 is not sensitive to inappropriate selection of prepositions for these three words (e.g., **have knowledge on history*, **to concentrate at science*). Of course, Word97 detects many kinds of errors that ALEK does not.

Research has been reported on grammar checkers specifically designed for an ESL population. These have been developed by hand, based on small training and test sets. Schneider and McCoy (1998) developed a system tailored to the error productions of American Sign Language signers. This system was tested on 79 sentences containing determiner and agreement errors, and 101 grammatical sentences. We calculate that their precision was 78% with 54% recall. Park, Palmer and Washburn (1997) adapted a categorial grammar to recognize "classes of errors [that] dominate" in the nine essays they inspected. This system was tested on eight essays, but precision and recall figures are not reported.

5 Conclusion

The unsupervised techniques that we have presented for inferring negative evidence are effective in recognizing grammatical errors in written text.

Preliminary results indicate that ALEK's error detection is predictive of TOEFL scores. If ALEK accurately detects usage errors, then it should report more errors in essays with lower scores than in those with higher scores. We have already seen in Table 1 that there is a negative correlation between essay score and two of ALEK's component measures, the general corpus n-grams. However, the data in Table 1 were not based on specific vocabulary items and do not reflect overall system performance, which includes the other measures as well.

Table 6 shows the proportion of test word occurrences that were classified by ALEK as containing errors within two positions of the target at each of 6 TOEFL score points. As predicted, the correlation is negative ($r_s = -1.00$, $n = 6$, $p < .001$, two-tailed). These data support the validity of the system as a detector of inappropriate usage, even when only a limited number of words are targeted and only the immediate context of each target is examined.

Score	ALEK	Human
1	.091	---
2	.085	.375
3	.067	.268
4	.057	.293
5	.048	.232
6	.041	.164

Table 6: Proportion of test word occurrences, by score point, classified as containing an error by ALEK and by a human judge

For comparison, Table 6 also gives the estimated proportions of inappropriate usage by score point based on the human judge's classification. Here, too, there is a negative correlation: $r_s = -.90$, $n = 5$, $p < .05$, two-tailed.

Although the system recognizes a wide range of error types, as Table 6 shows, it detects only about one-fifth as many errors as a human judge does. To improve recall, research needs to focus on the areas identified in section 3.2 and, to improve precision, efforts should be directed at reducing the false positives described in 3.3.

ALEK is being developed as a diagnostic tool for students who are learning English as a foreign language. However, its techniques could be incorporated into a grammar checker for native speakers.

Acknowledgments

We thank Susanne Wolff for evaluating the test sentences, and Robert Kantor, Ken Sheppard and 3 anonymous reviewers for their helpful suggestions.

References

Brill, E. 1994. Some advances in rule-based part-of-speech tagging. *Proceedings of the Twelfth National Conference on Artificial Intelligence*, Seattle, AAAI.

Choueka, Y. and S. Lusignan. 1985. Disambiguation by short contexts. *Computers and the Humanities*, 19:147-158.

Cohen, J. and P. Cohen. 1983. *Applied Multiple Regression/Correlation Analysis for the Behavioral Sciences*. Hillsdale, NJ: Erlbaum.

Francis, W. and H. Kučera. 1982. *Frequency Analysis of English Usage: Lexicon and Grammar*. Boston, Houghton Mifflin.

Golding, A. 1995. A Bayesian hybrid for context-sensitive spelling correction. *Proceedings of the 3rd Workshop on Very Large Corpora*. Cambridge, MA. 39—53.

Kilgarriff, A. and M. Palmer. 2000. Introduction to the special issue on SENSEVAL. *Computers and the Humanities*, 34:1—2.

Leacock, C., M. Chodorow and G.A. Miller. 1998. 1998. Using corpus statistics and WordNet's lexical relations for sense identification. *Computational Linguistics*, 24:1.

Lin, D. 1998. Extracting collocations from text corpora. *First Workshop on Computational Terminology*. Montreal, Canada.

Miller, G.A. and P. Gildea. 1987. How children learn words. *Scientific American*, 257.

Nation, I.S.P. 1990. *Teaching and learning vocabulary*. New York: Newbury House.

Nicholls, D. 1999. The Cambridge Learner Corpus – Error coding and analysis. Summer Workshop on Learner Corpora. Tokyo

Park, J.C., M. Palmer and G. Washburn. 1997. Checking grammatical mistakes for English-as-a-second-language (ESL) students. *Proceedings of KSEA-NERC*. New Brunswick, NJ.

Schneider, D.A. and K.F. McCoy. 1998. Recognizing syntactic errors in the writing of second language learners. *Proceedings of Coling-ACL-98*, Montréal.

Yarowsky, D. 1993. One sense per collocation. Proceedings of the ARPA Workshop on Human Language Technology. San Francisco. Morgan Kaufman.

Detecting Errors within a Corpus using Anomaly Detection

Eleazar Eskin
Department of Computer Science
Columbia University
eeskin@cs.columbia.edu

Abstract

We present a method for automatically detecting errors in a manually marked corpus using anomaly detection. Anomaly detection is a method for determining which elements of a large data set do not conform to the whole. This method fits a probability distribution over the data and applies a statistical test to detect anomalous elements. In the corpus error detection problem, anomalous elements are typically marking errors. We present the results of applying this method to the tagged portion of the Penn Treebank corpus.

1 Introduction

Manually marking corpora is a time consuming and expensive process. The process is subject to human error by the experts doing the marking. Unfortunately, many natural language processing methods are sensitive to these errors. In order to ensure accuracy in a corpus, typically several experts pass over the corpus to ensure consistency. For large corpora this can be a tremendous expense.

In this paper, we propose a method for automatically detecting errors in a marked corpus using an anomaly detection technique. This technique detects anomalies or elements which do not fit in with the rest of the corpus. When applied to marked corpora, the anomalies tend to be errors in the markings of the corpus.

To detect the anomalies, we first compute a probability distribution over the entire corpus. Then we apply a statistical test which identifies which elements are anomalies. In this case the anomalies are the elements with very low likelihood. These elements are marked as errors and are thrown out of the corpus. The model is recomputed on the remaining elements. At conclusion, we are left with two data sets: one the normal elements and the second the detected anomalous elements.

We evaluate this method over the part of speech tagged portion of the Penn Treebank corpus (Marcus et al., 1993). In one experiment, our method detected 1000 anomalies within a data set of 1.25 million tagged elements. Human judges evaluated the results of the application of this method and verified that 69% of identified anomalies are in fact tagging errors. In another experiment, our method detected 4000 anomalies of which 44% are tagging errors.

1.1 Related Work

The tagged portion of the Penn Treebank has been extensively utilized for construction and evaluation of taggers. This includes transformation-based tagging (Brill, 1994; Brill and Wu, 1998). Weischedel et al. (1993) applied Markov Models to tagging. Abney et al. (1999) applied boosting to part of speech tagging. Adwait Ratnaparkhi (1996) estimates a probability distribution for tagging using a maximum entropy approach.

Regarding error detection in corpora, Ratnaparkhi (1996) discusses inconsistencies in the Penn Treebank and relates them to interannotator differences in tagging style. Abney, Schapire and Singer (1999) discuss how to use boosting for cleaning data.

Much related work to the anomaly detection problem stems from the field of statistics in the study of outliers. This work examines detecting and dealing with outliers in univariate data, multivariate data, and structured data where the probability distribution over the data is given a priori. Statistics gives a set of discordancy tests which can be applied to any given element in the dataset to determine whether it is an outlier. A survey of outliers in statistics is given in Barnett and Lewis (1994).

Anomaly detection is extensively used within the field of computer security specifically in intrusion detection (Denning, 1987). Typically anomaly detection methods are applied to detect attacks by comparing the activity during an attack to the activity under normal use (Lane and Brodley, 1997; Warrender et al., 1999). The method used in this paper is based on a method for anomaly detection which detects anomalies in noisy data (Eskin, 2000).

The sparse Markov transducer probability modeling method is an extension of adaptive mixtures of probabilistic transducers (Singer, 1997; Pereira and Singer, 1999). Naive Bayes learning, which is used to estimate probabilities in this paper, is described in (Mitchell, 1997).

2 Anomaly Detection

More formally, *anomaly detection* is the process of determining when an element of data is an outlier. Given a set of training data without a probability distribution, we want to construct an automatic method for detecting anomalies. We are interested in detecting anomalies for two main reasons. One, we are interested in modeling the data and the anomalies can contaminate the model. And two, the anomalies themselves can be of interest as they may show rarely occurring events. For the purposes of this work, we are most interested in identifying mistagged elements, i.e. the second case.

In order to motivate a method for detecting anomalies, we must first make assumptions about how the anomalies occur in the data. We use a "mixture model" for explaining the presence of anomalies, one of several popular models in statistics for explaining outliers (Barnett and Lewis, 1994). In the mixture model, there are two probability distributions which generate the data. An element x_i is either generated from the majority distribution or with (small) probability λ from an alternate (anomalous) distribution. Our distribution for the data, $\mathbf{D}$, is then:

$$\mathbf{D} = (1-\lambda)\mathbf{M} + \lambda\mathbf{A} \tag{1}$$

where $\mathbf{M}$ is the majority distribution, and $\mathbf{A}$ is the anomalous distribution. The mixture framework for explaining anomalies is independent of the properties of the distributions $\mathbf{M}$ and $\mathbf{A}$. In other words, no assumptions about the nature of the probability distributions are necessary. The specific probability distributions, $\mathbf{M}$ and $\mathbf{A}$, are chosen based on prior knowledge of the problem. Typically $\mathbf{M}$ is a structured distribution which is estimated over the data using a machine learning technique, while $\mathbf{A}$ is a uniform (random) distribution representing elements which do not fit into $\mathbf{M}$.

In the corpus error detection problem, we are assuming that for each tag in the corpus with probability $(1-\lambda)$ the human annotator markes the corpus with the correct tag and with probability λ the human annotator makes an error. In the case of an error, we assume that the tag is chosen at random.

2.1 Detection of Anomalies

Detecting anomalies, in this framework, is equivalent to determining which elements were generated by the distribution $\mathbf{A}$ and which elements were generated by distribution $\mathbf{M}$. Elements generated by $\mathbf{A}$ are anomalies, while elements generated by $\mathbf{M}$ are not. In our case, we have probability distributions associated with the distributions $\mathbf{M}$ and $\mathbf{A}$, P_M and P_A respectively.

The algorithm partitions the data into two sets, the normal elements M and the anomalies A. For each element, we make a determination of whether it is an anomaly and should be included in A or a majority element in which it should be included in M. We measure the likelihood of the distribution under both cases to make this determination.

The likelihood, L, of distribution $\mathbf{D}$ with probability function P over elements $x_1,\ldots,x_N$ is defined as follows:

$$L(\mathbf{D}) = \prod_{i=1}^{N} P_D(x_i) = \tag{2}$$

$$\left((1-\lambda)^{|M|} \prod_{x_i \in M} P_M(x_i)\right)\left(\lambda^{|A|} \prod_{x_j \in A} P_A(x_j)\right)$$

Since the product of small numbers is difficult to compute, we instead compute the log likelihood, LL. The log likelihood for our case is:

$$LL(\mathbf{D}) = |M|\log(1-\lambda) + \sum_{x_i \in M} \log(P_M(x_i))$$
$$+|A|\log\lambda + \sum_{x_j \in A} \log(P_A(x_j)) \tag{3}$$

In order to determine which elements are anomalies, we use a general principal for determining outliers in multivariate data (Barnett, 1979). We measure how likely each element x_i is an outlier by comparing the difference between the log likelihood of the distribution if the element is removed from the majority distribution and included in the anomalous distribution. If this difference is sufficiently large, we declare the element an anomaly.

Specifically what this difference should be depends on the probability distributions and prior knowledge of the problem such as the rate of the anomalies, λ.

3 Methodology

3.1 Corpus

The corpus we use is the Penn Treebank tagged corpus. The corpus contains approximately 1.25 million manually tagged words from Wall Street Journal articles. For each word, a record is generated containing the following elements:

1. The tag of the current word T_i.
2. The current word W_i.
3. The previous tag T_{i-1}.
4. The next tag T_{i+1}.

Over records containing these 4 elements, we compute our probability distributions.

3.2 Probability Modeling Methods

The anomaly detection framework is independent of specific probability distributions. Different probability distributions have different properties. Since the anomaly detection framework does not depend on a specific probability distribution, we can choose the probability distribution to best model the data based on our intuitions about the problem.

To illustrate this, we perform two sets of experiments, each using a different probability distribution modeling method. The first set of experiments uses sparse Markov transducers as the probability modeling method, while the second uses a simple naive Bayes method.

3.3 Sparse Markov Transducers

Sparse Markov transducers compute probabilistic mappings over sparse data. A Markov transducer is defined to be a probability distribution conditional on a finite set of inputs. A Markov transducer of order L is the conditional probability distribution of the form:

$$P(Y_t | X_t X_{t-1} X_{t-2} X_{t-3} ... X_{t-(L-1)}) \quad (4)$$

where X_k are random variables over the input alphabet Σ_{in} and Y_k is a random variable over the output alphabet Σ_{out}. This probability distribution stochastically defines a mapping of strings over the input alphabet into the output alphabet. The mapping is conditional on the L previous input symbols.

In the case of sparse data, the probability distribution is conditioned on only some of the inputs. We use sparse Markov transducers to model these type of distributions. A sparse Markov transducer is a conditional probability of the form:

$$P(Y_t | \phi^{n_1} X_{t_1} \phi^{n_2} X_{t_2} ... \phi^{n_k} X_{t_k}) \quad (5)$$

where ϕ represents a wild card symbol and $t_i = t - \sum_{j=1}^{i} n_j - (i-1)$. The goal of the sparse Markov transducer estimation algorithm is to estimate a conditional probability of this form based upon a set of inputs and their corresponding outputs. However, the task is complicated due to the lack of knowledge *a priori* of which inputs the probability distribution is conditional on.

Intuitively, a fixed order Markov Chain of order L is equivalent to a n-gram with $n = L$. In a variable order Markov Chain, the value of n changes depending on the context. For example, some elements in the data may use a bigram, while others may use a trigram. The sparse Markov transducer uses a weighted sum of n-grams for different values of n and these weights depend on the context. In addition the weighted sum is over not only n-grams, but also n-grams with wild cards such as a trigram where only the first and last element is conditioned on.

In this case we are looking at the input sequence of the current word, W_t, the previous tag, T_{t-1}, and the next tag, T_{t+1}. The output is the set of all possible tags. The models that are in the weighted sum are the trigram, $W_t T_{t-1} T_{t+1}$; the bigrams $W_t T_{t-1}$, $W_t T_{t+1}$ and $T_{t-1} T_{t+1}$; and the unigrams W_t, T_{t-1} and T_{t+1}. The specific weights of each model depends on the context or the actual values of W_t, T_{t-1}, and T_{t+1}.

Sparse Markov transducers depend on a set of prior probabilities that incorporate prior knowledge about the importance of various elements in the input sequence. These prior probabilities are set based on the problem. For this problem, we use the priors to encode the information that the current word, W_t, is very important in determining the part of speech.

Each model in the weighted sum uses a pseudo-count predictor. This predictor computes the probability of an output (tag) by the number of times that a specific output was seen in a given context. In order to avoid probabilities of 0, we assume that we have seen each output at least once in every context. In fact, these predictors can be any probability distribution which can also depend on what works best for the task.

3.4 Naive Bayes

The probability distribution for the tags was also estimated using a straight forward naive Bayes approach.

We are interested in the probability of a tag, given the current word, the previous tag, and the next tag, or the probability distribution $P(T_i|W_i, T_{i-1}, T_{i+1})$ which using Bayes Rule is equivalent to:

$$P(T_i|W_i, T_{i-1}, T_{i+1}) = \frac{P(W_i, T_{i-1}, T_{i+1}|T_i) * P(T_i)}{P(W_i, T_{i-1}, T_{i+1})} \quad (6)$$

If we make the Naive Bayes independence assumption and we assume that the denominator is constant for all values this reduces to:

$$P(T_i|W_i, T_{i-1}, T_{i+1}) = \frac{P(W_i|T_i) * P(T_{i-1}|T_i) * P(T_{i+1}|T_i) * P(T_i)}{C} \quad (7)$$

where C is a normalization constant in order to have the probabilities sum to 1. Each of the values on the right side of the equation can easily be computed over the data estimating a probability distribution.

3.5 Computing Probability Distributions

Each probability distribution was trained over each record giving a model over the entire data. The probability model is then used to determine whether or not an element is an anomaly by applying the test in equation (3). Typically this can be done in an efficient manner because the approach does not require reestimating the model over the entire data set. If an element is designated as an anomaly, we remove it from the set of normal elements and efficiently reestimate the probability distribution to obtain more anomalous elements.

4 Results/Evaluation

The method was applied to the Penn Treebank corpus and a set of anomalies were generated. These anomalies were evaluated by human judges to determine if they are in fact tagging errors in the corpus. The human judges were natural language processing researchers (not the author) familiar with the Penn Treebank markings.

In the experiments involving the sparse Markov transducers, after applying the method, 7055 anomalies were detected. In the experiments involving the naive Bayes learning method, 6213 anomalies were detected.

Sample output from the system is shown in figure 1. The error is shown in the context marked with !!!. The likelihood of the tag is also given which is extremely low for the errors. The system also outputs a suggested tag and its likelihood which is the tag with the highest likelihood for that context. As we can see, these errors are clearly annotation errors.

Since the anomalies detected from the two probability modeling methods differed only slightly, we performed human judge verification of the errors over only the results of the sparse Markov transducer experiments.

The anomalies were ordered based on their likelihood. Using this ranking, the set of anomalies were broken up into sets of 1000 records. We examined the first 4000 elements by randomly selecting 100 elements out of each 1000.

Human judges were presented with the system output for four sets of 100 anomalies. The judges were asked to choose among three options for each example:

1. *Corpus Error* - The tag in the corpus sentence is incorrect.

2. *Unsure* - The judge is unsure whether or not the corpus tag is correct.

Error 0.000035: Its/PRP$ fast-food/NN restaurants/NNS –/: including/VBG Denny/NNP 's/POS ,/, Hardee/NNP 's/POS ,/, Quincy/NNP 's/POS and/CC El/NNP Pollo/NNP Loco/NNP (/("/" !!!the/NN!!! only/JJ significant/JJ fast-food/NN chain/NN to/TO specialize/VB in/IN char-broiled/JJ chicken/NN "/")/) –/: are/VBP stable/JJ ,/, recession-resistant/JJ and/CC growing/VBG ./.
Suggested Tag: DT (0.998262)

Error 0.019231: Not/RB even/RB Jack/NNP Lemmon/NNP 's/POS expert/JJ doddering/JJ !!!makes/NNS!!! this/DT trip/NN worth/NN taking/VBG ./.
Suggested Tag: VBZ (0.724359)

Error 0.014286: It/PRP also/RB underscores/VBZ the/DT difficult/JJ task/NN ahead/RB as/IN !!!Coors/NNS!!! attempts/VBZ to/TO purchase/VB Stroh/NNP Brewery/NNP Co./NNP and/CC fight/VB off/RP increasingly/RB tough/JJ competition/NN from/IN Anheuser-Busch/NNP Cos/NNP ./.
Suggested Tag: NNP (0.414286)

Figure 1: Sample output of anomalies in Penn Treebank corpus. The errors are marked with !!!.

3. *System Error* - The tag in the corpus sentence is correct and the system incorrectly marked it as an error.

The "unsure" choice was allowed because of the inherent subtleties in differentiating between types of tags such as "VB vs. VBP" or "VBD vs. VBN".

Over the 400 examples evaluated, 158 were corpus errors, 202 were system errors and the judges were unsure in 40 of the cases. The corpus error rate was computed by throwing out the unsure cases and computing:

$$\text{Corpus error rate} = \frac{\text{Corpus Errors}}{\text{System Errors} + \text{Corpus Errors}} \tag{8}$$

The total corpus error rate over the 400 manually checked examples was was 44%. As can be seen, many of the anomalies are in fact errors in the corpus.

For each error, we asked the human judge to determine if the correct tag is the systems suggested tag. Out of the total 158 corpus errors, the systems correct tag would have corrected the error in 145 cases.

Since the verified examples were random, we can assume that 91% of corpus errors would be automatically corrected if the system would replace the suspect tag with the suggested tag. Ignoring the "unsure" elements for the purposes of this analysis, if we attempted to automatically correct the first 1000 examples where the error rate was 69%, this method would have led to a reduction of the total number of errors in the corpus by 245.

5 Conclusion

This paper presents a fully automatic method for detecting errors in corpora using anomaly detection techniques. As shown, the anomalies detected in the Penn Treebank corpus tend to be tagging errors.

This method has some inherent limitations because not all errors in the corpus would manifest themselves as anomalies. In infrequent contexts or ambiguous situations, the method may not have enough information to detect an error. In addition, if there are inconsistencies between annotators, the method would not detect the errors because the errors would be manifested over a significant portion of the corpus.

Although this paper presents a fully automatic method for error detection in corpora, this method can also be used as a semi-automatic method for correcting errors. The method can guide an annotator to the elements which are most likely errors. The method can greatly reduce the number of elements that an annotator needs to examine.

Future work in this area involves modeling the corpora with other probability distributions.

Anomaly Rank	*Corpus Errors*	*System Error*	*Unsure*	*Corpus Error Rate*
1-1000	63	28	9	69%
1001-2000	36	54	10	40%
2001-3000	18	70	12	20%
3001-4000	41	50	9	45%
Totals	158	202	40	44%

Table 1: Results of error detection experiments on the tagged portion of the Penn Treebank

The method is very sensitive to the effectiveness of the probability model in modeling the normal elements. Extensions to the probability distributions presented here such as adding information about endings of words or using more features could increase the accuracy of the probability distribution and the overall performance of the anomaly detection system. Other future work involves applying this method to other marked corpora.

References

Steve Abney, Robert E. Schapire, and Yoram Singer. 1999. Boosting applied to tagging and PP attachment. In *Proceedings of the Joint SIGDAT Conference on Empirical Methods in Natural Language Processing Conference and Very Large Corpora.*

V. Barnett and T. Lewis. 1994. *Outliers in Statistical Data.* John Wiley and Sons.

V. Barnett. 1979. Some outlier tests for multivariate samples. *South African Statist*, 13:29–52.

Eric Brill and Jun Wu. 1998. Classifier combination for improved lexical disambiguation. In *Proceedings of COLING-ACL.*

Eric Brill. 1994. Some advances in transformation-based part of speech tagging. In *Proceedings of the Twelfth National Conference on Artificial Intelligence*, pages 722–727.

D.E. Denning. 1987. An intrusion detection model. *IEEE Transactions on Software Engineering*, SE-13:222–232.

Eleazar Eskin. 2000. Anomaly detection over noisy data using learned probability distributions. In *Proceedings of the Seventeenth International Conference on Machine Learning (ICML-2000) (to appear).*

T. Lane and C. E. Brodley. 1997. Sequence matching and learning in anomaly detection for computer security. In *AAAI Workshop: AI Approaches to Fraud Detection and Risk Management*, pages 43–49. AAAI Press.

Mitchell Marcus, Beatrice Santorini, and Mary Ann Marcinkiewicz. 1993. Building a large annotated corpus of english: The Penn Treebank. *Computational Linguistics*, 19(2):313–330.

Tom Mitchell. 1997. *Machine Learning.* McGraw Hill.

Fernando Pereira and Yoram Singer. 1999. An efficient extension to mixture techniques for prediction and decision trees. *Machine Learning*, 36(3):183–199.

Adwait Ratnaparkhi. 1996. A maximum entropy model part-of-speech tagger. In *Proceedings of the Empirical Methods in Natural Language Processing Conference.*

Yoram Singer. 1997. Adaptive mixtures of probalistic transducers. *Neural Computation*, 9(8):1711–1733.

Christina Warrender, Stephanie Forrest, and Barak Pearlmutter. 1999. Detecting intrusions using system calls: alternative data models. In *1999 IEEE Symposium on Security and Privacy*, pages 133–145. IEEE Computer Society.

Ralph Weischedel, Marie Meteer, Richard Schwartz, Lance Ramshaw, and Jeff Palmucci. 1993. Coping with ambiguity and unknown words through probabilistic models. *Computational Linguistics*, 19(2):359–382.

Exploiting auxiliary distributions in stochastic unification-based grammars

Mark Johnson*
Cognitive and Linguistic Sciences
Brown University
Mark_Johnson@Brown.edu

Stefan Riezler
Institut für Maschinelle Sprachverarbeitung
Universität Stuttgart
riezler@ims.uni-stuttgart.de

Abstract

This paper describes a method for estimating conditional probability distributions over the parses of "unification-based" grammars which can utilize auxiliary distributions that are estimated by other means. We show how this can be used to incorporate information about lexical selectional preferences gathered from other sources into Stochastic "Unification-based" Grammars (SUBGs). While we apply this estimator to a Stochastic Lexical-Functional Grammar, the method is general, and should be applicable to stochastic versions of HPSGs, categorial grammars and transformational grammars.

1 Introduction

"Unification-based" Grammars (UBGs) can capture a wide variety of linguistically important syntactic and semantic constraints. However, because these constraints can be non-local or context-sensitive, developing stochastic versions of UBGs and associated estimation procedures is not as straight-forward as it is for, e.g., PCFGs. Recent work has shown how to define probability distributions over the parses of UBGs (Abney, 1997) and efficiently estimate and use conditional probabilities for parsing (Johnson et al., 1999). Like most other practical stochastic grammar estimation procedures, this latter estimation procedure requires a parsed training corpus.

Unfortunately, large parsed UBG corpora are not yet available. This restricts the kinds of models one can realistically expect to be able to estimate. For example, a model incorporating lexical selectional preferences of the kind described below might have tens or hundreds of thousands of parameters, which one could not reasonably attempt to estimate from a corpus with on the order of a thousand clauses. However, statistical models of lexical selectional preferences can be estimated from very large corpora based on simpler syntactic structures, e.g., those produced by a shallow parser. While there is undoubtedly disagreement between these simple syntactic structures and the syntactic structures produced by the UBG, one might hope that they are close enough for lexical information gathered from the simpler syntactic structures to be of use in defining a probability distribution over the UBG's structures.

In the estimation procedure described here, we call the probability distribution estimated from the larger, simpler corpus an *auxiliary distribution*. Our treatment of auxiliary distributions is inspired by the treatment of reference distributions in Jelinek's (1997) presentation of Maximum Entropy estimation, but in our estimation procedure we simply regard the logarithm of each auxiliary distribution as another (real-valued) feature. Despite its simplicity, our approach seems to offer several advantages over the reference distribution approach. First, it is straight-forward to utilize several auxiliary distributions simultaneously: each is treated as a distinct feature. Second, each auxiliary distribution is associated with a parameter which scales its contribution to the final distribution. In applications such as ours where the auxiliary distribution may be of questionable relevance to the distribution we are trying to estimate, it seems reasonable to permit the estimation procedure to discount or even ignore the auxiliary distribution. Finally, note that neither Jelinek's nor our estimation procedures require that an auxiliary or reference distribution Q be a prob-

* This research was supported by NSF awards 9720368, 9870676 and 9812169.

ability distribution; i.e., it is not necessary that $Q(\Omega) = 1$, where Ω is the set of well-formed linguistic structures.

The rest of this paper is structured as follows. Section 2 reviews how exponential models can be defined over the parses of UBGs, gives a brief description of Stochastic Lexical-Functional Grammar, and reviews why maximum pseudo-likelihood estimation is both feasible and sufficient of parsing purposes. Section 3 presents our new estimator, and shows how it is related to the minimization of the Kullback-Leibler divergence between the conditional estimated and auxiliary distributions. Section 4 describes the auxiliary distribution used in our experiments, and section 5 presents the results of those experiments.

2 Stochastic Unification-based Grammars

Most of the classes of probabilistic language models used in computational linguistic are exponential families. That is, the probability $\mathrm{P}(\omega)$ of a well-formed syntactic structure $\omega \in \Omega$ is defined by a function of the form

$$\mathrm{P}_\lambda(\omega) \quad = \quad \frac{Q(\omega)}{Z_\lambda}\, e^{\lambda \cdot f(\omega)} \qquad (1)$$

where $f(\omega) \in \mathbb{R}^m$ is a vector of *feature values*, $\lambda \in \mathbb{R}^m$ is a vector of adjustable *feature parameters*, Q is a function of ω (which Jelinek (1997) calls a *reference distribution* when it is not an indicator function), and $Z_\lambda = \int_\Omega Q(\omega) e^{\lambda \cdot f(\omega)} d\omega$ is a normalization factor called the partition function. (Note that a feature here is just a real-valued function of a syntactic structure ω; to avoid confusion we use the term "attribute" to refer to a feature in a feature structure). If $Q(\omega) = 1$ then the class of exponential distributions is precisely the class of distributions with maximum entropy satisfying the constraint that the expected values of the features is a certain specified value (e.g., a value estimated from training data), so exponential models are sometimes also called "Maximum Entropy" models.

For example, the class of distributions obtained by varying the parameters of a PCFG is an exponential family. In a PCFG each rule or production is associated with a feature, so m is the number of rules and the jth feature value $f_j(\omega)$ is the number of times the j rule is used in the derivation of the tree $\omega \in \Omega$. Simple manipulations show that $\mathrm{P}_\lambda(\omega)$ is equivalent to the PCFG distribution if $\lambda_j = \log p_j$, where p_j is the rule emission probability, and $Q(\omega) = Z_\lambda = 1$.

If the features satisfy suitable Markovian independence constraints, estimation from fully observed training data is straight-forward. For example, because the rule features of a PCFG meet "context-free" Markovian independence conditions, the well-known "relative frequency" estimator for PCFGs both maximizes the likelihood of the training data (and hence is asymptotically consistent and efficient) and minimizes the Kullback-Leibler divergence between training and estimated distributions.

However, the situation changes dramatically if we enforce non-local or context-sensitive constraints on linguistic structures of the kind that can be expressed by a UBG. As Abney (1997) showed, under these circumstances the relative frequency estimator is in general inconsistent, even if one restricts attention to rule features. Consequently, maximum likelihood estimation is much more complicated, as discussed in section 2.2. Moreover, while rule features are natural for PCFGs given their context-free independence properties, there is no particular reason to use only rule features in Stochastic UBGs (SUBGs). Thus an SUBG is a triple $\langle G, f, \lambda \rangle$, where G is a UBG which generates a set of well-formed linguistic structures Ω, and f and λ are vectors of feature functions and feature parameters as above. The probability of a structure $\omega \in \Omega$ is given by (1) with $Q(\omega) = 1$. Given a base UBG, there are usually infinitely many different ways of selecting the features f to make a SUBG, and each of these makes an empirical claim about the class of possible distributions of structures.

2.1 Stochastic Lexical Functional Grammar

Stochastic Lexical-Functional Grammar (SLFG) is a stochastic extension of Lexical-Functional Grammar (LFG), a UBG formalism developed by Kaplan and Bresnan (1982). Given a base LFG, an SLFG is constructed by defining features which identify salient constructions in a linguistic structure (in LFG this is a c-structure/f-structure pair and its associated mapping; see Kaplan (1995)). Apart from the auxiliary distributions, we based our features on those used in Johnson et al. (1999), which should be consulted for further details. Most of these feature values range over the natural numbers, counting the number of times that a particular construction appears in a linguistic structure. For example, adjunct and argument features count the number of adjunct and argument attachments, permitting SLFG to capture a general argument attachment preference, while more specialized features count the number of attachments to each grammatical function (e.g., SUBJ, OBJ, COMP, etc.). The flexibility of features in stochastic UBGs permits us to include features for relatively complex constructions, such as date expressions (it seems that date interpretations, if possible, are usually preferred), right-branching constituent structures (usually preferred) and non-parallel coordinate structures (usually dispreferred). Johnson et al. remark that they would have liked to have included features for lexical selectional preferences. While such features are perfectly acceptable in a SLFG, they felt that their corpora were so small that the large number of lexical dependency parameters could not be accurately estimated. The present paper proposes a method to address this by using an auxiliary distribution estimated from a corpus large enough to (hopefully) provide reliable estimates for these parameters.

2.2 Estimating stochastic unification-based grammars

Suppose $\tilde{\omega} = \omega_1, \ldots, \omega_n$ is a corpus of n syntactic structures. Letting $f_j(\tilde{\omega}) = \sum_{i=1}^{n} f_j(\omega_i)$ and assuming each $\omega_i \in \Omega$, the likelihood of the corpus $\mathrm{L}_\lambda(\tilde{\omega})$ is:

$$\begin{aligned} \mathrm{L}_\lambda(\tilde{\omega}) &= \prod_{i=1}^{n} \mathrm{P}_\lambda(\omega_i) \\ &= e^{\lambda \cdot f(\tilde{\omega})} Z_\lambda^{-n} \qquad (2) \\ \frac{\partial}{\partial \lambda_j} \log \mathrm{L}_\lambda(\tilde{\omega}) &= f_j(\tilde{\omega}) - n \mathrm{E}_\lambda(f_j) \qquad (3) \end{aligned}$$

where $\mathrm{E}_\lambda(f_j)$ is the expected value of f_j under the distribution P_λ. The maximum likelihood estimates are the λ which maximize (2), or equivalently, which make (3) zero, but as Johnson et al. (1999) explain, there seems to be no practical way of computing these for realistic SUBGs since evaluating (2) and its derivatives (3) involves integrating over all syntactic structures Ω.

However, Johnson et al. observe that parsing applications require only the *conditional* probability distribution $\mathrm{P}_\lambda(\omega|y)$, where y is the terminal string or *yield* being parsed, and that this can be estimated by maximizing the *pseudo-likelihood* of the corpus $\mathrm{PL}_\lambda(\tilde{\omega})$:

$$\begin{aligned} \mathrm{PL}_\lambda(\tilde{\omega}) &= \prod_{i=1}^{n} \mathrm{P}_\lambda(\omega_i|y_i) \\ &= e^{\lambda \cdot f(\tilde{\omega})} \prod_{i=1}^{n} Z_\lambda^{-1}(y_i) \qquad (4) \end{aligned}$$

In (4), y_i is the yield of ω_i and

$$Z_\lambda(y_i) = \int_{\Omega(y_i)} e^{\lambda \cdot f(\omega)} d\omega,$$

where $\Omega(y_i)$ is the set of all syntactic structures in Ω with yield y_i (i.e., all parses of y_i generated by the base UBG). It turns out that calculating the pseudo-likelihood of a corpus only involves integrations over the sets of parses of its yields $\Omega(y_i)$, which is feasible for many interesting UBGs. Moreover, the maximum pseudo-likelihood estimator is asymptotically consistent for the conditional distribution $\mathrm{P}(\omega|y)$. For the reasons explained in Johnson et al. (1999) we actually estimate λ by maximizing a regularized version of the log pseudo-likelihood (5), where σ_j is 7 times the maximum value of f_j found in the training corpus:

$$\log \mathrm{PL}_\lambda(\tilde{\omega}) - \sum_{j=1}^{m} \frac{\lambda_j^2}{2\sigma_j^2} \qquad (5)$$

See Johnson et al. (1999) for details of the calculation of this quantity and its derivatives, and the conjugate gradient routine used to calculate the λ which maximize the regularized log pseudo-likelihood of the training corpus.

3 Auxiliary distributions

We modify the estimation problem presented in section 2.2 by assuming that in addition to the corpus $\tilde{\omega}$ and the m feature functions f we are given k auxiliary distributions $Q_1, \ldots, Q_k$ whose support includes Ω that we suspect may be related to the joint distribution $\mathrm{P}(\omega)$ or conditional distribution $\mathrm{P}(\omega|y)$ that we wish to estimate. We do not require that the Q_j be probability distributions, i.e., it is not necessary that $\int_\Omega Q_j(\omega)d\omega = 1$, but we do require that they are strictly positive (i.e., $Q_j(\omega) > 0, \forall\omega \in \Omega$). We define k new features $f_{m+1}, \ldots, f_{m+k}$ where $f_{m+j}(\omega) = \log Q_j(\omega)$, which we call *auxiliary features*. The $m+k$ parameters associated with the resulting $m+k$ features can be estimated using any method for estimating the parameters of an exponential family with real-valued features (in our experiments we used the pseudo-likelihood estimation procedure reviewed in section 2.2). Such a procedure estimates parameters $\lambda_{m+1}, \ldots, \lambda_{m+k}$ associated with the auxiliary features, so the estimated distributions take the form (6) (for simplicity we only discuss joint distributions here, but the treatment of conditional distributions is parallel).

$$\mathrm{P}_\lambda(\omega) = \frac{\prod_{j=1}^{k} Q_j(\omega)^{\lambda_{m+j}}}{Z_\lambda} e^{\sum_{j=1}^{m} \lambda_j f_j(\omega)} \quad (6)$$

Note that the auxiliary distributions Q_j are treated as fixed distributions for the purposes of this estimation, even though each Q_j may itself be a complex model obtained via a previous estimation process. Comparing (6) with (1) on page 2, we see that the two equations become identical if the reference distribution Q in (1) is replaced by a geometric mixture of the auxiliary distributions Q_j, i.e., if:

$$Q(\omega) = \prod_{j=1}^{k} Q_j(\omega)^{\lambda_{m+j}}.$$

The parameter associated with an auxiliary feature represents the weight of that feature in the mixture. If a parameter $\lambda_{m+j} = 1$ then the corresponding auxiliary feature Q_j is equivalent to a reference distribution in Jelinek's sense, while if $\lambda_{m+j} = 0$ then Q_j is effectively ignored. Thus our approach can be regarded as a smoothed version Jelinek's reference distribution approach, generalized to permit multiple auxiliary distributions.

4 Lexical selectional preferences

The auxiliary distribution we used here is based on the probabilistic model of lexical selectional preferences described in Rooth et al. (1999). An existing broad-coverage parser was used to find shallow parses (compared to the LFG parses) for the 117 million word British National Corpus (Carroll and Rooth, 1998). We based our auxiliary distribution on 3.7 million $\langle g, r, a\rangle$ tuples (belonging to 600,000 types) we extracted these parses, where g is a lexical governor (for the shallow parses, g is either a verb or a preposition), a is the head of one of its NP arguments and r is the the grammatical relationship between the governor and argument (in the shallow parses r is always OBJ for prepositional governors, and r is either SUBJ or OBJ for verbal governors).

In order to avoid sparse data problems we smoothed this distribution over tuples as described in (Rooth et al., 1999). We assume that governor-relation pairs $\langle g, r\rangle$ and arguments a are independently generated from 25 hidden classes C, i.e.:

$$\widehat{\mathrm{P}}(\langle g, r, a\rangle) = \sum_{c \in C} \mathrm{P}_e(\langle g, r\rangle|c)\widehat{\mathrm{P}}_e(a|c)\mathrm{P}_e(c)$$

where the distributions P_e are estimated from the training tuples using the Expectation-Maximization algorithm. While the hidden classes are not given any prior interpretation they often cluster semantically coherent predicates and arguments, as shown in Figure 1. The smoothing power of a clustering model such as this can be calculated explicitly as the percentage of possible tuples which are assigned a non-zero probability. For the 25-class model we get a smoothing power of 99%, compared to only 1.7% using the empirical distribution of the training data.

5 Empirical evaluation

Hadar Shemtov and Ron Kaplan at Xerox PARC provided us with two LFG parsed corpora called the Verbmobil corpus and the Homecentre corpus. These contain parse forests for each sentence (packed according to scheme described in Maxwell and Kaplan (1995)), together with a manual annotation as to which parse is correct. The Verbmobil corpus contains 540 sentences relating to appointment planning, while the Homecentre corpus contains 980 sentences from Xerox documentation on their "homecentre" multifunction devices. Xerox did not provide us with the base LFGs for intellectual property reasons, but from inspection of the parses

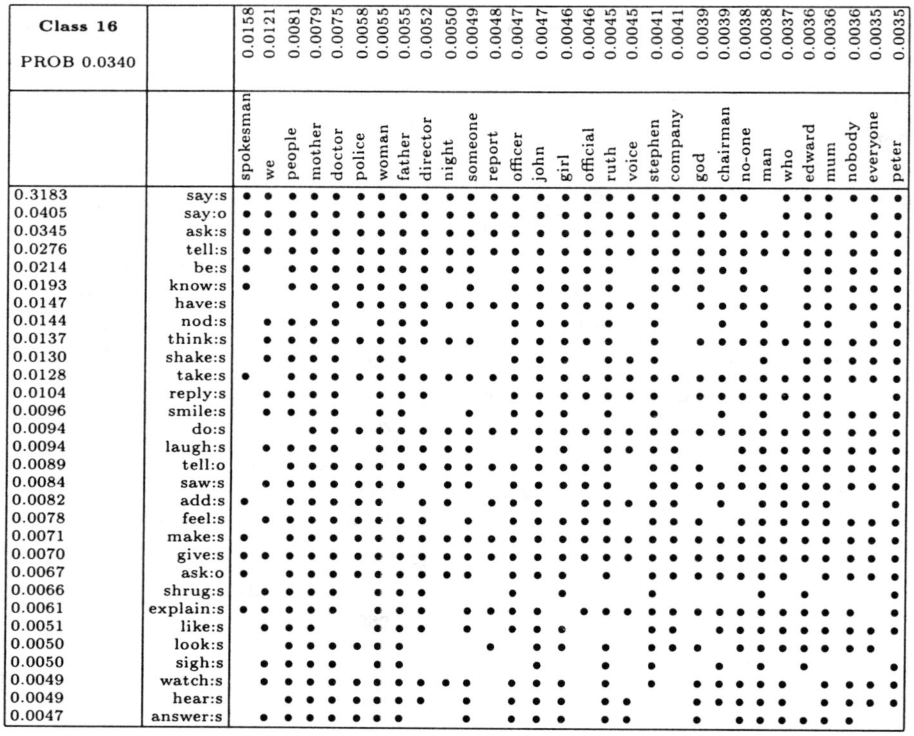

Figure 1: A depiction of the highest probability predicates and arguments in Class 16. The class matrix shows at the top the 30 most probable nouns in the $P_e(a|16)$ distribution and their probabilities, and at the left the 30 most probable verbs and prepositions listed according to $Pr_e(\langle g, r\rangle|16)$ and their probabilities. Dots in the matrix indicate that the respective pair was seen in the training data. Predicates with suffix $: s$ indicate the subject slot of an intransitive or transitive verb; the suffix $: o$ specifies the nouns in the corresponding row as objects of verbs or prepositions.

it seems that slightly different grammars were used with each corpus, so we did not merge the corpora. We chose the features of our SLFG based solely on the basis of the Verbmobil corpus, so the Homecentre corpus can be regarded as a held-out evaluation corpus.

We discarded the unambiguous sentences in each corpus for both training and testing (as explained in Johnson et al. (1999), pseudo-likelihood estimation ignores unambiguous sentences), leaving us with a corpus of 324 ambiguous sentences in the Verbmobil corpus and 481 sentences in the Homecentre corpus; these sentences had a total of 3,245 and 3,169 parses respectively.

The (non-auxiliary) features used in were based on those described by Johnson et al. (1999). Different numbers of features were used with the two corpora because some of the features were generated semi-automatically (e.g., we introduced a feature for every attribute-value pair found in any feature structure), and "pseudo-constant" features (i.e., features whose values never differ on the parses of the same sentence) are discarded. We used 172 features in the SLFG for the Verbmobil corpus and 186 features in the SLFG for the Homecentre corpus.

We used three additional auxiliary features derived from the lexical selectional preference model described in section 4. These were defined in the following way. For each governing predicate g, grammatical relation r and argument a, let $n_{\langle g,r,a\rangle}(\omega)$ be the number of times that the f-structure:

$$\begin{bmatrix} \text{PRED} = g \\ r = [\text{PRED} = a] \end{bmatrix}$$

appears as a subgraph of the f-structure of ω, i.e., the number of times that a fills the grammatical role r of g. We used the lexical model described in the last section to estimate $\widehat{\mathrm{P}}(a|g,r)$, and defined our first auxiliary feature as:

$$f_l(\omega) = \log \widehat{\mathrm{P}}(g_0) + \sum_{\langle g,r,a \rangle} n_{\langle g,r,a \rangle}(\omega) \log \widehat{\mathrm{P}}(a|g,r)$$

where g_0 is the predicate of the root feature structure. The justification for this feature is that if f-structures were in fact a tree, $f_l(\omega)$ would be the (logarithm of) a probability distribution over them. The auxiliary feature f_l is defective in many ways. Because LFG f-structures are DAGs with reentrancies rather than trees we double count certain arguments, so f_l is certainly not the logarithm of a probability distribution (which is why we stressed that our approach does not require an auxiliary distribution to be a distribution).

The number of governor-argument tuples found in different parses of the same sentence can vary markedly. Since the conditional probabilities $\widehat{\mathrm{P}}(a|g,r)$ are usually very small, we found that $f_l(\omega)$ was strongly related to the number of tuples found in ω, so the parse with the smaller number of tuples usually obtains the higher f_l score. We tried to address this by adding two additional features. We set $f_c(\omega)$ to be the number of tuples in ω, i.e.:

$$f_c(\omega) = \sum_{\langle g,r,a \rangle} n_{\langle g,r,a \rangle}(\omega).$$

Then we set $f_n(\omega) = f_l(\omega)/f_c(\omega)$, i.e., $f_n(\omega)$ is the average log probability of a lexical dependency tuple under the auxiliary lexical distribution. We performed our experiments with f_l as the sole auxiliary distribution, and with f_l, f_c and f_n as three auxiliary distributions.

Because our corpora were so small, we trained and tested these models using a 10-fold cross-validation paradigm; the cumulative results are shown in Table 1. On each fold we evaluated each model in two ways. The *correct parses measure* simply counts the number of test sentences for which the estimated model assigns its maximum parse probability to the correct parse, with ties broken randomly. The *pseudo-likelihood measure* is the pseudo-likelihood of test set parses; i.e., the conditional probability of the test parses given their yields. We actually report the negative log of this measure, so a smaller score corresponds to better performance here. The correct parses measure is most closely related to parser performance, but the pseudo-likelihood measure is more closely related to the quantity we are optimizing and may be more relevant to applications where the parser has to return a certainty factor associated with each parse.

Table 1 also provides the number of *indistinguishable sentences* under each model. A sentence y is indistinguishable with respect to features f iff $f(\omega_c) = f(\omega')$, where ω_c is the correct parse of y and $\omega_c \neq \omega' \in \Omega(y)$, i.e., the feature values of correct parse of y are identical to the feature values of some other parse of y. If a sentence is indistinguishable it is not possible to assign its correct parse a (conditional) probability higher than the (conditional) probability assigned to other parses, so all else being equal we would expect a SUBG with with fewer indistinguishable sentences to perform better than one with more.

Adding auxiliary features reduced the already low number of indistinguishable sentences in the Verbmobil corpus by only 11%, while it reduced the number of indistinguishable sentences in the Homecentre corpus by 24%. This probably reflects the fact that the feature set was designed by inspecting only the Verbmobil corpus.

We must admit disappointment with these results. Adding auxiliary lexical features improves the correct parses measure only slightly, and degrades rather than improves performance on the pseudo-likelihood measure. Perhaps this is due to the fact that adding auxiliary features increases the dimensionality of the feature vector f, so the pseudo-likelihood scores with different numbers of features are not strictly comparable.

The small improvement in the correct parses measure is typical of the improvement we might expect to achieve by adding a "good" non-auxiliary feature, but given the importance usually placed on lexical dependencies in statistical models one might have expected more improvement. Probably the poor performance is due in part to the fairly large differences between the parses from which the lexical dependencies were estimated and the parses produced by the LFG. LFG parses are very detailed, and many ambiguities depend on the precise grammatical

Verbmobil corpus (324 sentences, 172 non-auxiliary features)

Auxiliary features used	Indistinguishable	Correct	- log PL
(none)	9	180	401.3
f_l	8	183	401.6
f_l, f_c, f_n	8	180.5	404.0

Homecentre corpus (481 sentences, 186 non-auxiliary features)

Auxiliary features used	Indistinguishable	Correct	- log PL
(none)	45	283.25	580.6
f_l	34	284	580.6
f_l, f_c, f_n	34	285	582.2

Table 1: The effect of adding auxiliary lexical dependency features to a SLFG. The auxiliary features are described in the text. The column labelled "indistinguishable" gives the number of indistinguishable sentences with respect to each feature set, while "correct" and "– log PL" give the correct parses and pseudo-likelihood measures respectively.

relationship holding between a predicate and its argument. It could also be that better performance could be achieved if the lexical dependencies were estimated from a corpus more closely related to the actual test corpus. For example, the verb *feed* in the Homecentre corpus is used in the sense of "insert (paper into printer)", which hardly seems to be a prototypical usage.

Note that overall system performance is quite good; taking the unambiguous sentences into account the combined LFG parser and statistical model finds the correct parse for 73% of the Verbmobil test sentences and 80% of the Homecentre test sentences. On just the ambiguous sentences, our system selects the correct parse for 56% of the Verbmobil test sentences and 59% of the Homecentre test sentences.

6 Conclusion

This paper has presented a method for incorporating auxiliary distributional information gathered by other means possibly from other corpora into a Stochastic "Unification-based" Grammar (SUBG). This permits one to incorporate dependencies into a SUBG which probably cannot be estimated directly from the small UBG parsed corpora available today. It has the virtue that it can incorporate several auxiliary distributions simultaneously, and because it associates each auxiliary distribution with its own "weight" parameter, it can scale the contributions of each auxiliary distribution toward the final estimated distribution, or even ignore it entirely. We have applied this to incorporate lexical selectional preference information into a Stochastic Lexical-Functional Grammar, but the technique generalizes to stochastic versions of HPSGs, categorial grammars and transformational grammars. An obvious extension of this work, which we hope will be persued in the future, is to apply these techniques in broad-coverage feature-based TAG parsers.

References

Steven P. Abney. 1997. Stochastic Attribute-Value Grammars. *Computational Linguistics*, 23(4):597–617.

Glenn Carroll and Mats Rooth. 1998. Valence induction with a head-lexicalized PCFG. In *Proceedings of EMNLP-3*, Granada.

Frederick Jelinek. 1997. *Statistical Methods for Speech Recognition.* The MIT Press, Cambridge, Massachusetts.

Mark Johnson, Stuart Geman, Stephen Canon, Zhiyi Chi, and Stefan Riezler. 1999. Estimators for stochastic "unification-based" grammars. In *The Proceedings of the 37th Annual Conference of the Association for Computational Linguistics*, pages 535–541, San Francisco. Morgan Kaufmann.

Ronald M. Kaplan and Joan Bresnan. 1982. Lexical-Functional Grammar: A formal system for grammatical representation. In Joan Bresnan, editor, *The Mental Representation of Grammatical Relations*, chapter 4, pages 173–281. The MIT Press.

Ronald M. Kaplan. 1995. The formal architecture of LFG. In Mary Dalrymple, Ronald M. Kaplan, John T. Maxwell III, and Annie Zaenen, editors, *Formal Issues in Lexical-Functional Grammar*, number 47 in CSLI Lecture Notes Series, chapter 1, pages 7–28. CSLI Publications.

John T. Maxwell III and Ronald M. Kaplan. 1995. A method for disjunctive constraint satisfaction. In Mary Dalrymple, Ronald M. Kaplan, John T. Maxwell III, and Annie Zaenen, editors, *Formal Issues in Lexical-Functional Grammar*, number 47 in CSLI Lecture Notes Series, chapter 14, pages 381–481. CSLI Publications.

Mats Rooth, Stefan Riezler, Detlef Prescher, Glenn Carroll, , and Franz Beil. 1999. Inducing a semantically annotated lexicon via EM-based clustering. In *Proceedings of the 37th Annual Meeting of the Association for Computational Linguistics*, San Francisco. Morgan Kaufmann.

Ambiguity Packing in Constraint-based Parsing — Practical Results

Stephan Oepen
Computational Linguistics
Saarland University
66041 Saarbrücken, Germany
oe@coli.uni-sb.de

John Carroll
Cognitive and Computing Sciences
University of Sussex
Brighton BN1 9QH, UK
johnca@cogs.susx.ac.uk

Abstract

We describe a novel approach to 'packing' of local ambiguity in parsing with a wide-coverage HPSG grammar, and provide an empirical assessment of the interaction between various packing and parsing strategies. We present a linear-time, bidirectional subsumption test for typed feature structures and demonstrate that (a) subsumption- and equivalence-based packing is applicable to large HPSG grammars and (b) average parse complexity can be greatly reduced in bottom-up chart parsing with comprehensive HPSG implementations.

1 Background

The ambiguity inherent in natural language means that during parsing, some segments of the input string may end up being analysed as the same type of linguistic object in several different ways. Each of these different ways must be recorded, but subsequent parsing steps must treat the set of analyses as a single entity, otherwise the computation becomes theoretically intractable. Earley's algorithm (Earley, 1970), for example, avoids duplication of parse items by maintaining pointers to alternative derivations in association with the item. This process has been termed 'local ambiguity packing' (Tomita, 1985), and the structure built up by the parser, a 'parse forest' (Billot & Lang, 1989). Context free (CF) grammars represent linguistic objects in terms of atomic category symbols. The test for duplicate parse items—and thus being able to pack the sub-analyses associated with them—is equality of category symbols. In the final parse forest every different combination of packed nodes induces a distinct, valid parse tree.

Most existing unification-based parsing systems either implicitly or explicitly contain a context-free core. For example, in the CLE (Alshawi, 1992) the (manually-assigned) functors of the Prolog terms forming the categories constitute a CF 'backbone'. In the Alvey Tools system (Carroll, 1993) each distinct set of features is automatically given a unique identifier and this is associated with every category containing those features. The packing technique has been shown to work well in practice in these and similar unification-augmented CF systems: the parser first tests for CF category equality, and then either (a) checks that the existing feature structure subsumes the newly derived one (Moore & Alshawi, 1992), or (b) forms an efficiently processable disjunction of the feature structures (Maxwell and Kaplan, 1995). Extracting parses from the parse forest is similar to the CF case, except that a global check for consistency of feature values between packed nodes or between feature structure disjuncts is required (this global validation is not required if the subsumption test is strengthened to feature structure equivalence).

In contrast, there is essentially no CF component in systems which directly interpret HPSG grammars. Although HPSG feature structures are *typed*, an initial CF category equality test cannot be implemented straightforwardly in terms of the top-level types of feature structures since two compatible types need not be equal, but could stand in a subtype-supertype relationship. In addition, the feature structure subsumption test is potentially expensive since feature structures are large, typically containing hundreds of nodes. It is therefore an open question whether parsing systems using grammars of this type can gain any advantage from local ambiguity packing.

The question is becoming increasingly important, though, as wide-coverage HPSG grammars are starting to be deployed in practical applications—for example for 'deep' analysis in the VerbMobil speech-to-speech translation system (Wahlster, 1997; Kiefer, Krieger, Carroll, & Malouf, 1999).[1] In this paper we answer the question by demonstrating that (a) subsumption- and equivalence-based feature structure packing is applicable to large HPSG grammars, and (b) average complexity and time taken for the parsing task can be greatly reduced. In Section 2 we present a new, linear-time, bidirec-

[1] A significant body of work on efficient processing with such grammars has been building up recently, with investigations into efficient feature structure operations, abstract-machine-based compilation, CF backbone computation, and finite-state approximation of HPSG derivations, amongst others (Flickinger, Oepen, Uszkoreit, & Tsujii, 2000).

tional subsumption test for typed feature structures, which we use in a bottom-up, chart-based parsing algorithm incorporating novel, efficient accounting mechanisms to guarantee minimal chart size (Section 3). We present a full-scale evaluation of the techniques on a large corpus (Section 4), and complete the picture with an empirically-based discussion of grammar restrictors and parsing strategies (Section 5).

2 Efficient Subsumption and Equivalence Algorithms

Our feature structure subsumption algorithm[2] assumes totally well-typed structures (Carpenter, 1992) and employs similar machinery to the quasi-destructive unification algorithm described by Tomabechi (1991). In particular, it uses temporary pointers in dag nodes, each pointer tagged with a *generation counter*, to keep track of intermediate results in processing; incrementing the generation counter invalidates all temporary pointers in a single operation. But whereas quasi-destructive unification makes two passes (determining whether the unification will be successful and then copying out the intermediate representation) the subsumption algorithm makes only one pass, checking reentrancies and type-supertype relationships at the same time.[3] The algorithm, shown in Figure 1, also simultaneously tests if both feature structures subsume each other (i.e. they are equivalent), if either subsumes the other, or if there is no subsumption relation between them in either direction.

The top-level entry point *dag-subsumes-p()* and subsidiary function *dag-subsumes-p0()* each return two values, held in variables *forwardp* and *backwardp*, both initially true, recording whether it is possible that the first dag subsumes the second and/or vice-versa, respectively. When one of these possibilities has been ruled out the appropriate variable is set to false; in the statement of the algorithm the two returned values are notated as a pair, i.e. *(forwardp, backwardp)*. If at any stage both variables have become set to false the possibility of subsumption in both directions has been ruled out so the algorithm exits.

The (recursive) subsidiary function *dag-subsumes-p0()* does most of the work, traversing the two input dags in step. First, it checks whether the current node in either dag is involved in a reentrancy that is not present in the other: for each node visited in one dag it adds a temporary pointer (held in the 'copy' slot) to the corresponding node in the other dag. If a node is reached that already has a pointer then this is a point of reentrancy in the dag, and if the pointer is not identical to the other dag node then this reentrancy is not present in the other dag. In this case the possibility that the former dag subsumes the latter is ruled out. After the reentrancy check the type-supertype relationship between the types at the current nodes in the two dags is determined, and if one type is not equal to or a supertype of the other then subsumption cannot hold in that direction. Finally, after successfully checking the type-supertype relationships, the function recurses into the arcs outgoing from each node that have the same label. Since we are assuming totally well-typed feature structures, it must be the case that either the sets of arc labels in the two dags are the same, or one is a strict superset of the other. Only arcs with the same labels need be processed; extra arcs need not since the type-supertype check at the two nodes will already have determined that the feature structure containing the extra arcs must be subsumed by the other, and they merely serve to further specify it and cannot affect the final result.

Our implementation of the algorithm contains extra redundant but cheap optimizations which for reasons of clarity are not shown in figure 1; these include tests that *forwardp* is true immediately before the first supertype check and that *backwardp* is true before the second.[4]

The use of temporary pointers means that the space complexity of the algorithm is linear in the sum of the sizes of the feature structures. However, in our implementation the 'copy' slot that the pointers occupy is already present in each dag node (it is required for the final phase of unification to store new nodes representing equivalence classes), so in practice the subsumption test does not allocate any new storage. All pointer references take constant time since there are no chains of 'forwarded' pointers (forwarding takes place only during the course of unification and no forwarded pointers are left afterwards). Assuming the supertype tests can be carried

[2]Although independently-developed implementations of essentially the same algorithm can be found in the source code of The Attribute Logic Engine (ALE) version 3.2 (Carpenter & Penn, 1999) and the SICStus Prolog term utilities library (Penn, personal communication), we believe that there is no previous published description of the algorithm.

[3]Feature structure F subsumes feature structure G iff: (1) if path p is defined in F then p is also defined in G and the type of the value of p in F is a supertype or equal to the value in G, and (2) all paths that are reentrant in F are also reentrant in G.

[4]There is scope for further optimisation of the algorithm in the case where *dag1* and *dag2* are identical: full processing inside the structure is not required (since all nodes inside it will be identical between the two dags and any strictly internal reentrancies will necessarily be the same), but we would still need to assign temporary pointers inside it so that any external reentrancies into the structure would be treated correctly. In our tests we have found that as far as constituents that are candidates for local ambiguity packing are concerned there is in fact little equality of structures between them, so special equality processing does not justify the extra complication.

```
procedure dag-subsumes-p(dag1, dag2) ≡
  (forwardp, backwardp) ←                                      {establish context for non-local exit}
    catch with tag 'fail' dag-subsumes-p0(dag1, dag2, true, true);
  invalidate-temporary-pointers();                              {reset temporary 'copy' pointers}
  return (forwardp, backwardp);
end
procedure dag-subsumes-p0(dag1, dag2, forwardp, backwardp) ≡
  if (dag1.copy is empty) then dag1.copy ← dag2;                {check reentrancies}
  else if(dag1.copy ≠ dag2) then forwardp ← false; fi
  if (dag2.copy is empty) then dag2.copy ← dag1;
  else if (dag2.copy ≠ dag1) then backwardp ← false; fi
  if (forwardp = false and backwardp = false) then
    throw (false, false) with tag 'fail';                       {reentrancy check failed}
  fi
  if (not supertype-or-equal-p(dag1.type, dag2.type)) then forwardp ← false; fi     {check types}
  if (not supertype-or-equal-p(dag2.type, dag1.type)) then backwardp ← false; fi
  if (forwardp = false and backwardp = false) then
    throw (false, false) with tag 'fail';                       {no subtype relations}
  fi
  for each arc in intersect(dag1.arcs, dag2.arcs) do            {check shared arcs recursively}
    (forwardp, backwardp) ←
      dag-subsumes-p0(destination of arc for dag1, destination of arc for dag2, forwardp, backwardp);
  od
  return (forwardp, backwardp);                                 {signal result to caller}
end
```

Figure 1: Bidirectional, linear-time feature structure subsumption (and equivalence) algorithm.

out in constant time (e.g. by table lookup), and that the grammar allows us to put a small constant upper bound on the intersection of outgoing arcs from each node, the processing in the body of *dag-subsumes-p0()* takes unit time. The body may be executed up to N times where N is the number of nodes in the smaller of the two feature structures. So overall the algorithm has linear time complexity. In practice, our implementation (in the environment described in Section 4) performs of the order of 34,000 top-level feature structure subsumption tests per second.

3 Ambiguity Packing in the Parser

Moore and Alshawi (1992) and Carroll (1993) have investigated local ambiguity packing for unification grammars with CF backbones, using CF category equality and feature structure subsumption to test if a newly derived constituent can be packed. If a new constituent is equivalent to or subsumed by an existing constituent, then it can be packed into the existing one and will take no further part in processing. However, if the new constituent *subsumes* an existing one, the situation is not so straightforward: either (a) no packing takes place and the new constituent forms a separate edge (Carroll, 1993), or (b) previous processing involving the old constituent is undone or invalidated, and it is packed into the new one (Moore & Alshawi, 1992; however, it is unclear whether they achieve maximal compactness in practice: see Table 1). In the former case the parse forest produced will not be optimally compact; in the latter it will be, but maintaining chart consistency and parser correctness becomes a non-trivial problem. Packing of a new edge into an existing one we call *proactive* (or forward) packing; for the more complex situation involving a new edge subsuming an existing one we introduce the term *retroactive* (or backward) packing.

Several issues arise when packing an old edge (*old*) into one that was newly derived (*new*) retroactively: (i) everything derived from *old* (called *derivatives* of *old* in the following) must be invalidated and excluded from further processing (as *new* is known to generate more general derivatives); and (ii) all pending computation involving *old* and its derivatives has to be blocked efficiently. Derivatives of *old* that are invalidated because of retroactive packing may already contain packed analyses, however, which still represent valid ambiguity. These need to be repacked into corresponding derivatives of *new* when those become available. In turn, derivatives of *old* may have been packed already, such that they need not be available in the chart for subsequent subsumption tests. Therefore, the parser cannot simply delete everything derived from *old* when it is packed; instead, derivatives must be preserved (but blocked)

```
procedure block(edge, mark) ≡
  if (edge.frozen = false or mark = freeze) then edge.frozen ← mark; fi         {mark current edge}
  for each parent in edge.parents do block(parent, freeze); od       {recursively freeze derivatives}
end

procedure packed-edge-p(new) ≡
  for each old in chart[new.start][new.end] do                          {passive edges with same span}
    (forwardp, backwardp) ← dag-subsumes-p(old.dag, new.dag);             {test category subsumption}
    if (forwardp = true and old.frozen = false) then                  {equivalent or proactive packing}
      old.packed ← (new | old.packed);                                          {pack 'new' into 'old'}
      return true;                                                {return to caller; signal success}
    fi
    if (backwardp) then                                                           {retroactive packing}
      new.packed ← (new.packed ⊕ old.packed);                       {raise all packings into new host}
      old.packed ← ();
      if (old.frozen = false) then new.packed ← (old | new.packed); fi          {pack 'old' into 'new'}
      block(old, frost);                                             {frost 'old' and freeze derivatives}
      delete(old, chart);                                                 {remove 'old' from the chart}
    fi
  od
  return false;                                               {signal failure to pack 'new' to caller}
end
```

Figure 2: Algorithm called on each newly derived edge to achieve maximal packing.

until the derivations have been recomputed on the basis of *new*.[5] As *new* is equivalent to or more general than *old* it is guaranteed to derive at least the same set of edges; furthermore, the derivatives of *new* will again be equivalent to or more general than the corresponding edges derived from *old*.

The procedure *packed-edge-p()*, sketched in Figure 2, achieves pro- and retroactive packing without significant overhead in the parser; the algorithm can be integrated with arbitrary bottom-up (chart-based) parsing strategies. The interface assumes that the parser calls *packed-edge-p()* on each new edge *new* as it is derived; a return value of *true* indicates that *new* was packed proactively and requires no further processing. Conversely, a *false* return value from *packed-edge-p()* signals that *new* should subsequently undergo regular processing. The second part of the interface builds on notions we call *frosting* and *freezing*, meaning temporary and permament invalidation of edges, respectively. As a side-effect of calls to *packed-edge-p()*, a new edge can cause retroactive packing, resulting in the deletion of one or more existing edges from the chart and blocking of derivatives. Whenever the parser accesses the chart (i.e. in trying to combine edges) or retrieves a task from the agenda, it is expected to ignore all edges and parser tasks involving such edges that have a non-null 'frozen' value. When an existing edge *old* is packed retroactively, it is *frosted* and ignored by the parser; as *old* now represents local ambiguity, it still has to be taken into account when the parse forest is unpacked. Derivatives of *old*, on the other hand, need to be invalidated in both further parsing and later unpacking, since they would otherwise give rise to spurious analyses; accordingly, such derivatives are *frozen* permanently. Frosting and freezing is done in the subsidiary procedure *block()* that walks up the parent link recursively, storing a *mark* into the 'frozen' slot of edges that distinguishes between temporary frosting (in the top-level call) and permanent freezing (in recursive calls).

For a newly derived edge *new*, *packed-edge-p()* tests mutual subsumption against all passive edges that span the same portion of the input string. When forward subsumption (or equivalence) is detected and the existing edge *old* is not blocked, regular proactive packing is performed (adding *new* to the packing list for *old*) and the procedure returns immediately.[6] In the case of backward subsump-

[5]The situation is simpler in the CLE parser (Moore & Alshawi, 1992) because constituents and dominance relations are separated in the chart. The CLE encoding, in fact, does not record the actual daughters used in building a phrase (e.g. as unique references or pointers, as we do), but instead preserves the category information (i.e. a description) of those daughters. Hence, in extracting complete parses from the chart, the CLE has to perform (a limited) search with re-unification of categories; in this respect, the CLE parse forest still is an underspecified representation of the set of analyses, whereas our encoding (see below) facilitates unpacking without extra search.

[6]Packing an edge e_1 into another edge e_2 logically means that e_2 will henceforth serve as a representative for e_1 and the derivation(s) that it encodes. In practice, e_1 is removed from the chart and ignored in subsequent parser action and subsumption tests. Only in unpacking the parse forest will

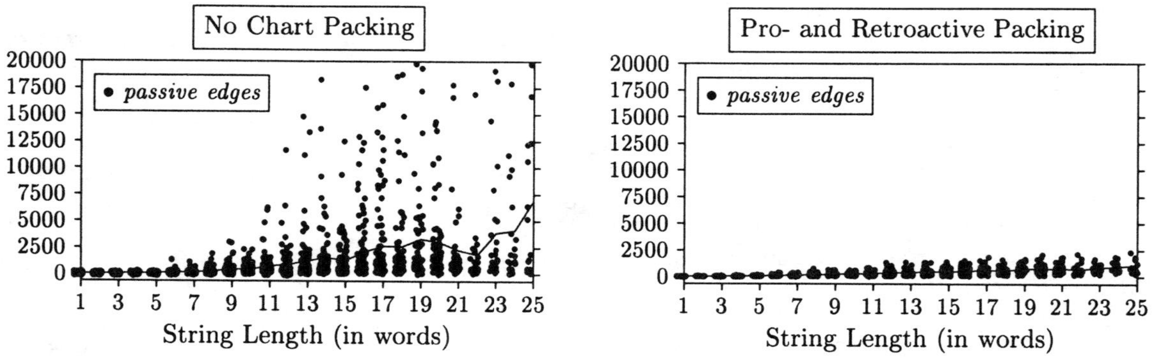

Figure 3: Effects of maximal ambiguity packing on the total chart size (truncated above 25 words).

tion, analyses packed into *old* are raised into *new* (using the append operator '$\oplus$' because *new* can attract multiple existing edges in the loop); *old* itself is only packed into *new* when it is not blocked already. Finally, *old* is frosted, its derivatives are recursively frozen, and *old* is deleted from the chart. In contrast to proactive packing, the top-level loop in the procedure continues so that *new* can pick up additional edges retroactively. However, once a backward subsumption is detected, it follows that no proactive packing can be achieved for *new*, as the chart cannot contain an edge that is more general than *old*.

4 Empirical Results

We have carried out an evaluation of the algorithms presented above using the LinGO grammar (Flickinger & Sag, 1998), a publicly-available, multipurpose, broad-coverage HPSG of English developed at CSLI Stanford. With roughly 8,000 types, an average feature structure size of around 300 nodes, and 64 lexical and grammar rules (fleshing out the interaction of HPSG ID schemata, wellformedness principles, and LP constraints), LinGO is among the largest HPSG grammars available. We used the LKB system (Copestake, 1992, 1999) as an experimentation platform since it provides a parameterisable bottom-up chart parser and precise, fine-grained profiling facilities (Oepen & Flickinger, 1998).[7] All of our results were obtained in this environment, running on a 300 Mhz UltraSparc, and using a balanced test set of 2,100 sentences extracted from VerbMobil corpora of transcribed speech: input lengths from 1 to 20 words are represented with 100 test items each; although sentences in the corpus range up to 36 words in length there are relatively few longer than 20 words.

Figure 3 compares total chart size (in all-paths mode) for the regular LKB parser and our variant with pro- and retroactive packing enabled. Factoring ambiguity reduces the number of passive edges by a factor of more than three on average, while for a number of cases the reduction is by a factor of 30 and more. Compared to regular parsing, the rate of increase of passive chart items with respect to sentence length is greatly diminished.

To quantify the degree of packing we achieve in practice, we re-ran the experiment reported by Moore and Alshawi (1992): counting the number of nodes required to represent all readings for a simple declarative sentence containing zero to six prepositional phrase (PP) modifiers. The results reported by Moore and Alshawi (1992) (using the CLE grammar of English) and those obtained using pro- and retroactive packing with the LinGO grammar are presented in Table 1.[8] Although the comparison involves different grammars we believe it to be instructive, since (i) both grammars have comprehensive coverage, (ii) derive the same numbers of readings for all test sentences in this experiment, (iii) require (almost) the same number of nodes for the basic cases (zero and one PP), (iv) exhibit a similar size in nodes for one core PP (measured by the increment from $n = 0$ to $n = 1$), and (v) the syntactic simplicity of the test material hardly allows crosstalk

the category of e_1 and its decomposition(s) in daughter edges (and corresponding subtrees) be used again, to multiply out and project local ambiguity.

[7] The LinGO grammar and LKB software are publicly available at '`http://lingo.stanford.edu/`'.

[8] Moore and Alshawi (1992) use the terms 'node' and 'record' interchangeably in their discussion of packing, where the CLE chart is comprised of separate **con**(stituent) and **ana**(lysis) entries for category and dominance information, respectively. It is unclear whether the counting of 'packed nodes' in Moore and Alshawi (1992) includes **con** records or not, since only **ana** records are required in parse tree recovery. In any case, both types of chart record need to be checked by subsumption as new entries are added to the chart. Conversely, in our setup each edge represents not only the node category, but also pointers to the daughter(s) that gave rise to this edge, and moreover, where applicable, a list of packed edges that are subsumed by the category (but not necessarily by the daughters). For the LKB, the column 'result edges' in Table 1 refers to the total number of edges in the chart that contribute to at least one complete analysis.

Kim saw a cat (in the hotel)^n									
n	**readings**	**Moore & Alshawi packed nodes**		**Our Method result edges**		**CPU Time**		
		♯	÷	♯	÷	**parse** msec	**unpack** msec	**plain** msec
0	1	10	1·0	11	1·0	210	10	180
1	2	21	2·1	23	2·1	340	40	290
2	5	38	3·8	38	3·5	460	80	530
3	14	62	6·2	56	5·1	600	200	1,180
4	42	94	9·4	77	7·0	870	590	2,990
5	132	135	13·5	101	9·2	1,150	1,860	8,790
6	429	186	18·6	128	11·6	1,460	5,690	28,160

Table 1: Comparison of retroactive packing vs. the method used by Moore and Alshawi (1992); columns labeled '÷' show the relative increase of packed nodes (result edges) normalised to the $n = 0$ baseline.

with other grammatical phenomena. Comparing relative packing efficiency with increasing ambiguity (the columns labeled '÷' in Table 1), our method appears to produce a more compact representation of ambiguity than the CLE, and at the same time builds a more specific representation of the parse forest that can be unpacked without search. To give an impression of parser throughput, Table 1 includes timings for our parsing and unpacking (validation) phases, contrasted with the plain, non-packing LKB parser: as would be expected, parse time increases linearly in the number of edges, while unpacking costs reflect the exponential increase in total numbers of analyses; the figures show that our packing scheme achieves a very significant speedup, even when unpacking time is included in the comparison.

5 Choosing the Grammar Restrictor and Parsing Strategy

In order for the subsumption relation to apply meaningfully to HPSG signs, two conditions must be met. Firstly, parse tree construction must not be duplicated in the feature structures (by means of the HPSG DTRS feature) but be left to the parser (i.e. recorded in the chart); this is achieved in a standard way by feature structure restriction (Shieber, 1985) applied to all passive edges. Secondly, the processing of constraints that do not restrict the search space but build up new (often semantic) structure should be postponed, since they are likely to interfere with subsumption. For example, analyses that differ only with respect to PP attachment would have the same syntax, but differences in semantics may prevent them being packed. This problem can be overcome by using restriction to (temporarily) remove such (semantic) attributes from lexical entries and also from the rule set, before they are input to the parser in the initial parse forest construction phase. The second, unpacking phase of the parser reverts to the unrestricted constraint set, so we can allow overgeneration in the first phase and filter globally inconsistent analyses during unpacking. Thus, the right choice of grammar restrictor can be viewed as an empirical rather than analytical problem.

Table 2 summarizes packing efficiency and parser performance for three different restrictors (labeled *no*, *partial*, and *full* semantics, respectively); to gauge effects of input complexity, the table is further subdivided by sentence length into two groups (of around 1,000 sentences each). Compared to regular parsing, packing with the full semantics in place is not effective: the chart size is reduced slightly, but the extra cost for testing subsumption increases total parse times by a factor of more than four. Eliminating all semantics (i.e. the entire HPSG CONT value), on the other hand, results in overgeneralisation: with less information in the feature structures we achieve the highest number of packings, but at the same time rules apply much more freely, resulting in a larger chart compared to parsing with a partial semantics; moreover, unpacking takes longer because the parse forest now contains inconsistent analyses. Restricting compositional semantics but preserving attributes that participate in selection and agreement results in minimal chart size and parsing time (shown in the *partial semantics* figures) for both divisions of the test corpus.

The majority of packings involve equivalent feature structures which suggests that unpacking could be greatly simplified if the grammar restrictor was guaranteed to preserve the generative capacity of the grammar (in the first parsing phase); then, only packings involving actual subsumption would have to be validated in the unpacking phase.[9] Finally,

[9] There is room for further investigation here: partly for theory-internal reasons, current development of the LinGO grammar is working towards a stricter separation of restrictive (selectional) and constructive (compositional) constraints in

	Parser	Passive Edges	Packed Trees	Packings				CPU Time (sec)	
				$\equiv$	$\sqsupset$	$\sqsubset$	$\perp$	parse	unpack
1 − 10 words	*no semantics*	116	0·9	15·5	4·1	2·6	1·8	0·37	0·05
	partial semantics	111	0·8	12·0	3·6	2·4	1·4	0·33	0·05
	full semantics	149	2·8	2·1	0·4	0·2	0·1	0·60	0·04
	no packing	160	5·6	–	–	–	–	0·44	–
> 10 words	*no semantics*	622	1·2	179·0	42·1	23·8	26·0	2·37	0·70
	partial semantics	575	1·0	134·9	35·0	20·6	18·9	1·97	0·63
	full semantics	1693	33·9	38·3	3·4	2·9	3·2	29·40	0·56
	no packing	2075	99·9	–	–	–	–	6·46	–

Table 2: Contrasting various grammar restrictors on short (top) and medium-length (bottom) inputs; all numbers are averaged over 1,000 items per class; packings are, from left to right: equivalence ('$\equiv$'), pro- ('$\sqsupset$') and retroactive ('$\sqsubset$') packings, and the number of edges that were frozen ('$\perp$').

we note that the number of retroactive packings is relatively small, and on average each such packing leads to only one previously derived edge being invalidated. This, of course, is a function of the order in which edges are derived, i.e. the parsing strategy.

All the results in Table 2 were obtained with a 'right corner' strategy which aims to exhaust computation for any suffix of the input string before moving the input pointer to the left; this is achieved by means of a scoring function $end - \frac{start}{n}$ (where *start* and *end* are the vertices of the derivation that would result from the computation, and n is the total input length) that orders parser tasks in the agenda. However, we have observed (Oepen & Callmeier, 2000) that HPSG-type, highly lexicalized grammars benefit greatly from a bidirectional, 'key'-driven, active parsing regime, since they often employ rules with underspecified arguments that are only instantiated by coreference with other daughters (where the 'key' daughter is the linguistic head in many but not all constructions). This requirement and the general non-predictability of categories derived for any token substring (in particular with respect to unary rule applications), means that a particular parsing strategy may reduce retroactive packing but cannot avoid it in general. With pro- and retroactive packing and the minimal accounting overhead, we find overall parser throughput to be very robust against variation in the parsing strategy. Lavie and Rosé (2000) present heuristics for ordering parser actions to achieve maximally compact parse forests—though only with respect to a CF category backbone—in the absence of retroactive packing; however, the techniques we have presented here allow local ambiguity packing and parser tuning—possibly including priority-driven best-first search—to be carried out mostly independently of each other.

the grammar and underlying semantic theory. We expect that our approach to packing will benefit from these developments.

6 Conclusions

We have presented novel algorithms for efficient subsumption checking and pro- and retroactive local ambiguity packing with large feature structures, and have provided strong empirical evidence that our approach can be applied beneficially to chart parsing with a large, broad-coverage HPSG of English. By comparison to previous work in unification-based parsing we have demonstrated that pro- and retroactive packing are well-suited to achieve optimal packing; furthermore, experimental results obtained with a publicly-available HPSG processing platform confirm that ambiguity packing can greatly reduce average parse complexity for this type of grammars.

In related work, Miyao (1999) describes an approach to packing in which alternative feature structures are represented as packed, distributed disjunctions of feature structure fragments. Although the approach may have potential, the shifting of complex accounting into the unification algorithm is at variance with the findings of Kiefer et al. (1999), who report large speed-ups from the elimination of disjunction processing during unification. Unfortunately, the reported evaluation measures and lack of discussion of parser control issues are insufficient to allow a precise comparison.

We intend to develop the approach presented in this paper in several directions. Firstly, we will enhance the unpacking phase to take advantage of the large number of equivalence packings we observe. This will significantly reduce the amount of work it needs to do. Secondly, many application contexts and subsequent layers of semantic processing will not require unfolding the entire parse forest; here, we need to define a selective, incremental unpacking procedure. Finally, applications like VerbMobil favour prioritized best-first rather than all-paths parsing. Using slightly more sophisticated accounting in the agenda, we plan to investigate priority propagation in a best-first variant of our parser.

Acknowledgements

We are grateful to Ulrich Callmeier, Ann Copestake, Dan Flickinger, and three anonymous reviewers for comments on a draft of the paper, to Bob Moore for a detailed explanation of the workings of the CLE parser, and to Gerald Penn for information about related implementations of the subsumption algorithm. The research was supported by the *Deutsche Forschungsgemeinschaft* as part of the Collaborative Research Division *Resource-Adaptive Cognitive Processes*, project B4 (PERFORM); and by a UK EPSRC Advanced Fellowship to the second author.

References

Alshawi, H. (Ed.). (1992). *The Core Language Engine.* Cambridge, MA: MIT Press.

Billot, S., & Lang, B. (1989). The structure of shared forests in ambiguous parsing. In *Proceedings of the 27th Meeting of the Association for Computational Linguistics* (pp. 143 – 151). Vancouver, BC.

Carpenter, B. (1992). *The logic of typed feature structures.* Cambridge, UK: Cambridge University Press.

Carpenter, B., & Penn, G. (1999). *ALE. The Attribute Logic Engine. User's guide version 3.2.* (Universität Tübingen: `http://wwww.sfs.nphil.uni-tuebingen.de/~gpenn/ale.html`)

Carroll, J. (1993). *Practical unification-based parsing of natural language* (Technical Report # 314). Cambridge, UK: Computer Laboratory, Cambridge University. (Online at: `ftp://ftp.cl.cam.ac.uk/papers/reports/TR314-jac-practical-unif-parsing.ps.gz`)

Copestake, A. (1992). The ACQUILEX LKB. Representation issues in semi-automatic acquisition of large lexicons. In *Proceedings of the 3rd ACL Conference on Applied Natural Language Processing* (pp. 88 – 96). Trento, Italy.

Copestake, A. (1999). *The (new) LKB system. User's guide.* (CSLI, Stanford University: `http://www-csli.stanford.edu/~aac/lkb.html`)

Earley, J. (1970). An efficient context-free parsing algorithm. *Communications of the ACM, 13 (2)*, 94 – 102.

Flickinger, D., Oepen, S., Uszkoreit, H., & Tsujii, J. (Eds.). (2000). *Journal of Natural Language Engineering. Special Issue on Efficient processing with HPSG: Methods, systems, evaluation.* Cambridge, UK: Cambridge University Press. (in preparation)

Flickinger, D. P., & Sag, I. A. (1998). Linguistic Grammars Online. A multi-purpose broad-coverage computational grammar of English. In *CSLI Bulletin 1999* (pp. 64 – 68). Stanford, CA: CSLI Publications.

Kiefer, B., Krieger, H.-U., Carroll, J., & Malouf, R. (1999). A bag of useful techniques for efficient and robust parsing. In *Proceedings of the 37th Meeting of the Association for Computational Linguistics* (pp. 473 – 480). College Park, MD.

Lavie, A., & Rosé, C. (2000). Optimal ambiguity packing in context-free parsers with interleaved unification. In *Proceedings of the 6th International Workshop on Parsing Technologies* (pp. 147 – 158). Trento, Italy.

Maxwell III, J. T., & Kaplan, R. M. (1995). A method for disjunctive constraint satisfaction. In M. Dalrymple, R. M. Kaplan, J. T. Maxwell III, & A. Zaenen (Eds.), *Formal issues in Lexical-Functional Grammar* (pp. 381 – 401). Stanford, CA: CSLI Publications.

Miyao, Y. (1999). Packing of feature structures for efficient unification of disjunctive feature structures. In *Proceedings of the 37th Meeting of the Association for Computational Linguistics* (pp. 579 – 84). College Park, MD.

Moore, R. C., & Alshawi, H. (1992). Syntactic and semantic processing. In H. Alshawi (Ed.), *The Core Language Engine* (pp. 129 – 148). Cambridge, MA: MIT Press.

Oepen, S., & Callmeier, U. (2000). Measure for measure: Parser cross-fertilization. Towards increased component comparability and exchange. In *Proceedings of the 6th International Workshop on Parsing Technologies* (pp. 183 – 194). Trento, Italy.

Oepen, S., & Flickinger, D. P. (1998). Towards systematic grammar profiling. Test suite technology ten years after. *Journal of Computer Speech and Language, 12 (4) (Special Issue on Evaluation)*, 411 – 436.

Shieber, S. M. (1985). Using restriction to extend parsing algorithms for complex feature-based formalisms. In *Proceedings of the 23rd Meeting of the Association for Computational Linguistics* (pp. 145 – 152). Chicago, IL.

Tomabechi, H. (1991). Quasi-destructive graph unification. In *Proceedings of the 29th Meeting of the Association for Computational Linguistics* (pp. 315 – 322). Berkeley, CA.

Tomita, M. (1985). An efficient context-free parsing algorithm for natural languages. In *Proceedings of the 9th International Joint Conference on Artificial Intelligence* (pp. 756 – 764). Los Angeles, CA.

Wahlster, W. (1997). *VerbMobil — Erkennung, Analyse, Transfer, Generierung und Synthese von Spontansprache* (VerbMobil Report # 198). Saarbrücken, Germany: Deutsches Forschungszentrum für Künstliche Intelligenz GmbH.

Forest-Based Statistical Sentence Generation

Irene Langkilde
Information Sciences Institute
University of Southern California
Marina del Rey CA 90292
ilangkil@isi.edu

Abstract

This paper presents a new approach to statistical sentence generation in which alternative phrases are represented as packed sets of trees, or forests, and then ranked statistically to choose the best one. This representation offers advantages in compactness and in the ability to represent syntactic information. It also facilitates more efficient statistical ranking than a previous approach to statistical generation. An efficient ranking algorithm is described, together with experimental results showing significant improvements over simple enumeration or a lattice-based approach.

1 Introduction

Large textual corpora offer the possibility of a statistical approach to the task of sentence generation. Like any large-scale NLP or AI task, the task of sentence generation requires immense amounts of knowledge. The knowledge needed includes lexicons, grammars, ontologies, collocation lists, and morphological tables. Acquiring and applying accurate, detailed knowledge of this breadth poses difficult problems.

Knight and Hatzivassiloglou (1995) suggested overcoming the knowledge acquisition bottleneck in generation by tapping the information inherent in textual corpora. They performed experiments showing that automatically-acquired, corpus-based knowledge greatly reduced the need for deep, hand-crafted knowledge. At the same time, this approach to generation improved scalability and robustness, offering the potential in the future for higher quality output.

In their approach, K & H adapted techniques used in speech recognition. Corpus-based statistical knowledge was applied to the generation process after encoding many alternative phrasings into a structure called a *lattice* (see Figure 1). A lattice was able to represent large numbers alternative phrases without requiring the large amount of space that an explicitly enumerated list of individual alternatives would require. The alternative sentences in the lattice were then ranked according to a statistical language model, and the most likely sentence was chosen as output. Since the number of phrases that needed be considered typically grew exponentially with the length of the phrase, the lattice was usually too large for an exhaustive search, and instead an n-best algorithm was used to heuristically narrow the search.

The lattice-based method, though promising, had several drawbacks that will be discussed shortly. This paper presents a different method of statistical generation based on a *forest* structure (a packed set of trees). A forest is more compact than a lattice, and it offers a hierarchical organization that is conducive to representing syntactic information. Furthermore, it facilitates dramatically more efficient statistical ranking, since constraints can be localized, and the combinatorial explosion of possibilities that need be considered can be reduced. In addition to describing the forest data structure we use, this paper presents a forest-based ranking algorithm, and reports experimental results on its efficiency in both time and space. It also favorably compares these results to the performance of a lattice-based approach.

2 Representing Alternative Phrases

2.1 Enumerated lists and lattices

The task of sentence generation involves mapping from an abstract representation of meaning or syntax to a linear ordering of words. Subtasks of generation usually include choosing content words, determining word order,

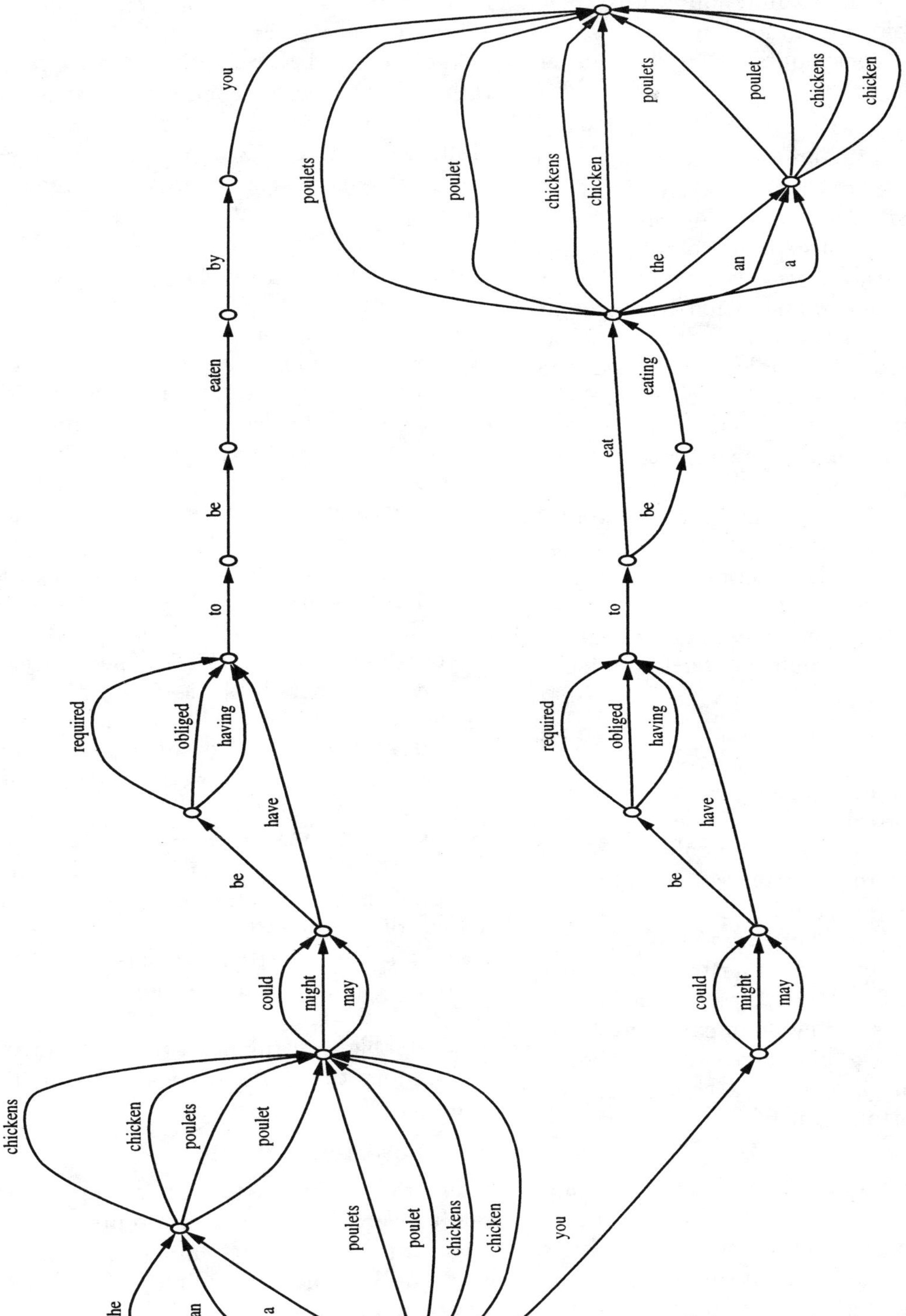

Figure 1: A lattice representing 576 different sentences, including "You may have to eat chicken", "The chicken may have to be eaten by you", etc.

deciding when to insert function words, performing morphological inflections, and satisfying agreement constraints, as well as other tasks.

One way of leveraging corpus-based knowledge is to explicitly enumerate many alternate possibilities and select the most likely according to a corpus-based statistical model. Since many subphrases and decisions will be common across proposed sentences, a lattice is a more efficient way than one-by-one enumeration to represent them. A lattice is a graph where each arc is labeled with a word. A complete path from the left-most node to right-most node through the lattice represents a possible sentence. Multiple arcs leaving a particular node represent alternate paths. A lattice thus allows structure to be shared between sentences. An example of a lattice is shown in Figure 1. This lattice encodes 576 unique sentences. In practice, a lattice may represent many trillions of sentences. Without a compact representation for so many sentences, statistical generation would be much less feasible.

The lattice in Figure 1 illustrates several types of decisions that need to be made in generation. For example, there is a choice between the root words "chicken" and "poulet", the choice of whether to use singular or plural forms of these words, the decision whether to use an article or not, and if so, which one—definite or indefinite. There are also other word choice decisions such as whether to use the auxiliary verb "could", "might", or "may", and whether to express the mode of eating with the predicate "have to", "be obliged to", or "be required to". Finally, there is a choice between active voice (bottom half of lattice), and passive voice (top half).

Inspection of the lattice reveals some unavoidable duplication, however. For example, the word "chicken" occurs four times, while the sublattice for the noun phrase containing "chicken" is repeated twice. So is the verb phrase headed by the auxiliaries "could", "might", and "may". Such repetition is common in a lattice representation for text generation, and has a negative impact on the efficiency of the ranking algorithm because the same set of score calculations end up being made several times. Another drawback of the duplication is that the representation consumes more storage space than necessary.

Yet another drawback of the lattice representation is that the independence between many choices cannot be fully exploited. Stolcke et al. (1997) noted that 55% of all word dependencies occur between adjacent words. This means that most choices that must be made in non-adjacent parts of a sentence are independent. For example, in Figure 1, the choice between "may", "might", or "could" is independent of the choice between "a", "an" or "the" to precede "chicken" or "poulet". Independence reduces the combination of possibilities that must be considered, and allows some decisions to be made without taking into account the rest of the context. Even adjacent words are sometimes independent of each other, such as the words "tail" and "ate" in the sentence "The dog with the short tail ate the bone". A lattice does not offer any way of representing which parts of a sentence are independent of each other, and thus cannot take advantage of this independence. This negatively impacts both the amount of processing needed and the quality of the results. In contrast, a forest representation, which we will discuss shortly, does allow the independence to be explicitly annotated.

A final difficulty with using lattices is that the search space grows exponentially with the length of the sentence(s), making an exhaustive search for the most likely sentence impractical for long sentences. Heuristic-based searches offer only a poor approximation. Any pruning that is done renders the solution theoretically inadmissable, and in practice, frequently ends up pruning the mathematically optimal solution.

2.2 Forests

These weaknesses of the lattice representation can be overcome with a forest representation. If we assign a label to each unique arc and to each group of arcs that occurs more than once in a lattice, a lattice becomes a forest, and the problems with duplication in a lattice are eliminated. The resulting structure can be represented as a set of context-free rewrite rules. Such a forest need not necessarily comply with a particular theory of syntactic structure, but it can if one wishes. It also need not be derived specifically from a lattice, but can be generated directly from a semantic input.

With a forest representation, it is quite natural to incorporate syntactic information. Syntactic information offers some potentially significant advantages for statistical language modeling. However, this paper will not discuss statistical modeling of syntax beyond making mention of it, leaving it instead for future work. Instead we focus on the nature of the forest representation itself and describe a general algorithm for ranking alternative trees that can be used with any language model.

A forest representation corresponding to the lattice in Figure 1 is shown in Figure 3. This forest structure is an AND-OR graph, where the AND nodes represent sequences of phrases, and the OR nodes represent mutually exclusive alternate phrasings for a particular relative position in the sentence. For example, at the top level of the forest, node S.469 encodes the choice between active and passive voice versions of the sentence. The active voice version is the left child node, labelled S.328, and the passive voice version is the right child node, S.358. There are eight OR-nodes in the forest, corresponding to the eight distinct decisions mentioned earlier that need to be made in deciding the best sentence to output.

The nodes are uniquely numbered, so that repeated references to the same node can be identified as such. In the forest diagram, only the first (left-most) reference to a node is drawn completely. Subsequent references only show the node name written in italics. This eases readability and clarifies which portions of the forest actually need to have scores computed during the ranking process. Nodes N.275, NP.318, VP.225 and PRP.3 are repeated in the forest of Figure 3.

S.469	$\Longrightarrow$	S.328
S.469	$\Longrightarrow$	S.358
S.328	$\Longrightarrow$	PRP.3 VP.327
PRP.3	$\Longrightarrow$	"you"
VP.327	$\Longrightarrow$	VP.248 NP.318
S.358	$\Longrightarrow$	NP.318 VP.357
NP.318	$\Longrightarrow$	NP.317
NP.318	$\Longrightarrow$	N.275

Figure 2: Internal representation of top nodes in forest

Figure 2 illustrates how the forest is represented internally, showing context-free rewrite rules for some of the top nodes in the forest. OR-nodes are indicated by the same label occuring more than once on the left-hand side of a rule. This sample of rules includes an example of multiple references to a node, namely node NP.318, which occurs on the right-hand side of two different rules.

A generation forest differs from a parse forest in that a parse forest represents different possible hierarchical structures that cover a single phrase. Meanwhile a generation forest generally represents one (or only a few) heirarchical structures for a given phrase, but represents many different phrases that generally express the same meaning.

2.3 Previous work on packed generation trees

There has been previous work on developing a representation for a packed generation forest structure. Shemtov (1996) describes extensions to a chart structure for generation originally presented in (Kay, 1996) that is used to generate multiple paraphrases from a semantic input. A prominent aspect of the representation is the use of boolean vector expressions to associate each sub-forest with the portions of the input that it covers and to control the unification-based generation process. A primary goal of the representation is to guarantee that each part of the semantic input is expressed once and only once in each possible output phrase.

In contrast, the packed forest in this paper keeps the association between the semantic input and nodes in the forest separate from the forest representation itself. (In our system, these mappings are maintained via an external cache mechanism as described in (Langkilde and Knight, 1998)). Once-and-only-once coverage of the semantic input is implicit, and is achieved by the process that maps from the input to a forest.

3 Forest ranking algorithm

The algorithm proposed here for ranking sentences in a forest is a bottom-up dynamic programming algorithm. It is analogous to a chart parser, but performs an inverse comparison. Rather than comparing alternate syntactic structures indexed to the same positions of an

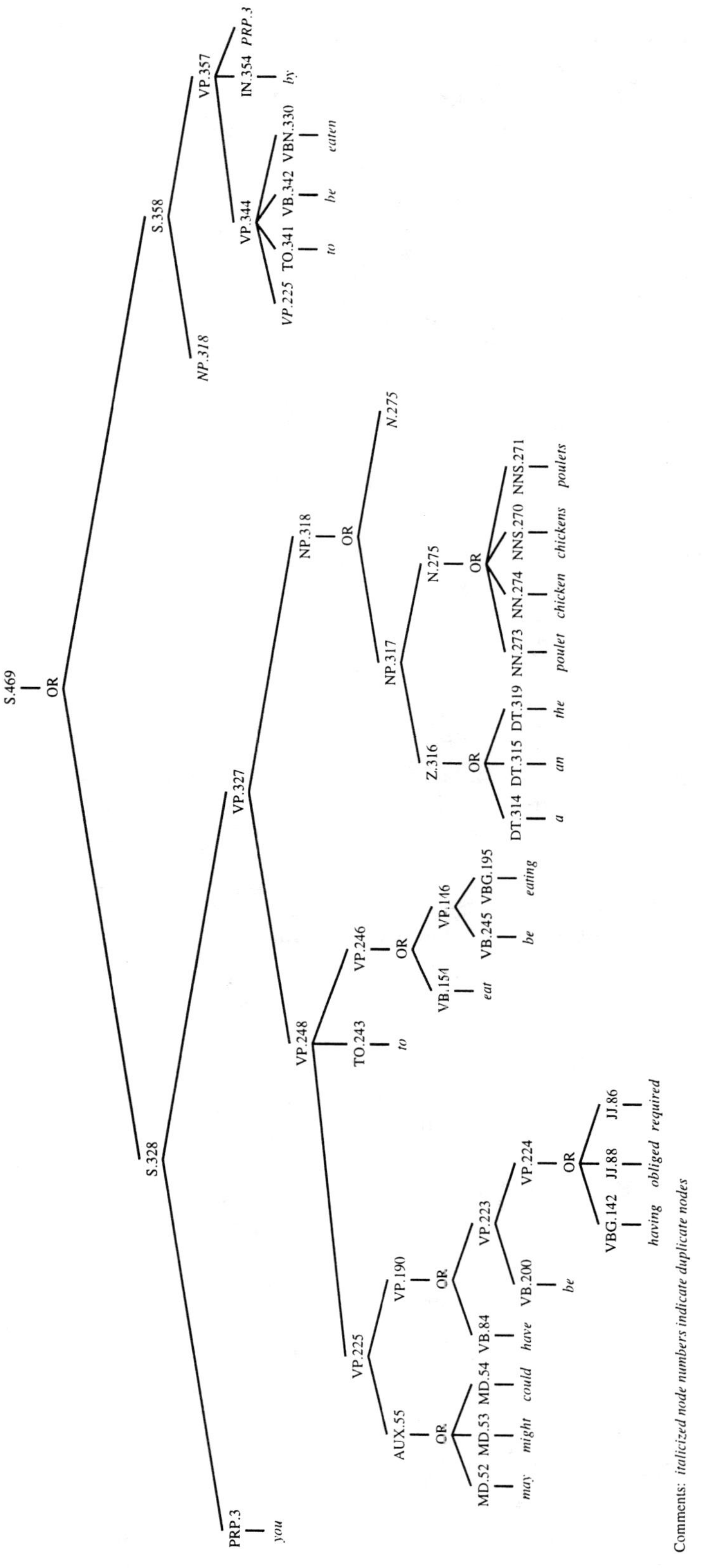

Figure 3: A generation forest

input sentence, it compares alternate phrases corresponding to the same semantic input.

As in a probabilistic chart parser, the key insight of this algorithm is that the score for each of the phrases represented by a particular node in the forest can be decomposed into a context-independent (internal) score, and a context-dependent (external) score. The internal score, once computed, is stored with the phrase, while the external score is computed in combination with other sibling nodes.

In general, the internal score for a phrase associated with a node p can be defined recursively as:

$$I(p) = \prod_{j=1}^{J} I(c_j) * E(c_j|context(c_1..c_{j-1}))$$

where I stands for the internal score, E the external score, and c_j for a child node of p. The specific formulation of I and E, and the precise definition of the *context* depends on the language model being used. As an example, in a bigram model,[1] I=1 for leaf nodes, and E can be expressed as:

$$E = P(FirstWord(c_j)|LastWord(c_{j-1}))$$

Depending on the language model being used, a phrase will have a set of externally-relevant *features*. These features are the aspects of the phrase that contribute to the context-dependent scores of sibling phrases. In the case of the bigram model, the features are the first and last words of the phrase. In a trigram model it is the first and last *two* words. In more elaborate language models, features might include elements such as head word, part-of-speech tag, constituent category, etc.

A crucial advantage of the forest-based method is that at each node only the best internally scoring phrase for each unique combination of externally relevant features needs to be maintained. The rest can be pruned without sacrificing the guarantee of obtaining the overall optimal solution. This pruning reduces exponentially the total number of phrases that need to be considered. In effect, the ranking algorithm exploits the independence that exists between most disjunctions in the forest.

[1]A bigram model is based on conditional probabilities, where the likelihood of each word in a phrase is assumed to depend on only the immediately previous word. The likelihood of a whole phrase is the product of the conditional probabilities of each of the words in the phrase.

VP.344 $\Longrightarrow$ VP.225 TO.341 VB.342 VBN.330			
225:	341:	342:	330:
might have	to	be	eaten
may have			
could have			
might be required			
may be required			
could be required			
might be having			
may be having			
could be having			
might be obliged			
may be obliged			
could be obliged			
344:			
might ... eaten			
may ... eaten			
could ... eaten			

Figure 4: Pruning phrases from a forest node, assuming a bigram model

To illustrate this, Figure 4 shows an example of how phrases in a node are pruned, assuming a bigram model. The rule for node VP.344 in the forest of Figure 3 is shown, together with the phrases corresponding to each of the child nodes. If every possible combination of phrases is considered for the sequence of nodes on the right-hand side, there are three unique first words, namely "might", "may" and "could", and only one unique final word, "eaten". Given that only the first and last words of a phrase are externally relevant features in a bigram model, only the three best scoring phrases (out of the 12 total) need to be maintained for node VP.344—one for each unique first-word and last-word pair. The other nine phrases can never be ranked higher, no matter what constituents VP.344 later combines with.

Pseudocode for the ranking algorithm is shown below. "Node" is assumed to be a record composed at least of an array of child nodes, "Node->c[1..N]," and best-ranked phrases, "Node->p[1..M]." The function ConcatAndScore concatenates two strings together, and computes a new score for it based on the formula given above. The function Prune guarantees that only the best phrase for each unique set of features values is maintained. The core loop in the algorithm considers the children of the node one-by-one, concatenating and scoring the phrases of the first two children and pruning the results, before considering the phrases of the third child, and concatenating them with the intermediate results, and so on. From the pseudocode, it can be seen that the complexity of the algorithm is dominated by the number of phrases associated with a node (not the number of rules used to represent the forest, nor the number of children in a an AND node). More specifically, because of the pruning, it depends on the number of features associated with the language model, and the average number of unique combinations of feature values that are seen. If f is the number of features, v the average number of unique values seen in a node for each feature, and N the number of N best being maintained for each unique set of feature values (but not a cap on the number of phrases), then the algorithm has the complexity $O((vN)^{2f})$ (assuming that children of AND nodes are concatenated in pairs). Note that f=2 for the bigram model, and f=4 for the trigram model.

In comparison, the complexity of an exhaustive search algorithm on a lattice is $O((vN)^{l})$, where l is approximately the length of the longest sentence in the lattice. The forest-based algorithm thus offers an exponential reduction in complexity while still guaranteeing an optimal solution. A capped N-best heuristic search algorithm on the other hand has complexity O(vNl). However, as mentioned earlier, it typically fails to find the optimal solution with longer sentences.

```
RankForest( Node)
{
  if ( Leafp( Node)) LeafScore( Node);
  for j=1 to J {
      if ( not( ranked?(Node->c[j])))
          RankForest(Node->c[j]);
  }
  for m=1 to NumberOfPhrasesIn( Node->c[1])
      Node->p[m] = (Node->c[1])->p[m];
  k=0for j=2 to J {
      for m=1 to NumberOfPhrasesIn( Node)
          for n=1 to NumberOfPhrasesIn(
                      Node->c[j])
              temp[k++] = ConcatAndScore(
                      Node->p[m],
                      (Node->c[j])->p[n]);
      Prune( temp);
      for m=1 to NumberOfPhrasesIn( temp)
          Node->p[m] = (temp[m]);
  }
}
```

In conclusion, the tables in Figure 5 and Figure 6 show experimental results comparing a forest representation to a lattice in terms of the time and space used to rank sentences. These results were generated from 15 test set inputs, whose average sentence length ranged from 14 to 36 words. They were ranked using a bigram model. The experiments were run on a Sparc Ultra 2 machine. Note that the time results for the lattice are not quite directly comparable to those for a forest because they include overhead costs for loading portions of a hash table. It was not possible to obtain timing measurements for the search algorithm alone. We estimate that roughly 80% of the time used in processing the lattice was used for search alone. Instead, the results in Figure 5 should be interpreted as a comparison between different kinds of systems.

In that respect, it can be observed from Table 5 that the forest ranking program performs at least 3 or 4 seconds faster, and that the time needed does *not* grow linearly with the number of paths being considered as it does with the lattice program. Instead it remains fairly constant. This is consistent with the theoretical result that the forest-based algorithm does not depend on sentence length, but only on the number of different alternatives being considered at each position in the sentence.

From Table 6 it can be observed that when there are a relatively moderate number of sentences being ranked, the forest and the lattice are fairly comparable in their space consumption. The forest has a little extra overhead in representing hierarchical structure. However, the space requirements of a forest do not grow linearly with the number of paths, as do those of the lattice. Thus, with very large numbers of paths, the forest offers significant savings in space.

The spike in the graphs deserves particular

comment. Our current system for producing forests from semantic inputs generally produces OR-nodes with about two branches. The particular input that triggered the spike produced a forest where some high-level OR-nodes had a much larger number of branches. In a lattice, any increase in the number of branches exponentially increases the processing time and storage space requirements. However, in the forest representation, the increase is only polynomial with the number of branches, and thus did not produce a spike.

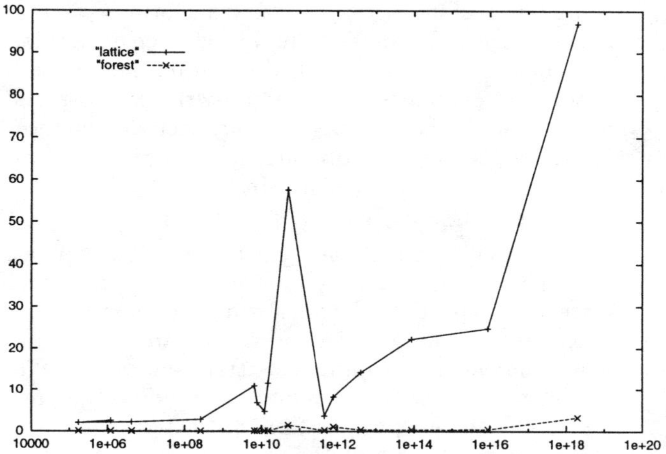

Figure 5: Time required for the ranking process using a lattice versus a forest representation. The X-axis is the number of paths (log_{10} scale), and the Y-axis is the time in seconds.

4 Future Work

The forest representation and ranking algorithm have been implemented as part of the Nitrogen generator system. The results shown in the previous section illustrate the time and space advantages of the forest representation which make calculating the mathematically optimal sentence in the forest feasible (particularly for longer sentences). However, obtaining the mathematically optimal sentence is only valuable if the mathematical model itself provides a good fit. Since a forest representation makes it possible to add syntactic information to the mathematical model, the next question to ask is whether such a model can provide a better fit for natural English than the ngram models we have used previously. In future work, we plan to modify the forests our system produces

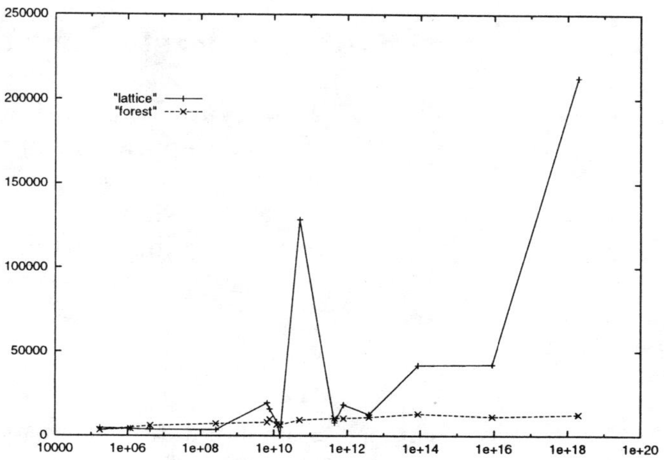

Figure 6: Size of the data structure for a lattice versus a forest representation. The X-axis is the number of paths (log_{10} scale), and the Y-axis is the size in bytes.

so they conform to the Penn Treebank corpus (Marcus et al., 1993) annotation style, and then do experiments using models built with Treebank data.

5 Acknowledgments

Special thanks go to Kevin Knight, Daniel Marcu, and the anonymous reviewers for their comments. This research was supported in part by NSF Award 9820291.

References

M. Kay. 1996. Chart generation. In *Proc. ACL*.

K. Knight and V. Hatzivassiloglou. 1995. Two-level, many-paths generation. In *Proc. ACL*.

I. Langkilde and K. Knight. 1998. Generation that exploits corpus-based statistical knowledge. In *Proc. COLING-ACL*.

M. Marcus, B. Santorini, and M. Marcinkiewicz. 1993. Building a large annotated corpus of english: the Penn treebank. *Computational Linguistics*, 19(2).

H. Shemtov. 1996. Generation of paraphrases from ambiguous logical forms. In *Coling'96*.

A. Stolcke. 1997. Linguistic knowledge and empirical methods in speech recognition. *AI Magazine*, 18(4):25–31.

Cut and Paste Based Text Summarization

Hongyan Jing and Kathleen R. McKeown
Department of Computer Science
Columbia University
New York, NY 10027, USA
hjing, kathy@cs.columbia.edu

Abstract

We present a cut and paste based text summarizer, which uses operations derived from an analysis of human written abstracts. The summarizer edits extracted sentences, using reduction to remove inessential phrases and combination to merge resulting phrases together as coherent sentences. Our work includes a statistically based sentence decomposition program that identifies where the phrases of a summary originate in the original document, producing an aligned corpus of summaries and articles which we used to develop the summarizer.

1 Introduction

There is a big gap between the summaries produced by current automatic summarizers and the abstracts written by human professionals. Certainly one factor contributing to this gap is that automatic systems can not always correctly identify the important topics of an article. Another factor, however, which has received little attention, is that automatic summarizers have poor text generation techniques. Most automatic summarizers rely on extracting key sentences or paragraphs from an article to produce a summary. Since the extracted sentences are disconnected in the original article, when they are strung together, the resulting summary can be inconcise, incoherent, and sometimes even misleading.

We present a cut and paste based text summarization technique, aimed at reducing the gap between automatically generated summaries and human-written abstracts. Rather than focusing on how to identify key sentences, as do other researchers, we study how to generate the text of a summary once key sentences have been extracted.

The main idea of cut and paste summarization is to reuse the text in an article to generate the summary. However, instead of simply extracting sentences as current summarizers do, the cut and paste system will "smooth" the extracted sentences by editing them. Such edits mainly involve cutting phrases and pasting them together in novel ways.

The key features of this work are:

(1) The identification of cutting and pasting operations. We identified six operations that can be used alone or together to transform extracted sentences into sentences in human-written abstracts. The operations were identified based on manual and automatic comparison of human-written abstracts and the original articles. Examples include sentence reduction, sentence combination, syntactic transformation, and lexical paraphrasing.

(2) Development of an automatic system to perform cut and paste operations. Two operations - sentence reduction and sentence combination - are most effective in transforming extracted sentences into summary sentences that are as concise and coherent as in human-written abstracts. We implemented a sentence reduction module that removes extraneous phrases from extracted sentences, and a sentence combination module that merges the extracted sentences or the reduced forms resulting from sentence reduction. Our sentence reduction model determines what to cut based on multiple sources of information, including syntactic knowledge, context, and statistics learned from corpus analysis. It improves the conciseness of extracted sentences, making them concise and on target. Our sentence combination module implements combination rules that were identified by observing examples written by human professionals. It improves the coherence of extracted sentences.

(3) Decomposing human-written summary sentences. The cut and paste technique we propose here is a new computational model which we based on analysis of human-written abstracts. To do this analysis, we developed an automatic system that can match a phrase in a human-written abstract to the corresponding phrase in the article, identifying its most likely location. This decomposition program allows us to analyze the construction of sentences in a human-written abstract. Its results have been used to train and test the sentence reduction and sentence combination module.

In Section 2, we discuss the cut and paste technique in general, from both a professional and computational perspective. We also describe the six cut and paste operations. In Section 3, we describe the system architecture. The major components of the system, including sentence reduction, sentence combination, decomposition, and sentence selection, are described in Section 4. The evaluation results are shown in Section 5. Related work is discussed in Section 6. Finally, we conclude and discuss future work.

2 Cut and paste in summarization

2.1 Related work in professional summarizing

Professionals take two opposite positions on whether a summary should be produced by cutting and pasting the original text. One school of scholars is opposed; "(use) your own words... Do not keep too close to the words before you", states an early book on abstracting for American high school students (Thurber, 1924). Another study, however, shows that professional abstractors actually rely on cutting and pasting to produce summaries: "Their professional role tells abstractors to avoid inventing anything. They follow the author as closely as possible and reintegrate the most important points of a document in a shorter text" (Endres-Niggemeyer et al., 1998). Some studies are somewhere in between: "summary language may or may not follow that of author's" (Fidel, 1986). Other guidelines or books on abstracting (ANSI, 1997; Cremmins, 1982) do not discuss the issue.

Our cut and paste based summarization is a *computational* model; we make no claim that humans use the same cut and paste operations.

2.2 Cut and paste operations

We manually analyzed 30 articles and their corresponding human-written summaries; the articles and their summaries come from different domains (15 general news reports, 5 from the medical domain, 10 from the legal domain) and the summaries were written by professionals from different organizations. We found that reusing article text for summarization is almost universal in the corpus we studied. We defined six operations that can be used alone, sequentially, or simultaneously to transform selected sentences from an article into the corresponding summary sentences in its human-written abstract:

(1) sentence reduction

Remove extraneous phrases from a selected sentence, as in the following example [1]:

> Document sentence: *When it arrives sometime next year in new TV sets,* the V-chip will give parents a *new and potentially revolutionary* device to block out programs they don't want their children to see.
> Summary sentence: The V-chip will give parents a device to block out programs they don't want their children to see.

The deleted material can be at any granularity: a word, a phrase, or a clause. Multiple components can be removed.

(2) sentence combination

Merge material from several sentences. It can be used together with sentence reduction, as illustrated in the following example, which also uses paraphrasing:

> Text Sentence 1: But it also raises serious questions about the privacy of such highly personal information *wafting about the digital world.*
> Text Sentence 2: The issue thus fits squarely into the broader debate about privacy and security on the internet, *whether it involves protecting credit card number or keeping children from offensive information.*
> Summary sentence: But it also raises the issue of privacy of such personal information *and* this issue hits the head on the nail in the broader debate about privacy and security on the internet.

(3) syntactic transformation

In both sentence reduction and combination, syntactic transformations may be involved. For example, the position of the subject in a sentence may be moved from the end to the front.

(4) lexical paraphrasing

Replace phrases with their paraphrases. For instance, the summaries substituted *point out* with *note*, and *fits squarely into* with a more picturesque description *hits the head on the nail* in the previous examples.

(5) generalization or specification

Replace phrases or clauses with more general or specific descriptions. Examples of generalization and specification include:

> Generalization: *"a proposed new law that would require Web publishers to obtain parental consent before collecting personal information from children"* → *"legislation to protect children's privacy on-line"*
> Specification: *"the White House's top drug official"* → *"Gen. Barry R. McCaffrey, the White House's top drug official"*

[1] All the examples in this section were produced by human professionals

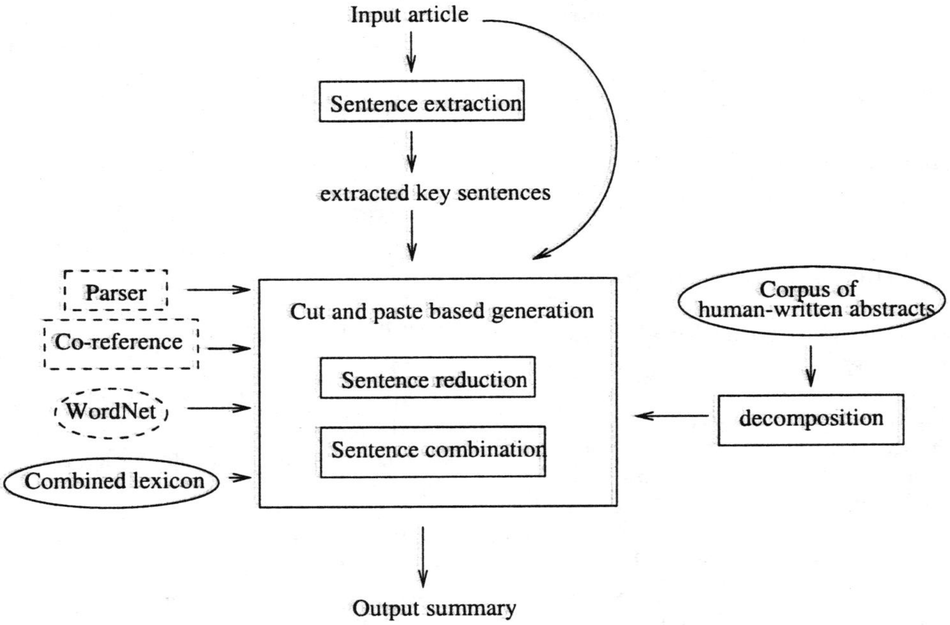

Figure 1: System architecture

(6) reordering
Change the order of extracted sentences. For instance, place an ending sentence in an article at the beginning of an abstract.

In human-written abstracts, there are, of course, sentences that are not based on cut and paste, but completely written from scratch. We used our decomposition program to automatically analyze 300 human-written abstracts, and found that 19% of sentences in the abstracts were written from scratch. There are also other cut and paste operations not listed here due to their infrequent occurrence.

3 System architecture

The architecture of our cut and paste based text summarization system is shown in Figure 1. Input to the system is a single document from any domain. In the first stage, *extraction*, key sentences in the article are identified, as in most current summarizers. In the second stage, *cut and paste based generation*, a sentence reduction module and a sentence combination module implement the operations we observed in human-written abstracts.

The cut and paste based component receives as input not only the extracted key sentences, but also the original article. This component can be ported to other single-document summarizers to serve as the generation component, since most current summarizers extract key sentences - exactly what the extraction module in our system does.

Other resources and tools in the summarization system include a corpus of articles and their human-written abstracts, the automatic decomposition program, a syntactic parser, a co-reference resolution system, the WordNet lexical database, and a large-scale lexicon we combined from multiple resources. The components in dotted lines are existing tools or resources; all the others were developed by ourselves.

4 Major components

The main focus of our work is on decomposition of summaries, sentence reduction, and sentence combination. We also describe the sentence extraction module, although it is not the main focus of our work.

4.1 Decomposition of human-written summary sentences

The decomposition program, see (Jing and McKeown, 1999) for details, is used to analyze the construction of sentences in human-written abstracts. The results from decomposition are used to build the training and testing corpora for sentence reduction and sentence combination.

The decomposition program answers three questions about a sentence in a human-written abstract: (1) Is the sentence constructed by cutting and pasting phrases from the input article? (2) If so, what phrases in the sentence come from the original article? (3) Where in the article do these phrases come from?

We used a Hidden Markov Model (Baum, 1972) solution to the decomposition problem. We first mathematically formulated the problem, reducing it to a problem of finding, for each word in a summary

Summary sentence:
(F0:S1 **arthur b sackler vice president for law and public policy of time warner inc**) (F1:S-1 *and*) (F2:S0 **a member of the direct marketing association told**) (F3:S2 **the communications subcommittee of the senate commerce committee**) (F4:S-1 *that legislation*) (F5:S1**to protect**) (F6:S4 **children' s**) (F7:S4 **privacy**) (F8:S4 **online**) (F9:S0 **could destroy the spontaneous nature that makes the internet unique**)

Source document sentences:
Sentence 0: a proposed new law that would require web publishers to obtain parental consent before collecting personal information from children **(F9 could destroy the spontaneous nature that makes the internet unique) (F2 a member of the direct marketing association told)** a senate panel thursday
Sentence 1: **(F0 arthur b sackler vice president for law and public policy of time warner inc)** said the association supported efforts **(F5 to protect)** children online but he urged lawmakers to find some middle ground that also allows for interactivity on the internet
Sentence 2: for example a child's e-mail address is necessary in order to respond to inquiries such as updates on mark mcguire's and sammy sosa's home run figures this year or updates of an online magazine sackler said in testimony to **(F3 the communications subcommittee of the senate commerce committee)**
Sentence 4: the subcommittee is considering the **(F6 children's) (F8 online) (F7 privacy)** protection act which was drafted on the recommendation of the federal trade commission

Figure 2: Sample output of the decomposition program

sentence, a document position that it most likely comes from. The position of a word in a document is uniquely identified by the position of the sentence where the word appears, and the position of the word within the sentence. Based on the observation of cut and paste practice by humans, we produced a set of general heuristic rules. Sample heuristic rules include: two adjacent words in a summary sentence are most likely to come from two adjacent words in the original document; adjacent words in a summary sentence are not very likely to come from sentences that are far apart in the original document. We use these heuristic rules to create a Hidden Markov Model. The Viterbi algorithm (Viterbi, 1967) is used to efficiently find the most likely document position for each word in the summary sentence.

Figure 2 shows sample output of the program. For the given summary sentence, the program correctly identified that the sentence was combined from four sentences in the input article. It also divided the summary sentence into phrases and pinpointed the exact document origin of each phrase. A phrase in the summary sentence is annotated as *(FNUM:SNUM actual-text)*, where *FNUM* is the sequential number of the phrase and *SNUM* is the number of the document sentence where the phrase comes from. SNUM = -1 means that the component does not come from the original document. The phrases in the document sentences are annotated as *(FNUM actual-text)*.

4.2 Sentence reduction

The task of the sentence reduction module, described in detail in (Jing, 2000), is to remove extraneous phrases from extracted sentences. The goal of reduction is to "reduce without major loss"; that is, we want to remove as many extraneous phrases as possible from an extracted sentence so that it can be concise, but without detracting from the main idea that the sentence conveys. Ideally, we want to remove a phrase from an extracted sentence *only if it is irrelavant to the main topic.*

Our reduction module makes decisions based on multiple sources of knowledge:

(1) Grammar checking. In this step, we mark which components of a sentence or a phrase are obligatory to keep it grammatically correct. To do this, we traverse the sentence parse tree, produced by the English Slot Grammar(ESG) parser developed at IBM (McCord, 1990), in top-down order and mark for each node in the parse tree, which of its children are obligatory. The main source of knowledge the system relies on in this step is a large-scale, reusable lexicon we combined from multiple resources (Jing and McKeown, 1998). The lexicon contains subcategorizations for over 5,000 verbs. This information is used to mark the obligatory arguments of verb phrases.

(2) Context information. We use an extracted sentence's local context in the article to decide which components in the sentence are likely to be most relevant to the main topic. We link the words in the extracted sentence with words in its local context, if they are repetitions, morphologically related, or linked with each other in WordNet through certain type of lexical relation, such as synonymy, antonymy, or meronymy. Each word in the extracted sentence gets an importance score, based on the number of links it has with other words and the types of links. Each phrase in the sentence is then assigned a score

Example 1:
Original sentence : *When it arrives sometime next year in new TV sets,* **the V-chip will give parents a new and potentially revolutionary device to block out programs they don't want their children to see.**
Reduction program: The V-chip will give parents a new and potentially revolutionary device to block out programs they don't want their children to see.
Professionals : The V-chip will give parents a device to block out programs they don't want their children to see.

Example 2:
Original sentence : **Som and Hoffman's creation would allow broadcasters to insert multiple ratings into a show,** *enabling the V-chip to filter out racy or violent material but leave unexceptional portions of a show alone.*
Reduction Program: Som and Hoffman's creation would allow broadcasters to insert multiple ratings into a show.
Professionals : Som and Hoffman's creation would allow broadcasters to insert multiple ratings into a show.

Figure 3: Sample output of the sentence reduction program

by adding up the scores of its children nodes in the parse tree. This score indicates how important the phrase is to the main topic in discussion.

(3) Corpus evidence. The program uses a corpus of input articles and their corresponding reduced forms in human-written abstracts to learn which components of a sentence or a phrase can be removed and how likely they are to be removed by professionals. This corpus was created using the decomposition program. We compute three types of probabilities from this corpus: the probability that a phrase is removed; the probability that a phrase is reduced (i.e., the phrase is not removed as a whole, but some components in the phrase are removed); and the probability that a phrase is unchanged at all (i.e., neither removed nor reduced). These corpus probabilities help us capture human practice.

(4) Final decision. The final reduction decision is based on the results from all the earlier steps. A phrase is removed only if it is not grammatically obligatory, not the focus of the local context (indicated by a low context importance score), and has a reasonable probability of being removed by humans. The phrases we remove from an extracted sentence include clauses, prepositional phrases, gerunds, and to-infinitives.

The result of sentence reduction is a shortened version of an extracted sentence [2]. This shortened text can be used directly as a summary, or it can be fed to the sentence combination module to be merged with other sentences.

Figure 3 shows two examples produced by the reduction program. The corresponding sentences in human-written abstracts are also provided for comparison.

[2] It is actually also possible that the reduction program decides no phrase in a sentence should be removed, thus the result of reduction is the same as the input.

4.3 Sentence combination

To build the combination module, we first manually analyzed a corpus of combination examples produced by human professionals, automatically created by the decomposition program, and identified a list of combination operations. Table 1 shows the combination operations.

To implement a combination operation, we need to do two things: decide when to use which combination operation, and implement the combining actions. To decide when to use which operation, we analyzed examples by humans and manually wrote a set of rules. Two simple rules are shown in Figure 4. Sample outputs using these two simple rules are shown in Figure 5. We are currently exploring using machine learning techniques to learn the combination rules from our corpus.

The implementation of the combining actions involves joining two parse trees, substituting a subtree with another, or adding additional nodes. We implemented these actions using a formalism based on Tree Adjoining Grammar (Joshi, 1987).

4.4 Extraction Module

The extraction module is the front end of the summarization system and its role is to extract key sentences. Our method is primarily based on lexical relations. First, we link words in a sentence with other words in the article through repetitions, morphological relations, or one of the lexical relations encoded in WordNet, similar to step 2 in sentence reduction. An importance score is computed for each word in a sentence based on the number of lexical links it has with other words, the type of links, and the directions of the links.

After assigning a score to each word in a sentence, we then compute a score for a sentence by adding up the scores for each word. This score is then normal-

Categories	Combination Operations
Add descriptions or names for people or organizations	add description (see Figure 5)
	add name
Aggregations	extract common subjects or objects (see Figure 5)
	change one sentence to a clause
	add connectives (e.g., *and* or *while*)
	add punctuations (e.g., ";")
Substitute incoherent phrases	substitute dangling anaphora
	substitute dangling noun phrases
	substitute adverbs (e.g., *here*)
	remove connectives
Substitute phrases with more general or specific information	substitute with more general information
	substitute with more specific information
Mixed operations	combination of any of above operations (see Figure 2)

Table 1: Combination operations

Rule 1:
IF: ((a person or an organization is mentioned the first time) and (the full name or the full description of the person or the organization exists somewhere in the original article but is missing in the summary))
THEN: replace the phrase with the full name plus the full description

Rule 2:
IF: ((two sentences are close to each other in the original article) and (their subjects refer to the same entity) and (at least one of the sentences is the reduced form resulting from sentence reduction))
THEN: merge the two sentences by removing the subject in the second sentence, and then combining it with the first sentence using connective "and".

Figure 4: Sample sentence combination rules

ized over the number of words a sentence contains. The sentences with high scores are considered important.

The extraction system selects sentences based on the importance computed as above, as well as other indicators, including sentence positions, cue phrases, and tf*idf scores.

5 Evaluation

Our evaluation includes separate evaluations of each module and the final evaluations of the overall system.

We evaluated the decomposition program by two experiments, described in (Jing and McKeown, 1999). In the first experiment, we selected 50 human-written abstracts, consisting of 305 sentences in total. A human subject then read the decomposition results of these sentences to judge whether they are correct. 93.8% of the sentences were correctly decomposed. In the second experiment, we tested the system in a summary alignment task. We ran the decomposition program to identify the source document sentences that were used to construct the sentences in human-written abstracts. Human subjects were also asked to select the document sentences that are semantic-equivalent to the sentences in the abstracts. We compared the set of sentences identified by the program with the set of sentences selected by the majority of human subjects, which is used as the gold standard in the computation of precision and recall. The program achieved an average 81.5% precision, 78.5% recall, and 79.1% f-measure for 10 documents. The average performance of 14 human judges is 88.8% precision, 84.4% recall, and 85.7% f-measure. Recently, we have also tested the system on legal documents (the headnotes used by Westlaw company), and the program works well on those documents too.

The evaluation of sentence reduction (see (Jing, 2000) for details) used a corpus of 500 sentences and their reduced forms in human-written abstracts. 400 sentences were used to compute corpus probabilities and 100 sentences were used for testing. The results show that 81.3% of the reduction decisions made by the system agreed with those of humans. The humans reduced the length of the 500 sentences by 44.2% on average, and the system reduced the length of the 100 test sentences by 32.7%.

The evaluation of sentence combination module is not as straightforward as that of decomposition or reduction since combination happens later in the pipeline and it depends on the output from prior

Example 1: add descriptions or names for people or organization
Original document sentences:
"We're trying to prove that there are big benefits to the patients by involving them more deeply in their treatment", **said Paul Clayton, Chairman of the Department dealing with computerized medical information at Columbia.**
"The economic payoff from breaking into health care records is a lot less than for banks", *said Clayton at Columbia.*
Combined sentence:
"The economic payoff from breaking into health care records is a lot less than for banks", said Paul Clayton, Chairman of the Department dealing with computerized medical information at Columbia.
Professional: *(the same)*

Example 2: extract common subjects
Original document sentences:
The new measure is an echo of the original bad idea, *blurred just enough to cloud prospects both for enforcement and for court review.*
Unlike the 1996 act, **this one applies only to commercial Web sites** *– thus sidestepping 1996 objections to the burden such regulations would pose for museums, libraries and freewheeling conversation deemed "indecent" by somebody somewhere.*
The new version also replaces the vague "indecency" standard, *to which the court objected, with the better-defined one of material ruled "harmful to minors."*
Combined sentences:
The new measure is an echo of the original bad idea.
The new version applies only to commercial web sites and replaces the vague "indecency" standard with the better-defined one of material ruled "harmful to minors."
Professional:
While the new law replaces the "indecency" standard with "harmful to minors" and now only applies to commercial Web sites, the "new measure is an echo of the original bad idea."

Figure 5: Sample output of the sentence combination program

modules. To evaluate just the combination component, we assume that the system makes the same reduction decision as humans and the co-reference system has a perfect performance. This involves manual tagging of some examples to prepare for the evaluation; this preparation is in progress. The evaluation of sentence combination will focus on the accessment of combination rules.

The overall system evaluation includes both intrinsic and extrinsic evaluation. In the intrinsic evaluation, we asked human subjects to compare the quality of extraction-based summaries and their revised versions produced by our sentence reduction and combination modules. We selected 20 documents; three different automatic summarizers were used to generate a summary for each document, producing 60 summaries in total. These summaries are all extraction-based. We then ran our sentence reduction and sentence combination system to revise the summaries, producing a revised version for each summary. We presented human subjects with the full documents, the extraction-based summaries, and their revised versions, and asked them to compare the extraction-based summaries and their revised versions. The human subjects were asked to score the conciseness of the summaries (extraction-based or revised) based on a scale from 0 to 10 – the higher the score, the more concise a summary is. They were also asked to score the coherence of the summaries based on a scale from 0 to 10. On average, the extraction-based summaries have a score of 4.2 for conciseness, while the revised summaries have a score of 7.9 (an improvement of 88%). The average improvement for the three systems are 78%, 105%, and 88% respectively. The revised summaries are on average 41% shorter than the original extraction-based summaries. For summary coherence, the average score for the extraction-based summaries is 3.9, while the average score for the revised summaries is 6.1 (an improvement of 56%). The average improvement for the three systems are 69%, 57%, and 53% respectively.

We are preparing a task-based evaluation, in which we will use the data from the Summarization Evaluation Conference (Mani et al., 1998) and compare how our revised summaries can influence humans' performance in tasks like text categorization and ad-hoc retrieval.

6 Related work

(Mani et al., 1999) addressed the problem of revising summaries to improve their quality. They suggested three types of operations: elimination, aggregation, and smoothing. The goal of the elimination operation is similar to that of the sentence reduction operation in our system. The difference is that while elimination always removes parentheticals, sentence-initial PPs and certain adverbial phrases for every extracted sentence, our sentence reduction module aims to make reduction decisions according to each case and removes a sentence component only if it considers it appropriate to do so. The goal of the aggregation operation and the smoothing operation is similar to that of the sentence combination operation in our system. However, the combination operations and combination rules that we derived from corpus analysis are significantly different from those used in the above system, which mostly came from operations in traditional natural language generation.

7 Conclusions and future work

This paper presents a novel architecture for text summarization using cut and paste techniques observed in human-written abstracts. In order to automatically analyze a large quantity of human-written abstracts, we developed a decomposition program. The automatic decomposition allows us to build large corpora for studying sentence reduction and sentence combination, which are two effective operations in cut and paste. We developed a sentence reduction module that makes reduction decisions using multiple sources of knowledge. We also investigated possible sentence combination operations and implemented the combination module. A sentence extraction module was developed and used as the front end of the summarization system.

We are preparing the task-based evaluation of the overall system. We also plan to evaluate the portability of the system by testing it on another corpus. We will also extend the system to query-based summarization and investigate whether the system can be modified for multiple document summarization.

Acknowledgment

We thank IBM for licensing us the ESG parser and the MITRE corporation for licensing us the co-reference resolution system. This material is based upon work supported by the National Science Foundation under Grant No. IRI 96-19124 and IRI 96-18797. Any opinions, findings, and conclusions or recommendations expressed in this material are those of the authors and do not necessarily reflect the views of the National Science Foundation.

References

ANSI. 1997. Guidelines for abstracts. Technical Report Z39.14-1997, NISO Press, Bethesda, Maryland.

L. Baum. 1972. An inequality and associated maximization technique in statistical estimation of probabilistic functions of a markov process. *Inequalities*, (3):1–8.

Edward T. Cremmins. 1982. *The Art of Abstracting.* ISI Press, Philadelphia.

Brigitte Endres-Niggemeyer, Kai Haseloh, Jens Müller, Simone Peist, Irene Santini de Sigel, Alexander Sigel, Elisabeth Wansorra, Jan Wheeler, and Brünja Wollny. 1998. *Summarizing Information.* Springer, Berlin.

Raya Fidel. 1986. Writing abstracts for free-text searching. *Journal of Documentation*, 42(1):11–21, March.

Hongyan Jing and Kathleen R. McKeown. 1998. Combining multiple, large-scale resources in a reusable lexicon for natural language generation. In *Proceedings of the 36th Annual Meeting of the Association for Computational Linguistics and the 17th International Conference on Computational Linguistics*, volume *1*, pages 607–613, Université de Montréal, Quebec, Canada, August.

Hongyan Jing and Kathleen R. McKeown. 1999. The decomposition of human-written summary sentences. In *Proceedings of the 22nd International ACM SIGIR Conference on Research and Development in Information Retrieval(SIGIR'99)*, pages 129–136, University of Berkeley, CA, August.

Hongyan Jing. 2000. Sentence reduction for automatic text summarization. In *Proceedings of ANLP 2000.*

Aravind.K. Joshi. 1987. Introduction to tree-adjoining grammars. In A. Manaster-Ramis, editor, *Mathematics of Language.* John Benjamins, Amsterdam.

Inderjeet Mani, David House, Gary Klein, Lynette Hirschman, Leo Obrst, Therese Firmin, Michael Chrzanowski, and Beth Sundheim. 1998. The TIPSTER SUMMAC text summarization evaluation final report. Technical Report MTR 98W0000138, The MITRE Corporation.

Inderjeet Mani, Barbara Gates, and Eric Bloedorn. 1999. Improving summaries by revising them. In *Proceedings of the 37th Annual Meeting of the Association for Computational Linguistics(ACL'99)*, pages 558–565, University of Maryland, Maryland, June.

Michael McCord, 1990. *English Slot Grammar.* IBM.

Samuel Thurber, editor. 1924. *Précis Writing for American Schools.* The Atlantic Monthly Press, INC., Boston.

A.J. Viterbi. 1967. Error bounds for convolution codes and an asymptotically optimal decoding algorithm. *IEEE Transactions on Information Theory*, 13:260–269.

Minimizing Word Error Rate in Textual Summaries of Spoken Language

Klaus Zechner and **Alex Waibel**
Language Technologies Institute
Carnegie Mellon University
5000 Forbes Avenue
Pittsburgh, PA 15213, USA
{zechner,waibel}@cs.cmu.edu

Abstract

Automatic generation of text summaries for spoken language faces the problem of containing incorrect words and passages due to speech recognition errors. This paper describes comparative experiments where passages with higher speech recognizer confidence scores are favored in the ranking process. Results show that a relative word error rate reduction of over 10% can be achieved while at the same time the accuracy of the summary improves markedly.

1 Introduction

The amount of audio data on-line has been growing rapidly in recent years, and so methods for efficiently indexing and retrieving non-textual information have become increasingly important (see, e.g., the TREC-7 branch for "Spoken Document Retrieval" (Garofolo et al., 1999)).

One way of compressing audio information is the automatic creation of textual summaries which can be skimmed much faster and stored much more efficiently than the audio itself. There has been plenty of research in the area of summarizing *written* language (see (Mani and Maybury, 1999) for a comprehensive overview). So far, however, very little attention has been given to the question how to create and evaluate a summary of spoken audio based on automatically generated transcripts from a speech recognizer. One fundamental problem with those summaries is that they contain incorrectly recognized words, i.e., the original text is to some extent "distorted".

Several research groups have developed interactive "browsing" tools, where audio (and possibly video) can be accessed together with various types of textual information (transcripts, summaries) via a graphical user interface (Waibel et al., 1998; Valenza et al., 1999; Hirschberg et al., 1999). With these tools, the problem of misrecognitions is alleviated in the sense that the user can always easily listen to the audio recording corresponding to a passage in a textual summary. In some instances, however, this approach may not be feasible or too expensive to pursue, and a short, stand-alone textual representation of the spoken audio may be preferred or even required. This paper addresses in particular this latter case and (a) explores means of making textual summaries less distorted (i.e., reducing their word error rate (WER)), and (b) assesses how the accuracy of the summaries changes when methods for word error rate reduction are applied. Summary accuracy will be a function of how much relevant information is present in the summary.

Our results from experiments on four television shows with multiple speakers show that it is possible to reduce word error rate while at the same time also improving the accuracy of the summary. Furthermore, this paper presents a novel method for evaluation of textual summaries from spoken language data.

The paper is organized as follows: In the next section, we review related work on spoken language summarization. In section 3 we describe our summarizer. Next, we present and discuss our proposal for an audio summarization evaluation metric (section 4). In section 5 we describe the corpus that we use for our experiments and how it was annotated. Sections 6 and 7 describe experiments on both human and machine generated transcripts of the audio data. Finally, we discuss and summarize the results in sections 8 and 9.

2 Related work

(Waibel et al., 1998) report results of their summarization system on automatically transcribed SWITCHBOARD data (Godfrey et al., 1992), the word error rate being about 30%. In a question-answer test with summaries of five dialogues, subjects could identify most of the key concepts using a summary size of only five turns. However, the results vary widely across five different dialogues tested in this experiment (between 20% and 90% accuracy).

(Valenza et al., 1999) went one step further and report that they were able to reduce the word error rate in summaries (as opposed to full texts) by using speech recognizer confidence scores. They combined inverse frequency weights with confidence scores for each recognized word. Using summaries composed of one 30-gram per minute (approximately 15% length of the full text), the WER dropped from 25% for the full text to 10% for these summaries. They also conducted a qualitative study where human subjects were given summaries of n-grams of different length and also summaries with speaker utterances as minimal units, either giving a high weight to the inverse frequency scores or to the confidence scores. The utterance summaries were considered best, followed closely by 30-gram summaries, both using high confidence score weights. This suggests that not only does the WER drop by extracting passages that are more likely to be correctly recognized but also do summaries seem to be "better" which are generated that way.

While the results of (Valenza et al., 1999) are *indicative* for their approach, we want to investigate the benefits of using speech recognizer confidence scores in more detail and particularly find out about the *trade-off* between WER and summarization accuracy when we vary the influence of the confidence scores. To our knowledge, this paper addresses this trade-off for the first time in a clear, numerically describable way. To be able to obtain numerical values for summary accuracy, we had our corpus annotated for relevance (section 5) and devised an evaluation scheme that allows the calculation of summary accuracy for both human and machine generated transcripts (section 4).

3 Summarization system

Prior to summarizing, the input text is cleaned up for disfluencies, such as hesitations, filled pauses, and repetitions.[1] In the context of multi-topical recordings we use for our experiments, summaries are generated for each topical segment separately. The segment boundaries were determined to be at those places where the majority (at least half) of the human annotators agreed (see section 5). Intercoder agreement for topical boundaries is fairly good (and higher than the agreement on relevant words or passages).[2]

To determine the content of the summaries, we use a "maximal marginal relevance" (MMR) based summarizer with speaker turns as minimal units (cf. (Carbonell and Goldstein, 1998)).

The MMR formula is given in equation 1. It generates a list of turns ranked by their relevance and states that the next turn to be put in this ranked list will be taken from the turns which were not yet ranked (t_{nr}) and has the following properties: it is (a) maximally similar to a "query" and (b) maximally dissimilar to the turns which were already ranked (t_r). As "query" we use a frequency vector for all content words within a topical segment. The λ-parameter ($0.0 \le \lambda \le 1.0$) is used to trade off the influence of (a) vs. (b).

Both similarity metrics (sim_1, sim_2) are inner vector products of (stemmed) term frequencies (see equations 2 to 4); $\vec{tf_t}$ is a vector of stem frequencies in a turn; f_s are in-segment frequencies of a stem; f_{smax} are maximal segment frequencies of any stem in the topical segment. sim_1 can be normalized or not. The formulae for tf_s (equation 4) are inspired from Cornell's SMART system (Salton, 1971); we will call these parameters "smax", "log", and "freq", respectively.

$$nextturn = \arg\max_{t_{nr,j}}(\lambda sim_1(t_{nr,j}, query) - (1-\lambda)\max_{t_{r,k}} sim_2(t_{nr,j}, t_{r,k})) \quad (1)$$

$$sim_1 = \vec{tf_s}\vec{tf_t} \quad \text{or} \quad \frac{\vec{tf_s}\vec{tf_t}}{|\vec{tf_s}||\vec{tf_t}|} \quad (2)$$

$$sim_2 = \frac{\vec{tf_{t1}}\vec{tf_{t2}}}{|\vec{tf_{t1}}||\vec{tf_{t2}}|} \quad (3)$$

$$tf_{i,s} = 0.5 + 0.5\frac{f_{i,s}}{f_{smax}} \quad \text{or} \quad 1 + \log f_{i,s} \quad \text{or} \quad f_{i,s} \quad (4)$$

Using the MMR algorithm, we obtain a list of ranked turns for each topical segment. We compute this both for human and machine generated transcripts of the audio files ("reference text" vs. "hypothesis text").[3]

4 Evaluation metrics

The challenge of devising a meaningful evaluation metric for the task of audio summarization is that it has to be applicable to both the reference (human transcript) and the hypothesis transcripts (automatic speech recognizer (ASR) transcripts). We want to be able to assess the quality of the summary with respect to the relevance markings of the human annotators (see section 5), as well as to relate this "summary accuracy" to the word error rate present in the ASR transcripts.

The approach we take is to *align* the words in the summary with the words in the reference transcript (w_a). For ASR transcripts, word substitutions are aligned with their "true original" and word insertions are aligned with a NIL dummy. That way,

[1] More details about this component and other parts of the summarization system can be found in (Zechner and Waibel, 2000).

[2] For details see (Zechner, 2000).

[3] The human reference is considered to be an "optimal" or "ideal" rendering of the words which were actually said in a conversation. Human transcription errors do occur, but are marginal and hence ignored in the context of this paper.

we can determine *for each* individual word w_a in the summary (a) whether it occurs in a "relevant phrase" and (b) whether it is correctly recognized or a recognition error (for ASR transcripts).

We define word error rate as WER $= (S + I + D)/(S + I + C)$ (I=insertion, D=deletion, S=substitution, C=correct).

Each word's relevance score r is the average number it occurs in the human annotators' relevant phrases ($0.0 \leq r \leq 1.0$). Relevance scores for insertions and substitutions are always 0.0.

We choose to define the summary accuracy sa ("relevance") as the sum of relevance scores of all n aligned words $\sum_{w_a} r_{w_a}$ divided by the *maximum achievable relevance score* with the same number of n words *somewhere* in the text (i.e., $0.0 \leq sa \leq 1.0$). Word deletions obviously do not show up in the summary, but are accounted for, as well, to make the WER computation sound.

To better illustrate how these metrics work, we demonstrate them on a simplified example of only two speaker turns (Figure 1). The first line represents the relevance score r for each word (the number this word was within a "relevant phrase" divided by the number of annotators for that text). In turn 1, "this is to illustrate" was only marked relevant by two annotators, whereas "the idea" by 3 out of 4 annotators. The second line provides the reference transcript, the third line the ASR transcript. Line 4 gives the type of word error, and line 5 the confidence score of the speech recognizer (between 0.0 and 1.0, 1.0 meaning maximal confidence).

Now let us assume that turn 2 shows up in the summary. The scores are computed as follows:

- When summarizing the *reference*: Here, the word error rate is trivially 0.0; the summary accuracy sa is the sum of all relevance scores (=6.0) divided by the *maximal achievable score* with the same number of words ($n = 7$). Turn 2 has 6 words which were marked relevant by all coders ($r = 1.0$), turn 1's highest score is $r = 0.75$. Therefore: $sa_2 = 6.0/(6.0 + 0.75) = 0.89$. This is higher than the summary accuracy for turn 1: $sa_1 = 3.5/6.0 = 0.58 (n = 6)$.
- When summarizing the *ASR transcript* ("hypothesis"): Selecting turn 2 will give $sa_2 = 0.0/2.25 = 0.0$ ($n = 5$). For turn 1, $sa_1 = 2.25/(0.75 + 0.5 + 0.5 + 0.5 + 0.0 + 0.0) = 1.0$ ($n = 6$; the sum in the denominator can only use relevance scores based on the *aligned* words w_a which were *correctly* recognized, therefore the 1.0-scores in turn 2 cannot be used). Turn 2 has WER=6/5=1.2, turn 1 has WER=3/6=0.5.

Obviously, when summarizing the ASR output, we would rather have turn 1 showing up in the summary than turn 2, because turn 2 is completely off from the truth and turn 1 only partially. The fact that turn 2 was considered to be more relevant by human coders cannot, in our opinion, be used to favor its inclusion in the summary. An exception would be a situation where the user has immediate access to the audio as well and is able to listen to selected passages from the summary (see section 1). In our case, where we focus on text-only summaries to be used stand-alone, we have to minimize their word error rate.

Given that, turn 1 has to be favored over turn 2, both because of its lower WER and because of its higher accuracy with respect to the relevance annotations.

In order to increase the likelihood that turns with lower WER are selected over turns with higher WER, we make use of the speech recognizer's confidence scores which are attached to every word hypothesis and can be viewed as probabilities: they are in [0.0,1.0], high values reflecting a high confidence in the correctness of the respective word.[4] Following (Valenza et al., 1999) we conjecture that we can use these confidence scores to increase the probability of passages with lower WER to show up in the summary. To test how far this assumption is justified, we correlated the WER with various metrics of confidence scores: (i) sum of scores, (ii) average of scores, (iii) number of scores above a threshold, (iv) the latter normalized by the number of all scores, and (v) the geometric mean of scores. Table 1 shows the correlation coefficients (Pearson r) for the four ASR transcripts we used in our experiments (see section 5). To prevent the influence of large differences in turn length, those computations were done for subsequent "buckets" of 50 words each.

Since in most cases we achieve the highest correlation coefficient (absolute value) for method (iv = avgth) (average number of words whose confidence score is greater than a threshold of 0.95), we apply this metric to the computation of turn-query similarities (sim_1 in equation 1). We use the two following formulae to adjust the similarity-scores. (We shall call these adjustments MULT and EXP in the following.)

$$[mult] \quad sim_1' = sim_1(1 + \alpha \text{avgth}) \qquad (5)$$

$$[exp] \quad sim_1'' = sim_1 \text{avgth}^{\alpha} \qquad (6)$$

For both equations it holds that if $\alpha = 0.0$, the scores don't change, whereas if $\alpha > 0.0$, we enhance the weights of turns with many high confidence scores ("boosting") and hence increase their likelihood of showing up earlier in the summary.[5]

Even though our evaluation method looks like it would "guarantee" an increase in summary accu-

[4] The speech recognizer computes these scores based on the acoustic stability of words during lattice rescoring.

[5] For EXP, we define $0^0 = 0$.

```
TURN 1:
rel:     0.5  0.5 0.5   0.5                0.75  0.75  ***
REF:     this is  to    illustrate         the   idea  ***
HYP:     this is  to    ILLUMINATE         ***   idea  AND
err:     C    C   C     S                  D     C     I
con:     1    1   1     0.9                -     0.8   0.8

TURN 2:
rel:     0   1    1 1       1     1           1
REF:     and here we have   very  relevant    information
HYP:     and HE   ** BEHAVES **** IRREVERENT  FORMATION
err:     C   S    D  S      D     S           S
con:     0.8 0.7  -  0.8    -     0.8         0.9
```

Figure 1: Simplified example of two turns (for score computation)

	BACK	19CENT	BUCHANAN	GRAY
(i) sum	-0.43	-0.51	-0.12	-0.03
(ii) average	-0.53	-0.52	-0.43	-0.42
(iii) scores > 0.95	-0.55	-0.48	-0.35	-0.25
(iv) normalized (iii)	**-0.58**	-0.48	**-0.48**	**-0.44**
(v) geometric mean	-0.53	**-0.53**	-0.42	-0.38

Table 1: Pearson r correlation between WER and confidence scores

racy when the word error rate is reduced, this is *not* necessarily the case. For example, it could turn out that while we can reduce WER by "boosting" passages with higher confidence scores, those passages might have (much) fewer words marked relevant than those being present in the summary without boosting. This way, it would be conceivable to create low word error summaries that contain also very few *relevant* pieces of information. However, as we will see later, WER reduction goes hand in hand with an increase of summary accuracy.

5 Data characteristics and annotation

Table 2 describes the main features of the corpus we used for our experiments: we selected four audio excerpts from four television shows, together with human generated textual transcripts. All these shows are conversations between multiple speakers. The audio was sampled at 16kHz and then also automatically transcribed using a gender independent, vocal tract length normalized, large vocabulary speech recognizer which was trained on about 80 hours of Broadcast News data (Yu et al., 1999). The average word error rates for our 4 recordings ranged from 25% to 50%.

The reference transcripts of the four recordings were given to six human annotators who had to segment them into topically coherent regions and to decide on the "most relevant phrases" to be included in a summary for each topical region. Those phrases usually do not coincide exactly with speaker turns and the annotators were encouraged to mark sections of text freely such that they would form meaningful, concise, and informative phrases. Three annotators could listen to the audio while annotating the corpus, the other three only had the human generated transcripts available. 2 of the 6 annotators only finished the NewsHour data, so we have the opinion of 4 annotators for the recordings BUCHANAN and GRAY and of 6 annotators for BACK and 19CENT.

6 Experiments on human generated transcripts

We created summaries of the reference transcripts using different parameters for the MMR computation: For tf we used "freq", "log", and "smax"; further, we did or did not normalize these weights; finally, we varied the MMR-λ from 0.85 to 1.0. Summarization accuracy was determined at 5%, 10%, 15%, 20%, and 25% of the text length of each summarized topical segment and then averaged over all sample points in all segments. Since these were *word-based* lengths, words were added incrementally to the summary in the order of the turns ranked via MMR; turns were cut off when the length limit was reached. As explained in the example in section 4, the accuracy score is defined as the fraction of the sum of all individual word relevance scores (as de-

	BACK	19CENT	BUCHANAN	GRAY
TV show	NewsHour	NewsHour	Crossfire	Crossfire
number of speakers	5	2	4	5
speaker turns	24	27	69	70
words in transcript	1216	1281	3252	2205
length in minutes	8.6	8.6	17.3	11.9
topical segments	4	4	4	3
word error rate (in %)	25.6	32.6	32.5	49.8

Table 2: Characteristics of the corpus

BACK	19CENT	BUCHANAN	GRAY	average
0.533	0.596	0.513	0.443	0.522

Table 3: Reference summarization accuracy of MMR summaries

termined by human annotators) over the *maximum possible* score given the current number of words in the summary.

Table 3 shows the summary accuracy results for the best parameter setting (tf=log, no normalization)[6].

7 Experiments on automatically generated transcripts

Using the same summarizer as before, we now created summaries from ASR transcripts. Additionally to the summary accuracy, we evaluate now also the WER for each evaluation point. Again, we ran a series of experiments for different parameters of the MMR formula (tf=log, smax, freq; with/without normalization). As before, we achieved the best results for non normalized scores and tf=log. We varied α from 0.0 to 10.0 to see how much of an effect we would get from the "boosting" of turns with many high confidence scores (see equations 5 and 6).

The EXP formula yielded better results than MULT (Table 4), the optimum for EXP was reached for $\alpha = 3.0$ with a WER of 26.6%, an absolute improvement of over 8% over the average of WER=35.1% for the complete ASR transcripts (non-summarized). The summarization accuracy peaks at 0.47, a 9% absolute improvement over the $\alpha = 0.0$-baseline and only about 5% absolute lower than for reference summaries (Table 4 and Figure 2).

When we compare the baseline of $\alpha = 0.0$ (i.e., no "boosting" of high confidence turns) to the best result ($\alpha = 3.0$), we see that the WER drops markedly by about 12% relative from 30.1 to 26.6%. At the same time, the summarization accuracy *increases* by about 18% relative form 0.401 to 0.472.

[6] If we use non-normalized scores, the value of the MMR-λ does not have any measurable effect; we assigned it to be 0.95 for all subsequent experiments.

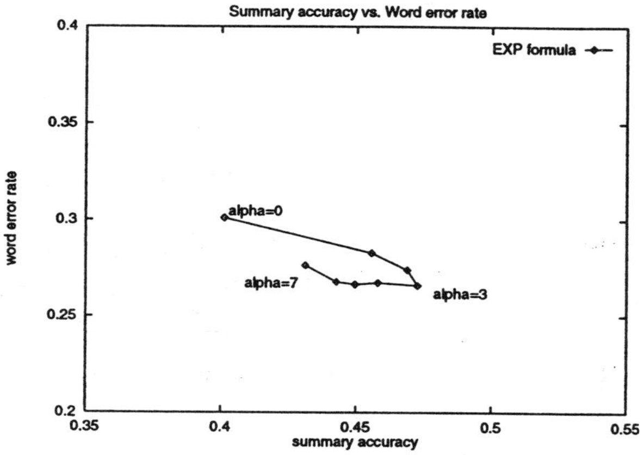

Figure 2: Summary accuracy vs. word error rates with EXP boosting ($0 \leq \alpha \leq 7$)

Results for the MULT formula confirm this trend, but it is considerably weaker: approximately 6% WER reduction and 14% accuracy improvement for $\alpha = 10.0$ over the $\alpha = 0.0$ baseline.

An appendix (section 11) provides an example of actual summaries generated by our system for the first topical segment of the BACK conversation. It illustrates how WER reduction and summary accuracy improvement can be achieved by using our confidence boosting method.

8 Discussion

The most significant result of our experiments is, in our opinion, the fact that the trade-off between *word* and *summary* accuracy indeed leads to an optimal parameter setting for the creation of textual summaries for spoken language (Figure 2). Using a formula which emphasizes turns containing many high confidence scores leads to an average WER reduction of over 10% and to an average improvement in summary accuracy of over 15%, compared to the baseline of a standard MMR-based summary.

Comparing our results to those reported in (Valenza et al., 1999), we find that their relative

	BACK		19CENT		BUCHANAN		GRAY		average	
	acc	WER	acc	WER	acc	WER	acc	WER	acc	WER
$\alpha = 0.0$	0.411	26.2	0.501	26.7	0.412	30.6	0.280	36.9	0.401	30.1
EXP ($\alpha = 3.0$)	0.648	18.8	0.501	26.7	0.444	26.9	0.296	34.0	**0.472**	**26.6**
MULT ($\alpha = 10.0$)	0.575	21.5	0.501	26.7	0.429	29.6	0.317	35.7	0.456	28.3

Table 4: Effect of α on summary accuracy vs. WER (in %) transcripts with EXP and MULT boosting methods

	BACK	19CENT	BUCHANAN	GRAY
avgth	-0.79	-0.11	-0.43	-0.03

Table 5: Correlation between WER and confidence scores on a turn basis

WER reduction for summaries over full texts was considerably larger than ours (60% vs. 24%). We conjecture that reasons for this may be due to the different nature and quality of the confidence scores, and (not unrelated), to the different absolute WER of the two corpora (25% vs. 35%): in transcripts with higher WER, the confidence scores are usually less reliable (cf. Table 1).

Looking at the four audio recordings individually, we see that the improvements vary strongly across different recordings. We conjecture that one reason for this fact may be due to the high variation in the correlation between WER and confidence scores on a *turn* basis (Table 5). This would explain why, e.g., BACK's improvements are much stronger than those of the BUCHANAN recording or why there are no improvements for the 19CENT recording. However, GRAY *does* improve despite its very low absolute correlation.

9 Summary

In this paper, we presented experiments on summaries of both human and machine generated transcripts from four recordings of spoken language. We explored the trade-off of word accuracy vs. summary accuracy (relevance) using speech recognizer confidence scores to rank passages with lower word error rate higher in the summarization process.

Results comparing our approach to a simple MMR ranking show that while the WER can be reduced by over 10%, summarization accuracy improves by over 15% as measured against transcripts with relevance annotations.

10 Acknowledgements

We thank the six human annotators for their tedious work of annotating the corpus with topical segment boundaries and relevance information. We also want to thank Alon Lavie and the three anonymous reviewers for useful feedback and comments on earlier drafts of this paper.

This work was funded in part by ATR – Interpreting Telecommunications Research Laboratories of Japan, and the US Department of Defense.

References

Jaime Carbonell and Jade Goldstein. 1998. The use of MMR, diversity-based reranking for reordering documents and producing summaries. In *Proceedings of the 21st ACM-SIGIR International Conference on Research and Development in Information Retrieval, Melbourne, Australia.*

John S. Garofolo, Ellen M. Voorhees, Cedric G. P. Auzanne, and Vincent M. Stanford. 1999. Spoken document retrieval: 1998 evaluation and investigation of new metrics. In *Proceedings of the ESCA workshop: Accessing information in spoken audio*, pages 1–7. Cambridge, UK, April.

J. J. Godfrey, E. C. Holliman, and J. McDaniel. 1992. SWITCHBOARD: telephone speech corpus for research and development. In *Proceedings of the ICASSP-92*, volume 1, pages 517–520.

Julia Hirschberg, Steve Whittaker, Don Hindle, Fernando Pereira, and Amit Singhal. 1999. Finding information in audio: A new paradigm for audio browsing/retrieval. In *Proceedings of the ESCA workshop: Accessing information in spoken audio*, pages 117–122. Cambridge, UK, April.

Inderjeet Mani and Mark T. Maybury, editors. 1999. *Advances in automatic text summarization*. MIT Press, Cambridge, MA.

Gerard Salton, editor. 1971. *The SMART Retrieval System — Experiments in Automatic Text Processing*. Prentice Hall, Englewood Cliffs, New Jersey.

Robin Valenza, Tony Robinson, Marianne Hickey, and Roger Tucker. 1999. Summarisation of spoken audio through information extraction. In *Proceedings of the ESCA workshop: Accessing information in spoken audio*, pages 111–116. Cambridge, UK, April.

Alex Waibel, Michael Bett, and Michael Finke. 1998. Meeting browser: Tracking and summarizing meetings. In *Proceedings of the DARPA Broadcast News Workshop*.

Hua Yu, Michael Finke, and Alex Waibel. 1999. Progress in automatic meeting transcription. In *Proceedings of EUROSPEECH-99, Budapest, Hungary, September.*

α	relative sa	WER in %	turns in summary
0.0	0.428	29.2	2, 1[beginning]
3.0	0.885	11.8	1, 5[beginning]

Table 6: Relative summary accuracy, WER, and selected turns by the summarizer for (a) no boosting and (b) EXP boosting.

turn	avg. relevance score	WER in %	avgth
1	0.663	9.5	0.84
2	0.369	27.5	0.40
3	0.149	26.9	0.39
4	0.212	11.1	0.08
5	0.274	27.7	0.17

Table 7: Average relevance scores, WER, and confidence values for the five turns of BACK's first topical segment.

Klaus Zechner and Alex Waibel. 2000. Diasumm: Flexible summarization of spontaneous dialogues in unrestricted domains. Available from http://www.cs.cmu.edu/~zechner/publications.html.

Klaus Zechner. 2000. A word-based annotation and evaluation scheme for summarization of spontaneous speech. Available from http://www.cs.cmu.edu/~zechner/publications.html.

11 Appendix: Example summaries

This appendix provides summaries for the first topical segment of the BACK conversation. The contents of this conversation revolves around former Illinois congressman Dan Rostenkowski who had been released from prison and was ready to re-enter public life.

Figure 3 shows the human transcript of this segment which is about two minutes long and consists of 5 speaker turns. Figure 4 contrasts the machine generated summaries for this segment (a) without confidence boosting ($\alpha = 0.0$) and (b) using the optimal confidence boosting ($\alpha = 3.0$, method EXP). Insertions and substitutions are capitalized and marked with I- or S- prefixes. Table 6 compares the relative summary accuracies (sa) and word error rates (WER in %) for these two summaries (average over the 5 sample points from 5% to 25% summary length). Additionally, the turns that show up in the summaries are listed in their ranking order. Table 7 provides the average relevance scores, word error rates, and confidence scores ("avgth") for each turn of this topical segment.

We observe that the most relevant turn is turn 1 which has, incidentally, also the lowest WER. Whereas in case (a) ($\alpha = 0.0$), turn 2 is ranked first and therefore dominates the lower relevance and higher WER scores, case (b) ($\alpha = 3.0$) successfully ranks turn 1 first due to its higher confidence scores and hence both summary accuracy and WER scores improve.

1 elizabeth: it has been eight months since dan rostenkowski walked out of a wisconsin federal prison six months since he left a halfway house in chicago the former chairman of the house ways and means committee is ready to step back into the public eye
2 elizabeth: the reception was warm the banquet hall packed with the city's movers and shakers the thirty five dollars a plate invitation referred to rostenkowski as mr. chairman rostenkowski made no reference to his conviction for misusing federal funds only a brief reference to his fifteen months of prison time
3 dan: i graduated from oxford and i really had a rhodes scholarship the past three years have been a constantly challenging time for me change never comes easily and given the circumstances of my situation that was particularly true for me at times things have been downright bleak and i wouldn't want to wish my experience on my worst enemy but there were some silver linings i've had an opportunity to read and reflect in a way that wasn't possible when i was in constant moment in these remarks today i'd like to share some of my conclusions
4 elizabeth: the conclusions did not dwell on the demise of dan rostenkowski's career but the demise of party politics
5 dan: those who say that the president's political power has been weakened by scandal have truly short memories the sad fact is that president clinton has never had a democratic base in congress a group of people whom one could support the white house on any given issue are not there

Figure 3: Human transcript of first topical segment (BACK)

1 elizabeth: has been eight months since dan rostenkowski walked out of wisconsin federal prison I-MAYBE
2 elizabeth: was S-ALARMED the banquet hall packed with the city's S-COMMUTERS S-IN S-CHAMBERS S-WHICH thirty five S-DOLLAR a plate S-IMITATION referred to rostenkowski as S-MR. chairman I-LET I-ME I-ASK rostenkowski made no reference to his conviction for I-MIS S-USING federal funds only a brief reference to S-IS fifteen months of prison time

1 elizabeth: has been eight months since dan rostenkowski walked out of wisconsin federal prison I-MAYBE six months since he left S-THE halfway house in chicago the former chairman of the house ways and means committee ready to step back into the public eye
5 dan: S-ALSO say that the president's political power has been weakened by scandal S-RIGHT S-ESPECIALLY short S-MEMORY S-THAT S-DISSATISFACTION that president clinton has never

Figure 4: Machine generated summaries for (a) $\alpha = 0.0$ and (b) $\alpha = 3.0$ (25% of text length)

Trainable Methods for Surface Natural Language Generation

Adwait Ratnaparkhi
IBM TJ Watson Research Center
P.O. Box 218
Yorktown Heights, NY 10598
aratnapa@us.ibm.com

Abstract

We present three systems for surface natural language generation that are trainable from annotated corpora. The first two systems, called NLG1 and NLG2, require a corpus marked only with domain-specific semantic attributes, while the last system, called NLG3, requires a corpus marked with both semantic attributes and syntactic dependency information. All systems attempt to produce a grammatical natural language phrase from a domain-specific semantic representation. NLG1 serves a baseline system and uses phrase frequencies to generate a whole phrase in one step, while NLG2 and NLG3 use maximum entropy probability models to individually generate each word in the phrase. The systems NLG2 and NLG3 learn to determine both the word choice and the word order of the phrase. We present experiments in which we generate phrases to describe flights in the air travel domain.

1 Introduction

This paper presents three trainable systems for surface natural language generation (NLG). Surface NLG, for our purposes, consists of generating a grammatical natural language phrase that expresses the meaning of an input semantic representation. The systems take a "corpus-based" or "machine-learning" approach to surface NLG, and learn to generate phrases from semantic input by statistically analyzing examples of phrases and their corresponding semantic representations. The determination of the content in the semantic representation, or "deep" generation, is not discussed here. Instead, the systems assume that the input semantic representation is fixed and only deal with how to express it in natural language.

This paper discusses previous approaches to surface NLG, and introduces three trainable systems for surface NLG, called NLG1, NLG2, and NLG3. Quantitative evaluation of experiments in the air travel domain will also be discussed.

2 Previous Approaches

Templates are the easiest way to implement surface NLG. A template for describing a flight noun phrase in the air travel domain might be `flight departing from $city-fr at $time-dep and arriving in $city-to at $time-arr` where the words starting with "$" are actually variables — representing the departure city, and departure time, the arrival city, and the arrival time, respectively— whose values will be extracted from the environment in which the template is used. The approach of writing individual templates is convenient, but may not scale to complex domains in which hundreds or thousands of templates would be necessary, and may have shortcomings in maintainability and text quality (e.g., see (Reiter, 1995) for a discussion).

There are more sophisticated surface generation packages, such as FUF/SURGE (Elhadad and Robin, 1996), KPML (Bateman, 1996), MUMBLE (Meteer et al., 1987), and RealPro (Lavoie and Rambow, 1997), which produce natural language text from an abstract semantic representation. These packages require linguistic sophistication in order to write the abstract semantic representation, but they are flexible because minor changes to the input can accomplish major changes to the generated text.

The only trainable approaches (known to the author) to surface generation are the purely statistical machine translation (MT) systems such as (Berger et al., 1996) and the corpus-based generation system described in (Langkilde and Knight, 1998). The MT systems of (Berger et al., 1996) learn to generate text in the target language straight from the source language, without the aid of an explicit semantic representation. In contrast, (Langkilde and Knight, 1998) uses corpus-derived statistical knowledge to rank plausible hypotheses from a grammar-based surface generation component.

3 Trainable Surface NLG

In trainable surface NLG, the goal is to learn the mapping from semantics to words that would otherwise need to be specified in a grammar or knowledge base. All systems in this paper use *attribute-value* pairs as a semantic representation, which suffice as a representation for a limited domain like air travel. For example, the set of attribute-value pairs { \$city-fr = New York City, \$city-to = Seattle , \$time-dep = 6 a.m., \$date-dep = Wednesday } represent the meaning of the noun phrase "a flight to Seattle that departs from New York City at 6 a.m. on Wednesday". The goal, more specifically, is then to learn the optimal *attribute ordering* and *lexical choice* for the text to be generated from the attribute-value pairs. For example, the NLG system should automatically decide if the attribute ordering in "flights to New York in the evening" is better or worse than the ordering in "flights in the evening to New York". Furthermore, it should automatically decide if the lexical choice in "flights departing to New York" is better or worse than the choice in "flights leaving to New York". The motivation for a trainable surface generator is to solve the above two problems in a way that reflects the observed usage of language in a corpus, but without the manual effort needed to construct a grammar or knowledge base.

All the trainable NLG systems in this paper assume the existence of a large corpus of phrases in which the values of interest have been replaced with their corresponding attributes, or in other words, a corpus of *generation templates*. Figure 1 shows a sample of training data, where only words marked with a "\$" are attributes. All of the NLG systems in this paper work in two steps as shown in Table 2. The systems NLG1, NLG2 and NLG3 all implement step 1; they produce a sequence of words intermixed with attributes, i.e., a template, from the the attributes alone. The values are ignored until step 2, when they replace their corresponding attributes in the phrase produced by step 1.

3.1 NLG1: the baseline

The surface generation model NLG1 simply chooses the most frequent template in the training data that corresponds to a given set of attributes. Its performance is intended to serve as a baseline result to the more sophisticated models discussed later. Specifically, $nlg_1(A)$ returns the phrase that corresponds to the attribute set A:

$$nlg_1(A) = \begin{cases} \text{argmax}_{phrase \in T_A} \; C(phrase, A) & T_A \neq \emptyset \\ \text{[empty string]} & T_A = \emptyset \end{cases}$$

where T_A are the phrases that have occurred with A in the training data, and where $C(phrase, A)$ is the training data frequency of the natural language phrase *phrase* and the set of attributes A. NLG1 will fail to generate anything if A is a novel combination of attributes.

3.2 NLG2: n-gram model

The surface generation system NLG2 assumes that the best choice to express any given attribute-value set is the word sequence with the highest probability that mentions all of the input attributes exactly once. When generating a word, it uses local information, captured by word n-grams, together with certain non-local information, namely, the subset of the original attributes that remain to be generated. The local and non-local information is integrated with use of features in a maximum entropy probability model, and a highly pruned search procedure attempts to find the best scoring word sequence according to the model.

3.2.1 Probability Model

The probability model in NLG2 is a conditional distribution over $V \cup *\texttt{stop}*$, where V is the generation vocabulary and where `*stop*` is a special "stop" symbol. The generation vocabulary V consists of all the words seen in the training data. The form of the maximum entropy probability model is identical to the one used in (Berger et al., 1996; Ratnaparkhi, 1998):

$$p(w_i|w_{i-1}, w_{i-2}, attr_i) = \frac{\prod_{j=1}^{k} \alpha_j^{f_j(w_i, w_{i-1}, w_{i-2}, attr_i)}}{Z(w_{i-1}, w_{i-2}, attr_i)}$$

$$Z(w_{i-1}, w_{i-2}, attr_i) = \sum_{w'} \prod_{j=1}^{k} \alpha_j^{f_j(w', w_{i-1}, w_{i-2}, attr_i)}$$

where w_i ranges over $V \cup *\texttt{stop}*$ and $\{w_{i-1}, w_{i-2}, attr_i\}$ is the history, where w_i denotes the ith word in the phrase, and $attr_i$ denotes the attributes that remain to be generated at position i in the phrase. The f_j, where $f_j(a, b) \in \{0, 1\}$, are called *features* and capture any information in the history that might be useful for estimating $p(w_i|w_{i-1}, w_{i-2}, attr_i)$. The features used in NLG2 are described in the next section, and the feature weights α_j, obtained from the Improved Iterative Scaling algorithm (Berger et al., 1996), are set to maximize the likelihood of the training data. The probability of the sequence $W = w_1 \ldots w_n$, given the attribute set A, (and also given that its length is n) is:

$$Pr(W = w_1 \ldots w_n | len(W) = n, A) = \prod_{i=1}^{n} p(w_i|w_{i-1}, w_{i-2}, attr_i)$$

3.2.2 Feature Selection

The feature patterns, used in NLG2 are shown in Table 3. The actual features are created by matching the patterns over the training data, e.g., an actual feature derived from the word bi-gram template might be:

$$f(w_i, w_{i-1}, w_{i-2}, attr_i) = \begin{cases} 1 & \text{if } w_i = \texttt{from} \\ & \text{and } w_{i-1} = \texttt{flight} \\ & \text{and } \texttt{\$city-fr} \in attr_i \\ 0 & \text{otherwise} \end{cases}$$

```
flights on $air from $city-fr to $city-to the $time-depint of $date-dep
$trip flights on $air from $city-fr to $city-to leaving after $time-depaft on $date-dep
flights leaving from $city-fr going to $city-to after $time-depaft on $date-dep
flights leaving from $city-fr to $city-to the $time-depint of $date-dep
$air flight $fltnum from $city-fr to $city-to on $date-dep
$city-fr to $city-to $air flight $fltnum on the $date-dep
$trip flights from $city-fr to $city-to
```

Table 1: Sample training data

Input to Step 1:	{ \$city-fr, \$city-to, \$time-dep, \$date-dep }
Output of Step 1:	"a flight to \$city-to that departs from \$city-fr at \$time-dep on \$date-dep"
Input to Step 2:	"a flight to \$city-to that departs from \$city-fr at \$time-dep on \$date-dep", { \$city-fr = New York City, \$city-to = Seattle , \$time-dep = 6 a.m., \$date-dep = Wednesday }
Output of Step 2:	"a flight to Seattle that departs from New York City at 6 a.m. on Wednesday"

Table 2: Two steps of NLG process

Low frequency features involving word $n-$grams tend to be unreliable; the NLG2 system therefore only uses features which occur K times or more in the training data.

3.2.3 Search Procedure

The search procedure attempts to find a word sequence $w_1 \dots w_n$ of any length $n \leq M$ for the input attribute set A such that

1. w_n is the stop symbol `*stop*`
2. All of the attributes in A are mentioned at least once
3. All of the attributes in A are mentioned at most once

and where M is an heuristically set maximum phrase length.

The search is similar to a left-to-right breadth-first-search, except that only a fraction of the word sequences are considered. More specifically, the search procedure implements the recurrence:

$$\begin{aligned} W_{N,1} &= top(N, \{w \mid w \in V\}) \\ W_{N,i+1} &= top(N, next(W_{N,i})) \end{aligned}$$

The set $W_{N,i}$ is the top N scoring sequences of length i, and the expression $next(W_{N,i})$ returns all sequences $w_1 \dots w_{i+1}$ such that $w_1 \dots w_i \in W_{N,i}$, and $w_{i+1} \in V \cup$ `*stop*`. The expression $top(N, next(W_{N,i}))$ finds the top N sequences in $next(W_{N,i})$. During the search, any sequence that ends with `*stop*` is removed and placed in the set of completed sequences. If N completed hypotheses are discovered, or if $W_{N,M}$ is computed, the search terminates. Any incomplete sequence which does not satisfy condition (3) is discarded and any complete sequence that does not satisfy condition (2) is also discarded.

When the search terminates, there will be at most N completed sequences, of possibly differing lengths. Currently, there is no normalization for different lengths, i.e., all sequences of length $n \leq M$ are equiprobable:

$$\begin{aligned} Pr(len(W) = n) &= \tfrac{1}{M} \quad n \leq M \\ &= 0 \quad n > M \end{aligned}$$

NLG2 chooses the best answer to express the attribute set A as follows:

$$nlg_2(A) = \operatorname{argmax}_{W \in W_{nlg2}} \; Pr(len(W) = n) \cdot Pr(W \mid len(W) = n, A)$$

where W_{nlg2} are the completed word sequences that satisfy the conditions of the NLG2 search described above.

3.3 NLG3: dependency information

NLG3 addresses a shortcoming of NLG2, namely that the previous two words are not necessarily the best informants when predicting the next word. Instead, NLG3 assumes that conditioning on *syntactically related* words in the history will result on more accurate surface generation. The search procedure in NLG3 generates a syntactic dependency tree from

Description	Feature $f(w_i, w_{i-1}, w_{i-2}, attr_i) = \ldots$
No Attributes remaining	1 if $w_i =?$ and $attr_i = \{\}$, 0 otherwise
Word bi-gram with attribute	1 if $w_i =?$ and $w_{i-1} =?$ and $? \in attr_i$, 0 otherwise
Word tri-gram with attribute	1 if $w_i =?$ and $w_{i-1}w_{i-2} =??$ and $? \in attr_i$, 0 otherwise

Table 3: Features patterns for NLG2. Any occurrence of "?" will be instantiated with an actual value from training data.

top-to-bottom instead of a word sequence from left-to-right, where each word is predicted in the context of its syntactically related parent, grandparent, and siblings. NLG3 requires a corpus that has been annotated with tree structure like the sample dependency tree shown in Figure 1.

3.3.1 Probability Model

The probability model for NLG3, shown in Figure 2, conditions on the parent, the two closest siblings, the direction of the child relative to the parent, and the attributes that remain to be generated.

Just as in NLG2, p is a distribution over $V \cup$ `*stop*`, and the Improved Iterative Scaling algorithm is used to find the feature weights α_j. The expression $ch_i(w)$ denotes the ith closest child to the headword w, $par(w)$ denotes the parent of the headword w, $dir \in \{\texttt{left}, \texttt{right}\}$ denotes the direction of the child relative to the parent, and $attr_{w,i}$ denotes the attributes that remain to be generated in the tree when headword w is predicting its ith child. For example, in Figure 1, if w = "flights", then $ch_1(w)$ = "evening" when generating the left children, and $ch_1(w)$ = "from" when generating the right children. As shown in Figure 3, the probability of a dependency tree that expresses an attribute set A can be found by computing, for each word in the tree, the probability of generating its left children and then its right children.[1] In this formulation, the left children are generated independently from the right children. As in NLG2, NLG3 assumes the uniform distribution for the length probabilities $Pr(\#$ of left children $= n)$ and $Pr(\#$ of right children $= n)$ up to a certain maximum length $M' = 10$.

3.3.2 Feature Selection

The feature patterns for NLG3 are shown in Table 4. As before, the actual features are created by matching the patterns over the training data. The features in NLG3 have access to syntactic information whereas the features in NLG2 do not. Low frequency features involving word $n-$grams tend to be unreliable; the NLG3 system therefore only uses features which occur K times or more in the training data. Furthermore, if a feature derived from Table 4 looks at a particular word $ch_i(w)$ and attribute a, we only allow it if a has occurred as a descendent of $ch_i(w)$ in some dependency tree in the training set. As an example, this condition allows features that look at $ch_i(w)$ = "to" and \$city-to$\in attr_{w,i}$ but disallows features that look at $ch_i(w)$ = "to" and \$city-fr$\in attr_{w,i}$.

[1]We use a dummy ROOT node to generate the top most head word of the phrase

3.4 Search Procedure

The idea behind the search procedure for NLG3 is similar to the search procedure for NLG2, namely, to explore only a fraction of the possible trees by continually sorting and advancing only the top N trees at any given point. However, the dependency trees are not built left-to-right like the word sequences in NLG2; instead they are built from the current head (which is initially the root node) in the following order:

1. Predict the next left child (call it x_l)
2. If it is `*stop*`, jump to (4)
3. Recursively predict children of x_l. Resume from (1)
4. Predict the next right child (call it x_r)
5. If it is `*stop*`, we are done predicting children for the current head
6. Recursively predict children of x_r. Resume from (4)

As before, any incomplete trees that have generated a particular attribute twice, as well as completed trees that have not generated a necessary attribute are discarded by the search. The search terminates when either N complete trees or N trees of the maximum length M are discovered. NLG3 chooses the best answer to express the attribute set A as follows:

$$nlg_3(A) = \operatorname*{argmax}_{T \in T_{nlg3}} Pr(T|A)$$

where T_{nlg3} are the completed dependency trees that satisfy the conditions of the NLG3 search described above.

4 Experiments

The training and test sets used to evaluate NLG1, NLG2 and NLG3 were derived semi-automatically from a pre-existing annotated corpus of user queries in the air travel domain. The annotation scheme used a total of 26 attributes to represent flights.

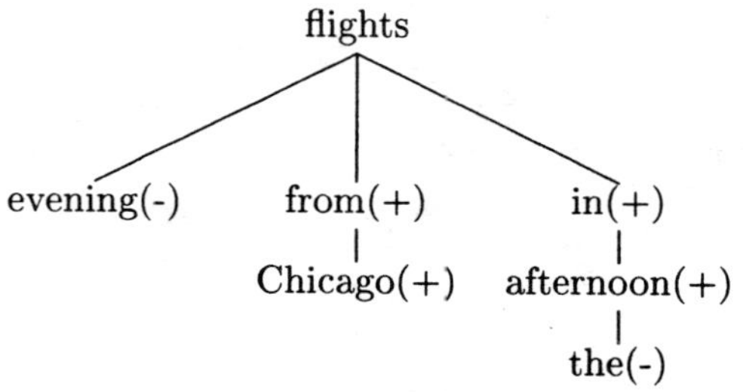

Figure 1: Sample dependency tree for the phrase *evening flights from Chicago in the afternoon.* - and + signs indicate left or right child, respectively.

$$p(ch_i(w)|w, ch_{i-1}(w), ch_{i-2}(w), par(w), dir, attr_{w,i}) = \frac{\prod_{j=1}^{k} \alpha_j^{f_j(ch_i(w),w,ch_{i-1}(w),ch_{i-2}(w),par(w),dir,attr_{w,i})}}{Z(w,ch_{i-1}(w),ch_{i-2}(w),par(w),dir,attr_{w,i})}$$

$$Z(w, ch_{i-1}(w), ch_{i-2}(w), par(w), dir, attr_{w,i}) = \sum_{w'} \prod_{j=1}^{k} \alpha_j^{f_j(w',w,ch_{i-1}(w),ch_{i-2}(w),par(w),dir,attr_{w,i})}$$

Figure 2: NLG3: Equations for the probability of the ith child of head word w, or $ch_i(w)$

$$Pr(T|A) = \prod_{w \in T} Pr_{left}(w|A) Pr_{right}(w|A)$$

$$Pr_{left}(w|A) = Pr(\#\text{ of left children} = n) \prod_{i=1}^{n} p(ch_i(w)|w, ch_{i-1}(w), ch_{i-2}(w), par(w), dir = \texttt{left}, attr_{w,i})$$

$$Pr_{right}(w|A) = Pr(\#\text{ of right children} = n) \prod_{i=1}^{n} p(ch_i(w)|w, ch_{i-1}(w), ch_{i-2}(w), par(w), dir = \texttt{right}, attr_{w,i})$$

Figure 3: NLG3: Equations for the probability of a dependency tree T

Description	Feature $f(ch_i(w), w, ch_{i-1}(w), ch_{i-2}(w), par(w), dir, attr_{w,i}) = \ldots$
Siblings	1 if $ch_i(w) =?$ and $ch_{i-1}(w) =?$ and $ch_{i-2}(w) =?$ and $dir =?$ and $? \in attr_{w,i}$, 0 otherwise
Parent + sibling	1 if $ch_i(w) =?$ and $ch_{i-1}(w) =?$ and $w =?$ and $dir =?$ and $? \in attr_{w,i}$, 0 otherwise
Parent + grandparent	1 if $ch_i(w) =?$ and $w =?$ and $par(w) =?$ and $dir =?$ and $? \in attr_{w,i}$, 0 otherwise

Table 4: Features patterns for NLG3. Any occurrence of "?" will be instantiated with an actual value from training data.

System	Parameters	% Correct	% OK	% Bad	% No output	% error reduction from NLG1
NLG1	-	84.9	4.9	7.2	3.0	-
NLG2	N=10,M=30,K=3	88.2	4.7	6.4	0.7	22
NLG3	N=5,M=30,K=10	89.9	4.4	5.5	0.2	33

Table 5: Weighted evaluation of trainable surface generation systems by judge A

System	Parameters	% Correct	% OK	% Bad	% No output	% error reduction from NLG1
NLG1	-	81.6	8.4	7.0	3.0	-
NLG2	N=10,M=30,K=3	86.3	5.8	7.2	0.7	26
NLG3	N=5,M=30,K=10	88.4	4.0	7.4	0.2	37

Table 6: Weighted evaluation of trainable surface generation systems by judge B

System	Parameters	% Correct	% OK	% Bad	% No output	% error reduction from NLG1
NLG1	-	48.4	6.8	24.2	20.5	-
NLG2	N=10,M=30,K=3	64.7	12.1	22.6	0.5	32
NLG3	N=5,M=30,K=10	63.1	11.6	23.7	1.6	29

Table 7: Unweighted evaluation of trainable surface generation systems by judge A

System	Parameters	% Correct	% OK	% Bad	% No output	% error reduction from NLG1
NLG1	-	41.1	8.9	29.5	20.5	-
NLG2	N=10,M=30,K=3	62.1	13.7	23.7	0.5	36
NLG3	N=5,M=30,K=10	65.3	11.1	22.1	1.6	41

Table 8: Unweighted evaluation of trainable surface generation systems by judge B

The training set consisted of 6000 templates describing flights while the test set consisted of 1946 templates describing flights. All systems used the same training set, and were tested on the attribute sets extracted from the phrases in the test set. For example, if the test set contains the template "flights to $city-to leaving at $time-dep", the surface generation systems will be told to generate a phrase for the attribute set { $city-to, $time-dep }. The output of NLG3 on the attribute set { $city-to, $city-fr, $time-dep } is shown in Table 9.

There does not appear to be an objective *automatic* evaluation method[2] for generated text that correlates with how an actual person might judge the output. Therefore, two judges — the author and a colleague — manually evaluated the output of all three systems. Each judge assigned each phrase from each of the three systems one of the following rankings:

Correct: Perfectly acceptable

OK: Tense or agreement is wrong, but word choice is correct. (These errors could be corrected by post-processing with a morphological analyzer.)

Bad: Words are missing or extraneous words are present

No Output: The system failed to produce any output

While there were a total 1946 attribute sets from the test examples, the judges only needed to evaluate the 190 *unique* attribute sets, e.g., the attribute set { $city-fr $city-to } occurs 741 times in the test data. Subjective evaluation of generation output is not ideal, but is arguably superior than an automatic evaluation that fails to correlate with human linguistic judgement.

[2] Measuring word overlap or edit distance between the system's output and a "reference" set would be an automatic scoring method. We believe that such a method does not accurately measure the correctness or grammaticality of the text.

The results of the manual evaluation, as well as the values of the search and feature selection parameters for all systems, are shown in Tables 5, 6, 7, and 8. (The values for N, M, and K were determined by manually evaluating the output of the 4 or 5 most common attribute sets in the training data). The *weighted* results in Tables 5 and 6 account for multiple occurrences of attribute sets, whereas the *unweighted* results in Tables 7 and 8 count each unique attribute set once, i.e., { $city-fr $city-to } is counted 741 times in the weighted results but once in the unweighted results. Using the weighted results, which represent testing conditions more realistically than the unweighted results, both judges found an improvement from NLG1 to NLG2, and from NLG2 to NLG3. NLG3 cuts the error rate from NLG1 by at least 33% (counting anything without a rank of **Correct** as wrong). NLG2 cuts the error rate by at least 22% and underperforms NLG3, but requires far less annotation in its training data. NLG1 has no chance of generating anything for 3% of the data — it fails completely on novel attribute sets. Using the unweighted results, both judges found an improvement from NLG1 to NLG2, but, surprisingly, judge A found a slight decrease while judge B found an increase in accuracy from NLG2 to NLG3. The unweighted results show that the baseline NLG1 does well on the common attribute sets, since it correctly generates only less than 50% of the unweighted cases but over 80% of the weighted cases.

5 Discussion

The NLG2 and NLG3 systems automatically attempt to generalize from the knowledge inherent in the training corpus of templates, so that they can generate templates for novel attribute sets. There

Probability	Generated Text
0.107582	$time-dep flights from $city-fr to $city-to
0.00822441	$time-dep flights between $city-fr and $city-to
0.00564712	$time-dep flights $city-fr to $city-to
0.00343372	flights from $city-fr to $city-to at $time-dep
0.0012465	$time-dep flights from $city-fr to to $city-to

Table 9: Sample output from NLG3. (Dependency tree structures are not shown.) Typical values for attributes: $time-dep = "10 a.m.", $city-fr = "New York", $city-to = "Miami"

is some additional cost associated with producing the syntactic dependency annotation necessary for NLG3, but virtually no additional cost is associated with NLG2, beyond collecting the data itself and identifying the attributes.

The trainable surface NLG systems in this paper differ from grammar-based systems in how they determine the attribute ordering and lexical choice. NLG2 and NLG3 automatically determine attribute ordering by simultaneously searching multiple orderings. In grammar-based approaches, such preferences need to be manually encoded. NLG2 and NLG3 solve the lexical choice problem by learning the words (via features in the maximum entropy probability model) that correlate with a given attribute and local context, whereas (Elhadad et al., 1997) uses a rule-based approach to decide the word choice.

While trainable approaches avoid the expense of crafting a grammar to determine attribute ordering and lexical choice, they are less accurate than grammar-based approaches. For short phrases, accuracy is typically 100% with grammar-based approaches since the grammar writer can either correct or add a rule to generate the phrase of interest once an error is detected. Whereas with NLG2 and NLG3, one can tune the feature patterns, search parameters, and training data itself, but there is no guarantee that the tuning will result in 100% generation accuracy.

Our approach differs from the corpus-based surface generation approaches of (Langkilde and Knight, 1998) and (Berger et al., 1996). (Langkilde and Knight, 1998) maps from semantics to words with a concept ontology, grammar, and lexicon, and ranks the resulting word lattice with corpus-based statistics, whereas NLG2 and NLG3 automatically learn the mapping from semantics to words from a corpus. (Berger et al., 1996) describes a statistical machine translation approach that generates text in the target language directly from the source text. NLG2 and NLG3 are also statistical learning approaches but generate from an actual semantic representation. This comparison suggests that statistical MT systems could also generate text from an "interlingua", in a way similar to that of knowledge-based translation systems.

We suspect that our statistical generation approach should perform accurately in domains of similar complexity to air travel. In the air travel domain, the length of a phrase fragment to describe an attribute is usually only a few words. Domains which require complex and lengthy phrase fragments to describe a single attribute will be more challenging to model with features that only look at word n-grams for $n \in \{2, 3\}$. Domains in which there is greater ambiguity in word choice will require a more thorough search, i.e., a larger value of N, at the expense of CPU time and memory. Most importantly, the semantic annotation scheme for air travel has the property that it is both rich enough to accurately represent meaning in the domain, but simple enough to yield useful corpus statistics. Our approach may not scale to domains, such as freely occurring newspaper text, in which the semantic annotation schemes do not have this property.

Our current approach has the limitation that it ignores the values of attributes, even though they might strongly influence the word order and word choice. This limitation can be overcome by using features on values, so that NLG2 and NLG3 might discover — to use a hypothetical example — that "flights leaving $city-fr" is preferred over "flights from $city-fr" when $city-fr is a particular value, such as "Miami".

6 Conclusions

This paper presents the first systems (known to the author) that use a statistical learning approach to produce natural language text directly from a semantic representation. Information to solve the attribute ordering and lexical choice problems— which would normally be specified in a large handwritten grammar— is automatically collected from data with a few feature patterns, and is combined via the maximum entropy framework. NLG2 shows that using just local n-gram information can outperform the baseline, and NLG3 shows that using syntactic information can further improve generation accuracy. We conjecture that NLG2 and NLG3 should work in other domains which have a complexity similar to air travel, as well as available annotated data.

7 Acknowledgements

The author thanks Scott McCarley for serving as the second judge, and Scott Axelrod, Kishore Papineni, and Todd Ward for their helpful comments on this work. This work was supported in part by DARPA Contract # MDA972-97-C-0012.

References

John Bateman. 1996. Kpml development environment – multilingual linguistic resource development and sentence generation. Technical report, German Centre for Information Technology (GMD), Institute for Integrated Information and Publication Systems (IPSI), Darmstadt, Germany.

Adam Berger, Stephen A. Della Pietra, and Vincent J. Della Pietra. 1996. A Maximum Entropy Approach to Natural Language Processing. *Computational Linguistics*, 22(1):39–71.

Michael Elhadad and Jacques Robin. 1996. An overview of surge: a reusable comprehensive syntactic realization component. Technical Report 96-03, Ben Gurion University, Beer Sheva, Israel.

Michael Elhadad, Kathleen McKeown, and Jacques Robin. 1997. Floating constraints in lexical choice. *Computational Linguistics*, pages 195–239.

Irene Langkilde and Kevin Knight. 1998. Generation that exploits corpus-based statistical knowledge. In *Proceedings of the 36th Annual Meeting of the Association for Computational Linguistics and 17th International Conference on Computational Linguistics*, University of Montreal, Montreal, Quebec, Canada.

Benoit Lavoie and Owen Rambow. 1997. A fast and portable realizer for text generation systems. In *Proceedings of the Fifth Conference on Applied Natural Language Processing*, pages 265–268, Washington D.C., March 31–April 3.

M. W. Meteer, D. D. McDonald, S.D. Anderson, D. Forster, L.S. Gay, A.K. Huettner, and P. Sibun. 1987. Mumble-86: Design and implementation. Technical Report Technical Report COINS 87-87, University of Massachusetts at Amherst.

Adwait Ratnaparkhi. 1998. *Maximum Entropy Models for Natural Language Ambiguity Resolution*. Ph.D. thesis, University of Pennsylvania.

Ehud Reiter. 1995. Nlg vs. Templates. In *Proceedings of the 5th European Workshop on Natural Language Generation*, Leiden, The Netherlands.

Evaluating Automatic Dialogue Strategy Adaptation for a Spoken Dialogue System

Jennifer Chu-Carroll
Lucent Technologies Bell Laboratories
600 Mountain Avenue
Murray Hill, NJ 07974, U.S.A.
jencc@research.bell-labs.com

Jill Suzanne Nickerson
Harvard University
Cambridge, MA 02138, U.S.A.
nickerso@eecs.harvard.edu

Abstract

In this paper, we describe an empirical evaluation of an adaptive mixed initiative spoken dialogue system. We conducted two sets of experiments to evaluate the mixed initiative and automatic adaptation aspects of the system, and analyzed the resulting dialogues along three dimensions: performance factors, discourse features, and initiative distribution. Our results show that 1) both the mixed initiative and automatic adaptation aspects led to better system performance in terms of user satisfaction and dialogue efficiency, and 2) the system's adaptation behavior better matched user expectations, more efficiently resolved dialogue anomalies, and resulted in higher overall dialogue quality.

1 Introduction

Recent advances in speech technologies have enabled spoken dialogue systems to employ mixed initiative dialogue strategies (e.g. (Allen et al., 1996; Sadek et al., 1996; Meng et al., 1996)). Although these systems interact with users in a manner more similar to human-human interactions than earlier systems employing system initiative strategies, their response strategies are typically selected using only local dialogue context, disregarding dialogue history. Therefore, their gain in naturalness and performance under optimal conditions is often overshadowed by their inability to cope with anomalies in dialogues by automatically adapting dialogue strategies. In contrast, Figure 1 shows a dialogue in which the system automatically adapts dialogue strategies based on the current user utterance and dialogue history.[1] After failing to obtain a valid response to an information-seeking query in utterance (4), the system adapted dialogue strategies to provide additional information in (6) that assisted the user in responding to the query. Furthermore, after the user responded to a limited system prompt in (10) with a fully-specified query in (11), implicitly indicating her intention to take charge of the problem-solving process, the system again adapted strategies, hence providing an open-ended prompt in (13).

Previous work has shown that dialogue systems in which users can explicitly change the system's dialogue strategies result in better performance than non-adaptable systems (Litman and Pan, 1999). However, no earlier system allowed for initiative-oriented automatic strategy adaptation based on information dynamically extracted from the user's spoken input. In this paper, we briefly introduce MIMIC, a *mixed initiative* spoken dialogue system that *automatically adapts* dialogue strategies. We then describe two experiments that evaluated the effectiveness of MIMIC's mixed initiative and automatic adaptation capabilities. Our results show that, when analyzed along the *performance* dimension, MIMIC's mixed initiative and automatic adaptation features lead to more efficient dialogues and higher user satisfaction. Moreover, when analyzed along the *discourse* and *initiative* dimensions, MIMIC's adaptation capabilities result in dialogues in which system behavior better matches user expectations and dialogue anomalies are resolved more efficiently.

2 MIMIC: An Adaptive Mixed Initiative Dialogue System

MIMIC is a voice-enabled, telephone-based dialogue system that provides movie showtime information. Two main features distinguish MIMIC from other existing spoken dialogue systems. First, MIMIC automatically adapts dialogue strategies based on dialogue characteristics and thus tailors its behavior to the dialogue context. Second, MIMIC's initiative module is decoupled from the dialogue manager's goal and strategy selection processes, thereby enabling the system's adaptation behavior to be easily modified. We outline characteristics of MIMIC relevant to our experiments and analyses. For further details about the system, see (Chu-Carroll, 2000).

2.1 Adaptation of Dialogue Strategies

Figure 1 showed an actual interaction between MIMIC and a user. The *task* and *dialogue* initiative holders annotated for each system turn are the factors that affect MIMIC's dialogue strategy adaptation. Following (Chu-Carroll and Brown, 1998), *task initiative* tracks the

[1] S and U indicate system and user utterances, respectively. The words appearing in square brackets are the output from the Lucent Automatic Speech Recognizer (Reichl and Chou, 1998; Ortmanns et al., 1999), configured to use class-based probabilistic n-gram language models. The task and dialogue initiative annotations are explained in Section 2.1.

		Utterance	Task Initiative	Dialogue Initiative
(1)	S:	Hello, this is MIMIC, the movie information system.	User	System
(2)		How can I help you?		
(3)	U:	What time is Analyze This playing in Montclair?		
		[what time is analyze this playing in montclair]		
(4)	S:	What theater would you like?	User	System
(5)	U:	Montclair.		
		[montclair]		
(6)	S:	Choices for theater are Wellmont Theater and Clearviews Screening Zone.	System	System
(7)		What theater would you like?		
(8)	U:	Clearviews Screening Zone.		
		[um movie screening zone]		
(9)	S:	Analyze This is playing at Clearviews Screening Zone in Montclair at 1:15pm, 4:10pm, and 6:30pm.	System	System
(10)		Please say the name of the movie or theater or town you would like information about.		
(11)	U:	What time is Analyze This playing at the Wellmont Theater?		
		[what time is analyze this playing at the wellmont theater]		
(12)	S:	Analyze this is playing at Wellmont Theater in Montclair at 3:15pm, 5:45pm, 8:20pm, and 10:10pm.	User	System
(13)		Can I help you with anything else?		

Figure 1: An Adaptive Mixed Initiative Dialogue with MIMIC

lead in the process toward achieving the dialogue participants' domain goal, while *dialogue initiative* models the lead in determining the current discourse focus. In our information query application domain, MIMIC has task (and thus dialogue) initiative when its utterances are intended to provide helpful guidance toward achieving the user's domain goal, while it has dialogue but not task initiative if its utterances only specify the current discourse goal.[2] For example, as a result of MIMIC taking over task initiative in (6), helpful guidance, in the form of valid response choices, was provided in its attempt to obtain a theater name after the user failed to answer an earlier question intended to solicit this information. In (4), MIMIC specified the current discourse goal (requesting information about a missing theater) but did not suggest valid response choices since it only had dialogue initiative.

MIMIC's ability to automatically adapt dialogue strategies is achieved by employing an initiative module that determines initiative distribution based on participant roles, cues detected during the current user utterance, and dialogue history (Chu-Carroll and Brown, 1998). This initiative framework utilizes the Dempster-Shafer theory (Shafer, 1976; Gordon and Shortliffe, 1984), and represents the current initiative distribution as two *basic probability assignments (bpas)* that signify the overall amount of evidence supporting each agent having task and dialogue initiatives. The effects that a cue has on changing the current task and dialogue initiative distribution are also represented as bpas, obtained using an iterative training procedure on a corpus of transcribed and annotated human-human dialogues. At the end of each user turn, the bpas representing the effects of cues detected during that turn are combined with the bpas representing the current initiative distribution to obtain the initiative distribution for the system's next turn.

In Figure 1, utterance (3) triggered the cue *AmbiguousAction* since the town of Montclair has multiple theaters. Although *AmbiguousAction* contributed to the system having both initiatives in the next turn, the effect of this cue, when combined with the initiative distribution of (3), resulted in MIMIC having dialogue but not task initiative in (4). However, in addition to triggering *AmbiguousAction*, utterance (5) also triggered *NoNewInfo*, since it did not contribute any new information. The effect of these two cues, combined with the initiative distribution in (5), was enough to lead MIMIC to take over task initiative in (6).

2.2 Modification of Adaptation Behavior

MIMIC employs an initiative module which is decoupled from its goal selection process, while allowing the outcome of both processes to guide its response strategy selection. A major advantage of this design is that changes in the system's strategy selection behavior, and thus its adaptation behavior, can be achieved by modifying parameters in the initiative module, while leaving the goal and strategy selection processes intact. The initiative module determines initiative distribution based on participant roles, cues observed in the current user utterance, and dialogue history. Although all three factors may play a role in modifying MIMIC's adaptation behavior, we discuss how the effects of participant roles and dialogue history are modified to create systems used as bases of comparison in our experiments.

Participant roles affect the default initiative distribu-

[2] In the dialogues collected in our experiments, which are described in Section 3, there are system turns in which MIMIC had neither task nor dialogue initiative. However, such cases are rare in this domain and will not be discussed in this paper.

		Utterance	Task Initiative	Dialogue Initiative
(14)	S:	Hello, this is MIMIC, the movie information system.	System	System
(15)		Please say the name of the movie or theater or town you would like information about.		
(16)	U:	Analyze This. *[analyze this]*		
(17)	S:	Choices for task are when and where.	System	System
(18)		What would you like to know about Analyze This?		
(19)	U:	When. *[when is]*		
(20)	S:	Choices for theater are Middlebrook Galeria, Loews East Hanover, Montgomery Cinemas, Atlantic Triplex Cinema, and others.	System	System
(21)		What theater would you like?		
(22)	U:	Montclair. *[montclair]*		
(23)	S:	Choices for theater are Wellmont Theater and Clearviews Screening Zone.	System	System
(24)		What theater would you like?		
(25)	U:	Wellmont. *[wellmont]*		
(26)	S:	Analyze This is playing at Wellmont Theater in Montclair at 3:15pm, 5:45pm, 8:20pm, and 10:10pm.	System	System
(27)		Please say the name of the movie or theater or town you would like information about.		
(28)	U:	Analyze This in Montclair. *[analyze this in montclair]*		
(29)	S:	Choices for task are location, what, where, and when.	System	System
(30)		What would you like to know about Montclair?		
(31)	U:	When.		
(32)		*[when]*		
(33)	S:	Choices for theater are Wellmont Theater and Clearviews Screening Zone	System	System
(34)		What theater would you like?		
(35)	U:	Clearviews Screening Zone. *[screening zone]*		
(36)	S:	Analyze This is playing at Clearviews Screening Zone in Montclair at 1:15pm, 4:10pm, and 6:30pm.	System	System
(37)		Please say the name of the movie or theater or town you would like information about.		

Figure 2: A System Initiative Dialogue with MIMIC-SI

tion for MIMIC's initial utterance. For naive users, it may be more appropriate for MIMIC to employ system-initiative strategies. This system, MIMIC-SI, can be achieved by setting the default initiative distribution to provide definite evidence for the system having both task and dialogue initiatives.[3] Figure 2 shows a dialogue in which a user interacts with MIMIC-SI to obtain the same information as in Figure 1. MIMIC-SI prompts the user for one piece of information at a time and provides (sometimes unnecessary) assistance, in the form of valid dialogue moves, during each turn.

Taking into account dialogue history allows MIMIC to determine the initiative distribution based on the cumulative effect of previously observed cues. This effect can be disabled so that only local dialogue context affects the initiative distribution for the next turn. Based on MIMIC's parameter settings, this adjustment results in MIMIC-MI, a system which always has dialogue initiative but never has task initiative. MIMIC-MI behaves similarly to many existing non-adaptive mixed initiative dialogue systems (e.g., (Bennacef et al., 1996; Papineni et al., 1999)). Figure 3 shows a dialogue involving MIMIC-MI in which the user again attempts to acquire the same information as in the previous two dialogues. Notice that (41)-(49) constitute a failed attempt to solicit a theater name from the user. Instead of providing helpful information as in (6) in Figure 1, MIMIC-MI relied on the user to change her problem-solving strategy in (50) to obtain the information needed to answer the system's question.

3 Experimental Design

Our main goal in evaluating MIMIC is to determine whether users find the mixed initiative and automatic adaptation aspects of its dialogue strategies useful. We compared MIMIC to two control systems: MIMIC-SI and MIMIC-MI, since they employ dialogue management strategies similar to those in many existing systems. The comparison between MIMIC and MIMIC-SI

[3]Based on the Dempster-Shafer theory, if the bpas of the default initiative distribution or those of a detected cue provide definite evidence for drawing a certain conclusion, then no subsequent cues have any effect on changing that conclusion.

		Utterance	Task Initiative	Dialogue Initiative
(38)	S:	Hello, this is MIMIC, the movie information system.	User	System
(39)		How can I help you?		
(40)	U:	When is Analyze This playing in Montclair? *[when analyze this playing in montclair]*		
(41)	S:	What theater would you like?	User	System
(42)	U:	 *[]*		
(43)	S:	What theater would you like?	User	System
(44)	U:	Um. *[um]*		
(45)	S:	What theater would you like?	User	System
(46)	U:	Montclair. *[montclair]*		
(47)	S:	What theater would you like?	User	System
(48)	U:	Any. *[any]*		
(49)	S:	What theater would you like?	User	System
(50)	U:	Where in Montclair is Analyze This playing? *[where in montclair is analyze this playing]*		
(51)	S:	Analyze This is playing at Wellmont Theater and Clearviews Screening Zone in Montclair.	User	System
(52)	U:	When is Analyze This playing at Wellmont Theater? *[when is analyze this playing at wellmont theater in]*		
(53)	S:	Analyze This is playing at Wellmont Theater in Montclair at 3:15pm, 5:45pm, 8:20pm, and 10:10pm.	User	System
(54)		Can I help you with anything else?		
(55)	U:	When is it playing at Clearviews Screening Zone? *[when is it playing at movie screening zone]*		
(56)	S:	Analyze This is playing at Clearviews Screening Zone in Montclair at 1:15pm, 4:10pm, and 6:30pm.	User	System
(57)		Can I help you with anything else?		

Figure 3: A Non-Adaptive Mixed Initiative Dialogue with MIMIC-MI

focused on the contribution of mixed-initiative dialogue management, while the comparison between MIMIC and MIMIC-MI emphasized the contribution of automatic strategy adaptation. The following three factors were controlled in our experiments:

1. **System version**: For each experiment, two systems were used: MIMIC and a control system. In the first experiment MIMIC was compared with MIMIC-SI, and in the second experiment, with MIMIC-MI.

2. **Order**: For each experiment, all subjects were randomly divided into two groups. One group performed tasks using MIMIC first, and the other group used the control system first.

3. **Task difficulty**: 3-4 tasks which highlighted differences between systems were used for each experiment. Based on the amount of information to be acquired, we divided the tasks into two groups: *easy* and *difficult*; an example of each is shown in Figure 4.

Town	Theater (if playing)	Movie	Times after 5:10pm (if playing)
Hoboken		Antz	

(a) Easy Task

Town	Theater (if playing)	Movie	Two Times (if playing)
Millburn		Analyze This	
Berkeley Hgts		Analyze This	
Mountainside		Analyze This	
Madison		True Crime	
Hoboken		True Crime	

(b) Difficult Task

Figure 4: Sample Tasks for Evaluation Experiments

Eight subjects[4] participated in each experiment. Each of the subjects interacted with both systems to perform

[4]The subjects were Bell Labs researchers, summer students, and their friends. Most of them are computer scientists, electrical engi-

all tasks. The subjects completed one task per call so that the dialogue history for one task did not affect the next task. Once they had completed all tasks in sequence using one system, they filled out a questionnaire to assess **user satisfaction** by rating 8-9 statements, similar to those in (Walker et al., 1997), on a scale of 1-5, where 5 indicated highest satisfaction. Approximately two days later, they attempted the same tasks using the other system.[5] These experiments resulted in 112 dialogues with approximately 2,800 dialogue turns.

In addition to user satisfaction ratings, we automatically logged, derived, and manually annotated a number of features (shown in boldface below). For each task/subject/system triplet, we computed the **task success rate** based on the percentage of slots correctly filled in on the task worksheet, and counted the **# of calls** needed to complete each task.[6] For each call, the user-side of the dialogue was recorded, and the **elapsed time** of the call was automatically computed. All user utterances were logged as recognized by our automatic speech recognizer (ASR) and manually transcribed from the recordings. We computed the **ASR word error rate**, **ASR rejection rate**, and **ASR timeout rate**, as well as **# of user turns** and **average sentence length** for each task/subject/system triplet. Additionally, we recorded the **cues** that the system automatically detected from each user utterance. All system utterances were also logged, along with the **initiative distribution** for each system turn and the **dialogue acts** selected to generate each system response.

Performance Feature	MIMIC	SI	p
# of user turns	*10.3*	*13.6*	*0.0075*
Elapsed time (sec.)	*229.5*	*277.5*	*0.0162*
ASR timeout (%)	*12.5*	*6.9*	*0.0239*
User satisfaction (n=8)	*21.9*	*19.8*	*0.0447*
ASR rejection (%)	5.4	8.1	0.1911
Task success (%)	100	98.8	0.3251
# of calls	1.0	1.1	0.572
ASR word error (%)	28.1	31.1	0.8475

(a) MIMIC vs. MIMIC-SI (n=32)

Performance Feature	MIMIC	MI	p
ASR timeout (%)	*5.7*	*15.6*	*0.001*
# of user turns	*10.3*	*14.3*	*0.0199*
User satisfaction (n=8)	*29.5*	*24.4*	*0.0364*
Elapsed time (sec.)	*200.6*	*246.4*	*0.0457*
ASR word error (%)	23.0	30.6	0.0588
Task success (%)	100	98.4	0.1639
# of calls	1.21	1.21	0.5
ASR rejection (%)	8.4	7.7	0.8271

(b) MIMIC vs. MIMIC-MI (n=24)

Table 1: Comparison of Performance Features

4 Results and Discussion

Based on the features described above, we compared MIMIC and the control systems, MIMIC-SI and MIMIC-MI, along three dimensions: *performance features*, in which comparisons were made using previously proposed features relevant to system performance (e.g., (Price et al., 1992; Simpson and Fraser, 1993; Danieli and Gerbino, 1995; Walker et al., 1997)); *discourse features*, in which comparisons were made using characteristics of the resulting dialogues; and *initiative distribution*, where initiative characteristics of all dialogues involving MIMIC from both experiments were examined.

4.1 Performance Features

For our performance evaluation, we first applied a three-way analysis of variance (ANOVA) (Cohen, 1995) to each feature using three factors: system version, order, and task difficulty.[7] If no interaction effects emerged, we compared system versions using paired sample t-tests.[8]

Following the PARADISE evaluation scheme (Walker et al., 1997), we divided performance features into four groups:

- Task success: task success rate, # of calls.
- Dialogue quality: ASR rejection rate, ASR timeout rate, ASR word error rate.
- Dialogue efficiency: # of user turns, elapsed time.
- System usability: user satisfaction.

For both experiments, the ANOVAs showed no interaction effects among the controlled factors. Tables 1(a) and 1(b) summarize the results of the paired sample t-tests based on performance features, where features that differed significantly between systems are shown in italics.[9] These results show that, when compared with either

neers, or linguists, and none had prior knowledge of MIMIC.

[5]We used the exact same set of tasks rather than designing tasks of similar difficulty levels because we intended to compare all available features between the two system versions, including ASR word error rate, which would have been affected by the choice of movie/theater names in the tasks.

[6]Although the vast majority of tasks were completed in one call, some subjects, when unable to make progress, did not change strategies as in (41)-(49) in Figure 3; instead, they hung up and started the task over.

[7]User satisfaction was a per subject as opposed to a per task performance feature; thus, we performed a two-way ANOVA using the factors system version and order.

[8]This paper focuses on evaluating the effect of MIMIC's mixed initiative and automatic adaptation capabilities. We assess these effects based on comparisons between system version when no interaction effects emerged from the ANOVA tests using the factors system version, order, and task difficulty. Effects based on system order and task difficulty alone are beyond the scope of this paper.

[9]Typically $p<0.05$ is considered statistically significant (Cohen, 1995).

control system, users were more satisfied with MIMIC[10] and that MIMIC helped users complete tasks more efficiently. Users were able to complete tasks in fewer turns and in a more timely manner using MIMIC.

When comparing MIMIC and MIMIC-MI, dialogues involving MIMIC had a lower timeout rate. When MIMIC detected cues signaling anomalies in the dialogue, it adapted strategies to provide assistance, which in addition to leading to fewer timeouts, saved users time and effort when they did not know what to say. In contrast, users interacting with MIMIC-MI had to iteratively reformulate questions until they obtained the desired information from the system, leading to more timeouts (see (41)-(49) in Figure 3). However, when comparing MIMIC and MIMIC-SI, even though users accomplished tasks more efficiently with MIMIC, the resulting dialogues contained more timeouts. As opposed to MIMIC-SI, which always prompted users for one piece of information at a time, MIMIC typically provided more open-ended prompts when the user had task initiative. Even though this required more effort on the user's part in formulating utterances and led to more timeouts, MIMIC quickly adapted strategies to assist users when recognized cues indicated that they were having trouble.

To sum up, our experiments show that both MIMIC's mixed initiative and automatic adaptation aspects resulted in better performance along the *dialogue efficiency* and *system usability* dimensions. Moreover, its adaptation capabilities contributed to better performance in terms of *dialogue quality*. MIMIC, however, did not contribute to higher performance in the *task success* dimension. In our movie information domain, the tasks were sufficiently simple; thus, all but one user in each experiment achieved a 100% task success rate.

4.2 Discourse Features

Our second evaluation dimension concerns characteristics of resulting dialogues. We analyzed features of user utterances in terms of utterance length and cues observed and features of system utterances in terms of dialogue acts. For each feature, we again applied a three-way ANOVA test, and if no interaction effects emerged, we performed a paired sample t-test to compare system versions.

The cues detected in user utterances provide insight into both user intentions and system capabilities. The cues that MIMIC automatically detects are a subset of those discussed in (Chu-Carroll and Brown, 1998):[11]

- *TakeOverTask*: triggered when the user provides more information than expected; an implicit indication that the user wants to take control of the problem-solving process.
- *NoNewInfo*: triggered when the user is unable to make progress toward task completion, either when the user does not know what to say or the ASR engine fails to recognize the user's utterance.
- *InvalidAction/InvalidActionResolved*: triggered when the user utterance makes an invalid assumption about the domain and when the invalid assumption is corrected, respectively.
- *AmbiguousAction/AmbiguousActionResolved*: triggered when the user query is ambiguous and when the ambiguity is resolved, respectively.

Discourse Feature	MIMIC	SI	p
Cue: TakeOverTask	*1.84*	*5*	*0*
Cue: AmbiguousActResolved	*1.69*	*4.59*	*0*
Cue: AmbiguousAction	*3*	*6.59*	*0.0008*
Avg sentence length (words)	*6.82*	*5.45*	*0.0016*
Cue: InvalidAction	1.16	0.94	0.1738
Cue: NoNewInfo	1.28	1.38	0.766

(a) MIMIC vs. MIMIC-SI (n=32)

Discourse Feature	MIMIC	MI	p
Cue: TakeOverTask	*2.33*	*0*	*0*
Cue: InvalidAction	*2.04*	*3.75*	*0.0011*
Cue: NoNewInfo	*2.25*	*4.79*	*0.0161*
Cue: AmbiguousActResolved	*2.08*	*1.13*	*0.0297*
Avg sentence length (words)	5.26	5.63	0.1771
Cue: AmbiguousAction	4.13	4.38	0.8767

(b) MIMIC vs. MIMIC-MI (n=24)

Table 2: Comparison of User Utterance Features

Tables 2(a) and (b) summarize the results of the paired sample t-tests based on user utterance features where features whose numbers of occurrences were significantly different according to system version used are shown in italics.[12] Table 2(a) shows that users expected the system to adapt its strategies when they attempted to take control of the dialogue. Even though MIMIC-SI did not behave as expected, the users continued their attempts, resulting in significantly more occurrences of *TakeOverTask* in dialogues with MIMIC-SI than with MIMIC. Furthermore, the average sentence length in dialogues with MIMIC was only 1.5 words per turn longer than in dialogues with MIMIC-SI, providing further evidence that users

[10]The range of user satisfaction scores was 8-40 for experiment one and 9-45 for experiment two.

[11]A subset of these cues corresponds loosely to previously proposed evaluation metrics (e.g., (Danieli and Gerbino, 1995)). However, our system automatically detects these features instead of requiring manual annotation by experts.

[12]Since system dialogue acts are often selected based on cues detected in user utterances, we only discuss results of our user utterance feature analysis, using dialogue act analysis results as additional support for our conclusions.

preferred to provide free-formed queries, regardless of system version used.

Table 2(b) shows that MIMIC was more effective at resolving dialogue anomalies than MIMIC-MI. More specifically, there were significantly fewer occurrences of *NoNewInfo* in dialogues with MIMIC than with MIMIC-MI. In addition, while the number of occurrences of *AmbiguousAction* was not significantly different for the two systems, the number that were resolved (*AmbiguousActionResolved*) was significantly higher in interactions with MIMIC than with MIMIC-MI. Since *NoNewInfo* and *AmbiguousAction* both prompted MIMIC to adapt strategies and, as a result, provide additional useful information, the user was able to quickly resolve the problem at hand. This is further supported by the higher frequency of the system dialogue act *GiveOptions* in MIMIC (p=0), which provides helpful information based on dialogue context.

In sum, the results of our discourse feature analysis further confirm the usefulness of MIMIC's adaptation capabilities. Comparisons with MIMIC-SI provide evidence that MIMIC's ability to give up initiative better matched user expectations. Moreover, comparisons with MIMIC-MI show that MIMIC's ability to opportunistically take over initiative resulted in dialogues in which anomalies were more efficiently resolved and progress toward task completion was more consistently made.

4.3 Initiative Analysis

Our final analysis concerns the task initiative distribution in our adaptive system in relation to the features previously discussed. For each dialogue involving MIMIC, we computed the percentage of turns in which MIMIC had task initiative and the *correlation coefficient (r)* between the initiative percentage and each performance/discourse feature. To determine if this correlation was significant, we performed *Fisher's r to z transform*, upon which a conventional Z test was performed (Cohen, 1995).

Tables 3(a) and (b) summarize the correlation between the performance and discourse features and the percentage of turns in which MIMIC has task initiative, respectively.[13] Again, those correlations which are statistically significant are shown in italics. Table 3(a) shows a strong positive correlation between task initiative distribution and the number of user turns as well as the elapsed time of the dialogues. Although earlier results (Table 1(a)) show that dialogues in which the system always had task initiative tended to be longer, we believe that this correlation also suggests that MIMIC took over task initiative more often in longer dialogues, those in which the user was more likely to be having difficulty. Table 3(a) further shows moderate correlation between task initiative distribution and ASR rejection rate as well as ASR word error rate. It is possible that such a correlation exists

[13]This test was not performed for user satisfaction, since user satisfaction was a per subject and not a per dialogue feature.

Performance Feature	r	p
# of user turns	*0.71*	*0*
ASR rejection	*0.55*	*0*
Elapsed time	*0.51*	*0.00002*
ASR word error	*0.46*	*0.00012*
# of calls	0.15	0.1352
ASR timeout	-0.003	0.4911
Task success rate	0	0.5

(a) Performance Features

Discourse Feature	r	p
Cue: AmbiguousActionResolved	*0.61*	*0*
Cue: NoNewInfo	*0.59*	*0*
Cue: TakeOverTask	*0.44*	*0.00028*
Cue: InvalidAction	*0.42*	*0.00057*
Average sentence length	*-0.40*	*0.00099*
Cue: AmbiguousAction	*0.38*	*0.00169*

(b) Discourse Features

Table 3: Correlation Between Task Initiative Distribution and Features (n=56)

because ASR performance worsens when MIMIC takes over task initiative. However, in that case, we would have expected the results in Section 4.1 to show that the ASR rejection and word error rates for MIMIC-SI are significantly greater than those for MIMIC, which are in turn significantly greater than those for MIMIC-MI, since in MIMIC-SI the system always had task initiative and in MIMIC-MI the system never took over task initiative. To the contrary, Tables 1(a) and 1(b) showed that the differences in ASR rejection rate and ASR word error rate were not significant between system versions, and Table 1(b) showed that ASR word error rate for MIMIC-MI was in fact quite substantially higher than that for MIMIC. This suggests that the causal relationship is the other way around, i.e., MIMIC's adaptation capabilities allowed it to opportunistically take over task initiative when ASR performance was poor.

Table 3(b) shows that all cues are positively correlated with task initiative distribution. For *AmbiguousAction*, *InvalidAction*, and *NoNewInfo*, this correlation exists because observation of these cues contributed to MIMIC having task initiative. However, note that *AmbiguousActionResolved* has a stronger positive correlation with task initiative distribution than does *AmbiguousAction*, again indicating that MIMIC's adaptive strategies contributed to more efficient resolution of ambiguous actions.

In brief, our initiative analysis lends additional support to the conclusions drawn in our performance and discourse feature analyses and provides new evidence for the advantages of MIMIC's adaptation capabilities.

In addition to taking over task initiative when previously identified dialogue anomalies were encountered (e.g., detection of ambiguous or invalid actions), our analysis shows that MIMIC took over task initiative when ASR performance was poor, allowing the system to better constrain user utterances.[14]

5 Conclusions

This paper described an empirical evaluation of MIMIC, an adaptive mixed initiative spoken dialogue system. We conducted two experiments that focused on evaluating the mixed initiative and automatic adaptation aspects of MIMIC and analyzed the results along three dimensions: performance features, discourse features, and initiative distribution. Our results showed that both the mixed initiative and automatic adaptation aspects of the system led to better performance in terms of user satisfaction and dialogue efficiency. In addition, we found that MIMIC's adaptation behavior better matched user expectations, more efficiently resolved anomalies in dialogues, and led to higher overall dialogue quality.

Acknowledgments

We would like to thank Bob Carpenter and Christine Nakatani for their help on experimental design, Jan van Santen for discussion on statistical analysis, and Bob Carpenter for his comments on an earlier draft of this paper. Support for the second author is provided by an NSF graduate fellowship and a Lucent Technologies GRPW grant.

References

James F. Allen, Bradford W. Miller, Eric K. Ringger, and Teresa Sikorski. 1996. A robust system for natural spoken dialogue. In *Proceedings of the 34th Annual Meeting of the Association for Computational Linguistics*, pages 62–70.

S. Bennacef, L. Devillers, S. Rosset, and L. Lamel. 1996. Dialog in the RAILTEL telephone-based system. In *Proceedings of the 4th International Conference on Spoken Language Processing*.

Jennifer Chu-Carroll and Michael K. Brown. 1998. An evidential model for tracking initiative in collaborative dialogue interactions. *User Modeling and User-Adapted Interaction*, 8(3-4):215–253.

Jennifer Chu-Carroll. 2000. MIMIC: An adaptive mixed initiative spoken dialogue system for information queries. In *Proceedings of the 6th ACL Conference on Applied Natural Language Processing*. To appear.

Paul R. Cohen. 1995. *Empirical Methods for Artificial Intelligence*. MIT Press.

Morena Danieli and Elisabetta Gerbino. 1995. Metrics for evaluating dialogue strategies in a spoken language system. In *Proceedings of the AAAI Spring Symposium on Empirical Methods in Discourse Interpretation and Generation*, pages 34–39.

Jean Gordon and Edward H. Shortliffe. 1984. The Dempster-Shafer theory of evidence. In Bruce Buchanan and Edward Shortliffe, editors, *Rule-Based Expert Systems: The MYCIN Experiments of the Stanford Heuristic Programming Project*, chapter 13, pages 272–292. Addison-Wesley.

Diane J. Litman and Shimei Pan. 1999. Empirically evaluating an adaptable spoken dialogue system. In *Proceedings of the 7th International Conference on User Modeling*, pages 55–64.

H. Meng, S. Busayaponchai, J. Glass, D. Goddeau, L. Hetherington, E. Hurley, C. Pao, J. Polifroni, S. Seneff, and V. Zue. 1996. WHEELS: A conversational system in the automobile classifieds domain. In *Proceedings of the International Conference on Spoken Language Processing*, pages 542–545.

Stefan Ortmanns, Wolfgang Reichl, and Wu Chou. 1999. An efficient decoding method for real time speech recognition. In *Proceedings of the 5th European Conference on Speech Communication and Technology*.

K.A. Papineni, S. Roukos, and R.T. Ward. 1999. Free-flow dialog management using forms. In *Proceedings of the 6th European Conference on Speech Communication and Technology*, pages 1411–1414.

Patti Price, Lynette Hirschman, Elizabeth Shriberg, and Elizabeth Wade. 1992. Subject-based evaluation measures for interactive spoken language systems. In *Proceedings of the DARPA Speech and Natural Language Workshop*, pages 34–39.

Wolfgang Reichl and Wu Chou. 1998. Decision tree state tying based on segmental clustering for acoustic modeling. In *Proceedings of the International Conference on Acoustics, Speech, and Signal Processing*.

M.D. Sadek, A. Ferrieux, A. Cozannet, P. Bretier, F. Panaget, and J. Simonin. 1996. Effective human-computer cooperative spoken dialogue: The AGS demonstrator. In *Proceedings of the International Conference on Spoken Language Processing*.

Glenn Shafer. 1976. *A Mathematical Theory of Evidence*. Princeton University Press.

Andrew Simpson and Norman M. Fraser. 1993. Black box and glass box evaluation of the SUNDIAL system. In *Proceedings of the 3rd European Conference on Speech Communication and Technology*, pages 1423–1426.

Gert Veldhuijzen van Zanten. 1999. User modelling in adaptive dialogue management. In *Proceedings of the 6th European Conference on Speech Communication and Technology*, pages 1183–1186.

Marilyn A. Walker, Diane J. Litman, Candance A. Kamm, and Alicia Abella. 1997. PARADISE: A framework for evaluating spoken dialogue agents. In *Proceedings of the 35th Annual Meeting of the Association for Computational Linguistics*, pages 271–280.

[14]Although not currently utilized, the ability to adapt dialogue strategies when ASR performance is poor enables the system to employ dialogue strategy specific language models for ASR.

Learning to Predict Problematic Situations in a Spoken Dialogue System: Experiments with How May I Help You?

Marilyn Walker, Irene Langkilde, Jerry Wright, Allen Gorin, Diane Litman
AT&T Labs—Research
180 Park Avenue
Florham Park, NJ 07932-0971 USA
walker,jwright,algor,diane@research.att.com, ilangkil@isi.edu

Abstract

Current spoken dialogue systems are deficient in their strategies for preventing, identifying and repairing problems that arise in the conversation. This paper reports results on learning to automatically identify and predict problematic human-computer dialogues in a corpus of 4774 dialogues collected with the *How May I Help You* spoken dialogue system. Our expectation is that the ability to predict problematic dialogues will allow the system's dialogue manager to modify its behavior to repair problems, and even perhaps, to prevent them. We train a problematic dialogue classifier using automatically-obtainable features that can identify problematic dialogues significantly better (23%) than the baseline. A classifier trained with only automatic features from the first exchange in the dialogue can predict problematic dialogues 7% more accurately than the baseline, and one trained with automatic features from the first two exchanges can perform 14% better than the baseline.

1 Introduction

Spoken dialogue systems promise efficient and natural access to a large variety of information sources and services from any phone. Systems that support short utterances to select a particular function (through a statement such as "Say credit card, collect or person-to-person") are saving companies millions of dollars. Research prototypes exist for applications such as personal email and calendars, travel and restaurant information, and personal banking (Baggia et al., 1998; Walker et al., 1998; Seneff et al., 1995; Sanderman et al., 1998; Chu-Carroll and Carpenter, 1999) *inter alia*. Yet there are still many research challenges: current systems are limited in the interaction they support and brittle in many respects. We show how spoken dialogue systems can *learn* to support more natural interaction on the basis of their previous experience.

One way that current spoken dialogue systems are quite limited is in their strategies for detecting and repairing problems that arise in conversation. If a problem can be detected, the system can either transfer the call to a human operator or modify its dialogue strategy in an attempt to repair the problem. We can train systems to improve their ability to detect problems by exploiting dialogues collected in interactions with human users. The initial segments of these dialogues can be used to *predict* that a problem is likely to occur. We expect that the ability to predict that a dialogue is likely to be problematic will allow the system's dialogue manager to apply more sophisticated strategies to repairing problems, and even perhaps, to prevent them.

This paper reports experiments on predicting problems in spoken dialogue interaction by training a problematic dialogue predictor on a corpus of 4774 dialogues collected in an experimental trial of AT&T's *How May I Help You* (HMIHY) spoken dialogue system (Gorin et al., 1997; Riccardi and Gorin, to appear; E. Ammicht and Alonso, 1999). In this trial, the HMIHY system was installed at an AT&T customer care center. HMIHY answered calls from live customer traffic and successfully automated a large number of customer requests. An example of a dialogue that HMIHY completed successfully is shown in Figure 1.[1]

S1: AT&T How may I help you?
U1: I need to [uh] put a call on my calling card please
S2: May I have your card number, please?
U2: 7 6 5 4 3 2 1 0 9 8 7 6 5 4
S3: What number would you like to call?
U3: 8 1 4 7 7 7 6 6 6 6 (*misrecognized*)
S4: May I have that number again?
U4: 8 1 4 7 7 7 6 6 6 6
S5: Thank you.

Figure 1: Sample TASKSUCCESS Dialogue

We shall refer to the dialogues with a TASKSUCCESS outcome, in which HMIHY successfully automates the customer's call, as the TASKSUCCESS dialogues. In addition to the TASKSUCCESS dialogues, there are several other call outcomes, to be described in detail below, which we consider problematic.

[1] The phone numbers, card numbers, and pin numbers in the sample dialogues are artificial.

This paper reports results from a set of experiments that test whether we can learn to automatically predict that a dialogue will be problematic on the basis of information the system has: (1) early on in the dialogue; and (2) in real time. We train an automatic classifer for predicting problematic dialogues from features that can be automatically extracted from the HMIHY corpus. The results show that we can learn to predict problematic dialogues using fully automatic features with an accuracy ranging from 72% to 87%, depending on how much of the dialogue the system has seen so far. Section 2 describes HMIHY and the dialogue corpus which the experiments are based on. Section 3 details the encoding of the dialogues and the methods used for utilizing the machine learning program RIPPER to train an automatic problematic dialogue predictor (Cohen, 1996). Section 4 presents the results and section 5 summarizes the paper and describes future work.

2 Experimental System and Data

HMIHY is a spoken dialogue system based on the notion of *call routing* (Gorin et al., 1997; Chu-Carroll and Carpenter, 1999). In the HMIHY call routing system, services that the user can access are classified into 14 categories, plus a category called *other* for calls that cannot be automated and must be transferred to a human operator (Gorin et al., 1997).[2] Each category describes a different task, such as person-to-person dialing, or receiving credit for a misdialed number. The system determines which task the caller is requesting on the basis of its understanding of the caller's response to the open-ended system greeting *AT&T, How May I Help You?*. Once the task has been determined, the information needed for completing the caller's request is obtained using dialogue submodules that are specific for each task (Abella and Gorin, 1999).

In addition to the TASKSUCCESS dialogues in which HMIHY successfully automates the customer's call, illustrated in Figure 1, and the calls that are transferred to a human operator, there are three other possible outcomes for a call, all of which are problematic. The first category, which we call HANGUP, results from a customer's decision to hang up on the system. A sample HANGUP dialogue is in Figure 2. A caller may hang up because s/he is frustrated with the system; our goal is to learn from the corpus which system behaviors led to the caller's frustration.

The second problematic category (WIZARD), results from a human customer care agent's decision to take over the call from the system. Because HMIHY is experimental, each call was monitored by a human

[2] One potential use of our results is to provide better rules for making the transfer decision.

S1: AT&T How may I help you?
U1: I need credit please.
S2: Okay. What is the reason for the credit?
U2: Miss, uh, Miss, different area code than I needed.
S3: Sorry. I need to know whether you need credit for a wrong number, bad connection or a call that was cut off.
U3: It is a wrong number. (*impatient humming*)
S4: What was the number that you dialed?
USER HANGS UP

Figure 2: Sample HANGUP Dialogue

agent serving as a wizard who could override the system. There were a number of agents who participated as wizards during the trial of HMIHY and each wizard was simply told to take over the call if s/he perceived problems with the system's performance. The wizard's decision was logged by the experimental setup, resulting in labelling the call as one that the wizard took over.[3] A dialogue where the wizard decided that the dialogue was problematic and took over the call is shown in Figure 3.

S1: AT&T How may I help you?
U1: (*silence*)
S2: Sorry. Please briefly tell me how I may help you?
U2: I'm trying to call 1 8 hundred call A T T.
S3: Do you want to place a call?
U3: Through my calling card.
S4: May I have your card number, please?
U4: It's 8 7 6 5 4 3 2 1 0 and then my pin number is 8 7 6 5. (*misrecognized*)
S5: Sorry. Please enter or say your card number again.
WIZARD STEPS IN

Figure 3: Sample WIZARD Dialogue

The third problematic category, the TASKFAILURE dialogues, are cases where the system completed the call, but carried out a task that was not the task that the customer was actually requesting. An example TASKFAILURE dialogue is given in Figure 4: HMIHY interpreted utterance U2 as a request to make a third-party call e.g. to *bill it to my home phone*. HMIHY then asked the caller for the information it needed to carry out this task, the caller complied, and the system completed the call.

The corpus of 4774 dialogues used in our experiments was collected in several experimental trials of HMIHY on live customer traffic (Riccardi and Gorin, to appear; E. Ammicht and Alonso, 1999), and is referred to as HM2 in (Riccardi and Gorin, to appear)). During the trial, all of the system behaviors were automatically recorded in a log file, and later the dialogues were transcribed by humans and labelled with a semantic category representing the

[3] Of course we can only infer what might have motivated the wizard to take over the call, but we assume that the wizard had good reason for doing so.

S1: AT&T How may I help you?
U1: (*silence*)
S2: Sorry. Please briefly tell me how I may help you?
U2: I wanta find out how much my bill's worth.
S3: What phone number would you like the call billed to?
U3: *Um* the access number.
S4: Sorry. Could I have that phone number again?
U4: 1 8 hundred 2 2 5 5 2 8 8.
S5: What number would you like to call?
U5: 800 225 5288 (*touchtone input*)
S6: Thank you.

Figure 4: Sample TASKFAILURE Dialogue

task that the caller was asking HMIHY to perform, on a per utterance basis. The logfiles also included labels indicating whether the wizard had taken over the call or the user had hung up.

3 Training an Automatic Problematic Dialogue Predictor

Our experiments apply the machine learning program RIPPER (Cohen, 1996) to automatically induce a "problematic dialogue" classification model. RIPPER takes as input the names of a set of *classes* to be learned, the names and ranges of values of a fixed set of *features*, and *training data* specifying the class and feature values for each example in a training set. Its output is a *classification model* for predicting the class of future examples. In RIPPER, the classification model is learned using greedy search guided by an information gain metric, and is expressed as an ordered set of if-then rules.

To apply RIPPER, the dialogues in the corpus must be encoded in terms of a set of classes (the output classification) and a set of input features that are used as predictors for the classes. We start with the dialogue categories described above, but since our goal is to develop algorithms that predict/identify problematic dialogues, we treat HANGUP, WIZARD and TASKFAILURE as equivalently problematic. Thus we train the classifier to distinguish between two classes: TASKSUCCESS and PROBLEMATIC. Note that our categorization is inherently noisy because we do not know the real reasons why a caller hangs up or a wizard takes over the call. The caller may hang up because she is frustrated with the system, or she may simply dislike automation, or her child may have started crying. Similarly, one wizard may have low confidence in the system's ability to recover from errors and use a conservative approach that results in taking over many calls, while another wizard may be more willing to let the system try to recover. Nevertheless we take these human actions as a human labelling of these calls as problematic. Given this classification, approximately 36% of the calls in the corpus of 4774 dialogues are PROBLEMATIC and 64% are TASKSUCCESS.

Next, we encoded each dialogue in terms of a set of 196 features that were either automatically logged by one of the system modules, hand-labelled by humans, or derived from raw features. We use the hand-labelled features to produce a TOPLINE, an estimation of how well a classifier could do that had access to perfect information. The entire feature set is summarized in Figure 5.

- **Acoustic/ASR Features**
  - recog, recog-numwords, ASR-duration, dtmf-flag, rg-modality, rg-grammar
- **NLU Features**
  - a confidence measure for all of the possible tasks that the user could be trying to do
  - salience-coverage, inconsistency, context-shift, top-task, nexttop-task, top-confidence, diff-confidence
- **Dialogue Manager Features**
  - sys-label, utt-id, prompt, reprompt, confirmation, subdial
  - running tallies: num-reprompts, num-confirms, num-subdials, reprompt%, confirmation%, subdialogue%
- **Hand-Labelled Features**
  - tscript, human-label, age, gender, user-modality, clean-tscript, cltscript-numwords, rsuccess
- **Whole-Dialogue Features**
  - num-utts, num-reprompts, percent-reprompts, num-confirms, percent-confirms, num-subdials, percent-subdials, dial-duration.

Figure 5: Features for spoken dialogues.

There are 8 features that describe the whole dialogue, and 47 features for each of the first four exchanges. We encode features for the first four exchanges because we want to *predict* failures before they happen. Since 97% of the dialogues in our corpus are five exchanges or less, in most cases, any potential problematic outcome will have occurred by the time the system has participated in five exchanges. Because the system needs to be able to *predict* whether the dialogue will be problematic using information it has available in the initial part of the dialogue, we train classifiers that only have access to input features from exchange 1, or only the features from exchange 1 and exchange 2. To see whether our results generalize, we also experiment with a subset of features that are task-independent. We compare results for *predicting* problematic dialogues, with results for *identifying* problematic dialogues, when the classifier has access to features representing the whole dialogue.

We utilized features logged by the system because they are produced automatically, and thus could be used during runtime to alter the course of the dialogue. The system modules that we collected information from were the acoustic processer/automatic speech recognizer (ASR) (Riccardi and Gorin, to appear), the natural language understanding (NLU) module (Gorin et al., 1997), and the dialogue manager (DM) (Abella and Gorin, 1999). Below we describe each module and the features obtained from it.

ASR takes as input the acoustic signal and outputs a potentially errorful transcription of what it believes the caller said. The ASR features for each of the first four exchanges were the output of the speech recognizer (*recog*), the number of words in the recognizer output (*recog-numwords*), the duration in seconds of the input to the recognizer (*asr-duration*), a flag for touchtone input (*dtmf-flag*), the input modality expected by the recognizer (*rg-modality*) (one of: none, speech, touchtone, speech+touchtone, touchtone-card, speech+touchtone-card, touchtone-date, speech+touchtone-date, or none-final-prompt), and the grammar used by the recognizer (*rg-grammar*).

The motivation for the ASR features is that any one of them may have impacted performance. For example, it is well known that longer utterances are less likely to be recognized correctly, thus *asr-duration* could be a clue to incorrect recognition results. In addition, the larger the grammar is, the more likely an ASR error is, so the name of the grammar *rg-grammar* could be a predictor of incorrect recognition.

The natural language understanding (NLU) module takes as input a transcription of the user's utterance from ASR and produces 15 confidence scores representing the likelihood that the caller's task is one of the 15 task types. It also extracts other relevant information, such as phone or credit card numbers. Thus 15 of the NLU features for each exchange represent the 15 confidence scores. There are also features that the NLU module calculates based on processing the utterance. These include an intra-utterance measure of the inconsistency between tasks that the user appears to be requesting (*inconsistency*), a measure of the coverage of the utterance by salient grammar fragments (*salience-coverage*), a measure of the shift in context between utterances (*context-shift*), the task with the highest confidence score (*top-task*), the task with the second highest confidence score (*nexttop-task*), the value of the highest confidence score (*top-confidence*), and the difference in values between the top and next-to-top confidence scores (*diff-confidence*).

The motivation for these NLU features is to make use of information that the NLU module has based on processing the output of ASR and the current discourse context. For example, for utterances that follow the first utterance, the NLU module knows what task it believes the caller is trying to complete. If it appears that the caller has changed her mind, then the NLU module may have misunderstood a previous utterance. The *context-shift* feature indicates the NLU module's belief that it may have made an error (or be making one now).

The dialogue manager (DM) takes the output of NLU and the dialogue history and decides what it should say to the caller next. It decides whether it believes there is a single unambiguous task that the user is trying to accomplish, and how to resolve any ambiguity. The DM features for each of the first four exchanges are the task-type label which includes a label that indicates task ambiguity (*sys-label*), utterance id within the dialogue (implicit in the encoding), the name of the prompt played before the user utterance (*prompt*), and whether that prompt was a reprompt (*reprompt*), a confirmation (*confirm*), or a subdialogue prompt (*subdial*), a superset of the reprompts and confirmation prompts.

The DM features are primarily motivated by previous work. The task-type label feature is to capture the fact that some tasks may be harder than others. The utterance id feature is motivated by the idea that the length of the dialogue may be important, possibly in combination with other features like task-type. The different prompt features for initial prompts, reprompts, confirmation prompts and subdialogue prompts are motivated by results indicating that reprompts and confirmation prompts are frustrating for callers and that callers are likely to hyperarticulate when they have to repeat themselves, which results in ASR errors (Shriberg et al., 1992; Levow, 1998).

The DM features also include running tallies for the number of reprompts (*num-reprompts*), number of confirmation prompts (*num-confirms*), and number of subdialogue prompts (*num-subdials*), that had been played up to each point in the dialogue, as well as running percentages (*percent-reprompts, percent-confirms, percent-subdials*). The use of running tallies and percentages is based on the assumption that these features are likely to produce generalized predictors (Litman et al., 1999).

The features obtained via hand-labelling were human transcripts of each user utterance (*tscript*), a set of semantic labels that are closely related to the system task-type labels (*human-label*), age (*age*) and gender (*gender*) of the user, the actual modality of the user utterance (*user-modality*) (one of: nothing, speech, touchtone, speech+touchtone, non-speech), and a cleaned transcript with non-word noise information removed (*clean-tscript*). From these features we calculated two derived features. The first was the number of words in the cleaned transcript (*cltscript numwords*), again on the assumption that utterance length is strongly correlated with ASR and NLU errors. The second derived feature was based on calculating whether the *human-label* matches the *sys-label* from the dialogue manager (*rsuccess*). There were four values for *rsuccess*: rcorrect, rmismatch, rpartial-match and rvacuous-match, indicating respectively correct understanding, incorrect understanding, partial understanding, and the fact that there had been no input for ASR and NLU to operate on, either because the user didn't say anything or because she used touch-tone.

The whole-dialogue features derived from the per-utterance features were: *num-utts*, *num-reprompts*, *percent-reprompts*, *num-confirms*, *percent-confirms*, *num-subdials*, and *per-cent-subdials* for the whole dialogue, and the duration of the entire dialogue in seconds (*dial-duration*).

In the experiments, the features in Figure 5 except the Hand-Labelled features are referred to as the AUTOMATIC feature set. We examine how well we can identify or predict problematic dialogues using these features, compared to the full feature set including the Hand-Labelled features. As mentioned earlier, we wish to generalize our problematic dialogue predictor to other systems. Thus we also discuss how well we can predict problematic dialogues using only features that are both automatically acquirable during runtime and independent of the HMIHY task. The subset of features from Figure 5 that fit this qualification are in Figure 6. We refer to them as the AUTO, TASK-INDEP feature set.

The output of each RIPPER experiment is a classification model learned from the training data. To evaluate these results, the error rates of the learned classification models are estimated using the resampling method of *cross-validation*. In 5-fold cross-validation, the total set of examples is randomly divided into 5 disjoint test sets, and 5 runs of the learning program are performed. Thus, each run uses the examples not in the test set for training and the remaining examples for testing. An estimated error rate is obtained by averaging the error rate on the testing portion of the data from each of the 5 runs.

Since we intend to integrate the rules learned by RIPPER into the HMIHY system, we examine the precision and recall performance of specific hypotheses. Because hypotheses from different cross-validation experiments cannot readily be combined together, we apply the hypothesis learned on one randomly selected training set (80% of the data) to that set's respective test data. Thus the precision and recall results reported below are somewhat less reliable than the error rates from cross-validation.

- **Acoustic/ASR Features**
  - recog, recog-numwords, ASR-duration, dtmf-flag, rg-modality
- **NLU Features**
  - salience-coverage, inconsistency, context-shift, top-confidence, diff-confidence
- **Dialogue Manager Features**
  - utt-id, reprompt, confirmation, subdial
  - running tallies: num-reprompts, num-confirms, num-subdials, reprompt%, confirmation%, subdialogue%

Figure 6: Automatic task independent (AUTO, TASK-INDEP) features available at runtime.

4 Results

We present results for both predicting and identifying problematic dialogues. Because we are interested in predicting that a dialogue will be problematic at a point in the dialogue where the system can do something about it, we compare prediction accuracy after having only seen the first exchange of the dialogue with prediction accuracy after having seen the first two exchanges, with identification accuracy after having seen the whole dialogue. For each of these situations we also compare results for the AUTOMATIC and AUTO, TASK-INDEP feature sets (as described earlier), with results for the whole feature set including hand-labelled features. Table 1 summarizes the results.

The baseline on the first line of Table 1 represents the prediction accuracy from always guessing the majority class. Since 64% of the dialogues are TASKSUCCESS dialogues, we can achieve 64% accuracy from simply guessing TASKSUCCESS without having seen any of the dialogue yet.

The first EXCHANGE 1 row shows the results of using the AUTOMATIC features from only the *first* exchange to predict whether the dialogue outcome will be TASKSUCCESS or PROBLEMATIC. The results show that the machine-learned classifier can predict problematic dialogues 8% better than the baseline after having seen only the first user utterance. Using only task-independent automatic features (Figure 6) the EXCHANGE 1 classifier can still do nearly as well. The ALL row for EXCHANGE 1 indicates that even if we had access to human perceptual ability (the hand-labelled features) we would still only be able to distinguish between TASKSUCCESS and PROBLEMATIC dialogues with 77% accuracy after having seen the first exchange.

Features Used		Accuracy	(SE)
BASELINE (majority class)		64.0 %	
EXCHANGE 1	AUTOMATIC	72.3 %	1.04 %
	AUTO, TASK-INDEP	71.6 %	1.05 %
	ALL	77.0 %	0.56 %
EXCHANGES 1&2	AUTOMATIC	79.9 %	0.58 %
	AUTO, TASK-INDEP	78.6 %	0.37 %
	ALL	86.7 %	0.33 %
FULL DIALOGUE	AUTOMATIC	87.0 %	0.72 %
	AUTO, TASK-INDEP	86.7 %	0.82 %
TOPLINE	ALL	92.3 %	0.72 %

Table 1: Results for predicting and identifying problematic dialogues (SE = Standard Error)

The EXCHANGE 1&2 rows of Table 1 show the results using features from the first *two* exchanges in the dialogue to predict the outcome of the dialogue.[4] The additional exchange gives roughly an additional 7% boost in predictive accuracy using either of the AUTOMATIC feature sets. This is only 8% less than the accuracy we can achieve using these features after having seen the whole dialogue (see below). The ALL row for EXCHANGE 1&2 shows that we could achieve over 86% accuracy if we had the ability to utilize the hand-labelled features.

The FULL DIALOGUE row in Table 1 for AUTOMATIC and AUTO, TASK-INDEP features shows the ability of the classifier to *identify* problematic dialogues, rather than predict them, using features for the whole dialogue. The ALL row for the FULL DIALOGUE shows that we could correctly identify over 92% of the outcomes accurately if we had the ability to utilize the hand-labelled features.

Note that the task-independent automatic features always perform within 2% error of the automatic features, and the hand-labelled features consistently perform with accuracies ranging from 6-8% greater.

The rules that RIPPER learned on the basis of the Exchange 1 automatic features are below.

Exchange 1, Automatic Features:
if (e1-top-confidence $\leq$ .924) $\wedge$ (e1-dtmf-flag = '1') **then** *problematic*,
if (e1-diff-confidence $\leq$ .916) $\wedge$ (e1-asr-duration $\geq$ 6.92) **then** *problematic*,
default is *tasksuccess*.

According to these rules, a dialogue will be problematic if the confidence score for the top-ranked task (given by the NLU module) is moderate or low and there was touchtone input in the user utterance. The second rule says that if the difference between the top confidence score and the second-ranked confidence score is moderate or low, and the duration of the user utterance is more than 7 seconds, predict PROBLEMATIC.

The performance of these rules is summarized in Table 2. These results show that given the first exchange, this ruleset predicts that 22% of the dialogues will be problematic, while 36% of them actually will be. Of the dialogues that actually will be problematic, it can predict 41% of them. Once it predicts that a dialogue will be problematic, it is correct 69% of the time. As mentioned earlier, this reflects an overall improvement in accuracy of 8% over the baseline.

The rules learned by training on the automatic task-independent features for exchanges 1 and 2 are given below. As in the first rule set, the features that the classifier appears to be exploiting are primarily those from the ASR and NLU modules.

Exchanges 1&2, Automatic Task-Independent Features:
if (e2-recog-numwords $\leq$ 0) $\wedge$ (e1-diff-confidence $\leq$ .95) **then** *problematic*.
if (e1-salience-coverage $\leq$ .889) $\wedge$ (e2-recog contains "I") $\wedge$ (e2-asr-duration $\geq$ 7.48) **then** *problematic*.
if (e1-top-confidence $\leq$ .924) $\wedge$ (e2-asr-duration $\geq$ 5.36) $\wedge$ (e1-asr-duration $\geq$ 8.6) **then** *problematic*.
if (e2-recog is blank) $\wedge$ (e2-asr-duration $\geq$ 2.8) **then** *problematic*.
if (e1-salience-coverage $\leq$ .737) $\wedge$ (e1-recog contains "help") $\wedge$ (e1-asr-duration $\leq$ 7.04) **then** *problematic*.
if (e1-diff-confidence $\leq$ .924) $\wedge$ (e1-dtmf-flag = '1') $\wedge$ (e1-asr-duration $\leq$ 6.68) **then** *problematic*.
default is *tasksuccess*.

The performance of this ruleset is summarized in Table 3. These results show that, given the first two exchanges, this ruleset predicts that 26% of the

[4] Since 23% of the dialogues consisted of only two exchanges, we exclude the second exchange features for those dialogues where the second exchange consists only of the system playing a closing prompt. We also excluded any features that indicated to the classifier that the second exchange was the last exchange in the dialogue.

Class	Occurred	Predicted	Recall	Precision
Success	64.1 %	78.3 %	89.44 %	73.14 %
Problematic	35.9 %	21.7 %	41.47 %	68.78 %

Table 2: Precision and Recall with Exchange 1 Automatic Features

Class	Occurred	Predicted	Recall	Precision
Success	64.1 %	75.3 %	91.42 %	77.81 %
Problematic	35.9 %	24.7 %	53.53 %	77.78 %

Table 3: Precision and Recall with Exchange 1&2 Automatic, Task-Independent Features

dialogues will be problematic, while 36% of them actually will be. Of the problematic dialogues, it can predict 57% of them. Once it predicts that a dialogue will be problematic, it is correct 79% of the time. Compared with the classifier for the first utterance alone, this classifier has an improvement of 16% in recall and 10% in precision, for an overall improvement in accuracy of 7% over using the first exchange alone.

One observation from these hypotheses is the classifier's preference for the *asr-duration* feature over the feature for the number of words recognized (*recog-numwords*). One would expect longer utterances to be more difficult, but the learned rulesets indicate that duration is a better measure of utterance length than the number of words. Another observation is the usefulness of the NLU confidence scores and the NLU salience-coverage in predicting problematic dialogues. These features seem to provide good general indicators of the system's success in recognition and understanding. The fact that the main focus of the rules is detecting ASR and NLU errors and that none of the DM behaviors are used as predictors also indicates that, in all likelihood, the DM is performing as well as it can, given the noisy input that it is getting from ASR and NLU.

To identify potential improvements in the problematic dialogue predictor, we analyzed which hand-labelled features made large performance improvements, under the assumption that future work can focus on developing automatic features that approximate the information provided by these hand-labelled features. The analysis indicated that the *rsuccess* feature alone improves the performance of the TOPLINE from 88.5%, as reported in (Langkilde et al., 1999), to 92.3%. Using *rsuccess* as the only feature results in 73.75% accuracy for exchange 1, 81.9% accuracy for exchanges 1&2 and 85.3% accuracy for the full dialogue. In addition, for Exchanges 1&2, the accuracy of the AUTOMATIC, TASK-INDEP feature set plus the *rsuccess* feature is 86.5%, which is only 0.2% less than the accuracy of ALL the features for Exchanges 1&2 as shown in Table 1. The rules that RIPPER learns for Exchanges 1&2 when the AUTOMATIC, TASK-INDEP feature set is augmented with the single hand-labelled *rsuccess* feature is shown below.

Exchanges 1&2, Rsuccess + Automatic Task-Independent Features:

if e2-salience-coverage $\leq$ 0.651 $\wedge$ e2-asr-duration $\geq$ 0.04 $\wedge$ e2-rsuccess=Rvacuous-match **then** ***problematic,***
if e2-rsuccess=Rmismatch $\wedge$ e1-top-confidence $\leq$ 0.909 **then** ***problematic,***
if e2-rsuccess=Rmismatch $\wedge$ e2-context-shift $\leq$ 0.014 $\wedge$ e2-salience-coverage $\geq$ 0.2 $\wedge$ e2-recog-numwords $\leq$ 12 (**then** ***problematic,***
if e2-rsuccess=Rmismatch $\wedge$ e1-rsuccess=Rmismatch **then** ***problematic,***
if e2-rsuccess=Rmismatch $\wedge$ e2-top-confidence $\leq$ 0.803 $\wedge$ e2-asr-duration $\geq$ 2.68 $\wedge$ e2-asr-duration $\leq$ 6.32 **then** ***problematic,***
if e1-rsuccess=Rmismatch $\wedge$ e1-diff-confidence $\geq$ 0.83 **then** ***problematic,***
if e2-rsuccess=Rmismatch $\wedge$ e2-context-shift $\geq$ 0.54 **then** ***problematic,***
if e2-asr-duration $\geq$ 5.24 $\wedge$ e2-salience-coverage $\leq$ 0.833 $\wedge$ e2-top-confidence $\leq$ 0.801 $\wedge$ e2-recog-numwords $\leq$ 7 $\wedge$ e2-asr-duration $\leq$ 16.08 **then** ***problematic,***
if e1-diff-confidence $\leq$ 0.794 $\wedge$ e1-asr-duration $\geq$ 7.2 $\wedge$ e1-inconsistency $\geq$ 0.024 $\wedge$ e1-inconsistency $\geq$ 0.755 **then** ***problematic,***
default is ***tasksuccess***

Note that the *rsuccess* feature is frequently used in the rules and that RIPPER learns rules that combine the *rsuccess* feature with other features, such as the *confidence*, *asr-duration*, and *salience-coverage* features.

5 Discussion and Future Work

In summary, our results show that: (1) All feature sets significantly improve over the baseline; (2) Using automatic features from the whole dialogue, we can identify problematic dialogues 23% better than the baseline; (3) Just the first exchange provides significantly better prediction (8%) than the baseline; (4) The second exchange provides an additional significant (7%) improvement, (5) A classifier based on task-independent automatic features performs with less than 1% degradation in error rate relative to the automatic features. Even with current accuracy rates, the improved ability to predict problematic dialogues means that it may be possible to field the system without human agent oversight, and we expect to be able to improve these results.

The research reported here is the first that we know of to automatically analyze a corpus of logs from a spoken dialogue system for the purpose of learning to *predict* problematic situations. Our work builds on earlier research on learning to *identify* dialogues in which the user experienced poor speech recognizer performance (Litman et al., 1999). However, that work was based on a much smaller set of experimental dialogues where the notion of a good or bad dialogue was automatically approximated rather than being labelled by humans. In addition, because that work was based on features synthesized over the entire dialogues, the hypotheses that were learned could not be used for prediction during runtime.

We are exploring several ways to improve the performance of and test the problematic dialogue predictor. First, we noted above the extent to which the hand-labelled feature *rsuccess* improves classifier performance. In other work we report results from training an *rsuccess* classifier on a per-utterance level (Walker et al., 2000), where we show that we can achieve 85% accuracy using only fully automatic features. In future work we intend to use the (noisy) output from this classifier as input to our problematic dialogue classifier with the hope of improving the performance of the fully automatic feature sets. In addition, since it is more important to minimize errors in predicting PROBLEMATIC dialogues than errors in predicting TASKSUCCESS dialogues, we intend to experiment with RIPPER's loss ratio parameter, which instructs RIPPER to achieve high accuracy for the PROBLEMATIC class, while potentially reducing overall accuracy. Finally, we plan to integrate the learned rulesets into the HMIHY dialogue system to improve the system's overall performance.

References

A. Abella and A.L. Gorin. 1999. Construct algebra: An analytical method for dialog management. In *Proc. of the Association for Computational Linguistics*.

P. Baggia, G. Castagneri, and M. Danieli. 1998. Field trials of the Italian Arise Train Timetable System. In *Interactive Voice Technology for Telecommunications Applications, IVTTA*, pages 97–102.

J. Chu-Carroll and R. Carpenter. 1999. Vector-based natural language call routing. *Computational Linguistics*, 25-3:361–387.

W. Cohen. 1996. Learning trees and rules with set-valued features. In *14th Conference of the American Association of Artificial Intelligence, AAAI.*

A.L. Gorin E. Ammicht and T. Alonso. 1999. Knowledge collection for natural language spoken dialog systems. In *Proc. of EUROSPEECH 99.*

A.L. Gorin, G. Riccardi, and J.H. Wright. 1997. How may I Help You? *Speech Communication*, 23:113–127.

I. Langkilde, M. Walker, J. Wright, A. Gorin, and D. Litman. 1999. Automatic prediction of problematic human-computer dialogues in How May I Help You? In *Proc. IEEE Workshop on Automatic Speech Recognition and Understanding.*

G. A. Levow. 1998. Characterizing and recognizing spoken corrections in human-computer dialogue. In *Proc. of the 36th Annual Meeting of the Association of Computational Linguistics, COLING/ACL 98*, pages 736–742.

D. J. Litman, M. A. Walker, and M. J. Kearns. 1999. Automatic detection of poor speech recognition at the dialogue level. In *Proc. of the 37th Annual Meeting of the Association of Computational Linguistics , ACL99*, pages 309–316.

G. Riccardi and A.L. Gorin. to appear. Spoken language adaptation over time and state in a natural spoken dialog system. *IEEE Transactions on Speech and Audio.*

A. Sanderman, J. Sturm, E. den Os, L. Boves, and A. Cremers. 1998. Evaluation of the Dutch Train Timetable Information System developed in the ARISE project. In *Interactive Voice Technology for Telecommunications Applications*, pages 91–96.

S. Seneff, V. Zue, J. Polifroni, C. Pao, L. Hetherington, D. Goddeau, and J. Glass. 1995. The preliminary development of a displayless PEGASUS system. In *ARPA SLT Workshop.*

E. Shriberg, E. Wade, and P. Price. 1992. Human-machine problem solving using spoken language systems (SLS): Factors affecting performance and user satisfaction. In *Proc. of the DARPA Speech and NL Workshop*, pages 49–54.

M. A. Walker, J. C. Fromer, and S. Narayanan. 1998. Learning optimal dialogue strategies: A case study of a spoken dialogue agent for email. In *Proc. of the 36th Annual Meeting of the Association of Computational Linguistics, COLING/ACL 98*, pages 1345–1352.

M. Walker, I. Langkilde, and J. Wright. 2000. Using NLP and Discourse features to identify understanding errors in the How May I Help You spoken dialogue system. *In Submission.*

Predicting Automatic Speech Recognition Performance Using Prosodic Cues

Diane J. Litman and **Julia B. Hirschberg**
AT&T Labs — Research
Florham Park, NJ 07932-0971 USA
{diane,julia}@research.att.com

Marc Swerts
IPO, Center for User-System Interaction
Eindhoven, The Netherlands
swerts@ipo.tue.nl

Abstract

In spoken dialogue systems, it is important for a system to know how likely a speech recognition hypothesis is to be correct, so it can reprompt for fresh input, or, in cases where many errors have occurred, change its interaction strategy or switch the caller to a human attendant. We have discovered prosodic features which more accurately predict when a recognition hypothesis contains a word error than the acoustic confidence score thresholds traditionally used in automatic speech recognition. We present analytic results indicating that there are significant prosodic differences between correctly and incorrectly recognized turns in the TOOT train information corpus. We then present machine learning results showing how the use of prosodic features to automatically predict correct versus incorrectly recognized turns improves over the use of acoustic confidence scores alone.

1 Introduction

One of the central tasks of the dialogue manager in most current spoken dialogue systems (SDSs) is error handling. The automatic speech recognition (ASR) component of such systems is prone to error, especially when the system has to operate in noisy conditions or when the domain of the system is large. Given that it is impossible to fully prevent ASR errors, it is important for a system to know how likely a speech recognition hypothesis is to be correct, so it can take appropriate action, since users have considerable difficulty correcting incorrect information that is presented by the system as true (Krahmer et al., 1999). Such action may include verifying the user's input, reprompting for fresh input, or, in cases where many errors have occurred, changing the interaction strategy or switching the caller to a human attendant (Smith, 1998; Litman et al., 1999; Langkilde et al., 1999). Traditionally, the decision to **reject** a recognition hypothesis is based on acoustic confidence score thresholds, which provide a reliability measure on the hypothesis and are set in the application (Zeljkovic, 1996). However, this process often fails, as there is no simple one-to-one mapping between low confidence scores and incorrect recognitions, and the setting of a rejection threshold is a matter of trial and error (Bouwman et al., 1999). Also, some incorrect recognitions do not necessarily lead to misunderstandings at a conceptual level (e.g. "a.m." recognized as "in the morning").

The current paper looks at prosody as one possible predictor of ASR performance. ASR performance is known to vary based upon speaking style (Weintraub et al., 1996), speaker gender and age, native versus non-native speaker status, and, in general, the deviation of new speech from the training data. Some of this variation is linked to prosody, as prosodic differences have been found to characterize differences in speaking style (Blaauw, 1992) and idiosyncratic differences (Kraayeveld, 1997). Several other studies (Wade et al., 1992; Oviatt et al., 1996; Swerts and Ostendorf, 1997; Levow, 1998; Bell and Gustafson, 1999) report that hyperarticulated speech, characterized by careful enunciation, slowed speaking rate, and increase in pitch and loudness, often occurs when users in human-machine interactions try to correct system errors. Still others have shown that such speech also decreases recognition performance (Soltau and Waibel, 1998). Prosodic features have also been shown to be effective in ranking recognition hypotheses, as a post-processing filter to score ASR hypotheses (Hirschberg, 1991; Veilleux, 1994; Hirose, 1997).

In this paper we present results of empirical studies testing the hypothesis that prosodic features provide an important clue to ASR performance. We first present results comparing prosodic analyses of correctly and incorrectly recognized speaker turns in TOOT, an experimental SDS for obtaining train information over the phone. We then describe machine learning experiments based on these results that explore the predictive power of prosodic features alone and in combination with other automatically available information, including ASR confidence scores and recognized string. Our results indicate that there are significant prosodic differences between correctly and incorrectly recognized utterances. These differences can in fact be used to predict whether an utterance has been misrecognized, with a high degree of accuracy.

2 The TOOT Corpus

Our corpus consists of a set of dialogues between humans and TOOT, an SDS for accessing train schedules from the web via telephone, which was collected to study both variations in SDS strategy and user-adapted interaction (Litman and Pan, 1999). TOOT is implemented on a platform combining ASR, text-to-speech, a phone interface, a finite-state dialogue manager, and application functions (Kamm et al., 1997). The speech recognizer is a speaker-independent hidden Markov model system with context-dependent phone models for telephone speech and constrained grammars for each dialogue state. Confidence scores for recognition were available only at the turn, not the word, level (Zeljkovic, 1996). An example TOOT dialogue is shown in Figure 1.

Subjects performed four tasks with one of several versions of TOOT, that differed in terms of locus of initiative (system, user, or mixed), confirmation strategy (explicit, implicit, or none), and whether these conditions could be changed by the user during the task. Subjects were 39 students, 20 native speakers of standard American English and 19 non-native speakers; 16 subjects were female and 23 male. Dialogues were recorded and system and user behavior logged automatically. The *concept accuracy* (CA) of each turn was manually labeled by one of the experimenters. If the ASR output correctly captured all the task-related information in the turn (e.g. time, departure and arrival cities), the turn was given a CA score of 1 (a *semantically correct recognition*). Otherwise, the CA score reflected the percentage of correctly recognized task information in the turn. The dialogues were also transcribed by hand and these transcriptions automatically compared to the ASR recognized string to produce a *word error rate* (WER) for each turn. Note that a concept can be correctly recognized even though all words are not, so the CA metric does not penalize for errors that are unimportant to overall utterance interpretation.

For the study described below, we examined 1994 user turns from 152 dialogues in this corpus. The speech recognizer was able to generate a recognized string and an associated acoustic confidence score per turn for 1975 of these turns.[1] 1410 of these 1975 turns had a CA score of 1 (for an overall conceptual accuracy score of 71%) and 961 had a WER of 0 (for an overall transcription accuracy score of 49%, with a mean WER per turn of 47%).

[1]For the remaining turns, ASR output "no speech" (and TOOT played a timeout message) or "garbage" (TOOT played a rejection message).

3 Distinguishing Correct from Incorrect Recognitions

We first looked for distinguishing prosodic characteristics of misrecognitions, defining misrecognitions in two ways: a) as turns with WER>0; and b) as turns with CA<1. As noted in Section 1, previous studies have speculated that hyperarticulated speech (slower and louder speech which contains wider pitch excursions) may be associated with recognition failure. So, we examined the following features for each user turn:[2]

- maximum and mean fundamental frequency values (F0 Max, F0 Mean)
- maximum and mean energy values (RMS Max, RMS Mean)
- total duration
- length of pause preceding the turn (Prior Pause)
- speaking rate (Tempo)
- amount of silence within the turn (% Silence)

F0 and RMS values, representing measures of pitch excursion and loudness, were calculated from the output of Entropic Research Laboratory's pitch tracker, *get_f0*, with no post-correction. Timing variation was represented by four features. Duration within and length of pause between turns was computed from the temporal labels associated with each turn's beginning and end. Speaking rate was approximated in terms of syllables in the recognized string per second, while % Silence was defined as the percentage of zero frames in the turn, i.e., roughly the percentage of time within the turn that the speaker was silent. These features were chosen based upon previous findings (see Section 1) and observations from our data.

To ensure that our results were speaker independent, we calculated mean values for each speaker's recognized turns and their misrecognized turns for every feature. Then, for each feature, we created vectors of speaker means for recognized and misrecognized turns and performed paired t-tests on the vectors. For example, for the feature "F0 max", we calculated mean maxima for misrecognized turns and for correctly recognized turns for each of our thirty-nine speakers. We then performed a paired t-test on these thirty-nine pairs of means to derive speaker-independent results for differences in F0 maxima between correct and incorrect recognitions.

Tables 1 and 2 show results of these comparisons when we calculate misrecognition in terms of

[2]While the features were automatically computed, turn beginnings and endings were hand segmented in dialogue-level speech files, as the turn-level files created by TOOT were not available.

Toot:	Hi, this is AT&T Amtrak schedule system. This is TOOT. How may I help you?
User:	I want the trains from New York City to Washington DC on Monday at 9:30 in the evening.
Toot:	Do you want me to find the trains from New York City to Washington DC on Monday approximately at 9:30 in the evening now?
User:	Yes.
Toot:	I am going to get the train schedule for you ...

Figure 1: Example Dialogue Excerpt with TOOT.

Table 1: Comparison of Misrecognized (WER>0) vs. Recognized Turns by Prosodic Feature Across Speakers.

Feature	T-stat	Mean Misrec'd - Rec'd	P
*F0 Max	7.83	30.31 Hz	0
*F0 Mean	3.66	4.12 Hz	0
*RMS Max	5.70	235.93	0
RMS Mean	-.57	-8.50	.57
*Duration	10.30	2.20 sec	0
*Prior Pause	5.55	.35 sec	0
Tempo	-.05	.15 sps	.13
*% Silence	-5.15	-.06%	0
*significant at a 95% confidence level ($p \leq .05$)			

Table 2: Comparison of Misrecognized (CA<1) vs. Recognized Turns by Prosodic Feature Across Speakers.

Feature	T-stat	Mean Misrec'd - Rec'd	P
*F0 Max	5.60	29.64 Hz	0
F0 Mean	1.70	2.10 Hz	.10
*RMS Max	2.86	173.87	.007
RMS Mean	-1.85	-27.75	.07
*Duration	9.80	2.15 sec	0
*Prior Pause	4.05	.38 sec	0
*Tempo	-4.21	-.58 sps	0
% Silence	-1.42	-.02%	.16
*significant at a 95% confidence level ($p \leq .05$)			

WER>0 and CA<1, respectively. These results indicate that misrecognized turns do differ from correctly recognized ones in terms of prosodic features, although the features on which they differ vary slightly, depending upon the way "misrecognition" is defined. Whether defined by WER or CA, misrecognized turns exhibit significantly higher F0 and RMS maxima, longer durations, and longer preceding pauses than correctly recognized speaker turns. For a traditional WER definition of misrecognition, misrecognitions are slightly higher in mean F0 and contain a lower percentage of internal silence. For a CA definition, on the other hand, tempo is a significant factor, with misrecognitions spoken at a faster rate than correct recognitions — contrary to our hypothesis about the role of hyperarticulation in recognition error.

While the comparisons in Tables 1 and 2 were made on the means of raw values for all prosodic features, little difference is found when values are normalized by value of first or preceding turn, or by converting to z scores.[3] From this similarity between the performance of raw and normalized values, it would seem to be relative differences in speakers' prosodic values, not deviation from some 'acceptable' range, that distinguishes recognition failures from successful recognitions. A given speaker's turns that are higher in pitch or loudness, or that are longer, or that follow longer pauses, are less likely to be recognized correctly than that same speaker's turns that are lower in pitch or loudness, shorter, and follow shorter pauses — however correct recognition is defined.

It is interesting to note that the features we found to be significant indicators of failed recognitions (F0 excursion, loudness, long prior pause, and longer duration) are all features previously associated with hyperarticulated speech. Since prior research has suggested that speakers may respond to failed recognition attempts by hyperarticulating, which itself may lead to more recognition failures, had we in fact simply identified a means of characterizing and identifying hyperarticulated speech prosodically?

Since we had independently labeled all speaker turns for evidence of hyperarticulation (two of the authors labeled each turn as "not hyperarticulated", "some hyperarticulation in the turn", and "hyperarticulated", following Wade et al. (1992)), we were able to test this possibility. We excluded any turn either labeler had labeled as partially or fully hyperarticulated, and again performed paired t-tests on mean values of misrecognized versus recognized turns for each speaker. Results show that for both WER-defined and CA-defined misrecognitions, not only are the same features significant differentiators when hyperarticulated turns are excluded from the analysis, but in addition, tempo also is significant for WER-defined misrecognition. So, our findings

[3] The only differences occur for CA defined misrecognition, where normalizing by first utterance results in significant differences in mean RMS, and normalizing by preceding turn results in no significant differences in tempo.

for the prosodic characteristics of recognized and of misrecognized turns hold even when perceptibly hyperarticulated turns are excluded from the corpus.

4 Predicting Misrecognitions Using Machine Learning

Given the prosodic differences between misrecognized and correctly recognized utterances in our corpus, is it possible to predict accurately when a particular utterance will be misrecognized or not? This section describes experiments using the machine learning program RIPPER (Cohen, 1996) to automatically induce prediction models, using prosodic as well as additional features. Like many learning programs, RIPPER takes as input the classes to be learned, a set of feature names and possible values, and training data specifying the class and feature values for each training example. RIPPER outputs a classification model for predicting the class of future examples. The model is learned using greedy search guided by an information gain metric, and is expressed as an ordered set of if-then rules.

Our predicted classes correspond to correct recognition (T) or not (F). As in Section 3, we examine both WER-defined and CA-defined notions of correct recognition, and represent each user turn as a set of features. The features used in our learning experiments include the raw prosodic features in Tables 1 and 2 (which we will refer to as the feature set "Prosody"), the hyperarticulation score discussed in Section 3, and the following additional potential predictors of misrecognition (described in Section 2):

- ASR grammar
- ASR confidence
- ASR string
- system adaptability
- dialogue strategy
- task number
- subject
- gender
- native speaker

The first three features are derived from the ASR process (the context-dependent grammar used to recognize the turn, the turn-level acoustic confidence score output by the recognizer, and the recognized string). We included these features as a baseline against which to test new methods of predicting misrecognitions, although, currently, we know of no ASR system that includes recognized string in its rejection calculations.[4] TOOT itself used only the first two features to calculate rejections and ask the user to repeat the utterance, whenever the confidence score fell below a pre-defined grammar-specific threshold. The other features represent the experimental conditions under which the data was collected (whether users could adapt TOOT's dialogue strategies, TOOT's initial initiative and confirmation strategies, experimental task, speaker's name and characteristics). We included these features to determine the extent to which particulars of task, subject, or interaction influenced ASR success rates or our ability to predict them; previous work showed that these factors impact TOOT's performance (Litman and Pan, 1999; Hirschberg et al., 1999). Except for the task, subject, gender, native language, and hyperarticulation scores, all of our features are automatically available.

Table 3 shows the relative performance of a number of the feature sets we examined; results here are for misrecognition defined in terms of WER.[5] A baseline classifier for misrecognition, predicting that ASR is always wrong (the majority class of F), has an error of 48.66%. The best performing feature set includes only the raw prosodic and ASR features and reduces this error to an impressive 6.53% +/- .63%. Note that this performance is not improved by adding manually labeled features or experimental conditions: the feature set corresponding to ALL features yielded the statistically equivalent 6.68% +/- 0.63%.

With respect to the performance of prosodic features, Table 3 shows that using them in conjunction with ASR features (error of 6.53%) significantly outperforms prosodic features alone (error of 12.76%), which, in turn, significantly outperforms any single prosodic feature; duration, with an error of 17.42%, is the best such feature. Although not shown in the table, the **un**normalized prosodic features significantly outperform the normalized versions by 7-13%. Recall that prosodic features normalized by first task utterance, by previous utterance, or by z scores showed little performance difference in the analyses performed in Section 3. This difference may indicate that there are indeed limits on the ranges in features such as F0 and RMS maxima, duration and preceding pause within which recognition performance is optimal. It seems reasonable that extreme deviation from characteristics of the acoustic training material should in fact impact ASR performance, and our experiments may have uncovered, if not the critical variants, at least important acoustic correlates of them. However, it is difficult to com-

[4] Note that, while the entire recognized string is provided to the learning algorithm, RIPPER rules test for the presence of particular words in the string.

[5] The errors and standard errors (SE) result from 25-fold cross-validation on the 1975 turns where ASR yielded a string and confidence. When two errors plus or minus twice the standard error do not overlap, they are statistically significantly different.

Table 3: Estimated Error for Predicting Misrecognized Turns (WER>0).

Features Used	Error	SE
Prosody, ASR Confidence, ASR String, ASR Grammar	6.53%	.63
ALL	6.68%	.63
Prosody, ASR String	7.34%	.75
ASR Confidence, ASR String, ASR Grammar	9.01%	.70
Prosody, ASR Confidence, ASR Grammar	10.63%	.88
Prosody, ASR Confidence	10.99%	.87
Prosody	12.76%	.79
ASR String	15.24%	1.11
Duration	17.42%	.88
ASR Confidence, ASR Grammar	17.77%	.72
ASR Confidence	22.23%	1.16
ASR Grammar	26.28%	.84
Tempo	32.76%	1.03
Hyperarticulation	35.24%	1.46
% Silence	36.46%	.79
Prior Pause	36.61%	.97
F0 Max	38.73%	.82
RMS Max	42.23%	.96
F0 Mean	46.33%	1.10
RMS Mean	48.35%	1.15
Majority Baseline	48.66%	

pare our machine learning results with the statistical analyses, since a) the statistical analyses looked at only a single prosodic variable at a time, and b) data points for that analysis were means calculated per speaker, while the learning algorithm operated on all utterances, allowing for unequal contributions by speaker.

We now address the issue of what prosodic features are contributing to misrecognition identification, relative to the more traditional ASR techniques. Do our prosodic features simply correlate with information already in use by ASR systems (e.g., confidence score, grammar), or at least available to them (e.g., recognized string)? First, the error using ASR confidence score alone (22.23%) is significantly worse than the error when prosodic features are combined with ASR confidence scores (10.99%) — and is also significantly worse than the use of prosodic features alone (12.76%). Similarly, the error using ASR confidence scores and the ASR grammar (17.77%) is significantly worse than prosodic features alone (12.76%). Thus, prosodic features, either alone or in conjunction with traditional ASR features, significantly outperform these traditional features alone for predicting WER-based misrecognitions.

Another interesting finding from our experiments is the predictive power of information available to current ASR systems but not made use of in calculating rejection likelihoods, the identity of the recognized string. This feature is in fact the best performing single feature in predicting our data (15.24%). And, at a 95% confidence level, the error using ASR confidence scores, the recognized string, and grammar (9.01%) matches the performance of our best performing feature set (6.53%). It seems that, at least in our task and for our ASR system, the appearance of particular words in the recognized strings is an extremely useful cue to recognition accuracy. So, even by making use of information currently available from the traditional ASR process, ASR systems could improve their performance on identifying rejections by a considerable margin. A caveat here is that this feature, like grammar state, is unlikely to generalize from task to task or recognizer to recognizer, but these findings suggest that both should be considered as a means of improving rejection performance in stable systems.

The classification model learned from the best performing feature set in Table 3 is shown in Figure 2.[6] The first rule RIPPER finds with this feature set is that if the user turn is less than .9 seconds and the recognized string contains the word "yes" (and possibly other words as well), with an acoustic confidence score $\geq$ -2.6, then predict that the turn will be correctly recognized.[7] Note that all of the prosodic fea-

[6] Rules are presented in order of importance in classifying data. When multiple rules are applicable, RIPPER uses the first rule.

[7] The confidence scores observed in our data ranged from a high of -0.087662 to a low of -9.884418.

if (duration $\leq$ 0.897073) $\wedge$ (confidence $\geq$ -2.62744) $\wedge$ (string contains 'yes') **then** T
if (duration $\leq$ 1.03872) $\wedge$ (confidence $\geq$ -2.69775) $\wedge$ (string contains 'no') **then** T
if (duration $\leq$ 0.982051) $\wedge$ (confidence $\geq$ -1.99705) $\wedge$ (tempo $\geq$ 3.1147) **then** T
if (duration $\leq$ 0.813633) $\wedge$ (duration $\geq$ 0.642652) $\wedge$ (confidence $\geq$ -3.33945) $\wedge$ (F0 Mean $\geq$ 176.794) **then** T
if (duration $\leq$ 1.30312) $\wedge$ (confidence $\geq$ -3.37301) $\wedge$ (% silences $\geq$ 0.647059) **then** T
if (duration $\leq$ 0.610734) $\wedge$ (confidence $\geq$ -3.37301) $\wedge$ (% silences $\geq$ 0.521739) **then** T
if (duration $\leq$ 1.09537) $\wedge$ (string contains 'Baltimore') **then** T
if (duration $\leq$ 0.982051) $\wedge$ (string contains 'no') **then** T
if (duration $\leq$ 1.1803) $\wedge$ (confidence $\geq$ -2.93085) $\wedge$ (grammar = date) **then** T
if (duration $\leq$ 1.09537) $\wedge$ (confidence $\geq$ -2.30717) $\wedge$ (% silences $\geq$ 0.356436) $\wedge$ (F0 Max $\geq$ 249.225) **then** T
if (duration $\leq$ 0.868743) $\wedge$ (confidence $\geq$ -4.14926) $\wedge$ (% silences $\geq$ 0.51923) $\wedge$ (F0 Max $\geq$ 205.296) **then** T
if (duration $\leq$ 1.18036) $\wedge$ (string contains 'Philadelphia') **then** T
else F

Figure 2: Ruleset for Predicting Correctly Recognized Turns (WER = 0) from Prosodic and ASR Features.

tures except for RMS mean, max, and prior pause appear in at least one rule, and that the features shown to be significant in our statistical analyses (Section 3) are not the same features as in the rules. But, as noted above, our data points in these two experiments differ. It is useful to note though, that while this ruleset contains all three ASR features, none of the experimental parameters was found to be a useful predictor, suggesting that our results are not specific to the particular conditions of and participants in the corpus collection, although they are specific to the lexicon and grammars.

Results of our learning experiments with misrecognition defined in terms of CA rather than WER show the overall role of the features which predict WER-defined misrecognition to be less successful in predicting CA-defined error. Table 4 shows the relative performance of the same feature sets discussed above, with misrecognition now defined in terms of CA<1. As with the WER experiments, the best performing feature set makes use of prosodic and ASR-derived features. However, the predictive power of prosodic over ASR features decreases when misrecognition is defined in terms of CA — which is particularly interesting since ASR confidence scores are intended to predict WER rather than CA; the error rate using ASR confidence scores alone (13.52%) is now significantly lower than the error obtained using prosody (18.18%). However, prosodic features still improve the predictive power of ASR confidence scores, to 11.34%, although this difference is not significant at a 95% confidence level. And the error rate of the three ASR features combined (11.70%) is reduced to the lowest error rate in our table when prosodic features are added (10.43%); this error rate is (just) significantly different from the use of ASR confidence scores alone. Thus, for CA-defined misrecognitions, our experiments have uncovered only minor improvements over traditional ASR rejection calculation procedures.

5 Discussion

A statistical comparison of recognized versus misrecognized utterances indicates that F0 excursion, loudness, longer prior pause, and longer duration are significant prosodic characteristics of both WER and CA-defined failed recognition attempts. Results from a set of machine learning experiments show that prosodic differences can in fact be used to improve the prediction of misrecognitions with a high degree of accuracy (12.76% error) for WER-based misrecognitions — and an even higher degree (6.53% error) when combined with information currently available from ASR systems. The use of ASR confidence scores alone had a predicted WER of 22.23%, so the improvement over traditional methods is quite considerable. For CA-defined misrecognitions, the improvement provided by prosodic features is considerably less. One of our future research directions will be to understand this difference.

Another future direction will be to address the issue of just **why** prosodic features provide such useful indicators of recognition failure. Do the features themselves make recognition difficult, or are they instead indirect correlates of other phenomena not captured in our study? While the negative influence of speaking rate variation on ASR has been reported before (e.g. (Ostendorf et al., 1996), it is traditionally assumed that ASR is impervious to differences in F0 and RMS; yet, it is known that F0 and RMS variations co-vary to some extent with spectral characteristics (e.g. (Swerts and Veldhuis, 1997; Fant et al., 1995)), so that it is not unlikely that utterances with extreme values for these may differ critically from the training data. Other prosodic features may be more indirect indicators of errors. Longer utterances may simply provide more chance for error than shorter ones, while speakers who pause longer before utterances and take more time making them may also produce more disfluencies than others.

We are currently replicating our experiment on a new domain with a new speech recognizer. We are examining the W99 corpus, which was collected in a

Table 4: Estimated Error for Predicting Misrecognized Turns (CA<1).

Features Used	Error	SE
Prosody, ASR Confidence, ASR String, ASR Grammar	10.43%	.63
ALL	10.68%	.71
Prosody, ASR Confidence, ASR Grammar	11.24%	.68
Prosody, ASR Confidence	11.34%	.64
ASR Confidence, ASR String, ASR Grammar	11.70%	.68
ASR Confidence	13.52%	.82
ASR Confidence, ASR Grammar	13.52%	.84
ASR String	13.62%	.83
Prosody, ASR String	15.04%	.84
Prosody	18.18%	.85
Duration	18.38%	.90
ASR Grammar	22.73%	.96
Tempo	24.61%	1.28
Hyperarticulation	25.27%	1.05
F0 Mean	28.61%	1.19
F0 Max	28.76%	.90
RMS Mean	28.86%	1.17
% Silence	28.91%	1.23
RMS Max	29.01%	1.16
Prior Pause	29.22%	1.26
Majority Baseline	28.61%	

spoken dialogue system that supported registration, checking paper status, and information access for the IEEE Automatic Speech Recognition and Understanding Workshop (ASRU99) (Rahim et al., 1999). This system employed the AT&T WATSON speech recognition technology (Sharp et al., 1997). Preliminary results indicate that our TOOT results do in fact hold up across recognizers. We also are extending our TOOT corpus analysis to include prosodic analyses of turns in which users become aware of misrecognitions and correct them. In addition, we are exploring whether prosodic differences can help explain the "goat" phenomenon — the fact that some voices are recognized much more poorly than others (Doddington et al., 1998; Hirschberg et al., 1999). Our ultimate goal is to provide prosodically-based mechanisms for identifying and reacting to ASR failures in SDS systems.

Acknowledgements

We would like to thank Jennifer Chu-Carroll, Candy Kamm, participants in the AT&T "SLUG" seminar series, and participants in the 1999 JHU Summer Language Engineering Workshop, for providing us with useful comments on this research and on earlier versions of this paper.

References

Linda Bell and Joakim Gustafson. 1999. Repetition and its phonetic realizations: Investigating a Swedish database of spontaneous computer-directed speech. In *Proceedings of ICPhS-99*, San Francisco. International Congress of Phonetic Sciences.

E. Blaauw. 1992. Phonetic differences between read and spontaneous speech. In *Proceedings of ICSLP92*, volume 1, pages 751–758, Banff.

A. G. Bouwman, J. Sturm, and L. Boves. 1999. Incorporating confidence measures in the dutch train timetable information system developed in the ARISE project. In *Proc. International Conference on Acoustics, Speech and Signal Processing*, volume 1, pages 493–496, Phoenix.

William Cohen. 1996. Learning trees and rules with set-valued features. In *14th Conference of the American Association of Artificial Intelligence, AAAI*.

George Doddington, Walter Liggett, Alvin Martin, Mark Przybocki, and Douglas Reynolds. 1998. Sheep, goats, lambs and wolves: A statistical analysis of speaker performance in the NIST 1998 speaker recognition evaluation. In *Proceedings of ICSLP-98*.

G. Fant, J. Liljencrants, I. Karlsson, and M. Båvegård. 1995. Time and frequency domain aspects of voice source modelling. BR Speechmaps 6975, ESPRIT. Deliverable 27 WP 1.3.

Keikichi Hirose. 1997. Disambiguating recognition results by prosodic features. In *Computing*

Prosody: Computational Models for Processing Spontaneous Speech, pages 327–342. Springer.

Julia Hirschberg, Diane Litman, and Marc Swerts. 1999. Prosodic cues to recognition errors. In *Proceedings of the Automatic Speech Recognition and Understanding Workshop (ASRU'99)*.

Julia Hirschberg. 1991. Using text analysis to predict intonational boundaries. In *Proceedings of the Second European Conference on Speech Communication and Technology*, Genova. ESCA.

C. Kamm, S. Narayanan, D. Dutton, and R. Ritenour. 1997. Evaluating spoken dialog systems for telecommunication services. In *5th European Conference on Speech Technology and Communication, EUROSPEECH 97*.

Hans Kraayeveld. 1997. *Idiosyncrasy in prosody. Speaker and speaker group identification in Dutch using melodic and temporal information.* Ph.D. thesis, Nijmegen University.

E. Krahmer, M. Swerts, M. Theune, and M. Weegels. 1999. Error spotting in human-machine interactions. In *Proceedings of EUROSPEECH-99*.

Irene Langkilde, Marilyn Walker, Jerry Wright, Al Gorin, and Diane Litman. 1999. Automatic prediction of problematic human-computer dialogues in 'how may i help you?'. In *Proceedings of the Automatic Speech Recognition and Understanding Workshop (ASRU'99)*.

Gina-Anne Levow. 1998. Characterizing and recognizing spoken corrections in human-computer dialogue. In *Proceedings of the 36th Annual Meeting of the Association of Computational Linguistics, COLING/ACL 98*, pages 736–742.

Diane J. Litman and Shimei Pan. 1999. Empirically evaluating an adaptable spoken dialogue system. In *Proceedings of the 7th International Conference on User Modeling (UM)*.

Diane J. Litman, Marilyn A. Walker, and Michael J. Kearns. 1999. Automatic detection of poor speech recognition at the dialogue level. In *Proceedings of the 37th Annual Meeting of the Association of Computational Linguistics , ACL99*, pages 309–316.

M. Ostendorf, B. Byrne, M. Bacchiani, M. Finke, A. Gunawardana, K. Ross, S. Roweis, E. Shriberg, D. Talkin, A. Waibel, B. Wheatley, and T. Zeppenfeld. 1996. Modeling systematic variations in pronunciation via a language-dependent hidden speaking mode. Report on 1996 CLSP/JHU Workshop on Innovative Techniques for Large Vocabulary Continuous Speech Recognition.

S. L. Oviatt, G. Levow, M. MacEarchern, and K. Kuhn. 1996. Modeling hyperarticulate speech during human-computer error resolution. In *Proceedings of ICSLP-96*, pages 801–804, Philadelphia.

M. Rahim, R. Pieracini, W. Eckert, E. Levin, G. Di Fabbrizio, G. Riccardi, C. Lin, and C. Kamm. 1999. W99 - a spoken dialogue system for the asru'99 workshop. In *Proc. ASRU'99*.

R.D. Sharp, E. Bocchieri, C. Castillo, S. Parthasarathy, C. Rath, M. Riley, and J Rowland. 1997. The watson speech recognition engine. In *Proc. ICASSP97*, pages 4065–4068.

Ronnie W. Smith. 1998. An evaluation of strategies for selectively verifying utterance meanings in spoken natural language dialog. *International Journal of Human-Computer Studies*, 48:627–647.

Hagen Soltau and Alex Waibel. 1998. On the influence of hyperarticulated speech on recognition performance. In *Proceedings of ICSLP-98*, Sydney. International Conference on Spoken Language Processing.

M. Swerts and M. Ostendorf. 1997. Prosodic and lexical indications of discourse structure in human-machine interactions. *Speech Communication*, 22:25–41.

Marc Swerts and Raymond Veldhuis. 1997. Interactions between intonation and glottal-pulse characteristics. In A. Botinis, G. Kouroupetroglou, and G. Carayiannis, editors, *Intonation: Theory, Models and Applications*, pages 297–300, Athens. ESCA.

Nanette Veilleux. 1994. *Computational Models of the Prosody/Syntax Mapping for Spoken Language Systems.* Ph.D. thesis, Boston University.

E. Wade, E. E. Shriberg, and P. J. Price. 1992. User behaviors affecting speech recognition. In *Proceedings of ICSLP-92*, volume 2, pages 995–998, Banff.

M. Weintraub, K. Taussig, K. Hunicke-Smith, and A. Snodgrass. 1996. Effect of speaking style on LVCSR performance. In *Proceedings of ICSLP-96*, Philadelphia. International Conference on Spoken Language Processing.

Ilija Zeljkovic. 1996. Decoding optimal state sequences with smooth state likelihoods. In *International Conference on Acoustics, Speech, and Signal Processing, ICASSP 96*, pages 129–132.

A Novel Use of Statistical Parsing to Extract Information from Text

Scott Miller, Heidi Fox, Lance Ramshaw, and Ralph Weischedel
BBN Technologies
70 Fawcett Street, Cambridge, MA 02138
szmiller@bbn.com

Abstract

Since 1995, a few statistical parsing algorithms have demonstrated a breakthrough in parsing accuracy, as measured against the UPenn TREEBANK as a gold standard. In this paper we report adapting a lexicalized, probabilistic context-free parser to information extraction and evaluate this new technique on MUC-7 template elements and template relations.

1 Introduction

Since 1995, a few statistical parsing algorithms (Magerman, 1995; Collins, 1996 and 1997; Charniak, 1997; Rathnaparki, 1997) demonstrated a breakthrough in parsing accuracy, as measured against the University of Pennsylvania TREEBANK as a gold standard. Yet, relatively few have embedded one of these algorithms in a task. Chiba, (1999) was able to use such a parsing algorithm to reduce perplexity with the long term goal of improved speech recognition.

In this paper, we report adapting a lexicalized, probabilistic context-free parser with head rules (LPCFG-HR) to information extraction. The technique was benchmarked in the Seventh Message Understanding Conference (MUC-7) in 1998.

Several technical challenges confronted us and were solved:

• How could the limited semantic interpretation required in information extraction be integrated into the statistical learning algorithm? We were able to integrate both syntactic and semantic information into the parsing process, thus avoiding potential errors of syntax first followed by semantics.

• Would TREEBANKing of the variety of news sources in MUC-7 be required? Or could the University of Pennsylvania's TREEBANK on Wall Street Journal adequately train the algorithm for New York Times newswire, which includes dozens of newspapers? Manually creating source-specific training data for syntax was not required. Instead, our parsing algorithm, trained on the UPenn TREEBANK, was run on the New York Times source to create unsupervised syntactic training which was constrained to be consistent with semantic annotation.

• Would semantic annotation require computational linguists? We were able to specify relatively simple guidelines that students with no training in computational linguistics could annotate.

2 Information Extraction Tasks

We evaluated the new approach to information extraction on two of the tasks of the Seventh Message Understanding Conference (MUC-7) and reported in (Marsh, 1998). The Template Element (TE) task identifies organizations, persons, locations, and some artifacts (rocket and airplane-related artifacts). For each organization in an article, one must identify all of its names as used in the article, its type (corporation, government, or other), and any significant description of it. For each person, one must find all of the person's names within the document, his/her type (civilian or military), and any significant descriptions (e.g., titles). For each location, one must also give its type (city, province, county, body of water, etc.). For the following example, the template element in Figure 1 was to be generated: "...according to the report by Edwin Dorn, under secretary of defense for personnel and readiness. ...Dorn's conclusion that Washington..."

<ENTITY-9601020516-13> :=
ENT_NAME: "Edwin Dorn"
"Dorn"
ENT_TYPE: PERSON
ENT_DESCRIPTOR: "under secretary of defense for personnel and readiness"
ENT_CATEGORY: PER_CIV

Figure 1: An example of the information to be extracted for TE.

The Template Relations (TR) task involves identifying instances of three relations in the text:

- the products made by each company
- the employees of each organization,
- the (headquarters) location of each organization.

TR builds on TE in that TR reports binary relations between elements of TE. For the following example, the template relation in Figure 2 was to be generated: "Donald M. Goldstein, a historian at the University of Pittsburgh who helped write..."

<EMPLOYEE_OF-9601020516-5> :=
PERSON: <ENTITY-9601020516-18>
ORGANIZATION: <ENTITY-9601020516-9>
<ENTITY-9601020516-9> :=
ENT_NAME: "University of Pittsburgh"
ENT_TYPE: ORGANIZATION
ENT_CATEGORY: ORG_CO
<ENTITY-9601020516-18> :=
ENT_NAME: "Donald M. Goldstein"
ENT_TYPE: PERSON
ENT_DESCRIPTOR: "a historian at the University of Pittsburgh"

Figure 2: An example of information to be extracted for TR

3 Integrated Sentential Processing

Almost all approaches to information extraction – even at the sentence level – are based on the divide-and-conquer strategy of reducing a complex problem to a set of simpler ones. Currently, the prevailing architecture for dividing sentential processing is a four-stage pipeline consisting of:

1. part-of-speech tagging
2. name finding
3. syntactic analysis, often limited to noun and verb group chunking
4. semantic interpretation, usually based on pattern matching

Since we were interested in exploiting recent advances in parsing, replacing the syntactic analysis stage of the standard pipeline with a modern statistical parser was an obvious possibility. However, pipelined architectures suffer from a serious disadvantage: errors accumulate as they propagate through the pipeline. For example, an error made during part-of-speech-tagging may cause a future error in syntactic analysis, which may in turn cause a semantic interpretation failure. There is no opportunity for a later stage, such as parsing, to influence or correct an earlier stage such as part-of-speech tagging.

An integrated model can limit the propagation of errors by making all decisions jointly. For this reason, we focused on designing an integrated model in which tagging, name-finding, parsing, and semantic interpretation decisions all have the opportunity to mutually influence each other.

A second consideration influenced our decision toward an integrated model. We were already using a generative statistical model for part-of-speech tagging (Weischedel *et al.* 1993), and more recently, had begun using a generative statistical model for name finding (Bikel *et al.* 1997). Finally, our newly constructed parser, like that of (Collins 1997), was based on a generative statistical model. Thus, each component of what would be the first three stages of our pipeline was based on the same general class of statistical model. Although each model differed in its detailed probability structure, we believed that the essential elements of all three models could be generalized in a single probability model.

If the single generalized model could then be extended to semantic analysis, all necessary sentence level processing would be contained in that model. Because generative statistical models had already proven successful for each of the first three stages, we were optimistic that some of their properties – especially their ability to learn from large amounts of data, and their robustness when presented with unexpected inputs – would also benefit semantic analysis.

4 Representing Syntax and Semantics Jointly

Our integrated model represents syntax and semantics jointly using augmented parse trees. In these trees, the standard TREEBANK structures are augmented to convey semantic information, that is, entities and relations. An example of an augmented parse tree is shown in Figure 3. The five key facts in this example are:

- "Nance" is the name of a person.
- "A paid consultant to ABC News" describes a person.
- "ABC News" is the name of an organization.
- The person described as "a paid consultant to ABC News" is employed by ABC News.
- The person named "Nance" and the person described as "a paid consultant to ABC News" are the same person.

Here, each "reportable" name or description is identified by a "-r" suffix attached to its semantic label. For example, “per-r” identifies “Nance” as a named person, and "per-desc-r" identifies "a paid consultant to ABC News" as a person description. Other labels indicate relations among entities. For example, the co-reference relation between "Nance" and "a paid consultant to ABC News" is indicated by "per-desc-of.” In this case, because the argument does not connect directly to the relation, the intervening nodes are labeled with semantics “-ptr” to indicate the connection. Further details are discussed in the section Tree Augmentation.

5 Creating the Training Data

To train our integrated model, we required a large corpus of augmented parse trees. Since it was known that the MUC-7 evaluation data would be drawn from a variety of newswire sources, and that the articles would focus on rocket launches, it was important that our training corpus be drawn from similar sources and that it cover similar events. Thus, we did not consider simply adding semantic labels to the existing Penn TREEBANK, which is drawn from a single source – the Wall Street Journal – and is impoverished in articles about rocket launches.

Instead, we applied an information retrieval system to select a large number of articles from the desired sources, yielding a corpus rich in the desired types of events. The retrieved articles would then be annotated with augmented tree structures to serve as a training corpus.

Initially, we tried to annotate the training corpus by hand marking, for each sentence, the entire augmented tree. It soon became painfully obvious that this task could not be performed in the available time. Our annotation staff found syntactic analysis particularly complex and slow going. By necessity, we adopted the strategy of hand marking only the semantics.

Figure 4 shows an example of the semantic annotation, which was the only type of manual annotation we performed.

To produce a corpus of augmented parse trees, we used the following multi-step training procedure which exploited the Penn TREEBANK

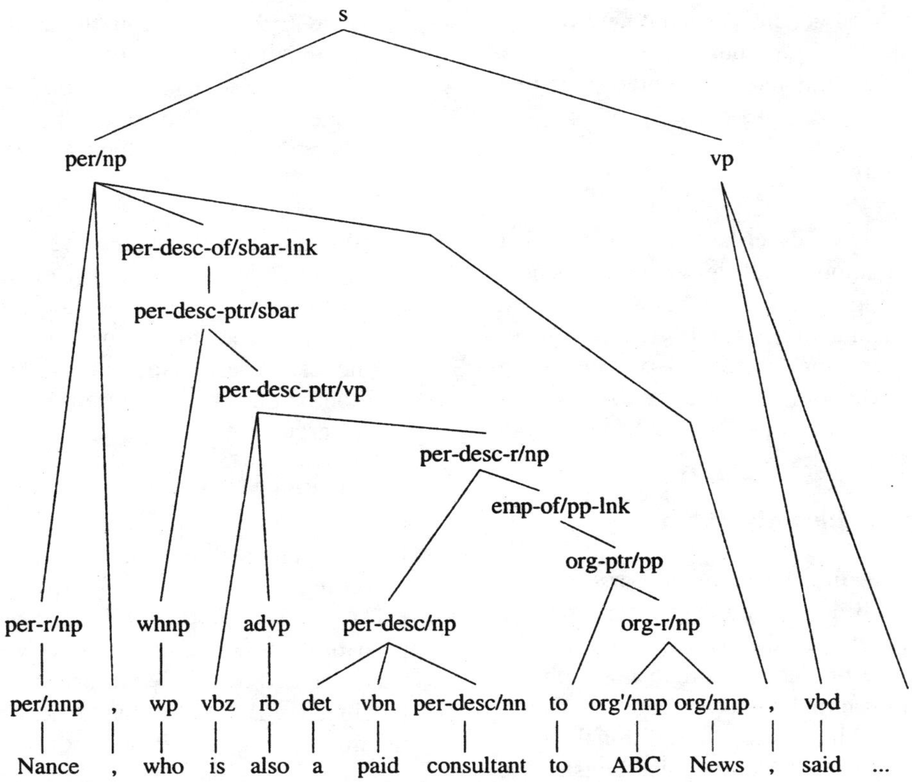

Figure 3: An example of an augmented parse tree.

1. The model (see Section 7) was first trained on purely syntactic parse trees from the TREEBANK, producing a model capable of broad-coverage syntactic parsing.

2. Next, for each sentence in the semantically annotated corpus:

   a. The model was applied to parse the sentence, constrained to produce only parses that were consistent with the semantic annotation. A parse was considered consistent if no syntactic constituents crossed an annotated entity or description boundary.

   b. The resulting parse tree was then augmented to reflect semantic structure in addition to syntactic structure.

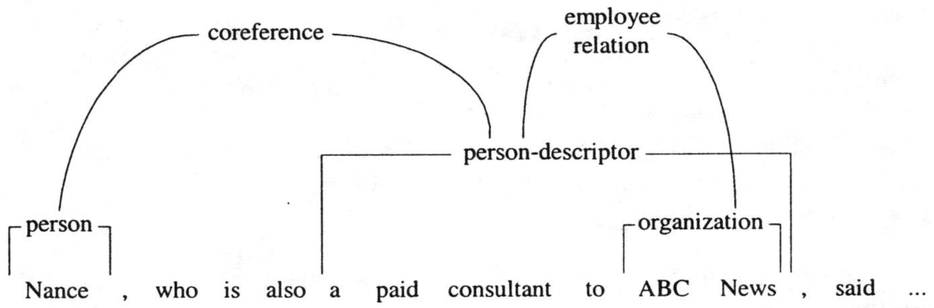

Figure 4: An example of semantic annotation.

Applying this procedure yielded a new version of the semantically annotated corpus, now annotated with complete augmented trees like that in Figure 3.

6 Tree Augmentation

In this section, we describe the algorithm that was used to automatically produce augmented trees, starting with a) human-generated semantic annotations and b) machine-generated syntactic parse trees. For each sentence, combining these two sources involved five steps. These steps are given below:

Tree Augmentation Algorithm

1. Nodes are inserted into the parse tree to distinguish names and descriptors that are not bracketed in the parse. For example, the parser produces a single noun phrase with no internal structure for "Lt. Cmdr. David Edwin Lewis". Additional nodes must be inserted to distinguish the description, "Lt. Cmdr.," and the name, "David Edwin Lewis."

2. Semantic labels are attached to all nodes that correspond to names or descriptors. These labels reflect the entity type, such as person, organization, or location, as well as whether the node is a proper name or a descriptor.

3. For relations between entities, where one entity is not a syntactic modifier of the other, the lowermost parse node that spans both entities is identified. A semantic tag is then added to that node denoting the relationship. For example, in the sentence "Mary Fackler Schiavo is the inspector general of the U.S. Department of Transportation," a co-reference semantic label is added to the *S* node spanning the name, "Mary Fackler Schiavo," and the descriptor, "the inspector general of the U.S. Department of Transportation."

4. Nodes are inserted into the parse tree to distinguish the arguments to each relation. In cases where there is a relation between two entities, and one of the entities is a syntactic modifier of the other, the inserted node serves to indicate the relation as well as the argument. For example, in the phrase "Lt. Cmdr. David Edwin Lewis," a node is inserted to indicate that "Lt. Cmdr." is a descriptor for "David Edwin Lewis."

5. Whenever a relation involves an entity that is not a direct descendant of that relation in the parse tree, semantic *pointer labels* are attached to all of the intermediate nodes. These labels serve to form a continuous chain between the relation and its argument.

7 Model Structure

In our statistical model, trees are generated according to a process similar to that described in (Collins 1996, 1997). The detailed probability structure differs, however, in that it was designed to jointly perform part-of-speech tagging, name finding, syntactic parsing, and relation finding in a single process.

For each constituent, the head is generated first, followed by the modifiers, which are generated from the head outward. Head words, along with their part-of-speech tags and features, are generated for each modifier as soon as the modifier is created. Word features are introduced primarily to help with unknown words, as in (Weischedel *et al.* 1993).

We illustrate the generation process by walking through a few of the steps of the parse shown in Figure 3. At each step in the process, a choice is made from a statistical distribution, with the probability of each possible selection dependent on particular features of previously generated elements. We pick up the derivation just after the topmost *S* and its head word, *said*, have been produced. The next steps are to generate in order:

1. A head constituent for the S, in this case a *VP*.

2. Pre-modifier constituents for the *S*. In this case, there is only one: a *PER/NP*.

3. A head part-of-speech tag for the *PER/NP*, in this case *PER/NNP*.

4. A head word for the *PER/NP*, in this case *nance*.

5. Word features for the head word of the *PER/NP*, in this case *capitalized*.

6. A head constituent for the *PER/NP*, in this case a *PER-R/NP*.

7. Pre-modifier constituents for the *PER/NP*. In this case, there are none.

8. Post-modifier constituents for the *PER/NP*. First a comma, then an *SBAR* structure, and then a second comma are each generated in turn.

This generation process is continued until the entire tree has been produced.

We now briefly summarize the probability structure of the model. The categories for head constituents, c_h, are predicted based solely on the category of the parent node, c_p:

$$P(c_h \mid c_p)\text{, e.g. } P(vp \mid s)$$

Modifier constituent categories, c_m, are predicted based on their parent node, c_p, the head constituent of their parent node, c_{hp}, the previously generated modifier, c_{m-1}, and the head word of their parent, w_p. Separate probabilities are maintained for left (pre) and right (post) modifiers:

$$P_L(c_m \mid c_p, c_{hp}, c_{m-1}, w_p)\text{, e.g.}$$
$$P_L(per/np \mid s, vp, null, said)$$
$$P_R(c_m \mid c_p, c_{hp}, c_{m-1}, w_p)\text{, e.g.}$$
$$P_R(null \mid s, vp, null, said)$$

Part-of-speech tags, t_m, for modifiers are predicted based on the modifier, c_m, the part-of-speech tag of the head word, t_h, and the head word itself, w_h:

$$P(t_m \mid c_m, t_h, w_h)\text{, e.g.}$$
$$P(per/nnp \mid per/np, vbd, said)$$

Head words, w_m, for modifiers are predicted based on the modifier, c_m, the part-of-speech tag of the modifier word , t_m, the part-of-speech tag of the head word , t_h, and the head word itself, w_h:

$$P(w_m \mid c_m, t_m, t_h, w_h)\text{, e.g.}$$
$$P(nance \mid per/np, per/nnp, vbd, said)$$

Finally, word features, f_m, for modifiers are predicted based on the modifier, c_m, the part-of-speech tag of the modifier word , t_m, the part-of-speech tag of the head word , t_h, the head word itself, w_h, and whether or not the modifier head word, w_m, is known or unknown.

$$P(f_m \mid c_m, t_m, t_h, w_h, known(w_m))\text{, e.g.}$$
$$P(cap \mid per/np, per/nnp, vbd, said, true)$$

The probability of a complete tree is the product of the probabilities of generating each element in the tree. If we generalize the tree components (constituent labels, words, tags, etc.) and treat them all as simply elements, e, and treat all the conditioning factors as the history, h, we can write:

$$P(tree) = \prod_{e \in tree} P(e \mid h)$$

8 Training the Model

Maximum likelihood estimates for the model probabilities can be obtained by observing frequencies in the training corpus. However, because these estimates are too sparse to be relied upon, we use interpolated estimates consisting of mixtures of successively lower-order estimates (as in Placeway *et al.* 1993).

For modifier constituents, the mixture components are:

$$P'(c_m \mid c_p, c_{hp}, c_{m-1}, w_p) = \lambda_1\, P(c_m \mid c_p, c_{hp}, c_{m-1}, w_p) + \lambda_2\, P(c_m \mid c_p, c_{hp}, c_{m-1})$$

For part-of-speech tags, the mixture components are:

$$P'(t_m \mid c_m, t_h, w_h) = \lambda_1\, P(t_m \mid c_m, w_h) + \lambda_2\, P(t_m \mid c_m, t_h) + \lambda_3\, P(t_m \mid c_m)$$

For head words, the mixture components are:

$$P'(w_m \mid c_m, t_m, t_h, w_h) = \lambda_1\, P(w_m \mid c_m, t_m, w_h) + \lambda_2\, P(w_m \mid c_m, t_m, t_h) + \lambda_3\, P(w_m \mid c_m, t_m) + \lambda_4\, P(w_m \mid t_m)$$

Finally, for word features, the mixture components are:

$$P'(f_m \mid c_m, t_m, t_h, w_h, known(w_m)) = \lambda_1\ P(f_m \mid c_m, t_m, w_h, known(w_m)) + \lambda_2\ P(f_m \mid c_m, t_m, t_h, known(w_m)) + \lambda_3\ P(f_m \mid c_m, t_m, known(w_m)) + \lambda_4\ P(f_m \mid t_m, known(w_m))$$

9 Searching the Model

Given a sentence to be analyzed, the search program must find the most likely semantic and syntactic interpretation. More precisely, it must find the most likely augmented parse tree. Although mathematically the model predicts tree elements in a top-down fashion, we search the space bottom-up using a chart-based search. The search is kept tractable through a combination of CKY-style dynamic programming and pruning of low probability elements.

9.1 Dynamic Programming

Whenever two or more constituents are equivalent relative to all possible later parsing decisions, we apply dynamic programming, keeping only the most likely constituent in the chart. Two constituents are considered equivalent if:

1. They have identical category labels.
2. Their head constituents have identical labels.
3. They have the same head word.
4. Their leftmost modifiers have identical labels.
5. Their rightmost modifiers have identical labels.

9.2 Pruning

Given multiple constituents that cover identical spans in the chart, only those constituents with probabilities within a threshold of the highest scoring constituent are maintained; all others are pruned. For purposes of pruning, and only for purposes of pruning, the prior probability of each constituent category is multiplied by the generative probability of that constituent (Goodman, 1997). We can think of this prior probability as an estimate of the probability of generating a subtree with the constituent category, starting at the topmost node. Thus, the scores used in pruning can be considered as the product of:

1. The probability of generating a constituent of the specified category, starting at the topmost node.
2. The probability of generating the structure beneath that constituent, having already generated a constituent of that category.

Given a new sentence, the outcome of this search process is a tree structure that encodes both the syntactic and semantic structure of the sentence. The semantics – that is, the entities and relations – can then be directly extracted from these sentential trees.

10 Experimental Results

Our system for MUC-7 consisted of the sentential model described in this paper, coupled with a simple probability model for cross-sentence merging. The evaluation results are summarized in Table 1.

In both Template Entity (TE) and Template Relation (TR), our system finished in second place among all entrants. Nearly all of the work was done by the sentential model; disabling the cross-sentence model entirely reduced our overall F-Score by only 2 points.

Task	*Recall*	*Precision*	*F-Score*
Entities (TE)	83%	84%	83.49%
Relations (TR)	64%	81%	71.23%

Table 1: MUC-7 scores.

Task	*Score*
Part-of-Speech Tagging	95.99 (% correct)
Parsing (sentences < 40 words)	85.06 (F-Score)
Name Finding	92.28 (F-Score)

Table 2: Component task performance.

While our focus throughout the project was on TE and TR, we became curious about how well the model did at part-of-speech tagging, syntactic parsing, and at name finding. We evaluated part-of-speech tagging and parsing accuracy on the Wall Street Journal using a now standard procedure (see Collins 97), and evaluated name finding accuracy on the MUC-7 named entity test. The results are summarized in Table 2.

While performance did not quite match the best previously reported results for any of these three tasks, we were pleased to observe that the scores were at or near state-of-the-art levels for all cases.

11 Conclusions

We have demonstrated, at least for one problem, that a lexicalized, probabilistic context-free parser with head rules (LPCFG-HR) can be used effectively for information extraction. A single model proved capable of performing all necessary sentential processing, both syntactic and semantic. We were able to use the Penn TREEBANK to estimate the syntactic parameters; no additional syntactic training was required. The semantic training corpus was produced by students according to a simple set of guidelines. This simple semantic annotation was the only source of task knowledge used to configure the model.

Acknowledgements

The work reported here was supported in part by the Defense Advanced Research Projects Agency. Technical agents for part of this work were Fort Huachucha and AFRL under contract numbers DABT63-94-C-0062, F30602-97-C-0096, and 4132-BBN-001. The views and conclusions contained in this document are those of the authors and should not be interpreted as necessarily representing the official policies, either expressed or implied, of the Defense Advanced Research Projects Agency or the United States Government.

We thank Michael Collins of the University of Pennsylvania for his valuable suggestions.

References

Bikel, Dan; S. Miller; R. Schwartz; and R. Weischedel. (1997) "NYMBLE: A High-Performance Learning Name-finder." In *Proceedings of the Fifth Conference on Applied Natural Language Processing*, Association for Computational Linguistics, pp. 194-201.

Collins, Michael. (1996) "A New Statistical Parser Based on Bigram Lexical Dependencies." In *Proceedings of the 34th Annual Meeting of the Association for Computational Linguistics*, pp. 184-191.

Collins, Michael. (1997) "Three Generative, Lexicalised Models for Statistical Parsing." In *Proceedings of the 35th Annual Meeting of the Association for Computational Linguistics*, pp. 16-23.

Marcus, M.; B. Santorini; and M. Marcinkiewicz. (1993) "Building a Large Annotated Corpus of English: the Penn Treebank." *Computational Linguistics*, 19(2):313-330.

Goodman, Joshua. (1997) "Global Thresholding and Multiple-Pass Parsing." In *Proceedings of the Second Conference on Empirical Methods in Natural Language Processing*, Association for Computational Linguistics, pp. 11-25.

Placeway, P., R. Schwartz, et al. (1993). "The Estimation of Powerful Language Models from Small and Large Corpora." IEEE ICASSP

Weischedel, Ralph; Marie Meteer; Richard Schwartz; Lance Ramshaw; and Jeff Palmucci. (1993) "Coping with Ambiguity and Unknown Words through Probabilistic Models." *Computational Linguistics*, 19(2):359-382.

Assigning Function Tags to Parsed Text*

Don Blaheta and Eugene Charniak
{dpb,ec}@cs.brown.edu
Department of Computer Science
Box 1910 / 115 Waterman St.—4th floor
Brown University
Providence, RI 02912

Abstract

It is generally recognized that the common non-terminal labels for syntactic constituents (NP, VP, etc.) do not exhaust the syntactic and semantic information one would like about parts of a syntactic tree. For example, the Penn Treebank gives each constituent zero or more 'function tags' indicating semantic roles and other related information not easily encapsulated in the simple constituent labels. We present a statistical algorithm for assigning these function tags that, on text already parsed to a simple-label level, achieves an F-measure of 87%, which rises to 99% when considering 'no tag' as a valid choice.

1 Introduction

Parsing sentences using statistical information gathered from a treebank was first examined a decade ago in (Chitrao and Grishman, 1990) and is by now a fairly well-studied problem ((Charniak, 1997), (Collins, 1997), (Ratnaparkhi, 1997)). But to date, the end product of the parsing process has for the most part been a bracketing with simple constituent labels like `NP`, `VP`, or `SBAR`. The Penn treebank contains a great deal of additional syntactic and semantic information from which to gather statistics; reproducing more of this information automatically is a goal which has so far been mostly ignored. This paper details a process by which some of this information—the function tags—may be recovered automatically.

In the Penn treebank, there are 20 tags (figure 1) that can be appended to constituent labels in order to indicate additional information about the syntactic or semantic role of the constituent. We have divided them into four categories (given in figure 2) based on those in the bracketing guidelines (Bies et al., 1995). A constituent can be tagged with multiple tags, but never with two tags from the same category.[1] In actuality, the case where a constituent has tags from all four categories never happens, but constituents with three tags do occur (rarely).

At a high level, we can simply say that having the function tag information for a given text is useful just because any further information would help. But specifically, there are distinct advantages for each of the various categories. Grammatical tags are useful for any application trying to follow the thread of the text—they find the 'who does what' of each clause, which can be useful to gain information about the situation or to learn more about the behaviour of the words in the sentence. The form/function tags help to find those constituents behaving in ways not conforming to their labelled type, as well as further clarifying the behaviour of adverbial phrases. Information retrieval applications specialising in describing events, as with a number of the MUC applications, could greatly benefit from some of these in determining the where-when-why of things. Noting a topicalised constituent could also prove useful to these applications, and it might also help in discourse analysis, or pronoun resolution. Finally, the 'miscellaneous' tags are convenient at various times; particularly the `CLR` 'closely related' tag, which among other things marks phrasal verbs and prepositional ditransitives.

To our knowledge, there has been no attempt so far to recover the function tags in parsing treebank text. In fact, we know of only

* This research was funded in part by NSF grants LIS-SBR-9720368 and IGERT-9870676.

[1] There is a single exception in the corpus: one constituent is tagged with `-LOC-MNR`. This appears to be an error.

ADV	Non-specific adverbial	HLN	Headline	PUT	Locative complement of 'put'
BNF	Benefactive	LGS	Logical subject	SBJ	Subject
CLF	It-cleft	LOC	Location	TMP	Temporal
CLR	'Closely related'	MNR	Manner	TPC	Topic
DIR	Direction	NOM	Nominal	TTL	Title
DTV	Dative	PRD	Predicate	VOC	Vocative
EXT	Extent	PRP	Purpose		

Figure 1: Penn treebank function tags

Grammatical		**53.%**	**Form/Function**		**37.%**	**Topicalisation**		**2.2%**	**Miscellaneous**		**9.5%**
DTV	0.48%	0.25%	NOM	6.8%	2.5%	TPC	100%	2.2%	CLR	94.%	8.8%
LGS	3.0%	1.5%	ADV	11.%	4.2%				CLF	0.34%	0.03%
PRD	18.%	9.3%	BNF	0.072%	0.026%				HLN	2.6%	0.25%
PUT	0.26%	0.13%	DIR	8.3%	3.0%				TTL	3.1%	0.29%
SBJ	78.%	41.%	EXT	3.2%	1.2%						
VOC	0.025%	0.013%	LOC	25.%	9.2%						
			MNR	6.2%	2.3%						
			PRP	5.2%	1.9%						
			TMP	33.%	12.%						

Figure 2: Categories of function tags and their relative frequencies

one project that used them at all: (Collins, 1997) defines certain constituents as complements based on a combination of label and function tag information. This boolean condition is then used to train an improved parser.

2 Features

We have found it useful to define our statistical model in terms of *features*. A 'feature', in this context, is a boolean-valued function, generally over parse tree nodes and either node labels or lexical items. Features can be fairly simple and easily read off the tree (e.g. 'this node's label is X', 'this node's parent's label is Y'), or slightly more complex ('this node's head's part-of-speech is Z'). This is concordant with the usage in the maximum entropy literature (Berger et al., 1996).

When using a number of known features to guess an unknown one, the usual procedure is to calculate the value of each feature, and then essentially look up the empirically most probable value for the feature to be guessed based on those known values. Due to sparse data, some of the features later in the list may need to be ignored; thus the probability of an unknown feature value would be estimated as

$$P(f|f_1, f_2, \ldots, f_n) \approx \hat{P}(f|f_1, f_2, \ldots, f_j), \quad j \leq n\,, \qquad (1)$$

where $\hat{P}$ refers to an empirically observed probability. Of course, if features 1 through i only co-occur a few times in the training, this value may not be reliable, so the empirical probability is usually smoothed:

$$P(f|f_1, f_2, \ldots, f_i) \approx \lambda_i \hat{P}(f|f_1, f_2, \ldots, f_i) + (1-\lambda_i) P(f|f_1, f_2, \ldots, f_{i-1})\,. \qquad (2)$$

The values for λ_i can then be determined according to the number of occurrences of features 1 through i together in the training.

One way to think about equation 1 (and specifically, the notion that j will depend on the values of $f_1 \ldots f_n$) is as follows: We begin with the prior probability of f. If we have data indicating $\hat{P}(f|f_1)$, we multiply in that likelihood, while dividing out the original prior. If we have data for $\hat{P}(f|f_1, f_2)$, we multiply that in while dividing out the $\hat{P}(f|f_1)$ term. This is repeated for each piece of feature data we have; at each point, we are *adjusting* the probability

$$P(f|f_1,f_2,\ldots,f_n) \approx \hat{P}(f)\frac{\hat{P}(f|f_1)}{\hat{P}(f)}\frac{\hat{P}(f|f_1,f_2)}{\hat{P}(f|f_1)}\cdots\frac{\hat{P}(f|f_1,f_2,\ldots,f_j)}{\hat{P}(f|f_1,f_2,\ldots,f_{j-1})}, \quad j \le n$$
$$\approx \prod_{i=0}^{j}\frac{\hat{P}(f|f_1,\ldots,f_{i-1},f_i)}{\hat{P}(f|f_1,\ldots,f_{i-1})} \quad (3)$$

we already have estimated. If knowledge about feature f_i makes f more likely than with just $f_1 \ldots f_{i-1}$, the term where f_i is added will be greater than one and the running probability will be adjusted upward. This gives us the new probability shown in equation 3, which is exactly equivalent to equation 1 since everything except the last numerator cancels out of the equation. The value of j is chosen such that features $f_1 \ldots f_j$ are sufficiently represented in the training data; sometimes all n features are used, but often that would cause sparse data problems. Smoothing is performed on this equation exactly as before: each term is interpolated between the empirical value and the prior estimated probability, according to a value of λ_i that estimates confidence. But aside from perhaps providing a new way to think about the problem, equation 3 is not particularly useful as it is—it is exactly the same as what we had before. Its real usefulness comes, as shown in (Charniak, 1999), when we move from the notion of a feature *chain* to a feature *tree*.

These feature chains don't capture everything we'd like them to. If there are two independent features that are each relatively sparse but occasionally carry a lot of information, then putting one before the other in a chain will effectively block the second from having any effect, since its information is (uselessly) conditioned on the first one, whose sparseness will completely dilute any gain. What we'd really like is to be able to have a feature *tree*, whereby we can condition those two sparse features independently on one common predecessor feature. As we said before, equation 3 represents, for each feature f_i, the probability of f based on f_i and all its predecessors, divided by the probability of f based only on the predecessors. In the chain case, this means that the denominator is conditioned on every feature from 1 to $i-1$, but if we use a feature tree, it is conditioned only on those features along the path to the root of the tree.

A notable issue with feature trees as opposed to feature chains is that the terms do *not* all cancel out. Every leaf on the tree will be repre-

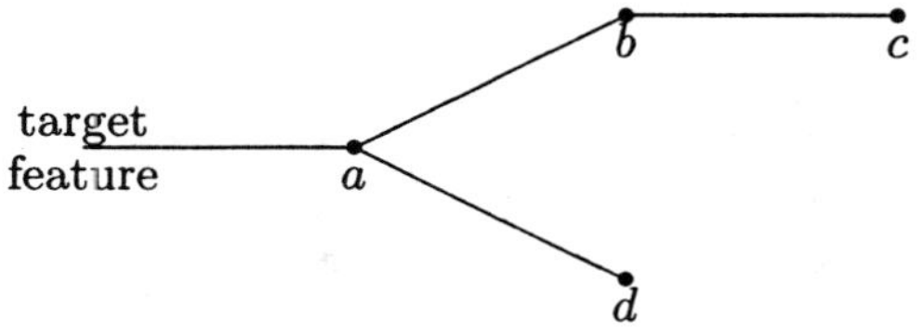

Figure 3: A small example feature tree

sented in the numerator, and every fork in the tree (from which multiple nodes depend) will be represented at least once in the denominator. For example: in figure 3 we have a small feature tree that has one target feature and four conditioning features. Features b and d are independent of each other, but each depends on a; c depends directly only on b. The unsmoothed version of the corresponding equation would be

$$P(f|a,b,c,d) \approx \hat{P}(f)\frac{\hat{P}(f|a)}{\hat{P}(f)}\frac{\hat{P}(f|a,b)}{\hat{P}(f|a)}\frac{\hat{P}(f|a,b,c)}{\hat{P}(f|a,b)}\frac{\hat{P}(f|a,d)}{\hat{P}(f|a)},$$

which, after cancelling of terms and smoothing, results in

$$P(f|a,b,c,d) \approx \frac{P(f|a,b,c)P(f|a,d)}{P(f|a)}. \quad (4)$$

Note that strictly speaking the result is not a probability distribution. It could be made into one with an appropriate normalisation—the so-called partition function in the maximum-entropy literature. However, if the independence assumptions made in the derivation of equation 4 are good ones, the partition function will be close to 1.0. We assume this to be the case for our feature trees.

Now we return the discussion to function tagging. There are a number of features that seem

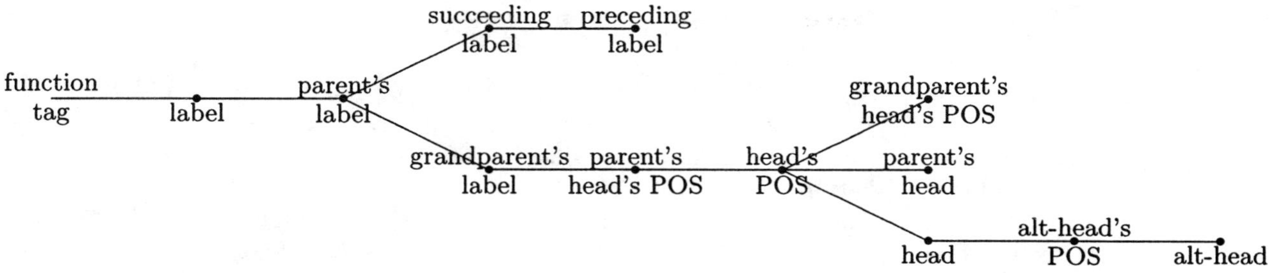

Figure 4: The feature tree used to guess function tags

to condition strongly for one function tag or another; we have assembled them into the feature tree shown in figure 4.[2] This figure should be relatively self-explanatory, except for the notion of an 'alternate head'; currently, an alternate head is only defined for prepositional phrases, and is the head of the object of the prepositional phrase. This data is very important in distinguishing, for example, 'by John' (where John might be a logical subject) from 'by next year' (a temporal modifier) and 'by selling it' (an adverbial indicating manner).

3 Experiment

In the training phase of our experiment, we gathered statistics on the occurrence of function tags in sections 2-21 of the Penn treebank. Specifically, for every constituent in the treebank, we recorded the presence of its function tags (or lack thereof) along with its conditioning information. From this we calculated the empirical probabilities of each function tag referenced in section 2 of this paper. Values of λ were determined using EM on the development corpus (treebank section 24).

To test, then, we simply took the output of our parser on the test corpus (treebank section 23), and applied a postprocessing step to add function tags. For each constituent in the tree, we calculated the likelihood of each function tag according to the feature tree in figure 4, and for each category (see figure 2) we assigned the most likely function tag (which might be the null tag).

[2]The reader will note that the 'features' listed in the tree are in fact not boolean-valued; each node in the given tree can be assumed to stand for a chain of boolean features, one per potential value at that node, exactly one of which will be true.

4 Evaluation

To evaluate our results, we first need to determine what is 'correct'. The definition we chose is to call a constituent correct if there exists in the correct parse a constituent with the same start and end points, label, and function tag (or lack thereof). Since we treated each of the four function tag categories as a separate feature for the purpose of tagging, evaluation was also done on a per-category basis.

The denominator of the accuracy measure should be the maximum possible number we could get correct. In this case, that means excluding those constituents that were already wrong in the parser output; the parser we used attains 89% labelled precision-recall, so roughly 11% of the constituents are excluded from the function tag accuracy evaluation. (For reference, we have also included the performance of our function tagger directly on treebank parses; the slight gain that resulted is discussed below.)

Another consideration is whether to count non-tagged constituents in our evaluation. On the one hand, we could count as correct any constituent with the correct tag as well as any correctly non-tagged constituent, and use as our denominator the number of all correctly-labelled constituents. (We will henceforth refer to this as the 'with-null' measure.) On the other hand, we could just count constituents with the correct tag, and use as our denominators the total number of *tagged*, correctly-labelled constituents. We believe the latter number ('no-null') to be a better performance metric, as it is not overwhelmed by the large number of untagged constituents. Both are reported below.

Table 1: Baseline performance

Category	Baseline 1	Baseline 2 (always choose most likely tag)			
	(never tag)	Tag	Precision	Recall	F-measure
Grammatical	86.935%	SBJ	10.534%	80.626%	18.633%
Form/Function	91.786%	TMP	3.105%	37.795%	5.738%
Topicalisation	99.406%	TPC	0.594%	100.00%	1.181%
Miscellaneous	98.436%	CLR	1.317%	84.211%	2.594%
Overall	94.141%	—	3.887%	66.345%	7.344%

Table 2: Performance within each category

	With-null	———No-null———		
Category	Accuracy	Precision	Recall	F-measure
Grammatical	98.909%	95.472%	95.837%	95.654%
Form/Function	97.104%	80.415%	77.595%	78.980%
Topicalisation	99.915%	92.195%	93.564%	92.875%
Miscellaneous	98.645%	55.644%	65.789%	60.293%

5 Results

5.1 Baselines

There are, it seems, two reasonable baselines for this and future work. First of all, most constituents in the corpus have no tags at all, so obviously one baseline is to simply guess no tag for any constituent. Even for the most common type of function tag (grammatical), this method performs with 87% accuracy. Thus the with-null accuracy of a function tagger needs to be very high to be significant here.

The second baseline might be useful in examining the no-null accuracy values (particularly the recall): always guess the most common tag in a category. This means that every constituent gets labelled with '-SBJ-TMP-TPC-CLR' (meaning that it is a topicalised temporal subject that is 'closely related' to its verb). This combination of tags is in fact entirely illegal by the treebank guidelines, but performs adequately for a baseline. The precision is, of course, abysmal, for the same reasons the first baseline did so well; but the recall is (as one might expect) substantial. The performances of the two baseline measures are given in Table 1.

5.2 Performance in individual categories

In table 2, we give the results for each category. The first column is the with-null accuracy, and the precision and recall values given are the no-null accuracy, as noted in section 4.

Grammatical tagging performs the best of the four categories. Even using the more difficult no-null accuracy measure, it has a 96% accuracy. This seems to reflect the fact that grammatical relations can often be guessed based on constituent labels, parts of speech, and high-frequency lexical items, largely avoiding sparse-data problems. Topicalisation can similarly be guessed largely on high-frequency information, and performed almost as well (93%).

On the other hand, we have the form/function tags and the 'miscellaneous' tags. These are characterised by much more semantic information, and the relationships between lexical items are very important, making sparse data a real problem. All the same, it should be noted that the performance is still far better than the baselines.

5.3 Performance with other feature trees

The feature tree given in figure 4 is by no means the only feature tree we could have used. In-

Table 3: Overall performance on different inputs

	With-null	——	No-null	——
Category	Accuracy	Precision	Recall	F-measure
Parsed	98.643%	87.173%	87.381%	87.277%
Treebank	98.805%	88.450%	88.493%	88.472%

deed, we tried a number of different trees on the development corpus; this tree gave among the best overall results, with no category performing too badly. However, there is no reason to use only one feature tree for all four categories; the best results can be got by using a separate tree for each one. One can thus achieve slight (one to three point) gains in each category.

5.4 Overall performance

The overall performance, given in table 3, appears promising. With a tagging accuracy of about 87%, various information retrieval and knowledge base applications can reasonably expect to extract useful information.

The performance given in the first row is (like all previously given performance values) the function-tagger's performance on the correctly-labelled constituents output by our parser. For comparison, we also give its performance when run directly on the original treebank parse; since the parser's accuracy is about 89%, working directly with the treebank means our statistics are over roughly 12% more constituents. This second version does slightly better.

The main reason that tagging does worse on the parsed version is that although the constituent itself may be correctly bracketed and labelled, its exterior conditioning information can still be incorrect. An example of this that actually occurred in the development corpus (section 24 of the treebank) is the 'that' clause in the phrase 'can swallow the premise that the rewards for such ineptitude are six-figure salaries', correctly diagrammed in figure 5. The function tagger gave this `SBAR` an `ADV` tag, indicating an unspecified adverbial function. This seems extremely odd, given that its conditioning information (nodes circled in the figure) clearly show that it is part of an `NP`, and hence probably modifies the preceding `NN`. Indeed, the statistics give the probability of an `ADV` tag in this conditioning environment as vanishingly small.

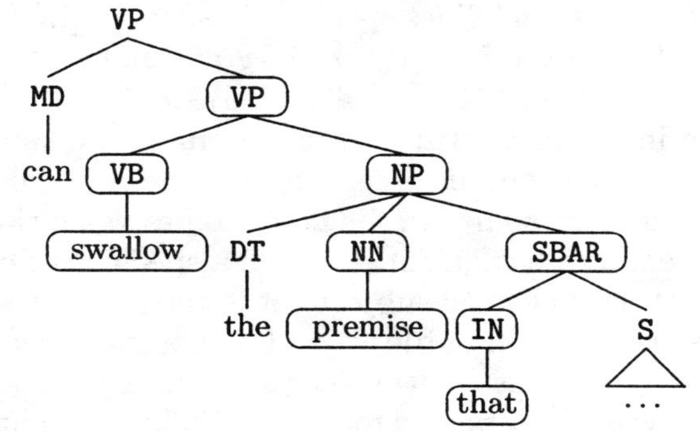

Figure 5: SBAR and conditioning info

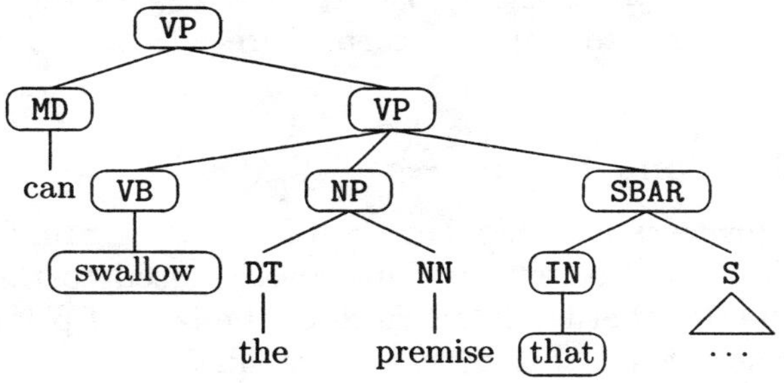

Figure 6: SBAR and conditioning info, as parsed

However, this was not the conditioning information that the tagger received. The parser had instead decided on the (incorrect) parse in figure 6. As such, the tagger's decision makes much more sense, since an `SBAR` under two `VP`s whose heads are `VB` and `MD` is rather likely to be an `ADV`. (For instance, the 'although' clause of the sentence 'he can help, although he doesn't want to.' has exactly the conditioning environment given in figure 6, except that its predecessor is a comma; and this `SBAR` would be correctly tagged `ADV`.) The `SBAR` itself is correctly bracketed and labelled, so it still gets counted in the statistics. Happily, this sort of case seems to be relatively rare.

Another thing that lowers the overall performance somewhat is the existence of error and inconsistency in the treebank tagging. Some tags seem to have been relatively easy for the human treebank taggers, and have few errors. Other tags have explicit caveats that, however well-justified, proved difficult to remember for the taggers—for instance, there are 37 instances of a PP being tagged with LGS (logical subject) in spite of the guidelines specifically saying, '[LGS] attaches to the NP object of *by* and not to the PP node itself.' (Bies et al., 1995) Each mistagging in the test corpus can cause up to two spurious errors, one in precision and one in recall. Still another source of difficulty comes when the guidelines are vague or silent on a specific issue. To return to logical subjects, it is clear that 'the loss' is a logical subject in 'The company was hurt by the loss', but what about in 'The company was unperturbed by the loss'? In addition, a number of the function tags are authorised for 'metaphorical use', but what exactly constitutes such a use is somewhat inconsistently marked. It is as yet unclear just to what degree these tagging errors in the corpus are affecting our results.

6 Conclusion

This work presents a method for assigning function tags to text that has been parsed to the simple label level. Because of the lack of prior research on this task, we are unable to compare our results to those of other researchers; but the results do seem promising. However, a great deal of future work immediately suggests itself:

- Although we tested twenty or so feature trees besides the one given in figure 4, the space of possible trees is still rather unexplored. A more systematic investigation into the advantages of different feature trees would be useful.
- We could add to the feature tree the values of other categories of function tag, or the function tags of various tree-relatives (parent, sibling).
- One of the weaknesses of the lexical features is sparse data; whereas the part of speech is too coarse to distinguish 'by John' (LGS) from 'by Monday' (TMP), the lexical information may be too sparse. This could be assisted by clustering the lexical items into useful categories (names, dates, etc.), and adding those categories as an additional feature type.
- There is no reason to think that this work could not be integrated directly into the parsing process, particularly if one's parser is already geared partially or entirely towards feature-based statistics; the function tag information could prove quite useful within the parse itself, to rank several parses to find the most plausible.

References

Adam L. Berger, Stephen A. Della Pietra, and Vincent J. Della Pietra. 1996. A maximum entropy approach to natural language processing. *Computational Linguistics*, 22(1):39–71.

Ann Bies, Mark Ferguson, Karen Katz, and Robert MacIntyre, 1995. *Bracketing Guidelines for Treebank II Style Penn Treebank Project*, January.

Eugene Charniak. 1997. Statistical parsing with a context-free grammar and word statistics. In *Proceedings of the Fourteenth National Conference on Artificial Intelligence*, pages 598–603, Menlo Park. AAAI Press/MIT Press.

Eugene Charniak. 1999. A maximum-entropy-inspired parser. Technical Report CS-99-12, Brown University, August.

Mahesh V. Chitrao and Ralph Grishman. 1990. Statistical parsing of messages. In *DARPA Speech and Language Workshop*, pages 263–266.

Michael Collins. 1997. Three generative, lexicalised models for statistical parsing. In *Proceedings of the 35th Annual Meeting of the Association for Computational Linguistics*, pages 16–23.

Adwait Ratnaparkhi. 1997. A linear observed time statistical parser based on maximum entropy models. In *Proceedings of the Second Annual Conference on Empirical Methods in Natural Language Processing*, pages 1–10.

Mostly-Unsupervised Statistical Segmentation of Japanese: Applications to Kanji

Rie Kubota Ando and Lillian Lee
Department of Computer Science
Cornell University
Ithaca, NY 14853-7501
{kubotar,llee}@cs.cornell.edu

Abstract

Given the lack of word delimiters in written Japanese, word segmentation is generally considered a crucial first step in processing Japanese texts. Typical Japanese segmentation algorithms rely either on a lexicon and grammar or on pre-segmented data. In contrast, we introduce a novel statistical method utilizing *unsegmented* training data, with performance on kanji sequences comparable to and sometimes surpassing that of morphological analyzers over a variety of error metrics.

1 Introduction

Because Japanese is written without delimiters between words,[1] accurate *word segmentation* to recover the lexical items is a key step in Japanese text processing. Proposed applications of segmentation technology include extracting new technical terms, indexing documents for information retrieval, and correcting optical character recognition (OCR) errors (Wu and Tseng, 1993; Nagao and Mori, 1994; Nagata, 1996a; Nagata, 1996b; Sproat et al., 1996; Fung, 1998).

Typically, Japanese word segmentation is performed by morphological analysis based on lexical and grammatical knowledge. This analysis is aided by the fact that there are three types of Japanese characters, *kanji*, *hiragana*, and *katakana*: changes in character type often indicate word boundaries, although using this heuristic alone achieves less than 60% accuracy (Nagata, 1997).

Character sequences consisting solely of kanji pose a challenge to morphologically-based segmenters for several reasons. First and most importantly, kanji sequences often contain domain terms and proper nouns: Fung (1998) notes that 50-85% of the terms in various technical dictionaries are composed at least partly of kanji. Such words tend to be missing from general-purpose lexicons, causing an *unknown word* problem for morphological analyzers; yet, these terms are quite important for information retrieval, information extraction, and text summarization, making correct segmentation of these terms critical. Second, kanji sequences often consist of compound nouns, so grammatical constraints are not applicable. For instance, the sequence *sha-choh|ken|gyoh-mu|bu-choh* (president|and|business|general manager = "a president as well as a general manager of business") could be incorrectly segmented as: *sha-choh|ken-gyoh|mu|bu-choh* (president|subsidiary business|Tsutomu [a name]|general manager); since both alternatives are four-noun sequences, they cannot be distinguished by part-of-speech information alone. Finally, heuristics based on changes in character type obviously do not apply to kanji-only sequences.

Sequence length	# of characters	% of corpus
1 - 3 kanji	20,405,486	25.6
4 - 6 kanji	12,743,177	16.1
more than 6 kanji	3,966,408	5.1
Total	37,115,071	46.8

Figure 1: Statistics from 1993 Japanese newswire (NIKKEI), 79,326,406 characters total.

Although kanji sequences are difficult to segment, they can comprise a significant portion of Japanese text, as shown in Figure 1. Since sequences of more than 3 kanji generally consist of more than one word, at least 21.2% of 1993 Nikkei newswire consists of kanji sequences requiring segmentation. Thus, accuracy on kanji sequences is an important aspect of the total segmentation process.

As an alternative to lexico-grammatical and supervised approaches, we propose a simple, effi-

[1] The analogous situation in English would be if words were written without spaces between them.

cient segmentation method which learns mostly from very large amounts of *unsegmented* training data, thus avoiding the costs of building a lexicon or grammar or hand-segmenting large amounts of training data. Some key advantages of this method are:

- No Japanese-specific rules are employed, enhancing portability to other languages.
- A very small number of pre-segmented training examples (as few as 5 in our experiments) are needed for good performance, as long as large amounts of unsegmented data are available.
- For long kanji strings, the method produces results rivalling those produced by Juman 3.61 (Kurohashi and Nagao, 1998) and Chasen 1.0 (Matsumoto et al., 1997), two morphological analyzers in widespread use. For instance, we achieve 5% higher *word precision* and 6% better *morpheme recall*.

2 Algorithm

Our algorithm employs counts of character n-grams in an unsegmented corpus to make segmentation decisions. We illustrate its use with an example (see Figure 2).

Let "A B C D W X Y Z" represent an eight-kanji sequence. To decide whether there should be a word boundary between D and W, we check whether n-grams that are adjacent to the proposed boundary, such as the 4-grams s_1 ="A B C D" and s_2 ="W X Y Z", tend to be more frequent than n-grams that straddle it, such as the 4-gram t_1 = "B C D W". If so, we have evidence of a word boundary between D and W, since there seems to be relatively little cohesion between the characters on opposite sides of this gap.

The n-gram orders used as evidence in the segmentation decision are specified by the set N. For instance, if $N = \{4\}$ in our example, then we pose the six questions of the form, "Is $\#(s_i) > \#(t_j)$?", where $\#(x)$ denotes the number of occurrences of x in the (unsegmented) training corpus. If $N = \{2, 4\}$, then two more questions (Is "#(C D) > #(D W)?" and "Is #(W X) > #(D W)?") are added.

More formally, let s_1^n and s_2^n be the non-straddling n-grams just to the left and right of location k, respectively, and let t_j^n be the straddling n-gram with j characters to the right of location k.

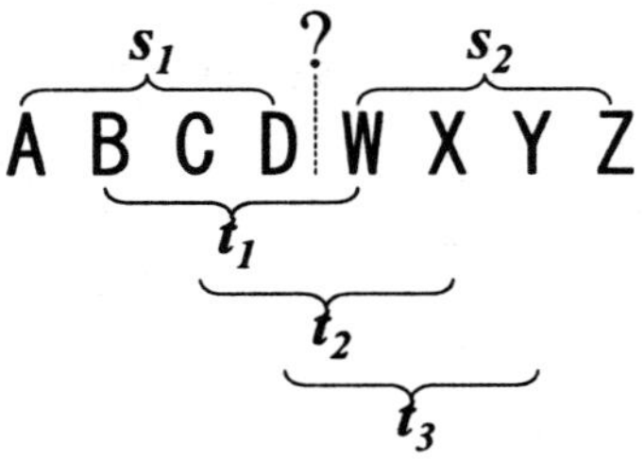

Figure 2: Collecting evidence for a word boundary – are the non-straddling n-grams s_1 and s_2 more frequent than the straddling n-grams t_1, t_2, and t_3?

Let $I_>(y, z)$ be an indicator function that is 1 when $y > z$, and 0 otherwise.[2] In order to compensate for the fact that there are more n-gram questions than $(n-1)$-gram questions, we calculate the fraction of affirmative answers separately for each n in N:

$$v_n(k) = \frac{1}{2(n-1)} \sum_{i=1}^{2} \sum_{j=1}^{n-1} I_>(\#(s_i^n), \#(t_j^n))$$

Then, we average the contributions of each n-gram order:

$$v_N(k) = \frac{1}{|N|} \sum_{n \in N} v_n(k)$$

After $v_N(k)$ is computed for every location, boundaries are placed at all locations ℓ such that either:

- $v_N(\ell) > v_N(\ell - 1)$ and $v_N(\ell) > v_N(\ell + 1)$ (that is, ℓ is a local maximum), or
- $v_N(\ell) \geq t$, a threshold parameter.

The second condition is necessary to allow for single-character words (see Figure 3). Note that it also controls the granularity of the segmentation: low thresholds encourage shorter segments.

Both the count acquisition and the testing phase are efficient. Computing n-gram statistics for all possible values of n simultaneously can be done in $O(m \log m)$ time using suffix arrays, where m is the training corpus size (Manber and Myers, 1993; Nagao and Mori, 1994). However, if the set N of n-gram orders is known in advance, conceptually simpler algorithms suffice. Memory allocation for

[2]Note that we do not take into account the magnitude of the difference between the two frequencies; see section 5 for discussion.

Figure 3: Determining word boundaries. The X- Y boundary is created by the threshold criterion, the other three by the local maximum condition.

count tables can be significantly reduced by omitting n-grams occurring only once and assuming the count of unseen n-grams to be one. In the application phase, the algorithm is clearly linear in the test corpus size if $|N|$ is treated as a constant.

Finally, we note that some pre-segmented data is necessary in order to set the parameters N and t. However, as described below, very little such data was required to get good performance; we therefore deem our algorithm to be "mostly unsupervised".

3 Experimental Framework

Our experimental data was drawn from 150 megabytes of 1993 Nikkei newswire (see Figure 1). Five 500-sequence *held-out* subsets were obtained from this corpus, the rest of the data serving as the unsegmented corpus from which to derive character n-gram counts. Each held-out subset was hand-segmented and then split into a 50-sequence parameter-training set and a 450-sequence test set. Finally, any sequences occurring in both a test set and its corresponding parameter-training set were discarded from the parameter-training set, so that these sets were disjoint. (Typically no more than five sequences were removed.)

3.1 Held-out set annotation

Each held-out set contained 500 randomly-extracted kanji sequences at least ten characters long (about twelve on average), lengthy sequences being the most difficult to segment (Takeda and Fujisaki, 1987). To obtain the gold-standard annotations, we segmented the sequences by hand, using an observation of Takeda and Fujisaki (1987) that many kanji compound words consist of two-character *stem* words together with one-character prefixes and suffixes. Using this terminology, our two-level bracketing annotation may be summarized as follows.[3] At the *word level*, a stem and its affixes are bracketed together as a single unit. At the *morpheme level*, stems are divided from their affixes. For example, although both *naga-no* (Nagano) and *shi* (city) can appear as individual words, *naga-no-shi* (Nagano city) is bracketed as [[*naga-no*][*shi*]], since here *shi* serves as a suffix. Loosely speaking, word-level bracketing demarcates discourse entities, whereas morpheme-level brackets enclose strings that cannot be further segmented without loss of meaning.[4] For instance, if one segments *naga-no* in *naga-no-shi* into *naga* (long) and *no* (field), the intended meaning disappears. Here is an example sequence from our datasets:

[小学校][屋内][[運動][場]][建設]

Three native Japanese speakers participated in the annotation: one segmented all the held-out data based on the above rules, and the other two reviewed 350 sequences in total. The percentage of agreement with the first person's bracketing was 98.42%: only 62 out of 3927 locations were contested by a verifier. Interestingly, all disagreement was at the morpheme level.

3.2 Baseline algorithms

We evaluated our segmentation method by comparing its performance against Chasen 1.0[5] (Matsumoto et al., 1997) and Juman 3.61,[6] (Kurohashi and Nagao, 1998), two state-of-the-art, publically-available, user-extensible morphological analyzers. In both cases, the grammars were used as distributed without modification. The sizes of Chasen's and Juman's default lexicons are approximately 115,000 and 231,000 words, respectively.

Comparison issues An important question that arose in designing our experiments was how to enable morphological analyzers to make use of the parameter-training data, since they do not have parameters to tune. The only significant way that they can be updated is by changing their grammars or lexicons, which is quite tedious (for instance, we had to add part-of-speech information to new entries by hand). We took what we felt to be a reasonable, but not too time-consuming, course of creating new lexical entries for all the bracketed words in the parameter-training data. Evidence that this

[3]A complete description of the annotation policy, including the treatment of numeric expressions, may be found in a technical report (Ando and Lee, 1999).

[4]This level of segmentation is consistent with Wu's (1998) *Monotonicity Principle* for segmentation.

[5]http://cactus.aist-nara.ac.jp/lab/nlt/chasen.html

[6]http://pine.kuee.kyoto-u.ac.jp/nl-resource/juman-e.html

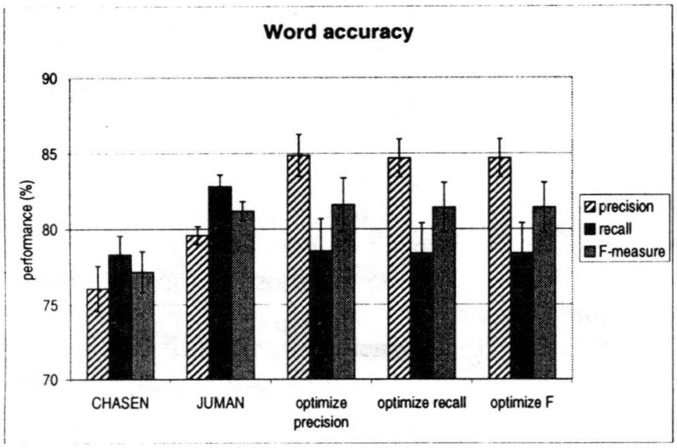

Figure 4: Word accuracy. The three rightmost groups represent our algorithm with parameters tuned for different optimization criteria.

was appropriate comes from the fact that these additions never degraded test set performance, and indeed improved it by one percent in some cases (only small improvements are to be expected because the parameter-training sets were fairly small).

It is important to note that in the end, we are comparing algorithms with access to different sources of knowledge. Juman and Chasen use lexicons and grammars developed by human experts. Our algorithm, not having access to such pre-compiled knowledge bases, must of necessity draw on other information sources (in this case, a very large unsegmented corpus and a few pre-segmented examples) to compensate for this lack. Since we are interested in whether using simple statistics can match the performance of labor-intensive methods, we do not view these information sources as conveying an unfair advantage, especially since the annotated training sets were small, available to the morphological analyzers, and disjoint from the test sets.

4 Results

We report the average results over the five test sets using the optimal parameter settings for the corresponding training sets (we tried all nonempty subsets of $\{2, 3, 4, 5, 6\}$ for the set of n-gram orders N and all values in $\{.05, .1, .15, \ldots, 1\}$ for the threshold t)[7]. In all performance graphs, the "error bars" represent one standard deviation. The results for Chasen and Juman reflect the lexicon additions described in section 3.2.

[7]For simplicity, ties were deterministically broken by preferring smaller sizes of N, shorter n-grams in N, and larger threshold values, in that order.

Word and morpheme accuracy The standard metrics in word segmentation are word precision and recall. Treating a proposed segmentation as a non-nested bracketing (e.g., "|AB|C|" corresponds to the bracketing "[AB][C]"), *word precision* (P) is defined as the percentage of proposed brackets that exactly match word-level brackets in the annotation; *word recall* (R) is the percentage of word-level annotation brackets that are proposed by the algorithm in question; and *word F* combines precision and recall: $F = 2PR/(P + R)$.

One problem with using word metrics is that morphological analyzers are designed to produce morpheme-level segments. To compensate, we altered the segmentations produced by Juman and Chasen by concatenating stems and affixes, as identified by the part-of-speech information the analyzers provided. (We also measured morpheme accuracy, as described below.)

Figures 4 and 8 show word accuracy for Chasen, Juman, and our algorithm for parameter settings optimizing word precision, recall, and F-measure rates. Our algorithm achieves 5.27% higher precision and 0.26% better F-measure accuracy than Juman, and does even better (8.8% and 4.22%, respectively) with respect to Chasen. The recall performance falls (barely) between that of Juman and that of Chasen.

As noted above, Juman and Chasen were designed to produce morpheme-level segmentations. We therefore also measured *morpheme precision, recall*, and *F measure*, all defined analogously to their word counterparts.

Figure 5 shows our morpheme accuracy results. We see that our algorithm can achieve better recall (by 6.51%) and F-measure (by 1.38%) than Juman, and does better than Chasen by an even wider margin (11.18% and 5.39%, respectively). Precision was generally worse than the morphological analyzers.

Compatible Brackets Although word-level accuracy is a standard performance metric, it is clearly very sensitive to the test annotation. Morpheme accuracy suffers the same problem. Indeed, the authors of Juman and Chasen may well have constructed their standard dictionaries using different notions of word and morpheme than the definitions we used in annotating the data. We therefore developed two new, more robust metrics to measure the number of proposed brackets that would be incor-

[[data][base]][system] **(annotation brackets)**

Proposed segmentation	word errors	morpheme errors	compatible-bracket errors	
			crossing	morpheme-dividing
[data][base] [system]	2	0	0	0
[data][basesystem]	2	1	1	0
[database] [sys][tem]	2	3	0	2

Figure 6: Examples of word, morpheme, and compatible-bracket errors. The sequence "data base" has been annotated as "[[data][base]]" because "data base" and "database" are interchangeable.

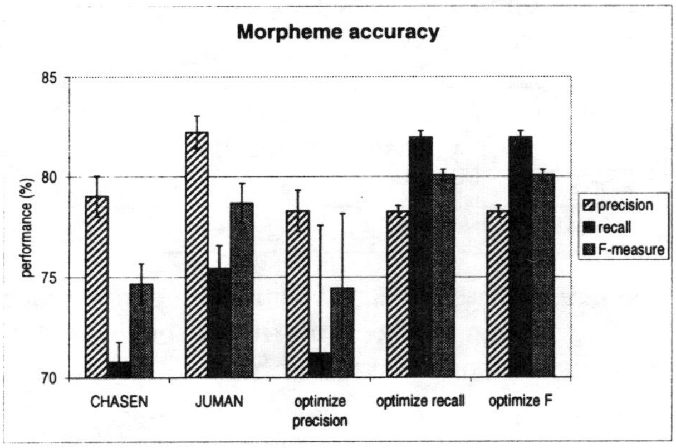

Figure 5: Morpheme accuracy.

rect with respect to *any* reasonable annotation.

Our novel metrics account for two types of errors. The first, a *crossing bracket*, is a proposed bracket that overlaps but is not contained within an annotation bracket (Grishman et al., 1992). Crossing brackets cannot coexist with annotation brackets, and it is unlikely that another human would create such brackets. The second type of error, a *morpheme-dividing bracket*, subdivides a morpheme-level annotation bracket; by definition, such a bracket results in a loss of meaning. See Figure 6 for some examples.

We define a *compatible bracket* as a proposed bracket that is neither crossing nor morpheme-dividing. The *compatible brackets rate* is simply the compatible brackets precision. Note that this metric accounts for different levels of segmentation simultaneously, which is beneficial because the granularity of Chasen and Juman's segmentation varies from morpheme level to compound word level (by our definition). For instance, well-known university names are treated as single segments by virtue of being in the default lexicon, whereas other university names are divided into the name and the word "university". Using the compatible brackets rate, both segmentations can be counted as correct.

We also use the *all-compatible brackets rate*, which is the fraction of sequences for which *all* the proposed brackets are compatible. Intuitively, this function measures the ease with which a human could correct the output of the segmentation algorithm: if the all-compatible brackets rate is high, then the errors are concentrated in relatively few sequences; if it is low, then a human doing post-processing would have to correct many sequences.

Figure 7 depicts the compatible brackets and all-compatible brackets rates. Our algorithm does better on both metrics (for instance, when F-measure is optimized, by 2.16% and 1.9%, respectively, in comparison to Chasen, and by 3.15% and 4.96%, respectively, in comparison to Juman), regardless of training optimization function (word precision, recall, or F — we cannot directly optimize the compatible brackets rate because "perfect" performance is possible simply by making the entire sequence a single segment).

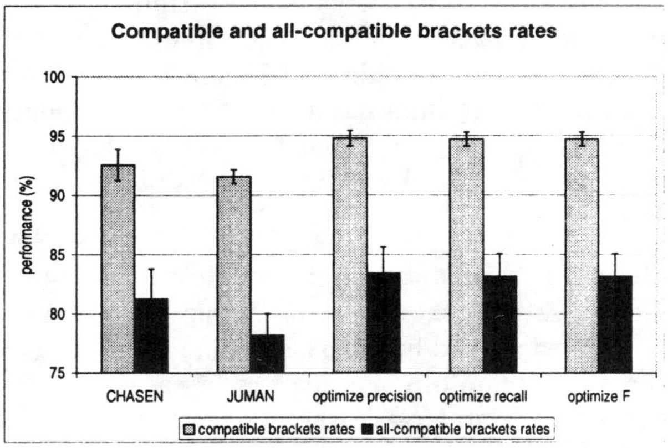

Figure 7: Compatible brackets and all-compatible bracket rates when word accuracy is optimized.

	Juman5 vs. Juman50	Our50 vs Juman50	Our5 vs. Juman5	Our5 vs. Juman50
precision	-1.04	+5.27	+6.18	+5.14
recall	-0.63	-4.39	-3.73	-4.36
F-measure	-0.84	+0.26	+1.14	+0.30

Figure 8: Relative word accuracy as a function of training set size. "5" and "50" denote training set size *before* discarding overlaps with the test sets.

4.1 Discussion

Minimal human effort is needed. In contrast to our mostly-unsupervised method, morphological analyzers need a lexicon and grammar rules built using human expertise. The workload in creating dictionaries on the order of hundreds of thousands of words (the size of Chasen's and Juman's default lexicons) is clearly much larger than annotating the small parameter-training sets for our algorithm. We also avoid the need to segment a large amount of parameter-training data because our algorithm draws almost all its information from an unsegmented corpus. Indeed, the only human effort involved in our algorithm is pre-segmenting the five 50-sequence parameter training sets, which took only 42 minutes. In contrast, previously proposed supervised approaches have used segmented training sets ranging from 1000-5000 sentences (Kashioka et al., 1998) to 190,000 sentences (Nagata, 1996a).

To test how much annotated training data is actually necessary, we experimented with using miniscule parameter-training sets: five sets of only *five* strings each (from which any sequences repeated in the test data were discarded). It took only 4 minutes to perform the hand segmentation in this case. As shown in Figure 8, relative word performance was *not degraded* and sometimes even slightly better. In fact, from the last column of Figure 8 we see that even if our algorithm has access to only five annotated sequences when Juman has access to ten times as many, we still achieve better precision and better F measure.

Both the local maximum and threshold conditions contribute. In our algorithm, a location k is deemed a word boundary if $v_N(k)$ is either (1) a local maximum or (2) at least as big as the threshold t. It is natural to ask whether we really need two conditions, or whether just one would suffice.

We therefore studied whether optimal performance could be achieved using only one of the conditions. Figure 9 shows that in fact both contribute to producing good segmentations. Indeed, in some cases, both are needed to achieve the best performance; also, each condition when used in isolation yields suboptimal performance with respect to some performance metrics.

accuracy	optimize precision	optimize recall	optimize F-measure
word	M	M & T	M
morpheme	M & T	T	T

Figure 9: Entries indicate whether best performance is achieved using the local maximum condition (M), the threshold condition (T), or both.

5 Related Work

Japanese Many previously proposed segmentation methods for Japanese text make use of either a pre-existing lexicon (Yamron et al., 1993; Matsumoto and Nagao, 1994; Takeuchi and Matsumoto, 1995; Nagata, 1997; Fuchi and Takagi, 1998) or pre-segmented training data (Nagata, 1994; Papageorgiou, 1994; Nagata, 1996a; Kashioka et al., 1998; Mori and Nagao, 1998). Other approaches bootstrap from an initial segmentation provided by a baseline algorithm such as Juman (Matsukawa et al., 1993; Yamamoto, 1996).

Unsupervised, non-lexicon-based methods for Japanese segmentation do exist, but they often have limited applicability. Both Tomokiyo and Ries (1997) and Teller and Batchelder (1994) explicitly avoid working with kanji charactes. Takeda and Fujisaki (1987) propose the *short unit model*, a type of Hidden Markov Model with linguistically-determined topology, to segment kanji compound words. However, their method does not handle three-character stem words or single-character stem words with affixes, both of which often occur in proper nouns. In our five test datasets, we found that 13.56% of the kanji sequences contain words that cannot be handled by the short unit model.

Nagao and Mori (1994) propose using the heuristic that high-frequency character n-grams may represent (portions of) new collocations and terms, but the results are not experimentally evaluated, nor is a general segmentation algorithm proposed. The work of Ito and Kohda (1995) similarly relies on high-frequency character n-grams, but again, is more concerned with using these frequent n-grams as pseudo-lexicon entries; a standard segmentation algorithm is then used on the basis of the induced lexicon. Our algorithm, on the hand, is fundamentally different in that it incorporates no explicit notion of word, but only "sees" locations between characters.

Chinese According to Sproat et al. (1996), most prior work in Chinese segmentation has exploited lexical knowledge bases; indeed, the authors assert that they were aware of only one previously published instance (the mutual-information method of Sproat and Shih (1990)) of a purely statistical approach. In a later paper, Palmer (1997) presents a transformation-based algorithm, which requires pre-segmented training data.

To our knowledge, the Chinese segmenter most similar to ours is that of Sun et al. (1998). They also avoid using a lexicon, determining whether a given location constitutes a word boundary in part by deciding whether the two characters on either side tend to occur together; also, they use thresholds and several types of local minima and maxima to make segmentation decisions. However, the statistics they use (mutual information and t-score) are more complex than the simple n-gram counts that we employ.

Our preliminary reimplementation of their method shows that it does not perform as well as the morphological analyzers on our datasets, although we do not want to draw definite conclusions because some aspects of Sun et al's method seem incomparable to ours. We do note, however, that their method incorporates numerical differences between statistics, whereas we only use indicator functions; for example, once we know that one trigram is more common than another, we do not take into account the difference between the two frequencies. We conjecture that using absolute differences may have an adverse effect on rare sequences.

6 Conclusion

In this paper, we have presented a simple, mostly-unsupervised algorithm that segments Japanese sequences into words based on statistics drawn from a large unsegmented corpus. We evaluated performance on kanji with respect to several metrics, including the novel compatible brackets and all-compatible brackets rates, and found that our algorithm could yield performances rivaling that of lexicon-based morphological analyzers.

In future work, we plan to experiment on Japanese sentences with mixtures of character types, possibly in combination with morphological analyzers in order to balance the strengths and weaknesses of the two types of methods. Since our method does not use any Japanese-dependent heuristics, we also hope to test it on Chinese or other languages as well.

Acknowledgments

We thank Minoru Shindoh and Takashi Ando for reviewing the annotations, and the anonymous reviewers for their comments. This material was supported in part by a grant from the GE Foundation.

References

Rie Ando and Lillian Lee. 1999. Unsupervised statistical segmentation of Japanese kanji strings. Technical Report TR99-1756, Cornell University.

Takeshi Fuchi and Shinichiro Takagi. 1998. Japanese morphological analyzer using word co-occurrence - JTAG. In *Proc. of COLING-ACL '98*, pages 409–413.

Pascale Fung. 1998. Extracting key terms from Chinese and Japanese texts. *Computer Processing of Oriental Languages*, 12(1).

Ralph Grishman, Catherine Macleod, and John Sterling. 1992. Evaluating parsing strategies using standardized parse files. In *Proc. of the 3rd ANLP*, pages 156–161.

Akinori Ito and Kasaki Kohda. 1995. Language modeling by string pattern N-gram for Japanese speech recognition. In *Proc. of ICASSP*.

Hideki Kashioka, Yasuhiro Kawata, Yumiko Kinjo, Andrew Finch, and Ezra W. Black. 1998. Use of mutual information based character clusters in dictionary-less morphological analysis of Japanese. In *Proc. of COLING-ACL '98*, pages 658–662.

Sadao Kurohashi and Makoto Nagao. 1998. Japanese morphological analysis system JUMAN version 3.6 manual. In Japanese.

Udi Manber and Gene Myers. 1993. Suffix arrays:

A new method for on-line string searches. *SIAM Journal on Computing*, 22(5):935–948.

T. Matsukawa, Scott Miller, and Ralph Weischedel. 1993. Example-based correction of word segmentation and part of speech labelling. In *Proc. of the HLT Workshop*, pages 227–32.

Yuji Matsumoto and Makoto Nagao. 1994. Improvements of Japanese morphological analyzer JUMAN. In *Proc. of the International Workshop on Sharable Natural Language Resources*, pages 22–28.

Yuji Matsumoto, Akira Kitauchi, Tatsuo Yamashita, Yoshitaka Hirano, Osamu Imaichi, and Tomoaki Imamura. 1997. Japanese morphological analysis system ChaSen manual. Technical Report NAIST-IS-TR97007, Nara Institute of Science and Technology. In Japanese.

Shinsuke Mori and Makoto Nagao. 1998. Unknown word extraction from corpora using n-gram statistics. *Journal of the Information Processing Society of Japan*, 39(7):2093–2100. In Japanese.

Makoto Nagao and Shinsuke Mori. 1994. A new method of N-gram statistics for large number of n and automatic extraction of words and phrases from large text data of Japanese. In *Proc. of the 15th COLING*, pages 611–615.

Masaaki Nagata. 1994. A stochastic Japanese morphological analyzer using a forward-DP backward-A* n-best search algorithm. In *Proc. of the 15th COLING*, pages 201–207.

Masaaki Nagata. 1996a. Automatic extraction of new words from Japanese texts using generalized forward-backward search. In *Proc. of the Conference on Empirical Methods in Natural Language Processing*, pages 48–59.

Masaaki Nagata. 1996b. Context-based spelling correction for Japanese OCR. In *Proc. of the 16th COLING*, pages 806–811.

Masaaki Nagata. 1997. A self-organizing Japanese word segmenter using heuristic word identification and re-estimation. In *Proc. of the 5th Workshop on Very Large Corpora*, pages 203–215.

David Palmer. 1997. A trainable rule-based algorithm for word segmentation. In *Proc. of the 35th ACL/8th EACL*, pages 321–328.

Constantine P. Papageorgiou. 1994. Japanese word segmentation by hidden Markov model. In *Proc. of the HLT Workshop*, pages 283–288.

Richard Sproat and Chilin Shih. 1990. A statistical method for finding word boundaries in Chinese text. *Computer Processing of Chinese and Oriental Languages*, 4:336–351.

Richard Sproat, Chilin Shih, William Gale, and Nancy Chang. 1996. A stochastic finite-sate word-segmentation algorithm for Chinese. *Computational Linguistics*, 22(3).

Maosong Sun, Dayang Shen, and Benjamin K. Tsou. 1998. Chinese word segmentation without using lexicon and hand-crafted training data. In *Proc. of COLING-ACL '98*, pages 1265–1271.

Koichi Takeda and Tetsunosuke Fujisaki. 1987. Automatic decomposition of kanji compound words using stochastic estimation. *Journal of the Information Processing Society of Japan*, 28(9):952–961. In Japanese.

Kouichi Takeuchi and Yuji Matsumoto. 1995. HMM parameter learning for Japanese morphological analyzer. In *Proc. of the 10th Pacific Asia Conference on Language, Information and Computation (PACLING)*, pages 163–172.

Virginia Teller and Eleanor Olds Batchelder. 1994. A probabilistic algorithm for segmenting non-kanji Japanese strings. In *Proc. of the 12th AAAI*, pages 742–747.

Laura Mayfield Tomokiyo and Klaus Ries. 1997. What makes a word: learning base units in Japanese for speech recognition. In *Proc. of the ACL Special Interest Group in Natural Language Learning (CoNLL97)*, pages 60–69.

Zimin Wu and Gwyneth Tseng. 1993. Chinese text segmentation for text retrieval: Achievements and problems. *Journal of the American Society for Information Science*, 44(9):532–542.

Dekai Wu. 1998. A position statement on Chinese segmentation. http://www.cs.ust.hk/~dekai/papers/segmentation.html. Presented at the Chinese Language Processing Workshop, University of Pennsylvania.

Mikio Yamamoto. 1996. A re-estimation method for stochastic language modeling from ambiguous observations. In *Proc. of the 4th Workshop on Very Large Corpora*, pages 155–167.

J. Yamron, J. Baker, P. Bamberg, H. Chevalier, T. Dietzel, J. Elder, F. Kampmann, M. Mandel, L. Manganaro, T. Margolis, and E. Steele. 1993. LINGSTAT: An interactive, machine-aided translation system. In *Proc. of the HLT Workshop*, pages 191–195.

Removing Left Recursion from Context-Free Grammars

Robert C. Moore
Microsoft Research
One Microsoft Way
Redmond, Washington 98052
bobmoore@microsoft.com

Abstract

A long-standing issue regarding algorithms that manipulate context-free grammars (CFGs) in a "top-down" left-to-right fashion is that left recursion can lead to nontermination. An algorithm is known that transforms any CFG into an equivalent non-left-recursive CFG, but the resulting grammars are often too large for practical use. We present a new method for removing left recursion from CFGs that is both theoretically superior to the standard algorithm, and produces very compact non-left-recursive CFGs in practice.

1 Introduction

A long-standing issue regarding algorithms that manipulate context-free grammars (CFGs) in a "top-down" left-to-right fashion is that left recursion can lead to nontermination. This is most familiar in the case of top-down recursive-descent parsing (Aho et al., 1986, pp. 181–182). A more recent motivation is that off-the-shelf speech recognition systems are now available (e.g., from Nuance Communications and Microsoft) that accept CFGs as language models for constraining recognition; but as these recognizers process CFGs top-down, they also require that the CFGs used be non-left-recursive.

The source of the problem can be seen by considering a directly left-recursive grammar production such as $A \rightarrow A\alpha$. Suppose we are trying to parse, or recognize using a speech recognizer, an A at a given position in the input. If we apply this production top-down and left-to-right, our first subgoal will be to parse or recognize an A at the same input position. This immediately puts us into an infinite recursion. The same thing will happen with an indirectly left-recursive grammar, via a chain of subgoals that will lead us from the goal of parsing or recognizing an A at a given position to a descendant subgoal of parsing or recognizing an A at that position.

In theory, the restriction to non-left-recursive CFGs puts no additional constraints on the languages that can be described, because any CFG can in principle be transformed into an equivalent non-left-recursive CFG. However, the standard algorithm for carrying out this transformation (Aho et al., 1986, pp. 176–178) (Hopcroft and Ullman, 1979, p. 96)—attributed to M. C. Paull by Hopcroft and Ullman (1979, p. 106)—can produce transformed grammars that are orders of magnitude larger than the original grammars. In this paper we develop a number of improvements to Paull's algorithm, which help somewhat but do not completely solve the problem. We then go on to develop an alternative approach based on the left-corner grammar transform, which makes it possible to remove left recursion with no significant increase in size for several grammars for which Paull's original algorithm is impractical.

2 Notation and Terminology

Grammar nonterminals will be designated by "low order" upper-case letters (A, B, etc.); and terminals will be designated by lower-case letters. We will use "high order" upper-case letters (X, Y, Z) to denote single symbols that could be either terminals or nonterminals, and Greek letters to denote (possibly empty) sequences of terminals and/or nonterminals. Any production of the form $A \rightarrow \alpha$ will be said to be an *A-production*, and α will be said to be an *expansion* of A.

We will say that a symbol X is a *direct left corner* of a nonterminal A, if there is an A-production with X as the left-most symbol on the right-hand side. We define the *left-corner* relation to be the reflexive transitive closure of the direct-left-corner relation, and we define the *proper-left-corner* relation to be the transitive closure of the direct-left-corner relation. A nonterminal is *left recursive* if it is a proper left corner of itself; a nonterminal is *directly left recursive* if it is a direct left corner of itself; and a nonterminal is *indirectly left recursive* if it is left recursive, but not directly left recursive.

3 Test Grammars

We will test the algorithms considered here on three large, independently-motivated, natural-language grammars. The CT grammar[1] was compiled into a CFG from a task-specific unification grammar

[1]Courtesy of John Dowding, SRI International

	Toy Grammar	CT Grammar	ATIS Grammar	PT Grammar
Grammar size	88	55,830	16,872	67,904
Terminals	40	1,032	357	47
Nonterminals	16	3,946	192	38
Productions	55	24,456	4,592	15,039
LR nonterminals	4	535	9	33
Productions for LR nonterminals	27	2,211	1,109	14,993

Table 1: Grammars used for evaluation.

written for CommandTalk (Moore et al., 1997), a spoken-language interface to a military simulation system. The ATIS grammar was extracted from an internally generated treebank of the DARPA ATIS3 training sentences (Dahl et al., 1994). The PT grammar[2] was extracted from the Penn Treebank (Marcus et al., 1993). To these grammars we add a small "toy" grammar, simply because some of the algorithms cannot be run to completion on any of the "real" grammars within reasonable time and space bounds.

Some statistics on the test grammars are contained in Table 1. The criterion we use to judge effectiveness of the algorithms under test is the size of the resulting grammar, measured in terms of the total number of terminal and nonterminal symbols needed to express the productions of the grammar. We use a slightly nonstandard metric, counting the symbols as if, for each nonterminal, there were a single production of the form $A \to \alpha_1 \mid \ldots \mid \alpha_n$. This reflects the size of files and data structures typically used to store grammars for top-down processing more accurately than counting a separate occurrence of the left-hand side for each distinct right-hand side.

It should be noted that the CT grammar has a very special property: none of the 535 left recursive nonterminals is indirectly left recursive. The grammar was designed to have this property specifically because Paull's algorithm does not handle indirect left recursion well.

It should also be noted that none of these grammars contains empty productions or cycles, which can cause problems for algorithms for removing left recursion. It is relatively easy to trasform an arbitrary CFG into an equivalent grammar which does not contain any of the probelmatical cases. In its initial form the PT grammar contained cycles, but these were removed at a cost of increasing the size of the grammar by 78 productions and 89 total symbols. No empty productions or cycles existed anywhere else in the original grammars.

[2]Courtesy of Eugene Charniak, Brown University

4 Paull's Algorithm

Paull's algorithm for eliminating left recursion from CFGs attacks the problem by an iterative procedure for transforming indirect left recursion into direct left recursion, with a subprocedure for eliminating direct left recursion. This algorithm is perhaps more familiar to some as the first phase of the textbook algorithm for transfomrming CFGs to Greibach normal form (Greibach, 1965).[3] The subprocedure to eliminate direct left recursion performs the following transformation (Hopcroft and Ullman, 1979, p. 96):

Let

$$A \to A\alpha_1 \mid \ldots \mid A\alpha_r$$

be the set of all directly left recursive A-productions, and let

$$A \to \beta_1 \mid \ldots \mid \beta_s$$

be the remaining A-productions. Replace all these productions with

$$A \to \beta_1 \mid \beta_1 A' \mid \ldots \mid \beta_s \mid \beta_s A',$$

and

$$A' \to \alpha_1 \mid \alpha_1 A' \mid \ldots \mid \alpha_s \mid \alpha_s A',$$

where A' is a new nonterminal not used elsewhere in the grammar.

This transformation is embedded in the full algorithm (Aho et al., 1986, p. 177), displayed in Figure 1.

The idea of the algorithm is to eliminate left recursion by transforming the grammar so that all the direct left corners of each nonterminal strictly follow that nonterminal in a fixed total ordering, in which case, no nonterminal can be left recursive. This is accomplished by iteratively replacing direct left corners that precede a given nonterminal with all their expansions in terms of other nonterminals that are greater in the ordering, until the nonterminal has only itself and greater nonterminals as direct left

[3]This has led some readers to attribute the algorithm to Greibach, but Greibach's original method was quite different and much more complicated.

```
Assign an ordering A_1, ..., A_n to the nonterminals of the grammar.

for i := 1 to n do begin
    for j := 1 to i − 1 do begin
        for each production of the form A_i → A_j α do begin
            remove A_i → A_j α from the grammar
            for each production of the form A_j → β do begin
                add A_i → βα to the grammar
            end
        end
    end
    transform the A_i-productions to eliminate direct left recursion
end
```

Figure 1: Paull's algorithm.

Grammar Description	Grammar Size
original toy grammar	88
PA, "best" ordering	156
PA, lexicographical ordering	970
PA, "worst" ordering	5696

Table 2: Effect of nonterminal ordering on Paull's algorithm.

corners. Any direct left recursion for that nonterminal is then eliminated by the first transformation discussed.

The difficulty with this approach is that the iterated substitutions can lead to an exponential increase in the size of the grammar. Consider the grammar consisting of the productions $A_1 \rightarrow 0 \mid 1$, plus $A_{i+1} \rightarrow A_i 0 \mid A_i 1$ for $1 \leq i < n$. It is easy to see that Paull's algorithm will transform the grammar so that it consists of all possible A_i-productions with a binary sequence of length i on the right-hand side, for $1 \leq i \leq n$, which is exponentially larger than the original grammar. Notice that the efficiency of Paull's algorithm crucially depends on the ordering of the nonterminals. If the ordering is reversed in the grammar of this example, Paull's algorithm will make no changes, since the grammar will already satisfy the condition that all the direct left corners of each nonterminal strictly follow that nonterminal in the revised ordering. The textbook discussions of Paull's algorithm, however, are silent on this issue.

In the inner loop of Paull's algorithm, for nonterminals A_i and A_j, such that $i > j$ and A_j is a direct left corner of A_i, we replace all occurrences of A_j as a direct left corner of A_i with all possible expansions of A_j. This only contributes to elimination of left recursion from the grammar if A_i is a left-recursive nonterminal, and A_j lies on a path that makes A_i left recursive; that is, if A_i is a left corner of A_j (in addition to A_j being a left corner of A_i). We could eliminate replacements that are useless in removing left recursion if we could order the nonterminals of the grammar so that, if $i > j$ and A_j is a direct left corner of A_i, then A_i is also a left corner of A_j. We can achieve this by ordering the nonterminals in decreasing order of the number of distinct left corners they have. Since the left-corner relation is transitive, if C is a direct left corner of B, every left corner of C is also a left corner of B. In addition, since we defined the left-corner relation to be reflexive, B is a left corner of itself. Hence, if C is a direct left corner of B, it must follow B in decreasing order of number of distinct left corners, unless B is a left corner of C.

Table 2 shows the effect on Paull's algorithm of ordering the nonterminals according to decreasing number of distinct left corners, with respect to the toy grammar.[4] In the table, "best" means an ordering consistent with this constraint. Note that if a grammar has indirect left recursion, there will be multiple orderings consistent with our constraint, since indirect left recursion creates cycles in the the left-corner relation, so every nonterminal in one of these cycles will have the same set of left corners. Our "best" ordering is simply an arbitrarily chosen

[4]As mentioned previously, grammar sizes are given in terms of total terminal and nonterminal symbols needed to express the grammar.

	CT Grammar	ATIS Grammar	PT Grammar
original grammar	55,830	16,872	67,904
PA	62,499	$> 5,000,000$	$> 5,000,000$
LF	54,991	11,582	37,811
LF+PA	59,797	2,004,473	$> 5,000,000$
LF+NLRG+PA	57,924	72,035	$> 5,000,000$

Table 3: Grammar size comparisons with Paull's algorithm variants

ordering respecting the constraint; we are unaware of any method for finding a unique best ordering, other than trying all the orderings respecting the constraint.

As a neutral comparison, we also ran the algorithm with the nonterminals ordered lexicographically. Finally, to test how bad the algorithm could be with a really poor choice of nonterminal ordering, we defined a "worst" ordering to be one with *increasing* numbers of distinct left corners. It should be noted that with either the lexicographical or worst ordering, on all of our three large grammars Paull's algorithm exceeded a cut-off of 5,000,000 grammar symbols, which we chose as being well beyond what might be considered a tolerable increase in the size of the grammar.

Let PA refer to Paull's algorithm with the nonterminals ordered according to decreasing number of distinct left corners. The second line of Table 3 shows the results of running PA on our three large grammars. The CT grammar increases only modestly in size, because as previously noted, it has no indirect left recursion. Thus the combinatorial phase of Paull's algorithm is never invoked, and the increase is solely due to the transformation applied to directly left-recursive productions. With the ATIS grammar and PT grammar, which do not have this special property, Paull's algorithm exceeded our cut-off, even with our best ordering of nonterminals.

Some additional optimizations of Paull's aglorithm are possible. One way to reduce the number of substitutions made by the inner loop of the algorithm is to "left factor" the grammar (Aho et al., 1986, pp. 178–179). The left-factoring transformation (LF) applies the following grammar rewrite schema repeatedly, until it is no longer applicable:

> **LF**: For each nonterminal A, let α be the longest nonempty sequence such that there is more than one grammar production of the form $A \rightarrow \alpha\beta$. Replace the set of all productions
>
> $$A \rightarrow \alpha\beta_1, \ \ldots, \ A \rightarrow \alpha\beta_n$$
>
> with the productions
>
> $$A \rightarrow \alpha A', \ A' \rightarrow \beta_1, \ \ldots, \ A' \rightarrow \beta_n,$$
>
> where A' is a new nonterminal symbol.

With left factoring, for each nonterminal A there will be only one A-production for each direct left corner of A, which will in general reduce the number of substitutions performed by the algorithm.

The effect of left factoring by itself is shown in the third line of Table 3. Left factoring actually reduces the size of all three grammars, which may be unintuitive, since left factoring necessarily increases the number of productions in the grammar. However, the transformed productions are shorter, and the grammar size as measured by total number of symbols can be smaller because common left factors are represented only once.

The result of applying PA to the left-factored grammars is shown in the fourth line of Table 3 (LF+PA). This produces a modest decrease in the size of the non-left-recursive form of the CT grammar, and brings the non-left-recursive form of the ATIS grammar under the cut-off size, but the non-left-recursive form of the PT grammar still exceeds the cut-off.

The final optimization we have developed for Paull's algorithm is to transform the grammar to combine all the non-left-recursive possibilities for each left-recursive nonterminal under a new nonterminal symbol. This transformation, which we might call "non-left-recursion grouping" (NLRG), can be defined as follows:

> **NLRG**: For each left-recursive nonterminal A, let $\alpha_1, \ldots, \alpha_n$ be all the expansions of A that do not have a left recursive nonterminal as the left most symbol. If $n > 1$, replace the set of productions
>
> $$A \rightarrow \alpha_1, \ \ldots, \ A \rightarrow \alpha_n$$
>
> with the productions
>
> $$A \rightarrow A', \ A' \rightarrow \alpha_1, \ \ldots, \ A' \rightarrow \alpha_n,$$
>
> where A' is a new nonterminal symbol.

Since all the new nonterminals introduced by this transformation will be non-left-recursive, Paull's algorithm with our best ordering will never substitute the expansions of any of these new nonterminals into the productions for any other nonterminal, which in general reduces the number of substitutions the algorithm makes. We did not empirically measure

	CT Grammar	ATIS Grammar	PT Grammar
original grammar	55,830	16,872	67,904
LF	54,991	11,582	37,811
LF+NLRG+PA	57,924	72,035	$> 5,000,000$
LC	762,576	287,649	1,567,162
LC_{LR}	60,556	40,660	1,498,112
$LF+LC_{LR}$	58,893	13,641	67,167
$LF+NLRG+LC_{LR}$	57,380	12,243	50,277

Table 4: Grammar size comparisons for LC transform variants

the effect on grammar size of applying the NLRG transformation by itself, but it is easy to see that it increases the grammar size by exactly two symbols for each left-recursive nonterminal to which it is applied. Thus an addition of twice the number of left-recursive nonterminals will be an upper bound on the increase in the size of the grammar, but since not every left-recursive nonterminal necessarily has more than one non-left-recursive expansion, the increase may be less than this.

The fifth line of Table 3 (LF+NLRG+PA) shows the result of applying LF, followed by NLRG, followed by PA. This produces another modest decrease in the size of the non-left-recursive form of the CT grammar and reduces the size of the non-left-recursive form of the ATIS grammar by a factor of 27.8, compared to LF+PA. The non-left-recursive form of the PT grammar remains larger than the cut-off size of 5,000,000 symbols, however.

5 Left-Recursion Elimination Based on the Left-Corner Transform

An alternate approach to eliminating left-recursion is based on the left-corner (LC) grammar transform of Rosenkrantz and Lewis (1970) as presented and modified by Johnson (1998). Johnson's second form of the LC transform can be expressed as follows, with expressions of the form $A\text{–}a$, $A\text{–}X$, and $A\text{–}B$ being new nonterminals in the transformed grammar:

1. If a terminal symbol a is a proper left corner of A in the original grammar, add $A \rightarrow aA\text{–}a$ to the transformed grammar.
2. If B is a proper left corner of A and $B \rightarrow X\beta$ is a production of the original grammar, add $A\text{–}X \rightarrow \beta A\text{–}B$ to the transformed grammar.
3. If X is a proper left corner of A and $A \rightarrow X\beta$ is a production of the original grammar, add $A\text{–}X \rightarrow \beta$ to the transformed grammar.

In Rosenkrantz and Lewis's original LC transform, schema 2 applied whenever B is a left corner of A, including all cases where $B = A$. In Johnson's version schema 2 applies when $B = A$ only if A is a proper left corner of itself. Johnson then introduces schema 3 handle the residual cases, without introducing instances of nonterminals of the form $A\text{–}A$ that need to be allowed to derive the empty string.

The original purpose of the LC transform is to allow simulation of left-corner parsing by top-down parsing, but it also eliminates left recursion from any noncyclic CFG.[5] Furthermore, in the worst case, the total number of symbols in the transformed grammar cannot exceed a fixed multiple of the square of the number of symbols in the original grammar, in contrast to Paull's algorithm, which exponentiates the size of the grammar in the worst case.

Thus, we can use Johnson's version of the LC transform directly to eliminate left-recursion. Before applying this idea, however, we have one general improvement to make in the transform. Johnson notes that in his version of the LC transform, a new nonterminal of the form $A\text{–}X$ is useless unless X is a proper left corner of A. We further note that a new nonterminal of the form $A\text{–}X$, as well as the orginal nonterminal A, is useless in the transformed grammar, unless A is either the top nonterminal of the grammar or appears on the right-hand side of an original grammar production in other than the left-most position. This can be shown by induction on the length of top-down derivations using the productions of the transformed grammar. Therefore, we will call the original nonterminals meeting this condition "retained nonterminals" and restrict the LC transform so that productions involving nonterminals of the form $A\text{–}X$ are created only if A is a retained nonterminal.

Let LC refer to Johnson's version of the LC transform restricted to retained nonterminals. In Table 4 the first three lines repeat the previously shown sizes for our three original grammars, their left-factored form, and their non-left-recursive form using our best variant of Paull's algorithm (LF+NLRG+PA). The fourth line shows the results of applying LC to the three original grammars. Note that this produces a non-left-recursive form of the PT grammar smaller than the cut-off size, but the non-left-recursive forms of the CT and ATIS grammars are

[5] In the case of a cyclic CFG, the schema 2 fails to guarantee a non-left-recursive transformed grammar.

considerably larger than the most compact versions created with Paull's algorithm.

We can improve on this result by noting that, since we are interested in the LC transform only as a means of eliminating left-recursion, we can greatly reduce the size of the transformed grammars by applying the transform only to left-recursive nonterminals. More precisely, we can retain in the transformed grammar all the productions expanding non-left-recursive nonterminals of the original grammar, and for the purposes of the LC transform, we can treat non-left-recursive nonterminals as if they were terminals:

1. If a terminal symbol or non-left-recursive nonterminal X is a proper left corner of a retained left-recursive nonterminal A in the original grammar, add $A \rightarrow XA\text{–}X$ to the transformed grammar.
2. If B is a left-recursive proper left corner of a retained left-recursive nonterminal A and $B \rightarrow X\beta$ is a production of the original grammar, add $A\text{–}X \rightarrow \beta A\text{–}B$ to the transformed grammar.
3. If X is a proper left corner of a retained left-recursive nonterminal A and $A \rightarrow X\beta$ is a production of the original grammar, add $A\text{–}X \rightarrow \beta$ to the transformed grammar.
4. If A is a non-left-recursive nonterminal and $A \rightarrow \beta$ is a production of the original grammar, add $A \rightarrow \beta$ to the transformed grammar.

Let LC_{LR} refer to the LC transform restricted by these modifications so as to apply only to left-recursive nonterminals. The fifth line of Table 4 shows the results of applying LC_{LR} to the three original grammars. LC_{LR} greatly reduces the size of the non-left-recursive forms of the CT and ATIS grammars, but the size of the non-left-recursive form of the PT grammar is only slightly reduced. This is not surprising if we note from Table 1 that almost all the productions of the PT grammar are productions for left-recursive nonterminals. However, we can apply the additional transformations that we used with Paull's algorithm, to reduce the number of productions for left-recursive nonterminals before applying our modified LC transform. The effects of left factoring the grammar before applying LC_{LR} (LF+LC_{LR}), and additionally combining non-left-recursive productions for left-recursive nonterminals between left factoring and applying LC_{LR} (LF+NLRG+LC_{LR}), are shown in the sixth and seventh lines of Table 4.

With all optimizations applied, the non-left-recursive forms of the ATIS and PT grammars are smaller than the originals (although not smaller than the left-factored forms of these grammars), and the non-left-recursive form of the CT grammar is only slightly larger than the original. In all cases, LF+NLRG+LC_{LR} produces more compact grammars than LF+NLRG+PA, the best variant of Paull's algorithm—slightly more compact in the case of the CT grammar, more compact by a factor of 5.9 in the case of the ATIS grammar, and more compact by at least two orders of magnitude in the case of the PT grammar.

6 Conclusions

We have shown that, in its textbook form, the standard algorithm for eliminating left recursion from CFGs is impractical for three diverse, independently-motivated, natural-language grammars. We apply a number of optimizations to the algorithm—most notably a novel strategy for ordering the nonterminals of the grammar—but one of the three grammars remains essentially intractable. We then explore an alternative approach based on the LC grammar transform. With several optimizations of this approach, we are able to obtain quite compact non-left-recursive forms of all three grammars. Given the diverse nature of these grammars, we conclude that our techniques based on the LC transform are likely to be applicable to a wide range of CFGs used for natural-language processing.

References

A. V. Aho, R. Sethi, and J. D. Ullman. 1986. *Compilers: Principles, Techniques, and Tools.* Addison-Wesley Publishing Company, Reading, Massachusetts.

D. A. Dahl et al. 1994. Expanding the scope of the ATIS task: the ATIS-3 corpus. In *Proceedings of the Spoken Language Technology Workshop*, pages 3–8, Plainsboro, New Jersey. Advanced Research Projects Agency.

S. A. Greibach. 1965. A new normal-form theorem for context-free phrase structure grammars. *Journal of the Association for Computing Machinery*, 12(1):42–52, January.

J. E. Hopcroft and J. D. Ullman. 1979. *Introduction to Automata Theory, Languages, and Computation.* Addison-Wesley Publishing Company, Reading, Massachusetts.

M. Johnson. 1998. Finite-state approximation of constraint-based grammars using left-corner grammar transforms. In *Proceedings, COLING-ACL '98*, pages 619–623, Montreal, Quebec, Canada. Association for Computational Linguistics.

M. P. Marcus, B. Santorini, and M. A. Marcinkiewicz. 1993. Building a large annotated corpus of English: The Penn Treebank. *Computational Linguistics*, 19(2):313–330, June.

R. Moore, J. Dowding, H. Bratt, J. M. Gawron, Y. Gorfu, and A. Cheyer. 1997. Commandtalk:

A spoken-language interface for battlefield simulations. In *Proceedings of the Fifth Conference on Applied Natural Language Processing*, pages 1–7, Washington, DC. Association for Computational Linguistics.

S. J. Rosenkrantz and P. M. Lewis. 1970. Deterministic left corner parser. In *IEEE Conference Record of the 11th Annual Symposium on Switching and Automata Theory*, pages 139–152.

Using Semantic Preferences to Identify Verbal Participation in Role Switching Alternations.

Diana McCarthy
Cognitive & Computing Sciences,
University of Sussex
Brighton BN1 9QH, UK
dianam@cogs.susx.ac.uk

Abstract

We propose a method for identifying diathesis alternations where a particular argument type is seen in slots which have different grammatical roles in the alternating forms. The method uses selectional preferences acquired as probability distributions over WordNet. Preferences for the target slots are compared using a measure of distributional similarity. The method is evaluated on the causative and conative alternations, but is generally applicable and does not require a priori knowledge specific to the alternation.

1 Introduction

Diathesis alternations are alternate ways in which the arguments of a verb are expressed syntactically. The syntactic changes are sometimes accompanied by slight changes in the meaning of the verb. An example of the causative alternation is given in (1) below. In this alternation, the object of the transitive variant can also appear as the subject of the intransitive variant. In the conative alternation, the transitive form alternates with a prepositional phrase construction involving either *at* or *on*. An example of the conative alternation is given in (2).

1. The boy broke the window ↔ The window broke.
2. The boy pulled at the rope ↔ The boy pulled the rope.

We refer to alternations where a particular semantic role appears in different grammatical roles in alternate realisations as "role switching alternations" (RSAs). It is these alternations that our method applies to.

Recently, there has been interest in corpus-based methods to identify alternations (McCarthy and Korhonen, 1998; Lapata, 1999), and associated verb classifications (Stevenson and Merlo, 1999). These have either relied on a priori knowledge specified for the alternations in advance, or are not suitable for a wide range of alternations. The fully automatic method outlined here is applied to the causative and conative alternations, but is applicable to other RSAs.

2 Motivation

Diathesis alternations have been proposed for a number of NLP tasks. Several researchers have suggested using them for improving lexical acquisition. Korhonen (1997) uses them in subcategorization frame (SCF) acquisition to improve the performance of a statistical filter which determines whether a SCF observed for a particular verb is genuine or not. They have also been suggested for the recovery of predicate argument structure, necessary for SCF acquisition (Briscoe and Carroll, 1997; Boguraev and Briscoe, 1987). And Ribas (1995) showed that selectional preferences acquired using alternations performed better on a word sense disambiguation task compared to preferences acquired without alternations. He used alternations to indicate where the argument head data from different slots can be combined since it occupies the same semantic relationship with the predicate.

Different diathesis alternations give different emphasis and nuances of meaning to the same basic content. These subtle changes of meaning are important in natural language generation (Stede, 1998).

Alternations provide a means of reducing redundancy in the lexicon since the alternating SCFs need not be enumerated for each individual verb if a marker is used to specify which verbs the alternation applies to. Alternations also provide a means of generalizing patterns of behaviour over groups of verbs, typically the group members are semantically related. Levin (1993) provides a classification of over 3000 verbs according to their participation in alternations involving NP and PP constituents. Levin's classification is not intended to be exhaustive. Automatic identification of alternations would be a useful tool for extending the classification with new participants. Levin's taxonomy might also be used alongside observed behaviour, to predict unseen behaviour.

Levin's classification has been extended by other NLP researchers (Dorr and Jones, 1996; Dang et al.,

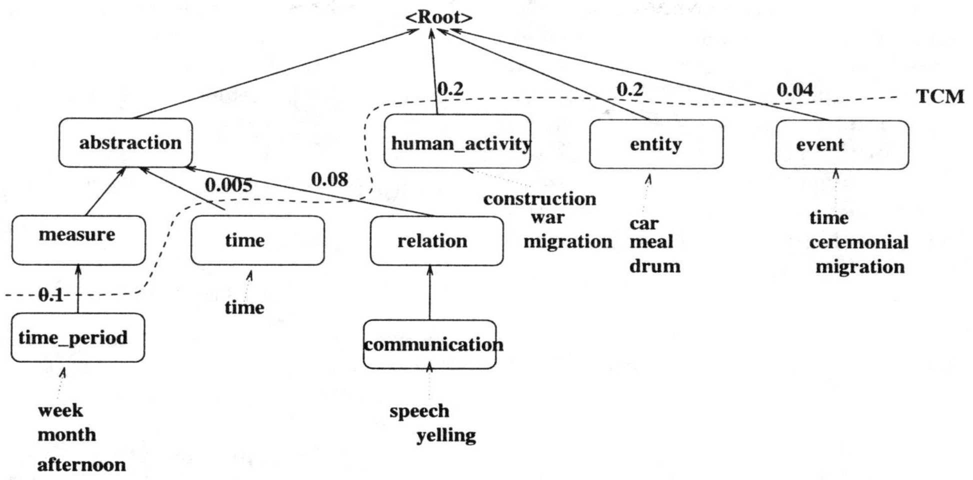

Figure 1: TCM for the object slot of the transitive frame of *start*.

1998). Dang et al. (1998) modify it by adding new classes which remove the overlap between classes from the original scheme. Dorr and Jones (1996) extend the classification by using grammatical information in LDOCE alongside semantic information in WordNet. What is missing is a way of classifying verbs when the relevant information is not available in a manmade resource. Using corpora by-passes reliance on the availability and adequacy of MRDs. Additionally, the frequency information in corpora is helpful for estimating alternation productivity (Lapata, 1999). Estimations of productivity have been suggested for controlling the application of alternations (Briscoe and Copestake, 1996). We propose a method to acquire knowledge of alternation participation directly from corpora, with frequency information available as a by-product.

3 Method

We use both syntactic and semantic information for identifying participants in RSAs. Firstly, syntactic processing is used to find candidates taking the alternating SCFs. Secondly, selectional preference models are acquired for the argument heads associated with a specific slot in a specific SCF of a verb.

We use the SCF acquisition system of Briscoe and Carroll (1997), with a probabilistic LR parser (Inui et al., 1997) for syntactic processing. The corpus data is POS tagged and lemmatised before the LR parser is applied. Subcategorization patterns are extracted from the parses, these include both the syntactic categories and the argument heads of the constituents. These subcategorization patterns are then classified according to a set of 161 SCF classes. The SCF entries for each verb are then subjected to a statistical filter which removes SCFs that have occurred with a frequency less than would be expected by chance. The resulting SCF lexicon lists each verb with the SCFs it takes. Each SCF entry includes a frequency count and lists the argument heads at all slots.

Selectional preferences are automatically acquired for the slots involved in the role switching. We refer to these as the target slots. For the causative alternation, the slots are the direct object slot of the transitive SCF and the subject slot of the intransitive. For the conative, the slots are the direct object of the transitive and the PP of the `np v pp` SCF.

Selectional preferences are acquired using the method devised by Li and Abe (1995). The preferences for a slot are represented as a tree cut model (TCM). This is a set of disjoint classes that partition the leaves of the WordNet noun hypernym hierarchy. A conditional probability is attached to each of the classes in the set. To ensure the TCM covers all the word senses in WordNet, we modify Li and Abe's original scheme by creating hyponym leaf classes below all WordNet's hypernym (internal) classes. Each leaf holds the word senses previously held at the internal class. The nominal argument heads from a target slot are collected and used to populate the WordNet hierarchy with frequency information. The head lemmas are matched to the classes which contain them as synonyms. Where a lemma appears as a synonym in more than one class, its frequency count is divided between all classes for which it has direct membership. The frequency counts from hyponym classes are added to the count for each hypernym class. A root node, created above all the WordNet roots, contains the total frequency count for all the argument head lemmas found within WordNet. The minimum description length principle (MDL) (Rissanen, 1978) is used to find the best TCM by considering the cost (in bits) of describing both the model and the argument head data encoded in the model. The cost (or description length) for a TCM is calculated according to equation 1. The number of parameters of the model is given by k, this is the number of classes in the TCM minus one. S is the sample size of the argument head data. The cost of describing each argument head (n) is calculated using the log of the probability estimate for the classes on the TCM that n belongs to (c_n).

$$description\ length = \frac{k}{2} \times \log |S| - \sum_{n \in S} \log p(c_n) \quad (1)$$

A small portion of the TCM for the object slot of *start* in the transitive frame is displayed in figure 1. WordNet classes are displayed in boxes with a label which best reflects the sense of the class. The probability estimates are shown for the classes along the TCM. Examples of the argument head data are displayed below the WordNet classes with dotted lines indicating membership at a hyponym class beneath these classes.

We assume that verbs which participate will show a higher degree of similarity between the preferences at the target slots compared with non-participating verbs. To compare the preferences we compare the probability distributions across WordNet using a measure of distributional similarity. Since the probability distributions may be at different levels of WordNet, we map the TCMs at the target slots to a common tree cut, a "base cut". We experiment with two different types of base cut. The first is simply a base cut at the eleven root classes of WordNet. We refer to this as the "root base cut" (RBC). The second is termed the "union base cut" (UBC). This is obtained by taking all classes from the union of the two TCMs which are not subsumed by another class in this union. Duplicates are removed. Probabilities are assigned to the classes of a base cut using the estimates on the original TCM. The probability estimate for a hypernym class is obtained by combining the probability estimates for all its hyponyms on the original cut. Figure 2 exemplifies this process for two TCMs (TCM1 and TCM2) in an imaginary hierarchy. The UBC is at the classes B, C and D.

To quantify the similarity between the probability distributions for the target slots we use the α-skew divergence (αSD) proposed by Lee (1999). [1] This measure, defined in equation 2, is a smoothed version of the Kulback-Liebler divergence. $p1(x)$ and $p2(x)$ are the two probability distributions which are being compared. The α constant is a value between 0 and 1 which smooths $p1(x)$ with $p2(x)$ so that αSD is always defined. We use the same value (0.99) for α as Lee. If α is set to 1 then this measure is equivalent to the Kulback-Liebler divergence.

$$\alpha sd(p1(x), p2(x)) = D(p2(x) || ((\alpha \times p1(x)) + ((1 - \alpha) \times p2(x)))) \quad (2)$$

4 Experimental Evaluation

We experiment with a SCF lexicon produced from 19.3 million words of parsed text from the BNC (Leech, 1992). We used the causative and conative alternations, since these have enough candidates in our lexicon for experimentation. Evaluation is performed on verbs already filtered by the syntactic processing. The SCF acquisition system has been evaluated elsewhere (Briscoe and Carroll, 1997).

We selected candidate verbs which occurred with 10 or more nominal argument heads at the target slots. The argument heads were restricted to those which can be classified in the WordNet hypernym hierarchy. Candidates were selected by hand so as to obtain an even split between candidates which did participate in the alternation (positive candidates) and those which did not (negative candidates). Four human judges were used to determine the "gold standard". The judges were asked to specify a *yes* or *no* decision on participation for each verb. They were also permitted a *don't know* verdict. The kappa statistic (Siegel and Castellan, 1988) was calculated to ensure that there was significant agreement between judges for the initial set of candidates. From these, verbs were selected which had 75% or more agreement, i.e. three or more judges giving the same *yes* or *no* decision for the verb.

For the causative alternation we were left with 46 positives and 53 negatives. For the conative alternation we had 6 of each. In both cases, we used the Mann Whitney U test to see if there was a significant relationship between the similarity measure and participation. We then used a threshold on the similarity scores as the decision point for participation to determine a level of accuracy. We experimented with both the mean and median of the scores as a threshold. Seven of the negative causative candidates were randomly chosen and removed to ensure an even split between positive and negative candidates for determining accuracy using the mean and median as thresholds.

The following subsection describes the results of the experiments using the method described in section 3 above. Subsection 4.2 describes an experiment on the same data to determine participation using a similarity measure based on the intersection of the lemmas at the target slots.

[1] We also experimented with euclidian distance, the L1 norm, and cosine measures. The differences in performance of these measures were not statistically significant.

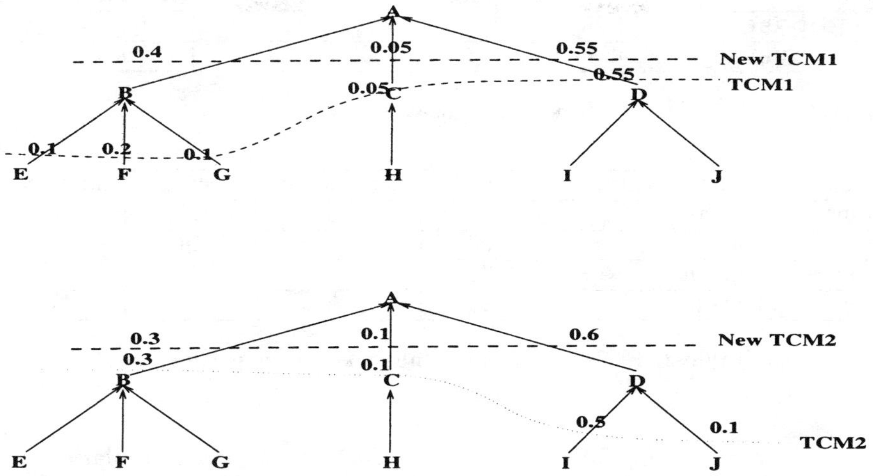

Figure 2: New TCMs at the union base cut

4.1 Using Syntax and Selectional Preferences

The results for the causative alternation are displayed in table 1 for both the RBC and the UBC. The relationship between participation and αSD is highly significant in both cases, with values of p well below 0.01. Accuracy for the mean and median thresholds are displayed in the fourth and fifth columns. Both thresholds outperform the random baseline of 50%. The results for the UBC are slightly improved, compared to those for the RBC, however the improvement is not significant.

The numbers of false negative (FN) and false positive (FP) errors for the mean and median thresholds are displayed in table 2, along with the threshold and accuracy. The outcomes for each individual verb for the experiment using the RBC and the mean threshold are as follows:

- True negatives:
  add admit answer believe borrow cost declare demand expect feel imagine know notice pay perform practise proclaim read remember sing survive understand win write
- True positives:
  accelerate bang bend boil break burn change close cook cool crack decrease drop dry end expand fly improve increase match melt open ring rip rock roll shatter shut slam smash snap spill split spread start stop stretch swing tilt turn wake
- False negatives:
  flood land march repeat terminate
- False positives:
  ask attack catch choose climb drink eat help kick knit miss outline pack paint plan prescribe pull remain steal suck warn wash

The results for the UBC experiment are very similar.

If the median is used, the number of FPs and FNs are evenly balanced. This is because the median threshold is, by definition, taken midway between the test items arranged in order of their similarity scores. There are an even number of items on either side of the decision point, and an even number of positive and negative candidates in our test sample. Thus, the errors on either side of the decision point are equal in number.

For both base cuts, there are a larger number of false positives than false negatives when the mean is used. The mean produces a higher accuracy than the median, but gives an increase in false positives. Many false positives arise where the preferences at both target slots are near neighbours in WordNet. For example, this occurred for *eat* and *drink*. There verbs have a high probability mass (around 0.7) under the **entity** class in both target slots, since both *people* and types of *food* occur under this class. In cases like these, the probability distributions at the RBC, and frequently the UBC, are not sufficiently distinctive.

The polysemy of the verbs may provide another explanation for the large quantity of false positives. The SCFs and data of different senses should not ideally be combined, at least not for coarse grained sense distinctions. We tested the false positive and true negative candidates to see if there was a relationship between the polysemy of a verb and its misclassification. The number of senses (according to WordNet) was used to indicate the polysemy of a verb. The Mann Whitney U test was performed on

	Mann Whitney z	significance (p)	mean	median
RBC	-4.03	0.0003	71	63
UBC	-4.3	0.00003	73	70

Table 1: Causative results

base cut	threshold type	threshold	accuracy %	num FPs	num FNs
UBC	mean	0.38	73	21	4
UBC	median	0.20	70	14	14
RBC	mean	0.32	71	22	5
RBC	median	0.15	63	17	17

Table 2: Error analysis for the causative experiments

the verbs found to be true negative and false positive using the RBC. A significant relationship was not found between participation and misclassification. Both groups had an average of 5 senses per verb. This is not to say that distinguishing verb senses would not improve performance, provided that there was sufficient data. However, verb polysemy does not appear to be a major source of error, from our preliminary analysis. In many cases, such as *read* which was classified both by the judges, and the system as a negative candidate, the predominant sense of the verb provides the majority of the data. Alternate senses, for example, *the book reads well*, often do not contribute enough data so as to give rise to a large proportion of errors. Finding an appropriate inventory of senses would be difficult, since we would not wish to separate related senses which occur as alternate variants of one another. The inventory would therefore require knowledge of the phenomena that we are endeavouring to acquire automatically.

To show that our method will work for other RSAs, we use the conative. Our sample size is rather small since we are limited by the number of positive candidates in the corpus having sufficient frequency for both SCFs. The sparse data problem is acute when we look at alternations with specific prepositions. A sample of 12 verbs (6 positive and 6 negative) remained after the selection process outlined above. For this small sample we obtained a significant result ($p = 0.02$) with a mean accuracy of 67% and a median accuracy of 83%. On this occasion, the median performed better than the mean. More data is required to see if this difference is significant.

4.2 Using Syntax and Lemmas

This experiment was conducted using the same data as that used in the previous subsection. In this experiment, we used a similarity score on the argument heads directly, instead of generalizing the argument heads to WordNet classes. The venn diagram in figure 3 shows a subset of the lemmas at the transitive and intransitive SCFs for the verb *break*.

The lemma based similarity measure is termed lemma overlap (LO) and is given in equation 3, where A and B represent the target slots. LO is the size of the intersection of the multisets of argument heads at the target slots, divided by the size of the smaller of the two multisets. The intersection of two multisets includes duplicate items only as many times as the item is in both sets. For example, if one slot contained the argument heads {*person, person, person, child, man, spokeswoman*}, and the other slot contained {*person, person, child, chair, collection*}, then the intersection would be {*person, person, child*}, and LO would be $\frac{3}{5}$. This measure ranges between zero (no overlap) and 1 (where one set is a proper subset of that at the other slot).

$$\text{LO}(A, B) = \frac{|multiset\ intersection(A\ B)|}{|smallest\ set(A, B)|} \quad (3)$$

Using the Mann Whitney U test on the LO scores, we obtained a z score of 2.00. This is significant to the 95% level, a lower level than that for the class-based experiments. The results using the mean and median of the LO scores are shown in table 3. Performance is lower than that for the class-based experiments. The outcome for the individual verbs using the mean as a threshold was:-

- True negatives:
  add admit answer borrow choose climb cost declare demand drink eat feel imagine notice outline pack paint perform plan practise prescribe proclaim read remain sing steal suck survive understand wash win write
- True positives:
  bend boil burn change close cool dry end fly improve increase match melt open ring roll shut slam smash start stop tilt wake
- False negatives:
  accelerate bang break cook crack decrease drop expand flood land march repeat rip rock shatter

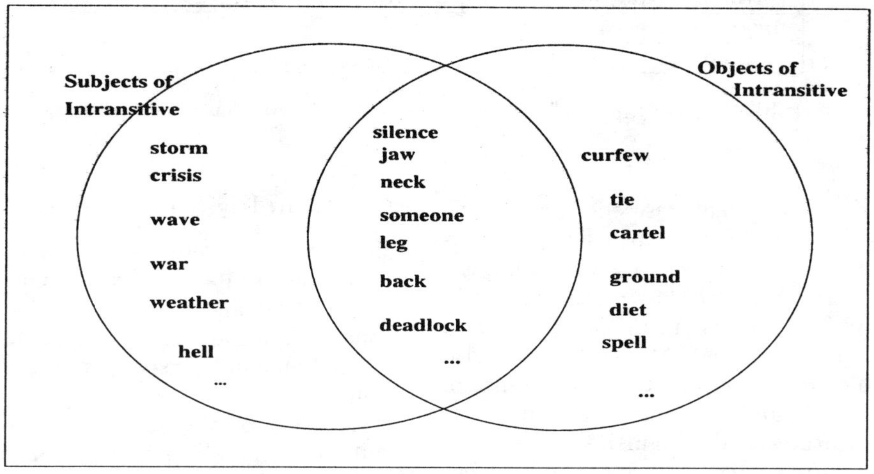

Figure 3: Lemmas at the causative target slots of *break*

snap spill split spread stretch swing terminate turn

- False positives:
  ask attack believe catch expect help kick knit know miss pay pull remember warn

Interestingly, the errors for the LO measure tend to be false negatives, rather than false positives. The LO measure is much more conservative than the approach using the TCMs. In this case the median threshold produces better results.

For the conative alternation, the lemma based method does not show a significant relationship between participation and the LO scores. Moreover, there is no difference between the sums of the ranks of the two groups for the Mann Whitney U test. The mean produces an accuracy of 58% whilst the median produces an accuracy of 50%.

5 Related Work

There has been some recent interest in observing alternations in corpora (McCarthy and Korhonen, 1998; Lapata, 1999) and predicting related verb classifications (Stevenson and Merlo, 1999). Earlier work by Resnik (1993) demonstrated a link between selectional preference strength and participation in alternations where the direct object is omitted. Resnik used syntactic information from the bracketing within the Penn Treebank corpus. Research into the identification of other diathesis alternations has been advanced by the availability of automatic syntactic processing. Most work using corpus evidence for verb classification has relied on a priori knowledge in the form of linguistic cues specific to the phenomena being observed (Lapata, 1999; Stevenson and Merlo, 1999). Our approach, whilst being applicable only to RSAs, does not require human input specific to the alternation at hand.

Lapata (1999) identifies participation in the dative and benefactive alternations. Lapata's strategy is to identify participants using a shallow parser and various linguistic and semantic cues, which are specified manually for these two alternations. PP attachments are resolved using Hindle and Rooth's (1993) lexical association score. Compound nouns, which could be mistaken for the double object construction, were filtered using the log-likelihood ratio test. The semantic cues were obtained by manual analysis. The relative frequency of a SCF for a verb, compared to the total frequency of the verb, was used for filtering out erroneous SCFs.

Lapata does not report recall and precision figures against a gold standard. The emphasis is on the phenomena actually evident in the corpus data. Many of the verbs listed in Levin as taking the alternation were not observed with this alternation in the corpus data. This amounted to 44% of the verbs for the benefactive, and 52% for the dative. These figures only take into account the verbs for which at least one of the SCFs were observed. 54% of the verbs listed for the dative and benefactive by Levin were not acquired with either of the target SCFs. Conversely, many verbs not listed in Levin were identified as taking the benefactive or dative alternation using Lapata's criteria. Manual analysis of these verbs revealed 18 false positives out of 52 candidates.

Stevenson and Merlo (1999) use syntactic and lexical cues for classifying 60 verbs in three verb classes: unergative, unaccusative and verbs with an optional direct object. These three classes were chosen be-

threshold type	threshold	accuracy %	num FPs	num FNs
mean	0.26	60	14	23
median	0.23	63	17	17

Table 3: Accuracy and error analysis for lemma based experiments

cause a few well defined features, specified a priori, can distinguish the three groups. Twenty verbs from Levin's classification were used in each class. They were selected by virtue of having sufficient frequency in a combined corpus (from the Brown and the WSJ) of 65 million words. The verbs were also chosen for having one predominant intended sense in the corpus. Stevenson and Merlo used four linguistically motivated features to distinguish these groups. Counts from the corpus data for each of the four features were normalised to give a score on a scale of 1 to 100. One feature was the causative non-causative distinction. For this feature, a measure similar to our LO measure was used. The four features were identified in the corpus using automatic POS tagging and parsing of the data. The data for half of the verbs in each class was subject to manual scrutiny, after initial automatic processing. The rest of the data was produced fully automatically. The verbs were classified automatically using the four features. The accuracy of automatic classification was 52% using all four features, compared to a baseline of 33%. The best result was obtained using a combination of three features. This gave an accuracy of 66%.

McCarthy and Korhonen (1998) proposed a method for identifying RSAs using MDL. This method relied on an estimation of the cost of using TCMs to encode the argument head data at a target slot. The sum of the costs for the two target slots was compared to the cost of a TCM for encoding the union of the argument head data over the two slots. Results are reported for the causative alternation with 15 verbs. This method depends on there being similar quantities of data at the alternating slots, otherwise the data at the more frequent slot overwhelms the data at the less frequent slot. However, many alternations involve SCFs with substantially different relative frequencies, especially when one SCF is specific to a particular preposition. We carried out some experiments using the MDL method and our TCMs. For the causative, we used a sample of 110 verbs and obtained 63% accuracy. For the conative, a sample of 16 verbs was used and this time accuracy was only 56%. Notably, only one negative decision was made because of the disparate frame frequencies, which reduces the cost of combining the argument head data.

6 Conclusion

We have discovered a significant relationship between the similarity of selectional preferences at the target slots, and participation in the causative and conative alternations. A threshold, such as the mean or median can be used to obtain a level of accuracy well above the baseline. A lemma based similarity score does not always indicate a significant relationship and generally produces a lower accuracy.

There are patterns of diathesis behaviour among verb groups (Levin, 1993). Accuracy may be improved by considering several alternations collectively, rather than in isolation. Complementary techniques to identify alternations, for example (Resnik, 1993), might be combined with ours.

Although we have reported results on only two RSAs, our method is applicable to other such alternations. Furthermore, such application requires no human endeavour, apart from that required for evaluation. However, a considerably larger corpus would be required to overcome the sparse data problem for other RSA alternations.

7 Acknowledgements

Some funding for this work was provided by UK EPSRC project GR/L53175 'PSET: Practical Simplification of English Text'. We also acknowledge Gerald Gazdar for his helpful comments on this paper.

References

Bran Boguraev and Ted Briscoe. 1987. Large lexicons for natural language processing: Utilising the grammar coding system of LDOCE. *Computational Linguistics*, 13(3-4):203–218.

Ted Briscoe and John Carroll. 1997. Automatic extraction of subcategorization from corpora. In *Fifth Applied Natural Language Processing Conference*, pages 356–363.

Ted Briscoe and Ann Copestake. 1996. Controlling the application of lexical rules. In E Viegas, editor, *SIGLEX Workshop on Lexical Semantics - ACL 96 Workshop.*

Hoa Trang Dang, Karin Kipper, Martha Palmer, and Joseph Rosensweig. 1998. Investigating regular sense extensions based on intersective Levin classes. In *Proceedings of the 17th International Conference on Computational Linguistics and the 36th Annual Meeting of the Association for Computational Linguistics*, volume 1, pages 293–299.

Bonnie J. Dorr and Doug Jones. 1996. Role of word sense disambiguation in lexical acquisition: Predicting semantics from syntactic cues. In *Proceedings of the 16th International Conference on Computational Linguistics, COLING-96*, pages 322–327.

Donald Hindle and Mats Rooth. 1993. Structural ambiguity and lexical relations. *Computational Linguistics*, 19(1):103–120.

Kentaro Inui, Virach Sornlertlamvanich, Hozumi Tanaka, and Takenobu Tokunaga. 1997. A new formalization of probabilistic glr parsing. In *5th ACL/SIGPARSE International Workshop on Parsing Technologies*, pages 123–134, Cambridge, MA.

Anna Korhonen. 1997. *Acquiring Subcategorisation from Textual Corpora.* Master's thesis, University of Cambridge.

Maria Lapata. 1999. Acquiring lexical generalizations from corpora: A case study for diathesis alternations. In *Proceedings of the 37th Annual Meeting of the Association for Computational Linguistics*, pages 397–404.

Lillian Lee. 1999. Measures of distributional similarity. In *Proceedings of the 37th Annual Meeting of the Association for Computational Linguistics*, pages 25–32.

Geoffrey Leech. 1992. 100 million words of English: the British National Corpus. *Language Research*, 28(1):1–13.

Beth Levin. 1993. *English Verb Classes and Alternations: a Preliminary Investigation.* University of Chicago Press, Chicago and London.

Hang Li and Naoki Abe. 1995. Generalizing case frames using a thesaurus and the MDL principle. In *Proceedings of the International Conference on Recent Advances in Natural Language Processing*, pages 239–248, Bulgaria.

Diana McCarthy and Anna Korhonen. 1998. Detecting verbal participation in diathesis alternations. In *Proceedings of the 17th International Conference on Computational Linguistics and the 36th Annual Meeting of the Association for Computational Linguists.*, volume 2, pages 1493–1495.

Philip Resnik. 1993. *Selection and Information: A Class-Based Approach to Lexical Relationships.* Ph.D. thesis, University of Pennsylvania.

Francesc Ribas. 1995. *On Acquiring Appropriate Selectional Restrictions from Corpora Using a Semantic Taxonomy.* Ph.D. thesis, University of Catalonia.

Jorma. Rissanen. 1978. Modeling by shortest data description. *Automatica*, 14:465–471.

Sidney Siegel and N. John Castellan, editors. 1988. *Non-Parametric Statistics for the Behavioural Sciences.* McGraw-Hill, New York.

Manfred Stede. 1998. A generative perspective on verb alternations. *Computational Linguistics*, 24(3):401–430.

Suzanne Stevenson and Paola Merlo. 1999. Automatic verb classification using distributions of grammatical features. In *Proceedings of the Ninth Conference of the European Chapter of the Association for Computational Linguistics*, pages 45–52.

Tagging Sentence Boundaries

Andrei Mikheev
Xanalys Inc. and The University of Edinburgh
2 Buccleuch Place, Edinburgh EH8 9LW, UK
mikheev@harlequin.co.uk

Abstract

In this paper we tackle sentence boundary disambiguation through a part-of-speech (POS) tagging framework. We describe necessary changes in text tokenization and the implementation of a POS tagger and provide results of an evaluation of this system on two corpora. We also describe an extension of the traditional POS tagging by combining it with the document-centered approach to proper name identification and abbreviation handling. This made the resulting system robust to domain and topic shifts.

1 Introduction

Sentence boundary disambiguation (SBD) is an important aspect in developing virtually any practical text processing application – syntactic parsing, Information Extraction, Machine Translation, Text Alignment, Document Summarization, etc. Segmenting text into sentences in most cases is a simple matter – a period, an exclamation mark or a question mark usually signal a sentence boundary. However, there are cases when a period denotes a decimal point or is a part of an abbreviation and thus it does not signal a sentence break. Furthermore, an abbreviation itself can be the last token in a sentence, in which case its period acts at the same time as part of this abbreviation and as the end-of-sentence indicator (fullstop).

The first large class of sentence boundary disambiguators uses manually built rules which are usually encoded in terms of regular expression grammars supplemented with lists of abbreviations, common words, proper names, etc. For instance, the Alembic workbench (Aberdeen et al., 1995) contains a sentence splitting module which employs over 100 regular-expression rules written in Flex. To put together a few rules which do a job is fast and easy, but to develop a good rule-based system is quite a labour consuming enterprise. Another potential shortcoming is that such systems are usually closely tailored to a particular corpus and are not easily portable across domains.

Automatically trainable software is generally seen as a way of producing systems quickly re-trainable for a new corpus, domain or even for another language. Thus, the second class of SBD systems employs machine learning techniques such as decision tree classifiers (Riley, 1989), maximum entropy modeling (MAXTERMINATOR) (Reynar and Ratnaparkhi, 1997), neural networks (SATZ) (Palmer and Hearst, 1997), etc.. Machine learning systems treat the SBD task as a classification problem, using features such as word spelling, capitalization, suffix, word class, etc., found in the local context of potential sentence breaking punctuation. There is, however, one catch - all machine learning approaches to the SBD task known to us require labeled examples for training. This implies an investment in the annotation phase.

There are two corpora normally used for evaluation and development in a number of text processing tasks and in the SBD task in particular: the Brown Corpus and the Wall Street Journal (WSJ) corpus – both part of the Penn Treebank (Marcus, Marcinkiewicz, and Santorini, 1993). Words in both these corpora are annotated with part-of-speech (POS) information and the text is split into documents, paragraphs and sentences. This gives all necessary information for the development of an SBD system and its evaluation. State-of-the-art machine-learning and rule-based SBD systems achieve the error rate of about 0.8-1.5% measured on the Brown Corpus and the WSJ. The best performance on the WSJ was achieved by a combination of the SATZ system with the Alembic system – 0.5% error rate. The best performance on the Brown Corpus, 0.2% error rate, was reported by (Riley, 1989), who trained a decision tree classifier on a 25 million word corpus.

1.1 Word-based vs. Syntactic Methods

The first source of ambiguity in end-of-sentence marking is introduced by abbreviations: if we know that the word which precedes a period is *not* an abbreviation, then almost certainly this period denotes a sentence break. However, if this word is an abbreviation, then it is not that easy to make a clear decision. The second major source of information for approaching the SBD task comes from the word which follows the period or other sentence splitting punctuation. In general, when the following word is punctuation, number or a lowercased word – the abbreviation is not sentence terminal. When the following word is capitalized the situation is less clear. If this word is a capitalized common word – this signals start of another sentence, but if this word is a proper name and the previous word is an abbreviation, then the situation is truly ambiguous.

Most of the existing SBD systems are word-based. They employ only lexical information (word capitalization, spelling, suffix, etc.) to predict whether a capitalized word-token which follows a period is a proper name or is a common word. Usually this is implemented by applying the lexical lookup method where a word is assigned its category according to which word-list it belongs to. This, however, is clearly an oversimplification. For instance, the word "Black" is a frequent surname and at the same time it is a frequent common word, thus the lexical information is not very reliable in this case. But by employing local context one can more robustly predict that in the context "Black described.." this word acts as a proper name and in the context "Black umbrella.." this word acts as a common word.

It is almost impossible to robustly estimate contexts larger than single focal word using word-based methods – even bigrams of words are too sparse. For instance, there are more than 50,000 distinct words in the Brown Corpus, thus there are $2^{50,000}$ potential word bigrams, but only a tiny fraction of them can be observed in the corpus. This is why words are often grouped into semantic classes. This, however, requires large manual effort, is not scalable and still covers only a fraction of the lexica. *Syntactic* context is much easier to estimate because the number of syntactic categories is much smaller than the number of distinct words.

A standard way to identify syntactic categories for word-tokens is part-of-speech (POS) tagging. There syntactic categories are represented as POS tags e.g. `NNS` - plural noun, `VBD` - verb past form, `JJR` - comparative adjective, etc. There exist several tag-sets which are currently in use – some of them reflect only the major syntactic information such as part-of-speech, number, tense, etc., whereas others reflect more refined information such as verb subcategorization, distinction between mass and plural nouns, etc.

Depending on the level of detail one tag-set can incorporate a few dozen tags where another can incorporate a few hundred, but still such tags will be considerably less sparse than individual words. For instance, there are only about 40 POS tags in the Penn Treebank tag-set, therefore there are only 2^{40} potential POS bigrams. Of course, not every word combination and POS tag combination is possible, but these numbers give a rough estimation of the magnitude of required data for observing necessary contexts for words and POS tags. This is why the "lexical lookup" method is the major source of information for word-based methods.

The "lexical lookup" method for deciding whether a capitalized word in a position where capitalization is expected (e.g. after a fullstop) is a proper name or a common word gives about an 8% error rate on the Brown Corpus. We developed and trained a POS tagger which reduced this error more than by half – achieving just above a 3% error rate. On the WSJ corpus the POS tagging advantage was even greater: our tagger reduced the error rate from 15% of the lexical lookup approach to 5%. This suggests that the error rate of a sentence splitter can be reduced proportionally by using the POS tagging methodology to predict whether a capitalized word after a period is a proper name or a common word.

1.2 The SATZ System

(Palmer and Hearst, 1997) described an approach which recognized the potential of the local syntactic context for the SBD problem. Their system, SATZ, used POS information for words in the local context of potential sentence splitting punctuation. However, what is interesting is that they found difficulty in applying a standard POS tagging framework for determining POS information for the words: "However, requiring a single part-of-speech assignment for each word introduces a processing circularity: because most part-of-speech taggers require predetermined sentence boundaries, the boundary disambiguation must be done before tagging. But if the disambiguations done before tagging, no part-of-speech assignments are available for the boundary determination system".

Instead, they applied a simplified method. The SATZ system mapped Penn Treebank POS tags into a set of 18 generic POS categories such as noun, article, verb, proper noun, preposition, etc. Each word was replaced with a set of these generic categories that it can take on. Such sets of generic syntactic categories for three tokens before and three tokens after the period constituted a context which was then fed into two kinds of classifiers (decision trees and neural networks) to make the predictions.

This system demonstrated reasonable accuracy (1.0% error rate on the WSJ corpus) and also exhibited robustness and portability when applied to other domains and languages. However, the N-grams of syntactic category sets have two important disadvantages in comparison to the traditional POS tagging which is usually largely based (directly or indirectly) on the N-grams of POS tags. First, syntactic category sets are much sparser than syntactic categories (POS tags) and, thus, require more data for training. Second, in the N-grams-only method

```
...<W C='RB' A='N'>soon</W><W C='.'>.</W> <W A='Y' C='NNP'>Mr</W><W C='A'>.</W>...

...<W C='VBD'>said</W> <W C='NNP' A='Y'>Mr</W><W C='A'>.</W>  <W C='NNP'>Brown</W>...

...<W C=','>,</W> <W C='NNP' A='Y'>Tex</W><W C='*'>.</W> <W C='DT'>The</W>...
```

Figure 1: Example of tokenization and markup. Text is tokenized into tokens represented as XML elements with attributes: `A='Y'` - abbreviation, `A='N'`- not abbreviation, `C` – part-of-speech tag attribute, `C='.'` - fullstop, `C='A'` - part of abbreviation, `C='*'` - a fullstop and part of abbreviation at the same time.

no influence from the words outside the N-grams can be traced, thus, one has to adopt N-grams of sufficient length which in its turn leads either to sparse contexts or otherwise to sub-optimal discrimination. The SATZ system adopted N-grams of length six. In contrast to this, POS taggers can capture influence of the words beyond an immediate N-gram and, thus, usually operate with N-grams of length two (bi-grams) or three (three-grams). Furthermore, in the POS tagging field there exist standard methods to cope with N-gram sparseness and unknown words. Also there have been developed methods for *unsupervised* training for some classes of POS taggers.

1.3 This Paper

In this paper we report on the integration of the sentence boundary disambiguation functionality into the POS tagging framework. We show that sentence splitting can be handled *during* POS tagging and the above mentioned "circularity" can be tackled by using a non-traditional tokenization and markup conventions for the periods. We also investigate reducing the importance of pre-existing abbreviation lists and describe guessing strategies for unknown abbreviations.

2 New Handling of Periods

In the traditional Treebank schema, abbreviations are tokenized *together* with their trailing periods and, thus, stand-alone periods unambiguously signal end-of-sentence. For handling the SBD task we suggest tokenizing periods *separately* from their abbreviations and treating a period as an ambiguous token which can be marked as a fullstop (`'.'`), part-of-abbreviation (`'A'`) or both (`'*'`). An example of such markup is displayed on Figure 1. Such markup allows us to treat the period similarly to all other words in the text: a word can potentially take on one of a several POS tags and the job of a tagger is to resolve this ambiguity.

In our experiments we used the Brown Corpus and the Wall Street Journal corpus both taken from the Penn Treebank (Marcus, Marcinkiewicz, and Santorini, 1993). We converted both these corpora from the original format to our XML format (as displayed on Figure 1), split the final periods from the abbreviations and assigned them with `C='A'` and `C='*'` tags according to whether or not the abbreviation was the last token in a sentence. There were also quite a few infelicities in the original tokenization and tagging of the Brown Corpus which we corrected by hand.

Using such markup it is straightforward to train a POS tagger which also disambiguates sentence boundaries. There is, however, one difference in the implementation of such tagger. Normally, a POS tagger operates on a text-span which forms a sentence and this requires performing the SBD before tagging. However, we see no good reason why such a text-span should necessarily be a sentence, because almost all the taggers do not attempt to parse a sentence and operate only in the local window of two to three tokens.

The only reason why the taggers traditionally operate on the sentence level is because there exists a technical issue of handling long text spans. Sentence length of 30-40 tokens seems to be a reasonable limit and, thus, having sentences pre-chunked before tagging simplifies life. This issue, however, can be also addressed by breaking the text into short text-spans at positions where the previous tagging history does not affect current decisions. For instance, a bigram tagger operates within a window of two tokens, and thus a sequence of word-tokens can be terminated at an unambiguous word because this unambiguous word token will be the only history used in tagging of the next token. A trigram tagger operates within a window of three tokens, and thus a sequence of word-tokens can be terminated when two unambiguous words follow each other.

3 Tagging Experiment

Using the modified treebank we trained a tri-gram POS tagger (Mikheev, 1997) based on a combination of Hidden Markov Models (HMM) and Maximum Entropy (ME) technologies. Words were clustered into ambiguity classes (Kupiec, 1992) according to sets of POS tags they can take on. This is a standard technique that was also adopted by the SATZ system[1]. The tagger predictions were based on the ambiguity class of the current word together with

[1] The SATZ system operated with a reduced set of 18 generic categories instead of 40 POS tags of the Penn Treebank tag-set.

Table 1: POS Tagging on sentence splitting punctuation and ambiguously capitalized words

Tagger Feature Set	*Error on Sentence Punct.*		*Error on Words in Mandatory Pos.*	
	Brown Corpus	WSJ Corpus	Brown Corpus	WSJ Corpus
Upper Bound	0.01	0.13	–	–
POS Tagger	0.25%	0.39%	3.15%	4.72%
POS Tagger Enhanced	0.20%	0.31%	1.87%	3.22%
POS Tagger/ No abbr. list	0.98%	1.95%	3.19%	5.29%
POS Tagger Enhanced/ No abbr. list	0.65%	1.39%	1.91%	3.28%

the POS trigrams: hypothesized current POS tag and partially disambiguated POS tags of two previous word-tokens. We also collected a list of abbreviations as explained later in this paper and used the information about whether a word is an abbreviation, ordinary word or potential abbreviation (i.e. a word which could not be robustly classified in the first two categories). This tagger employed Maximum Entropy models for tag transition and emission estimates and Viterbi algorithm (Viterbi, 1967) for the optimal path search.

Using the forward-backward algorithm (Baum, 1972) we trained our tagger in the *unsupervised* mode i.e. without using the annotation available in the Brown Corpus and the WSJ. For evaluation purposes we trained our tagger on the Brown Corpus and applied it to the WSJ corpus and vice versa. We preferred this method to ten-fold cross-validation because this allowed us to produce only two tagging models instead of twenty and also this allowed us to test the tagger in harsher conditions when it is applied to texts which are very distant from the ones it was trained on.

In this research we concentrated on measuring the performance only on two categories of word-tokens: on periods and other sentence-ending punctuation and on word-tokens in mandatory positions. Mandatory positions are positions which might require a word to be capitalized e.g. after a period, quotes, brackets, in all-capitalized titles, etc. At the evaluation we considered proper nouns (`NNP`), plural proper nouns (`NNPS`) and proper adjectives[2] (`JJP`) to signal a proper name, all all other categories were considered to signal a common word or punctuation. We also did not consider as an error the mismatch between "." and "*" categories because both of them signal that a period denotes the end of sentence and the difference between them is only whether this period follows an abbreviation or a regular word.

In all our experiments we treated embedded sentence boundaries in the same way as normal sentence boundaries. The embedded sentence boundary occurs when there is a sentence inside a sentence. This can be a quoted direct speech sub-sentence inside a sentence, this can be a sub-sentence embedded in brackets, etc. We considered closing punctuation of such sentences equal to closing punctuation of ordinary sentences.

There are two types of error the tagger can make when disambiguating sentence boundaries. The first one comes from errors made by the tagger in identifying proper names and abbreviations. The second one comes from the limitation of the POS tagging approach to the SBD task. This is when an abbreviation is followed by a proper name: POS information normally is not sufficient to disambiguate such cases and the tagger opted to resolve all such cases as "not sentence boundary". There are about 5-7% of such cases in the Brown Corpus and the WSJ and the majority of them, indeed, do not signal a sentence boundary.

We can estimate the upper bound for our approach by pretending that the tagger was able to identify all abbreviations and proper names with perfect accuracy. We can simulate this by using the information available in the treebank. It turned out that the tagger marked all the cases when an abbreviation is followed by a proper name, punctuation, non-capitalized word or a number as "not sentence boundary". All other periods were marked as sentence-terminal. This produced 0.01% error rate on the Brown Corpus and 0.13% error rate on the WSJ as displayed in the first row of Table 1.

In practice, however, we cannot expect the tagger to be 100% correct and the second row of Table 1 displays the actual results of applying our POS tagger to the Brown Corpus and the WSJ. General tagging performance on both our corpora was a bit better than a 4% error rate which is in line with the standard performance of POS taggers reported on these two corpora. On the capitalized words in mandatory positions the tagger achieved a 3.1-4.7% error rate which is an improvement over the lexical lookup approach by 2-3 times. On the sentence breaking punctuation the tagger performed extremely well – an error rate of 0.39% on the WSJ and 0.25% on the Brown Corpus. If we compare these results with the upper bound we see that the errors made by the tagger on the capitalized words and abbreviations

[2]These are adjectives like "American" which are always written capitalized. We identified and marked them in the WSJ and Brown Corpus.

instigated about a 0.25% error rate on the sentence boundaries.

We also applied our tagger to single-case texts. We converted the WSJ and the Brown Corpus to upper-case only. In contrast to the mixed case texts where capitalization together with the syntactic information provided very reliable evidence, syntactic information without capitalization is not sufficient to disambiguate sentence boundaries. For the majority of POS tags there is no clear preference as to whether they are used as sentence starting or sentence internal. To minimize the error rate on single case texts, our tagger adopted a strategy to mark all periods which follow abbreviations as "non-sentence boundaries". This gave a 1.98% error rate on the WSJ and a 0.51% error rate on the Brown Corpus. These results are in line with the results reported for the SATZ system on single case texts.

4 Enhanced Feature Set

(Mikheev, 1999) described a new approach to the disambiguation of capitalized words in mandatory positions. Unlike POS tagging, this approach does not use local syntactic context, but rather it applies the so-called *document-centered approach*. The essence of the document-centered approach is to scan the entire document for the contexts where the words in question are used unambiguously. Such contexts give the grounds for resolving ambiguous contexts.

For instance, for the disambiguation of capitalized words in mandatory positions the above reasoning can be crudely summarized as follows: if we detect that a word has been used capitalized in an unambiguous context (not in a mandatory position), this increases the chances for this word to act as a proper name in mandatory positions in the same document. And, conversely, if a word is seen only lowercased, this increases the chances to downcase it in mandatory positions of the same document. By collecting sequences and unigrams of unambiguously capitalized and lowercased words in the document and imposing special ordering of their applications (Mikheev, 1999) reports that the document-centered approach achieved a 0.4-0.7% error rate with coverage of about 90% on the disambiguation of capitalized words in mandatory positions.

We decided to combine this approach with our POS tagging system in the hope of achieving better accuracy on capitalized words after the periods and therefore improving the accuracy of sentence splitting. Although the document-centered approach to capitalized words proved to be more accurate than POS tagging, the two approaches are complimentary to each other since they use different types of information. Thus, the hybrid system can bring at least two advantages. First, unassigned by the document-centered approach 10% of the ambiguously capitalized words can be assigned using a standard POS tagging method based on the local syntactic context. Second, the local context can correct some of the errors made by the document-centered approach. To implement this hybrid approach we incorporated the assignments made by the document-centered approach to the words in mandatory positions to our POS tagging model by simple linear interpolation.

The third row of Table 1 displays the results of the application of the extended tagging model. We see an improvement on proper name recognition by about 1.5%: overall error rate of 1.87% on the Brown Corpus and overall error rate 3.22% on the WSJ. This in its turn allowed for better tagging of sentence boundaries : a 0.20% error rate on the Brown Corpus and a 0.31% error rate on the WSJ, which corresponds to about 20% cut in the error rate in comparision to the standard POS tagging.

5 Handling of Abbreviations

Information about whether a word is an abbreviation or not is absolutely crucial for sentence splitting. Unfortunately, abbreviations do not form a closed set, i.e., one cannot list all possible abbreviations. It gets even worse – abbreviations can coincide with ordinary words, i.e., "in" can denote an abbreviation for "inches", "no" can denote an abbreviation for "number", "bus" can denote an abbreviation for "business", etc.

Obviously, a practical sentence splitter which in our case is a POS tagger, requires a module that can guess unknown abbreviations. First, such a module can apply a well-known heuristic that single-word abbreviations are short and normally do not include vowels (Mr., Dr., kg.). Thus a word without vowels can be guessed to be an abbreviation unless it is written in all capital letters which can be an acronym (e.g. RPC). A span of single letters, separated by periods forms an abbreviation too (e.g. Y.M.C.A.). Other words shorter than four characters and unknown words shorter than five characters should be treated as *potential* abbreviations. Although these heuristics are accurate they manage to identify only about 60% of all abbreviations in the text which translates at 40% error rate as shown in the first row of Table 2.

These surface-guessing heuristics can be supplemented with the *document-centered approach* (DCA) to abbreviation guessing, which we call Positional Guessing Strategy (PGS). Although a short word which is followed by a period can potentially be an abbreviation, the same word when occurring in the same document in a different context can be unambiguously classified as an ordinary word if it is used without a trailing period, or it can be unambiguously classified as an abbreviation if it is used with a

Table 2: Error rate for different abbreviation identification methods

Corpus	*WSJ*	*Brown*
surface guess	39%	40%
surface guess and DCA	8.4%	9.5%
surface guess and DCA and abbr. list	0.8%	1.2%

trailing period and is followed by a lowercased word or a comma. This allows us to assign such words accordingly even in ambiguous contexts of the same document, i.e., when they are followed by a period.

For instance, the word "Kong" followed by a period and then by a capitalized word cannot be safely classified as a regular word (non-abbreviation) and therefore it is a potential abbreviation. But if in the same document we detect a context *"lived in Hong Kong in 1993"* this indicates that "Kong" is normally written without a trailing period and hence is not an abbreviation. Having established that, we can apply this findings to the non-evident contexts and classify "Kong" as a regular word (non-abbreviation) throughout the document. However, if we detect a context such as *"Kong., said"* this indicates that in this document "'Kong" is normally written with a trailing period and hence is an abbreviation. This gives us grounds to classify "Kong" as an abbreviation in all its occurrences within the same document.

The positional guessing strategy relies on the assumption that there is a consistency of writing within the same document. Different authors can write "Mr" or "Dr" with or without trailing period but we assume that the same author (the author of a document) will write consistently. However, there can occur a situation when a potential abbreviation is used as a regular word and as an abbreviation within the same document. This is usually the case when an abbreviation coincides with a regular word e.g. "Sun." (meaning Sunday) and "Sun" (the name of a newspaper). To tackle this problem, our strategy is to collect not only unigrams of potential abbreviations in unambiguous contexts as explained earlier but also their bigrams with the preceding word. Now the positional guessing strategy can assign ambiguous instances on the basis of the bigrams it collected from the document.

For instance, if in a document the system found a context *"vitamin C is"* it stores the bigram "vitamin C" and the unigram "C" with the information that it is a regular word. If in the same document the system also detects a context *"John C. later said"* it stores the bigram "John C." and the unigram "C" with the information that it is an abbreviation. Here we have conflicting information for the word "C" – it was detected as acting as a regular word and as an abbreviation within the same document – so there is not enough information to resolve ambiguous cases purely using the unigram. However, some cases can be resolved on the basis of the bigrams e.g. the system will assign "C" as an abbreviation in an ambiguous context *"... John C. Research ..."* and it will assign "C" as a regular word (non-abbreviation) in an ambiguous context *"... vitamin C. Research ..."*.

When neither unigrams nor bigrams can help to resolve an ambiguous context for a potential abbreviation, the system decides in favor of the more frequent category deduced from the current document for this potential abbreviation. Thus if the word "In" was detected as acting as a non-abbreviation (preposition) five times in the current document and two times as abbreviation (for the state Indiana), in a context where neither of the bigrams collected from the document can be applied, "In" is assigned as a regular word (non-abbreviation). The last resort strategy is to assign all non-resolved cases as non-abbreviations.

Apart from the ability of finding abbreviations beyond the scope of the surface guessing heuristics, the document-centered approach also allows for the classification of some potential abbreviations as ordinary words, thus reducing the ambiguity for the sentence splitting module. The second row of Table 2 shows the results when we supplemented the surface guessing heuristics with the document-centered approach. This alone gave a huge improvement over the surface guessing heuristics.

Using our abbreviation guessing module and an unlabeled corpus from New York Times 1996 of 300,000 words, we compiled a list of 270 abbreviations which we then used in our tagging experiments together with the guessing module. In this list we included abbreviations which were identified by our guesser and which had a frequency of five or greater. When we combined the guessing module together with the induced abbreviation list and applied it to the Brown Corpus and the WSJ we measured about 1% error rate on the identification of abbreviation as can be seen in the third row of Table 2.

We also tested our POS tagger and the extended tagging model in conjunction with the abbreviation guesser only, when the system was not equipped with the list of abbreviations. The error rate on capitalized words went just a bit higher while the error rate on the sentence boundaries increased by two-three times but still stayed reasonable. In terms of absolute numbers, the tagger achieved a 0.98% error rate on the Brown Corpus and a 1.95% error rate on the WSJ when disambiguating sentence boundaries. The extended system without the abbreviation list was about 30% more accurate and achieved a 0.65% error rate on sentence splitting on the Brown Corpus and 1.39% on the WSJ corpus as shown in the last row of Table 1. The larger impact on the WSJ corpus can be explained by the fact that it has a higher proportion of abbreviations than the Brown Corpus. In the Brown Corpus, 8% of potential sentence boundaries come after abbreviations. The WSJ is richer in abbreviations and 17% of potential sentence boundaries come after abbreviations. Thus, unidentified abbreviations had a higher impact on the error rate in the WSJ.

6 Conclusion

In this paper we presented an approach which treats the sentence boundary disambiguation problem as part of POS tagging. In its "vanilla" version the system performed above the results recently quoted in the literature for the SBD task. When we combined the "vanilla" model with the *document-centered approach* to proper name handling we measured about a 20% further improvement in the performance on sentence splitting and about a 40% improvement on capitalized word assignment.

POS tagging approach to sentence splitting produces models which are highly portable across different corpora: POS categories are much more frequent than individual words and less affected by unseen words. This differentiates our approach from word-based sentence splitters. In contrast to (Palmer and Hearst, 1997), which also used POS categories as predictive features, we relied on a proper POS tagging technology, rather than a shortcut to POS tag estimation. This ensured higher accuracy of the POS tagging method which cut the error rate of the SATZ system by 69%. On the other hand because of its simplicity the SATZ approach is probably easier to implement and faster to train than a POS tagger.

On single-case texts the syntactic approach did not show a considerable advantage to the word-based methods: all periods which followed abbreviations were assigned as "sentence internal" and the results achieved by our system on the single-case texts were in line with that of the other systems.

The abbreviation guessing module which combines the surface guessing heuristics with the document centered approach makes our system very robust to new domains. The system demonstrated strong performance even without being equipped with a list of known abbreviations which, to our knowledge, none of previously described SBD systems could achieve.

Another important advantage of our approach we see is that it requires potentially a smaller amount of training data and this training data does not need to be labeled in any way. In training a conventional sentence splitter one usually collects periods with the surrounding context and these samples have to be manually labeled. In our case a POS tagging model is trained on all available words, so syntactic dependencies between words which can appear in a local context of a period can be established from other parts of the text. Our system does not require annotated data for training and can be *unsupervisedly* trained from raw texts of approximately 300,000 words or more.

There are ways for further improvement of the performance of our system by combining it with a word-based system which encodes specific behavior for individual words. This is similar to how the SATZ system was combined with the Alembic system. This addresses the limitation of our syntactic approach in treating cases when an abbreviation is followed by a proper name always as "non sentence boundary". In fact we encoded one simple rule that an abbreviation which stands for an American state (e.g. Ala. or Kan.) always is sentence terminal if followed by a proper name. This reduced the error rate on the WSJ from 0.31% to 0.25%. Another avenue for further development is to extend the system to other languages.

References

Aberdeen, J., J Burger, D. Day, L. Hirschman, P. Robinson, and M. Vilain. 1995. Mitre: Description of the alembic system used for muc-6. In *The Proceedings of the Sixth Message Understanding Conference (MUC-6)*, Columbia, Maryland. Morgan Kaufmann.

Baum, L.E. 1972. An inequality and associated maximization techique in statistical estimation for probabilistic functions of a Markov process. *Inequalities* 3 (1972) 1-8.

Kupiec, Julian. 1992. Robust part-of-speech tagging using a hidden markov model. *Computer Speech and Language.*

Marcus, Mitchell, Mary Ann Marcinkiewicz, and Beatrice Santorini. 1993. Building a large annotated corpus of english: The penn treebank. *Computational Linguistics*, 19(2):313–329.

Mikheev, A. 1999. A knowledge-free method for capitalized word disambiguation. In *Proceedings of the 37th Conference of the Association for Computational Linguistics (ACL'99)*, pages 159–168. University of Maryland.

Mikheev, A., 1997. *LT POS – the LTG part of speech tagger.* Language Technology Group, University of Edinburgh. www.ltg.ed.ac.uk/software/pos.

Palmer, D. D. and M. A. Hearst. 1997. Adaptive multilingual sentence boundary disambiguation. *Computational Linguistics.*

Reynar, J. C. and A. Ratnaparkhi. 1997. A maximum entropy approach to identifying sentence boundaries. In *Proceedings of the Fifth ACL Conference on Applied Natural Language Processing (ANLP'97)*, Washington, D.C.

Riley, M.D. 1989. Some applications of tree-based modeling to speech and language indexing. In *Proceedings of the DARPA Speech and Natural Language Workshop*, pages 339–352. Morgan Kaufman.

Viterbi, A.J. 1967. Error bounds for convolutional codes and an asymptotically optimal decoding algorithm. *IEEE Transactions on Information Theory.*

Left-To-Right Parsing and Bilexical Context-Free Grammars

Mark-Jan Nederhof
DFKI
Stuhlsatzenhausweg 3
D-66123 Saarbrücken
Germany
nederhof@dfki.de

Giorgio Satta
Dipartimento di Elettronica e Informatica
Università di Padova
via Gradenigo, 6/A
I-35131 Padova, Italy
satta@dei.unipd.it

Abstract

We compare the asymptotic time complexity of left-to-right and bidirectional parsing techniques for bilexical context-free grammars, a grammar formalism that is an abstraction of language models used in several state-of-the-art real-world parsers. We provide evidence that left-to-right parsing cannot be realised within acceptable time-bounds if the so called correct-prefix property is to be ensured. Our evidence is based on complexity results for the representation of regular languages.

1 Introduction

Traditionally, algorithms for natural language parsing process the input string strictly from left to right. In contrast, several algorithms have been proposed in the literature that process the input in a bidirectional fashion; see (van Noord, 1997; Satta and Stock, 1994) and references therein. The issue of parsing efficiency for left-to-right vs. bidirectional methods has longly been debated. On the basis of experimental results, it has been argued that the choice of the most favourable strategy should depend on the grammar at hand. With respect to grammar formalisms based upon context-free grammars, and when the rules of these formalisms strongly depend on lexical information, (van Noord, 1997) shows that bidirectional strategies are more efficient than left-to-right strategies. This is because bidirectional strategies are most effective in reducing the parsing search space, by activating as early as possible the maximum number of lexical constraints available in the grammar.

In this paper we present mathematical arguments in support of the above empirically motivated thesis. We investigate a class of lexicalized grammars that, in their probabilistic versions, have been widely adopted as language models in state-of-the-art real-world parsers. The size of these grammars usually grows with the square of the size of the working lexicon, and thus can be very large. In these cases, the primary goal in the design of a parsing algorithm is to achieve asymptotic time performance sublinear in the size of the working grammar and independent of the size of the lexicon. These desiderata are met by existing bidirectional algorithms (Alshawi, 1996; Eisner, 1997; Eisner and Satta, 1999). In contrast, we show the following two main results for the asymptotic time performance of left-to-right algorithms satisfying the so called correct-prefix property.

- In case off-line compilation of the working grammar is not allowed, left-to-right parsing cannot be realised within time bounds independent of the size of the lexicon.
- In case polynomial-time, off-line compilation of the working grammar is allowed, left-to-right parsing cannot be realised in polynomial time, and independently of the size of the lexicon, unless a strong conjecture based on complexity results for the representation of regular languages is falsified.

The first result implies that the well known Earley algorithm and related standard parsing techniques that do not require grammar precompilation cannot be directly extended to process the above mentioned grammars (resp. language models) within an acceptable time bound. The second result provides evidence that well known parsing techniques as left-corner parsing, requiring polynomial-time preprocessing of the grammar, also cannot be directly extended to process these formalisms within an acceptable time bound.

The grammar formalisms we investigate are based upon context-free grammars and are called bilexical context-free grammars. Bilexical context-free grammars have been presented in (Eisner and Satta, 1999) as an abstraction of language models that have been adopted in several recent real-world parsers, improving state-of-the-art parsing accuracy (Alshawi, 1996; Eisner, 1996; Charniak, 1997; Collins, 1997). Our results directly transfer to all these language models. In a bilexical context-free grammar, possible arguments of a word are always specified along with possible head words for those arguments. Therefore a bilexical grammar requires the grammar writer to make stipulations about the compatibility of particular pairs of words in particular roles, something that was not necessarily true of general context-free grammars.

The remainder of this paper is organized as follows. We introduce bilexical context-free grammars in Section 2, and discuss parsing with the correct-prefix property in Section 3. Our results for parsing with on-line and off-line grammar compilation are presented in Sections 4 and 5, respectively. To complete the presentation, Appendix A shows that left-to-right parsing in time independent of the size of the lexicon is indeed possible when an off-line compilation of the working grammar is allowed that has an exponential time complexity.

2 Bilexical context-free grammars

In this section we introduce the grammar formalism we investigate in this paper. This formalism, originally presented in (Eisner and Satta, 1999), is an abstraction of the language models adopted by several state-of-the-art real-world parsers (see Section 1). We specify a non-stochastic version of the formalism, noting that probabilities may be attached to the rewrite rules exactly as in stochastic CFG (Gonzales and Thomason, 1978; Wetherell, 1980). We assume that the reader is familiar with context-free grammars. Here we follow the notation of (Harrison, 1978; Hopcroft and Ullman, 1979).

A context-free grammar (CFG) is a tuple $G = (V_N, V_T, P, S)$, where V_N and V_T are finite, disjoint sets of nonterminal and terminal symbols, respectively, $S \in V_N$ is the start symbol, and P is a finite set of productions having the form $A \rightarrow \alpha$, where $A \in V_N$ and $\alpha \in (V_N \cup V_T)^*$. A "derives" relation, written $\Rightarrow$, is associated with a CFG as usual. We use the reflexive and transitive closure of $\Rightarrow$, written $\Rightarrow^*$, and define $L(G)$ accordingly. The size of a CFG G is defined as $|G| = \Sigma_{(A \rightarrow \alpha) \in P} |A\alpha|$. If every production in P has the form $A \rightarrow BC$ or $A \rightarrow a$, for $A, B, C \in V_N, a \in V_T$, then G is said to be in Chomsky Normal Form (CNF).

A CFG $G = (V_N, V_T, P, S[\$])$ in CNF is called a **bilexical context-free grammar** if there exists a set V_D, called the set of **delexicalized nonterminals**, such that nonterminals from V_N are of the form $A[a]$, consisting of $A \in V_D$ and $a \in V_T$, and every production in P has one of the following two forms:

(i) $A[a] \rightarrow B[b]\ C[c]$, $a \in \{b, c\}$;

(ii) $A[a] \rightarrow a$.

A nonterminal $A[a]$ is said to have terminal symbol a as its **lexical head**. Note that in a parse tree for G, the lexical head of a nonterminal is always "inherited" from some daughter symbol (i.e., from some symbol in the right-hand side of a production). In the sequel, we also refer to the set V_T as the **lexicon** of the grammar.

A bilexical CFG can encode lexically specific preferences in the form of binary relations on lexical items. For instance, one might specify P as to contain the production VP[solve] $\rightarrow$ V[solve] NP[puzzles] but not the production VP[eat] $\rightarrow$ V[eat] NP[puzzles]. This will allow derivation of some VP constituents such as "solve two puzzles", while forbidding "eat two puzzles". See (Eisner and Satta, 1999) for further discussion.

The cost of this expressiveness is a very large grammar. Indeed, we have $|G| = \mathcal{O}(|V_D|^3 \cdot |V_T|^2)$, and in practical applications $|V_T| \gg |V_D| > 1$. Thus, the grammar size is dominated in its growth by the square of the size of the working lexicon. Even if we conveniently group lexical items with distributional similarities into the same category, in practical applications the resulting grammar might have several thousand productions. Parsing strategies that cannot work in sublinear time with respect to the size of the lexicon *and* with respect to the size of the whole input grammar are very inefficient in these cases.

3 Correct-prefix property

So called left-to-right strategies are standardly adopted in algorithms for natural language parsing. Although intuitive, the notion of left-to-right parsing is a concept with no precise mathematical meaning. Note that in fact, in a pathological way, one could read the input string from left-to-right, storing it into some data structure, and then perform syntactic analysis with a non-left-to-right strategy. In this paper we focus on a precise definition of left-to-right parsing, known in the literature as correct-prefix property parsing (Sippu and Soisalon-Soininen, 1990). Several algorithms commonly used in natural language parsing satisfy this property, as for instance Earley's algorithm (Earley, 1970), tabular left-corner and PLR parsing (Nederhof, 1994) and tabular LR parsing (Tomita, 1986).

Let V_T be some alphabet. A generic string over V_T is denoted as $w = a_1 \cdots a_n$, with $n \geq 0$ and $a_i \in V_T$ $(1 \leq i \leq n)$; in case $n = 0$, w equals the empty string ε. For integers i and j with $1 \leq i \leq j \leq n$, we write $w[i, j]$ to denote string $a_i a_{i+1} \cdots a_j$; if $i > j$, we define $w[i, j] = \varepsilon$.

Let $G = (V_N, V_T, P, S)$ be a CFG and let $w = a_1 \cdots a_n$ with $n \geq 0$ be some string over V_T. A **recognizer** for the CFG class is an algorithm R that, on input $\langle G, w \rangle$, decides whether $w \in L(G)$. We say that R satisfies the **correct-prefix property** (CPP) if the following condition holds. Algorithm R processes the input string from left-to-right, "consuming" one symbol a_i at a time. If for some i, $0 \leq i \leq n$, the set of derivations in G having the form $S \Rightarrow^* w[1, i]\gamma$, $\gamma \in (V_N \cup V_T)^*$, is empty, then R rejects and halts, and it does so before consuming symbol a_{i+1}, if $i < n$. In this case, we say that R

has detected an error at position i in w. Note that the above property forces the recognizer to do relevant computation for each terminal symbol that is consumed.

We say that $w[1,i]$ is a **correct-prefix** for a language L if there exists a string z such that $w[1,i]z \in L$. In the natural language parsing literature, the CPP is sometimes defined with the following condition in place of the above. If for some i, $0 \leq i \leq n$, $w[1,i]$ is not a correct prefix for $L(G)$, then R rejects and halts, and it does so before consuming symbol a_{i+1}, if $i < n$. Note that the latter definition asks for a stronger condition, and the two definitions are equivalent only in case the input grammar G is reduced.[1] While the above mentioned parsing algorithms satisfy the former definition of CPP, they do not satisfy the latter. Actually, we are not aware of any practically used parsing algorithm that satisfies the latter definition of CPP.

One needs to distinguish CPP parsing from some well known parsing algorithms in the literature that process symbols in the right-hand sides of each grammar production from left to right, but that do not exhibit any left-to-right dependency between different productions. In particular, processing of the right-hand side of some production may be initiated at some input position without consultation of productions or parts of productions that may have been found to cover parts of the input to the left of that position. These algorithms may also consult input symbols from left to right, but the processing that takes place to the right of some position i does not strictly depend on the processing that has taken place to the left of i. Examples are pure bottom-up methods, such as left-corner parsing without top-down filtering (Wiren, 1987).

Algorithms that do satisfy the CPP make use of some form of top-down prediction. Top-down prediction can be implemented at parse-time as in the case of Earley's algorithm by means of the "predictor" step, or can be precompiled, as in the case of left-corner parsing (Rosenkrantz and Lewis, 1970), by means of the left-corner relation, or as in the case of LR parsers (Sippu and Soisalon-Soininen, 1990), through the closure function used in the construction of LR states.

4 Recognition without precompilation

In this section we consider recognition algorithms that do not require off-line compilation of the input grammar. Among algorithms that satisfy the CPP, the most popular example of a recognizer that does not require grammar precompilation is perhaps Earley's algorithm (Earley, 1970). We show here that methods in this family cannot be extended to work in time independent of the size of the lexicon, in contrast with bidirectional recognition algorithms.

The result presented below rests on the following, quite obvious, assumption. There exists a constant c, depending on the underlying computation model, such that in $k \geq 0$ elementary computation steps any recognizer can only read up to $c \cdot k$ productions from set P. In what follows, and without any loss of generality, we assume $c = 1$. Apart from this assumption, no other restriction is imposed on the representation of the input grammar or on the access to the elements of sets V_{N}, V_{T} and P.

Theorem 1 *Let f be any function of two variables defined on natural numbers. No recognizer for bilexical context-free grammars that satisfies the* CPP *can run on input $\langle G, w\rangle$ in an amount of time bounded by $f(|V_{\mathrm{D}}|, |w|)$, where V_{D} is the set of delexicalized nonterminals of G.*

Proof. Assume the existence of a recognizer R satisfying the CPP and running in $f(|V_{\mathrm{D}}|, |w|)$ steps or less. We show how to derive a contradiction.

Let $q \geq 1$ be an integer. Define a bilexical CFG $G_q = (V_{\mathrm{N}}^q, V_{\mathrm{T}}^q, P^q, A[b_1])$ where V_{T}^q contains $q+2$ distinct symbols $\{b_1, \ldots, b_{q+2}\}$ and

$$V_{\mathrm{N}}^q = \{A[b_i] \mid 1 \leq i \leq q+1\} \cup \{T[b] \mid b \in V_{\mathrm{T}}^q\},$$

and where set P^q contains all and only the following productions:

(i) $A[b_i] \rightarrow A[b_{i+1}]\ T[b_i], \quad 1 \leq i \leq q;$

(ii) $A[b_{q+1}] \rightarrow T[b_{q+2}]\ T[b_{q+1}];$

(iii) $T[b] \rightarrow b, \quad b \in V_{\mathrm{T}}^q.$

Productions in (i) are called bridging productions. Note that there are q bridging productions in G_q. Also, note that $V_{\mathrm{D}}^q = \{A, T\}$ does not depend on the choice of q. Thus, we will simply write V_{D}.

Choose $q > \max\{f(|V_{\mathrm{D}}|, 2), 1\}$. On input $\langle G_q, b_{q+2}b_{q+1}\rangle$, R does not detect any error at position 1, that is after having read the first symbol b_{q+2} of the input string. This is because $A[b_1] \Rightarrow^* b_{q+2}\gamma$ with $\gamma = T[b_{q+1}]T[b_q]T[b_{q-1}]\cdots T[b_1]$ is a valid derivation in G. Since R executes no more than $f(|V_{\mathrm{D}}|, 2)$ steps, from our assumption that reading a production takes unit time it follows that there must be an integer k, $1 \leq k \leq q$, such that bridging production $A[b_k] \rightarrow A[b_{k+1}]\ T[b_k]$ is not read from G_q. Construct then a new grammar G'_q by replacing in G_q the production $A[b_k] \rightarrow A[b_{k+1}]\ T[b_k]$ with the new production $A[b_k] \rightarrow T[b_k]\ A[b_{k+1}]$, leaving everything else unchanged. It follows that, on input $\langle G'_q, b_{q+2}b_{q+1}\rangle$, R behaves exactly as before and does not detect any error at position 1. But this is

[1] A context-free grammar G is reduced if every nonterminal of G can be part of at least one derivation that rewrites the start symbol into some string of terminal symbols.

a contradiction, since there is no derivation in G'_q of the form $A[b_1] \Rightarrow^* b_{q+2}\gamma$, $\gamma \in (V_N \cup V_T)^*$, as can be easily verified. ∎

We can use the above result in the comparison of left-to-right and bidirectional recognizers. The recognition of bilexical context-free languages can be carried out by existing bidirectional algorithms in time independent of the size of the lexicon and without any precompilation of the input bilexical grammar. For instance, the algorithms presented in (Eisner and Satta, 1999) allow recognition in time $\mathcal{O}(|V_D|^3 |w|^4)$.[2] Theorem 1 states that this time bound cannot be met if we require the CPP and if the input grammar is not precompiled. In the next section, we will consider the possibility that the input grammar is in a precompiled form.

5 Recognition with precompilation

In this section we consider recognition algorithms that satisfy the CPP and allow off-line, polynomial-time compilation of the working grammar. We focus on a class of bilexical context-free grammars where recognition requires the stacking of a number of unresolved lexical dependencies that is proportional to the length of the input string. We provide evidence that the above class of recognizers perform much less efficiently for these grammars than existing bidirectional recognizers.

We assume that the reader is familiar with the notions of deterministic and nondeterministic finite automata. We follow here the notation in (Hopcroft and Ullman, 1979). A nondeterministic finite automaton (FA) is a tuple $M = (Q, \Sigma, \delta, q_0, F)$, where Q and Σ are finite, disjoint sets of state and alphabet symbols, respectively, $q_0 \in Q$ and $F \subseteq Q$ are the initial state and the set of final states, respectively, and δ is a total function mapping $Q \times \Sigma$ to 2^Q, the power-set of Q. Function δ represents the transitions of the automaton. Given a string $w = a_1 \cdots a_n$, $n \geq 0$, an **accepting computation** in M for w is a sequence $q_0, a_1, q_1, a_2, q_2, \ldots, a_n, q_n$ such that $q_i \in \delta(q_{i-1}, a_i)$ for $1 \leq i \leq n$, and $q_n \in F$. The language $L(M)$ is the set of all strings in Σ^* that admit at least one accepting computation in M. The size of M is defined as $|M| = \Sigma_{q \in Q, a \in \Sigma} |\delta(q, a)|$. The automaton M is deterministic if, for every $q \in Q$ and $a \in \Sigma$, we have $|\delta(q, a)| = 1$.

We call **quasi-determinizer** any algorithm A that satisfies the following two conditions:

1. A takes as input a nondeterministic FA $M = (Q, \Sigma, \delta, q_0, F)$ and produces as output a device D_M that, when given a string w as input, decides whether $w \in L(M)$; and
2. there exists a polynomial p_A such that every D_M runs in an amount of time bounded by $p_A(|w|)$.

We remark that, given a nondeterministic FA M specified as above, known algorithms allow simulation of M on an input string w in time $\mathcal{O}(|M|\,|w|)$ (see for instance (Aho et al., 1974, Thm. 9.5) or (Sippu and Soisalon-Soininen, 1988, Thm. 3.38)). In contrast, a quasi-determinizer produces a device that simulates M in an amount of time independent of the size of M itself.

A standard example of a quasi-determinizer is the so called power-set construction, used to convert a nondeterministic FA into a language-equivalent deterministic FA (see for instance (Hopcroft and Ullman, 1979, Thm. 2.1) or (Sippu and Soisalon-Soininen, 1988, Thm. 3.30)). In fact, there exist constants c and c' such that any deterministic FA can be simulated on input string w in an amount of time bounded by $c\,|w| + c'$. This requires function δ to be stored as a $|Q| \times |\Sigma|$, 2-dimensional array with values in Q. This is a standard representation for automata-like structures; see (Gusfield, 1997, Sect. 6.5) for discussion.

We now pose the question of the time efficiency of a quasi-determinizer, and consider the amount of time needed in the construction of D_M. In (Meyer and Fisher, 1971; Stearns and Hunt, 1981) it is shown that there exist (infinitely many) nondeterministic FAs with state set Q, such that any language-equivalent deterministic FA must have at least $2^{|Q|}$ states. This means that the power-set construction cannot work in polynomial time in the size of the input FA. Despite of much effort, no algorithm has been found, up to the authors' knowledge, that can simulate a nondeterministic FA on an input string w in linear time in $|w|$ and independently of $|M|$, if only polynomial-time precompilation of M is allowed. Even in case we relax the linear-time restriction and consider recognition of w in polynomial time, for some fixed polynomial, it seems unlikely that the problem can be solved if only polynomial-time precompilation of M is allowed. Furthermore, if we consider precompilation of nondeterministic FAs into "partially determinized" FAs that would allow recognition in polynomial (or even exponential) time in $|w|$, it seems unlikely that the analysis required for this precompilation could consider less than exponentially many combinations of states that may be active at the same time for the original nondeterministic FA. Finally, although more powerful formalisms have been shown to represent *some* regular languages much more succinctly than FAs (Meyer and Fisher, 1971), while allowing polynomial-time parsing, it seem unlikely that this could hold for regular languages in general.

[2]More precisely, the running time for these algorithms is $\mathcal{O}(|V_D|^3 |w|^3 \min\{|V_T|, |w|\})$. In cases of practical interest, we always have $|w| < |V_T|$.

Conjecture *There is no quasi-determinizer that works in polynomial time in the size of the input automaton.*

Before turning to our main result, we need to develop some additional machinery. Let $M = (Q, \Sigma, \delta, q_0, F)$ be a nondeterministic FA and let $w = a_1 \cdots a_n \in L(M)$, where $n \geq 0$. Let $q_0, a_1, q_1, \ldots, a_n, q_n$ be an accepting computation for w in M, and choose some symbol $\$ \notin \Sigma$. We can now encode the accepting computation as

$$(\$, q_0)(a_1, q_1) \cdots (a_n, q_n)$$

where we pair alphabet symbols to states, prepending \$ to make up for the difference in the number of alphabet symbols and states. We now provide a construction that associates M with a bilexical CFG G_M. Strings in $L(G_M)$ are obtained by pairing strings in $L(M)$ with encodings of their accepting computations (see below for an example).

Definition 1 *Let $M = (Q, \Sigma, \delta, q_0, F)$ be a nondeterministic* FA. *Choose two symbols $\$, \# \notin \Sigma$, and let $\Delta = \{(a, q) \mid a \in \Sigma \cup \{\$\},\ q \in Q\}$. A bilexical* CFG *$G_M = (V_N, V_T, P, C[(\$, q_0)])$ is specified as follows:*

(i) $V_N = \{T[\sigma] \mid \sigma \in V_T\} \cup \{C[\sigma], C'[\sigma] \mid \sigma \in \Delta\}$;

(ii) $V_T = \Delta \cup \Sigma \cup \{\#\}$;

(iii) *P contains all and only the following productions:*

(a) *for each $\sigma \in V_T$,*
$T[\sigma] \to \sigma$;

(b) *for each $(a, q), (a', q') \in \Delta$ such that $q' \in \delta(q, a')$,*
$C[(a, q)] \to C'[(a', q')]\ T[(a, q)]$;

(c) *for each $(a, q) \in \Delta$,*
$C'[(a, q)] \to T[a]\ C[(a, q)]$;

(d) *for each $(a, q) \in \Delta$ such that $q \in F$,*
$C[(a, q)] \to T[\#]\ T[(a, q)]$.

We give an example of the above construction. Consider an automaton M and a string $w = a_1 a_2 a_3$ such that $w \in L(M)$. Let $(\$, q_0)(a_1, q_1)(a_2, q_2)(a_3, q_3)$ be the encoding of an accepting computation in M for w. Then the string $a_1 a_2 a_3 \#(a_3, q_3)(a_2, q_2)(a_1, q_1)(\$, q_0)$ belongs to $L(G_M)$. The tree depicted in Figure 1 represents a derivation in G_M of such a string.

The following fact will be used below.

Lemma 1 *For each $w \in \Sigma^*$, $w\#$ is a correct-prefix for $L(G_M)$ if and only if $w \in L(M)$.*

Outline of the proof. We claim the following fact. For each $k > 0$, $a_1, a_2, \ldots, a_k \in \Sigma$ and $q_0, q_1, \ldots, q_k \in Q$ we have

$$q_i \in \delta(q_{i-1}, a_i), \quad \text{for all i } (1 \leq i \leq k),$$

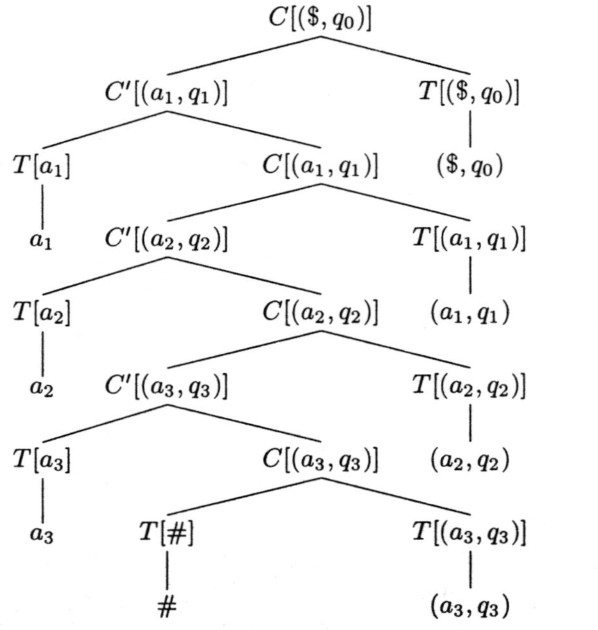

Figure 1: A derivation in G_M for string $a_1 a_2 a_3 \#(a_3, q_3)(a_2, q_2)(a_1, q_1)(\$, q_0)$.

if and only if

$$C[(\$, q_0)] \Rightarrow^* a_1 \cdots a_k C[(a_k, q_k)](a_{k-1}, q_{k-1}) \cdots (\$, q_0).$$

The claim can be proved by induction on k, using productions (a) to (c) from Definition 1.

Let R denote the reverse operator on strings.[3] From the above claim and using production (d) from Definition 1, one can easily show that

$$L(G_M) = \{w\#u \mid w \in L(M),\ u^R \text{ encodes an accepting computation for } w\}.$$

The lemma directly follows from this relation. ∎

We can now provide the main result of this section. To this end, we refine the definition of recognizer presented in Section 3. A recognizer for the CFG class is an algorithm R that has random access to some data structure $C(G)$ obtained by means of some off-line precompilation of a CFG G. On input w, which is a string on the terminal symbols of G, R decides whether $w \in L(G)$. The definition of the CPP extends in the obvious way to recognizers working with precompiled grammars.

Theorem 2 *Let p be any polynomial in two variables. If the conjecture about quasi-determinizers holds true, then no recognizer exists that*

[3]Note that R does not affect individual symbols in a string. Thus $(a, q)^R = (a, q)$.

(i) *has random access to data structure $C(G)$ precompiled from a bilexical CFG G in polynomial time in $|G|$,*

(ii) *runs in an amount of time bounded by $p(|V_D|, |w|)$, where V_D is the set of delexicalized nonterminals of G and w is the input string, and*

(iii) *satisfies the* CPP.

Proof. Assume there exists a recognizer R that satisfies conditions (i) to (iii) in the statement of the theorem. We show how this entails that the conjecture about quasi-determinizers is false.

We use algorithm R to specify a quasi-determinizer A. Given a nondeterministic FA M, A goes through the following steps.

1. A constructs grammar G_M as in Definition 1.
2. A precompiles G_M as required by R, producing data structure $C(G_M)$.
3. A returns a device D_M specified as follows. Given a string w as input, D_M runs R on string $w\#$. If R detects an error at any position i, $0 \leq i \leq |w\#|$, then D_M rejects and halts, otherwise D_M accepts and halts.

From Lemma 1 we have that D_M accepts w if and only if $w \in L(M)$. Since R runs in time $p(|V_D|, |w|)$ and since G_M has a set of delexicalized nonterminals independent of M, we have that there exists a polynomial p_A such that every D_M works in an amount of time bounded by $p_A(|w|)$. We therefore conclude that A is a quasi-determinizer.

It remains to be shown that A works in polynomial time in $|M|$. Step 1 can be carried out in time $\mathcal{O}(|M|)$. The compilation at Step 2 takes polynomial time in $|G_M|$, following our hypotheses on R, and hence polynomial time in $|M|$, since $|G_M| = \mathcal{O}(|M|)$. Finally, the construction of D_M at Step 3 can easily be carried out in time $\mathcal{O}(|M|)$ as well. ■

In addition to Theorem 1, Theorem 2 states that, even in case the input grammar is compiled offline and in polynomial time, we cannot perform CPP recognition for bilexical context-free grammars in time polynomial in the grammar and the input string but independent of the lexicon size. This is true with at least the same evidence that supports the conjecture on quasi-determinizers. Again, this should be contrasted with the time performance of existing bidirectional algorithms, allowing recognition for bilexical context-free grammars in time $\mathcal{O}(|V_D|^3 |w|^4)$.

In order to complete our investigation of the above problem, in Appendix A we show that, when we drop the polynomial-time restriction on the grammar precompilation, it is indeed possible to get rid of any $|V_T|$ factor from the running time of the recognizer.

6 Conclusion

Empirical results presented in the literature show that bidirectional parsing strategies can be more time efficient in cases of grammar formalisms whose rules are specialized for one or more lexical items. In this paper we have provided an original mathematical argument in favour of this thesis. Our results hold for bilexical context-free grammars and directly transfer to several language models that can be seen as stochastic versions of this formalism (see Section 1). We perceive that these results can be extended to other language models that properly embed bilexical context-free grammars, as for instance the more general history-based models used in (Ratnaparkhi, 1997) and (Chelba and Jelinek, 1998). We leave this for future work.

Acknowledgements

We would like to thank Jason Eisner and Mehryar Mohri for fruitful discussions. The first author is supported by the German Federal Ministry of Education, Science, Research and Technology (BMBF) in the framework of the VERBMOBIL Project under Grant 01 IV 701 V0, and was employed at AT&T Shannon Laboratory during a part of the period this paper was written. The second author is supported by MURST under project *PRIN: BioInformatica e Ricerca Genomica* and by University of Padua, under project *Sviluppo di Sistemi ad Addestramento Automatico per l'Analisi del Linguaggio Naturale.*

References

A. V. Aho, J. E. Hopcroft, and J. D. Ullman. 1974. *The Design and Analysis of Computer Algorithms.* Addison-Wesley, Reading, MA.

H. Alshawi. 1996. Head automata and bilingual tiling: Translation with minimal representations. In *Proc. of the 34th ACL*, pages 167–176, Santa Cruz, CA.

E. Charniak. 1997. Statistical parsing with a context-free grammar and word statistics. In *Proc. of AAAI-97*, Menlo Park, CA.

C. Chelba and F. Jelinek. 1998. Exploiting syntactic structure for language modeling. In *Proc. of the 36th ACL*, Montreal, Canada.

M. Collins. 1997. Three generative, lexicalised models for statistical parsing. In *Proc. of the 35th ACL*, Madrid, Spain.

J. Earley. 1970. An efficient context-free parsing algorithm. *Communications of the Association for Computing Machinery*, 13(2):94–102.

J. Eisner and G. Satta. 1999. Efficient parsing for bilexical context-free grammars and head automaton grammars. In *Proc. of the 37th ACL*, pages 457–464, College Park, Maryland.

J. Eisner. 1996. An empirical comparison of probability models for dependency grammar. Technical Report IRCS-96-11, IRCS, Univ. of Pennsylvania.

J. Eisner. 1997. Bilexical grammars and a cubic-time probabilistic parser. In *Proceedings of the 4th Int. Workshop on Parsing Technologies*, MIT, Cambridge, MA, September.

R. C. Gonzales and M. G. Thomason. 1978. *Syntactic Pattern Recognition.* Addison-Wesley, Reading, MA.

D. Gusfield. 1997. *Algorithms on Strings, Trees and Sequences.* Cambridge University Press, Cambridge, UK.

M. A. Harrison. 1978. *Introduction to Formal Language Theory.* Addison-Wesley, Reading, MA.

J. E. Hopcroft and J. D. Ullman. 1979. *Introduction to Automata Theory, Languages and Computation.* Addison-Wesley, Reading, MA.

A. R. Meyer and M. J. Fisher. 1971. Economy of description by automata, grammars and formal systems. In *12th Annual Symp. on Switching and Automata Theory*, pages 188–190, New York. IEEE.

M.-J. Nederhof and G. Satta. 1996. Efficient tabular LR parsing. In *Proc. of the 34th ACL*, pages 239–246, Santa Cruz, CA.

M.-J. Nederhof. 1994. An optimal tabular parsing algorithm. In *Proc. of the 32nd ACL*, pages 117–124, Las Cruces, New Mexico.

A. Ratnaparkhi. 1997. A linear observed time statistical parser based on maximum entropy models. In *Second Conference on Empirical Methods in Natural Language Processing*, Brown University, Providence, Rhode Island.

D. J. Rosenkrantz and P. M. Lewis. 1970. Deterministic left corner parsing. In *IEEE Conf. Record 11th Annual Symposium on Switching and Automata Theory*, pages 139–152.

G. Satta and O. Stock. 1994. Bidirectional context-free grammar parsing for natural language processing. *Artificial Intelligence*, 69:123–164.

S. Sippu and E. Soisalon-Soininen. 1988. *Parsing Theory: Languages and Parsing*, volume 1. Springer-Verlag, Berlin, Germany.

S. Sippu and E. Soisalon-Soininen. 1990. *Parsing Theory: LR(k) and LL(k) Parsing*, volume 2. Springer-Verlag, Berlin, Germany.

R. E. Stearns and H. B. Hunt. 1981. On the equivalence and containment problem for unambiguous regular expressions, grammars, and automata. In *22nd Annual Symp. on Foundations of Computer Science*, pages 74–81, New York. IEEE.

M. Tomita. 1986. *Efficient Parsing for Natural Language.* Kluwer, Boston, Mass.

G. van Noord. 1997. An efficient implementation of the head-corner parser. *Computational Linguistics*, 23(3):425–456.

C. S. Wetherell. 1980. Probabilistic languages: A review and some open questions. *Computing Surveys*, 12(4):361–379.

M. Wiren. 1987. A comparison of rule-invocation strategies in parsing. In *Proc. of the 3rd EACL*, pages 226–233, Copenhagen, Denmark.

A Recognition in time independent of the lexicon

In Section 5 we have shown that it is unlikely that correct-prefix property parsing for a bilexical CFG can be carried out in polynomial time and independently of the lexicon size, when only polynomial-time off-line compilation of the grammar is allowed. To complete our presentation, we show here that correct-prefix property parsing in time independent of the lexicon size is indeed possible if we spend exponential time on grammar precompilation.

We first consider tabular LR parsing (Tomita, 1986), a technique which satisfies the correct-prefix property, and apply it to bilexical CFGs. Our presentation relies on definitions from (Nederhof and Satta, 1996). Let $w \in V_T^*$ be some input string. A property of LR parsing is that any state that can be reached after reading prefix $w[1,j]$, $j \leq |w|$, must be of the form

$$goto(goto(\ldots(goto(q_{in}, X_1), \ldots), X_{m-1}), X_m)$$

where q_{in} is the initial LR state, and $X_1, \ldots, X_m$ are terminals or nonterminals such that $X_1 \cdots X_m \Rightarrow^* w[1,j]$. For a bilexical CFG, each X_i is of the form b_i or of the form $B_i[b_i]$, where $b_1, \ldots, b_m$ is some subsequence of $w[1,j]$. This means that there are at most $(2+|V_D|)^n$ distinct states that can be reached by the recognizer, apart from q_{in}. In the algorithm, the tabulation prevents repeated manipulation of states for a triple of input positions, leading to a time complexity of $\mathcal{O}(n^3\ |V_D|^n)$, where $n = |w|$. Hence, when we apply precompilation of the grammar, we can carry out recognition in time exponential in the length of the input string, yet independent of the lexicon size. Note however that the precompilation for LR parsing takes exponential time.

The second algorithm with the CPP we will consider can be derived from Earley's algorithm (Earley, 1970). For this new recognizer, we achieve a time complexity completely independent of the size of the whole grammar, not merely independent of the size of the lexicon as in the case of tabular LR parsing. Furthermore, the input grammar can be any general CFG, not necessarily a bilexical one. In terms of the length of the input, the complexity is polynomial rather than exponential.

Earley's algorithm is outlined in what follows, with minor modifications with respect to its original presentation. An **item** is an object of the form

$[A \rightarrow \alpha \bullet \beta]$, where $A \rightarrow \alpha\beta$ is a production from the grammar. The recognition algorithm consists in an incremental construction of a $(n+1) \times (n+1)$, 2-dimensional table T, where n is the length of the input string. At each stage, each entry $T[i, j]$ in the table contains a set of items, which is initially the empty set. After an initial item is added to entry $T[0, 0]$ in the table, other items in other entries are derived from it, directly or indirectly, using three steps called predictor, scanner and completer. When no more new items can be derived, the presence of a final item in entry $T[0, n]$ indicates whether the input is recognized.

The recognition process can be precompiled, based on the observation that for any grammar the set of all possible items is finite, and thereby all potential contents of T's entries can be enumerated. Furthermore, the dependence of entries on one another is not cyclic; one item in $T[i, j]$ may be derived from a second item in the same entry, but it is not possible that, for example, an item in $T[i, j]$ is derived from an item in $T[i', j']$, with $(i, j) \neq (i', j')$, which is in turn derived from an item in $T[i, j]$.

A consequence is that entries can be computed in a strict order, and an operation that involves the combination of, say, the items from two entries $T[i, j]$ and $T[j, k]$ by means of the completer step can be implemented by a simple table lookup. More precisely, each set of items is represented by an atomic state, and combining two sets of items according to the completer step is implemented by indexing a 2-dimensional array by the two states representing those two sets, yielding a third state representing the resulting set of items. Similarly, the scanner and predictor steps and the union operation on sets of items can all be implemented by table lookup.

The time complexity of recognition can straightforwardly be shown to be $\mathcal{O}(n^3)$, independent of the size of the grammar. However, massive precompilation is involved in enumerating all possible sets of items and precomputing the operations on them. The motivation for discussing this algorithm is therefore purely theoretical: it illustrates the unfavourable complexity properties that Theorem 2, together with the conjecture about quasi-determinizers, attributes to the recognition problem if the correct-prefix property is to be ensured.

Acknowledgments in Human-Computer Interaction

Karen Ward and Peter A. Heeman
Center for Spoken Language Understanding
Oregon Graduate Institute of Science & Technology
20000 NW Walker Road
Beaverton, Oregon 97006
wardk@cse.ogi.edu, heeman@cse.ogi.edu

Abstract

Acknowledgments are relatively rare in human-computer interaction. Are people unwilling to use this human convention when talking to a machine, or is their scarcity due to the way that spoken-language interfaces are designed? We found that, given a simple spoken-language interface that provided opportunities for and responded to acknowledgments, about half of our subjects used acknowledgments at least once and nearly 30% used them extensively during the interaction.

1 Introduction

As our ability to build robust and flexible spoken-language interfaces increases, it is worthwhile to ask to what extent we should incorporate various human-human discourse phenomena into our dialogue models. Many studies have shown that people alter their dialogue techniques when they believe that they are talking to a computer (e.g., Brennan, 1991), so it is not clear that observations of human-human conversation will provide us with the guidance we need. At the same time, we cannot always look to current systems to determine which discourse phenomena should be supported. Current-generation interfaces are still relatively fragile, and so designers of spoken-language systems go to some effort to structure dialogues and create prompts that guide the user toward short, contentful, in-vocabulary responses (e.g., Basson et al, 1996; Cole, et al, 1997; Oviatt et al, 1994). One result of this approach is the suppression of meta-dialogue acts such as acknowledgement and repetition.

The term "acknowledgment" is from Clark and Schaefer (1989), who describe a hierarchy of methods by which one conversant may signal that another's contribution has been understood well enough to allow the conversation to proceed. Acknowledgments often appear in American English conversation as an "okay" or "uh-huh" that signals understanding but not necessarily agreement. These are also called "back channels" or "prompts" (e.g., Chu-Carroll & Brown, 1997),

Closely related to acknowledgments are repetitions, in which the conversant provides a stronger signal that a contribution has been understood by repeating part or all of the other's contribution. Repetitions are also referred to as "paraphrases" (Traum & Heeman, 1996), "echoing" (Swerts et al, 1998), and "demonstration" (Clark & Schaefer, 1989). Repetitions are often seen when one is conveying complex information, such as when one copies an address or telephone number.

Neither acknowledgments nor repetitions contribute new domain information to the conversation, but they serve to assure the speaker that information has been conveyed successfully. Acknowledgments also play a role in managing turn-taking in mixed-initiative dialogue; although acknowledgments may preface a new contribution by the same speaker (Novick & Sutton, 1994), often they occur alone as a single-phrase turn that appears to serve the purpose of explicitly declining an opportunity to take a turn (Sacks et al, 1974).

Acknowledgments and repetitions are ubiquitous in many types of human-human conversation. In a corpus of problem-solving spoken dialogues, for example, Traum and Heeman (1996) found that 51% of turns began with or consisted of an explicit acknowledgment. Given this, one would expect that acknowledgments should be modeled in dialogue models for spoken-language systems, and indeed some research models are beginning to incorporate acknowledgments, e.g., Kita et al (1996), Aist, (1998), Iwase & Ward (1998).

Typical human-computer dialogue models are structured in ways that suppress the use of acknowledgments. In many systems turn-taking is completely controlled by one conversant, e.g., the user responds to system prompts, which tends to eliminate the need for acknowledgments as a turn-taking mechanism. In other systems, the use of barge-in defeats the common interpretation of an acknowledgment; if the user speaks, the system contribution is cut off before the user utterance is interpreted. If that utterance was intended to signal that the contribution should continue, the effect is exactly the opposite of the one desired.

Thus, current design practices both discourage and render meaningless the standard uses of acknowledgments. If these impediments were removed, would people choose to use acknowledgments when interacting with a computer interface?

2 Experiment

This study was designed as a pilot to our larger investigation into the effects of incorporating acknowledgement behavior in dialogue models for spoken-language interfaces. Before we attempted to compare interfaces with and without acknowledgement behavior, we wanted to understand whether people are willing to use this sort of meta-dialogue behavior when interacting with a computer.

2.1 Approach

In this study we hypothesized that subjects will choose to use acknowledgments in human-computer interaction if they are given an interface that provides opportunities for and responds to acknowledgments.

In designing the study, we assumed that it would not immediately occur to subjects that they could use acknowledgments to a computer. At the same time, we did not want to explicitly instruct or require subjects to use acknowledgment behavior, as that would tell us nothing about their preferences. We therefore decided against a comparison/control-group experimental design for this initial study and instead focused on creating a situation in which subjects would have a reason to use acknowledgments, perhaps even gain an advantage from doing so, while still keeping the behavior optional.

We decided to focus on a somewhat narrow use of acknowledgments. Conversants are especially likely to offer acknowledgments and repetitions when complex information is being presented, especially when the conversant is copying the information. While this is certainly explainable in terms of mutuality of understanding, this particular use of acknowledgment may be viewed from a more mechanical standpoint as regulating the pace at which information is presented. This insight suggested to us that a fruitful task for this study might be one in which the subject is asked to write down verbally-presented information, as when taking messages over the telephone.

2.2 Task

We selected the domain of telephone interface to email and designed a task in which subjects were asked to transcribe items of information from the messages. Writing is slow in comparison to speaking, so we anticipated that subjects would require a slower pace of information presentation when they were writing. The messages included information not asked for on the question list to simulate "uninteresting" material that the subject would want to move through at a faster pace. In this way we hoped to motivate subjects to try to control the pace at which information was presented.

The email was presented in segments roughly corresponding to a long phrase. After each segment, the system paused to give the subject time to make notes. If the subject said nothing, the system would continue by presenting the next message segment. Subjects could accept—and perhaps make use of—this delay, or they could reduce it by acknowledging the contribution, e.g., "okay," or by commanding the system to continue, e.g., "go on." The system signalled the possibility of controlling the delay by prompting the subject "Are you ready to go on?" after the first pause. This prompting was repeated for every third pause in which the subject said nothing. In this way we hoped to suggest to the subjects that they could control the wait time if desired without explicitly telling them how to do so.

On the surface, there is no functional difference in system behavior between a subject's use of a command to move the system onward (e.g., "go on," "next", "continue") and the use of an acknowledgment ("okay," "uh-huh", or a repetition). In either case, the system responds by presenting the next message segment, and in fact it eventually presents the next segment even if the subject says nothing at all. Thus, the design allows the subject to choose freely between accepting the system's pace (system initiative), or commanding the system to continue (user initiative), or acknowledging the presentations in a fashion more typical of mixed-initiative human conversation. In this way, we hoped to understand how the subject preferred to interact with the computer.

2.3 Subjects

Subjects were told that the study's purpose was to assess the understandability and usability of the interface, and that their task was to find the answers to a list of questions. They were given no instructions in the use of the program beyond the information that they could talk to it using normal, everyday speech.

The 14 volunteers were native speakers of North American English, and most were staff at a research university. Ten were female, four were male. Ages ranged from 13 to 57. All used computers, typically office software and games, but none had significant programming experience. Each session lasted about 45 minutes total, and each subject was paid $10.00. One subject declined payment.

2.4 Interface

As mentioned earlier, one difficulty with recognizing acknowledgements in spoken-language interfaces is that the use of barge-in tends to defeat the purpose of acknowledgments when they occur in overlapped speech. We used a Wizard of Oz protocol as a simple way to allow the system to respond to such utterances and to provide robustness in handling repetitions.

The wizard's interface was constructed using the Rapid Application Developer in the Center for Spoken Language Understanding Toolkit (Sutton, et al, 1998). A simple button panel allowed the wizard to select the appropriate response from the actions supported by the application. The application functionality was deliberately limited to suggest realistic abilities for a current spoken-language interface. Using messages pre-recorded in a synthesized voice, the wizard was able to direct the system to:

- Read a list of all messages.
- Begin reading a particular message.
- Read the next message segment.
- Repeat the current message segment.
- Repeat the previous message segment.
- Ask the subject whether the program should continue reading the current message.
- Ask the subject to what to do next.
- End the program.
- Play one of several error and help messages.

The texts of the email messages were presented in phrases of varying lengths, with each phrase followed by a pause of about five seconds. Preliminary tests showed that the combined response time of the wizard and the interface was between one and two seconds, and that pauses of less than five seconds were not obviously different from the normal pace of system response. Five seconds is a long response time, uncomfortably so for human-human conversation, so we hoped that this lengthy pause would encourage the subjects to take the initiative in controlling the pace of the interaction.

The messages were divided into segments by hand. The divisions were intended to simulate a phrase-level presentation, although some short phrases were combined to make the presentation less choppy. An example of one message and its division into phrases may be seen in Figure 1.

Synthesized speech from the Festival speech synthesizer (Taylor, et al, 1998) was used throughout the interface. The message texts were presented in a synthesized male voice, while the control portions of the interface used a synthesized female voice. Default pronunciations were used except when the default was incorrect, e.g., "read" defaulted to the past-tense pronunciation in all contexts. Also, there was minor use of the SABLE markup language (Wouters, et al, 1999) to flatten the pitch range at the end of phrases in list items; the intent was to suggest the prosody of list continuation rather than the default sentence-final drop.

Message six is from Jo at teleport dot com, about, please stop by store on your way home.
I'm going to be late getting home tonight, so would you please stop by the store on your way home?
We need milk,
eggs,
a bunch of spinach,
fresh ginger,
green onions,
maple syrup,
a pound of coos-coos,
mild curry powder,
a pound of coffee,
and a package of seventy five watt light bulbs.
Thanks! See you tonight.

Figure 1. Text of a sample message.
The subject's list of questions included "What items are you supposed to pick up at the store?"

To improve the understandability, both voices were slowed slightly to 90% of the default speaking rate.

2.5 Measures

The central question to be answered is: will the subject use acknowledgments in interacting with the program? A subject can show one of several patterns of response:

- The subject may make no attempt to control the pacing of the interface, instead allowing the interaction to proceed via time-outs.
- The subject may use only commands to control the pacing.
- The subject may use only acknowledgments to control the pacing.
- The subject may use a mixture of commands and acknowledgments.

The determination as to whether a particular utterance constituted an acknowledgment or a command was based primarily on word choice and dialogue context; this approach is consistent with definitions of this behavior, e.g., Chu-Carroll and Brown (1997). For example, "yes" in the context of a system inform (a segment of an email message) was considered an acknowledgment, but "yes" in the context of a system question was not. The words "okay," "uh-huh," and "yes" (immediately following an inform) were taken as evidence of acknowledgments, and phrases such as "go on," "continue," "next" following an inform were taken as evidence of commands. The interpretation was confirmed during the post-experiment interview by questioning the subjects about their word choice.

2.6 Post-Experiment Interview

A post-experiment interview was conducted to gather subject feedback and to answer subjects' questions. The experimenter took notes and thus could have introduced bias in the record of responses. No tape recording was made.

The subject was first invited to comment on the interface and the interaction in an open-ended fashion. When the subject had finished, the experimenter asked several specific questions to assess their understanding of the interface functionality. During this time, the experimenter reminded the subjects of the words that they had used most frequently to prompt the system to continue during pauses and asked the subjects why they had selected those words.

Finally, the experimenter explained the true purpose and hypothesis of the experiment, verified that the subject was unaware that they had been interacting with a Wizard-of-Oz interface, and asked the subject to comment on the notion of using acknowledgments when interacting with a computer. The responses to this question, especially, must be assumed to be somewhat optimistic, as it is likely that at least some subjects would be reluctant to disagree with the experimenter.

3 Results

Results are summarized in Table 1.Because the subject pool was not balanced for gender, results for male and female subjects are reported separately. Due to the small number of male subjects in

Table 1. Summary of Acknowledgment Behavior

Behavior	Subjects		Total (14)
	Female 10 subjects	Male. 4 subjects	
Used acknowledgment/repetition at least once	4 (40%)	4 (100%)	8 (57%)
Used acknowledgment/repetition more than command	3 (30%)	1 (25%)	4 (29%)
Used acknowledgment but no commands	1 (10%)	0	1 (7%)
Described acknowledgment to computer as strange	2 (20%)	0	2 (14%)

this pilot study, no tests of statistical significance of differences in the rates of acknowledgment behavior were made.

Eight of the fourteen subjects used an acknowledgment or repetition at least once, and four used acknowledgment/repetitions more frequently than they used commands. Only one subject used acknowledgments exclusively, while five subjects never used acknowledgments. No subject relied exclusively on time-outs to allow the system to proceed at its own pace, although one subject did use that as her predominant method (42 times, while using acknowledgments only six times and commands three times). Only one subject used repetition, and he reported during the interview that he was unaware of having done so.

It is interesting to note that while all of the male subjects in this sample exhibited acknowledgment behavior at least once, only one preferred acknowledgment over command. One of the male subjects used acknowledgments only three times, in all cases as prefaces to commands. Conversely, although a lower percentage of women used acknowledgments (40%), a higher percentage of them (30%) used acknowledgments in preference to commands. Because of the small numbers of subjects, however, we do not conclude that these differences are significant.

During the post-experiment interview, two subjects (both female) described the idea of using acknowledgments to the computer as strange and stated that they didn't feel that they would do this unless directed to—and even then, they would regard it as simply an alternate command. Two other subjects, both females who had used acknowledgments 2-6 times during the task, each reported that she had felt silly when she had caught herself saying "please" and "okay" to a computer but had been pleased when it had worked. The remainder of the subjects either expressed no strong opinion (two, both female) or expressed a positive attitude toward being able to use acknowledgments when interacting with a computer. Two subjects who had not used acknowledgments commented that they would probably be more likely to use human-like conversation if the synthesized voice were more human-like.

Again, this report of the subjects' attitudes should be interpreted with caution; at this point in the interview they knew the experimenter's hypothesis and so may have been reluctant to disagree.

3.1 Other Dialogue Behaviors

Although we had not formed any hypothesis about other dialogue behaviors, we noticed several interesting dialogue behaviors that we had not anticipated.

We were surprised at the number of subjects who exhibited politeness behavior toward the interface, either saying "please" when issuing commands to the computer or responding to the program's "good-bye" at the end of the session. One subject used "please" throughout the interaction, but a more common pattern was to use "please" at the beginning of the session and to drop the behavior as the interface became more familiar. Politeness did not seem to be strongly associated with a willingness to use acknowledgments, however; four of the nine subjects who exhibited politeness did not use any acknowledgments in their interaction.

Despite the deliberately-artificial interface, several subjects responded at least once to the message content as if they were talking to the message

System: I could come to your office now or at any of the following times. one thirty
SUBJECT: continue
System: three o clock
SUBJECT: continue
System: or five fifteen
SUBJECT: continue
System: thank you. I look forward to your prompt reply
SUBJECT: thank you- uh ((laugh)) continue

Figure 2. Excerpt of transcript.
Subject thanks the interface. The system is reading the text of one of the messages.

sender. In the excerpt shown in Figure 2., for example, the subject replied "Thank you" to the message text's "thank you." This did not appear to be a matter of misunderstanding the capabilities of the interface; the subject later reported that despite the synthesized voices she had briefly forgotten that she wasn't talking to her secretary.

Three subjects also made one or more meta-comments, e.g., "ah, there it is" when finding a particular piece of information. These may have been at least partially an artifact of the "treasure hunt" nature of the task. When questioned in the post-experiment interview, subjects didn't seem aware that they'd made these comments. All but one of these instances were followed immediately by a command, so the wizard responded to the command and ignored the meta-comment. The one stand-alone meta-comment was treated as an unrecognized command (an error message was played).

4 Discussion

Subjects were provided with three methods for controlling the pace at which information was presented: silence, command, or acknowledgment/ repetition. The majority of the subjects used commands more than they used acknowledgments, but over one half used an acknowledgment or repetition at least once during their interaction and nearly 30% used acknowledgments in preference to commands. This occurred despite the fact that subjects were given no reason to think that this behavior would be effective: the interface was deliberately limited in functionality, and voice synthesis was used instead of recorded voice to emphasize the artificial nature of the interaction. Furthermore, the interface did not offer acknowledgments to the subjects, and the subjects were given no instructions suggesting that the interface understood acknowledgments. In fact two subjects who did use acknowledgments expressed surprise that they had worked, and two who had not used acknowledgments reported that they would probably have used them if they had known it would work.

It is interesting to consider these results in light of those reported by Okato et al (1998). They describe a Japanese-language Wizard-of-Oz study in which the subjects were given some instruction on using the system, and in which the system both presented and accepted back-channel feedback. They found that even when the interface offered back channels itself the rate of subject back-channels was somewhat lower in human-computer interaction than in comparable human-human conversation. This makes the fact that our interface elicited acknowledgments without offering them even more encouraging. Clearly, some people are willing to utilize this human conversational convention in human-computer dialogue. Our post-experiment interviews suggest, however, that some people will find the use of acknowledgements strange or uncomfortable in human-computer interaction. While self-reports of attitudes toward hypothetical situations must be treated with some caution, it seems reasonable to assume that even when such interfaces become available there will be users who will prefer to interact with computers using commands.

Will attitudes and conversational behavior change as people gain experience with more advanced spoken-language interfaces? Despite the relatively short duration of this test—most subjects completed the task itself in 15-20 minutes—some changes in behavior could be observed over the course of the dialogue. In particular, politeness behaviors were likely to be seen early in the dialogues and then diminish as the subjects became more comfortable with their interaction. We speculate that the use of politeness words did not reflect a strong underlying politeness toward the computer so much as a falling back on human conventions when faced with an unfamiliar dialogue situation. One subject who had used "please" 21 times during the interaction, for example, simply hung up without warning when she had finished. This contrasts, however, with the findings of Nass et al (1999) that people do offer socially-desirable behavior to computers.

Would a better voice increase the incidence of acknowledgment behavior? Several subjects thought it would, and even with the current synthesized voices we saw several examples of subjects seemingly forgetting briefly that they were not talking to a human. We plan to explore this question in future work.

4.1 Conclusions and Future Work

We conducted a preliminary study to examine the willingness of subjects to use a particular dialogue act, acknowledgment, in human-computer interaction. Although the number of subjects was small, we saw that about half of our subjects used acknowledgements or repetition at least occasionally to control the pace at which information was presented, and about 29% used acknowledgments more frequently than they used commands for that purpose.

Our immediate plans include extending this study to a larger and gender-balanced group of subjects so that we can draw firmer quantitative conclusions about the percentage of people who are likely to prefer this style of interaction. In particular, we cannot conclude from the current study's small sample how strong the preference for using acknowledgment might be, especially among male subjects. Also, in our current study the subject achieved no functional benefit in using acknowledgments. With better estimates of subject preferences, we can then proceed to our larger goal of comparing the usefulness and user acceptability of spoken language dialogue models with and without acknowledgment behavior (c.f. Walker, 1993). We also plan to explore the effect of the quality of the synthesized voice on the incidence of acknowledgment behavior.

Acknowledgments

This work was partially supported by a grant from Intel Research Council. The authors gratefully acknowledge and thank David G. Novick and the anonymous reviewers for their helpful comments and suggestions.

References

Gregory Aist. 1998. Expanding a Time-Sensitive Conversational Architecture for Turn-Taking to Handle Content-Driven Interruption. In *Proceedings of ICSLP 98 Fifth International Conference on Spoken Language Processing*, pages 413-417.

Sara Basson, Stephen Springer, Cynthia Fong, Hong Leung, Ed Man, Michele Olson, John Pitrelli, Ranvir Singh, and Suk Wong. 1996. User Participation and Compliance in Speech Automated Telecommunications Applications. In *Proceedings of ICSLP 96 Fourth International Conference on Spoken Language Processing*, pages 1676-1679.

Susan E. Brennan. 1991. Conversation With and Through Computers. *User Modeling and User-Adapted Interaction*. 1:67-86.

Jennifer Chu-Carroll and Michael K. Brown. 1997. Tracking Initiative in Collaborative Dialogue Interactions. In *Proceedings of the 35th Annual Meeting of the Association for Computational Linguistics*, pages 262-270.

Herbert H. Clark and Edward F. Schaefer. 1989. Contributing to Discourse. *Cognitive Science*, 13:259-294.

Ronald A. Cole, David G. Novick, Pieter J. E. Vermeulen, Stephen Sutton, Mark Fanty, L. F. A. Wessels, Jacques H. de Villiers, Johan Schalkwyk, Brian Hansen and Daniel Burnett. 1997. Experiments with a Spoken Dialogue System for Taking the U.S. Census. *Speech Communications*, Vol. 23.

Peter A. Heeman, Michael Johnston, Justin Denney and Edward Kaiser. 1998. Beyond Structured Dialogues: Factoring out Grounding. In

Proceedings of ICSLP 98 Fifth International Conference on Spoken Language Processing, pages 863-867.

Tatsuya Iwase, and Nigel Ward. 1998. Pacing Spoken Directions to Suit the Listener. In *Proceedings of ICSLP 98 Fifth International Conference on Spoken Language Processing*, Vol. 4, page 1203-1207.

K. Kita, Y. Fukui, M. Jagata and T. Morimoto. 1996. Automatic Acquisition of Probabilistic Dialogue Models. In *Proceedings of ICSLP 96 Fourth International Conference on Spoken Language Processing*, pages 196-199.

Clifford Nass, Youngme Moon and Paul Carney. 1999. Are Respondents Polite to Computers? Social Desirability and Direct Responses to Computers. *Journal of Applied Social Psychology*, 29:5, pages 1093-1110.

H. Noguchi and Yasuharu Den. 1998. Prosody-Based Detection of the Context of Backchannel Responses. In *Proceedings of ICSLP 98 Fifth International Conference on Spoken Language Processing*, Vol. 2, pages 487-490.

David G. Novick and S. Sutton. 1994. An Empirical Model of Acknowledgment for Spoken-Language Systems. In *Proceedings of the 32nd Annual Meeting of the Association for Computational Linguistics*, pages 96-101.

Yohei Okato, Keiji Kato, Mikio Yamamoto and Shuichi Itahashi. 1998. System-User Interaction and Response Strategy in Spoken Dialogue System. *Proceedings of ICSLP 98 Fifth International Conference on Spoken Language Processing*, Vol. 2, pages 495-498.

S. L. Oviatt and P. R. Cohen and M. Wang. 1994. Toward Interface Design for Human Language Technology: Modality and Structure as Determinants of Linguistic Complexity. In *Speech Communication*, 15:3-4, pages 283-300.

H. Sacks, E. Schegloff and G. Jefferson. 1974. A Simplest Systematics for the Organization of Turn-Taking in Conversation. *Language*, 50:696-735.

Stephen Sutton, Ronald Cole, Jacques de Villiers, Johan Schalkwyk, Pieter Vermeulen, Mike Macon, Yonghong Yan, Ed Kaiser, Brian Rundle, Khaldoun Shobaki, Paul Hosom, Alex Kain, Johan Wouters, Dominic Massaro and Michael Cohen. 1998. Universal Speech Tools: the CSLU Toolkit. In *Proceedings of the International Conference on Spoken Language Processing*, pages 3221-3224.

Marc Swerts, Hanae Koiso, Atsushi Shimojima and Yasuhiro Katagiri. 1998. On Different Functions of Repetitive Utterances. In *Proceedings of ICSLP 98 Fifth International Conference on Spoken Language Processing*, Vol. 2, pages 483-487.

Paul Taylor, Alan W. Black and Richard Caley. 1998. The Architecture of the Festival Speech Synthesis System. In The Third ESCA/ COCOSDA Workshop on Speech Synthesis, pages 147-151.

David R. Traum and Peter A. Heeman. 1996. Utterance Units and Grounding in Spoken Dialogue. In *Proceedings of ICSLP 96 Fourth International Conference on Spoken Language Processing*, pages 1884-1887.

Marilyn A. Walker. 1993. *Informational Redundancy and Resource Bounds in Dialogue*. Doctoral dissertation, University of Pennsylvania.

Johan Wouters, Brian Rundle and Michael W. Macon. 1996. Authoring Tools for Speech Synthesis using the Sable Markup Standard. In *Proceedings of Eurospeech '99*.

Nigel Ward. 1996. Using Prosodic Clues to Decide When to Produce Back-Channel Utterances. In *Proceedings of ICSLP 96 Fourth International Conference on Spoken Language Processing*, page 1724-1727.

A New Algorithm for the Alignment of Phonetic Sequences

Grzegorz Kondrak
Department of Computer Science
University of Toronto
Toronto, Ontario, Canada M5S 3G4
kondrak@cs.toronto.edu

Abstract

Alignment of phonetic sequences is a necessary step in many applications in computational phonology. After discussing various approaches to phonetic alignment, I present a new algorithm that combines a number of techniques developed for sequence comparison with a scoring scheme for computing phonetic similarity on the basis of multivalued features. The algorithm performs better on cognate alignment, in terms of accuracy and efficiency, than other algorithms reported in the literature.

1 Introduction

Identification of the corresponding segments in sequences of phones is a necessary step in many applications in both diachronic and synchronic phonology. Usually we are interested in aligning sequences that represent forms that are related in some way: a pair of cognates, or the underlying and the surface forms of a word, or the intended and the actual pronunciations of a word. Alignment of phonetic sequences presupposes transcription of sounds into discrete phonetic segments, and so differs from matching of utterances in speech recognition. On the other hand, it has much in common with the alignment of proteins and DNA sequences. Many methods developed for molecular biology can be adapted to perform accurate phonetic alignment.

Alignment algorithms usually contain two main components: a metric for measuring distance between phones, and a procedure for finding the optimal alignment. The former is often calculated on the basis of phonological features that encode certain properties of phones. An obvious candidate for the latter is a well-known dynamic programming (DP) algorithm for string alignment (Wagner and Fischer, 1974), although other algorithms can used as well. The task of finding the optimal alignment is closely linked to the task of calculating the distance between two sequences. The basic DP algorithm accomplishes both tasks. Depending on the application, either of the results, or both, can be used.

Within the last few years, several different approaches to phonetic alignment have been reported. Covington (1996) used depth-first search and a special distance function to align words for historical comparison. In a follow-up paper (Covington, 1998), he extended the algorithm to align words from more than two languages. Somers (1998) proposed a special algorithm for aligning children's articulation data with the adult model. Gildea and Jurafsky (1996) applied the DP algorithm to pre-align input and output phonetic strings in order to improve the performance of their transducer induction system. Nerbonne and Heeringa (1997) employed a similar procedure to compute relative distance between words from various Dutch dialects. Some characteristics of these implementations are juxtaposed in Table 1.

In this paper, I present a new algorithm for the alignment of cognates. It combines various techniques developed for sequence comparison with an appropriate scoring scheme for computing phonetic similarity on the basis of multivalued features. The new algorithm performs better, in terms of accuracy and efficiency, than comparable algorithms reported by Covington (1996) and Somers (1999). Although the main focus of this paper is diachronic phonology, the techniques proposed here can also be applied in other contexts where it is necessary to align phonetic sequences.

2 Comparing Phones

To align phonetic sequences, we first need a function for calculating the distance between individual phones. The numerical value assigned by the function to a pair of segments is referred to as the cost, or penalty, of substitution. The function is often extended to cover pairs consisting of a segment and the null character, which correspond to the opera-

Algorithm	Calculation of alignment	Calculation of distance	Dynamic programming	Phonological features
Covington (1996)	explicit	implicit	no	no
Somers (1998)	explicit	no	no	multivalued
Nerbonne and Heeringa (1997)	implicit	explicit	yes	binary
Gildea and Jurafsky (1996)	explicit	implicit	yes	binary

Table 1: Comparison of alignment algorithms.

tions of insertion and deletion (also called *indels*). A distance function that satisfies the following axioms is called a *metric*:

1. $\forall a,b : d(a,b) \geq 0$ (*nonnegative property*)
2. $\forall a,b : d(a,b) = 0 \Leftrightarrow a = b$ (*zero property*)
3. $\forall a,b : d(a,b) = d(b,a)$ (*symmetry*)
4. $\forall a,b,c : d(a,b) + d(b,c) \geq d(a,c)$ (*triangle inequality*)

2.1 Covington's Distance Function vs. Feature-Based Metrics

Covington (1996), for his cognate alignment algorithm, constructed a special distance function. It was developed by trial and error on a test set of 82 cognate pairs from various related languages. The distance function is very simple; it uses no phonological features and distinguishes only three types of segments: consonants, vowels, and glides. Many important characteristics of sounds, such as place or manner of articulation, are ignored. For example, both *yacht* and *will* are treated identically as a glide-vowel-consonant sequence. The function's values for substitutions are listed in the "penalty" column in Table 2. The penalty for an indel is 40 if it is preceded by another indel, and 50 otherwise. Covington (1998) acknowledges that his distance function is "just a stand-in for a more sophisticated, perhaps feature-based, system".[1]

Both Gildea and Jurafsky (1996) and Nerbonne and Heeringa (1997) use distance functions based on binary features. Such functions have the ability to distinguish a large number of different phones. The underlying assumption is that the number of binary features by which two given sounds differ is a good indication of their proximity. Phonetic segments are represented by binary vectors in which every entry stands for a single articulatory feature. The penalty for a substitution is defined as the Hamming distance between two feature vectors. The penalty for indels is established more or less arbitrarily.[2] A distance function defined in such a way satisfies all metric axioms.

It is interesting to compare the values of Covington's distance function with the average Hamming distances produced by a feature-based metric. Since neither Gildea and Jurafsky (1996) nor Nerbonne and Heeringa (1997) present their feature vectors in sufficient detail to perform the calculations, I adopted a fairly standard set of 17 binary features from Hartman (1981).[3] The average feature distances between pairs of segments corresponding to every clause in Covington's distance function are given in Table 2, next to Covington's "penalties". By definition, the Hamming distance between identical segments is zero. The distance between the segments covered by clause #3 is also constant and equal to one (the feature in question being [long] or [syllabic]). The remaining average feature distances were calculated using a set of most frequent phonemes represented by 25 letters of the Latin alphabet (all but *q*). In order to facilitate comparison, the rightmost column of Table 2 contains the average distances interpolated between the minimum and the maximum value of Covington's distance function. The very high correlation (0.998) between Covington's penalties and the average distances demonstrates that feature-based phonology provides a theoretical basis for Covington's manually constructed distance function.

[1] Covington's distance function is not a metric. The zero property is not satisfied because the function's value for two identical vowels is greater than zero. Also, the triangle inequality does not hold in all cases; for example: $p(e,i) = 30$ and $p(i,y) = 10$, but $p(e,y) = 100$, where $p(x,y)$ is the penalty for aligning [x] with [y].

[2] Nerbonne and Heeringa (1997) fix the penalty for indels as half the average of the values of all substitutions. Gildea and Jurafsky (1996) set it at one fourth of the maximum substitution cost.

[3] In order to handle all the phones in Covington's data set, two features were added: [tense] and [spread glottis].

	Clause in Covington's distance function	Covington's penalty	Average Hamming distance	Interpolated average distance
1	*"identical consonants or glides"*	0	0.0	0.0
2	*"identical vowels"*	5	0.0	0.0
3	*"vowel length difference only"*	10	1.0	12.4
4	*"non-identical vowels"*	30	2.2	27.3
5	*"non-identical consonants"*	60	4.81	58.1
6	*"no similarity"*	100	8.29	100.0

Table 2: The clause-by-clause comparison of Covington's distance function (column 3) and a feature-based distance function (columns 4 and 5).

2.2 Binary vs. Multivalued Features

Although binary features are elegant and widely used, they might not be optimal for phonetic alignment. Their primary motivation is to classify phonological oppositions rather than to reflect the phonetic characteristics of sounds. In a strictly binary system, sounds that are similar often differ in a disproportionately large number of features. It can be argued that allowing features to have several possible values results in a more natural and phonetically adequate system. For example, there are many possible places of articulation, which form a near-continuum ranging from [labial] to [glottal].

Ladefoged (1995) devised a phonetically-based multivalued feature system. This system has been adapted by Connolly (1997) and implemented by Somers (1998). It contains about 20 features with values between 0 and 1. Some of them can take as many as ten different values (e.g. [place]), while others are basically binary oppositions (e.g. [nasal]). Table 3 contains examples of multivalued features.

The main problem with both Somers's and Connolly's approaches is that they do not differentiate the weights, or *saliences*, that express the relative importance of individual features. For example, they assign the same salience to the feature [place] as to the feature [aspiration], which results in a smaller distance between [p] and [k] than between [p] and [p^h]. I found that in order to avoid such incongruous outcomes, the salience values need to be carefully differentiated; specifically, the features [place] and [manner] should be assigned significantly higher saliences than other features (the actual values used in my algorithm are given in Table 4). Nerbonne and Heeringa (1997) experimented with weighting each feature by information gain but found it had an adverse effect on the quality of the alignments. The question of how to derive salience values in a principled manner is still open.

2.3 Similarity vs. Distance

Although all four algorithms listed in Table 1 measure relatedness between phones by means of a *distance* function, such an approach does not seem to be the best for dealing with phonetic units. The fact that Covington's distance function is not a metric is not an accidental oversight; rather, it reflects certain inherent characteristics of phones. Since vowels are in general more volatile than consonants, the preference for matching identical consonants over identical vowels is justified. This insight cannot be expressed by a metric, which, by definition, assigns a zero distance to all identical pairs of segments. Nor is it certain that the triangle inequality should hold for phonetic segments. A phone that has two different places of articulation, such as labio-velar [w], can be close to two phones that are distant from each other, such as labial [b] and velar [g].

In my algorithm, below, I employ an alternative approach to comparing segments, which is based on the notion of *similarity*. A similarity scoring scheme assigns large positive scores to pairs of related segments; large negative scores to pairs of dissimilar segments; and small negative scores to indels. The optimal alignment is the one that maximizes the overall score. Under the similarity approach, the score obtained by two identical segments does not have to be constant. Another important advantage of the similarity approach is the possibility of performing *local alignment* of phonetic sequences, which is discussed in the following section.

3 Tree Search vs. Dynamic Programming

Once an appropriate function for measuring similarity between pairs of segments has been designed,

Feature name	Phonological term	Numerical value
Place	[bilabial]	1.0
	[labiodental]	0.95
	[dental]	0.9
	[alveolar]	0.85
	[retroflex]	0.8
	[palato-alveolar]	0.75
	[palatal]	0.7
	[velar]	0.6
	[uvular]	0.5
	[pharyngeal]	0.3
	[glottal]	0.1
Manner	[stop]	1.0
	[affricate]	0.9
	[fricative]	0.8
	[approximant]	0.6
	[high vowel]	0.4
	[mid vowel]	0.2
	[low vowel]	0.0
High	[high]	1.0
	[mid]	0.5
	[low]	0.0
Back	[front]	1.0
	[central]	0.5
	[back]	0.0

Table 3: Multivalued features and their values.

we need an algorithm for finding the optimal alignment of phonetic sequences. While the DP algorithm, which operates in quadratic time, seems to be optimal for the task, both Somers and Covington opt for exhaustive search strategies. In my opinion, this is unwarranted.

Somers's algorithm is unusual because the selected alignment is not necessarily the one that minimizes the sum of distances between individual segments. Instead, it recursively selects the most similar segments, or "anchor points", in the sequences being compared. Such an approach has a serious flaw. Suppose that the sequences to be aligned are *tewos* and *divut*. Even though the corresponding segments are slightly different, the alignment is straightforward. However, an algorithm that looks for the best matching segments first, will erroneously align the two *t*'s. Because of its recursive nature, the algorithm has no chance of recovering from such an error.[4]

Syllabic	5	Place	40
Voice	10	Nasal	10
Lateral	10	Aspirated	5
High	5	Back	5
Manner	50	Retroflex	10
Long	1	Round	5

Table 4: Features used in ALINE and their salience settings.

Covington, who uses a straightforward depth-first search to find the optimal alignment, provides the following arguments for eschewing the DP algorithm.

> First, the strings being aligned are relatively short, so the efficiency of dynamic programming on long strings is not needed. Second, dynamic programming normally gives only one alignment for each pair of strings, but comparative reconstruction may need the *n* best alternatives, or all that meet some criterion. Third, the tree search algorithm lends itself to modification for special handling of metathesis or assimilation.[5] (Covington, 1996)

The efficiency of the algorithm might not be relevant in the simple case of comparing two words, but if the algorithm is to be of practical use, it will have to operate on large bilingual wordlists. Moreover, combining the alignment algorithm with some sort of strategy for identifying cognates on the basis of phonetic similarity is likely to require comparing thousands of words against one another. Having a polynomially bound algorithm in the core of such a system is crucial. In any case, since the DP algorithm involves neither significantly larger overhead nor greater programming effort, there is no reason to avoid using it even for relatively small data sets.

The DP algorithm is also sufficiently flexible to accommodate most of the required extensions without compromising its polynomial complexity. A simple modification will produce all alignments that are within ε of the optimal distance (Myers, 1995). By applying methods from the operations research literature (Fox, 1973), the algorithm can be adapted to deliver the *n* best solutions. Moreover, the basic set of editing operations (substitutions and indels)

[4] The criticism applies regardless of the method of choosing the best matching segments (see also Section 5).

[5] Covington does not elaborate on the nature of the modifications.

can be extended to include both transpositions of adjacent segments (metathesis) (Lowrance and Wagner, 1975) and compressions and expansions (Oommen, 1995). Other extensions of the DP algorithm that are applicable to the problem of phonetic alignment include affine gap scores and local comparison.

The motivation for generalized gap scores arises from the fact that in diachronic phonology not only individual segments but also entire morphemes and syllables are sometimes deleted. In order to take this fact into account, the penalty for a gap can be calculated as a function of its length, rather than as a simple sum of individual deletions. One solution is to use an *affine* function of the form $gap(x) = r + sx$, where r is the penalty for the introduction of a gap, and s is the penalty for each symbol in the gap. Gotoh (1982) describes a method for incorporating affine gap scores into the DP alignment algorithm. Incidentally, Covington's penalties for indels can be expressed by an affine gap function with $r = 10$ and $s = 40$.

Local comparison (Smith and Waterman, 1981) is made possible by using both positive and negative similarity scores. In local, as opposed to global, comparison, only similar subsequences are matched, rather than entire sequences. This often has the beneficial effect of separating inflectional and derivational affixes from the roots. Such affixes tend to make finding the proper alignment more difficult. It would be unreasonable to expect affixes to be stripped before applying the algorithm to the data, because one of the very reasons to use an automatic aligner is to avoid analyzing every word individually.

4 The algorithm

Many of the ideas discussed in previous sections have been incorporated into the new algorithm for the alignment of phonetic sequences (ALINE). Similarity rather than distance is used to determine a set of best local alignments that fall within ε of the optimal alignment.[6] The set of operations contains insertions/deletions, substitutions, and expansions/compressions. Multivalued features are employed to calculate similarity of phonetic segments. Affine gaps were found to make little difference when local comparison is used and they were subsequently removed from ALINE.[7] The algorithm has been implemented in C++ and will be made available in the near future.

```
algorithm Alignment
    input: phonetic sequences x and y
    output: alignment of x and y
    define S(i, j) = −∞ when i < 0 or j < 0

    for i ← 0 to |x| do
        S(i, 0) ← 0
    for j ← 0 to |y| do
        S(0, j) ← 0
    for i ← 1 to |x| do
        for j ← 1 to |y| do
            S(i, j) ← max(
                S(i−1, j) + σ_skip(x_i),
                S(i, j−1) + σ_skip(y_j),
                S(i−1, j−1) + σ_sub(x_i, y_j),
                S(i−1, j−2) + σ_exp(x_i, y_{j−1}y_j),
                S(i−2, j−1) + σ_exp(x_{i−1}x_i, y_j),
                0)

    T ← (1 − ε) × max_{i,j} S(i,j)

    for i ← 1 to |x| do
        for j ← 1 to |y| do
            if S(i, j) > T then
                Retrieve(i, j, 0)
```

Figure 1: The algorithm for computing the alignment of two phonetic sequences.

Figure 1 contains the main components of the algorithm. First, the DP approach is applied to compute the similarity matrix S using the σ scoring functions. The optimal score is the maximum entry in the whole matrix. A recursive procedure *Retrieve* (Figure 2) is called on every matrix entry that exceeds the threshold score T. The alignments are retrieved by traversing the matrix until a zero entry is encountered. The scoring functions for indels, substitutions and expansions are defined in Figure 3. C_{skip}, C_{sub}, and C_{exp} are the maximum scores for indels, substitutions, and expansions, respectively. C_{vwl} determines the relative weight of consonants and vowels. The default values are $C_{skip} = -10$, $C_{sub} = 35$, $C_{exp} = 45$ and $C_{vwl} = 10$. The *diff* function returns the difference between segments p and q for a given feature f. Set R_V contains features relevant for comparing two vowels: Syllabic, Nasal, Retroflex, High, Back, Round, and Long. Set

[6] Global and semiglobal comparison can also be used. In a semiglobal comparison, the leading and trailing indels are assigned a score of zero.

[7] They may be necessary, however, when dealing with languages that are rich in infixes.

procedure Retrieve(i, j, s)

```
if S(i, j) = 0 then
    print(Out)
    print("alignment score is s")
else
    if S(i−1, j−1) + σ_sub(x_i, y_j) + s ≥ T then
        push(Out, "align x_i with y_j")
        Retrieve(i−1, j−1, s + σ_sub(x_i, y_j))
        pop(Out)
    if S(i, j−1) + σ_skip(y_j) + s ≥ T then
        push(Out, "align null with y_j")
        Retrieve(i, j−1, s + σ_skip(y_j))
        pop(Out)
    if S(i−1, j−2) + σ_exp(x_i, y_{j−1}y_j) + s ≥ T then
        push(Out, "align x_i with y_{j−1}y_j")
        Retrieve(i−1, j−2, s + σ_exp(x_i, y_{j−1}y_j))
        pop(Out)
    if S(i−1, j) + σ_skip(x_j) + s ≥ T then
        push(Out, "align x_i with null")
        Retrieve(i−1, j, s + σ_skip(x_j))
        pop(Out)
    if S(i−2, j−1) + σ_exp(y_j, x_{i−1}x_i) + s ≥ T then
        push(Out, "align x_i x_{i−1} with y_j")
        Retrieve(i−2, j−1, s + σ_exp(y_j, x_{i−1}x_i))
        pop(Out)
```

Figure 2: The procedure for retrieving alignments from the similarity matrix.

$$\sigma_{skip}(p) = C_{skip}$$

$$\sigma_{sub}(p,q) = C_{sub} - \delta(p,q) - V(p) - V(q)$$

$$\sigma_{exp}(p,q_1q_2) = C_{exp} - \delta(p,q_1) - \delta(p,q_2) - V(p) - max(V(q_1),V(q_2))$$

where

$$V(p) = \begin{cases} 0 & \text{if } p \text{ is a consonant} \\ C_{vwl} & \text{otherwise} \end{cases}$$

$$\delta(p,q) = \sum_{f \in R} \text{diff}(p,q,f) \times \text{salience}(f)$$

where

$$R = \begin{cases} R_C & \text{if } p \text{ or } q \text{ is a consonant} \\ R_V & \text{otherwise} \end{cases}$$

Figure 3: Scoring functions.

R_C contains features for comparing other segments: Syllabic, Manner, Voice, Nasal, Retroflex, Lateral, Aspirated, and Place. When dealing with double-articulation consonantal segments, only the nearest places of articulation are used. For a more detailed description of the algorithm see (Kondrak, 1999).

ALINE represents phonetic segments as vectors of feature values. Table 4 shows the features that are currently used by ALINE. Feature values are encoded as floating-point numbers in the range $[0.0, 1.0]$. The numerical values of four principal features are listed in Table 3. The numbers are based on the measurements performed by Ladefoged (1995). The remaining features have exactly two possible values, 0.0 and 1.0. A special feature 'Double', which has the same values as 'Place', indicates the second place of articulation. Thanks to its continuous nature, the system of features and their values can easily be adjusted and augmented.

5 Evaluation

The best alignments are obtained when local comparison is used. For example, when aligning English *grass* with Latin *grāmen*, it is important to match only the first three segments in each word; the remaining segments are unrelated. ALINE obviously does not know the particular etymologies, but it can make a guess because [s] and [m] are not very similar phonetically. Only local alignment is able to distinguish between the essential and non-essential correspondences in this case (Table 5).

The operations of compression and expansion prove to be very useful in the case of complex correspondences. For example, in the alignment of Latin *factum* with Spanish *hecho*, the affricate [ʧ] should be linked with both [k] and [t] rather than with just one of them, because it originates from the merger of the two consonants. Note that taking a se-

g	r	-	-	æ	s	
g	r	ā	m	e	n	
‖	g	r	æ	s	‖	
‖	g	r	ā	m	‖	en
‖	g	r	æ	‖	s	
‖	g	r	ā	‖	men	

Table 5: Three alignments of English *grass* and Latin *grāmen* obtained with global, semiglobal, and local comparison. The double bars delimit the aligned subsequences.

	Covington's alignments	*ALINE's alignments*
three : trēs	θ r i y	‖ θ r iy ‖
	t r ē s	‖ t r ē ‖ s
blow : flāre	b l - - o w	‖ b l o ‖ w
	f l ā r e -	‖ f l ā ‖ re
full : plēnus	f - - - u l	‖ f u l ‖
	p l ē n u s	‖ p - l ‖ ēnus
fish : piscis	f - - - i š	‖ f i š ‖
	p i s k i s	‖ p i s ‖ kis
I : ego	- - a y	‖ ay ‖
	e g o -	‖ e ‖ go
tooth : dentis	- - - t u w θ	‖ t uw θ ‖
	d e n t i - s	den ‖ t i s ‖

Table 6: Examples of alignments of English and Latin cognates.

quence of substitution and deletion as compression is unsatisfactory because it cannot be distinguished from an actual sequence of substitution and deletion. ALINE posits this operation particularly frequently in cases of diphthongization of vowels (see the alignments in Table 6).

Covington's data set of 82 cognates provides a convenient test for the algorithm. His English/Latin set is particularly interesting, because these two languages are not closely related. Some of the alignments produced by Covington's algorithm and ALINE are shown in Table 6. ALINE accurately discards inflectional affixes in *piscis* and *flāre*. In *fish/piscis*, Covington's aligner produces four alternative alignments, while ALINE selects the correct one. Both algorithms are technically wrong on *tooth/dentis*, but this is hardly an error considering that only the information contained in the phonetic string is available to the aligners. On Covington's Spanish/French data, ALINE does not make any mistakes. Unlike Covington's aligner, it properly aligns [l] in *arbol* with the second [r] in *arbre*. On his English/German data, it selects the correct alignment in those cases where Covington's aligner produces two alternatives. In the final, mixed set, ALINE makes a single mistake in *daughter/thugatēr*, in which it posits a dropped prefix rather than a syncopated syllable; in all other cases, it is right on target. Overall, ALINE clearly performs better than Covington's aligner.

Somers (1999) tests one version of his algorithm, CAT, on the same set of cognates. CAT employs binary, rather than multivalued, features. Another important characteristic is that it pre-aligns the stressed segments in both sequences. Since CAT distinguishes between individual consonants, in some cases it produces more accurate alignments than Covington's aligner. However, because of its pre-alignment strategy, it is guaranteed to produce wrong alignments in all cases when the stress has moved in one of the cognates. For example, in the Spanish/French pair *cabeza/cap*, it aligns [p] with [θ] rather than [b] and fails to align the two [a]'s. The problem is even more acute for closely related languages that have different stress rules.[8] In contrast, ALINE does not even consider stress, which, in the context of diachronic phonology, is too volatile to depend on. Except for the single case of *daughter/thugatēr*, ALINE produces better alignments than Somers's algorithm.

6 Future Directions

The goal of my current research is to combine the new alignment algorithm with a cognate identification procedure. The alignment of cognates is possi-

[8]For example, stress regularly falls on the initial syllable in Czech and on the penultimate syllable in Polish, while in Russian it can fall anywhere in the word.

ble only after the pairs of words that are suspected of being cognate have been identified. Identification of cognates is, however, an even more difficult task than the alignment itself. Moreover, it is hardly feasible without some kind of pre-alignment between candidate lexemes. A high alignment score of two words should indicate whether they are related. An integrated cognate identification algorithm would take as input unordered wordlists from two or more related languages, and produce a list of aligned cognate pairs as output. Such an algorithm would be a step towards developing a fully automated language reconstruction system.

Acknowledgments

I would like to thank Graeme Hirst, Elan Dresher, Steven Bird, and Carole Bracco for their comments. This research was supported by Natural Sciences and Engineering Research Council of Canada.

References

John H. Connolly. 1997. Quantifying target-realization differences. *Clinical Linguistics & Phonetics*, 11:267–298.

Michael A. Covington. 1996. An algorithm to align words for historical comparison. *Computational Linguistics*, 22(4):481–496.

Michael A. Covington. 1998. Alignment of multiple languages for historical comparison. In *Proceedings of COLING-ACL'98: 36th Annual Meeting of the Association for Computational Linguistics and 17th International Conference on Computational Linguistics*, pages 275–280.

Bennett L. Fox. 1973. Calculating the *K*th shortest paths. *INFOR – Canadian Journal of Operational Research and Information Processing*, 11(1):66–70.

Daniel Gildea and Daniel Jurafsky. 1996. Learning bias and phonological-rule induction. *Computational Linguistics*, 22(4):497–530.

Osamu Gotoh. 1982. An improved algorithm for matching biological sequences. *Journal of Molecular Biology*, 162:705–708.

Steven Lee Hartman. 1981. A universal alphabet for experiments in comparative phonology. *Computers and the Humanities*, 15:75–82.

Grzegorz Kondrak. 1999. Alignment of phonetic sequences. Technical Report CSRG-402, University of Toronto. Available from ftp.cs.toronto.edu/csri-technical-reports.

Joseph B. Kruskal. 1983. An overview of sequence comparison. In David Sankoff and Joseph B. Kruskal, editors, *Time warps, string edits, and macromolecules: the theory and practice of sequence comparison*, pages 1–44. Reading, Mass.: Addison-Wesley.

Peter Ladefoged. 1995. *A Course in Phonetics*. New York: Harcourt Brace Jovanovich.

Roy Lowrance and Robert A. Wagner. 1975. An extension of the string-to-string correction problem. *Journal of the Association for Computing Machinery*, 22:177–183.

Eugene W. Myers. 1995. Seeing conserved signals. In Eric S. Lander and Michael S. Waterman, editors, *Calculating the Secrets of Life*, pages 56–89. Washington, D.C.: National Academy Press.

John Nerbonne and Wilbert Heeringa. 1997. Measuring dialect distance phonetically. In *Proceedings of the Third Meeting of the ACL Special Interest Group in Computational Phonology (SIGPHON-97)*. Available at http://www.cogsci.ed.ac.uk/sigphon/.

B. John Oommen. 1995. String alignment with substitution, insertion, deletion, squashing, and expansion operations. *Information Sciences*, 83:89–107.

T. F. Smith and Michael S. Waterman. 1981. Identification of common molecular sequences. *Journal of Molecular Biology*, 147:195–197.

Harold L. Somers. 1998. Similarity metrics for aligning children's articulation data. In *Proceedings of COLING-ACL'98: 36th Annual Meeting of the Association for Computational Linguistics and 17th International Conference on Computational Linguistics*, pages 1227–1231.

Harold L. Somers. 1999. Aligning phonetic segments for children's articulation assessment. *Computational Linguistics*, 25(2):267–275.

Robert A. Wagner and Michael J. Fischer. 1974. The string-to-string correction problem. *Journal of the Association for Computing Machinery*, 21(1):168–173.

Finite-State Reduplication in One-Level Prosodic Morphology

Markus Walther
University of Marburg
FB09/IGS, Wilhelm-Röpke-Str. 6A, D-35032 Marburg, Germany
Markus.Walther@mailer.uni-marburg.de

Abstract

Reduplication, a central instance of prosodic morphology, is particularly challenging for state-of-the-art computational morphology, since it involves copying of some part of a phonological string. In this paper I advocate a finite-state method that combines enriched lexical representations via intersection to implement the copying. The proposal includes a resource-conscious variant of automata and can benefit from the existence of lazy algorithms. Finally, the implementation of a complex case from Koasati is presented.

1 Introduction

In the past two decades computational morphology has been quite successful in dealing with the challenges posed by natural language word patterns. Using finite-state methods, it has been possible to describe both word formation and the concomitant phonological modifications in many languages, ranging from straightforward concatenative combination (Koskenniemi, 1983) over Semitic-style nonconcatenative intercalation (Beesley (1996), Kiraz (1994)) to circumfixional long-distance dependencies (Beesley, 1998).

However, Sproat (1992) observes that, despite the existence of "working systems that are capable of doing a great deal of morphological analysis", "there are still outstanding problems and areas which have not received much serious attention" (ibid., 123). Problem areas in his view include subtractive morphology, infixation, the proper inclusion of prosodic structure and, in particular, reduplication: "From a computational point of view, one point cannot be overstressed: the copying required in reduplication places reduplication in a class apart from all other morphology." (ibid., 60). Productive reduplication is so troublesome for a formal account based on regular languages (or regular relations) because unbounded total instances like Indonesian noun plural (*orang-orang* 'men') are isomorphic to the copy language ww, which is context-sensitive.

In the rest of this paper I will lay out a proposal for handling reduplication with finite-state methods. As a starting point, I adopt Bird & Ellison (1994)'s One-Level Phonology, a monostratal constraint-based framework where phonological representations, morphemes and generalizations are all finite-state automata (FSAs) and constraint combination is accomplished via automata intersection. While it is possible to transfer much of the present proposal to the transducer-based setting that is often preferred nowadays, the monostratal approach still offers an attractive alternative due to its easy blend with monostratal grammars such as HPSG and the good prospects for machine learning of its surface-true constraints (Ellison (1992), Belz (1998)).

After a brief survey of important kinds of reduplication in §2, section §3 explains the necessary extensions of One-Level Phonology to deal with the challenges presented by reduplication, within the larger domain of prosodic morphology in general. A worked-out example from Koasati in §4 illustrates the interplay of the various components in an implemented analysis, before some conclusions are drawn in section §5.

2 Reduplication

A well-known case from the context-sensitivity debate of the eighties is the N-o-N reduplicative construction from Bambara (Northwestern Mande, (Culy, 1985)):

(1) a. wulu-o-**wulu** 'whichever dog'
b. wulunyinina-o-**wulunyinina** 'whichever dog searcher'
c. wulunyininafilèla-o-**wulunyininafilèla** 'whoever watches dog searchers'

Beyond total copying, (1) also illustrates the possibility of so-called fixed-melody parts in reduplication: a constant /o/ intervenes between base (i.e. original) and reduplicant (i.e. copied part, in bold print).[1]

The next case from Semai expressive minor reduplication (Mon-Khmer, Hendricks (1998)) highlights the possibility of an interaction between reduplication and internal truncation:

(2) a. cʔɛːt **ct**-cʔɛːt 'sweet'
b. dŋɔh **dh**-dŋɔh 'appearance of nodding constantly'
c. cfaːl **cl**-cfaːl 'appearance of flickering red object'

Reduplication copies the initial and final segment of the base, skipping all of its interior segments, which may be of arbitrary length.

A final case comes from Koasati punctual-aspect reduplication (Muscogean, (Kimball, 1988)):

(3) a. ta.hás.pin t$_1$ahas-**t**$_1$óː-pin
'to be light in weight'
b. la.pát.kin l$_1$apat-**l**$_1$óː-kin
'to be narrow
c. ak.lát.lin a$_1$k-**h**$_1$o-látlin
'to be loose'
d. ok.cák.kon o$_1$k-**h**$_1$o-cákkon
'to be green or blue'

Koasati is particularly interesting, because it shows that copy and original need not always be adjacent – here the reduplicant is infixed into its own base – and also because it illustrates that the copy may be phonologically modified: the /h/ in the copied part of (3).c,d is best analysed as a voiceless vowel, i.e. the phonetically closest *consonantal* expression of its source. Moreover, the locus of the infixed reduplicant is predictable on prosodic grounds, as it is inserted after the first heavy syllable of the base. Heavy syllables in Koasati are long (C)VV or closed (C)VC. Prosodic influence is also responsible for the length alternation of its fixed-melody part /o(o)/, since the heaviness requirement for the penultimate, stressed, syllable of the word causes long [oː] iff the reduplicant constitutes that syllable.

[1]Culy (1985), who presents a superset of the data under (1) in the context of a formal proof of context-sensitivity, shows that the reduplicative construction in fact can copy the outcome of a *recursive* agentive construction, thereby becoming truly unbounded. He emphasizes the fact that it is "very productive, with few, if any restrictions on the choice of the noun" (p.346).

3 Finite-State Methods

The present proposal differs from the state-labelled automata employed in One-Level Phonology by returning to conventional arc-labelled ones, but shares the idea that labels denote *sets*, which is advantageous for compact automata.

3.1 Enriched Representations

As motivated in §2, an appropriate automaton representation of morphemes that may undergo reduplication should provide generic support for three key operations: (i) copying or repetition of symbols, (ii) truncation or skipping, and (iii) infixation.

For *copying*, the idea is to enrich the FSA representing a morpheme by encoding stepwise repetition locally. For every content arc $i \stackrel{c}{\rightarrow} j$ we add a reverse **repeat arc** $j \stackrel{repeat}{\longrightarrow} i$. Following repeat arcs, we can now move backwards within a string, as we shall see in more detail below.

For *truncation*, a similar local encoding is available: For every content arc $i \stackrel{c}{\rightarrow} j$, add another **skip arc** $i \stackrel{skip}{\longrightarrow} j$. This allows us to move forward while suppressing the spellout of c.

A generic recipe for *infixation* ensures that segmental material can be inserted anywhere within an existing morpheme FSA. A possible representational enrichment therefore adds a **self loop** $i \stackrel{\Sigma}{\rightarrow} i$ labelled with the symbol alphabet Σ to every state i of the FSA.[2]

Each of the three enrichments presupposes an epsilon-free automaton in order to be wellbehaved. This requirement in particular ensures that technical arcs ($skip$, $repeat$) are in 1:1 correspondence with content arcs, which is essential for unambiguous positional movement: e.g. $add\_skips(a\,\epsilon\,b)$ would ambiguously require 1 *or* 2 skips to supress the spellout of b, because it creates a disjunction of the empty string ϵ with $skip$. It is perhaps worth emphasizing that there is no special interpretation whatsoever for these technical arcs: the standard automaton semantics is unaffected. As a consequence, $skip$ and $repeat$ will be a visible part of the output in word form generation and must be allowed in the input for parsing as well.

Taken together, the three enrichments yield an automaton for Bambara *wulu*, shown in figure 1.a. While skipping is not necessary for this example, $4 \stackrel{\Sigma}{\rightarrow} 4$ is: it will host the fixed-melody /o/. The

[2]This can be seen as an application of the *ignore* operator of Kaplan and Kay (1994), where Σ^* is being ignored.

repeat arcs will of course facilitate copying, as we shall see in a moment.

a.

b.

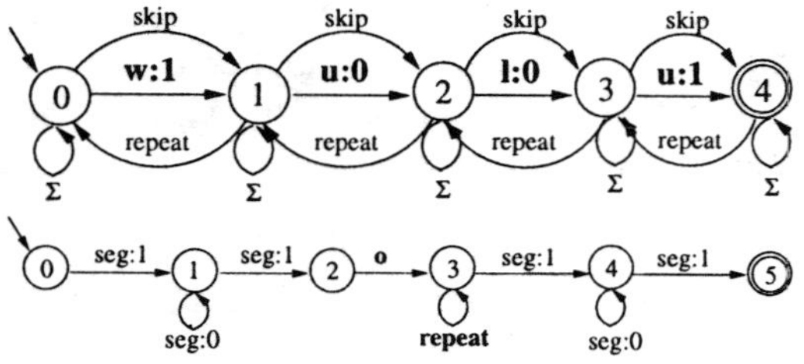

Figure 1: Enriched automata for *wulu* (a.), Bambara N-o-N reduplication (b.)

3.2 Copying as Intersection

Bird & Ellison (1992) came close to discovering a useful device for reduplication when they noted that automaton intersection has at least indexed-grammar power (ibid., p.48). They demonstrated their claim by showing that odd-length strings of indefinite length like the one described by the regular expression $(a\,b\,c\,d\,e\,f\,g)^{+}$ can be repeated by intersecting them with an automaton accepting only strings of even length: the result is $(a\,b\,c\,d\,e\,f\,g\,a\,b\,c\,d\,e\,f\,g)^{+}$.

Generalizing from their artifical example, let us first make one additional minor enrichment by tagging the edges of the reduplicative portion of a base with **synchronization bits :1**, while using the opposite value **:0** for the interior part (see figure 1.a). This gives us a segment-independent handle on those edges and a regular expression $seg_{:1}seg_{:0}{}^{*}seg_{:1}$ for the whole synchronized portion (*seg* abbreviates the set of phonological segments).

Assuming repeat-enriched bases, a total reduplication morpheme can now be seen as a partial word specification which mentions two synchronized portions separated by an arbitrary-length move backwards:

(4) $seg_{:1}seg_{:0}{}^{*}seg_{:1}\ \boldsymbol{repeat}^{*}\ seg_{:1}seg_{:0}{}^{*}seg_{:1}$

Moreover, total **reduplicative copying** now simply **is intersection** of the base and (4), or – in the Bambara case – a simple variant that adds the /o/ (figure 1.b). Disregarding self loops for the moment, the reader may verify that no expansion of the kleene-starred *repeat* that traverses less than $|base|$ segments will satisfy the demand for *two* synchronized portions. Semai requires another slight variant of (4) which *skips* the interior of the base in the reduplicant:

(5) $seg_{:1}\ \boldsymbol{skip}^{*}seg_{:1}\ repeat^{*}\ seg_{:1}seg_{:0}{}^{*}seg_{:1}$

The identification of copying with intersection not only allows for great flexibility in describing the full range of actual reduplicative constructions with regular expressions, it also *reuses* the central operation for constraint combination that is independently required for one-level morphology and phonology. Any improvement in efficient implementation of intersection therefore has immediate benefits for grammar computation as a whole. In contrast, a hypothetical setup where a dedicated total copy device is sandwiched between finite-state transducers seems much less elegant and may require additional machinery to detect copies during parsing.

Note that it is in fact possible to compute reduplication-as-intersection over an entire lexicon of bases (see figure 3 for an example), provided that repeat arcs are added individually to each base. Enriched base FSAs can then be unioned together and undergo further automaton transformations such as determinization or minimization. This restriction is necessary because our finite-state method cannot express token identity as normally required in string repetition. Rather than identifying the same token, it addresses the same string position, using the weaker notion of type identity. Therefore, application of the method is only safe if strings are effectively isolated from one another, which is exactly what per-base enrichment achieves. See §3.4 for a suggestion on how to lift the restriction in practice.

3.3 Resource Consciousness

One pays a certain price for allowing general repetition and infixation: because of its self loops and technical arcs, the automaton of figure 1.a overgenerates wildly. Also, during intersection, self loops can absorb other morphemes in unexpected ways. A possible diagnosis of the underlying defect is that we need to distinguish between **producers and consumers of information**. In analogy to LFG's constraint vs constraining equations, information may only be consumed if it has been produced at least once.

For automata, let us spend a P/C bit per arc, with P/C=1 for producers and P/C=0 for consumer arcs. In *open interpretation* mode, then, intersection combines the P/C bits of compatible arcs via logical OR, making producers dominant. It follows that a resource may be multiply consumed, which has obvious advantages for our application, the multiple realization of string symbols. A final step of *closed in-*

terpretation prunes all consumer-only arcs that survived constraint interaction, in what may be seen as intersection with the universal producer language under logical-AND combination of P/C bits.

Using these resource-conscious notions, we can now model both the default absence of material and purely contextual requirements as consumer-type information: unless satisfied by lexical resources that have been explicitly produced, the corresponding arcs will not be part of the result. By convention, producers are displayed in bold. Thus, the exact result of figure 1.a ∩ 1.b after closed interpretation is:

$$w_{:1}\, u_{:0}\, l_{:0}\, u_{:0}\, \mathbf{o}\ \mathbf{repeat^4}\ \mathbf{repeat^*}\ w_{:1}\, u_{:0}\, l_{:0}\, u_{:1}$$

This expression also illustrates that, for parsing, strings like *wuluowulu* need to be consumer-self-loop-enriched via a small preprocessing step, because intersection with the grammar would otherwise fail due to unmentioned technical arcs such as $repeat$. Because our proposal is fully declarative, parsing then reduces to intersecting the enriched parse string with the grammar-and-lexicon automaton (whose construction will itself involve intersection) in closed interpretation mode, followed by a check for nonemptiness of the result. Whereas the original parse string was underspecified for morphological categories, the parse result for a realistic morphology system will, in addition to technical arcs, contain fully specified category arcs in some predefined linearization order, which can be efficiently retrieved if desired.

3.4 On-demand Algorithms

It is clear that the above method is particularly attractive if some of its operations can be performed online, since a fullform lexicon of productive reduplications is clearly undesirable e.g. for Bambara. I therefore consider briefly questions of efficient implementation of these operations.

Mohri et al. (1998) identify the existence of a *local* computation rule as the main precondition[3] for a *lazy* implementation of automaton operations, i.e. one where results are only computed when demanded by subsequent operations. Such implementations are very advantageous when large intermediate automata may be constructed but only a small part of them is visited for any particular input. They show that such a rule exists for composition $\circ$, hence also for our operation of intersection $(A \cap B \equiv range(identity(A) \circ identity(B)))$.

Fortunately, the three enrichment steps all have local computation rules as well:

(6) a. $q_1 \xrightarrow{c} q_2 \;\Rightarrow\; q_2 \xrightarrow{repeat} q_1$

b. $q_1 \xrightarrow{c} q_2 \;\Rightarrow\; q_1 \xrightarrow{skip} q_2$

c. $q \;\Rightarrow\; q \xrightarrow{\Sigma} q$

The impact of the existence of lazy implementations for enrichment operations is twofold: we can (a) now maintain minimized base lexicons for storage efficiency and add enrichments lazily *to the currently pursued string hypothesis* only, possibly modulated by exception diacritics that control when enrichment should or should not happen.[4] And (b), laziness suffices to make the proposed reduplication method reasonably time-efficient, despite the larger number of online operations. Actual benchmarks from a pilot implementation are reported elsewhere (Walther, submitted).

4 A Worked Example

In this section I show how to implement the Koasati case from (3) using the FSA Utilities toolbox (van Noord, 1997). FSA Utilities is a Prolog-based finite-state toolkit and extendible regular expression compiler. It is freely available and encourages rapid prototyping.

Figure 2 displays the regular expression operators that will be used (italicized operators are modifications or extensions). The grammar will be presented below in a piecewise fashion, with line numbers added for easy reference.

`[]`	empty string
`[E1,E2, ... ,En]`	concatenation of E_i
`{E1,E2, ... ,En}`	union of E_i
`E*`	Kleene closure
`E^`	optionality
`E1 & E2`	intersection
X --> (Y / Z)	monotonic rule $X \rightarrow Y \subseteq X\ /\ \_\_\ Z$
$\sim S$	complement set of S
Head(arg1, ... , argN) := Body	(parametrized) macro definition

Figure 2: Regular expression operators

[3] A second condition is that no state is visited that has not been discovered from the start state. It is easy to implement (6) so that this condition is fulfilled as well.

[4] See Walther (submitted) for further details. With deterministic automata, the question of how to recover from a wrong string hypothesis during parsing is not an issue.

Starting with the definition of stems (line 1), we add the three enrichments to the bare phonological string (2). However, the innermost producer-type string constructed by `stringToAutomaton` (3) is intersected with phonological constraints (5,6) that need to see the string only, minus its enrichments. This is akin to lexical rule application.

```
1 stem(FirstSeg, String) :=
2  add_repeats(add_skips(add_self_loops(
3  [FirstSeg, stringToAutomaton(String)]
4    & ignore_technical_symbols_in(
5 moraification&mark_first_heavy_syllable
6    & positional_classification)))).
7
8 underspecified_for_voicing(BaseSpec) :=
9         { producer(BaseSpec & vowel),
10          [producer(h),consumer(skip)] }.
11
12 tahaspin    := stem([], "tahaspin").
13 aklatlin    := stem(underspecified_for_
14                voicing(low),"klatlin").
```

Lines 8-10 capture the V/h alternation that is characteristic for vowel-initial stems under reduplication, with the vocalic alternant constituting the default used in isolated pronunciation. In contrast, the /h/ alternant is concatenated with a `consumer`-type `skip` that requires a producer from elsewhere. Lines 12-14 define two example stems.

The following constraint (15-18) enriches a prosodically underspecified string with moras μ – abstract units of syllable weight (Hayes, 1995) –, a prerequisite to locating (20-24) and synchronization-marking (25-31) the first heavy syllable after which the reduplicative infix will be inserted.

```
15 moraification :=
16 ( vowel     --> ( mora / sigma ) )&
17 ( consonant --> ( mora / consonant ) )&
18 ( consonant --> ( (~ mora) / vowel ) ).
19
20 first_(X) := [not_contains(X), X].
21 heavy_rime := [consumer(mora),
22               consumer(mora)].
23 heavy_syllable := [consumer(~ mora),
24                    heavy_rime].
25 mark_first_heavy_syllable :=
26 [first_(heavy_rime)&synced_constituent,
27          synced_constituent].
28 right_synced := [consumer(~':1'&seg) *,
29                  consumer(':1'&seg)].
30 synced_constituent :=
31   [consumer(':1'&seg), right_synced].
32 positional_classification :=
33  [consumer(initial),consumer(medial) *,
34   consumer(final)].
```

Note that both the constituent before ($t_{:1}\ \overset{\mu}{a}\ h\ \overset{\mu}{a}\ \overset{\mu}{s}_{:1}$) and *after* ($p_{:1}\ \overset{\mu}{i}\ \overset{\mu}{n}_{:1}$) the infixation site need to be marked. Also, it turns out to be useful to classify base string positions for easy reference in the reduplicative morpheme, which motivates lines 32-34.

The main part now is the reduplicative morpheme itself (35), which looks like a mixture of Bambara and Semai: the spellout of the base is followed by iterated repeats (36) to move back to its synchronized initial position (37), which – recall /h/ – is required to be consonantal. The rest of the base is skipped before insertion of the fixed-melody part /o(o)/ occurs (38, 42-44). Proceeding with the interrupted realization of the base, we identify its beginning as a synchronized syllable onset (∼ `mora`), followed by a right-synchronized string (39-40).

```
35 punctual_aspect_reduplication :=
36 [synced_constituent, producer(repeat)*,
37  consumer(':1' & initial & consonant),
38  producer(skip) *, fixed_melody,
39  consumer(':1' & seg & ~ mora),
40  right_synced].
41
42 fixed_melody :=
43 [producer(o & ~ ':1' & medial & mora),
44  producer(o & ~ ':1' & medial & mora)^].
```

Finally, some obvious `word_level_constraints` need to be defined (45-54), before the central intersection of `Stem` and punctual-aspect reduplication (57) completes our Koasati fragment:

```
45 word_level_constraints :=
46 last_segment_is_moraic &
47 last_two_sylls_are_heavy.
48
49 last_segment_is_moraic :=
50   [consumer(sigma) *, consumer(mora)].
51
52 last_two_sylls_are_heavy :=
53   [consumer(sigma) *,
54    heavy_syllable,heavy_syllable].
55
56 wordform(Stem):=closed_interpretation(
57   word_level_constraints & Stem &
58   punctual_aspect_reduplication).
```

The result of `wordform({tahaspin,aklatlin})` is shown in figure 3 (`[` and `]` are aliases for initial and final position).

Space precludes the description of a final automaton operation called Bounded Local Optimization (Walther, 1999) that turns out to be useful here to

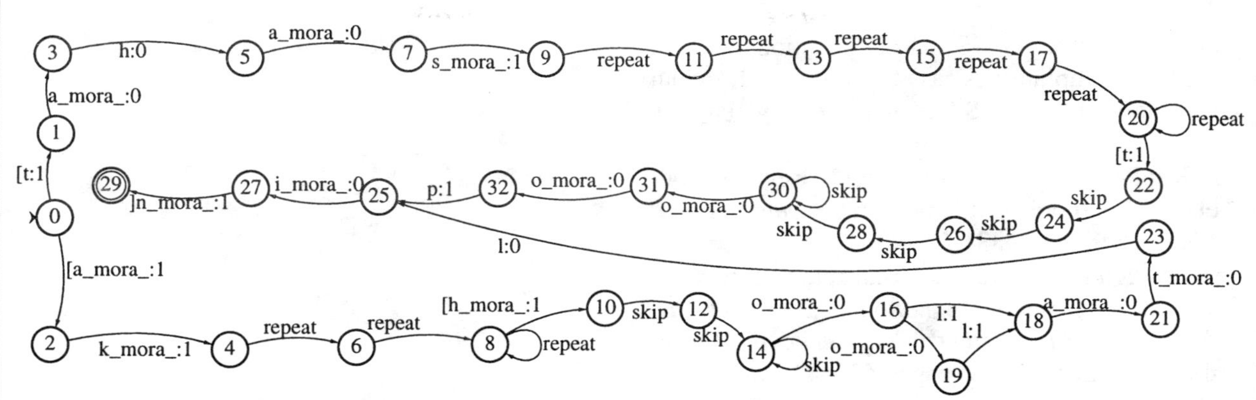

Figure 3: Koasati reduplications *tahas-too-pin, ak-ho(o)-latlin*

ban unattested free length variation, as found e.g. in *ak-ho(o)-latlin* where the length of *o* is yet to be determined. Suffice to say that a parametrization of Bounded Local Optimization would prune the moraic arc 16 → 19 in figure 3 by considering it costlier than the non-moraic arc 16 → 18, thereby eliminating the last source of indeterminacy.

5 Conclusion

This paper has presented a novel finite-state method for reduplication that is applicable for both unbounded total cases, truncated or otherwise phonologically modified types and infixing instances. The key ingredients of the proposal are suitably enriched automaton representations, the identification of reduplicative copying with automaton intersection and a resource-conscious interpretation that differentiates between two types of arc symbols, namely producers and consumers of information. After demonstrating the existence of efficient on-demand algorithms to reduplication's central operations, a case study from Koasati has shown that all of the above ingredients may be necessary in the analysis of a single complex piece of prosodic morphology.

It is worth mentioning that our method can be transferred into a two-level transducer setting without major difficulties (Walther, 1999, appendix B).

I conclude that the one-level approach to reduplicative prosodic morphology presents an attractive way of extending finite-state techniques to difficult phenomena that hitherto resisted elegant computational analyses.

Acknowledgements

The research in this paper has been funded by the German research agency DFG under grant WI 853/4-1. Particular thanks go to the anonymous reviewers for very useful comments.

References

Kenneth R. Beesley. 1996. Arabic finite-state morphological analysis and generation. In *Proceedings of COLING-96*, volume I, pages 89–94.

Kenneth R. Beesley. 1998. Constraining separated morphotactic dependencies in finite-state grammars. In *Proceedings of FSMNLP'98, Bilkent University, Turkey.*

Anja Belz. 1998. Discovering phonotactic finite-state automata by genetic search. In *Proceedings of COLING-ACL '98*, volume II, pages 1472–74.

Steven Bird and T. Mark Ellison. 1992. One-Level Phonology: Autosegmental representations and rules as finite-state automata. Technical report, Centre for Cognitive Science, University of Edinburgh. EUCCS/RP-51.

Steven Bird and T. Mark Ellison. 1994. One-Level Phonology. *Computational Linguistics*, 20(1):55–90.

Chris Culy. 1985. The complexity of the vocabulary of Bambara. *Linguistics and Philosophy*, 8:345–351.

T. Mark Ellison. 1992. *Machine Learning of Phonological Representations.* Ph.D. thesis, University of Western Australia, Perth.

Bruce Hayes. 1995. *Metrical stress theory: prin-*

ciples and case studies. University of Chicago Press.

Sean Hendricks. 1998. Reduplication without prosodic templates: A case from Semai. Handout from talk given at LSA annual meeting, January 8.

Ron Kaplan and Martin Kay. 1994. Regular models of phonological rule systems. *Computational Linguistics*, 20(3):331–78.

Geoffrey Kimball. 1988. Koasati reduplication. In W. Shipley, editor, *In honour of Mary Haas: from the Haas Festival Conference on Native American Linguistics*, pages 431–42. Mouton de Gruyter, Berlin.

George Anton Kiraz. 1994. Multi-tape two-level morphology: a case study in Semitic nonlinear morphology. In *Proceedings of COLING '94*, volume 1, pages 180–186.

Kimmo Koskenniemi. 1983. *Two-Level Morphology: A General Computational Model for Word-Form Recognition and Production*. Ph.D. thesis, University of Helsinki.

Mehryar Mohri, Fernando Pereira, and Michael Riley. 1998. A rational design for a weighted finite-state transducer library. In D. Wood and S. Yu, editors, *Automata Implementation. Second International Workshop on Implementing Automata, WIA '97*, volume 1436 of *Lecture Notes in Computer Science*, pages 144–58. Springer Verlag.

Richard Sproat. 1992. *Morphology and Computation*. MIT Press, Cambridge, Mass.

Gertjan van Noord. 1997. FSA Utilities: A toolbox to manipulate finite-state automata. In Darrell Raymond, Derrick Wood, and Sheng Yu, editors, *Automata Implementation*, volume 1260 of *Lecture Notes in Computer Science*, pages 87–108. Springer Verlag. (Software under `http://grid.let.rug.nl/~vannoord/Fsa/`).

Markus Walther. 1999. One-Level Prosodic Morphology. Marburger Arbeiten zur Linguistik 1, University of Marburg. 64 pp. (http://www.uni-marburg.de/linguistik/mal).

Markus Walther. submitted. On finite-state reduplication. In *COLING-2000*.

A Finite State and Data-Oriented Method for Grapheme to Phoneme Conversion

Gosse Bouma
Alfa-informatica
Rijksuniversiteit Groningen
Postbus 716
9700 AS Groningen
The Netherlands
gosse@let.rug.nl

Abstract

A finite-state method, based on leftmost longest-match replacement, is presented for segmenting words into graphemes, and for converting graphemes into phonemes. A small set of hand-crafted conversion rules for Dutch achieves a phoneme accuracy of over 93%. The accuracy of the system is further improved by using transformation-based learning. The phoneme accuracy of the best system (using a large rule and a 'lazy' variant of Brill's algoritm), trained on only 40K words, reaches 99%.

1 Introduction

Automatic grapheme to phoneme conversion (i.e. the conversion of a string of characters into a string of phonemes) is essential for applications of text to speech synthesis dealing with unrestricted text, where the input may contain words which do not occur in the system dictionary. Furthermore, a transducer for grapheme to phoneme conversion can be used to generate candidate replacements in a (pronunciation-sensitive) spelling correction system. When given the pronunciation of a misspelled word, the inverse of the grapheme to phoneme transducer will generate all identically pronounced words. Below, we present a method for developing such grapheme to phoneme transducers based on a combination of hand-crafted conversion rules, implemented using finite state calculus, and automatically induced rules.

The hand-crafted system is defined as a two-step procedure: segmentation of the input into a sequence of graphemes (i.e. sequences of one or more characters typically corresponding to a single phoneme) and conversion of graphemes into (sequences of) phonemes. The composition of the transducer which performs segmentation and the transducer defined by the conversion rules, is a transducer which converts sequences of characters into sequences of phonemes.

Specifying the conversion rules is a difficult task. Although segmentation of the input can in principle be dispensed with, we found that writing conversion rules for segmented input substantially reduces the context-sensitivity and order-dependence of such rules. We manually developed a grapheme to phoneme transducer for Dutch data obtained from CELEX (Baayen et al., 1993) and achieved a word accuracy of 60.6% and a phoneme accuracy of 93.6%.

To improve the performance of our system, we used transformation-based learning (TBL) (Brill, 1995). Training data are obtained by aligning the output of the hand-crafted finite state transducer with the correct phoneme strings. These data can then be used as input for TBL, provided that suitable rule templates are available. We performed several experiments, in which the amount of training data, the algorithm (Brill's original formulation and 'lazy' variants (Samuel et al., 1998)), and the number of rule templates varied. The best experiment (40K words, using a 'lazy' strategy with a large set of rule templates) induces over 2000 transformation rules, leading to 92.6% word accuracy and 99.0% phoneme accuracy. This result, obtained using a relatively small set of training data, compares well with that of other systems.

2 Finite State Calculus

As argued in Kaplan and Kay (1994), Karttunen (1995), Karttunen et al. (1997), and elsewhere, many of the rules used in phonology and morphology can be analysed as special cases of regular expressions. By extending the language of regular expressions with operators which capture the interpretation of linguistic rule systems, high-level linguistic descriptions can be compiled into finite state automata directly. Furthermore, such automata can be combined with other finite state automata performing low-level tasks such as tokenization or lexical-lookup, or more advanced tasks such as shallow parsing. Composition of the individual components into a single transducer may lead to highly efficient processing.

The system described below was implemented using FSA Utilities,[1] a package for implementing and manipulating finite state automata, which provides possibilities for defining new regular expression oper-

[1] `www.let.rug.nl/~vannoord/fsa/`

`[]`	the empty string
`[R1,...,Rn]`	concatenation
`{R1,...,Rn}`	disjunction
`R^`	optionality
`ignore(A,B)`	ignore: A interspersed with elements of B
`A x B`	cross-product: the transducer which maps all strings in A to all strings in B.
`identity(A)`	identity: the transducer which maps each element in A onto itself.
`T o U`	composition of the transducers T and U.
`macro(Term,R)`	use Term as an abbreviation for R (where Term and R may contain variables).

Figure 1: A fragment of FSA regular expression syntax. A and B are regular expressions denoting recognizers, T and U transducers, and R can be either.

ators. The part of FSA's built-in regular expression syntax relevant to this paper, is listed in figure 1.

One particular useful extension of the basic syntax of regular expressions is the replace-operator. Karttunen (1995) argues that many phonological and morphological rules can be interpreted as rules which replace a certain portion of the input string. Although several implementations of the replace-operator are proposed, the most relevant case for our purposes is so-called 'leftmost longest-match' replacement. In case of overlapping rule targets in the input, this operator will replace the leftmost target, and in cases where a rule target contains a prefix which is also a potential target, the longer sequence will be replaced. Gerdemann and van Noord (1999) implement leftmost longest-match replacement in FSA as the operator

```
replace(Target, LeftContext,RightContext),
```

where Target is a transducer defining the actual replacement, and LeftContext and RightContext are regular expressions defining the left- and rightcontext of the rule, respectively.

An example where leftmost replacement is useful is hyphenation. Hyphenation of (non-compound) words in Dutch amounts to segmenting a word into syllables, separated by hyphens. In cases where (the written form of) a word can in principle be segmented in several ways (i.e. the sequence `alfabet` can be segmented as `al-fa-bet`, `al-fab-et`, `alf-a-bet`, or `alf-ab-et`), the segmentation which maximizes onsets is in general the correct one (i.e. `al-fa-bet`). This property of hyphenation is captured by leftmost replacement:

```
macro(hyphenate,
   replace([] x -, syllable, syllable)).
```

Leftmost replacement ensures that hyphens are introduced 'eagerly', i.e. as early as possible. Given a suitable definition of `syllable`, this ensures that wherever a consonant can be final in a coda or initial in the next onset, it is in fact added to the onset.

The segmentation task discussed below makes crucial use of longest match.

3 A finite state method for grapheme to phoneme conversion

Grapheme to phoneme conversion is implemented as the composition of four transducers:

```
macro(graph2phon,
   segmentation       % segment the input
 o mark_begin_end     % add '#'
 o conversion         % apply rules
 o clean_up       ).  % remove markers
```

An example of conversion including the intermediate steps is given below for the word `aanknopingspunt` (*connection-point*).

```
input:  aanknopingspunt
s:      aa-n-k-n-o-p-i-ng-s-p-u-n-t-
m:      #-aa-n-k-n-o-p-i-ng-s-p-u-n-t-#
co:     #-a+N+k-n-o-p-I+N+s-p-}+n-t-#
cl:     aNknopINsp}nt
```

The first transducer (**segmentation**) takes as its input a sequence of characters and groups these into segments. The second transducer (**mark_begin_end**) adds a marker ('#') to the beginning and end of the sequence of segments. The third transducer (**conversion**) performs the actual conversion step. It converts each segment into a sequence of (zero or more) phonemes. The final step (**clean_up**) removes all markers. The output is a list of phonemes in the notation used by CELEX (which can be easily translated into the more common SAMPA-notation).

3.1 Segmentation

The goal of segmentation is to divide a word into a sequence of graphemes, providing a convenient input level of representation for the actual grapheme to phoneme conversion rules.

While there are many letter-combinations which are realized as a single phoneme (ch, ng, aa, bb, ..), it is only rarely the case that a single letter is mapped onto more than one phoneme (x), or that a letter receives no pronunciation at all (such as word-final n in Dutch, which is elided if it is proceeded by a schwa). As the number of cases where multiple letters have to be mapped onto a single phoneme is relatively high, it is natural to model a letter to phoneme system as involving two subtasks: segmentation and conversion. Segmentation splits an input string into graphemes, where each grapheme typically, but not necessarily, corresponds to a single phoneme.

Segmentation is defined as:

```
macro(segmentation,
 replace(
  [identity(graphemes), [] x - ],[],[])
        ).
```

The macro graphemes defines the set of graphemes. It contains 77 elements, some of which are:

```
a, aa, au, ai, aai, e, ee, ei, eu, eau,
eeu, i, ie, iee, ieu, ij, o, oe, oei,..
```

Segmentation attaches the marker '-' to each grapheme. Segmentation, as it is defined here, is not context-sensitive, and thus the second and third arguments of replace are simply empty. As the set of graphemes contains many elements which are substrings of other graphemes (i.e. e is a substring of ei, eau, etc.), longest-match is essential: the segmentation of beiaardier (*carillon player*) should be b-ei-aa-r-d-ie-r- and not b-e-i-a-a-r-d-i-e-r-. This effect can be obtained by making the segment itself part of the target of the replace statement. Targets are identified using leftmost longest-match, and thus at each point in the input, only the longest valid segment is marked.

The set of graphemes contains a number of elements which might seem superfluous. The grapheme aai, for instance, translates as aj, a sequence which could also be derived on the basis of two graphemes aa and i. However, if we leave out the segment aai, segmentation (using leftmost longest match) of words such as waaien (*to blow*) would lead to the segmentation w-aa-ie-n, which is unnatural, as it would require an extra conversion rule for ie. Using the grapheme aai allows for two conversion rules which always map aai to aj and ie goes to i.

Segmentation as defined above provides the intuitively correct result in almost all cases, given a suitably defined set of graphemes. There are some cases which are less natural, but which do not necessarily lead to errors. The grapheme eu, for instance, almost always goes to '|', but translates as 'e,j,}' in (loan-) words such as museum and petroleum. One might argue that a segmentation e-u- is therefore required, but a special conversion rule which covers these exceptional cases (i.e. eu followed by m) can easily be formulated. Similarly, ng almost always translates as N, but in some cases actually represents the two graphemes n-g-, as in aaneengesloten (*connected*), where it should be translated as NG. This case is harder to detect, and is a potential source of errors.

3.2 The Conversion Rules

The g2p operator is designed to facilitate the formulation of conversion rules for segmented input:

```
macro(g2p(Target,LtCont,RtCont),
  replace([Target, - x +],
             [ignore(LtCont,{+,-}), {-,+}],
                ignore(RtCont,{+,-})
          )
     ).
```

The g2p-operator implements a special purpose version of the replace-operator. The replacement of the marker '-' by '+' in the target ensures that g2p-conversion rules cannot apply in sequence to the same grapheme.[2] Second, each target of the g2p-operator must be a grapheme (and not some substring of it). This is a consequence of the fact that the final element of the left-context must be a marker and the target itself ends in '-'. Finally, the ignore statements in the left and right context imply that the rule contexts can abstract over the potential presence of markers.

An overview of the conversion rules we used for Dutch is given in Figure 2. As the rules are applied in sequence, exceptional rules can be ordered before the regular cases, thus allowing the regular cases to be specified with little or no context. The special_vowel_rules deal with exceptional translations of graphemes such as eu or cases where i or ij goes to '@'. The short_vowel_rules treat single vowels preceding two consonants, or a word final consonant. One problematic case is e, which can be translated either as 'E' or '@'. Here, an approximation is attempted which specifies the context where e goes 'E', and subsumes the other case under the general rule for short vowels. The special_consonant_rules address devoicing and a few other exceptional cases. The default_rules supply a default mapping for a large number of

[2]Note that the input and output alphabet are not disjoint, and thus rules applying in sequence to the same part of the input are not excluded in principle.

graphemes. The target of this rule is a long disjunction of grapheme-phoneme mappings. As this ruleset applies after all more specific cases have been dealt with, no context restrictions need to be specified.

Depending somewhat on how one counts, the full set of conversion rules for Dutch contains approximately 80 conversion rules, more than 40 of which are default mappings requiring no context.[3] Compilation of the complete system results in a (minimal, deterministic) transducer with 747 states and 20,123 transitions.

3.3 Test results and discussion

The accuracy of the hand-crafted system was evaluated by testing it on all of the words wihtout diacritics in the CELEX lexical database which have a phonetic transcription. After several development cycles, we achieved a word accuracy of 60.6% and a phoneme accuracy (measured as the edit distance between the phoneme string produced by the system and the correct string, divided by the number of phonemes in the correct string) of 93.6%.

There have been relatively few attempts at developing grapheme to phoneme conversion systems using finite state technology alone. Williams (1994) reports on a system for Welsh, which uses no less than 700 rules implemented in a rather restricted environment. The rules are also implemented in a two-level system, PC-KIMMO, (Antworth, 1990), but this still requires over 400 rules. Möbius et al. (1997) report on full-fledged text-to-speech system for German, containing around 200 rules (which are compiled into a weighted finite state transducer) for the grapheme-to-phoneme conversion step. These numbers suggest that our implementation (which contains around 80 rules in total) benefits considerably from the flexibility and high-level of abstraction made available by finite state calculus.

One might suspect that a two-level approach to grapheme to phoneme conversion is more appropriate than the sequential approach used here. Somewhat surprisingly, however, Williams concludes that a sequential approach is preferable. The formulation of rules in the latter approach is more intuitive, and rule ordering provides a way of dealing with exceptional cases which is not easily available in a two-level system.

While further improvements would definitely have been possible at this point, it becomes increasingly difficult to do this on the basis of linguistic knowledge alone. That is, most of the rules which have to be added deal with highly idiosyncratic cases (often related to loan-words) which can only be discovered by browsing through the test results of previous runs. At this point, switching from a linguistics-oriented to a data-oriented methodology, seemed appropriate.

4 Transformation-based grapheme to phoneme conversion

Brill (1995) demonstrates that accurate part-of-speech tagging can be learned by using a two-step process. First, a simple system is used which assigns the most probable tag to each word. The results of the system are aligned with the correct tags for some corpus of training data. Next, (context-sensitive) transformation rules are selected from a pool of rule patterns, which replace erroneous tags by correct tags. The rule with the largest benefit on the training data (i.e. the rule for which the number of corrections minus the number of newly introduced mistakes, is the largest) is learned and applied to the training data. This process continues until no more rules can be found which lead to improvement (above a certain threshold).

Transformation-based learning (TBL) can be applied to the present problem as well.[4] In this case, the base-line system is the finite state transducer described above, which can be used to produce a set of phonemic transcriptions for a word list. Next, these results are aligned with the correct transcriptions. In combination with suitable rule patterns, these data can be used as input for a TBL process.

4.1 Alignment

TBL requires aligned data for training and testing. While alignment is mostly trivial for part-of-speech tagging, this is not the case for the present task. Aligning data for grapheme-to-phoneme conversion amounts to aligning each part of the input (a sequence of characters) with a part of the output (a sequence of phonemes). As the length of both sequences is not guaranteed to be equal, it must be possible to align more than one character with a single phoneme (the usual case) or a single character with more than one phoneme (the exceptional case, i.e. 'x'). The alignment problem is often solved (Dutoit, 1997; Daelemans and van den Bosch, 1996) by allowing 'null' symbols in the phoneme string, and introducing 'compound' phonemes, such as 'ks' to account for exceptional cases where a single character must be aligned with two phonemes.

As our finite state system already segments the input into graphemes, we have adopted a strategy where *graphemes* instead of characters are aligned with phoneme strings (see Lawrence and Kaye (1986) for a similar approach). The correspondence

[3] It should be noted that we only considered words which do not contain diacritics. Including those is unproblematic in principle, but would lead to a slight increase of the number of rules.

[4] Hoste et al. (2000b) compare TBL to C5.0 (Quinlan, 1993) on a similar task, i.e. the mapping of the pronunciation of one regional variant of Dutch into another.

```
macro(conversion,      special_vowel_rules o short_vowel_rules
                     o special_consonant_rules o default_rules  ).
macro(special_vowel_rules,
    g2p([e,u] x [e,j,}], [],  m)  %% museum
  o g2p(i     x @,       [],  g)  %% moedig(st)
  o g2p([i,j] x @,       l,   k)  %% mogelijkheid
  .... ).
macro(short_vowel_rules,
    g2p(e x 'E', [], {[t,t],[k,k],x,...})
    g2p({ a x 'A' , e x @, i x 'I' , o x 'O', u x '}' }, [], [cons, {cons , #}] )
    ).
macro(special_consonant_rules,
     g2p(b x p,          [], {s,t,#})
   o g2p([d,t^] x t,     [], {s,g,k,j,v,h,z,#})
   o g2p({ f x v, s x z},  [], {b,d})
   o g2p(g x 'G',        vowel, vowel)
   o g2p(n x 'N',        [], {k,q})
   o g2p(n x [],         [@],[#])
   ...).
macro(default_rules,
  g2p({ [a,a] x a, [a,a,i] x [a,j], [a,u] x 'M',  [e,a,u] x o, ....,
          [b,b] x b, [d,d] x d, ...., [c,h] x 'x', [s,c,h] x [s,x], [n,g] x 'N', ...
     }, [], [] )
    ).
```

Figure 2: Conversion Rules

between graphemes and phonemes is usually one to one, but it is no problem to align a grapheme with two or more phonemes. Null symbols are only introduced in the output if a grapheme, such as word-final 'n', is not realized phonologically.

For TBL, the input actually has to be aligned both with the system output as well as with the correct phoneme string. The first task can be solved trivially: since our finite state system proceeds by first segmenting the input into graphemes (sequences of characters), and then transduces each grapheme into a sequence of phonemes, we can obtain aligned data by simply aligning each grapheme with its corresponding phoneme string. The input is segmented into graphemes by doing the segmentation step of the finite state transducer only. The corresponding phoneme strings can be identified by applying the conversion transducer to the segmented input, while keeping the boundary symbols '-' and '+'. As a consequence of the design of the conversion-rules, the resulting sequence of separated phonemes sequences stands in a one-to-one relationship to the graphemes. An example is shown in figure 3, where GR represents the grapheme segmented string, and SP the (system) phoneme strings produced by the finite state transducer. Note that the final SP cell contains only a boundary marker, indicating that the grapheme 'n' is translated into the null phoneme.

Word	aalbessen (*currants*)						
GR	aa -	l -	b -	e -	ss -	e -	n -
SP	a +	l -	b -	@ +	s +	@ +	+
CP	a	l	b	E	s	@	

Figure 3: Alignment

For the alignment between graphemes (and, idirectly, the system output) and the correct phoneme strings (as found in Celex), we used the 'hand-seeded' probabilistic alignment procedure described by Black et al. (1998). From the finite state conversion rules, a set of possible *grapheme → phoneme sequence* mappings can be derived. This *allowables*-set was extended with (exceptional) mappings present in the correct data, but not in the hand-crafted system. We computed all possible alignments between (segmented) words and correct phoneme strings licenced by the *allowables*-set. Next, probabilities for all allowed mappings were estimated on the basis of all possible alignments, and the data was parsed again, now picking the most probable alignment for each word. To minimize the number of words that could not be aligned, a maximum of one unseen mapping (which was assigned a low probability) was allowed per word. With this modification, only one out of 1000 words on average could not be aligned.[5] These words were discarded.The aligned phoneme

[5]Typical cases are loan words (*umpires*) and letter words (i.e. abbreviations) (*abc*).

method	training data (words)	phoneme accuracy	word accuracy	induced rules	CPU time (in minutes)
Base-line		93.6	60.6		
Brill	20K	98.0	86.1	447	162
Brill	40K	98.4	88.9	812	858
lazy(5)	20K	97.6	83.5	337	43
lazy(5)	40K	98.2	87.0	701	190
lazy(5)	60K	98.4	88.3	922	397
lazy(10)	20K	97.7	84.3	368	83
lazy(10)	40K	98.2	87.5	738	335
lazy(10)	60K	98.4	88.9	974	711
lazy(5)+	20K	98.6	89.8	1225	186
lazy(5)+	40K	99.0	92.6	2221	603

Figure 4: Experimental Results using training data produced by graph2phon

string for the example in figure 3 is shown in the bottom line. Note that the final cell is empty, representing the null phoneme.

4.2 The experiments

For the experiments with TBL we used the μ-TBL-package (Lager, 1999). This Prolog implementation of TBL is considerably more efficient (up to ten times faster) than Brill's original (C) implementation. The speed-up results mainly from using Prolog's first-argument indexing to access large quantities of data efficiently.

We constructed a set of 22 rule templates which replace a predicted phoneme with a (corrected) phoneme on the basis of the underlying segment, and a context consisting either of phoneme strings, with a maximum length of two on either side, or a context consisting of graphemes, with a maximal length of 1 on either side. Using only 20K words (which corresponds to almost 180K segments), and Brill's algorithm, we achieved a phoneme accuracy of 98.0% (see figure 4) on a test set of 20K words of unseen data.[6] Going to 40K words resulted in 98.4% phoneme accuracy. Note, however, that in spite of the relative efficiency of the implementation, CPU time also goes up sharply.

The heavy computation costs of TBL are due to the fact that for each error in the training data, all possible instantiations of the rule templates which correct this error are generated, and for each of these instantiated rules the score on the whole training set has to be computed. Samuel et al. (1998) therefore propose an efficient, 'lazy', alternative, based on Monte Carlo sampling of the rules. For each error in the training set, only a sample of the rules is considered which might correct it. As rules which correct a high number of errors have a higher chance of being sampled at some point, higher scoring rules are more likely to be generated than lower scoring rules, but no exhaustive search is required. We experimented with sampling sizes 5 and 10. As CPU requirements are more modest, we managed to perform experiments on 60K words in this case, which lead to results which are comparable with Brill's algoritm applied to 40K words.

Apart from being able to work with larger data sets, the 'lazy' strategy also has the advantage that it can cope with larger sets of rule templates. Brill's algorithm slows down quickly when the set of rule templates is extended, but for an algorithm based on rule sampling, this effect is much less severe. Thus, we also constructed a set of 500 rule templates, containing transformation rules which allowed up to three graphemes or phoneme sequences as left or right context, and also allowed for disjunctive contexts (i.e. the context must contain an `'a'` at the first or second position to the right). We used this rule set in combination with a 'lazy' strategy with sampling size 5 (lazy(5)+ in figure 4). This led to a further improvement of phoneme accuracy to 99.0%, and word accuracy of 92.6%, using only 40K words of training material.

Finally, we investigated what the contribution was of using a relatively accurate training set. To this end, we constructed an alternative training set, in which every segment was associated with its most probable phoneme (where frequencies were obtained from the aligned CELEX data). As shown in figure 5, the initial accuracy for such as system is much lower than that of the hand-crafted system. The experimental results, for the 'lazy' algorithm with sampling size 5, show that the phoneme accuracy for training on 20K words is 0.3% less than for the corresponding experiment in figure 4. For 40K words, the difference is still 0.2%, which, in both cases, corresponds to a difference in error rate of around 10%. As might be expected, the number of induced rules

[6]The statistics for less time consuming experiments were obtained by 10-fold cross-validation and for the more expensive experiments by 5-fold cross-validation.

method	training data (words)	phoneme accuracy	word accuracy	induced rules	CPU time (in minutes)
Base-line		72.9	10.8		
lazy(5)	20K	97.3	81.6	691	133
lazy(5)	40K	98.0	86.0	1075	705

Figure 5: Experimental results using data based on frequency.

is much higher now, and thus CPU-requirements also increase substantially.

5 Concluding remarks

We have presented a method for grapheme to phoneme conversion, which combines a hand-crafted finite state transducer with rules induced by a transformation-based learning. An advantage of this method is that it is able to achieve a high level of accuracy using relatively small training sets. Busser (1998), for instance, uses a memory-based learning strategy to achieve 90.1% word accuracy on the same task, but used 90% of the CELEX data (over 300K words) as training set and a (character/phoneme) window size of 9. Hoste et al. (2000a) achieve a word accuracy of 95.7% and a phoneme accuracy of 99.5% on the same task, using a combination of machine learning techniques, as well as additional data obtained from a second dictionary.

Given the result of Roche and Schabes (1997), an obvious next step is to compile the induced rules into an actual transducer, and to compose this with the hand-crafted transducer. It should be noted, however, that the number of induced rules is quite large in some of the experiments, so that the compilation procedure may require some attention.

References

Evan L. Antworth. 1990. *PC-KIMMO : a two-level processor for morphological analysis.* Summer Institute of Linguistics, Dallas, Tex.

R. H. Baayen, R. Piepenbrock, and H. van Rijn. 1993. *The CELEX Lexical Database (CD-ROM).* Linguistic Data Consortium, University of Pennsylvania, Philadelphia, PA.

Alan Black, Kevin Lenzo, and Vincent Pagel. 1998. Issues in building general letter to sound rules. In *Proceedings of the 3rd ESCA/COCSADA Workshop on Speech Synthesis*, pages 77–81, Jenolan Caves, Australia.

Eric Brill. 1995. Transformation-based error-driven learning and natural language processing: A case study in part-of-speech tagging. *Computational Linguistics*, 21:543–566.

Bertjan Busser. 1998. TreeTalk-D: a machine learning approach to Dutch word pronunciation. In *Proceedings TSD Conference*, pages 3–8, Masaryk University, Czech Republic.

W. Daelemans and A. van den Bosch. 1996. Language-independent data-oriented grapheme-to-phoneme conversion. In *Progress in Speech Synthesis*, pages 77–90, New York. Springer Verlag.

Thierry Dutoit. 1997. *An Introduction to Text-to-Speech Synthesis.* Kluwer, Dordrecht.

Dale Gerdemann and Gertjan van Noord. 1999. Transducers from rewrite rules with backreferences. In *Proceedings of the Ninth Conference of the European Chapter of the Association for Computational Linguistics*, pages 126–133, Bergen.

Veronique Hoste, Walter Daelemans, Erik Tjong Kim Sang, and Steven Gillis. 2000a. Meta-learning of phonemic annotation of corpora. ms., University of Antwerp.

Veronique Hoste, Steven Gillis, and Walter Daelemans. 2000b. A rule induction approach to modelling regional pronunciation variation. ms., University of Antwerp.

Ronald Kaplan and Martin Kay. 1994. Regular models of phonological rule systems. *Computational Linguistics*, 20(3).

L. Karttunen, J.P. Chanod, G. Grefenstette, and A. Schiller. 1997. Regular expressions for language engineering. *Natural Lanuage Engineering*, pages 1–24.

Lauri Karttunen. 1995. The replace operator. In *33th Annual Meeting of the Association for Computational Linguistics*, pages 16–23, Boston, Massachusetts.

Torbjörn Lager. 1999. The μ-TBL System: Logic programming tools for transformation-based learning. In *Proceedings of the Third International Workshop on Computational Natural Language Learning (CoNLL'99)*, pages 33–42, Bergen.

S. C. G. Lawrence and G. Kaye. 1986. Alignment of phonemes with their corresponding orthography. *Computer Speech and Language*, 1(2):153–165.

Bernd Möbius, Richard Sproat, Jan van Santen, and Joseph Olive. 1997. The Bell Labs German text-to-speech system: An overview. In *Proceedings of the European Conference on Speech Communication and Technology*, pages 2443–2446, Rhodes.

J. R. Quinlan. 1993. *C4.5: programs for machine learning.* Morgan Kaufmann Publishers, San Mateo.

Emmanuel Roche and Yves Schabes. 1997. Deterministic part-of-speech tagging with finite-state transducers. In Emmanuel Roche and Yves Schabes, editors, *Finite state language processing*, pages 205–239. MIT Press, Cambridge, Mass.

Ken Samuel, Sandra Carberry, and K. Vijay-Shanker. 1998. Dialogue act tagging with transformation-based learning. In *Proceedings of the 17th International Conference on Computational Linguistics (COLING-ACL '98)*, Montreal.

Briony Williams. 1994. Welsh letter-to-sound rules: rewrite rules and two-level rules compared. *Computer Speech and Language*, 8:261–277.

A Framework for Robust Semantic Interpretation

Carolyn P. Rosé
Learning Research and Development Center
University of Pittsburgh
Pittsburgh, PA 15260
rosecp@pitt.edu

Abstract

This paper describes AUTOSEM, a robust semantic interpretation framework that can operate both at parse time and repair time. The evaluation demonstrates that AUTOSEM achieves a high level of robustness efficiently and without requiring any hand coded knowledge dedicated to repair.

1 Introduction

In order for an approach to robust interpretation to be practical it must be efficient, address the major types of disfluencies that plague spontaneously produced language input, and be domain independent so that achieving robustness in a particular domain does not require an additional knowledge engineering effort. This paper describes AUTOSEM, a semantic interpretation framework that possesses these three qualities. While previous approaches to robust interpretation have offered robust parsers paired with separate repair modules, with separate knowledge sources for each, AUTOSEM is a single unified framework that can operate both at parse time and repair time. AUTOSEM is integrated with the LCFLEX robust parser (Rosé and Lavie, to appear; Lavie and Rosé, 2000). Together AUTOSEM and LCFLEX constitute the robust understanding engine within the CARMEL natural language understanding component developed in the context of the Atlas intelligent tutoring project (Freedman at al., to appear). The evaluation reported here demonstrates that AUTOSEM's repair approach operates 200 times faster than the most similar competing approach while producing hypotheses of better quality.

AUTOSEM provides an interface to allow semantic interpretation to operate in parallel with syntactic interpretation at parse time in a lexicon driven fashion. Domain specific semantic knowledge is encoded declaratively within a meaning representation specification. Semantic constructor functions are compiled automatically from this specification and then linked into lexical entries as in the Glue Language Semantics approach to interpretation (Dalrymple, 1999). Based on syntactic head/argument relationships assigned at parse time, the constructor functions enforce semantic selectional restrictions and assemble meaning representation structures by composing the meaning representation associated with the constructor function with the meaning representation of each of its arguments.

AUTOSEM first attempts to construct analyses that satisfy both syntactic and semantic well-formedness conditions. The LCFLEX parser has the ability to efficiently relax syntactic constraints as needed and as allowed by its parameterized flexibility settings. For sentences remaining beyond the parser's coverage, AUTOSEM's repair algorithm relies entirely on semantic knowledge to compose the partial analyses produced by the parser. Each semantic representation built by AUTOSEM's interpretation framework contains a pointer to the constructor function that built it. Thus, each partial analysis can be treated as a constructor function with built in knowledge about how the associated partial analysis can be combined with other partial analyses in a semantically meaningful way. Genetic programming search (Koza, 1992; Koza, 1994) is used to efficiently compose the fragments produced by the parser. The function definitions compiled from the meaning representation specification allow the genetic search to use semantic constraints to make effective use of its search space. Thus, AUTOSEM operates efficiently, free of any hand coded repair rules or any knowledge specifically dedicated to repair unlike other approaches to recovery from parser failure (Danieli and Gerbino, 1995; Van Noord, 1997; Kasper et al., 1999).

2 The Meaning Representation Specification

At the heart of AUTOSEM is its interpretation framework composed of semantic constructor functions compiled from a meaning representation specification. These semantic constructor functions can be used at parse time to build up semantic representations. These same constructor functions can then be used in a repair stage to compose the fragments returned by the parser in the cases where the parser is not able to obtain a complete analysis for an ex-

```
(:type <*state>
 :isa (<>)
 :instances nil
 :vars (entity time duration polarity)
 :spec ((who <*entity> entity)
        (when <*when> time)
        (how-long <*time-length> duration)
        (negation [+/-] polarity)))

(:type <*personal-state>
 :isa (<*state>)
 :instances nil
 :vars ()
 :spec ((who <*who> entity)))

(:type <busy>
 :isa (<*personal-state>)
 :instances nil
 :vars (activity)
 :spec ((frame *busy)
        (event <*event> activity)))

(:type [+/-]
 :isa (<>)
 :instances (+ -)
 :vars nil
 :spec nil)
```

Figure 1: **Sample meaning representation specification entries**

tragrammatical input sentence.

The meaning representation specification provides a venue for expressing domain specific semantic information declaratively. AUTOSEM produces frame-based meaning representation structures. Thus, each domain specific meaning representation specification must define a set of semantic types that together specify the set of frames and atomic feature values that make up the domain specific frame-based language, which slots are associated with each frame, and what range of frames and atomic feature values may fill each of those slots.

AUTOSEM provides a simple formalism for defining meaning representations. Each entry corresponds to a semantic type and contains five fields: `:type`, `:isa`, `:instances`, `:vars`, and `:spec`. Some sample entries for the appointment scheduling domain are displayed in Figure 1. Some details are omitted for simplicity. The `:type` field simply contains the name of the type. The `:vars` field contains a list of variables, each corresponding to a semantic role. The `:spec` field associates a frame and set of slots with a type. For each slot, the `:spec` field contains the name of the slot, the most general type restriction on the slot, and a specification of where the slot filler comes from. This third piece of information can be either a variable name, indicating that whatever is bound to that variable is what should fill that slot, or a function call to another semantic constructor function, allowing types to specify constraints at more than one level of embedding. Similar to the `:spec` field, the `:instances` field associates a list of atomic values with a type. Inheritance relations are defined via the `:isa` field. Types inherit the values of each subsuming type's `:instances`, `:vars`, and `:spec` fields.

3 Semantic Interpretation at Parse Time

```
(:type <cancel>
 :isa (<*event>)
 :instances nil
 :vars (agent activity time polarity)
 :spec ((frame *cancel)
        (engagement <*event> activity)))
```

Figure 2: **Meaning representation definition of <cancel>**

```
(:morph cancel
 :syntax ((cat vlex) (root cancel)
          (vform bare) (irreg-past +)
          (irreg-pastpart +)
          (irreg-prespart +)
          (subcat (*or* intrans np))
          (semtag cancel1))
 :semantics (cancel1 <cancel>
             ((subject agent)
              (object activity)
              (tempadjunct time)
              (negation polarity))))
```

Figure 3: **Lexical entry for the verb "cancel"**

As an extension to LCFLEX's LFG-like pseudo-unification grammar formalism, AUTOSEM provides the `insert-role` function as an interface to allow semantic interpretation to operate in parallel with syntactic interpretation at parse time. When the `insert-role` function is used to insert a child constituent into the slot corresponding to its syntactic functional role in a parent constituent, the child constituent's semantic representation is passed in to the parent constituent's semantic constructor function as in the Glue Language Semantics approach to interpretation (Dalrymple, 1999). AUTOSEM's lexicon formalism allows semantic constructor functions to be linked into lexical entries by means of the `semtag` feature. Each `semtag` feature value corresponds to a semantic constructor function and mappings between syntactic functional roles such as **subject**, **direct object**, and **indirect object** and semantic roles such as **agent**, **activity**, or **time**. See Figures 2 and 3 discussed further below. Note that the syntactic features that appear in this example are taken from the COMLEX lexicon (Grishman et al., 1994). In order to provide consistent input to the semantic constructor functions, AUTOSEM assumes a syntactic approach in which deep syntactic functional roles are assigned as in CARMEL's syntactic parsing grammar evaluated in (Freedman et al., to appear). In this way, for example, the roles assigned within an active sentence and its corresponding passive sentence remain the same.

Since the same constructor function is called with different arguments a number of times in order to construct an analysis incrementally, an argument is included in every constructor function that allows a "result so far" to be passed in and augmented. Its default value, which is used the first time the constructor function is executed, is the representation associated with the corresponding type in the absence of any arguments being instantiated. Each time the constructor function is executed, each of its arguments that are instantiated are first checked to be certain that the structures they are instantiated with match all of the type restrictions on all of the slots that are bound to that argument. If they are, the instantiated arguments' structures are inserted into the corresponding slots in the "result so far". Otherwise the constructor function fails.

Take as an example the sentence "The meeting I had scheduled was canceled by you." as it is processed by AUTOSEM using the CARMEL grammar and lexicon, which is built on top of the COMLEX lexicon (Grishman et al., 1994). The grammar assigns deep syntactic functional roles to constituents. Thus, "you" is the deep subject of "cancel", and "the meeting" is the direct object both of "cancel" and of "schedule". The detailed subcategorization classes associated with verbs, nouns, and adjectives in COMLEX make it possible to determine what these relationships should be. The meaning representation entry for <cancel> as well as the lexical entry for the verb "cancel" are found in Figures 2 and 3 respectively. Some details are left out for simplicity. When "the meeting I had scheduled" is analyzed as the surface subject of "was canceled", it is assigned the deep syntactic role of object since "was canceled" is passive. The verb "cancel" has `cancel1` as its semtag value in the lexicon. `cancel1` is defined there as being associated with the type <cancel>, and the `object` syntactic role is associated with the `activity` argument. Thus, the <cancel> function is called with its `activity` argument instantiated with the meaning of "the meeting I had scheduled". Next, when "by you" is attached, "you" is assigned the deep syntactic role of subject of "cancel". The `subject` role is associated with the `agent` argument in the definition of `cancel1`. Thus, <cancel> is called a again, this time with "you" instantiating the `agent` argument and the result from the last call to <cancel> passed in through the "result so far" argument.

4 Semantic Interpretation for Repair

While the LCFLEX parser has been demonstrated to robustly parse a variety of disfluencies found in spontaneously generated language (Rosé and Lavie, to appear), sentences still remain that are beyond its coverage. Previous research involving the earlier GLR* parser (Lavie, 1995) and an earlier repair module (Rosé, 1997) has demonstrated that dividing the task of robust interpretation into two stages, namely parsing and repair, provides a better trade off between run time and coverage than attempting to place the entire burden of robustness on the parser alone (Rosé, 1997). Thus, when the flexibility allowed at parse time is not sufficient to construct an analysis of an entire sentence for any reason, a fragmentary analysis is passed into the repair module. For each pair of vertices in the chart the best single clause level and noun phrase level analysis according to LCFLEX's statistical disambiguation scores is included in the set of fragmentary analyses passed on to the repair stage. An example[1] is displayed in Figure 4. Here the sentence "Why don't we make it from like eleven to one?" failed to parse. In this case, the problem is that the insertion of "like" causes the sentence to be ungrammatical. When the parser's flexibility settings are such that it is constrained to build analyses only for contiguous portions of text, such an insertion would prevent the parser from constructing an analysis covering the entire sentence. Nevertheless, it is able to construct analyses for a number of grammatical subsets of it.

Genetic programming search (Koza, 1992; Koza, 1994) is used to search for different ways to combine the fragments. Genetic programming is an opportunistic search algorithm used for constructing computer programs to solve particular problems. Among its desirable properties is its ability to search a large space efficiently by first sampling widely and shallowly, and then narrowing in on the regions surrounding the most promising looking points.

[1] This example was generated with the grammar used in the evaluation. See Section 6. The AUTOSEM repair algorithm can be used with grammars that do not make use of AUTOSEM's parse-time interface by using a simple conversion program that automatically builds a function for each partial analysis corresponding to its semantic type.

```
Sentence: Why don't we make it from like eleven to one?

Functions:

(<SCHEDULE> NIL T NIL NIL NIL NIL NIL NIL T
            NIL NIL
  :STR ((FRAME *SCHEDULE) (ATTITUDE *LET-S)
        (WHAT ((FRAME *IT))))
  :COV (6 5 4 3 2 1)
  :SCORE 1.4012985e-45)

(<SCHEDULE> NIL NIL NIL NIL NIL NIL NIL
            NIL T NIL NIL
  :STR ((FRAME *SCHEDULE) (ATTITUDE *LET-S))
  :COV (5 4 3 2 1)
  :SCORE 1.4012985e-45)

 (<INTERVAL> NIL T T T
 :STR ((END ((FRAME *SIMPLE-TIME)
             (HOUR 1)))
       (START ((FRAME *SIMPLE-TIME)
               (HOUR 11)))
       (INCL-EXCL INCLUSIVE)
       (FRAME *INTERVAL))
 :COV (11 10 9)
 :SCORE 1.2102125e-38)

(<PRO> NIL NIL NIL
 :STR ((FRAME *PRO))
 :COV (11)
 :SCORE 2.2223547e-18)

(<SIMPLE-TIME> NIL NIL NIL NIL NIL NIL
               T NIL
  :STR ((FRAME *SIMPLE-TIME) (HOUR 11))
  :COV (9)
  :SCORE 1.0090891e-22)

(<SCHEDULE> NIL T NIL NIL NIL T T NIL NIL
            NIL NIL
           :STR ((FRAME *SCHEDULE)
                 (WHAT ((FRAME *IT))) (NEGATIVE +)
                 (WHO ((FRAME *WE))))
           :COV (6 5 4 3 2) :SCORE 3.05483e-43)

(<SCHEDULE> NIL NIL NIL NIL NIL T T NIL NIL
            NIL NIL
  :STR ((FRAME *SCHEDULE) (NEGATIVE +)
        (WHO ((FRAME *WE))))
  :COV (5 4 3 2)
  :SCORE 2.2584231e-37)

(<SCHEDULE> NIL T NIL NIL NIL T NIL NIL NIL
            NIL NIL
  :STR ((FRAME *SCHEDULE) (WHAT ((FRAME *IT)))
   (WHO ((FRAME *WE))))
  :COV (6 5 4)
  :SCORE 1.861576e-27)

 (<SIMPLE-TIME> NIL NIL NIL NIL NIL NIL T NIL
  :STR ((FRAME *SIMPLE-TIME) (HOUR 1))
  :COV (11)
  :SCORE 2.2223547e-18)

 (<IT>
  :STR ((FRAME *IT))
  :COV (6)
  :SCORE 2.593466e-13)

Ideal Program:

            (<SCHEDULE> NIL NIL NIL NIL NIL NIL NIL
                          (<INTERVAL> NIL NIL NIL NIL
                            :STR ((END ((FRAME *SIMPLE-TIME) (HOUR 1)))
                                  (START
                                   ((FRAME *SIMPLE-TIME) (HOUR 11)))
                                  (INCL-EXCL INCLUSIVE)
                                  (FRAME *INTERVAL))
                            :COV (11 10 9)
                            :SCORE 1.2102125e-38)
                          NIL NIL NIL
               :STR ((FRAME *SCHEDULE) (ATTITUDE *LET-S)
                     (WHAT ((FRAME *IT))))
               :COV (6 5 4 3 2 1)
               :SCORE 1.4012985e-45)

Interpretation: Let's schedule it for from eleven o'clock till one o'clock
```

Figure 4: **Repair example**

It first takes a list of functions and terminal symbols and randomly generates a population of programs. It then evaluates each program for its "fitness" according to some predetermined set of criteria. The most fit programs are then paired up and used to produce the next generation by means of a crossover operation whereby a pair of subprograms, one from each parent program, are swapped. The new generation is evaluated for its fitness, and the process continues for a preset number of generations.

As mentioned earlier, because each semantic representation built by AUTOSEM contains a pointer to the constructor function that built it, each partial analysis can itself be treated as a constructor function. Thus, the function set made available to the genetic programming search for each sentence needing repair is derived from the set of partial analyses extracted from the parser's chart. A number of the functions produced for the example are displayed in Figure 4. Some functions have been omitted for brevity. The functions are displayed as function calls, with the name of the function followed by its arguments. The name of each function corresponds to the semantic type from the meaning representation that corresponds to the associated partial analysis. Following this is a list of place holders corresponding to each argument position associated with the semantic type, as described in Section 2. Each place holder is either `nil` if it is an open place holder, or `t` if the position has already been filled in the corresponding partial analysis. The `STR` field contains the corresponding partial analysis. This is the "result so far" parameter discussed in Section 3. The `COV` field lists the positions in the sentence covered by the partial analysis. Note that in the example sentence, the word "don't" covers both positions 2 and 3 since the parser expands the contraction before parsing. The `SCORE` field contains the statistical score assigned by the parser's statistical disambiguation procedure described in (Rosé and Lavie, to appear).

The repair process begins as the genetic programming algorithm composes the function definitions into programs that assemble the fragments produced by the parser. The genetic programming algorithm has access to a list of type restrictions that are placed on each argument position by the meaning representation specification. Thus, the algorithm ensures that the programs that are generated do not violate any of the meaning representation's type restrictions.

Once a population of programs is generated randomly, each program is evaluated for its fitness. A simple function implements a preference for programs that cover more of the sentence with fewer steps while using the analyses the parser assigned the best statistical scores to. A score between 0 and 1 is first assigned to each program corresponding to the percentage of the input sentence it covers. A second score between 0 and 1 estimates how complicated the program is by dividing the number of function calls by the length of the sentence and subtracting this number from 1. A third score is assigned the average of the statistical scores assigned by the parser to the fragments used in the program. Using coefficients based on an intuitive assignment of relative importance to the three scores, the final fitness value of each program is $1 - [(.55 * coverageS) + (.25 * complexityS) + (.2 * statisticalS)]$.

A typed version of the original crossover algorithm described in (Koza, 1992; Koza, 1994) was used to ensure that new programs would not violate any type restrictions or include more than one partial analysis covering the same span of text. This was accomplished by first making for each subprogram a list of the subprograms from the alternate program it could be inserted into without violating any semantic constraints. From these two lists it is possible to generate a list of all quadruples that specify a subprogram from each parent program to be removed and which subprogram from the alternate parent program they could be inserted into. From this list, all quadruples were removed that would either cause a span of text to be covered more than once in a resulting program or would require a subprogram to be inserted into a subprogram that would have been removed. From the remaining list, a quadruple was selected randomly. The corresponding crossover operation was then executed and the resulting two new programs were returned. While this typed version of crossover is more complex than the original crossover operation, it can be executed very rapidly in practice because the programs are relatively small and the semantic type restrictions ensure than the initial lists generated are correspondingly small.

5 Related Work

Recent approaches to robust parsing focus on shallow or partial parsing techniques (Van Noord, 1997; Worm, 1998; Ait-Mokhtar and Chanod, 1997; Abney, 1996). Rather than attempting to construct a parse covering an entire ungrammatical sentence as in (Lehman, 1989; Hipp, 1992), these approaches attempt to construct analyses for maximal contiguous portions of the input. The weakness of these partial parsing approaches is that part of the original meaning of the utterance may be discarded with the portion(s) of the utterance that are skipped in order to find a parsable subset. Information communicated by the relationships between these fragments within the original text is lost if these fragments are not combined. Thus, these less powerful algorithms essentially trade effectiveness for efficiency. Their goal is to introduce enough flexibility to gain an acceptable level of coverage at an acceptable computational expense.

Some partial parsing approaches have been coupled with a post-parsing repair stage (Danieli and Gerbino, 1995; Rosé and Waibel, 1994; Rosé, 1997; Van Noord, 1997; Kasper et al., 1999) The goal behind these two stage approaches is to increase the coverage over partial parsing alone at a reasonable computational cost. Until the introduction of AUTOSEM, the ROSE approach, introduced in (Rosé, 1997), was unique in that it achieved this goal without either requiring hand coded knowledge specifically dedicated to repair or excessive amounts of interaction with the user. However, although (Rosé, 1997) demonstrates that the two stage ROSE approach is significantly faster than attempting to achieve the same quality of results in a single stage parsing approach, our evaluation demonstrates that it remains computationally intractable, requiring on average 67 seconds to repair a single parse on a 330 MHz Gateway 2000. In contrast, we demonstrate that AUTOSEM is on average 200 times faster, taking only .33 seconds on average to repair a single parse while achieving results of superior quality.

6 Evaluation

An experiment was conducted to evaluate AUTOSEM's robustness by comparing the effectiveness and efficiency of AUTOSEM's repair approach with that of the alternative ROSE approach. The test set used for this evaluation contains 750 sentences extracted from a corpus of spontaneous scheduling dialogues collected in English. For both repair approaches we used the meaning representation developed for the appointment scheduling domain that was used in previous evaluations of the ROSE approach (Rosé, 1997). It consists of 260 semantic types, each expressing domain specific concepts for the appointment scheduling domain such as `busy`, `cancel`, and `out-of-town`. The ROSE meaning representation specification was easily converted to the format used in AUTOSEM. Because a pre-existing semantic grammar was available that parsed directly onto this meaning representation, that grammar was used in the parsing stage to construct analyses. The final meaning representation structures for the first 300 sentences were then passed to a generation component, and the resulting texts were graded by a human judge not involved in developing the research reported here. Each result was graded as either Bad, Okay, or Perfect, where Perfect indicates that the result was fluent and communicated the idea from the original sentence. A grade of Okay indicates that the result communicated the correct information, but not fluently. Those graded Bad either communicated incorrect information or were missing part or all of the information communicated in the original sentence.

Each sentence was parsed in two different modes. In `LC w/restarts` mode, the parser was allowed to construct analyses for contiguous portions of input starting at any point in the sentence. In LCFLEX mode, the parser was allowed to start an analysis at any point and skip up to three words within the analysis. Because the AUTOSEM repair algorithm runs significantly faster than the ROSE repair algorithm, repair was attempted after every parse rather than only when a parse quality heuristic indicated a need as in the ROSE approach (Rosé, 1997). We compared the results of both AUTOSEM and ROSE in conjunction with the `LC w/restarts` parsing mode. The results are displayed in Figures 5 and 7. Because the ROSE approach only runs the full repair algorithm when its parse quality heuristic indicates a need and the parser returns more than one partial analysis, it only attempted repair for 14% of the sentences in the corpus. Nevertheless, although the AUTOSEM repair algorithm ran for each sentence, Figure 5 demonstrates that processing time for parsing plus repair in the AUTOSEM condition was dramatically faster on average than with ROSE. Average processing time for the ROSE algorithm was 200 times slower than that for AUTOSEM on sentences where both repair algorithms were used. In addition to the advantage in terms of speed, the AUTOSEM repair approach achieved an acceptable grade (Okay or Perfect) on approximately 4% more sentences.

Parsing in `LC w/restarts` mode plus repair was also compared with parsing in LCFLEX mode with skipping up to three words. Again, `LC w/restarts` + AUTOSEM repair achieved a slightly higher number of acceptable grades, although LCFLEX achieved a slightly higher number of Perfect grades. On long sentences (between 15 and 20 words), LCFLEX mode required almost three times as much time as `LC w/restarts` mode plus AUTOSEM repair. This evaluation confirms our previous results that two stage approaches offer a better processing time versus robustness trade-off.

The primary difference between ROSE and AUTOSEM is that ROSE uses a single repair function, `MY-COMB`, to combine any two fragments by referring to the meaning representation specification. While it is possible to obtain the same set of repair hypotheses with ROSE as with AUTOSEM, the ROSE approach insulates the genetic search from the semantic restrictions imposed by the meaning representation. These restrictions are visible only locally within individual applications of the `MY-COMB` function. Thus, `MY-COMB` must be able to cope with the case where the arguments passed in cannot be combined. Large portions of the programs generated by ROSE as repair hypotheses do not end up contributing to the resulting structure. The programs gener-

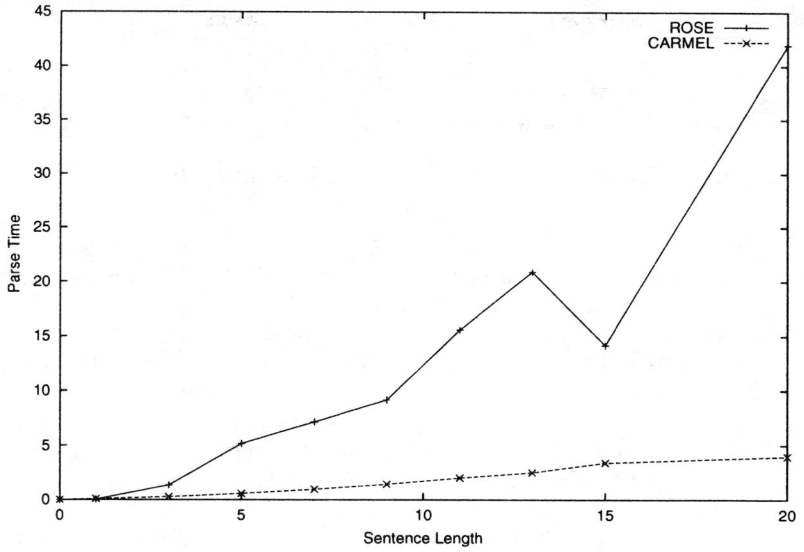

Figure 5: **Processing Times for Alternative Strategies**

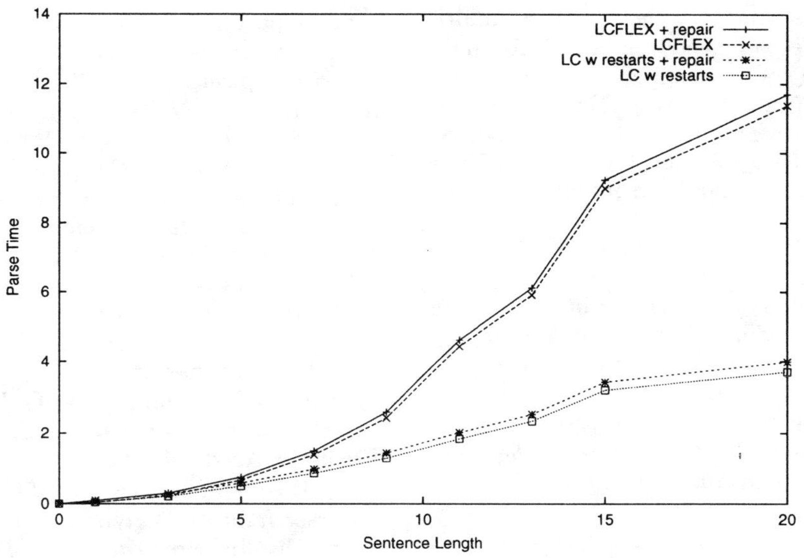

Figure 6: **Processing Times for Alternative Strategies**

ated by ROSE must therefore be much larger than in AUTOSEM in order to obtain the same results. Furthermore, the fitness of each repair hypothesis can only be computed by executing the program to obtain a result. The combination of all of these things makes the process of fitness evaluation in ROSE far more costly than in AUTOSEM. In contrast, AUTOSEM's constructor function definitions make it possible for the genetic search to make use of semantic restrictions to speed up the process of converging on a high quality repair hypothesis. The tremendous speed-up offered by the AUTOSEM approach makes it practical to apply repair more often and to use a larger generation size (50 individuals as opposed to 32) and a larger number of generations (5 as opposed to 4) for the genetic search.

7 Current Directions

In this paper we described AUTOSEM, a new robust semantic interpretation framework. Our evaluation demonstrates that AUTOSEM achieves a greater level of robustness 200 times more efficiently than the most similar competing approach.

In AUTOSEM, the mapping between syntactic

	Bad	Okay	Perfect	Total Acceptable
LC w/restarts	92 (30.7%)	61 (20.3%)	147 (49.0%)	209 (69.3%)
LCFLEX	72 (24.0%)	67 (22.3%)	161 (53.7%)	228 (76.0%)
LC w/restarts + ROSE	75 (25.0%)	68 (22.7%)	157 (52.3%)	225 (75.0%)
LC w/restarts + AUTOSEM	64 (21.3%)	84 (28.0%)	152 (50.7%)	236 (78.7%)
LCFLEX + AUTOSEM	64 (21.3%)	78 (26.0%)	158 (52.7%)	236 (78.7%)

Figure 7: **Interpretation quality with and without repair**

functional roles and semantic arguments is completely determined in the current version. In some cases, such as with copular constructions and with adjunct prepositional phrases, it would be useful to introduce some non-determinism so that, for example, semantic selectional restrictions between the object of the preposition and the semantic structure that the prepositional phrase is attaching to can more easily play a role in selecting the appropriate semantic relationship. Exploring approaches for achieving this non-determinism efficiently is one of our current objectives.

8 Acknowledgements

Special thanks are due to the JANUS multilingual speech-to-speech translation project for making their interlingua specification and semantic parsing and generation grammars available for the evaluation reported here. This research was supported by NSF Grant IRI-94-57637 and Grant 9720359 to CIRCLE, a center for research on intelligent tutoring.

References

S. Abney. 1996. Partial parsing via finite-state cascades. In *Proceedings of the Eighth European Summer School In Logic, Language and Information, Prague, Czech Republic.*

S. Ait-Mokhtar and J. Chanod. 1997. Incremental finite-state parsing. In *Proceedings of the Fifth Conference on Applied Natural Language Processing.*

M. Dalrymple. 1999. *Semantics and Syntax in Lexical Functional Grammar.* The MIT Press.

M. Danieli and E. Gerbino. 1995. Metrics for evaluating dialogue strategies in a spoken language system. In *Working Notes of the AAAI Spring Symposium on Empirical Methods in Discourse Interpretation and Generation.*

R. Freedman, C. P. Rosé, M. A. Ringenberg, and K. VanLehn. to appear. Its tools for natural language dialogue: A domain-independent parser and planner. In *Proceedings of the Intelligent Tutoring Systems Conference.*

R. Grishman, C. Macleod, and A. Meyers. 1994. COMLEX syntax: Building a computational lexicon. In *Proceedings of the 15th International Conference on Computational Linguistics (COLING-94).*

D. R. Hipp. 1992. *Design and Development of Spoken Natural-Language Dialog Parsing Systems.* Ph.D. thesis, Dept. of Computer Science, Duke University.

W. Kasper, B. Kiefer, H. Krieger, C. Rupp, and K. Worm. 1999. Charting the depths of robust speech parsing. In *Proceedings of the 37th Annual Meeting of the Association for Computational Linguistics.*

J. Koza. 1992. *Genetic Programming: On the Programming of Computers by Means of Natural Selection.* MIT Press.

J. Koza. 1994. *Genetic Programming II.* MIT Press.

A. Lavie and C. P. Rosé. 2000. Optimal ambiguity packing in unification-augmented context-free grammars. In *Proceedings of the International Workshop on Parsing Technologies.*

A. Lavie. 1995. *A Grammar Based Robust Parser For Spontaneous Speech.* Ph.D. thesis, School of Computer Science, Carnegie Mellon University.

J. F. Lehman. 1989. *Adaptive Parsing: Self-Extending Natural Language Interfaces.* Ph.D. thesis, School of Computer Science, Carnegie Mellon University.

C. P. Rosé and A. Lavie. to appear. Balancing robustness and efficiency in unification augmented context-free parsers for large practical applications. In J. C. Junqua and G. Van Noord, editors, *Robustness in Language and Speech Technologies.* Kluwer Academic Press.

C. P. Rosé and A. Waibel. 1994. Recovering from parser failures: A hybrid statistical/symbolic approach. In *Proceedings of The Balancing Act: Combining Symbolic and Statistical Approaches to Language workshop at the 32nd Annual Meeting of the ACL.*

C. P. Rosé. 1997. *Robust Interactive Dialogue Interpretation.* Ph.D. thesis, School of Computer Science, Carnegie Mellon University.

G. Van Noord. 1997. An efficient implementation of the head-corner parser. *Computational Linguistics*, 23(3).

K. Worm. 1998. A model of robust processing of spontaneous speech by integrating viable fragments. In *Proceedings of COLING-ACL 98.*

Understanding "Each Other"

Claire Gardent
Computational Linguistics
University of the Saarland
Saarbrücken, Germany
claire@coli.uni-sb.de

Karsten Konrad
Computer Science
University of the Saarland
Saarbrücken, Germany
konrad@ags.uni-sb.de

Abstract

Although natural language is ambiguous, various linguistic and extra-linguistic factors often help determine a preferred reading. In this paper, we show that model generation can be used to model this process in the case of reciprocal statements. The proposed analysis builds on insights from Dalrymple et al. 98 and is shown to provide an integrated, computational account of the interplay between model theoretic interpretation, knowledge-based reasoning and preferences that characterises the interpretation of reciprocals.

1 Introduction

Although there is widespread agreement that inference is an essential component of natural language processing, little work has been done so far on whether existing automated reasoning systems such as theorem provers and model builders could be fruitfully put to work in the area of natural language interpretation.

In this paper, we focus on the inference problems raised by the reciprocal expression *each other* and show that model generation provides an adequate tool for modeling them.

The paper is structured as follows. Section 3 discusses the meaning of reciprocal statements and proposes a formal semantics for *each other*. Section 2 shows how model generation can be used to provide this semantics with a computational interpretation. Section 4 compares our approach with the account of reciprocals which inspired it in the first place namely, (Dalrymple et al., 1998). Section 5 concludes with pointers for further research.

2 The meaning of reciprocal statements

In the linguistic literature, the reciprocal expression *each other* is often taken to denote a dyadic quantifier over a first-order set, which we will call the **antecedent set**, and a binary first-order relation, which we will call the **scope relation**. In what follows, we assume an approach of this type and will use the symbol RCP for such reciprocal quantifiers so that the semantic representation of e.g. *Jon and Bill saw each other* will be:

(1) $\textsc{Rcp}(\{jon, bill\})(\lambda y \lambda x\ \mathit{saw}(x, y))$

When antecedent sets of just two members are considered, each set member is required to stand in the scope relation to each other member. For larger sets however, research on reciprocal statements has uncovered a variety of logical contributions that the reciprocal can provide. Here are some examples.

(2) The students like each other.
$\forall x\ (\mathit{std}(x) \rightarrow \forall y\ (x \neq y \wedge \mathit{std}(y) \rightarrow \mathit{like}(x, y))$

(3) The students stare at each other in surprise.
$\forall x\ (\mathit{std}(x) \rightarrow \exists y\ (x \neq y \wedge \mathit{std}(y) \wedge \mathit{stare\_at}(x, y))$

(4) The students gave each other measles.
$\forall x\ (\mathit{std}(x) \rightarrow \exists y\ (x \neq y \wedge \mathit{std}(y) \wedge (\mathit{gave\_measles}(x, y) \vee \mathit{gave\_measle}(y, x))))$

We can accept (2) to be true only if for each pair x and y of two students it holds that x likes y. But an analogous interpretation would be invalid in the case of (3) and (4) where not all pairs in the antecedent set *the students* can consistently stand in the scope relation (one can only stare at most at one person at a time, and one can only get measles from at most one person). More generally, (Langendoen, 1978; Dalrymple et al., 1998) convincingly argues that different reciprocal statements can have very different truth conditions. The challenge to be addressed is thus the following: How can we determine a (computational) semantics for the reciprocal expressions *each other* that accounts for these multiplicity of meanings while predicting the specific meaning of a particular reciprocal statement?

Clearly knowledge based reasoning plays an important role: only those readings are possible that are consistent with our knowledge about the situation and the world. Specifically, knowledge based reasoning constrains the strength of the truth conditions of a reciprocal statement. Thus if we abstract away from the specific scope relations, the truth conditions of examples such as (2),(3) and (4) are ordered through entailment as follows (with A the antecedent set and R the scope relation):

$$\forall x\ (A(x)\ \rightarrow \forall y\ (A(y) \rightarrow R(xy))$$
$$\models\ \forall x\ (A(x)\ \rightarrow \exists y\ (A(y) \wedge R(xy))$$
$$\models\ \forall x\ (A(x)\ \rightarrow \exists y\ (A(y) \wedge (R(xy) \vee (R(yx)))$$

Specifically, example (2), which does not involve any strong knowledge based constraint, has the strongest truth–conditions of the three examples. By contrast in (3), the knowledge that one can stare at most at one person, forces a $\forall\exists$ reading while in (4), a weaker meaning still is imposed by knowledge based constraints: the *x gave y measles* relation is asymmetric hence the $\forall\forall$ reading is ruled out; moreover, since one cannot be infected twice, some students in the group will be infected but not pass on the disease to anyone. Hence the strongest truth conditions that can be assigned the sentence are the $\forall\exists$ disjunctive reading indicated in (4).

But are there any other constraints on the interpretation process than these knowledge based constraints? And which meaning shall we assign a reciprocal expression? The computational semantics we will propose is inspired from (Dalrymple et al., 1998) and relies on the following observations.

First, we note that (Dalrymple et al., 1998) identifies a lower bound for the truth conditions of reciprocal sentences which they dub Inclusive Alternative Ordering (IAO). It is exemplified by sentence (4) above and corresponds to the following definition of RCP.

(5) $\text{RCP}_{IAO} \equiv \lambda P \lambda R\ (|P| \geq 2 \wedge \forall x\ (P(x) \Rightarrow \exists y\ P(y) \wedge x \neq y \wedge (R(x,y) \vee R(y,x))))$

This definition only adequately characterises examples such as (4). It does not cover the stronger meanings of the reciprocal in sentences such as (2) and (3). However, each known form of reciprocity entails RCP_{IAO}'s truth conditions, and RCP_{IAO} therefore provides us with a minimal semantics for reciprocals.

Further, we observe that given a particular reciprocal statement, there seems to be a preference for consistent interpretations where the number of pairs that are in the scope relation is as large as possible. For instance in (3), not every student can stare at every other student (one can stare at at most one person), but intuitively, the sentence requires that *every* student stares at some other student. While such an interpretation is much weaker than that of (2), this maximisation of the scope relation yields a reading that is also much stronger than the minimal IAO interpretation of (4). More generally, while IAO provides us with a lower bound for the interpretation of reciprocal statements, we will see in section 3 that the maximisation of the scope relation that is consistent with contextual knowledge yields the upper bound for the interpretation of a particular reciprocal statement i.e., its meaning.

Based on these observations, the principle determining the actual logical contribution of a reciprocal statement can be stated as follows:

> **Maximise Meaning Hypothesis (MMH)**: The valid interpretations of a reciprocal sentence S in a context Γ (where Γ includes knowledge about the previous discourse, the discourse situation and the world) are those which (a) are consistent both with the IAO form of reciprocity and the information provided by Γ, and (b) whose contributions to the scope relation are the strongest.

The MMH selects from the set of interpretations that are consistent with IAO and contextual knowledge, those that maximise the scope relation. Crucially, this view of reciprocals leads to an inference method that can actually compute the preferred interpretations of reciprocal sentences. We now turn to this.

3 Interpretation as Model Generation

In Discourse Representation Theory (DRT, (Kamp, 1981; Kamp and Reyle, 1993)), a sentence with semantic representation Φ is true with respect to a model **M** iff there is an embedding of Φ onto **M**. Intuitively, this requirement says that a sub–model **M**' of **M** must be found which satisfies Φ. So for instance, sentence (6a) is true in **M** iff there are two individuals *bugs* and *bunny* in **M** such that *bugs* and *bunny* stand in the *love* relation; or in other words, iff the partial model sketched in (6b) is part of **M**.

(6) a. Bugs likes Bunny.
b. $\{\mathit{love}(\mathit{bugs}, \mathit{bunny})\}$

As shown in (Gardent and Konrad, To appear), model generators (i.e., programs that compute some of the models satisfying a finite set of logical formulas) can be used to provide DRT, and more generally model–theoretic approaches to natural language semantics, with a procedural interpretation: Given the semantic representation of a discourse and the relevant world knowledge Φ (i.e., a finite set of logical formulas), a model generator proves that Φ is satisfiable by generating some of its models.

Intuitively, satisfying models explain how discourses can be made true. They give an abstract representation of how (part of) the world should be for a discourse to be true. Concretely, satisfying models can be seen as capturing the meaning of discourses: databases that can be queried e.g. as part of a query/answer system or to interpret subsequent discourse. Satisfying models are also remininiscent of Johnson-Laird's *mental models* (Johnson-Laird and Byrne, 1991) and in essence, mental models are very much like the Herbrand models we are making use of here.

Formally, a **model** is a mathematical structure that describes how the symbols of a logical theory are interpreted. Given a first-order language $\mathcal{L}$, a model is a pair $\langle I, D\rangle$ with D a non-empty set of entities (the **domain of individuals**) and I an interpretation function which maps relation symbols in $\mathcal{L}$ to relations of appropriate arity in D and constant symbols in $\mathcal{L}$ to elements of D. Here we identify these models with sets of positive assumptions that unambiguously define the interpretation of the relation symbols and fix the interpretation of terms to first-order entities that carry a unique name. These are known in the literature as *Herbrand models.*

The set (7c) is such a model for the logical form (7b) which is a semantic representation of the sentence (7a).

(7) a. Jon likes his cousin.
b. $\exists x\ \mathit{cousin\_of}(x, jon) \wedge \mathit{like}(jon, x)$
c. $\mathcal{M}_1 = \{\mathit{cousin\_of}(c_1, jon),$
$\mathit{like}(jon, c_1)\}$

The model $\mathcal{M}_1$ defines an interpretation of the predicates *cousin* and *like* over the universe of discourse $\mathcal{D} = \{jon, c_1\}$. It can also be taken as a valid interpretation of (7a).There are, however, infinitely many models for (7b) that do not correspond to such interpretations e.g.

(8) $\mathcal{M}_2 = \{\mathit{cousin\_of}(jon, jon), \mathit{like}(jon, jon)\}$

(9) $\mathcal{M}_3 = \{\mathit{cousin\_of}(c_1, jon), \mathit{like}(jon, c_1),$
$\mathit{like}(c_1, jon)\}$

The model $\mathcal{M}_2$ explains the truth of (7a) by declaring Jon as his own cousin. This is a result of the inappropriate semantic representation (7b) which fails to specify that the relation expressed by the noun *cousin* is irreflexive. In the case of $\mathcal{M}_3$, the model contains superfluous information. While it is consistent to assume $\mathit{like}(c_1, jon)$ it is not necessary for explaining the truth of the input.

3.1 Minimality

For applications to natural-language, we are interested in exactly those models that capture the meaning of a discourse, or at least capture the preferred interpretations that a hearer associates with it. As discussed in (Gardent and Webber, January 2000), obtaining only these models requires eliminating both models that are "too small" (e.g. $\mathcal{M}_2$) and models that are "too big" (e.g. $\mathcal{M}_3$).

Models such as $\mathcal{M}_2$ can be eliminated simply by using more appropriate truth conditions for NL expressions (e.g. $\exists x\ \mathit{cousin}(x) \wedge \mathit{of}(x, jon) \wedge x \neq jon \wedge \mathit{like}(jon, x)$ for (7a)). In general however, eliminating models that are "too small" is a non-trivial task which involves the interaction of model-theoretic interpretation not only with world knowledge reasoning but also with syntax, prosody and pragmatics. The issue is discussed at some length (though not solved) in (Gardent and Webber, January 2000).

To eliminate models that are "too big", some notion of minimality must be resorted to. For instance, (Gardent and Konrad, 1999; Gardent and Konrad, To appear) argues that *local minimality* is an adequate form of minimality for interpreting definite descriptions. Local minimality is defined as follows.

Local Minimality: *Let Φ be a set of first-order formulas and **D** be the set of Herbrand models of Φ that use some finite domain D whose size is minimal. Then a model $\langle I, D\rangle \in$ **D** is **locally minimal** iff there is no other model $\langle I', D'\rangle \in$ **D** such that $I' \subseteq I$.*

Locally minimal models are models that satisfy some input Φ within a minimal domain $\mathcal{D}$ of individuals *and* are subset-minimal with respect to all other domain minimal models. These models are the simplest in the sense of Occam's Razor and often the best explanation for the truth of an observation. In particular, if we assume that $\mathcal{M}_2$ is ruled out by a more appropriate semantics for the word *cousin*, local minimality rules out $\mathcal{M}_3$ as non locally minimal and therefore $\mathcal{M}_1$ is correctly identified as giving the preferred interpretation for example (7).

3.2 The MMH as a Minimality Constraint

In the case of reciprocals, local minimality is clearly not a characterisation of preferred interpretations. Our semantic representation RCP_{IAO} will only capture a reciprocal's meaning if the reciprocal group has exactly two members or if the input meets IAO, the weakest form of reciprocity. For instance, the locally minimal model (10c) of formula (10b) is too weak to constitute an acceptable interpretation of (10a). Instead, the model capturing the meaning of (10a) is the model given in (10d).

(10) a. Jon, Bill and Dan like each other.
b. $\text{RCP}_{IAO}(\{jon, bill, dan\})(\lambda y \lambda x\ \mathsf{like}(x, y))$
c. $\{\mathsf{like}(jon, bill), \mathsf{like}(bill, dan)\}$
d. $\{\mathsf{like}(jon, bill), \mathsf{like}(jon, dan), \mathsf{like}(bill, dan), \mathsf{like}(bill, jon), \mathsf{like}(dan, bill), \mathsf{like}(dan, jon)\}$

Since the MMH maximises rather than minimises the logical contribution of formulas, it seems at first sight incompatible with local minimality. However, a simple method to combine the MMH and model minimality is to consider the maximisation of reciprocal relations as a minimisation of their complement sets. After all, the difference in acceptability between (10c) and (10d) as models for (10a) is due to exactly those pairs $\langle x, y\rangle$ (with $x \neq y$) that are *not* in the *like* relation. To capture this intuition, we introduce a special predicate **$R** that indicates assumptions whose truth is considered "costly". In our case, these assumptions correspond to the pairs of individuals that are not in the scope relation. The semantic representation of reciprocal *each other* is then as follows.

(11) $\text{RCP} \equiv \lambda P \lambda R\ (\text{RCP}_{IAO}(P)(R) \wedge \forall x \forall y\ (P(x) \wedge P(y) \wedge x \neq y \wedge \neg R(x, y) \Leftrightarrow \$R(x, y)))$

The first conjunct says that a reciprocal sentence has as weakest possible meaning an IAO reading. Since IAO is entailed by other identified meaning for reciprocal statements, this is compatible with the fact that reciprocal sentences can have other, stronger meanings. The second conjunct says that each pair $\langle x, y\rangle$ (with $x \neq y$) that is **not** in the *like* relation is in the **$R** relation. This encoding leads to models like (12b) and (12c) for (12a). We say that model (12b) has a **$R**-cost of 4 (**$R4**), while model (12c) has a cost of 0.

(12) a. $\text{RCP}(\{jon, bill, dan\})(\lambda y \lambda x\ \mathsf{like}(x, y))$
b. $\{\mathsf{like}(jon, bill), \mathsf{like}(jon, dan), \$R(bill, dan), \$R(bill, jon), \$R(dan, bill), \$R(dan, jon)\}$
$R4
c. $\{\mathsf{like}(jon, bill), \mathsf{like}(jon, dan), \mathsf{like}(bill, dan), \mathsf{like}(bill, jon), \mathsf{like}(dan, bill), \mathsf{like}(dan, jon)\}$
$R0

We now introduce a new form of minimality whose definition is as follows.

Conservative Minimality: *Let Φ be a set of first-order formulas and **D** be the set of Herbrand models of Φ with a minimal domain $\mathcal{D}$. Then **D** has a subset **C** of models that carry a minimal cost. A model $\langle I, D\rangle \in$ **C** is conservative minimal iff there is no other model $\langle I', D'\rangle \in$ **C** such that $I' \subseteq I$.*

Conservative minimality is a conservative extension of local minimality: if there are no costs at all, then all local minimal models are also conservative models. Conservative minimality is a combination of local minimality and cost minimisation that correctly identifies the preferred interpretation of reciprocal sentences. For instance since (12c) carries a minimal cost, it is a conservative minimal model for (12a) whereas (12b) isn't. Intuitively the approach works as follows: the more pairs there are that do not stand in the scope relation of the reciprocal, the bigger the $\$R$ predicate and the more costly (i.e. the least preferred) the model. That is, the combined use of a $\$R$-predicate and of conservative minimality allows us to enforce a preference for interpretations (i.e. models) maximising R.

3.3 The System

KIMBA (Konrad and Wolfram, 1999) is a finite model generator for first-order and higher-order logical theories that is based on a translation of logics into constraint problems over finite-domain integer variables. KIMBA uses an efficient constraint solver to produce solutions that can be translated back into Herbrand models of the input.

We have tailored KIMBA such that it enumerates the conservative models of its input. Intuitively, this works as follows. First, KIMBA searches for some arbitrary model of the input that mentions a minimum number of individuals. Then, it takes the $\$R$-cost of this model as an upper bound for the cost of all successor models and further minimises the cost as far as possible by branch-and-bound search. After KIMBA has determined the lowest cost possible, it restarts the model search and eliminates those models from the search space that have a non-minimal cost. For each model $\mathcal{M}$ that it identifies as a cost-minimal one, it proves by refutation that there is no other cost-minimal model $\mathcal{M}'$ that uses only a subset of the positive assumptions in $\mathcal{M}$. Each succesful proof yields a conservative minimal model.

All the examples discussed in this paper have been tested on Kimba and can be tried out at:

```
http://www.coli.uni-sb.de/cl/
projects /lisa/kimba.html
```

3.4 A spectrum of possible meanings

Let us see in more detail what the predictions of our analysis are. As we saw in section 2, reciprocal statements can have very different truth conditions. Intuitively, these truth-conditions lie on a spectrum from the weakest IAO interpretation (A is the antecedent set and R the scope relation):

$$|A| \geq 2 \wedge \forall x \in A(x)\ \exists y\ (A(y) \wedge x \neq y \wedge (R(x,y) \vee R(y,x))$$

to the strongest so-called Strong Reciprocity (SR) interpretation namely:

$$|A| \geq 2 \wedge \forall x\ A(x) \forall y\ A(y)(x \neq y \Rightarrow R(x,y))$$

We now see how the MMH allows us to capture this spectrum.

Let us start with example (2) whose truth-conditions are the strongest Strong Reciprocity conditions: every distinct x and y in the antecedent set are related to each other by the scope relation. In this case, there is no constraining world knowledge hence the content of the *like* relation can be fully maximised. For instance if there are five students, the cheapest model is one in which the cardinality of *like* is twenty (and consequently the cardinatity of $\$R$ is zero).

(13) $\{like(s1,s2), like(s1,s3), like(s1,s4), like(s1,s5), like(s2,s1), like(s2,s3), like(s2,s4), like(s2,s5), like(s3,s1), like(s3,s2), like(s3,s4), like(s3,s5), like(s4,s1), like(s4,s3), like(s4,s2), like(s4,s5), like(s5,s1), like(s5,s3), like(s5,s2), like(s5,s4)\}$ $\$R0$

By contrast, example (3) has a much weaker meaning. In this case there is a strong world knowledge constraint at work, namely that one can stare at only one other person at some time. The cheapest models compatible with this knowledge are models in which *every* student stare at exactly *one* other student. Thus in a universe with five students, the preferred interpretations are models in which the cardinality of the scope relation *x stares at y in surprise* is five. The following are example models. For simplicity we ommit the $\$R$ propositions and give the cost of the model instead (i.e. the cardinality of the complement set of the scope relation).

(14) $\{stare\_at(s1,s2), stare\_at(s2,s3), stare\_at(s3,s4), stare\_at(s4,s5), stare\_at(s5,s3)\}$ $\$R15$

(15) $\{stare\_at(s1, s2), stare\_at(s2, s3),$
$stare\_at(s3, s4), stare\_at(s4, s5),$
$stare\_at(s5, s1)\}$ $\$R15$

Sentence (4) illustrates an intermediate case with respect to strength of truth conditions. World knowledge implies that the scope relation *x give y measles* is assymetric and further that every individual is given measles by at most one other individual. Given a set of five students, model (16) and (17) are both acceptable interpretations of (4), (16) being the preferred interpretation.

(16) $\{gave\_measles(s1, s2), gave\_measles(s1, s3),$
$gave\_measles(s2, s4), gave\_measles(s3, s5)\}$
$\$R16$

(17) $\{gave\_measles(s1, s2), gave\_measles(s2, s4),$
$gave\_measles(s3, s5)\}$ $\$R17$

In short, these examples show the MMH at work. They show how given a *single* semantic representation for reciprocals, a variety of meanings can be derived as required by each specific reciprocal statement. Two elements are crucial to the account: the use of model building, and that of minimality as an implementation of preferences. Model building allows us to compute all the finite interpretations of a sentence that are consistent with contextual knowledge and with an IAO interpretation of the reciprocal expression. Preferences on the other hand (i.e. the use of the cost predicate $\$R$ and the search for conservative mininal models), permits choosing among these interpretations the most likely one(s) namely, the interpretation(s) maximising the scope relation.

4 Related Work

(Dalrymple et al., 1998) (henceforth DKKMP) proposes the following taxonomy of meanings for reciprocal statements (A stands for the antecedent set and R for the scope relation):

Strong Reciprocity (SR)
$\forall x, y \in A(x \neq y \rightarrow xRy)$.

Intermediate reciprocity (IR)
$\forall x, y \in A\ \exists z_1, \ldots \exists z_m \in A(x \neq y \rightarrow xRz_1 \wedge \ldots \wedge z_mRy)$

One-way Weak Reciprocity (OWR)
$\forall x \in A\ \exists y \in A\ (xRy)$

Intermediate Alternative Reciprocity (IAR)
$\forall x, y \in A \exists z_1, \ldots \exists z_m \in A(x \neq y \rightarrow (xRz_1 \vee z_1Rx) \wedge \ldots \wedge (z_mRy \vee yRz_m))$

Inclusive Alternative Ordering (IAO)
$\forall x \in A\ \exists y \in A(xRy \vee yRx)$

To predict the meaning of a specific reciprocal sentence, DKKMP then postulate the *Strongest Meaning Hypothesis* which says that the meaning of a reciprocal sentence is the logically strongest meaning consistent with world and contextual knowledge.

The main difference between the DKKMP approach and the present approach lies in how the best reading is determined: it is the logically strongest of the five postulated meanings in DKKMP, whereas in our approach, it is that reading which maximises the scope relation of the reciprocal. This difference has both empirical and computational consequences.

Empirically, the predictions are the same in most cases because maximising the scope relation often results in yielding a logically stronger meaning. In particular, as is illustrated by the examples in section 2, the present approach captures the five meanings postulated by DKKMP. Thus model (13) exemplifies an SR reading, model (15) an IR reading and model (14) an OWR reading. Further, model (16) is an IAR interpretation while model (17) shows an IAO reading.

But as the examples also show there are cases where the predictions differ. In particular, in the DKKMP approach, sentence (3) is assigned the IR reading represented by model (15). However as they themselves observe, the sentence also has a natural OWR interpretation namely, one as depicted in model (14), in which some pairs of students reciprocally stare at each other. This is predicted by the present approach which says that models (14) and (15) are equally plausible since they both maximise the *stare at* relation to cardinality five.

On the other hand, the DKKMP account is more appropriate for examples such as:

(18) The students sat next to each other
a. forming a nice cercle.

b. filling the bench.
c. some to the front and others to the back of the church.

An IR interpretation is predicted for (18) which is compatible with both continuation (18a) and continuation (18b). By contrast, the model generation approach predicts that the preferred interpretation is a model in which the students form a circle, an interpretation compatible with continuation (18a) but not with continuations (18b-c).

However, both approaches fail to predict the reading made explicit by continuation (18c) since this corresponds to the weaker OWR interpretation under the DKKMP account and to a model which fails to maximise the scope relation under the present approach. More generally, both approaches fail to capture the semantic vagueness of reciprocal statements illustrated by the following examples[1]:

(19) a. The students often help each other with their homework.
b. In the closing minutes of the game, the members of the losing team tried to encourage each other.

In both cases, the sentences can be true without maximising either the strength of its truth conditions (Strong Reciprocity) or the scope relation. This suggests that an empirically more correct analysis of reciprocals should involve prototypical and probabilistic knowledge – as it is essentially a computational approximation of the DKKMP approach, the present account does not integrate such information though it is compatible with it: just as we restrict the set of generated models to the set of conservative minimal models, we could restrict it to the set of models having some minimal probability.

Computationally, the difference between the DKKMP and the present approach is as follows. In essence, the DKKMP approach requires that each of the five possible readings (together with the relevant world knoweldge) be checked for consistency: some will be consistent, others will not. Since the first order consistency and validity problems are not decidable, we know that there can be no method guaranteed to always return a result. In order to implement the DKKMP approach, one must therefore resort to the technique advocated in (Blackburn et al., 1999) and use both a theorem prover and a model builder: for each possible meaning M_i, the theorem is asked to prove $\neg M_i$ and the model builder to satisfy M_i. M_i is inconsistent if the theorem prover succeeds, and consistent if the model builder does. Theoretically however, cases may remain where neither theorem proving nor model building will return an answer. If these cases occur in practice, the approach simply is not an option. Further, the approach is linguistically unappealing as it in essence requires the reciprocal *each other* to be five–way ambiguous.

By contrast, the model generation approach assigns a single semantic representation to *each other*. The approach strengthens the logical contribution of the weak semantic representation as a process based on *computational* constraints on a set of effectively enumerable models. As a result, we will never encounter undecidable logical problems as long as the represented discourse is consistent. The model generator is the only computational tool that we need for determining preferable readings, and our experiment shows that for the examples discussed in this paper, it returns preferred readings in a few seconds on standard PCs as long as the background theory and the size of the domain remain managably small.

5 Conclusion

We have argued that model building can be used to provide a computational approximation of DKKMP's analysis of reciprocals.

One crucial feature of the account is that it permits building, comparing and ranking of natural-language interpretations against each other. In the case of reciprocals, the ranking is given by the size of the scope relation, but other ranking criteria have already been identified in the literature as well. For instance, (Gardent and Konrad, To appear) shows that in the case of definite descriptions, the ranking defined by local minimality permits capturing the preference of binding over bridging, over accomodation. Similarly (Baumgartner and Kühn, 1999) shows that a predicate minimisation together with a preference for logically consequent reso-

[1] I am thankful to an anonymous NAACL referree for these examples.

lutions can be used to model the interpretation of pronominal anaphora.

This suggests that one of the most promising application of model generators is as a device for developing and testing *preference systems* for the interpretation of natural language. Inference and knowledge based reasoning are needed in NLP not only to check for consistency and informativity (as illustrated in e.g. (Blackburn et al., 1999)), but also to express preferences between, or constraints on, possible interpretations. For this, finite model builders are natural tools.

Another area that deserves further investigation concerns the use of minimality for disambiguation. In this paper, conservative minimality is used to choose among the possible interpretations of a particular reciprocal statement. On the other hand, (Gardent and Webber, January 2000) shows that minimality is also an important tool for disambiguating noun-compounds, logical metonymy and definite descriptions. As the paper shows though, many questions remains open about this use of minimality for disambiguation which are well worth investigating.

In further work, we intend to look at other ambiguous natural language constructs and to identify and model the ranking criteria determining their preferred interpretation. Plurals are a first obvious choice. But more generally, we hope that looking at a wider range of data will unveil a broader picture of what the general biases are which help determine a preferred reading — either in isolation, as here, or in context, as in (Gardent and Webber, January 2000) — and of how these biases can be modelled using automated reasoning systems.

Acknowledgements

We are grateful to audiences from ITRI-Brighton, the Edinburgh School of Cognitive Science, the Paris VI TALANA seminar and the Amsterdam DIP colloquium for helpful comments and discussion on the material presented here as well as to the three NAACL anonymous referrees for constructive feedback. This work was partially supported by the Project C2 (LISA) in SFB–378, grant by the Deutsche Forschungsgemeinschaft to the University of Saarbrücken.

References

Peter Baumgartner and Michael Kühn. 1999. Abductive coreference by model construction. In *ICoS-1 Inference in Computational Semantics*, Institute for Logic, Language and Computation, University of Amsterdam, August.

P. Blackburn, J. Bos, M. Kohlhase, and H. de Neville. 1999. Inference and Computational Semantics. In *Third International Workshop on Computational Semantics (IWCS-3)*, Tilburg, The Netherlands.

Mary Dalrymple, Makoto Kanasawa, Yookyung Kim, Sam Mchombo, and Stanley Peters. 1998. Reciprocal expressions and the concept of reciprocity. *Linguistics and Philosophy*, 21(2):159–210, April.

Claire Gardent and Karsten Konrad. 1999. Definites and the proper treatment of rabbits. In *Proceedings of ICOS*. Also CLAUS Report 111, http://www.coli.uni-sb.de/claus/.

Claire Gardent and Karsten Konrad. To appear. Interpreting Definites using Model Generation. *Journal of Language and Computation*.

Claire Gardent and Bonnie Webber. January 2000. Automated deduction and discourse disambiguation. Submitted for Publication. Also CLAUS Report 113, http://www.coli.uni-sb.de/claus/.

P.N. Johnson-Laird and Ruth M.J. Byrne. 1991. *Deduction*. Lawrence Erlbaum Associates Publishers.

Hans Kamp and Uwe Reyle. 1993. *From Discourse to Logic*. Kluwer, Dordrecht.

Hans Kamp. 1981. A theory of truth and semantic representation. In J. Groenendijk, Th. Janssen, and M. Stokhof, editors, *Formal Methods in the Study of Language*, pages 277 – 322. Mathematisch Centrum Tracts, Amsterdam.

Karsten Konrad and D. A. Wolfram. 1999. Kimba, a model generator for many-valued first-order logics. In *Proc., 16th International Conference on Automated Deduction, CADE 99*, LNCS, forthcoming, Trento, Italy. Springer.

D. Terence Langendoen. 1978. The logic of reciprocity. *Linguistic Inquiry*, 9(2):177–197.

An Empirical Assessment of Semantic Interpretation

Martin Romacker & Udo Hahn
Text Understanding Lab, CLIF Group,
Freiburg University, Freiburg, D-79085, Germany
{mr,hahn}@coling.uni-freiburg.de

Abstract

We introduce a framework for semantic interpretation in which dependency structures are mapped to conceptual representations based on a parsimonious set of interpretation schemata. Our focus is on the empirical evaluation of this approach to semantic interpretation, i.e., its quality in terms of recall and precision. Measurements are taken with respect to two real-world domains, *viz.* information technology test reports and medical finding reports.

1 Introduction

Semantic interpretation has been an actively investigated issue on the research agenda of the logic-based paradigm of NLP in the late eighties (e.g., Charniak and Goldman (1988), Moore (1989), Pereira and Pollack (1991)). With the emergence of empirical methodologies in the early nineties, attention has almost completely shifted away from this topic. Since then, semantic issues have mainly been dealt with under a lexical perspective, *viz.* in terms of the resolution of lexico-semantic ambiguities (e.g., Schütze (1998), Pedersen and Bruce (1998)) and the generation of lexical hierarchies from large text corpora (e.g., Li and Abe (1996), Hirakawa et al. (1996)) massively using statistical techniques.

The research on semantic interpretation that was conducted in the pre-empiricist age of NLP was mainly driven by an interest in logical formalisms as carriers for appropriate semantic representations of NL utterances. With this representational bias, computational matters — how can semantic representation structures be properly derived from parse trees for a *large* variety of linguistic phenomena? — became a secondary issue. In particular, this research lacked entirely quantitative data reflecting the accuracy of the proposed semantic interpretation mechanisms on real-world language data.

One might be tempted to argue that recent evaluation efforts within the field of information extraction (IE) systems (Chinchor et al., 1993) are going to remedy this shortcoming. Given, however, the fixed number of knowledge templates and the restricted types of entities, locations, and events they encode as target information to be extracted, one readily realizes that such an evaluation framework provides, at best, a considerably biased, overly selective test environment for judging the understanding potential of text analysis systems which are not tuned for this special application.

On the other hand, the IE experiments clearly indicate the need for a quantitative assessment of the interpretative performance of natural language understanding systems. We will focus on this challenge and propose such a general evaluation framework. We first outline the model of semantic interpretation underlying our approach and then focus on its empirical assessment for two basic syntactic structures of the German language, *viz.* genitives and auxiliary constructions, in two domains.

2 The Basic Model for Semantic Interpretation

The problem of semantic interpretation can be described as the mapping from syntactic to semantic (or conceptual) representation structures. In our approach, the syntactic representation structures are given as dependency graphs (Hahn et al., 1994). Unlike constituency-based syntactic descriptions, dependency graphs consist of lexical nodes only, and these nodes are connected by vertices, each one of which is labeled by a particular dependency relation (cf. Figure 1).

For the purpose of semantic interpretation, dependency graphs can be decomposed into *semantically interpretable subgraphs.*[1] Basically, two types of semantically interpretable subgraphs can be distinguished. The first one consists of lexical nodes which are labeled by content words only (lexical instances of verbs, nouns, adjectives or adverbs) and which are *directly* linked by a *single* dependency relation of any type whatsoever. Such a subgraph is illustrated in Figure 1 by ***Speicher*** – genatt – ***Computers***. The second type of subgraph is also delimited by labels of content words but, in addition, a series of $n = 1 \ldots 4$ intermediary lexical nodes may

[1]This notion and all subsequent criteria for interpretation are formally described in Romacker et al. (1999).

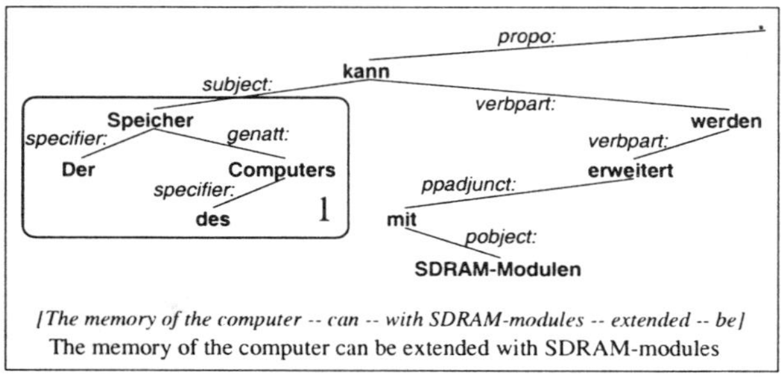

Figure 1: Dependency Graph for a Sample Sentence

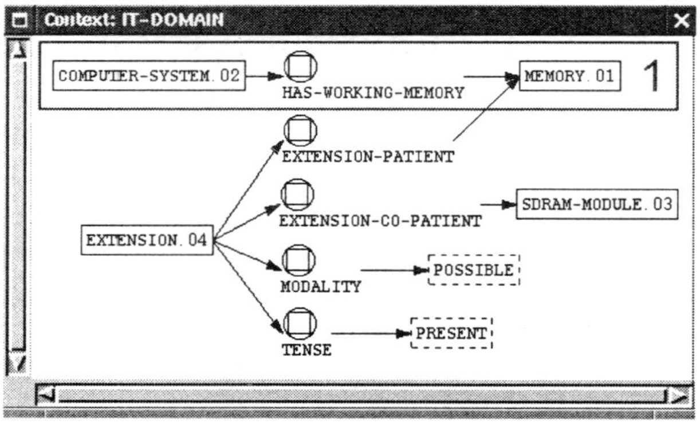

Figure 2: Concept Graph for a Sample Sentence

appear between these content words, all of which are labeled by non-content words (such as auxiliary or modal verbs, prepositions). Hence, in contrast to direct linkage we speak here of *indirect* linkage between content words. Such a subgraph, with two intervening non-content words – the modal *"kann"* and the auxiliary *"werden"* –, is given in Figure 1 by ***Speicher*** – subject – ***kann*** – verbpart – ***werden*** – verbpart – ***erweitert***. Another subgraph with just one intervening non-content word – the preposition *"mit"* – is illustrated by ***erweitert*** – ppadjunct – ***mit*** – pobject – ***SDRAM-Modulen***. From these considerations follows that, e.g., the subgraph spanned by ***Speicher*** and ***SDRAM-Modulen*** does not form a semantically interpretable subgraph, since the content word ***erweitert*** intervenes on the linking path.

Our approach to semantic interpretation subscribes to the principles of locality and compositionality. It operates on discrete and well-defined units (subgraphs) of the parse tree, and the results of semantic interpretation are incrementally combined by fusing semantically interpretable subgraphs.

As semantic target language we have chosen the framework of KL-ONE-type description logics (DL) (Woods and Schmolze, 1992). Since these logics are characterized by a settheoretical semantics we stay on solid formal ground. Furthermore, we take advantage of the powerful inference engine of DL systems, the description classifier, which turns out to be essential for embedded reasoning during the semantic interpretation process. By equating the semantic representation language with the conceptual one, we follow arguments discussed by Allen (1993).

The basic idea for semantic interpretation is as follows: Each lexical surface form of a content word is associated with a set of concept identifiers representing its (different) lexical meanings. This way, lexical ambiguity is accounted for. These conceptual correlates are internal to the domain knowledge base, where they are described by a list of attributes or conceptual roles, and corresponding restrictions on permitted attribute values or role fillers are associated with them.

As an example, consider the description for the concept COMPUTER-SYSTEM. It may be characterized by a set of roles, such as HAS-HARD-DISK or HAS-WORKING-MEMORY, with corresponding restrictions on the concept types of potential role fillers. HAS-WORKING-MEMORY, e.g., sanctions only fillers of the concept type MEMORY. These conceptual constraints are used for semantic filtering, i.e., for the elimination of syntactically admissible dependency graphs which, nevertheless, do not have a valid semantic interpretation.

Semantic interpretation, in effect, boils down to finding appropriate conceptual relations in the domain knowledge that link the conceptual correlates of the two content words spanning the semantically interpretable subgraph, irrespective of whether a direct or an indirect linkage holds at the syntactic level. Accordingly, Figure 2 depicts the semantic/conceptual interpretation of the dependency structure given in Figure 1. Instances representing the concrete discourse entities and events in the sample sentence are visualized as solid rectangles containing a unique identifier (e.g., COMPUTER-SYSTEM.02). Labeled and directed edges indicate instance roles. Dashed rectangles characterize symbols used as makers for tense and modality.[2]

Note that in Figure 2 each tuple of content words which configures a minimal subgraph in Figure 1 has already received an interpretation in terms of a relation linking the conceptual correlates. For example, ***Speicher*** – genatt – ***Computers*** (cf. Figure 1, box 1) is mapped to COMPUTER-SYSTEM.02 HAS-WORKING-MEMORY MEMORY.01 (cf. Figure 2, box 1). However, the search for a valid conceptual relation is not only limited to a simple one-link slot-filler structure. We rather may determine conceptual relation paths between conceptual correlates of lexical items, the length of which may be greater than 1.

[2]We currently do not further interpret the information contained in tense or modality markers.

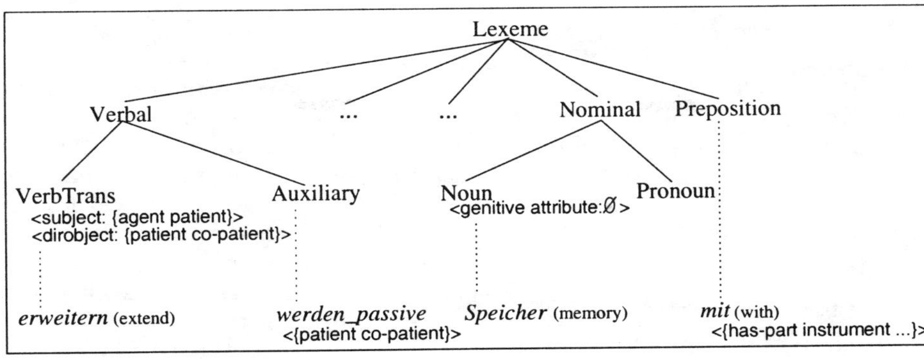

Figure 3: Fragment of the Lexeme Class Hierarchy

(Thus, the need for role composition in the DL language becomes evident.) The directed search in the concept graph of the domain knowledge requires sophisticated structural and topological constraints to be manageable at all. These constraints are encapsulated in a special path finding and path evaluation algorithm specified in Markert and Hahn (1997).

Besides these conceptual constraints holding in the domain knowledge, we further attempt to reduce the search space for finding relation paths by two kinds of syntactic criteria. First, the search may be constrained by the type of dependency relation holding between the content words of the currently considered semantically interpretable subgraph (direct linkage), or it may be constrained by the intervening lexical material, *viz.* the non-content words (indirect linkage). Each of these syntactic constraints has an immediate mapping to conceptual ones.

For some dependency configurations, however, no syntactic constraints may apply. Such a case of unconstrained semantic interpretation (e.g., for genitive attributes directly linked by the genatt relation) leads to an exhaustive directed search in the knowledge base in order to find all conceptually compatible role fillings among the two concepts involved.

Syntactic restrictions on semantic interpretation either come from lexeme classes or concrete lexemes. They are organized in terms of the lexeme class hierarchy superimposed on the fully lexicalized dependency grammar we use (Hahn et al., 1994). In the fragment depicted in Figure 3, the lexeme class of transitive verbs, VERBTRANS, requires that whenever a subject dependency relation is encountered, semantic interpretation is constrained to the conceptual roles AGENT or PATIENT and all their subrelations (such as EXTENSION-PATIENT). All other conceptual roles are excluded from the subsequent semantic interpretation. Exploiting the property inheritance mechanisms provided by the hierarchic organization of the lexicalized dependency grammar, all concrete lexemes subsumed by the lexeme class VERBTRANS, like *"erweitern" (extend)*, inherit the corresponding constraint. However, there are lexeme classes such as NOUN which do not render any constraints for dependency relations such as evidenced by *gen[itive] att[ribute]* (cf. Fig. 3).

It may even happen that such restrictions can only be attached to concrete lexemes in order to avoid overgeneralization. Fortunately, we observed that this only happened to be the case for closed-class, i.e., non-content words. Accordingly, in Figure 3 the preposition *"with"* is characterized by the constraint that only the conceptual roles HAS-PART, INSTRUMENT, etc. must be taken into consideration for semantic interpretation.

Since the constraints at the lexeme class or the lexeme level are hard-wired in the class hierarchy, we refer to the mapping of dependency relations (or idiosyncratic lexemes) to a set of conceptual relations (expanded to their transitive closure) as *static* interpretation. In contradistinction, the computation of relation paths for tuples of concepts during the sentence analysis process is called *dynamic* interpretation, since the latter process incorporates additional conceptual constraints on the fly.

The above-mentioned conventions allow the specification of high-level semantic interpretation schemata covering a large variety of different syntactic constructions by a single schema. For instance, each syntactic construction for which no conceptual constraints apply (e.g., the interpretation of genitives, most adjectives, etc.) receives its semantic interpretation by instantiating *the same* interpretation schema (Romacker et al., 1999). The power of this approach comes from the fact that these high-level schemata are instantiated in the course of the parsing process by exploiting the dense specifications of the inheritance hierarchies both at the grammar level (the lexeme class hierarchy), as well as the conceptual level (the concept and role hierarchies).

We currently supply up to ten semantic interpretation schemata for declaratives, relatives, and passives at the clause level, complement subcategorization via PPs, auxiliaries, all tenses at the VP level, pre- and and postnominal modifiers at the NP level, and anaphoric expressions. We currently do not account for control verbs (work in progress), coordination and quantification.

3 The Evaluation of Semantic Interpretation

In this section, we want to discuss, for two particular types of German language phenomena, the adequacy of our approach in the light of concrete language data taken from the two corpora we work with. This part of the enterprise, the empirical assessment of semantic interpretation, is almost entirely neglected in the literature (for two notable exceptions, cf. Bonnema et al. (1997) and Bean et al. (1998)).

Though similarities exist (*viz.* dealing with the performance of NLP systems in terms of their ability to generate semantic/conceptual structures), the semantic interpretation (SI) task has to be clearly distinguished from the information extraction (IE) task and its standard evaluation settings (Chinchor et al., 1993). In the IE task, a small *subset* of the templates from the entire domain is selected into which information from the texts are mapped. Also, the design of these templates focus on particularly *interesting* facets (roles, in our terminology), so that an IE system does not have to deal with the full range of qualifications that might occur — even relating to relevant, selected concepts. Note that in any case, *a priori* relevance decisions limit the range of *a posteriori* fact retrieval.

The SI task, however, is far less restricted. We here evaluate the adequacy of the conceptual representation structures relating, in principle (only restricted, of course, by the limits of the knowledge acquisition devices), to the *entire* domain of discourse, with *all* qualifications mentioned in a text. Whether these are relevant or not for a particular application has to be determined by subsequent data/knowledge cleansing. In this sense, semantic interpretation might deliver the raw data for transformation into appropriate IE target structures. Only because of feasibility reasons, the designers of IE systems equate IE with SI. The cross-linking of IE and SI tasks, however, bears the risk of having to determine, in advance, what will be relevant or not for later retrieval processes, assumptions which are likely to be flawed by the dynamics of domains and the unpredictability of the full range of interests of prospective users.

3.1 Methodological Issues

Our methodology to deal with the evaluation of semantic interpretation is based on a triple division of test conditions. The first category relates to checks whether so-called *static* constraints, effected by the mapping from a single dependency relation to one or more conceptual relations, are valid (cf. Figure 3 for restrictions of this type). Second, one may investigate the appropriateness of the results from the search of the domain knowledge base, i.e., whether a relation between two concepts can be determined at all, and, if so, whether that relation (or role chain) is adequate. The conceptual constraints which come into play at this stage of processing are here referred to as *dynamic* constraint propagation, since they are to be computed on the fly, while judging the validity of the role chain in question.[3] Third, interactions between the above-mentioned static constraints and dynamic constraint propagation may occur. This is the case for the interpretation of auxiliaries or prepositions, where intervening lexical material and associated constraints have to be accounted for simultaneously.

In our evaluation study, we investigated the effects of category II and category III phenomena by considering genitives and modal as well as auxiliary verbs, respectively. The knowledge background is constituted by a domain ontology that is divided into an upper generic part (containing about 1,500 concepts and relations) and domain-specific extensions. We here report on the two specialized domains we deal with — a hardware-biased information technology (IT) domain model and an ontology covering parts of anatomical medicine (MED). Each of these two domain models adds roughly about 1,400 concepts and relations to the upper model. Corresponding lexeme entries in the lexicon provide linkages to the entire ontology. In order to avoid error chaining, we always assume a correct parse to be delivered for the semantic interpretation process.

We took a random selection of 54 texts (comprising 18,500 words) from the two text corpora, *viz.* IT test reports and MEDical finding reports. For evaluation purposes (cf. Table 1), we concentrated on the interpretation of genitives (as an instance of direct linkage; GEN) and on the interpretation of periphrastic verbal complexes, i.e., passive, temporal and modal constructions (as instances of indirect linkage; MODAUX).

The choice of these two grammatical patterns allows us to ignore the problems caused by syntactic ambiguity, since in our data no structural am-

[3] Note that computations at the domain knowledge level which go beyond mere type checking are usually located outside the scope the semantic considerations. This is due to the fact that encyclopedic knowledge and its repercussions on the understanding process are typically not considered part of the semantic interpretation task proper. While this may be true from a strict linguistic point of view, from the computational perspective of NLP this position cannot seriously be maintained. Even more so, when semantic and conceptual representations are collapsed.

biguities occurred. If one were to investigate the combined effects of syntactic ambiguity and semantic interpretation the evaluation scenario had to be changed. Methodologically, the first step were to explore the precision of a semantic interpretation task without structural ambiguities (as we do) and then, in the next step, incorporate the treatment of syntactic ambiguities (e.g., by semantic filtering devices, cf. Bonnema et al. (1997)).

Several guidelines were defined for the evaluation procedure. A major issue dealt with the correctness of a semantic interpretation. In cases *with* interpretation, we considered a semantic interpretation to be a *correct* one, if the conceptual relation between the two concepts involved was considered adequate by introspection (otherwise, *incorrect*). This qualification is not as subjective as it may sound, since we applied really strict conditions adjusted to the fine-grained domain knowledge.[4] Interpretations were considered to be correct in those cases which contained exactly one relation, as well as cases of semantical/conceptual ambiguities (up to three readings, the most), presumed the relation set contained the correct one.[5] A special case of incorrectness, called *nil*, occurred when no relation path could be determined though the two concepts under scrutiny were contained in the domain knowledge base and an interpretation should have been computed.

We further categorized the cases where the system failed to produce an interpretation due to at least one concept specification missing (with respect to the two linked content words in a semantically interpretable subgraph). In all those cases *without* interpretation, insufficient coverage of the *upper model* was contrasted with that of the two *domain models* in focus, MED and IT, and with cases in which concepts referred to *other domains*, e.g., fashion or food. Ontological subareas that could neither be assigned to the upper model nor to particular domains were denoted by phrases referring to *time* (e.g., "the beginning of the year"), *space* (e.g., "the surface of the storage medium"), and *abstract* notions (e.g., "the acceptance of IT technology"). Finally, we further distinguished *evaluative* expressions (e.g., "the advantages of plasma display") from *figurative* language, including idiomatic expressions (e.g., "the heart of the notebook").

At first glance, the choice of genitives may appear somewhat trivial. From a syntactic point of view, genitives are directly linked and, indeed, constitute an easy case to deal with at the dependency level. From a conceptual perspective, however, they provide a real challenge. Since *no static* constraints are involved in the interpretation of genitives (cf. Figure 3, lexeme class NOUN) and, hence, no prescriptions of (dis)allowed conceptual relations are made, an unconstrained search (apart from connectivity conditions imposed on the emerging role chains) of the domain knowledge base is started. Hence, the main burden rests on the *dynamic* constraint processing part of semantic interpretation, i.e., the path finding procedure muddling through the complete domain knowledge base in order to select the adequate conceptual reading(s). Therefore, genitives make a strong case for test category II mentioned above.

Dependency graphs involving modal verbs or auxiliaries are certainly more complex at the syntactic level, since the corresponding semantically interpretable subgraphs may be composed of up to six lexical nodes. However, all intervening non-content-word nodes accumulate constraints for the search of a valid relation for semantic interpretations and, hence, allows us to test category III phenomena. The search space is usually pruned, since only those relations that are sanctioned by the intervening nodes have to be taken into consideration.

3.2 Evaluation Data

We considered a total of almost 250 genitives in all these texts, from which about 59%/33% (MED/IT) received an interpretation.[6] Out of the total loss due to incomplete conceptual coverage, 56%/58% (23 of 41 genitives/57 of 98 genitives) can be attributed to insufficient coverage of the domain models. Only the remaining 44%/42% are due to the residual factors listed in Table 1.

In our sample, the number of syntactic constructions containing modal verbs or auxiliaries amout to 292 examples. Compared to genitives, we obtained a more favorable recall for both domains: 66% for MED and 40% for IT. As for genitives, lacking interpretations, in the majority of cases, can be attributed to insufficient conceptual coverage. For the IT domain, however, a dramatic increase in the number of missing concepts is due to gaps in the upper model (78 or 63%) indicating that a large number of

[4]The majority of cases were easy to judge. For instance, *"the infiltration of the stroma"* resulted in a correct reading – STROMA being the PATIENT of the INFILTRATION event –, as well as in an incorrect one – being the AGENT of the INFILTRATION. Among the incorrect semantic interpretations we also categorized, e.g., the interpretation of the expression *"the prices of the manufacturers"* as a conceptual linkage from PRICE via PRICE-OF to PRODUCT via HAS-MANUFACTURER to MANUFACTURER (this type of role chaining can be considered an intriguing example of the embedded reasoning performed by the description logic inference engine), since it did not account for the interpretation that MANUFACTURERS fix PRICES as part of their marketing strategies. After all, correct interpretations always boiled down to entirely evident cases, e.g., HARD-DISK PART-OF COMPUTER.

[5]At the level of semantic interpretation, the notion of semantic ambiguity relates to the fact that the search algorithm for valid conceptual relation paths retrieves more than a single relation (chain).

[6]Confidence intervals at a 95% reliability level are given in brackets in Table 1.

	MED-GEN	IT-GEN	MED-MODAUX	IT-MODAUX
# texts	29	25	29	25
# words	4,300	14,200	4,300	14,200
recall	57%	31%	66%	40%
precision	97%	94%	95%	85%
# occurrences ...	100	147	58	234
... **with interpretation**	59 (59%)	49 (33%)	40 (69%)	111 (47%)
[confidence intervals]	[48%-67%]	[24%-41%]	[56%-81%]	[40%-53%]
...... correct (single reading)	53 (53%)	28 (19%)	38 (66%)	88 (38%)
...... correct (multiple readings)	4 (4%)	18 (12%)	0 (0%)	6 (3%)
...... incorrect	0	3	0	14
...... nil	2	0	2	3
... **without interpretation**	41 (41%)	98 (67%)	18 (31%)	123 (53%)
...... domain model (MED/IT)	23 (23%)	57 (39%)	11 (19%)	42 (34%)
...... upper model	3	23	5	78
...... other domains	0	4	0	0
...... time	0	15	0	1
...... space	7	8	0	5
...... abstracta, generics	11	12	0	16
...... evaluative expressions	0	8	0	3
...... figurative language	1	17	2	24
...... miscellaneous	0	1	0	3

Table 1: Empirical Results for the Semantic Interpretation of Genitives (GEN) and Modal Verbs and Auxiliaries (MODAUX) in the IT and MED domains

essential concepts for verbs were not modeled. Also, figurative speech plays a more important role in IT with 24 occurrences. Both observations mirror the fact that IT reports are linguistically far less constrained and are rhetorically more advanced than their MED counterparts.

Another interesting observation which is not made explicit in Table 1 concerns the distribution of modal verbs and auxiliaries. In MED, we encountered 57 passives and just one modal verb and no temporal auxiliaries, i.e., our data are in line with prevailing findings about the basic patterns of medical sublanguage (Dunham, 1986). For the IT domain, corresponding occurrences were far less biased, *viz.* 80 passives, 131 modal verbs, and 23 temporal auxiliaries. Finally, for the two domains 25 samples contained both modal verbs and auxiliaries, thus forming semantically interpretable subgraphs with four word nodes.

One might be tempted to formulate a null hypothesis concerning the detrimental impact of the length of semantically interpretable subgraphs (i.e., the number of intervening lexical nodes carrying non-content words) on the quality of semantic interpretation. In order to assess the role of the length of the path in a dependency graph, we separately investigated the results for these subclasses of combined verbal complexes. From the entire four-node set (cf. Table 2) with 25 occurrences (3 for MED and 22 for IT), 16 received an interpretation (3 for MED, 13 for IT). While we neglect the MED data due to the small absolute numbers, the IT domain revealed

	MED 4-nodes	IT 4-nodes
recall	–	59%
precision	–	85%
# occurrences ...	3	22
... **with interpretation**	3	13
...... correct	3	11

Table 2: Interpretation Results for Semantically Interpretable Graphs Consisting of Four Nodes

59% recall and 85% precision. If we compare this to the overall figures for recall (40%) and precision (85%), the data might indicate a gain in recall for longer subgraphs, while precision keeps stable.

The results we have worked out are just a first step into a larger series of broader and deeper evaluation efforts. The concrete values we present, sobering as they may be for recall (57%/31% for genitives and 66%/40% for modal verbs and auxiliaries), encouraging, however, for precision (97%/94% for genitives and 95%/85% for modal verbs and auxiliaries), can only be interpreted relative to other data still lacking on a broader scale.

As with any such evaluation, idiosyncrasies of the coverage of the knowledge bases are inevitably tied with the results and, thus, put limits on too far-reaching generalizations. However, our data reflect the intention to submit a knowledge-intensive text understander to a realistic, i.e., conceptually unconstrained and therefore "unfriendly" test environment.

Judged from the figures of our recall data, there is no doubt, whatsoever, that conceptual coverage of the domain constitutes *the* bottleneck for any knowledge-based approach to NLP.[7] Sublanguage differences are also mirrored systematically in these data, since medical texts adhere more closely to well-established concept taxonomies and writing standards than magazine articles in the IT domain.

4 Related Work

After a period of active research within the logic-based paradigm (e.g., Charniak and Goldman (1988), Moore (1989), Pereira and Pollack (1991)), work on semantic interpretation has almost ceased with the emergence of the empiricist movement in NLP (cf. Bos et al. (1996) for one of the more recent studies dealing with logic-based semantic interpretation in the framework of the VERBMOBIL project). Only few methodological proposals for semantic computations were made since then (e.g., higher-order colored unification as a mechanism to avoid over-generation inherent to unconstrained higher-order unification (Gardent and Kohlhase, 1996)). An issue which has lately received more focused attention are ways to cope with the tremendous complexity of semantic interpretations in the light of an exploding number of (scope) ambiguities. Within the underspecification framework of semantic representations, e.g., Dörre (1997) proposes a polynomial algorithm which constructs packed semantic representations directly from parse forests.

All the previously mentioned studies (with the exception of the experimental setup in Dörre (1997)), however, lack an empirical foundation of their various claims. Though the MUC evaluation rounds (Chinchor et al., 1993) yield the flavor of an empirical assessment of semantic structures, their scope is far too limited to count as an adequate evaluation platform for semantic interpretation. Nirenburg et al. (1996) already criticize the 'black-box' architecture underlying MUC-style evaluations, which precludes to draw serious conclusions from the shortcomings of MUC-style systems as far as single linguistic modules are concerned. More generally, in this paper the rationale underlying *size* (of the lexicons, knowledge or rule bases) as the major assessment category is questioned. Rather dimensions relating to the *depth* and *breadth* of the knowledge sources involved in complex system behavior should be taken more seriously into consideration. This is exactly what we intended to provide in this paper.

As far as evaluation studies are concerned dealing with the assessment of semantic interpretations, few have been carried out, some of which under severe restrictions. For instance, Bean et al. (1998) narrow semantic interpretation down to a very limited range of spatial relations in anatomy, while Gomez et al. (1997) bias the result by preselecting only those phrases that were already covered by their domain models, thus optimizing for precision while shunting aside recall considerations.

A recent study by Bonnema et al. (1997) comes closest to a serious confrontation with a wide range of real-world data (Dutch dialogues on a train travel domain). This study proceeds from a corpus of annotated parse trees to which are assigned type-logical formulae which express the corresponding semantic interpretation. The goal of this work is to compute the most probable semantic interpretation for a given parse tree. Accuracy (i.e., precision) is rather high and ranges between 89,2%–92,3% depending on the training size and depth of the parse tree. Our accuracy criterion is weaker (the intended meaning must be included in the set of all readings), which might explain the slightly higher rates we achieve for precision. However, this study does not distinguish between different syntactic constructions that undergo semantic interpretation, nor does it consider the level of *conceptual* interpretation (we focus on) as distinguished from the level of *semantic* interpretation to which Bonnema et al. refer.

5 Conclusions

The evaluation of the quality and adequacy of semantic interpretation data is still in its infancy. Our approach which confronts semantic interpretation devices with a random sample of textual real-world data, without intentionally constraining the selection of these language data, is a real challenge for the proposed methodology and it is unique in its experimental rigor.

However, our work is just a step in the right direction rather than giving a complete picture or allowing final conclusions. Two reasons may be given for the lack of such experiments. First, interest in the deeper conceptual aspects of text interpretation has ceased in the past years, with almost all efforts devoted to robust and shallow syntactic processing of large data sets. This also results in a lack of sophisticated semantic and conceptual specifications, in particular, for larger text analysis systems. Second, providing a gold standard for semantic interpretation is, in itself, an incredibly underconstrained and time-consuming process for which almost no resources have been allocated in the NLP community up to now.

Acknowledgements. We want to thank the members of the CLIF group for close cooperation. Martin Romacker is supported by a grant from DFG (Ha 2097/5-1).

[7] At least for the medical domain, we are currently actively pursuing research on the semiautomatic creation of large-scale ontologies from weak knowledge sources (medical terminologies); cf. Schulz and Hahn (2000).

References

James F. Allen. 1993. Natural language, knowledge representation, and logical form. In M. Bates and R. M. Weischedel, editors, *Challenges in Natural Language Processing*, pages 146–175. Cambridge: Cambridge University Press.

Carol A. Bean, Thomas C. Rindflesch, and Charles A. Sneiderman. 1998. Automatic semantic interpretation of anatomic spatial relationships in clinical text. In *Proceedings of the 1998 AMIA Annual Fall Symposium.*, pages 897–901. Orlando, Florida, November 7-11, 1998.

Remko Bonnema, Rens Bod, and Remko Scha. 1997. A DOP model for semantic interpretation. In *Proceedings of the 35th Annual Meeting of the Association for Computational Linguistics & 8th Conference of the European Chapter of the ACL*, pages 159–167. Madrid, Spain, July 7-12, 1997.

Johan Bos, Björn Gambäck, Christian Lieske, Yoshiki Mori, Manfred Pinkal, and Karsten Worm. 1996. Compositional semantics in VERBMOBIL. In *COLING'96 – Proceedings of the 16th International Conference on Computational Linguistics*, pages 131–136. Copenhagen, Denmark, August 5-9, 1996.

Eugene Charniak and Robert Goldman. 1988. A logic for semantic interpretation. In *Proceedings of the 26th Annual Meeting of the Association for Computational Linguistics*, pages 87–94. Buffalo, New York, U.S.A., 7-10 June 1988.

Nancy Chinchor, Lynette Hirschman, and David D. Lewis. 1993. Evaluating message understanding systems: an analysis of the third Message Understanding Conference (MUC-3). *Computational Linguistics*, 19(3):409–447.

Jochen Dörre. 1997. Efficient construction of underspecified semantics under massive ambiguity. In *Proceedings of the 35th Annual Meeting of the Association for Computational Linguistics & 8th Conference of the European Chapter of the ACL*, pages 386–393. Madrid, Spain, July 7-12, 1997.

George Dunham. 1986. The role of syntax in the sublanguage of medical diagnostic statements. In R. Grishman and R. Kittredge, editors, *Analyzing Language in Restricted Domains: Sublanguage Description and Processing*, pages 175–194. Hillsdale, NJ & London: Lawrence Erlbaum.

Claire Gardent and Michael Kohlhase. 1996. Higher-order coloured unification and natural language semantics. In *ACL'96 – Proceedings of the 34th Annual Meeting of the Association for Computational Linguistics*, pages 1–9. Santa Cruz, California, U.S.A., 24-27 June 1996.

Fernando Gomez, Carlos Segami, and Richard Hull. 1997. Determining prepositional attachment, prepositional meaning, verb meaning and thematic roles. *Computational Intell.*, 13(1):1–31.

Udo Hahn, Susanne Schacht, and Norbert Bröker. 1994. Concurrent, object-oriented natural language parsing: the PARSETALK model. *International Journal of Human-Computer Studies*, 41(1/2):179–222.

Hideki Hirakawa, Zhonghui Xu, and Kenneth Haase. 1996. Inherited feature-based similarity measure based on large semantic hierarchy and large text corpus. In *COLING'96 – Proceedings of the 16th International Conference on Computational Linguistics*, pages 508–513. Copenhagen, Denmark, August 5-9, 1996.

Hang Li and Naoki Abe. 1996. Clustering words with the MDL principle. In *COLING'96 – Proceedings of the 16th International Conference on Computational Linguistics*, pages 4–9. Copenhagen, Denmark, August 5-9, 1996.

Katja Markert and Udo Hahn. 1997. On the interaction of metonymies and anaphora. In *IJCAI'97 – Proceedings of the 15th International Joint Conference on Artificial Intelligence*, pages 1010–1015. Nagoya, Japan, August 23-29, 1997.

Robert C. Moore. 1989. Unification-based semantic interpretation. In *Proceedings of the 27th Annual Meeting of the Association for Computational Linguistics*, pages 33–41. Vancouver, B.C., Canada, 26-29 June 1989.

Sergei Nirenburg, Kavi Mahesh, and Stephen Beale. 1996. Measuring semantic coverage. In *COLING'96 – Proceedings of the 16th International Conference on Computational Linguistics*, pages 83–88. Copenhagen, Denmark, August 5-9, 1996.

Ted Pedersen and Rebecca Bruce. 1998. Knowledge lean word-sense disambiguation. In *AAAI'98 – Proceedings of the 15th National Conference on Artificial Intelligence*, pages 800–805. Madison, Wisconsin, July 26-30, 1998.

Fernando C.N. Pereira and Martha E. Pollack. 1991. Incremental interpretation. *Artificial Intelligence*, 50(1):37–82.

Martin Romacker, Katja Markert, and Udo Hahn. 1999. Lean semantic interpretation. In *IJCAI'99 – Proceedings of the 16th International Joint Conference on Artificial Intelligence*, pages 868–875. Stockholm, Sweden, July 31 - August 6, 1999.

Stefan Schulz and Udo Hahn. 2000. Knowledge engineering by large-scale knowledge reuse: experience from the medical domain. In *Proceedings of the 7th International Conference on Principles of Knowledge Representation and Reasoning*. Breckenridge, CO, USA, April 12-15, 2000.

Hinrich Schütze. 1998. Automatic word sense discrimination. *Computational Linguistics*, 24(1):97–124.

William A. Woods and James G. Schmolze. 1992. The KL-ONE family. *Computers & Mathematics with Applications*, 23(2/5):133–177.

Association for Computational Linguistics

Proceedings of the ANLP-NAACL 2000 Student Research Workshop

April 29—May 4, 2000
Seattle, Washington, USA

Preface to the Student Research Workshop

This was the inaugural year of the Student Research Workshop, which remodeled the traditional student session into a new format that allows students to present their research to a panel of scientific advisors in addition to the audience of workshop attendees. Panelists have an opportunity to prepare questions and comments prior to the workshop, so we hope this format will provide student authors with more detailed feedback and suggestions for further development of their research than would be possible in the traditional setting. The new format also allows a longer time for presentations (25 minutes) and for discussion of each paper by the panelists and audience members (15 minutes). We received 18 submissions and accepted 8 (44%) for inclusion in the workshop. These papers describe original unpublished work in progress in which all authors are students.

We would first like to acknowledge and thank the panelists:

James Allen, *University of Rochester (USA)*
Claire Cardie, *Cornell University (USA)*
Jennifer Chu-Carroll, *Bell Labs (USA)*
Deborah Dahl, *Unisys Corporation (USA)*
Barbara Di Eugenio, *University of Chicago (USA)*
Jan Hajic, *Johns Hopkins University (USA)*
Mary Harper, *Purdue University (USA)*
Eduard Hovy, *USC Information Sciences Institute (USA)*
James Lester, *North Carolina State University (USA)*
Scott Miller, *BBN Technologies (USA)*
Donia Scott, *University of Brighton (UK)*

Each submission was reviewed blind by one non-student and two student researchers. We would like to thank all members of the review committee for their thoughtful comments and for their timely completion of the reviews:

David Ahn, *University of Rochester (USA)*
Timothy Baldwin, *Tokyo Institute of Technology (Japan)*
Melanie Baljko, *University of Toronto (Canada)*
Sabine Buchholz, *Tilburg University (Netherlands)*
Patrick Caudal, *Université Paris 7 (France)*
Yllias Chali, *University of Lethbridge (Canada)*
Hsin-Hsi Chen, *National Taiwan University (Taiwan)*
Freddy Choi, *University of Manchester (UK)*
Sherri Condon, *University of Louisiana (USA)*
Deborah Dahl, *Unisys (USA)*
Paul Davis, *Ohio State University (USA)*
Jonathan DeCristofaro, *University of Delaware (USA)*
Mona Diab, *University of Maryland College/UMIACS (USA)*
Mark Dras, *University of Pennsylvania (USA)*
Richard Evans, *University of Wolverhampton (UK)*
Martha Evens, *Illinois Institute of Technology (USA)*
Eileen Fitzpatrick, *Montclair State University (USA)*
Mary Harper, *Purdue University (USA)*
Woody Haynes, *Illinois Institute of Technology (USA)*
Barbora Hladka, *Charles University (Czech Republic)*
Kristiina Jokinen, *Flanders Language Valley (Belgium)*
Vlado Keselj, *University of Waterloo (Canada)*
Rodger Kibble, *University of Brighton/ITRI (UK)*
Adam Kilgariff, *University of Brighton/ITRI (UK)*
Anna Korhonen, *University of Cambridge (UK)*
Irene Langkilde, *University of Southern California/ISI (USA)*
Christophe Luc, *Université Paul Sabatier (France)*
Diana Maynard, *Manchester Metropolitan University (UK)*
Lisa Michaud, *University of Delaware (USA)*
Derek Walker, *University of Geneva (Switzerland)*
Teresa Zollo, *University of Rochester (USA)*

We would like to acknowledge and thank Mary Harper, our Faculty Advisor and also the Principal Investigator on the NSF grant, for her considerable help and advice. We received much helpful guidance from the ACL Executive Board and the NAACL/ANLP 2000 Conference Executive Committee -- in particular Janyce Wiebe, Kathleen McCoy, Priscilla Rasmussen and Marie Meteer. Also, we extend a heart-felt thanks to last year's Student Session Co-Chairs, Anna Korhonen and Melanie Baljko, for their friendly and helpful replies to our many questions. Finally, we would like to thank the National Science Foundation for their generous support of this workshop under grant number 0001350-IIS.[1] The NSF grant allowed students who might have had no other means of support to travel to the workshop and interact with the scientific community.

Student Research Workshop Co-Chairs:
Donna Byron, *University of Rochester (USA)*
Peter Vanderheyden, *University of Waterloo (Canada)*

---

[1] Any opinions, findings, and conclusions or recommendations expressed in this material are those of the authors and do not necessarily reflect the views of the granting institution.

ANLP-NAACL 2000 Student Research Workshop Table of Contents

Section 3: ANLP-NAACL 2000 Student Research Workshop (SRW)

Experimenting with the Interaction between Aggregation and Text Structuring

Hua Cheng
Division of Informatics
University of Edinburgh
80 South Bridge, Edinburgh EH1 1HN, UK
Email: huac@dai.ed.ac.uk

Abstract

In natural language generation, different generation tasks often interact with each other in a complex way, which is hard to capture in the pipeline architecture described by Reiter (Reiter, 1994). This paper focuses on the interaction between a specific type of aggregation and text planning, in particular, maintaining local coherence, and tries to explore what preferences exist among the factors related to the two tasks. The evaluation result shows that it is these preferences that decide the quality of the generated text and capturing them properly in a generation system could lead to coherent text.

1 Introduction

In automatic natural language generation (NLG), various versions of the pipeline architecture specified by Reiter and Dale ((Reiter, 1994) and (Reiter and Dale, 1997)) are usually adopted. They successfully modularise the generation problem, but fail to capture the complex interactions between different modules. Take aggregation as an example. It combines simple representations to form a complex one, which in the mean time leads to a shorter text as a whole. There is no consensus as to where aggregation should happen and how it is related to other generation processes ((Wilkinson, 1995) and (Reape and Mellish, 1999)).

We think that the effect of aggregation spreads from text planning to sentence realisation. The task of text planning is to select the relevant information to be expressed in the text and organise it into a hierarchical structure which captures certain discourse preferences such as preferences for global coherence (e.g. the use of RST relations (Mann and Thompson, 1987)) and local coherence (e.g. center transitions as defined in Centering Theory (Grosz et al., 1995)). Aggregation affects text planning by taking away facts from a sequence featuring preferred center movements for subordination. As a result, the preferred center transitions in the sequence are cut off. For example, comparing the two descriptions of a necklace in Figure 1, *2* is less coherent than *1* because of the shifting from the description of the necklace to that of the designer. To avoid this side effect, aggregation should be considered in text planning, which might produce a different planning sequence.

Aggregation is also closely related to the task of referring expression generation. A referring expression is used not only for identifying a referent, but also for providing additional information about the referent and expressing the speaker's emotional attitude toward the referent (Appelt, 1985). The syntactic form of a referring expression affects how much additional information can be expressed, but it can only be determined after sentence planning, when the ordering between sentences and sentence components has been decided. This demands that the factors relevant to referring expression generation and aggregation be considered at the same time rather than sequentially to generate referring expressions capable of serving multiple goals.

In this paper, we are concerned with a specific type of aggregation called embedding, which shifts one clause to become a component within the structure of an NP in another clause. We focus on the interaction between maintaining local coherence and embedding, and describe how to capture this interaction as preferences among related factors. We believe that if these preferences are used properly, we would be able to generate more flexible texts without sacrificing quality. We implemented the preferences

1. This necklace is in the Arts and Crafts style. Arts and Crafts style jewels usually have an elaborate design. They tend to have floral motifs. For instance, this necklace has floral motifs. It was designed by Jessie King. King once lived in Scotland.

2. This necklace, which was designed by Jessie King, is in the Arts and Crafts style. Arts and Crafts style jewels usually have an elaborate design. They tend to have floral motifs. For instance, this necklace has floral motifs. King once lived in Scotland.

Figure 1: An aggregation example

in an experimental generation system based on a Genetic Algorithm to produce museum descriptions, which describe museum objects on display. The result shows that the system can generate a number texts of similar qualities to human written texts.

2 Embedding in a GA Text Planner

To experiment with the interaction between maintaining local coherence and embedding, we adopt the text planner based on a Genetic Algorithm (GA) as described in (Mellish et al., 1998). The task is, given a set of facts and a set of relations between facts, to produce a legal rhetorical structure tree using all the facts and some relations. A fragment of the possible input is given in Figure 2.

A genetic algorithm is suitable for such a problem because the number of possible combinations is huge, the search space is not perfectly smooth and unimodal, and the generation task does not require a global optimum to be found. The algorithm of (Mellish et al., 1998) is basically a repeated two step process - first sequences of facts are generated by applying GA operators (crossover and mutation) and then the RS trees built from these sequences are evaluated. This provides a mechanism to integrate various planning factors in the evaluation function and search for the best combinations of them.

To explore the whole space of embedding, we did not perform embedding on structured facts or on adjacent facts in a linear sequence because these might restrict the possibilities and even miss out good candidates. Instead, we defined an operator called *embedding mutation*. It randomly selects two units (say U_i and U_k) mentioning a common entity from a sequence $[U_1,U_2,...,U_i,...,U_k,...,U_n]$ to form a list $[U_i,U_k]$ representing an embedding. The list substitutes the original unit U_i to produce a new sequence $[U_1,U_2,...,[U_i,U_k],...,U_n]$, which is then evaluated and ordered in the population.

3 Capturing the Interactions as Preferences

A key requirement of the GA approach is the ability to evaluate the quality of a possible solution. We claim that it is the relative preferences among factors rather than each individual factor that play the crucial role in deciding the quality. Therefore, if we can capture these preferences in a generation system properly, we would be able to produce coherent text. In this section, we first discuss the preferences among factors related to text planning, based on which those for embedding can be introduced.

3.1 Preferences for global coherence

Following the assumption of RST, a text is globally coherent if a hierarchical structure like an RST tree can be constructed from the text. In addition to the semantic relations and the *Joint* relation[1] used in (Mellish et al., 1998), we assume a *Conjunct* or *Disjunct* relation between two facts with at least two identical components, so that semantic parataxis can be treated as a combining operation on two subtrees connected by the relation.

Embedding a *Conjunct* relation inside another semantic relation is not preferred because this could convey wrong information, for example, in Figure 3, *2* cannot be used to substitute *1*. Also a semantic relation is preferred to be used whenever possible. Here is the preferences concerning the use of relations, where "A>B" means that A is preferred over B:

[1]In (Mellish et al., 1998), a *Joint* relation is used to connect every two text spans that do not have a normal semantic relation in between.

```
fact(choker,is,broad,fact_node-1).
fact('Queen Alexandra',wore,choker,fact_node-2).
fact(choker,'can cover',scar,fact_node-3).
fact(band,'might be made of',plaques,fact_node-4).
fact(band,'might be made of',panels,fact_node-5).
fact(scar,is,'on her neck',fact_node-6).
...
rel(in_that_reln,fact_node-2,fact_node-3,[]).
rel(conjunct,fact_node-4,fact_node-5,[]).
```

Figure 2: A fragment of the input to the GA text planner

1. The necklace is set with jewels in that it features cabuchon stones. Indeed, an Arts and Crafts style jewel usually uses cabuchon stones. An Arts and Crafts style jewel usually uses oval stones.

2. The necklace is set with jewels in that it features cabuchon stones. Indeed, an Arts and Crafts style jewel usually uses cabuchon stones and oval stones.

Figure 3: Conjunct and semantic relations

Heuristic 1 *Preferences among features for global coherence:*
a semantic relation > Conjunct > Joint > parataxis in a semantic relation

3.2 Preferences for local coherence

In Centering Theory, Rule 2 specifies preferences among center transitions in a locally coherent discourse segment: sequences of *continuation* are preferred over sequences of *retaining*, which are then preferred over sequences of *shifting*. Instead of claiming that this is the best model, we use it simply as an example of a linguistic model being used for evaluating factors for text planning.

Another type of center transition that appears frequently in museum descriptions is *associate shifting*, where the description starts with an object and then moves to a closely associated object or perspectives of that object. Our observation from museum descriptions shows that *associate shifting* is preferred by human writers to all other types of movements except for *center continuation*.

Oberlander et al. (1999) define yet another type of transition called *resuming*, where an utterance mentions an entity not in the immediate previous utterance, but in the previous discourse. The following is the preferences among features for local coherence:

Heuristic 2 *Preferences among center transitions and semantic relations:*
Continuation > Associate shifting > Retaining > Shifting > Resuming
a semantic relation > Joint + Continuation

3.3 Preferences for embedding

For a randomly produced embedding, we must be able to judge its quality. We distinguish between a *good, normal* and *bad embedding* based on the features it bears[2]. A *good embedding* is one satisfying all following conditions:

1. The referring expression is an indefinite, a demonstrative or a bridging description (as defined in (Poesio et al., 1997)).
2. The embedded part can be realised as an adjective or a prepositional phrase (Scott and de Souza, 1990)[3].
3. The embedded part does not lie between text spans connected by semantic parataxis or hypotaxis (Cheng, 1998).
4. There is an available syntactic slot to hold the embedded part.

---

[2]We do not claim that the set of features is complete. In a different context, more criteria might have to be considered.

[3]We assume that syntactic constraints have been inserted before in text planning, using Meteer's Text Structure (Meteer, 1992) for example.

A *good embedding* is highly preferred and should be performed whenever possible. A *normal embedding* is one satisfying condition 1, 3 and 4 and the embedded part is a relative clause. A *bad embedding* consists of all those left.

To decide the preferences among embeddings and center transitions, let's look at the paragraphs in Figure 1 again. The only difference between them is the position of the sentence "*This necklace was designed by Jessie King*", which can be represented in terms of features of local coherence and embedding as follows:

> *the last three sentences in 1: Joint + Continuation + Joint + Shifting*
> *the last two sentences plus embedding in 2: Joint + Resuming + Normal embedding*

Since *1* is preferred over *2*, we have the following heuristics:

Heuristic 3 *Preferences among features for embedding and center transition:*
Continuation + Shifting + Joint > Resuming + Normal embedding
Good embedding > Normal embedding > Joint > Bad embedding
Good embedding > Continuation + Joint

4 Justifying the Evaluation Function

We have illustrated the linguistic theories that can be used to evaluate a text. However, they only give evidence in qualitative terms. For a GA-based planner to work, we have to come up with actual numbers that can be used to evaluate an RS tree.

We extended the existing scoring scheme of (Mellish et al., 1998) to account for features for local coherence, embedding and semantic parataxis. This resulted in the rater 1 in Table 1[4], which satisfied all the heuristics introduced in Section 3.

We manually broke down four human written museum descriptions into individual facts and relations and reconstructed sequences of facts with the same orderings and aggregations as in the original texts. We then used the evaluation function of the GA planner to score the RS trees built from these sequences. In the meantime, we ran the GA algorithm for 5000 iterations on the facts and relations for 10 times. All human texts were scored among the highest and machine generated texts can get scores very close to human ones sometimes (see Table 2 for the actual scores of the four texts). Since the four human texts were written and revised by museum experts, they can be treated as "nearly best texts". The result shows that the evaluation function based on our heuristics can find good combinations.

To justify our claim that it is the preferences among generation factors that decide the coherence of a text, we fed the heuristics into a constraint-based program, which produced a lot of raters satisfying the heuristics. One of them is given in Table 1 as the rater 2. We then generated all possible combinations, including embedding, of seven facts from a human text and used the two raters to score each of them. The two distributions are shown in Figure 4.

The qualities of the generated texts are normally distributed according to both raters. The two raters assign different scores to a text as the means of the two distributions are quite different. There is also slight difference in standard deviations, where the deviation of Rater 2 is bigger and therefore it has more distinguishing power. Despite these differences, the behaviours of the two raters are indeed very similar as the two histograms are of roughly the same shape, including the two right halves which tell us how many good texts there are and if they can be distinguished from the rest. The difference in standard deviations is not significant at all. So the distributions of the scores from the two raters show that they behave very similarly in distinguishing the qualities of texts from the same population.

As to what extent the two raters agree with each other, we drew the scatterplot of the scores, which showed a strong positive linear correlation between the variables representing the two scores. That is, the higher the score from rater 1 for a given text of the population, the higher the score from rater 2 tends to be. We also calculated the Pearson correlation coefficient between the two raters and the corre-

[4]The table only shows the features we are concerned with in this paper.

Features/Factors	Values 1	Values 2
Semantic relations		
a Joint	-20	-46
a Conjunct or Disjunct	10	11
a relation other than Joint, Conjunct or Disjunct	21	69
a Conjunct inside another semantic relation	-50	-63
a precondition not satisfied	-30	-61
Center transitions		
a Continuation	20	7
an Associate shifting	16	1
a Shifting	14	-3
resuming a previous center	6	-43
Embedding		
a Good embedding	6	3
a Normal embedding	3	0
a Bad embedding	-30	-64
Others		
topic not mentioned in the first sentence	-10	-12

Table 1: Two different raters satisfying the same constraints

	text 1	text 2	text 3	text 4
scores of the human texts	170	22	33	24
highest scores of the generated texts	167	24	31	25
average scores of the generated texts	125.7	18.9	26.1	9.3

Table 2: The scores of four human written texts

lation was .9567. So we can claim that for this data, the scores from rater 1 and rater 2 correlate, and we have fairly good chance to believe our hypothesis that the two raters, randomly produced in a sense, agree with each other on evaluating the text and they measure basically the same thing.

Since the two raters are derived from the heuristics in Section 3, the above result partially validates our claim that it is the relevant preferences among factors that decide the quality of the generated text.

5 Summary and Future work

This paper focuses on the complex interactions between embedding and planning local coherence, and tries to capture the interactions as preferences among related features. These interactions cannot be easily modelled in a pipeline architecture, but the GA-based architecture offers a mechanism to coordinate them in the planning of a coherent text. The result shows to some extent that capturing the interactions properly in an NLG system is important to the generation of coherence text.

Our experiment could be extended in many aspects, for example, validating the evaluation function through empirical analysis of human assessments of the generated texts, and experimenting with the interaction between aggregation and referring expression generation. The architecture based on the Genetic Algorithm can also be used for testing interactions between or within other text generation modules. To generalise our claim, a larger scale experiment is needed.

Acknowledgement This research is supported by a University of Edinburgh Studentship.

References

Douglas Appelt. 1985. Planning english referring expressions. *Artificial Intelligence*, 26:1–33.

Hua Cheng. 1998. Embedding new information into referring expressions. In *Proceedings*

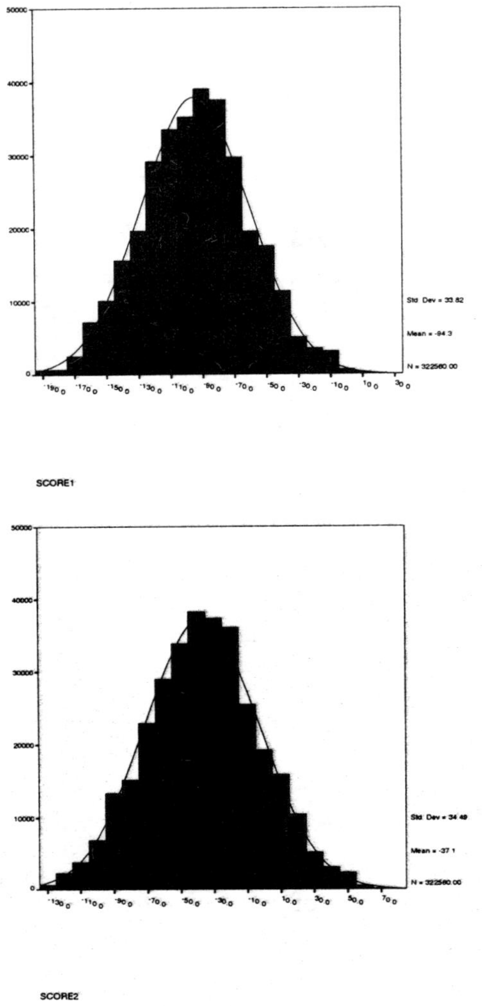

Figure 4: Histogram of the scores from rater 1 (top) and rater 2 (bottom)

of COLING-ACL'98, pages 1478–1480, Montreal, Canada.

Barbara Grosz, Aravind Joshi, and Scott Weinstein. 1995. Centering: A framework for modelling the local coherence of discourse. *Computational Linguistics*, 21(2):203–226.

William Mann and Sandra Thompson. 1987. Rhetorical Structure Theory: A Theory of Text Organization. Technical Report ISI/RR-87-190, Information Sciences Institute, University of Southern California.

Chris Mellish, Alistair Knott, Jon Oberlander, and Mick O'Donnell. 1998. Experiments using stochastic search for text planning. In *Proceedings of the 9th International Workshop on Natural Language Generation*, Ontario, Canada.

Marie Meteer. 1992. *Expressibility and The Problem of Efficient Text Planning.* Communication in Artificial Intelligence. Pinter Publishers Limited, London.

Jon Oberlander, Alistair Knott, Mick O'Donnell, and Chris Mellish. 1999. Beyond elaboration: Generating descriptive texts containing it-clefts. In T Sanders, J Schilperoord, and W Spooren, editors, *Text Representation: Linguistic and Psycholinguistic Aspects.* Benjamins, Amsterdam.

Massimo Poesio, Renata Vieira, and Simone Teufel. 1997. Resolving bridging references in unrestricted text. Research paper hcrc-rp87, Centre for Cognitive Science, University of Edinburgh.

Michael Reape and Chris Mellish. 1999. Just what is aggregation anyway? In *Proceedings of the 7th European Workshop on Natural Language Generation*, pages 20–29, Toulouse, France.

Ehud Reiter and Robert Dale. 1997. Building applied natural language generation systems. *Natural Language Engineering*, 3(1):57–87.

Ehud Reiter. 1994. Has a consensus nl generation architecture appeared, and is it psycholinguistically plausible? In *Proceedings of the 7th International Workshop on Natural Language Generation.*

Donia Scott and Clarisse Sieckenius de Souza. 1990. Getting the Message Across in RST-based Text Generation. In R. Dale, C. Mellish, and M. Zock, editors, *Current Research in Natural Language Generation*, pages 47–73. Academic Press.

John Wilkinson. 1995. Aggregation in Natural Language Generation: Another Look. Technical report, Computer Science Department, University of Waterloo.

Efficient parsing strategies for syntactic analysis of closed captions

Krzysztof Czuba
kczuba@cs.cmu.edu
Language Technologies Institute
Carnegie Mellon University
Pittsburgh, PA 15213, USA

Abstract

We present an efficient multi-level chart parser that was designed for syntactic analysis of closed captions (subtitles) in a real-time Machine Translation (MT) system. In order to achieve high parsing speed, we divided an existing English grammar into multiple levels. The parser proceeds in stages. At each stage, rules corresponding to only one level are used. A constituent pruning step is added between levels to insure that constituents not likely to be part of the final parse are removed. This results in a significant parse time and ambiguity reduction. Since the domain is unrestricted, out-of-coverage sentences are to be expected and the parser might not produce a single analysis spanning the whole input. Despite the incomplete parsing strategy and the radical pruning, the initial evaluation results show that the loss of parsing accuracy is acceptable. The parsing time favorable compares with a Tomita parser and a chart parser parsing time when run on the same grammar and lexicon.

1 Introduction

In this paper we present on-going research on parsing closed captions (subtitles) from a news broadcast. The research has been conducted as part of an effort to build a prototype of a real-time Machine Translation (MT) system translating news captions from English into Cantonese (Nyberg and Mitamura, 1997). We describe an efficient multi-level chart parser that was designed to handle the kind of language used in our domain within a time that allows for a real-time automatic translation. In order to achieve high parsing speed, we divided an existing English grammar into multiple levels. The parser proceeds in stages. At each stage, rules corresponding to only one level are used. A constituent pruning step is added between levels to insure that constituents not likely to be part of the final parse are removed. This results in a significant parse time and ambiguity reduction. Since the domain is unrestricted, out-of-coverage sentences are to be expected and the parser might not produce a single analysis spanning the whole input. Thus, the set of final constituents has to be extracted from the chart. Despite the incomplete parsing strategy and the radical pruning, the initial evaluation results show that the loss of parsing accuracy is acceptable. The parsing time favorable compares with a Tomita parser and a chart parser parsing time when run on the same grammar and lexicon.

The outline of the paper is as follows. In Section 2 we describe the syntactic and semantic characteristics of the input domain. Section 3 provides a short summary of previous published research. Section 4 gives an overview of requirements on the parsing algorithm posed by our application. Section 5 describes how the grammar was partitioned into levels. Section 6 describes the constituent pruning algorithm that we used. In Section 7 we present the method for extracting final constituents from the chart. Section 8 presents the results of an initial evaluation. Finally, we close with future research in Section 9.

2 Captioning domain

Translation of closed captions has been attempted before. (Popowich et al., 1997) describe a system that translates closed captions taken from North American prime time TV. In their approach, (Popowich et al., 1997) assume a shallow parsing method that proves effective in achieving broad system coverage required for translation of closed captions from, e.g., movies. As reported by (Popowich et al., 1997), the shallow analysis performed by the system combined with the transfer-based translation strategy results in a number of sentences that are understandable only in conjunction with the broadcast images. The number of sentences that are translated incorrectly is also significant.

The parsing scheme described below was used in a pilot Machine Translation system for translation of news captions. The following requirements were posed: a) the translations should not be misleading, b) they can be telegraphic since the input is often in a telegraphic style, c) partial translations are acceptable, d) if no correct translation can be produced then it is preferable to not output any.

The closed captions were taken from a financial news segment. Although the language in this segment is not strongly domain-restricted, it is centered around the financial aspects of the described events, which makes certain tasks such as sense disambiguation feasible.

In order to address the translation quality problems found by (Popowich et al., 1997), (Nyberg and Mitamura, 1997) propose a multi-engine MT system architechture to handle the task of translating closed captions. The parser described in this paper, was developed for the knowledge-based module (Nyberg and Mitamura, 1992) in the system and it was required to produce "deep" analyses with the level of detail sufficient for creating interlingua.

The stream of closed captions we worked with shows many interesting characteristics that influence the design of the parsing algorithm and the whole MT system. In the paper, we consider only the issues that are related to the syntactic analysis of closed captions. The stream contains long sentences taken from interviews, short phrases making the program more lively, and telegraphic style sentences used to report the latest stock market news. It has unrestricted syntax in long descriptive sentences, which resembles written language, with some phenomena like omission of function words that are characteristic of spoken language. It is likely to contain words not present in the lexicon, such as company names. Although not considered here directly, a caption stream usually also contains some typos and corrections made by the captioner. It is however different from, e.g., a speech recognizer output since the human captioner usually provides the correct transcription and there is no immediate need to model recognition errors.

3 Partial, robust and fast parsing

The kind of input described above requires robust parsing methods. Since our goal was real-time translation, the parsing module had to be very efficient. We concentrated on reducing the amount of work done by the parser at the potential cost of lowering the quality of the resulting analysis[1]. Similar methods have been adopted elsewhere, although in most cases the goal was a shallow parse. (Abney, 1996) describes a chunking approach based on cascades of finite transducers in which the parser finds "islands of certainty" at multiple analysis levels. Only maximal constituents (in terms of length) found by transducers at lower levels are the input to the transducers at higher levels, which results in constituent pruning and ambiguity containment, and low parsing times.

(Ciravegna and Lavelli, 1997) introduce additional controlling strategies to a chart parser. (Ciravegna and Lavelli, 1997) experiment with chunks and add a preprocessing step that uses a finite-state machine to identify potential chunks in the input. The chart parser control strategy is augmented so that constituents found during parsing that align with chunk boundaries are processed with a higher priority in the hope that they are more likely to become part of the final parse. Constituents that do not align with chunk boundaries are assigned lower priorities and remain in the agenda. The resulting algorithm can avoid pruning of useful constituents that can happen in Abney's cascading approach.

Explicit pruning of constituents is another strategy that can be used to improve the efficiency of a parser as shown, e.g., by (Rayner and Carter, 1996). (Rayner and Carter, 1996) experimented with a bottom-up parser with three levels: lexical level, phrasal level and full parsing level. Constituents are pruned before the phrasal and full parsing levels using statistical scores based on how likely is a constituent with a certain property to be part of the final solution.

4 Requirements on the algorithm

Given the characteristics of the input and previously published results described above, we decided to design a parsing strategy with the following characteristics:

1. bottom-up: this allows for partial parses to be identified;
2. multi-level: combined with pruning provides additional control over created constituents;
3. pruning: constituents not likely to contribute to the final parse should be removed early.

In what follows we will describe some initial results of experiments in applying a multi-level chart parser with a radical pruning strategy to the captioning domain.

5 Introducing levels to the grammar

The parsing proceeds in multiple levels. The grammar is split into groups of rules corresponding to the different levels. At a given level, only rules assigned to this level are allowed to fire. They use as input all the constituents the parser created so far (only inactive edges, all active edges are currently pruned between levels). In a sense, this corresponds to parsing with multiple grammars, although the grammar partitioning can be done once the grammar is complete and fine tuning is performed to achieve the right balance between ambiguity, output fragmentation and parsing speed. This approach makes it also possible to test the improvement introduced by the special processing scheme in comparison to some

[1] Dealing with typos, out-of-coverage lexical item, etc, was not considered here, although the parser offers some robustness in skipping unknown words, see Section 7.

other parsing scheme since the grammar is kept in a general form.

The grammar that we are currently using has been adapted from a general English grammar written for the Tomita parser. The grammar does not follow any particular theoretical framework, although it has been strongly influenced by both LFG (Bresnan, 1982) and HPSG (Polard and Sag, 1994). It consists currently of about 300 general rules with some general attachment preference constraints that have been fine tuned on various kinds of text, including news broadcasts and written texts. One important characteristic of the grammar is the use of subcategorization information (at the syntactic level, with values such as `subject+object`, `subject+complement`, `subject+object+oblique("of")`, etc.), and some broad semantic classification of adjuncts to help prevent ambiguity. The lexicalist character of the grammar requires that subcategorization and simple semantic information (temporal expressions, location expressions, etc) be present in the lexicon. The grammar coverage (Czuba et al., 1998) is quite broad, but it is not sufficient, e.g., to cover some types of clause attachment that are present in long sentences found in the input.

The changes that were introduced to the grammar, in comparison to the original version without levels, concentrated on a simple addition of levels to the rules and duplicating some rules at multiple levels. In the current grammar, the following levels have been introduced:

1. lexical level: lexicon lookup, idioms and fixed phrases;
2. nominal phrases without adjuncts;
3. verb phrases with obligatory complements;
4. noun and verb phrases with adjuncts;
5. clausal constituents; noun and verb phrases with obligatory clausal complements;
6. top level with preferences for attachment and well-formedness of constituents (e.g., prefer finite clauses, prefer ungapped constituents, etc).

Although some motivation for the above partitioning can be found on X-bar theory, we mostly used our intuition for choosing the number of levels and deciding how to assign rules to different levels. These are parameters of the algorithm and they can be tuned in further experiments. See the next section for examples of rules that were added to multiple levels.

6 Constituent pruning

We will refer to constituents that were created using grammar rules with the nonterminal `<X>` on their LHS as `<X>` *constituents*. Two constituents will be *similar* if they were created using rules with the same nonterminal on the LHS. E.g., two `<NP>` constituents are similar, regardless of their positions and spanned input.

The pruning phase was added to the usual chart parsing algorithm in a way that makes it invisible to the grammar writer. The pruning algorithm is called on the chart whenever no more rules are allowed to fire at the current level and no active arcs can be extended. In the initial implementation, the pruning algorithm was based on a simple subsumption relation: only the maximal(i.e., covering the longest number of input tokens) constituents from a set of similar constituents remain in the chart and are added to the agenda for the next level. E.g., if the chart contained two `<NP>` constituents, only the one spanning more input would be retained.

Although the original pruning strategy resulted in many reasonable parses, we noticed a few general problems. The parser is very sensitive to wrongly created long constituents. This means that the grammar has to be relatively tight for a successful application with the described parser since no global optimization is performed. However, this also means that if in a particular context the parser builds a constituent C that is not correct in this context but the rules that were used to build the constituent cannot be removed from the grammar since they are useful in general, the pruning step will wrongly remove all, potentially correct, similar constituents subsumed by C.

We observed this kind of behavior in practice and at least two cases can be distinguished. Some constituents are added to the chart early in the analysis and they form bigger constituents as the analysis progresses. Consequently, if a similar constituent is created, the original constituent will be pruned and will not be available at higher levels. This behavior can be observed, e.g., for the string *that help*, in which *that* is supposed to be a pronoun and *help* is supposed to have a verbal reading. Since *that help* is a well-formed `<NP>` constituent according to our grammar, it will be created and it will subsume the pronoun *that*. This means that the pronoun *that* will be pruned and it will not be available at a higher level that tries to create a correct parse incorporating *that* as an object of a preceding verb and *help* as the main verb. In order to solve this problem we allowed some rules to be repeated at multiple levels. The rules introducing pronouns were added at two levels. The rules involving verbal complements were also introduced twice. Since verbal phrases are created relatively late in the analysis, verbal complements on, e.g., noun phrases are not available yet. Because of that, e.g., the rule that attaches the direct object to a verb is present twice in the grammar:

one version of it takes care of nominal objects without complements, the other one is specific for objects with a verbal complements. Since the second version of the rule contains a check for the presence of a verbal complement, no work is repeated.

The second case that we noticed involved large noun phrases created as the result of applying the rules for nominal apposition (e.g., *the U.S. president, Bill Clinton*) and coordination. Since the parser does not use any semantic information, it is difficult to prevent such rules from applying in some wrong contexts. Examples include noun phrases at clause boundaries as in the following sentence: *BTM says it will issue new shares to strengthen its capital base, BTM plans to raise 300 billion yen via the issue.* In this case, an apposition *its capital base, BTM* is created and the phrases *its capital base* and *BTM* are pruned, preventing the parser from finding the correct analysis consisting of two finite clauses.

In order to solve that problem, we introduced an option of relaxing the pruning constraint. Currently, such relaxing is allowed only for phrases containing appositions and coordination. All constituents that are subsumed by similar ones containing apposition or coordination are marked and they can never be pruned. As a result, both *its capital base* and *BTM* remain in the chart and can be used to create the required clauses at higher levels.

The pruning algorithm that we implemented can be potentially quite costly since it involves many comparisons between constituents. Although its worst-case cost is quadratic, in practice the equivalence classes of similar constituents are small and they are pruned quickly. As a result, in our experiments the pruning time was below 0.01% of the total parse time.

In addition to the actual removal of constituent, the function implementing the pruning algorithm performed local ambiguity packing: it removes constituents that have the same feature structures as a constituent already present in the chart and it creates constituents with disjunction of feature structures in case similar constituents spanning the same chunk of input but having different feature structures are found.

7 Extraction from the chart

After the parser finished creating constituents at the highest level, the final result has to be extracted from the chart. Since the parser might not be able to produce a single analysis spanning the whole input, the best sequence of constituents needs to be extracted.

Currently, a simple best-first beam search through the chart is used to find a sequence (path) of constituents spanning the whole input. Paths are allowed to have gaps, i.e., they do not have to be contiguous, although we do not allow for overlapping constituents. The algorithm prefers shorter paths. The length of a path is computed as a weighted sum of the lengths of constituents in the path. We experimented with two different ways of assigning weights and lengths to constituents. In the first method, each constituent was assigned the length of 1 that was weighted by a factor depending of the "quality" of the constituent. Paths can be extended by a gap spanning one input token at a time. Such a gap is weighted with the factor of 3. Constituents that are created by rules with the nonterminal `<OUTPUT>` on their LHS are assumed to be of the highest quality and they are weighted with the factor of 1. All remaining constituents can also be added to the path and are weighted with the factor of 1.5. So a path consisting of an `<OUTPUT>` constituent spanning input tokens 1 to 3, a gap spanning input tokens 4 and 5, and a `<V1>` constituent spanning input tokens 6 to 10 would receive the length of $1 + 6 + 1.5 = 8.5$. This algorithm shows a strong preference for contiguous paths and assigns lengths depending on the number of constituents in the path, ignoring their length.

The second weighting scheme we tried was based on the actual length of constituents. `<OUTPUT>` constituents were assigned their actual length multiplied by 1. Other constituents had their actual length multiplied by 1.5, and gaps were weighted with the factor of 2. The path described in the previous paragraph was thus assigned the length of $3 + 4 + 7.5 = 14.5$.

Although the first weighting scheme seems rather crude, it resulted in a very good performance both in terms of the quality of paths found and the time required to find the best path. The best-first search was implemented using a binary heap priority queue in an array, and the extraction time for the first weighting scheme was below 5% of the total time required for both parsing and extraction. We also did not notice any cases in which the returned path was not the optimal one given the constituents found by the parser. The second weighting scheme is more fine-grained and might turn out to be better on a bigger corpus. However, it required about 15 as much time to complete the search as the first scheme.

Finally, in case of ambiguity, the first feature structure returned by the parser was chosen.

8 Preliminary results

The algorithm has been applied to a sample of 42 sentences from a real TV broadcast. The sentences were picked from a contiguous transcript that was cleaned up for captioner mistakes. Since the parser was designed for use in a real-time multi-engine MT system, we concentrated on sentences which were likely to be translated by the knowledge-based part of the system. Sentences that were likely to be

Sentence 1, 17 tokens:
[[Well] [[Japan] [is [unlikely to adopt [any more stimulus spending measures]] soon [despite [that U.S. pressure.]]]]]

algorithm	#arcs	#constituents	time (s)
chart	20410	6680	76.6
Tomita	–	–	28.0
multi-level	891	191	1.0

Sentence 2, 49 tokens:
[[Reform legislation] [is quite good]] [because [it [[puts up] [public money]] [which] [[financial institutions] [can get]] [to protect [depositors]] [but only if], [[[they] [[[recycle] [or if you will,] [write off]] [their bad loans]]] [and] [[clean up] [their balance sheets]]] [[so] [they] [can start [to loan [money]] again.]]

algorithm	#arcs	#constituents	time (s)
chart	13530	4849	43.7
Tomita	–	–	22.0
multi-level	3101	388	3.0

Figure 1: Sample sentences with bracketing found the parser

translated by a translation memory look-up, such as greetings and short canned phrases, were not added to the test corpus. The resulting corpus consisted of relatively long sentences, with the average length of 23.5 tokens (including punctuation).

The parser was compared to a Tomita parser and a chart parser with local ambiguity packing. All the parsers were implemented in lisp and used the same unification package, which made the parsing results easily comparable. They also used the same grammar and lexicon with about 8000 entries. The grammar was preprocessed for the Tomita parser and the chart parser by removing the rules that were present at multiple levels. The chart parser was set up to quit after finding the first parse covering the whole input. All times given below were obtained on the same machine (SPARCStation 5). Care was taken to disable lisp garbage collection during parsing.

As it was expected, the pruning strategy resulted in a significant reduction of execution time. In Figure 1 we present a few measurements to illustrate the time improvement for two example sentences. For the first one, all parsers produced a complete analysis spanning the whole input. For the second one, due to the lack of grammar coverage, no single analysis can be found. Figure 1 shows the bracketing that the multi-level parser found. It also produced correct feature structures for all the chunks that can be used by an MT system.

As can be seen from Table 1, the time improvement is significant. The improvement in the number of elements in the final chart is crucial for good performance of the extraction algorithm that chooses constituents to be output by the parser in case there is no single analysis spanning the whole input. Also, the multilevel parser did not produce ambiguous feature-structures (ambiguity containment). The Tomita parser produced two packed f-structures for the first sentence that would have to be unpacked and disambiguated for further processing. For the second sentence, the Tomita parser did not find any full parse. The multilevel parser produced chunks that are usable in an MT system and can be translated giving at least partial translation to the user.

The results on the whole test set were as follows. The Tomita parser needed 652 seconds to analyze all the sentences. It produced a complete analysis for 31 sentences, returning no analysis for 11. The chart parser run till the first solution spanning the whole input was found needed 937 seconds to analyze the same 31 sentences, failing on the rest. In the case of the Tomita parser, the average ambiguity level was 3.7 analyses per sentence. The Tomita parser produced an acceptable[2] parse for all the 31 sentences it could analyze in full. However, the acceptable analysis would still have to be distilled from all the parses it returned. The time needed by the chart parser was prohibitively high for any attempt at extracting constituents in the cases when no single parse was found. The total time required by the multi-level parser was 60.7 sec, 10.7 times less than the Tomita parser and 15.4 times less than the chart parser. Figure 2 illustrates the parsing and extraction time as function of sentence length. Although clearly dependent on the syntactic complexity of the input sentence, the parsing time appears to be linearly related to the input length.

[2] An analysis with, e.g., wrong PP-attachment that could be potentially repaired using lexical selection rules during translation, was marked as acceptable.

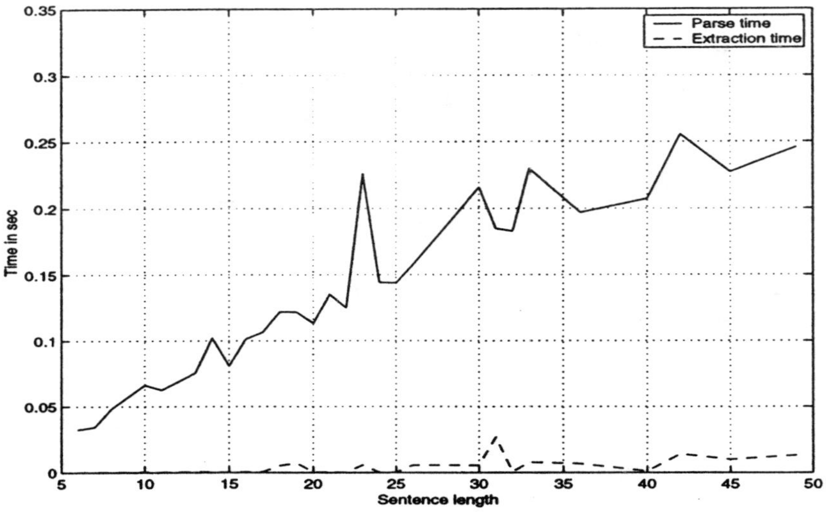

Figure 2: Parse and extraction time as function of sentence length

Since the parser's ability to attach constituents is limited, it produced 114 chunks for all the input sentences, average 2.71 per sentence. The chunks fully covered the input sentences. They were compared to a bracketing that was assigned by a human and corresponded to linguistically motivated phrases. Out of these, 11 corresponded to a wrong bracketing as judged by a human. This affected 8 sentences in the corpus. The remaining chunks were acceptable (as defined in the footnote on the previous page). Although an evaluation in terms of precision/recall would be possible, we have not done it for this paper. We believe that an end-to-end evaluation using, e.g., an MT or Information Extraction system that would be able to handle the parser output would be more meaningful, since it would also be a way to evaluate the effect of the large number of small chunks the parser produced.

9 Future research

There are a number of research issues that we are planning to address soon. First, a more thorough evaluation is required, as described in the previous section. We are currently looking for ways to perform such an evaluation. We are also looking into replacing the fixed pruning and constituent extraction strategy with one learned from training data. We are also investigating ways of learning the number of levels and grammar rule partitioning among levels.

10 Acknowledgements

We would like to thank Eric Nyberg and Teruko Mitamura for providing support for this research and useful discussion, Alon Lavie for helpful comments about the research and earlier versions of the paper, and the anonymous NAACL Student Workshop reviewers for their constructive comments.

References

S. Abney. 1991. Parsing by chunks. In Berwick, Abney, and Tenny, editors, *Principle-Based Parsing*. Kluwer.

S. Abney. 1996. Partial parsing via finite-state cascades. In *Proceedings of Workshop on Robust Parsing, ESSLI-96*.

J. Bresnan, editor. 1982. *The mental representation of grammatical relations*. MIT Press.

F. Ciravegna and A. Lavelli. 1997. Controlling bottom-up chart parser through text chunking. In *Proceedings of IWPT'97*.

K. Czuba, T. Mitamura, and E. Nyberg. 1998. Can practical interlinguas be used for difficult analysis problems? In *Proceedings of AMTA-98 Workshop on Interlinguas*.

E. Nyberg and T. Mitamura. 1992. The kant system: Fast, accurate, high-quality translation in practical domains. In *Proceedings of COLING-92*.

E. Nyberg and T. Mitamura. 1997. A real-time MT system for translating broadcast captions. In *Proceedings of MT Summit VI*.

C. Polard and I. Sag. 1994. *Head-Driven Phrase Structure Grammar*. University of Chicago Press.

F. Popowich, D. Turcato, O. Laurens, and P. McFetridge. 1997. A lexicalist approach to the translation of colloquial text. In *Proceedings of TMI-97*.

M. Rayner and D. Carter. 1996. Fast parsing using pruning and grammar specialization. In *Proceedings of ACL'96*.

Generating Text with a Theorem Prover

Iván I. Garibay
School of Computer Science
University of Central Florida
Orlando, FL
igaribay@cs.ucf.edu

Abstract

The process of documenting designs is tedious and often error-prone. We discuss a system that automatically generates documentation for the single step transition behavior of Statecharts with particular focus on the correctness of the result in the sense that the document will present all and only the facts corresponding to the design being documented.

Our approach is to translate the Statechart into a propositional formula, then translate this formula into a natural language report. In the later translation pragmatic effects arise due to the way the information is presented. Whereas such effects can be difficult to quantify, we account for them within an abstract framework by applying a series of transformations on the structure on the report while preserving soundness and completeness of the logical content. The result is an automatically generated hypertext report that is both logically correct and, to a relatively high degree of confidence, free of misleading implicatures.

1 Introduction

Producing technical documentation is a time-consuming and expensive task. For instance, Reiter et al. (1995), report cases of engineers expending five hours on documentation for each hour spent on design and of airplane documentation sets which weigh more than the actual airplane being documented. Part of the reason for this problem is the gap between Computer Aided Design (CAD) tools and similar tools for assisting the documentation of those designs. Since research efforts focus primarily in the former, this situation is likely to get worse as the CAD tools get more powerful while documentation tools lag far behind.

In this paper we address the matter of automatic generation of technical documentation (Reiter et al., 1992; Reiter et al., 1995; Rösner and Stede, 1992; Svenberg, 1994; Punshon et al., 1997) by studying the problem of automatically generating documents describing the single step transition behavior of Statecharts.

From a natural language generation (NLG) perspective, this problem is distinguished in that the formal correctness of the document being generated is crucial while felicitousness of the style is relatively unimportant. This leads us to a solution based on formally verifiable theorem-proving techniques which allows us to approach strategic NLG issues within a highly abstract and conceptually clear framework.

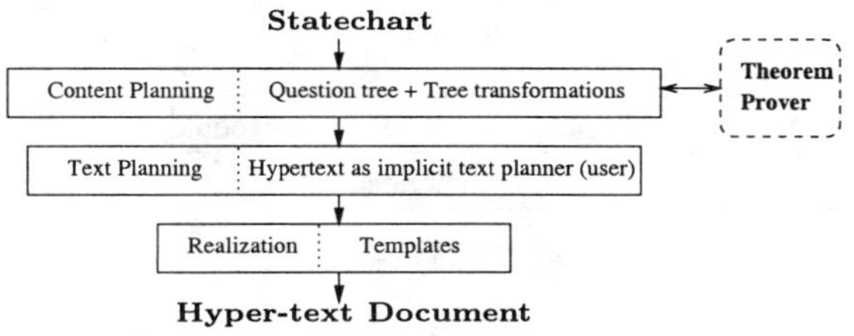

Figure 1: Conceptual view of the system.

The system takes a statechart in the form of a labeled directed graph and translates it into a set of propositional formulae defining its transition behavior. A hyper-text natural language document is generated on-demand from this set of formulae in response to the reader's interaction with the application.

Figure 1 depicts a comparative (Moore and Paris, 1993; Paris et al., 1991; Hovy, 1988) conceptual view of the system while Fig. 2 shows the system architecture. A prototype has been fully implemented with the exception of the statechart axiomatization module. [1]

2 A Logical Semantics for Statecharts

The graphical language of statecharts as proposed by David Harel (Harel et al., 1987; Harel and Naamad, 1996), has been widely recognized as a important tool for analyzing complex reactive systems. It has been implemented in commercial applications like STATEMATE (Harel and Politi, 1998)

[1] A full description of this algorithmic translation of a statechart from its graphical formalism to the propositional logic input format used in this work is described in Garibay (2000).

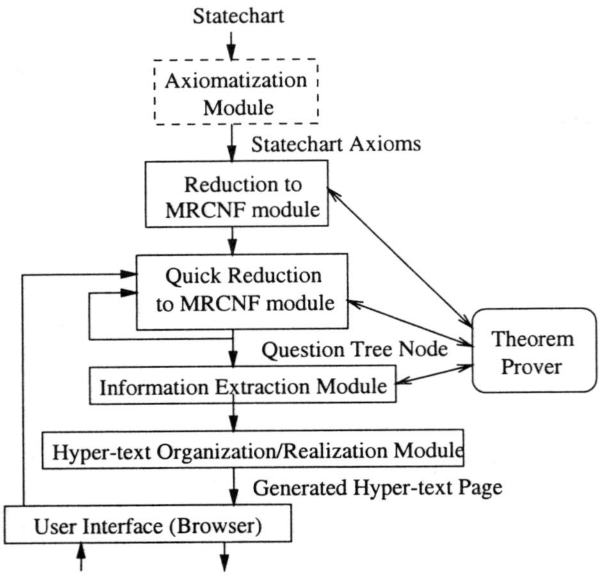

Figure 2: System architecture of the theorem prover based generator. The dotted box is not implemented.

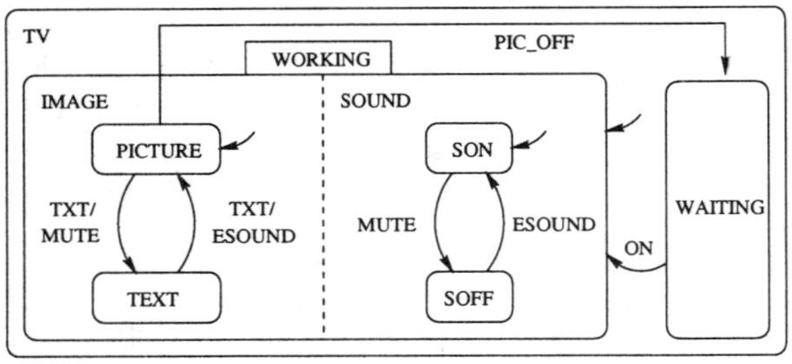

Figure 3: Example Statechart.

and RHAPSODY from ilogix (I-Logix Inc., 2000) and has been adopted as a part of the Unified Modeling Language (UML Revision Task Force, 1999; Booch, 1999), an endeavor to standardize a language of blueprints for software.

Statecharts (Fig. 3) are an extension of conventional finite state machines in which the states may have a hierarchical structure. A *configuration* is defined as a maximal set of non-conflicting states which are active at a given time. A *transition* connects states and is labeled with the set of events that trigger it, and a second set of events that are generated when the transition is taken. A *step* of the statechart relates the current configuration and the events that are active to the next configuration and the events that are generated. A configuration and the set of events that are active is referred to as a *status*.

We capture a step of a statechart as a pair of propositional models, one for the current status and

```
((TV ⟺ WORKING ∨ WAITING)
 (TV.next ⟺ WORKING.next ∨ WAITING.next)
 (WORKING → ¬ WAITING)
 (WORKING.next → ¬ WAITING.next)
 (WAITING → ¬ WORKING)
 (WAITING.next → ¬ WORKING.next)
 (WORKING ⟺ IMAGE ∧ SOUND)
 (WORKING.next ⟺ IMAGE.next ∧ SOUND.next)
...   )
((TV) ∧
 ((WORKING ∧ PICTURE ∧ PIC-OFF ∧ WAITING.next) ∨
  (WORKING ∧¬ (PICTURE ∧ PIC-OFF) ∧
      ((IMAGE ∧ PICTURE ∧ PIC-OFF ∧ WAITING.next) ∨
       (IMAGE ∧¬ (PICTURE ∧ PIC-OFF) ∧
          ((PICTURE ∧ PIC-OFF ∧ WAITING.next) ∨
           (PICTURE ∧ TXT ∧ MUTE.next ∧ TEXT.next) ∨
           (PICTURE ∧¬ OFF ∧¬ TXT ∧ PICTURE.next)
          )
...   )))
```

Figure 4: Section of the propositional logic translation of the example statechart (Fig. 3).

one for the next status. In practice, we incorporate this into a single model with two versions of each propositional variable: P for the truth value in the current status and Pn for the truth value in the next status [2]. A full description of the algorithm for translating statecharts to sets of formulae can be found in Garibay (2000). For a example of this translation see Fig. 4.

3 The Minimum Clausal Theory of the Statecharts

At this point, we have a formula that entails the theory of the single step transition behavior of a Statechart. We can fulfill our requirement of generating a sound and complete report just by translating this formula into English. However, this approach presents a number of problems. For instance, the AND and OR connectives do not in general have the same meaning in English as they do in logic (Gazdar, 1979), furthermore, unlike in the logical formula the scope of the connectives in English is not, in general, well defined (Holt and Klein, 1999). To minimize the ambiguity, we need to take the formula to a form with minimal nesting of operators.

Potentially a more significant problem is the fact that much of the theory (the formula plus all its logical consequences) is obtainable only via complicated inferences. Since the reader understands the translation of the formula at an intuitive level, making only limited inferences, a direct translation will fail to communicate the entire theory. Hence, we would like to take the formula to a form that is closed, in some sense, under logical consequences.

We address both issues by using what we refer to as *minimal (fully) resolved conjunctive normal form (MRCNF)*. A formula is in a MRCNF if and only if

[2] These single step models will form the basis for a temporal model capturing the full behavior of the statecharts as described by Harel and Naamad (1996).

it is in conjunctive normal form (CNF) and is closed under resolution, absorption and tautology (Fitting, 1990; Rogers and Vijay-Shanker, 1994). The closure under resolution is effectively a finite approximation of closure under consequence, that is, every clause that is a logical consequence of the theory entailed by the formula is a direct consequence of some clause in the MRCNF. The other two operations guarantee minimality in size by removing clauses that are trivially true (tautology), and those that are proper super-sets of another (absorption). Hence, the translation will communicate not only the initial facts but also those inferred by resolution. Moreover, a formula in this form is just a conjunction of disjunctions—eliminating the scoping problem. If we interpret the disjunctions as implications, the translation into English will be just a sequence of implicative sentences that are to be interpreted conjunctively—a typical structure for such information in English.

4 Organizing the Hyper-text Report: The Question Tree

A formula in MRCNF is organized in a way that resembles a sequence of implicative sentences. The problem now is the size of this sequence. Large to begin with, its size is increased by the transformation to CNF and closure under resolution. Hence, the translation of MRCNF directly into a sequence of statements would present an uninterpretable sequence of facts. If they are going to be understood by the reader there is a need for some kind of structure. The correct organization depends heavily on the reader's goals and expectations. However, beyond the assumption that the reader's generic goal is to obtain information about the transition behavior of the statechart under consideration, we do not make any assumptions about what the particular reader's goals may be. Instead we present the report as a hyper-text document and allow the reader to interactively refine their goal by following hyper-links. Effectively, the reader's queries focus the theory of the statechart in a particular aspect of its behavior[3].

In this way, as in Reiter et al. (1992) and Levine et al. (1991), we use hyper-text as an implicit text planner, in the sense that we account for every possible model of the user/system interaction and let the actual reader decide which goal to pursue.

We will call the reader's selections *choices*. Each choice the reader makes narrows the information we have to convey, limiting it to all and only the part that is logically consistent with that choice. We will say that the reader *refines* the theory by making the choice. At each point, the choices available to the reader are all the propositional variables that the theory is contingent upon. The reader effectively fixes the valuation of one of these variables to true or false. The system then adds the reader's choice to the theory and recalculates the MRCNF. If the newly obtained theory remains contingent upon some variables, the reader then will have available a new set of choices. If not, the reader will have reached a set of *non-contingent facts* (henceforth *facts*) which are consequences of all the previous choices.

While this process makes the information more accessible by giving it a logical structure, it does nothing to reduce the size of the report. We resolve this by generating the document on demand. While the refinement process (the core computation for on-demand generation) can potentially be very expensive in terms of time, the fact that we are adding singleton clauses to an already minimum set of clausal consequences allows us to use a simplified form of the theorem prover with asymptotic time complexity linear in the number of clauses.

We can visualize the process of the reader making choices as navigating a *question tree*, in which each branch is labeled with a choice and each node contains the theory of the Statechart as refined by the path of choices from the root to that node. In this tree, a reader's choice is equivalent to the question: "What are the circumstances/situations if X is true/false?." The root is the full theory of the transition behavior of the Statechart. The children of a node are obtained by fixing the valuation of each of its contingent propositional variables in turn and recomputing the MRCNF. The leaves are non-contingent theories (those containing only facts) [4].

Conceptually, the labels of each path from the root to a leaf together with each one of the facts in that leaf corresponds to all and only the valuations which are models of the original theory. Therefore, the question tree is sound and complete in the logical sense.

5 Generating the Hyper-text Page under Pragmatic Considerations: Information Extraction Module

This tree turns out to provide a useful framework to address pragmatic issues—those that arise principally from the structure of the report itself (Gazdar, 1979). By addressing these issues in the context of the question tree, rather than in its realization as a report, we abstract away from a great deal of subtle semantic detail that would otherwise obscure the analysis. Our approach consists of applying a series of transformations that resolve these issues while

[3]In a process that will be precisely described shortly.

[4]In general this structure is a directed acyclic graph which Reiter *et al.* call the *question space* (Reiter et al., 1995), but since we work with a tree that spans it, we prefer *question tree*.

preserving logical soundness and completeness of the document.

5.1 Promoting facts

In the question tree, the facts are either reported at the end of a chain of choices or are encoded in the choices themselves. A sequence of these choices is analogous to a chain of nested implications in which the antecedents are the choices made by the user and the consequence is the theory as refined by the choices. This refinement continues until we obtain a non-contingent theory—one in which all variables have valuations. Thus, the chain of implications eventually leads to a set of facts as its final consequence. The pragmatic problem in this case relates to the amount of information to be provided (Grice's *Maxim of Quantity* (Grice, 1975)). This maxim states that speakers will make their contribution as informative as is required, but not more informative than that (Gazdar, 1979). Under this assumption, reporting a fact as a consequence of a sequence of choices explicitly denies that this fact is a consequence of any prefix of that sequence, in contrast to the logical semantics of implication. Such implicatures, while not consequences of the logical content, are valid inferences that people make on the basis of well established expectations about the communicative act.

To avoid this false implicature, we present the facts to the reader as soon as they become available, that is, as soon as they become non-contingent in the theory. The transformation, in this case, moves the facts from the leaves to the interior nodes. This transformation does not change the set of models represented in the tree simply because the movement of facts does not eliminate any path of the tree. Hence, the transformation preserves soundness and completeness of the tree.

In practice, the facts are just the singleton clauses of a theory, therefore we can realize this transformation by simply reporting singleton clauses as soon as they appear in the theory.

5.2 Reporting facts only once

On the other hand, facts in a theory are also facts in every consistent refinement of that theory. Hence, reporting all the facts at each node of the question tree leads us to report many of them repeatedly. In effect, every fact reported in a node will be reported in each of its children as well. This repetition of facts violates the "upper-bound" of Quantity—it reports more than is relevant. In this case Quantity requires us to report only information that is "new".

In general, what is new will depend not only on what is reported but on inferences the reader is likely to have made (McDonald, 1992). We have, however, already committed to being explicit; our assumption is that the reader makes essentially no inferences, that they know all and only what we have explicitly reported. Therefore, we can satisfy the upper bound of Quantity by reporting each fact exactly once on each branch—when it first becomes non-contingent. To do this, we simply keep a list of all facts that have been reported in the current branch; this is the extent of our model of the user.

This transformation does not change the set of models represented in the tree, since it only eliminates repeated literals.

5.3 Promoting single level implications

One of the difficulties in using Quantity is to determine what information is "required". At each node of the question tree we have a current theory to report. The issue, in essence, is what to report at that node and what to report at its descendents. On one hand, it seems clear that we are, at least, required to report the non-contingent facts at each node. On the other hand, we don't want to report the whole theory at the root.

Our intuition is that the degree to which facts are relevant is inversely proportional to the difficulty of interpreting them. Under these circumstances, un-nested implications (i.e., binary disjunctions) are simple enough that the reader is likely to expect them to be reported. From the perspective of the question tree, this suggest, that in addition to the facts at a node, we should also report, as implications, the facts at its non-contingent children (those that are leaves). We refer to the choices leading to non-contingent theories as *conclusive choices.* These are reported as single-level implications ("If X then ⟨some sequence of facts⟩"). This has the effect of promoting the leaves of the tree to their parent pages.

Note that a choice that is conclusive at some page will also be conclusive at each page in the subtree rooted at that page (or, rather, at each page reached by a sequence of choices consistent with that choice). In keeping with the principle of reporting a fact exactly once along each path, we must avoid reporting the implication at the descendent pages. To this end, after reporting each of the conclusive choices on a page, we report the remainder of the tree below that page under an "Otherwise" choice in which the theory has been refined with the complements of the conclusive choices. This has the effect of dramatically restructuring the tree: each of the non-contingent leaves is promoted to the highest page at which the choice that selects it becomes conclusive.

Once again this transformation reorganizes the branches of the question tree without changing the set of models it represents.

To find the conclusive choices we run the theorem prover on the current theory extended, in turn, with each literal upon which it is contingent. If the resulting theory is non-contingent, then that literal is a

```
So far:
 * (the current configuration does not include the state WORKING)
 * (the event OFF is not active).

Facts:
 * the next configuration will not include the state WORKING.

Independent off whether:
 * the event PIC-OFF is active.

Depends on whether:
 * the current configuration includes the states SON and SOF.
 * the event MUTE is active.

Choices:
 * If the current configuration includes the state SON [ then...  ]
 * If the current configuration does not include the state SON [ then...  ]
 * If the current configuration includes the state SOF [ then...  ]
 * If the current configuration does not include the state SOF [ then...  ]
 * If the event MUTE is active [ then...  ]
 * If the event MUTE is not active [ then...  ]
```

Figure 5: Example of generated hyper-text page.

```
The following choices are conclusive:

 * If the event OFF is active then:
 - the next configuration will include the state WAITING,
   but will not include the states PICTURE or TEXT.
 - the event MUTE will not be generated.

 * If the next configuration includes the state WAITING then:
 - the event OFF is active.
 - the next configuration will not include the states PICTURE or TEXT
 - the event MUTE will not be generated.
---------------------------------------------------------------------
[Otherwise ...]
```

Figure 6: Conclusive choices section (up), non-conclusive otherwise section (bottom).

conclusive choice. To find the remainder of the tree to be reported under the "Otherwise" case we extend the current theory with the negation of each of the conclusive choices. If the resulting theory is inconsistent we will say that the conclusive choices are *exhaustive*, if the result is a contingent theory we will say that the conclusive choices are *non-exhaustive with non-conclusive otherwise*, and if the result is a non-contingent theory we will say that the conclusive choices, in this case, are *non-exhaustive with conclusive otherwise.*

5.4 Aggregating pairs of single conditionals

It frequently happens that, at some page, two conclusive choices lead to the same model. In this case, we would report that each implies (among other things) the other. However, these two implications can be aggregated to form a biconditional. Furthermore, Quantity requires us to select the strongest connective that applies in any such case because if a weaker connective is selected it suggests that no stronger one applies (a *scalar implicature*). Consequently, we are actually compelled to aggregate these two facts into a single biconditional.

In practice, we use the theorem prover to either prove or disprove, for every implication, whether its converse is a theorem of the current theory. If proved then the biconditional is reported.

```
Biconditional Implications:
 - the next configuration will include the state SOFF if and only if
   the next configuration will not include the state SON.
One of the following must be the case:

Either:
 - the current configuration includes the state SOFF,
   but does not include the state TEXT.
 - the event ESOUND is not active.
 - the next configuration will include the state SOFF,
   but will not include the state SON.
 - the event ESOUND will not be generated.

Or:the current configuration includes the state SOFF,
   but does not include the state TEXT.
 - the event ESOUND is active.
 - the next configuration will include the state SON,
   but will not include the state SOFF.
 - the event ESOUND will not be generated.
```

Figure 7: Biconditional implications and models sections.

```
Otherwise:
        - the current configuration does not include the state TEXT
        - the next configuration will not include the state SON.
```

Figure 8: Conclusive otherwise section.

6 Hyper-text Organization and Realization Module

The organization of the hyper-text page generated from each node of the question tree visited by the user is shown in Fig. 5. At the top of the page we report (parenthetically) the set of choices that have led to this page. Next we report all of the new facts obtained from the current theory as described in sections 5.1 and 5.2. Then, the propositions that the theory is no longer dependent on (those which no longer occur in the theory) followed by the list of propositions on which it does depend. Finally we present the choices or, if there are any, the conclusive choices. In the first (Fig. 5), each choice is presented as an implicative sentence with a hyper-text link leading to another page (another node of the question tree). In the second (Fig. 6 top), we present the set of conclusive choices followed by one of the three possible cases (described in Section 5.3) for the "Otherwise" case. If the conclusive choices are exhaustive (the otherwise case is inconsistent), we report the biconditional implications (Section 5.4) followed by the final models (Fig 7). If they are exhaustive with a conclusive otherwise, we report the otherwise as another conclusive choice (Fig 8). Finally, if they are exhaustive with a non-conclusive otherwise, we report only an otherwise hyper-link (Fig 6 bottom).

The realization module is, in essence, a pattern matching and template filling process. It's basic component simply translates facts into fixed English language sentences.[5] Facts are represented by literals. These are classified into the following categories: *current state, current event, next state,* and *next event* and the literals in each category are syn-

[5]With added html mark-up.

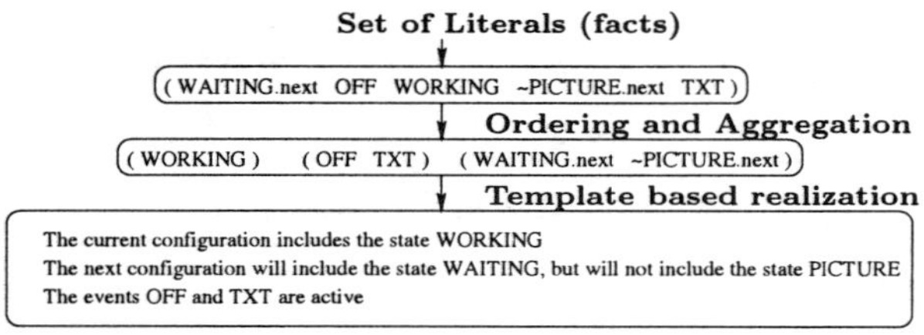

Figure 9: Example of realization.

tactically aggregated (Dalianis, 1999). The process is illustrated in Figure 9.

References

Grady Booch. 1999. UML in action. *Communications of the ACM*, 42(10).

Hercules Dalianis. 1999. Aggregation in natural language generation. *Computational Intelligence*, 15(4):384–414.

Melvin Fitting. 1990. *First-order Logic and Automated Theorem Proving.* Springer-Verlag, New York.

Iván Ibargüen Garibay. 2000. Automatic generation of natural language documentation from statecharts. Master's thesis, University of Central Florida.

Gerald Gazdar. 1979. *Pragmatics: Implicature, Presupposition, and Logical Form.* Academic Press.

H. Paul Grice. 1975. Logic and conversation. In Peter Cole and Jerry L. Morgan, editors, *Syntax and Semantics: Speech Acts*, volume 3, pages 41–58. Academic Press.

David Harel and Amnon Naamad. 1996. The STATEMATE semantics of statecharts. *ACM Transactions on Software Engineering and Methodology*, 5(4):293–333, Oct.

David Harel and Machal Politi. 1998. *Modeling Reactive Systems with Statecharts: The STATEMATE Approach.* McGraw-Hill. QA 76.9 .S88 H3677 1998.

D. Harel, A. Pnueli, J. P. Schmidt, and R. Sherman. 1987. On the formal semantics of statecharts. In *Symposium on Logic in Computer Science*, pages 54–64. Computer Society of the IEEE, Computer Society Press, June.

Alexander Holt and Ewan Klein. 1999. A semantically-derived subset of english for hardware verification. In *Proceedings of the 37th Annual Meeting of the Association for Computational Linguistics.*

Eduard H. Hovy. 1988. *Generating Natural Language under Pragmatic Constraints.* Lawrence Erlbaum Associates.

I-Logix Inc. 2000. http://www.ilogix.com.

John Levine, Alison Cawsey, Chris Mellish, Lawrence Poynter, Ehud Reiter, Paul Tyson, and John Walker. 1991. IDAS: Combining hypertext and natural language generation. In *Third European Workshop on Natural Language Generation*, pages 55–62, Innsbruck, Austria.

David D. McDonald. 1992. Type-driven suppression of redundancy in the generation of inference-rich reports. In R. Dale, E. Hovy, D. Rösner, and O. Stock, editors, *Aspects of Automated Natural Language Generation*, volume 587 of *Lecture Notes in Artificial Intelligence*, pages 73–88. Springer-Velag.

Johanna D. Moore and Cécile L. Paris. 1993. Planning text for advisory dialogues: Capturing intentional and rhetorical information. *Computational Linguistics*, 19(4):651–694.

Cécile L. Paris, William R. Swartout, and William C. Mann, editors. 1991. *Natural Language Generation in Artificial Intelligence and Computational Linguistics.* Kluwer Academic Publishers.

J. M. Punshon, J. P. Tremblay, P. G. Sorenson, and P. S. Findeisen. 1997. From formal specifications to natural language: A case of study. In *12th IEEE International Conference Automated Software Engineering*, pages 309–310, Incline Village, Nevada; USA, November. IEEE Computer Society.

Ehud Reiter, Chris Mellish, and John Levine. 1992. Automatic generation of on-line documentation in the IDAS project. In *Third Conference on Applied Natural Language Processing (ANLP-1992)*, pages 64–71, Trento, Italy.

Ehud Reiter, Chris Mellish, and John Levine. 1995. Automatic generation of technical documentation. *Applied Artificial Intelligence*, 9(3):259–287.

James Rogers and K. Vijay-Shanker. 1994. Obtaining trees from their descriptions: An application to tree-adjoining grammars. *Computational Intelligence*, 10:401–421.

D. Rösner and M. Stede. 1992. Customizing rst for the automatic production of technical manuals. In R. Dale et al., editors, *Aspects of Automated Natural Language Generation*, number 587 in Lecture Notes in Artificial Intelligence, pages 199–214, Berlin. Springer Verlag.

S. Svenberg. 1994. Representing conceptual and linguistic knowledge for multi-lingual generation in a technical domain. In *Proceedings of the 7th International Workshop on Natural Language Generation*, pages 245–248, Kennebunkport.

UML Revision Task Force, 1999. *OMG Unified Modeling Language Specification , v. 1.3. Document ad/99-06-09.* Object Management Group, June.

A Weighted Robust Parsing Approach to Semantic Annotation

Hatem Ghorbel and Vincenzo Pallotta
LITH-MEDIA group
Swiss Federal Institute of Technology
IN Ecublens, 1015 Lausanne, Switzerland
{ghorbel,pallotta}@di.epfl.ch

Abstract

This paper proposes a grammar-based approach to semantic annotation which combines the notions of robust parsing and fuzzy grammars. We present an overview of a preliminary research aimed to generalize some results from a recent project on interaction through speech with information systems where techniques based on the above notions have been successfully applied. The goal of the article is to give a development environment to linguists.

1 Introduction

In this article we are mainly interested in semantic annotation (Sperberg-McQueen and Burnard, 1994). We are considering the Information Extraction (I.E.) problem as a semantic annotation problem: extracting information is finding the relevant terms that contribute to describe an appropriate semantic structure of the text. Some of the most important works in I.E. have been dealing with domain dependent documents like (Moll et al., 1998; Hobbs et al., 1996). Both systems employ complex analysis schemas. Assigning semantic field tags is in general a difficult task. This is due at least to the crucial need of the domain knowledge and also of the linguistic knowledge. Our approach considers that for some specific domains a semantic annotation can be achieved by a *light parsing* of the text which is based on the user of certain *cue-words* as a heuristic for describing its semantic structure.

1.1 A case study in query generation

The availability of a large collection of annotated telephone calls for querying the Swiss phone-book database (i.e the Swiss French PolyPhone corpus) allowed us to experiment our recent findings in robust text analysis obtained in the context of the Swiss National Fund research project ROTA (Robust Text Analysis), and in the recent Swisscom funded project ISIS (Interaction through Speech with Information Systems)[1] (Chappelier et al., 1999). This database contains 4293 simulated recordings related to the "111" Swisscom service calls. For instance a query call like:

```
Bonjour j'aimerais un numéro de
   téléphone à Saignelegier c'est
   Mottaz m o deux ta z Monique rue du
   printemps numéro quatre
```

would produce the following query frame filling for the Swiss Phone-book database:

```
Nom de famille / Firme: MOTTAZ
Prénom / Autres informations: MONIQUE
Rue, numéro: rue du PRINTEMPS, 4
NPA, localité: SAIGNELEGIER.
```

The goal of semantic annotation is to provide a tree structure which can be superposed over the flat sentence. This structure can be supported by a PROLOG compound term consisting of "tag" functors and list arguments. Moreover this same structure can also be supported by the SGML structural representation. The translation between the two models is an intuitive task and an example of such translation is provided by the two following corresponding representations for a possible query call schema.

PROLOG:

```
s([...,announce([...]),
   query([...,
      name([...,
         fam_name([...]),...,
         first_name([...]),
        ...]),...,
      address([...,
         street([...]),...,
         city([...]),
          ...]),
     ...])
 ...]).
```

SGML:

```
...
<announce>
...
</announce>
<query>
    <name>
```

[1]The final report of ISIS project is available at http://lithwww.epfl.ch/~pallotta/isis.html

```
        ...
        <fam_name> ... </fam_name>
        ...
        <first_name> ... </first_name>
        ...
    </name>
    ...
    <address>
         ...
         <street> ... </street>
         ...
          <city> ... </city>
         ...
    </address>
    ...
</query>
...
```

1.1.1 Processing phases

The processing of the corpus data is performed at various linguistic levels by modules organized into a pipeline. Each module assumes as input the output of the preceding module. The main goal of this architecture is to understand how far it is possible to go without using any kind of feedback and interactions among different linguistic modules. At a first stage, morphologic and syntactic processing[2] is applied to the output from the *speech recognizer* module which usually produces a huge word-graph hypothesis. Thus the forest of syntactic trees produced by this phase have been used to achieve two goals:

1. The n-best analyses are used to disambiguate speech recognizer hypotheses
2. They served as supplementary input for the robust semantic analysis that we performed, that had as goal the production of query frames for the information system.

Although robustness can be considered as being applied at either a syntactic or semantic level, we believe it is generally at the semantic level that it is most effective. This robust analysis needs a model of the domain in which the system operates, and a way of linking this model to the lexicon used by the other components. The degree of detail required of the domain model used by the robust analyzer depends upon the ultimate task that must be performed — in our case, furnishing a query to an information system. The results of the processing phase of the previous example is represented below as an SGML annotation:

```
<announce>
 Bonjour j'aimerais un
</announce>
<query> numéro de téléphone à Saignelegier
   <name>
        <fam_name> c'est Mottaz m o deux ta z
        </fam_name>
        <first_name> Monique </first_name>
   </name>
   <address>
        <street> rue du printemps </street>
        <number> numéro quatre </number>
        <city> </city>
   </address>
</query>
```

2 Methodology

In this section we propose the use of a "light-parser" for doing sentence-level semantic annotation. The main idea comes from the observation that annotation does not always need to rely on the deep structure of the sentence (e.g. at morpho-syntactic level). It is sometimes sufficient to find some *cue-words* which allow us to locate the logical sub-structures of the sentence. If the domain is simple enough, this task can be easily mechanized. A similar approach, using finite state parsing technology, has been proposed by Grefenstette in (Grefenstette, 1996) where the main applications are slanted to the extraction of syntactic information.

2.1 Robust Definite Clause Grammars

LHIP (Left-corner Head-driven Island Parser) (Ballim and Russell, 1994; Lieske and Ballim, 1998) is a system which performs robust analysis of its input, using a grammar defined in an extended form of the PROLOG Definite Clause Grammars (DCGs). The chief modifications to the standard PROLOG 'grammar rule' format are of two types: one or more right-hand side (RHS) items may be marked as 'heads' (e.g. using a leading '*'), and one or more RHS items may be marked as 'ignorable' (e.g. using a leading '-'). LHIP employs a different control strategy from that used by PROLOG DCGs, in order to allow it to cope with ungrammatical or unforeseen input. The behavior of LHIP can best be understood in terms of the complementary notions of **span** and **cover**. A grammar rule is said to produce an island which **spans** input terminals t_i to t_{i+n} if the island starts at the ith terminal, and the $i+n^{th}$ terminal is the terminal immediately to the right of the last terminal of the island. A rule is said to **cover** m items if m terminals are consumed in the span of the rule.

[2] Our partner institution ISSCO (Institute Dalle Molle, University of Geneva) performed this analysis phase using tools that were developed in the European Linguistics Engineering project MULTEXT. For syntactic analysis, ISSCO developed a Feature Unification Grammar based on a small sample of the Polyphone data. This grammar was taken by another of our partners (the Laboratory for Artificial Intelligence of the Swiss Federal Institute of Technology, Lausanne) and converted into a probabilistic context-free grammar, which was then applied to a sample of 500 entries from the Polyphone data.

Thus $m \leq n$. If $m = n$ then the rule has completely covered the span. As implied here, rules need not cover all of the input in order to succeed.

2.1.1 Weighted LHIP rules

The main goal of introducing weights into LHIP rules is to induce a partial order over the generated hypotheses. The following schema illustrate how to build a simple weighted rule in a compositional fashion where the resulting weight is computed from the sub-constituents using the minimum operator. Weights are real numbers in the interval $[0, 1]$.

```
cat(cat(Hyp),Weight) ~~>
          sub_cat1(H1,W1),
           ...,
          sub_catn(Hn,Wn),
          {app_list([H1,...,Hn],Hyp),
           min_list([W1,...,Wn],Weight)}.
```

This strategy is not the only possible since the LHIP formalism allows a greater flexibility. Without entering into formal details we can observe that if we strictly follow the above schema and we impose a cover threshold of 1 we are dealing with *fuzzy DCG grammars* (Lee and Zadeh, 1969; Asveld, 1996). We actually extend this class of grammars with a notion of *fuzzy-robustness* where weights are used to compute confidence factors for the membership of islands to categories[3]. The order of constituents may play an important role in assigning weights for different rules having the same number and type of constituents. Each LHIP rule returns a weight together with a term which will contribute to build the resulting structure. The confidence factor for a pre-terminal rule has been assigned statically on the basis of the rule designer's domain knowledge.

2.2 The methodology at work

In our case study we try to integrate the above principles in order to effectively compute annotation hypotheses for the query generation task. This can be done by building a lattice of *annotation hypotheses* and possibly selecting the best one. This lattice is generated by means of a LHIP *weighted grammar* which is used to extract and assemble what we called *semantic constituents.* At the end of this process we presumably obtain suitable annotations from which we will able to extract the content of the query (e.g. name, address, city, etc.). The rules are designed taking into consideration the following kind of knowledge:

Domain Knowledge is exploited to provide quantitative support (or confidence factor) to our rules.

Linguistic Knowledge (as for instance previous POS tagging or syntactic analysis) is used for determining constraints in order to prune the hypotheses space.

Lexical knowledge: As pointed out in (Basili and M.T., 1997), lexical knowledge plays an important role in Information Extraction since it can contribute in guiding the analysis process at various linguistic level. In our case we are concerned with lexical knowledge when we need to specify lexical LHIP rules which represent the building blocks of our parsing system. *Semantic markers* are domain-dependent word patterns and must be defined for a given corpus. They identify *cue-words* serving both as *separators* among logical subparts of the same sentence and as *introducers* of *semantic constituents.* In our specific case they allow us to search for the content of the query only in interesting parts of the sentence. One of the most important separators is the *announcement-query separator.* The LHIP clauses defining this separator can be one or more words covering rule like for instance:

```
ann_query_separator([X],0.7) #1.0 ~~>
          @terminal(X),
          {X='téléphone'}.
ann_query_separator([X,Y],1) #1.0 ~~>
          @terminal(X),
          @terminal(Y),
          {[X = 'numéro',Y = 'de']}.
```

As an example of semantic constituents introducers we propose here the following rule:

```
street_intro([T,Prep],1) #1.0 ~~>
          * street_type(T),
          preposition(Prep).
```

which make use of some word knowledge about street types coming from an external thesaurus like:

```
street_type(X) ~~>
          @terminal(X),
          {thesaurus(street,W),member(X,W)}.
```

It should be noted that we mix weighted and non-weighted rules, simply because non-weighted rules are rules with the highest weight 1.

2.2.1 Generation of hypotheses

The generation of annotation hypotheses is performed by: composing weighted rules, assembling constituents and filtering possible hypotheses. In this case the grammar should provide a means to provide an empty constituent when all possible hypothesis rules have failed. The highest level constituent is represented by the whole sentence structure which simply specifies the possible orders of constituents relative to annotation hypotheses.

[3]Development of this notion is currently under investigation and not yet formalized.

```
s(s([Ann,Query]), W) ~~>
                   ann(Ann),
                   query(Query,W2).

ann(ann(Ann)) ~~> closK(word(Ann)).

query(query(Q),W) ~~>
          * ann_query_separator(QSep,W1),
           target(Target,W2),
           address(Addr,W3)
           {app_list([Qsep,[Target],
           [Addr]],Q),
            min_list([W1,W2,W3],W)}.
```

In the *ann* rule we have made use of the Kleene closure operator *closK* which allow LHIP to simply formulate regular expressions. In the *query* rule we have specified a possible order of constituents interleaved by semantic markers (e.g. separators and introducers). In this case we did not provide any linguistic constraint (e.g. preferring names belonging to the minimal common syntactic sub-tree or those having the longest sequence of proper names belonging to the same sub-tree).

3 Conclusions and future works

In this paper we summarized a proposal for a framework for designing grammar-based automated annotation applications. Starting with a case study and following an approach which combines the notions of fuzziness and robustness in sentence parsing, we showed how to build practical domain-dependent rules which can be applied whenever it is possible to superimpose a sentence-level semantic structure to a text without relying on a previous deep syntactical analysis. Even if the query generation problem may not seem a critical application one should bear in mind that the sentence processing must be done on-line.

As we have previously seen, the cue-words used as semantic markers are domain-dependent. Even their relevance disposal and their weight within the rules depends on their linguistic usage. Therefore, a complete automatic annotation system based on the approach proposed in this article seems to be adequate to give precise results. However, a semi-automatic system could satisfy our needs. This system should be based on the following techniques to achieve a high level of performance:

1. For each annotation, the system offers a list of propositions based on standard grammars as well as on external knowledge (ontologies, knowledge bases ...)
2. According to the grammar initially proposed, the user may change the annotation according to his needs. These modifications are held within the system to change the grammar rules as well as their weights. This makes the system interactive and enhanced by a learning phase.
3. We could imagine that rule design process can be partially automated and we intend to pursue some research on developing methods for both assisted rule design and corpus based rule induction.

References

Peter. R.J. Asveld. 1996. Towards robustness in parsing - fuzzifying context-free language recognition. In J. Dassow, G. Rozemberg, and A. Salomaa, editors, *Developments in Language Theory II - At the Crossroad of Mathematics*, Computer Science and Biology, pages 443–453. World Scientific, Singapore.

A. Ballim and G. Russell. 1994. LHIP: Extended DCGs for Configurable Robust Parsing. In *Proceedings of the 15th International Conference on Computational Linguistics*, pages 501 – 507, Kyoto, Japan. ACL.

R. Basili and Pazienza M.T. 1997. Lexical acquisitiion and information extraction. In Pazienza M.T., editor, *Information Extraction – A multidiciplinary approach to an ermerging information technology*, volume 1299 of *LNAI*, pages 44–72. Springer Verlag.

J-C. Chappelier, M. Rajman, P. Bouillon, S. Armstrong, V. Pallotta, and A Ballim. 1999. Isis project: final report. Technical report, Computer Science Department - Swiss Federal Institute of Technology, September.

G. Grefenstette. 1996. Light parsing as finite-state filtering. In Kornai A., editor, *Proceedings of the ECAI 96 Workshop on Extended Finite State Models of Language*, pages 20–25.

J. Hobbs, D. Appelt, J. Bear, D. Israel, M. Kameyama, M. Stickel, and M. Tyson. 1996. Fastus: a cascaded finite-state transducer for extracting information from natural-language text. In E. Roche and Y. Schabes, editors, *Finite State Devices for Natural Language Processing*. MIT Press, Cambridge MA.

E.T. Lee and L.A. Zadeh. 1969. Note on fuzzy languages. *Information Science*, 1:421–434.

C. Lieske and A. Ballim. 1998. Rethinking natural language processing with prolog. In *Proceedings of Practical Applications of Prolog and Practical Applications of Constraint Technology (PAPPACTS98)*, London,UK. Practical Application Company.

D. Moll, J. Berri, and M. Hess. 1998. A real world implementation of answer extraction. In *Proc. of the 9th International Conference and Workshop on Database and Expert Systems. Workshop on Natural Language and Information Systems*, volume NLIS'98, pages 143–148, Vienna.

C.M. Sperberg-McQueen and L. Burnard, editors. 1994. *Guidelines for Electronic Text Encoding and Interchange, Text Encoding Initiative.* Chicago and Oxford.

Corpus-Based Syntactic Error Detection Using Syntactic Patterns

Koldo Gojenola, Maite Oronoz
Informatika Fakultatea, 649 P. K., Euskal Herriko Unibertsitatea,
20080 Donostia (Euskal Herria)
jipgogak@si.ehu.es, jiboranm@si.ehu.es

Abstract

This paper presents a parsing system for the detection of syntactic errors. It combines a robust partial parser which obtains the main sentence components and a finite-state parser used for the description of syntactic error patterns. The system has been tested on a corpus of real texts, containing both correct and incorrect sentences, with promising results.

Introduction

The problem of syntactic error detection and correction has been addressed since the early years of natural language processing. Different techniques have been proposed for the treatment of the significant portion of errors (typographic, phonetic, cognitive and grammatical) that result in valid words (Weischedel and Sondheimer 1983; Heidorn *et al.* 1982). However, although most currently used word-processors actually provide a grammar checking module, little work has been done on the evaluation of results. There are several reasons for this:

- Incomplete coverage. Some of the best parsers at the moment can analyze only a subset of the sentences in real texts. Compared to syntactic valid structures, the set of syntactically incorrect sentences can be considered almost infinite. When a sentence cannot be parsed it is difficult to determine whether it corresponds to a syntactic error or to an uncovered syntactic construction. In the literature, syntactic errors have been defined mostly with respect to their corresponding correct constructions. The use of unrestricted corpora confronts us with the problem of flagging a correct structure as erroneous (false alarms). These facts widen the scope of the problem, as not only incorrect structures but also correct ones must be taken into account.

  On the other hand, robust parsing systems (e.g., statistical ones) are often unable to distinguish ungrammatical structures from correct ones.

- The need for big corpora. Each kind of syntactic error occurs with very low frequency and, therefore, big corpora are needed for testing. Even if such corpora were available, the task of recognizing error instances for evaluation is a hard task, as there are no syntactically annotated treebanks with error marks for the purposes of evaluation and testing. Thus, to obtain naturally occurring test data, hundreds of texts must be automatically and manually examined and marked.

The aim of the present work is to examine the feasibility of corpus-based syntactic error detection, with methods that are sensitive enough to obtain high correction rates and discriminating enough to maintain low false alarm rates. The system will be applied to Basque, an agglutinative language with relative free order among sentence components. Its recent standardization makes it necessary to develop a syntactic checking tool.
The remainder of this paper is organized as follows. After commenting on the literature on syntactic error detection in section 2, section 3 presents a description of the linguistic resources we have used. Section 4 describes the error types we have treated, while section 5 gives the evaluation results.

1 Background

Kukich (1992) surveys the state of the art in syntactic error detection. She estimates that a proportion of all the errors varying between 25% and over 50%, depending on the application, are valid words. Atwell and Elliott (1987) made a manual study concluding that 55% of them are local syntactic errors (detectable by an examination of the local syntactic context), 18% are due to global syntactic errors (involving long-distance syntactic dependencies, which need a full parse of the sentence), and 27% are semantic errors. Regarding their treatment, different approaches have been proposed:

- The relaxation of syntactic constraints (Douglas and Dale 1992). This grammar-based method allows the analysis of sentences

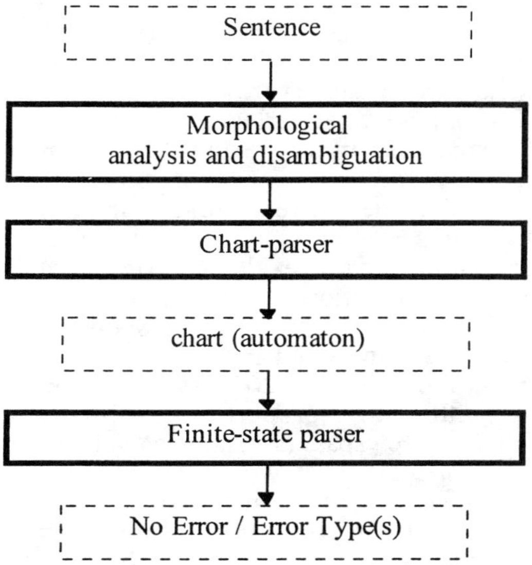

Figure 1. Overview of the system.

that do not fulfill some of the constraints of the language by identifying a rule that might have been violated, determining whether its relaxation might lead to a successful parse. Its main disadvantage is the need of a full-coverage grammar, a problem not solved at the moment, except for restricted environments (Menzel and Schröder 1999).

- Error patterns (Kukich 1992; Golding and Schabes 1996; Mangu and Brill 1997), in the form of statistical information, hand-coded rules or automatically learned ones.
- Charts have been used in grammar-based systems as a source of information; they can be resorted to if no complete analysis is found, so as to detect a syntactic error (Mellish 1989; Min-Wilson 1998).

2 Linguistic resources

We have used a parsing system (Aldezabal *et al.* 1999, 2000) divided in three main modules (see figure 1):

- Morphological analysis and disambiguation. A robust morphological analyzer (Alegria *et al.* 1996) obtains for each word its segmentation(s) into component morphemes. After that, morphological disambiguation (Ezeiza *et al.* 1998) is applied, reducing the high word-level ambiguity from 2.65 to 1.19 interpretations.
- Unification-based chart-parsing. After morphological analysis and disambiguation, a PATR-II unification grammar is applied bottom-up to each sentence, giving a chart as a result. The grammar is partial but it gives a complete coverage of the main sentence elements, such as noun phrases, prepositional phrases, sentential complements and simple sentences. The result is a shallow parser (Abney 1997) that can be used for subsequent processing (see figure 2). In this figure, dashed lines are used to indicate lexical elements (lemmas and morphemes), while plain lines define syntactic constituents. Bold circles represent word-boundaries, and plain ones delimit morpheme-boundaries. The figure has been simplified, as each arc is actually represented by its morphological and syntactic information, in the form of a sequence of feature-value pairs.
- Finite-state parsing. A tool is needed that will allow the definition of complex linguistic error patterns over the chart. For that reason, we view the chart as an automaton to which finite-state constraints can be applied encoded in the form of automata and transducers (we use the Xerox Finite State Tool, XFST, (Karttunen *et al.* 1997)). Finite-state rules provide a modular, declarative and flexible workbench to deal with the resulting chart. Among the finite-state operators used, we apply composition, intersection and union of regular expressions and relations.

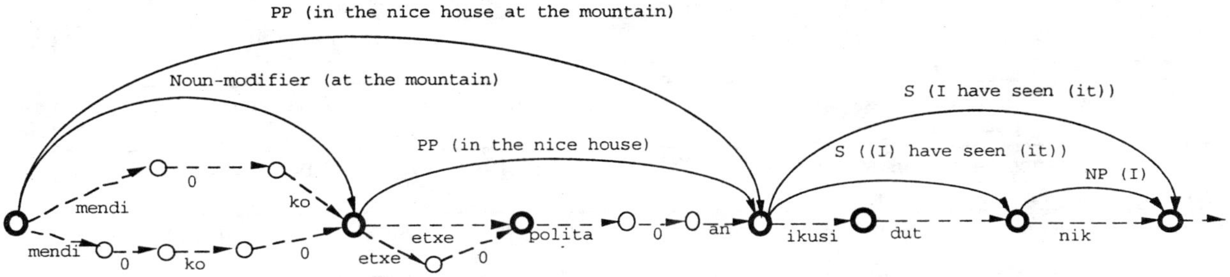

Figure 2. State of the chart after the analysis of *Mendiko etxe politean ikusi dut nik* ('I have seen (it) in the nice house at the mountain').

Durangon,	*1999ko*	*martxoaren*	*7an*
In Durango,	1999,	March	the 7th
(Durango, inessive, sing)	(1999 genitive)	(March, genitive, sing)	(7, inessive sing)

Example 1. Format of a valid date expression.

The full system provides a robust basis, necessary for any treatment based on corpora. In the case of error detection, a solid base is indispensable.

3 Error detection

As a test, we chose the case of date expressions due to several reasons:

- It was relatively easy to obtain test data compared to other kinds of errors. Although the data must be obtained mostly manually, date expressions contain several cues (month names, year numbers) that help in the process of finding semiautomatically test sentences. In any case, manual marking is needed for all the retrieved sentences.
- The context of application is wide, that is, date expressions contain morphologically and syntactically rich enough phenomena where several types of errors can be found. These can be viewed as representative of the set of local syntactic errors so that the same procedure can be used when dealing with other kinds of errors. Example 1 shows one of the formats of a date expression.

Basque being an agglutinative language, most of the elements appearing in date expressions (year numbers, months and days) must be inflected, attaching to them the corresponding number and case morphemes. Moreover, each different date format requires that the elements involved appear in fixed combinations. This is a common source of errors, not detectable by a spelling-checker, as each isolated word-form is correct.

For evaluation, we collected 267 essays written by students (with a high proportion of errors) and texts from newspapers and magazines, totaling more than 500,000 words. From them we chose 658 sentences, including correct dates, incorrect dates, and also structures 'similar' to dates (those sentences containing months and years, which could be mistaken for a date), in order to test false positives (see table 1). As a result of the selection procedure, the proportion of errors is higher than in normal texts. We divided our data into two groups. One of them was used for development, leaving the second one for the final test. The proportion of correct dates is higher in the case of test data with respect to those in the development corpus, so that the effect of false positives will be evaluated with more accuracy.

	Development corpus		**Test corpus**	
Number of sentences	411		247	
Correct dates	65		39	
Structures 'similar' to dates	255		171	
Incorrect dates	91		37	
Incorrect dates with 1 error	43	% 47	6	% 16
Incorrect dates with 2 errors	42	% 46	27	% 73
Incorrect dates with 3 errors	6	% 7	4	% 11

Table 1. Test data.

Error type	**Example**
1. The year number cannot be inflected using a hyphen	Donostian, 1995-eko martxoaren 14an
2. The month (*martxoak*) must appear in lowercase	1997ko martxoak 14
3. The optional locative preceding dates (*Frantzia*) must be followed by a comma	Frantzia 1997ko irailaren 8an
4. The day number after a month in genitive case (*martxoaren*) must have a case mark	Donostian, 19995eko martxoaren 22
5. The day number after a month in absolutive case (*ekainak*) cannot have a case mark	1998.eko ekainak 14ean argitaratua
6. The month (*martxoan*) must be inflected in genitive or absolutive case	Donostian, 1995.eko martxoan 28an
Combination of errors (2, 3 and 4)	karrera bukatu nuenean 1997ko Ekainaren 30an

Table 2. Most frequent error types in dates.

```
define NP_Month_Absolutive_or_Ergative   ...
define PP_Year_Genitive   ...
define Error_Type_5         NP_Month_Absolutive_or_Ergative   Inflected_Number;
define Mark_Error_Type_5    [Error_Type_5]   @->   BEGINERRORTYPE5   "..."   ENDERRORTYPE5
                            || Optional_Place_Name   Optional_Comma   PP_Year_Genitive   _  ;
```

Example 2. Regular expressions for an error pattern.

After examining different instances of errors, we chose the six most frequent error types (see table 2). In a first phase, one or more patterns were defined for each error type. However, we soon realized that this approach failed because quite often two or three errors might appear in the same expression. This phenomenon asked for a kind of 'gradual relaxation' approach, which had to consider that several mistakes could co-occur. Instead of treating each error independently, we had to design error patterns bearing in mind not only the correct expression, but its erroneous versions as well. For example, the last sentence in table 2 contains three different errors, so that the error pattern for the second error should consider the possibility of also containing errors 3 and 4. This relaxation on what could be considered a correct date had the risk of increasing the number of false positives. As the number of interactions among errors grows exponentially with the number of errors (there are potentially 2^6 combinations of the six error types), we based our error patterns on the combinations actually found in the corpus, so that in practice that number can be considerably reduced (we did not find any expression containing more than three errors in the corpus).

The error pattern for the fifth kind of error (see example 2[1]) is defined in two steps. First, the syntactic pattern of the error is defined (an NP consisting of a month in ergative or absolutive case followed by an inflected number), and named *Error_Type5*. Second, a transducer (*Mark_Error_Type_5*) is defined which surrounds the incorrect pattern (represented by "...") by two error tags (BEGINERRORTYPE5 and ENDERRORTYPE5). To further restrict the application of the rule, left and right contexts for the error can be defined (in a notation reminiscent of two-level morphology), mostly to assure that the rule is only applied to dates, thus preventing the possibility of obtaining false positives.

Concerning the definition of error patterns, equal care must be taken for correct and incorrect dates. In a first phase, we devised rules for the errors but, after testing them on correct dates from the development corpus, we had to extend the rules so as to eliminate false positives. As a result, more than 60 morphosyntactic patterns (each corresponding to a finite-state automata or transducer) were needed for the definition of the six basic error patterns. They range from small local constraints (45 automata with less than 100 states) to the most complex patterns (a transducer with 10,000 states and 475,000 arcs).

4 Evaluation

Table 3 shows the results. As the development corpus could be inspected during the refinement of the parser, the results in the second and third columns can be understood as an upper limit of the parser in its current state, with 100% precision (no false alarms) and 91% recall.

The system obtains 84% recall over the corpus of previously unseen 247 sentences. 31 errors out of 37 are detected giving the exact cause of the error (in cases with multiple errors almost all of them were found).

	Development corpus		Test corpus	
Number of sentences	411		247	
Undetected date errors	7	9%	6	16%
Detected date errors	84	91%	31	84%
False alarms	0		5	

Table 3. Evaluation results.

[1] For more information on XFST regular expressions, see (Karttunen *et al.* 1997).

Example	Cause of the error
atxiloketa 1998ko urtarriletik irailaren 16ra ... *the imprisonment from January 1998 till the 16th of September*	Structure similar to a date incorrectly interpreted as a date and flagged as erroneous.
Donostian 1960ko Urtarrilaren jaioa *born in Donostia in the January of 1960*	Incorrect Basque construction that is interpreted as a date.
etorriko da 1997ko irailaren 26ko 1:15etan *it will come the 26 of September 1997 at 1:15*	The system takes the hour number (1:15) as the day of the month.
atzotik 1999ko abenduaren 31 arte *from yesterday until the 31st of December*	The grammar does not cover the *arte* (until) particle, so a correct date is flagged as ungrammatical.
Primakovek 1998ko irailaren 11n hartu zuen ... *Primakov took it on the 11th of September 1998*	The unknown word *Primakov* is interpreted as a locative.

Table 4. False alarms.

Regarding precision, there are 5 false alarms, that is, correct dates or sentences similar to dates flagged as erroneous. If these false positives are divided by the number of sentences (247) of the test corpus, we can estimate the false alarm rate to be 2.02% over the number of dates in real texts. Table 4 examines some of the false alarms, two of them due to expressions similar to dates that are mistaken for dates, other two relate to constructions not taken into account in the design of the partial grammar, and the last one is due to insufficient lexical coverage.

Although the results are promising, more corpus data will be needed in order to maximize precision.

Conclusions

This work presents the application of a parsing system to syntactic error detection. The reported experiment has as its main features:

- It is corpus-based. If a system is to be useful, it must be tested on real examples of both correct and incorrect sentences. Although this may seem evident, it has not been the case for most of the previous work on syntactic errors. This implies the existence of big corpora and, for most of the errors, manual annotation.
- The most successful methods for error detection, i.e., relaxation of syntactic constraints and error patterns over a chart, have been combined with good results. On the other hand, the relaxation is not applied dynamically at parsing time, but it has been manually coded. This implies a considerable amount of work, as we had to consider the formats for valid sentences as well as for all their incorrect variants.
- A partial robust parsing architecture provides a powerful way to consider simultaneously information at the morphemic and syntactic levels. The unification grammar is necessary to treat aspects like complex agreement and word order variations, currently unsolvable using finite-state networks. It constructs all the possible syntactic components. On the other hand, regular expressions in the form of automata and transducers are suitable for the definition of complex error patterns based on linguistic units.

We are currently exploring new extensions to the system:

- Adding new kinds of errors. Our system, as well as any system dealing with syntactic errors, suffers the problem of scaling up, as the addition of new types of errors will suppose an increment in the number of error patterns that involves a considerable amount of work in the process of hand-coding the rules. The possible interaction among rules for different error types must be studied, although we expect that the rule sets will be mostly independent. Another interesting aspect is the reusability of the linguistic patterns: in the process of treating errors in dates some patterns describe general linguistic facts that can be reused, while others pertain to idiosyncratic facts of dates.

  We plan to extend the system to other qualitatively different types of errors, such as those involving agreement between the main components of the sentence, which is very rich in Basque, errors due to incorrect use of subcategorization and errors in post-positions. Although the number of potential syntactic errors is huge, we think that the treatment of the most frequent kinds of error with high recall and precision can result in useful grammar-checking tools.
- Automatic acquisition of error detecting patterns. Although manual examination seems unavoidable we think that, with a corpus of errors big enough, machine learning techniques could be applied to the

problem of writing error patterns (Golding and Roth 1996; Mangu and Brill 1997). This solution would be even more useful in the case of combinations of different errors. In any case, it must be examined whether automatic methods reach the high precision and reliability obtained by hand-coded rules.

- Using either hand-coded rules or automatically learned ones, both methods have still the problem of obtaining and marking big test corpora, a process that will have to be made mostly manually (except for some limited cases like word confusion (Golding and Roth 1996)). This is one of the major bottlenecks.

Acknowledgements

This research is supported by the Basque Government, the University of the Basque Country and the Interministerial Commission for Science and Technology (CICYT). Thanks to Gorka Elordieta for his help writing the final version of the paper.

References

Agirre E., Gojenola K., Sarasola K., Voutilainen A. (1998) *Towards a Single Proposal in Spelling Correction.* COLING-ACL'98, Montreal.

Abney S. (1997) *Part-of-Speech Tagging and Partial Parsing.* In Corpus-Based Methods in Language and Speech Processing, Kluwer, Dordrecht, 1997.

Aldezabal I., Gojenola K., Oronoz M. (1999) *Combining Chart-Parsing and Finite State Parsing.* Proceedings of the Student Session of the European Summer School in Logic, Language and Computation (ESSLLI'99), Utrecht.

Aldezabal I., Gojenola K., Sarasola K. (2000) *A Bootstrapping Approach to Parser* Development. Sixth International Workshop on Parsing Technologies, Trento.

Alegria I., Artola X., Sarasola K., Urkia. M. (1996) *Automatic morphological analysis of Basque.* Literary & Linguistic Computing, Vol. 11.

Atwell E., Elliott S. (1987) *Dealing with Ill-Formed English Text.* In The Computational Analysis of English: a Corpus-Based Approach, De. Longman.

Douglas, S., Dale R. 1992. *Towards Robust PATR.* COLING'92, Nantes.

Ezeiza N., Alegria I., Arriola J.M., Urizar R., Aduriz I. (1998) *Combining Stochastic and Rule-Based Methods for Disambiguation in Agglutinative Languages.* COLING-ACL-98, Montreal.

Golding A. and Schabes. Y. (1996) *Combining trigram-based and feature-based methods for context-sensitive spelling correction.* In Proc. of the 34th ACL Meeting, Santa Cruz, CA.

Golding A., Roth. D. (1996) *A Winnow-based Approach to Spelling Correction.* Proceedings of the 13th International Conference on Machine Learning, ICML'96.

Heidorn G. E., Jensen K., Miller L. A., Byrd R. J., Chodorow M. S. (1982) *The EPISTLE text-critiquing system.* IBM Systems Journal, Vol. 21, No. 3.

Karttunen L., Chanod J-P., Grefenstette G., Schiller A. (1997) *Regular Expressions For Language Engineering.* Journal of Natural Language Engineering.

Kukich K. (1992) *Techniques for automatically correcting words in text.* In ACM Computing Surveys, Vol. 24, N. 4, December, pp. 377-439.

Mangu L., Brill E. (1997) *Automatic Rule Acquisition for Spelling Correction.* Proceedings of the 14th International Conference on Machine Learning, ICML'97.

Mellish C. (1989) *Some Chart-Based Techniques for Parsing Ill-Formed Input.* EACL'89.

Menzel W., Schröder I. (1999) *Error Diagnosis for Language Learning Systems.* ReCALL, special edition, May 1999.

Min K., Wilson W. (1998) *Integrated Control of Chart Items for Error Repair.* COLING-ACL'98, Montreal.

Roche E., Schabes Y. (1997) *Finite-State Language Processing.* MIT Press.

Weischedel R.M., Sondheimer N.K. (1983) *Meta-rules as a Basis for Processing Ill-Formed Input.* American Journal of Computational Linguistics, 9.

The use of error tags in ARTFL's *Encyclopédie*: Does good error identification lead to good error correction?

Derrick Higgins
Department of Linguistics
University of Chicago

Abstract

Many corpora which are prime candidates for automatic error correction, such as the output of OCR software, and electronic texts incorporating markup tags, include information on which portions of the text are most likely to contain errors.

This paper describes how the error markup tag <?> is being incorporated in the spell-checking of an electronic version of Diderot's *Encyclopédie*, and evaluates whether the presence of this tag has significantly aided in *correcting* the errors which it marks. Although the usefulness of error tagging may vary from project to project, even as the precise way in which the tagging is done varies, error tagging does *not necessarily* confer any benefit in attempting to correct a given word. It may, of course, nevertheless be useful in marking errors to be fixed manually at a later stage of processing the text.

1 The *Encyclopédie*

1.1 Project Overview

The goal of this project is ultimately to detect and correct all errors in the electronic version of the 18th century French encyclopedia of Diderot and d'Alembert, a corpus of ca. 18 million words. This text is currently under development by the Project for American and French Research on the Treasury of the French Language (ARTFL); a project overview and limited sample of searchable text from the *Encyclopédie* are available at:
`http://humanities.uchicago.edu/ARTFL/projects/encyc/`.
Andreev et al. (1999) also provides a thorough summary of the goals and status of the project.

The electronic text was largely transcribed from the original, although parts of it were produced by optical character recognition on scanned images. Unfortunately, whether a section of text was transcribed or produced by OCR was not recorded at the time of data capture, so that the error correction strategy cannot be made sensitive to this parameter. Judging from a small hand-checked section of the text, the error rate is fairly low; about one word in 40 contains an error. It should also be added that the version of the text with which I am working has already been subjected to some corrective measures after the initial data capture stage. For example, common and easily identifiable mistakes such as the word *enfant* showing up as *ensant* were simply globally repaired throughout the text. (The original edition of the *Encyclopédie* made use of the sharp 's', which was often confused with an 'f' during data entry—cf. Figure 1.)

At present, my focus is on non-word error detection and correction, although use of word n-grams seems to be a fairly straightforward extension to allow for the kind of context-sensitivity in error correction which has been the focus of much recent work (cf. Golding and Roth (1999), Mays et al. (1991), Yarowsky (1995)).

The approach I am pursuing is an application of Bayesian statistics. We treat the process by which the electronic text was produced as a noisy channel, and take as our goal the maximization of the probability of each input word, given a string which is the

Figure 1: Example text from the *Encyclopédie.* Note the similarity between the 'f' and the problematic sharp 's' in *signifie*

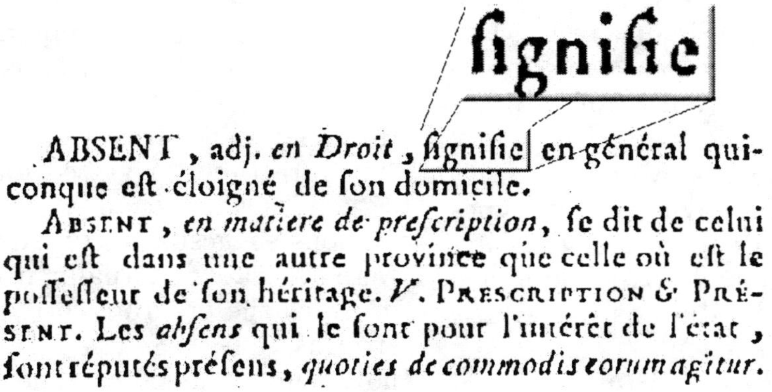
ſignifie

ABSENT, adj. *en Droit*, ſignifie en général quiconque eſt éloigné de ſon domicile.

ABSENT, *en matiere de preſcription*, ſe dit de celui qui eſt dans une autre province que celle où eſt le poſſeſſeur de ſon héritage. *V.* PRESCRIPTION & PRÉSENT. Les *abſens* qui le ſont pour l'intérêt de l'état, ſont réputés préſens, *quoties de commodis eorum agitur.*

output of the noisy channel. If we represent the correct form by w_c, and the observed form by w_o, our goal can be described as finding the w_c which maximizes $p(w_c|w_o)$, the probability that w_c is the intended form, given that w_o is the observed form.

By Bayes' rule, this can be reduced to the problem of maximizing $\frac{p(w_o|w_c)p(w_c)}{p(w_o)}$. Of course, the probability of the observed string will be constant across all candidate corrections, so the same w_c will also maximize $p(w_o|w_c)p(w_c)$.

The term $p(w_c)$ (the *prior* probability) can be estimated by doing frequency counts on a corpus. In this case, I am using an interpolated model of Good-Turing smoothed word and letter probabilities as the prior.

The term $p(w_o|w_c)$ is called the *error model.* Intuitively, it quantifies the probability of certain kinds of errors resulting from the noisy channel. It is implemented as a confusion matrix, which associates a probability with each input/output character pair, representing the probability of the input character being replaced by the output character. These probabilities can be estimated from a large corpus tagged for errors, but since I do not have access to such a source for this project, I needed to train the matrix as described in Kernighan et al. (1990).

Cf. Jurafsky and Martin (1999) for an introduction to spelling correction using confusion matrices, and Kukich (1992) for a survey of different strategies in spelling correction.

1.2 Treatment of <?>

A number of different SGML-style tags are currently used in the encoding of the *Encyclopédie*, ranging from form-related tags such as `<i>` (for italic text), to semantic markup tags such as `<article>`, to the error tag `<?>`, the treatment of which is the focus of this article. The data entry specification for the project prescribes the use of `<?>` in all cases in which the keyboard operator has any doubt as to the identity of a printed character, and also when symbols appear in the text which cannot be represented in the Latin-1 codepage (except for Greek text, which is handled by other means). Other instances of the `<?>` tag were produced as indications of mistakes in OCR output.

Some examples of the use of the error tag from the actual corpus include the following:

`<?>`	for a Hebrew א
`<?>dans`	for *dans*
`J'<?>i`	for *J'ai*
`ab<?>ci<?><?>es`	for *abscisses*
`d'autre<?>aladies`	for *d'autres maladies*

The first is a case where `<?>` was used to mark an untypeable character. In the second case, it was somehow inserted superfluously (most likely by OCR). In the third row, <?> stands in for a single missing character, and in the fourth it does the same, but three times in a single word. Finally, in the last row the error tag indicates the omission of multiple characters, and even a word boundary.

In fact, as Table 1 shows, words which include the error tag generally have error types which are more difficult to correct than average. Our confusion matrix-based approach is best at handling substitutions (e.g., *onfin* → *enfin*), deletions (*apellent* → *appellent*), and insertions (*asselain* → *asselin*), and cannot correct words with multiple errors at all.[1] "Unrecoverable" errors are those in which no "correction" is possible, for example, when non-ASCII symbols occur in the original.

The fact that the error tag is used to code such a wide variety of irregularities in the corpus makes it difficult to incorporate into our general error correction strategy. Since <?> so often occurred as a replacement for a single, missing character, however, I treated it as a character in the language model, but one with an extremely low probability, so that any suggested correction would have to get rid of it in order to appreciably increase the probability of the word.

In short, <?> is included in the confusion matrix as a character which may occur as the result of interference from the noisy channel, but is highly unlikely to appear independently in the language. This approach ignores the many cases of multiple errors indicated by the error tag, but these probably pose too difficult a problem for this stage of the project anyhow. The funding available for the project does not currently allow us to pursue the possibility of computer-aided error correction; rather, the program must correct as many errors as it can without human intervention. Toward this end, we are willing to sacrifice the ability to cope with more esoteric error types in order to improve the reliability of the system on other error types.

The actual performance of the spelling correction algorithm on words which include the error tag, while comparable to the performance on other words, is perhaps not as high as we might initially have hoped, given that they were already tagged as errors. Of the corrections suggested for words without <?>, 47% were accurate, while of the corrections suggested for words with <?>, 29% were accurate.[2] Actually, if we include cases in which the program correctly identified an error as "unrecoverable", and opted to make no change, the percentage for <?> suggestions rises to 71%.

It may seem that these numbers in fact undermine the thesis that the error tagging in the *Encyclopédie* was not useful in error correction. I.e., if the correction algorithm exhibits the correct behavior on 47% of untagged errors, and on 71% of tagged errors, it seems that the tags are helping out somewhat. Actually, this is not the case. First, we should not give the same weight to correct behavior on unrecoverable errors (which means giving up on correction) and correct behavior on other errors (which means actually finding the correct form). Second, the tagged errors are often simply 'worse' than untagged errors, so that even if the OCR or keyboard operator had made a guess at the correct form, they would have easily been identifiable as errors, and even errors of a certain type. For example, I maintain that the form ab<?>ci<?><?>es would have been no more difficult to correct had it occurred instead as abfciffes.

2 Conclusion

In sum, the errors which are marked with the <?> tag in the electronic version of the

[1] Actually, it does have a mechanism for dealing with cases such as ab<?>ci<?><?>es, in which the error tag occurs multiple times, but stands for a single letter in each case.

[2] I admit that these numbers may seem low, but bear in mind that the percentage reflects the accuracy of the *first guess* made by the system, since its operation is required to be entirely automatic. Furthermore, the correction task is made more difficult by the fact that the corpus is an encyclopedia, which contains more infrequent words and proper names than most corpora.

	Substitution	Deletion	Insertion	Word-breaking	Multiple	Unrecoverable
Contains <?>	37.4%	0%	2.2%	0%	16.5%	44%
Does not contain <?>	58.5%	11.6%	6.8%	12.9%	10.2%	0%

Table 1: Breakdown of error types, according to whether the word contains <?>

Encyclopédie encompass so many distinct error types, and errors of such difficulty, that it is hard to come up with corrections for many of them without human intervention. For this reason, experience with the *Encyclopédie* project suggests that error tagging is not necessarily a great aid in performing automatic error correction.

There is certainly a great deal of room for further investigation into the use of metadata in spelling correction in general, however. While the error tag is a somewhat unique member of the tagset, in that it typically flags a subpart of a word, rather than a string of words, this should not be taken to mean that it is the only tag which could be employed in spelling correction. If nothing else, "wider-scope" markup tags can be helpful in determining when certain parts of the corpus should not be seen as representative of the language model, or should be seen as representative of a distinct language model. (For example, the italic tag <i>. often marks Latin text in the *Encyclopédie*.)

Ultimately, I believe that what is needed in order for text tagging to be useful in error correction is a recognition that the tagset will influence the correction process. Tags which are applied in such a way as to delimit sections of text which are relevant to correction (such as names, equations, and foreign language text), will be of greater use than tags which represent a mixture of such classes. Error tagging in particular should be most useful if it does not conflate quite distinct things that may be "wrong" with a text, such as illegibility of the original, unrenderable symbols, and OCR inaccuracies. Such considerations are certainly relevant in the evaluation of emerging text encoding standards, such as the specification of the Text Encoding Initiative.

References

Leonid Andreev, Jack Iverson, and Mark Olsen. 1999. Re-engineering a war-machine: *ARTFL's Encyclopédie*. *Literary and Linguistic Computing*, 14(1):11–28.

Denis Diderot and Jean Le Rond d'Alembert, editors. 1976 [1751–1765]. *Encyclopédie, ou Dictionnaire raisonné des sciences, des arts et des métiers*. Research Publications, New Haven, Conn. Microfilm.

Andrew R. Golding and Dan Roth. 1999. A winnow-based approach to context-sensitive spelling correction. *Machine Learning*, 34(1):107–130.

Daniel Jurafsky and James Martin. 1999. *Speech and Language Processing: An Introduction to Speech Recognition, Natural Language Processing and Computational Linguistics*. Prentice Hall.

M. D. Kernighan, K. W. Church, and W. A. Gale. 1990. A spelling correction program based on a noisy channel model. In *Proceedings of the 13th International Conference on Computational Linguistics (COLING '90)*, volume 2, pages 205–211.

Karen Kukich. 1992. Techniques for automatically correcting words in text. *ACM Computing Surveys*, 24(4):377–439.

Eric Mays, Fred J. Damerau, and Robert L. Mercer. 1991. Context based spelling correction. *Information Processing & Management*, 27(5):517–522.

David Yarowsky. 1995. Unsupervised word sense disambiguation rivaling supervised methods. In *Proceedings of the 33rd An-*

nual Meeting of the Association for Computational Linguistics, volume 33, pages 189–196.

Word Sense Disambiguation for Cross-Language Information Retrieval

Mary Xiaoyong Liu, **Ted Diamond,** and **Anne R. Diekema**

School of Information Studies
Syracuse University
Syracuse, NY 13244
xliu03@mailbox.syr.edu
tdiamon1@twcny.rr.com
diekemar@mailbox.syr.edu

Abstract

We have developed a word sense disambiguation algorithm, following Cheng and Wilensky (1997), to disambiguate among WordNet synsets. This algorithm is to be used in a cross-language information retrieval system, CINDOR, which indexes queries and documents in a language-neutral concept representation based on WordNet synsets. Our goal is to improve retrieval precision through word sense disambiguation. An evaluation against human disambiguation judgements suggests promise for our approach.

1 Introduction

The CINDOR cross-language information retrieval system (Diekema et al., 1998) uses an information structure known as "conceptual interlingua" for query and document representation. This conceptual interlingua is a hierarchically organized multilingual concept lexicon, which is structured following WordNet (Miller, 1990). By representing query and document terms by their WordNet synset numbers we arrive at essentially a language neutral representation consisting of synset numbers representing concepts. This representation facilitates cross-language retrieval by matching term synonyms in English as well as across languages. However, many terms are polysemous and belong to multiple synsets, resulting in spurious matches in retrieval. The noun *figure* for example appears in 13 synsets in WordNet 1.6. This research paper describes the early stages[1] of our efforts to develop a word sense disambiguation (WSD) algorithm aimed at improving the precision of our cross-language retrieval system.

2 Related Work

To determine the sense of a word, a WSD algorithm typically uses the context of the ambiguous word, external resources such as machine-readable dictionaries, or a combination of both. Although dictionaries provide useful word sense information and thesauri provide additional information about relationships between words, they lack pragmatic information as can be found in corpora. Corpora contain examples of words that enable the development of statistical models of word senses and their contexts (Ide and Veronis, 1998; Leacock and Chodorow, 1998).

There are two general problems with using corpora however; 1) corpora typically do not come pre-tagged with manually disambiguated senses, and 2) corpora are often not large nor diverse enough for all senses of a word to appear often enough for reliable statistical models (data sparseness). Although researchers have tried sense-tagging corpora automatically by using either supervised or unsupervised training methods, we have adopted a WSD algorithm which avoids the necessity for a sense-tagged training corpus.

[1] Please note that the disambiguation research described in this paper has not yet been extended to multiple language areas.

$$P(\text{synset}|\text{context}(w)) = \frac{P(\text{context}(w) \mid \text{synset})\, P(\text{synset})}{P(\text{context}(w))} \quad (1)$$

The problem of data sparseness is usually solved by using either smoothing methods, class-based methods, or by relying on similarity-based methods between words and co-occurrence data. Since we are using a WordNet-based resource for retrieval, using class-based methods seems a natural choice. Appropriate word classes can be formed by synsets or groups of synsets. The evidence of a certain sense (synset) is then no longer dependent on one word but on all the members of a particular synset.

Yarowsky (1992) used Rogets Thesaurus categories as classes for WSD. His approach was based on selecting the most likely Roget category for nouns given their context of 50 words on either side. When any of the category indicator words appeared in the context of an ambiguous word, the indicator weights for each category were summed to determine the most likely category. The category with the largest sum was then selected.

A similar approach to that of Yarowsky was followed by Cheng and Willensky (1997) who used a training matrix of associations of words with a certain category. Their algorithm was appealing to us because it requires no human intervention, and more importantly, it avoids the use of sense-tagged data. Our methodology described in the next section is therefore based on Cheng and Wilensky's approach.

Methods to reduce (translation) ambiguity in cross-language information retrieval have included using part-of-speech taggers to restrict the translation options (Davis 1997), applying pseudo-relevance feedback loops to expand the query with better terms aiding translation (Ballesteros and Croft 1997), using corpora for term translation disambiguation (Ballesteros and Croft, 1998), and weighted Boolean models which tend to have a self-disambiguating quality (Hull, 1997; Diekema et al., 1999; Hiemstra and Kraaij, 1999).

3 Methodology

To disambiguate a given word, we would like to know the probability that a sense occurs in a given context, i.e., P(sense|context). In this study, WordNet synsets are used to represent word senses, so P(sense|context) can be rewritten as P(synset|context), for each synset of which that word is a member. For nouns, we define the context of word w to be the occurrence of words in a moving window of 100 words (50 words on each side) around w[2].

By Bayes Theorem, we can obtain the desired probability by inversion (see equation (1)). Since we are not specifically concerned with getting accurate probabilities but rather relative rank order for sense selection, we ignore P(context(w)) and focus on estimating P(context(w)|synset)P(synset). The event space from which "context(w)" is drawn is the set of sets of words that ever appear with each other in the window around w. In other words, w induces a partition on the set of words. We define "context(w)" to be true whenever any of the words in the set appears in the window around w, and conversely to be false whenever none of the words in the set appears around w. If we assume independence of appearance of any two words in a given context, then we get:

$$P(\text{synset}) \times (1 - \prod_{w_i \in context} (1 - P(w_i \mid \text{synset}))) \quad (2)$$

Due to the lack of sense-tagged corpora, we are not able to directly estimate P(synset) and $P(w_i|\text{synset})$. Instead, we introduce "noisy estimators" ($P_e(\text{synset})$ and $P_e(w_i|\text{synset})$) to approximate these probabilities. In doing so, we make two assumptions: 1) The presence of any word w_k that belongs to synset s_i signals the presence of s_i; 2) Any word w_k belongs to all its synsets simultaneously, and with equal probability. Although the assumptions underlying the "noisy estimators" are not strictly true, it is our belief that the "noisy estimators" should work reasonably well if:

- The words that belong to synset s_i tend to appear in similar contexts when s_i is their intended sense;
- These words do not completely overlap with the words belonging to some synset s_j ($i \neq j$) that partially overlaps with s_i;

[2] For other parts of speech, the window size should be much smaller as suggested by previous research.

- The common words between s_i and s_j appear in different contexts when s_i and s_j are their intended senses.

4 The WSD Algorithm

We chose as a basis the algorithms described by Yarrowsky (1992) and by Cheng and Wilensky (1997). In our variation, we use the synset numbers in WordNet to represent the senses of a word. Our algorithm learns associations of WordNet synsets with words in a surrounding context to determine a word sense. It consists of two phases.

During the training phase, the algorithm reads in all training documents in collection and computes the distance-adjusted weight of co-occurrence of each word with each corresponding synset. This is done by establishing a 100-word window around a target word (50 words on each side), and correlating each synset to which the target word belongs with each word in the surrounding window. The result of the training phase is a matrix of associations of words with synsets.

In the sense prediction phase, the algorithm takes as input randomly selected testing documents or sentences that contain the polysemous words we want to disambiguate and exploits the context vectors built in the training phase by adding up the weighted "votes". It then returns a ranked list of probability values associated with each synset, and chooses the synset with the highest probability as the sense of the ambiguous word.

Figure 1 and Figure 2 show an outline of the algorithm.

In this algorithm, "noisy estimators" are employed in the sense prediction phase. They are calculated using following formulas:

$$P_e(w_i|x) = \frac{M[w_i][x]}{\sum_{w \in W} M[w][x]} \quad (3)$$

where w_i is a stem, x is a given synset, M[w][x] is a cell in the correlation matrix that corresponds to word w and synset x, and

$$P_e(x) = \frac{\sum_{w \in W} M[w][x]}{\sum_{w \in W, y \in Y} M[w][y]} \quad (4)$$

where w is any stem in the collection, x is a given synset, y is any synset ever occurred in collection.

```
For each document d in collection
        read in a  noun stem w from d
        for each synset s in which w occurs
                get the column b in the association matrix M that corresponds to s if the column already
                                exists; create a new column for s otherwise
                for each word stem j appearing in the 100-word window around w
                        get the row a in M that corresponds to j if the row already exists;  create a new
                                row for j otherwise
                        add a distance-adjusted weight to M[a][b]
```

Figure 1: WSD Algorithm: the training phase

```
Set value = 1
For each word w to be disambiguated
        get synsets of w
        for each synset x of w
                for each wi in the context of w (within the 100-window around w)
                        calculate Pe(wi|x)
                         value *= ( 1 - Pe(wi|x))
                P(context(w)|x) = 1 - value
               Calculate pe(x)
               P(x|context(w)) = pe(x)* P(context(w)|x)
        display a ranked list of the synsets arranged according to their P(x|context(w)) in decreasing
order
```

Figure 2: WSD Algorithm: the sense prediction phase

5 Evaluation

As suggested by the WSD literature, evaluation of word sense disambiguation systems is not yet standardized (Resnik and Yarowsky, 1997). Some WSD evaluations have been done using the Brown Corpus as training and testing resources and comparing the results against SemCor[3], the sense-tagged version of the Brown Corpus (Agirre and Rigau, 1996; Gonzalo et al., 1998). Others have used common test suites such as the 2094-word *line* data of Leacock et al. (1993). Still others have tended to use their own metrics. We chose an evaluation with a user-based component that allowed a ranked list of sense selection for each target word and enabled a comprehensive comparison between automatic and manual WSD results. In addition we wanted to base the disambiguation matrix on a corpus that we use for retrieval. This approach allows for a much richer evaluation than a simple hit-or-miss test. For validation purpose, we will conduct a fully automatic evaluation against SemCor in our future efforts.

We use *in vitro* evaluation in this study, i.e. the WSD algorithm is tested independent of the retrieval system. The population consists of all the nouns in WordNet, after removal of monosemous nouns, and after removal of a problematic class of polysemous nouns.[4] We drew a random sample of 87 polysemous nouns[5] from this population.

In preparation, for each noun in our sample we identified all the documents containing that noun from the Associated Press (AP) newspaper corpus. The testing document set was then formed by randomly selecting 10 documents from the set of identified documents for each of the 87 nouns. In total, there are 867 documents in the testing set. The training document set consists of all the documents in the AP corpus excluding the above-mentioned 867 documents. For each noun in our sample, we selected all its corresponding WordNet noun synsets and randomly selected 10 sentence occurrences with each from one of the 10 random documents.

After collecting 87 polysemous nouns with 10 noun sentences each, we had 870 sentences for disambiguation. Four human judges were randomly assigned to two groups with two judges each, and each judge was asked to disambiguate 275 word occurrences out of which 160 were unique and 115 were shared with the other judge in the same group. For each word occurrence, the judge put the target word's possible senses in rank order according to their appropriateness given the context (ties are allowed).

Our WSD algorithm was also fed with the identical set of 870 word occurrences in the sense prediction phase and produced a ranked list of senses for each word occurrence.

Since our study has a matched-group design in which the subjects (word occurrences) receive both the treatments and control, the measurement of variables is on an ordinal scale, and there is no apparently applicable parametric statistical procedure available, two nonparametric procedures -the Friedman two-way analysis of variance and the Spearman rank correlation coefficient -were originally chosen as candidates for the statistical analysis of our results. However, the number of ties in our results renders the Spearman coefficient unreliable. We have therefore concentrated on the Friedman analysis of our experimental results. We use the two-alternative test with α=0.05.

The first tests of interest were aimed at establishing inter-judge reliability across the 115 shared sentences by each pair of judges. The null hypothesis can be generalized as "There is no difference in judgments on the same word occurrences between two judges in the same group". Following general steps of conducting a Friedman test as described by Siegel (1956), we cast raw ranks in a two-way table having 2 conditions/columns (K = 2) with each of the human judges in the pair serving as one condition and 365 subjects/rows (N = 365) which are all the senses of the 115 word occurrences that were judged by both human judges. We then ranked

[3] SemCor is a semantically sense-tagged corpus comprising approximately 250, 000 words. The reported error rate is around 10% for polysemous words.

[4] This class of nouns refers to nouns that are in synsets in which they are the sole word, or in synsets whose words were subsets of other synsets for that noun. This situation makes disambiguation extremely problematic. This class of noun will be dealt with in a future version of our algorithm but for now it is beyond the scope of this evaluation.

[5] A polysemous noun is defined as a noun that belongs to two or more synsets.

	N	K	X_r^2	df	Rejection region	Reject H_0?
First pair of judges	365	2	.003	1	3.84	No
Second pair of judges	380	2	2.5289	1	3.84	No

Figure 3: Statistics for significance tests of inter-judge reliability (α=.05, 2-alt. Test)

	N	K	X_r^2	df	Rejection region	Reject H_0?
Auto WSD vs man. WSD vs sense pooling	2840	3	73.217	2	5.99	Yes
Auto WSD vs man. WSD	2840	2	3.7356	1	3.84	No
Auto WSD vs sense pooling	2840	2	5.9507	1	3.84	Yes
Man. WSD vs sense pooling	2840	2	126.338	1	3.84	Yes

Figure 4: Statistics for significance tests among automatic WSD, manual WSD, and sense pooling (α=.05, 2-alt. Test)

the scores in each row from 1 to K (in this case K is 2), summed the derived ranks in each column, and calculated X_r^2 which is .003. For α=0.05, degrees of freedom df = 1 (df = K –1), the rejection region starts at 3.84. Since .003 is smaller than 3.84, the null hypothesis is not rejected. Similar steps were used for analyzing reliability between the second pair of judges. In both cases, we did not find significant difference between judges (see Figure 3).

Our second area of interest was the comparison of automatic WSD, manual WSD, and "sense pooling". Sense pooling equates to no disambiguation, where each sense of a word is considered equally likely (a tie). The null hypothesis (H_0) is "There is no difference among manual WSD, automatic WSD, and sense pooling (all the conditions come from the same population)". The steps for Friedman analysis were similar to what we did for the inter-judge reliability test while the conditions and subjects were changed in each test according to what we would like to compare. Test results are summarized in Figure 4. In the three-way comparison shown in the first row of the table, we rejected H_0 so there was at least one condition that was from a different population. By further conducting tests which examined each two of the above three conditions at a time we found that it was sense pooling that came from a different population while manual and automatic WSD were not significantly different. We can therefore conclude that our WSD algorithm is better than no disambiguation.

6 Concluding Remarks

The ambiguity of words may negatively impact the retrieval performance of a concept-based information retrieval system like CINDOR. We have developed a WSD algorithm that uses all the words in a WordNet synset as evidence of a given sense and builds an association matrix to learn the co-occurrence between words and senses. An evaluation of our algorithm against human judgements of a small sample of nouns demonstrated no significant difference between our automatic ranking of senses and the human judgements. There was, however, a significant difference between human judgement and rankings produced with no disambiguation where all senses were tied.

These early results are such as to encourage us to continue our research in this area. In our future work we must tackle issues associated with the fine granularity of some WordNet sense distinctions, synsets which are proper subsets of other synsets and are therefore impossible to distinguish, and also extend our evaluation to multiple languages and to other parts of speech. The next step in our work will be to evaluate our WSD algorithm against the manually sense-tagged SemCor Corpus for validation, and then integrate our WSD algorithm into CINDOR's processing and evaluate directly the impact on retrieval performance. We hope to verify that word sense disambiguation leads to improved precision in cross-language retrieval.

Acknowledgements

This work was completed under a research practicum at MNIS-TextWise Labs, Syracuse, NY. We thank Paraic Sheridan for many useful discussions and the anonymous reviewers for constructive comments on the manuscript.

References

Agirre, E., and Rigau, G. (1996). Word sense disambiguation using conceptual density. In: *Proceedings of the 16th International Conference on Computational Linguistics*, Copenhagen,1996.

Ballesteros, L., and Croft, B. (1997). Phrasal Translation and Query Expansion Techniques for Cross-Language Information Retrieval. In: *Proceedings of the Association for Computing Machinery Special Interest Group on Information Retrieval (ACM/SIGIR) 20th International Conference on Research and Development in Information Retrieval*; 1997 July 25-31; Philadelphia, PA. New York, NY: ACM, 1997. 84-91.

Ballesteros, L., and Croft, B. (1998). Resolving Ambiguity for Cross-language Retrieval. In: *Proceedings of the Association for Computing Machinery Special Interest Group on Information Retrieval (ACM/SIGIR) 21st International Conference on Research and Development in Information Retrieval*; 1998 August 24-28; Melbourne, Australia. New York, NY: ACM, 1998. 64-71.

Cheng, I., and Wilensky, R. (1997). An Experiment in Enhancing Information Access by Natural Language Processing. UC Berkeley Computer Science Technical Report UCB/CSD UCB//CSD-97-963.

Davis, M. (1997). New Experiments in Cross-Language Text Retrieval at NMSU's Computing Research Lab. In: D.K. Harman, Ed. *The Fifth Text Retrieval Conference (TREC-5).* 1996, November. National Institute of Standards and Technology (NIST), Gaithersburg, MD.

Diekema, A., Oroumchian, F., Sheridan, P., and Liddy, E. D. (1999). TREC-7 Evaluation of Conceptual Interlingua Document Retrieval (CINDOR) in English and French. In: E.M. Voorhees and D.K. Harman (Eds.) *The Seventh Text REtrieval Conference (TREC-7).* 1998, November 9-11; National Institute of Standards and Technology (NIST), Gaithersburg, MD. 169-180.

Gonzalo, J., Verdejo, F., Chugur, I., and Cigarran, J. (1998). Indexing with WordNet synsets can improve text retrieval. In: *Proceedings of the COLING/ACL Workshop on Usage of WordNet in Natural Language Processing Systems*, Montreal, 1998.

Hiemstra, D., and Kraaij, W. (1999). Twenty-One at TREC-7: Ad-hoc and Cross-language Track. In: E.M. Voorhees and D.K. Harman (Eds.) *The Seventh Text REtrieval Conference (TREC-7).* 1998, November 9-11; National Institute of Standards and Technology (NIST), Gaithersburg, MD. 227-238.

Hull, D. A. (1997). Using Structured Queries for Disambiguation in Cross-Language Information Retrieval. In: *American Association for Artificial Intelligence (AAAI) Symposium on Cross-Language Text and Speech Retrieval*; 1997 March 24-26; Palo Alto, CA 1997. 84-98.

Ide, N., and Veronis, J. (1998). Introduction to the Special Issue on Word Sense Disambiguation: The State of the Art. *Computational Linguistics*, Vol. 24, No. 1, 1-40.

Leacock, C., and Chodorow, M. (1998). Combining Local Context and WordNet Similarity for Word Sense Identification. In: Christiane Fellbaum (Eds.) *WordNet: An Electronic Lexical Database.* Cambridge, MA: MIT Press.

Leacock, C., Towell, G., and Voorhees, E. (1993). Corpus-based Statistical Sense Resolution. In: *Proceedings, ARPA Human Language Technology Workshop*, Plainsboro, NJ. 260-265.

Miller, G. (1990). WordNet: An On-line Lexical Database. *International Journal of Lexicography*, Vol. 3, No. 4, Special Issue.

Resnik, P., and Yarowsky, D. (1997). A Perspective on Word Sense Disambiguation Methods and Their Evaluation, position paper presented at *the ACL SIGLEX Workshop on Tagging Text with Lexical Semantics: Why, What, and How?,* held April 4-5, 1997 in Washington, D.C., USA in conjunction with ANLP-97.

Siegel, S. (1956). Nonparametric Statistics for the Behavioral Sciences. New York: McGraw-Hill, 1956.

Yarowsky, D. (1992). Word-Sense Disambiguation Using Statistical Models of Roget's Categories Trained on Large Corpora. In: *Proceedings of the Fourteenth International Conference on Computational Linguistics.* Nantes, France. 454-460.

Multiple Discourse Marker Occurrence: Creating Hierarchies for Natural Language Generation

Sarah Louise Oates*
University of Brighton.
Sarah.Oates@itri.brighton.ac.uk

Abstract

Most studies on discourse markers implicitly assume that only one marker or discourse relation will occur in a sentence. In reality, more than one relation may hold between text spans and may be cued by multiple discourse markers. We describe here a method for hierarchically organising discourse markers. The hierarchies are intended for use by a generation system to enable the selection and placement of more than one marker in a single text span.

1 Introduction

The majority of studies on discourse markers implicitly assume that only one marker or discourse relation will occur in a sentence or that the presence of multiple markers will not affect the choice and placement of others. However, in reality, more than one relation may hold between text spans which may be cued by multiple markers. The available rules describing the occurrence, choice and placement of a given marker do not account for multiple marker occurrence (Grote et al., 1995; Webber and Joshi, 1998; Power et al., 1999, e.g.,). We have found that the choice and placement of discourse markers is greatly affected, not only by the presence and number of other markers, but also by the style of the text and the strength of other markers in the text span. We describe here a method for hierarchically organising discourse markers which takes account of these factors. The hierarchies are intended for use by a generation system to enable the selection and placement of multiple markers.

* The author would like to thank the Engineering and Physical Sciences Research Council for funding

2 Defining Discourse Markers

Although precise definitions of discourse markers differ between studies, it is generally accepted that their role is to signal how one proposition should be interpreted given the other(s) in the discourse (Millis et al., 1995; Moore and Pollack, 1992). Most researchers in this field also agree that the relation between these propositions may exist regardless of whether a discourse marker is used (Scott and de Souza, 1990; Knott, 1995): a discourse marker is simply an explicit signal of a specific relation between two or more propositions. The non-occurrence of a marker does not mean that a discourse relation is absent:

(1) *no marker, 1 relation:* The museum does not intend to sponsor a particular aspect of modern art; it intends to make a report to the public by offering material for study and comparison.

By the same token, the presence of more than one discourse marker does not always signal a multitude of relations:

(2) *2 markers, 1 relation*: The museum does not intend to sponsor a particular aspect of modern art, **but rather** to make a report to the public by offering material for study and comparison. (BNC)[1]

Previous studies have accounted for a wide range of phenomena, from choosing between similar discourse markers (Fraser, 1998; Sanders et al., 1992) to abstracting away from discourse markers and using syntax to signal underlying discourse relations (Delin et al., 1996). However, the issue of multiple markers, like those in the example above, is only now beginning

[1]British National Corpus (Leech et al., 1994)

to be addressed. Recent work in computational linguistics has provided possible solutions for the use of correlative markers (Webber and Joshi, 1998) and embedded clauses (Power et al., 1999). However, these solutions are incomplete and further research is needed if we are to account for all examples of multiple discourse markers.

3 Multiple Markers

The present project focuses on *all* cases of *multiple discourse markers*, in other words, all cases where more than one marker occurs within two spans of text which are expressed either (a) within the same *text sentence* (Nunberg, 1990) covering one or more discourse relations (e.g., examples 3 and 4);

(3) **Having said that, if** you weigh only 60 kg (132lb) **and yet** still manage to sit your 90 kg (198lb) opponent down with a solid thump to his mid-section, **then** the refereeing panel may well applaud your fervour with a full point. (BNC)

(4) **Since** the question turns on the meaning of the word "appropriate" in section 1(1) of the Act of 1968, the problem is **therefore** one of statutory interpretation. (BNC)

or (b) in different text sentences but covering only one relation, the so-called *correlative markers* (Quirk et al., 1985) (e.g., example 5):

(5) The job of being an Acorn Project leader is an unenviable one. **For a start**, they don't get paid, though they do receive a petrol allowance; **for another thing**, it's a bit like being in a group of unruly children for the week... (BNC)

The work described here focuses solely on *multiple discourse markers cueing a single relation*, paying attention, when possible, to embedded discourse relations and their markers.

4 Single Relations — Multiple Markers

Preliminary tests using the British National Corpus (BNC) and Knott's (1995) taxonomy of discourse markers suggested that the order of multiple markers cueing a single relation is affected by their position in the taxonomy; those higher in the taxonomy always precede those lower in the taxonomy (see figure 1 and examples 6-7);

(6) This blood-line was particularly helpful to the early breeders because the line was in-bred, his parents being brother and sister of excellent breeding **and so consequently** true to type. (BNC)

(7) The difficulty is that the sites which have been extensively excavated, **and so** produced the largest quantities of pottery, such a Corbridge and Newstead, are multi-period, and the stratification of the excavations early in the century, **consequently** suspect. (BNC)

However, since Knott's taxonomy only allows us to view hierarchies of markers of a single relation, improvements were necessary in order to account for multiple markers. Using the BNC, a list of at least 350 English discourse markers and Mann and Thompson's (1988) original 23 rhetorical relations, we created a database on the number and type of relations each marker can cue (see figure 2). From this a hierarchy was built, similar to Knott's (1995), but benefiting from a wider range of markers and allowing more than one relation to be expressed at a time, thus reducing the redundancy present in Knott's taxonomy. Furthermore, in contrast to Knott's study in which examples were fabricated, all examples of discourse marker usage in our database are taken from the British National Corpus (BNC). Thus, all of our examples are taken from real, natural texts and are, therefore, representative of discourse marker occurrence in natural language.

5 Constructing the Hierarchy

Our hierarchies are constructed on the assumption that (a) some discourse markers may be used to cue more than one relation and (b) when more than one marker is needed, the number of relations a marker can cue will affect the choice and position of that marker. In our hierarchy, those discourse markers which can cue many relations appear at the top and those marking only a single relation occur at the bottom. Markers may also have additional constraints on their usage depending upon the text style, other relations being marked simultaneously and the content of the related propositions.

6 Strong & Weak Markers

Figure 3 is an example of our hierarchy for the family of contrastive relations. Here we see that 'but' can mark four discourse relations

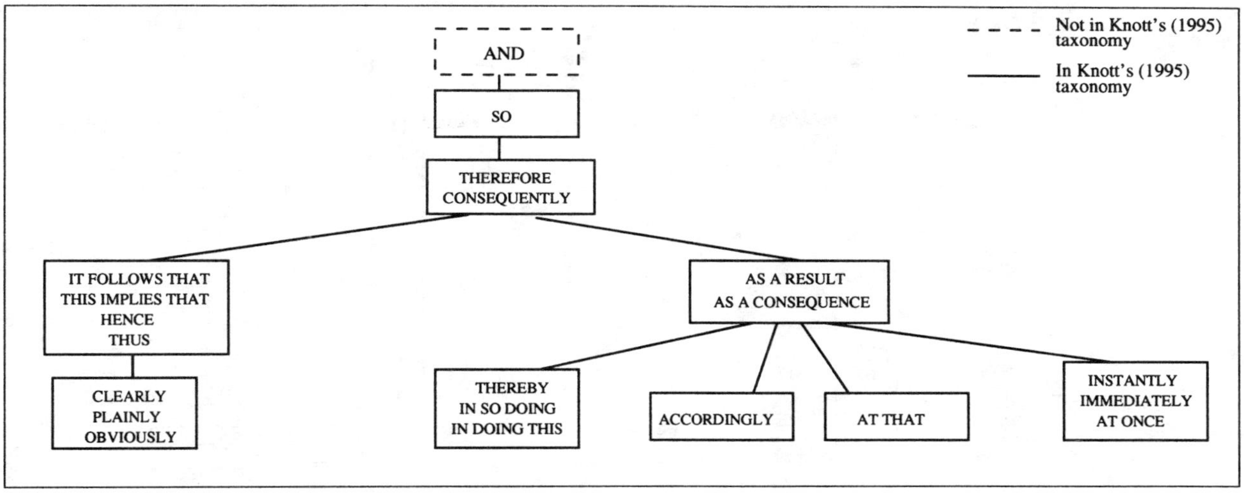

Figure 1: Example of Knott's (1995) Taxonomy

DISCOURSE MARKER	CATEGORY	DISCOURSE RELATION	SAT/ NUC*	EXAMPLE IN USE
so	subordinator	vol-cause	(n)	He had no chance of winning SO he pretended he wasn't trying (BNC)
		non-vol-cause	(n)	While deciding to stay as independent as possible, I contacted ACET who I knew provided practical care at home. I had previously spent about 2 years asking local services and friends for help and not having it happen, SO my flat had become pretty run down. (BNC)
		non-vol-result	(s)	While wanting to dismiss the stereotyping and silly superstition, the snag remains that within all the ballyhoo there are elements of truth. SO instead of being outraged, one is left with a resigned smirk. (BNC)
		enablement	(n)	Loosen the cord SO you can remove the curtains easily. (BNC)
		evaluation	(s)	Nor is this feeling only provoked by the sight or the thought of art, he wrote. I also experienced it when I signed the marriage register as well as when I saw the pig slaughtered...a feeling of the heart leaping and the blood pumping.....SO, wrote Harsnet, there is continuity as well as discontinuity. (BNC)
		justify	(n)	If you went on strike they didn't pay you off. You got sacked and you just didn't get any money. So people had no other option but to work. (BNC)
		sequence	multi-nuclear	.....that's what I guessed so I said "no" , I said they're fine, SO she said "oh, I'm ever so sorry". I said "don't be". (BNC)
		purpose	(s)	He'll remind her SO she'll remember. (BNC)

*SAT/NUC = The text span upon which the discourse marker occurs - SAT(satellite), NUC(nucleus).

Figure 2: Extract from Database of Discourse Markers & Relations

(contrast, antithesis, concession and exception) without constraint. When discourse markers can be used for a large number of relations, we refer to them as 'weak' markers since there is only a weak correlation between the marker and the relation being signalled. In contrast, when a discourse marker can only cue a single relation, we refer to it as a 'strong' marker, since there is a strong correlation between the relation and the explicit lexical cue. In the hierarchy 'notwithstanding that' is a highly constrained, strong discourse marker since it can only mark one relation (concession) and occur only when the text is formal, legal or both.

Our tests on the BNC show that the choice and placement of a marker will be affected by its strength or weakness; the weakest markers always precede the stronger ones. We find that this rule not only applies to single relations cued by multiple markers:

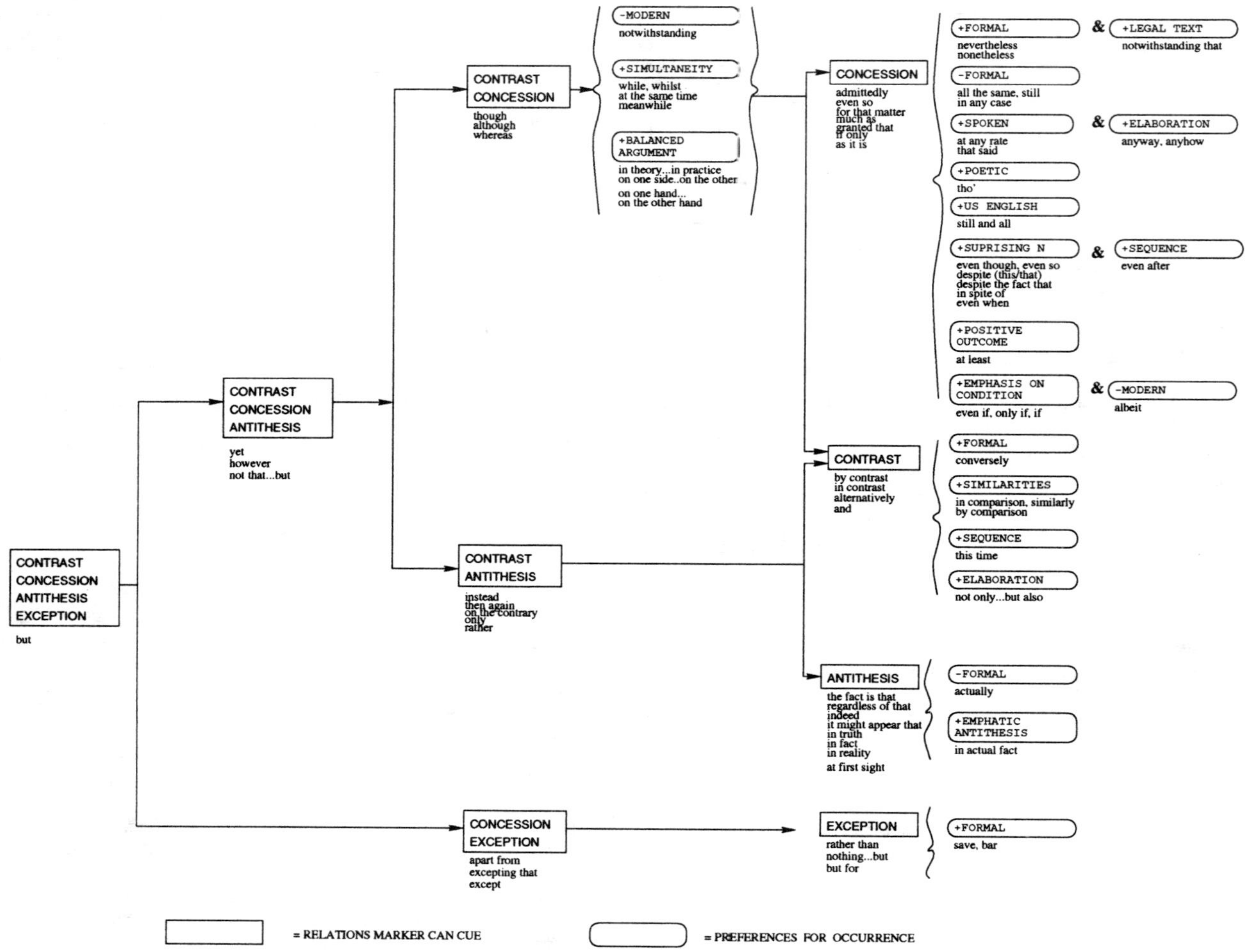

Figure 3: Hierarchy of Contrastive Family of Relations

(8) (a) The pores in the skin are a classic example: they can not become perceptible to us by themselves, **but yet** (b) their presence in the skin can be deduced from sweat. (BNC)

but also, to a certain extent, to embedded relations cued by two markers in the same text span. In the following example, we have two relations and two markers of contrast. The superordinate relation, marked by 'however', holds between proposition (a) and propositions (b) and (c), whilst the subordinate relation, marked by 'whereas', holds between propositions (b) and (c);

(9) Indeed , (a) so strong have the differential views on advantageous locations become that one recent assessment of the total stock of foreign capital in developing countries suggests that it is less today than it was in 1900. **However, whereas** (b) the G-5 countries now account for 75 per cent of the world's FDI flow, (c) their position as the five major exporters is a much less concentrated 45 per cent.(BNC)

In both cases, the weakest marker precedes the stronger marker and neither could be reversed and remain grammatical. Thus, working through the hierarchy from the weakest to the strongest markers, a generation system can determine which discourse marker should occur in a particular position on the basis that the weakest markers always precede the stronger ones.

Decisions are based on the relation(s) to be marked, any other relation(s) already present, the style of the text, the content of the text spans, and the strength or weakness of other discourse markers present.

7 Conclusions

Thus far, we have developed hierarchies for the family of contrastive relations in English and French and the family of causal relations in English. Ultimately, we intend to establish a complete hierarchy of all the markers of discourse relations; this will not only allow us to choose between different markers, regardless of whether one or more are used, but will also help to determine their order when multiple markers are necessary. In the final version of the hierarchy, we intend to provide the generation system with statistical information on the likelihood of one marker following another. Such information will take account of the fact that certain markers tend to occur together more often than others. These statistics are currently being derived from tests on the International Corpus of English (Nelson, 1995).

References

J. Delin, D. R. Scott, and A. Hartley. 1996. Language Specific Mappings from Semantics to Syntax. In *Proceedings of the 16th International Conference on Computational Linguistics*, pages 292–297. COLING96.

B. Fraser. 1998. Contrastive Discourse Markers in English. In A. H. Jucker and Y. Ziv, editors, *Discourse Markers: Descriptions and Theory*, pages 301–326. John Benjamins, Amsterdam.

B. Grote, N. Lenke, and M. Stede. 1995. Ma(r)king Concessions in English and German. In *Proceedings of the 5th European Workshop on Natural Language Generation*, pages 11–32, Leiden, May. Leiden University.

A. Knott. 1995. *A Data-Driven Methodology for Motivating a Set of Coherence Relations.* Ph.D. thesis, University of Edinburgh.

G. Leech, R. Garside, and M. Bryant. 1994. CLAWS4: The tagging of the British National Corpus. In *Proceedings of the 15th International Conference on Computational Linguistics (COLING)*, pages 622–628, Kyoto, Japan.

W. Mann and S. Thompson. 1988. Rhetorical structure theory: Toward a functional theory of text organisation. *Text*, 8:243–281.

K. K. Millis, J. M. Golding, and G. Barker. 1995. Causal Connectives Increase Inference Generation. *Discourse Processes*, 20(1):29–50.

J. D. Moore and M. E. Pollack. 1992. A Problem for RST: The need for multi-level discourse analysis. *Computational Linguistics*, 18(4):537–544.

G Nelson. 1995. The International Corpus of English: Markup & Transcription. In G. N. Leech, G. Myers, and J. A. Thomas, editors, *Spoken English on Computer: Transcription, mark-up and application*, pages 220–223. Longman, London.

G. Nunberg. 1990. The Linguistics of Punctuation. CSLI Lecture Notes, no.18. Center for the study of Language and information, Stanford.

R. Power, D. Scott, and C. Doran. 1999. Generating Embedded Discourse Markers from Rhetorical Structure. In *Proceedings from the European Workshop on Natural Language Generation EWNLG'99*, pages 30–38, Toulouse.

R. Quirk, S. Greenbaum, S. Leech, and J. Svartvik. 1985. *A Comprehensive Grammar of the English Language.* Longman, London.

T. Sanders, W. Spooren, and L. Noordman. 1992. Toward a Taxonomy of Coherence Relations. *Discourse Processes*, 15:1–35.

D.R. Scott and C.S. de Souza. 1990. Getting the Message Across in RST-based Text Generation. In R. Dale, C. Mellish, and M. Zock, editors, *Current Research in Natural Language Generation*, pages 47–73. Academic Press, London.

B. L. Webber and A. K. Joshi. 1998. Anchoring a Lexicalised Tree-Adjoining Grammar for Discourse. In M. Stede, L. Warner, and E. Hovy, editors, *Discourse Relations and Discourse Markers. Proceedings from the Workshop. COLING-ACL'98*, pages 86–92, Montreal.

Association for Computational Linguistics

Author Index to the Proceedings of ANLP-NAACL 2000 and the Student Research Workshop

April 29—May 4, 2000
Seattle, Washington, USA

Author Index

Section 1: Applied Natural Language Processing Conference (ANLP)

Section 2: North American Chapter of the Association for Computational Linguistics (NAACL)

Section 3: ANLP-NAACL 2000 Student Research Workshop (SRW)